with MyEconLab

$$P = c + dQ_S$$

- **NEW: Math Review Exercises in MyEconLab**—MyEconLab now offers an array of assignable and auto-graded exercises that cover fundamental math concepts. Geared specifically toward principles and intermediate economics students, these exercises aim to increase student confidence and success in these courses. Our new Math Review is accessible from the assignment manager and contains over 150 graphing, algebra, and calculus exercises for homework, quiz, and test use.

- **Real-Time Data Analysis Exercises**—Using current macro data to help students understand the impact of changes in economic variables, Real-Time Data Analysis Exercises communicate directly with the Federal Reserve Bank of St. Louis's FRED® site and update as new data are available.

- **Current News Exercises**—Every week, current microeconomic and macroeconomic news articles or videos, with accompanying exercises, are posted to MyEconLab. Assignable and auto-graded, these multi-part exercises ask students to recognize and apply economic concepts to real-world events.

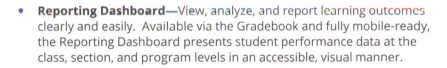

- **Experiments**—Flexible, easy-to-assign, auto-graded, and available in Single Player and Multiplayer versions, Experiments in MyEconLab make learning fun and engaging.

- **Reporting Dashboard**—View, analyze, and report learning outcomes clearly and easily. Available via the Gradebook and fully mobile-ready, the Reporting Dashboard presents student performance data at the class, section, and program levels in an accessible, visual manner.

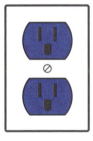

- **LMS Integration**—Link from any LMS platform to access assignments, rosters, and resources, and synchronize MyLab grades with your LMS gradebook. For students, new direct, single sign-on provides access to all the personalized learning MyLab resources that make studying more efficient and effective.

- **Mobile Ready**—Students and instructors can access multimedia resources and complete assessments right at their fingertips, on any mobile device.

ALWAYS LEARNING

FOUNDATIONS OF ECONOMICS

delivers a complete, hands-on learning system designed around active learning.

A Learning-by-Doing Approach

The **Checklist** that begins each chapter highlights the key topics covered and the chapter is divided into sections that directly correlate to the Checklist.

The **Checkpoint** that ends each section provides a full page of practice problems to encourage students to review the material while it is fresh in their minds.

Each chapter opens with a question about a central issue that sets the stage for the material.

Eye On boxes apply theory to important issues and problems that shape our global society and individual decisions.

Confidence-Building Graphs

use color to show the direction of shifts and detailed, numbered captions guide students step-by-step through the action.

100% of the figures are animated in MyEconLab, with step-by-step audio narration.

Why did the price of coffee rise in 2014?

Demand and Supply

4

CHAPTER CHECKLIST

When you have completed your study of this chapter, you will be able to

1 Distinguish between quantity demanded and demand, and explain what determines demand.

2 Distinguish between quantity supplied and supply, and explain what determines supply.

3 Explain how demand and supply determine price and quantity in a market, and explain the effects of changes in demand and supply.

MyEconLab **Big Picture Video**

CHECKPOINT 4.1

MyEconLab Study Plan 4.1
Key Terms Quiz
Solutions Video

Distinguish between quantity demanded and demand, and explain what determines demand.

Practice Problems

The following events occur one at a time in the market for smartphones:

- The price of a smartphone falls.
- Producers announce that the price of a smartphone will fall next month.
- The price of a call made from a smartphone falls.
- The price of a call made from a land-line phone increases.
- An increase in memory makes smartphones more popular.

1. Explain the effect of each event on the demand for smartphones.
2. Use a graph to illustrate the effect of each event.
3. Does any event (or events) illustrate the law of demand?

In the News

Airline profits soar yet no relief for passengers

EYE on the PRICE OF COFFEE

MyEconLab **Critical Thinking Exercise**

Why Did the Price of Coffee Rise in 2014?

When a fungus called coffee rust swept through Brazil and other countries of South America in 2014, world coffee production decreased and the price of coffee beans increased.

The table below provides some data on the quantity and price of coffee in 2013 and 2014. What does the data table tell us?

It tells us that the quantity of coffee

You can answer this question from the information provided. You know that an increase in demand brings a rise in the price and an increase in the quantity bought, while a decrease in supply brings a rise in the price and a decrease in the quantity bought.

Because the quantity of coffee decreased and the price increased, there must have been a decrease in the sup-

The figure illustrates the global market for coffee in 2013 and 2014. The demand curve D shows the demand for coffee, which we will assume was the same in both years.

In 2013, the supply curve was S_{2013}, the equilibrium price was \$1.04 per pound and the equilibrium quantity traded was 19.4 billion pounds.

In 2014, decreased coffee produc-

■ **FIGURE 4.4**

Change in Quantity Demanded Versus Change in Demand

MyEconLab **Animation**

❶ **A decrease in the quantity demanded**
The quantity demanded decreases and there is a movement up along the demand curve D_0 if the price of the good rises and other things remain the same.

❸ **A decrease in demand**
Demand decreases and the demand curve shifts leftward (from D_0 to D_1) if

- The price of a substitute falls or the price of a complement rises.
- The price of the good is expected to fall.
- Income decreases.*
- Expected future income or credit decreases.
- The number of buyers decreases.

* Bottled water is a normal good.

Price (dollars per bottle)

❷ **An increase in the quantity demanded**
The quantity demanded increases and there is a movement down along the demand curve D_0 if the price of the good falls and other things remain the same.

❹ **An increase in demand**
Demand increases and the demand curve shifts rightward (from D_0 to D_2) if

- The price of a substitute rises or the price of a complement falls.
- The price of the good is expected to rise.
- Income increases.
- Expected future income or credit increases.
- The number of buyers increases.

Quantity (millions of bottles per day)

Foundations of
ECONOMICS

Robin Bade

Michael Parkin
University of Western Ontario

EIGHTH EDITION

330 Hudson Street, NY NY 10013

Vice President, Business Publishing: Donna Battista
Director of Portfolio Management: Adrienne
  D'Ambrosio
Portfolio Manager: Ashley Bryan
Editorial Assistant: Michelle Zeng
Vice President, Product Marketing: Roxanne McCarley
Director of Strategic Marketing: Brad Parkins
Strategic Marketing Manager: Deborah Strickland
Product Marketer: Tricia Murphy
Field Marketing Manager: Ramona Elmer
Field Marketing Assistant: Kristen Compton
Product Marketing Assistant: Jessica Quazza
Vice President, Production and Digital Studio, Arts
  and Business: Etain O'Dea
Director of Production, Business: Jeff Holcomb
Managing Producer, Business: Alison Kalil
Content Producer: Nancy Freihofer

Operations Specialist: Carol Melville
Creative Director: Blair Brown
Manager, Learning Tools: Brian Surette
Managing Producer, Digital Studio, Arts and
  Business: Diane Lombardo
Digital Studio Producer: Melissa Honig
Digital Studio Producer: Alana Coles
Digital Content Team Lead: Noel Lotz
Digital Content Project Lead: Noel Lotz
Full-Service Project Management and
  Composition: Integra Software Services
Interior Design: Integra Software Services
Cover Design: Jon Boylan
Cover Art: Rosalie Kreulen/www.shutterstock.com
Technical Illustrator: Richard Parkin
Printer/Binder: LSC Communications
Cover Printer: LSC Communications

To Erin, Tessa, Jack, Abby, and Sophie

About the Authors

Robin Bade was an undergraduate at the University of Queensland, Australia, where she earned degrees in mathematics and economics. After a spell teaching high school math and physics, she enrolled in the Ph.D. program at the Australian National University, from which she graduated in 1970. She has held faculty appointments at the University of Edinburgh in Scotland, at Bond University in Australia, and at the Universities of Manitoba, Toronto, and Western Ontario in Canada. Her research on international capital flows appears in the *International Economic Review* and the *Economic Record*.

Robin first taught the principles of economics course in 1970 and has taught it (alongside intermediate macroeconomics and international trade and finance) most years since then. She developed many of the ideas found in this text while conducting tutorials with her students at the University of Western Ontario.

Michael Parkin studied economics in England and began his university teaching career immediately after graduating with a B.A. from the University of Leicester. He learned the subject on the job at the University of Essex, England's most exciting new university of the 1960s, and at the age of 30 became one of the youngest full professors. He is a past president of the Canadian Economics Association and has served on the editorial boards of the *American Economic Review* and the *Journal of Monetary Economics*. His research on macroeconomics, monetary economics, and international economics has resulted in more than 160 publications in journals and edited volumes, including the *American Economic Review*, the *Journal of Political Economy*, the *Review of Economic Studies*, the *Journal of Monetary Economics*, and the *Journal of Money, Credit, and Banking*. He is author of the best-selling textbook, *Economics* (Pearson), now in its Twelfth Edition.

Robin and Michael are a wife-and-husband team. Their most notable joint research created the Bade-Parkin Index of central bank independence and spawned a vast amount of research on that topic. They don't claim credit for the independence of the new European Central Bank, but its constitution and the movement toward greater independence of central banks around the world were aided by their pioneering work. Their joint textbooks include *Macroeconomics* (Prentice-Hall), *Modern Macroeconomics* (Pearson Education Canada), and *Economics: Canada in the Global Environment*, the Canadian adaptation of Parkin, *Economics* (Addison-Wesley). They are dedicated to the challenge of explaining economics ever more clearly to a growing body of students.

Music, the theater, art, walking on the beach, and five grandchildren provides their relaxation and fun.

ECONOMICS

Brief Contents

PART 1 INTRODUCTION
1 Getting Started   1
2 The U.S. and Global Economies   33
3 The Economic Problem   59
4 Demand and Supply   83

PART 2 A CLOSER LOOK AT MARKETS
5 Elasticities of Demand and Supply   113
6 Efficiency and Fairness of Markets   139

PART 3 HOW GOVERNMENTS INFLUENCE THE ECONOMY
7 Government Actions in Markets   169
8 Taxes   191
9 Global Markets in Action   215

PART 4 MARKET FAILURE AND PUBLIC POLICY
10 Externalities   243
11 Public Goods and Common Resources   267
12 Private Information and Healthcare Markets   293

PART 5 A CLOSER LOOK AT DECISION MAKERS
13 Consumer Choice and Demand   319
14 Production and Cost   347

PART 6 PRICES, PROFITS, AND INDUSTRY PERFORMANCE
15 Perfect Competition   375
16 Monopoly   403
17 Monopolistic Competition   435
18 Oligopoly   459

PART 7 INCOMES AND INEQUALITY
19 Markets for Factors of Production   487
20 Economic Inequality   511

PART 8   MONITORING THE MACROECONOMY
21   **GDP: A Measure of Total Production and Income**   537
22   **Jobs and Unemployment**   567
23   **The CPI and the Cost of Living**   589

PART 9   THE REAL ECONOMY
24   **Potential GDP and the Natural Unemployment Rate**   613
25   **Economic Growth**   637
26   **Finance, Saving, and Investment**   665

PART 10   THE MONEY ECONOMY
27   **The Monetary System**   691
28   **Money, Interest, and Inflation**   721

PART 11   ECONOMIC FLUCTUATIONS
29   **Aggregate Supply and Aggregate Demand**   749
30   **Aggregate Expenditure Multiplier**   775
31   **The Short-Run Policy Tradeoff**   801

PART 12   MACROECONOMIC POLICY
32   **Fiscal Policy**   823
33   **Monetary Policy**   849
34   **International Finance**   877

Glossary   G-1
Index   I-1
Credits   C-1

Contents

PART 1   INTRODUCTION

CHAPTER 1
Getting Started   1
CHAPTER CHECKLIST   1

1.1   Definition and Questions   2
Scarcity   2
Economics Defined   2
What, How, and For Whom?   3
Can the Pursuit of Self-Interest Be in the Social Interest?   4
CHECKPOINT 1.1   7

1.2   The Economic Way of Thinking   8
A Choice Is a Tradeoff   8
Cost: What You *Must* Give Up   8
Benefit: What You Gain   9
Rational Choice   9
How Much? Choosing at the Margin   10
Choices Respond to Incentives   11
CHECKPOINT 1.2   13

1.3   Economics as a Life Skill   14
Economics as a Decision Tool   14
Economics as a Social Science   14
Economics as an Aid to Critical Thinking   16
CHECKPOINT 1.3   18

CHAPTER SUMMARY   19

CHAPTER CHECKPOINT   20

Appendix: Making and Using Graphs   23
Basic Idea   23
Interpreting Data Graphs   24
Interpreting Graphs Used in Economic Models   26
The Slope of a Relationship   29
Relationships Among More Than Two Variables   30
APPENDIX CHECKPOINT   32
■ **EYE on the BENEFIT AND COST OF SCHOOL**
Did You Make the Right Decision?   12

■ **EYE on YOUR LIFE**
Your Time Allocation   17
■ **EYE on the PAST**
Adam Smith and the Birth of Economics as a Social Science   18

CHAPTER 2
The U.S. and Global Economies   33
CHAPTER CHECKLIST   33

2.1   What, How, and for Whom?   34
What Do We Produce?   34
How Do We Produce?   36
For Whom Do We Produce?   39
CHECKPOINT 2.1   40

2.2   The Global Economy   41
The People   41
The Economies   41
What in the Global Economy   42
How in the Global Economy   44
For Whom in the Global Economy   44
CHECKPOINT 2.2   47

2.3   The Circular Flows   48
Households and Firms   48
Markets   48
Real Flows and Money Flows   48
Governments   50
Governments in the Circular Flow   51
Circular Flows in the Global Economy   52
CHECKPOINT 2.3   54

CHAPTER SUMMARY   55

CHAPTER CHECKPOINT   56

■ **EYE on the U.S. ECONOMY**
What We Produce   35

■ **EYE on the PAST**
Changes in What We Produce 36

■ **EYE on the U.S. ECONOMY**
Changes in How We Produce in the Information
Economy 38

■ **EYE on the DREAMLINER**
Who Makes the Dreamliner? 43

■ **EYE on the GLOBAL ECONOMY**
Differences in How We Produce 45

■ **EYE on YOUR LIFE**
The U.S. and Global Economies in Your Life 47

■ **EYE on the PAST**
Growing Government 52

■ **EYE on the GLOBAL ECONOMY**
The Ups and Downs in International Trade 54

CHAPTER **3**

The Economic Problem 59

CHAPTER CHECKLIST 59

3.1 Production Possibilities 60
Production Possibilities Frontier 60
How the *PPF* Illustrates Scarcity and Its
Consequences 61
CHECKPOINT 3.1 65

3.2 Opportunity Cost 66
The Opportunity Cost of a Smartphone 66
Opportunity Cost and the Slope of the *PPF* 67
Opportunity Cost Is a Ratio 67
Increasing Opportunity Costs Are Everywhere 68
Your Increasing Opportunity Cost 68
CHECKPOINT 3.2 69

3.3 Economic Growth 70
CHECKPOINT 3.3 72

3.4 Specialization and Trade 73
Absolute Advantage and Comparative Advantage 73
Comparative Advantage: A Model 74
Achieving Gains from Trade 76
The Economy's Production Possibilities Frontier 77
CHECKPOINT 3.4 78

CHAPTER SUMMARY 79

CHAPTER CHECKPOINT 80

■ **EYE on YOUR LIFE**
Your Production Possibilities Frontier 64

■ **EYE on the ENVIRONMENT**
Is Wind Power Free? 68

■ **EYE on the U.S. ECONOMY**
Expanding Our Production Possibilities 71

■ **EYE on the GLOBAL ECONOMY**
Hong Kong's Rapid Economic Growth 72

■ **EYE on the U.S. ECONOMY**
No One Knows How to Make a Pencil 73

■ **EYE on YOUR LIFE**
Your Comparative Advantage 77

CHAPTER **4**

Demand and Supply 83

CHAPTER CHECKLIST 83

Competitive Markets 84

4.1 Demand 85
The Law of Demand 85
Demand Schedule and Demand Curve 85
Individual Demand and Market Demand 87
Changes in Demand 88
Change in Quantity Demanded Versus Change in
Demand 90
CHECKPOINT 4.1 91

4.2 Supply 92
The Law of Supply 92
Supply Schedule and Supply Curve 92
Individual Supply and Market Supply 94
Changes in Supply 95
Change in Quantity Supplied Versus Change in
Supply 97
CHECKPOINT 4.2 99

4.3 Market Equilibrium 100
Price: A Market's Automatic Regulator 100
Predicting Price Changes: Three Questions 101
Effects of Changes in Demand 102
Effects of Changes in Supply 104
Effects of Changes in Both Demand and
Supply 106
CHECKPOINT 4.3 108

CHAPTER SUMMARY 109

CHAPTER CHECKPOINT 110

■ **EYE on YOUR LIFE**
Understanding and Using Demand and Supply 98

■ **EYE on the GLOBAL ECONOMY**
The Markets for Cocoa and Chocolate 103

■ **EYE on the PRICE OF COFFEE**
Why Did the Price of Coffee Rise in 2014? 105

PART 2   A CLOSER LOOK AT MARKETS

CHAPTER 5
Elasticities of Demand and Supply   113
CHAPTER CHECKLIST   113

5.1   The Price Elasticity of Demand   114
Percentage Change in Price   114
Percentage Change in Quantity Demanded   115
Comparing the Percentage Changes in Price and Quantity   115
Elastic and Inelastic Demand   116
Influences on the Price Elasticity of Demand   116
Computing the Price Elasticity of Demand   118
Interpreting the Price Elasticity of Demand Number   119
Elasticity Along a Linear Demand Curve   120
Total Revenue and the Price Elasticity of Demand   122
CHECKPOINT 5.1   125

5.2   The Price Elasticity of Supply   126
Elastic and Inelastic Supply   126
Influences on the Price Elasticity of Supply   126
Computing the Price Elasticity of Supply   128
CHECKPOINT 5.2   130

5.3   Cross Elasticity and Income Elasticity   131
Cross Elasticity of Demand   131
Income Elasticity of Demand   132
CHECKPOINT 5.3   134

CHAPTER SUMMARY   135

CHAPTER CHECKPOINT   136

■ **EYE on the GLOBAL ECONOMY**
Price Elasticities of Demand   121
■ **EYE on ELASTICITY AT THE COFFEE SHOP**
What Do You Do When Starbucks Raises the Price of a Latte?   123
■ **EYE on the U.S. ECONOMY**
Two Applications of the Price Elasticity of Demand   124
■ **EYE on YOUR LIFE**
Your Price Elasticities of Demand   133

CHAPTER 6
Efficiency and Fairness of Markets   139
CHAPTER CHECKLIST   139

6.1   Allocation Methods and Efficiency   140
Resource Allocation Methods   140
Using Resources Efficiently   143
CHECKPOINT 6.1   147

6.2   Value, Price, and Consumer Surplus   148
Demand and Marginal Benefit   148
Consumer Surplus   149
CHECKPOINT 6.2   150

6.3   Cost, Price, and Producer Surplus   151
Supply and Marginal Cost   151
Producer Surplus   152
CHECKPOINT 6.3   153

6.4   Are Markets Efficient?   154
Marginal Benefit Equals Marginal Cost   154
Total Surplus Is Maximized   155
The Invisible Hand   155
Market Failure   157
Sources of Market Failure   158
Alternatives to the Market   159
CHECKPOINT 6.4   160

6.5   Are Markets Fair?   161
It's Not Fair If the *Rules* Aren't Fair   161
It's Not Fair If the *Result* Isn't Fair   161
Compromise   163
CHECKPOINT 6.5   164

CHAPTER SUMMARY   165

CHAPTER CHECKPOINT   166

■ **EYE on the U.S. ECONOMY**
The Invisible Hand and e-Commerce   156
■ **EYE on PRICE GOUGING**
Should Price Gouging Be Illegal?   162
■ **EYE on YOUR LIFE**
Allocation Methods, Efficiency, and Fairness   163

PART 3   HOW GOVERNMENTS INFLUENCE THE ECONOMY

CHAPTER 7
Government Actions in Markets   169
CHAPTER CHECKLIST   169

7.1   Price Ceilings   170
A Rent Ceiling   170
Are Rent Ceilings Efficient?   173
Are Rent Ceilings Fair?   174
If Rent Ceilings Are So Bad, Why Do We
    Have Them?   174
CHECKPOINT 7.1   175

7.2   Price Floors   176
The Minimum Wage   177
Is the Minimum Wage Efficient?   180
Is the Minimum Wage Fair?   181
If the Minimum Wage Is So Bad, Why Do We
    Have It?   181
CHECKPOINT 7.2   182

7.3   Production Quotas   183
Production Quota: An Example   183
CHECKPOINT 7.3   186

CHAPTER SUMMARY   187

CHAPTER CHECKPOINT   188

■   **EYE on the U.S. ECONOMY**
Minimum Wages and Employment   179
■   **EYE on PRICE REGULATION**
Can Congress Repeal the Law of Market Forces?   181
■   **EYE on the GLOBAL ECONOMY**
Production Quotas   183
■   **EYE on YOUR LIFE**
Price Ceilings and Price Floors You Encounter   185

CHAPTER 8
Taxes   191
CHAPTER CHECKLIST   191

8.1   Taxes on Buyers and Sellers   192
Tax Incidence   192
Taxes and Efficiency   193
Tax Burden   194

Incidence, Inefficiency, and Elasticity   194
Incidence, Inefficiency, and the Elasticity of
    Demand   195
Incidence, Inefficiency, and the Elasticity of
    Supply   196
CHECKPOINT 8.1   197

8.2   Income Taxes and Social Security Taxes   198
The Effects of the Income Tax   198
The Social Security Tax   202
CHECKPOINT 8.2   205

8.3   Fairness and the Big Tradeoff   206
The Benefits Principle   206
The Ability-to-Pay Principle   206
Ability to Pay and Tax Progressivity   207
The Big Tradeoff and Alternative Tax
    Proposals   207
CHECKPOINT 8.3   210

CHAPTER SUMMARY   211

CHAPTER CHECKPOINT   212

■   **EYE on the U.S. ECONOMY**
Taxes in the United States Today   199
■   **Eye on CONGRESS**
Does Congress Decide Who Pays the Taxes?   203
■   **EYE on the PAST**
The Origins and History of the U.S.
    Income Tax   204
■   **EYE on YOUR LIFE**
Tax Freedom Day   204
■   **EYE on the U.S. ECONOMY**
The Progressive Income Tax   208

CHAPTER 9
Global Markets in Action   215
CHAPTER CHECKLIST   215

9.1   How Global Markets Work   216
International Trade Today   216
What Drives International Trade?   216
Why the United States Imports T-Shirts   218
Why the United States Exports Airplanes   219
CHECKPOINT 9.1   220

9.2 Winners, Losers, and Net Gains From Trade 221
Gains and Losses from Imports 222
Gains and Losses from Exports 223
CHECKPOINT 9.2 224

9.3 International Trade Restrictions 225
Tariffs 225
Import Quotas 229
Other Import Barriers 231
Export Subsidies 231
CHECKPOINT 9.3 232

9.4 The Case Against Protection 233
Three Traditional Arguments for Protection 233
Four Newer Arguments for Protection 235

Why Is International Trade Restricted? 236
CHECKPOINT 9.4 238

CHAPTER SUMMARY 239

CHAPTER CHECKPOINT 240

■ **EYE on the U.S. ECONOMY**
U.S. Exports and Imports 217

■ **Eye on GLOBALIZATION**
Who Wins and Who Loses from Globalization? 221

■ **EYE on the PAST**
The History of U.S. Tariffs 225

■ **EYE on YOUR LIFE**
International Trade 237

PART 4   MARKET FAILURE AND PUBLIC POLICY

CHAPTER 10
Externalities 243
CHAPTER CHECKLIST 243

Externalities in our Daily Lives 244
Negative Production Externalities 244
Positive Production Externalities 244
Negative Consumption Externalities 245
Positive Consumption Externalities 245

10.1 Negative Externalities: Pollution 246
Private Costs and Social Costs 246
Production and Pollution: How Much? 248
Establish Property Rights 249
Mandate Clean Technology 251
Tax or Cap and Price Pollution 251
CHECKPOINT 10.1 256

10.2 Positive Externalities: Education 257
Private Benefits and Social Benefits 257
Government Actions in the Face of External Benefits 259
CHECKPOINT 10.2 262

CHAPTER SUMMARY 263

CHAPTER CHECKPOINT 264

■ **EYE on YOUR LIFE**
Externalities in Your Life 245

■ **EYE on the U.S. ECONOMY**
U.S. Air Pollution Trends 253

■ **EYE on CLIMATE CHANGE**
How Can We Limit Carbon Emissions? 254

CHAPTER 11
Public Goods and Common Resources 267
CHAPTER CHECKLIST 267

11.1 Classifying Goods and Resources 268
Excludable 268
Rival 268
A Fourfold Classification 268
CHECKPOINT 11.1 270

11.2 Public Goods and The Free-Rider Problem 271
The Free-Rider Problem 271
The Marginal Benefit from a Public Good 272
The Marginal Cost of a Public Good 272
The Efficient Quantity of a Public Good 274
Private Provision: Underproduction 274
Public Provision: Efficient Production 275
Obstacles to Efficient Public Provision 276
CHECKPOINT 11.2 279

11.3 The Tragedy of The Commons 280
Unsustainable Use of a Common Resource 280
Inefficient Use of a Common Resource 281
Using the Commons Efficiently 284
CHECKPOINT 11.3 288

CHAPTER SUMMARY 289

CHAPTER CHECKPOINT 290

■ **EYE on the PAST**
Is a Lighthouse a Public Good? 270

■ **EYE on YOUR LIFE**
A Student's Free-Rider Problem and a Market
Solution 271

■ **EYE on the U.S. INFRASTRUCTURE**
Should America Spend More on Transportation
Infrastructure? 278

■ **EYE on the PAST**
The Commons of England's Middle Ages 280

■ **EYE on the GLOBAL ECONOMY**
The North Atlantic Cod Tragedy of the Commons 282

■ **EYE on the GLOBAL ECONOMY**
ITQs Work 287

CHAPTER 12
Private Information and Healthcare
Markets 293
CHAPTER CHECKLIST 293

12.1 The Lemons Problem and its Solution 294
A Market for Used Cars with a Lemons Problem 294
A Used-Car Market with Dealers' Warranties 298
CHECKPOINT 12.1 300

**12.2 Information Problems in Insurance
Markets** 301
Insurance Markets 301
Asymmetric Information in Insurance 302
Screening in Insurance Markets 304
Separating Equilibrium with Screening 304
CHECKPOINT 12.2 306

12.3 The Economics of Healthcare 307
Healthcare Market Failure 307
Alternative Public Choice Solutions 310
A Reform Idea? 312
CHECKPOINT 12.3 314

CHAPTER SUMMARY 315

CHAPTER CHECKPOINT 316

■ **EYE on the MARKET FOR USED CARS**
How Do You Avoid Buying a Lemon? 298

■ **EYE on the U.S. ECONOMY**
Insurance in the United States 301

■ **EYE on the U.S. ECONOMY**
Healthcare in the United States: A Snapshot 308

■ **EYE on the GLOBAL ECONOMY**
Healthcare Expenditures and Health Outcomes 311

■ **EYE on YOUR LIFE**
Signaling Your Ability 313

PART 5   A CLOSER LOOK AT DECISION MAKERS

CHAPTER 13
Consumer Choice and
Demand 319
CHAPTER CHECKLIST 319

13.1 Consumption Possibilities 320
The Budget Line 320
A Change in the Budget 321
Changes in Prices 322
Prices and the Slope of the Budget Line 323
CHECKPOINT 13.1 325

13.2 Marginal Utility Theory 326
Total Utility 326
Marginal Utility 326
Graphing Tina's Utility Schedules 328

Maximizing Total Utility 328
Finding an Individual Demand Curve 330
CHECKPOINT 13.2 332

13.3 Efficiency, Price, and Value 333
Consumer Efficiency 333
The Paradox of Value 333
CHECKPOINT 13.3 336

CHAPTER SUMMARY 337

CHAPTER CHECKPOINT 338

Appendix: Indifference Curves 341
An Indifference Curve 341
Marginal Rate of Substitution 342
Consumer Equilibrium 343
Deriving the Demand Curve 344

APPENDIX CHECKPOINT 346

   ■ **EYE on the U.S. ECONOMY**
Relative Prices on the Move 324

   ■ **EYE on the PAST**
Jeremy Bentham, William Stanley Jevons,
   and the Birth of Utility 327

   ■ **EYE on SONG DOWNLOADS AND
   STREAMING**
How Much Would You Pay for a Song? 334

   ■ **EYE on YOUR LIFE**
Do You Maximize Your Utility? 336

■ **CHAPTER 14**
Production and Cost 347
   CHAPTER CHECKLIST 347

14.1 Economic Cost and Profit 348
The Firm's Goal 348
Accounting Cost and Profit 348
Opportunity Cost 348
Economic Profit 349
   CHECKPOINT 14.1 351

Short Run and Long Run 352

14.2 Short-Run Production 353
Total Product 353
Marginal Product 354
Average Product 356
   CHECKPOINT 14.2 358

14.3 Short-Run Cost 359
Total Cost 359
Marginal Cost 360
Average Cost 361
Why the Average Total Cost Curve Is U-Shaped 363
Cost Curves and Product Curves 364
Shifts in the Cost Curves 364
   CHECKPOINT 14.3 366

14.4 Long-Run Cost 367
Plant Size and Cost 367
The Long-Run Average Cost Curve 368
   CHECKPOINT 14.4 370

CHAPTER SUMMARY 371

CHAPTER CHECKPOINT 372

   ■ **EYE on YOUR LIFE**
Your Average and Marginal Grades 357

   ■ **EYE on RETAILERS' COSTS**
Which Store Has the Lower Costs: Walmart or
   7-Eleven? 369

PART 6   PRICES, PROFITS, AND INDUSTRY PERFORMANCE

■ **CHAPTER 15**
Perfect Competition 375
   CHAPTER CHECKLIST 375

Market Types 376
Perfect Competition 376
Other Market Types 376

15.1 A Firm's Profit-Maximizing Choices 377
Price Taker 377
Revenue Concepts 377
Profit-Maximizing Output 378
Marginal Analysis and the Supply Decision 380
Temporary Shutdown Decision 381
The Firm's Short-Run Supply Curve 382
   CHECKPOINT 15.1 384

15.2 Output, Price, and Profit In The Short Run 385
Market Supply in the Short Run 385
Short-Run Equilibrium in Normal Times 386
Short-Run Equilibrium in Good Times 387
Short-Run Equilibrium in Bad Times 388
   CHECKPOINT 15.2 389

15.3 Output, Price, and Profit In The Long Run 390
Entry and Exit 391
The Effects of Exit 392
Change in Demand 393
Technological Change 393
Is Perfect Competition Efficient? 396
Is Perfect Competition Fair? 397
   CHECKPOINT 15.3 398

CHAPTER SUMMARY 399

CHAPTER CHECKPOINT 400

   ■ **EYE on RECORD STORES**
Where Have All the Record Stores Gone? 394

   ■ **EYE on YOUR LIFE**
The Perfect Competition That You Encounter 397

CHAPTER 16
Monopoly 403
CHAPTER CHECKLIST 403

16.1 Monopoly and How it Arises 404
No Close Substitute 404
Barrier to Entry 404
Monopoly Price-Setting Strategies 406
CHECKPOINT 16.1 407

16.2 Single-Price Monopoly 408
Price and Marginal Revenue 408
Marginal Revenue and Elasticity 409
Output and Price Decision 410
CHECKPOINT 16.2 412

16.3 Monopoly and Competition Compared 413
Output and Price 413
Is Monopoly Efficient? 414
Is Monopoly Fair? 415
Rent Seeking 415
CHECKPOINT 16.3 417

16.4 Price Discrimination 418
Price Discrimination and Consumer Surplus 418
Profiting by Price Discriminating 419
Perfect Price Discrimination 420
Price Discrimination and Efficiency 422
CHECKPOINT 16.4 423

16.5 Monopoly Regulation 424
Efficient Regulation of a Natural Monopoly 424
Second-Best Regulation of a Natural Monopoly 425
CHECKPOINT 16.5 430

CHAPTER SUMMARY 431

CHAPTER CHECKPOINT 432

■ **EYE on the U.S. ECONOMY**
Information-Age Monopolies 406
■ **EYE on the U.S. ECONOMY**
Airline Price Discrimination 422
■ **EYE on MICROSOFT**
Are Microsoft's Prices Too High? 427
■ **EYE on YOUR LIFE**
Monopoly in Your Everyday Life 428

CHAPTER 17
Monopolistic Competition 435
CHAPTER CHECKLIST 435

17.1 What is Monopolistic Competition? 436
Describing Monopolistic Competition 436
Identifying Monopolistic Competition 437
CHECKPOINT 17.1 441

17.2 Output and Price Decisions 442
The Firm's Profit-Maximizing Decision 442
Profit Maximizing Might Be Loss Minimizing 443
Long Run: Zero Economic Profit 444
Monopolistic Competition and Perfect Competition 445
Is Monopolistic Competition Efficient? 446
CHECKPOINT 17.2 447

17.3 Innovation and Advertising 448
Design and Quality Decision 448
Advertising 448
The Demand for Advertising 449
The Supply of Advertising 453
Equilibrium and Efficiency in the Advertising Market 453
CHECKPOINT 17.3 454

CHAPTER SUMMARY 455

CHAPTER CHECKPOINT 456

■ **EYE on the U.S. ECONOMY**
Examples of Monopolistic Competition 440
■ **EYE on SMARTPHONES**
Which Smartphone? 451
■ **EYE on YOUR LIFE**
Some Selling Costs You Pay 452

CHAPTER 18
Oligopoly 459
CHAPTER CHECKLIST 459

18.1 What is Oligopoly? 460
Small Number of Firms 460
Barriers to Entry 460
Identifying Oligopoly 462
CHECKPOINT 18.1 463

18.2 The Oligopolists' Dilemma 464
  Monopoly Outcome 464
  Perfect Competition Outcome 465
  Other Possible Cartel Breakdowns 465
  The Oligopoly Cartel Dilemma 466
  CHECKPOINT 18.2 468

18.3 Game Theory 469
  What Is a Game? 469
  The Prisoners' Dilemma 469
  The Duopolists' Dilemma 471
  The Payoff Matrix 471
  Advertising and Research Games in Oligopoly 472
  Repeated Games 474
  Is Oligopoly Efficient? 475
  CHECKPOINT 18.3 476

18.4 Antitrust Law 477
  The Antitrust Laws 477
  Three Antitrust Policy Debates 477

Recent Antitrust Showcase: The United States Versus
  Microsoft 479
  Merger Rules 480
  CHECKPOINT 18.4 482

CHAPTER SUMMARY 483

CHAPTER CHECKPOINT 484

■ **EYE on the U.S. ECONOMY**
Examples of Oligopoly 462

■ **EYE on the GLOBAL ECONOMY**
The OPEC Global Oil Cartel 467

■ **EYE on YOUR LIFE**
A Game You Might Play 474

■ **EYE on the WIRELESS OLIGOPOLY**
Is Four Too Few? 475

■ **EYE on the U.S. ECONOMY**
No Wireless Service Merger 481

PART 7   INCOMES AND INEQUALITY

CHAPTER 19
Markets for Factors of Production 487
  CHAPTER CHECKLIST 487

  The Anatomy of Factor Markets 488

19.1 The Demand for A Factor of Production 489
  Value of Marginal Product 489
  A Firm's Demand for Labor 490
  A Firm's Demand for Labor Curve 491
  Changes in the Demand for Labor 492
  CHECKPOINT 19.1 493

19.2 Labor Markets 494
  The Supply of Labor 494
  Influences on the Supply of Labor 495
  Competitive Labor Market Equilibrium 496
  Labor Unions 498
  CHECKPOINT 19.2 500

19.3 Capital and Natural Resource Markets 501
  Capital Markets 501
  Land Markets 502
  Nonrenewable Natural Resource Markets 503
  CHECKPOINT 19.3 506

CHAPTER SUMMARY 507

CHAPTER CHECKPOINT 508

■ **EYE on the COACH**
Why Is a Coach Worth $7 Million? 497

■ **EYE on YOUR LIFE**
Job Choice and Income Prospects 499

■ **EYE on the GLOBAL ECONOMY**
Oil and Metal Prices 504

CHAPTER 20
Economic Inequality 511
  CHAPTER CHECKLIST 511

20.1 Measuring Economic Inequality 512
  Lorenz Curves 513
  Inequality over Time 514
  Poverty 515
  Economic Mobility 516
  CHECKPOINT 20.1 519

20.2 How economic Inequality Arises 520
  Human Capital 520
  Discrimination 523

Financial and Physical Capital   524
Entrepreneurial Ability   524
Personal and Family Characteristics   524
CHECKPOINT 20.2   525

20.3 Income Redistribution   526
How Governments Redistribute Income   526
The Scale of Income Redistribution   527
Why We Redistribute Income   529
The Major Welfare Challenge   530
CHECKPOINT 20.3   532

CHAPTER SUMMARY   533

CHAPTER CHECKPOINT   534

■ **EYE on the GLOBAL ECONOMY**
Global Inequality   517

■ **Eye on INEQUALITY**
Who Are the Rich and the Poor?   518

■ **EYE on the U.S. ECONOMY**
Does Education Pay?   522

■ **EYE on the U.S. ECONOMY**
Sex and Race Earnings Differences   523

■ **EYE on YOUR LIFE**
What You Pay and Gain Through
    Redistribution   531

PART 8   MONITORING THE MACROECONOMY

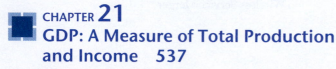

CHAPTER **21**
GDP: A Measure of Total Production and Income   537
CHAPTER CHECKLIST   537

21.1 GDP, Income, and Expenditure   538
GDP Defined   538
Circular Flows in the U.S. Economy   539
Expenditure Equals Income   540
CHECKPOINT 21.1   542

21.2 Measuring U.S. GDP   543
The Expenditure Approach   543
The Income Approach   545
GDP and Related Measures of Production and Income   547
Real GDP and Nominal GDP   548
Calculating Real GDP   548
Using the Real GDP Numbers   549
CHECKPOINT 21.2   550

21.3 The Uses and Limitations of Real GDP   551
The Standard of Living Over Time   551
Tracking the Course of the Business Cycle   552
The Standard of Living Among Countries   554
Goods and Services Omitted from GDP   555
Other Influences on the Standard of Living   556
CHECKPOINT 21.3   558

CHAPTER SUMMARY   559

CHAPTER CHECKPOINT   560

Appendix: Measuring Real GDP   563
The Problem With Base Year Prices   563
Value Production in the Prices of Adjacent Years   563
APPENDIX CHECKPOINT   566

■ **EYE on the U.S. ECONOMY**
Is a Computer Program an Intermediate Good or a
    Final Good?   544

■ **EYE on BOOMS AND BUSTS**
How Do We Track Economic Booms and Busts?   554

■ **EYE on YOUR LIFE**
Making GDP Personal   556

■ **EYE on the GLOBAL ECONOMY**
Which Country Has the Highest Standard of
    Living?   557

CHAPTER **22**
Jobs and Unemployment   567
CHAPTER CHECKLIST   567

22.1 Labor Market Indicators   568
Current Population Survey   568
Population Survey Criteria   568
Three Labor Market Indicators   569
Alternative Measures of Unemployment   570
CHECKPOINT 22.1   572

22.2 Labor Market Trends and Fluctuations   573
Unemployment Rate   573
The Participation Rate   574

Alternative Measures of Unemployment   576

CHECKPOINT 22.2   577

22.3 Unemployment and Full Employment   578

Frictional Unemployment   578
Structural Unemployment   578
Cyclical Unemployment   579
"Natural" Unemployment   579
Unemployment and Real GDP   581

CHECKPOINT 22.3   584

CHAPTER SUMMARY   585

CHAPTER CHECKPOINT   586

■ **EYE on the U.S. ECONOMY**
The Current Population Survey   571

■ **EYE on the GLOBAL ECONOMY**
Unemployment and Labor Force Participation   575

■ **EYE on the U.S. ECONOMY**
How Long Does it Take to Find a Job?   579

■ **EYE on FULL EMPLOYMENT**
Are We Back at Full Employment?   580

■ **EYE on YOUR LIFE**
Your Labor Market Status and Activity   583

CHAPTER 23
The CPI and the Cost of Living   589

CHAPTER CHECKLIST   589

23.1 The Consumer Price Index   590

Reading the CPI Numbers   590
Constructing the CPI   590
The CPI Market Basket   590
The Monthly Price Survey   591
Calculating the CPI   592

Measuring Inflation and Deflation   593
The Price Level, Inflation, and Deflation in the United States   593

CHECKPOINT 23.1   595

23.2 The CPI and Other Price Level Measures   596

Sources of Bias in the CPI   596
The Magnitude of the Bias   597
Two Consequences of the CPI Bias   598
Alternative Consumer Price Indexes   598

CHECKPOINT 23.2   601

23.3 Nominal and Real Values   602

Dollars and Cents at Different Dates   602
Nominal and Real Values in Macroeconomics   603
Nominal GDP and Real GDP   603
Nominal Wage Rate and Real Wage Rate   604
Nominal Interest Rate and Real Interest Rate   606

CHECKPOINT 23.3   608

CHAPTER SUMMARY   609

CHAPTER CHECKPOINT   610

■ **EYE on the PAST**
700 Years of Inflation and Deflation   594

■ **EYE on the U.S. ECONOMY**
Measuring and Forecasting Inflation: The Sticky-Price CPI   600

■ **EYE on the U.S. ECONOMY**
Deflating the GDP Balloon   603

■ **EYE on the PAST**
The Nominal and Real Wage Rates of Presidents of the United States   605

■ **EYE on BOX OFFICE HITS**
Which Movie *Really* Was the Biggest Box Office Hit?   606

■ **EYE on YOUR LIFE**
A Student's CPI   607

PART 9   THE REAL ECONOMY

CHAPTER 24
Potential GDP and the Natural Unemployment Rate   613

CHAPTER CHECKLIST   613

Macroeconomic Approaches and Pathways
The Three Main Schools of Thought   614
Today's Consensus   615
The Road Ahead   616

24.1 Potential GDP   617

The Production Function   618
The Labor Market   619

CHECKPOINT 24.1   625

24.2 The Natural Unemployment Rate   626

Job Search   627
Job Rationing   628

CHECKPOINT 24.2   632

CHAPTER SUMMARY 633

CHAPTER CHECKPOINT 634

■ **EYE on the U.S. ECONOMY**
The Lucas Wedge and the Okun Gap 616

■ **EYE on the GLOBAL ECONOMY**
Potential GDP in the United States and the European Union 617

■ **EYE on POTENTIAL GDP**
Why Do Americans Earn More and Produce More Than Europeans? 624

■ **EYE on the PAST**
The Natural Unemployment Rate Over Seven Decades 626

■ **EYE on the GLOBAL ECONOMY**
Unemployment Benefits and the Natural Unemployment Rate 628

■ **EYE on the U.S. ECONOMY**
The Federal Minimum Wage 631

■ **EYE on YOUR LIFE**
Natural Unemployment 631

CHAPTER 25
Economic Growth 637
CHAPTER CHECKLIST 637

25.1 The Basics of Economic Growth 638
Calculating Growth Rates 638
The Magic of Sustained Growth 640
CHECKPOINT 25.1 641

25.2 Labor Productivity Growth 642
Labor Productivity 642
Saving and Investment in Physical Capital 642
Expansion of Human Capital and Discovery of New Technologies 644
Combined Influences Bring Labor Productivity Growth 646
CHECKPOINT 25.2 649

25.3 Causes and Effects of Economic Growth 650
Old Growth Theory 650
New Growth Theory 650
Economic Growth and the Distribution of Income 652
CHECKPOINT 25.3 655

25.4 Achieving Faster Growth 656
Preconditions for Economic Growth 656
Policies to Achieve Faster Growth 657
How Much Difference Can Policy Make? 658
CHECKPOINT 25.4 660

CHAPTER SUMMARY 661

CHAPTER CHECKPOINT 662

■ **EYE on the PAST**
How Fast Has Real GDP per Person Grown? 639

■ **EYE on the U.S. ECONOMY**
U.S. Growth Is Slowing 640

■ **EYE on the U.S. ECONOMY**
U.S. Labor Productivity Growth Since 1960 648

■ **EYE on the U.S. ECONOMY**
The Changing Shares in the Gains from Economic Growth 653

■ **EYE on YOUR LIFE**
How You Influence and Are Influenced by Economic Growth 654

■ **EYE on RICH AND POOR NATIONS**
Why Are Some Nations Rich and Others Poor? 659

CHAPTER 26
Finance, Saving, and Investment 665
CHAPTER CHECKLIST 665

26.1 Financial Institutions and Financial Markets 666
Some Finance Definitions 666
Markets for Financial Capital 667
Financial Institutions 669
Insolvency and Illiquidity 670
Interest Rates and Asset Prices 670
CHECKPOINT 26.1 671

26.2 The Loanable Funds Market 672
Flows in the Loanable Funds Market 672
The Demand for Loanable Funds 672
The Supply of Loanable Funds 675
Equilibrium in the Loanable Funds Market 678
Changes in Demand and Supply 679
CHECKPOINT 26.2 681

26.3 Government in Loanable Funds Market 682

A Government Budget Surplus 682

A Government Budget Deficit 683

CHECKPOINT 26.3 686

CHAPTER SUMMARY 687

CHAPTER CHECKPOINT 688

■ **EYE on the U.S. ECONOMY**
Interest Rate Patterns 668

■ **EYE on the U.S. ECONOMY**
The Loanable Funds Market in a Financial Crisis 680

■ **EYE on YOUR LIFE**
Your Participation in the Loanable Funds Market 684

■ **EYE on FINANCIAL MARKETS**
Why Have Interest Rates Been So Low? 685

PART 10   THE MONEY ECONOMY

■ **CHAPTER 27**
The Monetary System 691
CHAPTER CHECKLIST 691

27.1 What is Money? 692

Definition of Money 692

The Functions of Money 692

Money Today 694

Official Measures of Money: M1 and M2 694

Checks, Credit Cards, Debit Cards, and Mobile Wallets 695

An Embryonic New Money: E-Cash 696

CHECKPOINT 27.1 697

27.2 The Banking System 698

Commercial Banks 698

Thrift Institutions 701

Money Market Funds 701

CHECKPOINT 27.2 702

27.3 The Federal Reserve System 703

The Structure of the Federal Reserve 703

The Fed's Policy Tools 704

How the Fed's Policy Tools Work 705

CHECKPOINT 27.3 706

27.4 Regulating the Quantity of Money 707

Creating Deposits by Making Loans 707

How Open Market Operations Change the Monetary Base 709

The Multiplier Effect of an Open Market Operation 712

The Money Multiplier 713

CHECKPOINT 27.4 716

CHAPTER SUMMARY 717

CHAPTER CHECKPOINT 718

■ **EYE on the PAST**
The "Invention" of Banking 699

■ **EYE on the U.S. ECONOMY**
Commercial Banks Under Stress in the Financial Crisis 701

■ **EYE on YOUR LIFE**
Money and Your Role in Its Creation 707

■ **EYE on CREATING MONEY**
How Does the Fed Create Money and Regulate Its Quantity? 714

■ **CHAPTER 28**
Money, Interest, and Inflation 721
CHAPTER CHECKLIST 721

Where We are and Where We're Heading 722

The Real Economy 722

The Money Economy 722

Real and Money Interactions and Policy 722

28.1 Money and the Interest Rate 723

The Demand for Money 723

Changes in the Demand for Money 725

The Supply of Money 726

The Nominal Interest Rate 726

Changing the Interest Rate 728

CHECKPOINT 28.1 730

28.2 Money, the Price Level, and Inflation 731

The Money Market in the Long Run 731

A Change in the Quantity of Money 733

The Price Level in a Baby-Sitting Club 734

The Quantity Theory of Money 734

Inflation and the Quantity Theory of Money 736

Hyperinflation 739

CHECKPOINT 28.2 740

28.3 The Cost of Inflation 741
Tax Costs 741
Shoe-Leather Costs 742
Confusion Costs 742
Uncertainty Costs 743
How Big Is the Cost of Inflation? 743
CHECKPOINT 28.3 744

CHAPTER SUMMARY 745

CHAPTER CHECKPOINT 746

■ **EYE on the U.S. ECONOMY**
Credit Cards and Money 728
■ **EYE on YOUR LIFE**
Money Holding and Fed Watching 729
■ **EYE on INFLATION**
What Causes Inflation? 738
■ **EYE on the PAST**
Hyperinflation in Germany in the 1920s 739

PART 11   ECONOMIC FLUCTUATIONS

CHAPTER **29**
Aggregate Supply and Aggregate Demand 749
CHAPTER CHECKLIST 749

29.1 Aggregate Supply 750
Aggregate Supply Basics 750
Changes in Aggregate Supply 753
CHECKPOINT 29.1 755

29.2 Aggregate Demand 756
Aggregate Demand Basics 756
Changes in Aggregate Demand 758
The Aggregate Demand Multiplier 760
CHECKPOINT 29.2 761

29.3 Explaining Economic Trends and Fluctuations 762
Macroeconomic Equilibrium 762
Three Types of Macroeconomic Equilibrium 763
Economic Growth and Inflation Trends 764
The Business Cycle 765
Inflation Cycles 766
Deflation and the Great Depression 768
CHECKPOINT 29.3 770

CHAPTER SUMMARY 771

CHAPTER CHECKPOINT 772

■ **EYE on the U.S. ECONOMY**
U.S. Economic Growth, Inflation, and the Business Cycle 764
■ **EYE on YOUR LIFE**
Using the *AS-AD* Model 768
■ **EYE on the BUSINESS CYCLE**
Why Did the U.S. Economy Go into Recession in 2008? 769

CHAPTER **30**
Aggregate Expenditure Multiplier 775
CHAPTER CHECKLIST 775

30.1 Expenditure Plans and Real GDP 776
The Consumption Function 776
Imports and Real GDP 780
CHECKPOINT 30.1 781

30.2 Equilibrium Expenditure 782
Induced Expenditure and Autonomous Expenditure 782
Aggregate Planned Expenditure and Real GDP 782
Equilibrium Expenditure 784
Convergence to Equilibrium 785
CHECKPOINT 30.2 787

30.3 Expenditure Multipliers 788
The Basic Idea of the Multiplier 788
The Size of the Multiplier 789
The Multiplier and the *MPC* 789
The Multiplier, Imports, and Income Taxes 790
Business-Cycle Turning Points 792
CHECKPOINT 30.3 793

30.4 The *AD* Curve and Equilibrium Expenditure 794
Deriving the *AD* Curve from Equilibrium Expenditure 794
CHECKPOINT 30.4 796

CHAPTER SUMMARY 797

CHAPTER CHECKPOINT 798

■ **EYE on the U.S. ECONOMY**
The U.S. Consumption Function 780

■ **EYE on the PAST**
Say's Law and Keynes' Principle of Effective
  Demand   786

■ **EYE on YOUR LIFE**
Looking for Multipliers   791

■ **EYE on the MULTIPLIER**
How Big Is the Government Expenditure
  Multiplier?   792

 **CHAPTER 31**
The Short-Run Policy Tradeoff   801
  CHAPTER CHECKLIST   801

31.1 The Short-Run Phillips Curve   802
  Aggregate Supply and the Short-Run Phillips
    Curve   803
  Aggregate Demand Fluctuations   805
  Why Bother with the Phillips Curve?   806
  CHECKPOINT 31.1   807

31.2 Short-Run and Long-Run Phillips Curves   808
  The Long-Run Phillips Curve   808
  Expected Inflation   809
  The Natural Rate Hypothesis   810

Changes in the Natural Unemployment Rate   811
Have Changes in the Natural Unemployment Rate
  Changed the Tradeoff?   812
  CHECKPOINT 31.2   814

**31.3 Influencing Inflation and
  Unemployment**   815
  Influencing the Expected Inflation Rate   815
  Targeting the Unemployment Rate   816
  CHECKPOINT 31.3   818

CHAPTER SUMMARY   819

CHAPTER CHECKPOINT   820

■ **EYE on the GLOBAL ECONOMY**
Inflation and Unemployment   805

■ **EYE on the PAST**
The U.S. Phillips Curve   806

■ **EYE on the PAST**
A Live Test of the Natural Rate Hypothesis   811

■ **EYE on the TRADEOFF**
Can We Have Low Unemployment *and* Low
  Inflation?   813

■ **EYE on YOUR LIFE**
The Short-Run Tradeoff in Your Life   817

PART 12   MACROECONOMIC POLICY

 **CHAPTER 32**
Fiscal Policy   823
  CHAPTER CHECKLIST   823

32.1 The Federal Budget   824
  The Institutions and Laws   824
  Budget Balance and Debt   824
  The Federal Budget in Fiscal 2017   825
  A Fiscal Policy Challenge   828
  Generational Accounting   828
  CHECKPOINT 32.1   830

32.2 Fiscal Stimulus   831
  Fiscal Policy and Aggregate Demand   831
  Automatic Fiscal Policy   831
  Cyclical and Structural Budget Balances   832
  Discretionary Fiscal Policy   833
  A Successful Fiscal Stimulus   834
  Limitations of Discretionary Fiscal Policy   836
  CHECKPOINT 32.2   837

**32.3 The Supply Side: Potential GDP and
  Growth**   838
  Full Employment and Potential GDP   838
  Fiscal Policy, Employment, and Potential GDP   838
  Fiscal Policy and Potential GDP: A Graphical
    Analysis   840
  Taxes, Deficits, and Economic Growth   841
  The Supply-Side Debate   842
  Long-Run Fiscal Policy Effects   843
  CHECKPOINT 32.3   844

CHAPTER SUMMARY   845

CHAPTER CHECKPOINT   846

■ **EYE on the GLOBAL ECONOMY**
The U.S. Budget in Global Perspective   826

■ **EYE on the PAST**
Federal Tax Revenues, Outlays, Deficits, and Debt   827

■ **EYE on the U.S. ECONOMY**
Fiscal and Generational Imbalances   829

■ **EYE on the U.S. ECONOMY**
The U.S. Structural and Cyclical Budget Balances   832

■ **EYE on FISCAL STIMULUS**
Can Fiscal Stimulus End a Recession?   835

■ **EYE on the GLOBAL ECONOMY**
Some Real-World Tax Wedges   839

■ **EYE on YOUR LIFE**
Your Views on Fiscal Policy and How Fiscal Policy
   Affects You   843

CHAPTER **33**
Monetary Policy   849
CHAPTER CHECKLIST   849

33.1 How The Fed Conducts Monetary Policy   850
Monetary Policy Objectives   850
Operational "Maximum Employment" Goal   851
Operational "Stable Prices" Goal   851
Responsibility for Monetary Policy   852
Policy Instrument   852
Hitting the Federal Funds Rate Target   854
Restoring Financial Stability in a Financial Crisis   855
CHECKPOINT 33.1   857

33.2 Monetary Policy Transmission   858
Quick Overview   858
Interest Rate Changes   858
Exchange Rate Changes   860
Money and Bank Loans   860
The Long-Term Real Interest Rate   861
Expenditure Plans   861
The Fed Fights Recession   862
The Fed Fights Inflation   864
Loose Links and Long and Variable Lags   866
A Final Reality Check   866
CHECKPOINT 33.2   867

33.3 Alternative Monetary Policy Strategies   868
An Interest Rate Rule   868
A Monetary Base Rule   868
Inflation Targeting   869
Money Targeting Rule   871
CHECKPOINT 33.3   872

CHAPTER SUMMARY   873

CHAPTER CHECKPOINT   874

■ **EYE on the FED IN A CRISIS**
Did the Fed Save Us From Another Great
   Depression?   856

■ **EYE on the U.S. ECONOMY**
The Fed's Decisions Versus Two Rules   869

■ **EYE on the GLOBAL ECONOMY**
Inflation Targeting Around the World   870

■ **EYE on YOUR LIFE**
Your Views on Monetary Policy and How Monetary
   Policy Affects You   871

CHAPTER **34**
International Finance   877
CHAPTER CHECKLIST   877

34.1 Financing International Trade   878
Balance of Payments Accounts   878
Borrowers and Lenders, Debtors and Creditors   880
Current Account Balance   881
CHECKPOINT 34.1   884

34.2 The Exchange Rate   885
Demand in the Foreign Exchange Market   886
The Law of Demand for Foreign Exchange   886
Changes in the Demand for Dollars   887
Supply in the Foreign Exchange Market   889
The Law of Supply of Foreign Exchange   889
Changes in the Supply of Dollars   890
Market Equilibrium   892
Exchange Rate Expectations   894
Purchasing Power Parity   894
Monetary Policy and the Exchange Rate   896
Pegging the Exchange Rate   896
The People's Bank of China in the Foreign Exchange
   Market   897
CHECKPOINT 34.2   900

CHAPTER SUMMARY   901

CHAPTER CHECKPOINT   902

■ **EYE on the U.S. ECONOMY**
The U.S. Balance of Payments   879

■ **EYE on the GLOBAL ECONOMY**
Current Account Balances Around the World   883

■ **EYE on the DOLLAR**
Why Does Our Dollar Fluctuate?   893

■ **EYE on the GLOBAL ECONOMY**
Purchasing Power Parity   895

■ **EYE on the GLOBAL ECONOMY**
The Managed Yuan   899

■ **EYE on YOUR LIFE**
Your Foreign Exchange Transactions   899

Glossary   G-1
Index   I-1
Credits   C-1

Preface

Students know that throughout their lives they will make economic decisions and be influenced by economic forces. They want to understand the economic principles that can help them navigate these forces and guide their decisions. *Foundations of Economics* is our attempt to satisfy this want.

The response to our earlier editions from hundreds of colleagues across the United States and throughout the world tells us that most of you agree with our view that the principles course must do four things well. It must

- Motivate with compelling issues and questions
- Focus on core ideas
- Steer a path between an overload of detail and too much left unsaid
- Encourage and aid learning by doing

The Foundations icon with its four blocks (on the cover and throughout the book) symbolizes this four-point approach that has guided all our choices in writing this text and creating its comprehensive teaching and learning supplements.

WHAT'S NEW IN THE EIGHTH EDITION

New in this Eighth Edition revision are: A further fine-tuning of the content; an enhanced focus on outcome-driven teaching and learning; and a further large investment in enhanced digital features to bring economics to life and provide an exciting interactive experience for the student on all platforms and devices.

■ Fine-Tuning the Content

The content of this revision is driven by the drama of the extraordinary period of economic history in which we are living and its rich display of events and forces through which students can be motivated to discover the economic way of thinking. Persistent slow economic growth; increasing concentration of wealth; headwinds from Europe's stagnant economy and the UK decision to leave the economic union (Brexit); ongoing tensions arising from the loss of American jobs to offshore outsourcing and the political popularity of trade protection; a slowing pace of China's expansion; enhanced concern about carbon emission and climate change; relentless pressure on the federal budget from the demands of an aging population and a sometimes dysfunctional Congress with its associated rising government debt; the dilemma posed by slow, almost decade-long recovery from the global financial crisis and recession and the related question of when and how fast to exit an era of extreme monetary stimulus. These are just a few of these interest-arousing events. All of them feature at the appropriate points in our new edition.

Every chapter contains many small changes, all designed to enhance clarity and currency, and the text and examples are all thoroughly updated to reflect the most recently available data and events.

Because the previous edition's revision was so extensive and well-received, we have limited our interventions and changes in this Eighth Edition to addressing the small number of issues raised by our reviewers and users, ensuring that we are thoroughly up-to-date, and focusing on the new digital tools that we've just described. Nonetheless, some changes that we now summarize are worth noting.

■ Notable Content Changes in Micro

In Chapter 1, Getting Started, we have added a new section, *Economics as a Life Skill*, which explains how economics is used as a decision tool, the scientific method the subject employs, and economics as an aid to critical thinking. A new *Eye on Your Life* looks at the BLS data on student time allocation (which contains some surprises).

In Chapter 3, The Economic Problem, we show explicitly how the outward-bowed production possibilities frontier arises from exploiting comparative advantage.

Chapter 7, Government Actions in Markets, has a new section on production quotas, which explains why producers like them and illustrates how a quota expands producer surplus.

Chapter 8, Taxes, explains the Flat Tax and Fair Tax proposals and compares their efficiency and equity properties with those of the existing tax code.

In Chapter 10, Externalities, we have expanded our discussion of carbon emissions and the global challenge of achieving an efficient use of energy resources.

Chapter 11, Public Goods and Common Resources, now uses the efficient provision of transportation infrastructure as its motivating example and discusses the underprovision that results from limited revenue sources.

Chapter 12, retitled Private Information and Healthcare Markets, has a new and expanded coverage of the economics of healthcare insurance and services. It identifies the sources of healthcare market failure and describes and compares alternative solutions including Obamacare and the healthcare systems of Canada and Europe.

In Chapter 20, Economic Inequality, we have broadened our examination of inequality trends with a focus on the income share of the top one percent—the great compression through the mid-1970s and the great divergence of the past 40 years. We have also expanded our coverage of mobility up and down the income quintiles.

■ Notable Content Changes in Macro

Chapter 22, Jobs and Unemployment, is motivated by the question of whether we are back at full employment. In seeking an answer, the chapter adds to the standard list of job market indicators the new Z-Pop measure of the percentage of the population that is fully occupied.

Chapter 23, The CPI and the Cost of Living, explains and presents data on the new "Sticky Price CPI" and its related "Flexible Price CPI" as an attempt to measure the underlying inflation rate.

In Chapter 25, Economic Growth, we have added an account of who gets the benefits of economic growth with a dramatic demonstration of the gains by the top one percent compared with the gains of the other 99 percent.

Chapter 32, Fiscal Policy, has a new and expanded explanation of the concepts of fiscal imbalance and generational imbalance and the magnitudes of these imbalances in the United States today.

Chapter 33, Monetary Policy, has a new discussion of the rules versus discretion dichotomy and a description of both the Taylor interest rate rule and the McCallum monetary base growth rate rule.

Outcome-Driven Teaching and Learning

An overarching revision message is that this text, its customized MyEconLab, and classroom resources are built to support an outcome-driven teaching and learning program in which the principles of economics course strengthens

- Problem solving
- Critical thinking
- Decision making
- Citizenship

Problem solving is central to the *Foundations* story. A Checkpoint at the end of each topic, typically three per chapter, provides a pause and opportunity to check understanding with problems, one of which is driven by a recent news clip, and worked solutions. A series of MyEconLab Solutions Videos then give the student an alternative way of reviewing the solutions to these problems.

Critical thinking is encouraged and supported through a series of interactive exercises in MyEconLab. In each chapter, there is one exercise that is based on the question or issue that opens and motivates the chapter, and a second that builds from an *Economics in Your Life* feature.

Enhanced eText

The new Enhanced Pearson eText gives students access to their textbook anytime, anywhere. In addition to note-taking, highlighting, and bookmarking, the Pearson eText offers interactive and sharing features. Students actively read and learn through embedded and auto-graded practice, real-time data-graphs, animations, author videos, and more. Instructors can share comments or highlights, and students can add their own, for a tight community of learners in any class.

The new eText includes:

- A Big Picture Video that motivates and summarizes each chapter and provides an outline answer to the chapter's motivating question.
- A series of Concept Videos that illustrate and explain the key ideas in each section of a chapter. These videos also contain animations and explanations of each figure, which can be played separately.
- A series of Solutions Videos that walk the student through the solutions to the Practice Problems and In the News exercises in each Checkpoint.
- Interactive data graphs that display real-time data from the St. Louis Federal Reserve data base, FRED.

- Study Plan links that provide opportunities for more practice with problems similar to those in the text, some with real-time FRED data, that give targeted feedback to guide the student in answering the exercises.
- Key Terms Quiz links that provide opportunities for students to check their knowledge of the definitions and uses of the key terms.

THE FOUNDATIONS VISION

■ Focus on Core Concepts

Each chapter of *Foundations* concentrates on a manageable number of main ideas (most commonly three or four) and reinforces each idea several times throughout the chapter. This patient, confidence-building approach guides students through unfamiliar terrain and helps them to focus their efforts on the most important tools and concepts of our discipline.

■ Many Learning Tools for Many Learning Styles

Foundations' integrated print and electronic package builds on the basic fact that students have a variety of learning styles. Students have powerful tools at their fingertips: Within the eText, they can get an immediate sense of the content of a chapter by playing the Big Picture video; learn the key ideas by playing the Concept videos; and get a quick walkthrough of the Checkpoint Practice Problems and In the News exercises with the Solutions videos.

In MyEconLab, students can complete all Checkpoint problems and In the News exercises online and get instant feedback; work with interactive graphs and real-time data graphs; assess their skills by taking Practice Tests; receive a personalized Study Plan; and step-by-step help through the learning aid called "Help Me Solve This."

■ Diagrams That Tell the Whole Story

We developed the style of our diagrams with extensive feedback from faculty focus-group participants and student reviewers. All of our figures make consistent use of color to show the direction of shifts and contain detailed, numbered captions designed to direct students' attention step-by-step through the action.

Because beginning students of economics are often apprehensive about working with graphs, we have made a special effort to present material in as many as three ways—with graphs, words, and tables—in the same figure. In an innovation that seems necessary, but is to our knowledge unmatched, nearly all of the information supporting a figure appears on the same page as the figure itself. No more flipping pages back and forth!

■ Real-World Connections That Bring Theory to Life

Students learn best when they can see the purpose of what they are studying, apply it to illuminate the world around them, and use it in their lives.

Eye On boxes offer fresh new examples to help students see that economics is everywhere. Current and recent events appear in *Eye on the U.S. Economy* boxes; we place current U.S. economic events in global and historical perspectives in our *Eye on the Global Economy* and *Eye on the Past* boxes; and we show how students can use economics in day-to-day decisions in *Eye on Your Life* boxes.

Each chapter-opening question is answered in an Eye On box that helps students see the economics behind a key issue facing the world and highlights a major aspect of the chapter's story.

ORGANIZATION

We have organized the sequence of material and chapters in what we think is the most natural order in which to cover the material. But we recognize that there are alternative views on the best order. We have kept this fact and the need for flexibility firmly in mind throughout the text. Many alternative sequences work, and the Flexibility Charts on pp. xxxiv–xxxv explains the alternative pathways through the chapters. In using the flexibility information, keep in mind that the best sequence is the one in which we present the material. And even chapters that the flexibility charts identify as strictly optional are better covered than omitted.

MYECONLAB   MyEconLab

MyEconLab has been designed and refined with a single purpose in mind: to create those moments of understanding that transform the difficult into the clear and obvious. With comprehensive homework, quiz, test, activity, and tutorial options, instructors can manage all their assessment needs in one program.

- All of the Checkpoint and Chapter Checkpoint Problems and Applications can be assigned and automatically graded in MyEconLab.
- Extra problems and applications, including algorithmic, draw-graph, and numerical exercises can be used for student practice or instructor assignment.
- Problems and applications that use real-time data continuously update directly from a feed to the Federal Reserve Bank of St. Louis.
- Test Item File questions can be assigned in quiz, test, or homework.
- The Custom Exercise Builder gives instructors the flexibility to create their own problems for assignment.
- The Gradebook records each student's performance and time spent on the Tests and Study Plan and generates reports by student or by chapter.

New for the Eighth Edition is an Enhanced Pearson eText, which includes embedded and auto-graded practice, real-time data graphs, animations, videos, and more. Instructors can share comments or highlights, and students can add their own, for a tight community of learners in any class.

   With the Pearson eText 2.0 mobile app students can access the Enhanced eText and all its functionality from their computer, tablet, or cell phone. Because the student's progress is synced across all of their devices, they can stop what they're doing on one device and pick up again later on another one—without breaking their stride.

■ Features of the Enhanced eText

Big Picture Videos   Big Picture videos, tied to the Chapter Checklist, set the stage for the main concept that will be introduced throughout the chapter. Students can use these videos to prepare for today's lecture or to help them focus on main chapter ideas.

DEMAND and SUPPLY: THE BIG PICTURE

Buyers like a low price, and the lower the price, the greater is the quantity they plan to buy—the **law of demand**.

Sellers like a high price, and the higher the price, the greater is the quantity they plan to sell—the **law of supply**.

Too high a price brings a surplus, and too low a price brings a shortage.

When there is a surplus, the price falls; and when there is a shortage, the price rises—the **law of market forces**.

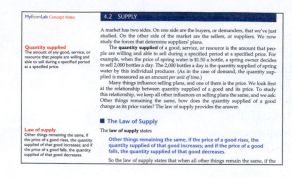

Concept Videos Concept videos accompany every major section of each chapter and are designed to briefly present the major concepts and graphical tools covered within key sections. Using text, audio, and animation, Concept videos enable students with different learning styles to efficiently study and review key concepts of the chapter.

Animations Every textbook figure includes a step-by-step animation, with audio, to help students learn the intuition behind reading and interpreting graphs. These animations may be used for review, or as an instructional aid in the classroom. Figures labeled *MyEconLab Real-Time Data* update using the most recent data available from the Federal Reserve Bank of St. Louis's FRED site.

Embedded MyEconLab Assessment Every Checkpoint Practice Problem, every In the News problem, and every Study Plan Problem and Application in the enhanced eText can be worked by the student directly from the eText page on which it occurs. These problems are auto-graded and feed into the MyEconLab's Study Plan, where students receive recommendations based upon their performance.

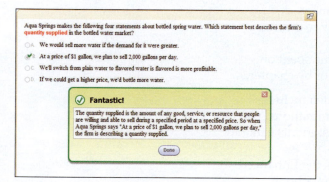

Key Terms Quiz The Key Terms Quiz, accessible from each Checkpoint, allows students to check their understanding of key chapter concepts before moving onto the next section. The Interactive Glossary that supports the enhanced eText provides the key term definition, an example, and related terms.

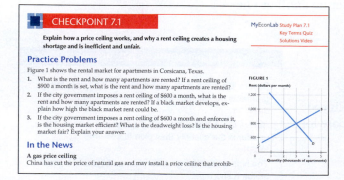

Solutions Videos Every Checkpoint Practice problem and In the News problem is supported by a Solutions video that provides a step-by-step working of the problem, including graphical analysis. Text, audio, and animation ensure that a student understands how to set-up and solve each of the problems.

■ MyEconLab also includes:

Economics in the News   Economics in the News is a turn-key solution to bringing current news into the classroom. Updated daily during the academic year, we upload two relevant articles (one micro, one macro) and provide questions that may be assigned for homework or for classroom discussion.

Current News   Each week during the academic year, we upload multi-part microeconomic and macroeconomic exercises, with links to relevant articles, into the MyEconLab assignment manager. These enable instructors to bring current issues and events into the course with easy to assign and auto-graded exercises.

Real-Time Data Analysis Exercises (FRED)   Easy to assign and automatically graded, Real-Time Data Analysis exercises use up-to-the-minute, real-time macroeconomic data. These exercises communicate directly with the Federal Reserve Bank of St. Louis's FRED site, so every time FRED posts new data, students see new data. As a result, Real-Time Data Analysis exercises offer a no-fuss solution for instructors who want to make the most recent data a central part of their macro course. End-of-chapter exercises accompanied by the Real-Time Data Analysis icon (●) include Real-Time Data versions in MyEconLab. Select in-text figures, labeled Real-time data, update in the eText using FRED data.

Digital Interactives: Economic principles are not static ideas, and learning them shouldn't be either! Digital Interactives are dynamic and engaging assessment activities that promote critical thinking and application of key economic principles.

   Each Digital Interactive has 3 to 5 progressive levels and requires approximately 20 minutes to explore, apply, compare, and analyze each topic. Many Digital Interactives include real-time data from FRED™ allowing professors and students to display, in graph and table form, up-to-the-minute data on key macro variables.

   Digital Interactives can be assigned and graded within MyEconLab, or used as a lecture tool to encourage engagement, classroom conversation, and group work.

   Topics include:

Comparative Advantage
Opportunity Cost
Unemployment
Consumer Price Index/Inflation
Monetary Policy
Elasticity
GDP
Demand & Supply

Math Review Exercises in MyEconLab—MyEconLab now offers an array of assignable and auto-graded exercises that cover fundamental math concepts. Geared specifically toward principles economics students, these exercises aim to increase student confidence and success in these courses. Our new Math Review is accessible from the assignment manager and contains more than 150 exercises for homework, quiz, and test use.

Learning Catalytics   Learning Catalytics helps you generate class discussion, customize your lecture, and promote peer-to-peer learning with real-time analytics. As a student response tool, Learning Catalytics uses students' smartphones, tablets, or laptops to engage them in more interactive tasks and thinking.

- NEW! Upload a full PowerPoint® deck for easy creation of slide questions.
- Help your students develop critical thinking skills.
- Monitor responses to find out where your students are struggling.
- Rely on real-time data to adjust your teaching strategy.
- Automatically group students for discussion, teamwork, and peer-to-peer learning.

Experiments in MyEconLab   Experiments are a fun and engaging way to promote active learning and mastery of important economic concepts. Pearson's Experiments program is flexible and easy for instructors to assign and students to use.

- Single-player experiments, available to assign, allow your students to play against virtual players from anywhere at anytime so long as they have an internet connection.
- Multiplayer experiments allow you to assign and manage a real-time experiment with your class.
- Pre and post-questions for each experiment are available for assignment in MyEconLab.
- Experiments are auto-graded using algorithms that objectively evaluate a student's economic gain and performance during the experiment.

AACSB and Learning Outcomes   All end-of-chapter and Test Item File questions are tagged in two ways: to AACSB standards and to discipline-specific Learning Outcomes. These two separate tagging systems allow professors to build assessments around desired departmental and course outcomes and track results in MyEconLab's gradebook.

Personalized Study Plan   The Personalized Study Plan provides recommendations for each of your students based on his or her ability to master the learning objectives in your course. This allows students to focus their study time by pinpointing the precise areas they need to review and allowing them to use customized practice and learning aids—such as videos, eText, tutorials, and more—to get them back on track. The Study Plan also ensures that your students are mastering the concepts, not just guessing the answers.

Using the report available in the Gradebook, you can then tailor course lectures to prioritize the content where students need the most support—offering you better insight into classroom and individual performance.

Dynamic Study Modules   Dynamic Study Modules help students study effectively on their own by continuously assessing their activity and performance in real time. Here's how it works: students complete a set of questions with a unique answer format that also asks them to indicate their confidence level. Questions repeat until the student can answer them all correctly and confidently. Once completed, Dynamic Study Modules explain the concept using materials from the text. These are available as graded assignments prior to class, and accessible on smartphones, tablets, and computers.

NEW! Instructors can now remove questions from Dynamic Study Modules to better fit their course.

SUPPORT MATERIALS FOR INSTRUCTORS AND STUDENTS

Foundations of Economics is accompanied by the most comprehensive set of teaching and learning tools ever assembled. Each component of our package is organized by Checkpoint topic for a tight, seamless integration with both the textbook and the other components. In addition to authoring the MyEconLab Study Plan and Assignment problems, PowerPoint resources, and Video scripts, we have helped in the reviewing and revising of the Solutions Manual, Instructor's Manual, and Test Item Files to ensure that every element of the package achieves the consistency that students and teachers need.

■ PowerPoint Resources

We have created the PowerPoint resources based on our 24 years of experience using this tool in our own classrooms. We have created four sets of PowerPoint presentations for instructors. They are:

- Lecture notes with full-color, animated figures, and tables from the textbook
- Figures and tables from the textbook, animated with step-by-step walk-through for instructors to use in their own personal slides
- *Eye On* features
- Alternative micro lecture notes with full-color, animated figures and tables that use examples different from those in the textbook

A student version of the lecture notes is also available on MyEconLab.

■ Instructor's Manual

The Instructor's Manual, written by Luke Armstrong and reviewed by Mark Rush, contains chapter outlines and road maps, additional exercises with solutions, a comprehensive Chapter Lecture resource, and a virtual encyclopedia of suggestions on how to enrich class presentation and use class time efficiently. The Instructor's Manual has been updated to reflect changes in the main text as well as infused with a fresh and intuitive approach to teaching this course. The Instructor's Manual is available for download in Word and PDF formats.

■ Solutions Manual

The Solutions Manual, written by Mark Rush and checked for accuracy by Jeannie Gillmore, contains the solutions to all Chapter Checkpoint Study Plan Problems and Applications, Instructor Assignable Problems and Applications, and the Multiple Choice Quiz. The Solutions Manual is available for download in Word and PDF formats.

■ Three Test Item Files and TestGen

More than 12,000 multiple-choice, numerical, fill-in-the-blank, short answer, essay, and integrative questions make up the three Test Item Files that support *Foundations of Economics*. Mark Rush reviewed and edited the updated and new questions from three dedicated principles instructors to form one of the most comprehensive testing systems on the market. Our microeconomics questions were written by Carol Dole (Jackson University); and our macroeconomics questions were written by Svitlana. Maksymenko (University of Pittsburgh) and David Black (University of

Toledo). The entire set of questions is available for download in Word, PDF, and TestGen formats.

All three Test Item Files are available in test generator software (TestGen with QuizMaster). TestGen's graphical interface enables instructors to view, edit, and add questions; transfer questions to tests; and print different forms of tests. Instructors also have the option to reformat tests with varying fonts and styles, margins, and headers and footers, as in any word-processing document. Search and sort features let the instructor quickly locate questions and arrange them in a preferred order. QuizMaster, working with your school's computer network, automatically grades the exams, stores the results on disk, and allows the instructor to view and print a variety of reports.

■ Instructor's Resource Center

This page on the Pearson Higher Education website (www.pearsonhighered.com/IRC) contains the Instructor's Manual, Solutions Manual, and Test Item Files in Word and PDF formats. It also contains the Computerized Test Item Files (with a TestGen program installer) and PowerPoint resources. It is compatible with both Windows and Macintosh operating systems.

For access or more information, contact your local Pearson representative or request access online at the Instructor Resource Center.

ACKNOWLEDGMENTS

Working on a project such as this one generates many debts that can never be repaid. But they can be acknowledged, and it is a special pleasure to be able to do so here and to express our heartfelt thanks to each and every one of the following long list, without whose contributions we could not have produced *Foundations*.

Mark Rush again coordinated, managed, and contributed to our Solutions Manual, Instructor's Manual, and Test Item Files. He assembled, polished, wrote, and rewrote these materials to ensure their close consistency with the text. He and we were in constant contact as all the elements of our text and package came together. Mark also made many valuable suggestions for improving the text and the Checkpoint Problems. His contribution went well beyond that of a reviewer, and his effervescent sense of humor kept us all in good spirits along the way.

Working closely with Mark, Luke Armstrong wrote content for the Instructor's Manual. Carol Dole, Svitlana Maksymenko and David Black authored new questions for the Test Item Files.

Luke Armstrong and Carol Dole recorded the narrations that accompany the Big Picture, Concept, and Solutions Videos in the eText. The engaging style and clarity of these outstanding teachers makes these videos a powerful learning tool.

Fred Bounds (Georgia Perimeter College) and Carol Dole provided outstanding reviews of the Study Plan and Assessment problems in MyEconLab that helped to make our exercises as effective as possible.

The ideas from which *Foundations* grew began to form over dinner at the Andover Inn in Andover, Massachusetts, with Denise Clinton and Sylvia Mallory. We gratefully acknowledge Sylvia's role not only at the birth of this project but also in managing its initial development team. Denise was an ongoing inspiration for 15 years, and we are privileged to have had the benefit of her enormous experience.

The success of *Foundations* owes much to its outstanding editors: Director of Portfolio Management, Adrienne D'Ambrosio, and Portfolio Manager, Ashley Bryan. Adrienne's acute intelligence and sensitive understanding of the market have helped sharpen our vision of this text and package over several editions, and Ashley has brought a fresh perspective to this Eight edition revision. The value-added of Adrienne and Ashley is huge. It has been, and we hope it will for many future editions remain, a joy to work with them.

Jonathan Boylan created the new impressive cover design and converted the raw ideas of our brainstorms into an outstandingly designed text.

Melissa Honig, Digital Studio Producer, and Noel Lotz, Digital Content Team Lead have set a new standard for online learning and teaching resources. They have been sources of high energy, good sense, and level-headed advice and quickly found creative solutions to all our technology problems.

Nancy Freihofer, our outstanding, ever calm, Content Producer, worked with a talented team at Integra, Project Editor, Heather Johnson, and designer, art coordinator, and typesetter. Our copy editor, Catherine Baum, gave our work a thorough review and helpful polish, and our proofreader ensured the most error-free text we have yet produced.

Our marketing team, comprised of Ramona Elmer, Tricia Murphy, and Brad Parkins, has been an integral part of this revision process. They have provided great knowledge and strategies to help continuously improve our suite of materials and keep them relevant and valuable in these ever-changing times.

Richard Parkin, our technical illustrator, created the figures in the text, the dynamic figures in the eText, the animated figures in the PowerPoint presentations, created the animations for and assembled the enhanced eText videos, and contributed many ideas to improving the clarity of our illustrations in all media.

Jeannie Gillmore, our long-standing personal assistant, worked closely with us to create MyEconLab Study Plan and Assignment problems and to ensure the highest standards for our feedbacks and "help me solve this" question help.

Finally, our reviewers, whose names appear on the following pages, have made an enormous contribution to this text and MyEconLab resources. Once again we find ourselves using superlatives, but they are called for. In the many texts that we've written, we've not seen reviewing of the quality that we enjoyed on this revision. It has been a pleasure (if at times a challenge) to respond constructively to their many excellent suggestions.

Robin Bade
Michael Parkin
London, Ontario, Canada
robin@econ100.com
mparkin@uwo.ca

FOUNDATIONS OF ECONOMICS: FLEXIBILITY CHART

Micro Flexibility

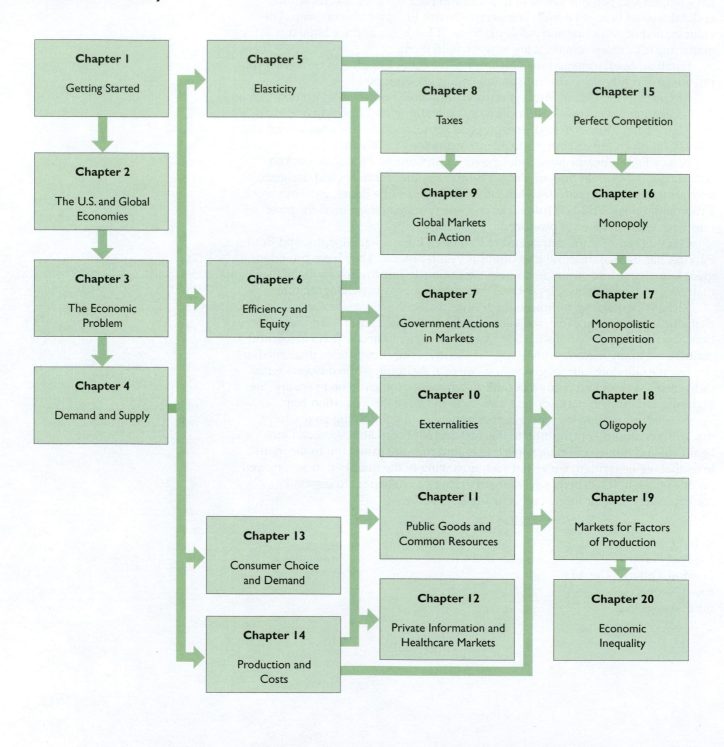

Start here ...   **... then jump to
any of these ...**   **... and jump to any of these after
doing the prerequisites indicated**

Macro Flexibility

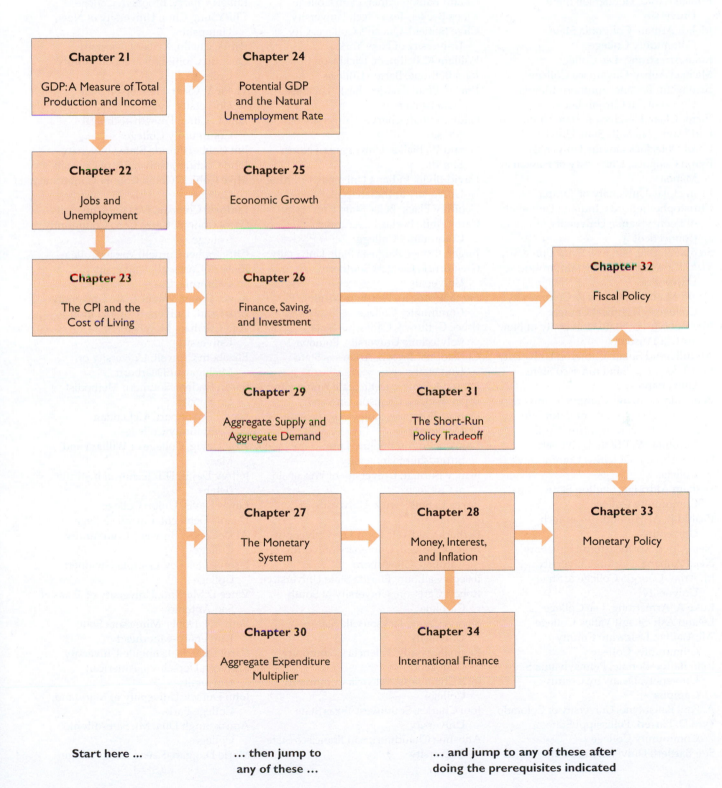

Start here ...

... then jump to
any of these ...

... and jump to any of these after
doing the prerequisites indicated

Reviewers

Eunice Akoto, Henderson State University

Mehdi Arman, Columbia State Community College

Luke Armstrong, Lee College

Michael Aubry, Cuyamaca College

Bizuayehu Bedane, Southern Illinois University at Carbondale

Victor Claar, Henderson State University

Earl Davis, Nicholls State University

Carol Dole, Jacksonville University

Byron Gangnes, University of Hawaii at Manoa

Leon Hoke, University of Tampa

Christopher Jeffords, Indiana University of Pennsylvania; University of Connecticut

Stephen Jerbic, San Jose State University

Vicki King-Skinner, Coastal Carolina University

David Manifold, Caldwell Community College & Technical Center

Michael Nuwer, State University of New York at Potsdam

Abdulhamid Sukar, Cameron University

Lisa Takeyama, San Francisco State University

Benjamin Zamzow, Campbell University

Ting Zhang, University of Baltimore

Alfredo A. Romero Aguirre, North Carolina A&T State University

Seemi Ahmad, Dutchess Community College

William Aldridge, Shelton State Community College

Rashid B. Al-Hmoud, Texas Tech University

Neil Alper, Northeastern University

Nejat Anbarci, Deakin University

J.J. Arias, Georgia College & State University

Luke A. Armstrong, Lee College

Leland Ash, Skagit Valley College

Ali Ataiifar, Delaware County Community College

John Baffoe-Bonnie, Pennsylvania State University, Delaware County Campus

A. Paul Ballantyne, University of Colorado

Tyra D. Barrett, Pellissippi State Community College

Sue Bartlett, University of South Florida

Gerald Baumgardner, Penn College

Klaus Becker, Texas Tech University

Clive Belfield, Queen's College, City University of New York

William K. Bellinger, Dickinson College

John Bethune, Barton College

Prasun Bhattacharjee, East Tennessee State University

Gautam Bhattacharya, University of Kansas

Gerald W. Bialka, University of North Florida

David Bivin, Indiana University–Purdue University at Indianapolis

Geoffrey Black, Boise State University

Carey Anne Borkoski, Arundel Community College

Jurgen Brauer, Augusta State University

Greg Brock, Georgia Southern University

Barbara Brogan, Northern Virginia Community College

Bruce C. Brown, California State Polytechnic University, Pomona

Christopher Brown, Arkansas State University

James O. Brown, Delta State University

Brian Buckley, Clemson University

Donald Bumpass, Sam Houston State University

Seewoonundun Bunjun, East Stroudsburg University

Nancy Burnett, University of Wisconsin at Oshkosh

James L. Butkiewicz, University of Delaware

Barbara Caldwell, Saint Leo University

Bruce Caldwell, University of North Carolina, Greensboro

Joseph Calhoun, Florida State University

Robert Carlsson, University of South Carolina

Shawn Carter, Jacksonville State University

Regina Cassady, Valencia Community College

Jack Chambless, Valencia Community College

Joni Charles, Southwest Texas State University

Anoshua Chaudhuri, San Francisco State University

Robert Cherry, Brooklyn College

Chi-Young Choi, University of New Hampshire

Paul Cichello, Xavier University

Quentin Ciolfi, Brevard Community College

Victor V. Claar, Henderson State University

Jane L. Cline, Forsyth Technical Community College

Jim Cobbe, Florida State University

John Cochran, University of Chicago

Mike Cohick, Collin County Community College

Ludovic Comeau, De Paul University

Carol Conrad, Cerro Coso Community College

Christopher Cornell, Vassar College

Richard Cornwall, University of California, Davis

Kevin Cotter, Wayne State University

Erik Craft, University of Richmond

Tom Creahan, Morehead State University

Elizabeth Crowell, University of Michigan at Dearborn

Susan Dadres, Southern Methodist University

David Davenport, McLennan Community College

Troy Davig, College of William and Mary

Jeffrey Davis, ITT Technical Institute (Utah)

Lewis Davis, Union College

Dennis Debrecht, Carroll College

Al DeCooke, Broward Community College

Jason J. Delaney, Georgia Gwinnett College

Vince DiMartino, University of Texas at San Antonio

Vernon J. Dobis, Minnesota State University–Moorhead

Carol Dole, Jacksonville University

Kathleen Dorsainvil, American University

John Dorsey, University of Maryland, College Park

Amrik Singh Dua, Mt. San Antonio College

Marie Duggan, Keene State College

Allen Dupont, North Carolina State University

David Eaton, Murray State University

Kevin J. Egan, University of Toledo

Harold W. Elder, University of Alabama

Harry Ellis, University of North Texas

Stephen Ellis, North Central Texas College

Carl Enomoto, New Mexico State University

Chuen-mei Fan, Colorado State University

Chris Fant, Spartanburg Community College

Elena Ermolenko Fein, Oakton Community College

Gary Ferrier, University of Arkansas

Rudy Fichtenbaum, Wright State University

Donna K. Fisher, Georgia Southern University

Kaya Ford, Northern Virginia Community College

Robert Francis, Shoreline Community College

Roger Frantz, San Diego State University

Amanda S. Freeman, Kansas State University

Marc Fusaro, East Carolina University

Arthur Friedberg, Mohawk Valley Community College

Julie Gallaway, Southwest Missouri State University

Byron Gangnes, University of Hawaii

Gay GareschÈ, Glendale Community College

Neil Garston, California State University, Los Angeles

Lisa Geib-Gunderson, University of Maryland

Lisa M. George, City University of New York

Linda Ghent, Eastern Illinois University

Soma Ghosh, Bridgewater State College

Kirk Gifford, Ricks College

Scott Gilbert, Southern Illinois University

Maria Giuili, Diablo Valley Community College

Mark Gius, Quinnipiac College

Gregory E. Givens, University of Alabama

Randall Glover, Brevard Community College

Stephan Gohmann, University of Louisville

Richard Gosselin, Houston Community College

John Graham, Rutgers University

Patricia E. Graham, University of Northern Colorado

Warren Graham, Tulsa Community College

Homer Guevara, Jr., Northwest Vista College

Osman Gulseven, North Carolina State University

Jang-Ting Guo, University of California, Riverside

Dennis Hammett, University of Texas at El Paso

Leo Hardwick, Macomb Community College

Mehdi Haririan, Bloomsburg University

Paul Harris, Camden County Community College

Mark Healy, William Rainey Harper College

Rey Hernandez-Julian, Metropolitan State College of Denver

Gus Herring, Brookhaven College

Michael Heslop, Northern Virginia Community College

Steven Hickerson, Mankato State University

Frederick Steb Hipple, East Tennessee State University

Lee Hoke, University of Tampa

Andy Howard, Rio Hondo College

Yu Hsing, Southeastern Louisiana University

Greg Hunter, California State Polytechnic University, Pomona

Matthew Hyle, Winona State University

Todd Idson, Boston University

Harvey James, University of Hartford

Russell Janis, University of Massachusetts at Amherst

Ricot Jean, Valencia College

Jay A. Johnson, Southeastern Louisiana University

Ted Joyce, City University of New York, Baruch College

Ahmad A. Kader, University of Nevada, Las Vegas

Jonathan D. Kaplan, California State University, Sacramento

Arthur Kartman, San Diego State University

Chris Kauffman, University of Tennessee

Diane Keenan, Cerritos College

Brian Kench, University of Tampa

John Keith, Utah State University

Kristen Keith, University of Toledo

Joe Kerkvliet, Oregon State University

Randall Kesselring, Arkansas State University

Gary Kikuchi, University of Hawaii at Manoa

Douglas Kinnear, Colorado State University

Morris Knapp, Miami Dade Community College

Steven Koch, Georgia Southern University

Kate Krause, University of New Mexico

Stephan Kroll, California State University, Sacramento

Joyce Lapping, University of Southern Maine

Tom Larson, California State University, Los Angeles

Robert Lemke, Florida International University

J. Mark Leonard, University of Nebraska at Omaha

Tony Lima, California State University, Hayward

Joshua Long, Ivy Tech Community College

Kenneth Long, New River Community College

Noel Lotz, Middle Tennessee State University

Marty Ludlum, Oklahoma City Community College

Brian Lynch, Lake Land College

Michael Machiorlatti, Oklahoma City Community College

Roger Mack, De Anza College

Michael Magura, University of Toledo

Mark Maier, Glendale College

Svitlana Maksymenko, University of Pittsburgh

Paula Manns, Atlantic Cape Community College

Dan Marburger, Arkansas State University

Kathryn Marshall, Ohio State University

John V. Martin, Boise State University

Drew E. Mattson, Anoka-Ramsey Community College

Stephen McCafferty, Ohio State University

Thomas S. McCaleb, Florida State University

Katherine S. McCann, University of Delaware

William McLean, Oklahoma State University

Diego Mendez-Carbajo, Illinois Wesleyan University

Evelina Mengova, California State University, Fullerton

Thomas Meyer, Patrick Henry Community College

Meghan Millea, Mississippi State University

Michael Milligan, Front Range Community College

Jenny Minier, University of Miami

David Mitchell, Valdosta State University

Dr. Carl B. Montano, Lamar University

Christine Moser, Western Michigan University

William Mosher, Clark University

Mike Munoz, Northwest Vista College

John R. Mundy, St. Johns River State College

Kevin Murphy, Oakland University

Ronald Nate, Brigham Young University, Idaho

Nasrin Nazemzadeh, Rowan Cabarrus Community College

Michael Nelson, Texas A&M University

Rebecca Neumann, University of Wisconsin—Milwaukee

Charles Newton, Houston Community College Southwest

Melinda Nish, Salt Lake Community College

Lee Nordgren, Indiana University at Bloomington

Norman P. Obst, Michigan State University

Inge O'Connor, Syracuse University

William C. O'Connor, Western Montana College–University of Montana

Fola Odebunmi, Cypress College

Victor I. Oguledo, Florida A&M University

Charles Okeke, College of Southern Nevada

Lydia M. Ortega, St. Philip's College

P. Marcelo Oviedo, Iowa State University

Jennifer Pate, Ph.D., Loyola Marymount University

Sanjay Paul, Elizabethtown College

Ken Peterson, Furman University

Tim Petry, North Dakota State University

Charles Pflanz, Scottsdale Community College

Jonathon Phillips, North Carolina State University

Basharat Pitafi, Southern Illinois University

Anthony Plunkett, Harrison College

Paul Poast, Ohio State University

Greg Pratt, Mesa Community College

Fernando Quijano, Dickinson State University

Andy Radler, Butte Community College

Ratha Ramoo, Diablo Valley College

Karen Reid, University of Wisconsin, Parkside

Mary Rigdon, University of Texas, Austin

Helen Roberts, University of Illinois at Chicago

Greg Rose, Sacramento City College

Barbara Ross, Kapi'olani Community College

Elham Rouhani, Gwinnett Technical College

Jeffrey Rous, University of North Texas

June Roux, Salem Community College

Udayan Roy, Long Island University

Nancy C. Rumore, University of Louisiana–Lafayette

Mark Rush, University of Florida

Rolando Sanchez, Northwest Vista College

Joseph Santos, South Dakota State University

Roland Santos, Lakeland Community College

Mark Scanlan, Stephen F. Austin State University

Ted Scheinman, Mount Hood Community College

Buffie Schmidt, Augusta State University

Jerry Schwartz, Broward Community College

Gautam Sethi, Bard College

Margaret Anne Shannon, Georgia Southern University

Mushtaq Sheikh, Union County College

Michelle Sheran-Andrews, University of North Carolina at Greensboro

Virginia Shingleton, Valparaiso University

Steven S. Shwiff, Texas A & M University—Commerce

Charles Sicotte, Rock Valley College

Issoufou Soumaila, Texas Tech University

Martin Spechler, Indiana University

Leticia Starkov, Elgin Community College

Stela Stefanova, University of Delaware

John Stiver, University of Connecticut

Richard W. Stratton, The University of Akron

Abdulhamid Sukar, Cameron University

Terry Sutton, Southeast Missouri State University

Janet M. Thomas, Bentley College

Donna Thompson, Brookdale Community College

Deborah Thorsen, Palm Beach State College

James Thorson, Southern Connecticut State University

Marc Tomljanovich, Colgate University

Cynthia Royal Tori, Valdosta State University

Ngoc-Bich Tran, San Jacinto College South

Nora Underwood, University of California, Davis

Jogindar S. Uppal, State University of New York

Va Nee L. Van Vleck, California State University, Fresno

Victoria Vernon, Empire State College / SUNY

Christian Weber, Seattle University

Ethel Weeks, Nassau Community College

Jack Wegman, Santa Rosa Junior College

Jason White, Northwest Missouri State University

Benjamin Widner, Colorado State University

Barbara Wiens-Tuers, Pennsylvania State University, Altoona

Katherine Wolfe, University of Pittsburgh

Kristen Wolfe, St. Johns River State College

You're in school!
Did you make the right decision?

Getting Started

When you have completed your study of this chapter, you will be able to

1 Define economics and explain the kinds of questions that economists try to answer.

2 Explain the ideas that define the economic way of thinking.

3 Explain how economics is useful as a life skill.

MyEconLab Big Picture Video

1.1 DEFINITION AND QUESTIONS

Well, did you make the right decision? Is being in school the best use of your time? You'll soon know how an economist answers this question—for it is an economic question. It arises from the fact that you want more than you can get. You want to be in school. But you also want the time to enjoy your favorite sports and movies, to travel, and to hang out with friends—time that right now you don't have because you've got classes to attend and assignments due. Your time is scarce.

■ Scarcity

Scarcity
The condition that arises because wants exceed the ability of resources to satisfy them.

Our inability to satisfy all our wants is called **scarcity**. The ability of each of us to satisfy our wants is limited by the time we have, the incomes we earn, and the prices we pay for the things we buy. These limits mean that everyone has unsatisfied wants. The ability of all of us as a society to satisfy our wants is limited by the productive resources that exist. These resources include the gifts of nature, our labor and ingenuity, and the tools and equipment that we have made.

Everyone, poor and rich alike, faces scarcity. A student wants Taylor Swift's latest album and a paperback but has only $10.00 in his pocket. He faces scarcity. Gwen Stefani wants to spend a week on the set of *The Voice* in L.A., but she also wants to devote time and energy to her successful clothing line. She faces scarcity. The U.S. government wants to increase spending on homeland security and cut taxes. It faces scarcity. An entire society wants improved healthcare, an Internet connection in every classroom, clean lakes and rivers, and so on. Society faces scarcity. Scarcity is everywhere: Even parrots face scarcity!

Faced with scarcity, we must make choices. We must choose among the available alternatives. The student must choose the download or the paperback. Gwen Stefani must choose shooting episodes of *The Voice* or designing her next clothing collection. The government must choose greater security or tax cuts. And society must choose among healthcare, computers, the environment, and so on.

Not only do I want a cracker—we all want a cracker!

■ Economics Defined

Economics
The social science that studies the choices that individuals, businesses, governments, and entire societies make as they cope with *scarcity*, all the things that influence those choices, and the arrangements that coordinate them.

Economics is the social science that studies the choices that individuals, businesses, governments, and entire societies make as they cope with *scarcity*, all the things that influence those choices, and the arrangements that coordinate them.

The subject has two broad parts:

- Microeconomics, and
- Macroeconomics

Microeconomics

Microeconomics
The study of the choices that individuals and businesses make and the way these choices interact and are influenced by governments.

Microeconomics is the study of the choices that individuals and businesses make and the way these choices interact and are influenced by governments. Some examples of microeconomic questions are: Will you buy a 3-D TV or a standard one? Will Nintendo sell more units of Wii if it cuts the price? Will a cut in the income tax rate encourage people to work longer hours? Will a hike in the gas tax encourage more people to drive hybrid or smaller automobiles? Is music streaming killing song downloads?

Macroeconomics

Macroeconomics is the study of the aggregate (or total) effects on the national economy and the global economy of the choices that individuals, businesses, and governments make. Some examples of macroeconomic questions are: Why did production and jobs expand slowly in the United States during 2014 and 2015? Why are incomes growing much faster in China and India than in the United States? Why is unemployment in Europe so high? Why are Americans borrowing more than $1 billion a day from the rest of the world?

Two big questions define the scope of economics:

- How do choices end up determining *what, how,* and *for whom* goods and services get produced?
- When do choices made in the pursuit of *self-interest* also promote the *social interest*?

Macroeconomics
The study of the aggregate (or total) effects on the national economy and the global economy of the choices that individuals, businesses, and governments make.

■ What, How, and For Whom?

Goods and services are the objects and actions that people value and produce to satisfy human wants. Goods are *objects* that satisfy wants. Sports shoes and ketchup are examples. Services are *actions* that satisfy wants. Haircuts and rock concerts are examples. We produce a dazzling array of goods and services that range from necessities such as food, houses, and healthcare to leisure items such as Blu-ray players and roller coaster rides.

Goods and services
The objects (goods) and the actions (services) that people value and produce to satisfy human wants.

What?

What determines the quantities of corn we grow, homes we build, and healthcare services we produce? Sixty years ago, farm output was 5 percent of total U.S. production. Today, it is 1 percent. Over the same period, the output of mines, construction, and utilities slipped from 9 percent to 7 percent of total production and manufacturing fell from 28 percent to 12 percent. These decreases in output are matched by increases in the production of a wide range of services, up from 58 percent of total production 60 years ago to 80 percent today. How will these quantities change in the future as ongoing changes in technology make an ever-wider array of goods and services available to us?

How?

How are goods and services produced? In a vineyard in France, a hundred basket-carrying workers pick the annual grape crop by hand. In a vineyard in California, a huge machine and a few workers do the same job. Look around and you will see many examples of this phenomenon—the same job being done in different ways. In some stores, checkout clerks key in prices. In others, they use a laser scanner. One farmer keeps track of his livestock feeding schedules and inventories by using paper-and-pencil records, while another uses a computer. In some plants, GM hires workers to weld auto bodies and in others it uses robots to do the job.

Why do we use machines in some cases and people in others? Do mechanization and technological change destroy more jobs than they create? Do they make us better off or worse off?

In a California vineyard a machine and a few workers do the same job as a hundred grape pickers in France.

A doctor gets more of the goods and services produced than a nurse or a medical assistant gets.

For Whom?

For whom are goods and services produced? The answer depends on the incomes that people earn and the prices they pay for the goods and services they buy. At given prices, a person who has a high income is able to buy more goods and services than a person who has a low income. Doctors earn much higher incomes than do nurses and medical assistants, so doctors get more of the goods and services produced than nurses and medical assistants get.

You probably know about many other persistent differences in incomes. Men, on average, earn more than women. Whites, on average, earn more than minorities. College graduates, on average, earn more than high school graduates. Americans, on average, earn more than Europeans, who in turn earn more, on average, than Asians and Africans. But there are some significant exceptions. The people of Japan and Hong Kong now earn an average income similar to that of Americans. And there is a lot of income inequality throughout the world.

What determines the incomes we earn? Why do doctors earn larger incomes than nurses? Why do men earn more, on average, than women? Why do college graduates earn more, on average, than high school graduates? Why do Americans earn more, on average, than Africans?

Economics explains how the choices that individuals, businesses, and governments make and the interactions of those choices end up determining *what*, *how*, and *for whom* goods and services are produced. In answering these questions, we have a deeper agenda in mind. We're not interested in just knowing how many Blu-ray players are produced, how they are produced, and who gets to enjoy them. We ultimately want to know the answer to the second big economic question that we'll now explore.

■ Can the Pursuit of Self-Interest Be in the Social Interest?

Every day, you and 321 million other Americans, along with 7.2 billion people in the rest of the world, make economic choices that result in *"what," "how,"* and *"for whom"* goods and services are produced.

Are the goods and services produced, and the quantities in which they are produced, the right ones? Are the scarce resources used in the best possible way? Do the goods and services we produce go to those who benefit most from them?

Self-Interest and the Social Interest

Self-interest
The choices that are best for the individual who makes them.

Social interest
The choices that are best for society as a whole.

Choices that are the best for the individual who makes them are choices made in the pursuit of **self-interest**. Choices that are the best for society as a whole are said to be in the **social interest**. The social interest has two dimensions: *efficiency* and *equity*. We'll explore these concepts in later chapters. For now, think of efficiency as being achieved by baking the biggest possible pie, and think of equity as being achieved by sharing the pie in the fairest possible way.

You know that your own choices are the best ones for you—or at least you *think* they're the best at the time that you make them. You use your time and other resources in the way that you think is best. You might consider how your choices affect other people, but you order a home delivery pizza because you're hungry and want to eat, not because you're concerned that the delivery person or the cook needs an income. You make choices that are in your self-interest— choices that you think are best for you.

When you act on your economic decisions, you come into contact with thousands of other people who produce and deliver the goods and services that you decide to buy or who buy the things that you sell. These people have made their own decisions—what to produce and how to produce it, whom to hire or whom to work for, and so on. Like you, all these people make choices that they think are best for them. When the pizza delivery person shows up at your home, he's not doing you a favor. He's earning his income and hoping for a good tip.

Can it be possible that when each one of us makes choices that are in our own best interest—in our self-interest—it turns out that these choices are also the best choices for society as a whole—in the social interest?

Adam Smith, regarded as the founder of economic science, (see *Eye on the Past* on p. 18) said the answer is *yes*. He believed that when we pursue our self-interest, we are led by an *invisible hand* to promote the social interest.

Is Adam Smith correct? Can it really be possible that the pursuit of self-interest promotes the social interest? Much of the rest of this book helps you to learn what economists know about this question and its answer. To help you start thinking about the question, we're going to illustrate it with four topics that generate heated discussion in today's world. You're already at least a little bit familiar with each one of them. They are

- Globalization
- The information revolution
- Climate change
- Government budget deficit and debt

Globalization

Globalization—the expansion of international trade and the production of components and services by firms in other countries—has been going on for centuries. But in recent years, its pace has accelerated. Microchips, satellites, and fiber-optic cables have lowered the cost of communication and globalized production decisions. When Nike produces more sports shoes, people in Malaysia get more work. When Steven Spielberg makes a new movie, programmers in New Zealand write the code that makes magical animations. And when China Airlines wants a new airplane, Americans who work for Boeing build it.

Workers in Asia make our shoes.

Globalization is bringing rapid income growth, especially in Asia. But globalization is leaving some people behind. Jobs in manufacturing and routine services are shrinking in the United States, and some nations of Africa and South America are not sharing in the prosperity enjoyed in other parts of the world.

The owners of multinational firms benefit from lower production costs and consumers benefit from low-cost imported goods. But don't displaced American workers lose? And doesn't even the worker in Malaysia, who sews your new shoes for a few cents an hour, also lose? Is globalization in the social interest, or does globalization benefit just some at the expense of others?

The Information Revolution

We are living at a time of extraordinary economic change that has been called the *Information Revolution*. This name suggests a parallel with the *Industrial Revolution* of the 1800s and the *Agricultural Revolution* of 12,000 years ago.

The changes that have occurred during the last 35 years are based on one major technology: the microprocessor or computer chip. The spin-offs from faster and cheaper computing have been widespread in telecommunications, music, and the automation of millions of tasks that previously required human decisions. You encounter some of these tasks when you check out at the grocery store or use an ATM. Less visible, but larger in scope, are the robots that assemble cars and move goods around warehouses. Over the next 20 years, more than one third of today's jobs will be done by a new generation of robots.

Robots fill orders at Amazon.

The computing and robot revolution resulted from people pursuing their self-interest. Gordon Moore, the chip maker who set up Intel, and Bill Gates, who quit Harvard to set up Microsoft, weren't thinking how much easier it would be for you to turn in your essay on time if you had a computer. Moore and Gates and thousands of other entrepreneurs were in pursuit of big rewards. Yet their actions made many other people better off. They advanced the social interest.

But are resources used in the best possible way? Or do Intel and Microsoft set their prices too high and put their products out of reach for too many people? And is it in the social interest for robots to take people's jobs?

Climate Change

The Earth is getting hotter and the ice at the two poles is melting. Since the late nineteenth century, the Earth's surface temperature has increased about 1 degree Fahrenheit, and close to a half of that increase occurred over the past 25 years.

Human activity is raising the Earth's surface temperature.

Most climate scientists believe that the current warming has come at least in part from human economic activity—from self-interested choices—and that, if left unchecked, the warming will bring large future economic costs.

Are the individual energy choices that each of us makes damaging the social interest? What needs to be done to make our choices serve the social interest? Would the United States joining with other nations to limit carbon emissions serve the social interest? What other measures might be introduced?

Government Budget Deficit and Debt

Every year since 2000, the U.S. government has run a budget deficit. On average, the government has spent $2.3 billion a day more than it has received in taxes. The government's debt has increased each day by that amount. Over the 15 year period from 2000 to 2015, government debt increased by $12.5 trillion. Your personal share of this debt is $56,000.

A government budget time bomb is ticking as spending grows faster than tax revenues.

This large deficit and debt is just the beginning of an even bigger problem. From about 2020 onwards, the retirement and healthcare benefits to which older Americans are entitled are going to cost increasingly more than current taxes can cover. With no changes in tax or benefit rates, the budget deficit will increase and the debt will swell ever higher.

Deficits and the debts they create cannot persist indefinitely, and debts must somehow be repaid. They will most likely be repaid by you, not by your parents. When we make our voter choices, we pursue our self-interest. Do our choices serve the social interest? Do the choices made by politicians and bureaucrats in Washington and the state capitals promote the social interest, or do they only serve their own self-interests?

The four issues we've just reviewed raise questions that are hard to answer. We'll return to each of them at various points throughout this text and explain when the social interest is served and when there remain problems to be solved.

CHECKPOINT 1.1

MyEconLab Study Plan 1.1
Key Terms Quiz
Solutions Video

Define economics and explain the kinds of questions that economists try to answer.

Practice Problems

1. Economics studies choices that arise from one fact. What is that fact?
2. Provide three examples of wants in the United States today that are especially pressing but not satisfied.
3. In the following three news items, find examples of the *what, how*, and *for whom* questions: "With more research, we will cure cancer"; "A good education is the right of every child"; "Congress raises taxes to curb the deficit."
4. How does a new Starbucks in Beijing, China, influence self-interest and the social interest?
5. How does Facebook influence self-interest and the social interest?

In the News

1. The Bureau of Labor Statistics (BLS) reports that high-paying jobs in healthcare and jobs in leisure, hospitality, and education will expand quickly over the next five years. How does the BLS expect *what* and *for whom* goods and services are produced to change in the next five years?
2. Hewlett-Packard will cut 30,000 jobs and lower its cost by $2.7 billion a year.
   Source: *Fortune*, October 1, 2015

   Explain how Hewlett-Packard's decision made in its self-interest might also be in the social interest.

Solutions to Practice Problems

1. The fact is scarcity—human wants exceed the resources available.
2. Examples would include security from terrorism, cleaner air in our cities, better public schools, and better public infrastructure. (Think of others.)
3. More research is a *how* question, and a cure for cancer is a *what* question. Good education is a *what* question, and every child is a *for whom* question. Raising taxes is a *for whom* question.
4. Decisions made by Starbucks are in Starbucks' self-interest but they also serve the self-interest of its customers and so contribute to the social interest.
5. Facebook serves the self-interest of its investors, users, and advertisers. It also serves the social interest by enabling people to share information.

Solutions to In the News

1. The BLS expects the quantities of goods and services produced by workers in healthcare, leisure, hospitality, and education to increase. For whom they are produced depends on how people's incomes and the prices of goods and services will change in the next five years. The BLS expects workers in these high-paying jobs and expanding industries will get more of them.
2. Hewlett-Packard's product prices might fall and benefit its customers. The laid-off workers will find new jobs, some of which might pay higher wages.

1.2 THE ECONOMIC WAY OF THINKING

The definition of economics and the kinds of questions that economists try to answer give you a flavor of the scope of economics. But they don't tell you how economists *think* about these questions and how they go about seeking answers to them. You're now going to see how economists approach their work.

We'll break this task into two parts. First, we'll explain the ideas that economists use to frame their view of the world. These ideas will soon have you thinking like an economist. Second, we'll look at economics both as a social science and as a policy tool that governments, businesses, and *you* can use.

Six ideas define the *economic way of thinking*:

- A choice is a *tradeoff*
- *Cost* is what you *must give up* to get something.
- *Benefit* is what you gain from something.
- People make *rational choices* by comparing benefits and costs.
- Most choices are "*how much*" choices made at the *margin*.
- Choices respond to *incentives.*

■ A Choice Is a Tradeoff

Tradeoff
An exchange—giving up one thing to get something else.

A **tradeoff** is an exchange—giving up one thing to get something else. Because we face scarcity, we must make choices. And when we make a choice, we select from the available alternatives. You can think about choices as tradeoffs. When you choose one thing, you give up something else that you could have chosen.

Think about what you will do on Saturday night. You can spend the night studying for your next economics test or having fun with your friends, but you can't do both of these activities at the same time. You must choose how much time to devote to each. Whatever choice you make, you could have chosen something else. When you choose how to spend your Saturday night, you face a tradeoff between studying and hanging out with your friends. To get more study time, you must give up some time with your friends.

■ Cost: What You *Must* Give Up

Opportunity cost
The opportunity cost of something is the best thing you must give up to get it.

The **opportunity cost** of something is the best thing you must give up to get it. You most likely think about the cost of something as the money you must spend to get it. But dig a bit deeper. If you spend $10 on a movie ticket, you can't spend it on a sandwich. The movie ticket really costs a sandwich. The *cost* of something is what must be given up to get it, not the money spent on it. Economists use the term *opportunity cost* to emphasize this view of cost.

The biggest opportunity cost you face is that of being in school. This opportunity cost has two components: things you can't afford to buy and things you can't do with your time.

Start with the things you can't afford to buy. You've spent all your income on tuition, residence fees, books, and a laptop. If you weren't in school, you would have spent this money on tickets to ball games and movies and all the other things that you enjoy. But that's only the start of the things you can't afford to buy because you're in school. You've also given up the opportunity to get a job and buy the things that you could afford with your higher income. Suppose that the

The opportunity cost of being in school: things you can't buy and do.

best job you could get if you weren't in school is working as a convenience store manager earning $24,000 a year. Another part of your opportunity cost of being in school is all the things that you would buy with that extra $24,000.

Now think about the time that being a student eats up. You spend many hours each week in class, doing homework assignments, preparing for tests, and so on. To do all these school activities, you must give up what would otherwise be time spent playing your favorite sport, time watching movies, and leisure time spent with your friends.

The opportunity cost of being in school is the best alternative things that you can't afford and that you don't have the time to enjoy. You might put a dollar value on this cost but the cost is the goods and services and time that you give up, not dollars.

The opportunity cost of being in school includes forgone earnings.

■ Benefit: What You Gain

The **benefit** from something is the gain or pleasure that it brings, measured by what you are *willing to give up* to get it. Benefit is determined by personal *preferences*—by what a person likes and dislikes and the intensity of those feelings. If you get a huge kick out of Madden NFL, that video game brings you a large benefit. And if you have little interest in listening to Yo Yo Ma playing a Vivaldi cello concerto, that activity brings you a small benefit.

Some benefits are large and easy to identify, such as the benefit that you get from being in school. A big piece of that benefit is the goods and services that you will be able to enjoy with the boost to your earning power when you graduate. Some benefits are small, such as the benefit you receive from a slice of pizza.

Economists measure benefit as the most that a person is *willing to give up* to get something. You are willing to give up a lot for something that brings a large benefit. For example, because being in school brings a large benefit, you're *willing to give up* a lot of time and goods and services to get that benefit. But you're willing to give up very little for something that brings a small benefit. For example, you might be willing to give up one iTunes download to get a slice of pizza.

Benefit
The benefit from something is the gain or pleasure that it brings, measured by what you are *willing to give up* to get it.

■ Rational Choice

A basic idea of economics is that in making choices, people act rationally. A **rational choice** is one that uses the available resources to best achieve the objective of the person making the choice.

But how do people choose rationally? The answer is by comparing the *benefits* and *costs* of the alternative choices and choosing the alternative that makes *net benefit*—benefit minus cost—as large as possible.

You have chosen to be a student. If that choice is rational, as economists assume, your benefit from being in school exceeds the cost, so your net benefit is maximized by being in school. For an outstanding baseball player, a high earning potential makes the opportunity cost of school higher than the benefit from school, so for that person, net benefit is maximized by choosing full-time sport. (*Eye on the Benefit and Cost of School* on p. 12 explores these examples more closely.)

The benefit from a choice is determined by the preferences of the person making the choice, so two people can make different rational choices even if they face the same cost. For example, you might like chocolate ice cream more than vanilla ice cream, but your friend prefers vanilla. So it is rational for you to choose chocolate and for your friend to choose vanilla.

Rational choice
A choice that uses the available resources to best achieve the objective of the person making the choice.

A rational choice might turn out not to have been the best choice after the fact. For example, a farmer might decide to plant wheat rather than soybeans. Then, when the crop comes to market, the price of soybeans might be much higher than the price of wheat. The farmer's choice was rational when it was made, but subsequent events made it less profitable than the alternative choice.

All the rational choices we've just considered (school or not, chocolate or vanilla ice cream, soybeans or wheat) involve choosing between two things. One or the other is chosen. We call such choices *all-or-nothing* choices. Many choices are of this type, but most choices involve *how much* of an activity to do.

◼ How Much? Choosing at the Margin

You can allocate the next hour between studying and video chatting with your friends, but the choice is not all or nothing. You must decide how many minutes to allocate to each activity. To make this decision, you compare the benefit of a little bit more study time with its cost—you make your choice *at the margin*.

Other words for "margin" are "border" or "edge." You can think of a choice at the margin as one that adjusts the border or edge of a plan to determine the best course of action. Making a choice at the **margin** means comparing the relevant alternatives systematically and incrementally.

Marginal Cost

The opportunity cost of a one-unit increase in an activity is called **marginal cost**. The marginal cost of something is what you *must* give up to get *one additional* unit of it. Think about your marginal cost of going to the movies for a third time in a week. Your marginal cost of seeing the movie is what you must give up to see that one additional movie. It is *not* what you give up to see all three movies. The reason is that you've already given up something to see two movies, so you don't count that cost when making a decision to see the third movie.

The marginal cost of any activity increases as you do more of it. You know that going to the movies decreases your study time and lowers your grade. Suppose that seeing a second movie in a week lowers your grade by five percentage points. Seeing a third movie will lower your grade by more than five percentage points. Your marginal cost of moviegoing is increasing as you see more movies.

Marginal Benefit

The benefit of a one-unit increase in an activity is called **marginal benefit**. Marginal benefit is what you gain from having *one more* unit of something. But the marginal benefit from something is *measured* by what you *are willing* to give up to get that *one additional* unit of it.

A fundamental feature of marginal benefit is that it diminishes. Think about your marginal benefit from movies. If you've been studying hard and haven't seen a movie this week, your marginal benefit from seeing your next movie is large. But if you've been on a movie binge this week, you now want a break and your marginal benefit from seeing your next movie is small.

Because the marginal benefit from a movie decreases as you see more movies, you are willing to give up less to see one additional movie. For example, you know that going to the movies decreases your study time and lowers your grade. You pay for seeing a movie with a lower grade. You might be willing to give up ten percentage points to see your first movie in a week, but you won't be willing to take such a big hit on your grade to see a second movie in a week. Your willingness to pay to see a movie decreases as the number of movies increases.

Margin
A choice on the margin is a choice that is made by comparing *all* the relevant alternatives systematically and incrementally.

Marginal cost
The opportunity cost that arises from a one-unit increase in an activity. The marginal cost of something is what you *must* give up to get *one additional* unit of it.

Marginal benefit
The benefit that arises from a one-unit increase in an activity. The marginal benefit of something is *measured* by what you *are willing* to give up to get *one additional* unit of it.

Making a Rational Choice

So, will you go to the movies for that third time in a week? The answer is found by comparing marginal benefit and marginal cost.

If the marginal cost of the movie is less than the marginal benefit from it, seeing the third movie adds more to benefit than to cost. Your net benefit increases, so your rational choice is to see the third movie.

If the marginal cost of the movie exceeds the marginal benefit from it, seeing the third movie adds more to cost than to benefit. Your net benefit decreases, so your rational choice is to spend the evening studying.

When the marginal benefit from something equals its marginal cost, the choice is rational and it is not possible to make a better choice. Scarce resources are being used in the best possible way.

■ Choices Respond to Incentives

The choices we make depend on the incentives we face. An **incentive** is a reward or a penalty—a "carrot" or a "stick"—that encourages or discourages an action. We respond positively to "carrots" and negatively to "sticks." The carrots are marginal benefits; the sticks are marginal costs. A change in marginal benefit or a change in marginal cost changes the incentives that we face and leads us to change our actions.

Most students believe that the payoff from studying just before a test is greater than the payoff from studying a month before a test. In other words, as a test date approaches, the marginal benefit from studying increases and the incentive to study becomes stronger. For this reason, we observe an increase in study time and a decrease in leisure pursuits during the last few days before a test. And the more important the test, the greater is this effect.

A change in marginal cost also changes incentives. For example, suppose that last week, you found your course work easy and you scored 100 percent on your practice quizzes. You figured that the marginal cost of taking an evening off to enjoy a movie was low and that your grade on the next test would not suffer, so you headed to the Cineplex. But this week the going has gotten tough. You're just not getting it, and your practice test scores are low. If you take off even one evening this week, your grade on the next test will suffer. The marginal cost of seeing a movie is now high, so you decide to give the movies a miss.

A central idea of economics is that by observing *changes in incentives*, we can predict how *choices change*.

Incentive
A reward or a penalty—a "carrot" or a "stick"—that encourages or discourages an action.

Changes in marginal benefit and marginal cost change the incentive to study or to enjoy a movie.

EYE on the BENEFIT AND COST OF SCHOOL

Did You Make the Right Decision?

Your decision to be in school is an economic decision. You faced a tradeoff between school, a job, and leisure time. You compared benefits and costs, and you responded to incentives.

Did you make the right decision when you chose school over a full-time job? Or, if you have a full-time job and you're studying in what would be your leisure time, did you make the right choice? Does school provide a big enough benefit to justify its cost?

The Benefits of School

Being in school has many benefits for which people are willing to pay. They fall into two broad categories: present enjoyment and a higher future income.

You can easily make a list of all the fun things you do with your friends in school that would be harder to do if you didn't have these friends and opportunities for social interaction that school provides.

Putting a dollar value on the items in your list would be hard, but it is possible to put a dollar value, or rather an expected dollar value, on the other benefit—a higher future income.

A high-school graduate earns, on average, an annual income of $40,000 a year. A graduate with a bachelor's degree earns, on average, $76,000 a year.

So by being in school, you can expect (on average) to increase your annual earnings by $36,000 a year.

This number is likely to grow as the economy becomes more productive and prices and earnings rise.

The Costs of School

The opportunity cost of being in school is your best forgone alternative. It is all the things you would have been able to enjoy if you were not in school. An opportunity cost is goods and services and time that must be forgone. Putting a dollar value on opportunity cost for a full-time student includes

- Tuition
- Expenditure on books and other study aids
- Forgone earnings

For a student attending a state university in her or his home state, tuition is around $10,000 per year.

Books and other study aids cost around $1,000 per year.

Forgone earnings are the wage of a high-school graduate in a starter job, which is around $24,000 a year.

So the total cost of being in school is about $35,000 per year or $105,000 for a 3-year degree and $140,000 for a 4-year degree.

Net Benefit

The benefit of extra earnings alone brings in $36,000 a year or $360,000 in 10 years and $1,440,000 in a working life of 40 years.

But you are incurring the costs now while you won't enjoy the benefits until some time in the future. We need to lower the benefits to compare them properly with the costs. You'll learn how to do that later in your economics course. But even allowing for the fact that the costs are incurred now while the benefits are received in the future, the net benefit is big!

Is School Always Best?

At the age of 18, Clayton Kershaw was offered a baseball scholarship at Texas A & M. The scholarship wouldn't have covered all the costs of school, but it would have lowered them a long way below those that you face.

But Clayton had an alternative to school. He was considered the top high-schooler available entering the 2006 MLB Draft and he was offered a signing bonus by the Los Angeles Dodgers said to be $2.3 million.

Clayton turned down the baseball scholarship at Texas A & M and signed with the Dodgers.

As the starting pitcher, Clayton's value to the Dodgers is high and earned him a salary of $30 million in 2015.

Clayton Kershaw's opportunity cost of a college education vastly exceeded the benefit he could expect to get from it. So, like you, he made the right decision.

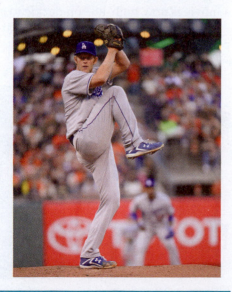

CHECKPOINT 1.2

MyEconLab Study Plan 1.2
Key Terms Quiz
Solutions Video

Explain the ideas that define the economic way of thinking.

Practice Problems

Every week, Kate plays tennis for two hours, and her grade on each math test is 70 percent. Last week, after playing for two hours, Kate considered playing for another hour. She decided to play for another hour and cut her study time by one hour. But last week, her math grade fell to 60 percent. Use this information to work Problems **1** to **4**.

1. What was Kate's opportunity cost of the third hour of tennis?
2. Given that Kate played the third hour, what can you conclude about her marginal benefit and marginal cost of the second hour of tennis?
3. Was Kate's decision to play the third hour of tennis rational?
4. Did Kate make her decision on the margin?

In the News

The *New York Times* reports that cruise lines have been slashing prices and cruise sales are up. It says this surge of interest tells us that despite the uncertain economic climate, people clearly need more fun in their lives and view their vacations as valuable and necessary.

1. In deciding whether to take a cruise, would you face a tradeoff?
2. How would you make a rational choice about taking a cruise?
3. What would be the marginal benefit from a cruise? What would be the marginal cost of a cruise?
4. Why would you expect a lower price to increase the number of people who decide to take a cruise?

Solutions to Practice Problems

1. Kate's opportunity cost of the third hour of tennis was the drop in her grade of ten percentage points.
2. The marginal benefit from the second hour of tennis must have exceeded the marginal cost of the second hour because Kate chose to play the third hour.
3. If marginal benefit exceeded marginal cost, Kate's decision was rational.
4. Kate made her decision on the margin because she compared the benefit and cost of one more hour (marginal benefit and marginal cost).

Solutions to In the News

1. You would face a tradeoff because you would have to forgo something else that you might otherwise do with your resources (time and budget).
2. You would make a rational choice by comparing the marginal benefit from a cruise and the marginal cost of taking one.
3. The marginal benefit from a cruise is the most you are willing to pay for one. The marginal cost is what you would have to pay to take a cruise.
4. With a lower price, more people will have a marginal benefit that exceeds the price and they will choose to take a cruise.

1.3 ECONOMICS AS A LIFE SKILL

Economics is a life skill. It is a decision-making toolkit and, as a social science, it is a platform on which you will build critical thinking skills that prepare you for your career and life.

■ Economics as a Decision Tool

Economics is useful. The economic way of thinking provides you with tools for making decisions in all aspects of your lives:

- Personal
- Business
- Government

Personal Decisions

Should you take a student loan? Should you get a weekend job? Should you rent an apartment or borrow and buy a condo? How should you allocate your time between study, working, volunteering, caring for others, and having fun?

Deciding the answers to these questions involves weighing a marginal benefit and a marginal cost. Although some of the numbers might be hard to pin down, you will make more solid decisions if you approach these questions with the tools of economics.

Business Decisions

Should Sony compete with Apple in the smartphone market? Should Texaco get more oil from the Gulf of Mexico or from Alaska? Should Marvel Studios produce Spider-Man 4, a sequel to Spider-Man 3?

Like personal economic questions, these business questions involve the evaluation of a marginal benefit and a marginal cost. So again, by approaching these questions with the tools of economics and by hiring economists as advisers, businesses can make better decisions.

Government Decisions

Should there be a special tax to penalize corporations that send jobs overseas? Should cheap foreign imports of furniture and textiles be limited? Should the farms that grow beets receive a subsidy?

These government policy questions call for decisions that involve the evaluation of a marginal benefit and a marginal cost and an investigation of the interactions of individuals and businesses. Yet again, by approaching these questions with the tools of economics, governments can make better decisions.

■ Economics as a Social Science

Economists try to understand and predict the effects of economic forces by using the *scientific method* first developed by physicists. The scientific method is a commonsense way of systematically checking what works and what doesn't work. It begins with a question about cause and effect arising from some observed facts. An economist might wonder why computers are getting cheaper and more computers are being used. Are computers getting cheaper because more people are buying them, or are more people buying computers because they are getting cheaper? Or is a third factor causing both the price fall and the quantity increase?

Economic Models

A scientist's second step is to build a model that provides a possible answer to the question of interest. All sciences use models. An **economic model** is a description of the economy or a part of the economy that includes only those features assumed necessary to explain the observed facts.

A model is like a map. If you want to know about valleys and mountains, you use a physical map; if you're studying nations, you use a political map; if you want to drive from *A* to *B* in an unfamiliar city, you use a street map; and if you're a city engineer, you use a map of the cables and conduit under the streets.

In economics, we use mathematical and graph-based models. The questions posed above about the price and quantity of computers bought are answered by a graph-based model called "demand and supply" that you will study in Chapter 4.

Economic model

A description of the economy or a part of the economy that includes only those features assumed necessary to explain the observed facts.

Check Predictions of Models Against Facts

A scientist's third step is to check the predictions of a proposed model against the facts. Physicists check whether their models correspond to the facts by doing experiments. For example, with a particle accelerator, a physicist can test a model of the structure of an atom.

Economists have a harder time than physicists, but they still approach the task in a scientific manner. To check predictions of a model against facts, economists use natural experiments, statistical investigations, and laboratory experiments.

A natural experiment is a situation that arises in the ordinary course of economic life in which the one factor of interest is different and other things are equal (or similar). For example, Canada has higher unemployment benefits than the United States, but the people in the two nations are similar. So to study the effect of unemployment benefits on the unemployment rate, economists might compare the United States with Canada.

A statistical investigation looks for a *correlation*—a tendency for the values of two variables to move together (either in the same direction or in opposite directions) in a predictable and related way. For example, cigarette smoking and lung cancer are correlated. Sometimes a correlation shows a causal influence of one variable on the other. Smoking causes lung cancer. But sometimes the direction of causation is hard to determine.

A laboratory experiment puts people (often students) in a decision-making situation and varies the influence of one factor at a time to discover how they respond to changed incentives. Some economists (neuroeconomists) are now studying what happens inside the brain of a decisionmaker.

Disagreement: Normative versus Positive

Economists sometimes disagree. Some disagreements can be settled by checking facts, but others cannot.

Disagreements that can't be settled by facts are *normative*—disagreements about what *should be*. These disagreements turn on subjective values and cannot be tested. The statement "We *should* burn less coal" is normative. You may agree or disagree with it, but you can't test it. It doesn't assert a fact that can be checked. Economists as social scientists try to steer clear of normative statements.

Disagreements that *can* be settled by facts are *positive*—disagreements about *what is*. These disagreements can be settled by careful observation of facts. "Burning coal raises the temperature of the planet" is a positive statement. It can be tested. Sometimes the facts are hard to get and sometimes they are hard to interpret, so disagreement persists. It is an ongoing feature of a healthy science.

■ Economics as an Aid to Critical Thinking

Throughout your career you will need to engage in *critical thinking*. And throughout your life, if you strive to approach personal and social issues as a critical thinker, you will make better decisions and be a better friend, neighbor, and citizen.

What is Critical Thinking?

Critical thinking is thinking that is logical and fact-based. It is thinking that

- begins with a question
- clarifies the question
- thinks with an open mind about how to answer the question
- identifies potential answers
- seeks the relevant facts to check the potential answers
- ends with a well-reasoned answer

Does this sequence of critical thinking activities seem familiar? It does if you have just read the previous page. You will recognize that critical thinking is just another name for approaching an issue like a scientist. Economic science begins with a question about some economic event or activity; uses the economic way of thinking to clarify the question, think about how to answer it, identify possible answers, and check them against the facts; and arrives at a well-reasoned answer.

As a student, you will have lots of opportunities to practice critical thinking. It will be a feature of almost all your courses, and it will be a major feature of your economics course. What you learn in this course and the critical thinking and economic thinking skills that you develop will enrich your career and your life.

Learning-by-Doing

A central theme of this textbook is that the best way to learn economics is to do it—*learning-by-doing*. The mantra is "work the problem" and "draw the graph." This same message applies to critical thinking. The best way to become skilled at critical thinking is to do it.

To get you started, look at the example of a critical thinking question in *Eye on Your Life* on p. 17. The question is a simple one about facts. It doesn't have a cause-and-effect dimension, but it illustrates the central role that facts play. Facts always trump guesses and beliefs. The question also suggests another valuable activity: cooperating and working with others. Teamwork enables data to be shared and brainstorming a question often triggers better ideas about other possible answers that should be checked.

Throughout this textbook, we present you with a wide variety of critical thinking opportunities. Some arise from your life experiences in *Eye on Your Life* boxes like the one in this chapter. Others arise from economic events and issues in the news. News clips and the critical thinking questions that they raise appear in every chapter.

Also, every chapter starts with a question that is answered with a critical thinking box later in the chapter. The question on the opening page of this chapter and the *Eye on the Benefit and Cost of School* box on p. 12 are examples. Studying these examples and using what you learn to answer the economic questions that arise in your life and in the news will strengthen your critical thinking. You will emerge from your economics course with not only the ability to think like an economist but also more generally to be a critical thinker.

EYE on YOUR LIFE
Your Time Allocation

MyEconLab Critical Thinking Exercise

Your time is a scarce resource and how you allocate it impacts the quality of your life. Your physical fitness depends on how much time you allocate to sports and exercise, and your grade depends on the amount of time you allocate to studying.

Sleeping, personal care, eating and drinking, and traveling take a large chunk of your time, but you have choices about how much time to allocate to each of these activities. You also have choices about how much time to spend working for an income, enjoying sports and other leisure activities, and on educational activities (attending class, doing assignments, and studying).

Do you know the number of hours per day that you allocate to sleeping, personal care, eating and drinking, traveling, working, sports and leisure, and educational activities?

Here is a critical thinking question for you: Who works harder, you or the average student?

This question is one of fact, but answering requires agreement on what we mean by "works harder" and requires some data (the facts).

Let's agree that we will measure how hard a person works as the average number of hours per weekday spent working and on educational activities.

Next, we need the facts about time allocation—data about your time use and the time use of an average student.

The table above has eight activities and two columns for data. Complete the first column based on your current best guess about your time use.

Now keep a calendar for a normal week, and calculate your actual average hours for each activity. At the end of the week, complete the second column of the table.

How do your actual numbers compare with your guesses? Are there any surprises?

Now we need to compare your time use with that of the average student. The Bureau of Labor Statistics has conducted a survey to get the facts and the figure below shows what it found.

So, what is the answer? Are there any more surprises? Who works more hours, you or the average student?

Does the answer make you want to change your time allocation?

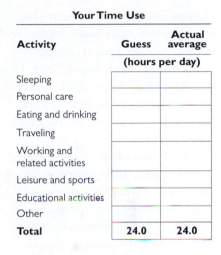

Your Time Use		
Activity	**Guess**	**Actual average**
	(hours per day)	
Sleeping		
Personal care		
Eating and drinking		
Traveling		
Working and related activities		
Leisure and sports		
Educational activities		
Other		
Total	**24.0**	**24.0**

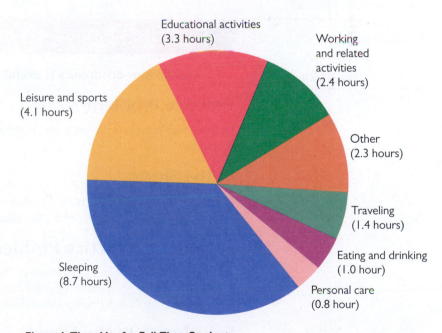

Figure 1 Time Use for Full-Time Students

SOURCE OF DATA: Bureau of Labor Statistics, American Time Use Survey, average on non-holiday weekdays for full-time university and college students 2010–2014.

EYE on the PAST
Adam Smith and the Birth of Economics as a Social Science

Many people had written about economics before Adam Smith did, but he made economics a social science.

Born in 1723 in Scotland, Smith became a full professor at 28 and published his masterpiece, *An Inquiry into the Nature and Causes of the Wealth of Nations,* in 1776.

Adam Smith asked: Why are some nations wealthy while others are poor? His answer: Through the division of labor and free markets, nations become wealthy. To illustrate his argument, he used the example of a pin factory. He guessed that one person, using the hand tools available in the 1770s, might make 20 pins a day. Yet,

he observed, by using the same hand tools but breaking the process into a number of individually small tasks in which people specialize—by the division of labor—ten people could make a staggering 48,000 pins a day.

But a large market is needed to support the division of labor: One factory employing ten workers would need to sell more than 15 million pins a year to stay in business!

Smith saw free competitive markets as a source of wealth. The self-interested pursuit of profit, led by an invisible hand, resulted in resources being used in ways that created the greatest possible value and wealth.

MyEconLab Study Plan 1.3
Key Terms Quiz
Solutions Video

 # CHECKPOINT 1.3

Explain how economics is useful as a life skill.

Practice Problem

Distinguish between positive and normative statements and provide an example of each.

In the News

The *New York Times* reports that China will end its one-child policy. How would an economist study the effect of this policy change?

Solution to Practice Problem

A positive statement is a statement of fact that can be checked, such as "grocery prices are rising." A normative statement is an opinion that cannot be checked, such as "tuition should be based on family income."

Solution to In the News

As a social scientist, an economist would construct a population model. As a policy adviser, an economist would evaluate the benefits and costs of the change.

CHAPTER SUMMARY

Key Points

1. Define economics and explain the kinds of questions that economists try to answer.

- Economics is the social science that studies the choices that we make as we cope with scarcity and the incentives that influence and reconcile our choices.
- Microeconomics is the study of individual choices and interactions, and macroeconomics is the study of the national economy and global economy.
- The first big question of economics is: How do the choices that people make end up determining *what, how,* and *for whom* goods and services are produced?
- The second big question is: When do choices made in the pursuit of *self-interest* also promote the *social interest*?

2. Explain the ideas that define the economic way of thinking.

- Six ideas define the economic way of thinking:
  1. A choice is a *tradeoff*.
  2. *Cost* is what you *must* give up to get something.
  3. *Benefit* is what you gain when you get something (measured by what you *are willing to* give up to get it).
  4. People make *rational* choices by comparing benefits and costs.
  5. A "how much" choice is made on the *margin* by comparing *marginal benefit* and *marginal cost*.
  6. Choices respond to *incentives*.

3. Explain how economics is useful as a life skill.

- Economics is a tool for personal, business, and government decisions.
- Economists use the *scientific method* to try to understand how the economic world works. They create economic models and test them using natural experiments, statistical investigations, and laboratory experiments.
- Economics and the economic way of thinking are foundations on which to build critical thinking skills.

Key Terms

MyEconLab Key Terms Quiz

Benefit, 9	Margin, 10	Scarcity, 2
Economic model, 15	Marginal benefit, 10	Self-interest, 4
Economics, 2	Marginal cost, 10	Social interest, 4
Goods and services, 3	Microeconomics, 2	Tradeoff, 8
Incentive, 11	Opportunity cost, 8	
Macroeconomics, 3	Rational choice, 9	

MyEconLab Chapter 1 Study Plan

CHAPTER CHECKPOINT

Study Plan Problems and Applications

1. Provide three examples of scarcity that illustrate why even the 1,826 billionaires in the world face scarcity.

2. Label each entry in List 1 as dealing with a microeconomic topic or a macroeconomic topic. Explain your answer.

Use the following information to work Problems **3** to **6**.

Jurassic World had world-wide box office receipts of $1.66 billion. The movie's production budget was $150 million with additional marketing costs. A successful movie brings pleasure to millions, creates work for thousands, and makes a few people rich.

3. What contribution does a movie like *Jurassic World* make to coping with scarcity? When you buy a movie ticket, are you buying a good or a service?

4. Who decides whether a movie is going to be a blockbuster? How do you think the creation of a blockbuster movie influences *what*, *how*, and *for whom* goods and services are produced?

5. What are some of the components of marginal cost and marginal benefit that the producer of a movie faces?

6. Suppose that Chris Pratt had been offered a part in another movie and that to hire him for *Jurassic World*, the producer had to double Chris Pratt's pay. What incentives would have changed? How might the changed incentives have changed the choices that people made?

7. What is the social interest? Distinguish it from self-interest. In your answer give an example of self-interest and an example of social interest.

8. Pam, Pru, and Pat are deciding how they will celebrate the New Year. Pam prefers to take a cruise, is happy to go to Hawaii, but does not want to go skiing. Pru prefers to go skiing, is happy to go to Hawaii, but does not want to take a cruise. Pat prefers to go to Hawaii or to take a cruise but does not want to go skiing. Their decision is to go to Hawaii. Is this decision rational? What is the opportunity cost of the trip to Hawaii for each of them? What is the benefit that each gets?

9. Label each of the entries in List 2 as a positive or a normative statement.

Use the following information to work Problems **10** to **12**.

REI is paying its employees to take Black Friday, Thanksgiving off
REI, the outdoor gear and apparel retailer, is paying employees to celebrate Thanksgiving 2015 by spending Black Friday outdoors with their families.
Source: Sustainable Brands, October 28, 2015

10. With Black Friday off with full pay, explain what is free and what is scarce.

11. What is REI's incentive to give its workers Black Friday off? Was REI's decision made in self-interest or in the social interest? Explain your answer.

12. Do you think that REI workers will shop or spend the day with family? Explain your answer.

13. Read *Eye on the Benefit and Cost of School* on p. 12 and explain why both you and Clayton Kershaw made the right decision.

LIST 1

- Motor vehicle production in China is growing by 10 percent a year.
- Coffee prices skyrocket.
- Globalization has reduced African poverty.
- The government must cut its budget deficit.
- Apple sells 20 million iPhone 6 smartphones a month.

LIST 2

- Low-income people pay too much for housing.
- The number of U.S. farms has decreased over the past 50 years.
- Toyota expands parts production in the United States.
- Imports from China are swamping U.S. department stores.
- The rural population in the United States is declining.

Instructor Assignable Problems and Applications

MyEconLab Homework, Quiz, or Test if assigned by instructor

1. Which of the following items are components of the opportunity cost of being a full-time college student who lives at home? The things that the student would have bought with
   - A higher income
   - Expenditure on tuition
   - A subscription to the *Rolling Stone* magazine
   - The income the student will earn after graduating

2. Think about the following news items and label each as involving a *what, how,* or *for whom* question:
   - Today, most stores use computers to keep their inventory records, whereas 20 years ago most stores used paper records.
   - Healthcare professionals and drug companies recommend that Medicaid drug rebates be made available to everyone in need.
   - An increase in the gas tax pays for low-cost public transit.

3. The headlines in List 1 appeared in *The Wall Street Journal*. Classify each headline as a signal that the news article is about a microeconomic topic or a macroeconomic topic. Explain your answers.

4. Your school decides to increase the intake of new students next year. To make its decision, what economic concepts would it have considered? Would the school have used the "economic way of thinking" in reaching its decision? Would the school have made its decision on the margin?

5. Provide examples of (a) a monetary incentive and (b) a non-monetary incentive, a carrot and a stick of each, that governments use to influence behavior.

6. Think about each of the items in List 2 and explain how they affect incentives and might change the choices that people make.

7. Does the decision to make a blockbuster movie mean that some other more desirable activities get fewer resources than they deserve? Is your answer positive or normative? Explain your answer.

8. Provide two examples of economics being used as a tool by (a) a student, (b) a business, and (c) a government. Classify your examples as dealing with microeconomic topics and macroeconomic topics.

LIST 1
- Job Gains Calm Slump Worries
- Washington Post's Profit Falls
- Overcapacity, Fuel Costs Hit Shipping
- U.S. Budget Deficit Expands

LIST 2
- A hurricane hits Central Florida.
- The World Series begins tonight, but a storm warning is in effect for the area around the stadium.
- The price of a personal computer falls to $50.
- Unrest in the Middle East sends the price of gas to $5 a gallon.

Use the following news clip to work Problems **9** to **12**.

Obama unveils major climate change policy
Obama's Clean Power Plan, which will set federal limits on carbon emissions from coal-fired power plants, will cost $8.4 billion and reap benefits of more than $34 billion. Opponents of the plan say it will drive up the cost of electricity for millions of Americans.

Source: CNN, August 3, 2015

9. What are the more than $34 billion of benefits from using less coal to produce electricity? Who receives these benefits: the users of electricity or the owners of power plants, or both the users and the owners?

10. What are the $8.4 billion of costs arising from using less coal to produce electricity? Who bears these costs: the users of electricity or the owners of power plants, or both the users and the owners?

11. Explain why someone might oppose the Clean Power Plan when its benefits exceed its costs.

12. Explain whether the Clean Power Plan has an opportunity cost.

Multiple Choice Quiz

1. Which of the following describes the reason why scarcity exists?

   A. Governments make bad economic decisions.
   B. The gap between the rich and the poor is too wide.
   C. Wants exceed the resources available to satisfy them.
   D. There is too much unemployment.

2. Which of the following defines economics?
Economics is the social science that studies _____.

   A. the best way of eliminating scarcity
   B. the choices made to cope with scarcity, how incentives influence those choices, and how the choices are coordinated
   C. how money is created and used
   D. the inevitable conflict between self-interest and the social interest

3. Of the three big questions, *what, how,* and *for whom,* which of the following is an example of a *how* question?

   A. Why do doctors and lawyers earn high incomes?
   B. Why don't we produce more small cars and fewer gas guzzlers?
   C. Why do we use machines rather than migrant workers to pick grapes?
   D. Why do college football coaches earn more than professors?

4. Which of the following is not a key idea in the economic way of thinking?

   A. People make rational choices by comparing costs and benefits.
   B. Poor people are discriminated against and should be treated more fairly.
   C. A rational choice is made at the margin.
   D. Choices respond to incentives.

5. A rational choice is _____.

   A. the best thing you must forgo to get something
   B. what you are willing to forgo to get something
   C. made by comparing marginal benefit and marginal cost
   D. the best for society

6. Which of the following best illustrates your marginal benefit from studying?

   A. The knowledge you gain from studying two hours a night for a month
   B. The best things forgone by studying two hours a night for a month
   C. What you are willing to give up to study for one additional hour
   D. What you must give up to be able to study for one additional hour

7. The scientific method uses models to _____.

   A. clarify normative disagreements
   B. avoid the need to study real questions
   C. replicate all the features of the real world
   D. focus on those features of reality assumed relevant for understanding a cause-and-effect relationship

8. Which of the following is a positive statement?

   A. We should stop using corn to make ethanol because it is raising the cost of food.
   B. You will get the most out of college life if you play a sport once a week.
   C. Competition among wireless service providers across the borders of Canada, Mexico, and the United States has driven roaming rates down.
   D. Bill Gates ought to spend more helping to eradicate malaria in Africa

APPENDIX: MAKING AND USING GRAPHS

When you have completed your study of this appendix, you will be able to

1 Interpret graphs that display data.

2 Interpret the graphs used in economic models.

3 Define and calculate slope.

4 Graph relationships among more than two variables.

Basic Idea

A graph represents a quantity as a distance and enables us to visualize the relationship between two variables. To make a graph, we set two lines called *axes* perpendicular to each other, like those in Figure A1.1. The vertical line is called the *y*-axis, and the horizontal line is called the *x*-axis. The common zero point is called the *origin*. In Figure A1.1, the *x*-axis measures temperature in degrees Fahrenheit. A movement to the right shows an increase in temperature, and a movement to the left shows a decrease in temperature. The *y*-axis represents ice cream consumption, measured in gallons per day.

To make a graph, we need a value of the variable on the *x*-axis and a corresponding value of the variable on the *y*-axis. For example, if the temperature is 40°F, ice cream consumption is 5 gallons a day at point *A* in Figure A1.1. If the temperature is 80°F, ice cream consumption is 20 gallons a day at point *B* in Figure A1.1. Graphs like that in Figure A1.1 can be used to show any type of quantitative data on two variables.

FIGURE A1.1

Making a Graph

MyEconLab Animation

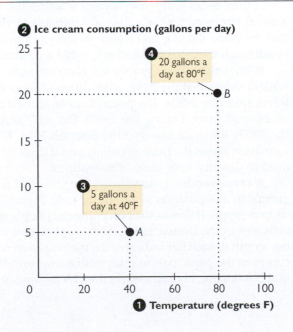

All graphs have axes that measure quantities as distances.

❶ The horizontal axis (*x*-axis) measures temperature in degrees Fahrenheit. A movement to the right shows an increase in temperature.

❷ The vertical axis (*y*-axis) measures ice cream consumption in gallons per day. A movement upward shows an increase in ice cream consumption.

❸ Point *A* shows that 5 gallons of ice cream are consumed on a day when the temperature is 40°F.

❹ Point *B* shows that 20 gallons of ice cream are consumed on a day when the temperature is 80°F.

■ Interpreting Data Graphs

Scatter diagram
A graph of the value of one variable against the value of another variable.

A **scatter diagram** is a graph of the value of one variable against the value of another variable. It is used to reveal whether a relationship exists between two variables and to describe the relationship. Figure A1.2 shows two examples.

Figure A1.2(a) shows the relationship between expenditure and income. Each point shows expenditure per person and income per person in the United States in a given year from 2000 to 2015. The points are "scattered" within the graph. The label on each point shows its year. The point marked 10 shows that in 2010, income per person was $36,183 and expenditure per person was $32,758. This scatter diagram reveals that as income increases, expenditure also increases.

Figure A1.2(b) shows the relationship during the 1990s between the percentage of Americans who own a cell phone and the average monthly cell-phone bill. This scatter diagram reveals that as the cost of using a cell phone falls, the number of cell-phone subscribers increases.

Time-series graph
A graph that measures time on the *x*-axis and the variable or variables in which we are interested on the *y*-axis.

A **time-series graph** measures time (for example, months or years) on the *x*-axis and the variable or variables in which we are interested on the *y*-axis. Figure A1.2(c) shows an example. In this graph, time (on the *x*-axis) is measured in years, which run from 1980 to 2016. The variable that we are interested in is the price of coffee, and it is measured on the *y*-axis.

A time-series graph conveys an enormous amount of information quickly and easily, as this example illustrates. It shows when the value is

1. High or low. When the line is a long way from the *x*-axis, the price is high, as it was in 1986. When the line is close to the *x*-axis, the price is low, as it was in 2001.

2. Rising or falling. When the line slopes upward, as in 2006, the price is rising. When the line slopes downward, as in 1997, the price is falling.

3. Rising or falling quickly or slowly. If the line is steep, then the price is rising or falling quickly. If the line is not steep, the price is rising or falling slowly. For example, the price rose quickly in 2006 and slowly in 2014. The price fell quickly in 1987 and slowly in 1996.

Trend
A general tendency for the value of a variable to rise or fall over time.

A time-series graph also reveals whether the variable has a trend. A **trend** is a general tendency for the value of a variable to rise or fall over time. You can see that the price of coffee had a general tendency to fall from 1980 to late in 2000. That is, although the price rose and fell, it had a general tendency to fall.

With a time-series graph, we can compare different periods quickly. Figure A1.2(c) shows that the 2000s were different from the 1990s, which in turn were different from the 1980s. The price of coffee started the 1980s high and then fell for a number of years. During the 1990s, the price was on a roller coaster. And during the 2000s, the price rose steadily through 2014. This graph conveys a wealth of information about the price of coffee, and it does so in much less space than we have used to describe only some of its features.

Cross-section graph
A graph that shows the values of an economic variable for different groups in a population at a point in time.

A **cross-section graph** shows the values of an economic variable for different groups in a population at a point in time. Figure A1.2(d) is an example of a cross-section graph. It shows the percentage of people who participate in selected sports activities in the United States. This graph uses bars rather than dots and lines, and the length of each bar indicates the participation rate. Figure A1.2(d) enables you to compare the participation rates in these ten sporting activities, and you can do so much more quickly and clearly than by looking at a list of numbers.

■ FIGURE A1.2

Data Graphs

MyEconLab Animation

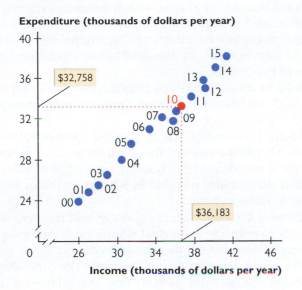

(a) Scatter Diagram: Expenditure and income

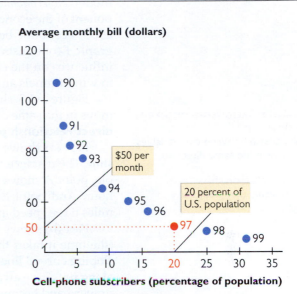

(b) Scatter Diagram: Subscribers and cost

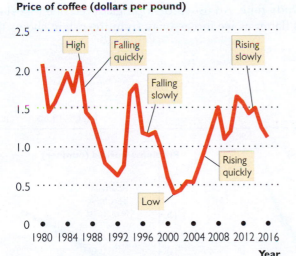

(c) Time Series: The price of coffee

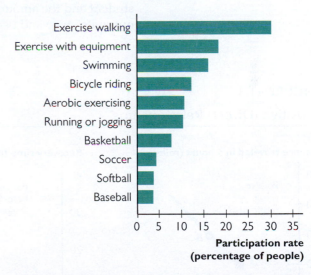

(d) Cross Section: Participation in selected sports activities

A scatter diagram reveals the relationship between two variables. In part (a), as income increases, expenditure almost always increases. In part (b), as the monthly cell-phone bill falls, the percentage of people who own a cell phone increases.

A time-series graph plots the value of a variable on the y-axis against time on the x-axis. Part (c) plots the price of coffee each

year from 1980 to 2016. The graph shows when the price of coffee was high and low, when it increased and decreased, and when it changed quickly and changed slowly.

A cross-section graph shows the value of a variable across the members of a population. Part (d) shows the participation rate in the United States in each of ten sporting activities.

■ Interpreting Graphs Used in Economic Models

We use graphs to show the relationships among the variables in an economic model. An *economic model* is a simplified description of the economy or of a component of the economy such as a business or a household. It consists of statements about economic behavior that can be expressed as equations or as curves in a graph. Economists use models to explore the effects of different policies or other influences on the economy in ways similar to those used to test model airplanes in wind tunnels and models of the climate.

Figure A1.3 shows graphs of the relationships between two variables that move in the same direction. Such a relationship is called a **positive relationship** or **direct relationship**.

Part (a) shows a straight-line relationship, which is called a **linear relationship**. The distance traveled in 5 hours increases as the speed increases. For example, point *A* shows that 200 miles are traveled in 5 hours at a speed of 40 miles an hour. And point *B* shows that the distance traveled in 5 hours increases to 300 miles if the speed increases to 60 miles an hour.

Part (b) shows the relationship between distance sprinted and recovery time (the time it takes the heart rate to return to its normal resting rate). An upward-sloping curved line that starts out quite flat but then becomes steeper as we move along the curve away from the origin describes this relationship. The curve slopes upward and becomes steeper because the extra recovery time needed from sprinting another 100 yards increases. It takes 5 minutes to recover from sprinting 100 yards but 15 minutes to recover from sprinting 200 yards.

Part (c) shows the relationship between the number of problems worked by a student and the amount of study time. An upward-sloping curved line that starts out quite steep and becomes flatter as we move away from the origin shows this

Positive relationship or direct relationship
A relationship between two variables that move in the same direction.

Linear relationship
A relationship that graphs as a straight line.

■ **FIGURE A1.3**

Positive (Direct) Relationships   MyEconLab Animation

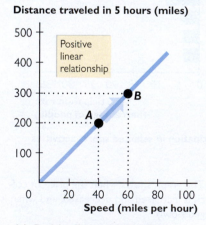

(a) **Positive linear relationship**

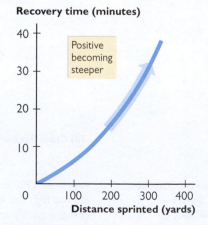

(b) **Positive becoming steeper**

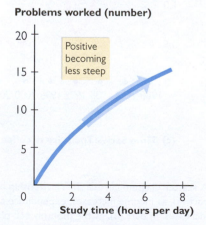

(c) **Positive becoming less steep**

Part (a) shows that as speed increases, the distance traveled in a given number of hours increases along a straight line.

Part (b) shows that as the distance sprinted increases, recovery time increases along a curve that becomes steeper.

Part (c) shows that as study time increases, the number of problems worked increases along a curve that becomes less steep.

relationship. Study time becomes less effective as you increase the hours worked and become more tired.

Figure A1.4 shows relationships between two variables that move in opposite directions. Such a relationship is called a **negative relationship** or **inverse relationship**.

Part (a) shows the relationship between the number of hours spent playing squash and the number of hours spent playing tennis when the total number of hours available is five. One extra hour spent playing tennis means one hour less playing squash and vice versa. This relationship is negative and linear.

Part (b) shows the relationship between the cost per mile traveled and the length of a journey. The longer the journey, the lower is the cost per mile. But as the journey length increases, the fall in the cost per mile becomes smaller. This feature of the relationship is shown by the fact that the curve slopes downward, starting out steep at a short journey length and then becoming flatter as the journey length increases. This relationship arises because some of the costs, such as auto insurance, are fixed, and as the journey length increases, the fixed costs are spread over more miles.

Part (c) shows the relationship between the amount of leisure time and the number of problems worked by a student. Increasing leisure time produces an increasingly large reduction in the number of problems worked. This relationship is a negative one that starts out with a gentle slope at a small number of leisure hours and becomes steeper as the number of leisure hours increases. This relationship is a different view of the idea shown in Figure A1.3(c).

Many relationships in economic models have a maximum or a minimum. For example, firms try to make the largest possible profit and to produce at the lowest possible cost. Figure A1.5 shows relationships that have a maximum or a minimum.

Negative relationship or **inverse relationship**
A relationship between two variables that move in opposite directions.

■ **FIGURE A1.4**

Negative (Inverse) Relationships   MyEconLab Animation

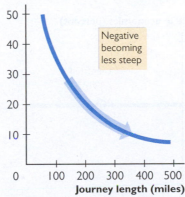
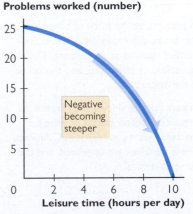

(a) **Negative linear relationship**

(b) **Negative becoming less steep**

(c) **Negative becoming steeper**

Part (a) shows that as the time playing tennis increases, the time playing squash decreases along a straight line.

Part (b) shows that as the journey length increases, the cost of the trip falls along a curve that becomes less steep.

Part (c) shows that as leisure time increases, the number of problems worked decreases along a curve that becomes steeper.

■ **FIGURE A1.5**

Maximum and Minimum Points

MyEconLab Animation

In part (a), as the rainfall increases, the curve ❶ slopes upward as the yield per acre rises, ❷ is flat at point *A*, the maximum yield, and then ❸ slopes downward as the yield per acre falls.

In part (b), as the speed increases, the curve ❶ slopes downward as the cost per mile falls, ❷ is flat at the minimum point *B*, and then ❸ slopes upward as the cost per mile rises.

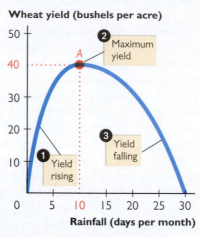

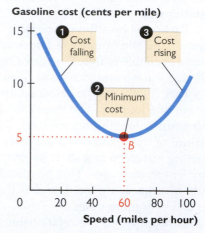

(a) **Relationship with a maximum**

(b) **Relationship with a minimum**

Part (a) shows a relationship that starts out sloping upward, reaches a maximum, and then slopes downward. Part (b) shows a relationship that begins sloping downward, falls to a minimum, and then slopes upward.

Finally, there are many situations in which, no matter what happens to the value of one variable, the other variable remains constant. Sometimes we want to show two variables that are unrelated in a graph. Figure A1.6 shows two graphs in which the variables are unrelated.

■ **FIGURE A1.6**

Variables That Are Unrelated

MyEconLab Animation

In part (a), as the price of bananas increases, the student's grade in economics remains at 75 percent. These variables are unrelated, and the curve is horizontal.

In part (b), the vineyards of France produce 3 billion gallons of wine no matter what the rainfall is in California. These variables are unrelated, and the curve is vertical.

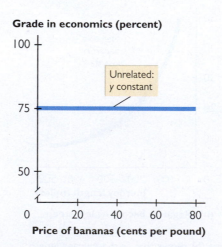

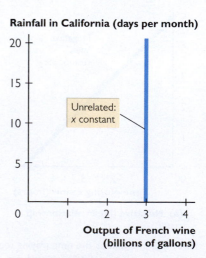

(a) **Unrelated: y constant**

(b) **Unrelated: x constant**

■ The Slope of a Relationship

We can measure the influence of one variable on another by the slope of the relationship. The **slope** of a relationship is the change in the value of the variable measured on the y-axis divided by the change in the value of the variable measured on the x-axis. We use the Greek letter Δ (delta) to represent "change in." So Δy means the change in the value of y, and Δx means the change in the value of x. The slope of the relationship is

$$\Delta y \div \Delta x.$$

If a large change in y is associated with a small change in x, the slope is large and the curve is steep. If a small change in y is associated with a large change in x, the slope is small and the curve is flat.

Figure A1.7 shows you how to calculate slope. The slope of a straight line is the same regardless of where on the line you calculate it—the slope is constant. In part (a), when x increases from 2 to 6, y increases from 3 to 6. The change in x is 4—that is, Δx is 4. The change in y is 3—that is, Δy is 3. The slope of that line is 3/4. In part (b), when x increases from 2 to 6, y *decreases* from 6 to 3. The change in y is *minus* 3—that is, Δy is -3 The change in x is plus 4—that is, Δx is 4. The slope of the curve is $-3/4$.

In part (c), we calculate the slope at a point on a curve. To do so, place a ruler on the graph so that it touches point A and no other point on the curve, then draw a straight line along the edge of the ruler. The slope of this straight line is the slope of the curve at point A. This slope is 3/4.

Slope
The change in the value of the variable measured on the y-axis divided by the change in the value of the variable measured on the x-axis.

■ **FIGURE A1.7**

Calculating Slope

MyEconLab Animation

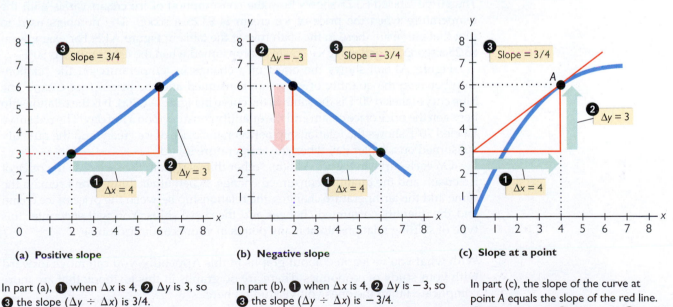

(a) Positive slope

(b) Negative slope

(c) Slope at a point

In part (a), ❶ when Δx is 4, ❷ Δy is 3, so ❸ the slope ($\Delta y \div \Delta x$) is 3/4.

In part (b), ❶ when Δx is 4, ❷ Δy is -3, so ❸ the slope ($\Delta y \div \Delta x$) is $-3/4$.

In part (c), the slope of the curve at point A equals the slope of the red line. ❶ When Δx is 4, ❷ Δy is 3, so ❸ the slope ($\Delta y \div \Delta x$) is 3/4.

■ Relationships Among More Than Two Variables

All the graphs that you have studied so far plot the relationship between two variables as a point formed by the x and y values. But most of the relationships in economics involve relationships among many variables, not just two. For example, the amount of ice cream consumed depends on the price of ice cream and the temperature. If ice cream is expensive and the temperature is low, people eat much less ice cream than when ice cream is inexpensive and the temperature is high. For any given price of ice cream, the quantity consumed varies with the temperature; and for any given temperature, the quantity of ice cream consumed varies with its price.

Figure A1.8 shows a relationship among three variables. The table shows the number of gallons of ice cream consumed per day at various temperatures and ice cream prices. How can we graph these numbers?

To graph a relationship that involves more than two variables, we use the *ceteris paribus* assumption.

Ceteris Paribus

The Latin phrase *ceteris paribus* means "other things remaining the same." Every laboratory experiment is an attempt to create *ceteris paribus* and isolate the relationship of interest. We use the same method to make a graph.

Figure A1.8(a) shows an example. This graph shows what happens to the quantity of ice cream consumed when the price of ice cream varies while the temperature remains constant. The curve labeled 90°F shows the relationship between ice cream consumption and the price of ice cream if the temperature is 90°F. The numbers used to plot that curve are those in the first and fifth columns of the table in Figure A1.8. For example, if the temperature is 90°F, 10 gallons of ice cream are consumed when the price is $3.25 a scoop.

We can also show the relationship between ice cream consumption and temperature while the price of ice cream remains constant, as shown in Figure A1.8(b). The curve labeled $3.25 shows how the consumption of ice cream varies with the temperature when the price of ice cream is $3.25 a scoop. The numbers used to plot that curve are those in the sixth row of the table in Figure A1.8. For example, at $3.25 a scoop, 10 gallons of ice cream are consumed when the temperature is 90°F.

Figure A1.8(c) shows the effect of a change in temperature on the relationship between the quantity of ice cream consumed and the price of ice cream. The blue curve labeled 90°F is the same as the curve in Figure A1.8(a). It is the relationship between the price of ice cream and the quantity consumed on a hot day. The red curve labeled 70°F shows the relationship between the price of ice cream and the quantity consumed on a cooler day when the temperature is 70°F.

On each curve in Figure A1.8(c), "other things remain the same" as the price of ice cream and the quantity consumed change. When other things don't remain the same and the termperature changes, the relationship between the price of ice cream and the quantity consumed changes and the curve shifts. You will encounter this type of shifting relationship at many points in your economics course.

With what you've learned about graphs in this Appendix, you can move forward with your study of economics. There are no graphs in this textbook that are more complicated than the ones you've studied here.

■ **FIGURE A1.8**

Graphing a Relationship Among Three Variables

Price (dollars per scoop)	Ice cream consumption (gallons per day)			
	30°F	50°F	70°F	90°F
2.00	12	18	25	50
2.25	10	12	18	37
2.50	7	10	13	27
2.75	5	7	10	20
3.00	3	5	7	14
3.25	2	3	5	10
3.50	1	2	3	6

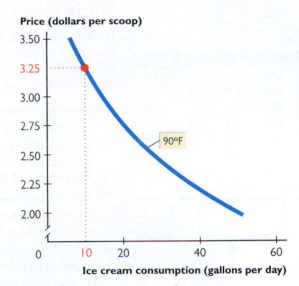

Price (dollars per scoop)

(a) Price and consumption at a given temperature

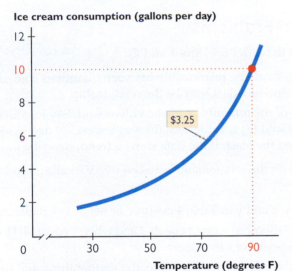

(b) Temperature and consumption of ice cream at a given price

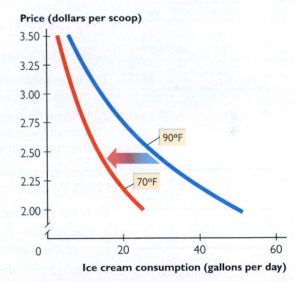

(c) A change in temperature shifts the curve

The table shows the quantity of ice cream consumed at different prices and different temperatures. For example, if the price is $3.25 a scoop and the temperature is 90°F, 10 gallons of ice cream are consumed. This set of values is highlighted in the table and in parts (a) and (b).

Part (a) shows the relationship between the price and consumption when the temperature is 90°F. The negative slope means that a higher price brings lower consumption.

Part (b) shows the relationship between the temperature and consumption when price is

$3.25 a scoop. The positive slope means that a higher temperature brings greater consumption

Part (c) shows the change in the relationship between price and consumption when the temperature falls from 90°F to 70°F.

MyEconLab Chapter 1 Study Plan

APPENDIX CHECKPOINT

Study Plan Problems

TABLE 1

	A	B	C	D
1	2004	767	33	139
2	2006	620	23	586
3	2008	385	13	1,033
4	2010	226	9	1,162
5	2012	211	11	1,392
6	2014	144	4	1,200

TABLE 2

x	0	1	2	3	4	5
y	32	31	28	23	16	7

TABLE 3

Price (dollars per ride)	Balloon rides (number per day)		
	50°F	70°F	90°F
5	32	50	40
10	27	40	32
15	18	32	27
20	10	27	18

MyEconLab Homework, Quiz, or Test if assigned by instructor

TABLE 4

x	0	1	2	3	4	5
y	0	1	4	9	16	25

TABLE 5

Price (dollars per cup)	Hot chocolate (cups per week)		
	50°F	70°F	90°F
2.00	40	30	20
2.50	30	20	10
3.00	20	10	0
3.50	10	0	0

The spreadsheet in Table 1 provides data on the U.S. economy: Column A is the year; the other columns are quantities sold in millions per year of compact discs (column B), music videos (column C), and singles downloads (column D). Use this spreadsheet to work Problems **1** and **2**.

1. Draw a scatter diagram to show the relationship between the quantities sold of compact discs and music videos. Describe the relationship.

2. Draw a time-series graph of the quantity of compact discs sold. Say in which year or years the quantity sold (a) was highest, (b) was lowest, (c) increased the most, and (d) decreased the most. If the data show a trend, describe it.

3. Is the relationship between x and y in Table 2 positive or negative? Calculate the slope of the relationship when x equals 2 and when x equals 4. How does the slope change as the value of x increases?

4. Table 3 provides data on the price of a balloon ride, the temperature, and the number of rides a day. Draw graphs to show the relationship between
   • The price and the number of rides, when the temperature is 70°F.
   • The number of rides and the temperature, when the price is $15 a ride.

Instructor Assignable Problems

Use the information in Table 1 to work Problems **1** and **2**.

1. Draw a scatter diagram to show the relationship between quantities sold of music videos and singles downloads. Describe the relationship.

2. Draw a time-series graph of the quantity of music videos sold. Say in which year or years the quantity sold (a) was highest, (b) was lowest, (c) decreased the most, and (d) decreased the least. If the data show a trend, describe it.

Use the information in Table 4 on the relationship between two variables x and y to work Problems **3** and **4**.

3. Is the relationship between x and y in Table 4 positive or negative? Explain.

4. Calculate the slope of the relationship when x equals 2 and when x equals 4. How does the slope change as the value of x increases?

5. Table 5 provides data on the price of hot chocolate, the temperature, and the cups of hot chocolate bought. Draw graphs to show the relationship between
   • The price and cups of hot chocolate bought, when the temperature is constant.
   • The temperature and cups of hot chocolate bought, when the price is constant.

Key Terms

MyEconLab Key Terms Quiz

Cross-section graph, 24
Direct relationship, 26
Inverse relationship, 27
Linear relationship, 26

Negative relationship, 27
Positive relationship, 26
Scatter diagram, 24
Slope, 29

Time-series graph, 24
Trend, 24

The U.S. and Global Economies

2

When you have completed your study of this chapter, you will be able to

1 Describe what, how, and for whom goods and services are produced in the United States.

2 Describe what, how, and for whom goods and services are produced in the global economy.

3 Explain the circular flow model of the U.S. economy and of the global economy.

MyEconLab Big Picture Video

33

2.1 WHAT, HOW, AND FOR WHOM?

Who makes the Dreamliner? Boeing, right? Not exactly right. You'll see in this chapter that 400 firms around the world produce components of this airliner.

Airplanes are one of the many millions of different goods and services produced in the United States today. To see some more, walk around a shopping mall and go inside some of the shops and check the labels to see where things are made. Some are made in the United States but many, perhaps most, are made in other countries. We're going to look at what goods and services get produced and where; how they are produced, and who gets to enjoy them. We begin with *what* we produce in the United States..

■ What Do We Produce?

We place the goods and services produced into two large groups:

- Consumption goods and services
- Capital goods

Consumption Goods and Services

Consumption goods and services are items that individuals and governments buy and use up in the current period. Consumption goods and services bought by households include items such as housing, automobiles, bottled water, ramen noodles, chocolate bars, Po' boy sandwiches, movies, downhill skiing lessons, and doctor and dental services. Consumption goods and services bought by governments include items such as police and fire services, garbage collection, and education.

Capital Goods

Capital goods are goods that businesses and governments buy to increase productive resources to use during future periods to produce other goods and services. Capital goods bought by businesses include items such as auto assembly lines, shopping malls, airplanes, and oil tankers. Capital goods bought by governments include missiles and weapons systems for national security, public schools and universities, and interstate highways.

Consumption goods and services represent 78.5 percent of U.S. production by value and that percentage doesn't fluctuate much. *Eye on the U.S. Economy* on p. 35 breaks the goods and services down into smaller categories.

Health services is the largest category, with 19.4 percent of the value of total production. Real estate services come next at 14.5 percent. The main components of this item are the services of rental and owner-occupied housing. Professional and business services, which include the services of accountants and lawyers, are 13.2 percent of total production. Other large components of services are education and retail and wholesale trades.

The manufacture of goods represents only 12.1 percent of total production and the largest category of goods produced, chemicals, accounts for less than 2 percent of total production.

Construction accounts for 3.7 percent of production, and utilities, mining, and agriculture together make up only 5.7 percent. The nation's farms produce only a bit more than 1 percent of total production.

Consumption goods and services

Goods and services that individuals and governments buy and use in the current period.

Capital goods

Goods bought by businesses and governments to increase productive resources and to use over future periods to produce other goods and services.

EYE on the U.S. ECONOMY
What We Produce

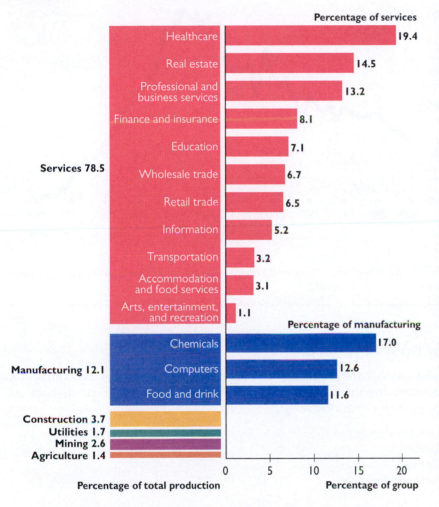

Percentage of services

Healthcare	19.4
Real estate	14.5
Professional and business services	13.2
Finance and insurance	8.1
Education	7.1
Wholesale trade	6.7
Retail trade	6.5
Information	5.2
Transportation	3.2
Accommodation and food services	3.1
Arts, entertainment, and recreation	1.1

Services 78.5

Percentage of manufacturing

Chemicals	17.0
Computers	12.6
Food and drink	11.6

Manufacturing 12.1

Construction 3.7
Utilities 1.7
Mining 2.6
Agriculture 1.4

Percentage of total production

0 5 10 15 20

Percentage of group

SOURCE OF DATA: Bureau of Economic Analysis.

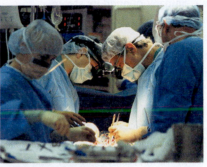

Healthcare services, …

education services, …

and retail trades are among the largest categories of services produced.

Chemicals, ….

computer chips, …

and food are the largest categories of goods produced in the United States.

EYE on the PAST
Changes in What We Produce

Freeport, Maine, became a shoemaking center in 1881 when the H.E. Davis Shoe Company opened its steam-powered factory in the town. Over the following years, many other shoemakers set up in Freeport and production steadily expanded. The town's shoe production peaked in 1968 after which it shrank rapidly. When the Freeport Shoe Company closed its factory in 1972, it became the fifteenth shoe factory to close in Freeport in four years. Today, the Freeport economy is based on shopping, not shoes.

Freeport's story of shoemaking was repeated across America and the figure tells this broader story. And as manufacturing has shrunk, retail and other services have expanded.

Leather shoe production (millions of pairs per year)

SOURCES OF DATA: *Historical Statistics of the United States Millennial Edition Online* and *Statistical Abstract of the United States*, 2012.

■ How Do We Produce?

Goods and services are produced by using productive resources. Economists call the productive resources **factors of production**. Factors of production are grouped into four categories:

- Land
- Labor
- Capital
- Entrepreneurship

Factors of production
The productive resources that are used to produce goods and services—land, labor, capital, and entrepreneurship.

Land

Land
The "gifts of nature," or *natural resources*, that we use to produce goods and services.

In economics, **land** includes all the "gifts of nature" that we use to produce goods and services. Land is what, in everyday language, we call *natural resources*. It includes land in the everyday sense, minerals, energy, water, air, and wild plants, animals, birds, and fish. Some of these resources are renewable, and some are non-renewable. The U.S. Geological Survey maintains a national inventory of the quantity and quality of natural resources and monitors changes to that inventory.

The United States covers almost 2 billion acres. About 45 percent of the land is forest, lakes, and national parks. In 2009, almost 50 percent of the land was used for agriculture and 5 percent was urban, but urban land use is growing and agricultural land use is shrinking.

Our land surface and water resources are renewable, and some of our mineral resources can be recycled. But many mineral resources can be used only once. They are nonrenewable resources. Of these, the United States has vast known reserves of coal, oil, and natural gas.

Labor

Labor is the work time and work effort that people devote to producing goods and services. Labor includes the physical and mental efforts of all the people who work on farms and construction sites and in factories, shops, and offices. The Census Bureau and Bureau of Labor Statistics measure the quantity of labor at work every month.

In the United States in October 2015, 157 million people had jobs or were available for work. Some worked full time, some worked part time, and some were unemployed but looking for an acceptable vacant job. The total amount of time worked during 2015 was about 282 billion hours.

The quantity of labor increases as the adult population increases. The quantity of labor also increases if a larger percentage of the population takes jobs. During the past 50 years, a larger proportion of women have taken paid work and this trend has increased the quantity of labor. At the same time, a slightly smaller proportion of men have taken paid work and this trend has decreased the quantity of labor.

The *quality* of labor depends on how skilled people are. A laborer who can push a hand cart but can't drive a truck is much less productive than one who can drive. An office worker who can use a computer is much more productive than one who can't. Economists use a special name for human skill: human capital. **Human capital** is the knowledge and skill that people obtain from education, on-the-job training, and work experience.

You are building your own human capital right now as you work on your economics course and other subjects. Your human capital will continue to grow when you get a full-time job and become better at it. Human capital improves the *quality* of labor and increases the quantity of goods and services that labor can produce.

Capital

Capital consists of the tools, instruments, machines, buildings, and other items that have been produced in the past and that businesses now use to produce goods and services. Capital includes hammers and screwdrivers, computers, auto assembly lines, office towers and warehouses, dams and power plants, airplanes, cookie factories, and shopping malls.

Capital also includes inventories of unsold goods or of partly finished goods on a production line. And capital includes what is sometimes called *infrastructure capital*, such as highways and airports.

Capital, like human capital, makes labor more productive. A truck driver can produce vastly more transportation services than someone pushing a hand cart; the Interstate highway system enables us to produce vastly more transportation services than was possible on the old highway system that preceded it.

The Bureau of Economic Analysis in the U.S. Department of Commerce keeps track of the total value of capital in the United States and how it grows over time. Today, the value of capital in the U.S. economy is around $50 trillion.

Financial Capital Is Not Capital In everyday language, we talk about money, stocks, and bonds as being capital. These items are *financial capital*, and they are not productive resources. Stocks and bonds enable people to provide businesses with financial resources, but they are *not* used to produce goods and services. They are not capital.

Labor
The work time and work effort that people devote to producing goods and services.

Human capital
The knowledge and skill that people obtain from education, on-the-job training, and work experience.

Capital
Tools, instruments, machines, buildings, and other items that have been produced in the past and that businesses now use to produce goods and services.

EYE on the U.S. ECONOMY
Changes in How We Produce in the Information Economy

The information economy consists of the jobs and businesses that produce and use computers and equipment powered by computer chips. This information economy is highly visible in your daily life.

The pairs of images here illustrate two examples. In each pair, a new technology enables capital to replace labor.

The top pair of pictures illustrate the replacement of bank tellers (labor) with ATMs (capital). Although the ATM was invented almost 50 years ago, when it made its first appearance, it was located only inside banks and was not able to update customers' accounts. It is only in the last decade that ATMs have spread to corner stores and enable us to get cash and check our bank balance from almost anywhere in the world.

The bottom pair of pictures illustrate a more recent replacement of labor with capital: self-check-in. Air passengers today issue their own boarding pass, often at their own computer before leaving home. For international flights, some of these machines now

even check passport details.

The number of bank teller and airport check-in clerk jobs is shrinking, but these new technologies are

creating a whole range of new jobs for people who make, program, install, and repair the vast number of machines.

Entrepreneurship
The human resource that organizes labor, land, and capital to produce goods and services.

Entrepreneurship

Entrepreneurship is the human resource that organizes land, labor, and capital to produce goods and services. Entrepreneurs are creative and imaginative. They come up with new ideas about what and how to produce, make business decisions, and bear the risks that arise from these decisions. If their ideas work out, they earn a profit. If their ideas turn out to be wrong, they bear the loss.

The quantity of entrepreneurship is hard to describe or measure. During some periods, there appears to be a great deal of imaginative entrepreneurship around. People such as Sam Walton, who created Wal-Mart, one of the world's largest retailers; Bill Gates, who founded the Microsoft empire; and Mark Zuckerberg, who founded Facebook, are examples of extraordinary entrepreneurial talent. But these highly visible entrepreneurs are just the tip of an iceberg that consists of hundreds of thousands of people who run businesses, large and small.

■ For Whom Do We Produce?

Who gets the goods and services depends on the incomes that people earn. A large income enables a person to buy large quantities of goods and services. A small income leaves a person with a small quantity of goods and services.

People earn their incomes by selling the services of the factors of production they own. **Rent** is paid for the use of land, **wages** are paid for the services of labor, **interest** is paid for the use of capital, and entrepreneurs receive a **profit** (or incur a **loss**) for running their businesses. What are the shares of these four factor incomes in the United States? Which factor receives the largest share?

Figure 2.1(a) answers these questions. It shows that wages were 63 percent of total income in 2014 and rent, interest, and profit were 37 percent of total income. These percentages remain remarkably constant over time. We call the distribution of income among the factors of production the *functional distribution of income.*

Figure 2.1(b) shows the *personal distribution of income*—the distribution of income among households—in 2014. Some households, like that of Clayton Kershaw, earn many millions of dollars a year. These households are in the richest 20 percent who earn 50 percent of total income. Households at the other end of the scale, like those of fast-food servers, are in the poorest 20 percent who earn only 3 percent of total income. The distribution of income has been changing and becoming more unequal. The rich have become richer. But it isn't the case, on the whole, that the poor have become poorer. They just haven't become richer as fast as the rich have.

Rent
Income paid for the use of land.

Wages
Income paid for the services of labor.

Interest
Income paid for the use of capital.

Profit (or loss)
Income earned by an entrepreneur for running a business.

■ FIGURE 2.1

For Whom in 2014   MyEconLab Animation

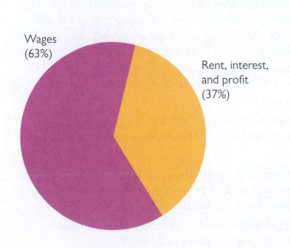

Wages (63%)

Rent, interest, and profit (37%)

(a) Functional distribution of income

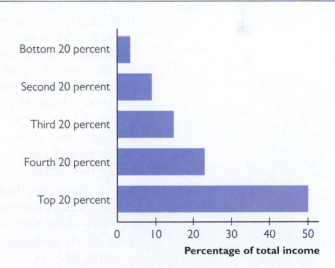

Bottom 20 percent
Second 20 percent
Third 20 percent
Fourth 20 percent
Top 20 percent

0   10   20   30   40   50
Percentage of total income

(b) Personal distribution of income

SOURCES OF DATA: Bureau of Economic Analysis, *National Income and Product Accounts,* Table 1.10 and U.S. Census Bureau, *Income and Poverty in the United States*: 2014, Current Population Reports P60-252, 2015.

In 2014, wages (the income from labor) were 63 percent of total income. Rent, interest, and profit (the income from the services of land, capital, and entrepreneurship) totaled the remaining 37 percent.

In 2014, the 20 percent of the population with the highest incomes received 50 percent of total income. The **20 percent** with the lowest incomes received only 3 percent of total income.

MyEconLab Study Plan 2.1

Key Terms Quiz

Solutions Video

CHECKPOINT 2.1

Describe what, how, and for whom goods and services are produced in the United States.

Practice Problems

1. What are the types of goods and services produced? Give an example of each (different from those in the chapter) and distinguish between them.
2. Name the four factors of production and the incomes they earn.
3. Distinguish between the functional distribution of income and the personal distribution of income.
4. In the United States, which factor of production earned the largest share of income in 2014 and what percentage did it earn?

In the News

The frustration that drives people to become entrepreneurs
A study by researchers at Stanford and the University of Chicago discovered that most of the people who quit their jobs and start their own business do so not because they have a billion-dollar idea but because they are frustrated in their jobs.
Source: Chad Brooks, *Business News Daily*, September 16, 2014

Why do people become entrepreneurs? What do we call the income earned by entrepreneurs? Are most people entrepreneurs? What is the factor of production supplied by people who are not entrepreneurs? What is their income called? What percentage of total income does their income represent?

Solutions to Practice Problems

1. The goods and services produced fall into two types: consumption goods and services and capital goods. A hamburger is a consumption good and a haircut is a consumption service. An oil rig and auto assembly line are capital goods. A consumption good or service is an item that is bought by individuals or the government and is used up in the current period. A capital good is bought by businesses or the government and it is used over and over again to produce other goods and services.
2. The factors of production are land, labor, capital, and entrepreneurship. Land earns rent; labor earns wages; capital earns interest; and entrepreneurship earns profit or incurs a loss.
3. The functional distribution of income shows the percentage of total income received by each factor of production. The personal distribution of income shows how total income is shared among households.
4. Labor is the factor of production that earns the largest share of income. In 2014, labor in the United States earned 63 percent of total income.

Solution to In the News

People become entrepreneurs because they are frustrated in their jobs. The income earned by entrepreneurs is called profit. Most people are suppliers of labor, for which they earn a wage. The data in Figure 2.1 show that wage income of labor represents 63 percent of total income.

2.2 THE GLOBAL ECONOMY	MyEconLab Concept Video

We're now going to look at *what, how,* and *for whom* goods and services get produced in the global economy. We'll begin with a brief overview of the people and countries that form the global economy.

■ The People

Visit the Web site of the U.S. Census Bureau and go to the population clocks to find out how many people there are today in both the United States and the entire world. On the day these words were written, November 8, 2015, the U.S. clock recorded a population of 322,115,000. The world clock recorded a global population of 7,284,290,000. The U.S. clock ticks along showing a population increase of one person every 15 seconds. The world clock spins faster, adding 30 people in the same 15 seconds.

■ The Economies

The world's 7.3 billion (and rising) population lives in 176 economies, which the International Monetary Fund classifies into two broad groups:

- Advanced economies
- Emerging market and developing economies

Advanced Economies

Advanced economies are the richest 29 countries (or areas). The United States, Japan, Italy, Germany, France, the United Kingdom, and Canada belong to this group. So do four new industrial Asian economies: Hong Kong, South Korea, Singapore, and Taiwan. The other advanced economies include Australia, New Zealand, and most of the rest of Western Europe. Almost 1 billion people (15 percent of the world's population) live in the advanced economies.

Emerging Market and Developing Economies

Emerging market economies are 28 countries in Central and Eastern Europe and Asia. Almost 500 million people live in these countries—about half of the number in the advanced economies. These countries are important because they are emerging (hence the name) from a system of state-owned production, central economic planning, and heavily regulated markets moving toward a system of free enterprise and unregulated markets.

Developing economies are the 119 countries in Africa, Asia, the Middle East, Europe, and Central and South America. More than 5.5 billion people—almost four out of every five people—live in the developing economies.

Developing economies vary enormously in size, the level of average income, and the rate of growth of production and incomes. But in all the developing economies, average incomes are much lower than those in the advanced economies, and in some cases, they are extremely low.

Five emerging market and developing economies, representing 3 billion people or 42 percent of the world's population and known as BRICS (Brazil, Russia, India, China, and South Africa), hold regular meetings to advance the interests of these nations and draw attention to their development problems.

■ *What* in the Global Economy

First, let's look at the big picture. Imagine that each year the global economy produces an enormous pie. In 2015, the pie was worth about $113 trillion! To give this number some meaning, if the pie were shared equally among the world's 7.3 billion people, each of us would get a slice worth a bit less than $15,500.

Where Is the Global Pie Baked?

Figure 2.2 shows us where in the world the pie is baked. The advanced economies produce 43 percent—16 percent in the United States, 17 percent in the European Union, and 10 percent in the other advanced economies. This 43 percent of global output (by value) is produced by 15 percent of the world's population.

The BRICS economies, highlighted in the figure, together produce 31 percent of the world's output. China, with 17 percent of world production, dominates this group and South Africa, the group's smallest member, produces barely 1 percent of global output. This 31 percent of the global pie is baked by 42 percent of the world's population.

The remaining 26 percent of the global pie comes from other emerging market and developing economies and is baked by 43 percent of the world's people.

Unlike the slices of an apple pie, those of the global pie have different fillings. Some slices have more oil, some more food, some more clothing, some more housing services, some more autos, and so on. Let's look at some of these different fillings and at some similarities too.

■ FIGURE 2.2

What in the Global Economy in 2015   MyEconLab Animation

If we show the value of production in the world economy as a pie, the United States produces a slice that is 16 percent of the total. The European Union produces 17 percent and other advanced economies 10 percent, so together, the advanced economies produce 43 percent of global output.

Another 31 percent of the global pie comes from the BRICS economies. China, which produces 17 percent of world output, dominates this group.

The remaining 26 percent of world output comes from other emerging market and developing economies in Africa, Asia, the Middle East, and the Western Hemisphere.

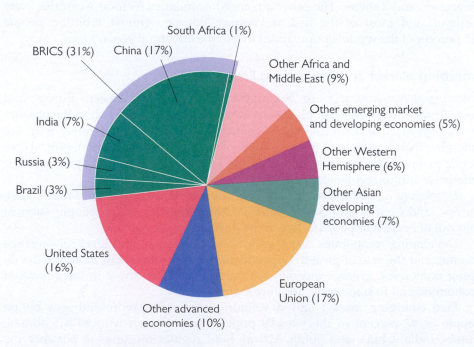

SOURCE OF DATA: International Monetary Fund, World Economic Outlook Database, April 2015.

EYE on the DREAMLINER

MyEconLab Critical Thinking Exercise

Who Makes the Dreamliner?

Boeing designed, assembles, and markets the Dreamliner, but the airplane is made by more than 400 firms on four continents that employ thousands of workers and millions of dollars' worth of specialized capital equipment. The graphic identifies some of the firms and the components they make.

Boeing and these firms make decisions and pay their workers, investors, and raw material suppliers to influence *what, how,* and *for whom* goods and services are produced. All these decisions are made in self-interest, and produce an airplane at the lowest possible cost.

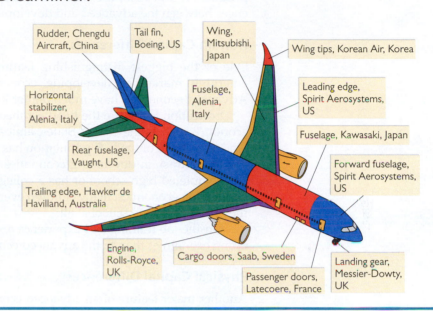

Rudder, Chengdu Aircraft, China

Tail fin, Boeing, US

Wing, Mitsubishi, Japan

Wing tips, Korean Air, Korea

Horizontal stabilizer, Alenia, Italy

Fuselage, Alenia, Italy

Leading edge, Spirit Aerosystems, US

Rear fuselage, Vaught, US

Fuselage, Kawasaki, Japan

Forward fuselage, Spirit Aerosystems, US

Trailing edge, Hawker de Havilland, Australia

Engine, Rolls-Royce, UK

Cargo doors, Saab, Sweden

Passenger doors, Latecoere, France

Landing gear, Messier-Dowty, UK

Some Differences in What Is Produced

What is produced in the developing economies contrasts sharply with that of the advanced economies. Manufacturing is the big story. Developing economies have large and growing industries, which produce textiles, footwear, sports gear, toys, electronic goods, furniture, steel, and even automobiles and airplanes.

Food production is a small part of the U.S. and other advanced economies and a large part of the developing economies such as Brazil, China, and India. But the advanced economies produce about one third of the world's food. How can this be? *Total* production is much larger in the advanced economies than in the developing economies, but a small percentage of a big number can be a *greater amount* than a large percentage of a small number!

Some Similarities in What Is Produced

If you were to visit a shopping mall in Canada, England, Australia, Japan, or any of the other advanced economies, you would wonder whether you had left the United States. You would see Starbucks, Burger King, Pizza Hut, Domino's Pizza, KFC, Kmart, Wal-Mart, Target, Gap, Tommy Hilfiger, Lululemon, Banana Republic, the upscale Louis Vuitton and Burberry, and a host of other familiar names. And, of course, you would see McDonald's golden arches. You would see them in any of the 119 countries in which one or more of McDonald's 30,000 restaurants are located.

The similarities among the advanced economies go beyond the view from main street and the shopping mall. The structure of *what* is produced is similar in these economies. As percentages of the total economy, agriculture and manufacturing are small and shrinking whereas services are large and expanding.

McDonald's in Shanghai.

■ *How* in the Global Economy

Goods and services are produced using land, labor, capital, and entrepreneurial resources, and the combinations of these resources used are chosen to produce at the lowest possible cost. Each country or region has its own blend of factors of production, but there are some interesting common patterns and crucial differences between the advanced and developing economies that we'll now examine.

Human Capital Differences

One of the biggest distinguishing features of an advanced economy from an emerging market or developing economy is its quantity of *human capital*. Advanced economies have much higher levels of human capital.

Education levels are the handiest measure of human capital. In an advanced economy such as the United States, almost everyone has completed high school. And 30 percent of the U.S. population has completed 4 years or more of college.

In contrast, in developing economies, the proportion of the population who has completed high school or has a college degree is small. In the poorest of the developing economies, many children even miss out on basic primary education—they just don't go to school at all.

On-the-job training and experience are also much less extensive in the developing economies than in the advanced economies.

Physical Capital Differences

Another major feature of an advanced economy that differentiates it from a developing economy is the amount of capital available for producing goods and services. The differences begin with the basic transportation systems. In the advanced economies, a well-developed highway system connects all the major cities and points of production. Open a map app on your phone. Contrast the U.S. interstate highway system in Texas with the sparse highways of Mexico. You would see a similar contrast if you swiped across the Atlantic Ocean and checked out the highway structures in Western Europe and Africa.

But it isn't the case that the developing economies have no highways and no modern trucks and cars. In fact, some of them have the newest and the best. But the new and best are usually inside and around the major cities—see *Eye on the Global Economy* on p. 45.

The contrasts in the transportation system are matched by those on farms and in factories. In general, the more advanced the economy, the greater are the amount and sophistication of the capital equipment used in production. But again, the contrast is not all or nothing. Some factories in India, China, and other parts of Asia use the very latest technologies. Furniture manufacturing is an example. To make furniture of a quality that Americans are willing to buy, firms in Asia use machines like those in the furniture factories of North Carolina.

The differences in human capital and physical capital between advanced and developing economies have a big effect on *who* gets the goods and services, which we'll now examine.

■ *For Whom* in the Global Economy

Who gets the world's goods and services depends on the incomes that people earn. We're now going to see how incomes are distributed within economies and across the world.

EYE on the GLOBAL ECONOMY
Differences in How We Produce

Big differences exist in how goods and services are produced and the images here illustrate three examples.

Laundry services (top), transportation services (center), and highway systems (bottom) can use a large amount of capital and almost no labor (left) or use almost no capital and a large amount of labor (right).

Capital-intensive automatic laundry equipment, big trucks, and multi-lane paved freeways are common in advanced economies but rare in poorer developing economies.

Riverside clothes washing, human pedal power, and unsealed dirt tracks are seen only in developing economies.

But we also see huge differences even within a developing economy. The bottom pictures contrast Beijing's capital-intensive highway system with the unpaved and sometimes hazardous roads of rural China.

Personal Distribution of Income

You saw earlier (on p. 39) that in the United States, the lowest-paid 20 percent of the population receives 3 percent of total income and the highest-paid 20 percent receives 50 percent of total income. The personal distribution of income in the world economy is much more unequal. According to World Bank data, the lowest-paid 20 percent of the world's population receives 2 percent of world income and the highest-paid 20 percent receives about 70 percent of world income.

International Distribution

Much of the greater inequality at the global level arises from differences in average incomes among countries. Figure 2.3 shows some of these differences. It shows the dollar value of what people can afford each day on average. You can see that in the United States, that number is $153 a day—an average person in the United States can buy goods and services that cost $153. This amount is around five times the world average. The European Union has an average income of around two thirds that of the United States at $104 per day. Income levels fall off quickly as we move farther down the graph, with Russia at $65 a day, China $39 a day, India $17 a day, and Africa only $11 a day.

As people have lost well-paid manufacturing jobs and found lower-paid service jobs, inequality has increased in the United States and in most other advanced economies. Inequality is also increasing in the developing economies. People with skills enjoy rapidly rising incomes but the incomes of the unskilled are falling.

A Happy Paradox and a Huge Challenge

Despite the increase in inequality inside most countries, inequality across the entire world has decreased during the past 20 years. And most important, according to Xavier Sala-i-Martin, an economics professor at Columbia University, extreme poverty has declined. Professor Sala-i-Martin estimates that between 1976 and 1998, the number of people who earn $1 a day or less fell by 235 million and the number who earn $2 a day or less fell by 450 million. This positive situation arises because in China, the largest nation, incomes have increased rapidly and lifted millions from extreme poverty. Incomes are growing quickly in India too.

Lifting Africa from poverty is today's big challenge. In 1960, 11 percent of the world's poor lived in Africa, but in 1998, 66 percent did. Between 1976 and 1998, the number of people in Africa who earn $1 a day or less rose by 175 million, and the number who earn $2 a day or less rose by 227 million.

■ **FIGURE 2.3**

For Whom in the Global Economy in 2015   MyEconLab Animation

In 2015, the average income per person per day in the United States was $153. It was $104 in the European Union and $65 in Russia. The number falls to $39 in China, $17 in India, and $11 in Africa.

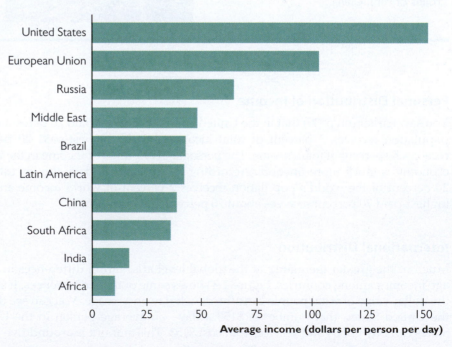

SOURCE OF DATA: International Monetary Fund, World Economic Outlook Database, October 2015.

EYE on YOUR LIFE
The U.S. and Global Economies in Your Life

MyEconLab Critical Thinking Exercise

You've encountered a lot of facts and trends about what, how, and for whom goods and services are produced in the U.S. economy and the global economy. How can you use this information? You can use it in two ways:

1. To inform your choice of career
2. To inform your stand on the politics of protecting U.S. jobs

Career Choices

As you think about your future career, you are now better informed about some of the key trends. You know that manufacturing is shrinking.

The U.S. economy is what is sometimes called a *post-industrial economy*. Industries that provided the backbone of the economy in previous generations have fallen to barely a fifth of

the economy today, and the trend continues. It is possible that by the middle of the current century, manufacturing will be as small a source of jobs as agriculture is today.

So, a job in a manufacturing business is likely to lead to some tough situations and possibly the need for several job changes over a working life.

As manufacturing shrinks, so services expand, and this expansion will continue. The provision of healthcare, education, communication, wholesale and retail trades, and entertainment are all likely to expand in the future and be sources of increasing employment and rising wages. A job in a service-oriented business is more likely to lead to steady advances in income.

Political Stand on Job Protection

As you think about the stand you will take on the political question of protecting U.S. jobs, you are better informed about the basic facts and trends.

When you hear that manufacturing jobs are disappearing to China, you will be able to place that news in historical perspective. You might reasonably be concerned, especially if you or a member of your family has lost a job. But you know that trying to reverse or even halt this process is flying in the face of stubborn historical trends.

In later chapters, you will learn that there are good economic reasons to be skeptical about any form of protection and placing limits on competition.

 CHECKPOINT 2.2

MyEconLab Study Plan 2.2
Solutions Video

Describe what, how, and for whom goods and services are produced in the global economy.

Practice Problems

1. Describe what, how, and for whom goods and services are produced in developing economies.

2. A Clinton Foundation success story is that it loaned $23,000 to Rwandan coffee growers to support improvements to coffee washing stations and provided technical support. What was the source of the success?

Solutions to Practice Problems

1. In developing countries, agriculture is the largest percentage, manufacturing is an increasing percentage, and services are a small percentage of total production. Most production does not use modern capital-intensive technologies, but some industries do. People who work in factories have rising incomes while those who work in rural industries are left behind.

2. The technical support allowed Rwandan coffee growers to improve their knowledge of coffee farming, which increased their human capital. The improvements to washing stations was a change in physical capital that allowed farmers to increase the quantity of washed coffee.

MyEconLab Concept Video

Circular flow model
A model of the economy that shows the circular flow of expenditures and incomes that result from decision makers' choices and the way those choices interact to determine what, how, and for whom goods and services are produced.

Households
Individuals or groups of people living together.

Firms
The institutions that organize the production of goods and services.

Market
Any arrangement that brings buyers and sellers together and enables them to get information and do business with each other.

Goods markets
Markets in which goods and services are bought and sold.

Factor markets
Markets in which the services of factors of production are bought and sold.

2.3 THE CIRCULAR FLOWS

We can organize the data you've just studied using the **circular flow model**—a model of the economy that shows the circular flow of expenditures and incomes that result from decision makers' choices and the way those choices interact to determine what, how, and for whom goods and services are produced. Figure 2.4 shows the circular flow model.

■ Households and Firms

Households are individuals or groups of people living together. The 124 million households in the United States own the factors of production—land, labor, capital, and entrepreneurship—and choose the quantities of these resources to provide to firms. Households also choose the quantities of goods and services to buy.

Firms are the institutions that organize the production of goods and services. The 28 million firms in the United States choose the quantities of the factors of production to hire and the quantities of goods and services to produce.

■ Markets

Households choose the quantities of the factors of production to provide to firms, and firms choose the quantities of the services of the factors of production to hire. Firms choose the quantities of goods and services to produce, and households choose the quantities of goods and services to buy. How are these choices coordinated and made compatible? The answer is: by markets.

A **market** is any arrangement that brings buyers and sellers together and enables them to get information and do business with each other. An example is the market in which oil is bought and sold—the world oil market. The world oil market is not a place. It is the network of oil producers, oil users, wholesalers, and brokers who buy and sell oil. In the world oil market, decision makers do not meet physically. They make deals by telephone, fax, and the Internet.

Figure 2.4 identifies two types of markets: goods markets and factor markets. Goods and services are bought and sold in **goods markets**; and the services of factors of production are bought and sold in **factor markets**.

■ Real Flows and Money Flows

When households choose the quantities of services of land, labor, capital, and entrepreneurship to offer in factor markets, they respond to the incomes they receive—rent for land, wages for labor, interest for capital, and profit for entrepreneurship. When firms choose the quantities of factor services to hire, they respond to the rent, wages, interest, and profits they must pay to households.

Similarly, when firms choose the quantities of goods and services to produce and offer for sale in goods markets, they respond to the amounts that they receive from the expenditures that households make. And when households choose the quantities of goods and services to buy, they respond to the amounts they must pay to firms.

Figure 2.4 shows the flows that result from these choices made by households and firms. The flows shown in orange are *real flows:* the flows of the factors of production that go from households through factor markets to firms and of the goods and services that go from firms through goods markets to households. The flows in the opposite direction are *money flows:* the flows of payments made in exchange for the services of factors of production (shown in blue) and of expenditures on goods and services (shown in red).

Lying behind these real flows and money flows are millions of individual choices about what to consume and what and how to produce. These choices result in buying plans by households and selling plans by firms in goods markets. And the choices result in selling plans by households and buying plans by firms in factor markets that interact to determine the prices that people pay and the incomes they earn, and so determine for whom goods and services are produced. You'll learn in Chapter 4 how markets coordinate the buying plans and selling plans of households and firms and make them compatible.

Firms produce most of the goods and services that we consume, but governments provide some of the services that we enjoy. Governments also play a big role in modifying for whom goods and services are produced by changing the personal distribution of income. We're now going to look at the role of governments in the U.S. economy and add them to the circular flow model.

■ **FIGURE 2.4**

The Circular Flow Model

MyEconLab Animation

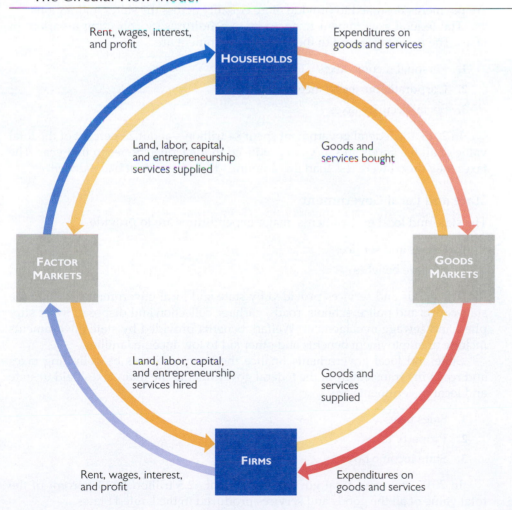

The orange flows are the services of factors of production that go from households through factor markets to firms and the goods and services that go from firms through goods markets to households. These flows are *real* flows.

The blue flow is the income earned by the factors of production, and the red flow is the expenditures on goods and services. These flows are *money* flows.

The choices that generate these real and money flows determine *what, how,* and *for whom* goods and services are produced.

■ Governments

More than 86,000 organizations operate as governments in the United States. Some are tiny like the Yuma, Arizona, school district and some are enormous like the U.S. federal government. We divide governments into two levels:

- Federal government
- State and local government

Federal Government

The federal government's major expenditures provide

1. Goods and services
2. Social Security and welfare payments
3. Transfers to state and local governments

The goods and services provided by the federal government include the legal system, which protects property and enforces contracts, and national defense. Social Security and welfare benefits, which include income for retired people and programs such as Medicare and Medicaid, are transfers from the federal government to households. Federal government transfers to state and local governments are payments designed to provide more equality across the states and regions.

The federal government finances its expenditures by collecting a variety of taxes. The main taxes paid to the federal government are

1. Personal income taxes
2. Corporate (business) income taxes
3. Social Security taxes

In 2015, the federal government spent $4 trillion—about 23 percent of the total value of all the goods and services produced in the United States in that year. The taxes they raised were less than this amount—the government had a deficit.

State and Local Government

The state and local governments' major expenditures are to provide

1. Goods and services
2. Welfare benefits

The goods and services provided by state and local governments include the state courts and police, schools, roads, garbage collection and disposal, water supplies, and sewage management. Welfare benefits provided by state governments include unemployment benefits and other aid to low-income families.

State and local governments finance these expenditures by collecting taxes and receiving transfers from the federal government. The main taxes paid to state and local governments are

1. Sales taxes
2. Property taxes
3. State income taxes

In 2015, state and local governments spent $2.5 trillion or 14 percent of the total value of all the goods and services produced in the United States.

■ Governments in the Circular Flow

Figure 2.5 adds governments to the circular flow model. As you study this figure, first notice that the outer circle is the same as in Figure 2.4. In addition to these flows, governments buy goods and services from firms. The red arrows that run from governments through the goods markets to firms show this expenditure.

Households and firms pay taxes to governments. The green arrows running directly from households and firms to governments show these flows. Also, governments make money payments to households and firms. The green arrows running directly from governments to households and firms show these flows. Taxes and transfers are direct transactions with governments and do not go through the goods markets and factor markets.

Not part of the circular flow and not visible in Figure 2.5, governments provide the legal framework within which all transactions occur. For example, governments operate the courts and legal system that enable contracts to be written and enforced.

■ **FIGURE 2.5**

Governments in the Circular Flow   MyEconLab Animation

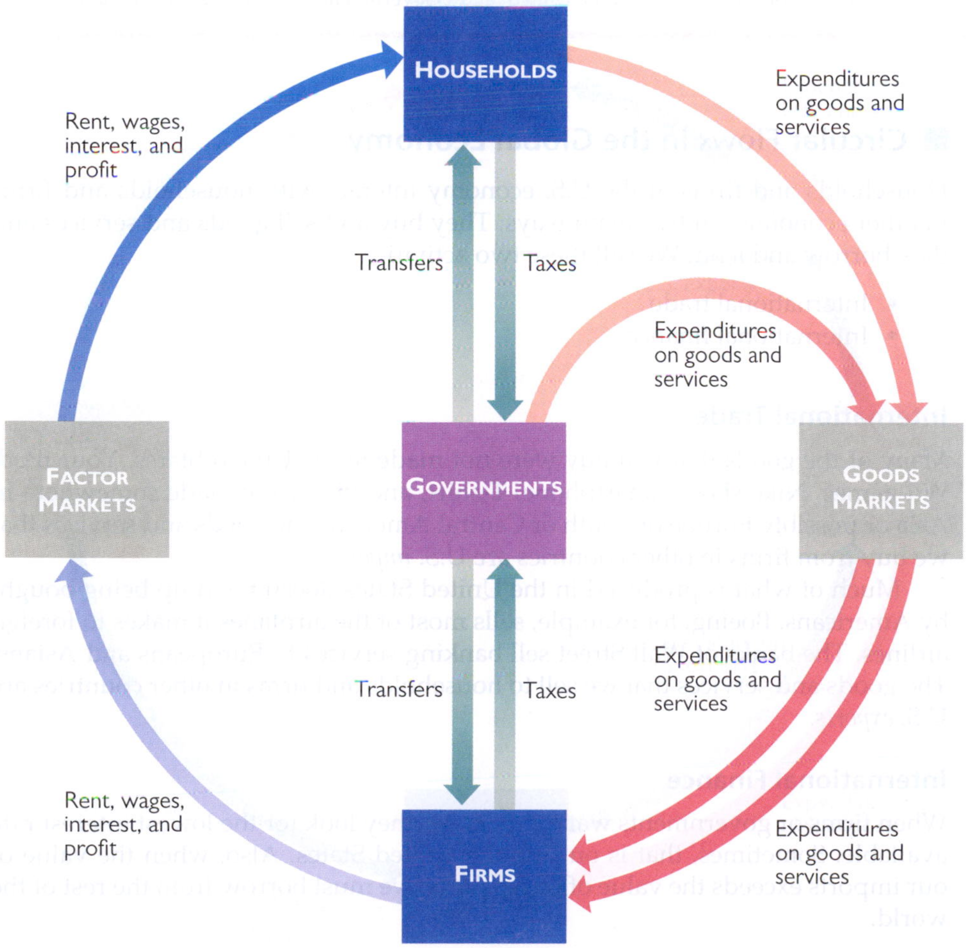

The green flows from households and firms to governments are taxes, and the green flows from governments to households and firms are money transfers.

The red flow from governments through the goods markets to firms is the expenditure on goods and services by governments.

EYE on the GLOBAL ECONOMY
The Ups and Downs in International Trade

International trade expanded rapidly after China became a powerful player in the global economy.

At an average growth rate of close to 7 percent a year, world trade has doubled every decade and increased as a percentage of world production.

A mini-recession in 2001 slowed the growth in world trade to a crawl and the 2009 global recession reduced world trade.

After the recession of 2009, world trade bounced back to 27 percent of global production, where it remained in 2015.

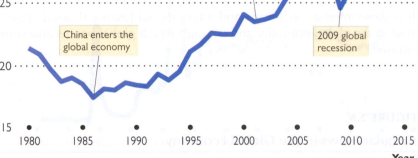

Global international trade (percentage of world GDP)

2001 mini-recession

China enters the global economy

2009 global recession

Source of data: International Monetary Fund, World Economic Outlook Database, October 2015.

MyEconLab Study Plan 2.3
Key Terms Quiz
Solutions Video

CHECKPOINT 2.3

Explain the circular flow model of the U.S. economy and of the global economy.

Practice Problems

1. Describe the flows in the circular flow model in which expenditure on consumption goods and services, purchases of new national defense equipment, and payments for labor services appear. Through which market does each flow pass?

2. Of the flows that run between households, firms, and governments in the circular flow model, which ones are real flows and which are money flows?

Solutions to Practice Problems

1. Expenditure on consumption goods and services flows from households to firms through the goods market. Purchases of national defense flow from governments to firms through the goods market. Payments for labor services flow from firms to households through the factor market.

2. The flow of services of factors of production from households to firms through factor markets is a real flow, as are the flows of goods and services from firms to households and from firms to governments through goods markets. The money flows are the flows of factor incomes, household and government expenditures on goods and services, taxes, and transfers.

CHAPTER SUMMARY

Key Points

1. **Describe what, how, and for whom goods and services are produced in the United States.**

   - Consumption goods and services represent 85 percent of total production; capital goods represent 15 percent.
   - Goods and services are produced by using the four factors of production: land, labor, capital, and entrepreneurship.
   - The incomes people earn (rent for land, wages for labor, interest for capital, and profit for entrepreneurship) determine who gets the goods and services produced.

2. **Describe what, how, and for whom goods and services are produced in the global economy.**

   - Forty-three percent of the world's production (by value) comes from the advanced industrial countries and 57 percent comes from the emerging market and developing economies.
   - Production in the advanced economies uses more capital (both machines and human), but some developing economies use the latest capital and technologies.
   - The global distribution of income is more unequal than the U.S. distribution. Poverty has fallen in Asia, but it has increased in Africa.

3. **Explain the circular flow model of the U.S. economy and of the global economy.**

   - The circular flow model of the U.S. economy shows the real flows of factors of production and goods and the corresponding money flows of incomes and expenditures.
   - Governments in the circular flow receive taxes, make transfers, and buy goods and services.
   - The circular flow model of the global economy shows the flows of U.S. exports and imports and the international financial flows that result from lending to and borrowing from other countries.

Key Terms

MyEconLab Key Terms Quiz

Capital, 37
Capital goods, 34
Circular flow model, 48
Consumption goods and services, 34
Entrepreneurship, 38
Factor markets, 48

Factors of production, 36
Firms, 48
Goods markets, 48
Households, 48
Human capital, 37
Interest, 39

Labor, 37
Land, 36
Market, 48
Profit (or loss), 39
Rent, 39
Wages, 39

MyEconLab Chapter 2 Study Plan

CHAPTER CHECKPOINT

Study Plan Problems and Applications

1. Which of the following items are *not* consumption goods and services? Explain why not.
   - A chocolate bar
   - A ski lift
   - A golf ball

2. Which of the following items are *not* capital goods? Explain why not.
   - An auto assembly line
   - A shopping mall
   - A golf ball

3. Which of the following items are *not* factors of production? Explain why not.
   - Vans used by a baker to deliver bread
   - 1,000 shares of Amazon.com stock
   - Undiscovered oil in the Arctic Ocean

4. Which factor of production earns the highest percentage of total U.S. income? Define that factor of production. What is the income earned by this factor of production called?

5. With more job training and more scholarships to poor American students, which special factor of production is likely to grow faster than in the past?

6. Define the factor of production called capital. Give three examples of capital, different from those in the chapter. Distinguish between the factor of production capital and financial capital.

7. The pace at which new businesses are created in the U.S. economy and the percentage of U.S. jobs in young firms has fallen.
   > Ryan Decker and others, "The Role of Entrepreneurship in U.S. Job Creation and Economic Dynamism."
   > *Journal of Economic Perspectives*, 2014.

   Explain how you would expect these facts to influence *what, how,* and *for whom* goods and services are produced in the United States.

8. In the circular flow model, explain the real flow and/or the money flow in which each item in List 1 belongs. Illustrate your answers on a circular flow diagram.

9. **Why you can get a free college education in Germany but not in California** Even American students can get a free college degree in Germany, where high taxes pay for colleges. Despite college being free, fewer students in Germany earn college degrees than in the United States and more enter vocational apprenticeships.
   > Source: *Los Angeles Times*, October 29, 2015

   If California adopted the German model of higher education, how would that change *for whom* goods and services are produced?

10. Read *Eye on the Dreamliner* on p. 43 and then answer the following questions:
    - How many firms are involved in the production of the Dreamliner and how many are identified in the figure on p. 43?
    - Is the Dreamliner a capital good or a consumption good? Explain why.
    - State the factors of production that make the Dreamliner and provide an example of each.
    - Explain how the production of the Dreamliner influences *what, how,* and *for whom* goods and services are produced.
    - Use a diagram to show where in the circular flow model of the global economy the flows of the components listed on p. 43 appear and where the sales of Dreamliners appear.

LIST 1

- You buy a coffee at Starbucks.
- The government buys some Dell computers.
- A student works at a FedEx office.
- Donald Trump rents a building to Marriott hotels.
- You pay your income tax.

Instructor Assignable Problems and Applications

MyEconLab Homework, Quiz, or Test if assigned by instructor

1. Boeing's Dreamliner has had a rocky start.
   - Why doesn't Boeing manufacture all the components of the Dreamliner at its own factory in the United States?
   - Describe some of the changes in *what, how*, and *for whom* that would occur if Boeing manufactured all the components of the Dreamliner at its own factories in the United States.
   - State some of the tradeoffs that Boeing faces in making the Dreamliner.
   - Why might Boeing's decisions in making the Dreamliner be in the social interest?

2. The global economy has seen a fall in the number of landlines and rapid growth in the number of smartphones. In the United States, 41 percent of households have no landline and 90 percent have a smartphone. In Africa, 33 percent have a smartphone. Describe the changes in *what, how,* and *for whom* telecommunication services are produced in the global economy.

3. Which of the entries in List 1 are consumption goods and services? Explain your choice.

4. Which of the entries in List 1 are capital goods? Explain your choice.

5. Which of the entries in List 1 are factors of production? Explain your choice.

6. In the African nation of Senegal, to enroll in school a child needs a birth certificate that costs $25. This price is several weeks' income for many families. Explain how this requirement is likely to affect the growth of human capital in Senegal.

7. **China's income gap widens**
   The income gap has widened in China. In 2014, the pay of workers in the coastal regions increased by 9.7 percent while that of workers in the inland regions grew by 9 percent.

   Source: *South China Morning Post*, May 28, 2015

   Explain how the distribution of personal income in China can be getting more unequal even though the poorest are getting richer.

8. Compare the scale of agricultural production in the advanced and developing economies. In which is the percentage higher? In which is the total amount produced greater?

9. On a diagram of the circular flow model, indicate in which real or money flow each entry in List 2 belongs.

Use the following information to work Problems **10** and **11**.

Poor India makes millionaires at fastest pace
India, with the world's largest population of poor people, also paradoxically created millionaires at the fastest pace in the world. Millionaires increased by 22.7 percent to 123,000. In contrast, the number of Indians living on less than a dollar a day is 350 million and those living on less than $2 a day is 700 million. In other words, there are 7,000 very poor Indians for every millionaire.

Source: *The Times of India*, June 25, 2008

10. How is the personal distribution of income in India changing?

11. Why might incomes of $1 a day and $2 a day underestimate the value of the goods and services that these households actually consume?

LIST 1

- An interstate highway
- An airplane
- A school teacher
- A stealth bomber
- A garbage truck
- A pack of bubble gum
- President of the United States
- A strawberry field
- A movie
- An ATM

LIST 2

- General Motors pays its workers wages.
- IBM pays a dividend to its stockholders.
- You buy your groceries.
- Southwest rents some aircraft.
- Nike pays Serena Williams for promoting its sports shoes.

MyEconLab Chapter 2 Study Plan

Multiple Choice Quiz

1. Which of the following classifications is correct?

A. City streets are consumption goods because they wear out with use.
B. Stocks are capital goods because when people buy and sell them they make a profit.
C. The coffee maker in the coffee shop at an airport is a consumption good because people buy the coffee it produces.
D. White House security is a government service because it is paid for by the government.

2. Which of the following statements about U.S. production is correct?

A. Construction accounts for a larger percentage of total production than does manufacturing.
B. Real estate services account for 14.5 percent of the value of total production, larger than any other item of services or goods.
C. Consumption goods and services represent 78.5 percent of U.S. production by value and that percentage doesn't fluctuate much.
D. The manufacture of goods represents more than 50 percent of total production.

3. Which of the following items is *not* a factor of production?

A. An oil rig in the Gulf of Mexico
B. A ski jump in Utah
C. A bank loan to a farmer
D. An orange grove in Florida

4. What is human capital?

A. A fruit picker
B. Unskilled labor
C. Your professor's knowledge of economics
D. An auto assembly line robot

5. Which of the following statements is correct?

A. Labor earns wages and entrepreneurship earns bonuses.
B. Land earns interest and capital earns rent.
C. Entrepreneurship earns interest and capital earns profit.
D. Capital earns interest and labor earns wages.

6. How are goods and services produced in the global economy?

A. Developing countries use less human capital but just as much physical capital as advanced economies.
B. Emerging economies use more capital-intensive technology than do developing economies.
C. Human capital in all economies is similar.
D. Advanced economies use less capital than developing economies.

7. In the circular flow model, which of the following items is a real flow?

A. The flow of government expenditures to firms for the goods bought
B. The flow of income from firms to households for the services of the factors of production hired
C. The flow of U.S. borrowing from the rest of the world
D. The flow of labor services from households to firms

Is wind power free?

The Economic Problem

3

When you have completed your study of this chapter, you will be able to

1 Explain and illustrate the concepts of scarcity, production efficiency, and tradeoff using the production possibilities frontier.

2 Calculate opportunity cost.

3 Explain what makes production possibilities expand.

4 Explain how people gain from specialization and trade.

MyEconLab Big Picture Video

MyEconLab Concept Video

3.1   PRODUCTION POSSIBILITIES

The wind is free, but wind power is not: it must be produced. It is one of the vast array of goods and services produced in the nation's farms, factories, stores, offices, and construction sites. In 2015, 280 billion hours of labor equipped with $55 trillion worth of capital produced $18 trillion worth of goods and services.

Our production capability is enormous, but it is limited by our available resources and by technology. At any given time, we have fixed quantities of the factors of production and a fixed state of technology, so there is a limit to what we can produce. The economic problem is that our wants exceed what it is possible for our resources to produce.

Your task in this chapter is to study a model of the economic problem. We begin with a piece of the model that describes the limits to production, which is called the production possibilities frontier.

■ Production Possibilities Frontier

Production possibilities frontier
The boundary between the combinations of goods and services that can be produced and the combinations that cannot be produced, given the available factors of production and the state of technology.

The **production possibilities frontier** is the boundary between the combinations of goods and services that can be produced and the combinations that cannot be produced, given the available factors of production—land, labor, capital, and entrepreneurship—and the state of technology.

Although we produce millions of different goods and services, we can visualize the limits to production most easily if we look at a model economy that produces just two goods. Imagine an economy that produces only bikes and smartphones. All the land, labor, capital, and entrepreneurship available gets used to produce these two goods.

Land can be used for bike factories or smartphone factories. Labor can be trained to work as bike makers or as smartphone makers. Capital can be used for building bike or smartphone assembly lines. Entrepreneurs can put their talents to making bikes or running smartphone businesses. In every case, the more resources that are used to produce bikes, the fewer are left to produce smartphones.

Suppose that if no factors of production are allocated to producing smartphones, the maximum number of bikes that can be produced is 15 million a year. So one production possibility is no smartphones and 15 million bikes. Another possibility is to allocate sufficient resources to produce 1 million smartphones a year. But these resources must be taken from bike factories. Suppose that the economy can now produce only 14 million bikes a year. As resources are moved from producing bikes to producing smartphones, the economy produces more smartphones but fewer bikes.

The table in Figure 3.1 illustrates these two combinations of smartphones and bikes as possibilities A and B. Suppose that C, D, E, and F are other combinations of the quantities of these two goods that the economy can produce. Possibility F uses all the resources to produce 5 million smartphones a year and allocates no resources to producing bikes. These six possibilities are alternative combinations of the quantities of the two goods that the economy can produce by *using all of its resources, given the technology.*

The graph in Figure 3.1 illustrates the production possibilities frontier, *PPF*, for smartphones and bikes. Each point on the graph labeled A through F represents the possibility in the table identified by the same letter. For example, point B represents the production of 1 million smartphones and 14 million bikes. These quantities also appear in the table as possibility B.

■ FIGURE 3.1

The Production Possibilities Frontier

MyEconLab Animation

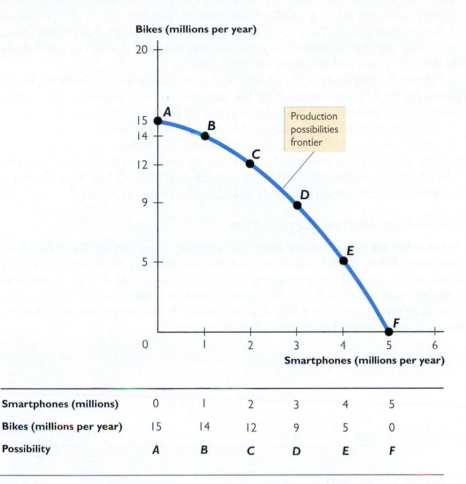

The table and the graph show the production possibilities frontier for smartphones and bikes.

Point *A* tells us that if the economy produces no smartphones, the maximum quantity of bikes it can produce is 15 million a year.

Each point *A*, *B*, *C*, *D*, *E*, and *F* on the graph represents the possibility in the table identified by the same letter.

The line passing through these points is the production possibilities frontier.

Smartphones (millions)	0	1	2	3	4	5
Bikes (millions per year)	15	14	12	9	5	0
Possibility	*A*	*B*	*C*	*D*	*E*	*F*

The *PPF* shows the limits to production *with the available resources and technology.* If either resources or technology change, the *PPF* shifts. If more resources or better technology become available, the *PPF* shifts outward. If resources are lost, for example in a natural disaster, the *PPF* shifts inward.

The *PPF* is a valuable tool for illustrating the effects of scarcity and its consequences. Let's see how.

■ How the *PPF* Illustrates Scarcity and Its Consequences

The *PPF* illustrates scarcity and some of its consequences by putting three distinctions in sharp focus. They are the distinctions between

- Attainable and unattainable combinations
- Efficient and inefficient production
- Tradeoffs and free lunches

Attainable and Unattainable Combinations

Because the *PPF* shows the *limits* to production, it separates attainable combinations from unattainable ones. The economy can produce combinations of smartphones and bikes that are smaller than those on the *PPF*, and it can produce any of the combinations *on* the *PPF*. These combinations of smartphones and bikes are attainable. But it is impossible to produce combinations that are larger than those on the *PPF*. These combinations are unattainable.

Figure 3.2 emphasizes the attainable and unattainable combinations. Only the points on the *PPF* and inside it (in the orange area) are attainable. The combinations of smartphones and bikes beyond the *PPF* (in the white area), such as the combination at point *G*, are unattainable. These points illustrate combinations that cannot be produced with the current resources and technology. The *PPF* tells us that the economy can produce 4 million smartphones and 5 million bikes at point *E or* 2 million smartphones and 12 million bikes at point *C*. But the economy cannot produce 4 million smartphones and 12 million bikes at point *G*.

Efficient and Inefficient Production

Production efficiency
A situation in which the economy is getting all that it can from its resources and cannot produce more of one good or service without producing less of something else.

Production efficiency occurs when the economy is getting all that it can from its resources. When production is efficient it is not possible to produce more of one good or service without producing less of something else. For production to be efficient, there must be full employment—not just of labor but of all the available factors of production—and each resource must be assigned to the task that it performs comparatively better than other resources can.

■ **FIGURE 3.2**

Attainable and Unattainable Combinations   MyEconLab Animation

---

The production possibilities frontier, *PPF*, separates attainable combinations from unattainable ones. The economy can produce at any point *inside* the *PPF* (the orange area) or at any point *on* the frontier. Any point outside the production possibilities frontier, such as point *G*, is unattainable.

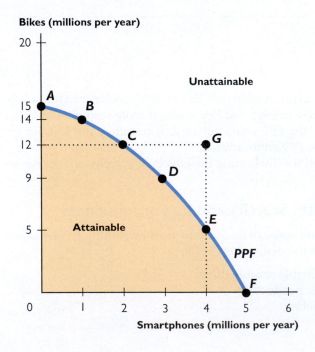

Figure 3.3 illustrates the distinction between efficient and inefficient production. With *inefficient* production, the economy might be producing 3 million smartphones and 5 million bikes at point *H*. With an *efficient* use of the economy's resources, it is possible to produce at a point on the *PPF* such as point *D* or *E*. At point *D*, there are more bikes and the same quantity of smartphones as at point *H*. And at point *E*, there are more smartphones and the same quantity of bikes as at point *H*. At points *D* and *E*, production is efficient.

Tradeoffs and Free Lunches

A **tradeoff** is an exchange—giving up one thing to get something else. You trade off income for a better grade when you decide to cut back on the hours you spend on your weekend job and allocate the time to extra study. The Ford Motor Company faces a tradeoff when it cuts the production of trucks and uses the resources saved to produce more hybrid SUVs. The federal government faces a tradeoff when it cuts NASA's space exploration program and allocates more resources to homeland security. As a society, we face a tradeoff when we decide to cut down a forest and destroy the habitat of the spotted owl.

The production possibilities frontier illustrates the idea of a tradeoff. The *PPF* in Figure 3.3 shows how. If the economy produces at point *E* and people want to produce more bikes, they must forgo some smartphones. In the move from point *E* to point *D*, people trade off smartphones for bikes.

Economists often express the central idea of economics—that choices involve a tradeoff—with the saying "There is no such thing as a free lunch." A *free lunch* is a gift—getting something without giving up something else. What does the

Tradeoff
An exchange—giving up one thing to get something else.

■ **FIGURE 3.3**

Efficient and Inefficient Production, Tradeoffs, and Free Lunches

MyEconLab Animation

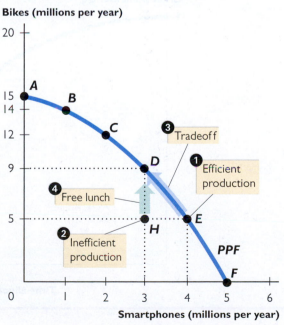

❶ When production occurs at a point on the *PPF*, such as point *E*, resources are used efficiently.

❷ When production occurs at a point inside the *PPF*, such as point *H*, resources are used inefficiently.

❸ When production is efficient—on the *PPF*—the economy faces a tradeoff. To move from point *E* to point *D* requires that some smartphones be given up for more bikes.

❹ When production is inefficient—inside the *PPF*—there is a free lunch. To move from point *H* inside the *PPF* to point *D* on the *PPF* does not involve a tradeoff.

famous saying mean? Suppose some resources are not being used or are not being used efficiently. Isn't it then possible to avoid a tradeoff and get a free lunch?

The answer is yes. You can see why in Figure 3.3. If production is taking place *inside* the *PPF* at point *H*, then it is possible to move to point *D* and increase the production of bikes by using currently unused resources or by using resources in their most productive way. Nothing is forgone to increase production—there is a free lunch.

When production is efficient—at a point on the *PPF*—choosing to produce more of one good involves a tradeoff. But if production is inefficient—at a point inside the *PPF*—there is a free lunch. More of some goods and services can be produced without producing less of any others.

So "there is no such thing as a free lunch" means that when resources are used efficiently, every choice involves a tradeoff. Because economists view people as making rational choices, they expect that resources will be used efficiently. That is why they emphasize the tradeoff idea and deny the existence of free lunches. We might *sometimes* get a free lunch, but we *almost always* face a tradeoff.

EYE on YOUR LIFE

MyEconLab Critical Thinking Exercise

Your Production Possibilities Frontier

Two "goods" that concern you a great deal are your grade point average (GPA) and the amount of time you have available for leisure or earning an income. You face a tradeoff. To get a higher GPA you must give up leisure or income. Your forgone leisure or forgone income is the opportunity cost of a higher GPA. Similarly, to get more leisure or more income, you must accept a lower grade. A lower grade is the opportunity cost of increased leisure or increased income.

The figure illustrates a student's *PPF*. Any point on or inside the *PPF* is attainable and any point outside the *PPF* is unattainable. A student who wastes time ends up with a lower GPA than the highest attainable from the time spent studying. But a student who works efficiently achieves a point *on* the *PPF* and achieves production efficiency.

The student in the figure allocates the scarce 168 hours a week between studying (class and study hours) and other activities (work, leisure, and sleep hours). The student attends class and studies for 48 hours each week and works or has fun (and sleeps) for the other 120 hours. With this allocation of time, and studying efficiently, the student's GPA is 3.

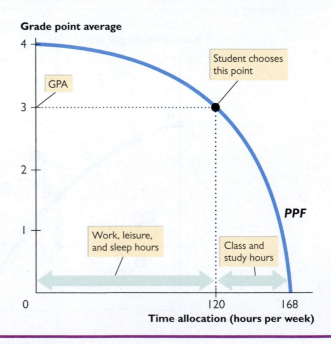

CHECKPOINT 3.1

MyEconLab Study Plan 3.1
Key Terms Quiz
Solutions Video

Explain and illustrate the concepts of scarcity, production efficiency, and tradeoff using the production possibilities frontier.

Practice Problems

1. Table 1 sets out the production possibilities of a small Pacific island economy. Draw the economy's *PPF*.

Figure 1 shows an economy's *PPF* and identifies some production points. Use this figure to work Problems **2** to **4**.

2. Which points are attainable? Explain why.

3. Which points are efficient and which points are inefficient? Explain why.

4. Which points illustrate a tradeoff? Explain why.

In the News

Honeybee decline linked to killer virus
In 2007, the killer virus arrived in Hawaii, where almost all the queen bees used in the United States are bred. Bees are used to pollinate crops that are used in a third of the food we eat.

Source: *The Guardian*, June 8, 2012

Explain how a decline in bee population affects the U.S. *PPF*.

Solutions to Practice Problems

1. The *PPF* is the boundary between attainable and unattainable combinations of goods. Figure 2 shows the economy's *PPF*. The graph plots each row of the table as a point with the corresponding letter.

2. Attainable points: Any point on the *PPF* is attainable and any point inside the *PPF* is attainable. Points outside the *PPF* (*F* and *G*) are unattainable. In Figure 1, the attainable points are *A*, *B*, *C*, *D*, and *E*.

3. Efficient points: Production is efficient when it is not possible to produce more of one good without producing less of another good. To be efficient, a point must be attainable, so points *F* and *G* can't be efficient. Points inside the *PPF* can't be efficient because more goods can be produced, so *D* and *E* are not efficient. The only efficient points are those *on* the *PPF*—*A*, *B*, and *C*.

   Inefficient points: Inefficiency occurs when resources are misallocated or unemployed. Such points are *inside* the *PPF*. These points are *D* and *E*.

4. Tradeoff: Begin by recalling that a tradeoff is an exchange—giving up something to get something else. A tradeoff occurs when moving along the *PPF* from one point to another point. So moving from any point *on* the *PPF*, point *A*, *B*, or *C*, to another point *on* the *PPF* illustrates a tradeoff.

Solution to In the News

Honeybees are a resource used in the production of many food crops. Before 2007, the United States was at a point on its *PPF*. During the following years, with fewer queen bees, the number of honeybees declined and the quantity of food produced decreased. With no change in other resources and technology, and no change in the quantity of other goods and services produced, the U.S. *PPF* rotated inward.

TABLE 1

Possibility	Fish (pounds)		Berries (pounds)
A	0	and	20
B	1	and	18
C	2	and	15
D	3	and	11
E	4	and	6
F	5	and	0

FIGURE 1

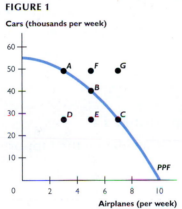

FIGURE 2

3.2 OPPORTUNITY COST

You've seen that moving from one point to another on the *PPF* involves a trade-off. But what are the terms of the tradeoff? *How much* of one item must be forgone to obtain an additional unit of another item—a large amount or a small amount? The answer is given by opportunity cost—the best thing you must give up to get something (see p. 8). We can use the *PPF* to calculate opportunity cost.

■ The Opportunity Cost of a Smartphone

The opportunity cost of producing a smartphone is the number of bikes forgone to get an additional smartphone. It is calculated as the number of bikes forgone divided by the number of smartphones gained.

Figure 3.4 illustrates the calculation. At point *A*, the quantities produced are zero smartphones and 15 million bikes; and at point *B*, the quantities produced are 1 million smartphones and 14 million bikes. To gain 1 million smartphones by moving from point *A* to point *B*, 1 million bikes are forgone, so the opportunity cost of 1 smartphone is 1 bike.

At point *C*, the quantities produced are 2 million smartphones and 12 million bikes. To gain 1 million smartphones by moving from point *B* to point *C*, 2 million bikes are forgone. Now the opportunity cost of 1 smartphone is 2 bikes.

If you repeat these calculations, moving from *C* to *D*, *D* to *E*, and *E* to *F*, you will obtain the opportunity costs shown in the table and the graph.

FIGURE 3.4

Calculating the Opportunity Cost of a Smartphone

Movement along *PPF*	Decrease in quantity of bikes	Increase in quantity of smartphones	Decrease in bikes divided by increase in smartphones
A to *B*	1 million	1 million	1 bike per phone
B to *C*	2 million	1 million	2 bikes per phone
C to *D*	3 million	1 million	3 bikes per phone
D to *E*	4 million	1 million	4 bikes per phone
E to *F*	5 million	1 million	5 bikes per phone

Along the *PPF* from *A* to *F*, the opportunity cost of a smartphone increases as the quantity of smartphones produced increases.

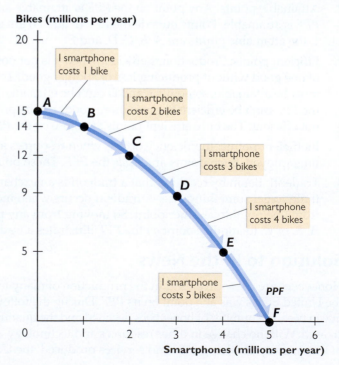

■ Opportunity Cost and the Slope of the *PPF*

Look at the numbers that we've just calculated for the opportunity cost of a smartphone and notice that they follow a striking pattern. The opportunity cost of a smartphone increases as the quantity of smartphones produced increases.

The magnitude of the *slope* of the *PPF* measures the opportunity cost. Because the *PPF* in Figure 3.4 is bowed outward, its slope changes and gets steeper as the quantity of smartphones produced increases.

When a small quantity of smartphones is produced—between points *A* and *B*—the *PPF* has a gentle slope and the opportunity cost of a smartphone is low. A given increase in the quantity of smartphones costs a small decrease in the quantity of bikes. When a large quantity of smartphones is produced—between points *E* and *F*—the *PPF* is steep and the opportunity cost of a smartphone is high. A given increase in the quantity of smartphones costs a large decrease in the quantity of bikes. Figure 3.5 shows the increasing opportunity cost of a smartphone.

■ Opportunity Cost Is a Ratio

The opportunity cost of a smartphone is the *ratio* of bikes forgone to smartphones gained. Similarly, the opportunity cost of a bike is the *ratio* of smartphones forgone to bikes gained. So the opportunity cost of producing a bike is equal to the inverse of the opportunity cost of producing a smartphone. For example, moving along the *PPF* in Figure 3.4 from *C* to *D* the opportunity cost of a smartphone is 3 bikes. Moving along the *PPF* in the opposite direction, from *D* to *C*, the opportunity cost of a bike is 1/3 of a smartphone.

■ FIGURE 3.5

The Opportunity Cost of a Smartphone

MyEconLab Animation

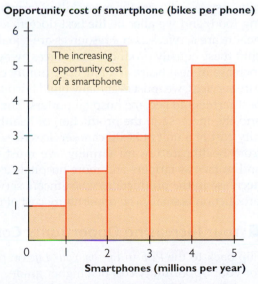

Opportunity cost of smartphone (bikes per phone)

The increasing opportunity cost of a smartphone

Smartphones (millions per year)

Because the *PPF* in Figure 3.4 is bowed outward, the opportunity cost of a smartphone increases as the quantity of smartphones produced increases.

Smartphones (millions)	0 to 1	1 to 2	2 to 3	3 to 4	4 to 5
Opportunity cost (bikes per phone)	1	2	3	4	5

EYE on the ENVIRONMENT

MyEconLab Critical Thinking Exercise

Is Wind Power Free?

Wind power is not free. To use it, we must give up other goods and services to build wind turbines and transmission lines.

Wind turbines can produce electricity only when the wind is strong enough, but advances in technology are enabling turbines to operate in lower wind conditions.

Some of the best wind farm locations are far from major population centers, so transmission lines can be long and power losses large.

If we produced most of our electricity using wind power, we would be operating inside the *PPF* at a point such as Z.

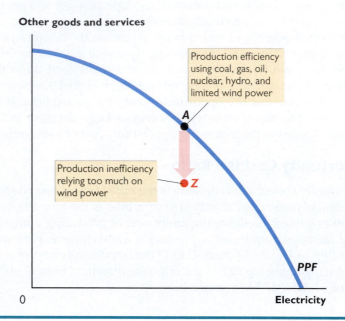

Other goods and services

Production efficiency using coal, gas, oil, nuclear, hydro, and limited wind power

A

Production inefficiency relying too much on wind power

Z

PPF

0   Electricity

■ Increasing Opportunity Costs Are Everywhere

Just about every production activity that you can think of has increasing opportunity cost. We allocate the most skillful farmers and the most fertile land to producing food, and we allocate the best doctors and the least fertile land to producing healthcare services. Some resources are equally productive in both activities. If we shift these equally productive resources away from farming to hospitals, we get an increase in healthcare at a low opportunity cost. But if we keep increasing healthcare services, we must eventually build hospitals on the most fertile land and get the best farmers to become hospital porters. The production of food drops drastically and the increase in the production of healthcare services is small. The opportunity cost of a unit of healthcare services rises. Similarly, if we shift resources away from healthcare toward farming, we must eventually use more skilled doctors and nurses as farmers and more hospitals as hydroponic vegetable factories. The decrease in the production of healthcare services is large, but the increase in food production is small. The opportunity cost of producing a unit of food rises.

■ Your Increasing Opportunity Cost

Flip back to the *PPF* in *Eye on Your Life* on p. 64 and think about its implications for your opportunity cost of a higher grade.

What is the opportunity cost of spending time with your friends in terms of the grade you might receive on your exam? What is the opportunity cost of a higher grade in terms of the activities you give up to study? Do you face increasing opportunity costs in these activities?

CHECKPOINT 3.2

MyEconLab Study Plan 3.2
Solutions Video

Calculate opportunity cost.

Practice Problems

Table 1 shows Robinson Crusoe's production possibilities.

1. What is his opportunity cost of a pound of berries when Crusoe increases the quantity of berries from 21 pounds to 26 pounds and production is efficient? Does this opportunity cost increase as he produces more berries?

2. If Crusoe is producing 10 pounds of fish and 21 pounds of berries, what is his opportunity cost of an extra pound of berries? And what is his opportunity cost of an extra pound of fish? Explain your answers.

In the News

Cost of meeting 2021 vehicle emission standards

Carbon dioxide emissions from cars must be cut from 130 grams to 95 grams per kilometer. To meet this new standard, the price of a car will rise by $1,350.

Source: *International Business Times*, November 9, 2015

Calculate the opportunity cost of reducing the carbon emission level by 1 gram.

TABLE 1

Possibility	Fish (pounds)		Berries (pounds)
A	0	and	36
B	4.0	and	35
C	7.5	and	33
D	10.5	and	30
E	13.0	and	26
F	15.0	and	21
G	16.5	and	15
H	17.5	and	8
I	18.0	and	0

Solutions to Practice Problems

1. If Crusoe's production is efficient, he is producing at a point *on* his *PPF*. His opportunity cost of an extra pound of berries is the quantity of fish he must give up to get the berries. It is calculated as the decrease in the quantity of fish divided by the increase in the quantity of berries as he moves along his *PPF*.

    To increase the quantity of berries from 21 pounds to 26 pounds (from row *F* to row *E* of Table 1), production of fish decreases from 15 pounds to 13 pounds. To gain 5 pounds of berries, Crusoe must forgo 2 pounds of fish. The opportunity cost of 1 pound of berries is the 2 pounds of fish forgone divided by 5 pounds of berries gained—2/5 of a pound of fish.

    Crusoe's opportunity cost of berries increases as he produces more berries. To see why, move Crusoe from row *E* to row *D* in Table 1. His production of berries increases by 4 pounds and his production of fish falls by 2.5 pounds. His opportunity cost of 1 pound of berries increases to 5/8 of a pound of fish.

2. Figure 1 graphs the data in Table 1 and shows Crusoe's *PPF*. If Crusoe is producing 10 pounds of fish and 21 pounds of berries, he is producing at point *Z*. Point *Z* is a point *inside* Crusoe's *PPF*. When Crusoe produces 21 pounds of berries, he has enough time available to produce 15 pounds of fish at point *F* on his *PPF*. To produce more fish, Crusoe can move from *Z* toward *F* on his *PPF* and forgo no berries. His opportunity cost of a pound of fish is zero. Similiarly, his opportunity cost of a pound of berries is zero.

FIGURE 1

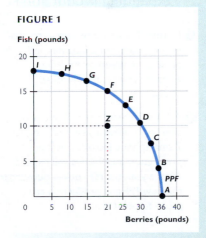

Solution to In the News

By spending $1,350 extra on a new car, you forgo $1,350 of other goods. With a new car, your emissions fall from 130 grams to 95 grams, a reduction of 35 grams. The opportunity cost of a 1-gram reduction in emissions is $1,350 of other goods divided by 35 grams, or $38.57 of other goods.

3.3 ECONOMIC GROWTH

Economic growth
The sustained expansion of production possibilities.

The *PPF* shows the limits to production with given resources and technology. But over time, resources and technology change and production possibilities expand. A process of sustained expansion of production possibilities is called **economic growth**. Our economy grows when we develop better technologies; improve the quality of labor by education, on-the-job training, and work experience; and acquire more machines (capital) to help us produce.

To study economic growth, we must look at the production possibilities for a consumption good—a smartphone—and a capital good—a smartphone factory. By using resources to produce smartphone factories, the economy can expand its future production possibilities. The greater the production of new capital—of new smartphone factories—the faster is the expansion of production possibilities.

Figure 3.6 shows how the *PPF* can expand. If no new factories are produced (at point *L*), production possibilities do not expand and the *PPF* stays at its original position. By producing fewer smartphones and using resources to produce 2 new smartphone factories (at point *K*), production possibilities expand once the new factories become operational. The *PPF* rotates outward to the new *PPF*.

But economic growth is *not* free. To make it happen, current consumption must decrease. The move from *L* to *K* in Figure 3.6 means forgoing 2 million smartphones now. The opportunity cost of producing new smartphone factories is the decrease in the number of smartphones produced today.

Also, economic growth does not end scarcity. It rotates the *PPF* outward, but on the new *PPF* we continue to face opportunity costs. To keep producing new capital, current consumption must be less than its maximum possible level.

FIGURE 3.6

Expanding Production Possibilities

MyEconLab Animation

❶ If firms allocate no resources to producing smartphone factories and produce 5 million smartphones a year at point *L*, the *PPF* doesn't change.

❷ If firms decrease smartphone production to 3 million a year and produce 2 smartphone factories, at point *K*, production possibilities will expand. After a year, the *PPF* rotates outward to the new *PPF* and production can move to point *K'*.

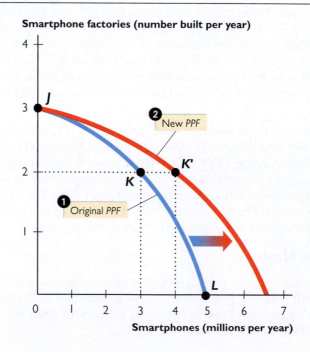

EYE on the U.S. ECONOMY
Expanding Our Production Possibilities

Horizontal drilling and hydraulic fracturing—fracking—combined with recent advances in remote sensing technology have made it possible to extract a large quantity of gas trapped in shale at low cost. The United States has an estimated 750 trillion cubic feet of this gas, enough for more than 90 years at today's extraction rate. The map below shows the locations of these gas deposits.

Figure I shows recent years of shale gas production. During 2010 and 2011, production doubled. The average growth rate since 2010 exceeds 30 percent per year.

Was this increase in gas production achieved by sliding along the *PPF* and producing less of other goods and servces? No! It was the result of advances in technology and the opening up of additional gas wells.

Figure 2 illustrates how these changes rotated the *PPF* outward from *PPF*$_{10}$ in 2010 to *PPF*$_{13}$ in 2013. Point *J* is the same on both curves because if we produced at that point (only other goods and services and no gas), we would not get the benefits of the technological advances in gas production. In 2010 we produced at point *K*, and in 2013 at point *K'*. Along *PPF*$_{13}$ the opportunity cost of gas is lower than along *PPF*$_{10}$.

Figure I Shale Gas Production

Natural Gas Shale Basins in the United States

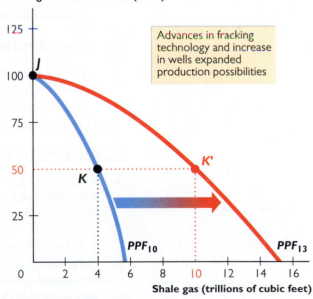

Figure 2 Shale Gas Versus Other Goods and Services

Source of data: Energy Information Administration.

EYE on the GLOBAL ECONOMY
Hong Kong's Rapid Economic Growth

Hong Kong's production possibilities per person were 25 percent of those of the United States in 1960. By 2015, they had grown to become equal to U.S. production possibilities per person. Hong Kong grew faster than the United States because it allocated more of its resources to accumulating capital and less to consumption than did the United States.

In 1960, the United States and Hong Kong produced at point A on their respective *PPF*s. In 2015, Hong Kong was at point *B* and the United States was at point *C*.

If Hong Kong continues to produce at any point on its *PPF* above *C*, it will grow more rapidly than the United States and its *PPF* will eventually shift out

beyond the *PPF* of the United States. But if Hong Kong produces at a point

below *B*, the pace of expansion of its *PPF* will slow.

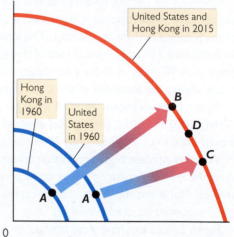

CHECKPOINT 3.3

Explain what makes production possibilities expand.

Practice Problems

1. Table 1 shows an economy that produces education services and consumption goods. If the economy currently produces 500 graduates a year and 2,000 units of consumption goods, what is the opportunity cost of one additional graduate?
2. How does an economy grow? Explain why economic growth is not free.

Solutions to Practice Problems

1. By increasing the number of graduates from 500 to 750, the quantity of consumption goods produced decreases from 2,000 to 1,000 units. The opportunity cost of a graduate is the decrease in consumption goods divided by the increase in the number of graduates. That is, the opportunity cost of a graduate is 1,000 units divided by 250, or 4 units of consumption goods.

2. An economy grows if it expands its production possibilities—if it develops better technologies; improves the quality of labor by education, on-the-job training, and work experience; and acquires more capital to use in production.

   Economic growth occurs when resources are used today to produce better technologies, higher-quality labor, or more machines. Those resources cannot be used to produce goods and services today, so the cost of economic growth is the goods and services forgone today. Economic growth is not free.

TABLE 1

Possibility	Education services (graduates)	Consumption goods (units)
A	1,000	0
B	750	1,000
C	500	2,000
D	0	3,000

3.4 SPECIALIZATION AND TRADE

MyEconLab Concept Video

The next time you visit your favorite fast-food restaurant, watch what the workers are doing. You might see one person re-stocking the bread, salad materials, meat, sauces, boxes, and wrappers; another working the grill and another the fry maker; another assembling meals; and yet another taking orders and payments. Imagine how long you would wait for your burger if each worker performed all the tasks needed to fill each customer's not-so-fast-food order.

Specialization makes people more productive in two ways: It brings absolute advantage and comparative advantage.

Specialization boosts productivity in a fast-food kitchen

■ Absolute Advantage and Comparative Advantage

A person has an **absolute advantage** if that person is more productive than another. Being more productive means using fewer inputs or taking less time to produce a good or perform a production task. Being more productive also means being able to produce more with given inputs in a given amount of time.

The specialized workers at McDonald's have an *absolute advantage* over the same number of workers each performing all the tasks needed to make a burger.

A person has a **comparative advantage** in an activity if that person can perform the activity at a lower opportunity cost than anyone else. Recall that the opportunity cost of something is what you must give up to get it.

Notice the contrast between *absolute advantage* and *comparative advantage*. Absolute advantage is about *productivity*—how long does it take to produce a unit of a good. Comparative advantage is about *opportunity cost*—how much of some other good must be forgone to produce a unit of a good.

Absolute advantage
When one person (or nation) is more productive than another—needs fewer inputs or takes less time to produce a good or perform a production task.

Comparative advantage
The ability of a person to perform an activity or produce a good or service at a lower opportunity cost than anyone else.

EYE on the U.S. ECONOMY
No One Knows How to Make a Pencil

Not many products in today's world are as simple as a pencil. Yet the story of how the pencil in your hand got there illustrates the astonishing power of specialization and trade.

When you hold a pencil, you're holding cedar grown in Oregon, graphite mined in Sri Lanka, clay from Mississippi, wax from Mexico, rapeseed oil grown in the Dutch East Indies, pumice from Italy, copper from Arizona, and zinc from Alaska.

These materials were harvested and mined by thousands of workers equipped with hundreds of specialized tools, all of which were manufactured by thousands of other workers using hundreds more specialized tools. These tools were in turn made of steel, itself made from iron ore, and from other minerals and materials.

Rail, road, and ocean transportation systems moved all these things to custom-built factories that made graphite "leads," erasers, brass to hold the erasers, paint, and glue.

Finally, all these components were bought by a pencil factory which, with its millions of dollars' worth of custom machinery, put them all together.

Millions of people contributed to making that pencil, many of whom don't even know what a pencil is and *not one of whom knows how to make a pencil*. No one directed all these people. Each worker and business went about its self-interested specialized task trading with each other in markets.

Adapted from *I Pencil*, by Leonard Read, Foundation for Economic Education, 1958.

TABLE 3.1 LIZ'S PRODUCTION POSSIBILITIES

Item	Minutes to produce 1	Quantity per hour
Smoothies	2	30
Salads	2	30

TABLE 3.2 JOE'S PRODUCTION POSSIBILITIES

Item	Minutes to produce 1	Quantity per hour
Smoothies	10	6
Salads	2	30

■ Comparative Advantage: A Model

We're going to explore the idea of comparative advantage and make it concrete by looking at a model economy with two smoothie bars: one operated by Liz and the other operated by Joe. You will see how we identify comparative advantage and how it creates an opportunity for Liz and Joe to gain from specialization and trade.

Liz's Smoothie Bar

Liz operates a high-tech bar. She can turn out *either* a smoothie *or* a salad every 2 minutes. If she spends all her time making smoothies, she produces 30 an hour. If she spends all her time making salads, she also produces 30 an hour (Table 3.1). If she splits her time equally between the two, she can produce 15 smoothies *and* 15 salads an hour. For each additional smoothie Liz produces, she must decrease her production of salads by one, and for each additional salad Liz produces, she must decrease her production of smoothies by one. So

Liz's opportunity cost of producing 1 smoothie is 1 salad,

and

Liz's opportunity cost of producing 1 salad is 1 smoothie.

Liz's customers buy smoothies and salads in equal quantities, so Liz splits her time equally between the items and produces 15 smoothies and 15 salads an hour.

Joe's Smoothie Bar

Joe produces smoothies and salads in a smaller bar than Liz's, and he has only one blender—a slow, old machine. Even if Joe uses all his resources to produce smoothies, he can produce only 6 an hour. But Joe is pretty good in the salad department. If he uses all his resources to make salads, he can produce 30 an hour (Table 3.2). Joe's ability to make smoothies and salads is the same regardless of how he splits an hour between the two tasks. He can make a salad in 2 minutes or a smoothie in 10 minutes. For each additional smoothie Joe produces, he must decrease his production of salads by 5. And for each additional salad Joe produces, he must decrease his production of smoothies by 1/5 of a smoothie. So

Joe's opportunity cost of producing 1 smoothie is 5 salads,

and

Joe's opportunity cost of producing 1 salad is 1/5 of a smoothie.

Joe's customers, like Liz's, buy smoothies and salads in equal quantities. Joe spends 50 minutes of each hour making smoothies and 10 minutes of each hour making salads. With this division of his time, Joe produces 5 smoothies and 5 salads an hour.

Liz's and Joe's *PPFs*

The *PPFs* in Figure 3.7 illustrate the situation we've just described. In part (a), Liz faces a *PPF* that enables her to produce 15 smoothies and 15 salads. In part (b), Joe faces a *PPF* that enables him to produce 5 smoothies and 5 salads. On Liz's *PPF*, 1 smoothie costs 1 salad. On Joe's *PPF*, 1 smoothie costs 5 salads.

The *PPFs* in Figure 3.7 contrast with the outward-bowed *PPFs* that you've seen earlier in this chapter, which capture the general rule that the opportunity cost of a good increases as we increase its rate of production. It is easier to identify

FIGURE 3.7

Production Possibilities Frontiers

MyEconLab Animation

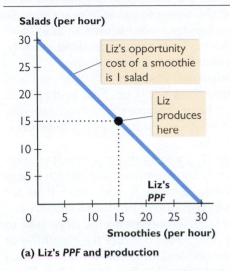

(a) Liz's *PPF* and production

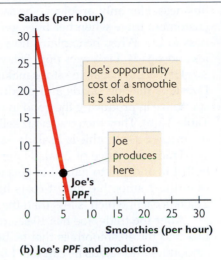

(b) Joe's *PPF* and production

Liz can produce 30 smoothies per hour or 30 salads per hour or any other combination along her *PPF* in part (a). Liz chooses to produce 15 smoothies and 15 salads per hour.

Joe can produce 6 smoothies per hour or 30 salads per hour or any other combination along his *PPF* in part (b). Joe chooses to produce 5 smoothies and 5 salads per hour.

comparative advantage and see the gains from trade when individuals have constant opportunity cost. And as you will soon see, the economy's *PPF* is outward-bowed even when individuals have constant opportunity cost and linear *PPF*s.

Liz's Greater Productivity

You can see from the production numbers that Liz is three times as productive as Joe—her 15 smoothies and 15 salads an hour are three times Joe's 5 smoothies and 5 salads. Liz is more productive than Joe in producing both smoothies and salads, but Liz has a comparative advantage in only one of the activities.

Liz's Comparative Advantage

In which of the two activities does Liz have a *comparative* advantage? Recall that comparative advantage is a situation in which one person's opportunity cost of producing a good is lower than another person's opportunity cost of producing that same good.

You've seen that Liz's opportunity cost of a smoothie is 1 salad, whereas Joe's opportunity cost of a smoothie is 5 salads. To produce 1 smoothie, Liz must forgo 1 salad while Joe must forgo 5 salads. So, because Liz forgoes fewer salads to make a smoothie, she has a comparative advantage in producing smoothies.

What about Joe? Doesn't he have a comparative advantage at anything? He does as you're about to see.

Joe's Comparative Advantage

Look at the opportunity costs of producing salads. For Liz, that opportunity cost is 1 smoothie. But for Joe, a salad costs only 1/5 of a smoothie. Because Joe's opportunity cost of a salad is less than Liz's, Joe has a comparative advantage in producing salads.

It is always true that if one person has a comparative advantage in producing a good, others have a comparative advantage in producing some other good.

■ Achieving Gains from Trade

Liz and Joe run into each other in a bar, where Liz tells Joe about her smoothie business. Her only problem, she says, is that she wants to produce more because customers leave when her lines get too long. Joe describes his own smaller business to Liz. When he explains how he divides his hour between making smoothies and salads, Liz's eyes pop. "Have I got a deal for you!" she exclaims.

Here's Liz's deal. Joe stops making smoothies and produces 30 salads per hour. Liz stops making salads and produces 30 smoothies per hour. That is, they both specialize in producing the good in which they have a comparative advantage—see Table 3.3(b). They then trade: Liz sells Joe 10 smoothies and Joe sells Liz 20 salads—the price of a smoothie is 2 salads—see Table 3.3(c).

Trade at a price of 2 salads per smoothie (1/2 a smoothie per salad) enables both Liz and Joe to gain. Liz gets salads for 1/2 a smoothie each, which is less than the 1 smoothie that it costs her to produce a salad. Joe gets smoothies for 2 salads each, which is less than the 5 salads it costs him to produce a smoothie.

After the trade, Joe has 10 salads (the 30 he produces minus the 20 he sells to Liz) and the 10 smoothies that he buys from Liz. So Joe doubles the quantities of smoothies and salads he can sell. Liz has 20 smoothies (the 30 she produces minus the 10 she sells to Joe) and the 20 salads she buys from Joe. See Table 3.3(d). From specialization and trade, each gains 5 smoothies and 5 salads—see Table 3.3(e).

Liz draws the graphs in Figure 3.8 to illustrate her idea. The blue *PPF* is Liz's and the red *PPF* is Joe's. They are each producing at the points marked *A*. Liz's proposal is that they each produce at the points marked *B*.

After trading, each moves to the point marked *C*. At these points, Liz has 20 smoothies and 20 salads, 5 more of each than she was producing only for herself. Joe has 10 smoothies and 10 salads, also 5 more of each than he was producing only for himself. Because of the gains from specialization and trade, total production increases by 10 smoothies and 10 salads.

Notice that the points *C* are *outside* Liz's and Joe's *PPF*s. Everyone gains and enjoys greater quantities of goods than they can produce on their own.

TABLE 3.3   LIZ AND JOE GAIN FROM TRADE

(a) Before Trade	Liz	Joe
Smoothies	15	5
Salads	15	5

(b) Specialization	Liz	Joe
Smoothies	30	0
Salads	0	30

(c) Trade		
Smoothies	sell 10	buy 10
Salads	buy 20	sell 20

(d) After Trade		
Smoothies	20	10
Salads	20	10

(e) Gains from Trade		
Smoothies	+5	+5
Salads	+5	+5

FIGURE 3.8

The Gains from Specialization and Trade

MyEconLab Animation

❶ Before trade, Liz and Joe each produce at point *A* on their respective *PPF*s.

❷ Liz specializes in smoothies and Joe specializes in salads, so they each move to point *B* on their respective *PPF*s.

❸ They exchange smoothies for salads at a price of 2 salads per smoothie. After trade, each goes to point *C*—a point *outside* their individual *PPF*s. They each gain 5 salads and 5 smoothies—the quantities at point *C* minus the quantities at point *A*.

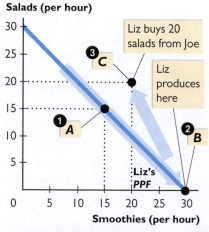

(a) Liz's gains from trade

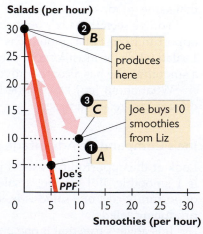

(b) Joe's gains from trade

■ The Economy's Production Possibilities Frontier

With specialization and trade, Liz and Joe get outside their individual *PPFs*, but they produce *on* the economy's *PPF*. Also, despite Liz and Joe having constant opportunity costs, along the economy's *PPF* opportunity cost is increasing—the economy's *PPF* is bowed outward. Figure 3.9 illustrates. The first 30 smoothies produced (by Liz) cost 1 salad each, but the 31st smoothie produced (by Joe) costs 5 salads. Similarly, the first 30 salads produced (by Joe) cost 1/5 smoothie each, but the 31st salad produced (by Liz) costs 1 smoothie. When Liz and Joe specialize, they produce efficiently on the economy's *PPF*. Without specialization and trade, they produce at an inefficient point *inside* the economy's *PPF*.

■ **FIGURE 3.9**

The Economy's Production Possibilities   MyEconLab Animation

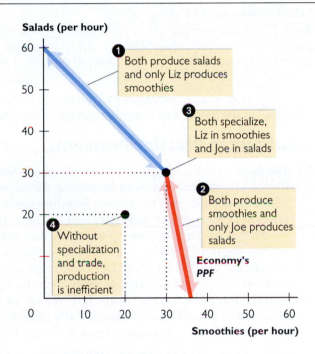

1 When the economy produces more than 30 salads per hour, both Liz and Joe produce salads but only Liz produces smoothies.

2 When the economy produces more than 30 smoothies per hour, both Liz and Joe produce smoothies but only Joe produces salads.

3 When Liz and Joe specialize in their comparative advantage, the economy produces 30 salads and 30 smoothies at an efficient point on the economy's *PPF*.

4 Without specialization and trade, Liz and Joe produce at an inefficient point inside the economy's *PPF*.

EYE on YOUR LIFE
Your Comparative Advantage

MyEconLab Critical Thinking Exercise

You are expanding your production possibilities by being in school and accumulating human capital.

By discovering your comparative advantage, you will be able to focus on producing the items that make you as well off as possible. Think hard about what you enjoy doing, and what you do comparatively better than others.

In today's world, it is a good idea to try to remain flexible so that you can switch jobs if you discover that your comparative advantage has changed.

Looking beyond your own self-interest, are you going to be a voice that supports or opposes offshore outsourcing?

You've learned in this chapter that

regardless of whether outsourcing remains inside the United States, as it does with Liz and Joe at their smoothie bars, or is global like the outsourcing of jobs by U.S. producers to India, both parties gain from trade.

Americans pay less for goods and services and Indians earn higher incomes.

MyEconLab Study Plan 3.4
Key Terms Quiz
Solutions Video

CHECKPOINT 3.4

Explain how people gain from specialization and trade.

Practice Problems

Tony and Patty produce skis and snowboards. Tables 1 and 2 show their production possibilities. Each week, Tony produces 5 snowboards and 40 skis and Patty produces 10 snowboards and 5 skis.

1. Who has a comparative advantage in producing snowboards? Who has a comparative advantage in producing skis?

2. If Tony and Patty specialize and trade, what are the gains from trade?

In the News

Sweet news after TPP sting

Trans-Pacific Partnership (TPP) trade deal has kept tight restrictions on Australia's sugar exports to the United States. In 2015, U.S. sugar producers received 22¢ per pound while Australian growers received the world price of 12¢ per pound.

Source: *The Land*, October 8, 2015

Which country has a comparative advantage in producing sugar? Explain why both the United States and Australia can gain from free trade in sugar.

TABLE 1 TONY'S PRODUCTION POSSIBILITIES

Snowboards (per week)		Skis (per week)
25	and	0
20	and	10
15	and	20
10	and	30
5	and	40
0	and	50

TABLE 2 PATTY'S PRODUCTION POSSIBILITIES

Snowboards (per week)		Skis (per week)
20	and	0
10	and	5
0	and	10

Solutions to Practice Problems

1. The person with a comparative advantage in snowboards is the one who has the lower opportunity cost of producing a snowboard. Tony's production possibilities show that to produce 5 more snowboards he must produce 10 fewer skis. So Tony's opportunity cost of a snowboard is 2 skis.

   Patty's production possibilities show that to produce 10 more snowboards, she must produce 5 fewer skis. So Patty's opportunity cost of a snowboard is 1/2 a ski. Patty has a comparative advantage in snowboards because her opportunity cost of a snowboard is less than Tony's. Tony's comparative advantage is in skis. For each ski produced, Tony must forgo making 1/2 a snowboard, whereas Patty must forgo making 2 snowboards for a ski. So Tony's opportunity cost of a ski is lower than Patty's.

2. Patty has a comparative advantage in snowboards, so she specializes in snowboards. Tony has a comparative advantage in skis, so he specializes in skis. Patty makes 20 snowboards and Tony makes 50 skis. Before specializing, they made 15 snowboards and 45 skis. By specializing, total output increases by 5 snowboards and 5 skis. They share this gain by trading.

Solution to In the News

The cost of producing sugar is less in Australia than in the United States, so Australia has a comparative advantage in producing sugar. If Australia specializes in producing sugar and the United States specializes in producing other goods (for example, movies or airplanes) and the two countries engage in free trade, each country can gain and get to a point outside its own *PPF*.

CHAPTER SUMMARY

Key Points

1. Explain and illustrate the concepts of scarcity, production efficiency, and tradeoff using the production possibilities frontier.

- The production possibilities frontier, *PPF*, describes the limits to what can be produced by using all the available resources efficiently.
- Points inside and on the *PPF* are attainable. Points outside the *PPF* are unattainable.
- Production at any point on the *PPF* achieves production efficiency. Production at a point inside the *PPF* is inefficient.
- When production is efficient—on the *PPF*—people face a tradeoff. If production is at a point inside the *PPF*, there is a free lunch to be had.

2. Calculate opportunity cost.

- Along the *PPF*, the opportunity cost of *X* (the item measured on the *x*-axis) is the decrease in *Y* (the item measured on the *y*-axis) divided by the increase in *X*.
- The opportunity cost of *Y* is the inverse of the opportunity cost of *X*.
- The opportunity cost of producing a good increases as the quantity of the good produced increases.

3. Explain what makes production possibilities expand.

- Technological change and increases in capital and human capital expand production possibilities.
- The opportunity cost of economic growth is the decrease in current consumption.

4. Explain how people gain from specialization and trade.

- A person has a comparative advantage in an activity if he or she can perform that activity at a lower opportunity cost than someone else.
- People gain by increasing the production of the item in which they have a comparative advantage and trading.

Key Terms

MyEconLab **Key Terms Quiz**

Absolute advantage, 73
Comparative advantage, 73
Economic growth, 70
Production efficiency, 62
Production possibilities frontier, 60
Tradeoff, 63

MyEconLab Chapter 3 Study Plan

CHAPTER CHECKPOINT

Study Plan Problems and Applications

TABLE 1

Corn (bushels)		Beef (pounds)
250	and	0
200	and	300
100	and	500
0	and	600

TABLE 2

Labor (hours)	Entertainment (units)		Good food (units)
0	0	or	0
10	20	or	30
20	40	or	50
30	60	or	60
40	80	or	65
50	100	or	67

FIGURE 1

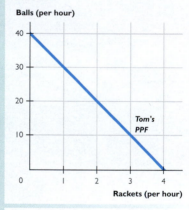

FIGURE 2

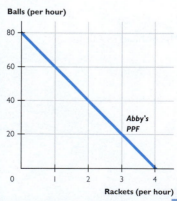

1. Table 1 shows the quantities of corn and beef that a farm can produce in a year. Draw a graph of the farm's *PPF*. Mark on the graph.
- An inefficient combination of corn and beef—label this point *A*.
- An unattainable combination of corn and beef—label this point *B*.
- An efficient combination of corn and beef—label this point *C*.

Use the following information to work Problems **2** and **3**.

The people of Leisure Island have 50 hours of labor a day that can be used to produce entertainment and good food. Table 2 shows the maximum quantity of *either* entertainment *or* good food that Leisure Island can produce with different quantities of labor.

2. Is an output of 50 units of entertainment and 50 units of good food attainable and efficient? With a production of 50 units of entertainment and 50 units of good food, do the people of Leisure Island face a tradeoff?

3. What is the opportunity cost of producing an additional unit of entertainment? Explain how the opportunity cost of producing a unit of entertainment changes as more entertainment is produced.

Use the following information to work Problems **4** and **5**.

Malaria can be controlled
The World Health Organization's malaria chief says that it is too costly to try to fully eradicate the disease. He says that by using nets, medicine, and DDT it is possible to eliminate 90 percent of malaria cases. But to eliminate 100 percent of cases would be extremely costly.

Source: *The New York Times*, March 4, 2008

4. Make a graph of the production possibilities frontier with malaria control on the *x*-axis and other goods and services on the *y*-axis.

5. Describe how the opportunity cost of controlling malaria changes as more resources are used to reduce the number of malaria cases.

6. Explain how the following events influence U.S. production possibilities:
- Some retail workers are re-employed building dams and wind farms.
- More people take early retirement.
- Drought devastates California's economy.

Use the following information to work Problems **7** and **8**.

Figures 1 and 2 show Tom's and Abby's production possibilities. Tom uses all his resources and produces 2 rackets and 20 balls an hour. Abby uses all her resources and produces 2 rackets and 40 balls an hour.

7. What is Tom's opportunity cost of producing a racket? What is Abby's opportunity cost of a racket? Who has a comparative advantage in producing rackets? Who has a comparative advantage in producing balls?

8. If Tom and Abby specialize and trade balls and rackets at the price of 15 balls per racket, what are Tom's and Abby's gains from trade?

9. Read *Eye on the Environment* on p. 68 and describe a tradeoff faced when deciding how to generate electricity and whether to use wind power.

Instructor Assignable Problems and Applications

MyEconLab Homework, Quiz, or Test if assigned by instructor

Use the following information to work Problems **1** to **4**.

Representatives Waxman of California and Markey of Massachusetts proposed a law to limit greenhouse gas emissions from electricity generation and require electricity producers to generate a minimum percentage of power using renewable fuels, with some emission rights to be auctioned. The Congressional Budget Office estimated that the government would receive $846 billion from auctions and would spend $821 billion on incentive programs and compensation for higher energy prices. Electricity producers would spend $208 million a year to comply with the new rules. (Think of these dollar amounts as dollars' worth of other goods and services.)

1. Would the Waxman-Markey law achieve production efficiency?

2. Is the $846 billion that electricity producers would pay for the right to emit greenhouse gasses part of the opportunity cost of producing electricity?

3. Is the $821 billion that the government would spend on incentive programs and compensation for higher energy prices part of the opportunity cost of producing electricity?

4. Is the $208 million that electricity producers will spend to comply with the new rules part of the opportunity cost of producing electricity?

5. The people of Foodland have 40 hours of labor a day to bake pizza and bread. Table 1 shows the maximum quantity of *either* pizza *or* bread that Foodland can bake with different quantities of labor. Can Foodland produce 30 pizzas and 30 loaves of bread a day? If it can, is this output efficient, do the people of Foodland face a tradeoff, and what is the opportunity cost of producing an additional pizza?

Use Table 2, which shows a farm's production possibilities, to work Problems **6** and **7**.

6. If the farm uses its resources efficiently, what is the opportunity cost of an increase in chicken production from 300 pounds to 500 pounds a year? Explain your answer.

7. If the farm adopted a new technology, which allows it to use fewer resources to fatten chickens, explain how the farm's production possibilities will change. Explain how the opportunity cost of producing a bushel of soybean will be affected.

8. In an hour, Sue can produce 40 caps or 4 jackets and Tessa can produce 80 caps or 4 jackets. Who has a comparative advantage in producing caps? If Sue and Tessa specialize and trade, who will gain?

Use the following opinion to work Problems **9** to **11**.

Free Internet?

Everyone should have free Internet access to education, news, jobs, and more.

9. Explain how Internet access has changed the production possibilities and the opportunity cost of producing education and news.

10. Sketch a *PPF* curve with education and news on the *x*-axis and other goods and services on the *y*-axis before and after the Internet.

11. Explain why it is not possible for everyone to have free Internet access to education, news, jobs, and more.

TABLE 1

Labor (hours)	Pizzas		Bread (loaves)
0	0	or	0
10	30	or	10
20	50	or	20
30	60	or	30
40	65	or	40

TABLE 2

Soybean (bushels per year)		Chicken (pounds per year)
500	and	0
400	and	300
200	and	500
0	and	600

Multiple Choice Quiz

1. Table 1 shows the production possibilities of an island community. Choose the best statement.

A. This community has enough resources to produce 2 pounds of fish and 36 pounds of berries.

B. This community cannot produce 2 pounds of fish and 36 pounds of berries because this combination is inefficient.

C. This community will waste resources if it produces 2 pounds of fish and 22 pounds of berries.

D. This community can produce 2 pounds of fish and 30 pounds of berries but this combination is inefficient.

2. Table 1 shows the production possibilities of an island community. Choose the best statement.

A. Suppose that this community produces 3 pounds of fish and 20 pounds of berries. If it decides to gather more berries, it faces a tradeoff.

B. When this community produces 4 pounds of fish and 12 pounds of berries it faces a tradeoff, but it is inefficient.

C. Suppose that this community produces 5 pounds of fish and 0 pounds of berries. If it decides to gather some berries, it will get a free lunch.

D. If this community produces 3 pounds of fish and 22 pounds of berries, production is efficient but to produce more fish it faces a tradeoff.

3. Table 1 shows the production possibilities of an island community. This community's opportunity cost of producing 1 pound of fish _____.

A. is the increase in the quantity of berries gathered as the quantity of fish increases by 1 pound

B. increases as the quantity of berries gathered increases

C. is 10 pounds of berries if the quantity of fish increases from 2 to 3 pounds

D. increases as the quantity of fish caught increases

4. Table 1 shows the production possibilities of an island community. Choose the best statement.

A. When a drought hits the island, its *PPF* rotates outward.

B. When the islanders discover a better way of catching fish, the island's *PPF* rotates outward.

C. When islanders reduce the time they spend gathering berries, the *PPF* rotates inward.

D. If the islanders decide to spend more time gathering berries but continue to spend the same amount of time fishing, they face a tradeoff.

5. Mary makes 10 pies and 20 cakes a day and her opportunity cost of producing a cake is 2 pies. Tim makes 20 pies and 10 cakes a day and his opportunity cost of producing a cake is 4 pies. If Mary and Tim specialize in producing the good in which each has a comparative advantage, _____.

A. Mary produces only pies

B. Tim produces both pies and cakes

C. Mary produces only cakes while Tim produces only pies

D. Tim produces only cakes while Mary produces only pies

TABLE 1

Possibility	Fish (pounds)		Berries (pounds)
A	0	and	40
B	1	and	36
C	2	and	30
D	3	and	22
E	4	and	12
F	5	and	0

Why did the price of coffee rise in 2014?

Demand and Supply

4

When you have completed your study of this chapter, you will be able to

CHAPTER CHECKLIST

1 Distinguish between quantity demanded and demand, and explain what determines demand.

2 Distinguish between quantity supplied and supply, and explain what determines supply.

3 Explain how demand and supply determine price and quantity in a market, and explain the effects of changes in demand and supply.

MyEconLab Big Picture Video

COMPETITIVE MARKETS

When you want a latte you go to a coffee shop. When a coffee shop needs to restock with beans and milk, it calls its suppliers of those items. You, your favorite coffee shop, and the shop's suppliers are trading in *markets*.

You learned in Chapter 2 that a market is any arrangement that brings buyers and sellers together. A market has two sides: demand (buyers) and supply (sellers). There are markets for *goods* such as a latte and a bagel, running shoes, apples, and hiking boots; for *services* such as airplane trips, haircuts, and tennis lessons; for *resources* such as coffee beans, computer programmers, and tractors; and for *manufactured components* such as memory chips and auto parts. There are also markets for money such as Japanese yen and for financial securities such as Facebook stock. Only imagination limits what can be traded in markets.

Some markets are physical places where buyers and sellers meet and where an auctioneer or a broker helps to determine the prices. Examples of this type of market are the New York Stock Exchange; wholesale fish, meat, and produce markets; and used car auctions.

Some markets are virtual spaces where buyers and sellers never meet face-to-face but connect over telephone lines or the Internet. Examples include currency markets, e-commerce Web sites such as Amazon.com and iTunes, auction sites such as eBay, and travel Web sites.

But most markets are unorganized collections of buyers and sellers. You do most of your trading in this type of market. An example is the market for coffee and snacks. The buyers in this $75-billion-a-year market are the more than 100 million Americans who regularly drink coffee. The sellers are the 55,000 coffee shops and snack bars. Each buyer can visit several different sellers, and each seller knows that the buyer has a choice of many alternatives.

Markets vary in the intensity of competition that buyers and sellers face. In this chapter, we're going to study a *competitive market* that has so many buyers and so many sellers that no single buyer or seller can influence the price.

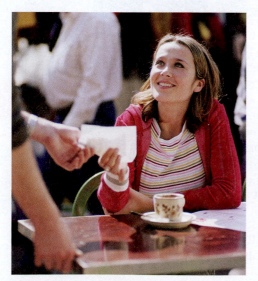

Markets for coffee and a bagel …

running shoes …

and airline travel.

4.1 DEMAND

MyEconLab Concept Video

First, we'll study the behavior of buyers in a competitive market. The **quantity demanded** of any good, service, or resource is the amount that people are willing and able to buy during a specified period at a specified price. For example, when spring water costs $1 a bottle, you decide to buy 2 bottles a day. The 2 bottles a day is your quantity demanded of spring water.

The quantity demanded is measured as an amount *per unit of time.* For example, your quantity demanded of water is 2 bottles *per day.* We could express this quantity as 14 bottles per week, or some other number per month or per year. A particular number of bottles without a time dimension has no meaning.

Many things influence buying plans, and one of them is price. We look first at the relationship between quantity demanded and price. To study this relationship, we keep all other influences on buying plans the same and we ask: How, other things remaining the same, does the quantity demanded of a good change as its price varies? The law of demand provides the answer.

Quantity demanded
The amount of any good, service, or resource that people are willing and able to buy during a specified period at a specified price.

■ The Law of Demand

The **law of demand** states

> **Other things remaining the same, if the price of a good rises, the quantity demanded of that good decreases; and if the price of a good falls, the quantity demanded of that good increases.**

So the law of demand states that when all other things remain the same, if the price of an iPhone falls, people will buy more iPhones; or if the price of a baseball ticket rises, people will buy fewer baseball tickets.

Why does the quantity demanded increase if the price falls, all other things remaining the same?

The answer is that, faced with a limited budget, people always have an incentive to find the best deals available. If the price of one item falls and the prices of all other items remain the same, the item with the lower price is a better deal than it was before, so some people buy more of this item. Suppose, for example, that the price of bottled water fell from $2 a bottle to $1.50 a bottle while the price of Gatorade remained at $2 a bottle. Wouldn't some people switch from Gatorade to water? By doing so, they save 50¢ a bottle, which they can spend on other things they previously couldn't afford.

Think about the things that you buy and ask yourself: Which of these items does *not* obey the law of demand? If the price of a new textbook were lower, other things remaining the same (including the price of a used textbook), would you buy more new textbooks? Then think about all the things that you do not buy but would if you could afford them. How cheap would a computer have to be for you to buy *both* a tablet and a laptop? There is a price that is low enough to entice you!

Law of demand
Other things remaining the same, if the price of a good rises, the quantity demanded of that good decreases; and if the price of a good falls, the quantity demanded of that good increases.

■ Demand Schedule and Demand Curve

Demand is the relationship between the quantity demanded and the price of a good when all other influences on buying plans remain the same. The quantity demanded is *one* quantity at *one* price. *Demand* is a *list of quantities at different prices* illustrated by a demand schedule and a demand curve.

Demand
The relationship between the quantity demanded and the price of a good when all other influences on buying plans remain the same.

Demand schedule

A list of the quantities demanded at each different price when all the other influences on buying plans remain the same.

Demand curve

A graph of the relationship between the quantity demanded of a good and its price when all the other influences on buying plans remain the same.

A **demand schedule** is a list of the quantities demanded at each different price when *all the other influences on buying plans remain the same*. The table in Figure 4.1 is one person's (Tina's) demand schedule for bottled water. This schedule tells us that if the price of water is $2.00 a bottle, Tina buys no water. Her quantity demanded is 0 bottles a day. If the price of water is $1.50 a bottle, her quantity demanded is 1 bottle a day. Tina's quantity demanded increases to 2 bottles a day at a price of $1.00 a bottle and to 3 bottles a day at a price of 50¢ a bottle.

A **demand curve** is a graph of the relationship between the quantity demanded of a good and its price when all the other influences on buying plans remain the same. The points on the demand curve labeled *A* through *D* represent the rows *A* through *D* of the demand schedule. For example, point *B* on the graph represents row *B* of the demand schedule and shows that the quantity demanded is 1 bottle a day when the price is $1.50 a bottle. Point *C* on the demand curve represents row *C* of the demand schedule and shows that the quantity demanded is 2 bottles a day when the price is $1.00 a bottle.

The downward slope of the demand curve illustrates the law of demand. Along the demand curve, when the price of the good *falls*, the quantity demanded *increases*. For example, in Figure 4.1, when the price of a bottle of water falls from $1.00 to 50 cents, the quantity demanded increases from 2 bottles a day to 3 bottles a day. Conversely, when the price *rises*, the quantity demanded *decreases*. For example, when the price rises from $1.00 to $1.50 a bottle, the quantity demanded decreases from 2 bottles a day to 1 bottle a day.

■ FIGURE 4.1

Demand Schedule and Demand Curve   MyEconLab Animation

The table shows Tina's demand schedule that lists the quantity of water demanded at each price if all other influences on buying plans remain the same. At a price of $1.50 a bottle, the quantity demanded is 1 bottle a day.

The demand curve shows the relationship between the quantity demanded and price, other things remaining the same. The downward-sloping demand curve illustrates the law of demand. When the price falls, the quantity demanded increases; and when the price rises, the quantity demanded decreases.

	Price (dollars per bottle)	Quantity demanded (bottles per day)
A	2.00	0
B	1.50	1
C	1.00	2
D	0.50	3

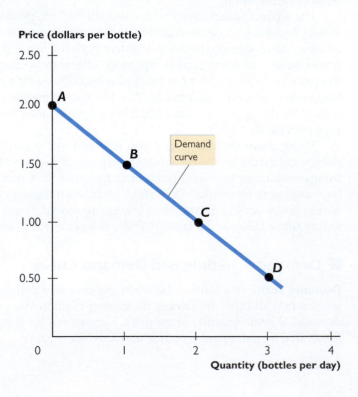

■ Individual Demand and Market Demand

The demand schedule and the demand curve that you've just studied are for one person. To study a market, we must determine the market demand.

Market demand is the sum of the demands of all the buyers in a market. To find the market demand, imagine a market in which there are only two buyers: Tina and Tim. The table in Figure 4.2 shows three demand schedules: Tina's, Tim's, and the market demand schedule. Tina's demand schedule is the same as before. It shows the quantity of water demanded by Tina at each different price. Tim's demand schedule tells us the quantity of water demanded by Tim at each price. To find the quantity of water demanded in the market, we sum the quantities demanded by Tina and Tim. For example, at a price of $1.00 a bottle, the quantity demanded by Tina is 2 bottles a day, the quantity demanded by Tim is 1 bottle a day, and so the quantity demanded in the market is 3 bottles a day.

Tina's demand curve in part (a) and Tim's demand curve in part (b) are graphs of the two individual demand schedules. The market demand curve in part (c) is a graph of the market demand schedule. At a given price, the quantity demanded on the market demand curve equals the horizontal sum of the quantities demanded on the individual demand curves.

■ FIGURE 4.2

Individual Demand and Market Demand

MyEconLab Animation

Price (dollars per bottle)	Quantity demanded (bottles per day)		
	Tina	Tim	Market
2.00	0	0	0
1.50	1	0	1
1.00	2 +	1 =	3
0.50	3	2	5

The market demand schedule is the sum of the individual demand schedules, and the market demand curve is the horizontal sum of the individual demand curves.

At a price of $1 a bottle, the quantity demanded by Tina is 2 bottles a day and the quantity demanded by Tim is 1 bottle a day, so the total quantity demanded in the market is 3 bottles a day.

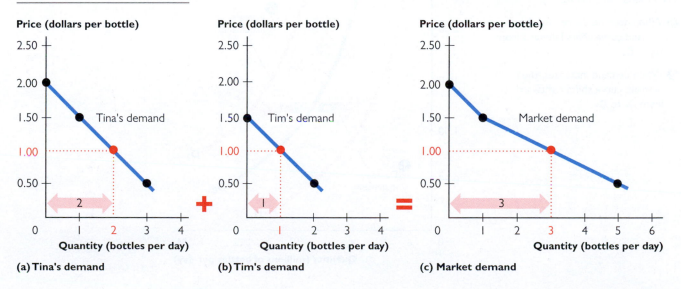

(a) Tina's demand

(b) Tim's demand

(c) Market demand

MyEconLab Concept Video

Change in demand

A change in the quantity that people plan to buy when any influence on buying plans other than the price of the good changes.

Changes in Demand

The demand curve shows how the quantity demanded changes when the price of the good changes but *all other influences on buying plans remain the same.* When any of these other influences on buying plans change, there is a **change in demand**, which means that there is a new demand schedule and new demand curve. *The demand curve shifts.*

Demand can either increase or decrease and Figure 4.3 illustrates the two cases. Initially, the demand curve is D_0. When demand decreases, the demand curve shifts leftward to D_1. On demand curve D_1, the quantity demanded at each price is smaller. When demand increases, the demand curve shifts rightward to D_2. On demand curve D_2, the quantity demanded at each price is greater.

The main influences on buying plans that change demand are

- Prices of related goods
- Expected future prices
- Income
- Expected future income and credit
- Number of buyers
- Preferences

Substitute

A good that can be consumed in place of another good.

Complement

A good that is consumed with another good.

Prices of Related Goods

Goods have substitutes and complements. A **substitute** for a good is another good that can be consumed in its place. Chocolate cake is a substitute for cheesecake, and bottled water is a substitute for Gatorade. A **complement** of a good is another good that is consumed with it. A helmet is a complement of a bike, and bottled water is a complement of fitness center services.

■ **FIGURE 4.3**

Changes in Demand

MyEconLab Animation

A change in any influence on buying plans, other than a change in the price of the good itself, changes demand and shifts the demand curve.

1 When demand decreases, the demand curve shifts leftward from D_0 to D_1.

2 When demand increases, the demand curve shifts rightward from D_0 to D_2.

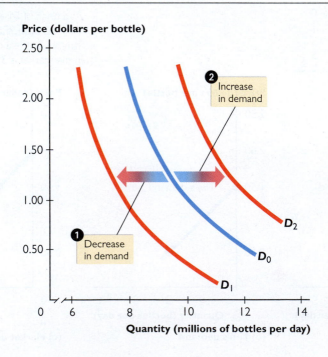

The demand for a good and the price of one of its substitutes move in the *same direction*. The demand for a good *increases* if the price of one of its substitutes *rises* and *decreases* if the price of one of its substitutes *falls*. For example, the demand for cheesecake increases when the price of chocolate cake rises.

The demand for a good and the price of one of its complements move in *opposite directions*. The demand for a good *decreases* if the price of one of its complements *rises* and *increases* if the price of one of its complements *falls*. For example, the demand for helmets decreases when the price of a bike rises.

Expected Future Prices

A rise in the expected *future* price of a good increases the *current* demand for that good and a fall in the expected *future* price decreases *current* demand. If you expect the price of noodles to rise next week, you buy a big enough stockpile to get you through the next few weeks. Your demand for noodles today has increased. If you expect the price of noodles to fall next week, you buy none now and plan to buy next week. Your demand for noodles today has decreased.

Income

A rise in income brings an increase in demand and a fall in income brings a decrease in demand for a **normal good**. A rise in income brings a *decrease* in demand and a fall in income brings an *increase* in demand for an **inferior good**. For example, if your income increases and you decide to buy more chicken and less pasta, for you, chicken is a normal good and pasta is an inferior good.

Normal good
A good for which demand increases when income increases and demand decreases when income decreases.

Inferior good
A good for which demand decreases when income increases and demand increases when income decreases.

Expected Future Income and Credit

When income is expected to increase in the future, or when credit is easy to get and the cost of borrowing is low, the demand for some goods increases. And when income is expected to decrease in the future, or when credit is hard to get and the cost of borrowing is high, the demand for some goods decreases.

Changes in expected future income and the availability and cost of credit have the greatest effect on the demand for big ticket items such as homes and automobiles. Modest changes in expected future income or credit availability bring large swings in the demand for these items.

Number of Buyers

The greater the number of buyers in a market, the larger is demand. For example, the demand for parking spaces, movies, bottled water, or just about anything is greater in New York City than it is in Boise, Idaho.

Preferences

Tastes or *preferences*, as economists call them, influence demand. When preferences change, the demand for one item increases and the demand for another item (or items) decreases. For example, preferences have changed as people have become better informed about the health hazards of tobacco. This change in preferences has decreased the demand for cigarettes and has increased the demand for nicotine patches. Preferences also change when new goods become available. For example, the development of smartphones has decreased the demand for landlines and has increased the demand for Internet service.

■ Change in Quantity Demanded Versus Change in Demand

The influences on buyers' plans that you've just seen bring a *change in demand.* These are all the influences on buying plans *except for the price of the good.* To avoid confusion, when *the price of the good changes* and all other influences on buying plans remain the same, we say there has been a **change in the quantity demanded**.

Change in the quantity demanded
A change in the quantity of a good that people plan to buy that results from a change in the price of the good with all other influences on buying plans remaining the same.

The distinction between a change in demand and a change in the quantity demanded is crucial for working out how a market responds to the forces that hit it. Figure 4.4 illustrates and summarizes the distinction:

- If the price of bottled water *rises* when other things remain the same, the quantity demanded of bottled water *decreases* and there is a *movement up* along the demand curve D_0. If the price *falls* when other things remain the same, the quantity demanded *increases* and there is a *movement down* along the demand curve D_0.
- If some influence on buyers' plans other than the price of bottled water changes, there is a change in demand. When the demand for bottled water *decreases*, the demand curve *shifts leftward* to D_1. When the demand for bottled water *increases*, the demand curve *shifts rightward* to D_2.

When you are thinking about the influences on demand, try to get into the habit of asking: Does this influence change the quantity demanded or does it change demand? The test is: Did the price of the good change or did some other influence change? If the price changed, then quantity demanded changed. If some other influence changed and the price remained constant, then demand changed.

■ **FIGURE 4.4**

Change in Quantity Demanded Versus Change in Demand   MyEconLab Animation

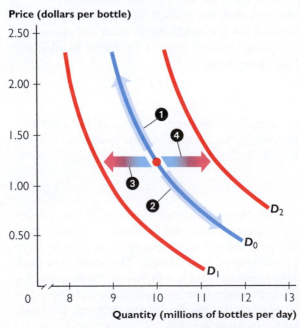

❶ **A decrease in the quantity demanded**
The quantity demanded decreases and there is a movement up along the demand curve D_0 if the price of the good rises and other things remain the same.

❷ **An increase in the quantity demanded**
The quantity demanded increases and there is a movement down along the demand curve D_0 if the price of the good falls and other things remain the same.

❸ **A decrease in demand**
Demand decreases and the demand curve shifts leftward (from D_0 to D_1) if

- The price of a substitute falls or the price of a complement rises.
- The price of the good is expected to fall.
- Income decreases.*
- Expected future income or credit decreases.
- The number of buyers decreases.

* Bottled water is a normal good.

❹ **An increase in demand**
Demand increases and the demand curve shifts rightward (from D_0 to D_2) if

- The price of a substitute rises or the price of a complement falls.
- The price of the good is expected to rise.
- Income increases.
- Expected future income or credit increases.
- The number of buyers increases.

CHECKPOINT 4.1

MyEconLab Study Plan 4.1
Key Terms Quiz
Solutions Video

Distinguish between quantity demanded and demand, and explain what determines demand.

Practice Problems

The following events occur one at a time in the market for smartphones:
- The price of a smartphone falls.
- Producers announce that the price of a smartphone will fall next month.
- The price of a call made from a smartphone falls.
- The price of a call made from a land-line phone increases.
- An increase in memory makes smartphones more popular.

1. Explain the effect of each event on the demand for smartphones.
2. Use a graph to illustrate the effect of each event.
3. Does any event (or events) illustrate the law of demand?

In the News

Airline profits soar yet no relief for passengers
Airplanes are more crowded than ever and fares are at a five-year high.
Source: *USA Today*, January 27, 2015

Does this news clip imply that the law of demand doesn't work in the real world? Explain why or why not.

Solutions to Practice Problems

1. A fall in the price of a smartphone increases the quantity of smartphones demanded but has no effect on the demand for smartphones.
   With the producers' announcement, the expected future price of a smartphone falls, which decreases the demand for smartphones today.
   A fall in the price of a call from a smartphone increases the demand for smartphones because a smartphone call and a smartphone are complements.
   A rise in the price of a call from a land-line phone increases the demand for smartphones because a land-line phone and a smartphone are substitutes.
   With smartphones more popular, the demand for smartphones increases.

2. Figure 1 illustrates the effect of a fall in the price of a smartphone as a movement along the demand curve D.
   Figure 2 illustrates the effect of an increase in the demand for smartphones as the shift of the demand curve from D_0 to D_1 and a decrease in the demand for smartphones as the shift of the demand curve from D_0 to D_2.

3. A fall in the price of a smartphone (other things remaining the same) illustrates the law of demand. Figure 1 illustrates the law of demand. The other events change demand and do not illustrate the law of demand.

Solution to In the News

The law of demand states: If the price of an airline ticket rises, other things remaining the same, the quantity demanded of airline tickets will decrease. The demand curve for airline tickets slopes downward. The law of demand does work in the real world. Airlines can fill planes at high fares because "other things" have not remained the same. The demand for air travel has increased.

FIGURE 1

FIGURE 2

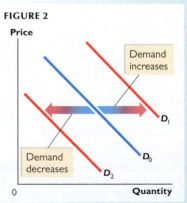

4.2 SUPPLY

Quantity supplied
The amount of any good, service, or resource that people are willing and able to sell during a specified period at a specified price.

A market has two sides. On one side are the buyers, or demanders, that we've just studied. On the other side of the market are the sellers, or suppliers. We now study the forces that determine suppliers' plans.

The **quantity supplied** of a good, service, or resource is the amount that people are willing and able to sell during a specified period at a specified price. For example, when the price of spring water is $1.50 a bottle, a spring owner decides to sell 2,000 bottles a day. The 2,000 bottles a day is the quantity supplied of spring water by this individual producer. (As in the case of demand, the quantity supplied is measured as an amount *per unit of time*.)

Many things influence selling plans, and one of them is the price. We look first at the relationship between quantity supplied of a good and its price. To study this relationship, we keep all other influences on selling plans the same, and we ask: Other things remaining the same, how does the quantity supplied of a good change as its price varies? The law of supply provides the answer.

■ The Law of Supply

Law of supply
Other things remaining the same, if the price of a good rises, the quantity supplied of that good increases; and if the price of a good falls, the quantity supplied of that good decreases.

The **law of supply** states

> **Other things remaining the same, if the price of a good rises, the quantity supplied of that good increases; and if the price of a good falls, the quantity supplied of that good decreases.**

So the law of supply states that when all other things remain the same, if the price of bottled water rises, spring owners will offer more water for sale; if the price of a flat-screen TV falls, Sony Corp. will offer fewer flat-screen TVs for sale.

Why, other things remaining the same, does the quantity supplied increase if the price rises and decrease if the price falls? Part of the answer lies in the principle of increasing opportunity cost (see p. 68). Because factors of production are not equally productive in all activities, as more of a good is produced, the opportunity cost of producing it increases. A higher price provides the incentive to bear the higher opportunity cost of increased production. Another part of the answer is that for a given cost, the higher price brings a larger profit, so sellers have greater incentive to increase production.

Think about the resources that you own and can offer for sale to others and ask yourself: Which of these items does *not* obey the law of supply? If the wage rate for summer jobs increased, would you have an incentive to work longer hours and bear the higher opportunity cost of forgone leisure? If the bank offered a higher interest rate on deposits, would you have an incentive to save more and bear the higher opportunity cost of forgone consumption? If the used book dealer offered a higher price for last year's textbooks, would you have an incentive to sell that handy math text and bear the higher opportunity cost of visiting the library (or finding a friend) whenever you needed the book?

■ Supply Schedule and Supply Curve

Supply
The relationship between the quantity supplied and the price of a good when all other influences on selling plans remain the same.

Supply is the relationship between the quantity supplied and the price of a good when all other influences on selling plans remain the same. The quantity supplied is *one* quantity at *one* price. *Supply is a list of quantities at different prices* illustrated by a supply schedule and a supply curve.

A **supply schedule** lists the quantities supplied at each different price when all the other influences on selling plans remain the same. The table in Figure 4.5 is one firm's (Agua's) supply schedule for bottled water. It tells us that if the price of water is 50¢ a bottle, Agua plans to sell no water. Its quantity supplied is 0 bottles a day. If the price of water is $1.00 a bottle, Agua's quantity supplied is 1,000 bottles a day. Agua's quantity supplied increases to 2,000 bottles a day at a price of $1.50 a bottle and to 3,000 bottles a day at a price of $2.00 a bottle.

A **supply curve** is a graph of the relationship between the quantity supplied of a good and its price when all the other influences on selling plans remain the same. The points on the supply curve labeled *A* through *D* represent the rows *A* through *D* of the supply schedule. For example, point *C* on the supply curve represents row *C* of the supply schedule and shows that the quantity supplied is 1,000 bottles a day when the price is $1.00 a bottle. Point *B* on the supply curve represents row *B* of the supply schedule and shows that the quantity supplied is 2,000 bottles a day when the price is $1.50 a bottle.

The upward slope of the supply curve illustrates the law of supply. Along the supply curve, when the price of the good *rises*, the quantity supplied *increases*. For example, in Figure 4.5, when the price of a bottle of water rises from $1.50 to $2.00, the quantity supplied increases from 2,000 bottles a day to 3,000 bottles a day. And when the price *falls*, the quantity supplied *decreases*. For example, when the price falls from $1.50 to $1.00 a bottle, the quantity supplied decreases from 2,000 bottles a day to 1,000 bottles a day.

Supply schedule
A list of the quantities supplied at each different price when all the other influences on selling plans remain the same.

Supply curve
A graph of the relationship between the quantity supplied of a good and its price when all the other influences on selling plans remain the same.

■ **FIGURE 4.5**

Supply Schedule and Supply Curve

MyEconLab Animation

	Price (dollars per bottle)	Quantity supplied (thousands of bottles per day)
A	2.00	3
B	1.50	2
C	1.00	1
D	0.50	0

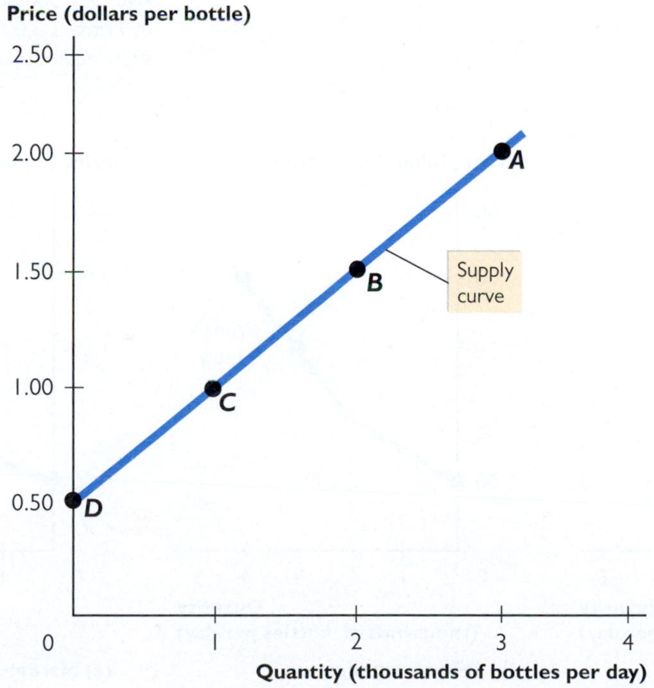

The table shows a supply schedule that lists the quantity of water supplied at each price if all other influences on selling plans remain the same. At a price of $1.50 a bottle, the quantity supplied is 2,000 bottles a day.

The supply curve shows the relationship between the quantity supplied and price, other things remaining the same. The upward-sloping supply curve illustrates the law of supply. When the price rises, the quantity supplied increases; and when the price falls, the quantity supplied decreases.

◼ Individual Supply and Market Supply

The supply schedule and the supply curve that you've just studied are for one seller. To study a market, we must determine the market supply.

Market supply is the sum of the supplies of all the sellers in the market. To find the market supply of water, imagine a market in which there are only two sellers: Agua and Prima. The table in Figure 4.6 shows three supply schedules: Agua's, Prima's, and the market supply schedule. Agua's supply schedule is the same as before. Prima's supply schedule tells us the quantity of water that Prima plans to sell at each price. To find the quantity of water supplied in the market, we sum the quantities supplied by Agua and Prima. For example, at a price of $1.00 a bottle, the quantity supplied by Agua is 1,000 bottles a day, the quantity supplied by Prima is 2,000 bottles a day, and the quantity supplied in the market is 3,000 bottles a day.

Agua's supply curve in part (a) and Prima's supply curve in part (b) are graphs of the two individual supply schedules. The market supply curve in part (c) is a graph of the market supply schedule. At a given price, the quantity supplied on the market supply curve equals the horizontal sum of the quantities supplied on the individual supply curves.

◼ **FIGURE 4.6**

Individual Supply and Market Supply   MyEconLab Animation

Price (dollars per bottle)	Quantity supplied (thousands of bottles per day)		
	Agua	Prima	Market
2.00	3	4	7
1.50	2	3	5
1.00	1 +	2 =	3
0.50	0	0	0

The market supply schedule is the sum of the individual supply schedules, and the market supply curve is the horizontal sum of the individual supply curves.

At a price of $1 a bottle, the quantity supplied by Agua is 1,000 bottles a day and the quantity supplied by Prima is 2,000 bottles a day, so the total quantity supplied in the market is 3,000 bottles a day.

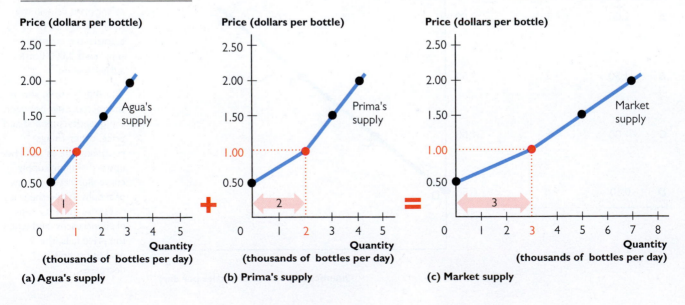

(a) Agua's supply   (b) Prima's supply   (c) Market supply

Changes in Supply

MyEconLab Concept Video

The supply curve shows how the quantity supplied changes when the price of the good changes but *all other influences on selling plans remain the same*. When any of these other influences on selling plans change, there is a **change in supply**, which means that there is a new supply schedule and new supply curve. *The supply curve shifts.*

Supply can either increase or decrease, and Figure 4.7 illustrates the two cases. Initially, the supply curve is S_0. When supply decreases, the supply curve shifts leftward to S_1. On supply curve S_1, the quantity supplied at each price is smaller. When supply increases, the supply curve shifts rightward to S_2. On supply curve S_2, the quantity supplied at each price is greater.

The main influences on selling plans that change supply are

- Prices of related goods
- Prices of resources and other inputs
- Expected future prices
- Number of sellers
- Productivity

Change in supply
A change in the quantity that suppliers plan to sell when any influence on selling plans other than the price of the good changes.

Prices of Related Goods

Related goods are either substitutes *in production* or complements *in production*. A **substitute in production** for a good is another good that can be produced in its place. Skinny jeans are substitutes in production for boot cut jeans in a clothing factory.

A **complement in production** of one good is another good that is produced along with it. Cream is a complement in production of skim milk in a dairy.

Substitute in production
A good that can be produced in place of another good.

Complement in production
A good that is produced along with another good.

■ FIGURE 4.7

Changes in Supply

MyEconLab Animation

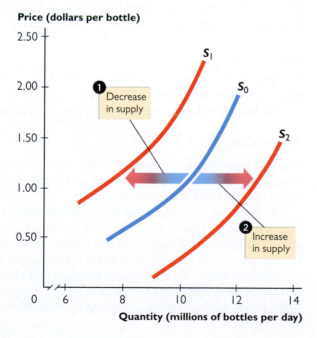

A change in any influence on selling plans other than a change in the price of the good itself changes supply and shifts the supply curve.

❶ When supply decreases, the supply curve shifts leftward from S_0 to S_1.

❷ When supply increases, the supply curve shifts rightward from S_0 to S_2.

A Change in the Price of a Substitute in Production   The supply of a good *decreases* if the price of one of its substitutes in production *rises;* and the supply of a good *increases* if the price of one of its substitutes in production *falls*. That is, the supply of a good and the price of one of its substitutes in production move in *opposite directions*. For example, a clothing factory can produce chinos or button-fly jeans, so these goods are substitutes in production. When the price of button-fly jeans rises, the clothing factory switches production from chinos to button-fly jeans, so the supply of chinos decreases.

A Change in the Price of a Complement in Production   The supply of a good *increases* if the price of one of its complements in production *rises;* and the supply of a good *decreases* if the price of one of its complements in production *falls*. That is, the supply of a good and the price of one of its complements in production move in the *same direction*. For example, when a dairy produces skim milk, it also produces cream, so these goods are complements in production. When the price of skim milk rises, the dairy produces more skim milk, so the supply of cream increases.

Prices of Resources and Other Inputs

Supply changes when the price of a resource or other input used to produce the good changes. The reason is that resource and input prices influence the cost of production. The more it costs to produce a good, the smaller is the quantity supplied of that good at each price (other things remaining the same). For example, if the wage rate of bottling-plant workers rises, it costs more to produce a bottle of water, so the supply of bottled water decreases.

Expected Future Prices

Expectations about future prices influence supply. For example, a severe frost that wipes out Florida's citrus crop doesn't change the production of orange juice today, but it does decrease production later in the year when the current crop would normally have been harvested. Sellers of orange juice will expect the price to rise in the future. To get the higher future price, some sellers will increase their inventory of frozen juice, and this action decreases the supply of juice today.

Number of Sellers

The greater the number of sellers in a market, the larger is the supply. For example, many new sellers have developed springs and water-bottling plants in the United States, and the supply of bottled water has increased.

Productivity

Productivity is output per unit of input. An increase in productivity lowers the cost of producing the good and increases its supply. A decrease in productivity has the opposite effect and decreases supply.

Technological change and the increased use of capital increase productivity. For example, advances in electronic technology have lowered the cost of producing a computer and increased the supply of computers. Technological change brings new goods such as the iPhone 6, the supply of which was previously zero.

Natural events such as severe weather and earthquakes decrease productivity and decrease supply. For example, the four-year drought in California decreased the supply of agricultural products including nuts, fruits, and vegetables in 2015.

■ Change in Quantity Supplied Versus Change in Supply

The influences on sellers' plans that you've just considered bring a *change in supply*. These are all the influences on sellers' plans *except the price of the good*. To avoid confusion, when the *price of the good changes* and all other influences on selling plans remain the same, we say there has been a **change in the quantity supplied**.

The distinction between a change in supply and a change in the quantity supplied is crucial for figuring out how a market responds to the forces that hit it. Figure 4.8 illustrates and summarizes the distinction:

- If the price of bottled water *falls* when other things remain the same, the quantity supplied of bottled water *decreases* and there is a *movement down* along the supply curve S_0. If the price *rises* when other things remain the same, the quantity supplied *increases* and there is a *movement up* along the supply curve S_0.
- If any influence on water bottlers' plans other than the price of bottled water changes, there is a change in the supply of bottled water. When the supply of bottled water *decreases*, the supply curve *shifts leftward* to S_1. When the supply of bottled water *increases*, the supply curve *shifts rightward* to S_2.

When you are thinking about the influences on supply, get into the habit of asking: Does this influence change the quantity supplied or does it change supply? The test is: Did the price change or did some other influence change? If the price of the good changed, then quantity supplied changed. If some other influence changed and the price of the good remained constant, then supply changed.

Change in the quantity supplied

A change in the quantity of a good that suppliers plan to sell that results from a change in the price of the good.

■ FIGURE 4.8

Change in Quantity Supplied Versus Change in Supply

MyEconLab Animation

❶ A decrease in the quantity supplied

The quantity supplied decreases and there is a movement down along the supply curve S_0 if the price of the good falls and other things remain the same.

❸ A decrease in supply

Supply decreases and the supply curve shifts leftward (from S_0 to S_1) if

- The price of a substitute in production rises.
- The price of a complement in production falls.
- A resource price or other input price rises.
- The price of the good is expected to rise.
- The number of sellers decreases.
- Productivity decreases.

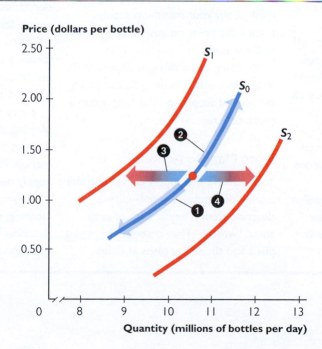

❷ An increase in the quantity supplied

The quantity supplied increases and there is a movement up along the supply curve S_0 if the price of the good rises and other things remain the same.

❹ An increase in supply

Supply increases and the supply curve shifts rightward (from S_0 to S_2) if

- The price of a substitute in production falls.
- The price of a complement in production rises.
- A resource price or other input price falls.
- The price of the good is expected to fall.
- The number of sellers increases.
- Productivity increases.

EYE on YOUR LIFE
Understanding and Using Demand and Supply

MyEconLab Critical Thinking Exercise

To truly understand the demand and supply model, it is a good idea to go beyond just memorizing the key terms and definitions and the lists of factors that change demand or change supply. Take ownership of the model by seeing how it explains your buying plans and your selling plans.

Your Buying Plans

Think about the things you buy: the quantities you buy and the prices you pay. These quantities and prices are points on your demand curves.

Now think about how some price changes would change your buying plans. How would your buying plans change if prices at the campus coffee shop increased? For which items would you change your quantity demanded? And for which items would you change your demand?

How would your buying plans change if you started a new job with a higher wage? What would you buy more of? What would you buy less of?

Suppose that you were just about to buy a new smartphone when Apple and Samsung announce plans to launch new phones next month. You figure that the prices of the older models will fall. How will this fall in the expected future price of a smartphone influence your buying plans?

For each thought experiment we've just described, think about whether you are sliding along a demand curve or shifting a demand curve.

Your Selling Plans

Most likely, you don't sell much stuff, but you own one precious resource that you might sell: your time.

If you have a job, think about the number of hours you work and the wage rate you earn. Are you working as many hours as you want to? If you are, you're at a point on the supply curve of your labor services.

How would you respond to a rise in the wage rate? Would you plan to work more hours or fewer hours?

Another thing you own is a pile of textbooks. Think about your selling plan for when your courses are over at the end of the semester. What is the lowest price at which you will sell this textbook? That price is a point on your supply curve of this book to the used book market.

You might also have a few old things that you'd like to sell on eBay. Again, think about your minimum supply-price—the point on your supply curve of these items.

By doing these thought experiments about your selling plans, you can make the idea of supply and the supply curve more concrete.

From Plans to Actions

Your demand and supply curves and the *market* demand and supply curves describe *plans*. They are statements about "what-if." They describe the buying plans and the selling plans at differ-

ent possible prices. But when you act on your plan and buy something, someone else must have a plan to sell that item. Your buying plan must match someone else's selling plan.

Neither demand nor supply on its own tells us what actually happens in a market. To find buying plans and selling plans that match, we must look at demand and supply together. That's what you will do in the final section of this chapter. You will see how prices adjust to balance the opposing forces of demand and supply.

The Rest of Your Life

The demand and supply model is going to be a big part of the rest of your life! You will use it again and again during your economics course, so having a firm grasp of it will bring an immediate payoff.

But much more important, by understanding the laws of demand and supply and being aware of how prices adjust to balance these two opposing forces, you will have a much better appreciation of how your economic world works.

Every time you hear someone complaining about a price hike and blaming it on someone's greed, think about the market forces and how demand and supply determine that price.

As you shop for your favorite clothing, music, and food items, try to describe how supply and demand influence the prices of these goods.

CHECKPOINT 4.2

Distinguish between quantity supplied and supply, and explain what determines supply.

Practice Problems

Lumber companies make timber beams from logs. In the process of making beams, the mill produces sawdust, which is made into pressed wood. In the market for timber beams, the following events occur one at a time:

- The wage rate of sawmill workers rises.
- The price of sawdust rises.
- The price of a timber beam rises.
- Next year's expected price of a timber beam rises.
- A new law reduces the amount of forest that can be cut for timber.
- A new technology lowers the cost of producing timber beams.

1. Explain the effect of each event on the supply of timber beams.

2. Use a graph to illustrate the effect of each event.

3. Does any event (or events) illustrate the law of supply?

In the News

Pump prices slide as crude oil falls to six-year low
The average price for regular gasoline at U.S. pumps fell almost 4¢ in March to $2.50 a gallon. The price of crude oil dropped to $43.46 per barrel on March 17, the lowest since March 2009.

Source: *Bloomberg Business*, March 23, 2015

Explain the effect of a lower crude oil price on the supply of gasoline.

Solutions to Practice Problems

1. A rise in workers' wage rates increases the cost of producing a timber beam and decreases the supply of timber beams. A rise in the price of sawdust increases the supply of timber beams because sawdust and timber beams are complements in production. A rise in the price of a timber beam increases the quantity of timber beams supplied but has no effect on the supply of timber beams. A rise in the expected price of a timber beam decreases the supply of timber beams today as producers hold back and wait for the higher price. The new law decreases the supply of timber beams. The new technology increases the supply of timber beams.

2. In Figure 1, an increase in the supply shifts the supply curve from S_0 to S_1, and a decrease in the supply shifts the supply curve from S_0 to S_2. In Figure 2, the rise in the price of a beam creates a movement along the supply curve.

3. A rise in the price of a beam, other things remaining the same, is the only event that illustrates the law of supply—see Figure 2.

Solution to In the News

Crude oil is refined to produce gasoline, so a fall in the price of crude oil lowers the cost of producing gasoline and increases the supply of gasoline.

FIGURE 1

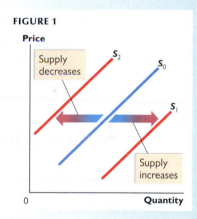

FIGURE 2

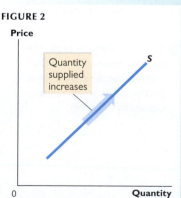

Market equilibrium
When the quantity demanded equals the quantity supplied—buyers' and sellers' plans are in balance.

Equilibrium price
The price at which the quantity demanded equals the quantity supplied.

Equilibrium quantity
The quantity bought and sold at the equilibrium price.

Law of market forces
When there is a surplus, the price falls; and when there is a shortage, the price rises.

4.3 MARKET EQUILIBRIUM

In everyday language, "equilibrium" means "opposing forces are in balance." In a market, demand and supply are the opposing forces. **Market equilibrium** occurs when the quantity demanded equals the quantity supplied—when buyers' and sellers' plans are in balance. At the **equilibrium price**, the quantity demanded equals the quantity supplied. The **equilibrium quantity** is the quantity bought and sold at the equilibrium price.

In the market for bottled water in Figure 4.9, equilibrium occurs where the demand curve and the supply curve intersect. The equilibrium price is $1.00 a bottle, and the equilibrium quantity is 10 million bottles a day.

■ Price: A Market's Automatic Regulator

When equilibrium is disturbed, market forces restore it. The **law of market forces** states

> **When there is a surplus, the price falls; and when there is a shortage, the price rises.**

A *surplus* is the amount by which the quantity supplied exceeds the quantity demanded. If there is a surplus, suppliers must cut the price to sell more. Buyers are pleased to take the lower price, so the price falls. Because a surplus arises when the price is above the equilibrium price, a falling price is exactly what the market needs to restore equilibrium.

A *shortage* is the amount by which the quantity demanded exceeds the quantity supplied. If there is a shortage, buyers must pay a higher price to get more. Sellers are pleased to take the higher price, so the price rises. Because a shortage arises when the price is below the equilibrium price, a rising price is exactly what is needed to restore equilibrium.

■ **FIGURE 4.9**

Equilibrium Price and Equilibrium Quantity   MyEconLab Animation

❶ Market equilibrium occurs at the intersection of the demand curve and the supply curve.

❷ The equilibrium price is $1.00 a bottle.

❸ At the equilibrium price, the quantity demanded and the quantity supplied are 10 million bottles a day, which is the equilibrium quantity.

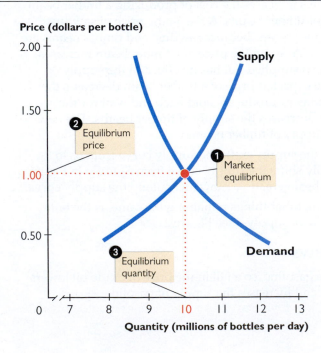

FIGURE 4.10

The Forces That Achieve Equilibrium

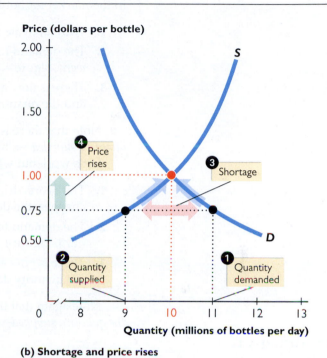

(a) Surplus and price falls

(b) Shortage and price rises

At $1.50 a bottle, ❶ the quantity supplied is 11 million bottles of water, ❷ the quantity demanded is 9 million bottles, ❸ the surplus is 2 million bottles, and ❹ the price falls.

At 75¢ a bottle, ❶ the quantity demanded is 11 million bottles of water, ❷ the quantity supplied is 9 million bottles, ❸ the shortage is 2 million bottles, and ❹ the price rises.

In Figure 4.10(a), at $1.50 a bottle, there is a surplus: The price falls, the quantity demanded increases, the quantity supplied decreases, and the surplus is eliminated at $1.00 a bottle.

In Figure 4.10(b), at 75¢ a bottle, there is a shortage of water: The price rises, the quantity demanded decreases, the quantity supplied increases, and the shortage is eliminated at $1.00 a bottle.

■ Predicting Price Changes: Three Questions

Because price adjustments eliminate shortages and surpluses, markets are normally in equilibrium. When an event disturbs an equilibrium, a new equilibrium soon emerges. To explain and predict changes in prices and quantities, we need to consider only changes in the *equilibrium* price and the *equilibrium* quantity. We can work out the effects of an event on a market by answering three questions:

1. Does the event influence demand or supply?
2. Does the event *increase* or *decrease* demand or supply—shift the demand curve or the supply curve *rightward* or *leftward*?
3. What are the new *equilibrium* price and *equilibrium* quantity and how have they changed?

■ Effects of Changes in Demand

Let's practice answering the three questions by working out the effects of an event in the market for bottled water: A new study says that tap water is unsafe.

1. With tap water unsafe, the demand for bottled water changes.

2. The demand for bottled water *increases*, and the demand curve *shifts rightward*. Figure 4.11(a) shows the shift from D_0 to D_1.

3. There is now a *shortage* at $1.00 a bottle. The *price rises* to $1.50 a bottle, and the quantity increases to 11 million bottles.

Note that there is *no change in supply*; the rise in price brings an *increase in the quantity supplied*—a movement along the supply curve.

Let's work out what happens if the price of a zero-calorie sports drink falls.

1. The sports drink is a substitute for bottled water, so when its price changes, the demand for bottled water changes.

2. The demand for bottled water *decreases*, and the demand curve *shifts leftward*. Figure 4.11(b) shows the shift from D_0 to D_2.

3. There is now a *surplus* at $1.00 a bottle. The price *falls* to 75¢ a bottle, and the quantity decreases to 9 million bottles.

Note again that there is *no change in supply*; the fall in price brings a *decrease in the quantity supplied*—a movement along the supply curve.

■ **FIGURE 4.11**

The Effects of a Change in Demand

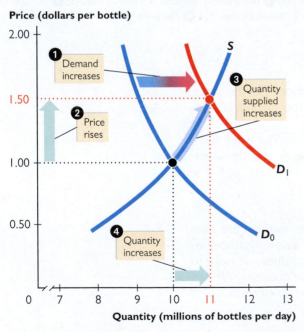

(a) An increase in demand

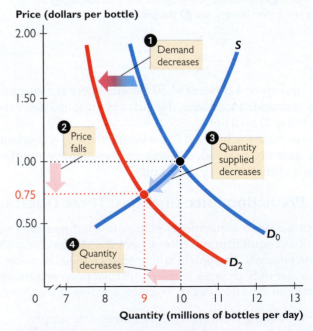

(b) A decrease in demand

❶ An increase in demand shifts the demand curve rightward to D_1 and creates a shortage of water. ❷ The price rises, ❸ the quantity supplied increases, and ❹ the equilibrium quantity increases.

❶ A decrease in demand shifts the demand curve leftward to D_2 and creates a surplus of water. ❷ The price falls, ❸ the quantity supplied decreases, and ❹ the equilibrium quantity decreases.

EYE on the GLOBAL ECONOMY
The Markets for Cocoa and Chocolate

Fast-rising incomes in China and other developing economies and the sweet tooth of millions of newly rich middle classes are sending the consumption of chocolate soaring. With chocolate made from cocoa, the price of cocoa is soaring too.

Look at the data table below. It shows the quantities and prices of cocoa in 2010 and 2014, and it tells us that both the quantity of cocoa produced and the price of cocoa increased.

The quantity produced increased by 25 percent from 4 million tons in 2010 to 5 million tons in 2014.

The price of cocoa doubled from $1,500 to $3,000.

Why did the price of cocoa increase? Was it because demand increased or supply decreased?

You can answer this question with the information in the table. You know that an increase in demand brings a rise in the price and an increase in the quantity bought, while a decrease in supply brings a rise in the price and a decrease in the quantity bought.

Because when the price of cocoa increased, the quantity of cocoa produced and consumed also increased, the demand for cocoa must have increased.

An increase in demand is consistent with the facts about rising incomes in China and other developing economies.

Cocoa is a normal good, so an increase in income brings an increase in the demand for cocoa. The fast-rising incomes in China and other developing economies brought an increase in the demand for cocoa.

The figure illustrates the global market for cocoa in 2010 and 2014. The supply curve S shows the supply of cocoa, which we will assume didn't change between 2010 and 2014.

In 2010, the demand curve for cocoa was D_{2010}, the equilibrium price was $1,500 per ton and the equilibrium quantity of cocoa traded was 4 million tons.

By 2014, the higher incomes in China and other developing economies had increased the demand for cocoa to D_{2014}. The equilibrium price rose to $3,000 per ton and the equilibrium quantity traded increased to 5 million tons.

The higher price of cocoa brought an increase in the quantity of cocoa supplied, which is shown in the figure by the movement up along the supply curve of cocoa.

Year	Quantity of Cocoa (millions of tons per year)	Price of Cocoa (dollars per ton)
2010	4	1,500
2014	5	3,000

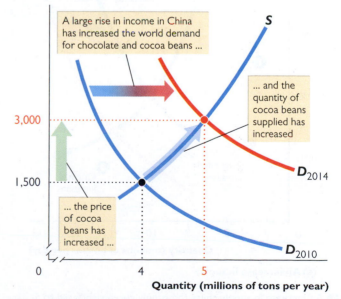

The Market for Cocoa Beans

MyEconLab Concept Video

■ Effects of Changes in Supply

You can get more practice working out the effects of another event in the market for bottled water: European water bottlers buy springs and open new plants in the United States.

1. With more suppliers of bottled water, the supply changes.

2. The supply of bottled water *increases*, and the supply curve *shifts rightward*. Figure 4.12(a) shows the shift from S_0 to S_1.

3. There is now a *surplus* at $1.00 a bottle. The *price falls* to 75¢ a bottle, and the quantity increases to 11 million bottles.

Note that there is *no change in demand*; the fall in price brings an *increase in the quantity demanded*—a movement along the demand curve.

What happens if a drought dries up some springs?

1. The drought is a change in productivity, so the supply of water changes.

2. With fewer springs, the supply of bottled water *decreases*, and the supply curve *shifts leftward*. Figure 4.12(b) shows the shift from S_0 to S_2.

3. There is now a *shortage* at $1.00 a bottle. The *price rises* to $1.50 a bottle, and the quantity decreases to 9 million bottles.

Again, there is *no change in demand*; the rise in price brings a *decrease in the quantity demanded*—a movement along the demand curve.

■ FIGURE 4.12

The Effects of a Change in Supply

MyEconLab Animation

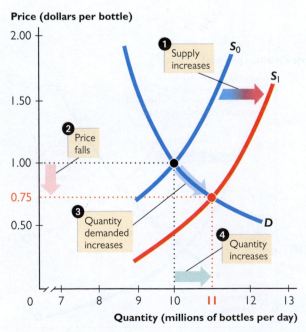

(a) An increase in supply

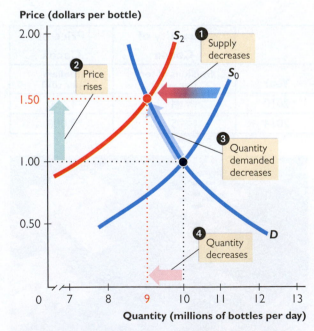

(b) A decrease in supply

❶ An increase in supply shifts the supply curve rightward to S_1 and creates a surplus of water. ❷ The price falls, ❸ the quantity demanded increases, and ❹ the equilibrium quantity increases.

❶ A decrease in supply shifts the supply curve leftward to S_2 and creates a shortage of water. ❷ The price rises, ❸ the quantity demanded decreases, and ❹ the equilibrium quantity decreases.

EYE on the PRICE OF COFFEE

MyEconLab Critical Thinking Exercise

Why Did the Price of Coffee Rise in 2014?

When a fungus called coffee rust swept through Brazil and other countries of South America in 2014, world coffee production decreased and the price of coffee beans increased.

The table below provides some data on the quantity and price of coffee in 2013 and 2014. What does the data table tell us?

It tells us that the quantity of coffee produced decreased by 3.6 percent from 19.4 billion pounds in 2013 to 18.7 billion pounds in 2014, and the price of coffee rose by more than 30 percent from $1.04 per pound to $1.35 per pound.

Did the price of coffee rise because demand increased or because supply decreased?

You can answer this question from the information provided. You know that an increase in demand brings a rise in the price and an increase in the quantity bought, while a decrease in supply brings a rise in the price and a decrease in the quantity bought.

Because the quantity of coffee decreased and the price increased, there must have been a decrease in the supply of coffee.

The supply of coffee decreases if the crop yields decrease or if producers decrease their plantings.

The information that coffee rust swept through Brazil and other countries of South America in 2014 suggests that coffee crop yields decreased, which decreased the supply.

The figure illustrates the global market for coffee in 2013 and 2014. The demand curve D shows the demand for coffee, which we will assume was the same in both years.

In 2013, the supply curve was S_{2013}, the equilibrium price was $1.04 per pound and the equilibrium quantity traded was 19.4 billion pounds.

In 2014, decreased coffee production in Brazil and other countries decreased the supply of coffee to S_{2014}.

The equilibrium price rose to $1.35 per pound and the quantity traded decreased to 18.7 billion pounds.

The higher price brought a decrease in the quantity of coffee demanded, which is shown by the movement up along the demand curve.

Year	Quantity of Coffee (billions of pounds per year)	Price of Coffee (dollars per pound)
2013	19.4	1.04
2014	18.7	1.35

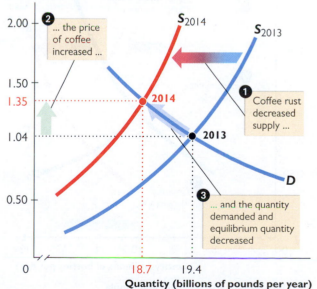

The Market for Coffee in 2013–2014

■ Effects of Changes in Both Demand and Supply

When events occur that change *both* demand and supply, you can find the resulting change in the equilibrium price and equilibrium quantity by combining the cases you've just studied.

Both Demand and Supply Change in the Same Direction

When demand and supply change in the same direction, the equilibrium quantity changes in that same direction, but we need to know the magnitudes of the changes in demand and supply to predict whether the price rises or falls. If demand increases by more than supply increases, the price rises. But if supply increases by more than demand increases, the price falls.

Figure 4.13(a) shows the case when both demand and supply increase and by the same amount. The equilibrium quantity increases. But because the increase in demand equals the increase in supply, neither a shortage nor a surplus arises so the price doesn't change. A bigger increase in demand would have created a shortage and a rise in the price; a bigger increase in supply would have created a surplus and a fall in the price.

Figure 4.13(b) shows the case when both demand and supply decrease by the same amount. Here the equilibrium quantity decreases and again the price might either rise or fall.

■ **FIGURE 4.13**

The Effects of Change in *Both* Demand and Supply in the *Same Direction*

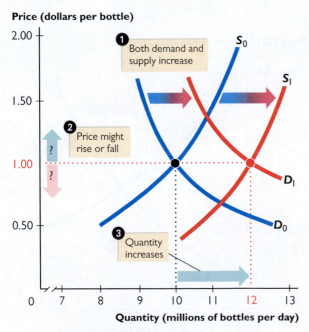

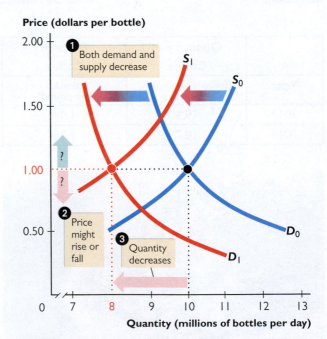

(a) Increase in both demand and supply

(b) Decrease in both demand and supply

❶ An increase in demand shifts the demand curve rightward to D_1 and an increase in supply shifts the supply curve rightward to S_1.
❷ The price might rise or fall, but ❸ the quantity increases.

❶ A decrease in demand shifts the demand curve leftward to D_1 and a decrease in supply shifts the supply curve leftward to S_1.
❷ The price might rise or fall, but ❸ the quantity decreases.

Both Demand and Supply Change in Opposite Directions

When demand and supply change in opposite directions, we can predict how the price changes, but we need to know the magnitudes of the changes in demand and supply to say whether the equilibrium quantity increases or decreases. If demand changes by more than supply, the equilibrium quantity changes in the same direction as the change in demand. But if supply changes by more than demand, the equilibrium quantity changes in the same direction as the change in supply.

Figure 4.14(a) illustrates what happens when demand decreases and supply increases by the same amount. At the initial price, there is a surplus, so the price falls. A decrease in demand decreases the quantity and an increase in supply increases the quantity, so when these changes occur together, we can't say what happens to the quantity unless we know the magnitudes of the changes.

Figure 4.14(b) illustrates what happens when demand increases and supply decreases by the same amount. In this case, at the initial price, there is a shortage, so the price rises. An increase in demand increases the quantity and a decrease in supply decreases the quantity, so again, when these changes occur together, we can't say what happens to the quantity unless we know the magnitudes of the changes in demand and supply.

For all the cases in Figures 4.13 and 4.14 where you "can't say" what happens to price or quantity, draw some examples that go in each direction.

■ **FIGURE 4.14**

The Effects of Change in *Both* Demand and Supply in *Opposite Directions*   MyEconLab Animation

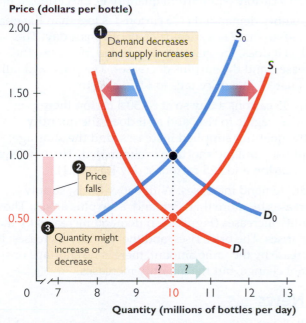

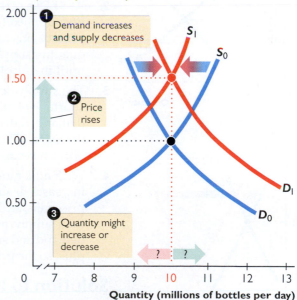

(a) Decrease in demand and increase in supply

(b) Increase in demand and decrease in supply

❶ A decrease in demand shifts the demand curve leftward to D_1 and an increase in supply shifts the supply curve rightward to S_1.
❷ The price falls, but ❸ the quantity might increase or decrease.

❶ An increase in demand shifts the demand curve rightward to D_1 and a decrease in supply shifts the supply curve leftward to S_1.
❷ The price rises, but ❸ the quantity might increase or decrease.

MyEconLab Study Plan 4.3
Key Terms Quiz
Solutions Video

CHECKPOINT 4.3

Explain how demand and supply determine price and quantity in a market, and explain the effects of changes in demand and supply.

Practice Problems

Table 1 sets out the demand and supply schedules for milk.

1. What is the equilibrium price and equilibrium quantity of milk?
2. Describe the situation in the milk market if the price were $1.75 a carton and explain how the market reaches equilibrium.
3. A drought decreases the quantity supplied by 45 cartons a day at each price. What is the new equilibrium and how does the market adjust to it?
4. If milk becomes more popular and better feeds increase milk production, describe how the equilibrium price and quantity of milk will change.

TABLE 1

Price (dollars per carton)	Quantity demanded	Quantity supplied
	(cartons per day)	
1.00	200	110
1.25	175	130
1.50	150	150
1.75	125	170
2.00	100	190

In the News

El Niño takes toll on U.S. rice farmers

Dry weather has delayed rice planting and harvests will be low. But wheat is enjoying a bumper crop.

Source: *The Guardian*, September 27, 2015

Using the demand and supply model, explain how the prices of rice and wheat will change and how the markets for rice and wheat will influence each other.

Solutions to Practice Problems

1. Equilibrium price is $1.50 a carton; equilibrium quantity is 150 cartons a day.
2. At $1.75 a carton, the quantity demanded (125 cartons) is less than the quantity supplied (170 cartons), so there is a surplus of 45 cartons a day. The price begins to fall, and as it does, the quantity demanded increases, the quantity supplied decreases, and the surplus decreases. The price will fall until the surplus is eliminated. The price falls to $1.50 a carton.
3. The supply decreases by 45 cartons a day so at $1.50 a carton there is a shortage of milk. The price begins to rise, and as it does, the quantity demanded decreases, the quantity supplied increases, and the shortage decreases. The price will rise until the shortage is eliminated. The new equilibrium occurs at $1.75 a carton and 125 cartons a day (Figure 1).
4. With milk more popular, demand increases. With better feeds, supply increases. If supply increases by more than demand, a surplus arises. The price falls, and the quantity increases (Figure 2). If demand increases by more than supply, a shortage arises. The price rises, and the quantity increases. If demand and supply increase by the same amount, there is no shortage or surplus, so the price does not change, but the quantity increases.

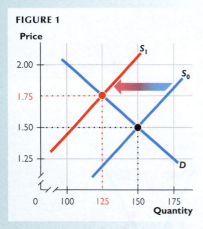

FIGURE 1

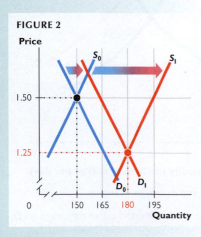

FIGURE 2

Solution to In the News

A fall in the rice harvest will decrease the supply of rice and raise its price. A bumper wheat harvest will increase the supply of wheat and lower its price. Wheat and rice are substitutes, so a higher price of rice will increase the demand for wheat and a lower price of wheat will decrease the demand for rice.

CHAPTER SUMMARY

Key Points

1. **Distinguish between quantity demanded and demand, and explain what determines demand.**

   - Other things remaining the same, the quantity demanded increases as the price falls and decreases as the price rises—the law of demand.
   - The demand for a good is influenced by the prices of related goods, expected future prices, income, expected future income and credit, the number of buyers, and preferences. A change in any of these influences changes the demand for the good.

2. **Distinguish between quantity supplied and supply, and explain what determines supply.**

   - Other things remaining the same, the quantity supplied increases as the price rises and decreases as the price falls—the law of supply.
   - The supply of a good is influenced by the prices of related goods, prices of resources and other inputs, expected future prices, the number of sellers, and productivity. A change in any of these influences changes the supply of the good.

3. **Explain how demand and supply determine price and quantity in a market, and explain the effects of changes in demand and supply.**

   - The law of market forces brings market equilibrium—the equilibrium price and equilibrium quantity at which buyers and sellers trade.
   - The price adjusts to maintain market equilibrium—to keep the quantity demanded equal to the quantity supplied. A surplus brings a fall in the price to restore market equilibrium; a shortage brings a rise in the price to restore market equilibrium.
   - Market equilibrium responds to changes in demand and supply. An increase in demand increases both the price and the quantity; a decrease in demand decreases both the price and the quantity. An increase in supply increases the quantity but decreases the price; and a decrease in supply decreases the quantity but increases the price.

Key Terms

MyEconLab Key Terms Quiz

Change in demand, 88

Change in the quantity demanded, 90

Change in the quantity supplied, 97

Change in supply, 95

Complement, 88

Complement in production, 95

Demand, 85

Demand curve, 86

Demand schedule, 86

Equilibrium price, 100

Equilibrium quantity, 100

Inferior good, 89

Law of demand, 85

Law of market forces, 100

Law of supply, 92

Market equilibrium, 100

Normal good, 89

Quantity demanded, 85

Quantity supplied, 92

Substitute, 88

Substitute in production, 95

Supply, 92

Supply curve, 93

Supply schedule, 93

CHAPTER CHECKPOINT

Study Plan Problems and Applications

1. Explain how each of the following events changes the demand for or supply of air travel.
   - Airfares tumble, while long-distance bus fares don't change.
   - The price of jet fuel rises.
   - Airlines reduce the number of flights each day.
   - People expect airfares to increase next summer.
   - The price of train travel falls.
   - The price of a pound of air cargo increases.

Use the laws of demand and supply to explain whether the statements in Problems **2** and **3** are true or false. In your explanation, distinguish between a change in demand and a change in the quantity demanded and between a change in supply and a change in the quantity supplied.

2. The United States does not allow oranges from Brazil (the world's largest producer of oranges) to enter the United States. If Brazilian oranges were sold in the United States, oranges and orange juice would be cheaper.

3. If the price of frozen yogurt falls, the quantity of ice cream consumed will decrease and the price of ice cream will rise.

4. Table 1 shows the demand and supply schedules for running shoes. What is the market equilibrium? If the price is $70 a pair, describe the situation in the market. Explain how market equilibrium is restored. If a rise in income increases the demand for running shoes by 100 pairs a day at each price, explain how the market adjusts to its new equilibrium.

5. "As more people buy fuel-efficient hybrid cars, the demand for gasoline will decrease and the price of gasoline will fall. The fall in the price of gasoline will decrease the supply of gasoline." Is this statement true? Explain.

6. **OPEC deadlocked on oil production hike**

   Oil prices exceeded the $100-a-barrel mark Wednesday after OPEC said it could not reach an agreement about raising crude production.

   Source: CNN Money, June 8, 2011

   Suppose that OPEC members had agreed to increase production. Use a graph of the oil market to show the effect of this decision on the market equilibrium.

Use the following information to work Problems **7** and **8**.

Rain delays to U.S. planting lift corn and soybean prices
Heavy rain has delayed the planting of corn and soybean and soggy conditions have slowed the winter wheat harvest.

   Source: *Financial Times*, June 25, 2015

7. Explain how heavy rain and soggy conditions will change the prices of corn, soybean, and wheat.

8. Use graphs to show how supply and demand will change in the markets for corn, soybean, and wheat.

9. Read *Eye on the Price of Coffee* on p. 105 and explain how we know that the price increased in 2014 because the supply of coffee decreased and not because the demand for coffee increased.

TABLE 1

Price (dollars per pair)	Quantity demanded	Quantity supplied
	(pairs per day)	
60	1,000	400
70	900	500
80	800	600
90	700	700
100	600	800
110	500	900

Instructor Assignable Problems and Applications

MyEconLab Homework, Quiz, or Test if assigned by instructor

1. Why can we be confident that the market for coffee is competitive and that a decrease in supply rather than the greed of coffee growers is the reason for the 2014 rise in price?

2. What is the effect on the equilibrium price and equilibrium quantity of orange juice if the price of apple juice decreases and the wage rate paid to orange grove workers increases?

3. What is the effect on the equilibrium in the orange juice market if orange juice becomes more popular and a cheaper robot is used to pick oranges?

4. Concerns over winter wheat may boost price
Concerns about the U.S. winter wheat crop and dry conditions in other wheat-producing nations have increased the price of wheat.
Source: Agweb.com, July 6, 2015

Explain how an upcoming harvest influences today's price of wheat.

Table 1 shows the demand and supply schedules for boxes of chocolates in an average week. Use this information to work Problems **5** and **6**.

5. If the price of chocolates is $17.00 a box, describe the situation in the market. Explain how market equilibrium is restored.

6. During Valentine's week, more people buy chocolates and chocolatiers offer their chocolates in special red boxes, which cost more to produce than the everyday box. Set out the three-step process of analysis and show on a graph the adjustment process to the new equilibrium. Describe the changes in the equilibrium price and the equilibrium quantity.

7. After a severe bout of foreclosures and defaults on home loans, banks made it harder for people to borrow. How does this change influence
- The demand for new homes?
- The supply of new homes?
- The price of new homes?
Illustrate your answer with a graphical analysis.

8. Bacon is 25 percent cheaper
Bacon is 25 percent cheaper now than a year ago and bacon sales are up 13 percent on the year. At the same time, the bird flu virus is killing millions of chickens, raising egg prices.
Source: *CNN Money*, May 20, 2015

Explain how this news clip illustrates: (a) the law of demand and why the price of bacon fell, and (b) how the markets for bacon and eggs influence each other. Draw a graph to illustrate your explanation.

9. "As more people buy smartphones, the demand for smartphone service increases and the price of smartphone service falls, which decreases the supply of smartphone service." Is this statement true or false? Explain.

10. China slowdown could bring good news
China's economic slowdown could help reduce the cost of steel used by U.S. auto makers.
Source: *The Wall Street Journal*, September 8, 2015

Explain how an economic slowdown in China influences the global steel market. What happens to the equilibrium price of steel?

TABLE 1

Price (dollars per box)	Quantity demanded	Quantity supplied
	(boxes per day)	
13.00	1,600	
14.00	1,500	1,300
15.00	1,400	1,400
16.00	1,300	1,500
17.00	1,200	1,600
18.00	1,100	1,700

Multiple Choice Quiz

1. Which of the following events illustrates the law of demand: Other things remaining the same, a rise in the price of a good will _____.

    A. decrease the quantity demanded of that good
    B. increase the demand for a substitute of that good
    C. decrease the demand for the good
    D. increase the demand for a complement of that good

2. In the market for jeans, which of the following events increases the demand for a pair of jeans?

    A. The wage rate paid to garment workers rises.
    B. The price of a denim skirt (a substitute for jeans) rises.
    C. The price of denim cloth falls.
    D. New technology reduces the time it takes to make a pair of jeans.

3. Other things remaining the same, a fall in the price of peanuts will _____.

    A. increase the supply of peanuts
    B. decrease the supply of peanut butter
    C. decrease the quantity supplied of peanuts
    D. decrease the supply of peanuts

4. In the market for smartphones, which of the following events increases the supply of smartphones?

    A. New technology lowers the cost of making a smartphone
    B. A rise in the price of an e-book reader (a substitute in production)
    C. An increase in people's incomes
    D. A rise in the wage rate paid to electronics workers

5. When floods wiped out the banana crop in Central America, the equilibrium price of bananas _____ and the equilibrium quantity of bananas _____.

    A. rose; increased
    B. rose; decreased
    C. fell; increased
    D. fell; decreased

6. A decrease in the demand for chocolate with no change in the supply of chocolate will create a _____ of chocolate at today's price, but gradually the price will _____.

    A. surplus; fall
    B. shortage; fall
    C. surplus; rise
    D. shortage; rise

7. Many Americans are selling their cars and buying new fuel-efficient hybrids. Other things remaining the same, in the market for used cars, _____ and in the market for hybrids _____.

    A. supply increases and the price falls; demand increases and the price rises
    B. demand decreases and the price rises; supply increases and the price falls
    C. both demand and supply decrease and the price might rise, fall, or not change; demand increases and the price rises
    D. demand decreases, supply increases, and the price falls; supply increases and the price falls

What do you do when Starbucks raises the price of a latte?

Elasticities of Demand and Supply

5

When you have completed your study of this chapter, you will be able to

1 Define and calculate the price elasticity of demand, and explain the factors that influence it.

2 Define and calculate the price elasticity of supply, and explain the factors that influence it.

3 Define the cross elasticity of demand and the income elasticity of demand, and explain the factors that influence them.

MyEconLab Big Picture Video

113

MyEconLab Concept Video

5.1 THE PRICE ELASTICITY OF DEMAND

Starbucks knows that if it raises the price of a latte and everything else remains the same, the quantity of lattes that it sells—the quantity demanded—will decrease. But by how much? To answer this question, Starbucks needs to know how responsive the quantity of latte demanded is to a change in its price. Elasticity provides this information.

Price elasticity of demand
A measure of the responsiveness of the quantity demanded of a good to a change in its price when all other influences on buyers' plans remain the same.

The **price elasticity of demand** is a measure of the responsiveness of the quantity demanded of a good to a change in its price when all other influences on buyers' plans remain the same.

To determine the price elasticity of demand, we compare the percentage change in the quantity demanded with the percentage change in price.

■ Percentage Change in Price

If Starbucks changes its price of a latte by $2, the percentage change in price depends on whether the price has gone up or down.

A Rise in Price

Suppose that Starbucks raises the price of a latte from $3 to $5. The percentage change is calculated as the change in price divided by the initial price, all multiplied by 100. The formula for the percentage change is

$$\text{Percentage change in price} = \left(\frac{\text{New price} - \text{Initial price}}{\text{Initial price}}\right) \times 100.$$

In this example, the initial price is $3 and the new price is $5, so

$$\text{Percentage change in price} = \left(\frac{\$5 - \$3}{\$3}\right) \times 100 = \left(\frac{\$2}{\$3}\right) \times 100 = 66.67 \text{ percent.}$$

A Fall in Price

Now suppose that Starbucks cuts the price of a latte from $5 to $3. The initial price is now $5 and the new price is $3, so the percentage change in price is

$$\text{Percentage change in price} = \left(\frac{\$3 - \$5}{\$5}\right) \times 100 = \left(\frac{-\$2}{\$5}\right) \times 100 = -40 \text{ percent.}$$

The same price change, $2, over the same interval, between $3 and $5, is a different absolute percentage change—66.67 percent if the price rises and 40 percent if the price falls.

Because elasticity compares the percentage change in the quantity demanded with the percentage change in price, we need a measure of percentage change that does not depend on the direction of the price change. The measure that economists use is called the *midpoint method*.

The Midpoint Method

To calculate the percentage change in price using the midpoint method, we divide the change in the price by the *average price*—the *average* of the new price and the initial price—and then multiply by 100. The average price is at the midpoint between the initial and the new price, hence the name *midpoint method*.

The formula for the percentage change using the midpoint method is

$$\text{Percentage change in price} = \left(\frac{\text{New price} - \text{Initial price}}{(\text{New price} + \text{Initial price}) \div 2} \right) \times 100.$$

In this formula, the numerator (New price − Initial price) is the same as before. The denominator, (New price + Initial price) ÷ 2, is the average of the new price and the initial price.

To calculate the percentage change in the price of a Starbucks latte using the midpoint method, put $5 for new price and $3 for initial price in the formula:

$$\begin{aligned}\text{Percentage change in price} &= \left(\frac{\$5 - \$3}{(\$5 + \$3) \div 2} \right) \times 100 = \left(\frac{\$2}{\$8 \div 2} \right) \times 100 \\ &= \left(\frac{\$2}{\$4} \right) \times 100 = 50 \text{ percent}.\end{aligned}$$

Because the average price is the same regardless of whether the price rises or falls, the percentage change in price calculated by the midpoint method is the same (magnitude) for a price rise and a price fall. In this example, it is 50 percent.

■ Percentage Change in Quantity Demanded

Suppose that when the price of a latte rises from $3 to $5, the quantity demanded decreases from 15 cups to 5 cups an hour. The percentage change in the quantity demanded using the midpoint method is

$$\begin{aligned}\text{Percentage change in quantity} &= \left(\frac{\text{New quantity} - \text{Initial quantity}}{(\text{New quantity} + \text{Initial quantity}) \div 2} \right) \times 100 \\ &= \left(\frac{5 - 15}{(5 + 15) \div 2} \right) \times 100 = \left(\frac{-10}{20 \div 2} \right) \times 100 \\ &= \left(\frac{-10}{10} \right) \times 100 = -100 \text{ percent}.\end{aligned}$$

When the price of a good *rises*, the quantity demanded of it *decreases*—a *positive* change in price brings a *negative* change in the quantity demanded. Similarly, when the price of a good *falls*, the quantity demanded of it *increases*—this time a *negative* change in price brings a *positive* change in the quantity demanded.

To compare the percentage changes in price and quantity demanded, we use the magnitudes of the percentage changes and we ignore the minus sign.

■ Comparing the Percentage Changes in Price and Quantity

To determine the responsiveness of the quantity of Starbucks lattes demanded to its price, we compare the two percentage changes we've just calculated. The percentage change in quantity demanded is 100 percent and the percentage change in price is 50 percent. In this case, the percentage change in the quantity of Starbucks lattes demanded is greater than the percentage change in its price. But it might have been equal or less. Let's see how we classify degrees of responsiveness.

MyEconLab Concept Video

Elastic demand
When the percentage change in the quantity demanded exceeds the percentage change in price.

Unit elastic demand
When the percentage change in the quantity demanded equals the percentage change in price.

Inelastic demand
When the percentage change in the quantity demanded is less than the percentage change in price.

Perfectly elastic demand
When the quantity demanded changes by a very large percentage in response to an almost zero percentage change in price.

Perfectly inelastic demand
When the percentage change in the quantity demanded is zero for any percentage change in the price.

■ Elastic and Inelastic Demand

If we collected data on the prices and quantities of Starbucks lattes and a number of other goods and services and we were careful to check that other things had remained the same, we could calculate lots of percentage changes in prices and quantities demanded. We could then classify the demands by their degree of responsiveness of quantity demanded to price.

Our calculations would fall into three groups: The percentage change in the quantity demanded might exceed the percentage change in price (as in the example of Starbucks lattes), be equal to the percentage change in price, or be less than the percentage change in price. Each of these three possibilities defines three ranges for the price elasticity of demand:

- When the percentage change in the quantity demanded exceeds the percentage change in price, demand is **elastic**.
- When the percentage change in the quantity demanded equals the percentage change in price, demand is **unit elastic**.
- When the percentage change in the quantity demanded is less than the percentage change in price, demand is **inelastic**.

Figure 5.1 shows the different types of demand curves that illustrate the range of possible price elasticities of demand. Part (a) shows an extreme case of an elastic demand called a **perfectly elastic demand**—an almost zero percentage change in the price brings a very large percentage change in the quantity demanded. Consumers are willing to buy any quantity of the good at a given price but none at a higher price. Part (b) shows an elastic demand—the percentage change in the quantity demanded exceeds the percentage change in price. Part (c) shows a unit elastic demand—the percentage change in the quantity demanded equals the percentage change in price. Part (d) shows an inelastic demand—the percentage change in the quantity demanded is less than the percentage change in price. Finally, part (e) shows an extreme case of an inelastic demand called a **perfectly inelastic demand**—the percentage change in the quantity demanded is zero for any percentage change in price.

■ Influences on the Price Elasticity of Demand

What makes the demand for some things elastic and the demand for others inelastic? The influences on the price elasticity of demand fall into two groups:

- Availability of substitutes
- Proportion of income spent

Availability of Substitutes

The demand for a good is elastic if a substitute for it is easy to find. Soft drink containers can be made of either aluminum or plastic and it doesn't matter which, so the demand for aluminum is elastic.

The demand for a good is inelastic if a substitute for it is hard to find. Oil has poor substitutes (imagine a coal-fueled car), so the demand for oil is inelastic.

Three main factors influence the ability to find a substitute for a good: whether the good is a luxury or a necessity, how narrowly the good is defined, and the amount of time available to find a substitute for it.

■ **FIGURE 5.1**

The Range of Price Elasticities of Demand

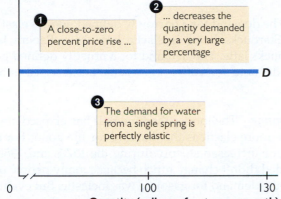

(a) Perfectly elastic demand

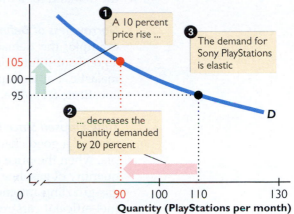

(b) Elastic demand

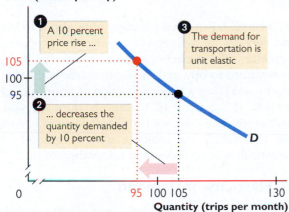

(c) Unit elastic demand

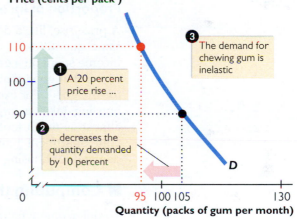

(d) Inelastic demand

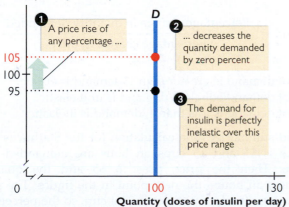

(e) Perfectly inelastic demand

① A price rise brings **②** a decrease in the quantity demanded. The relationship between the percentage change in the quantity demanded and the percentage change in price determines **③** the price elasticity of demand, which ranges from perfectly elastic (part a) to perfectly inelastic (part e).

Luxury Versus Necessity   We call goods such as food and housing *necessities* and goods such as exotic vacations *luxuries.* A necessity has poor substitutes—you must eat—so the demand for a necessity is inelastic. A luxury has many substitutes—you don't absolutely have to go to the Galapagos Islands this summer—so the demand for a luxury is elastic.

Narrowness of Definition   The demand for a narrowly defined good is elastic. For example, the demand for Starbucks lattes is elastic because a Panera latte is a good substitute for a Starbucks latte. The demand for a broadly defined good is inelastic. For example, the demand for coffee is inelastic because tea is a poor substitute for coffee.

Time Elapsed Since Price Change   The longer the time that has elapsed since the price of a good changed, the more elastic is the demand for the good. For example, when the price of gasoline increased steeply during the 1970s and 1980s, the quantity of gasoline demanded didn't change much because many people owned gas-guzzling automobiles—the demand for gasoline was inelastic. But eventually, fuel-efficient cars replaced gas guzzlers and the quantity of gasoline demanded decreased—the demand for gasoline became more elastic.

Proportion of Income Spent

A price rise, like a decrease in income, means that people cannot afford to buy the same quantities of goods and services as before. The greater the proportion of income spent on a good, the greater is the impact of a rise in its price on the quantity of that good that people can afford to buy and the more elastic is the demand for the good. For example, toothpaste takes a tiny proportion of your budget and housing takes a large proportion. If the price of toothpaste doubles, you buy almost as much toothpaste as before. Your demand for toothpaste is inelastic. If your apartment rent doubles, you shriek and look for more roommates. Your demand for housing is more elastic than is your demand for toothpaste.

MyEconLab Concept Video

■ Computing the Price Elasticity of Demand

To determine whether the demand for a good is elastic, unit elastic, or inelastic, we compute a numerical value for the price elasticity of demand by using the following formula:

$$\text{Price elasticity of demand} = \frac{\text{Percentage change in quantity demanded}}{\text{Percentage change in price}}.$$

- If the price elasticity of demand is greater than 1, demand is elastic.
- If the price elasticity of demand equals 1, demand is unit elastic.
- If the price elasticity of demand is less than 1, demand is inelastic.

Figure 5.2 illustrates and summarizes the calculation for the Starbucks latte example. Initially, the price is $3 and 15 cups an hour are demanded—the initial point in the figure. Then the price rises to $5 and the quantity demanded decreases to 5 cups an hour—the new point in the figure. The price rises by $2 a cup and the average (midpoint) price is $4 a cup, so the percentage change in price is 50. The quantity demanded decreases by 10 cups an hour and the average (midpoint) quantity is 10 cups an hour, so the percentage change in quantity demanded is 100.

FIGURE 5.2

Price Elasticity of Demand Calculation   MyEconLab Animation

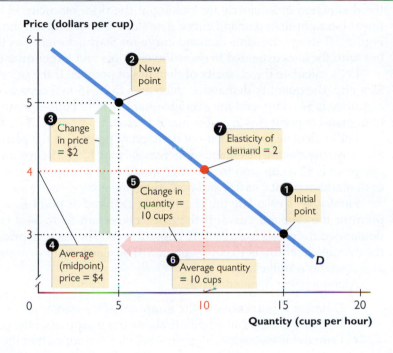

① At the initial point, the price is $3 and the quantity demanded is 15 cups an hour.

② At the new point, the price is $5 and the quantity demanded is 5 cups an hour.

③ The change in price is $2 and ④ the average price is $4, so the percentage change in price equals ($2 ÷ $4) × 100, which is 50 percent.

⑤ The change in the quantity demanded is 10 cups and ⑥ the average quantity demanded is 10 cups, so the percentage change in quantity demanded equals (10 ÷ 10) × 100, which is 100 percent.

⑦ The price elasticity of demand equals (100 percent ÷ 50 percent), which is 2.

Using the above formula, you can see that the price elasticity of demand for Starbucks lattes is

$$\text{Price elasticity of demand} = \frac{100 \text{ percent}}{50 \text{ percent}} = 2.$$

The price elasticity of demand is 2 at the midpoint between the initial price and the new price on the demand curve. Over this price range, the demand for Starbucks lattes is elastic.

■ Interpreting the Price Elasticity of Demand Number

The number we've just calculated for Starbucks lattes is only an example. We don't have real data on the price and quantity. But if we did have real data and we discovered that the price elasticity of demand for Starbucks lattes is 2, what does this number tell us?

It tells us three main things:

1. The demand for Starbucks lattes is elastic. Being elastic, the good has plenty of convenient substitutes (such as other brands of latte) and takes only a small proportion of buyers' incomes.

2. Starbucks must be careful not to charge too high a price for its latte. Pushing the price up brings in more revenue per cup but wipes out a lot of potential business.

3. The flip side of the second point: Even a slightly lower price could create a lot of potential business and end up bringing in more revenue.

■ Elasticity Along a Linear Demand Curve

Slope measures responsiveness. But elasticity is *not* the same as *slope*. You can see the distinction most clearly by looking at the price elasticity of demand along a linear (straight-line) demand curve. The slope is constant, but the elasticity varies. Figure 5.3 shows the same demand curve for Starbucks lattes as that in Figure 5.2 but with the axes extended to show lower prices and larger quantities demanded.

Let's calculate the elasticity of demand at point A. If the price rises from $3 to $5 a cup, the quantity demanded decreases from 15 to 5 cups an hour. The average price is $4 a cup, and the average quantity is 10 cups—point A. The elasticity of demand at point A is 2, and demand is elastic.

Let's calculate the elasticity of demand at point C. If the price falls from $3 to $1 a cup, the quantity demanded increases from 15 to 25 cups an hour. The average price is $2 a cup, and the average quantity is 20 cups—point C. The elasticity of demand at point C is 0.5, and demand is inelastic.

Finally, let's calculate the elasticity of demand at point B, which is the midpoint of the demand curve. If the price rises from $2 to $4 a cup, the quantity demanded decreases from 20 to 10 cups an hour. The average price is $3 a cup, and the average quantity is 15 cups—point B. The elasticity of demand at point B is 1, and demand is unit elastic.

Along a linear demand curve,

- Demand is unit elastic at the midpoint of the curve.
- Demand is elastic at all points above the midpoint of the curve.
- Demand is inelastic at all points below the midpoint of the curve.

■ **FIGURE 5.3**

Elasticity Along a Linear Demand Curve

On a linear demand curve, the slope is constant, but the elasticity decreases as the price falls and the quantity demanded increases.

❶ At point A, demand is elastic.

❷ At point B, which is the midpoint of the demand curve, demand is unit elastic.

❸ At point C, demand is inelastic.

Demand is elastic at all points above the midpoint of the demand curve and inelastic at all points below the midpoint of the demand curve.

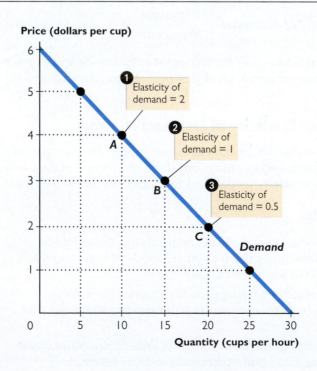

EYE on the GLOBAL ECONOMY
Price Elasticities of Demand

A wealthy American student is casual about her food. It costs only a few dollars a day, and she's going to have her burger, even at double the price. But a poor Tanzanian boy takes his food with deadly seriousness. He has a tough time getting, preparing, and even defending his food. A rise in the price of food means that he must cut back and eat even less.

The figure shows the percentage of income spent on food and the price elasticity of demand for food in ten countries. The larger the proportion of income spent on food, the larger is the price elasticity of demand for food.

As the low-income countries become richer, the proportion of income they spend on food will decrease and their demand for food will become more inelastic. Consequently, the world's demand for food will become more inelastic.

Harvests fluctuate and bring fluctuations in the price of food. As the world demand for food becomes more and more inelastic, the fluctuations in the prices of food items will become larger.

The table shows a few real-world price elasticities of demand. The numbers in the table range from 1.52 for metals to 0.12 for food. Metals have good substitutes, such as plastics, while food has virtually no substitutes. As we move down the list of items, they have fewer good substitutes and are more likely to be regarded as necessities.

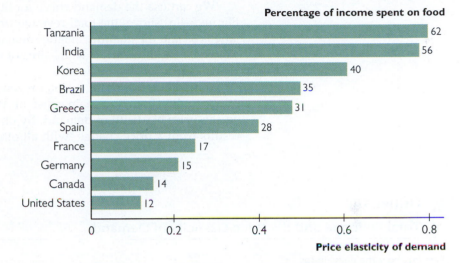

Percentage of income spent on food

Tanzania	62
India	56
Korea	40
Brazil	35
Greece	31
Spain	28
France	17
Germany	15
Canada	14
United States	12

Price elasticity of demand

Some Price Elasticities of Demand

Good or Service	Elasticity
Elastic Demand	
Metals	1.52
Electrical engineering products	1.39
Mechanical engineering products	1.30
Furniture	1.26
Motor vehicles	1.14
Instrument engineering products	1.10
Professional services	1.09
Transportation services	1.03
Inelastic Demand	
Gas, electricity, and water	0.92
Oil	0.91
Chemicals	0.89
Beverages (all types)	0.78
Clothing	0.64
Tobacco	0.61
Banking and insurance services	0.56
Housing services	0.55
Agricultural and fish products	0.42
Books, magazines, and newspapers	0.34
Food	0.12

SOURCES OF DATA: See p. C1.

■ Total Revenue and the Price Elasticity of Demand

Total revenue

The amount spent on a good and received by its seller and equals the price of the good multiplied by the quantity sold.

Total revenue is the amount spent on a good and received by its seller and equals the price of the good multiplied by the quantity of the good sold. For example, suppose that the price of a Starbucks latte is $3 and that 15 cups an hour are sold. Then total revenue is $3 a cup multiplied by 15 cups an hour, which equals $45 an hour.

We can use the demand curve for Starbucks lattes to illustrate total revenue. Figure 5.4(a) shows the total revenue from the sale of lattes when the price of a latte is $3 and the quantity of lattes demanded is 15 cups an hour. Total revenue is shown by the blue rectangle, the area of which equals $3, its height, multiplied by 15, its length, which equals $45.

When the price changes, total revenue can change in the same direction, the opposite direction, or remain constant. Which of these outcomes occurs depends on the price elasticity of demand. By observing the change in total revenue that results from a price change (with all other influences on the quantity remaining

■ **FIGURE 5.4**

Total Revenue and the Price Elasticity of Demand

MyEconLab Animation

Part (a) show the demand for Starbucks lattes. Total revenue equals price multiplied by quantity. When the price of a latte is $3, the quantity demanded is 15 cups an hour and total revenue equals $45 an hour. But when the price rises to $5, the quantity demanded decreases to 5 cups an hour and total revenue decreases to $25 an hour.

Starbucks' total revenue decreases when it raises its price because the demand for Starbucks lattes is elastic.

Part (b) shows the demand for textbooks. When the price is $50 a book, the quantity demanded is 5 million books a year and total revenue equals $250 million a year. When the price rises to $75 a book, the quantity demanded decreases to 4 million books a year and total revenue increases to $300 million a year.

When the textbook price rises, total revenue increases because the demand for textbooks is inelastic.

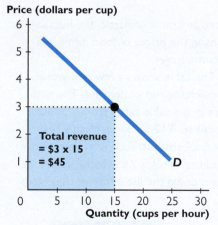

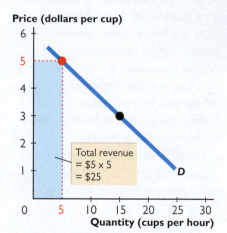

(a) Total revenue and elastic demand: Starbucks lattes

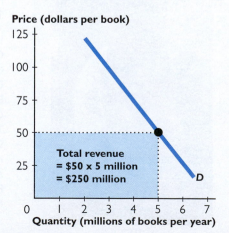

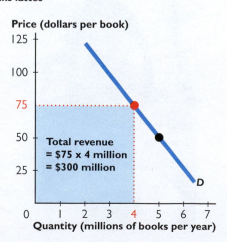

(b) Total revenue and inelastic demand: textbooks

unchanged), we can estimate the price elasticity of demand. This method of estimating the price elasticity of demand is called the **total revenue test**.

If demand is elastic, a given percentage rise in price brings a larger percentage decrease in the quantity demanded, so total revenue—price multiplied by quantity—decreases. Figure 5.4(a) shows this outcome. When the price of a latte is $3, the quantity demanded is 15 cups an hour, so total revenue ($3 × 15) equals $45. If the price of a latte rises to $5, the quantity demanded decreases to 5 cups an hour, so total revenue ($5 × 5) *decreases* to $25.

If demand is inelastic, a given percentage rise in price brings a smaller percentage decrease in the quantity demanded, so total revenue increases. Figure 5.4(b) shows this outcome. When the price of a textbook is $50, the quantity demanded is 5 million textbooks a year and total revenue ($50 × 5 million) is $250 million. If the price of a textbook rises to $75, the quantity demanded decreases to 4 million textbooks a year and total revenue ($75 × 4 million) *increases* to $300 million.

The relationship between the price elasticity of demand and total revenue is

- If price and total revenue change in opposite directions, demand is elastic.
- If a price change leaves total revenue unchanged, demand is unit elastic.
- If price and total revenue change in the same direction, demand is inelastic.

Total revenue test
A method of estimating the price elasticity of demand by observing the change in total revenue that results from a price change (with all other influences on the quantity sold remaining unchanged).

MyEconLab Critical Thinking Exercise

EYE on ELASTICITY AT THE COFFEE SHOP

What Do You Do When Starbucks Raises the Price of a Latte?

When Starbucks raises the price of a latte, the first thing to do is look at the price of lattes in other conveniently located coffee shops. Suppose they have not increased and you can get an acceptable latte for a lower price at Dunkin' Donuts. You decide to switch your allegiance and keep drinking the same quantity of latte.

Soon though, all the coffee shops in your neighborhood have raised their price. Your daily latte is more expensive, no matter how you satisfy your craving for it. You look at the dwindling change in your pocket and decide to return to Starbucks but trim your latte consumption by a cup a week.

Price Elasticity of Demand

We can translate this account of your possible response to a hike in Starbucks' price into some estimates of your price elasticity of demand for Starbucks latte and for latte in general.

Close Substitutes

When Starbucks alone has a higher price, you decrease the quantity of Starbucks latte to zero, so your price elasticity of demand for Starbucks latte is high—it is elastic.

A Starbucks latte and a Dunkin' Donuts latte are different, but for some people they are reasonably close substitutes. So when Starbucks alone

raises its price of a latte, the quantity sold by Starbucks changes a lot—the demand for a Starbucks latte is elastic.

Poor Substitutes

Later, when all the coffee shops have raised the price of a latte, you return to Starbucks but cut back a bit on your consumption of latte. Your price elasticity of demand for latte of all types is low—it is inelastic.

Latte, tea, water, juice, and other drinks are poor substitutes. So when the price of a latte rises, the quantity of latte bought decreases but not by very much—the demand for lattes of all types is inelastic.

EYE on the U.S. ECONOMY
Two Applications of the Price Elasticity of Demand

Orange Prices and Total Revenue

Is a Florida frost that damages the orange crop bad news or good news for orange growers? Does the frost decrease or increase growers' total revenue? Knowledge of the price elasticity of demand for oranges enables us to answer these questions.

If supply changes and demand doesn't change, the percentage change in the equilibrium quantity equals the percentage change in the quantity demanded. And the magnitude of the change in the price and quantity depends on the elasticity of demand.

Economists have estimated that the demand for oranges is inelastic. So if a frost in Florida decreases the orange harvest and decreases the equilibrium quantity of oranges by 1 percent, the price of oranges will rise by more than 1 percent.

Because the price rises by a larger percentage than the percentage decrease in quantity, total revenue increases.

A Florida frost is bad news for buyers of orange juice and for growers who lose their crops, but good news for other orange growers.

So when a Florida frost strikes, the price of oranges rises by a larger percentage than the percentage decrease in the quantity of oranges and the total revenue of the orange growers increases.

A frost is bad news for consumers and growers who lose their crops, but good news for other growers.

Addiction and Elasticity

We can gain insights that might help to design potentially effective policies for dealing with addiction to drugs, whether legal (such as tobacco and alcohol) or illegal (such as meth or heroin).

Nonusers' demand for addictive substances is elastic. A moderately higher price leads to a substantially smaller number of people trying a drug and so exposing themselves to the possibility of becoming addicted. But the existing users' demand for addictive substances is inelastic. Even a substantial price rise brings only a modest decrease in the quantity demanded.

These facts about the price elasticity of demand mean that high taxes on cigarettes and alcohol limit the number of young people who become habitual users of these products, but high taxes have only a modest effect on the quantities consumed by established users.

Similarly, effective policing of imports of an illegal drug that limits its supply leads to a large price rise and a substantial decrease in the number of new users but only a small decrease in the quantity consumed by addicts.

Expenditure on the drug by addicts increases. Further, because many drug addicts finance their purchases with crime, the amount of theft and burglary increases.

Because the price elasticity of demand for drugs is low for addicts, any successful policy to decrease drug use will be one that focuses on the demand for drugs and attempts to change preferences through rehabilitation programs.

Cracking down on imports of illegal drugs limits supply, which leads to a higher price. But it also increases the expenditure on drugs by addicts and increases the crime that finances addiction.

CHECKPOINT 5.1

MyEconLab Study Plan 5.1
Key Terms Quiz
Solutions Video

Define and calculate the price elasticity of demand, and explain the factors that influence it.

Practice Problems

When the price of a good increased by 10 percent, the quantity demanded of it decreased by 2 percent.

1. Is the demand for this good elastic, unit elastic, or inelastic?

2. Does this good have close substitutes or poor substitutes? Is this good more likely to be a necessity or a luxury and to be narrowly or broadly defined? Why?

3. Calculate the price elasticity of demand for this good; explain how the total revenue from the sale of the good has changed; and explain which of the following goods this good is most likely to be: orange juice, bread, toothpaste, theater tickets, clothing, blue jeans, or Super Bowl tickets.

In the News

Samsung and LG slash prices to take sales from Apple

Apple's new iPhone 6 sold out quickly in the United States and to avoid the same outcome in other national markets, Samsung and LG cut the prices of their Galaxy and V10 smartphones by over 10 percent.

Source: *International Business Times*, October 27, 2015

Will a price cut by Samsung and LG increase their total revenue? If Apple also cuts its prices, what will happen to the total revenue from all smartphone sales?

Solutions to Practice Problems

1. The demand for a good is *inelastic* if the percentage decrease in the quantity demanded is less than the percentage increase in its price. In this example, a 10 percent price rise brings a 2 percent decrease in the quantity demanded, so demand is inelastic.

2. Because the good has an inelastic demand, it most likely has poor substitutes, is a necessity rather than a luxury, and is broadly defined.

3. Price elasticity of demand equals the percentage change in the quantity demanded divided by the percentage change in price. In this example, the price elasticity of demand is 2 percent divided by 10 percent, or 0.2. An elasticity less than 1 means that demand is inelastic. When demand is inelastic, a price rise increases total revenue. This good is most likely a necessity (bread), or has poor substitutes (toothpaste), or is broadly defined (clothing).

Solution to In the News

The Apple 6s, Galaxy S6, and LG V10 offer similar features and functions, so they are close substitutes and the demand for any one of them alone is elastic. If the prices of only Samsung and LG fall by 10 percent, the quantity sold will increase by more than 10 percent and the two firms' total revenue will increase. But a smartphone has poor substitutes, so if Apple also cuts its prices, the total revenue of all three firms will decrease because the demand for smartphones is inelastic.

Price elasticity of supply
A measure of the responsiveness of the quantity supplied of a good to a change in its price when all other influences on sellers' plans remain the same.

Perfectly elastic supply
When the quantity supplied changes by a very large percentage in response to an almost zero percentage change in price.

Elastic supply
When the percentage change in the quantity supplied exceeds the percentage change in price.

Unit elastic supply
When the percentage change in the quantity supplied equals the percentage change in price.

Inelastic supply
When the percentage change in the quantity supplied is less than the percentage change in price.

Perfectly inelastic supply
When the percentage change in the quantity supplied is zero for any percentage change in the price.

5.2 THE PRICE ELASTICITY OF SUPPLY

You know that when demand increases, the equilibrium price rises and the equilibrium quantity increases. But does the price rise by a large amount and the quantity increase by a little? Or does the price barely rise and the quantity increase by a large amount? To answer this question, we need to know the price elasticity of supply.

The **price elasticity of supply** is a measure of the responsiveness of the quantity supplied of a good to a change in its price when all other influences on sellers' plans remain the same. We determine the price elasticity of supply by comparing the percentage change in the quantity supplied with the percentage change in price.

■ Elastic and Inelastic Supply

The supply of a good might be

- Elastic
- Unit elastic
- Inelastic

Figure 5.5 illustrates the range of supply elasticities. Figure 5.5(a) shows the extreme case of a **perfectly elastic supply**—an almost zero percentage change in price brings a very large percentage change in the quantity supplied. Figure 5.5(b) shows an **elastic supply**—the percentage change in the quantity supplied exceeds the percentage change in price. Figure 5.5(c) shows a **unit elastic supply**—the percentage change in the quantity supplied equals the percentage change in price. Figure 5.5(d) shows an **inelastic supply**—the percentage change in the quantity supplied is less than the percentage change in price. And Figure 5.5(e) shows the extreme case of a **perfectly inelastic supply**—the percentage change in the quantity supplied is zero when the price changes.

■ Influences on the Price Elasticity of Supply

What makes the supply of some things elastic and the supply of others inelastic? The two main influences on the price elasticity of supply are

- Production possibilities
- Storage possibilities

Production Possibilities

Some goods can be produced at a constant (or very gently rising) opportunity cost. These goods have an elastic supply. The silicon in your computer chips is an example of such a good. Silicon is extracted from sand at a tiny and almost constant opportunity cost, so the supply of silicon is perfectly elastic.

Some goods can be produced in only a fixed quantity. These goods have a perfectly inelastic supply. A beachfront home in Malibu can be built only on a unique beachfront lot, so the supply of these homes is perfectly inelastic.

Hotel rooms in New York City can't easily be used as office accommodation and office space cannot easily be converted into hotel rooms, so the supply of hotel rooms in New York City is inelastic. Paper and printing presses can be used to produce textbooks or magazines, and the supplies of these goods are elastic.

■ FIGURE 5.5

The Range of Price Elasticities of Supply

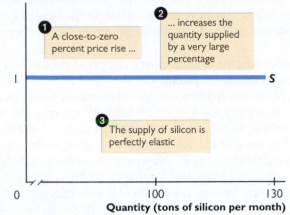

Price (dollars per ton)

① A close-to-zero percent price rise ...

② ... increases the quantity supplied by a very large percentage

③ The supply of silicon is perfectly elastic

S

0   100   130

Quantity (tons of silicon per month)

(a) Perfectly elastic supply

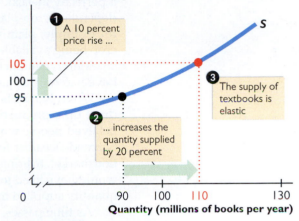

Price (dollars per book)

S

① A 10 percent price rise ...

③ The supply of textbooks is elastic

② ... increases the quantity supplied by 20 percent

105
100
95

0   90   100   110   130

Quantity (millions of books per year)

(b) Elastic supply

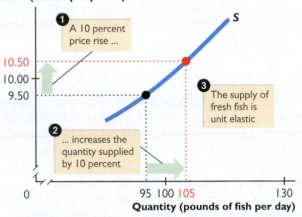

Price (dollars per pound)

S

① A 10 percent price rise ...

③ The supply of fresh fish is unit elastic

② ... increases the quantity supplied by 10 percent

10.50
10.00
9.50

0   95 100 105   130

Quantity (pounds of fish per day)

(c) Unit elastic supply

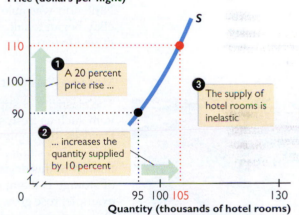

Price (dollars per night)

S

110
100
90

① A 20 percent price rise ...

③ The supply of hotel rooms is inelastic

② ... increases the quantity supplied by 10 percent

0   95 100 105   130

Quantity (thousands of hotel rooms)

(d) Inelastic supply

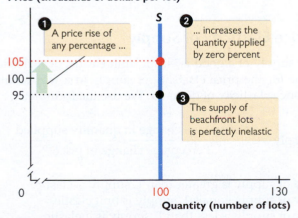

Price (thousands of dollars per lot)

S

① A price rise of any percentage ...

② ... increases the quantity supplied by zero percent

105
100
95

③ The supply of beachfront lots is perfectly inelastic

0   100   130

Quantity (number of lots)

(e) Perfectly inelastic supply

① A price rise brings **②** an increase in the quantity supplied. The relationship between the percentage change in the quantity supplied and the percentage change in price determines **③** the price elasticity of supply, which ranges from perfectly elastic (part a) to perfectly inelastic (part e).

Time Elapsed Since Price Change As time passes after a price change, it becomes easier to change production plans and supply becomes more elastic. For some items—fruits and vegetables are examples—it is difficult or perhaps impossible to change the quantity supplied immediately after a price change. These goods have a perfectly inelastic supply on the day of a price change. The quantities supplied depend on crop-planting decisions that were made earlier. In the case of oranges, for example, planting decisions have to be made many years in advance of the crop being available.

Many manufactured goods also have an inelastic supply if production plans have had only a short period in which to change. For example, before it launched the Wii in November 2006, Nintendo made a forecast of demand, set a price, and drew up a production plan to supply the United States with the quantity that it believed people would be willing to buy. It turned out that demand outstripped Nintendo's earlier forecast. The price of the Wii increased on eBay, an Internet auction market, to bring market equilibrium. At the high price that emerged, Nintendo would have liked to ship more units of Wii, but it could do nothing to increase the quantity supplied in the near term. The supply of Wii was inelastic.

As time passes, the elasticity of supply increases. After all the technologically possible ways of adjusting production have been exploited, supply is extremely elastic—perhaps perfectly elastic—for most manufactured items. In 2007, Nintendo was able to step up the production rate of Wii units and the price on eBay began to fall. The supply of Wii had become more elastic as production continued to expand.

Storage Possibilities

The elasticity of supply of a good that cannot be stored (for example, a perishable item such as fresh strawberries) depends only on production possibilities. But the elasticity of supply of a good that can be stored depends on the decision to keep the good in storage or to offer it for sale. A small price change can make a big difference to this decision, so the supply of a storable good is highly elastic. The cost of storage is the main influence on the elasticity of supply of a storable good. For example, rose growers in Colombia, anticipating a surge in demand on Valentine's Day in February, hold back supplies in late January and early February and increase their inventories of roses. They then release roses from inventory for Valentine's Day.

Fresh strawberries must be sold before they deteriorate, so their supply is inelastic.

■ Computing the Price Elasticity of Supply

To determine whether the supply of a good is elastic, unit elastic, or inelastic, we compute a numerical value for the price elasticity of supply in a way similar to that used to calculate the price elasticity of demand. We use the formula:

$$\text{Price elasticity of supply} = \frac{\text{Percentage change in quantity supplied}}{\text{Percentage change in price}}.$$

- If the price elasticity of supply is greater than 1, supply is elastic.
- If the price elasticity of supply equals 1, supply is unit elastic.
- If the price elasticity of supply is less than 1, supply is inelastic.

Let's calculate the price elasticity of the supply of roses. Suppose that in a normal month, the price of roses is $40 a bouquet and 6 million bouquets are supplied. And suppose that in February, the price rises to $80 a bouquet and the quantity supplied increases to 24 million bouquets. Figure 5.6 illustrates the supply of roses and summarizes the calculation. The figure shows the initial point at $40 a bouquet and the new point at $80 a bouquet. The price increases by $40 a bouquet and the average, or midpoint, price is $60 a bouquet, so the percentage change in the price is 66.67 percent. The quantity supplied increases by 18 million bouquets. and the average, or midpoint, quantity is 15 million bouquets, so the percentage change in the quantity supplied is 120 percent.

Using the above formula, you can see that the price elasticity of supply of roses is

$$\text{Price elasticity of supply} = \frac{120 \text{ percent}}{66.67 \text{ percent}} = 1.8.$$

The price elasticity of supply is 1.8 at the midpoint between the initial point and the new point on the supply curve. In this example, over this price range, the supply of roses is elastic.

FIGURE 5.6

Price Elasticity of Supply Calculation

MyEconLab Animation

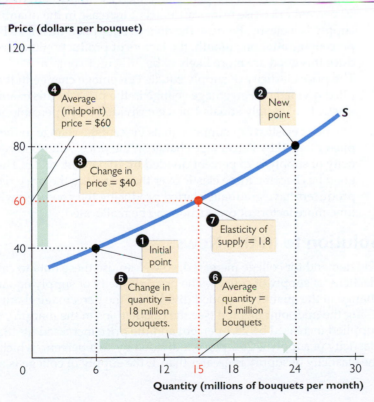

1 At the initial point, the price is $40 a bouquet and the quantity supplied is 6 million bouquets a month.

2 At the new point, the price is $80 a bouquet and the quantity supplied is 24 million bouquets a month.

3 The change in price is $40, and **4** the average price is $60, so the percentage change in the price equals ($40 ÷ $60) × 100, which is 66.67 percent.

5 The change in the quantity supplied is 18 million bouquets and **6** the average quantity supplied is 15 million bouquets, so the percentage change in quantity supplied is (18 million ÷ 15 million) × 100, which is 120 percent.

7 The price elasticity of supply is 120 percent ÷ 66.67 percent, which equals 1.8.

MyEconLab Study Plan 5.2
Key Terms Quiz
Solutions Video

CHECKPOINT 5.2

Define and calculate the price elasticity of supply, and explain the factors that influence it.

Practice Problems

A 10 percent increase in the price of a good increased the quantity supplied of the good by 1 percent after one month and by 25 percent after one year.

1. Is the supply of this good elastic, unit elastic, or inelastic? Is this good likely to be produced using factors of production that are easily obtained? What is the price elasticity of supply of this good?

2. What is the price elasticity of supply after one year? Has the supply of this good become more elastic or less elastic? Why?

In the News

Tuition and enrollment data
Enrollment increased from 15,539,000 in 2000 to 20,618,000 in 2013. The net cost of college (average for all types) increased from $12,357 to $14,860.

Source: trends.collegeboard.org, 2015

Calculate the price elasticity of supply of college. Is the supply of college elastic or inelastic?

Solutions to Practice Problems

1. The supply of a good is *inelastic* if the percentage increase in the quantity supplied is less than the percentage increase in price. In this example, a 10 percent price rise brings a 1 percent increase in the quantity supplied, so supply is inelastic. Because the quantity supplied increases by such a small percentage after one month, the factors of production that are used to produce this good are more likely to be difficult to obtain.
   The price elasticity of supply equals Percentage change in the quantity supplied divided by Percentage change in the price. In this example, the price elasticity of supply equals 1 percent divided by 10 percent, or 0.1.

2. The price elasticity of supply equals Percentage change in the quantity supplied divided by Percentage change in the price. After one year, the price elasticity of supply is 25 percent divided by 10 percent, or 2.5. The supply of the good has become more elastic over the year since the price rise. Possibly other producers have gradually started producing the good and with the passage of time more factors of production can be reallocated.

Calculations:

The change in price is $2,503, the average price is $13,609, so the percentage change in the price equals ($2,503 ÷ $13,609) × 100, which is 18.4 percent.

The change in the quantity supplied is 5,079,000, the average quantity supplied is 18,078,500, so the percentage change in quantity supplied is (5,079,000 ÷ 18,078,500) × 100, which is 28.1 percent.

Solution to In the News

The demand for college increased, so we can use these data to calculate the price elasticity of supply of college. The price elasticity of supply equals the percentage change in the quantity supplied divided by the percentage change in the price. Using the midpoint method (see the calculations in the margin), the quantity supplied increased by 28.1 percent and the price increased by 18.4 percent. The elasticity of supply is 28.1 percent divided by 18.4 percent, which is 1.53. Because the elasticity of supply is greater than 1, the supply of college is elastic.

5.3   CROSS ELASTICITY AND INCOME ELASTICITY

MyEconLab Concept Video

Domino's Pizza in Chula Vista has a problem. Burger King has just cut its prices. Domino's manager, Pat, knows that pizzas and burgers are substitutes. He also knows that when the price of a substitute for pizza falls, the demand for pizza decreases. But by how much will the quantity of pizza bought decrease if Pat maintains his current price?

Pat also knows that pizza and soda are complements. He knows that if the price of a complement of pizza falls, the demand for pizza increases. So he wonders whether he might keep his customers by cutting the price he charges for soda. But he wants to know by how much he must cut the price of soda to keep selling the same quantity of pizza with cheaper burgers all around him.

To answer these questions, Pat needs to calculate the cross elasticity of demand. Let's examine this elasticity measure.

■ Cross Elasticity of Demand

The **cross elasticity of demand** is a measure of the responsiveness of the demand for a good to a change in the price of a substitute or complement when other things remain the same. It is calculated by using the formula:

Cross elasticity of demand
A measure of the responsiveness of the demand for a good to a change in the price of a substitute or complement when other things remain the same.

$$\text{Cross elasticity of demand} = \frac{\text{Percentage change in quantity demanded of a good}}{\text{Percentage change in price of one of its substitutes or complements}}.$$

Suppose that when the price of a burger falls by 10 percent, the quantity of pizza demanded decreases by 5 percent.* The cross elasticity of demand for pizza with respect to the price of a burger is

$$\text{Cross elasticity of demand} = \frac{-5 \text{ percent}}{-10 \text{ percent}} = 0.5.$$

The cross elasticity of demand for a substitute is positive. A *fall* in the price of a substitute brings a *decrease* in the quantity demanded of the good. The quantity demanded of a good and the price of one of its substitutes change in the *same* direction.

Suppose that when the price of soda falls by 10 percent, the quantity of pizza demanded increases by 2 percent. The cross elasticity of demand for pizza with respect to the price of soda is

$$\text{Cross elasticity of demand} = \frac{+2 \text{ percent}}{-10 \text{ percent}} = -0.2.$$

The cross elasticity of demand for a complement is negative. A *fall* in the price of a complement brings an *increase* in the quantity demanded of the good. The quantity demanded of a good and the price of one of its complements change in *opposite* directions.

---

*As before, these percentage changes are calculated by using the midpoint method.

■ **FIGURE 5.7**

Cross Elasticity of Demand

MyEconLab Animation

❶ A burger is a *substitute* for pizza. When the price of a burger falls, the demand curve for pizza shifts leftward from D_0 to D_1. At the price of $10 a pizza, people plan to buy fewer pizzas. The cross elasticity of the demand for pizza with respect to the price of a burger is *positive*.

❷ Soda is a *complement* of pizza. When the price of soda falls, the demand for pizza increases and the demand curve for pizza shifts rightward from D_0 to D_2. At the price of $10 a pizza, people plan to buy more pizzas. The cross elasticity of the demand for pizza with respect to the price of soda is *negative*.

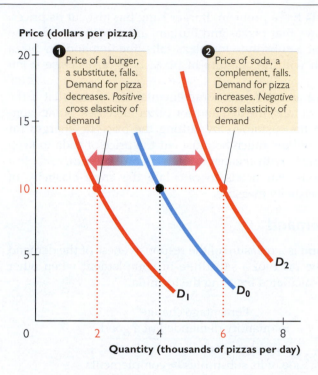

Figure 5.7 illustrates these two cross elasticities of demand for pizza. With the price of a pizza constant at $10, when the price of a burger falls, the demand for pizza decreases and the demand curve for pizza shifts leftward from D_0 to D_1. When the price of soda falls, the demand for pizza increases and the demand curve for pizza shifts rightward from D_0 to D_2. The magnitude of the cross elasticity determines how far the demand curve shifts.

■ **Income Elasticity of Demand**

The U.S. and global economies are expanding, and people are enjoying rising incomes. This increasing prosperity brings an increasing demand for most types of goods. But by how much will the demand for different items increase? Will the demand for some items increase so rapidly that we spend an increasing percentage of our incomes on them? And will the demand for some items decrease?

Income elasticity of demand
A measure of the responsiveness of the demand for a good to a change in income when other things remain the same.

The answer depends on the income elasticity of demand. The **income elasticity of demand** is a measure of the responsiveness of the demand for a good to a change in income when other things remain the same. It is calculated by using the following formula:

$$\text{Income elasticity of demand} = \frac{\text{Percentage change in quantity demanded}}{\text{Percentage change in income}}.$$

The income elasticity of demand falls into three ranges:

• Greater than 1 (normal good, income elastic)
• Between zero and 1 (normal good, income inelastic)
• Less than zero (inferior good)

As our incomes increase: items that have

- An income elastic demand take an increasing share of income
- An income inelastic demand take a decreasing share of income
- A negative income elasticity of demand take an absolutely smaller amount of income.

You can make some strong predictions about how the world will change over the coming years by knowing the income elasticities of demand of different goods and services. Table 5.1 provides a sampling of numbers.

These estimated income elasticities of demand tell us that we can expect air travel—both domestic and international—to become hugely more important; an increasing share of our incomes will be spent on watching movies, eating out in restaurants, using public transportation, and getting haircuts. Two other prominent items not shown in the table, items for which demand is income elastic, are healthcare and education. As our incomes grow, we can expect education and healthcare to take increasing shares of our incomes.

As our incomes grow, we'll spend a decreasing percentage on clothing, phone calls, and food. The income elasticity of demand for food is less than one, even for the poorest people. So we can predict a continuation of the trends of the past—shrinking agriculture and manufacturing, and expanding services.

TABLE 5.1

Some Income Elasticities of Demand

Good or Service	Elasticity
Income Elastic	
Airline travel	5.82
Movies	3.41
Foreign travel	3.08
Electricity	1.94
Restaurant meals	1.61
Local buses and trains	1.38
Haircuts	1.36
Income Inelastic	
Tobacco	0.86
Alcoholic beverages	0.62
Clothing	0.51
Newspapers	0.38
Telephone	0.32
Food	0.14

SOURCES OF DATA: See p. C1.

EYE on YOUR LIFE
Your Price Elasticities of Demand

MyEconLab Critical Thinking Exercise

Pay close attention the next time the price of something that you buy rises. Did you spend more, the same, or less on this item?

Your expenditure on a good is equal to the price of the good multiplied by the quantity that you buy.

But recall that a seller's total revenue is equal to the price of the good multiplied by the quantity sold.

Because your expenditure on a good is equal to the seller's total revenue, the total revenue test that the seller uses to estimate price elasticity of demand can also be used to estimate your price elasticity of demand.

You can determine whether your demand for a good is elastic, unit elastic,

or inelastic by noting how your total expenditure on a good changes when its price changes.

When the price of a good rises, your demand for that good is

- *Elastic* if your expenditure on it decreases.
- *Unit elastic* if your expenditure on it remains constant.
- *Inelastic* if your expenditure on it increases.

Think about why your demand for a good might be elastic, unit elastic, or inelastic by checking back to the list of influences on the price elasticity of demand on p. 116.

Most likely, as we noted in the *Eye on Elasticity at the Coffee Shop* on

p. 123, when the price of a latte rises, you drink almost as many lattes as you did at the lower price. A latte has poor substitutes and your demand for latte is inelastic.

What do you do if the price of smartphone service falls? Do you spend less on smartphone service, as you would if your demand for smartphone service is inelastic? Or do you spend more on smartphone service, which would indicate an elastic demand for smartphone service?

What about your iTunes and Hulu or Netflix? Is your demand for these items elastic or inelastic? Is your demand for textbooks elastic or inelastic? You can estimate all these elasticities.

MyEconLab Study Plan 5.3

Key Terms Quiz

Solutions Video

CHECKPOINT 5.3

Define the cross elasticity of demand and the income elasticity of demand, and explain the factors that influence them.

Practice Problems

1. The quantity demanded of good *A* increases by 5 percent when the price of good *B* rises by 10 percent and other things remain the same. Calculate the cross elasticity of demand. Are goods *A* and *B* complements or substitutes? Describe how the demand for good *A* changes.

2. When income rises by 5 percent and other things remain the same, the quantity demanded of good *C* increases by 1 percent. Calculate the income elasticity of demand for good *C*. Is good *C* a normal good or an inferior good? Describe how the demand for good *C* changes.

In the News

China is the world's fastest-growing market for "vanity" spending
China's market for the consumption of goods aimed at enhancing one's appearance or status grew an average of 15.6 percent a year for the past five years.
Source: qz.com, April 23, 2015

Given the information that incomes grew at about 7 percent a year, is the demand for "vanity" goods in China income elastic or income inelastic? Explain.

Solutions to Practice Problems

1. Cross elasticity of demand = Percentage change in the quantity demanded of good *A* ÷ Percentage increase in the price of good *B*.
   Cross elasticity of demand = 5 ÷ 10, or 0.5.
   Goods *A* and *B* are substitutes because the cross elasticity of demand is positive. When the price of good *B* rises, the quantity demanded of good *A* increases and people switch from good *B* to good *A*. The demand for good *A* increases (Figure 1).

2. Income elasticity of demand = Percentage change in the quantity demanded of good *C* ÷ Percentage increase in income.
   Income elasticity of demand = 1 ÷ 5, or 0.2.

   Income elasticity of demand is positive, so good *C* is a normal good.

   As income rises, the quantity demanded of good *C* increases. The demand for good *C* increases (Figure 2).

Solution to In the News

To know whether the demand for a good is income elastic, we need to calculate the income elasticity of demand. A good with an income elastic demand is one that has an income elasticity of demand greater than 1. If spending on "vanity" goods increased by 15.6 percent per year when incomes grew by 7 percent per year, the income elasticity of demand for "vanity" goods is 15.6 divided by 7, which equals 2.2. The income elasticity of demand for "vanity" goods is greater than 1, so the demand for "vanity" goods is income elastic.

FIGURE 1

Price of good *A*

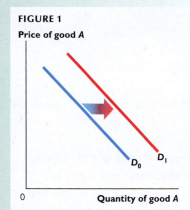

Quantity of good *A*

FIGURE 2

Price of good *C*

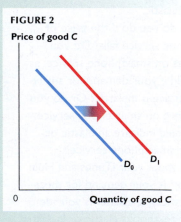

Quantity of good *C*

CHAPTER SUMMARY

Key Points

1. Define and calculate the price elasticity of demand, and explain the factors that influence it.

- The demand for a good is elastic if, when its price changes, the percentage change in the quantity demanded exceeds the percentage change in price.
- The demand for a good is inelastic if, when its price changes, the percentage change in the quantity demanded is less than the percentage change in price.
- The price elasticity of demand for a good depends on how easy it is to find substitutes for the good and on the proportion of income spent on it.
- Price elasticity of demand equals the percentage change in the quantity demanded divided by the percentage change in price.
- If demand is elastic, a rise in price leads to a decrease in total revenue. If demand is unit elastic, a rise in price leaves total revenue unchanged. And if demand is inelastic, a rise in price leads to an increase in total revenue.

2. Define and calculate the price elasticity of supply, and explain the factors that influence it.

- The supply of a good is elastic if, when its price changes, the percentage change in the quantity supplied exceeds the percentage change in price.
- The supply of a good is inelastic if, when its price changes, the percentage change in the quantity supplied is less than the percentage change in price.
- The main influences on the price elasticity of supply are the flexibility of production possibilities and storage possibilities.

3. Define the cross elasticity of demand and the income elasticity of demand, and explain the factors that influence them.

- Cross elasticity of demand shows how the demand for a good changes when the price of one of its substitutes or complements changes.
- Cross elasticity is positive for substitutes and negative for complements.
- Income elasticity of demand shows how the demand for a good changes when income changes. For a normal good, the income elasticity of demand is positive. For an inferior good, the income elasticity of demand is negative.

Key Terms

MyEconLab Key Terms Quiz

Cross elasticity of demand, 131
Elastic demand, 116
Elastic supply, 126
Income elasticity of demand, 132
Inelastic demand, 116
Inelastic supply, 126

Perfectly elastic demand, 116
Perfectly elastic supply, 126
Perfectly inelastic demand, 116
Perfectly inelastic supply, 126
Price elasticity of demand, 114
Price elasticity of supply, 126

Total revenue, 122
Total revenue test, 123
Unit elastic demand, 116
Unit elastic supply, 126

CHAPTER CHECKPOINT

Study Plan Problems and Applications

When the price of home heating oil increased by 20 percent, the quantity demanded decreased by 2 percent and the quantity of wool sweaters demanded increased by 10 percent. Use this information to work Problems **1** and **2**.

1. Use the total revenue test to determine whether the demand for home heating oil is elastic or inelastic.

2. If the price of a wool sweater did not change, calculate the cross elasticity of demand for wool sweaters with respect to the price of home heating oil. Are home heating oil and wool sweaters substitutes or complements? Why?

3. Figure 1 shows the demand for movie tickets. Is the demand for movie tickets elastic or inelastic over the price range $7 to $9 a ticket? If the price falls from $9 to $7 a ticket, explain how the total revenue from the sale of movie tickets will change. Calculate the price elasticity of demand for movie tickets when the price is $8 a ticket.

4. The price elasticity of demand for Pete's chocolate chip cookies is 1.5. Pete wants to increase his total revenue. Would you recommend that Pete raise or lower his price of cookies? Explain your answer.

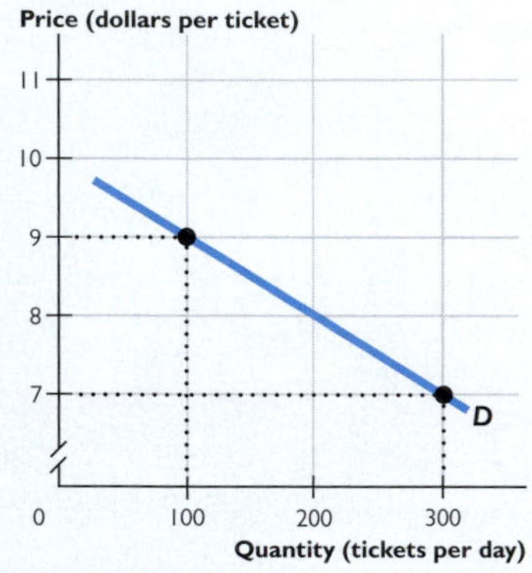

Use the following information to work Problems **5** and **6**.

The price of a plane ride rises by 10 percent. The price elasticity of demand for plane rides is 0.5 and the price elasticity of demand for train rides is 0.2. The cross elasticity of demand for train rides with respect to the price of a plane ride is 0.4.

5. Calculate the percentage changes in the quantity demanded of plane rides and train rides.

6. Given the rise in the price of a plane ride, what percentage change in the price of a train ride will leave the quantity demanded of train rides unchanged?

7. A survey found that when incomes increased by 10 percent, the following changes in quantities demanded occurred: spring water up by 5 percent; sports drinks down by 2 percent; cruises up by 15 percent. For which good is demand income elastic? For which good is demand income inelastic? Which goods are normal goods?

8. Did Starbucks start a pumpkin boom?
Ever since Starbucks introduced its famed pumpkin spice latte about a decade ago, pumpkin sales have skyrocketed.

Source: CNNMoney, October 1, 2014

The price of pumpkin increased from $286 per ton in 2000 to $732 per ton in 2014 (both prices in 2014 dollars) and the quantity produced increased from 423,000 tons in 2000 to 657,150 in 2014. Calculate the U.S. price elasticity of supply of pumpkin: Is its supply elastic?

9. Read *Eye on Elasticity at the Coffee Shop* on p. 123 and then explain why the demand for latte is inelastic while the demand for a Starbucks latte is elastic. Which demand is likely to be more inelastic: the demand for latte or the demand for coffee?

FIGURE 1

Price (dollars per ticket)

11

10

9

8

7

D

0   100   200   300

Quantity (tickets per day)

Instructor Assignable Problems and Applications

MyEconLab Homework, Quiz, or Test if assigned by instructor

Use the following data to work Problems **1** and **2**.

When Elle's Espresso Bar increased its prices by 10 percent, the quantity of coffee that Elle sold decreased by 40 percent. When Elle and all her competitors cut their prices by 10 percent, the quantity of coffee sold by Elle increased by only 4 percent.

1. Calculate the price elasticity of demand for Elle's Espresso Bar coffee and the price elasticity of demand for coffee.

2. Explain the difference between the responses to Elle's price hike and price cut. Why did the price increase bring a large response in the quantity sold while the price cut had only a small effect?

3. When rain ruined the banana crop in Central America, the price of bananas rose from $1 to $2 a pound. Growers sold fewer bananas, but their total revenue was unchanged. By what percentage did the quantity demanded of bananas change? Is the demand for bananas elastic, unit elastic, or inelastic?

4. The income elasticity of demand for haircuts is 1.5, and the income elasticity of demand for food is 0.14. You take a weekend job, and the income you have available to spend on food and haircuts doubles. If the prices of food and haircuts remain the same, will you double your expenditure on haircuts and double your expenditure on food? Explain why or why not.

5. Drought cuts the quantity of wheat grown by 2 percent. If the price elasticity of demand for wheat is 0.5, by how much will the price of wheat rise?

If pasta makers estimate that this change in the price of wheat will increase the price of pasta by 25 percent and decrease the quantity demanded of pasta by 8 percent, what is the pasta makers' estimate of the price elasticity of demand for pasta?

If pasta sauce makers estimate that, with the change in the price of pasta, the quantity of pasta sauce demanded will decrease by 5 percent, what is the pasta sauce makers' estimate of the cross elasticity of demand for pasta sauce with respect to the price of pasta?

6. "In a market in which demand is price inelastic, producers can gouge consumers and the government should set high standards of conduct for producers to ensure that consumers get a fair deal." Which parts of this statement are positive and which are normative? Explain how you might go about testing the positive part.

Use the following information to work Problems **7** and **8**.

Valentine roses

On Valentine's Day 2015, 257 million roses were sold for about double the normal price. On a normal day, 3 million roses are sold.

Source: aboutflowers.com, 2015

7. Does the information about the market for roses enable us to estimate an elasticity, and if so, which one: the price elasticity of demand, the price elasticity of supply, an income elasticity, or a cross elasticity? Explain your answer.

8. What is the magnitude of the elasticity that you can estimate using the information provided? Explain your answer.

MyEconLab Chapter 5 Study Plan

Multiple Choice Quiz

1. When the price of ice cream rises from $3 to $5 a scoop, the quantity of ice cream bought decreases by 10 percent. The price elasticity of demand for ice cream is _____.

A. 5
B. 0.2
C. 50
D. 2.5

2. In Pioneer Ville, the price elasticity of demand for bus rides is 0.5. When the price of a bus ticket rises by 5 percent, _____.

A. the demand for bus rides increases by 10 percent
B. the quantity of bus rides demanded increases by 2.5 percent
C. the demand for bus rides decreases by 2.5 percent
D. the quantity of bus rides demanded decreases by 2.5 percent

3. The price elasticity of demand for a good is 0.2. A 10 percent rise in the price will _____ the total revenue from sales of the good.

A. decrease
B. increase
C. decrease the quantity sold with no change in
D. not change

4. If the price of a good falls and expenditure on the good rises, the demand for the good is _____.

A. elastic
B. perfectly elastic
C. inelastic
D. unit elastic

5. When the price of a good rises from $5 to $7 a unit, the quantity supplied increases from 110 to 130 units a day. The price elasticity of supply is _____. The supply of the good is _____.

A. 60; elastic
B. 10; elastic
C. 0.5; inelastic
D. 2; inelastic

6. The cross elasticity of demand for good *A* with respect to good *B* is 0.2. A 10 percent change in the price of good *B* will lead to a _____ percent change in the quantity of good *A* demanded. Goods *A* and *B* are _____.

A. 2; substitutes
B. 0.5; complements
C. −2; complements
D. −0.5; substitutes

7. A 2 percent increase in income increases the quantity demanded of a good by 1 percent. The income elasticity of demand for this good is _____. The good is a _____ good.

A. 2; normal
B. −2; inferior
C. 1/2; normal
D. 2; inferior

Should price gouging be illegal?

Efficiency and Fairness of Markets

6

When you have completed your study of this chapter, you will be able to

CHAPTER CHECKLIST

1 Describe the alternative methods of allocating scarce resources, and define and explain the features of an efficient allocation.

2 Distinguish between value and price, and define consumer surplus.

3 Distinguish between cost and price, and define producer surplus.

4 Evaluate the efficiency of the alternative methods of allocating resources.

5 Explain the main ideas about fairness, and evaluate the fairness of the alternative methods of allocating scarce resources.

MyEconLab Big Picture Video

6.1 ALLOCATION METHODS AND EFFICIENCY

Because resources are scarce, they must be allocated among their competing uses. Doing nothing and leaving resource use to chance is one method of allocation. *Price gouging*—charging an unusually high price for an essential item following a natural disaster—is another. The goal of this chapter is to evaluate the ability of a market price to allocate resources efficiently and fairly.

But market price is only one of several methods of allocating resources. To know whether the market does a good job, we need to compare it with its alternatives. We also need to know what is meant by an efficient and fair allocation.

Economists have much more to say about efficiency than about fairness, so efficiency is the main focus of this chapter. We leave the difficult issue of fairness until the final section. We begin by describing the alternative ways in which resources might be allocated. Then we explain the characteristics of an efficient allocation.

■ Resource Allocation Methods

Resources might be allocated by using any one or some combination of the following methods:

- Market price
- Command
- Majority rule
- Contest
- First-come, first-served
- Sharing equally
- Lottery
- Personal characteristics
- Force

Let's see how each method works and look at an example of each.

Market price allocates resources to those who are willing and able to pay.

Market Price

When a market price allocates a scarce resource, the people who get the resource are those who are willing and able to pay the market price. People who don't value the resource as highly as the market price leave it for others to buy and use.

Most of the scarce resources that you supply get allocated by market price. For example, you sell your labor services in a market. And almost everything that you consume gets bought in a market.

Two kinds of people decide not to buy at the market price: those who can afford to buy but choose not to, and those who are too poor and can't afford to buy.

For many goods and services, distinguishing between those who choose not to buy and those who can't afford to buy doesn't matter. For a few items, that distinction does matter. For example, some poor people can't afford to pay school fees and doctor's fees. The inability of poor people to buy items that most people consider to be essential is not handled well by the market price method and is usually dealt with by one of the other allocation methods.

But for most goods and services, the market turns out to do a good job. We'll examine just how good a job it does later in this chapter.

Command

A **command system** allocates resources by the order (command) of someone in authority. Many resources get allocated by command. In the U.S. economy, the command system is used extensively inside firms and government bureaus. For example, if you have a job, it is most likely that someone tells you what to do. Your labor time is allocated to specific tasks by a command.

Sometimes, a command system allocates the resources of an entire economy. The former Soviet Union is an example. North Korea and Cuba are the only remaining command economies.

A command system works well in organizations in which the lines of authority and responsibility are clear and it is easy to monitor the activities being performed. But a command system works badly when applied to an entire economy. The range of activities to be monitored is just too large, and it is easy for people to fool those in authority. The system works so badly in North Korea that it fails even to deliver an adequate supply of food.

Majority Rule

Majority rule allocates resources in the way that a majority of voters choose. Societies use majority rule for some of their biggest decisions. For example, majority rule decides the tax rates that end up allocating scarce resources between private use and public use. And majority rule decides how tax dollars are allocated among competing uses such as national defense and healthcare for the aged.

Having 200 million people vote on every line in a nation's budget would be extremely costly, so instead of direct majority rule, the United States (and most other countries) use the system of representative government. Majority rule determines who will represent the people, and majority rule among the representatives decides the detailed allocation of scarce resources.

Majority rule works well when the decisions being made affect large numbers of people and self-interest must be suppressed to use resources most effectively.

Contest

A contest allocates resources to a winner (or a group of winners). The most obvious contests are sporting events. Serena Williams and Sloane Stephens do battle on a tennis court, and the winner gets twice as much in prize money as the loser.

But contests are much more general than those in a sports arena, though we don't call them contests in ordinary speech. For example, Bill Gates won a big contest to provide the world's personal computer operating system, and Jennifer Lawrence won a type of contest to rise to the top of the movie-acting business.

Contests do a good job when the efforts of the "players" are hard to monitor and reward directly. By dangling the opportunity to win a big prize, people are motivated to work hard and try to be the "winner." Even though only a few people end up with a big prize, many people work harder in the process of trying to win and so total production is much greater than it would be without the contest.

First-Come, First-Served

A first-come, first-served method allocates resources to those who are first in line. Most national parks allocate campsites in this way. Airlines use first-come, first-served to allocate standby seats at the departure gate. A freeway is an everyday example of first-come, first-served. This scarce transportation resource gets allocated

Command system
A system that allocates resources by the order of someone in authority.

A command allocates resources by the order of someone in authority.

Voting allocates resources in the way that the majority wants.

A contest allocates resources to the winner, in sport and business.

First-come, first-served allocates resources to the first in line.

to the first to arrive at the on-ramp. If too many vehicles enter the freeway, the speed slows and people, in effect, wait in line for a bit of the "freeway" to become free!

First-come, first-served works best when, as in the above examples, a scarce resource can serve just one user at a time in a sequence. By serving the user who arrives first, this method minimizes the time spent waiting in line for the resource to become free.

Sharing Equally

When a resource is shared equally, everyone gets the same amount of it. You perhaps use this method to share dessert at a restaurant. People sometimes jointly own a vacation apartment and share its use equally.

To make equal shares work, people must agree on how to use the resource and must make an arrangement to implement the agreement. Sharing equally can work for small groups who share a set of common goals and ideals.

Sharing allocates resources by mutual agreement.

Lottery

Lotteries allocate resources to those who pick the winning number, draw the lucky cards, or come up lucky on some other gaming system. State lotteries and casinos reallocate millions of dollars' worth of goods and services every year.

But lotteries are far more widespread than state jackpots and roulette wheels in casinos. They are used in a variety of situations to allocate scarce resources. For example, the Lawn Tennis Association operates ballots and draws to allocate Wimbledon tickets and some airports use them to allocate landing slots to airlines.

Lotteries work well when there is no effective way to distinguish among potential users of a scarce resource.

A lottery allocates resources to the one who draws the winning number.

Personal Characteristics

When resources are allocated on the basis of personal characteristics, people with the "right" characteristics get the resources. Some of the resources that matter most to you are allocated in this way. The people you like are the ones you spend the most time with. You try to avoid having to spend time with people you don't like. People choose marriage partners on the basis of personal characteristics. The use of personal characteristics to allocate resources is regarded as completely natural and acceptable.

But this method also gets used in unacceptable ways. Allocating the best jobs to white, Anglo-Saxon males and discriminating against minorities and women is an example.

Personal characteristics allocate resources based on whom we like.

Force

Force plays a crucial role, for both good and ill, in allocating scarce resources. Let's start with the ill.

War, the use of military force by one nation against another, has played an enormous role historically in allocating resources. The economic supremacy of European settlers in the Americas and Australia owes much to the use of this method.

Theft, the taking of the property of others without their consent, also plays a large role. Both large-scale organized crime and small-scale petty crime collectively allocate billions of dollars' worth of resources annually. A large amount of

Force protects the rule of law and facilitates economic activity.

theft today is conducted by using sophisticated electronic methods that move resources from banks and also from thousands of innocent people.

But force plays a crucial positive role in allocating resources. It provides an effective method for the government to transfer wealth from the rich to the poor and is the legal framework in which voluntary exchange in markets takes place.

Most income and wealth redistribution in modern societies occurs through a taxation and benefits system that is enforced by the power of the state. We vote for taxes and benefits—a majority vote allocation—but we use the power of the state to ensure that everyone complies with the rules and pays their allotted share.

A legal system is the foundation on which our market economy functions. Without courts to enforce contracts, it would be difficult to do business. But the courts could not enforce contracts without the ability to apply force if necessary. The state provides the ultimate force that enables the courts to do their work.

More broadly, the force of the state is essential to uphold the principle of the *rule of law*. This principle is the bedrock of civilized economic (and social and political) life. With the rule of law upheld, people can go about their daily economic lives with the assurance that their property will be protected—that they can sue for violations of their property (and be sued if they violate the property of others).

Free from the burden of protecting their property and confident in the knowledge that those with whom they trade will honor their agreements, people can get on with focusing on the activity at which they have a comparative advantage and trading for mutual gain.

In the next sections of this chapter, we're going to see how a market achieves an efficient use of resources, examine obstacles to efficiency, and see how sometimes, an alternative method might improve on the market. But first we need to be clear about the meaning of efficiency. What are the characteristics of an efficient allocation of resources?

■ Using Resources Efficiently

MyEconLab Concept Video

In everyday language, *efficiency* means getting the most out of something. An efficient automobile is one that gets the best possible gas mileage; an efficient furnace is one that uses as little fuel as possible to deliver its heat. In economics, efficiency means getting the most out of the entire economy.

Efficiency and the *PPF*

The *production possibilities frontier* (*PPF*) is the boundary between the combinations of goods and services that can be produced and those that cannot be produced given the available factors of production and state of technology (p. 60). Production is efficient when the economy is *on* its *PPF* (Chapter 3, pp. 62–63). Production at a point *inside* the *PPF* is *inefficient*.

Allocative efficiency is achieved when the quantities of goods and services produced are those that people *value most highly*. To put it another way, resources are allocated efficiently when we cannot produce more of one thing without giving up something else *that people value more highly*. If we can give up some units of one good to get more of something that is *valued more highly*, we haven't achieved the most valued point on the *PPF*.

The *PPF* tells us what it is *possible* to produce but it doesn't tell us about the *value* of what we produce. To find the *highest-valued* point on the *PPF*, we need some information about value. *Marginal benefit* provides that information.

Allocative efficiency
A situation in which the quantities of goods and services produced are those that people *value most highly*—it is not possible to produce more of a good or service without giving up some of another good that people *value more highly*.

Marginal Benefit

Marginal benefit is the benefit that people receive from consuming *one more unit* of a good or service. People's *preferences* determine marginal benefit and we can measure the marginal benefit from a good or service by what people *are willing to give* up to get *one more* unit of it.

The more we have of any good or service, the smaller is our marginal benefit from it—*the principle of decreasing marginal benefit*. Think about your own marginal benefit from pizza. You really enjoy the first slice. A second slice is fine, too, but not quite as satisfying as the first one. But eat three, four, five, six, and more slices, and each additional slice is less enjoyable than the previous one. You get diminishing marginal benefit from pizza. The more pizza you have, the less of some other good or service you are willing to give up to get one more slice.

Figure 6.1 illustrates the economy's marginal benefit schedule and marginal benefit curve for pizza. The schedule and curve show the same information. In the schedule and on the curve, the quantity of other goods that people *are willing to give up* to get one more pizza *decreases* as the quantity of pizza available *increases*.

Marginal Cost

To achieve allocative efficiency, we must compare the marginal benefit from pizza with its marginal cost. *Marginal cost* is the opportunity cost of producing one more unit of a good or service (see p. 10) and is measured by the slope of the production possibilities frontier (see pp. 66–67). The marginal cost of a good increases as the quantity produced of that good increases.

◼ FIGURE 6.1

Marginal Benefit from Pizza

MyEconLab Animation

The table and the graph show the marginal benefit from pizza.

Possibility A and point A tell us that if 2,000 pizzas a day are produced, people are willing to give up 15 units of other goods for a pizza. Each point A, B, and C on the graph represents the possibility in the table identified by the same letter.

The line passing through these points is the marginal benefit curve. The marginal benefit from pizza decreases as the quantity of pizza available increases.

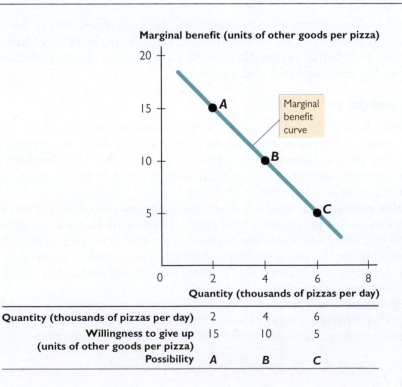

Quantity (thousands of pizzas per day)	2	4	6
Willingness to give up (units of other goods per pizza)	15	10	5
Possibility	A	B	C

Figure 6.2 illustrates the economy's marginal cost schedule and marginal cost curve. In the schedule and along the curve, which show the same information, the quantity of other goods that people *must give up* to get one more pizza *increases* as the quantity of pizza produced *increases*.

We can now use the concepts of marginal benefit and marginal cost to discover the efficient quantity of pizza to produce.

Efficient Allocation

The efficient allocation is the highest-valued allocation. To find this allocation, we compare marginal benefit and marginal cost.

If the marginal benefit from pizza exceeds its marginal cost, we're producing too little pizza (and too many units of other goods). If we increase the quantity of pizza produced, we incur a cost but receive a larger benefit from the additional pizza. Our allocation of resources becomes more efficient.

If the marginal cost of pizza exceeds its marginal benefit, we're producing too much pizza (and too little of other goods). Now if we decrease the quantity of pizza produced, we receive a smaller benefit from pizza but save an even greater cost of pizza. Again, our allocation of resources becomes more efficient.

Only when the marginal benefit and marginal cost of pizza are equal are we allocating resources efficiently. Figure 6.3 on the next page illustrates this efficient allocation and provides a graphical summary of the above description of allocative efficiency.

> ### FIGURE 6.2
>
> ### Marginal Cost of Pizza   MyEconLab Animation

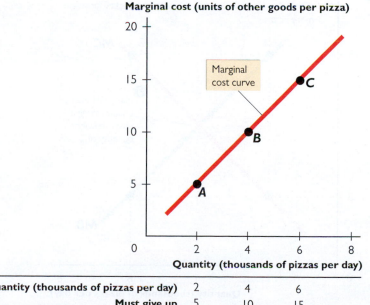

The table and the graph show the marginal cost of a pizza. Marginal cost is the opportunity cost of producing one more unit. It is derived from the *PPF* and is measured by the slope of the *PPF*.

Points *A*, *B*, and *C* on the graph represent the possibilities in the table. The marginal cost curve shows that the marginal cost of a pizza increases as the quantity of pizza produced increases.

Quantity (thousands of pizzas per day)	2	4	6
Must give up (units of other goods per pizza)	5	10	15
Possibility	A	B	C

■ **FIGURE 6.3**

The Efficient Quantity of Pizza

Production efficiency occurs at all points on the *PPF*, but *allocative efficiency* occurs at only one point on the *PPF*.

❶ When 2,000 pizzas are produced in part (a), the marginal benefit from pizza exceeds its marginal cost in part (b). Too few pizzas are being produced. If more pizzas and fewer other goods are produced, the value of production increases and resources are used more efficiently.

❷ When 6,000 pizzas are produced in part (a), the marginal cost of a pizza exceeds its marginal benefit in part (b). Too many pizzas are being produced. If fewer pizzas and more other goods are produced, the value of production increases and resources are used more efficiently.

❸ When 4,000 pizzas a day are produced in part (a), the marginal cost of a pizza equals its marginal benefit in part (b). The efficient quantity of pizzas is being produced. It is not possible to get greater value from the economy's scarce resources. If one less pizza and more other goods are produced, the value of the lost pizza exceeds the value of the additional other goods, so total value falls. And if one more pizza and fewer other goods are produced, the value of the gained pizza is less than the value of the lost other goods, so again total value falls.

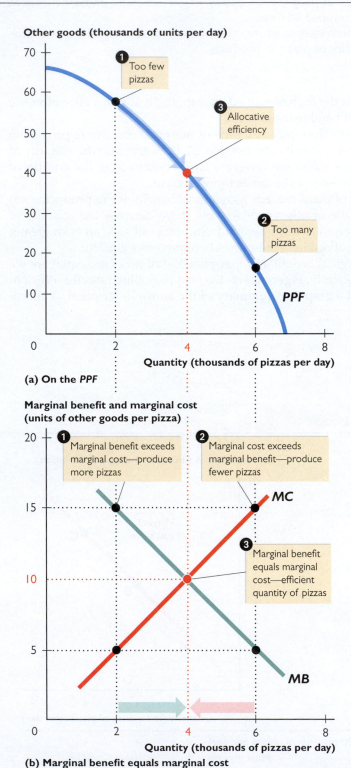

(a) On the *PPF*

(b) Marginal benefit equals marginal cost

CHECKPOINT 6.1

MyEconLab Study Plan 6.1
Key Terms Quiz
Solutions Video

Describe the alternative methods of allocating scarce resources, and define and explain the features of an efficient allocation.

Practice Problems

1. Which method is used to allocate the following scarce resources?
   - Campus parking space between student areas and faculty areas
   - A spot in a restricted student parking area
   - Textbooks
   - Host city for the Olympic Games

Use Figure 1, which shows a nation's *PPF*, and Table 1, which shows its marginal benefit and marginal cost schedules, to work Problems **2** and **3**.

2. What is the marginal benefit from bananas when 1 pound of bananas is grown? What is the marginal cost of growing 1 pound of bananas?

3. On Figure 1, mark two points: Point *A* at which production is efficient but too much coffee is produced for allocative efficiency; and point *B*, the point of allocative efficiency.

In the News

Jack White announces short run of shows—our best guesses as to where
Fresh off his scorching performance at Coachella Saturday night, rocker Jack White announced he'll do shows unannounced until day-of-show, with tickets priced at $3 and limited to one ticket per person, to be purchased only at the venue on a first-come, first-served basis.

Source: *Billboard Magazine*, April 14, 2015

What method was used to allocate Jack White concert tickets? Was it efficient?

Solutions to Practice Problems

1. Campus parking is allocated by command. The spot in a restricted student parking area is allocated by first-come, first-served. Textbooks are allocated by market price. The Olympic Games' host city is allocated by contest.

2. The marginal benefit from 1 pound of bananas is 3 pounds of coffee. Marginal benefit is the amount of coffee that the nation is *willing to give up* to get *one additional* pound of bananas. The marginal cost of growing 1 pound of bananas is 1 pound of coffee. Marginal cost is the amount of coffee that the nation *must give up* to get *one additional* pound of bananas.

3. Point *A* on Figure 2 shows production efficiency (on the *PPF*) but not allocative efficiency because from Table 1 marginal benefit from bananas exceeds the marginal cost—too few bananas are produced. Point *B* is the point of allocative efficiency: It is on the *PPF* and marginal benefit equals marginal cost.

Solution to In the News

The initial allocation used was first-come, first-served at the venue. But a person who gets a ticket can either use it or sell it at the going market price to someone in the ticket line at the venue. Only if the market price equals the organizer's marginal cost is the allocation of tickets efficient.

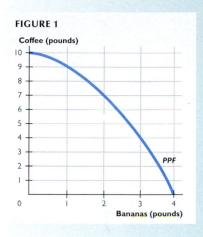

FIGURE 1

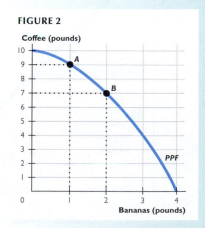

FIGURE 2

TABLE 1   MARGINAL BENEFIT AND MARGINAL COST

Bananas (pounds)	Willing to give up	Must give up
	(pounds of coffee per pound of bananas)	
1	3	1
2	2	2
3	1	3

6.2   VALUE, PRICE, AND CONSUMER SURPLUS

To investigate whether a market is efficient, we need to understand the connection between demand and marginal benefit and between supply and marginal cost.

■ Demand and Marginal Benefit

In everyday life, when we talk about "getting value for money," we're distinguishing between *value* and *price.* Value is what we get, and price is what we pay. In economics, the everyday idea of value is *marginal benefit,* which we measure as the maximum price that people are willing to pay for another unit of the good or service. The demand curve tells us this price. In Figure 6.4(a), the demand curve shows the quantity demanded at a given price—when the price is $10 a pizza, the quantity demanded is 10,000 pizzas a day. In Figure 6.4(b), the demand curve shows the maximum price that people are willing to pay when there is a given quantity—when 10,000 pizzas a day are available, the most that people are willing to pay for the 10,000th pizza is $10. The marginal benefit from the 10,000th pizza is $10. So:

A demand curve is a marginal benefit curve. The demand curve for pizza tells us the dollars' worth of other goods and services that people are willing to forgo to consume one more pizza.

■ **FIGURE 6.4**

Demand, Willingness to Pay, and Marginal Benefit

MyEconLab Animation

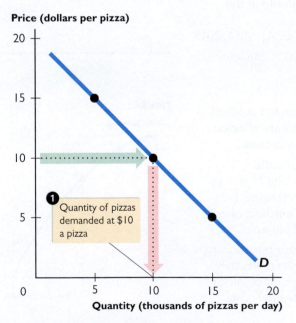

(a) Price determines quantity demanded

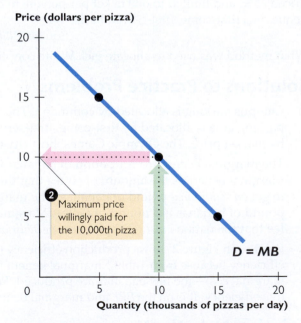

(b) Quantity determines willingness to pay

❶ The demand curve for pizza, *D,* shows the quantity of pizza demanded at each price, other things remaining the same. At $10 a pizza, the quantity demanded is 10,000 pizzas a day.

❷ The demand curve shows the maximum price willingly paid (marginal benefit) for a given quantity. If 10,000 pizzas are available, the maximum price willingly paid for the 10,000th pizza is $10. The demand curve is also the marginal benefit curve *MB.*

Consumer Surplus

We don't always have to pay as much as we're willing to pay. When people buy something for less than it is worth to them, they receive a consumer surplus. **Consumer surplus** is the excess of marginal benefit from a good over the price paid for it, summed over the quantity consumed.

Figure 6.5 illustrates consumer surplus. The demand curve for pizza tells us the quantity of pizza that people plan to buy at each price and the marginal benefit from pizza at each quantity. If the price of a pizza is $10, people buy 10,000 pizzas a day. Expenditure on pizza is $100,000, which is shown by the area of the blue rectangle.

To calculate consumer surplus, we must find the consumer surplus on each pizza and add these consumer surpluses together. For the 10,000th pizza, marginal benefit equals $10 and people pay $10, so the consumer surplus on this pizza is zero. For the 5,000th pizza (highlighted in the figure), marginal benefit is $15. So on this pizza, consumer surplus is $15 minus $10, which is $5. For the first pizza, marginal benefit is almost $20, so on this pizza, consumer surplus is almost $10.

Consumer surplus—the sum of the consumer surpluses on the 10,000 pizzas that people buy—is $50,000 a day, which is shown by the area of the green triangle. (The base of the triangle is 10,000 pizzas a day and its height is $10, so its area is ($10 × 10,000) ÷ 2 = $50,000.)

The total benefit is the amount paid, $100,000 (the area of the blue rectangle), plus consumer surplus, $50,000 (the area of the green triangle), and is $150,000. Consumer surplus is the total benefit minus the amount paid, or net benefit to consumers.

Consumer surplus
The marginal benefit from a good or service in excess of the price paid for it, summed over the quantity consumed.

FIGURE 6.5

Demand and Consumer Surplus

MyEconLab Animation

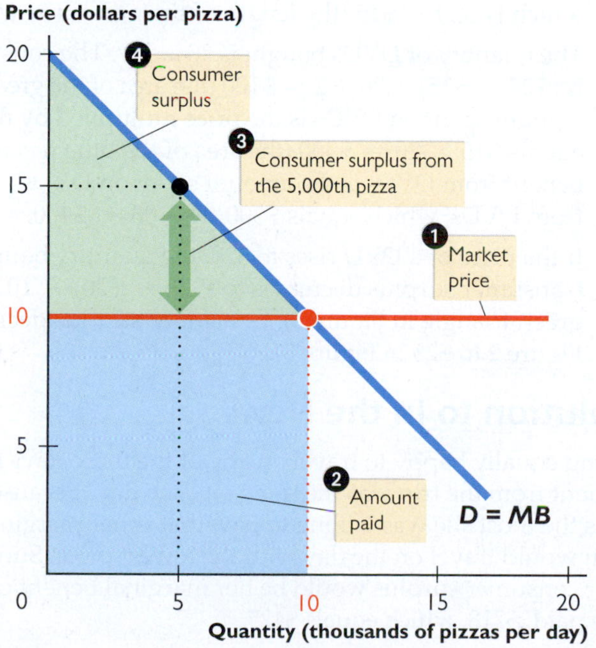

❶ The market price of a pizza is $10.

❷ At the market price, people buy 10,000 pizzas a day and spend $100,000 on pizza—the area of the blue rectangle.

❸ The demand curve tells us that people are willing to pay $15 for the 5,000th pizza, so consumer surplus on the 5,000th pizza is $5.

❹ Consumer surplus from the 10,000 pizzas that people buy is $50,000—the area of the green triangle.

The total benefit from pizza is the $100,000 that people pay plus the $50,000 consumer surplus they receive, or $150,000.

■⊢ CHECKPOINT 6.2

Distinguish between value and price, and define consumer surplus.

Practice Problems

Figure 1 shows the demand curve for DVDs and the market price of a DVD.

1. What is the willingness to pay for the 20th DVD? Calculate the value of the 10th DVD and the consumer surplus on the 10th DVD.

2. What is the quantity of DVDs bought? Calculate the consumer surplus, the amount spent on DVDs, and the total benefit from the DVDs bought.

3. If the price of a DVD rises to $20, what is the change in consumer surplus?

In the News

Airfares stacked against consumers
The airlines change prices from day to day. For example, the fare on one Delta flight from New York to Los Angeles jumped from $755 to $1,143 from a Friday to Saturday in April, then fell to $718 on Sunday.

Source: boston.com, June 22, 2011

Jodi planned a trip from New York to Los Angeles and was equally happy to travel on Friday, Saturday, or Sunday. The Saturday price was the most she was willing to pay. On which day do you predict she travelled and how much consumer surplus did she receive?

Solutions to Practice Problems

1. The willingness to pay for the 20th DVD is the price on the demand curve at 20 DVDs, which is $15 (Figure 2). The value of the 10th DVD is its marginal benefit, which is also the maximum price that someone is willing to pay for it. In Figure 2, the value of the 10th DVD is $20. The consumer surplus on the 10th DVD is its marginal benefit minus the price paid for the DVD, which is $20 − $15 (the length of the green arrow in Figure 2).

2. The quantity of DVDs bought is 20 a day. The consumer surplus from DVDs is ($25 − $15) × 20 ÷ 2 = $100 (the area of the green triangle in Figure 2). The amount spent on DVDs is the price multiplied by the quantity bought, which equals $15 × 20 = $300 (the area of the blue rectangle in Figure 2). The total benefit from DVDs is the amount spent on DVDs plus the consumer surplus from DVDs, which equals $300 + $100 = $400.

3. If the price of a DVD rises to $20, the quantity bought decreases to 10 a day. Consumer surplus decreases to ($25 − $20) × 10 ÷ 2 = $25 (the area of the green triangle in Figure 3). Consumer surplus decreases by $75 (from $100 in Figure 2 to $25 in Figure 3).

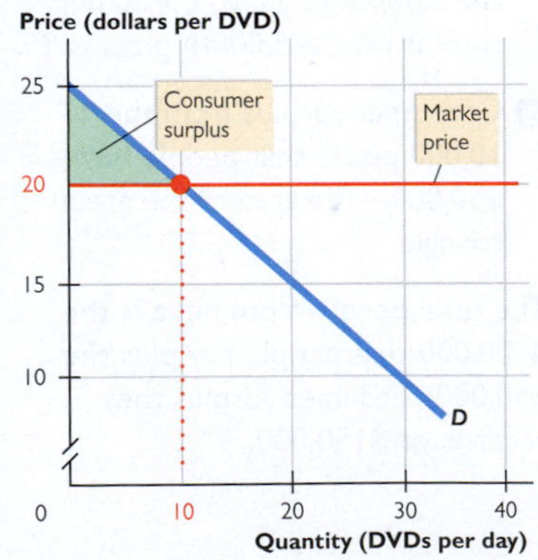

Solution to In the News

Being equally happy to travel on any of the three days means that Jodi's marginal benefit from the trip was the same on each day. Because Saturday's price of $1,143 was the most she was willing to pay, that is her marginal benefit. Being rational, Jodi would travel on the day with the lowest price, Sunday, and pay a fare of $718. Her consumer surplus would be her marginal benefit of $1,143 minus the price she paid, $718, which equals $425.

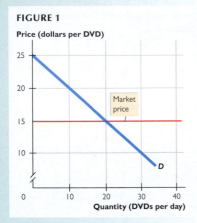

FIGURE 1
Price (dollars per DVD)

FIGURE 2
Price (dollars per DVD)

FIGURE 3
Price (dollars per DVD)

6.3   COST, PRICE, AND PRODUCER SURPLUS

MyEconLab Concept Video

You are now going to learn about cost, price, and producer surplus, which parallels what you've learned about value, price, and consumer surplus.

■ Supply and Marginal Cost

Just as buyers distinguish between *value* and *price,* so sellers distinguish between *cost* and *price.* Cost is what a seller must give up to produce the good, and price is what a seller receives when the good is sold. The cost of producing one more unit of a good or service is its *marginal cost.* It is just worth producing one more unit of a good or service if the price for which it can be sold equals marginal cost. The supply curve tells us this price. In Figure 6.6(a), the supply curve shows the quantity supplied at a given price—when the price of a pizza is $10, the quantity supplied is 10,000 pizzas a day. In Figure 6.6(b), the supply curve shows the minimum price that producers must receive to supply a given quantity—to supply 10,000 pizzas a day, producers must be able to get at least $10 for the 10,000th pizza. The marginal cost of the 10,000th pizza is $10. So:

> **A supply curve is a marginal cost curve. The supply curve of pizza tells us the dollars' worth of other goods and services that people must forgo if firms produce one more pizza.**

■ FIGURE 6.6

Supply, Minimum Supply Price, and Marginal Cost

MyEconLab Animation

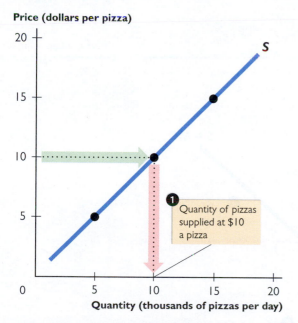

(a) Price determines quantity supplied

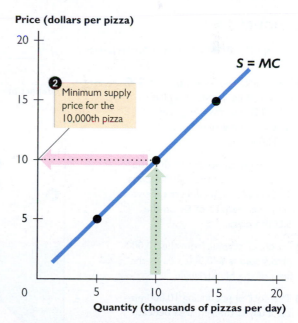

(b) Quantity determines minimum supply price

❶ The supply curve of pizza, *S,* shows the quantity of pizza supplied at each price, other things remaining the same. At $10 a pizza, the quantity supplied is 10,000 pizzas a day.

❷ The supply curve shows the minimum price that firms must be offered to supply a given quantity. The minimum supply price equals marginal cost, which for the 10,000th pizza is $10. The supply curve is also the marginal cost curve *MC.*

■ Producer Surplus

Producer surplus
The price of a good in excess of the marginal cost of producing it, summed over the quantity produced.

When the price exceeds marginal cost, the firm obtains a producer surplus. **Producer surplus** is the excess of the price of a good over the marginal cost of producing it, summed over the quantity produced.

Figure 6.7 illustrates the producer surplus for pizza producers. The supply curve of pizza tells us the quantity of pizza that producers plan to sell at each price. The supply curve also tells us the marginal cost of pizza at each quantity produced. If the price of a pizza is $10, producers plan to sell 10,000 pizzas a day. The total revenue from pizza is $100,000 per day.

To calculate producer surplus, we must find the producer surplus on each pizza and add these surpluses together. For the 10,000th pizza, marginal cost equals $10 and producers receive $10, so the producer surplus on this pizza is zero. For the 5,000th pizza (highlighted in the figure), marginal cost is $6. So on this pizza, producer surplus is $10 minus $6, which is $4. For the first pizza, marginal cost is $2, so on this pizza, producer surplus is $10 minus $2, which is $8.

Producer surplus—the sum of the producer surpluses on the 10,000 pizzas that firms produce—is $40,000 a day, which is shown by the area of the blue triangle. The base of the triangle is 10,000 pizzas a day and its height is $8, so its area is (10,000 × $8) ÷ 2 = $40,000.

The total cost of producing pizza is the amount received from selling it, $100,000, minus the producer surplus, $40,000 (the area of the blue triangle), and is $60,000 (the red area beneath the *MC* curve). Producer surplus is the total amount received minus the total cost, or net benefit to producers.

■ FIGURE 6.7

Supply and Producer Surplus

MyEconLab Animation

❶ The market price of a pizza is $10. At this price, producers plan to sell 10,000 pizzas a day and receive a total revenue of $100,000 a day.

❷ The supply curve shows that the marginal cost of the 5,000th pizza a day is $6, so producers receive a producer surplus of $4 on the 5,000th pizza.

❸ Producer surplus from the 10,000 pizzas sold is $40,000 a day—the area of the blue triangle.

❹ The cost of producing 10,000 pizzas a day is the red area beneath the marginal cost curve. It equals total revenue of $100,000 minus producer surplus of $40,000 and is $60,000 a day.

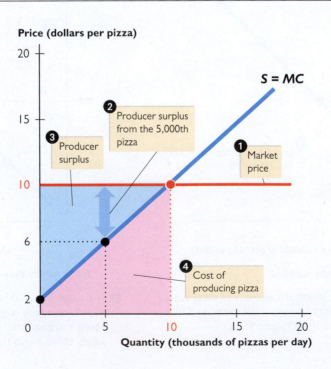

CHECKPOINT 6.3

MyEconLab Study Plan 6.3
Key Terms Quiz
Solutions Video

Distinguish between cost and price, and define producer surplus.

Practice Problems

Figure 1 shows the supply curve of DVDs and the market price of a DVD.

1. What is the minimum supply price of the 20th DVD? Calculate the marginal cost of the 10th DVD and the producer surplus on the 10th DVD.

2. What is the quantity of DVDs sold? Calculate the producer surplus, the total revenue from the DVDs sold, and the cost of producing the DVDs sold.

3. If the price of a DVD falls to $10, what is the change in producer surplus?

In the News

BlackBerry looks for reboot with Android

BlackBerry, the pioneer of smartphones, has almost vanished as Android and Apple phones have dominated the market. BlackBerry is now betting its future on using the Android operating system.

Source: *Financial Times*, November 6, 2015

As people have switched from BlackBerry to Android and Apple smartphones, how has BlackBerry's producer surplus changed? How has the producer surplus of Apple and the Android smartphone makers such as Samsung and LG changed?

Solutions to Practice Problems

1. The minimum supply price of the 20th DVD is the marginal cost of the 20th DVD, which is $15 (Figure 2). The marginal cost of the 10th DVD is equal to the minimum supply price for the 10th DVD, which is $10. The producer surplus on the 10th DVD is its market price minus the marginal cost of producing it, which is $15 − $10 = $5 (the blue arrow in Figure 2).

2. The quantity sold is 20 a day. Producer surplus equals ($15 − $5) × 20 ÷ 2, which is $100 (the area of the blue triangle in Figure 2). The total revenue is price multiplied by quantity sold, which equals $15 × 20 = $300. The cost of producing DVDs equals total revenue minus producer surplus, which is $300 − $100 = $200 (the red area in Figure 2).

3. If the price falls to $10, the quantity sold decreases to 10 a day. The producer surplus decreases to ($10 − $5) × 10 ÷ 2 = $25 (the area of the blue triangle in Figure 3). The change in producer surplus is a decrease of $75 (from $100 down to $25).

Solution to In the News

Producer surplus is the excess of the price of a good over the marginal cost of producing it, summed over the quantity produced.

For BlackBerry, the demand for its phones decreased, the price fell, and quantity sold decreased. BlackBerry's producer surplus decreased.

For Apple and the Android smartphone makers, demand increased, the quantity sold increased, and their producer surplus increased.

FIGURE 1

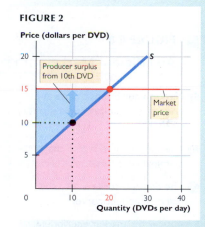

FIGURE 2

FIGURE 3

6.4 ARE MARKETS EFFICIENT?

You've seen (pp. 145–146) that an efficient allocation of resources is the highest-valued allocation, and it occurs when marginal benefit equals marginal cost. Continuing with the pizza example, the efficient quantity of pizza is the quantity that people value most highly, the quantity at which the marginal benefit of pizza equals its marginal cost.

The market forces that you studied in Chapter 4 (pp. 100–101) determine the equilibrium quantity and equilibrium price and coordinate the plans of buyers and sellers. Figure 6.8 shows the market for pizza in equilibrium. The demand curve is *D*, the supply curve is *S*, the equilibrium price is $10 a pizza, and the equilibrium quantity is 10,000 pizzas a day.

Does this competitive equilibrium deliver the efficient quantity of pizza?

■ Marginal Benefit Equals Marginal Cost

To check whether the equilibrium in Figure 6.8 is efficient, recall the interpretation of the demand curve as a marginal benefit curve and the supply curve as a marginal cost curve. The demand curve tells us the marginal benefit from pizza. The supply curve tells us the marginal cost of pizza. Where the demand curve and the supply curve intersect, marginal benefit equals marginal cost.

■ **FIGURE 6.8**

An Efficient Market for Pizza

❶ Market equilibrium occurs at a price of $10 a pizza and a quantity of 10,000 pizzas a day.

❷ The supply curve is also the marginal cost curve.

❸ The demand curve is also the marginal benefit curve.

Because at the market equilibrium, marginal benefit equals marginal cost, ❹ the efficient quantity of pizza is produced. The sum of the ❺ consumer surplus and ❻ producer surplus is maximized.

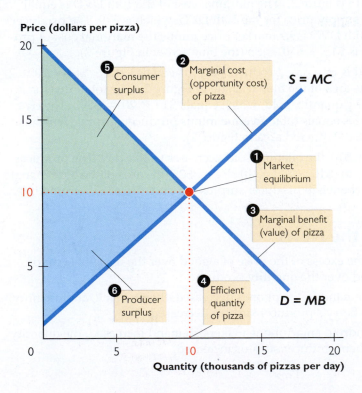

This condition—marginal benefit equals marginal cost—is the condition that delivers an efficient use of resources. Because a competitive equilibrium allocates resources to the activities that create the greatest possible value, it is efficient.

■ Total Surplus Is Maximized

Another way of checking that the equilibrium is efficient is to look at the total surplus that it generates. **Total surplus** is the sum of producer surplus and consumer surplus. A price above the equilibrium might increase producer surplus, but it would decrease consumer surplus by more. And a price below the equilibrium price might increase consumer surplus, but it would decrease producer surplus by more. The competitive equilibrium price maximizes total surplus.

> **Total surplus**
> The sum of producer surplus and consumer surplus.

In Figure 6.8, if production is less than 10,000 pizzas a day, someone is willing to buy a pizza for more than it costs to produce. Buyers and sellers will gain if production increases. If production exceeds 10,000 pizzas a day, it costs more to produce a pizza than anyone is willing to pay for it. Buyers and sellers will gain if production decreases. Only when 10,000 pizzas a day are produced is there no unexploited gain from changing the quantity of pizza produced, and total surplus is maximized.

Buyers and sellers each attempt to do the best they can for themselves—they pursue their self-interest. No one plans for an efficient outcome for society as a whole. No one worries about the social interest. Buyers seek the lowest possible price, and sellers seek the highest possible price. But as buyers and sellers pursue their self-interest, this astonishing outcome occurs: The social interest is served.

■ The Invisible Hand

Writing in his *Wealth of Nations* in 1776, Adam Smith was the first to suggest that competitive markets send resources to the uses in which they have the highest value. Smith believed that each participant in a competitive market is "led by an invisible hand to promote an end [the efficient use of resources] which was no part of his intention."

You can see the effects of the invisible hand at work every day. Your campus bookstore is stuffed with texts at the start of each term. It has the quantities that it predicts students will buy. The coffee shop has the variety and quantities of drinks and snacks that people plan to buy. Your local clothing store has the sweatpants and socks and other items that you plan to buy. Truckloads of textbooks, coffee and cookies, and sweatpants and socks roll along our highways and bring these items to where you and your friends want to buy them. Firms that don't know you anticipate your wants and work hard to help you satisfy them.

No government organizes all this production, and no government auditor monitors producers to ensure that they serve the social interest. The allocation of scarce resources is not planned. It happens because prices adjust to make buying plans and selling plans compatible, and it happens in a way that sends resources to the uses in which they have the highest value.

Adam Smith explained why all this amazing activity occurs. "It is not from the benevolence of the butcher, the brewer, or the baker that we expect our dinner," he wrote, "but from their regard to their own interest."

Publishing companies, coffee growers, garment manufacturers, and a host of other producers are led by their regard for *their* own interest to serve *your* interest.

EYE on the U.S. ECONOMY

The Invisible Hand and e-Commerce

You can see Adam Smith's invisible hand idea in the cartoon.

On a hot sunny day, a cold-drinks vendor approaches a man sitting in a park reading a newspaper (the top frame). The vendor has both cold drinks and shade and an opportunity cost and a minimum supply-price of each item. The park bench reader has a marginal benefit from a cold drink and from shade.

A transaction occurs and the invisible hand does its work (the middle frame). The park bench reader buys the vendor's sun shade. This transaction tells us that the reader's marginal benefit from shade exceeds the vendor's marginal cost of shade.

After the transaction (bottom frame), the vendor obtains a producer surplus from selling the shade for more than its opportunity cost, and the reader obtains a consumer surplus from buying the shade for less than its marginal benefit. Both the buyer of shade and the seller are better off.

The umbrella has moved to its highest-valued use and the resource is being used efficiently.

© The New Yorker Collection 1985
Mike Twohy from cartoonbank.com. All Rights Reserved.

The market economy performs activity similar to that illustrated in the cartoon to achieve an efficient allocation of resources. New technologies have cut the cost of using the Internet and during the past few years, hundreds of Web sites have been established that are dedicated to facilitating trade in all types of goods, services, and factors of production.

The electronic auction site eBay (http://www.ebay.com/) has brought a huge increase in consumer surplus and producer surplus, and helps to achieve ever-greater allocative efficiency.

■ Market Failure

You've seen that a competitive market in equilibrium delivers an efficient outcome. But not all markets are competitive and sometimes a competitive market is prevented from achieving an equilibrium. We call a situation in which a market delivers an inefficient outcome a **market failure**. Either too little of an item is produced—*underproduction*—or too much—*overproduction*.

Market failure
An inefficient market outcome.

Underproduction and Overproduction

When underproduction occurs, marginal benefit exceeds marginal cost. Items *not* produced are worth more than they cost. When overproduction occurs, marginal cost exceeds marginal benefit. Items produced cost more than they are worth.

Figure 6.9(a) illustrates underproduction at 5,000 pizzas a day. Every pizza between 5,000 and 9,999 is worth more than it costs to make but it is not produced. Figure 6.9(b) illustrates overproduction at 15,000 pizzas a day. Every pizza produced between 10,001 and 15,000 costs more to make than it is worth.

Deadweight Loss

A **deadweight loss** is the decrease in total surplus that results from inefficient underproduction or overproduction. It is a *social* loss.

The deadweight loss from underproduction equals the area of the gray triangle in Figure 6.9(a). That area is $22,500 [($15 − $6) × 5,000 ÷ 2 = $22,500]. Can you calculate the deadweight loss from overproduction in Figure 6.9(b)?

Deadweight loss
The decrease in total surplus that results from an inefficient underproduction or overproduction.

■ FIGURE 6.9

Inefficient Outcomes

MyEconLab Animation

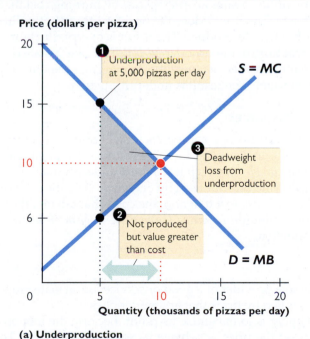

(a) Underproduction

❶ If production is 5,000 pizzas a day, ❷ pizzas not produced are worth more than they cost to make—there is inefficient underproduction. ❸ The gray triangle shows the deadweight loss that arises.

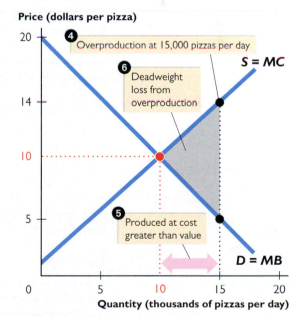

(b) Overproduction

❹ If production is 15,000 pizzas a day, ❺ pizzas produced cost more to make than they are worth—there is inefficient overproduction. ❻ The gray triangle shows the deadweight loss that arises.

■ Sources of Market Failure

Obstacles to efficiency that bring market failure and create deadweight losses are

- Price and quantity regulations
- Taxes and subsidies
- Externalities
- Public goods and common resources
- Monopoly
- High transactions costs

Price and Quantity Regulations

Price regulations that put a cap on the rent a landlord is permitted to charge and laws that require employers to pay a minimum wage sometimes block the price adjustments that balance the quantity demanded and the quantity supplied and lead to underproduction. *Quantity regulations* that limit the amount that a farm is permitted to produce also lead to underproduction.

Taxes and Subsidies

Taxes increase the prices paid by buyers and lower the prices received by sellers. So taxes decrease the quantity produced and lead to underproduction. *Subsidies*, which are payments by the government to producers, decrease the prices paid by buyers and increase the prices received by sellers. So subsidies increase the quantity produced and lead to overproduction.

Externalities

An *externality* is a cost or a benefit that affects someone other than the seller and the buyer of a good. An electric utility creates an *external cost* by burning coal that brings acid rain and crop damage. The utility doesn't consider the cost of pollution when it decides how much power to produce. The result is overproduction.

A condominium owner would provide an *external benefit* if she installed a smoke detector. But she doesn't consider her neighbor's marginal benefit and decides not to install a smoke detector. The result is underproduction.

Public Goods and Common Resources

A *public good* benefits everyone and no one can be excluded from its benefits. National defense is an example. It is in everyone's self-interest to avoid paying for a public good (called the *free-rider problem*), which leads to its underproduction.

A *common resource* is owned by no one but used by everyone. Atlantic salmon is an example. It is in everyone's self-interest to ignore the costs that fall on others as a result of their own use of a common resource (called the *tragedy of the commons*), which leads to overproduction.

Monopoly

A *monopoly* is a firm that is the sole provider of a good or service. Local water supply and cable television are supplied by firms that are monopolies.

The self-interest of a monopoly is to maximize its profit. Because the monopoly has no competitors, it can set the price to achieve its self-interested goal. To achieve its goal, a monopoly produces too little and charges too high a price, which leads to underproduction.

High Transactions Costs

Stroll around a shopping mall and observe the retail markets in which you participate. You'll see that these markets employ enormous quantities of scarce labor and capital resources. It is costly to operate any market. Economists call the opportunity costs of making trades in a market **transactions costs**.

To use market prices as the allocators of scarce resources, it must be worth bearing the opportunity cost of establishing a market. Some markets are just too costly to operate. For example, when you want to play tennis on your local "free" court, you don't pay a market price for your slot on the court. You hang around until the court becomes vacant, and you "pay" with your waiting time.

When transactions costs are high, the market might underproduce.

Transactions costs
The opportunity costs of making trades in a market.

■ Alternatives to the Market

When a market is inefficient, can one of the alternative non-market methods that we described at the beginning of this chapter do a better job? Sometimes it can.

Table 6.1 summarizes the sources of market failure and the possible remedies. Often, majority rule might be used, but majority rule has its own shortcomings. A group that pursues the self-interest of its members can become the majority. For example, price and quantity regulations that create deadweight loss are almost always the result of a self-interested group becoming the majority and imposing costs on the minority. Also, with majority rule, votes must be translated into actions by bureaucrats who have their own agendas.

Managers in firms issue commands and avoid the transactions costs that they would incur if they went to a market every time they needed a job done. First-come, first-served saves a lot of hassle in waiting lines. These lines could have markets in which people trade their place in the line—but someone would have to enforce the agreements. Can you imagine the hassle at a busy Starbucks if you had to buy your spot at the head of the line?

There is no one mechanism for allocating resources efficiently. But markets bypassed by command systems inside firms and supplemented by majority rule and first-come, first-served do an amazingly good job.

■ TABLE 6.1

Market Failure and Some Possible Remedies

Reason for market failure	Possible remedy
1. Price and quantity regulations	Remove regulation by majority rule
2. Taxes and subsidies	Minimize deadweight loss by majority rule
3. Externalities	Minimize deadweight loss by majority rule
4. Public goods	Allocate by majority rule
5. Common resources	Allocate by majority rule
6. Monopoly	Regulate by majority rule
7. High transactions costs	Command or first-come, first-served

MyEconLab Study Plan 6.4
Key Terms Quiz
Solutions Video

FIGURE 1

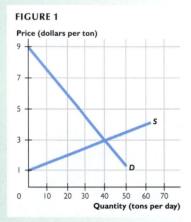

CHECKPOINT 6.4

Evaluate the efficiency of the alternative methods of allocating resources.

Practice Problems

Figure 1 shows the market for paper.

1. At the market equilibrium, what are consumer surplus, producer surplus, and total surplus? Is the market for paper efficient? Why or why not?

2. Lobbyists for a group of news magazines persuade the government to pass a law that requires producers to sell 50 tons of paper a day. Is the market for paper efficient? Explain your answer and illustrate it on the figure.

3. An environmental lobbying group persuades the government to pass a law that limits the quantity of paper that producers sell to 20 tons a day. Is the market for paper efficient? If not, what is the deadweight loss?

In the News

Milking taxpayers

American corn and soybean farmers receive subsidies of about $20 billion a year.

Source: *The Economist*, February 14, 2015

Because they receive subsidies, the price they receive for their crops exceeds the market price. Describe the efficiency of the markets for corn and soybean with subsidies in place. If the subsidies (and the taxes that pay them) were decreased, explain how the efficiency of the markets for corn and soybean would change.

FIGURE 2

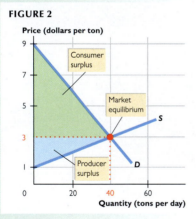

Solutions to Practice Problems

1. Market equilibrium is 40 tons a day at a price of $3 a ton (Figure 2). Consumer surplus is ($9 − $3) × 40 ÷ 2, which equals $120 (the area of the green triangle in Figure 2). Producer surplus is ($3 − $1) × 40 ÷ 2, which equals $40 (the area of the blue triangle in Figure 2). Total surplus is the sum of consumer surplus and producer surplus, which is $160.
   The market is efficient because marginal benefit (on the demand curve) equals marginal cost (on the supply curve) and total surplus (consumer surplus plus producer surplus) is maximized.

2. With producers required to sell 50 tons of paper a day, the market is inefficient because marginal cost exceeds marginal benefit. Deadweight loss equals the area of the gray triangle 1 in Figure 3.

3. With production limited to 20 tons a day, the market is inefficient because marginal benefit exceeds marginal cost. The deadweight loss equals the area of the gray triangle 2 in Figure 3.

FIGURE 3

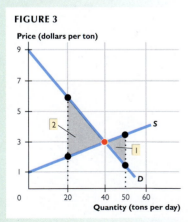

Solution to In the News

Subsidies to producers induce overproduction and increase the supply of the good. With no change in demand, the market price falls. The price received by producers equals the market price plus the subsidy. Market failure occurs and the market is inefficient. A deadweight loss arises. By decreasing the subsidies (and taxes), overproduction would decrease, the markets for corn and soybean would become more efficient, and the deadweight loss would decrease.

6.5 ARE MARKETS FAIR?

MyEconLab Concept Video

Following a severe winter storm or hurricane, the prices of many essential items jump. Is it fair that disaster victims should be hit with higher prices? Many low-skilled people work for a wage that is below what most would regard as a living wage. Is that fair? How do we decide whether something is fair or unfair?

Economists have a clear definition of efficiency but they do not have a similarly clear definition of fairness. Also, ideas about fairness are not exclusively economic ideas. They involve the study of ethics.

To study ideas about fairness, think of economic life as a game—a serious game—that has *rules* and a *result*. Two broad and generally conflicting approaches to fairness are

- It's not fair if the *rules* aren't fair.
- It's not fair if the *result* isn't fair.

■ It's Not Fair If the *Rules* Aren't Fair

Harvard philosopher Robert Nozick argued for the fair-rules view in a book entitled *Anarchy, State, and Utopia*, published in 1974. Nozick argued that fairness requires two rules:

- The state must establish and protect private property rights.
- Goods and services and the services of factors of production may be transferred from one person to another only by voluntary exchange with everyone free to engage in such exchange.

The first rule says that everything that is valuable—all scarce resources and goods—must be owned by individuals and that the state must protect private property rights. The second rule says that the only way a person can acquire something is to buy it in voluntary trade.

If these rules are followed, says Nozick, the outcome is fair. It doesn't matter how unequally the economic pie is shared provided that the people who bake it supply their services voluntarily in exchange for the share of the pie offered in compensation. Opportunity is equal but the result might be unequal. This fair-rules approach is consistent with allocative efficiency.

■ It's Not Fair If the *Result* Isn't Fair

Most people think that the fair-rules approach leads to too much inequality—to an unfair result: For example, it is unfair for a bank president to earn millions of dollars a year while a bank teller earns only thousands of dollars a year.

But what is "too unequal"? Is it fair for some people to receive twice as much as others but not ten times as much or a hundred times as much? Or is all that matters that the poorest people shouldn't be "too poor"?

There is no easy answer to these questions. Generally, greater equality is regarded as good but there is no measure of the most desirable shares.

The fair-result approach conflicts with allocative efficiency and leads to what is called the **big tradeoff**—a tradeoff between efficiency and fairness that recognizes the cost of making income transfers.

The big tradeoff is based on the fact that income can be transferred to people with low incomes only by taxing people with high incomes. But taxing people's

Big tradeoff
A tradeoff between efficiency and fairness that recognizes the cost of making income transfers.

EYE on PRICE GOUGING

MyEconLab Critical Thinking Exercise

Should Price Gouging Be Illegal?

Price gouging is the practice of selling an essential item for a much higher price than normal, and usually occurs following a natural disaster. In Florida and Texas, where hurricanes happen all too often, price gouging is illegal.

Whether price gouging *should* be illegal depends on the view of fairness employed and on the facts about whether the buyers or the sellers are the poorer group.

The standard view of economists is that price gouging should *not* be illegal and that it is the expected and *efficient* response to a change in demand.

After a hurricane, the demand for items such as generators, pumps, lamps, gasoline, and camp stoves increases and the prices of these items rise in a natural response to the change in demand.

The figure illustrates the market for camp stoves. The supply of stoves is the curve S, and in normal times, the demand for stoves is D_0. The price is $20 per stove and the equilibrium quantity is 5 stoves per day.

Following a hurricane that results in a lengthy power outage, the demand for camp stoves increases to D_1. Provided there is no price-gouging law, the equilibrium price of a stove jumps to $40 and the equilibrium quantity increases to 7 stoves per day.

This outcome is efficient because the marginal cost of a stove (on the supply curve) equals the marginal benefit from a stove (on the demand curve).

If a strict price-gouging law requires the price after the hurricane to be the *same* as the price before the hurricane, the price of a stove is stuck at $20.

At this price, the quantity of stoves supplied remains at 5 per day and a deadweight loss shown by the gray triangle arises. The price-gouging law is inefficient, and the price rise is efficient.

Whether a doubling of the price is *fair* depends on the idea of fairness used. On the *fair-rules* view, the price rise is fair. Trade is voluntary and both the buyer and the seller are better off. On the *fair-result* view, the price rise might be considered unfair if the buyers are poor and the sellers are rich. But if the buyers are rich and the sellers are poor, the price rise would be considered fair even on the fair-result view.

After Hurricane Katrina, John Shepperson bought 19 generators, loaded them into a rented U-Haul vehicle, and drove the 600 miles from his home in Kentucky to a place in Mississippi that had no power. He offered his generators to eager buyers for twice the price he had paid for them. But before he could complete a sale, the Mississippi police swooped in and arrested him. They confiscated his generators and put him in jail for four days. His crime: price gouging.

Was it efficient to stop Mr. Shepperson from selling his generators? Was it fair either to him or his deprived customers?

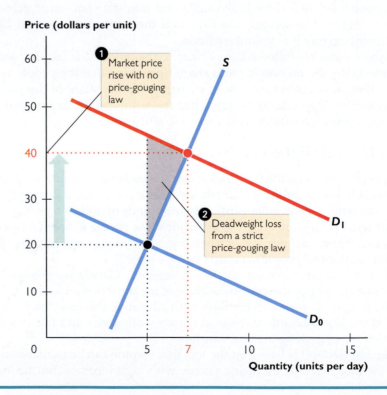

① Market price rise with no price-gouging law

② Deadweight loss from a strict price-gouging law

EYE on YOUR LIFE
Allocation Methods, Efficiency, and Fairness

MyEconLab Critical Thinking Exercise

You live in the national economy, your state economy, your regional economy, and your own household economy. The many decisions you must make affect efficiency and fairness at all these levels. Think about your household economy.

Make a spreadsheet and on it identify all the factors of production that your household owns. Count all the person-hours available and any capital.

Show how these resources are allocated.

By what methods are your household's scarce resources allocated? Identify those allocated by market price; by command; by first-come, first-served; and by equal shares. Are any resources allocated by majority vote?

Now the tough part: Are these resources allocated efficiently—is the value of your household's resources maximized? Think about how you can check whether marginal benefit equals marginal cost for each of your household's activities.

And now an even tougher question: Are your household's resources allocated fairly? Think about the two ideas of fairness and how they apply in your household.

---

income from employment discourages work. It results in the quantity of labor being less than the efficient quantity. Taxing the income people earn from capital discourages saving and results in the quantity of capital being less than the efficient quantity. With smaller quantities of both labor and capital, the quantity of goods and services produced is less than the efficient quantity. The economic pie shrinks.

Income redistribution creates a tradeoff between the size of the economic pie and the equality with which it is shared. The greater the scale of income redistribution through income taxes, the greater is the inefficiency—the smaller is the pie.

There is a second source of inefficiency: A dollar taken from a rich person does not end up as a dollar in the hands of a poorer person. Some of the dollar is spent on administration of the tax and transfer system, which includes the cost of accountants, auditors, and lawyers. These activities use skilled labor and capital resources that could otherwise be used to produce other goods and services that people value.

You can see that when all these costs are taken into account, transferring a dollar from a rich person does not give a dollar to a poor person. It is even possible that those with low incomes end up being worse off. For example, if a highly taxed entrepreneur decides to work less hard and shut down a business, low-income workers get fired and must seek other, perhaps even lower-paid, work.

■ Compromise

Most people, and probably most economists, have sympathy with the Nozick view but think it too extreme. They see a role for taxes and government income support schemes to transfer some income from the rich to the poor. Such transfers could be considered voluntary in the sense that they are decided by majority voting, and even those who vote against such transfers voluntarily participate in the political process.

Once we agree that using the tax system to make transfers from the rich to the poor is fair, we need to determine just what we mean by a fair tax. We'll look at this big question when we study the tax system in Chapter 8.

MyEconLab Study Plan 6.5
Key Terms Quiz
Solutions Video

CHECKPOINT 6.5

Explain the main ideas about fairness, and evaluate the fairness of the alternative methods of allocating scarce resources.

Practice Problems

A winter storm cuts the power supply and isolates a small town in the mountains. The people rush to buy candles from the town store, which is the only source of candles. The store owner decides to ration the candles to one per family but to keep the price of a candle unchanged.

1. Who gets to use the candles? Who receives the consumer surplus and who receives the producer surplus on candles?

2. Is the allocation efficient? Is the allocation fair?

In the News

Water wars are coming

Water use is growing at a faster pace than the rate of population growth. Earth has lots of water, but 97.5 percent of it is in the oceans and is salty. The problem is that a growing number of people have no clean fresh drinking water.

Source: PBS, November 16, 2015

Would a free world market in fresh water achieve a fair use of the world's water resources? Explain why or why not and be clear about the concept of fairness that you are using.

Solutions to Practice Problems

1. The people who buy candles from the town store are not necessarily the people who use the candles. A buyer from the town store can sell a candle and will do so if he or she can get a price that exceeds his or her marginal benefit. The people who value the candles most—who are willing to pay the most—will use the candles.

   Only the people who are willing to pay the most for candles receive the consumer surplus on candles, and the store owner receives the same producer surplus as normal. People who sell the candles they buy from the store receive additional producer surplus.

2. The allocation is efficient because the people who value the candles most use them. Whether the allocation is fair depends on which of the two views of fairness is adopted. In the fair-rules view, if the rule of one candle per family is followed and exchange is voluntary, then the outcome is fair. But in the fair-result view, if the candles are allocated unequally, then the allocation is unfair.

Solution to In the News

If the world market in fresh water were free, the market price would allocate the water. This allocation of water would be fair on the fair-rules view because the exchange of water would be voluntary, but it would not be fair on the fair-result view because poor people who own no water and those living in drought-stricken areas would not be able to afford water.

CHAPTER SUMMARY

Key Points

1. **Describe the alternative methods of allocating scarce resources, and define and explain the features of an efficient allocation.**

- The methods of allocating scarce resources are market price; command; majority rule; contest; first-come, first-served; sharing equally; lottery; personal characteristics; and force.
- Allocative efficiency occurs when resources are used to create the greatest value, which means that marginal benefit equals marginal cost.

2. **Distinguish between value and price, and define consumer surplus.**

- Marginal benefit is measured by the maximum price that consumers are willing to pay for another unit of a good or service.
- A demand curve is a marginal benefit curve.
- Value is what people are *willing to* pay; price is what they *must* pay.
- Consumer surplus equals the excess of marginal benefit over price, summed over the quantity consumed.

3. **Distinguish between cost and price, and define producer surplus.**

- Marginal cost is measured by the minimum price producers must be offered to increase production by one unit.
- A supply curve is a marginal cost curve.
- Opportunity cost is what producers *must* pay; price is what they *receive*.
- Producer surplus equals the excess of price over marginal cost, summed over the quantity produced.

4. **Evaluate the efficiency of the alternative methods of allocating resources.**

- In a competitive equilibrium, marginal benefit equals marginal cost and resource allocation is efficient.
- Price and quantity regulations, taxes, subsidies, externalities, public goods, common resources, monopoly, and high transactions costs lead to market failure and create deadweight loss.

5. **Explain the main ideas about fairness, and evaluate the fairness of the alternative methods of allocating scarce resources.**

- Ideas about fairness divide into two groups: fair *rules* and a fair *result*.
- Fair rules require private property rights and voluntary exchange, and a fair result requires income transfers from the rich to the poor.

Key Terms

Allocative efficiency, 143
Big tradeoff, 161
Command system, 141

Consumer surplus, 149
Deadweight loss, 157
Market failure, 157

Producer surplus, 152
Total surplus, 155
Transactions costs, 159

CHAPTER CHECKPOINT

Study Plan Problems and Applications

At McDonald's, no reservations are accepted; at the St. Louis Art Museum Restaurant, reservations are accepted; at Le Bernardin in New York, reservations are essential. Use this information to answer Problems **1** to **3**.

1. Describe the method of allocating table resources in these three restaurants.

2. Why do you think restaurants have different reservation policies, and why might each restaurant be using an efficient allocation method?

3. Why don't all restaurants use the market price to allocate their tables?

Table 1 shows the demand and supply schedules for sandwiches. Use Table 1 to work Problems **4** to **7**.

4. Calculate the equilibrium price of a sandwich, the consumer surplus, and the producer surplus. What is the efficient quantity of sandwiches?

5. If the quantity demanded decreases by 100 sandwiches an hour at each price, what is the equilibrium price and what is the change in total surplus?

6. If the quantity supplied decreases by 100 sandwiches an hour at each price, what is the equilibrium price and what is the change in total surplus?

7. If Sandwiches To Go, Inc., buys all the sandwich producers and cuts production to 100 sandwiches an hour, what is the deadweight loss that is created? If Sandwiches To Go, Inc., rations sandwiches to two per person, by what view of fairness would the allocation be unfair?

Use the following information to work Problems **8** and **9**.

Table 2 shows the demand and supply schedules for sandbags before and during a major flood. During the flood, suppose that the government gave all families an equal quantity of sandbags. Resale of sandbags is not permitted.

8. How would total surplus and the price of a sandbag change?

9. Would the outcome be more efficient than if the government took no action? Explain.

10. The winner of the men's or women's tennis singles at the U.S. Open is paid twice as much as the runner-up, but it takes two players to have a singles final. Is this compensation arrangement efficient? Is it fair? Explain why it might illustrate the big tradeoff.

11. eBay saves billions for bidders

On eBay, the bidder who places the highest bid wins the auction and pays only what the second highest bidder offered. Researchers Wolfgang Jank and Galit Shmueli reported that purchasers on eBay in 2003 paid $7 billion less than their winning bids. Because each bid shows the buyer's willingness to pay, the winner receives an estimated consumer surplus of $4 or more.

Source: *InformationWeek*, January 28, 2008

What method is used to allocate goods on eBay? How does an eBay auction influence consumer surplus from the good?

 12. Read *Eye on Price Gouging* on p. 162 and explain why it was inefficient to stop Mr. Shepperson from selling his generators.

TABLE 1

Price (dollars per sandwich)	Quantity demanded	Quantity supplied
	(sandwiches per hour)	
0	400	0
1	350	50
2	300	100
3	250	150
4	200	200
5	150	250
6	100	300
7	50	350
8	0	400

TABLE 2

Price (dollars per bag)	Quantity demanded before flood	Quantity demanded during flood	Quantity supplied
	(thousands of bags)		
0	40	70	0
1	35	65	5
2	30	60	10
3	25	55	15
4	20	50	20
5	15	45	25
6	10	40	30
7	5	35	35
8	0	30	40

Instructor Assignable Problems and Applications

MyEconLab Homework, Quiz, or Test if assigned by instructor

1. **Mets World Series ticket prices spike after NLCS win**
   Now that the New York Mets are in baseball's World Series for the first time in 15 years, fans who don't have a ticket will pay a hefty $1,667.82 to get one. That's the average asking price for a resold ticket, which is the highest since World Series price-tracking started in 2010.

   Source: CNBC.com, October 22, 2015

   Why is a $1,667.82 ticket price similar to "price gouging"? Is the high price an example of the market price method of allocating scarce resources? Is the market for tickets efficient? Is it fair?

Table 1 shows the demand schedule for haircuts and the supply schedule of haircuts. Use Table 1 to work Problems **2** and **3**.

2. What is the quantity of haircuts bought, the value of a haircut, and the total surplus from haircuts?

3. Suppose that all salons agree to charge $40 a haircut. How do consumer surplus and producer surplus change? What is the deadweight loss created?

In California, farmers pay a lower price for water than do city residents. Use this information to work Problems **4** to **6**.

4. What is this method of allocation of water resources? Is this allocation of water efficient? Is this use of scarce water fair? Why or why not?

5. If farmers were charged the same price as city residents pay, how would the price of agricultural produce, the quantity of produce grown, consumer surplus, and producer surplus change?

6. If all water in California is sold for the market equilibrium price, would the allocation of water be more efficient? Why or why not?

Use the following information to work Problems **7** and **8**.

The world's largest tulip and flower market
Every day over 19 million tulips and flowers are auctioned at the Dutch market called "The Bloemenveiling." These Dutch auctions match buyers and sellers.

Source: Tulip-Bulbs.com

In a Dutch auction, the auctioneer announces the highest price. If no one offers to buy the flowers, the auctioneer lowers the price until a buyer is found.

7. What method is used to allocate flowers at the Bloemenveiling?

8. How does a Dutch flower auction influence consumer surplus and producer surplus? Are the flower auctions at the Bloemenveiling efficient?

9. **Take pride in U.S. forests**
   U.S. forestland has been a constant 755 million acres for the past century, but the number of trees has increased by 20 percent since 1970, the volume of wood has doubled since 1953, and the United States is the world's largest supplier of forest products. Decisions by millions of private forest-land owners are responsible for this remarkable performance.

   Source: Frank Beidler letter, *Chicago Tribune*, October 23, 2015

   Is the U.S. timber industry efficient and do forest-land owners operate in the social interest or self-interest? What effect does private ownership have on the efficiency of the timber industry?

TABLE 1

Price (dollars per haircut)	Quantity demanded	supplied
	(haircuts per day)	
0	100	0
10	80	0
20	60	20
30	40	40
40	20	60
50	0	80

MyEconLab Chapter 6 Study Plan

Multiple Choice Quiz

1. The method of allocation that most stores use during Thanksgiving sales is:

 A. a combination of market price and lottery
 B. first-come, first-served
 C. a combination of contest and command
 D. a combination of market price and first-come, first-served

2. All of the following statements are correct *except* _____.

 A. the value of an additional unit of the good equals the marginal benefit from the good
 B. marginal benefit is the excess of value over the price paid, summed over the quantity consumed
 C. the maximum price willingly paid for a unit of a good is the marginal benefit from it
 D. price is what we pay for a good but value is what we get from it

3. Choose the best statement.

 A. An increase in the demand for a good increases producer surplus.
 B. If producers decrease the supply of the good, their producer surplus will increase.
 C. Producer surplus equals the total revenue from selling the good.
 D. Producer surplus is the excess of the value of the good over the market price, summed over the quantity produced.

4. The market for a good is efficient if _____.

 A. the marginal cost of producing the good is minimized
 B. the marginal benefit from the good is maximized
 C. the consumer surplus is maximized
 D. the total surplus is maximized

5. When the marginal benefit from a good exceeds its marginal cost, _____.

 A. there is overproduction of the good
 B. a deadweight loss, which is the excess of marginal benefit over marginal cost, arises
 C. producer surplus decreases and consumer surplus increases
 D. total production increases and efficiency increases

6. Market failure arises if _____.

 A. there is overproduction of the good but not if there is underproduction
 B. the deadweight loss is zero
 C. producer surplus exceeds consumer surplus
 D. total surplus is not maximized

7. The allocation of resources is fair _____.

 A. in the fair-rules view if everyone has equal opportunity
 B. in the fair-result view if most resources are distributed to the poorest people
 C. in the fair-rules view if owners of the resources are protected by property rights and all transfers of resources are voluntary
 D. in the fair-result view if resources are transferred voluntarily so that everyone has the same quantity

A Fair Shot for Everyone
$10.10
per hour
#RaiseTheWage

A Fair Shot for Everyone

Can Congress repeal the law of market forces?

Government Actions in Markets

7

When you have completed your study of this chapter, you will be able to

1 Explain how a price ceiling works, and why a rent ceiling creates a housing shortage and is inefficient and unfair.

2 Explain how a price floor works, and why the minimum wage creates unemployment and is inefficient and unfair.

3 Explain how a production quota works, and why it brings a higher price and is inefficient and unfair.

MyEconLab Big Picture Video

7.1 PRICE CEILINGS

Congress might want to set a price or a quantity at a level that it chooses rather than at the level determined by market forces. What are the effects of this type of government action in a market? You'll find the answer in this chapter, starting with a government attempt to place an upper limit on a price.

A government regulation that places an *upper* limit on the price at which a particular good, service, or factor of production may be traded is called a **price ceiling** (or a **price cap**). Trading at a higher price is illegal.

A price ceiling has been used in several markets, but the one that looms largest in everyone's budget is the housing market. The price of housing is the rent that people pay for a house or apartment.

Figure 7.1 illustrates the apartment rental market in Biloxi, Mississippi. The rent is $550 a month, and 4,000 apartments are rented.

▪ A Rent Ceiling

Suppose the mayor of Biloxi gets elected on a promise to impose a **rent ceiling**— a regulation that makes it illegal to charge more than a specified rent for housing.

The effect of a rent ceiling depends on whether it is imposed at a level above or below the equilibrium rent. In Figure 7.1, if the rent ceiling is set *above* $550 a month, nothing would change because people are already paying $550 a month.

But a rent ceiling that is set *below* the equilibrium rent has powerful effects on the market outcome. The reason is that the rent ceiling attempts to prevent the rent from rising high enough to regulate the quantities demanded and supplied. The law and the market are in conflict, and one (or both) of them must yield.

Price ceiling or **price cap**
A government regulation that places an *upper* limit on the price at which a particular good, service, or factor of production may be traded.

Rent ceiling
A regulation that makes it illegal to charge more than a specified rent for housing.

■ **FIGURE 7.1**

A Housing Market

The figure shows the demand curve, *D*, and the supply curve, *S*, for rental housing.

❶ The market is in equilibrium when the quantity demanded equals the quantity supplied.

❷ The equilibrium price (rent) is $550 a month.

❸ The equilibrium quantity is 4,000 units of housing.

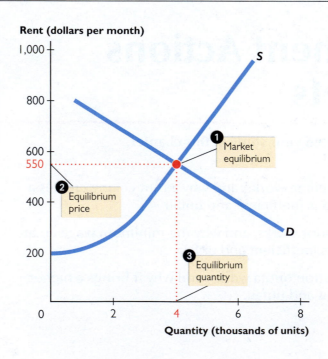

Figure 7.2 shows a rent ceiling that is set below the equilibrium rent at $400 a month. We've shaded the area *above* the rent ceiling because any rent in this region is illegal. The first effect of a rent ceiling is a housing shortage. At a rent of $400 a month, the quantity of housing supplied is 3,000 units and the quantity demanded is 6,000 units. So at $400 a month, there is a shortage of 3,000 units of housing.

But the story does not end here. The 3,000 units of housing that owners are willing to make available must somehow be allocated among people who are seeking 6,000 units. This allocation might be achieved in two ways:

- A black market
- Increased search activity

A Black Market

A **black market** is an illegal market that operates alongside a government-regulated market. A rent ceiling sometimes creates a black market in housing as frustrated renters and landlords try to find ways of raising the rent above the legally imposed ceiling. Landlords want higher rents because they know that renters are willing to pay more for the existing quantity of housing. Renters are willing to pay more to jump to the front of the line.

Because raising the rent is illegal, landlords and renters use creative tricks to get around the law. One of these tricks is for a new tenant to pay a high price for worthless fittings—perhaps paying $2,000 for threadbare drapes. Another is for the tenant to pay a high price for new locks and keys—called "key money."

Figure 7.3 shows how high the black market rent might go in Biloxi. With strict enforcement of the rent ceiling, the quantity of housing available is 3,000

Black market
An illegal market that operates alongside a government-regulated market.

■ **FIGURE 7.2**

A Rent Ceiling Creates a Shortage

MyEconLab Animation

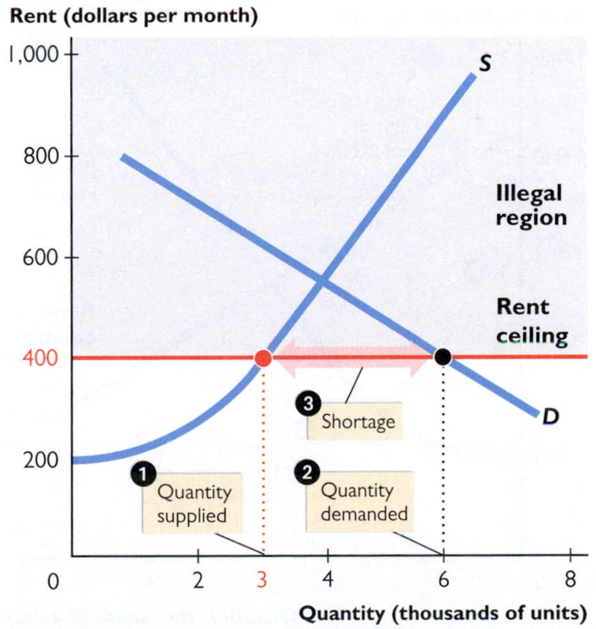

A rent ceiling is imposed below the equilibrium rent. In this example, the rent ceiling is $400 a month.

❶ The quantity of housing supplied decreases to 3,000 units.

❷ The quantity of housing demanded increases to 6,000 units.

❸ A shortage of 3,000 units arises.

units. But at this quantity, renters are willing to offer as much as $625 a month—the amount determined on the demand curve.

So a small number of landlords illegally offer housing for rents up to $625 a month. The black market rent might be at any level between the rent ceiling of $400 a month and the maximum that a renter is willing to pay of $625 a month.

Increased Search Activity

Search activity
The time spent looking for someone with whom to do business.

The time spent looking for someone with whom to do business is called **search activity**. We spend some time in search activity almost every time we buy something, and especially when we buy a big item such as a car or a home. When a price ceiling creates a shortage of housing, search activity *increases*. In a rent-controlled housing market, frustrated would-be renters do an Internet search or scan the newspapers. Keen apartment seekers race to be first on the scene when news of a possible apartment breaks.

The *opportunity cost* of a good is equal to its price *plus* the value of the search time spent finding the good. So the opportunity cost of housing is equal to the rent plus the value of the search time spent looking for an apartment. Search activity is costly. It uses time and other resources, such as telephones, automobiles, and gasoline that could have been used in other productive ways. In Figure 7.3, to find accommodation at $400 a month, someone who is willing to pay a rent of $625 a month would be willing to spend on search activity an amount that is equivalent to adding $225 a month to the rent ceiling.

A rent ceiling controls the rent portion of the cost of housing but not the search cost. So when the search cost is added to the rent, some people end up paying a higher opportunity cost for housing than they would if there were no rent ceiling.

FIGURE 7.3

A Rent Ceiling Creates a Black Market and Housing Search

MyEconLab Animation

With a rent ceiling of $400 a month,

❶ 3,000 units of housing are available.

❷ Someone is willing to pay $625 a month for the 3,000th unit of housing.

❸ Black market rent might be as high as $625 a month or search activity might be equivalent to adding $225 a month to the rent ceiling.

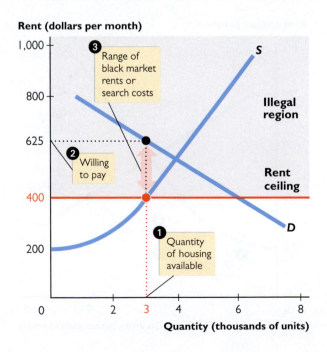

■ Are Rent Ceilings Efficient?

In a housing market with no rent ceiling, market forces determine the equilibrium rent. The quantity of housing demanded equals the quantity of housing supplied. In this situation, scarce housing resources are allocated efficiently because the marginal cost of housing equals the marginal benefit. Figure 7.4(a) shows this efficient outcome in the Biloxi apartment rental market. In this efficient market, total surplus—the sum of *consumer surplus* (the green area) and *producer surplus* (the blue area)—is maximized at the equilibrium rent and quantity of housing (see Chapter 6, pp. 154–155).

Figure 7.4(b) shows that with a rent ceiling, the outcome is inefficient. Marginal benefit from rented housing exceeds its marginal cost. Producer surplus and consumer surplus shrink, and a deadweight loss (the gray area) arises. This loss is borne by the people who can't find housing and by landlords who can't offer housing at the lower rent ceiling.

But the total loss *exceeds* the deadweight loss. Resources get used in costly search activity or in evading the law in the black market. The value of these resources might be as large as the area of the red rectangle. There is yet a further loss: the cost of enforcing the rent ceiling law. This loss, which is borne by taxpayers, is not visible in the figure.

■ **FIGURE 7.4**

The Inefficiency of a Rent Ceiling

MyEconLab Animation

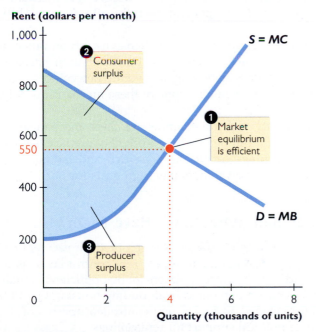

(a) Efficient housing market

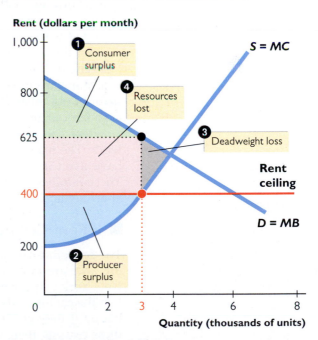

(b) Inefficient housing market

❶ The market equilibrium is efficient with marginal benefit equal to marginal cost. Total surplus, the sum of ❷ consumer surplus (green area) and ❸ producer surplus (blue area), is maximized.

A rent ceiling is inefficient. ❶ Consumer surplus and ❷ producer surplus shrink, a ❸ deadweight loss arises, and ❹ resources are lost in search activity and evading the rent ceiling law.

With rent ceilings, landlords have no incentive to maintain buildings, and both the quality and quantity of housing supplied decrease.

Although a rent ceiling creates inefficiency, not everyone loses. The people who pay the rent ceiling get an increase in consumer surplus, and landlords who charge a black market rent get an increase in producer surplus.

The costs of a rent ceiling that we've just considered are only the initial costs. With the rent below the market equilibrium rent, landlords have no incentive to maintain their buildings. So over time, both the quality and quantity of housing supplied *decrease* and the loss arising from a rent ceiling increases.

The size of the loss from a rent ceiling depends on the elasticities of supply and demand. If supply is inelastic, a rent ceiling brings a small decrease in the quantity of housing supplied. And if demand is inelastic, a rent ceiling brings a small increase in the quantity of housing demanded. So the more inelastic the supply or the demand, the smaller is the shortage of housing and the smaller is the deadweight loss.

■ Are Rent Ceilings Fair?

We've seen that rent ceilings prevent scarce resources from being allocated efficiently—resources do not flow to their highest-valued use. But don't they ensure that scarce housing resources are allocated more fairly?

You learned in Chapter 6 (pp. 161–163) that fairness is a complex idea about which there are two broad views: fair *rules* versus a fair *result*. Rent controls violate the fair-rules view of fairness because they block voluntary exchange. But do they deliver a fair result? Do rent ceilings ensure that scarce housing goes to the poor people whose need is greatest?

Blocking rent adjustments that bring the quantity of housing demanded into equality with the quantity supplied doesn't end scarcity. So when the law prevents the rent from adjusting and blocks the price mechanism from allocating scarce housing, some other allocation mechanism must be used. If that mechanism were one that provided the housing to the poorest, then the allocation might be regarded as fair.

But the mechanisms that get used do not usually achieve such an outcome. First-come, first-served is one allocation mechanism. Discrimination based on race, ethnicity, or sex is another. Discrimination against young newcomers and in favor of old established families is yet another. None of these mechanisms delivers a fair outcome.

Rent ceilings in New York City provide examples of these mechanisms at work. The main beneficiaries of rent ceilings in New York City are families who have lived in the city for a long time—including some rich and famous ones. These families enjoy low rents while newcomers pay high rents for hard-to-find apartments.

■ If Rent Ceilings Are So Bad, Why Do We Have Them?

The economic case against rent ceilings is now widely accepted, so *new* rent ceiling laws are rare. But when governments try to repeal rent control laws, as the New York City government did in 1999, current renters lobby politicians to maintain the ceilings. Also, people who are prevented from finding housing would be happy if they got lucky and managed to find a rent-controlled apartment. For these reasons, there is plenty of political support for rent ceilings.

Apartment owners who oppose rent ceilings are a minority, so their views are not a powerful influence on politicians. Because more people support rent ceilings than oppose them, politicians are sometimes willing to support them too.

CHECKPOINT 7.1

MyEconLab Study Plan 7.1
Key Terms Quiz
Solutions Video

Explain how a price ceiling works, and why a rent ceiling creates a housing shortage and is inefficient and unfair.

Practice Problems

Figure 1 shows the rental market for apartments in Corsicana, Texas.

1. What is the rent and how many apartments are rented? If a rent ceiling of $900 a month is set, what is the rent and how many apartments are rented?

2. If the city government imposes a rent ceiling of $600 a month, what is the rent and how many apartments are rented? If a black market develops, explain how high the black market rent could be.

3. If the city government imposes a rent ceiling of $600 a month and enforces it, is the housing market efficient? What is the deadweight loss? Is the housing market fair? Explain your answer.

In the News

A gas price ceiling
China has cut the price of natural gas and may install a price ceiling that prohibits a price rise of more than 20 percent above a benchmark.
Source: *Bloomberg News*, November 18, 2015

Explain how a cut in the price and a price ceiling will influence consumer surplus, producer surplus, and deadweight loss in China's natural gas market.

Solutions to Practice Problems

1. The equilibrium rent is $800 a month, and 3,000 apartments are rented. A rent ceiling of $900 a month is above the equilibrium rent, so the outcome is the market equilibrium rent of $800 a month with 3,000 apartments rented.

2. A rent ceiling at $600 a month is below the market equilibrium rent, so the number of apartments rented is 1,000 and the rent is $600 a month (Figure 2). In a black market, someone would be willing to rent an apartment for more than the rent ceiling. The highest rent that someone would offer is $1,200 a month. This rent equals someone's willingness to pay for the 1,000th apartment (Figure 2).

3. The housing market is not efficient. With 1,000 apartments rented, marginal benefit exceeds marginal cost and a deadweight loss arises (Figure 2). The deadweight loss is equal to the area of the gray triangle, which equals (1,200 − 600) × (3,000 − 1,000) ÷ 2. The deadweight loss is $600,000. The housing market is less fair on both views of fairness: It blocks voluntary transactions and does not provide more housing to those most in need.

Solution to In the News

If the price cut and price ceiling keeps the price below the market equilibrium price, then the quantity produced will decrease and a shortage of gas will arise. The marginal benefit from gas will exceed the marginal cost of producing gas, and resources will be used trying to obtain gas. The lower price and reduced quantity will decrease consumer surplus, decrease producer surplus, and create a deadweight loss.

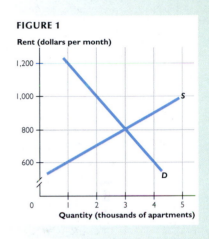

FIGURE 1
Rent (dollars per month)

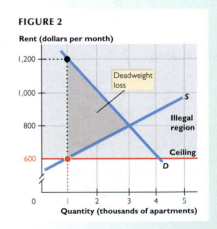

FIGURE 2
Rent (dollars per month)

Price floor

A government regulation that places a *lower* limit on the price at which a particular good, service, or factor of production may be traded.

7.2 PRICE FLOORS

You've seen the effects of a price ceiling. Let's now look at the effects of a **price floor**, a government regulation that places a *lower* limit on the price at which a particular good, service, or factor of production may be traded. Trading at a lower price than the price floor is illegal.

Price floors are used in many markets, but the one that looms largest is the labor market. The price of labor is the wage rate that people earn. Demand and supply in the labor market determine the wage rate and the quantity of labor employed.

Figure 7.5 illustrates the market for fast-food servers in Yuma, Arizona. In this market, the demand for labor curve is *D*. On this demand curve, at a wage rate of $13 an hour, the quantity of fast-food servers demanded is zero. If Subway, Burger King, Taco Bell, McDonald's, Wendy's, and the other fast-food places had to pay servers $13 an hour, they wouldn't hire any. They would replace servers with vending machines! But at wage rates below $13 an hour, they would hire servers. At a wage rate of $7 an hour, firms would hire 6,000 servers.

On the supply side of the market, no one is willing to work for $4 an hour. To attract servers, firms must pay more than $4 an hour.

Equilibrium in this market occurs at a wage rate of $7 an hour with 6,000 people employed as servers.

Suppose that the government thinks that no one should have to work for a wage rate as low as $7 an hour and decides that it wants to increase the wage rate. Can the government improve conditions for these workers by passing a minimum wage law? Let's find out.

■ **FIGURE 7.5**

A Market for Fast-Food Servers

The figure shows the demand curve, *D*, and the supply curve, *S*, for fast-food servers.

❶ The market is in equilibrium when the quantity demanded equals the quantity supplied.

❷ The equilibrium price (wage rate) is $7 an hour.

❸ The equilibrium quantity is 6,000 servers.

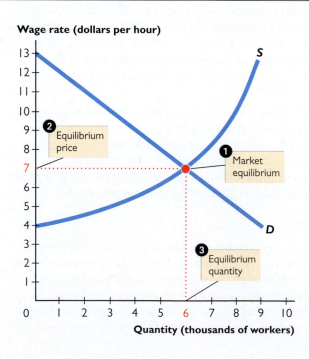

■ The Minimum Wage

A **minimum wage law** is a government regulation that makes hiring labor services for less than a specified wage illegal. Firms are free to pay a wage rate that exceeds the minimum wage but may not pay less than the minimum. A minimum wage is an example of a price floor.

The effect of a price floor depends on whether it is set below or above the equilibrium price. In Figure 7.5, the equilibrium wage rate is $7 an hour, and at this wage rate, firms hire 6,000 workers. If the government introduced a minimum wage below $7 an hour, nothing would change. The reason is that firms are already paying $7 an hour, and because this wage exceeds the minimum wage, the wage rate paid doesn't change. Firms continue to hire 6,000 workers.

But the aim of a minimum wage is to boost the incomes of low-wage earners. So in the markets for the lowest-paid workers, the minimum wage will exceed the equilibrium wage rate.

Suppose that the government introduces a minimum wage of $10 an hour. Figure 7.6 shows the effects of this law. Wage rates below $10 an hour are illegal, so we've shaded the illegal region *below* the minimum wage. Firms and workers are no longer permitted to operate at the equilibrium point in this market because it is in the illegal region. Market forces and political forces are in conflict.

The government can set a minimum wage, but it can't tell employers how many workers to hire. If firms must pay a wage rate of $10 an hour, they will hire only 3,000 workers. At the equilibrium wage rate of $7 an hour, firms hired 6,000 workers, so when the minimum wage is introduced, firms lay off 3,000 workers.

But at a wage rate of $10 an hour, 2,000 people who didn't want to work for $7 an hour will now try to find work as servers. So at $10 an hour, the quantity of

Minimum wage law
A government regulation that makes hiring labor services for less than a specified wage illegal.

A Minimum Wage Creates Unemployment

MyEconLab Animation

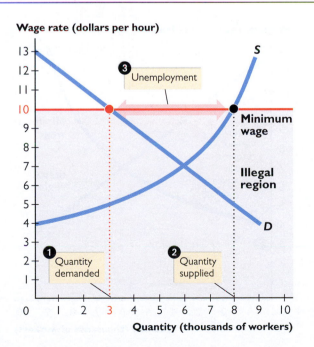

Wage rate (dollars per hour)

Quantity (thousands of workers)

A minimum wage is introduced above the equilibrium wage rate. In this example, the minimum wage rate is $10 an hour.

❶ The quantity of labor demanded decreases to 3,000 workers.

❷ The quantity of labor supplied increases to 8,000 people.

❸ 5,000 people are unemployed.

labor supplied is 8,000 people. With 3,000 workers fired and another 2,000 people looking for work at the higher wage rate, 5,000 people who would like to work as servers are unemployed.

The 3,000 jobs available must somehow be allocated among the 8,000 people who are willing to work as servers. How is this allocation achieved? The answer is by increased job-search activity and illegal hiring.

Increased Job-Search Activity

Finding a good job takes a great deal of time and other resources. With a minimum wage, more people are looking for jobs than the number of jobs available at that wage rate. Frustrated unemployed people spend time and other resources searching for hard-to-find jobs. In Figure 7.7, to find a job at $10 an hour, someone who is willing to work for $5 an hour (on the supply curve) would be willing to spend $5 an hour (the minimum wage rate of $10 an hour minus $5 an hour) on job-search activity. The amount is shown by the red arrow.

Illegal Hiring

With more people looking for work than the number of jobs available, some firms and workers might agree to do business at an illegal wage rate below the minimum wage in a black market. An illegal wage rate might be at any wage rate between the minimum wage of $10 an hour and the lowest wage rate at which someone is willing to work, $5 an hour.

FIGURE 7.7

A Minimum Wage Creates Job Search and Illegal Hiring

The minimum wage rate is set at $10 an hour:

❶ 3,000 jobs are available.

❷ The lowest wage rate for which someone is willing to work is $5 an hour. In a black market, illegal wage rates might be as low as $5 an hour.

❸ The maximum that might be spent on job search is an amount equivalent to $5 an hour—the $10 an hour they would receive if they found a job *minus* the $5 an hour at which they are willing to work.

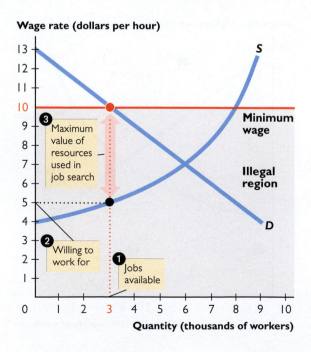

EYE on the U.S. ECONOMY
Minimum Wages and Employment

The *Fair Labor Standards Act* sets the federal minimum wage, but most states set their own minimum at a level higher than the federal minimum.

The figure shows the minimum wage since 1993 in terms of what it would buy at 2015 prices.

The minimum wage creates unemployment, but how much? Between 2007 and 2009, when the minimum wage increased by 38 percent (see the figure), the employment of 16- to 19-year-olds fell by 28 percent. How much of that decrease was caused by the rise in the minimum wage.

David Neumark, an economics professor at the University of California, Irvine, has reviewed all the most recent studies on the effects of a minimum wage on employment.

He reports that a 10 percent rise in the minimum wage reduces teen employment by between 1 percent and 3 percent, and 23 states have raised minimum wages to average 11.5 percent higher than the federal minimum.

He says that in 2014, "minimum wages ... reduced the number of jobs nationally by about 100,000 to 200,000, relative to the period just before the Great Recession."

Most economists agree with David Neumark. But David Card of the University of California at Berkeley and Alan Krueger of Princeton University have challenged this consensus view. They say that a rise in the minimum wage in California, New Jersey, and Texas *increased* the employment rate of low-income workers.

Most economists are skeptical about their conclusion and see other explanations for the employment increase that Card and Krueger found.

Daniel Hamermesh of the University of Texas at Austin says that Card and Krueger got the timing wrong. Firms anticipated the wage rise and so cut employment before it occurred. Looking at employment changes after the minimum wage increased missed its main effect. Finis Welch of Texas A&M University and Kevin Murphy of the University of Chicago say that the employment effects that Card and Krueger found are caused by regional differences in economic growth, not by changes in the minimum wage.

Pizza delivery people gain from the minimum wage.

Also, looking only at employment misses the supply-side effect of the minimum wage. It brings an increase in the number of people who drop out of high school to look for work.

Minimum wage (2015 dollars per hour)

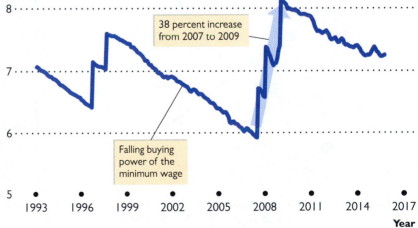

Source of data: Bureau of Labor Statistics.

■ Is the Minimum Wage Efficient?

The efficient allocation of a factor of production is similar to that of a good or service, which you studied in Chapter 6. The demand for labor tells us about the marginal benefit of labor to the firms that hire it. Firms benefit because the labor they hire produces the goods or services that they sell. Firms are willing to pay a wage rate equal to the benefit they receive from an additional hour of labor. In Figure 7.8(a), the demand curve for labor tells us the marginal benefit that the firms in Yuma receive from hiring fast-food servers. The marginal benefit minus the wage rate is a surplus for the firms.

The supply of labor tells us about the marginal cost of working. To work, people must forgo leisure or working in the home, activities that they value. The wage rate received *minus* the marginal cost of working is a surplus for workers.

An efficient allocation of labor occurs when the marginal benefit to firms equals the marginal cost borne by workers. Such an allocation occurs in the labor market in Figure 7.8(a). Firms enjoy a surplus (the blue area), and workers enjoy a surplus (the green area). Total surplus, the sum of these surpluses, is maximized.

Figure 7.8(b) shows the loss from a minimum wage. With a minimum wage of $10 an hour, 3,000 workers are hired. Marginal benefit exceeds marginal cost. The firms' surplus and workers' surplus shrink, and a deadweight loss (the gray area) arises. This loss falls on the firms that cut back employment and the people who can't find jobs at the higher wage rate.

■ FIGURE 7.8

The Inefficiency of the Minimum Wage

MyEconLab Animation

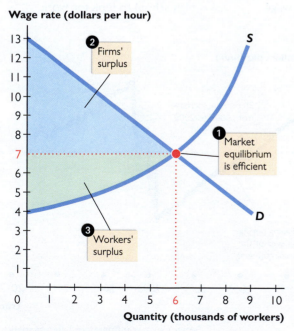

(a) Efficient labor market

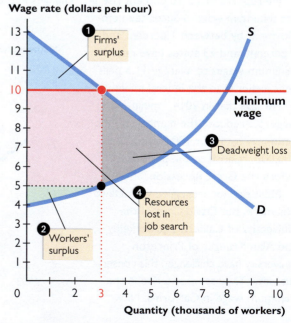

(b) Inefficient labor market

❶ The market equilibrium is efficient with marginal benefit equal to marginal cost. Total surplus, the sum of ❷ the firms' surplus (blue area) and ❸ workers' surplus (green area), is maximized.

A minimum wage is inefficient. ❶ The firms' surplus and ❷ workers' surplus shrink, a ❸ deadweight loss arises, and ❹ resources are lost in job search.

But the total loss exceeds the deadweight loss. As each unemployed person keeps looking for a job, resources are used in costly job-search activity—writing letters, sending emails, making phone calls, going to interviews, and so on. The value of these resources might be as large as the red rectangle.

■ Is the Minimum Wage Fair?

The minimum wage is unfair on both views of fairness: It delivers an unfair *result* and imposes unfair *rules*. The *result* is unfair because only those people who find jobs benefit. The people unemployed end up worse off than they would be with no minimum wage. And those who get jobs were probably not the least well off. Personal characteristics, which means discrimination, allocates jobs and is another source of unfairness. The minimum wage imposes unfair *rules* because it blocks voluntary exchange. Firms are willing to hire more labor and people are willing to work more, but they are not permitted by the minimum wage law to do so.

■ If the Minimum Wage Is So Bad, Why Do We Have It?

Although the minimum wage is inefficient, not everyone loses from it. The people who find jobs at the minimum wage rate are better off. Other supporters of the minimum wage believe that the elasticities of demand and supply in the labor market are low, so not much unemployment results. Labor unions support the minimum wage because it puts upward pressure on all wage rates, including those of union workers. Nonunion labor is a substitute for union labor, so when the minimum wage rises, the demand for union labor increases.

EYE on PRICE REGULATION

MyEconLab Critical Thinking Exercise

Can Congress Repeal the Law of Market Forces?

When Congress enacts a new law and the President signs it, the outcome is not always exactly what was intended. A mismatch between intention and outcome is almost inevitable when Congress seeks to block the law of market forces.

You've seen the problems created by a minimum wage law, which leaves teenagers without jobs. There would also be problems at the other extreme of the labor market if the law tried to place a cap on executive pay.

In the spring of 2009, the "Cap Executive Officer Pay Act of 2009" was introduced in the Senate. The goal of the Act was to limit the compensation of executives and directors of firms receiving government handouts. The Act defined compensation broadly as all forms of cash receipts, property, and any perks. The cap envisaged was an annual compensation no greater than that of the President of the United States.

This Act never made it into law, but you can see some of the problems that would have arisen if it had.

First, there is the difficult task of determining the President's compensation. Does it include the use of the White House and Air Force One?

Second, assuming the first problem could be solved, placing a cap on executive pay would work like putting a ceiling on home rents which you've studied in this chapter.

The quantity of executive services supplied would decrease and the most talented executives would seek jobs with the unregulated employers. The firms in the most difficulty—those receiving government funding—would face the added challenge of recruiting and keeping competent executives and directors. The deadweight loss from this action would be large. It is fortunate that the idea didn't have legs!

MyEconLab Study Plan 7.2
Key Terms Quiz
Solutions Video

CHECKPOINT 7.2

Explain how a price floor works, and why the minimum wage creates unemployment and is inefficient and unfair.

Practice Problems

Figure 1 shows the market for tomato pickers in southern California.

1. If California introduces a minimum wage of $4 an hour, how many tomato pickers are employed and how many are unemployed?

2. If California introduces a minimum wage of $8 an hour, how many tomato pickers are employed and how many are unemployed? What is the lowest wage that some workers might be able to earn if a black market develops?

3. If California introduces a minimum wage of $8 an hour, (a) is the minimum wage of $8 an hour efficient? (b) Who gains and who loses from the minimum wage of $8 an hour? Is it fair?

In the News

Will the United States raise the minimum wage to $15?
The labor movement is urging a minimum wage of $15 an hour. Currently, more than 40 percent of employees and 96 percent of fast-food workers earn less than $15 an hour. The U.S. Chamber of Commerce and the National Restaurant Association oppose the increase and say it will hurt small businesses and stifle job creation.

Source: *CBS News*, November 10, 2015

What will be the effects of a $15 an hour minimum wage?

Solutions to Practice Problems

1. The market equilibrium wage rate is $6 an hour, and 4,000 pickers are employed. The minimum wage of $4 an hour is below the equilibrium wage rate, so 4,000 tomato pickers are employed and no worker is unemployed.

2. The minimum wage of $8 an hour is above the equilibrium wage rate, so 3,000 pickers are employed (determined by the demand) and 5,000 people would like to work as pickers for $8 an hour (determined by the supply), so 2,000 are unemployed (Figure 2). If a black market developed, the lowest wage that someone might be able to earn would be $4 an hour (Figure 2).

3. The minimum wage of $8 an hour is not efficient because it creates a deadweight loss—the marginal benefit to growers exceeds the marginal cost to workers. Tomato pickers who find work at $8 an hour gain. Tomato growers and unemployed pickers lose. The minimum wage is unfair on both the fair-rules and fair-result views of fairness.

Solution to In the News

Given the information about how many workers currently earn less than $15 an hour, we can infer that a minimum wage of $15 an hour exceeds the equilibrium wage rate. Setting the minimum wage at $15 an hour will increase unemployment and create a deadweight loss. Some of this loss will be borne by employers whose profits will fall, but some will be borne by the workers who can't find jobs. Workers who do find jobs will gain.

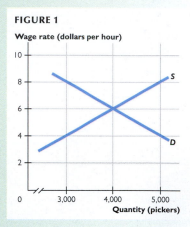

FIGURE 1

Wage rate (dollars per hour)

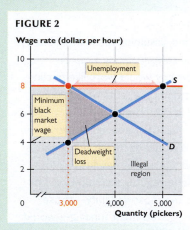

FIGURE 2

Wage rate (dollars per hour)

7.3   PRODUCTION QUOTAS

MyEconLab Concept Video

So far in this chapter, we have examined the effects of government actions that seek to prevent the price from moving toward the equilibrium price. In this final section, we look at a market intervention that aims to block the quantity supplied from moving toward the equilibrium quantity. The tool used for this purpose is a **production quota**, which is a government regulation in a market that places an upper limit on the quantity that may be supplied.

A government can't regulate the quantity supplied without isolating the domestic market from global competition. For this reason, production quotas usually are accompanied by *import quotas*—restrictions on the quantity that can be imported from other countries—that we study in Chapter 9.

To make a production quota effective—to successfully limit the quantity supplied—quotas must be allocated to each producer that sum to the market quota. Also, mechanisms must be used to prevent individual producers from exceeding their quotas.

An effective production quota (accompanied if needed by an import quota) decreases the quantity supplied below the equilibrium quantity. As a result, it raises the price. The higher price clearly damages the consumer, who pays more for a smaller quantity. Whether it benefits the producer depends on the elasticity of demand for the item. If the demand for the item subject to a quota is inelastic, the higher price brings an increase in total revenue and the producer gains. Not surprisingly, quotas are only used when demand is inelastic (see *Eye on the Global Economy*).

To see how consumers lose and producers gain and to see why a production quota is inefficient and unfair, we'll look at an example

Production quota
A government regulation in a market that places an upper limit on the quantity that may be supplied.

■ Production Quota: An Example

To illustrate the effects of a production quota, we'll use the example of the market for dairy products in California. Markets in milk, both liquid and powder, cheese, and other dairy products are regulated by the California Department of Food and Agriculture. A production quota for the market is set and allocations are made to each producer that sum to the market quota.

EYE on the GLOBAL ECONOMY
Production Quotas

What do cranberries, peanuts, sugar, chicken, eggs, milk, cheese, and tobacco have in common?

The answer is that production quotas have been used, either in the past or in the present, to regulate the markets for these items. Each item has an inelastic demand, so if its quantity supplied can be restricted to below the equilibrium quantity, its price rises by a larger percentage than the percentage decrease in the quantity supplied. As a result, producers end up with a greater total revenue and producer surplus.

Consumers lose. The loss incurred by each consumer is too small to complain about, but with millions of consumers, the total loss is large.

Some of what consumers lose is deadweight loss, but most of the consumers' loss is the producers' gain. And because there are many fewer producers than consumers, each producer ends up with a gain that is large enough to be worth paying for in political contributions to legislators who vote to sustain the quotas.

Figure 7.9 illustrates this market. The demand curve, *D*, tells us the quantity demanded at each price and the supply curve, *S*, tells us the quantity supplied at each price.

Free Market Reference Point

In Figure 7.9(a), with no production quota, the equilibrium price is 10 cents per pound and the equilibrium quantity of dairy products is 60 billion pounds per year. The market is efficient because marginal benefit on the demand curve equals marginal cost on the supply curve, and total surplus, the sum of consumer surplus (green triangle) and producer surplus (blue triangle) is maximized.

The Market with an Effective Production Quota

Figure 7.9(b) illustrates the effects of a production quota in this market. The government sets a production quota for the market of 40 billion pounds per year and allocates quotas to each producer that total the same 40 billion pounds. For now, we will assume that no one produces more than the allocated quota so the quantity supplied in the market is the quota quantity of 40 billion pounds.

FIGURE 7.9

The Inefficiency of a Production Quota

MyEconLab Animation

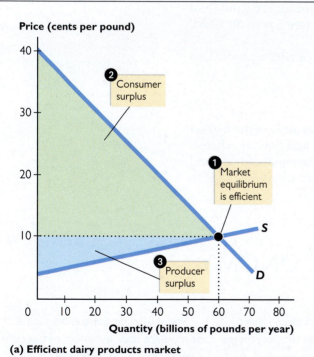

(a) Efficient dairy products market

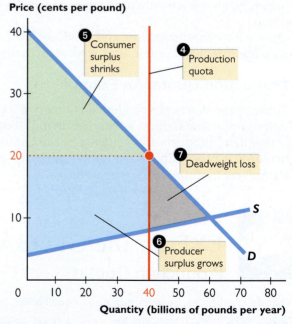

(b) Inefficient dairy products market with production quota

In the market for dairy products:

1 With no intervention, the market is competitive and the equilibrium price is 10 cents per pound and the equilibrium quantity of dairy products is 60 billion pounds per year.

2 Consumer surplus plus **3** producer surplus is maximized.

4 The government imposes a production quota of 40 billion pounds per year.

5 Consumer surplus shrinks, **6** producer surplus grows, and **7** a deadweight loss arises.

With no quota, the market is efficient. With a quota, it is inefficient.

At this quantity supplied, if the price remained at 10 cents per pound, there would be a shortage of dairy products. A shortage brings a rise in price and the market would achieve a new equilibrium at a price of 20 cents per pound.

At this smaller quantity and higher price, consumers are worse off. By how much they are worse off is shown by the shrinkage of consumer surplus.

Consumers lose, but dairy farmers gain. They produce a smaller quantity but sell it for a higher price. And the higher price more than counters the smaller quantity because the demand for dairy products is inelastic. Recall that when demand is inelastic, the percentage decrease in quantity is smaller than the percentage rise in price and a rise in price brings an incease in total revenue. You can see that total revenue increases from $6 billion to $8 billion. (Do the math and calculate the elasticity of demand between prices of 10 cents and 20 cents.)

Production Quota is Inefficient

The farmers' gain is smaller than the consumers' loss—the outcome is inefficient and a deadweight loss arises. The decreased quantity is valued on the demand curve more highly than its marginal cost on the supply curve. The area of the gray triangle shows the deadweight loss.

Production Quota is Unfair

A production quota is unfair on both views of fairness: It delivers an unfair *result* and imposes unfair *rules*. The result is unfair because well-off farmers benefit and consumers lose. A production quota imposes an unfair rule because it blocks voluntary exchange. Farmers are willing to produce a larger quantity and consumers are willing to buy the larger quantity, but they are not permitted by the quota to do so.

EYE on YOUR LIFE

MyEconLab Critical Thinking Exercise

Price Ceilings and Price Floors You Encounter

Price ceilings and price floors operate in many of the markets in which you trade, and they require you to take a stand as a citizen and voter.

Unless you live in New York City, you're not likely to live in a rent controlled house or apartment. Because economists have explained the unwanted effects of rent ceilings that you've learned about in this chapter, this type of market intervention is now rare.

But you run into a price ceiling almost every time you use a freeway.

The zero price for using a freeway is a type of price ceiling. The next time you're stuck in traffic and moving at a crawl, think about how a free market in road use would cut the congestion and allow you to zip along.

In Singapore, a transponder on your dashboard keeps track of your road use in dollars and cents as you drive around the city. The price varies with the time of day, the traffic density, and where in the city you are. As a result, you and other drivers are never stuck in slow-moving traffic.

You encounter a price floor in the labor market. Have you wanted a job and been willing and available to work, but unable to get hired? Would you have taken a job for a slightly lower wage if one had been available?

You also encounter price floors in markets for food. You pay more for tomatoes, sugar, oranges, and many other food items than the minimum cost of producing them.

Develop your own policy position on price floors and price ceilings.

MyEconLab Study Plan 7.3
Key Terms Quiz
Solutions Video

■ CHECKPOINT 7.3

Explain how a production quota works and why it brings a higher price and is inefficient and unfair.

Practice Problems

Figure 1 shows the market for cranberries.

1. What are the equilibrium price and quantity of cranberries? Is the market for cranberries efficient?

2. If the government sets a production quota of 20 billion pounds, what is the quantity of cranberries produced, the quantity demanded, and the price of a pound of cranberries?

3. If the government sets a production quota of 20 billion pounds, is the market for cranberries efficient? What is the deadweight loss created? Who gains and who loses from the production quota? Could the production quota be regarded as being fair?

In the News

Conditions sour for California's dairy farmers
California dairy farmers are being hit by falling prices, drought, and rising feed costs.

Source: *The Wall Street Journal*, October 8, 2015

How would the events in the news clip affect a competitive market in milk? How would a production quota change the effects of these events?

Solutions to Practice Problems

1. The equilibrium price is 10 cents a pound; the equilibrium quantity is 60 billion pounds. The market is efficient—marginal benefit equals marginal cost.

2. The production quota decreases the quantity supplied and the quantity demanded to 20 billion pounds and the price is 30 cents per pound (Figure 2).

3. With the production quota, the market is not efficient because at the quantity produced, the marginal benefit (on the demand curve) exceeds the marginal cost (on the supply curve). The deadweight loss equals $5 billion, of which $4 billion is a decrease in consumer surplus and $1 billion is a decrease in producer surplus. But another $2 billion of consumer surplus is transferred to producers, so consumer surplus decreases by $6 billion. Consumers lose. The change in producer surplus is an increase of $1 billion. Farmers gain. The outcome is unfair on both views of fairness unless farmers are poorer than consumers, in which case it might be fair to boost farmers' incomes.

Solution to In the News

In a competitive milk market, drought and rising feed costs would decrease supply. With no other changes, the price would rise and the equilibrium quantity would decrease. Because the price of milk fell, the demand for California milk must have decreased, most likely from competition with other sources of supply. An effective production quota combined with an import quota would have prevented or lessened the fall in price, but it would not have avoided the decrease in supply caused by drought and rising feed prices.

FIGURE 1

Price (cents per pound)

Quantity (billions of pounds per year)

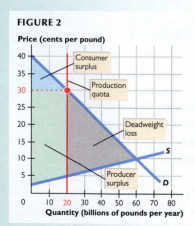

FIGURE 2

Price (cents per pound)

Quantity (billions of pounds per year)

CHAPTER SUMMARY

Key Points

1. Explain how a price ceiling works, and why a rent ceiling creates a housing shortage and is inefficient and unfair.

- A price ceiling set above the equilibrium price has no effects.
- A price ceiling set below the equilibrium price creates a shortage and increased search activity or a black market.
- A price ceiling is inefficient and unfair.
- A rent ceiling is an example of a price ceiling.

2. Explain how a price floor works, and why the minimum wage creates unemployment and is inefficient and unfair.

- A price floor set below the equilibrium price has no effects.
- A price floor set above the equilibrium price creates a surplus and increased search activity or illegal trading.
- A price floor is inefficient and unfair.
- A minimum wage is an example of a price floor.

3. Explain how a production quota works, and why it brings a higher price and is inefficient and unfair.

- A production quota decreases the quantity produced, decreases the quantity consumed, and raises the price.
- A production quota is used in the market for an item that has an inelastic demand.
- A production quota benefits the producer but costs the consumer more than the producer gains—it creates a deadweight loss.
- A production quota is inefficient and unfair.

Key Terms

MyEconLab Key Terms Quiz

Black market, 171
Minimum wage law, 177
Price cap, 170

Price ceiling, 170
Price floor, 176
Production quota, 183

Rent ceiling, 170
Search activity, 172

CHAPTER CHECKPOINT

Study Plan Problems and Applications

Table 1 shows the demand and supply schedules for on-campus housing. Use Table 1 to work Problems **1** to **3**.

1. If the college puts a rent ceiling on rooms of $650 a month, what is the rent, how many rooms are rented, and is the on-campus housing market efficient?

2. If the college puts a strictly enforced rent ceiling on rooms of $550 a month, what is the rent, how many rooms are rented, and is the on-campus housing market efficient? Explain why or why not.

3. Suppose that with a strictly enforced rent ceiling on rooms of $550 a month, a black market develops. How high could the black market rent be and would the on-campus housing market be fair? Explain your answer.

Table 2 shows the demand and supply schedules for student workers at on-campus venues. Use Table 2 to work Problems **4** to **6**.

4. If the college introduces a minimum wage of $10.50 an hour, how many students are employed at on-campus venues and how many are unemployed?

5. If the college introduces a strictly enforced minimum wage of $11.50 an hour, how many students are employed, how many are unemployed, and what is the lowest wage at which some students would be willing to work?

6. If the college introduces a strictly enforced minimum wage of $11.50 an hour, who gains and who loses from the minimum wage, and is the campus labor market efficient or fair?

Table 3 shows the demand and supply schedules for mushrooms. Use Table 3 to work Problems **7** and **8**.

7. Suppose that the government introduces a production quota for mushrooms and sets it at 3,000 pounds per week. What is the market price of mushrooms? Calculate the producer surplus and the deadweight loss created?

8. Suppose that the government introduces a production quota for mushrooms and sets it at 2,000 pounds a week. What is the market price of mushrooms? Calculate the producer surplus and the deadweight loss? Who gains and who loses?

Use the following news clip to work Problems **9** and **10**.

Venezuelans organize to overcome food shortages

The government of Venezuela controls the price of food and there are shortages of milk, rice, coffee, pasta, sugar, corn flour, and cooking oil. Eggs have disappeared from store shelves. While people stand in line for milk, cheese and yogurt are abundant. People who buy milk at the low price either sell it for a profit or exchange it for food items that other families stand in line to buy.

Source: www.teleSURtv.net/english, November 27, 2015

9. Are Venezuela's price controls price floors or price ceilings? Draw a graph to illustrate the shortages of food created by the price controls.

10. Explain how Venezuela's price controls have changed consumer surplus, producer surplus, total surplus, and the deadweight loss in the markets for milk and cheese. Draw a graph to illustrate your answer.

 11. Read *Eye on Price Regulation* on p. 181 and explain why a mismatch between intention and outcome is inevitable if a price regulation seeks to block the law of market forces.

TABLE 1

Rent (dollars per month)	Quantity demanded	Quantity supplied
	(rooms)	
500	2,500	2,000
550	2,250	2,000
600	2,000	2,000
650	1,750	2,000
700	1,500	2,000
750	1,250	2,000

TABLE 2

Wage rate (dollars per hour)	Quantity demanded	Quantity supplied
	(student workers)	
10.00	600	300
10.50	500	350
11.00	400	400
11.50	300	450
12.00	200	500
12.50	100	550

TABLE 3

Price (dollars per pound)	Quantity demanded	Quantity supplied
	(pounds per week)	
1.00	4,500	0
2.00	4,000	1,000
3.00	3,500	2,000
4.00	3,000	3,000
5.00	2,500	4,000
6.00	2,000	5,000

Instructor Assignable Problems and Applications

MyEconLab Homework, Quiz, or Test if assigned by instructor

1. Suppose that Congress caps executive pay at a level below the equilibrium.

   a. Explain how the quantity of executives demanded, the quantity supplied, and executive pay will change, and explain why the outcome is inefficient.

   b. Draw a graph of the market for corporate executives. On your graph, show the market equilibrium, the pay cap, the quantity of executives supplied and the quantity demanded at the pay cap, and the deadweight loss created. Also show the highest pay that an executive might be offered in a black market.

Use the following information to work Problems **2** to **4**.

Concerned about the political fallout from rising gas prices, the U.S. government imposes a price ceiling of $3.00 a gallon on gasoline.

2. Explain how the market for gasoline would react to this price ceiling if the oil-producing nations increased production and drove the equilibrium price of gasoline to $2.50 a gallon. Would the U.S. gasoline market be efficient?

3. Explain how the market for gasoline would react to this price ceiling if a global shortage of oil sent the equilibrium price of gasoline to $3.50 a gallon. Would the U.S. gasoline market be efficient?

4. Under what conditions would the price ceiling create lines at the pumps?

5. Suppose the government introduced a ceiling on lawyers' fees.

   a. How would the amount of work done by lawyers, the consumer surplus of people who hire lawyers, and the producer surplus of law firms change?

   b. Would this fee ceiling result in an efficient and fair use of resources? Why or why not?

Use the following information to work Problems **6** and **7**.

New York seals deal on $15 minimum fast-food wage
"Raising the minimum wage to $15 an hour will add fairness to our economy and bring dignity and respect to 2.2 million people, many of whom have been forced to live in poverty for too long," said Governor Andrew Cuomo. Between 135,000 and 200,000 workers will see their hourly wage rise gradually to $15 by the end of 2018 in New York City and by 2021 in the rest of the state.
                                                Source: CNNMoney, September 11, 2015

6. On a graph of the market for fast-food workers, show the effect of the $15 an hour minimum wage on employment of fast-food workers.

7. Explain the effects of the higher minimum wage on the workers' surplus and the firms' surplus. Will the $15 wage bring fairness, dignity, and respect?

Use the following information to work Problems **8** and **9**.

Canada's dairy industry is a rich, closed club
If you want to be a dairy farmer, you buy a plot of land and some cows and start to sell your milk. Not in Canada. There, farmers must buy a quota to produce a set amount of milk. The situation is similar in the markets for chicken and eggs.
                                                Source: *The Globe and Mail*, June 25, 2015

8. Draw a graph to illustrate the Canadian market for milk. With a production quota, show the quantity of milk produced, the price, consumer surplus, producer surplus, and the deadweight loss created.

9. In the Canadian market for milk with a production quota, explain what happens if a drought decreases supply.

MyEconLab Chapter 7 Study Plan

Multiple Choice Quiz

1. A rent ceiling creates a _____ of housing if it _____ the equilibrium rent.

A. surplus; is less than
B. shortage; is less than
C. surplus; exceeds
D. shortage; exceeds

2. A price ceiling imposed below the equilibrium price _____.

A. creates a black market in which the price might equal or exceed the equilibrium price
B. creates a black market in which the price equals the price ceiling
C. leads to increased search activity, which reduces the shortage of the good
D. increases the demand for the good, which makes the shortage even larger

3. A price ceiling is _____ if it is set _____ the market equilibrium price.

A. efficient and fair; below
B. unfair but efficient; equal to
C. efficient and unfair; above
D. inefficient and unfair; below

4. A price floor influences the outcome of a market if it is _____.

A. set below the equilibrium price
B. set above the equilibrium price
C. an incentive for buyers to increase demand for the good
D. an incentive for sellers to decrease supply of the good

5. A minimum wage set above the market equilibrium wage rate _____.

A. increases both employment and the quantity of labor supplied
B. decreases unemployment and raises the wage rate of those employed
C. raises the wage rate of those employed and increases the supply of jobs
D. increases unemployment and decreases employment

6. A minimum wage is _____.

A. efficient if the wage paid rises and more people look for jobs
B. inefficient if workers' surplus decreases and firms' surplus increases
C. inefficient if job search increases and total surplus decreases
D. efficient if workers' surplus increases and firms' surplus decreases

7. A production quota set below the market equilibrium quantity _____.

A. increases the price, increases producer surplus, and is inefficient
B. creates a shortage and increases farmers' total revenue but is unfair
C. is inefficient because farmers' marginal cost exceeds consumers' marginal benefit
D. is efficient because farmers' surplus increases

8. An effective production quota for peanuts with no imports of peanuts will _____.

A. lower the peanut growers' costs, raise the market price of peanuts, and decrease consumer surplus
B. raise the price of peanuts, which will decrease the demand for peanuts
C. make the peanut market more efficient if the demand for peanuts is inelastic
D. decrease the quantity of peanuts produced, decrease the quantity consumed, and increase the total surplus from peanuts

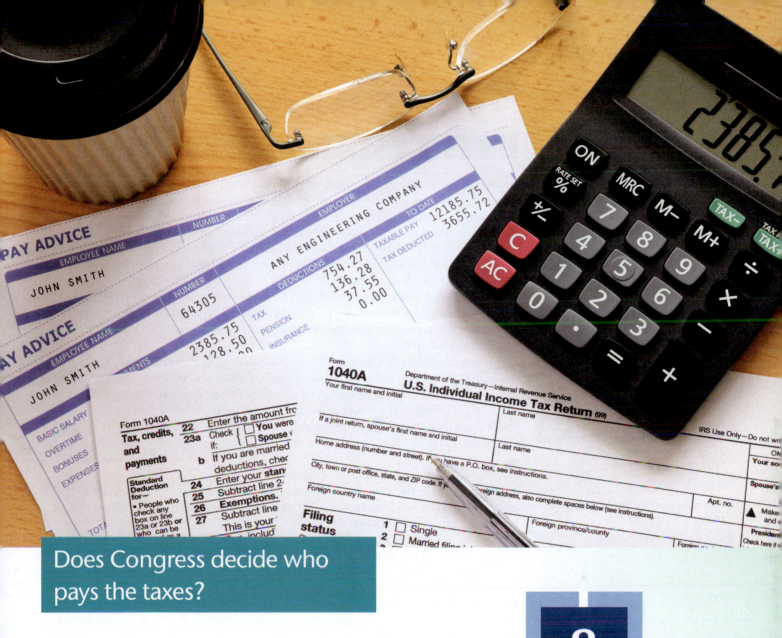

Does Congress decide who pays the taxes?

Taxes

When you have completed your study of this chapter, you will be able to

1 Explain how taxes change prices and quantities, are shared by buyers and sellers, and create inefficiency.

2 Explain how income taxes and Social Security taxes change wage rates and employment, are shared by employers and workers, and create inefficiency.

3 Review ideas about the fairness of the tax system and the tradeoff between efficiency and fairness.

8

CHAPTER CHECKLIST

MyEconLab Big Picture Video

Does "tax free" really mean that the seller pays the tax?

Tax incidence
The division of the tax between the buyer and the seller.

8.1 TAXES ON BUYERS AND SELLERS

Almost every time you buy something—a late-night order of chow mein, a plane ticket, a tank of gasoline—you pay a tax. On some items, you pay a sales tax that is added to the advertised price. On other items, you pay an excise tax—often at a high rate like the tax on gasoline—that is included in the advertised price.

But do you really pay these taxes? When a tax is added to the advertised price, isn't it obvious that *you* pay the tax? Isn't the price higher than it otherwise would be by an amount equal to the tax?

What about a tax that is buried in the price, such as that on gasoline? Who pays that tax? Does the seller just pass on the full amount of the tax to you, the buyer? Or does the seller pay the tax by taking a lower price and leaving the price you pay unchanged?

To answer these questions, let's suppose that TIFS, the Tax Illegal File Sharing lobby, has persuaded the government to collect a $10 tax on every new smartphone and to use the tax revenue to compensate artists. But an argument is raging between those who claim that the buyer benefits from using the smartphone and should pay the tax and those who claim that the seller profits and should pay the tax.

◼ Tax Incidence

Tax incidence is the division of the tax between the buyer and the seller. We're going to find the incidence of a $10 tax on smartphones with two different taxes: a tax on the buyer and a tax on the seller.

Figure 8.1 shows the market for smartphones. With no tax, the equilibrium price is $100 and the equilibrium quantity is 5,000 smartphones a week.

When a good is taxed, it has two prices: a price that excludes the tax and a price that includes the tax. Buyers respond only to the price that includes the tax, because that is the price they pay. Sellers respond only to the price that excludes the tax, because that is the price they receive. The tax is like a wedge between these two prices.

Figure 8.1(a) shows what happens if the government taxes the buyer. The tax doesn't change the buyer's willingness and ability to pay. The demand curve, *D*, tells us the *total* amount that buyers are willing and able to pay. Because buyers must pay $10 to the government on each item bought, the curve that tells us what buyers are willing to pay to sellers is the red curve labeled *D − tax*. This curve lies $10 *below* the blue demand curve.

Market equilibrium occurs where the red curve *D − tax* intersects the supply curve, *S*. Buyers pay the equilibrium net-of-tax price $95 plus the $10 tax: $105 per smartphone. Sellers receive the net-of-tax price $95 per smartphone. The government collects a tax revenue of $10 on each of the 2,000 smartphones, or $20,000 (shown by the purple rectangle).

Figure 8.1(b) shows what happens if the government taxes the seller. The tax acts like an increase in the suppliers' cost, so supply decreases and the supply curve shifts to the red curve labeled *S + tax*. This curve tells us what sellers are willing to accept, given that they must pay the government $10 on each item sold. The red curve, *S + tax*, lies $10 *above* the blue supply curve.

Market equilibrium occurs where the red curve *S + tax* intersects the demand curve, *D*. Buyers pay the equilibrium price $105 per smartphone. Sellers receive the net-of-tax price $95, and the government collects a tax revenue of $20,000.

FIGURE 8.1

A Tax on Smartphones

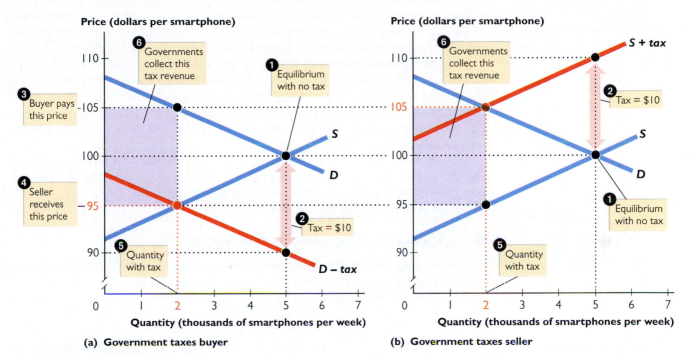

(a) Government taxes buyer

(b) Government taxes seller

❶ With no tax on smartphones, the price is $100 and 5,000 smartphones a week are bought—in both parts of the figure.

❷ In part (a), a $10 tax on buyers shifts the demand curve down to the red curve *D − tax* and in part (b), a $10 tax on sellers shifts the supply curve up to the red curve *S + tax*.

In both parts of the figure:

❸ The price paid by buyers rises to $105—an increase of $5;

❹ The price received by sellers falls to $95—a decrease of $5;

❺ The quantity bought decreases to 2,000 smartphones a week; and

❻ The government collects tax revenue of $20,000 a week—the purple rectangle.

In both cases, the tax is split equally between the buyer and the seller—each pays $5 per smartphone.

In both cases, the buyer and the seller split the $10 tax and pay $5 each. You can now see that the argument about making the buyer pay or the seller pay is futile. The price the buyer pays, the price the seller receives, and the tax revenue the government receives are the same, regardless of who the government taxes.

In this example, the tax is shared equally between the buyer and the seller. But in most cases, the tax will be shared unequally and might even fall entirely on one side of the market. We'll explore what determines the incidence of a tax, but first let's see how a tax creates inefficiency.

■ Taxes and Efficiency

You've seen that resources are used efficiently when marginal benefit equals marginal cost. You've also seen that a tax places a wedge between the price the buyer pays and the price the seller receives equal to the tax. The buyer's price equals marginal benefit and the seller's price equals marginal cost, so a tax puts a wedge between marginal benefit and marginal cost. The tax decreases the equilibrium quantity to less than the efficient quantity and creates a deadweight loss.

■ Tax Burden

Excess burden
The deadweight loss from a tax.

A tax creates a loss of consumer surplus and producer surplus—a deadweight loss. The amount of tax paid plus the deadweight loss that results from the tax is called the *burden of the tax*. And the deadweight loss is called the **excess burden** of the tax. Because the government uses the tax revenue to provide goods and services that people value, only the excess burden measures the inefficiency of a tax

Figure 8.2 shows the inefficiency of a tax. We'll assume that the government taxes the seller. In part (a), with no tax, marginal benefit equals marginal cost and the market is efficient. In part (b), with a tax, marginal benefit exceeds marginal cost. Consumer surplus and producer surplus shrink. Part of each surplus goes to the government as tax revenue—the purple area—and part becomes a deadweight loss—the gray area.

In this example, the excess burden is large. You can see how large by calculating the area of the deadweight loss triangle. This area equals ($10 × 3,000) ÷ 2, which is $15,000 per week. The tax revenue is $20,000 per week, so the excess burden of the tax is 75 percent of the tax revenue.

■ Incidence, Inefficiency, and Elasticity

In the example of a $10 tax on smartphones, buyers and sellers split the tax equally and the excess burden is large. What determines how the tax is split and the size of its excess burden?

FIGURE 8.2

Taxes and Efficiency

MyEconLab Animation

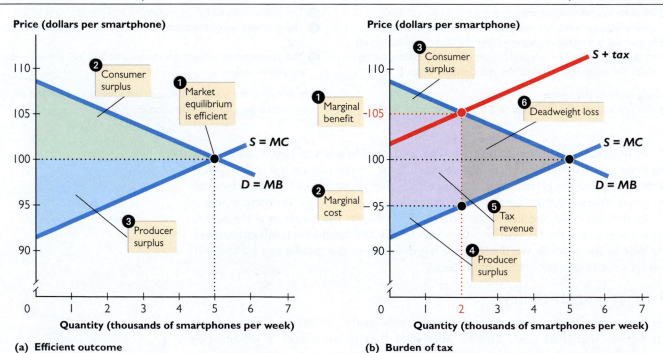

(a) Efficient outcome

(b) Burden of tax

❶ The market is efficient with marginal benefit equal to marginal cost. Total surplus—the sum of ❷ consumer surplus (green area) and ❸ producer surplus (blue area)—is at its maximum possible level.

A $10 tax drives a wedge between ❶ marginal benefit and ❷ marginal cost. ❸ Consumer surplus and ❹ producer surplus shrink by the amount of the ❺ tax revenue plus the ❻ deadweight loss. The deadweight loss is the excess burden of the tax.

The incidence of a tax and its excess burden depend on the elasticities of demand and supply in the following ways:

- For a given elasticity of supply, the more inelastic the demand for the good, the larger is the share of the tax paid by the buyer.
- For a given elasticity of demand, the more inelastic the supply of the good, the larger is the share of the tax paid by the seller.
- The excess burden is smaller, the more inelastic is demand *or* supply.

■ Incidence, Inefficiency, and the Elasticity of Demand

MyEconLab Concept Video

To see how the division of a tax between the buyer and the seller and the size of the excess burden depend on the elasticity of demand, we'll look at two extremes.

Perfectly Inelastic Demand: Buyer Pays and Efficient

Figure 8.3(a) shows the market for insulin, a vital daily medication of diabetics. Demand is perfectly inelastic at 100,000 doses a week, as shown by the vertical demand curve. With no tax, the price is $2 a dose. A tax of 20¢ a dose raises the price to $2.20, but the equilibrium quantity does not change. The tax leaves the price received by sellers unchanged but raises the price paid by buyers by the entire tax. Marginal benefit equals marginal cost, so the outcome is efficient and no deadweight loss arises.

Perfectly Elastic Demand: Seller Pays and Inefficient

Figure 8.3(b) shows the market for pink marker pens. Demand is perfectly elastic at $1 a pen, as shown by the horizontal demand curve. If pink pens are less expensive than other pens, everyone uses pink. If pink pens are more expensive than other pens, no one uses a pink pen. With no tax, the price of a pink pen is $1 and the quantity is 4,000 pens a week. A tax of 10¢ a pen leaves the price at $1 a pen,

■ FIGURE 8.3

Incidence, Inefficiency, and the Elasticity of Demand

MyEconLab Animation

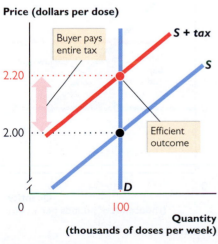

(a) Inelastic demand

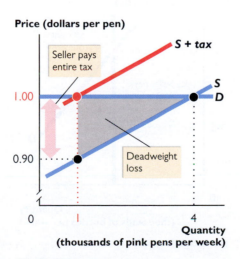

(b) Elastic demand

In part (a), the demand for insulin is perfectly inelastic. A tax of 20¢ a dose raises the price by 20¢, and the buyer pays all the tax. But marginal benefit still equals marginal cost, so the outcome is efficient.

In part (b), the demand for pink marker pens is perfectly elastic. A tax of 10¢ a pen lowers the price received by the seller by 10¢, and the seller pays all the tax. Marginal benefit exceeds marginal cost, so the outcome is inefficient. The deadweight loss is the excess burden of the tax and measures its inefficiency.

but the equilibrium quantity decreases to 1,000 pens a week. The price paid by the buyer is unchanged, and the seller pays the entire tax. The outcome is inefficient because marginal benefit exceeds marginal cost and a deadweight loss arises.

◼ Incidence, Inefficiency, and the Elasticity of Supply

To see how the division of a tax between the buyer and the seller depends on the elasticity of supply, we'll again look at two extremes.

Perfectly Inelastic Supply: Seller Pays and Efficient

Figure 8.4(a) shows the market for spring water that flows at a constant rate that can't be controlled. Supply is perfectly inelastic at 100,000 bottles a week, as shown by the vertical supply curve. With no tax, the price is 50¢ a bottle and the 100,000 bottles that flow from the spring are bought. A tax of 5¢ a bottle leaves the quantity unchanged at 100,000 bottles a week. Buyers are willing to buy 100,000 bottles a week only if the price is 50¢ a bottle. The price remains at 50¢ a bottle, but the tax lowers the price received by the seller by 5¢ a bottle. The seller pays the entire tax.

Because marginal benefit equals marginal cost, there is no deadweight loss and the outcome is efficient.

Perfectly Elastic Supply: Buyer Pays and Inefficient

Figure 8.4(b) shows the market for sand from which computer-chip makers extract silicon. Supply of this sand is perfectly elastic at a price of 10¢ a pound as shown by the horizontal supply curve. With no tax, the price is 10¢ a pound and 5,000 pounds a week are bought. A tax of 1¢ a pound raises the price to 11¢ a pound and the quantity decreases to 3,000 pounds a week. The buyer pays the entire tax.

Because marginal benefit exceeds marginal cost, a deadweight loss arises and the outcome is inefficient.

◼ FIGURE 8.4

Incidence, Inefficiency, and the Elasticity of Supply

MyEconLab Animation

In part (a), the supply of bottled spring water is perfectly inelastic. A tax of 5¢ a bottle lowers the price received by the seller by 5¢ a bottle, and the seller pays all the tax. Marginal benefit equals marginal cost, so the outcome is efficient.

In part (b), the supply of sand is perfectly elastic. A tax of 1¢ a pound increases the price by 1¢ a pound, and the buyer pays all the tax. Marginal benefit exceeds marginal cost, so the outcome is inefficient. The deadweight loss is the excess burden of the tax and measures its inefficiency.

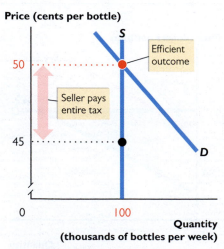

(a) Inelastic supply

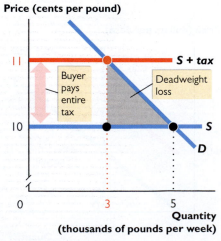

(b) Elastic supply

CHECKPOINT 8.1

MyEconLab Study Plan 8.1
Key Terms Quiz
Solutions Video

Explain how taxes change prices and quantities, are shared by buyers and sellers, and create inefficiency.

Practice Problems

Figure 1 shows the market for basketballs, when basketballs are not taxed.

1. If buyers of basketballs are taxed $6 a ball, what price does the buyer pay and how many basketballs do they buy? What is the tax revenue collected?

2. If sellers of basketballs are taxed $6 a ball, what price does the seller receive and how many basketballs do they sell? What is the tax revenue collected?

3. If basketballs are taxed at $6 a ball, what is the excess burden of the tax? Is the demand for basketballs or the supply of basketballs more inelastic? Explain your answer.

In the News

Gas tax increases by 7 cents in Washington State
Washington State gas taxes will rise by 7¢ a gallon now and by a further 4.9¢ a gallon next summer.

Source: *The Seattle Times*, August 1, 2015

If the demand for gasoline is inelastic and the supply of gasoline is elastic, who will pay more of the increase in Washington's gas tax: drivers or the gasoline companies? If there is a big switch to natural gas for big trucks, how will the tax incidence change?

Solutions to Practice Problems

1. With a $6 tax on buyers, the demand curve shifts downward by $6 a ball as shown in Figure 2. The price that the buyer pays is $16 a basketball and 8 million basketballs a week are bought. The tax revenue is $6 × 8 million, which is $48 million a week (the purple rectangle in Figure 2).

2. With a $6 tax on sellers, the supply curve shifts upward by $6 a ball as shown in Figure 3. The price that the seller receives is $10 a basketball and 8 million basketballs a week are sold. The tax revenue is $6 × 8 million, which is $48 million a week (the purple rectangle in Figure 3).

3. The excess burden of the tax is $12 million. Excess burden equals the deadweight loss, the area of the gray triangle, which is (4 million × $6) ÷ 2. The $6 tax increases the price paid by buyers by $1 and lowers the price received by sellers by $5. The seller pays the larger share of the tax because the supply of basketballs is more inelastic than the demand for basketballs.

Solution to In the News

If the demand for gasoline is inelastic and supply is elastic, drivers will pay more of the increase in Washington's gas tax than the gasoline companies will pay. Although the demand for gasoline is inelastic, the availability of natural gas and big trucks switching to natural gas makes the demand for gasoline (and diesel) less inelastic, so the share of the tax paid by drivers will fall and the share paid by the gasoline companies will rise.

FIGURE 1

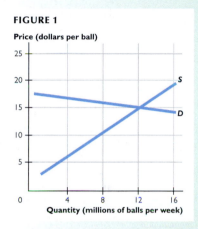

FIGURE 2

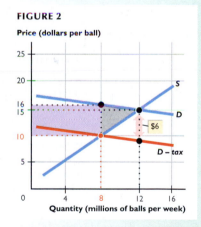

FIGURE 3

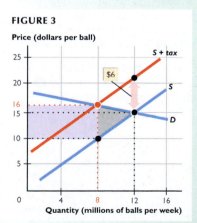

MyEconLab Concept Video

8.2 INCOME TAXES AND SOCIAL SECURITY TAXES

Income taxes and Social Security taxes raise two-thirds of total U.S. government revenue (see *Eye on the U.S. Economy* on p. 199). Who pays these taxes? Are they efficient? Let's find out.

■ The Effects of the Income Tax

An income tax is a tax on the sellers of the services of the factors of production— labor, capital, and land. You've just seen that who pays a tax—the incidence of a tax—depends on the elasticities of demand and supply. These same elasticities also influence the inefficiency created by a tax.

The elasticities of demand and supply are different for each factor of production, so to determine the incidence and inefficiency of an income tax, we must examine its effects on each factor of production separately. Let's look first at the effects of the tax on labor income.

Tax on Labor Income

Figure 8.5 shows the demand curve, *LD*, and the supply curve, *LS*, in a competitive labor market. The equilibrium in this market, with no income tax, occurs when workers earn $19 an hour and work 40 hours a week. This equilibrium is efficient. Firms are willing to pay $19 an hour because that is their marginal gain

---

■ **FIGURE 8.5**

A Tax on Labor Income

MyEconLab Animation

With no income tax, workers would earn $19 an hour and work 40 hours a week.

❶ With a 20 percent marginal tax on labor income, the supply of labor decreases. The supply curve becomes *LS + tax*, the wage rate rises, and the after-tax wage rate falls.

Because the demand for labor is elastic and the supply of labor is inelastic, ❷ the tax paid by the employer is less than ❸ the tax paid by the worker.

The quantity of labor employed is less than the efficient quantity, so ❹ a deadweight loss arises.

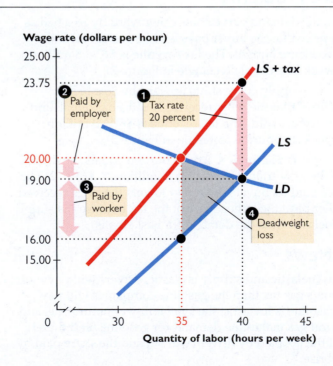

EYE on the U.S. ECONOMY
Taxes in the United States Today

Federal, state, and local governments in the United States have the six main revenue sources shown in the figure.

Personal income taxes at 39 percent of total tax revenue and Social Security taxes at 25 percent together account for almost two thirds of all tax revenue.

These two taxes fall more on workers than on employers.

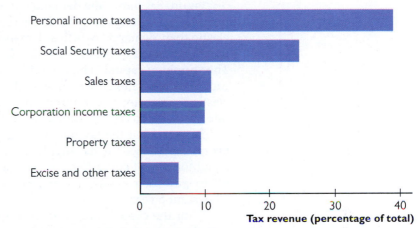

SOURCES OF DATA: Bureau of Economic Analysis, *National Income and Product Accounts*, Tables 1.1.5, 3.2, and 3.3.

from one extra hour of labor. And workers are willing to supply the 40th hour of labor for $19 because that compensates them for the marginal cost of working.

Before working out the effects of the income tax, look closely at the labor demand curve and labor supply curve. One point on the demand curve is the equilibrium 40 hours and $19 an hour. Another point on the demand curve is 35 hours and $20 an hour. The demand for labor is *elastic*. A small percentage rise in the wage rate from $19 to $20 brings a large percentage decrease in hours demanded from 40 to 35 per week. The demand for labor is elastic because firms can easily substitute machines for labor in many tasks. If labor costs too much, it gets replaced by a machine.

Now focus on the supply curve. Two points on that curve are the equilibrium 40 hours and $19 an hour and 35 hours and $16 an hour. The supply of labor is *inelastic*. It takes a large percentage fall in the wage rate from $19 to $16 to bring a large, but smaller percentage, decrease in hours supplied from 40 to 35 per week. The supply of labor is inelastic because most people have few good options other than to work for their income.

Now let's see what happens with a 20 percent marginal tax on labor income. The labor supply curve shifts to *LS + tax*. If workers are willing to supply the 40th hour a week for $19 with no tax, then with a 20 percent tax, they are willing to supply the 40th hour only if the wage is $23.75 an hour. That is, workers want to get the $19 they received before plus $4.75 (20 percent of $23.75) that they now must pay to the government.

The equilibrium wage rate rises to $20 an hour, but the after-tax wage rate falls to $16 an hour—the tax is $4 an hour. Employment decreases to 35 hours a week. The worker pays most of the tax—$3 compared to the $1 the employer pays—because the demand for labor is elastic and the supply of labor is inelastic. The tax creates a deadweight loss shown by the gray triangle.

Tax on Capital Income

Capital income in the form of interest on bonds and bank deposits is taxed at the normal income tax rate; and capital income in the form of dividends on stocks is taxed as a dividend at 15 percent and as corporate profit at the corporation income tax rate.

Figure 8.6 shows the demand curve, *KD*, and the supply curve, *KS*, in a competitive capital market. Both demand and supply are elastic, but supply is more elastic than demand. A firm's demand for capital is elastic for the same reason that the demand for labor is elastic: Many tasks can be done by machines or labor. The supply of capital is highly elastic, and in Figure 8.6 perfectly elastic, because capital is internationally mobile. In this example, the supply of capital is perfectly elastic at 6 percent a year. Firms can obtain all the capital they wish at this interest rate and with no capital income tax, they use $40 billion of capital.

Suppose that the tax rate on capital income is 40 percent. With a 40 percent tax on capital income, the supply of capital curve shifts to *KS + tax*. With the demand for capital curve *KD*, lenders want to receive an additional 4 percent interest to pay their capital income tax and are not willing to lend for less than 10 percent a year.

With the capital income tax, the quantity of capital decreases to $20 billion and the interest rate rises to 10 percent a year. Firms pay the entire capital income tax, and lenders receive the same after-tax interest rate as they receive in the absence of a capital income tax. The tax creates a deadweight loss shown by the gray triangle.

FIGURE 8.6

A Tax on Capital Income

MyEconLab Animation

❶ The supply of capital is highly elastic (here perfectly elastic). With no tax on capital income, the interest rate is 6 percent a year and firms use $40 billion of capital.

❷ With a 40 percent tax on capital income, the supply curve becomes *KS + tax*. The interest rate rises to 10 percent a year, and ❸ firms pay the entire tax.

The quantity of capital used is less than the efficient quantity, so ❹ a deadweight loss arises.

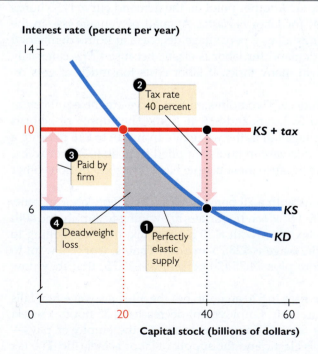

Tax on Income from Land and Other Unique Resources

Each plot of land is unique and its supply is perfectly inelastic. A fixed amount of the resource is supplied regardless of the rent offered for its use.

Figure 8.7(a) illustrates a tax on land income. In this example, a fixed 250 billion acres of land is supplied regardless of the rent. The equilibrium rent is determined by the demand for land. In this example, the equilibrium rent is $1,000 an acre.

When a 40 percent tax is imposed on rent income, landowners pay the entire tax. Their after-tax income falls to $600 an acre. The tax on income from land is efficient and it creates no deadweight loss (excess burden).

Figure 8.7(b) illustrates another example. Suppose that Bradley Cooper is willing to make three movies per year. His supply of services is perfectly inelastic at that quantity. Hollywood studios compete for his services, and the demand curve reflects the studios' willingness to pay for them. The equilibrium price is $20 million per movie. If Bradley pays a 40 percent tax on this income, he receives an after-tax income of $12 million per movie. Bradley pays the entire tax. The price paid by the studios is unaffected by this tax, and Bradley makes the same number of movies with the tax as without it. This tax creates no deadweight loss (excess burden).

■ **FIGURE 8.7**

A Tax on Land Income and Other Unique Resource Income   MyEconLab Animation

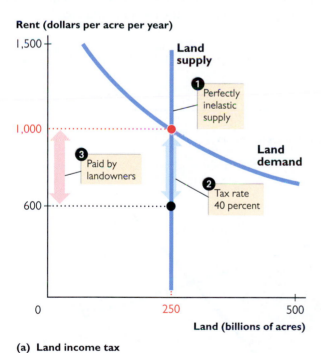

(a) Land income tax

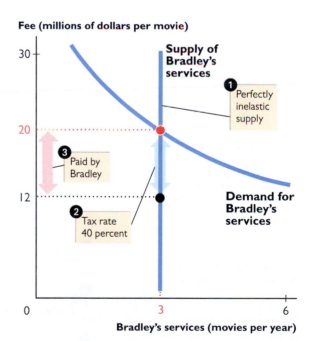

(b) Unique resource income tax

❶ In the markets for land and for the services of Bradley Cooper, supply is highly inelastic (here perfectly inelastic).

❷ With a 40 percent tax on income from these resources, the

equilibrium quantity and the market price remain unchanged,.

❸ Landowners and Bradley pay the entire tax. With no change in the quantity of the resource used, the tax is efficient.

■ The Social Security Tax

The law says that Social Security taxes fall equally on workers and employers. But does this outcome actually occur? You can probably guess that it does not. The Social Security tax is just like the other taxes you've studied in this chapter. Who pays the tax—its incidence—depends on the elasticities of demand and supply in the labor market and not on the wishes of Congress.

Figure 8.8 illustrates the effects of a Social Security tax. In this model labor market, with demand *LD* and supply *LS*, and with no taxes, the wage rate is $12 an hour and 4,000 people are employed. Congress now introduces a Social Security tax of $2.50 per hour and says that employers and workers must pay $1.25 each. Regardless of who sends the money to the government, the tax raises the cost of labor, lowers what workers earn, and lowers employment.

To find the new equilibrium, we find the level of employment at which the gap between what employers are willing to pay and workers are willing to accept equals the $2.50 tax. That employment level is 3,000 people at which employers pay $12.50 an hour and workers receive $10 an hour.

With the $2.50 Social Security tax, employers pay 50¢ an hour and workers pay $2 an hour. This division of the burden of the tax arises because the demand for labor is more elastic than the supply of labor.

The tax law could have required employers or workers to pay the entire tax or split the tax between them in any way, but the amounts of tax paid by workers and employers would remain the same. Congress cannot decide who pays the Social Security tax. When the laws of Congress come into conflict with the laws of economics, economics wins. Congress can't repeal the law of market forces!

■ **FIGURE 8.8**

The Social Security Tax

MyEconLab Animation

With no tax, 4,000 people are employed at a wage rate of $12 an hour.

1 A Social Security tax of $2.50 per hour puts a wedge between what employers pay and what workers receive and lowers employment to 3,000 workers.

2 Employers pay a higher wage rate of $12.50 an hour, an increase of 50¢ an hour.

3 Workers receive a lower wage rate of $10 an hour, a decrease of $2 an hour.

4 The government collects tax revenue shown by the purple rectangle.

Workers pay most of the tax because the demand for labor is more elastic than the supply of labor.

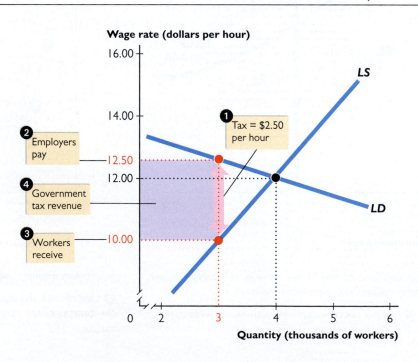

EYE on CONGRESS

MyEconLab Critical Thinking Exercise

Does Congress Decide Who Pays the Taxes?

Congress says that employers and workers pay the same Social Security tax contributions (7.65 percent each in 2015). But because the elasticity of demand for labor is much greater than the elasticity of supply of labor, workers end up paying most of the Social Security tax (see Figure 8.8).

Similarly, because the elasticity of demand for labor is greater than the elasticity of supply, the tax on wage income is paid mainly by workers. In contrast, the tax on capital income falls mainly on borrowers because the supply of capital is highly elastic.

But there is one thing that Congress can do to influence who pays a tax. It can pass a tax law (or tax rebate law) that doesn't impact the margin on which decisions turn.

Congress passed such a law in 2009 as part of the American Recovery and Reinvestment Act, an attempt to kickstart an economy that was struggling to recover from a global financial crisis. The tax rebate, called the "Making Work Pay Tax Credit" gave a single worker a $400 tax break and a couple $800.

A tax credit is a fixed reduction in the amount paid in personal income tax (in the current case, $400). For most people, a tax credit has no effect on their supply of labor. A worker gets the $400 tax credit regardless of how many hours he or she works. The tax credit doesn't influence the work-hours choice.

What influences the work-hours choice is the after-tax hourly wage rate, and that depends on the *marginal* income tax rate.

The figure illustrates the effects of a tax credit. The figure is similar to Figure 8.5 on p. 198. A 20 percent income tax rate shifts the labor supply curve from *LS* to *LS + tax*. With the demand for labor curve *LD*, the 20 percent tax raises the pre-tax wage rate by $1 to $20 per hour, lowers the after-tax wage rate by $3 to $16 per hour, and lowers the average workweek from 40 hours to 35 hours. With no tax credit, the worker pays 75 percent of the tax and the employer pays 25 percent.

Suppose that Congress now passes an Act that gives workers a tax credit of $30 a week. This credit has no effect on the supply of labor because it isn't a credit per hour worked. It is

Shaun Donovan, Director of the Office of Management and Budget

a fixed credit amount independent of the hours worked. Workers now pay only 68 percent of the tax, and employers pay 32 percent of the tax. Congress has worked around the elasticities! Unfortunately for workers, this tax credit is no longer available.

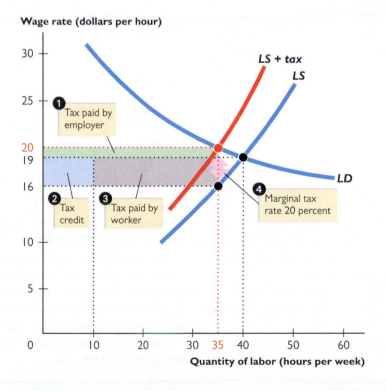

EYE on the PAST
The Origins and History of the U.S. Income Tax

1861 First federal income tax was 3 percent on all incomes above $800 a year.

1872 Income tax was repealed. (Tariffs on imports provided government revenue.)

1895 Income tax reestablished, but the Supreme Court ruled it unconstitutional.

1913 The 16th Amendment to the Constitution made the federal income tax legal.

1913– 2015 The top rate increased to 91 percent in World War II, fell to 28 percent during the Reagan era, and today is 39.6 percent.

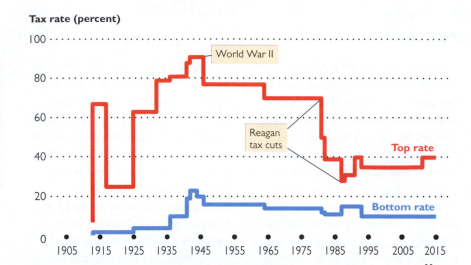

SOURCE OF DATA: Congressional Joint Committee on Taxation.

The bottom rate was below 5 percent until the 1940s when it increased to 20 percent. In 1963, the bottom rate decreased and since then, it has fluctuated between 10 percent and 15 percent. Today's bottom rate is 10 percent.

EYE on YOUR LIFE
Tax Freedom Day

MyEconLab Critical Thinking Exercise

The Tax Foundation is an organization that seeks to promote a tax system that is as simple, transparent, and stable as possible, that minimizes excess burden, and that promotes trade and income growth.

Each year, to make the level of taxes as transparent as possible, the Tax Foundation calculates and publicizes "Tax Freedom Day"—the date by when an average U.S. citizen has worked long enough to pay the year's tax bill.

In 2015, "Tax Freedom Day" for Americans was April 10, the 100th day of the year.

The 100 days Americans had to work to pay their taxes in 2015 break down as follows

Personal income taxes	39 days
Social Security taxes	25 days
Sales and excise taxes	17 days
Corporate income taxes	10 days
Property taxes	9 days

To work out your own "Tax Freedom Day," record all the taxes you pay in a year. Then express this number as a percentage of your annual income. Now find the number of days (as a percentage of 365) that this amount of tax represents and then work out your "Tax Freedom Day".

If you think taxes are high in the United States, think again.

Here are some "Tax Freedom Days" in a few other countries in 2015:

United Kingdom	May 28
Canada	June 6
Norway	July 4
Germany	July 8
Belgium	August 6

Of the advanced countries, only Australia has a similar tax freedom day to the United States. Down Under, they paid their taxes in 2015 by April 10.

The "Tax Freedom Day" is a dramatic way of drawing attention to high *average* taxes, but it is high *marginal* taxes that create inefficiency.

CHECKPOINT 8.2

MyEconLab Study Plan 8.2
Key Terms Quiz
Solutions Video

Explain how income taxes and Social Security taxes change wage rates and employment, are shared by employers and workers, and create inefficiency.

Practice Problems

1. Which income tax is the most efficient and which is the most inefficient, and why: a tax on labor income, a tax on capital income, or a tax on land income?

2. Comparing a tax on labor income, a tax on capital income, and a tax on land income, who pays more of each tax, and why?

3. Explain why Jordan Spieth pays his own Social Security tax and the PGA (the Professional Golfers' Association) pays none of it.

In the News

Want Arizona jobs? Phase out the state income tax
Arizona's state income taxes rank in the middle among U.S. states. The state can promote job creation by abolishing its income taxes.
Source: azcentral, November 30, 2015
Is the news clip correct? Explain the effects of abolishing the state personal income tax and corporation income tax. Will workers or employers benefit most?

Solutions to Practice Problems

1. The income tax that is most efficient is that on the income earned by the factor of production that has the lowest elasticity of demand or supply. The reason is that the deadweight loss from a tax (the excess burden) is smaller if the tax decreases the equilibrium quantity of the factor by a small amount. The supply of land is perfectly inelastic, while the supplies of labor and capital are elastic. So the tax on land income is the most efficient tax.
For a similar reason, the income tax that is most *inefficient* is that on the income earned by the factor of production that has the *highest* elasticity of demand or supply. The supply of capital is highly elastic, perhaps perfectly elastic, so the tax on capital income is the most inefficient.

2. Who pays more of a tax depends on the relative elasticities of demand and supply. The demand for labor is more elastic than the supply of labor, so workers bear a larger share of the tax on labor income than employers. The supply of capital is more elastic than the demand for capital, so business owners pay more of the tax on capital income than savers and lenders pay. The supply of land is less elastic than the demand for land, so land owners pay more of the tax on land income than renters pay.

3. Jordan Spieth pays his Social Security tax and the PGA pays none of it because the supply of Jordan Spieth's services is (most likely) perfectly inelastic. The elasticities of demand and supply determine who pays the tax.

Solution to In the News

Because the demand for labor is elastic and the supply of labor is inelastic, most of the personal tax cut will benefit workers and it will increase employment. Because the supply of capital is perfectly elastic, most of the corporation tax cut will benefit employers and it, too, will create jobs. So the news clip is correct.

MyEconLab Concept Video

8.3 FAIRNESS AND THE BIG TRADEOFF

We've examined the incidence and the efficiency of different types of taxes. These topics have occupied most of this chapter because they are the issues about taxes that economics can address. But when political leaders debate tax issues, it is fairness, not just incidence and efficiency, that gets the most attention. Democrats complain that Republican tax cuts are unfair because they give the benefits of lower taxes to the rich. Republicans counter that because the rich pay most of the taxes, it is fair that they get most of the tax cuts. No easy answers are available to the questions about the fairness of taxes. Economists have proposed two principles of fairness to apply to a tax system:

- The benefits principle
- The ability-to-pay principle

■ The Benefits Principle

Benefits principle
The proposition that people should pay taxes equal to the benefits they receive from public goods and services.

The **benefits principle** is the proposition that people should pay taxes equal to the benefits they receive from public goods and services. This arrangement is fair because those who benefit most pay the most. The benefits principle makes tax payments and the consumption of government-provided services similar to private consumption expenditures. If taxes are based on the benefits principle, the people who enjoy the largest benefits pay the most for them.

To implement the benefits principle, it would be necessary to have an objective method of measuring each individual's marginal benefit from government-provided goods. In the absence of such a method, the principle can be used to justify a wide range of different taxes.

For example, the benefits principle can justify high gasoline taxes to pay for public highways. Here, the argument would be that those who value the highways most are the people who use them most, and so they should pay most of the cost of providing them. Similarly, the benefits principle can justify high taxes on alcoholic beverages and tobacco products. Here, the argument would be that those who drink and smoke the most place the largest burden on public health-care services and so they should pay the greater part of the cost of those services.

The benefits principle can also be used to justify a higher income tax on those who earn larger incomes. Here, the argument would be that the rich receive a disproportionately large share of the benefit from law and order and security, so they should pay the largest share of providing these services.

■ The Ability-to-Pay Principle

Ability-to-pay principle
The proposition that people should pay taxes according to how easily they can bear the burden.

The **ability-to-pay principle** is the proposition that people should pay taxes according to how easily they can bear the burden. A rich person can more easily bear the burden of providing public goods than a poor person can, so the rich should pay higher taxes than the poor. The ability-to-pay principle involves comparing people along two dimensions: horizontally and vertically.

Horizontal Equity

Horizontal equity
The requirement that taxpayers with the same ability to pay should pay the same taxes.

If taxes are based on ability to pay, taxpayers with the same ability to pay should pay the same taxes, a situation called **horizontal equity**. While horizontal equity is easy to agree with in principle, it is difficult to implement in practice. If two people are identical in every respect, horizontal equity is easy to apply. But how do we compare people who are similar but not identical? The greatest difficulty arises in working out differences in ability to pay that arise from the state of a person's health and from a person's family responsibilities. The U.S. income tax has many special deductions and other rules that aim to achieve horizontal equity.

Vertical Equity

Vertical equity is the requirement that taxpayers with a greater ability to pay bear a greater share of the taxes. This proposition easily translates into the requirement that people with higher incomes should pay higher taxes. But it doesn't tell us how steeply taxes should increase as income increases.

Vertical equity
The requirement that taxpayers with a greater ability to pay bear a greater share of the taxes.

◼ Ability to Pay and Tax Progressivity

The relationship between tax rates and income levels—how steeply taxes increase as income increases—is called the degree of *tax progressivity*. To describe tax progressivity, we use two tax rate concepts, the *average* and the *marginal* tax rate.

An **average tax rate** is the percentage of income that is paid in tax. For example, if the tax paid on an income of $50,000 is $10,000, the average tax rate is 20 percent.

Average tax rate
The percentage of income that is paid in tax.

A **marginal tax rate** is the percentage of an *additional* dollar of income that is paid in tax. For example, if income increases from $50,000 to $50,001, and the tax paid increases from $10,000.00 to $10,000.30—increases by 30¢—the marginal tax rate is 30 percent.

Marginal tax rate
The percentage of an additional dollar of income that is paid in tax.

If the *average* tax rate increases as income increases, the tax is called a **progressive tax**. When a tax is progressive, the marginal tax rate exceeds the average tax rate. To illustrate, think about the above example. At an income of $50,000, the average tax rate is 20 percent. When income rises above $50,000, the marginal tax rate is 30 percent. Suppose that the marginal rate remains at 30 percent for all income levels up to $100,000. Then at $100,000, the average tax rate is 25 percent, an average of 20 percent on the first $50,000 and 30 percent on the second $50,0000.

Progressive tax
A tax whose average rate increases as income increases.

A progressive tax contrasts with a **proportional tax**, which has the same average tax rate at *all* income levels. When a tax is proportional, the marginal tax rate equals the average tax rate.

Proportional tax
A tax whose average rate is constant at *all* income levels.

A third possibility is a **regressive tax**, which has an average tax rate that decreases as income increases.

Regressive tax
A tax whose average rate decreases as income increases.

Should taxes be progressive, proportional, or regressive? All of these arrangements have higher-income people paying higher taxes, so they all satisfy the basic idea of vertical equity. But most people think that vertical equity can only be achieved with a progressive income tax. And the U.S. federal income tax code reflects this view of fairness as you can see in *Eye on the U.S. Economy* (p. 208).

◼ The Big Tradeoff and Alternative Tax Proposals

Questions about the fairness of taxes conflict with efficiency questions and create the *big tradeoff* that you met in Chapter 6. The taxes that generate the greatest deadweight loss are those on the income from capital. But most capital is owned by a relatively small number of people who have the greatest ability to pay taxes. So a conflict arises between efficiency and fairness. We want a tax system that is efficient, in the sense that it raises the revenue that the government needs to provide public goods and services, but we want a tax system that shares the burden of providing these goods and services fairly.

EYE on the U.S. ECONOMY
The Progressive Income Tax

The U.S. federal income tax is progressive. The average tax rate rises with income and the marginal rate exceeds the average rate. The table and the figure illustrate these facts. The table lists the marginal tax rates and the graph shows the average and marginal tax rates.

Using the numbers in the table, we can calculate the tax paid by a person who earns $50,000 a year. Taxable income is $39,700, which is total income minus deductions. The tax paid is 10 percent of the first $9,225 of taxable income ($923) plus 15 percent of the next $28,225 ($4,234) plus 25 percent of the remaining $2,250 ($563). The total tax equals $5,720, which is 11.4 percent of $50,000. The average tax rate is 11.4 percent.

You can see how the average tax rate rises with income by looking at someone who earns $100,000 a

Taxable income (dollars)	Marginal tax rate (percent)
$0 to $9,225	10.0
$9,226 to $37,450	15.0
$37,451 to $90,750	25.0
$90,751 to $189,300	28.0
$189,301 to $411,500	33.0
$411,501 to $413,200	35.0
$413,201 or more	39.6

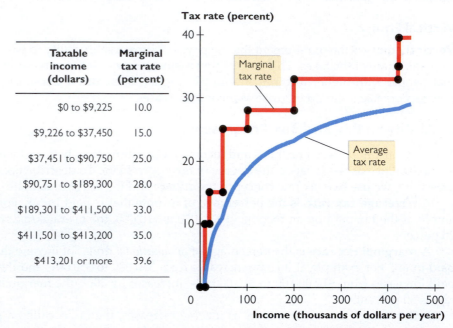

SOURCE OF DATA: Internal Revenue Service.

year. For this person, the tax paid on the first $50,000 is the same as for someone who earns that amount. But the taxes paid on the next $50,000 are $12,500—a 25 percent marginal tax rate. The total tax equals $18,219, which is 18.2 percent of $100,000. The average tax rate is 18.2 percent.

Our tax system is an evolving compromise that juggles these two goals. Part of that evolution is an ongoing conversation about reform proposals. Two of these proposals are

- A flat tax
- The FairTax

A Flat Tax

Flat tax

A tax system with a constant average and marginal tax rate: A proportional tax.

A **flat tax** is a tax system with a constant average and marginal rate. It is a proportional tax.

Eight U.S. states—Colorado, Illinois, Indiana, Massachusetts, Michigan, North Carolina, Pennsylvania, and Utah—tax household incomes at a single rate. Flat tax plans have been proposed for the U.S. federal income tax, but the idea has never had broad support.

The idea has received more support in some Eastern European countries— Albania, Bulgaria, Estonia, Latvia, Lithuania, Macedonia, Romania, Russia,

Slovakia, and Ukraine—where some form of flat tax has been introduced.

You've seen that all taxes are inefficient: They create deadweight loss. A flat tax is less inefficient than a progressive tax because the top tax rate is lower with a flat tax. So compared with a progressive tax, a flat tax strengthens the incentive to work, save, and invest. These productive activities increase income and boost the pace at which incomes grow.

The efficiency gain from a flat tax comes at the cost of placing a larger tax burden on people with low and average incomes and lessening the burden on those with the highest incomes. So the flat tax chooses a point on the big tradeoff that is more efficient but less fair than our current progressive tax system.

The second tax proposal that we examine seeks to replicate the efficiency of a flat tax while remaining a progressive tax and being as fair as our current taxes.

The FairTax

The **FairTax** is a proposal considered by the United States Congress in 1999 to tax the purchase of all consumption goods and services above the poverty level. It is a proposal for a radical reform of the entire U.S. federal tax system. All current federal taxes—personal and corporate income taxes, capital gains taxes, payroll taxes (including Social Security and Medicare taxes), gift taxes, and estate taxes—would be abolished. These taxes would be replaced by a single tax, initially at a 23 percent rate, on the purchase of all new goods and services for personal consumption.

The current federal tax is mainly a tax on income. Income is the *tax base*. The tax base of the FairTax is consumption expenditure, not income. People choose how to allocate their income between consumption and saving. Because the FairTax hits only consumption expenditure, it strengthens the incentive to save. And increased saving finances increased investment in productive business activities, which brings increased job opportunities and incomes. So the FairTax has the efficiency properties of the flat tax.

The "fair" component of the FairTax is that every household receives a monthly payment from the federal government equal to the tax on purchases up to the poverty level. In 2015, the poverty level for a family of two adults and two children was $24,250 per year, so a 23 percent tax on consumption at this level is $5,578 a year or $465 per month.

This monthly payment means that at low incomes, the FairTax is a progressive tax—the average tax rate increases with income. Families with incomes up to the poverty level pay no tax. And families with incomes of double the poverty level who spend all their income on consumption and have no saving pay an average tax equal to 11.5 percent of their income—the average of zero percent on the first $24,250 and 23 percent on the second $24,250.

The FairTax takes an increasing percentage of consumption expenditure, but it doesn't take an increasing percentage of income—it is a regressive tax. The reason is that although a higher income brings higher consumption, the percentage of income spent on consumption decreases with income. So the percentage of income paid in taxes decreases as income increases. This regressive feature of the FairTax makes it appear to be unfair.

So despite its name, the FairTax might be less inefficient than our current progressive taxes, but it could not be considered fairer.

We are left with the current progressive taxes as the best available compromise between efficiency and fairness. The conversation and the search for a better solution to the big tradeoff continues.

FairTax
A proposal to tax the purchase of consumption goods and services above the poverty level, considered by the United States Congress in 1999.

MyEconLab Study Plan 8.3
Key Terms Quiz
Solutions Video

CHECKPOINT 8.3

Review ideas about the fairness of the tax system and the tradeoff between efficiency and fairness.

Practice Problems

1. "Retired seniors should pay higher taxes than college students because government-funded healthcare for seniors costs more than government-funded tuition." Is this statement consistent with a principle of tax-system fairness?

2. Florida levies the following taxes: a 5.5 percent corporate income tax; a 6 percent sales tax; taxes of $0.34 a gallon on gasoline, $1.34 a pack on cigarettes, $0.48 a gallon on beer, and $2.25 a gallon on wine; and property taxes that vary across the counties and range from 1.4 percent to 2.0 percent of property values. Classify Florida's taxes into progressive, proportional, and regressive taxes.

3. What are the main differences between a flat tax and the FairTax? Which of the two taxes places a greater weight on efficiency and a smaller weight on fairness in the big tradeoff?

In the News

California voters overwhelmingly back $2-a-pack increase in the cigarette tax with the revenue being used to fund healthcare for the poor.

Source: *Los Angeles Times*, September 3, 2015

Which principle of fairness would California use to justify this big tax hike?

Solutions to Practice Problems

1. The statement "Retired seniors should pay higher taxes than college students because government-funded healthcare for seniors costs more than government-funded tuition." is consistent with the benefits principle of tax-system fairness, which is the proposition that people should pay taxes equal to the benefits they receive.

2. If counties with the higher rates are those with high property values, then Florida's property taxes are progressive. The corporate income tax does not vary with income, so this tax is a proportional tax. Because saving increases with income, expenditure as a fraction of income decreases as income increases. The taxes on expenditure (sales tax, gasoline tax, cigarette tax, beer tax, and wine tax) are regressive taxes.

3. The tax base for the flat tax is income and the tax base for the FairTax is expenditure on consumption goods and services. The flat tax is proportional while the FairTax is progressive at low income levels but regressive at high income levels because consumption expenditure decreases as a percentage of income as income increases. The FairTax places a greater weight on efficiency and a smaller weight on fairness.

Solution to In the News

The two principles of fairness are the benefits principle and the ability-to-pay principle. California will justify the tax on the benefits principle because the funds raised will pay for healthcare of the poor, who are most of the smokers.

CHAPTER SUMMARY

Key Points

1. **Explain how taxes change prices and quantities, are shared by buyers and sellers, and create inefficiency.**

- Regardless of whether a tax is imposed on buyers or sellers, it has the same effects: The price paid by the buyer rises and the price received by the seller falls.
- A tax creates inefficiency by driving a wedge between marginal benefit and marginal cost and creating a deadweight loss.
- The less elastic the demand or the more elastic the supply, the greater is the price increase and the larger is the share of the tax paid by the buyer.
- If demand is perfectly elastic or supply is perfectly inelastic, the seller pays all the tax; if demand is perfectly inelastic or supply is perfectly elastic, the buyer pays all the tax.
- If demand or supply is perfectly inelastic, the tax creates no deadweight loss and is efficient.

2. **Explain how income taxes and Social Security taxes change wage rates and employment, are shared by employers and workers, and create inefficiency.**

- The shares of the income tax paid by firms and households depend on the elasticity of demand and the elasticity of supply of the factors of production.
- The elasticities of demand and supply, not Congress, determine who pays the income tax and who pays the Social Security tax.
- The more elastic is either the demand or supply of a factor of production, the greater is the excess burden of an income tax.

3. **Review ideas about the fairness of the tax system and the tradeoff between efficiency and fairness.**

- The two main principles of fairness of taxes—the benefits principle and the ability-to-pay principle—do not deliver universally accepted ideas of fairness.
- Taxes can be progressive (the average tax rate rises with income), proportional (the average tax rate is constant), or regressive (the average tax rate falls with income). The U.S. income tax is progressive.
- A flat tax and the FairTax have been proposed as alternative solutions to the "big tradeoff" that are more efficient, but they are generally regarded as less fair than the current tax arrangements.

Key Terms

MyEconLab Key Terms Quiz

Ability-to-pay principle, 206
Average tax rate, 207
Benefits principle, 206
Excess burden, 194
FairTax, 209

Flat tax, 208
Horizontal equity, 206
Marginal tax rate, 207
Progressive tax, 207
Proportional tax, 207

Regressive tax, 207
Tax incidence, 192
Vertical equity, 207

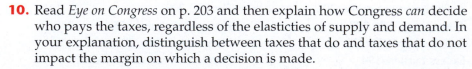

CHAPTER CHECKPOINT

Study Plan Problems and Applications

1. In Florida, sunscreen and sunglasses are vital items. If the tax on sellers of these items is doubled from 5.5 percent to 11 percent, who will pay most of the tax increase: the buyer or the seller? Will the tax increase halve the quantity of sunscreen and sunglasses bought?

2. Suppose that the government imposes a $2-a-cup tax on coffee. What determines by how much Starbucks will raise its price? How will the quantity of coffee bought in coffee shops change? Will this tax raise much revenue?

Concerned about the political fallout from rising gas prices, the government cuts the tax on gasoline. Use this information to work Problems **3** and **4**.

3. Explain the effect of this tax cut on the price of gasoline and the quantity bought if, at the same time, the oil-producing nations increase production.

4. Explain the effect of this tax cut on the price of gasoline and the quantity bought if, at the same time, a global shortage of oil sends the price up.

Table 1 illustrates the market for Internet service. Use the information in Table 1 and a demand-supply graph to work Problems **5** and **6**.

5. What is the market price of Internet service? If the government taxes Internet service $15 a month, what price would the buyer of Internet service pay? What price would the seller of Internet service receive?

6. If the government taxes Internet service $15 a month, does the buyer or the seller pay more of the tax? What is the tax revenue? What is the excess burden of the tax? Is the tax proportional, progressive, or regressive?

Figure 1 illustrates the labor market in a country that does not tax labor income. Suppose that the government introduces a Social Security tax on workers of $2 per hour. Use this information to work Problems **7** and **8**.

7. How many workers are employed? What is the wage rate paid by employers and what is the workers' after-tax wage rate? How many workers are no longer employed?

8. If the government splits the Social Security tax equally between workers and employers, how many workers are employed? What is the wage rate paid by employers and what is the workers' after-tax wage rate?

9. **What a big tax on soft drinks can do**
   A big tax on sugary drinks in Mexico has cut consumption. Sellers passed on the entire tax in higher prices. The largest consumers of sugary drinks are the poor who suffer from diabetes and obesity.
   Source: *The New York Times*, October 19, 2015

   What can we say about the incidence of Mexico's tax on sugary drinks and what can we infer about the elasticities of supply and demand for these drinks? Would this tax be a progressive tax or a regressive tax? On the basis of what principle would this tax be fair?

10. Read *Eye on Congress* on p. 203 and then explain how Congress *can* decide who pays the taxes, regardless of the elasticities of supply and demand. In your explanation, distinguish between taxes that do and taxes that do not impact the margin on which a decision is made.

TABLE 1

Price (dollars per month)	Quantity demanded	Quantity supplied
	(units per month)	
0	30	0
10	25	10
20	20	20
30	15	30
40	10	40
50	5	50
60	0	60

FIGURE 1

Wage rate (dollars per hour)

Instructor Assignable Problems and Applications

MyEconLab Homework, Quiz, or Test if assigned by instructor

Use the following information to work Problems **1** to **3**.

New York has the highest cigarette taxes in the country. The price of an average pack of cigarettes in New York City is $10.60. The combined state and city taxes are $5.95 a pack. The average income of smokers is less than that of non-smokers.

1. Draw a graph to show the effects of the $5.95 tax on the buyer's price, the seller's price, the quantity of cigarettes bought, and the tax revenue. Does the buyer or seller pay more of the tax? Why?

2. What is the effect of the tax on consumer surplus and producer surplus, and what is the excess burden of the tax?

3. Is this tax on cigarettes a progressive, regressive, or proportional tax?

4. The supply of luxury boats is perfectly elastic, the demand for luxury boats is unit elastic, and with no tax on luxury boats the price is $1 million and 240 luxury boats a week are bought.

   Now luxury boats are taxed at 20 percent. What is the price that buyers pay? How is the tax split between buyers and sellers? What is the government's tax revenue? On a graph, show the excess burden of this tax. Is this tax efficient?

5. Figure 1 illustrates the market for chocolate bars. If a new tax of $1.50 a chocolate bar is imposed, what is the change in the quantity of chocolate bars bought, who pays most of the tax, and what is the deadweight loss?

6. In an hour, a baker earns $10, a gas pump attendant earns $6, and a copy shop worker earns $7. Suppose that the government introduces an income tax of $1 an hour. Calculate the marginal tax rates for bakers, gas pump attendants, and copy shop workers. Is this tax progressive or regressive?

7. Larry earns $25,000 and pays $2,500 in tax, while Suzy earns $50,000 and pays $15,000 in tax. If Larry's income increases by $100, his tax increases by $12, but if Suzy's income increases by $100, her tax increases by $35. Calculate the average tax rate and marginal tax rate that Larry pays and that Suzy pays. Is this income tax fair? Explain.

8. A study of the Bush tax cuts of 2001 noted that the top 1 percent of income earners reaped the biggest benefits. What assumptions about the elasticities of demand and supply for high-wage labor and capital might be consistent with this assessment? What other facts about demand and supply and market outcomes would you need to know to verify this claim?

Use the following news clip to work Problems **9** and **10**.

The gas tax is running on empty
The federal gas tax has been stuck at 18.4¢ a gallon since 1993. Today, Americans are driving fewer miles and vehicles have become more fuel-efficient. Less gas consumption means less gas-tax revenue to repair the nation's roads.

Source: *Bloomberg News*, July 17, 2014

9. Would a tax per mile driven be more efficient or less efficient than a tax per gallon of gasoline? Which tax would be more regressive? Explain your answers.

10. Would a tax per mile driven be fairer than a tax per gallon of gasoline? Explain your answer.

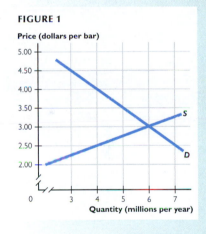

FIGURE 1

MyEconLab Chapter 8 Study Plan

Multiple Choice Quiz

1. If a tax of $1 a can is imposed on the buyers of sugary drinks, the demand for sugary drinks _____ and the price that buyers pay _____.

  A. doesn't change; doesn't change
  B. doesn't change; rises by $1 a can
  C. decreases; rises by more than $1 a can
  D. decreases; rises by less than $1 a can

2. A tax on sugar will be paid by only _____.

  A. buyers if the supply of sugar is perfectly elastic
  B. sellers if the demand for sugar is perfectly inelastic
  C. buyers if the demand for sugar is perfectly elastic
  D. sellers if the supply of sugar is perfectly elastic

3. If the government imposes a new tax on plastic bags, _____.

  A. total surplus from bags shrinks by more than the amount of tax collected
  B. total surplus from bags shrinks by the amount of the tax revenue collected
  C. a deadweight loss arises equal to the amount of tax revenue collected
  D. the market for plastic bags remains efficient if the tax is fair

4. The demand for labor is more elastic than the supply of labor. An income tax _____ the wage rate paid by employers and _____.

  A. lowers; workers pay all the tax
  B. raises; workers pay most of the tax
  C. does not change; employers pay all the tax
  D. raises; employers pay most of the tax

5. The supply of low-skilled workers in China is perfectly elastic. In 2011, when China cut the tax on these workers' incomes from 5 percent to zero, _____.

  A. employers cut the wage rate but hired the same number of workers
  B. employers cut the wage rate and hired more workers
  C. employers didn't change the wage rate but hired more workers
  D. employers didn't change the wage rate and hired the same number of workers

6. The supply of land is perfectly inelastic, so a tax on land rent is _____.

  A. efficient and the landowner pays all the tax
  B. inefficient because the renter pays all the tax
  C. inefficient if the tax is too high
  D. efficient and the renter pays all the tax

7. The demand for labor is more elastic than the supply of labor. A Social Security tax imposed equally on workers and employers _____.

  A. raises the wage rate by more than the Social Security tax
  B. decreases employment and workers pay most of the tax
  C. increases the wage rate paid by employers by the amount of the tax
  D. is fair because workers and employers pay the same amount of tax

8. The _____ principle of fairness is the proposition that _____.

  A. benefits; people should pay taxes equal to the benefits they receive from the public goods bought with the tax revenue
  B. benefits; people should receive benefits equal to their ability to pay
  C. ability-to-pay; people should pay taxes equal to the benefits they receive
  D. ability-to-pay; people should receive benefits equal to their ability to pay

Who wins and who loses
from globalization?

Global Markets in Action

9

When you have completed your study of this chapter, you will be able to

1 Explain how markets work with international trade.

2 Identify the gains from international trade and its winners and losers.

3 Explain the effects of international trade barriers.

4 Explain and evaluate arguments used to justify restricting international trade.

MyEconLab Big Picture Video

MyEconLab Concept Video

Imports
The goods and services that people and firms in one country buy from firms in other countries.

Exports
The goods and services that firms in one country sell to people and firms in other countries.

9.1   HOW GLOBAL MARKETS WORK

Because we trade with people in other countries, the goods and services that we buy and consume are not limited by what we produce. The goods and services that we buy from people and firms in other countries are our **imports**; the goods and services that we sell to people and firms in other countries are our **exports**.

■ International Trade Today

Global trade today is enormous. In 2015, global exports and imports (the two numbers are the same because what one country exports another imports) were about $23 trillion, which is 31 percent of the value of global production. The United States is the world's largest international trader and accounts for 10 percent of world exports and 12 percent of world imports. Germany and China, which rank 2 and 3 behind the United States, lag by a large margin.

In 2015, total U.S. exports were $2.3 trillion, which is about 13 percent of the value of U.S. production. Total U.S. imports were $2.8 trillion, which is about 16 percent of the value of total expenditure in the United States.

The United States trades both goods and services. In 2015, exports of services were $0.75 trillion (33 percent of total exports) and imports of services were $0.5 trillion (16 percent of total imports).

Our largest exports are private services such as banking, insurance, and business consulting. Our largest exports of goods are automobile parts. Our largest import used to be crude oil, and it remains a large item. But in 2015, computers were our largest import. *Eye on the U.S. Economy* (p. 217) provides a bit more detail on ten large exports and imports.

■ What Drives International Trade?

The fundamental force that drives international trade is *comparative advantage*. We defined comparative advantage in Chapter 3 (p. 73) as the ability of a person to perform an activity or produce a good or service at a lower opportunity cost than anyone else. This same idea applies to nations. We can define *national comparative advantage* as the ability of a *nation* to perform an activity or produce a good or service at a lower opportunity cost than *any other nation*.

The opportunity cost of producing a T-shirt is lower in China than in the United States, so China has a comparative advantage in producing T-shirts. The opportunity cost of producing an airplane is lower in the United States than in China, so the United States has a comparative advantage in producing airplanes.

You saw in Chapter 3 how Liz and Joe reaped gains from trade by specializing in the production of the good at which they have a comparative advantage and then trading. Both were better off. This same principle applies to trade among nations.

China has a comparative advantage at producing T-shirts and the United States has a comparative advantage at producing airplanes, so the people of both countries can gain from specialization and trade. China can buy airplanes from the United States at a lower opportunity cost than that at which it can produce them. Americans can buy T-shirts from China for a lower opportunity cost than that at which U.S. firms can produce them. Also, through international trade, Chinese producers can get higher prices for their T-shirts and Boeing can sell airplanes for a higher price. Both countries gain from international trade.

We're going to illustrate the gains from trade that we've just described by studying demand and supply in the global markets for T-shirts and airplanes.

EYE on the U.S. ECONOMY
U.S. Exports and Imports

The blue bars in part (a) of the figure show ten large U.S. exports and the red bars in part (b) show ten large U.S. imports. Some items appear in both parts (a) and (b) because the United States exports and imports items in many of the broad categories.

Three of the leading U.S. exports are services—private services, which include financial, business, professional and technical services (such as the sale of advertising by Google to Adidas, a European sportswear maker), and education (foreign students in our colleges and universities); travel (such as the expenditure on a Florida vacation by a visitor from England); and royalties and license fees (such as fees received by Hollywood movie producers on films shown abroad).

Computers such as laptops and tablets are the largest import. We also import large quantities of industrial ands service machinery, automobiles and parts, clothing, crude oil, and travel. Private services also feature as a large imports category.

Although we import a large quantity of computers, we export some too. We also export the semiconductors (computer chips) inside those imported computers. The Intel chip in a Lenovo laptop built in China and imported into the United States is an example. This chip is made in the United States and exported to China.

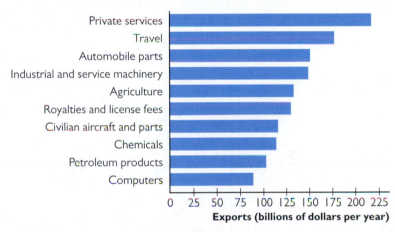

(a) Ten large U.S. exports

The United States exports airplanes …

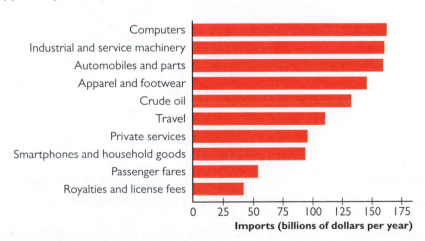

(b) Ten large U.S. imports

SOURCE OF DATA: Bureau of Economic Analysis.

and imports computers.

■ Why the United States Imports T-Shirts

Figure 9.1 illustrates the effects of international trade in T-shirts. The demand curve D_{US} and the supply curve S_{US} show the demand and supply in the U.S. domestic market only. The demand curve tells us the quantity of T-shirts that Americans are willing to buy at various prices. The supply curve tells us the quantity of T-shirts that U.S. garment makers are willing to sell at various prices.

Figure 9.1(a) shows what the U.S. T-shirt market would be like with no international trade. The price of a T-shirt would be $8 and 40 million T-shirts a year would be produced by U.S. garment makers and bought by U.S. consumers.

Figure 9.1(b) shows the market for T-shirts *with* international trade. Now the price of a T-shirt is determined in the world market, not the U.S. domestic market. The world price is *less than* $8 a T-shirt, which means that the rest of the world has a comparative advantage in producing T-shirts. The world price line shows the world price as $5 a T-shirt.

The U.S. demand curve, D_{US}, tells us that at $5 a T-shirt, Americans buy 60 million T-shirts a year. The U.S. supply curve, S_{US}, tells us that at $5 a T-shirt, U.S. garment makers produce 20 million T-shirts. To buy 60 million T-shirts when only 20 million are produced in the United States, we must import T-shirts from the rest of the world. The quantity of T-shirts imported is 40 million a year.

FIGURE 9.1

A Market with Imports   MyEconLab Animation

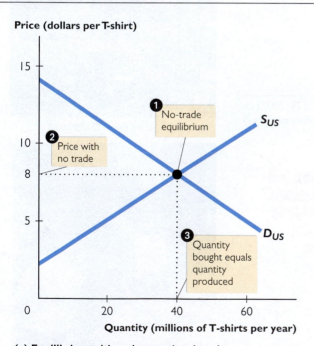

(a) Equilibrium with no international trade

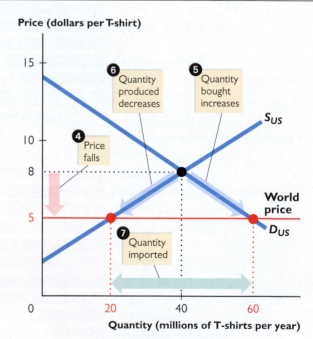

(b) Equilibrium in a market with imports

With no international trade, in part (a), ❶ domestic demand and domestic supply determine ❷ the equilibrium price at $8 a T-shirt and ❸ the quantity at 40 million T-shirts a year.
With international trade, in part (b), world demand and world supply

determine the world price, which is $5 per T-shirt. ❹ The domestic price falls to $5 a T-shirt. ❺ Domestic purchases increase to 60 million T-shirts a year, and ❻ domestic production decreases to 20 million T-shirts a year. ❼ 40 million T-shirts a year are imported.

■ Why the United States Exports Airplanes

Figure 9.2 illustrates the effects of international trade in airplanes. The demand curve D_{US} and the supply curve S_{US} show the demand and supply in the U.S. domestic market only. The demand curve tells us the quantity of airplanes that U.S. airlines are willing to buy at various prices. The supply curve tells us the quantity of airplanes that U.S. aircraft makers are willing to sell at various prices.

Figure 9.2(a) shows what the U.S. airplane market would be like with no international trade. The price of an airplane would be $100 million and 400 airplanes a year would be produced by U.S. aircraft makers and bought by U.S. airlines.

Figure 9.2(b) shows the U.S. airplane market *with* international trade. Now the price of an airplane is determined in the world market, not the U.S. domestic market. The world price is *higher than* $100 million, which means that the United States has a comparative advantage in producing airplanes. The world price line shows the world price as $150 million.

At $150 million per airplane, the U.S. demand curve, D_{US}, tells us that airlines in the United States buy 200 airplanes a year and the U.S. supply curve, S_{US}, tells us that U.S. aircraft makers produce 700 airplanes a year. The quantity produced in the United States (700 a year) minus the quantity purchased by U.S. airlines (200 a year) is the quantity of U.S. exports, which is 500 airplanes a year.

FIGURE 9.2

A Market with Exports   MyEconLab Animation

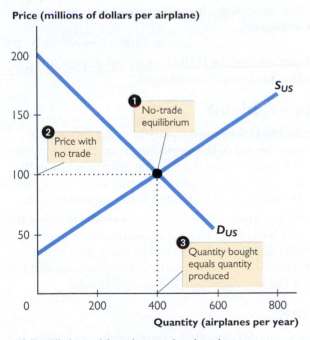

(a) Equilibrium with no international trade

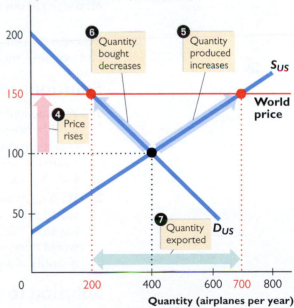

(b) Equilibrium in a market with exports

With no international trade, in part (a), ❶ domestic demand and domestic supply determine ❷ the equilibrium price at $100 million an airplane and ❸ the equilibrium quantity at 400 airplanes a year. With international trade, in part (b), world demand and world

supply determine the world price, which is $150 million an airplane. ❹ The domestic price rises. ❺ Domestic production increases to 700 airplanes a year, ❻ domestic purchases decrease to 200 airplanes a year, and ❼ 500 airplanes a year are exported.

MyEconLab Study Plan 9.1
Key Terms Quiz
Solutions Video

CHECKPOINT 9.1

Explain how markets work with international trade.

Practice Problems

1. Suppose that the world price of sugar is 10¢ a pound, the United States does *not* trade internationally, and the U.S. equilibrium price of sugar is 20¢ a pound. The United States then begins to trade internationally.
   • How does the price of sugar in the United States change?
   • Do U.S. consumers buy more or less sugar?
   • Do U.S. sugar growers produce more or less sugar?
   • Does the United States export or import sugar?

2. Suppose that the world price of steel is $100 a ton, India does *not* trade internationally, and the equilibrium price of steel in India is $60 a ton. India then begins to trade internationally.
   • How does the price of steel in India change?
   • How does the quantity of steel produced in India change?
   • How does the quantity of steel bought by India change?
   • Does India export or import steel?

In the News

The great American shale boom
In the past five years, U.S. oil output has doubled. In 2014, the United States and a few smaller countries added 2.4 million barrels a day to total world supply. Thanks to incredible advances in technology, instead of having to import more oil we've cut our reliance on foreign oil.

Source: Forbes, November 20, 2015

Describe the comparative advantage that the United States has in producing oil, and explain why its comparative advantage has changed.

Solutions to Practice Problems

1. With no international trade, the U.S. domestic price of sugar exceeds the world price so we know that the rest of the world has a comparative advantage at producing sugar. With international trade, the price of sugar in the United States falls to the world price, U.S. consumers buy more sugar, and U.S. sugar growers produce less sugar. The United States imports sugar.

2. With no international trade, the domestic price of steel in India is below the world price so we know that India has a comparative advantage at producing steel. With international trade, the price of steel in India rises to the world price, steel mills in India increase the quantity they produce, and the quantity of steel bought by Indians decreases. India exports steel.

Solution to In the News

Before new fracking technology was developed, the opportunity cost of producing oil in the United States was higher than the world market price, so the United States imported most of its oil. With the development of fracking, the cost of producing a barrel of oil in the United States is below the world price. Now the United States has a comparative advantage in the production of oil.

9.2   WINNERS, LOSERS, AND NET GAINS FROM TRADE

MyEconLab Concept Video

You've seen how international trade lowers the price of an imported good and raises the price of an exported good. Buyers of imported goods benefit from lower prices, and sellers of exported goods benefit from higher prices. But some people complain about international competition: Not everyone gains. We're now going to see who wins and who loses from free international trade. You will then be able to understand who complains about international competition and why.

We'll also see why we never hear the consumers of imported goods complaining and why we never hear exporters complaining, except when they want greater access to foreign markets. And we'll see why we *do* hear complaints from producers about cheap foreign imports.

EYE on GLOBALIZATION

MyEconLab Critical Thinking Exercise

Who Wins and Who Loses from Globalization?

Economists generally agree that the gains from globalization vastly outweigh the losses, but there are both winners and losers.

The U.S. consumer is a big winner. Globalization has brought iPads, Wii games, Nike shoes, and a wide range of other products to our shops at ever lower prices.

The Indian (and Chinese and other Asian) worker is another big winner. Globalization has brought a wider range of more interesting jobs and higher wages.

The U.S. (and European) textile workers and furniture makers are big losers. Their jobs have disappeared and many of them have struggled to find new jobs, even when they've been willing to take a pay cut.

But one of the biggest losers is the African farmer. Blocked from global agricultural markets by trade restrictions and subsidies in the United States and Europe, globalization is leaving much of Africa on the sidelines.

The U.S. consumer …

and Indian workers gain from globalization.

But some U.S. workers and …

African farmers lose.

■ Gains and Losses from Imports

We measure the gains and losses from imports by examining their effect on consumer surplus, producer surplus, and total surplus. The winners are those whose surplus increases and the losers are those whose surplus decreases.

Figure 9.3(a) shows what consumer surplus and producer surplus would be with no international trade. Domestic demand, D_{US}, and domestic supply, S_{US}, determine the price and quantity. The green area shows consumer surplus and the blue area shows producer surplus. Total surplus is the sum of consumer surplus and producer surplus.

Figure 9.3(b) shows how these surpluses change when the market opens to imports. The price falls to the world price. The quantity purchased increases to the quantity demanded at the world price, and consumer surplus expands to the larger green area $A + B + D$. The quantity produced decreases to the quantity supplied at the world price, and producer surplus shrinks to the smaller blue area C.

Part of the gain in consumer surplus, the area B, is a loss of producer surplus— a redistribution of total surplus. But the other part of the increase in consumer surplus, the area D, is a net gain. This increase in total surplus is the gain from imports and results from the lower price and increased purchases.

■ **FIGURE 9.3**

Gains and Losses in a Market with Imports

MyEconLab Animation

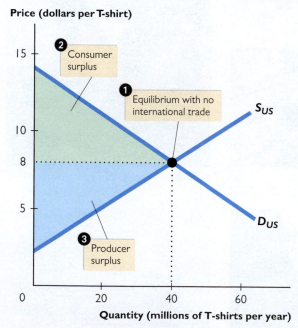

(a) Consumer surplus and producer surplus with no international trade

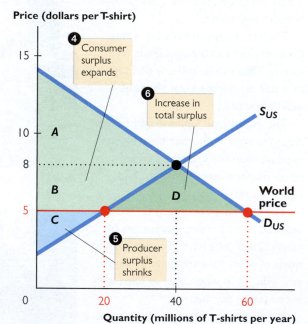

(b) Gains and losses from imports

With no international trade, ❶ equilibrium at the intersection of the domestic demand and domestic supply curves determines the price and quantity. ❷ The green area shows the consumer surplus and ❸ the blue area shows the producer surplus.

With international trade, the domestic price falls to the world price. ❹ Consumer surplus expands to the area $A + B + D$. Area B is a transfer of surplus from producers to consumers, and ❺ producer surplus shrinks to area C. ❻ Area D is an increase in total surplus.

■ Gains and Losses from Exports

We measure the gains and losses from exports just like we measured those from imports, by examining their effect on consumer surplus, producer surplus, and total surplus.

Figure 9.4(a) shows what the consumer surplus and producer surplus would be with no international trade. Domestic demand, D_{US}, and domestic supply, S_{US}, determine the price and quantity. The green area shows consumer surplus and the blue area shows producer surplus. The two surpluses sum to total surplus.

Figure 9.4(b) shows how the consumer surplus and producer surplus change when the good is exported. The price rises to the world price. The quantity bought decreases to the quantity demanded at the world price, and the consumer surplus shrinks to the green area A. The quantity produced increases to the quantity supplied at the world price, and the producer surplus expands from the blue area C to the larger blue area

Part of the gain in producer surplus, the area B, is a loss in consumer surplus—a redistribution of the total surplus. But the other part of the increase in producer surplus, the area D, is a net gain. This increase in total surplus is the gain from exports and results from the higher price and increased production.

■ FIGURE 9.4

Gains and Losses in a Market with Exports

MyEconLab Animation

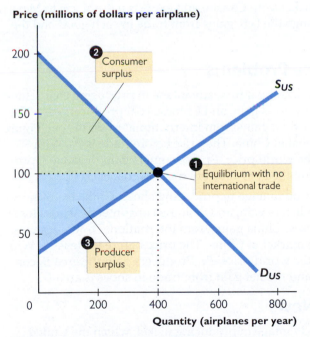

(a) Consumer surplus and producer surplus with no international trade

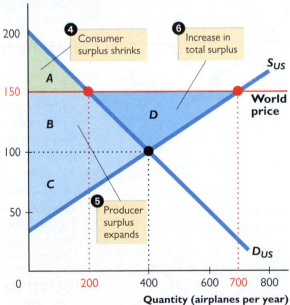

(b) Gains and losses from exports

With no international trade, ❶ equilibrium at the intersection of the domestic demand and domestic supply curves determines the price and quantity. ❷ The green area shows the consumer surplus and ❸ the blue area shows the producer surplus.

With international trade, the domestic price rises to the world price. ❹ Consumer surplus shrinks to the area A. ❺ Producer surplus expands to the area $B + C + D$. Area B is transferred from consumers to producers. ❻ Area D is an increase in total surplus.

MyEconLab Study Plan 9.2
Solutions Video

CHECKPOINT 9.2

Identify the gains from international trade and its winners and losers.

Practice Problems

Before the 1980s, China did not trade internationally: It was self-sufficient. Then China began to trade internationally in, among other items, coal and shoes. The world price of coal was less than China's domestic price and the world price of shoes was higher than its domestic price.

1. Does China import or export coal? Who in China gains and who loses from international trade in coal? Does China gain from this trade in coal? On a graph of the market for coal in China show the gains, losses, and net gain or loss from international trade in coal.

2. Does China import or export shoes? Who in China gains and who loses from international trade in shoes? Does China gain from this trade in shoes? On a graph of the market for shoes in China, show the gains, losses, and net gain or loss from international trade in shoes.

In the News

The commodity prices nightmare of 2015
Commodity prices have been decimated in 2015: natural gas down 38.5% and nickel down nearly 43%.

Source: *Money Morning*, December 3, 2015

The United States imports nickel from Canada and exports natural gas to Mexico. How do these price falls change the U.S. gains from trade in each good and the distribution of the gains?

Solutions to Practice Problems

1. The rest of the world has a comparative advantage in producing coal. China imports coal, Chinese coal users gain, and Chinese coal producers lose. The gains exceed the losses: China gains from international trade in coal. Figure 1 shows the market for coal in China. The price before trade is P_0. With trade, the price falls to the world price, P_1. Consumers gain the area B, producers lose the area B, and the net gain from trade in coal is D.

2. China has a comparative advantage in producing shoes. China exports shoes, Chinese shoe producers gain, and Chinese consumers of shoes lose. The gains exceed the losses: China gains from international trade in shoes. Figure 2 shows the shoe market in China. The price before trade is P_0. With trade, the price rises to the world price, P_1. Producers gain the area B, consumers lose the area B, and the net gain from trade in shoes is area D.

Solution to In the News

Canada has a comparative advantage in producing nickel, which the United States imports. A fall in the world price increases U.S. imports and increases U.S. consumer surplus and total surplus. The United States has a comparative advantage in producing natural gas, so the fall in the world price decreases U.S. production and exports. U.S. producer surplus decreases, consumer surplus increases, but producers lose more than consumers gain. Total surplus decreases.

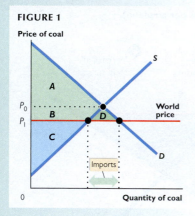

FIGURE 1

Price of coal

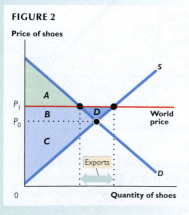

FIGURE 2

Price of shoes

9.3 INTERNATIONAL TRADE RESTRICTIONS

MyEconLab Concept Video

Governments use four sets of tools to influence international trade and protect domestic industries from foreign competition. They are

- Tariffs
- Import quotas
- Other import barriers
- Export subsidies

■ Tariffs

A **tariff** is a tax that is imposed on a good when it is imported. For example, the government of India imposes a 100 percent tariff on wine imported from California. When an Indian firm imports a $10 bottle of Californian wine, it pays the Indian government a $10 import duty.

The incentive for governments to impose tariffs is strong. First, they provide revenue to the government. Second, they enable the government to satisfy the self-interest of people who earn their incomes in import-competing industries. As you will see, tariffs and other restrictions on free international trade decrease the gains from trade and are not in the social interest. Let's see how.

Tariff
A tax imposed on a good when it is imported.

EYE on the PAST
The History of U.S. Tariffs

The figure shows the average tariff rate on U.S. imports since 1930. Tariffs peaked during the 1930s when Congress passed the Smoot-Hawley Act. With other nations, the United States signed the General Agreement on Tariffs and Trade (GATT) in 1947. In a series of rounds of negotiations, GATT achieved widespread tariff cuts for the United States and many other nations. Today, the World Trade Organization (WTO) continues the work of GATT and seeks to promote unrestricted trade among all nations.

The United States is a party to many trade agreements with individual countries or regions. These agreements include the North American Free Trade Agreement (NAFTA) and

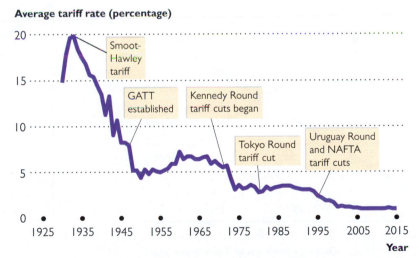

SOURCES OF DATA: The Budget for Fiscal Year 2015, Historical Tables, Table 2.5 and Bureau of Economic Analysis.

the Central American Free Trade Agreement (CAFTA). These agreements have eliminated tariffs on most goods traded between the United States and the countries of North and Central America.

The Effects of a Tariff

To see the effects of a tariff, let's return to the example in which, with free international trade, the United States imports T-shirts. The T-shirts are imported and sold at the world price. Then, under pressure from U.S. garment makers, the U.S. government imposes a tariff on imported T-shirts. Buyers of T-shirts must now pay the world price plus the tariff. Several consequences follow in the market for T-shirts. Figure 9.5 illustrates these consequences.

Figure 9.5(a) is the same as Figure 9.1(b) and shows the situation with free international trade. The United States produces 20 million T-shirts and imports 40 million T-shirts a year at the world price of $5 a T-shirt.

Figure 9.5(b) shows what happens with a tariff, which is set at $2 per T-shirt. The following changes occur in the U.S. market for T-shirts:

- The price of a T-shirt in the United States rises by $2.
- The quantity of T-shirts bought in the United States decreases.
- The quantity of T-shirts produced in the United States increases.
- The quantity of T-shirts imported into the United States decreases.
- The U.S. government collects a tariff revenue.

■ FIGURE 9.5

The Effects of a Tariff   MyEconLab Animation

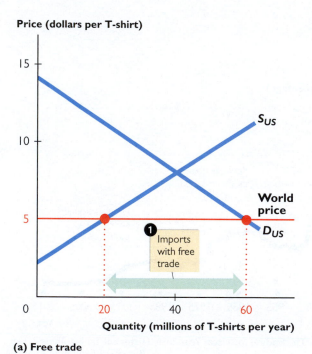

(a) Free trade

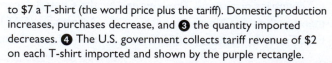

(b) Market with tariff

The world price of a T-shirt is $5. With free trade, in part (a), Americans buy 60 million T-shirts. The United States produces 20 million T-shirts and **❶** imports 40 million T-shirts. In part (b), **❷** with a tariff of $2 per T-shirt, the domestic price rises

to $7 a T-shirt (the world price plus the tariff). Domestic production increases, purchases decrease, and **❸** the quantity imported decreases. **❹** The U.S. government collects tariff revenue of $2 on each T-shirt imported and shown by the purple rectangle.

Rise in Price of a T-Shirt   To buy a T-shirt, Americans must pay the world price plus the tariff, so the price of a T-shirt rises by $2 to $7. Figure 9.5(b) shows the new domestic price line, which lies $2 above the world price line.

Decrease in Purchases   The higher price of a T-shirt brings a decrease in the quantity demanded, which Figure 9.5(b) shows as a movement along the demand curve from 60 million T-shirts at $5 a T-shirt to 45 million T-shirts at $7 a T-shirt.

Increase in Domestic Production   The higher price of a T-shirt stimulates domestic production, which Figure 9.5(b) shows as a movement along the supply curve from 20 million T-shirts at $5 a T-shirt to 35 million T-shirts at $7 a T-shirt.

Decrease in Imports   T-shirt imports decrease by 30 million from 40 million to 10 million a year. Both the decrease in purchases and the increase in domestic production contribute to this decrease in imports.

Tariff Revenue   The government's tariff revenue is $20 million—$2 per T-shirt on 10 million imported T-shirts—shown by the purple rectangle.

Winners, Losers, and the Social Loss from a Tariff

A tariff on an imported good creates winners and losers. When the U.S. government imposes a tariff on an imported good,

- U.S. producers of the good gain.
- U.S. consumers of the good lose.
- U.S. consumers lose more than U.S. producers gain.

U.S. Producers of the Good Gain   Because the price of an imported T-shirt rises by the tariff, U.S. T-shirt producers are now able to sell their T-shirts for a higher price—the world price plus the tariff. As the price of a T-shirt rises, U.S. producers increase the quantity supplied. Because the marginal cost of producing a T-shirt in the United States is less than the higher price of all the T-shirts sold, except for the marginal T-shirt, producer surplus increases. This increase in producer surplus is the gain to U.S. producers.

U.S. Consumers of the Good Lose   Because the price of a T-shirt in the United States rises, the quantity of T-shirts demanded decreases. The combination of a higher price and smaller quantity bought decreases consumer surplus. This loss of consumer surplus represents the loss to U.S. consumers that arises from a tariff.

U.S. Consumers Lose More Than U.S. Producers Gain   You've just seen that consumer surplus decreases and producer surplus increases, but which changes by more? Do consumers lose more than producers gain, or do producers gain more than consumers lose? Or is there just a straight transfer from consumers to producers? To answer these questions, we need to return to the demand and supply analysis of the market for T-shirts and compare the changes in consumer surplus and producer surplus.

Figure 9.6(a) is the same as Figure 9.3(b) and shows the consumer surplus and producer surplus with free international trade in T-shirts. The dark green area is the increase in total surplus that comes from free international trade. By comparing

■ **FIGURE 9.6**

The Winners and Losers from a Tariff

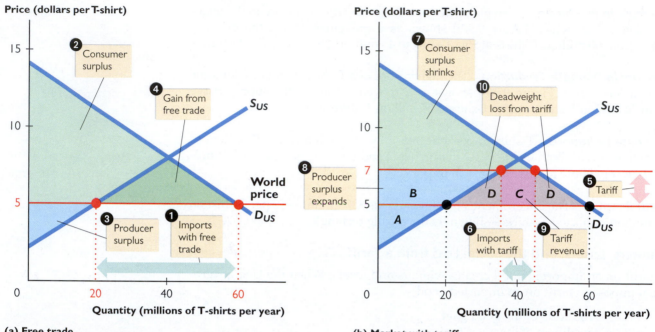

(a) Free trade

(b) Market with tariff

The world price of a T-shirt is $5. With free trade, ❶ the United States imports 40 million T-shirts. ❷ Consumer surplus, ❸ producer surplus, and ❹ the gains from free international trade are as large as possible. ❺ A tariff of $2 per T-shirt raises the price of a

T-shirt to $7. ❻ The quantity imported decreases. ❼ Consumer surplus shrinks by the areas B, C, and D. ❽ Producer surplus expands by area B. ❾ The government's tariff revenue is area C, and ❿ a deadweight loss equal to the two areas D is created.

Figure 9.6(b) with Figure 9.6(a), you can see how a $2 tariff on imported T-shirts changes the surpluses. Producer surplus—the blue area—increases by the area labeled *B*. The increase in producer surplus is the gain to U.S. producers from the tariff on T-shirts. Consumer surplus—the green area—shrinks.

The decrease in consumer surplus divides into three parts. First, some of the consumer surplus is transferred to producers. The blue area *B* represents this loss of consumer surplus (and gain of producer surplus). Second, part of the consumer surplus is transferred to the government. The purple area *C* represents this loss of consumer surplus (and gain of government revenue). When the tariff revenue is spent, both consumers and producers receive some benefit, but there is no expectation that the buyers of T-shirts will receive the benefits of the expenditure of this tariff revenue from T-shirts. The tariff revenue is a loss to buyers of T-shirts.

The third part of the loss of consumer surplus is a transfer to no one: it is a *deadweight loss*. Consumers buy a smaller quantity at a higher price. The two gray areas labeled *D* represent this loss of consumer surplus. Total surplus decreases by this amount, which is the social loss from the tariff.

Let's now look at the second tool for restricting trade: quotas.

Import Quotas

An **import quota** is a quantitative restriction on the import of a good that limits the maximum quantity of a good that may be imported in a given period. The United States imposes import quotas on many items, including sugar, bananas, beef, and textiles.

Quotas enable the government to satisfy the self-interest of people who earn their incomes in import-competing industries. You will see that like a tariff, a quota on imports decreases the gains from trade and is not in the social interest.

The Effects of an Import Quota

The effects of an import quota are similar to those of a tariff. The price rises, the quantity bought decreases, and the quantity produced in the United States increases. Figure 9.7 illustrates the effects.

Figure 9.7(a) shows the situation with free international trade. Figure 9.7(b) shows what happens with a quota that limits imports to 10 million T-shirts a year. The U.S. supply curve of T-shirts becomes the domestic supply curve, S_{US}, plus the quantity that the quota permits to be imported. So the U.S. supply curve becomes the curve labeled S_{US} + *quota*. The price of a T-shirt rises to $7, the

MyEconLab Concept Video

Import quota
A quantitative restriction on the import of a good that limits the maximum quantity of a good that may be imported in a given period.

FIGURE 9.7

The Effects of an Import Quota

MyEconLab Animation

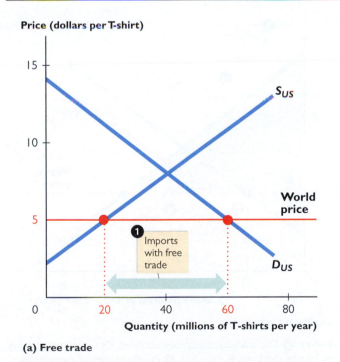

(a) Free trade

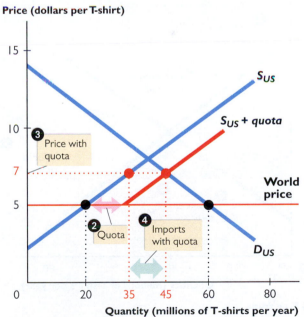

(b) Market with quota

With free trade, in part (a), Americans buy 60 million T-shirts at the world price. The United States produces 20 million T-shirts and ❶ imports 40 million T-shirts. In part (b), ❷ with an import quota

of 10 million T-shirts, the U.S. supply curve becomes S_{US} + *quota*. ❸ The price rises to $7 a T-shirt. Domestic production increases, purchases decrease, and ❹ the quantity imported decreases.

quantity of T-shirts bought in the United States decreases to 45 million a year, the quantity of T-shirts produced in the United States increases to 35 million a year, and the quantity of T-shirts imported into the United States decreases to the quota quantity of 10 million a year. All these effects of a quota are identical to the effects of a tariff set at $2 per T-shirt, as you can check in Figure 9.6(b).

Winners, Losers, and the Social Loss from an Import Quota

An import quota creates winners and losers that are similar to those of a tariff but with an interesting difference. When the government imposes an import quota,

- U.S. producers of the good gain.
- U.S. consumers of the good lose.
- Importers of the good gain.
- U.S. consumers lose more than U.S. producers and importers gain.

Figure 9.8 compares the gains from trade under free trade with those under a quota. Figure 9.8(a) shows the consumer surplus and producer surplus with free international trade in T-shirts. By comparing Figure 9.8(b) with Figure 9.8(a), you can see how an import quota of 10 million T-shirts changes the surpluses. Producer surplus—the blue area—increases by the area labeled B. The increase in

■ FIGURE 9.8

The Winners and Losers from an Import Quota

MyEconLab Animation

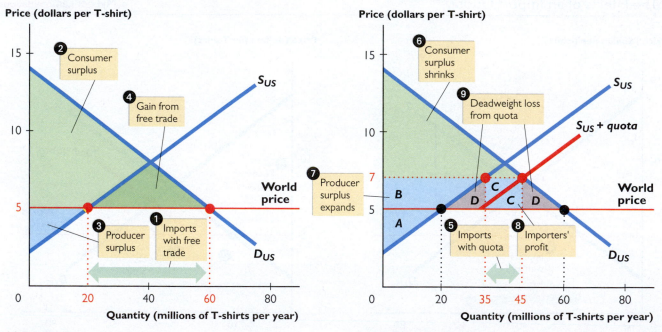

(a) Free trade

(b) Market with quota

The world price of a T-shirt is $5. With free trade, ❶ the United States imports 40 million T-shirts. ❷ Consumer surplus, ❸ producer surplus, and ❹ the gains from free trade are as large as possible. In part (b), an import quota raises the domestic price to $7 a

T-shirt. ❺ The quantity imported decreases. ❻ Consumer surplus shrinks by the areas B, C, and D. ❼ Producer surplus expands by area B. ❽ Importers' profit equals the two areas C, and the quota creates ❾ a deadweight loss equal to the two areas D.

producer surplus is the gain by U.S. producers from the import quota. Consumer surplus—the green area—shrinks. This decrease is the loss to consumers from the import quota.

The decrease in consumer surplus divides into three parts. First, some of the consumer surplus is transferred to producers. The blue area *B* represents this loss of consumer surplus (and gain of producer surplus). Second, part of the consumer surplus is transferred to importers who buy T-shirts for $5 (the world price) and sell them for $7 (the domestic price). The blue areas *C* represent this loss of consumer surplus and the importers' profit.

The third part of the loss of consumer surplus is a transfer to no one: it is a *deadweight loss*. Consumers buy a smaller quantity at a higher price. The two gray areas labeled *D* represent this loss of consumer surplus. Total surplus decreases by this amount, which is the social loss from the import quota.

You can now see the one difference between an import quota and a tariff. A tariff brings in revenue for the government while an import quota brings a profit for the importer. All the other effects are the same, provided the quota is set at the same level of imports that results from the tariff.

■ Other Import Barriers

Two sets of policies that influence imports are

- Health, safety, and regulation barriers
- Voluntary export restraints

Health, Safety, and Regulation Barriers

Thousands of detailed health, safety, and other regulations restrict international trade. For example, U.S. food imports are examined by the Food and Drug Administration to determine whether the food is "pure, wholesome, safe to eat, and produced under sanitary conditions." The discovery of BSE (mad cow disease) in just one U.S. cow in 2003 was enough to close down international trade in U.S. beef. The European Union bans imports of most genetically modified foods, such as U.S.-produced soybeans. Although regulations of the type we've just described are not designed to limit international trade, they have that effect.

Voluntary Export Restraints

A *voluntary export restraint* is like a quota allocated to a foreign exporter of the good. A voluntary export restraint decreases imports just like an import quota does, but the foreign exporter gets the profit from the gap between the domestic price and the world price.

■ Export Subsidies

An **export subsidy** is a payment by the government to the producer to cover part of the cost of production that is exported. The U.S. and European Union governments subsidize farm products. These subsidies stimulate the production and export of farm products, but they make it harder for producers in other countries, notably in Africa and Central and South America, to compete in global markets. Export subsidies bring gains to domestic producers, but they result in overproduction in the domestic economy and underproduction in the rest of the world and so create a deadweight loss (see Chapter 6, p. 157).

Export subsidy
A payment by the government to a producer to cover part of the cost of production that is exported.

MyEconLab Study Plan 9.3

Key Terms Quiz

Solutions Video

CHECKPOINT 9.3

Explain the effects of international trade barriers.

Practice Problems

Before 1995, the United States imposed tariffs on goods imported from Mexico and Mexico imposed tariffs on goods imported from the United States. In 1995, Mexico joined NAFTA. U.S. tariffs on imports from Mexico and Mexican tariffs on imports from the United States are gradually being removed.

1. Explain how the price that U.S. consumers pay for goods imported from Mexico and the quantity of U.S. imports from Mexico have changed. Who, in the United States, are the winners and losers from this free trade?

2. Explain how the quantity of U.S. exports to Mexico and the U.S. government's tariff revenue from trade with Mexico have changed.

3. Suppose that this year, tomato growers in Florida lobby the U.S. government to impose an import quota on Mexican tomatoes. Explain who, in the United States, would gain and who would lose from such a quota.

In the News

The Trans-Pacific Partnership (TPP)
If the TPP comes into effect, Canada will remove import quotas on American milk, Japan will free imports of American beef, and the United States will remove import tariffs on items such as steel, auto-parts, garments, and solar panels.

Source: *The New York Times*, October 6, 2015

Explain how the changes described in the news clip will change U.S. exports and imports and who in the United States will gain and lose from the TPP.

Solutions to Practice Problems

1. The price that U.S. consumers pay for goods imported from Mexico has fallen and the quantity of U.S. imports from Mexico has increased. The winners are U.S. consumers of goods imported from Mexico and the losers are U.S. producers of goods imported from Mexico.

2. The quantity of U.S. exports to Mexico has increased and the U.S. government's tariff revenue from trade with Mexico has fallen.

3. With an import quota, the price of tomatoes in the United States would rise and the quantity bought would decrease. Consumer surplus would decrease. Growers would receive a higher price, produce a larger quantity, and producer surplus would increase. The U.S. total surplus in the tomato market would be redistributed from consumers to producers, but it would decrease.

Solution to In the News

Removing trade barriers on milk and beef will raise the price at which U.S. farmers can sell each item and exports will increase. U.S. farmers will gain and U.S. consumers will lose. Removing U.S. tariffs on steel and other manufactures will lower their prices in the United States and increase U.S. imports. With the lower prices, U.S. consumer surplus increases—consumers gain. U.S. producer surplus decreases—producers lose. For both exports and imports, total surplus increases.

9.4   THE CASE AGAINST PROTECTION

MyEconLab Concept Video

For as long as nations and international trade have existed, people have debated whether free international trade or protection from foreign competition is better for a country. The debate continues, but most economists believe that free trade promotes prosperity for all countries while protection reduces the potential gains from trade. We've seen the most powerful case for free trade: All countries benefit from their comparative advantage. But there is a broader range of issues in the free trade versus protection debate. Let's review these issues.

■ Three Traditional Arguments for Protection

Three traditional arguments for protection and restricting international trade are

- The national security argument
- The infant-industry argument
- The dumping argument

Let's look at each in turn.

The National Security Argument

The national security argument is that a country must protect industries that produce defense equipment and armaments and those on which the defense industries rely for their raw materials and other intermediate inputs. This argument for protection can be taken too far.

First, it is an argument for international isolation, for in a time of war, there is no industry that does not contribute to national defense. Second, if the case is made for boosting the output of a strategic industry—say aerospace—it is more efficient to achieve this outcome with a subsidy financed out of taxes than with a tariff or import quota. A subsidy would keep the industry operating at the scale that is judged appropriate, and free international trade would keep the prices faced by consumers at their world market levels.

Should producers of national security equipment be protected from international competition?

The Infant-Industry Argument

The **infant-industry argument** is that it is necessary to protect a new industry to enable it to grow into a mature industry that can compete in world markets. The argument is based on an idea called *learning-by-doing*. By working repeatedly at a task, workers become better at that task and can increase the amount they produce in a given period.

There is nothing wrong with the idea of learning-by-doing. It is a powerful engine of human capital accumulation and economic growth. Learning-by-doing can change comparative advantage. If on-the-job experience lowers the opportunity cost of producing a good, a country might develop a comparative advantage in producing that good.

But learning-by-doing does not justify protection. It is in the self-interest of firms and workers who benefit from learning-by-doing to produce the efficient quantities. If the government protected these firms to boost their production, there would be an inefficient overproduction (just like the overproduction in Chapter 6, p. 157).

Historical evidence is against the protection of infant industries. Countries in East Asia that have not given such protection have performed well. Countries that have protected infant industries, as India once did, have performed poorly.

Infant-industry argument
The argument that it is necessary to protect a new industry to enable it to grow into a mature industry that can compete in world markets.

India's protection of manufacturing industries from international competition is generally regarded as a failure.

The Dumping Argument

Dumping

When a foreign firm sells its exports at a lower price than its cost of production.

Dumping occurs when a foreign firm sells its exports at a lower price than its cost of production. You might be wondering why a firm would ever want to sell any of its output at a price below the cost of production. Wouldn't such a firm be better off either selling nothing or, if it could do so, raising its price to at least cover its costs? Two possible reasons why a firm might sell at a price below cost and therefore engage in dumping are

- Predatory pricing
- Subsidy

China, a major producer of solar panels, is accused of dumping them on the U.S. and European markets.

Predatory Pricing   A firm that engages in *predatory pricing* sets its price below cost in the hope that it can drive its competitors out of the market. If a firm in one country tries to drive out competitors in another country, it will be *dumping* its product in the foreign market. The foreign firm sells its output at a price below its cost to drive domestic firms out of business. When the domestic firms have gone, the foreign firm takes advantage of its monopoly position and charges a higher price for its product. The higher price will attract new competitors, which makes it unlikely that this strategy will be profitable. For this reason, economists are skeptical that this type of dumping occurs.

Subsidy   A *subsidy* is a payment by the government to a producer. A firm that receives a subsidy is able to sell profitably for a price below cost. Subsidies are very common in almost all countries. The United States and the European Union subsidize the production of many agricultural products and dump their surpluses on the world market. This action lowers the prices that farmers in developing nations receive and weakens the incentive to expand farming in poor countries. India and Europe have been suspected of dumping steel in the United States.

Whatever its source, dumping is illegal under the rules of the WTO, NAFTA, and CAFTA and is regarded as a justification for temporary tariffs. Consequently, anti-dumping tariffs have become important in today's world.

But there are powerful reasons to resist the dumping argument for protection. First, it is virtually impossible to detect dumping because it is hard to determine a firm's costs. As a result, the test for dumping is whether a firm's export price is below its domestic price. This test is a weak one because it can be rational for a firm to charge a lower price in markets in which the quantity demanded is highly sensitive to price and a higher price in a market in which demand is less price-sensitive.

Second, it is hard to think of a good that is produced by a single firm. Even if all the domestic firms were driven out of business in some industry, it would always be possible to find several and usually many alternative foreign sources of supply and to buy at prices determined in competitive markets.

Third, if a good or service were a truly global natural monopoly, the best way to deal with it would be by regulation—just as in the case of domestic monopolies. Such regulation would require international cooperation.

The three arguments for protection that we've just examined have an element of credibility. The counterarguments are in general stronger, so these arguments do not make the case for protection. They are not the only arguments that you might encounter. There are many others, four of which we'll now examine.

■ Four Newer Arguments for Protection

Four newer and commonly made arguments for restricting international trade are that protection

- Saves jobs
- Allows us to compete with cheap foreign labor
- Brings diversity and stability
- Penalizes lax environmental standards

Saves Jobs

When Americans buy imported goods such as shoes from Brazil, U.S. workers who produce shoes lose their jobs. With no earnings and poor prospects, these workers become a drain on welfare and spend less, which creates a ripple effect of further job losses. The proposed solution is to protect U.S. jobs by banning imports of cheap foreign goods. The proposal is flawed for the following reasons.

First, free trade does cost some jobs, but it also creates other jobs. It brings about a global rationalization of labor and allocates labor resources to their highest-valued activities. Because of international trade in textiles, tens of thousands of workers in the United States have lost jobs because shoe factories and textile mills have closed. Tens of thousands of workers in other countries now have jobs because shoe factories and textile mills have opened there. And tens of thousands of U.S. workers now have better-paying jobs than as shoe makers or textile workers because other export industries have expanded and created more jobs than have been destroyed.

Second, imports create jobs. They create jobs for retailers that sell imported goods and for firms that service those goods. They also create jobs by creating incomes in the rest of the world, some of which are spent on imports of U.S.-made goods and services.

Protection saves some particular jobs, but it does so at a high cost. For example, until 2005, textile jobs in the United States were protected by import quotas imposed under an international agreement called the Multifiber Arrangement (or MFA). The U.S. International Trade Commission (ITC) estimated that because of import quotas, 72,000 jobs existed in textiles that would otherwise have disappeared and that the annual clothing expenditure in the United States was $15.9 billion ($160 per family) higher than it would be with free trade. An implication of the ITC estimate is that each textile job saved cost consumers $221,000 a year. The end of the MFA led to the destruction of a large number of textile jobs in the United States and Europe in 2005.

Few shoe factories remain in the United States and manufacturing jobs have been lost …

… but well-paid professional and service jobs have been created to replace the lost manufacturing jobs.

Allows Us to Compete with Cheap Foreign Labor

With the removal of protective tariffs in U.S. trade with Mexico, some people said that jobs would be sucked into Mexico and that the United States would not be able to compete with its southern neighbor. Let's see what's wrong with this view.

Labor costs depend on the wage rate and the quantity a worker produces. For example, if a U.S. auto worker earns $30 an hour and produces 15 units of output an hour, the average labor cost of a unit of output is $2. If a Mexican auto worker earns $3 an hour and produces 1 unit of output an hour, the average labor cost of a unit of output is $3. Other things remaining the same, the greater the output a worker produces, the higher is the worker's wage rate. High-wage workers produce a large output. Low-wage workers produce a small output.

Although high-wage U.S. workers are more productive, on the average, than lower-wage Mexican workers, there are differences across industries. U.S. labor is relatively more productive in some activities than in others. For example, the productivity of U.S. workers in producing movies, financial services, and customized computer chips is relatively higher than their productivity in the production of metals and some standardized machine parts. The activities in which U.S. workers are relatively more productive than their Mexican counterparts are those in which the United States has a comparative advantage. By engaging in free trade, increasing our production and exports of the goods and services in which we have a comparative advantage, and decreasing our production and increasing our imports of the goods and services in which our trading partners have a comparative advantage, we can make ourselves and the citizens of other countries better off.

Brings Diversity and Stability

A diversified investment portfolio is less risky than one that has "all of its eggs in one basket." The same is true for an economy's production. A diversified economy fluctuates less than an economy that produces only one or two goods.

Most economies—the rich advanced economies of the United States, Japan, and Europe and the developing economies of China and Brazil—have diversified production and do not have this type of stability problem. A few economies, such as Saudi Arabia, have a comparative advantage that leads to the specialized production of only one good. But even these economies can stabilize their income and consumption by investing in a wide range of production activities in other countries.

Penalizes Lax Environmental Standards

A new argument for protection is that many poorer countries, such as Mexico, do not have the same environmental standards that we have, and because they are willing to pollute and we are not, we cannot compete with them without tariffs. If these countries want free trade with the richer and "greener" countries, then they must raise their environmental standards.

This argument for trade restrictions is not entirely convincing. A poor country is less able than a rich one to devote resources to achieving high environmental standards. If free trade helps a poor country to become richer, then it will also help that country to develop the means to improve its environment. But there probably is a case for using the negotiation of free trade agreements such as NAFTA and CAFTA to hold member countries to higher environmental standards. There is an especially large payoff from using such bargaining to try to avoid irreversible damage to resources such as tropical rainforests.

So the four common arguments that we've just considered do not provide overwhelming support for protection. They all have flaws and leave the case for free international trade a strong one.

■ Why Is International Trade Restricted?

Why, despite all the arguments against protection, is international trade restricted? One reason that applies to developing nations is that the tariff is a convenient source of government revenue, but this reason does not apply to the United States where the government has access to income taxes and sales taxes.

Political support for international trade restrictions in the United States and most other developed countries arises from rent seeking. **Rent seeking** is lobbying and other political activity that seeks to capture the gains from trade. You've seen that free trade benefits consumers but shrinks the producer surplus of firms that compete in markets with imports.

The winners from free trade are the millions of consumers of low-cost imports, but the benefit per individual consumer is small. The losers from free trade are the producers of import-competing items. Compared to the millions of consumers, there are only a few thousand producers.

Now think about imposing a tariff on clothing. Millions of consumers will bear the cost in the form of a smaller consumer surplus and a few thousand garment makers and their employees will share the gain in producer surplus.

Because the gain from a tariff is large, producers have a strong incentive to incur the expense of lobbying *for* a tariff and *against* free trade. On the other hand, because each consumer's loss is small, consumers have little incentive to organize and incur the expense of lobbying *for* free trade. The gain from free trade for any one person is too small for that person to spend much time or money on a political organization to lobby for free trade. The loss from free trade will be seen as being so great by those bearing that loss that they will find it profitable to join a political organization to prevent free trade. Each group weighs benefits against costs and chooses the best action for themselves, but the anti-free-trade group will undertake more political lobbying than will the pro-free-trade group.

Rent seeking
Lobbying and other political activity that aims to capture the gains from trade.

EYE on YOUR LIFE
International Trade

MyEconLab Critical Thinking Exercise

International trade plays an extraordinarily large role in your life in three broad ways. It affects you as a

- Consumer
- Producer
- Voter

As a *consumer*, you benefit from the availability of a wide range of low-cost, high-quality goods and services that are produced in other countries.

Look closely at the labels on the goods that you buy. Where was your computer made? Where were your shirt and your shoes made? Where are the fruits and vegetables that you buy, especially in winter, grown?

The answers to all these questions are most likely Asia, Mexico, or South America. A few goods were produced in Europe, Canada, and the United States.

As a *producer* (or as a potential producer if you don't yet have a job), you benefit from huge global markets for U.S. products. Your job prospects would be much dimmer if the firm for which you work didn't have global markets in which to sell its products.

People who work in the aircraft industry, for example, benefit from the huge global market for large passenger jets. Airlines from Canada to China are buying Boeing 737 and 787 aircraft as fast as they can be pushed out of the production line.

Even if you were to become a college professor, you would benefit from international trade in education services when your school admits foreign students.

As a *voter*, you have a big stake in the politics of free trade versus protection. As a buyer, your self-interest is hurt by tariffs and quotas on imported goods. Each time you buy a $20 sweater, you contribute $5 to the government in tariff revenue. But as a worker, your self-interest might be hurt by freer access to U.S. markets for foreign producers.

So as you decide how to vote, you must figure out what trade policy serves your self-interest and what best serves the social interest.

MyEconLab Study Plan 9.4
Key Terms Quiz
Solutions Video

 # CHECKPOINT 9.4

Explain and evaluate arguments used to justify restricting international trade.

Practice Problems

1. Japan sets an import quota on rice. California rice growers would like to export more rice to Japan. What are Japan's arguments for restricting imports of Californian rice? Are these arguments correct? Who loses from this restriction in trade?

2. The United States has, from time to time, limited imports of steel from Europe. What argument has the United States used to justify this quota? Who wins from this restriction? Who loses?

3. The United States maintains an import quota on sugar. What is the argument for this import quota? Is this argument flawed? If so, explain why.

In the News

India looks at raising duty on steel imports to 20%
India's steel imports are 58 percent higher than a year ago and the country's steel producers have complained that cheap imports have driven market prices below their production costs.

Source: *The Financial Times*, September 10, 2015

What is the argument that Indian steel producers are using to support an increase in the tariff on steel imports? What is wrong with their argument?

Solutions to Practice Problems

1. The main arguments are that Japanese rice is a better quality rice and that the quota limits competition faced by Japanese farmers. The arguments are not correct. If Japanese consumers do not like the quality of Californian rice, they will not buy it. The quota does limit competition and the quota allows Japanese farmers to use their land less efficiently. The big losers are the Japanese consumers who pay about three times the U.S. price for rice.

2. The U.S. argument is that European producers dump steel on the U.S. market. With an import quota, U.S. steel producers will face less competition and U.S. jobs will be saved. Workers in the steel industry and owners of steel companies will win at the expense of U.S. buyers of steel.

3. The argument is that the import quota protects the jobs of U.S. workers. The argument is flawed because the United States does not have a comparative advantage in producing sugar and so an import quota allows the U.S. sugar industry to be inefficient. With free international trade in sugar, the U.S. sugar industry would exist but it would be much smaller and more efficient.

Solution to In the News

Indian steel producers are using the dumping argument: Protection is needed because foreign producers are selling steel in India at prices below the cost of production. What's wrong with this argument is that it is difficult to determine whether foreign producers are selling at prices below their costs and unlikely that they would want to do so. So foreign producers might have a comparative advantage in producing steel.

CHAPTER SUMMARY

Key Points

1. **Explain how markets work with international trade.**

   - Comparative advantage drives international trade.
   - When the world price of a good is lower than the price that balances domestic demand and supply, a country gains by decreasing production and importing the good.
   - When the world price of a good is higher than the price that balances domestic demand and supply, a country gains by increasing production and exporting the good.

2. **Identify the gains from international trade and its winners and losers.**

   - Compared to a no-trade situation, in a market with imports, consumer surplus is larger, producer surplus is smaller, and total surplus is larger with free international trade.
   - Compared to a no-trade situation, in a market with exports, consumer surplus is smaller, producer surplus is larger, and total surplus is larger with free international trade.

3. **Explain the effects of international trade barriers.**

   - Countries restrict international trade by imposing tariffs, import quotas, other import barriers, and export subsidies.
   - Trade restrictions raise the domestic price of imported goods, lower the quantity imported, decrease consumer surplus, increase producer surplus, and create a deadweight loss.

4. **Explain and evaluate arguments used to justify restricting international trade.**

   - The arguments that protection is necessary for national security, for infant industries, and to prevent dumping are weak.
   - Arguments that protection saves jobs, allows us to compete with cheap foreign labor, makes the economy diversified and stable, and is needed to penalize lax environmental standards are flawed.
   - Trade is restricted because protection brings small losses to a large number of people and large gains to a small number of people.

Key Terms

MyEconLab Key Terms Quiz

Dumping, 234
Export subsidy, 231
Exports, 216

Import quota, 229
Imports, 216
Infant-industry argument, 233

Rent seeking, 237
Tariff, 225

CHAPTER CHECKPOINT

Study Plan Problems and Applications

Use Figures 1 and 2 to work Problems **1** to **4**. Figure 1 and Figure 2 show the markets for shoes if there is no trade between the United States and Brazil.

FIGURE 1   U.S. SHOE MARKET

Price (dollars per pair)

Quantity (millions of pairs per year)

FIGURE 2   BRAZIL'S SHOE MARKET

Price (dollars per pair)

Quantity (millions of pairs per year)

1. Which country has a comparative advantage in producing shoes? With international trade, explain which country would export shoes and how the price of shoes in the importing country and the quantity produced by the importing country would change. Explain which country gains from this trade.

2. The world price of a pair of shoes is \$20. Explain how consumer surplus and producer surplus in the United States change as a result of international trade. On the graph, show the change in U.S. consumer surplus (label it *A*) and the change in U.S. producer surplus (label it *B*).

3. The world price of a pair of shoes is \$20. Explain how consumer surplus and producer surplus in Brazil change as a result of international trade. Show the change in Brazil's consumer surplus (label it *C*) and the change in Brazil's producer surplus (label it *D*).

4. Who in the United States loses from free trade in shoes with Brazil? Explain.

Use the following information to work Problems **5** to **7**.

5. The supply of roses in the United States is made up of U.S.-grown roses and imported roses. Draw a graph to illustrate the U.S. rose market with free international trade. On your graph, mark the price of roses and the quantities of roses bought, produced, and imported into the United States.

6. Who in the United States loses from this trade in roses and would lobby for a restriction on the quantity of imported roses? If the U.S. government put a tariff on rose imports, show on your graph the U.S. consumer surplus that is redistributed to U.S. producers and also the government's tariff revenue.

7. Suppose that the U.S. government puts an import quota on roses. Show on your graph the consumer surplus that is redistributed to producers and importers and also the deadweight loss created by the import quota.

Use the following information to work Problems **8** to **10**.

U.S. steelmakers seek antidumping action
Steelmakers want the United States to put restrictions on imports from five nations, alleging unfair pricing of steel for the automobile and construction industries.

Source: *Wall Street Journal*, June 3, 2015

8. Explain who in the United States gains and who loses from restrictions on steel imports. How do you expect the prices of automobiles and office towers to be affected?

9. What is dumping? Who in the United States loses from foreign firms' dumping of steel?

10. Explain what an antidumping tariff is. What argument might U.S. steelmakers use to get the government to raise the tariff on steel imports?

11. Read *Eye on Globalization* on p. 221 and draw two graphs to show how U.S. consumers gain from iPads manufactured in China and why Chinese workers also gain.

Instructor Assignable Problems and Applications

MyEconLab Homework, Quiz, or Test if assigned by instructor

Use the following information to work Problems **1** and **2**.

The future of U.S.–India relations

When she was Secretary of State, Hillary Clinton gave a major speech covering all the issues in U.S.–India relations. On economic and trade relations she noted that India maintains significant barriers to U.S. trade. The United States also maintains barriers against Indian imports such as textiles. Mrs. Clinton, President Obama, and Anand Sharma, the Indian Minister of Commerce and Industry, say they want to dismantle these trade barriers.

Source: www.state.gov

1. Explain who in the United States would gain and who might lose from dismantling trade barriers between the United States and India.

2. Draw a graph of the U.S. market for textiles and show how removing a tariff would change producer surplus, consumer surplus, and the deadweight loss from the tariff.

3. The United States exports wheat. Draw a graph to illustrate the U.S. wheat market if there is free international trade in wheat. On your graph, mark the price of wheat and the quantities bought, produced, and exported by the United States.

4. Suppose that the world price of sugar is 20¢ a pound, Brazil does not trade internationally, and the equilibrium price of sugar in Brazil is 10¢ a pound. Brazil then begins to trade internationally.
  - How does the price of sugar in Brazil change? Do Brazilians buy more or less sugar? Do Brazilian sugar growers produce more or less sugar?
  - Does Brazil export or import sugar and why?

5. The United States exports services and imports coffee. Why does the United States gain from exporting services and importing coffee? How do economists measure the net gain from this international trade?

6. In the 1950s, Ford and General Motors established a small car-producing industry in Australia and argued for a high tariff on car imports. The tariff has remained through the years. Until 2000, the tariff was 22.5 percent. What might have been Ford's and General Motors' argument for the high tariff? Is the tariff the best way to achieve the goals of the argument?

Use Figure 1 and the following information to work Problems **7** to **9**.

Figure 1 shows the car market in Mexico when Mexico places no restriction on the quantity of cars imported. The world price of a car is $10,000.

7. If the government of Mexico introduces a $2,000 tariff on car imports, what will be the price of a car in Mexico, the quantity of cars produced in Mexico, the quantity imported into Mexico, and the government's tariff revenue?

8. If the government of Mexico introduces an import quota of 4 million cars a year, what will be the price of a car in Mexico, the quantity of cars produced in Mexico, and the quantity imported?

9. What argument might be used to encourage the government of Mexico to introduce a $2,000 tariff on car imports from the United States? Who will gain and who will lose as a result of Mexico's tariff?

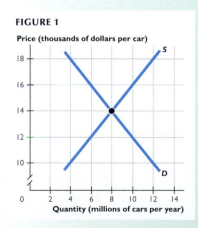

FIGURE 1

Price (thousands of dollars per car)

Quantity (millions of cars per year)

MyEconLab Chapter 9 Study Plan

Multiple Choice Quiz

1. The fundamental force driving international trade is comparative _____.

    A. advantage: a country exports those goods that have high prices
    B. abundance: the country that produces more than it needs exports the good
    C. advantage: the country with the lower opportunity cost of production exports the good
    D. cost: a country trades with other countries that produce cheaper goods

2. A country will export wheat if, with no international trade, _____.

    A. it produces a surplus of wheat
    B. its opportunity cost of producing wheat is below the world price
    C. its domestic price of wheat exceeds the world price
    D. other countries have a shortage of wheat

3. With free trade between the United States and Canada, the United States exports tomatoes and Canada exports maple syrup. U.S. consumers _____.

    A. of tomatoes gain and Canadian consumers of maple syrup lose
    B. of both tomatoes and maple syrup gain more than either producer
    C. of maple syrup gain more than U.S. producers of maple syrup lose
    D. of tomatoes gain more than U.S. producers of tomatoes lose

4. With free trade between China and the United States, the winners are _____ and the losers are _____.

    A. U.S. consumers of U.S. imports; U.S. producers of the U.S. import good
    B. China's consumers of China's imports; China's producers of its export good
    C. U.S. producers of the U.S. export good; U.S. consumers of U.S. imports
    D. China's consumers of China's export good; China's producers of its imported good

5. The U.S. tariff on paper _____ the U.S. price of paper, _____ U.S. production of paper and _____ the U.S. gains from trade.

    A. raises; increases; increases
    B. doesn't change; increases; increases
    C. doesn't change; doesn't change; decreases
    D. raises; increases; decreases

6. If Korea imposes an import quota on U.S. oranges, losers include Korean _____ of oranges and U.S. _____ of oranges.

    A. consumers; consumers
    B. consumers; producers
    C. producers; consumers
    D. producers; producers

7. The people who support restricted international trade say that _____.

    A. protection saves jobs, in both the United States and foreign economies
    B. U.S. firms won't be able to compete with low-wage foreign labor if trade is free
    C. outsourcing sends jobs abroad, which brings diversification and makes our economy more stable
    D. protection is needed to enable U.S. firms to produce the things at which they have a comparative advantage

How can we limit carbon emissions?

Externalities

10

When you have completed your study of this chapter, you will be able to

1 Explain why negative externalities lead to inefficient over-production and how property rights and pollution taxes can achieve a more efficient outcome.

2 Explain why positive externalities lead to inefficient under-production and how public provision, subsidies, and vouchers can achieve a more efficient outcome.

MyEconLab Big Picture Video

243

MyEconLab Concept Video

Externality
A cost or a benefit that arises from production and that falls on someone other than the producer; or a cost or benefit that arises from consumption and that falls on someone other than the consumer.

Negative externality
A production or consumption activity that creates an external cost.

Positive externality
A production or consumption activity that creates an external benefit.

Negative production externality.

EXTERNALITIES IN OUR DAILY LIVES

Climate change is an externality, and a huge one. You will learn what economists say about limiting it in this chapter. But first we need to build a foundation. We begin by classifying and illustrating the range of externalities in our daily lives.

An **externality** is a cost or a benefit that arises from production and that falls on someone other than the producer; or a cost or a benefit that arises from consumption and that falls on someone other than the consumer. An externality can arise from either a production activity or a consumption activity. It can be either a **negative externality**, which imposes an external cost, or a **positive externality**, which provides an external benefit. So there are four types of externalities:

- Negative production externalities
- Positive production externalities
- Negative consumption externalities
- Positive consumption externalities

■ Negative Production Externalities

Negative production externalities are among the most serious challenges faced by the world today. Starting in the Industrial Revolution of the eighteenth century, humans have poured billions of tons of pollutants in the air, oceans, lakes, and rivers.

Power generators, airplanes, and road vehicles are the biggest polluters. Burning coal to generate electricity emits carbon dioxide that warms the planet and it emits other chemicals that pollute the atmosphere. The coal-burning Navajo Generating Station near Page, Arizona, emits about 16 million tons of carbon into the atmosphere every year, an amount similar to that of 3.3 million passenger car miles each year.

Logging and the clearing of forests in California, Oregon, and Washington destroy the habitat of wildlife and also influence the amount of carbon dioxide in the atmosphere.

Noise is another negative production externality. When planes take off and land at LaGuardia airport in New York City, the noise they make imposes a large cost on the people who live under the flight paths. This noise is replicated at airports in every major city around the world.

All these activities are examples of production that brings negative externalities. The costs of these production activities are borne by everyone, and even by future generations.

■ Positive Production Externalities

Positive production externalities are a smaller problem than negative ones. But they pose interesting problems. A notable one arises in the production of fruit and vegetables and honey. To produce honey, bee-keepers locate their hives next to fruit orchards and vegetable farms. The honeybees collect pollen and nectar from the fruit and vegetable blossoms to make the honey. At the same time, they transfer pollen between the blossoms, which helps to fertilize the blossoms. Two positive production externalities are present in this example. Honey producers get a positive production externality from the owners of the orchards and farms; and the fruit growers and vegetable farmers get a positive production externality from the honey producer.

Positive production externality.

■ Negative Consumption Externalities

Negative consumption externalities are a source of irritation for most of us. Smoking tobacco in a confined space creates fumes that many people find unpleasant and that pose a health risk. So smoking in restaurants and on airplanes generates a negative externality. To avoid this negative externality, many restaurants and all airlines ban smoking. But while a smoking ban avoids a negative consumption externality for most people, it imposes a negative external cost on smokers who would prefer to enjoy the consumption of tobacco while dining or traveling by air.

Noisy parties and outdoor rock concerts are other examples of negative consumption externalities. They are also examples of the fact that a simple ban on an activity is not a solution. Banning noisy parties avoids the external cost on sleep-seeking neighbors, but it results in the sleepers imposing an external cost on the fun-seeking partygoers.

Leaving beer bottles on the beach, allowing a dog to bark loudly or to foul a neighbor's lawn, and letting a smartphone ring during a lecture are other examples of negative consumption externalities.

Negative consumption externality.

■ Positive Consumption Externalities

When you get a flu vaccination, you lower your risk of being infected. If you avoid the flu, your neighbor, who didn't get vaccinated, has a better chance of remaining healthy too. Flu vaccinations generate positive consumption externalities.

When the owner of a historic building restores it, everyone who sees the building gets pleasure. Similarly, when someone erects a spectacular home or other exciting construction or building such as the Walt Disney Concert Hall in Los Angeles, an external consumption benefit flows to everyone who has an opportunity to view it.

Education, which we examine in more detail in this chapter, is a major example of a positive consumption and production externality.

Positive consumption externality.

EYE on YOUR LIFE
Externalities in Your Life

MyEconLab Critical Thinking Exercise

Think about the externalities, both negative and positive, that play a huge part in *your* life; and think about the incentives that attempt to align your self-interest with the social interest.

You respond to the gasoline tax by buying a little less gas than you otherwise would. As you will see in *Eye on Climate Change* (p. 254), this incentive is small compared to that in some other countries. With a bigger gas tax, such

as that in the United Kingdom for example, you would find ways of getting by with a smaller quantity of gasoline and your actions and those of millions of others would make the traffic on our highways much lighter.

You are responding to the huge incentive of subsidized tuition by being in school. Without subsidized college education, fewer people would attend college and university and with fewer

college graduates, the benefits we all receive from living in a well-educated society would be smaller.

Think about your attitude as a citizen–voter to these two externalities. Should the gas tax be higher to discourage the use of the automobile? Should tuition be even lower to encourage even more people to enroll in school? Or have we got these incentives just right in the social interest?

10.1 NEGATIVE EXTERNALITIES: POLLUTION

Climate change is a *negative externality*. It is the unintended consequence of production and consumption activities that create carbon emissions and global warming. We'll address the challenge of limiting climate change in this chapter.

Although climate change from human actions is new, pollution and other environmental problems are not. Preindustrial towns in Europe had sewage disposal problems that brought cholera and plagues that killed millions. Nor is the desire to find solutions to environmental problems new. The fourteenth century development of a pure water supply and the hygienic disposal of garbage and sewage are examples of early efforts to improve the quality of the environment.

Popular discussions about climate change and pollution focus on physical aspects of the problem and not on costs and benefits. A common assumption is that activities that damage the environment are wrong and must cease. An economic study of the same problems emphasizes costs and benefits, and economists talk about the efficient amount of pollution. This emphasis on costs and benefits does not mean that economists have the right answers. Rather, economics provides a set of tools and principles that help to clarify the issues.

We illustrate the economics of a negative externality with the example of a paint factory that dumps waste into a river. The people who live by the river use it for fishing and boating and bear the cost of the pollution. The paint factory does not consider these costs when it decides the quantity of paint to produce. The factory's production decision is based on its own costs of production, not on the costs that it inflicts on others. You're going to see that when external costs are present, output exceeds the efficient quantity and we get more than the efficient quantity of pollution.

The starting point for an economic analysis of a negative externality is the distinction between private costs and social costs.

■ Private Costs and Social Costs

Marginal private cost
The cost of producing an additional unit of a good or service that is borne by the producer of that good or service.

A *private cost* of production is a cost that is borne by the producer of a good or service. *Marginal cost* is the cost of producing an *additional unit* of a good or service. So **marginal private cost** (*MC*) is the cost of producing an additional unit of a good or service that is borne by the producer of that good or service.

Marginal external cost
The cost of producing an additional unit of a good or service that falls on people other than the producer.

You've seen that an *external cost* is a cost of producing a good or service that is *not* borne by the producer but borne by other people. A **marginal external cost** is the cost of producing an additional unit of a good or service that falls on people other than the producer.

Marginal social cost
The marginal cost incurred by the entire society—by the producer and by everyone else on whom the cost falls. It is the sum of marginal private cost and marginal external cost.

Marginal social cost (*MSC*) is the marginal cost incurred by the entire society—by the producer and by everyone else on whom the cost falls—and is the sum of marginal private cost and marginal external cost. That is,

$$MSC = MC + \text{Marginal external cost}$$

We express costs in dollars, but we must always remember that a cost is an opportunity cost—the best thing we give up to get something. A marginal external cost is what someone other than the producer of a good or service must give up when the producer makes one more unit of the item. Something real that people value, such as a clean river or clean air, is given up.

Valuing an External Cost

Economists use market prices to put a dollar value on the cost of pollution. For example, suppose that there are two similar rivers, one polluted and the other clean, with identical homes along the side of each river. The homes on the clean river rent for $1,000 a month more than those on the polluted river. If pollution is the only detectable difference between the two locations, the $1,000 a month rent difference is the social cost per home of the pollution. The $1,000 multiplied by the number of homes on the polluted river is the total external cost of this pollution.

External Cost and Output

Figure 10.1 shows an example of the relationship between output and cost in a polluting paint industry. The marginal cost curve, MC, describes the private marginal cost borne by the firms that produce the paint. Marginal cost increases as the quantity of the paint produced increases. If the firms dump waste into a river, they impose an external cost that increases with the amount of the paint produced. The marginal social cost curve, MSC, is the sum of the marginal private cost and the marginal external cost. For example, when firms produce 4 million gallons of paint a month, marginal private cost is $1.00 a gallon, marginal external cost is $1.25 a gallon, and marginal social cost is $2.25 a gallon.

In Figure 10.1, as the quantity of the paint produced increases, the amount of pollution increases and the external cost of pollution increases. The quantity of the paint produced and the pollution created depend on how the market for the paint operates. First, we'll see what happens when the industry is free to pollute.

FIGURE 10.1

An External Cost

MyEconLab Animation

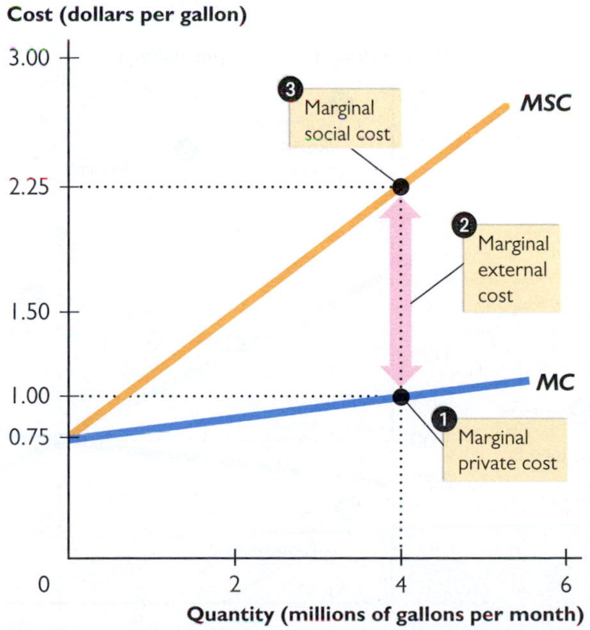

The MC curve shows the marginal private cost borne by the factories that produce paint. The MSC curve shows the sum of marginal private cost and marginal external cost.

When firms produce 4 million gallons of paint a month
① Marginal private cost is $1.00 per gallon.
② Marginal external cost is $1.25 per gallon.
③ Marginal social cost is $2.25 per gallon.

■ Production and Pollution: How Much?

When a polluting industry is unregulated, the market outcome is one of inefficient *overproduction.* In the pursuit of their self-interest, firms produce too much, and they pollute too much. Figure 10.2, which illustrates a market for paint in which the producers pollute, explains why.

The demand curve and marginal benefit curve for paint is $D = MB$ (see Chapter 6, p. 148). The supply curve and marginal private cost curve of producers of the paint is $S = MC$ (see Chapter 6, p. 151). The supply curve is the marginal *private* cost curve because when firms make their supply decisions, they pursue their self-interest and consider only the costs that they will bear. The market *equilibrium* occurs where marginal benefit equals marginal *private* cost. The price is $1.00 a gallon and the quantity is 4 million gallons of paint a month. This outcome is inefficient because marginal *social* cost exceeds marginal benefit.

The efficient outcome is when marginal benefit *equals* marginal *social* cost. In Figure 10.2, the efficient quantity is 2 million gallons of the paint a month, where marginal social cost and marginal benefit each equal $1.50 per gallon.

The equilibrium outcome is one of inefficient *overproduction* and the gray triangle shows the deadweight loss that arises in this situation.

If some method can be found to get paint factories to create less pollution and eliminate the deadweight loss, everyone—the owners of the factories and the residents of the riverside homes—can gain. So what can be done to fix the inefficiency? Three methods are available and we'll examine each of them. They are

- Establish property rights
- Mandate clean technology
- Tax or cap and price pollution

■ **FIGURE 10.2**

Inefficiency with an External Cost

MyEconLab Animation

The market supply curve is the marginal private cost curve, $S = MC$. The demand curve is the marginal benefit curve, $D = MB$. The marginal social cost curve is *MSC*.

❶ Market equilibrium at a price of $1.00 a gallon and 4 million gallons of paint a month is inefficient because ❷ marginal social cost exceeds ❸ marginal benefit.

❹ The efficient quantity of paint is 2 million gallons a month where marginal benefit equals marginal social cost.

❺ The area of the gray triangle shows the deadweight loss created by the pollution externality.

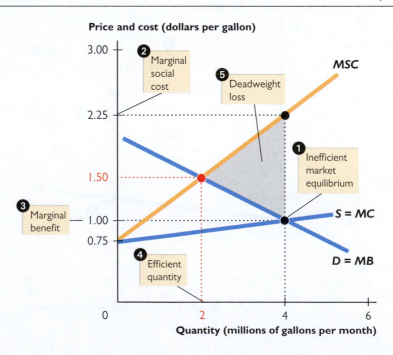

■ Establish Property Rights

Property rights are legally established titles to the ownership, use, and disposal of factors of production and goods and services that are enforceable in the courts. Establishing property rights where they do not currently exist can confront producers with the costs of their actions and provide them with an incentive to allocate resources efficiently.

To see how property rights work, suppose that the paint producers have property rights on a river and the homes alongside it—they own the river and the homes. The rental income that the paint producers earn on the homes depends on the amount of pollution they create. If people are willing to pay $1,000 a month more to live alongside a pollution-free river, the paint producers can earn that amount for each of the homes they own by not polluting the river.

The forgone rental income from homes alongside a polluted river is an opportunity cost of producing paint. It is part of the paint producers' marginal *private* cost and the paint producers must now decide how to respond to this cost. There are two things they might do:

- Use an abatement technology
- Produce less and pollute less

Use an Abatement Technology

An **abatement technology** is a production technology that reduces or prevents pollution. The catalytic converter in every U.S. car is an example of an abatement technology. Its widespread adoption, along with lead-free gasoline, has dramatically reduced pollution from highway vehicles and helped to achieve the trends in U.S. air quality shown on p. 253.

Abatement technologies are available to reduce carbon emissions from electricity generation and pollution from industrial processes and paint manufacture.

Produce Less and Pollute Less

An alternative to incurring the cost of using an abatement technology is to use the polluting technology but cut production, which will reduce pollution and result in higher income from renting homes by the river. Firms will choose the least-cost alternative method of lowering pollution.

The Coase Theorem

Does it matter whether the polluter or the victim of the pollution owns the resource that might be polluted? The Coase theorem (named for British economist Ronald Coase who was the first to have this remarkable insight) says it doesn't matter.

The **Coase theorem** is the proposition that if property rights exist and the costs of enforcing them are low, then the market outcome is efficient and it doesn't matter who has the property rights.

Application of the Coase Theorem

Suppose that the residents own their homes and the river. Now the factories must pay a fee to the homeowners for the right to dump waste into the river. The greater the quantity of waste dumped, the more the factories must pay. So again, the factories face the opportunity cost of the pollution they create as part of their marginal *private* cost. The quantity of paint produced and the amount of waste

Property rights
Legally established titles to the ownership, use, and disposal of factors of production and goods and services that are enforceable in the courts.

Abatement technology
A production technology that reduces or prevents pollution.

Coase theorem
The proposition that if property rights exist and the costs of enforcing them are low, then the market outcome is efficient and it doesn't matter who has the property rights.

dumped are the same whoever owns the homes and the river. If the factories own them, they bear the cost of pollution because they receive a lower income from home rents. If the residents own the homes and the river, the factories bear the cost of pollution because they must pay a fee to the homeowners. In both cases, the factories bear the cost of their pollution and dump the efficient amount of waste into the river.

Efficient Market Equilibrium With Property Rights

Figure 10.3 illustrates the efficient market outcome with property rights in place. The paint producers face the pollution costs or the abatement costs, whichever is lower. The *MSC* curve includes the cost of producing paint plus either the cost of abatement or the cost of pollution (forgone rent), whichever is lower. This curve, labeled $S = MC = MSC$, is now the market supply curve.

Market equilibrium occurs at a price of $1.50 per gallon and 2 million gallons of paint per month. This outcome is efficient.

If the forgone rent is less than the abatement cost, the factories will still create some pollution, but it will be the efficient quantity. If the abatement cost is lower than the forgone rent, the factories will stop polluting, but they will produce less paint because marginal cost includes the abatement cost.

The Coase property rights solution works only when the cost of reaching an agreement between property owners is low. In many situations, these negotiation costs are high, so this solution is not available and government action is needed. One such action is to mandate the use of a clean abatement technology.

■ **FIGURE 10.3**

Property Rights Achieve an Efficient Outcome   MyEconLab Animation

❶ With property rights, the marginal cost curve that excludes the cost of pollution shows only part of the producers' marginal cost.

The marginal private cost curve includes ❷ the cost of pollution, so the supply curve of paint is $S = MC = MSC$.

❸ Market equilibrium is at a price of $1.50 a gallon and a quantity of 2 million gallons of paint a month. The market outcome is efficient because ❹ marginal social cost equals marginal benefit.

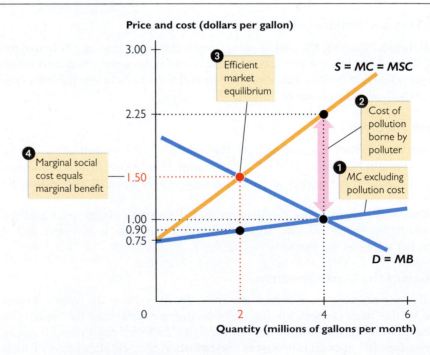

■ Mandate Clean Technology

The governments of most countries regulate what may be emitted into the atmosphere and dumped in rivers and lakes. The direct regulation of what is and is not legally permitted is called **command-and-control regulation**.

Command-and-control regulation
The direct regulation of what is and is not permitted.

Command-and-control environmental regulation in the United States is conducted under the provisions of the Clean Air Act of 1970 and the Clean Water Act of 1972. These Acts give the Environmental Protection Agency (EPA) the authority to issue regulations that limit emissions and achieve defined air and water quality standards.

The EPA has issued thousands of regulations that require chemical plants, utilities, and steel mills to adopt best-practice pollution-abatement technologies and to either eliminate or limit their emissions of specified pollutants. Other regulations have been issued that govern road vehicle emission limits, which must be met by vehicle manufacturers.

Command-and-control regulation works particularly well for keeping water resources clean because even a small breach of safety standards can bring a large catastrophic consequence. An example is what happened in Michigan when the state switched Flint's water supply from Lake Huron (clean) to the Flint River (polluted). Tap water became discolored and its lead level tripled, prompting residents to bring a class action against the state. But Flint's problem is rare because command-and-control water regulation is usually effective.

Although command-and-control regulation provides clean water and has improved air quality, economists see three problems with this approach. It doesn't confront individual producers with incentives to limit pollution. A one-size-fits-all solution is generally not the lowest-cost solution to a pollution problem. And lawmakers are subject to lobbying by the polluters whose actions they seek to control. The third approach for dealing with pollution directly addresses these three concerns.

A Supreme Court decision says greenhouse gas emissions are pollution— the EPA must regulate them.

■ Tax or Cap and Price Pollution

Governments use two main methods of confronting polluters with the costs of their decisions:

- Taxes
- Cap-and-trade

Taxes

Governments can use taxes as an incentive for producers to reduce the pollution they create. Taxes used in this way are called Pigovian taxes, (named for Arthur Cecil Pigou, the British economist who first worked out this method of dealing with external costs during the 1920s).

By setting the tax equal to the marginal external cost (or marginal abatement cost if it is lower), firms can be made to behave in the same way as they would if they bore the cost of the externality directly.

To see how government actions can change the outcome in a market with external costs, let's return to the example of paint factories and the river. Assume that the government has assessed the marginal external cost of pollution accurately and imposes a tax on the factories that exactly equals this cost. The producers are now confronted with the social cost of their actions. The market equilibrium is one in which price equals marginal social cost—an efficient outcome.

Figure 10.4 illustrates the effects of a Pigovian tax on pollution from paint factories. The curve $D = MB$ is the market demand for paint and the marginal benefit curve. The curve MC is the marginal private cost of producing paint. The tax equals the marginal external cost of the pollution. We add this tax to the marginal private cost to find the market supply curve, the curve labeled $S = MC + tax$. This curve is the market supply curve because it tells us the quantity of paint supplied at each price, given the factories' marginal cost and the tax they must pay. This curve is also the marginal social cost curve MSC because the pollution tax has been set equal to the marginal external cost at the quantity produced.

Demand and supply now determine the market equilibrium price at $1.50 per gallon and a quantity of 2 million gallons of paint a month. At this quantity of paint produced, the marginal social cost is $1.50 per gallon and the marginal benefit is $1.50 per gallon, so the market outcome is efficient. The factories incur a marginal private cost of 90¢ per gallon and pay a pollution tax of 60¢ per gallon. The government collects tax revenue of $1.2 million per month.

Cap-and-Trade

Cap-and-trade places a cap or ceiling on emissions and assigns or sells emission rights to individual producers who are then free to trade permits with each other. It is a tool that seeks to combine the power of government to limit total emissions with the power of the market to minimize cost and maximize benefit.

A government that uses this method must first estimate the efficient quantity of pollution and set the overall emissions cap to achieve the efficient outcome. Then the government must somehow allocate shares of the cap to individual

---

■ FIGURE 10.4

A Pollution Tax

MyEconLab Animation

❶ A pollution tax is imposed that is equal to the marginal external cost of pollution.

Because the pollution tax equals the marginal external cost, the supply curve is the marginal social cost curve:
$S = MC + tax = MSC$.

❷ Market equilibrium is efficient because ❸ marginal social cost equals marginal benefit.

❹ The government collects tax revenue equal to the area of the purple rectangle.

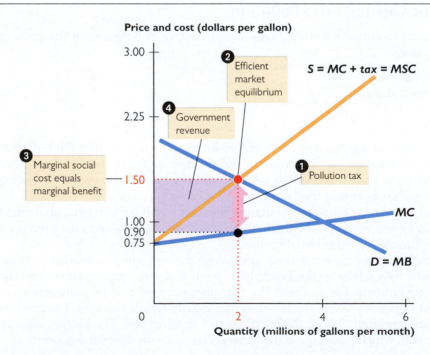

firms (and possibly even households). In an efficient allocation of emissions quotas to firms, each firm has the same marginal social cost of production and emissions abatement. So to allocate the cap efficiently across firms, the government would need to know a lot about each firm's production and abatement costs.

A Pigovian tax achieves an efficient allocation of pollution across firms because each firm chooses how much to produce and pollute by taking the tax into account, and then produces the quantity at which marginal social cost equals price. Because all firms face the same market price, they also incur the same marginal social cost.

The government solves the allocation problem by making an initial distribution of the cap across firms and then allows the firms to trade in a market for emission permits. Firms that have a low marginal abatement cost sell permits and make big cuts in pollution. Firms that have a high marginal abatement cost buy permits and make smaller cuts or perhaps even no cuts in pollution.

The market in permits determines the equilibrium price of emissions and each firm, confronted with that price, maximizes profit by setting its marginal pollution cost or marginal abatement cost, whichever is lower, equal to the market price of a permit. By confronting polluters with a price of pollution, trade in pollution permits can achieve the same efficient outcome as a Pigovian tax.

Cap-and-trade has been used by the EPA to address sulfur dioxide and lead emissions and has been very successful in reducing the levels of concentration of these pollutants in the atmosphere. (See *Eye on the U.S. Economy* below.)

EYE on the U.S. ECONOMY
U.S. Air Pollution Trends

Air quality in the United States has improved. The figure shows the trends for the atmospheric concentrations of five main air pollutants monitored by the Environmental Protection Agency (EPA) since 1980 and a sixth pollutant (suspended particulates) monitored since 1990.

By using a mix of regulation, pollution limits, economic incentives, and permit trading, the EPA has almost eliminated lead and has substantially decreased sulfur dioxide, carbon monoxide, nitrogen dioxide, and suspended particulates.

Ozone is harder to eliminate, but it has nonetheless fallen to 70 percent of its 1980 level.

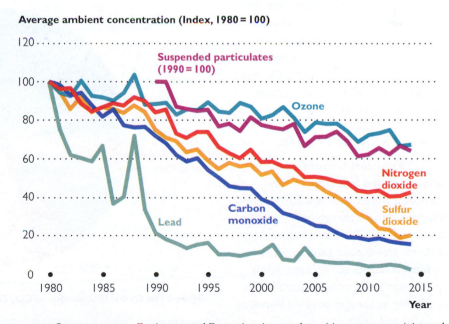

SOURCE OF DATA: Environmental Protection Agency, http://www.epa.gov/airtrends.

EYE on CLIMATE CHANGE

MyEconLab Critical Thinking Exercise

How Can We Limit Carbon Emissions?

The Problem

The Earth's temperature is rising and so is the amount of carbon dioxide, CO_2, in the atmosphere. Figure 1 shows these trends. The scientific consensus is that human economic activity is their major source.

Figure 2 shows that China, the United States, and Europe create 54 percent of carbon emissions and another eight large emitters create a further 25 percent.

On current trends, by 2050, three quarters of carbon emissions will come from developing economies and by 2100, the temperature will have increased by 3°C to a level that brings extreme weather and widespread coastal flooding.

Economist Nicholas Stern, principal author of *The Stern Review on the Economics of Climate Change*, says that carbon emission is "the greatest market failure the world has ever seen," and to avoid the risk of catastrophic climate change, the upward CO_2 trend must be stopped. Most economists agree with Stern and favor action.

Coping with the Problem

A global problem requires global action, and the first steps in this direction were taken at a 2015 United Nations climate change conference in Paris where 197 countries agreed to

1. Limit greenhouse gases emitted by human activity to the same levels that can be absorbed naturally, beginning as early as possible between 2050 and 2100.

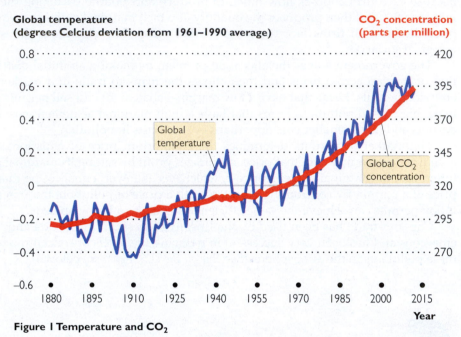

Figure 1 Temperature and CO$_2$

Sources of data: Met Office Hadley Centre and Scripps Institution of Oceanography.

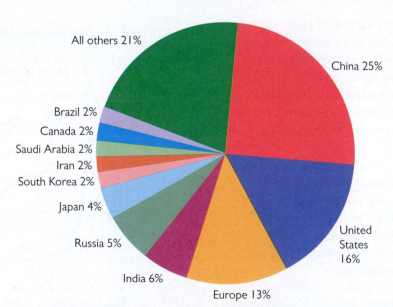

Figure 2 The Global Distribution of CO$_2$ Emissions

Sources of data: Energy Information Administration.

Greenhouse gas emission is "the greatest market failure the world has ever seen."

To avoid the risk of catastrophic climate change, the upward CO_2 trend must be stopped.

Nicholas Stern

2. Keep global temperatures "well below" 2°C above pre-industrial levels and to "endeavor to limit" them to 1.5°C above by 2100.
3. Provide "climate finance" payments by rich countries of at least $100 billion a year starting in 2020 and more by 2025 to help poorer countries leapfrog fossil fuels and move straight to renewables.
4. Review each country's voluntary contribution to cutting emissions every five years.

If carbon emissions are to be cut, incentives must change. The cost of carbon-emitting activities must rise and the cost of alternative clean-energy technologies must fall. Disagreement centers on how to change incentives.

Should countries use carbon taxes or should they cap emissions and introduce carbon trading? Should clean energy and the research to develop new green technologies be subsidized?

Carbon Taxes

The Canadian province of British Columbia, Ireland, and the United Kingdom are among those making their carbon footprints smaller by taxing carbon-emitting activities. British Columbia has a tax of $30 per ton of carbon emitted. Ireland and the United Kingdom have steep taxes on gasoline. Figure 3 shows the large U.K. gas tax and contrasts it with the very low U.S. gas tax.

Cap-and-Trade

Cap-and-trade—capping emissions and issuing tradeable emissions permits—has been used successfully by the EPA to cut local air pollutants, particularly lead. The system is also in use in Europe, but the cap is too large and the price is too low.

Subsidize Green Alternatives

Many countries provide subsidies to power utilities when they install wind farms or arrays of solar panels. The cost of these technologies is falling and they provide an increasing percentage of energy demand.

"For little environmental benefit, we could end up sacrificing growth, jobs, and opportunities for the big majority, especially in the developing world."

Bjørn Lomborg

Why Isn't More Being Done?

Why don't we have more aggressive caps and stronger incentives to encourage a larger reduction in carbon emissions? Four reasons are

1. Developing economies want to develop *and* want low-cost energy. With the currently available technologies, coal is an attractive choice for them.
2. Getting global agreement is hard. Paris 2015 was the first time that every country signed onto a plan.
3. The costs of lowering emissions are certain and are borne now while most of the benefits come in the future. Bjørn Lomborg, author of *The Skeptical Environmentalist*, says that "For little environmental benefit, we could end up sacrificing growth, jobs, and opportunities for the big majority, especially in the developing world."
4. Technology is advancing and the cost of cleaner energy is falling, so there is a temptation to rely on this trend continuing. An example is replacing coal with gas, which halves the carbon emissions from electricity generation and which fracking technology has made a cost-effective option.

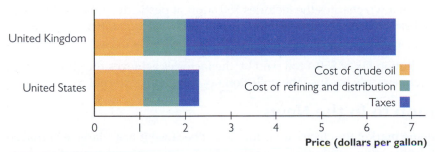

Figure 3 Gasoline Taxes

Sources of data: Energy Information Administration, Automobile Association, and authors' assumptions.

CHECKPOINT 10.1

Explain why negative externalities lead to inefficient overproduction and how property rights and pollution taxes can achieve a more efficient outcome.

Practice Problems

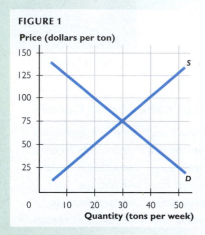

FIGURE 1

Figure 1 illustrates the unregulated market for a pesticide. When factories produce pesticide, they also create waste, which they dump into a lake on the edge of the town. The marginal external cost of the dumped waste is equal to the marginal private cost of producing the pesticide (that is, the marginal social cost of producing the pesticide is double the marginal private cost).

1. What is the quantity of pesticide produced if no one owns the lake and what is the efficient quantity of pesticide? What is the deadweight loss?

2. If the town owns the lake, what is the quantity of pesticide produced and how much does the town charge the factories to dump waste?

3. If the pesticide factories own the lake, how much pesticide is produced?

4. If no one owns the lake and the government levies a pollution tax, what is the tax per ton of pesticide that achieves the efficient outcome?

In the News

Could U.S. pollution regulations help smog-enshrouded China?
Beijing officials issued a "red alert" for air quality, closed schools, limited automobile traffic, and kept people indoors to avoid toxic smog. Most of Beijing's energy comes from carbon-emitting coal. The U.S. EPA is working with China to develop a national cap-and-trade system.
Source: *The Christian Science Monitor*, December 8, 2015

Explain the inefficiency in Beijing's market for electricity and contrast it with the U.S. market. How can cap-and-trade achieve an efficient outcome?

Solutions to Practice Problems

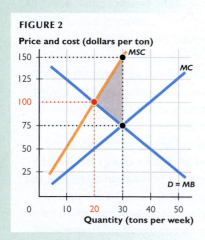

FIGURE 2

1. In Figure 2, production is 30 tons a week, the efficient quantity is 20 tons a week, and the deadweight loss is the area of the gray triangle.

2. The quantity of pesticide produced is the efficient quantity, 20 tons a week, and the town charges the factories $50 a ton of pesticide, which is the marginal external cost of the pollution produced by that quantity.

3. The factories produce the efficient quantity: 20 tons a week.

4. A pollution tax of $50 a ton paid by the factories achieves the efficient quantity of pesticide because the pollution tax equals the external cost.

Solution to In the News

The Beijing market for electricity is inefficient because it has a large external cost arising from carbon (and other) emissions from coal powered generators. The marginal social cost of electricity exceeds its marginal benefit by a large amount. The U.S. market for electricity is also inefficient but less so than Beijing's. Cap-and-trade can achieve an efficient outcome by confronting power utilities with the marginal *social* cost of their production.

10.2 POSITIVE EXTERNALITIES: EDUCATION

MyEconLab Concept Video

Education benefits the students who receive it, and the many other people with whom a well-educated person interacts. To study the economics of education, we must distinguish between its private benefits and its social benefits.

■ Private Benefits and Social Benefits

A *private benefit* is a benefit that the consumer of a good or service receives. The **marginal private benefit** (*MB*) is the benefit from an additional unit of a good or service that the consumer of that good or service receives.

An *external benefit* is a benefit from a good or service that someone other than the consumer receives. A **marginal external benefit** is the benefit from an additional unit of a good or service that people other than the consumer enjoy.

Marginal social benefit (*MSB*) is the marginal benefit enjoyed by society—by the consumers of a good or service (marginal private benefit) and by everyone else who benefits from it (the marginal external benefit). That is,

$$MSB = MB + \text{Marginal external benefit}$$

Figure 10.5 illustrates these benefit concepts. It uses college education as an example, but the same principles apply to all levels of education. The marginal benefit curve, *MB*, describes the marginal private benefit—such as expanded job opportunities and higher incomes—enjoyed by college graduates. Marginal private benefit decreases as the quantity of education increases.

Marginal private benefit
The benefit from an additional unit of a good or service that the consumer of that good or service receives.

Marginal external benefit
The benefit from an additional unit of a good or service that people other than the consumer of that good or service enjoy.

Marginal social benefit
The marginal benefit enjoyed by society—by the consumer of a good or service and by everyone else who benefits from it. It is the sum of marginal private benefit and marginal external benefit.

■ FIGURE 10.5

An External Benefit

MyEconLab Animation

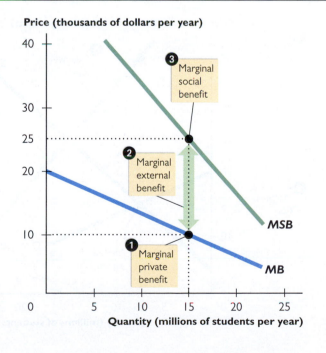

The *MB* curve shows the marginal private benefit enjoyed by the people who receive a college education. The *MSB* curve shows the sum of marginal private benefit and marginal external benefit.

When 15 million students attend college

❶ Marginal private benefit is $10,000 per year.

❷ Marginal external benefit is $15,000 per year.

❸ Marginal social benefit is $25,000 per year.

But college graduates generate external benefits. On the average, college graduates communicate more effectively with others and tend to be better citizens. Their crime rates are lower, and they are more tolerant of the views of others. A society with a large number of college graduates can support activities such as high-quality music, theater, and other organized social activities.

In the example in Figure 10.5, the marginal external benefit is $15,000 per year when 15 million students enroll in college. Marginal social benefit is the sum of marginal private benefit and marginal external benefit. For example, when 15 million students a year enroll in college, the marginal private benefit is $10,000 per year and the marginal external benefit is $15,000 per year, so the marginal social benefit is $25,000 per year.

The marginal social benefit curve, *MSB*, is the sum of marginal private benefit and marginal external benefit. It is steeper than the *MB* curve because marginal external benefit diminishes for the same reasons that *MB* diminishes.

When people make decisions about how much schooling to undertake, they consider only its private benefits and if education were provided by private schools that charged full-cost tuition, there would be too few college graduates.

Figure 10.6 shows the underproduction that would occur if all college education were left to the private market. The supply curve is the marginal cost curve of the private schools, *S = MC*. The demand curve is the marginal private benefit curve, *D = MB*. Market equilibrium is at a tuition of $15,000 per year and 7.5 million students enroll per year. At this equilibrium, the marginal social benefit is $38,000 per year, which exceeds the marginal cost by $23,000 per year. Too few students enroll in college. The efficient number of students is 15 million per year, with marginal social benefit equal to marginal cost. The gray triangle shows the deadweight loss created by the underproduction.

FIGURE 10.6

Underproduction with an External Benefit

MyEconLab Animation

The market demand curve is the marginal private benefit curve, *D = MB*. The supply curve is the marginal cost curve, *S = MC*.

❶ Market equilibrium is at a tuition of $15,000 per year with 7.5 million students per year enrolled.

The marginal social benefit curve is *MSB*, so the market equilibrium is inefficient because ❷ marginal social benefit exceeds ❸ marginal cost.

❹ The efficient number of students is 15 million a year.

❺ The gray triangle shows the deadweight loss created because too few students enroll in college.

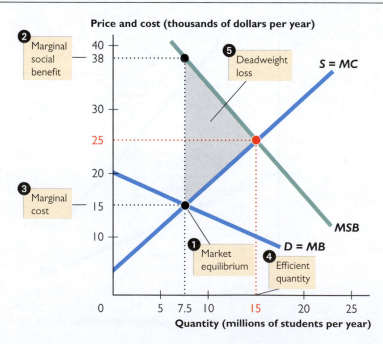

■ Government Actions in the Face of External Benefits

To get closer to producing the efficient quantity of a good or service that generates an external benefit, we make public choices through governments and modify the market outcome. To achieve a more efficient allocation of resources in the presence of external benefits, such as those that arise from education, governments can use three devices:

- Public provision
- Private subsidies
- Vouchers

Public Provision

Public provision is the production of a good or service by a public authority that receives most of its revenue from the government. Education services produced by public universities, colleges, and schools are examples of public provision.

Figure 10.7 shows how public provision might overcome the underproduction that arises in Figure 10.6. Public provision cannot lower the cost of production, so marginal cost is the same as before. Marginal private benefit, marginal external benefit, and marginal social benefit are also the same as in Figure 10.6.

The efficient quantity occurs where marginal social benefit equals marginal cost. In Figure 10.7, this quantity is 15 million students per year. Tuition is set to ensure that the efficient number of students enroll. That is, tuition is set at the level that equals the marginal private benefit at the efficient quantity. In Figure 10.7, tuition is $10,000 a year. The rest of the cost of the public college is borne by the taxpayers and, in this example, is $15,000 per student per year.

Public provision

The production of a good or service by a public authority that receives most of its revenue from the government.

■ **FIGURE 10.7**

Public Provision to Achieve an Efficient Outcome

MyEconLab Animation

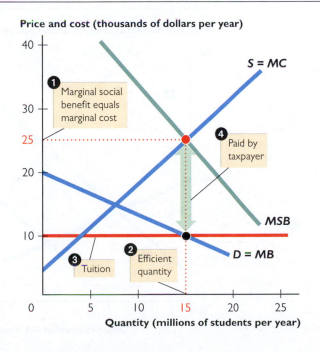

❶ Marginal social benefit equals marginal cost with 15 million students enrolled in college.

❷ The efficient quantity is 15 million students per year.

❸ Tuition is set at $10,000 per year.

❹ Taxpayers cover the remaining $15,000 of marginal cost per student per year.

Subsidy

A payment by the government to a producer to cover part of the costs of production.

Private Subsidies

A **subsidy** is a payment by the government to a producer to cover part of the costs of production. By giving producers a subsidy, the government can induce private decision makers to consider external benefits when they make their choices.

Figure 10.8 shows how a subsidy to private colleges works. In the absence of a subsidy, the marginal cost curve is the market supply curve of private college education, $S = MC$. The marginal benefit is the demand curve, $D = MB$. In this example, the government provides a subsidy to colleges of $15,000 per student per year. We must subtract the subsidy from the marginal cost of education to find the colleges' supply curve. That curve is $S = MC - subsidy$ in the figure. The equilibrium tuition (market price) is $10,000 per year, and the equilibrium number of students is 15 million per year. To educate 15 million students, colleges incur a marginal cost of a student of $25,000 per year. The marginal social benefit of a student is also $25,000 per year. So with marginal cost equal to marginal social benefit, the subsidy achieves an efficient outcome. The tuition and the subsidy just cover the colleges' marginal cost of a student per year.

Public Provision Versus Private Subsidy   In the two methods we've just studied, the number of students who enroll and the tuition are the same. So are these two methods of providing education services equally good? This question is difficult to resolve. The bureaucrats that operate public schools don't have as strong an incentive to minimize costs and maximize *quality* as those who run private schools. But for elementary and secondary education, charter schools might be an efficient compromise between traditional public schools and subsidized private schools.

FIGURE 10.8

Private Subsidy to Achieve an Efficient Outcome

MyEconLab Animation

With ❶ a subsidy of $15,000 per student per year, the supply curve is $S = MC - subsidy$.

❷ The equilibrium tuition is $10,000 per year and 15 million students per year enroll in college.

❸ The market equilibrium is efficient because with 15 million students enrolled in college, ❹ marginal social benefit equals marginal cost.

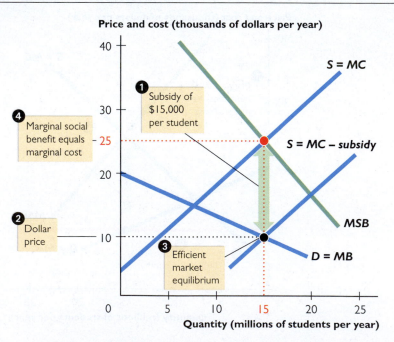

Vouchers

A **voucher** is a token that the government provides to households, which they can use to buy specified goods or services. The SNAP food stamp benefits provided by the U.S. Department of Agriculture to low-income households are an example of a voucher. Vouchers for college education could be provided to students.

Suppose that the government provides each student with a voucher. Students would choose the college to attend and use dollars plus the voucher to pay the tuition. Colleges would exchange the vouchers they receive for dollars from the government. If the government set the value of the voucher equal to the marginal external benefit of a year of college at the efficient number of students, then the outcome would be efficient.

Figure 10.9 illustrates an efficient voucher scheme. The government issues vouchers worth $15,000 per year, equal to the marginal external benefit at the efficient number of students. Each student pays $10,000 per year tuition and the government pays $15,000 per voucher, so the college collects $25,000 per student per year. The voucher scheme results in 15 million students attending college, the marginal cost equals the marginal social benefit, and the outcome is efficient.

Do Vouchers Beat Public Provision and Subsidy?   Vouchers provide public financial resources to the consumer rather than the producer. Economists generally believe that vouchers offer a more efficient outcome than public provision and subsidies because they combine the benefits of competition among private colleges with the injection of the public funds needed to achieve an efficient number of students. Also, students and their parents can monitor school performance more effectively than the government can.

Voucher
A token that the government provides to households, which they can use to buy specified goods or services.

■ **FIGURE 10.9**

Vouchers Achieve an Efficient Outcome

MyEconLab Animation

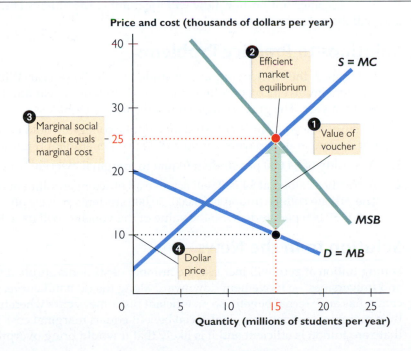

With vouchers for college, students are willing to pay *MB* plus the value of the voucher.

❶ The government issues vouchers to each student valued at $15,000, equal to the marginal external benefit of a year of college at the efficient number of students.

❷ The market equilibrium is efficient because with 15 million students enrolled in college, **❸** marginal social benefit equals marginal cost.

❹ Each student pays tuition of $10,000 (the dollar price) and the school collects $15,000 (the value of the voucher) from the government.

MyEconLab Study Plan 10.2
Key Terms Quiz
Solutions Video

CHECKPOINT 10.2

Explain why positive externalities lead to inefficient underproduction and how public provision, subsidies, and vouchers can achieve a more efficient outcome.

Practice Problems

Figure 1 shows the marginal private benefit from college education. The marginal cost of a college education is a constant $6,000 a year. The marginal external benefit from a college education is a constant $4,000 per student per year.

1. What is the efficient number of students? If colleges are private (no government involvement), how many people enroll, what is the tuition, and what is the deadweight loss?

2. If the government provides public colleges, what is the tuition that will achieve the efficient number of students? How much must taxpayers pay?

3. If the government subsidizes private colleges, what subsidy will achieve the efficient number of college students?

4. If the government offers each student a voucher, what value of the voucher will achieve the efficient number of students?

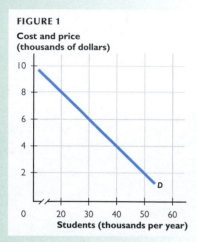

FIGURE 1

Cost and price
(thousands of dollars)

Students (thousands per year)

In the News

Students across America march for tuition-free college
Students at colleges and universities from Los Angeles to New York are demonstrating in support of free education. The website studentmarch.org says: "Education should be free. The United States is the richest country in the world, yet students have to take on crippling debt in order to get a college education."
Sources: *Reuters*, November 12, 2015, and www.studentmarch.org

If college becomes tuition-free, how will the number of students enrolled change and will the outcome be efficient?

Solutions to Practice Problems

1. In Figure 2, the efficient number of students is 50,000 a year. With no government involvement, enrollment is 30,000 students a year and tuition is $6,000 a year. The gray triangle shows the deadweight loss.

2. To enroll the efficient 50,000 students, public colleges would charge $2,000 per student and taxpayers would pay $4,000 per student (Figure 2).

3. A subsidy of $4,000 per student (equal to marginal external benefit).

4. A voucher valued at $4,000 will achieve an efficient enrollment of 50,000. The private college tuition is $6,000. 50,000 students will enroll if the dollar cost is $2,000 per student. So the value of the voucher will have to be $4,000.

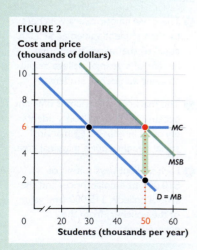

FIGURE 2

Cost and price
(thousands of dollars)

Students (thousands per year)

Solution to In the News

Setting tuition at zero will increase the number of students enrolled in colleges and universities—a movement downward along the demand curve. College education has an external benefit, so an efficient outcome occurs when tuition is less than marginal cost and marginal social benefit equals marginal cost. It is unlikely that zero tuition is efficient and it is likely that it would bring overproduction.

CHAPTER SUMMARY

Key Points

1. **Explain why negative externalities lead to inefficient overproduction and how property rights and pollution taxes can achieve a more efficient outcome.**

   - External costs are costs of production that fall on people other than the producer of a good or service. Marginal social cost equals marginal private cost plus marginal external cost.

   - Producers take account only of marginal private cost and produce more than the efficient quantity when there is a marginal external cost.

   - Sometimes it is possible to overcome a negative externality by assigning a property right.

   - When property rights cannot be assigned, governments might overcome a negative externality by mandating clean technologies (command-and-control), imposing pollution taxes, or using a cap-and-trade program.

2. **Explain why positive externalities lead to inefficient underproduction and how public provision, subsidies, and vouchers can achieve a more efficient outcome.**

   - External benefits are benefits that are received by people other than the consumer of a good or service. Marginal social benefit equals marginal private benefit plus marginal external benefit.

   - External benefits from education arise because better-educated people are better citizens, commit fewer crimes, and support social activities.

   - Vouchers or subsidies to private colleges or the provision of public education below cost can achieve a more efficient provision of education.

Key Terms

MyEconLab Key Terms Quiz

Abatement technology, 249
Coase theorem, 249
Command-and-control regulation, 251
Externality, 244
Marginal external benefit, 257
Marginal external cost, 246

Marginal private benefit, 257
Marginal private cost, 246
Marginal social benefit, 257
Marginal social cost, 246
Negative externality, 244
Positive externality, 244

Property rights, 249
Public provision, 259
Subsidy, 260
Voucher, 261

CHAPTER CHECKPOINT

Study Plan Problems and Applications

Table 1 shows the demand schedule for electricity from a coal-burning utility. Table 2 shows the utility's cost of producing electricity and the external cost of the pollution created. Use this information to work Problems **1** to **3**.

1. With no pollution control, calculate the quantity of electricity produced, the price of electricity, and the marginal external cost of the pollution generated.

2. With no pollution control, calculate the quantity of electricity produced, the marginal social cost of the electricity generated, and the deadweight loss.

3. If the government levies a pollution tax such that the utility generates the efficient quantity of electricity, calculate the quantity of electricity generated, the price of electricity, the size of the pollution tax, and the tax revenue.

Use the following information to work Problems **4** and **5**.

Tom and Larry must spend a day working together. Tom likes to smoke cigars and the price of a cigar is $2. Larry likes a smoke-free environment.

4. If Tom's marginal benefit from a cigar a day is $20 and Larry's marginal benefit from a smoke-free environment is $25 a day, what is the outcome if they meet at Tom's home? What is the outcome if they meet at Larry's home?

5. If Tom's marginal benefit from a cigar a day is $25 and Larry's marginal benefit from a smoke-free environment is $20 a day, what is the outcome if they meet at Tom's home? What is the outcome if they meet at Larry's home?

Use Table 3 and the following information to work Problems **6** to **8**.

The marginal cost of educating a college student is $5,000 a year. Table 3 shows the marginal benefit schedule from a college education. The marginal external benefit from a college education is a constant $2,000 per student per year. There are no public colleges.

6. With no government involvement in college education, how many students enroll, what is the tuition, and what is the deadweight loss created?

7. If the government subsidizes colleges and sets the subsidy so that the efficient number of students enroll, what is the subsidy per student, how many students enroll, and what is the cost to taxpayers?

8. If the government offers vouchers to students, what is the value of the voucher that will encourage the efficient number of students to enroll?

9. **Two Philadelphia highways waste a million hours**
   A study of highway use says that on two short stretches of expressway in Philadelphia, delays of 1 million hours a year cost $22 million in lost time and waste 375,700 gallons of fuel.

   Source: Bob McGovern, *PhillyVoice*, November 23, 2015

   What is the externality described in the news clip? How could road tolls and high parking levies reduce congestion on Philadelpia roads? If road tolls and parking charges cut commute times, would the Philadelphia road system be more efficient? Explain your answers.

 10. Read *Eye on Climate Change* on pp. 254–255 and then describe the government actions that could decrease carbon emissions. Explain why the government is not taking these actions more aggressively.

TABLE 1   DEMAND FOR ELECTRICITY

Price (cents per kilowatt)	Quantity demanded (kilowatts per day)
4	500
8	400
12	300
16	200
20	100
24	0

TABLE 2   PRIVATE AND EXTERNAL COSTS

Quantity (kilowatts per day)	Marginal cost	Marginal external cost
	(cents per kilowatt)	
0	0	0
100	2	2
200	4	4
300	6	6
400	8	8
500	10	10

TABLE 3

Students (millions per year)	Marginal benefit (dollars per student per year)
1	5,000
2	3,000
3	2,000
4	1,500
5	1,200
6	1,000
7	800
8	500

Instructor Assignable Problems and Applications

MyEconLab Homework, Quiz, or Test if assigned by instructor

1. The price of gasoline in Europe is about three times that in the United States, mainly because the European gas tax is higher than the U.S. gas tax. How would an increase in the gas tax in the United States to the European level change carbon emissions? Would this tax increase bring greater efficiency or would it increase deadweight loss?

2. **The warming Arctic affects us all**
   Arctic temperatures are rising twice as fast as the global average and receding sea ice threatens polar bears, walruses, and seals that exist nowhere else on earth and face an increased risk of extinction.
   Source: *Truthout*, December 4, 2015

   What is the externality described in the news clip? How could property rights influence the amount of damage done to the Arctic Sea and its wildlife?

Use the following information to work Problems **3** and **4**.

City ponders ban on plastic bags
Most plastic shopping bags end up in the landfill or as litter. Tacoma city officials are considering banning them or allowing them for a fee of 5 or 10 cents.
Source: *Tacoma Weekly*, December 8, 2015

3. Explain how a Tacoma charge will change the use of plastic bags and how the deadweight loss created by plastic bags will change.

4. Explain why a Tocoma ban on plastic bags would be inefficient.

Use the following information to work Problems **5** to **7**.

The marginal cost of educating a college student online is $3,000 a year. Table 1 shows the marginal private benefit schedule from a college education. The marginal external benefit is 50 percent of the marginal private benefit.

5. With no government involvement in college education, how many students enroll and what is the tuition? Calculate the deadweight loss created.

6. If the government subsidizes colleges so that the efficient number of students will enroll, what is the cost to taxpayers?

7. If the government offers vouchers to students and values them so that the efficient number of students will enroll, what is the value of the voucher?

8. **Worse than useless**
   Europe's Emissions Trading Scheme (ETS) has too many carbon emission permits trading at too low a price.
   Source: *The Economist*, January 25, 2014

   Explain the conditions under which the ETS, a cap-and-trade system, would reduce the amount of carbon emissions to the efficient quantity. Use a graph of the European market for electricity to illustrate your explanation. On your graph, show the effects of having too many emission permits.

9. **Carbon tax debate heats up in Montpelier, VT**
   Vermonters are debating the pros and cons of a state carbon tax—a new tax on gasoline, heating oil, and other fossil fuels sold in the state. Backers say the tax revenue would be used to cut other taxes and increase energy efficiency.
   Source: Watchdog.org, December 3, 2015

   Draw a graph of the market for gasoline in Vermont to show the effects of a state carbon tax.

TABLE 1

Students (millions per year)	Marginal private benefit (dollars per student per year)
1	6,000
2	5,000
3	4,000
4	3,000
5	2,000
6	1,000

MyEconLab Chapter 10 Study Plan

Multiple Choice Quiz

1. Electricity has a negative production externality because _____.

   A. its marginal benefit decreases as more of it is consumed
   B. the marginal private cost of producing it increases as more of it is produced
   C. the marginal social cost of producing it exceeds the marginal private cost of producing it
   D. a marginal external cost lowers the marginal benefit from consuming it

2. A steelmaking plant pollutes the air and water so _____.

   A. the marginal social cost of producing steel exceeds the marginal private cost by the amount of the marginal external cost
   B. the marginal social cost of producing steel is less than the marginal private cost by the amount of the marginal external cost
   C. the marginal private cost of producing steel equals the marginal external cost plus the marginal social cost
   D. the marginal private cost of producing steel minus the marginal social cost equals the marginal external cost

3. An unregulated paint factory that pollutes a river results in _____ and _____.

   A. overproduction; a price that exceeds the marginal benefit from the good
   B. underproduction; a price that equals the marginal benefit from the good
   C. the efficient quantity produced; a marginal benefit equal to the marginal social cost
   D. an inefficient quantity produced; a marginal benefit below the marginal social cost

4. Steel production creates pollution. If a tax is imposed on steel production equal to the marginal external cost of the pollution it creates, _____.

   A. steel producers will cut pollution to zero
   B. the deadweight loss created by steel producers will be cut to zero
   C. the market price of steel will rise by the amount of the tax
   D. steel producers will continue to produce the inefficient quantity of steel

5. A good or service with a positive externality is one which _____.

   A. everyone wants to have access to
   B. is produced in the social interest
   C. the marginal social benefit exceeds the marginal private benefit
   D. the marginal external benefit exceeds the marginal private benefit

6. Because education generates a positive externality, _____.

   A. everyone who wants a college education should get one
   B. graduates' marginal benefit exceeds the society's value of the education
   C. the quantity of education undertaken will achieve the social interest if it is free
   D. subsidies to colleges or vouchers to students are means of achieving the efficient number of graduates

Should America spend more on transportation infrastructure?

Public Goods and Common Resources

CHAPTER CHECKLIST

When you have completed your study of this chapter, you will be able to

1 Distinguish among private goods, public goods, and common resources.

2 Explain the free-rider problem and how public provision might help to overcome it and deliver an efficient quantity of public goods.

3 Explain the tragedy of the commons and review its possible solutions.   MyEconLab **Big Picture Video**

MyEconLab Concept Video

11.1 CLASSIFYING GOODS AND RESOURCES

Why do governments use tax dollars to build highways, bridges, and tunnels? Why don't profit-seeking private firms build and sell the services of the transportation infrastructure? What's the difference between fish in the Pacific Ocean and fish on East Point Seafood Company's Seattle fish farm? What's the difference between a live Taylor Swift concert and a concert on network television? What's the difference between education and fast food? Each pair differs in many ways, but key is the extent to which people can be *excluded* from enjoying the benefits from them and the extent to which their use by one person *rivals* their use by others.

■ Excludable

Excludable

A good, service, or resource is excludable if it is possible to prevent someone from enjoying its benefits.

A good, service, or resource is **excludable** if it is possible to prevent someone from enjoying its benefits. Brink's security services, East Point Seafood's fish, and Taylor Swift concerts are examples. You must pay to benefit from them.

A good, service, or resource is **nonexcludable** if it is impossible (or extremely costly) to prevent someone from benefiting from it. The services of the city police department, fish in the Pacific Ocean, and a concert on network television are examples. When a police cruiser slows the traffic on a highway to the speed limit, it lowers the risk of an accident to all the road users. It can't exclude some road users from the lower risk. Anyone with a boat can try to catch the fish in the ocean. Anyone with a television can watch a network broadcast.

Nonexcludable

A good, service, or resource is nonexcludable if it is impossible (or extremely costly) to prevent someone from enjoying its benefits.

■ Rival

Rival

A good, service, or resource is rival if its use by one person decreases the quantity available for someone else.

A good, service, or resource is **rival** if its use by one person decreases the quantity available for someone else. Brink's security might work for two banks, but one truck can't deliver cash to two banks at the same time. A fish, whether in the ocean or on a fish farm, can be consumed only once. One seat at a concert can hold only one person at a time. These items are rival.

A good, service, or resource is **nonrival** if its use by one person does not decrease the quantity available for someone else. The services of the city police department and a concert on network television are nonrival. The arrival of one more person in a neighborhood doesn't lower the level of police protection enjoyed by the community. When one additional person switches on the TV, no other viewer is affected.

Nonrival

A good, service, or resource is nonrival if its use by one person does not decrease the quantity available for someone else.

■ A Fourfold Classification

Figure 11.1 classifies goods, services, and resources into four types using the two criteria that we've just considered.

Private Goods

Private good

A good or service that can be consumed by only one person at a time and only by the person who has bought it or owns it.

A good or service that is both rival and excludable (top left of Figure 11.1) is a **private good**: It can be consumed by only one person at a time and only by the person who has bought it or owns it. The fish on East Point's farm are an example of a private good. One person's consumption of a fish rivals others', and everyone except the person who bought a fish is excluded from consuming it.

Public Goods

A good or service that is both nonrival and nonexcludable (bottom right of Figure 11.1) is a **public good**: It can be consumed simultaneously by everyone, and no one can be excluded from enjoying its benefits. A flood-control levee is an example of a public good. Everyone who lives in a protected floodplain enjoys the benefits, and no one can be excluded from receiving those benefits. The system of law and order provided by the courts and the body of laws is another example.

Common Resources

A resource that is rival and nonexcludable (top right of Figure 11.1) is a **common resource**: A unit of it can be used only once, but no one can be prevented from using what is available. Ocean fish and the Earth's atmosphere are examples of common resources. Ocean fish are rival because a fish taken by one person is not available for anyone else, and they are nonexcludable because it is difficult to prevent people from catching them. The Earth's atmosphere is rival because oxygen used by one person is not available for anyone else, and it is nonexcludable because we can't prevent people from breathing!

Natural Monopoly Goods

A good that is nonrival but excludable (bottom left of Figure 11.1) is a good produced by a *natural monopoly*. We define natural monopoly in Chapter 16 (p. 402). A natural monopoly is a firm that can produce at a lower cost than two or more firms can. Examples are the Internet, cable television, and a bridge or tunnel. One more user doesn't decrease the enjoyment of the other users, and people can be excluded with user codes, scramblers, and tollgates.

Public good
A good or service that can be consumed simultaneously by everyone and from which no one can be excluded.

Common resource
A resource that can be used only once, but no one can be prevented from using what is available.

■ **FIGURE 11.1**

Fourfold Classification of Goods

MyEconLab Animation

	Private goods	Common resources
Rival	Food and drink Car House	Fish in ocean Atmosphere National parks
	Natural monopoly goods	**Public goods**
Nonrival	Internet Cable television Bridge or tunnel	National defense The law Flood-control levees
	Excludable	**Nonexcludable**

Goods that are rival and excludable are private goods (top left).

Goods that are nonrival and nonexcludable are public goods (bottom right).

Goods and resources that are rival but nonexcludable are common resources (top right).

Goods that are nonrival but excludable are goods produced by a natural monopoly (bottom left).

SOURCE OF DATA: Adapted from and inspired by E. S. Savas, *Privatizing the Public Sector,* Chatham House Publishers, Inc., Chatham, NJ, 1982, p. 34.

EYE on the PAST
Is a Lighthouse a Public Good?

A lighthouse looks like a public good: *nonexcludable* and *nonrival*. But in the eighteenth century, lighthouses in England were built and operated by private companies that earned profits by charging tolls on ships docking at nearby ports. A ship that refused to pay the lighthouse toll was excluded from using the port. So even the services of a lighthouse, when it is near a port, are excludable! Such a lighthouse is an example of a natural monopoly good and not a public good.

CHECKPOINT 11.1

Distinguish among private goods, public goods, and common resources.

Practice Problems

1. Classify the following services for computer owners with an Internet connection as rival or nonrival and as excludable or nonexcludable:

    - eBay
    - A mouse
    - A Twitter page
    - MyEconLab Web site

2. Classify each of the following items as a public good, a private good, a natural monopoly good, or a common resource:

    - Fire protection
    - A seat at the final match of the U.S. Open (tennis)
    - A pay-per-view movie on television
    - The Ohio River

Solutions to Practice Problems

1. eBay is nonrival and nonexcludable. A mouse is rival and excludable. Twitter is nonrival and you can choose to make your feed excludable or nonexcludable. MyEconLab is nonrival and excludable.

2. Fire protection is nonrival and nonexcludable, so it is a public good. A seat at the U.S. Open final match is rival and excludable, so it is a private good. A pay-per-view movie is nonrival and excludable, so it is a natural monopoly good. The Ohio River is rival and nonexcludable, so it is a common resource.

11.2   PUBLIC GOODS AND THE FREE-RIDER PROBLEM

MyEconLab Concept Video

Why does the U.S. government provide our national defense and district court system? Why do the state governments provide flood-control levees? Why do our city governments provide fire and police services? Why don't we buy our national defense from North Pole Protection, Inc., a private firm that competes for our dollars in the marketplace in the same way that McDonald's does? Why don't private engineering firms provide levees? Why don't we buy our policing and fire services from Brink's and other private firms? The answer is that all of these goods are public goods—goods that are nonexcludable and nonrival—and such goods create a free-rider problem.

The Free-Rider Problem

A **free rider** is a person who enjoys the benefits from a good or service without paying for it. Because everyone consumes the same quantity of a public good and no one can be excluded from enjoying its benefits, no one has an incentive to pay for it. Everyone has an incentive to free ride. The *free-rider problem* is that the private market, left on its own, would provide too small a quantity of a public good. To produce the efficient quantity, government action is required.

To see how a private market would provide too little of a public good and how government might provide the efficient quantity, we need to consider the marginal benefit from a public good and its marginal cost. The marginal benefit from a public good is a little different from that of a private good, so we'll begin on the benefit side of the calculation.

Free rider
A person who enjoys the benefits of a good or service without paying for it.

EYE on YOUR LIFE

MyEconLab Critical Thinking Exercise

A Student's Free-Rider Problem and a Market Solution

A music file is nonrival because it can be copied at the click of a mouse. A duplicate file can be created at zero marginal cost. A music file is also effectively nonexcludable because it is extremely costly to prevent someone who wants to make an illegal copy from doing so.

Because a music file is nonrival and nonexcludable, it is a public good with a free-rider problem.

If everyone obtained their music by copying the files of their friends, you can see that it would not take long for the provision of songs to dry up. Professional writers and performers would not be able to generate an

income and only amateurs who write, perform, and record for fun would be left in the business.

This free-rider problem might be tackled by using the copyright laws that restrict the legal right to copy music files. What is wrong with this approach is that making something illegal isn't effective if it is difficult to detect and punish the illegal act. With the spread of ownership of smartphones, laptops, and fast Internet connections, free-riding became a big problem.

As almost always eventually happens, a market solution emerged. That solution is streaming.

Spotify, Apple Music, and others have created subscription services that give access to music but not to files. Subscriptions to streaming services have doubled each year, and singles downloads are now declining.

Illegal file sharing creates a free-rider problem, and streaming services solve it.

■ The Marginal Benefit from a Public Good

Lisa and Max (the only people in a society) share a common parking area that has no security lighting, a public good. Both of them would like some lights, but how many? The answer is determined by marginal benefit and marginal cost.

Lisa and Max know their own marginal benefit from different levels of security lighting, and the tables in parts (a) and (b) of Figure 11.2 show these marginal benefits. The curves MB_L and MB_M are Lisa's and Max's marginal benefit curves. As the quantity of the good increases, each person's marginal benefit from the public good diminishes—just as it does for a private good.

The table in part (c) of Figure 11.2 shows the marginal benefit for the entire economy. We obtain this curve by summing the individual marginal benefits at each quantity. For example, with 3 lights, the marginal benefit is $70 ($40 for Lisa plus $30 for Max). The curve MSB is the marginal social benefit curve.

Because we find the marginal benefit from a public good by summing the marginal benefits of all individuals at each quantity, we find the MSB curve for a public good by summing the individual marginal benefit curves *vertically*. In contrast, to obtain the MB curve for a private good—which is also the market demand curve—we sum the quantities demanded by all individuals at each price—we sum the individual demand curves *horizontally* (see Chapter 4, p. 87).

■ The Marginal Cost of a Public Good

The marginal cost of a public good is determined in exactly the same way as that of a private good. The principle of *increasing marginal cost* that you learned in Chapter 6 applies to the marginal cost of a public good. So the marginal cost curve of a public good slopes upward. A public good does not create an externality, so the marginal cost is also the marginal social cost.

We find the marginal social benefit curves of the law courts, flood-control levees, police protection, and firefighting service by summing the individual marginal benefit curves for these public goods.

FIGURE 11.2

Marginal Benefit from a Public Good

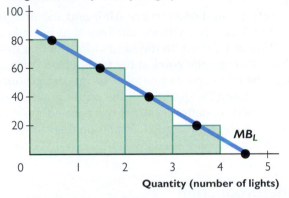

(a) Lisa's marginal benefit

The marginal benefit curves for a public good are MB_L for Lisa and MB_M for Max. The marginal benefit from the public good for the economy is the sum of the marginal benefits of all individuals at each quantity. The marginal social benefit curve for the economy is MSB.

Quantity of lights	0	1	2	3	4	5
Lisa's MB (dollars per light)		80	60	40	20	0

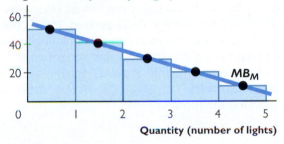

(b) Max's marginal benefit

Quantity of lights	0	1	2	3	4	5
Max's MB (dollars per light)		50	40	30	20	10

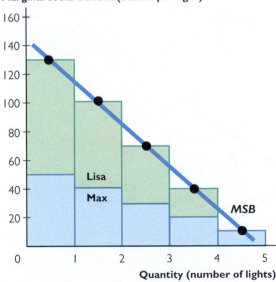

(c) Economy's marginal social benefit

Quantity of lights	0	1	2	3	4	5
Lisa's MB (dollars per light)		80	60	40	20	0
Max's MB (dollars per light)		50	40	30	20	10
Economy's MSB (dollars per light)		130	100	70	40	10

MyEconLab Concept Video

The Efficient Quantity of a Public Good

To determine the efficient quantity of a public good, we use the same principles that you learned in Chapter 10: We find the quantity at which marginal social benefit equals marginal social cost.

Figure 11.3 shows the marginal social benefit curve *MSB* and the marginal social cost curve *MSC* of a public good—surveillance satellites that provide national defense services. The *MSB* curve is based on the same principle that determines the marginal social benefit of the public good in the two-person (Lisa and Max) economy. If marginal social benefit exceeds marginal social cost, resources can be used more efficiently by increasing the quantity of the public good. If marginal social cost exceeds marginal social benefit, resources can be used more efficiently by decreasing the quantity of the public good. If marginal social benefit equals marginal social cost, resources are being used efficiently—in this example, 200 satellites.

Private Provision: Underproduction

Could a private firm—say, North Pole Protection, Inc.—deliver the efficient quantity of satellites? Most likely it couldn't, because no one would have an incentive to pay his or her share of the cost of the satellites. Everyone would reason as follows: "The number of satellites provided by North Pole Protection, Inc., is not affected by my decision to pay my share or not. My own private consumption will be greater if I free ride. If I do not pay, I enjoy the same level of security and I can buy more private goods. So I will free ride on the public good." Such reasoning is the free-rider problem. If everyone reasons the same way, North Pole Protection, Inc., has no revenue and so provides no satellites.

FIGURE 11.3

The Efficient Quantity and Private Underproduction of a Public Good   MyEconLab Animation

❶ With fewer than 200 satellites, marginal social benefit *MSB* exceeds marginal social cost *MSC*. An increase in the quantity will make resource use more efficient.

❷ With more than 200 satellites, marginal social cost exceeds marginal social benefit. A decrease in the quantity will make resource use more efficient.

❸ With 200 satellites, marginal social benefit *MSB* equals marginal social cost *MSC*. Resources are used efficiently.

❹ The efficient quantity of the public good is 200 satellites.

❺ Private provision leads to underproduction—in the extreme, to zero production.

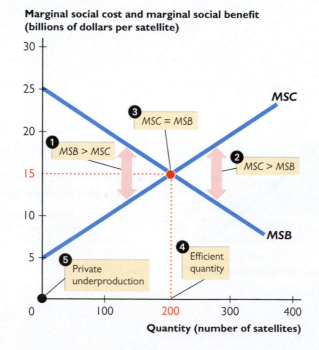

■ Public Provision: Efficient Production

The political outcome might be efficient or inefficient. We look first at an efficient outcome. There are two political parties, the Hawks and the Doves, and they agree on all issues except for the quantity of defense satellites. The Hawks prefer 300 satellites, and the Doves prefer 100 satellites. Both parties want to get elected, so they run a voter survey and discover the *MSB* curve of Figure 11.4. They also consult with satellite producers to establish the marginal cost schedule. The parties then do a "what-if" analysis. If the Hawks propose 300 satellites and the Doves propose 100 satellites, the voters will be equally unhappy with both parties. Compared to the efficient quantity of satellites, the Doves propose an underprovision of 100 satellites and the Hawks propose an overprovision of 100 satellites. The deadweight losses are equal, and an election would be too close to call.

Contemplating this outcome, the Hawks realize that they are too hawkish to get elected. They figure that if they scale back to 250 satellites, they will win the election if the Doves propose 100 satellites. The Doves reason in a similar way and figure that if they increase the number of satellites to 150, they can win the election if the Hawks propose 300 satellites. Each party knows how the other is reasoning, so they realize that their party must provide 200 satellites or it will lose the election. So both parties propose 200 satellites. The voters are indifferent between the parties, and each party receives 50 percent of the vote.

■ FIGURE 11.4

An Efficient Political Outcome

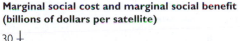
MyEconLab Animation

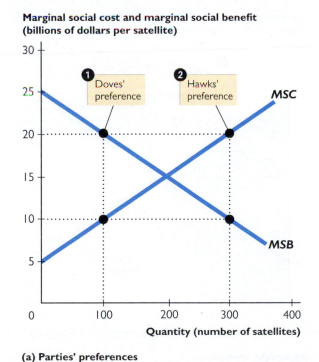

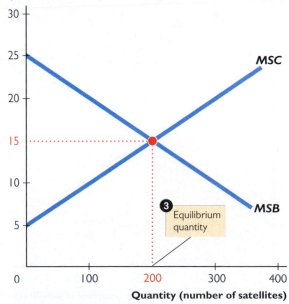

(a) Parties' preferences

(b) Political outcome

❶ The Doves would like to provide 100 satellites. ❷ The Hawks would like to provide 300 satellites.

❸ The political outcome is 200 satellites: Unless each party proposes 200 satellites, the other party can win an election.

■ Obstacles to Efficient Public Provision

Achieving an efficient political outcome is much harder than describing one. Three obstacles stand in its path:

- Determining benefits and costs
- Bureaucrats' goals and rationally uninformed voters
- Limited funds.

Determining Benefits and Costs

Elections are almost never about a single issue. Satellites compete with MRI scanners, education, and countless other public goods for the taxpayers' dollar. Bureaucrats help politicians to develop detailed proposals for a menu of items.

Benefit-cost analysis

An accounting exercise to determine the total benefit, total cost, and net benefit of a proposed project.

The tool that bureaucrats use in this process is called **benefit-cost analysis**, which is an accounting exercise to determine the total benefit, total cost, and net benefit of a proposed project. By pursuing projects with the highest net benefit, politicians hope to win and keep their seats.

Total benefit and cost are related to marginal benefit and cost and Figure 11.5 shows how. In part (a), at $15 billion each, 200 satellites cost $3 trillion, the area of the red rectangle. In part (b), with the benefit of each satellite shown by the *MSB* curve, the total benefit is $4 trillion, the green area. Net benefit equals total benefit minus total cost and is $1 trillion, the area of the green triangle.

■ FIGURE 11.5

Total Cost, Total Benefit, and Net Benefit

MyEconLab Animation

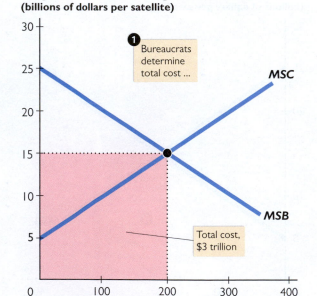

(a) Cost of satellites

❶ Total cost is the cost of each unit multiplied by the quantity bought. The total cost of 200 satellites is $3 trillion.

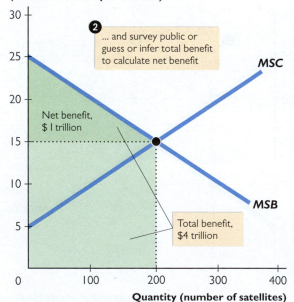

(b) Benefit of satellites

❷ Total benefit is marginal benefit summed over the 200 satellites bought and net benefit is total benefit minus total cost.

Bureaucrats can get a good estimate of total cost by consulting engineers and others who possess the relevant technical knowledge and by obtaining price quotations from potential suppliers. In the case of surveillance satellites, the price of a Lockheed Martin satellite can be determined and used as input in the benefit-cost analysis.

The benefit is hard to measure. When people buy a private good, they reveal their willingness to pay and their marginal benefit by the choices they make. But votes for packages containing hundreds of projects don't reveal the willingness of voters to pay for any individual project. Public policy planners can sometimes use surveys that ask people to report their valuations of a project. And sometimes they can make inferences. For example, if a transport project will save people time, the value of time might be inferred from wage rates. But sometimes, there is no information and an educated guess must be made.

Because benefits are hard to measure, there will be both underprovision and overprovision of individual public goods.

Bureaucrats' Goals and Rationally Uninformed Voters

Bureau heads have their own goals and one of them is to maximize their budgets to enhance their status and power. For the top Pentagon bureaucrats, the objective is to maximize the national defense budget. They might pursue this goal by trying to persuade politicians that more satellites or more costly satellites are needed.

But won't overpaying for or overproviding satellites cost votes and be opposed by politicians? It would if voters were well informed. But rational voters are not well informed. The reason is that it is rational for a voter to be ignorant about an issue when the cost of information exceeds its benefit.

Rational ignorance is the decision not to acquire information because the marginal cost of doing so exceeds the marginal benefit. Each voter knows that he or she can make no difference to national defense policy and that it would take an enormous amount of time and effort to become even moderately well informed about alternative defense technologies. So voters remain relatively uninformed about the technicalities of defense (and most other) issues, leaving open the opportunity for bureaucrats to overprovide public goods.

Rational ignorance
The decision not to acquire information because the marginal cost of doing so exceeds the marginal benefit.

Limited Funds

The tendency to overprovide public goods is countered by limited funds. Taxes pay for public goods and while voters like public goods, they don't like paying taxes. And overprovision of public goods would mean voters being over-taxed.

Because politicians don't get elected by promising higher taxes, the funds available for providing public goods can be lower than the level needed to provide the efficient quantity.

Eye on the U.S. Infrastructure on p. 278 describes a situation in which there appears to be a clear underprovision arising from limited funds. If there really is underprovision of transportation infrastructure, shouldn't a political party be able to secure more votes by proposing greater provision and higher taxes to pay the bill? If the tax and spend package could be offered with guarantees, that outcome would be feasible. But there is a disconnect in Congress and the state legislatures between higher taxes and improved public goods. Taxes are legislated before the underprovision of public goods is corrected, and politicians can't credibly commit to using the taxes to deliver the promised goods.

EYE on the U.S. INFRASTRUCTURE

Should America Spend More on Transportation Infrastructure?

The Problem

The road transportation infrastructure of the United States consists of 4 million miles of roads, 47,000 miles of interstate highways, and 607,000 bridges.

The gas tax is the main source of funds for maintaining this infrastructure. The federal gas tax has been stuck at 18.4¢ per gallon since 1997 and the last time most states changed the gas tax was before 2000.

Fixed tax rates, declining gas consumption due to more fuel-efficient vehicles, and rising costs of maintaining roads and bridges mean that the funds needed for repairs have outstripped the funds available. Gas tax revenue adjusted for rising prices—the real gas tax—has decreased.

With decreasing real tax revenue, expenditure on maintaining the transportation infrastructure has trended downward. Figure 1 shows the trends in expenditure and taxes, both adjusted for the cost of inflation.

The American Society of Civil Engineers says that 67,500 bridges are structurally deficient and a spending increase of $8 billion annually is needed to bring the nation's bridges to a safe standard by 2028.

Economic Analysis

Figure 2 shows a model of the problem. The x-axis measures the number of bridges repaired per year and the y-axis measures the marginal social benefit and marginal social cost of

repairing a bridge, shown by the *MSB* and *MSC* curves.

In the model economy, it is efficient to repair 6,000 bridges a year at a cost of $3 million per bridge, with a total expenditure of $18 billion per year.

Limited funds block this efficient outcome. The number of bridges repaired is 4,000 per year at a cost of $2.5 million per bridge, with a total expenditure of $10 billion per year.

Because the number of bridges repaired per year is less than the efficient quantity, a deadweight loss is created.

In Figure 2, *MSB* exceeds *MSC*, so voters will support higher taxes and a bigger bridge repair program. In the U.S. economy, politicians have not found that efficient outcome.

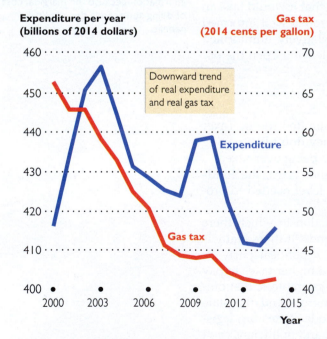

Figure 1 Public Expenditure and Gas Tax

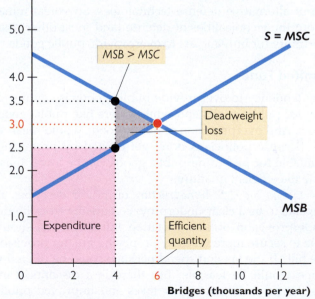

Figure 2 Underprovision of Infrastructure

CHECKPOINT 11.2

MyEconLab Study Plan 11.2
Key Terms Quiz
Solutions Video

Explain the free-rider problem and how public provision might help to overcome it and deliver an efficient quantity of public goods.

Practice Problems

1. For each of the following goods, explain whether there is a free-rider problem. If there is no such problem, how is it avoided?
   - Fire protection
   - A July 4th fireworks display
   - Interstate 80 in rural Wyoming

Use Table 1, which provides data about a mosquito control program, to work Problems **2** and **3**.

2. What quantity of spraying would a private control program provide? What is the efficient quantity of spraying? In a single-issue election on the quantity of spraying, what quantity would the winner of the election provide?

3. Suppose that the government sets up a Department of Mosquito Control and appoints a bureaucrat to run it. Would the department most likely underprovide, overprovide, or provide the efficient quantity of spraying?

TABLE 1

Quantity (square miles sprayed per day)	Marginal social cost	Marginal social benefit
	(dollars per day)	
0	0	6,000
1	1,000	5,000
2	2,000	4,000
3	3,000	3,000
4	4,000	2,000
5	5,000	1,000

In the News

The BBC is a cross between PBS and the IRS
Take a moment to thank the voluntary PBS fundraisers. The British Broadcasting Corporation (BBC) is funded by something called the "license fee," a tax of £145.50 ($245) per year on every household that has a television.

Source: *The Federalist*, August 7, 2014

Do the BBC and PBS produce a public good? Which one has a free-rider problem and how has the other one solved it?

Solutions to Practice Problems

1. Fire protection is a public good; a July 4th fireworks display is a public good. In both cases, the free-rider problem is avoided by public provision and financing through taxes. Interstate 80 in rural Wyoming is a public good. The public good creates a free-rider problem that is avoided because governments collect various taxes via the tax on gas and the vehicle registration fee.

2. A private program would provide zero spraying because the free-rider problem would prevail. The efficient quantity is 3 square miles a day—the quantity at which the marginal social benefit equals the marginal social cost. The winner will provide the efficient quantity: 3 square miles sprayed a day.

3. The Department of Mosquito Control would most likely overprovide because the bureau would try to maximize its budget.

Solution to In the News

Broadcast television is nonrival and nonexcludable, so it is a public good. PBS has a free-rider problem because only viewers who choose to contribute toward the cost of its service actually pay, while others free ride. The BBC has solved a free-rider problem by being funded by a compulsory fee that works like a tax.

MyEconLab Concept Video

11.3 THE TRAGEDY OF THE COMMONS

Overgrazing the pastures of a village in Middle Ages England and overfishing North Atlantic cod during recent decades are tragedies of the commons. The **tragedy of the commons** is the overuse of a common resource—a resource that is nonexcludable but rival—that arises because its users have no incentive to conserve it and use it sustainably.

To study the tragedy of the commons, its cause, and its possible remedies, we'll study the overfishing and depletion of the cod stock. You're about to discover that there are two problems that give rise to the tragedy of the commons:

- Unsustainable use of a common resource
- Inefficient use of a common resource

Tragedy of the commons
The overuse of a common resource that arises because its users have no incentive to conserve it and use it sustainably.

■ Unsustainable Use of a Common Resource

Renewable common resources such as fish and trees replenish themselves by the birth and growth of new members of the population.

Think about cod in the North Atlantic. At any given time, there is a *stock* of cod, a *rate of renewal*, and a rate of use—a *catch rate*. If the rate of renewal exceeds the catch rate, the cod stock grows and cod is being caught sustainably. The cod stock is also being used sustainably if its rate of renewal equals the catch rate and the stock remains constant. But if the catch rate exceeds the rate of renewal, the stock decreases and the cod stock is being used unsustainably.

The sustainable catch depends on the stock. With a small stock, few fish are born, so only a small quantity can be sustainably caught. With a large stock, many

EYE on the PAST
The Commons of England's Middle Ages

The term "the tragedy of the commons" comes from fourteenth century England, where areas of rough grassland surrounded villages. The commons were open to all and were used for grazing cows and sheep owned by the villagers.

Because the commons were open to everyone, no one had an incentive to ensure that the land was not overgrazed. The result was an overgrazing situation similar to that of overfishing in some of today's oceans.

During the sixteenth century, when the price of wool increased, England became a wool exporter to the world. Sheep farming became

profitable and sheep owners needed better control of the land they used, so the commons were gradually

enclosed and privatized. Overgrazing ended, and land use became more efficient.

fish are born but they must compete with each other for food, so only a few survive to reproduce and to grow large enough to be caught. So again, the sustainable catch is small. Between a small and a large stock is a stock at which, given the availability of food, the rate of renewal is at its maximum. At this stock, the sustainable catch rate is also at its maximum.

Figure 11.6 illustrates the relationship between the stock and sustainable catch. The *sustainable catch curve, SCC*, shows the sustainable catch rate at each stock size. As the stock increases, the sustainable catch increases to a maximum and then decreases.

If the catch rate is less than the sustainable catch rate, at a point such as *A*, the cod stock grows. If the quantity caught equals the sustainable catch, at any point on the *SCC*, the fish stock remains constant and is available for future generations of fishers in the same quantity that is available today. But if the quantity caught exceeds the sustainable catch, at a point such as *B*, the fish stock shrinks and, unchecked, eventually falls to zero.

You now understand the sustainable use of a resource, but another problem is its efficient use.

■ Inefficient Use of a Common Resource

Even if the catch is sustainable, it will exceed the efficient catch: overfishing occurs. Why does overfishing occur? The answer is that fishers face only their own *private* cost and don't face the cost they impose on others—the *external* cost. In pursuit of self-interest, the fishers ignore this external cost. Let's explore overfishing in more detail, starting with the marginal social cost of catching fish.

The pursuit of self-interest results in overfishing.

■ FIGURE 11.6

Sustainable Catch

MyEconLab Animation

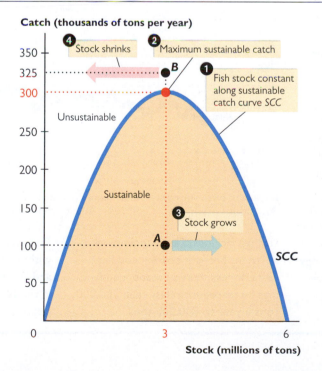

❶ Along the sustainable catch curve, *SCC*, the fish stock is constant.

❷ As the fish stock increases (on the *x*-axis), the sustainable catch (on the *y*-axis) increases to the maximum sustainable catch. As the stock increases further, the fish must compete for food and the sustainable catch falls.

❸ If the catch is less than the sustainable catch, such as at point *A*, the fish stock grows.

❹ If the catch exceeds the sustainable catch, such as at point *B*, the fish stock diminishes.

Marginal Social Cost

The *marginal social cost* of catching fish is the marginal private cost plus the marginal external cost.

The *marginal private cost* of catching fish is the fishers' cost of keeping a boat and crew at sea for long enough to increase the catch by one ton. The principle of increasing marginal cost applies to catching fish just as it applies to other production activities. Crew fatigue, overfull refrigerators, and a lower speed to conserve fuel decrease the catch per hour, so the marginal private cost of catching fish increases as the quantity caught increases.

The *marginal external cost* of catching fish is the cost per additional ton that one fisher's production imposes on all other fishers. This additional cost arises because one fisher's catch decreases the remaining stock, which in turn decreases the renewal rate of the stock and makes it harder for others to find and catch fish. Marginal external cost also increases as the quantity of fish caught increases.

Because both components of marginal social cost increase as the quantity caught increases, marginal social cost increases with the quantity of fish caught.

EYE on the GLOBAL ECONOMY
The North Atlantic Cod Tragedy of the Commons

Before 1970, Atlantic cod was abundant. It had been fished for many centuries and was a major food source for the first European settlers in North America. In 1812, there were more than 1,600 fishing boats in the waters off New England and Newfoundland, Canada. At that time, cod were huge fish, weighing in at more than 220 pounds and measuring up to 6 feet in length.

Fish were caught using lines and productivity was low. But low productivity limited the catch and enabled cod to be caught sustainably over hundreds of years.

The situation changed dramatically during the 1960s with the introduction of high-efficiency nets (called trawls, seines, and gill nets), sonar technology to find fish concentrations, and large ships with efficient processing and

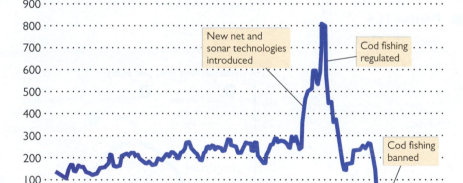

Fish landings (thousands of tons per year)

SOURCE OF DATA FOR GRAPH: Millennium Ecosystem Assessment.
SOURCE OF INFORMATION: Codfishes —Atlantic cod and its fishery, http://science.jrank.org/

storage facilities. These technological advances brought soaring cod harvests. In less than a decade, cod landings increased from less than 300,000 tons a year to 800,000 tons.

This volume of cod could not be taken without a serious collapse in the stock and in 1992, a total ban on cod fishing in the North Atlantic stabilized the population but at a very low level.

Marginal Social Benefit and Demand

The marginal social benefit from fish is the price that consumers are willing to pay for an additional pound of fish. Marginal social benefit decreases as the quantity of fish consumed increases, so the market demand curve, which is also the marginal social benefit curve, slopes downward.

Overfishing Equilibrium

Figure 11.7 illustrates overfishing and how it arises. The market demand curve for fish is the marginal social benefit curve, *MSB*. The market supply curve is the marginal private cost curve, *MC*. Market equilibrium occurs at the intersection point of these two curves. The equilibrium quantity is 800,000 tons of fish per year and the equilibrium price is $10 per pound. At the market equilibrium quantity, marginal social cost exceeds marginal social benefit.

Efficient Equilibrium

The efficient quantity is where marginal social benefit equals marginal social cost. In Figure 11.7, the efficient quantity of fish is 300,000 tons. At this quantity, the marginal social cost (on the *MSC* curve) and marginal social benefit (on the *MSB* curve) are equal.

Deadweight Loss from Overfishing

Deadweight loss measures the cost of overfishing. The gray triangle in Figure 11.7 illustrates this loss. It is the marginal social cost minus the marginal social benefit from all the fish caught in excess of the efficient quantity.

■ **FIGURE 11.7**

Why Overfishing Occurs   MyEconLab Animation

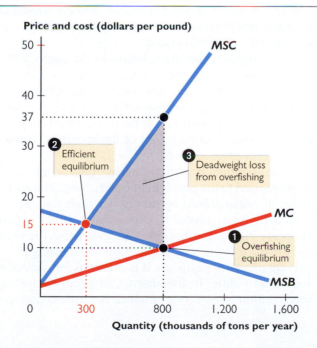

The market supply curve is the marginal private cost curve, *MC*, and the market demand curve is the marginal social benefit curve, *MSB*.

❶ The market equilibrium occurs at a quantity of 800,000 tons and a price of $10 a pound—an overfishing equilibrium.

❷ The marginal social cost curve is *MSC* and the efficient equilibrium is at a quantity of 300,000 tons a year.

❸ The market equilibrium quantity exceeds the efficient quantity and overfishing brings a deadweight loss.

MyEconLab Concept Video

■ Using the Commons Efficiently

It is easier to define the conditions under which a common resource is used efficiently than to deliver those conditions. To use a common resource efficiently, it is necessary to design an incentive mechanism that confronts the users of the resource with the marginal social consequences of their actions. The same principles apply to common resources as those that you met in Chapter 10 when you studied the external cost of pollution.

The three main methods that might be used to achieve the efficient use of a common resource are

- Property rights
- Production quotas
- Individual transferable quotas (ITQs)

Property Rights

A common resource that no one owns and that anyone is free to use contrasts with *private property*, which is a resource that someone owns and has an incentive to use in the way that maximizes its value. The resource is used efficiently. One way of overcoming the tragedy of the commons is to convert a common resource to private property. With private property rights, the owner of the resource faces the same conditions as society faces. It doesn't matter who owns the resource. The users of the resource that someone owns are confronted with the opportunity cost of using it. If the user is the owner, the opportunity cost of using it is forgone rental income. If the resource is used by someone who leases it from its owner, the opportunity cost of using it is the rent paid to the owner.

Figure 11.8 illustrates the efficient outcome when private property rights over a resource are established and enforced. The marginal private cost curve, *MC*, and the market supply curve, *S*, are the same as the marginal social cost curve, *MSC*: the curve labeled *S = MC = MSC*. The demand curve is the marginal social benefit curve, *MSB*. The market price and equilibrium quantity are determined by supply and demand at $15 per pound and an annual catch of 300,000 tons. At this quantity marginal social benefit equals marginal social cost, so the quantity produced is the efficient quantity.

The private property solution to the tragedy of the commons is available in some cases. It was the solution to the original tragedy of the commons in England's Middle Ages. It is also a solution that has been used to prevent overuse of the airwaves that carry smartphone services. The right to use this space (called the frequency spectrum) has been auctioned by governments to the highest bidders. The owner of each part of the spectrum is the only one permitted to use it (or to license someone else to use it).

But assigning private property rights is not always feasible and it isn't a practical solution to the problem of overfishing. The cost of policing millions of square miles of ocean would be far greater than the benefit arising from it. Also, there would be international disputes about which country had the right to enforce property rights. Further, in some cases and the ocean fish stock is one of them, people have an emotional objection to assigning private property rights. Critics of private property rights say it is immoral for someone to own a resource that they regard as public. In the absence of property rights, some form of government intervention is used, one of which is a production quota.

Wireless communications companies bid in government auctions to be the owners of the frequency spectrum.

FIGURE 11.8

Property Rights Achieve the Efficient Use of a Common Resource

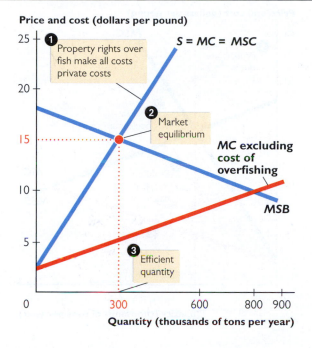

With property rights to the fish stock assigned, fishers pay the owner of the fish stock for permission to fish and face the marginal social cost of their decisions.

❶ The marginal cost curve, which is also the market supply curve, includes all the costs of fishing, so it is also the marginal social cost curve, $S = MC = MSC$.

❷ The market equilibrium occurs at the intersection of MSC and MSB and the resource use is efficient.

❸ The quantity caught, 300,000 tons, is the efficient quantity.

Production Quotas

A *production quota* is an upper limit to the quantity of a good that may be produced in a specified period. The quota is allocated to individual producers, so each producer has its own quota.

Figure 11.9 shows a production quota that achieves an efficient outcome. The quota limits the catch (production) to 300,000 tons, the efficient quantity at which marginal social benefit, *MSB*, equals marginal social cost, *MSC*. If everyone catches their own quota, the outcome is efficient. But implementing a production quota has two problems.

First, it is in every fisher's self-interest to catch more fish than the quantity permitted under the quota. The reason is that the market price exceeds marginal private cost, so by catching more fish, a fisher gets a higher income. If enough fishers break the quota, overfishing occurs and the tragedy of the commons remains.

Second, marginal cost is not, in general, the same for all producers—as we're assuming here. Some producers have a comparative advantage in using the resource. Efficiency requires that the quota be allocated to the producers with the lowest marginal cost. But the government department that allocates quotas does not have information about the marginal cost of individual producers. Even if the government tried to get this information, producers would have an incentive to lie about their costs so as to get a bigger quota.

A production quota can work, but only if the activities of every producer can be monitored and all producers have the same marginal cost. Where producers are difficult or very costly to monitor or where marginal cost varies across producers, a production quota cannot achieve an efficient outcome.

◼ **FIGURE 11.9**

A Production Quota to Use a Common Resource Efficiently

MyEconLab Animation

❶ A production quota is set at the efficient quantity and each fisher is assigned a share of the quota.

❷ The market equilibrium is efficient, but the price, $15 a pound, exceeds the fishers' marginal cost, $5 a pound.

❸ Fishers earn a profit on the marginal catch.

❹ With price exceeding marginal cost, fishers have an incentive to break the quota and overfish.

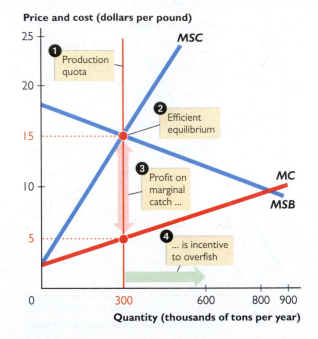

Individual Transferable Quotas

Individual transferable quota (ITQ)

A production limit assigned to an individual who is then free to transfer (sell) the quota to someone else.

Where producers are difficult to monitor or where marginal cost varies across producers, a more sophisticated quota system, called an individual transferable quota, can be effective. An **individual transferable quota (ITQ)** is a production limit assigned to an individual who is then free to transfer (sell) the quota to someone else. A market in ITQs emerges and ITQs are traded at their market price.

The market price of an ITQ is the highest price that someone is willing to pay for one. That price is marginal social benefit minus marginal cost. The price of an ITQ will rise to this level because fishers who don't have a quota would be willing to pay this amount to get one.

A fisher with an ITQ could sell it for the market price, so by not selling the ITQ the fisher incurs an opportunity cost. The marginal cost of fishing, which now includes the opportunity cost of the ITQ, equals the marginal social benefit from the efficient quantity.

Figure 11.10 illustrates how ITQs work. Each fisher receives an allocation of ITQs and the total catch permitted by the ITQs is 300,000 tons per year. Fishers trade ITQs: Those with low marginal cost buy ITQs from those with high marginal cost, and the market price of an ITQ settles at $10 per pound of fish. The marginal private cost of fishing now becomes the original marginal private cost, *MC*, plus the price of the ITQ. The marginal private cost curve shifts upward from *MC* to *MC* + *price of ITQ* and each fisher is confronted with the marginal social cost of fishing.

Now no one has an incentive to cheat and exceed the quota because to do so would send marginal cost above the market price and result in a loss on the marginal catch. The outcome is efficient.

EYE on the GLOBAL ECONOMY
ITQs Work

Economists agree that ITQs offer an effective tool for achieving an efficient use of the stock of ocean fish.

Iceland, the Netherlands, and Canada were the first countries to adopt ITQs in the late 1970s. New Zealand was the first country to adopt them as a national policy in 1986.

Today, 28 U.S. fisheries and 150 major fisheries and 100 smaller fisheries around the world, representing 10 percent of the world's marine life harvest, is managed by ITQs.

Marine biologists and economists agree that ITQs prevent fish stocks from collapsing and restore fisheries in critical decline.

Studies based on large data sets from more than 10,000 fisheries recorded for more than half a century have shown that without ITQs, there would be a major collapse of the global fish stock, but that with ITQs, a fish crisis has been averted.

One study found that ITQs even reverse a trend decline and turn it around to a trend recovery.

Fisheries that are managed with ITQs are half as likely to collapse as those that are not.

ITQs help maintain fish stocks, but they also reduce the size of the fishing industry. This consequence of adopting ITQs to restore fish

stocks pits the use of ITQs against the self-interest of fishers.

In all countries, the fishing industry opposes restrictions on its activities, but in the countries that pioneered ITQs, the opposition was not strong enough to block them.

In the United States the opposition to ITQs was so strong that the fishing industry persuaded Congress to outlaw them. In 1996, Congress passed the Sustainable Fishing Act that put a moratorium on ITQs that lasted until 2004. Since then, many U.S. fisheries have been managed by ITQs and have begun to see their benefits. ITQs are a success story.

FIGURE 11.10

An ITQ to Use a Common Resource Efficiently

MyEconLab Animation

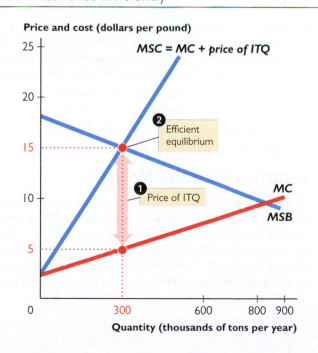

ITQs are issued such that the quantity of fish caught equals the efficient quantity.

❶ The market price of an ITQ equals the marginal external cost of fishing and confronts fishers with the marginal social cost of their decisions.

❷ The market equilibrium is efficient with 300,000 tons a year caught at the marginal social cost and market price of $15 a pound.

CHECKPOINT 11.3

Explain the tragedy of the commons and review its possible solutions.

Practice Problems

Cows graze on common pasture and can produce milk in the amounts shown in Table 1. The marginal private cost of producing milk is zero.

1. What is the quantity of milk produced if use of the common pasture is not regulated? Use a graph to illustrate your answer.

2. What is the efficient quantity of milk to produce? On a graph show the deadweight loss from overproduction.

3. If the common pasture were converted to private land and fenced off, what quantity of milk would be produced?

4. If ITQs were issued for the efficient quantity of milk production, what would be the market price of an ITQ?

TABLE 1

Quantity of milk (gallons per day)	Marginal external cost	Marginal social benefit
	(dollars per gallon)	
0	0	15
20	2	12
40	4	9
60	6	6
80	8	3
100	10	0

In the News

Can ecotourism help save endangered species?
Well-practiced ecotourism is helping to conserve the orangutan, humpback whale, African lion, snow leopard, and many other species and drawing dollars to the cause.

Source: www.thetravelworld.com, May 22, 2012

Explain how ecotourism changes incentives and might avoid the tragedy of the commons for many species, including those mentioned in the news clip.

Solutions to Practice Problems

1. The quantity of milk produced is 100 gallons a day—the quantity at which the marginal private cost equals the marginal social benefit. See Figure 1.

2. The efficient quantity of milk is 60 gallons a day—the quantity at which the marginal social cost equals the marginal social benefit. Marginal social cost equals marginal private cost plus marginal external cost. The gray area in Figure 2 shows the deadweight loss from overproduction.

3. If the common pasture were converted to private land and fenced off, the quantity of milk produced would be the efficient quantity—60 gallons a day.

4. The market price of an ITQ would be $6 a gallon, which equals the marginal external cost at the efficient quantity of milk.

Solution to In the News

There is a tradeoff between hunting and killing animals for their meat, skin, tusks, or other parts and maintaining a healthy population of animals to be viewed by curious and interested tourists. With a thriving ecotourist industry, communities living close to populations of orangutans, humpback whales, African lions, and snow leopards have an incentive to protect the animals, earn an income from ecotourists, and not overuse their natural resources.

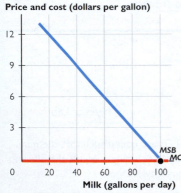

FIGURE 1

Price and cost (dollars per gallon)

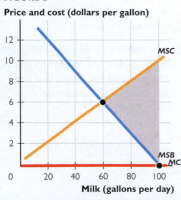

FIGURE 2

Price and cost (dollars per gallon)

CHAPTER SUMMARY

Key Points

1. Distinguish among private goods, public goods, and common resources.

- A private good is a good or service that is rival and excludable.
- A public good is a good or service that is nonrival and nonexcludable.
- A common resource is a resource that is rival but nonexcludable.

2. Explain the free-rider problem and how public provision might help to overcome it and deliver an efficient quantity of public goods.

- A public good creates a free-rider problem—no one has a private incentive to pay her or his share of the cost of providing a public good.
- The efficient level of provision of a public good is that at which marginal social benefit equals marginal social cost.
- Competition between political parties, each of which tries to appeal to the maximum number of voters, can lead to the efficient scale of provision of a public good and to both parties proposing the same policies.
- Obstacles to efficient political outcomes are the difficulty of estimating social benefit, bureaucrats' goals, and rational ignorance.
- When bureaucrats try to maximize their budgets, and if voters are rationally ignorant, public goods might be overprovided.

3. Explain the tragedy of the commons and review its possible solutions.

- Common resources create the tragedy of the commons—no one has a private incentive to conserve the resource and use it at an efficient rate.
- A common resource is used to the point at which the marginal private cost equals the marginal social benefit.
- The efficient use of a common resource is the point at which marginal social benefit equals marginal social cost.
- A common resource might be used efficiently by creating a private property right, setting a quota, or issuing individual transferable quotas.

Key Terms

MyEconLab **Key Terms Quiz**

Benefit-cost analysis, 276

Common resource, 269

Excludable, 268

Free rider, 271

Individual transferable quota (ITQ), 286

Nonexcludable, 268

Nonrival, 268

Private good, 268

Public good, 269

Rational ignorance, 277

Rival, 268

Tragedy of the commons, 280

CHAPTER CHECKPOINT

Study Plan Problems and Applications

Use the following list of items to work Problems **1** and **2**.

- New Year's Eve celebrations in Times Square, New York
- A city's sewer system
- New York subway system
- A skateboard
- Cable TV
- Niagara Falls

TABLE 1

Units of public good	Total benefit		
	Wendy	Sara	Tom
0	0	0	0
1	20	10	30
2	40	15	50
3	60	20	60
4	80	25	65
5	100	30	67

1. Classify each of the items in the list as a private good, a public good, a common resource, or a natural monopoly good. Explain each classification.

2. For each public good in the list, is there a free-rider problem? If not, how is the free-rider problem avoided?

3. Table 1 sets out total benefit from a public good for Wendy, Sara, and Tom, who are the only people in the society. If the government provided 3 units of the public good, calculate the marginal social benefit.

Use Figure 1 to work Problems **4** and **5**. It shows the marginal social benefit and marginal social cost of a waste disposal system in a city of 1 million people.

4. What is the efficient capacity of the system and how much would each person have to pay in taxes if the city installed the efficient capacity?

5. If voters are well informed about the costs and benefits of the waste disposal system, what capacity will voters choose? If voters are rationally ignorant, will bureaucrats install the efficient capacity? Explain your answer.

FIGURE 1

Marginal benefit and marginal cost (dollars per million gallons)

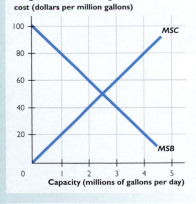

Use Figure 2, which shows the market for North Atlantic tuna, to work Problems **6** to **8**.

6. a. What is the quantity of tuna that fishers catch and the price of tuna? Is there overfishing? Explain why or why not.
   b. If the stock of tuna is used efficiently, what would be the price of fish?

7. a. With a quota of 40 tons a month for the tuna fishing industry, what is the equilibrium price of tuna and the quantity of tuna that fishers catch?
   b. Is the equilibrium an overfishing equilibrium?

8. If the government issues ITQs to individual fishers that limit the total catch to the efficient quantity, what is the market price of an ITQ?

9. **U.S. issues Arctic drilling permit to Royal Dutch Shell**
The U.S. government has given Royal Dutch Shell permission to drill for oil and natural gas in the Arctic Ocean. Environmentalists say it is the wrong decision.

Source: *The Wall Street Journal*, August 17, 2015

Are the oil and gas reserves public goods, private goods, or common resources? When an oil company receives a permit to develop a particular oil reserve, is that oil reserve a public good or a private good? Will the oil company produce an inefficient quantity or the efficient quantity? Explain.

FIGURE 2

Price and cost (dollars per ton)

10. Read *Eye on the U.S. Infrastructure* on p. 278 and then explain why it would be efficient to repair more bridges every year and why we don't do so.

Instructor Assignable Problems and Applications

1. a. What type of good is a highway bridge?

b. Why might a bridge be provided by government rather than privately?

c. Why might it be efficient to charge drivers a toll every time they use a bridge?

d. What information would be needed to determine the efficient number of bridges to repair each year?

Use Table 1, which provides data about a dandelion control program, to work Problems **2** and **3**.

2. What quantity of spraying would a private control program provide? What is the efficient quantity of spraying?

3. Two political parties, the Conservers and the Eradicators, fight an election in which the only issue is the quantity of spraying to undertake. The Conservers want no spraying and the Eradicators want to spray 2.5 square miles a day. The voters are well-informed about the benefits and costs of the program. What is the outcome of the election?

4. If hikers and others were required to pay a fee to use the Appalachian Trail, would the use of this common resource be more efficient? Would it be even more efficient if the most popular spots such as Annapolis Rock had more highly priced access? Why do you think we don't see more market solutions to the tragedy of the commons?

Use the following information to answer Problems **5** to **7**.

A natural spring runs under land owned by ten people. Each person has the right to sink a well and can take water from the spring at a constant marginal cost of $5 a gallon. Table 2 sets out the marginal external cost and the marginal social benefit from the water.

5. Draw a graph to illustrate the market equilibrium. On your graph, show the efficient quantity of water taken.

6. If the government sets a production quota on the total amount of water such that the spring is used efficiently, what would that quota be?

7. If the government issues ITQs to land owners that limit the total amount of water taken to the efficient quantity, what is the market price of an ITQ?

8. Waukesha deserves a shot at Great Lakes water supply

The city of Waukesha, Wis., has applied to borrow water from Lake Michigan under the Great Lakes Compact, an agreement between the states and Canadian provinces that border the Great Lakes designed to meet long-term drinking water needs for communities like Waukesha.

Source: www.startribune.com, December 11, 2015

Is water in the Great Lakes a public good, a private good, or a common resource? What are the goals of the Compact? How might they be achieved?

9. The Great Pacific Tuna Cartel

Eight small Pacific islands with control of 5.5 million square miles of prime tuna fishing waters, have tripled the access fee for U.S. tuna fishers from $21 million to $63 million and increased monitoring of these waters.

Source: *The Wall Street Journal*, March 20, 2013

Explain how the Pacific islands' action influences the efficiency of the use of tuna resources and illustrate your answer with a graph of the tuna market.

TABLE 1

Quantity (square miles sprayed per day)	Marginal social cost	Marginal social benefit
	(dollars per day)	
0.5	0	600
1.0	100	500
1.5	200	400
2.0	300	300
2.5	400	200
3.0	500	100

TABLE 2

Quantity of water (gallons per day)	Marginal external cost	Marginal social benefit
	(dollars per gallon)	
10	1	10
20	2	9
30	3	8
40	4	7
50	5	6
60	6	5
70	7	4

Multiple Choice Quiz

1. A good is _____ if it is possible to prevent someone from enjoying its benefits and such a good might be a _____ good.

   A. rival; private
   B. excludable; public
   C. excludable; private
   D. nonexcludable; common resource

2. A free-rider problem arises if a good is _____.

   A. nonrival and nonexcludable
   B. nonrival and excludable
   C. rival and nonexcludable
   D. rival and excludable

3. The marginal social benefit from a public good is _____.

   A. the quantity demanded by all the people at a given price
   B. the amount that all the people are willing to pay for a given quantity
   C. the amount that all the people are willing to pay at a given quantity for one more unit
   D. the quantity demanded by all the people at a given marginal social cost

4. The efficient quantity of a public good is most likely to be delivered by _____.

   A. an election contest between two parties that want different quantities
   B. highly trained bureaucrats
   C. efficient private companies
   D. an individual transferable quota

5. A renewable common resource is used sustainably if _____.

   A. private benefits and public benefits are equal
   B. private benefits equal private costs
   C. the rate of renewal of the resource equals its rate of use
   D. the rate of use of the resource equals the social benefit from its use

6. Overfishing occurs if, at the quantity caught, _____.

   A. marginal social cost equals marginal private cost plus marginal external cost
   B. marginal social benefit equals the fishers' marginal private cost
   C. marginal social benefit equals marginal social cost
   D. marginal social benefit equals marginal private cost plus marginal external cost

7. All the following can achieve an efficient use of a common resource *except* _____.

   A. a production quota equal to the marginal external cost
   B. individual transferable quotas that total the efficient quantity
   C. assigning property rights to convert the common resource to private use
   D. individual transferable quotas that trade at marginal external cost

8. When ITQs are assigned, the market price of an ITQ equals the _____.

   A. marginal benefit consumers receive from the fish caught
   B. marginal private cost of fishing
   C. marginal external cost of fishing
   D. marginal social cost of fishing

How do you avoid buying a lemon?

Private Information and Healthcare Markets

12

When you have completed your study of this chapter, you will be able to

1 Describe the lemons problem and explain how the used-car market solves it.

2 Describe the asymmetric information problems in the insurance market and explain how they are solved.

3 Explain the information problems and other economic problems in healthcare markets.

MyEconLab Big Picture Video

MyEconLab Concept Video

12.1 THE LEMONS PROBLEM AND ITS SOLUTION

In all the markets that you've studied so far, buyers and sellers are well informed about the features and the value of the item being traded. Buyers know the benefits they get and sellers know the costs they incur. The buyers' marginal benefit determines demand, the sellers' marginal cost determines supply, and demand and supply together determine the equilibrium price and quantity. If none of the obstacles to efficiency described in Chapter 6 (see p. 158) are present, then the market allocates resources efficiently.

In some markets, either the buyer or the seller has some relevant information to a transaction—**private information**—that the other lacks. One example of these markets is the market for used cars. In this market, each seller has private information about the quality of the vehicle offered for sale. When you buy a used car, you hope it isn't a lemon, but until you have driven it for a month or two, you won't know for sure. But the person who sells you the car knows. When one side of a market has private information, we call the situation one of **asymmetric information**—a situation in which *either* the buyer *or* the seller has *private information*. How does a market with asymmetric information work? What determines the equilibrium price and quantity? Is the market efficient or inefficient?

These are the questions we'll now answer.

■ A Market for Used Cars with a Lemons Problem

When a person buys a used car, it might turn out to be a lemon. If the car *is* a lemon, it is worth less to the buyer than if it has no defects. Does the used-car market have different prices reflecting different qualities—a low price for a lemon and a higher price for a car without defects? It turns out that it does. But the market needs some help in overcoming what is called the **lemons problem**—the problem that when it is not possible to distinguish reliable products from lemons, there are too many lemons—perhaps only lemons—and too few reliable products—perhaps none.

To see how the used-car market overcomes the lemons problem, we'll first look at a market that *does* have a lemons problem.

To explain the lemons problem as clearly as possible, we'll assume that there are only two kinds of cars: defective cars—*lemons*—and cars without defects, which we'll call *good cars*. Whether a car is a lemon is private information that is available only to the current owner. The buyer can't tell whether the car for sale is a lemon until after buying it, driving it for a few weeks, and learning as much about it as its current owner knows.

Buyers' Decisions and Demand

Even though the buyers of used cars don't know whether they are buying a good car or a lemon, the law of demand applies. The lower the price of a car, the greater is the quantity of cars demanded. But what determines demand and the willingness to pay is a bit different. To see why, let's think about the choice that a car buyer called Greg is about to make.

Greg wants to buy a used car and he would like to avoid buying a lemon. He knows that for him, the value of a good car—his marginal benefit—is $20,000. But Greg has a low income, some spare time, and he knows how to fix a car, so he would be willing to buy a lemon if he could get it for an appropriately low price—a price equal to his marginal benefit from a lemon, which he says is $10,000.

Private information
Information relevant to a transaction that is possessed by some market participants but not all.

Asymmetric information
A situation in which either the buyer or the seller has private information.

Lemons problem
The problem that when it is not possible to distinguish reliable products from lemons, there are too many lemons and too few reliable products.

George Akerlof of the University of California, Berkeley, and 2001 Nobel Laureate, was the first person to pose the lemons problem and the challenge that it presents for markets to allocate resources efficiently.

Now think about Greg's dilemma. He has found a car priced at $15,990 (in the photo). He likes the look of the car, but is it a good one or a lemon? If the car is a good one, he gets a marginal benefit of, and would be willing to pay, $20,000. So buying the car for $15,990 gives him a consumer surplus of $4,110. But if the car is a lemon, his marginal benefit is only $10,000, so paying $15,990 for the car leaves him with a negative consumer surplus (a consumer deficit!) of $5,990.

Will Greg pay $15,990? The answer depends on the odds of avoiding a lemon and how Greg regards taking risks. Although he doesn't know the quality of the car, he knows what all his friends have told him about the cars they've bought from the same dealer. If all his friends bought good cars, he will be thinking that this car is most likely a good one too. In this case, he is willing to pay $20,000 and at $15,990, he would buy this car.

But if all Greg's friends bought lemons, he will be thinking that this car is most likely a lemon too. In this case, he is willing to pay only $10,000, so $15,990 is much more than he would be willing to pay.

Other buyers are making decisions like Greg's and figuring out what they are willing to pay for a car of unknown quality. Some buyers are willing to pay more than Greg and some less. At higher prices, there are fewer buyers and at lower prices more buyers. The demand curve for used cars slopes downward.

Figure 12.1 illustrates the demand for used cars. If previous buyers say that they've never seen a lemon, buyers expect no lemons and the demand curve for used cars is D_G. If previous buyers say that they've never seen a good car, buyers expect only lemons and the demand curve is D_L. If previous buyers say that some cars were good ones and some were lemons, buyers expect to see some of each type of car and the demand curve will lie between D_G and D_L.

Is this car a good one with a marginal benefit of $20,000 and a consumer surplus of $4,110? Or is it a lemon with a marginal benefit of $10,000 and a consumer "deficit" of $5,990? Will Greg buy it?

■ **FIGURE 12.1**

The Demand for a Used Car of Unknown Quality

MyEconLab Animation

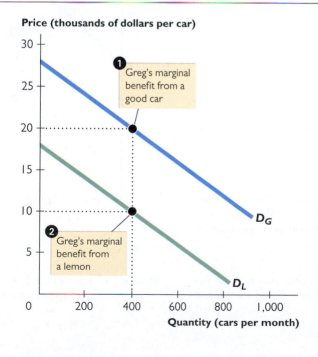

❶ If all Greg's friends bought good used cars, Greg might expect to buy a good one too and be willing to pay $20,000—his marginal benefit from a good car. The demand curve for good cars is D_G.

❷ If all Greg's friends bought lemons, Greg might expect to buy a lemon too and be willing to pay $10,000—his marginal benefit from a lemon. The demand curve for lemons is D_L.

The demand curve for used cars of unknown quality lies between D_L and D_G.

Sellers' Decisions and Supply

Now think about the sellers of used cars, who know the quality of their cars. There is nothing special about this supply: Sellers know their marginal cost, so they know the quantity they are willing to supply at a given price. The marginal cost of a lemon is less than that of a good car and over a range of low prices, only lemons are supplied. At higher prices, the quantity of lemons supplied falls off and good cars start to be supplied.

Figure 12.2 shows an example of what the supply curves might look like. In this example, lemons are offered for sale at prices up to $12,000 and at that price all the lemons available are supplied and good cars start to be offered for sale.

The Market Outcome

Demand and supply determine the price of a used car and the quantity traded, but the market doesn't work well. To explain, we'll focus on an extreme outcome in which only lemons get traded.

Suppose that buyers have learned from their friends that everyone who has bought a used car got a lemon. They assume that they, too, will get a lemon. Consequently, the demand for used cars is based on the willingness to pay for a lemon. The market demand is the demand for lemons, which delivers a low market price. At this low market price, good cars are worth more to their owners than

■ **FIGURE 12.2**

The Supply of Used Cars

MyEconLab Animation

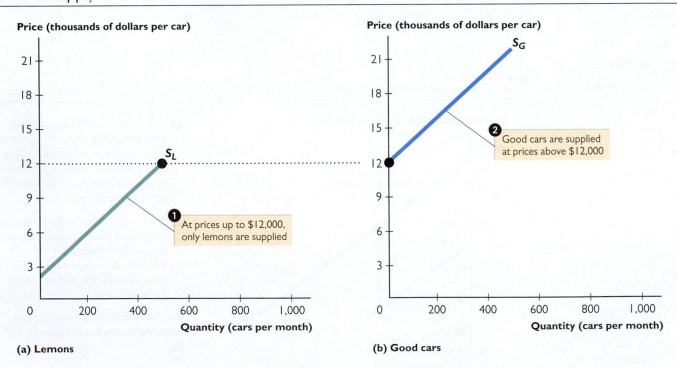

(a) Lemons

(b) Good cars

Suppliers of used cars know the quality of what they offer for sale.
❶ At prices below $12,000, only lemons are offered for sale and the supply curve of lemons is S_L.

❷ At prices above $12,000, good cars are offered for sale and the supply curve of good cars is S_G.

they would get from selling them, so no good cars are offered for sale: only lemons are available. So lemons are the only cars traded.

Figure 12.3 illustrates the used-car market that we've just described. The demand for used cars, D, is equal to the demand for lemons, D_L. The supply of used cars, S, is the supply of lemons up to $12,000 a car (the green segment of the supply curve) and the supply of lemons plus the supply of good cars at prices above $12,000 (the blue segment of the supply curve).

The equilibrium price is $10,000 per car and 400 lemons are traded each month.

Adverse Selection

This market suffers from adverse selection, a general problem that arises in markets with private information. **Adverse selection** is the tendency for people to enter into transactions that bring them benefits from their private information and impose costs on the uninformed party.

For example, Jackie hires salespeople and offers them a fixed wage contract. The only people Jackie attracts are lazy workers. Hardworking salespeople don't work for Jackie because they can earn more by working for someone who pays by results. Jackie's fixed-wage contract adversely selects those with private information—knowledge that they are lazy in this case—who use that knowledge to their own benefit and to impose costs on Jackie.

In the used-car market, the low price adversely selects lemons. The owners of lemons have a greater incentive to offer their cars for sale. In the extreme case (and in the above example), good cars disappear from the market. The owners of good cars have no incentive to offer them for sale. They hold on to their good cars because the market price is less than the owners' minimum supply price.

Adverse selection
The tendency for people to enter into transactions that bring them benefits from their private information and impose costs on the uninformed party.

■ FIGURE 12.3

The Lemons Problem in a Used-Car Market

MyEconLab Animation

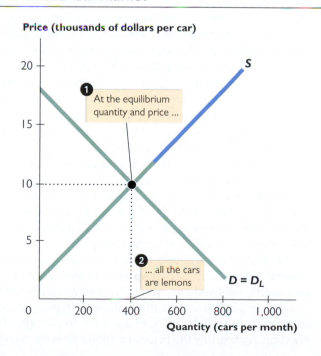

The demand for used cars is the demand for lemons, so the demand curve is labeled $D = D_L$. The supply curve of used cars is S. The green portion of the curve is the supply of lemons and the blue portion adds the supply of good cars.

❶ The equilibrium price of a used car is $10,000.

❷ 400 used cars a month are traded and they are all lemons. At the equilibrium price, no good cars are offered for sale.

EYE on the MARKET FOR USED CARS

How Do You Avoid Buying a Lemon?

The used-car market in the United States might have a lemons problem, but it definitely works: It is a very active and successful market.

In 2008 (the latest year for which data are available), 50,000 used-car dealers sold 37 million cars at an average price of $8,000 per car.

This scale of operation contrasts with the market for new cars in which around 40 domestic and foreign producers sold 13 million cars at an average price of $26,500 per car.

The stock of cars on U.S. roads is 250 million, so with 37 million being traded, more than one car in seven changes hands each year.

What makes this market work and helps it overcome the lemons problem? The answer is dealers' warranties and third-party inspection services.

By offering warranties, dealers *signal* that the cars they are selling are free from defects and, if a car should turn out to be a lemon, the dealer will bear the cost of fixing it.

MyEconLab Concept Video

Signaling
When an informed person takes an action that sends information to uninformed people.

■ A Used-Car Market with Dealers' Warranties

How can used-car dealers convince buyers that a car isn't a lemon and that it is worth more than a lemon? The answer is: By giving a guarantee in the form of a warranty, the dealer *signals* which cars are good ones and which cars are lemons.

Signaling occurs when an informed person takes actions that send information to uninformed people. The grades and degrees that a university awards students are signals. They inform potential (uninformed) employers about the abilities of the people they are considering hiring—see *Eye on Your Life* on p. 313.

In the market for used cars, dealers send signals by giving warranties on the used cars they offer for sale. The message in the signal is that the dealer agrees to pay the costs of repairing the car if it turns out to have a defect.

Buyers believe the signal because the cost of sending a false signal is high. A dealer who gives a warranty on a lemon ends up bearing a high cost of repairs—and gains a bad reputation. A dealer who gives a warranty only on good cars has few repair costs and a reputation that gets better and better. It pays dealers to send an accurate signal, and it is rational for buyers to believe the signal.

So a car with a warranty is a good car; a car without a warranty is a lemon. Buyers are now effectively as informed as sellers, so the demand for cars depends on whether the car is a good one or a lemon. Because the willingness to pay for a good car is greater than that for a lemon, the demand for good cars is greater than the demand for lemons. But there is still a demand for lemons from people with a low income and a skill at fixing faulty cars.

So there are now two markets for used cars: one for good cars and one for lemons and in each market there is a price. Warranties solve the lemons problem and enable the used-car market to function efficiently.

Figure 12.4 illustrates this outcome. In part (a), the demand for and supply of lemons determine the price of a lemon. In part (b), the demand for and supply of good cars determine the price of a good car. Both markets are efficient. The marginal

■ **FIGURE 12.4**

Warranties Make a Used-Car Market Efficient

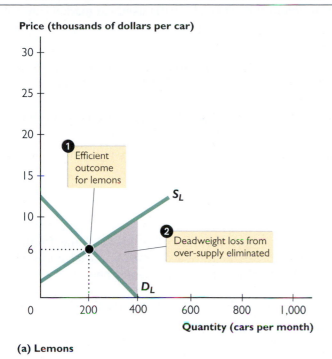

(a) Lemons

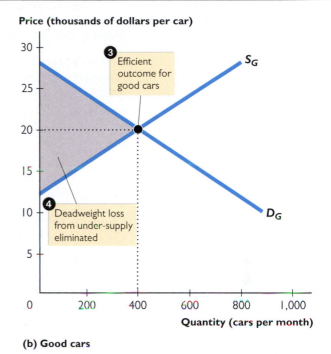

(b) Good cars

1 The demand for and supply of lemons determine the equilibrium price and quantity of lemons and **2** the deadweight loss from the oversupply of lemons (gray triangle) is eliminated.

3 The demand for and supply of good cars determine the equilibrium price and quantity of good cars and **4** the deadweight loss from the undersupply of good cars (gray triangle) is eliminated.

cost of each quality of car equals its marginal benefit and the deadweight loss that arises with asymmetric information is eliminated.

Pooling Equilibrium and Separating Equilibrium

You've seen two outcomes in the market for used cars. Without warranties, there is only one message visible to the buyer: All cars look the same. So there is one price regardless of whether the car is a good car or a lemon. It is as if all the cars, good ones and lemons, are in one big pool. We call the outcome in a market when only one message is available and an uninformed person cannot determine quality a **pooling equilibrium**. In the example above, only lemons were traded. But in such a market it is possible that a few good cars will be traded, though not enough to make buyers believe they will be lucky enough to get one.

In a used-car market with warranties, there are two messages. Good cars have warranties, and lemons don't. So there are two car prices for the two types of cars. The information created by warranties *separates* good cars and lemons. So the outcome in a market when signaling provides full information to a previously uninformed person is called a **separating equilibrium**.

Notice that no government action is needed to get the used-car market to work well. Dealers' warranties, voluntarily provided, do the job. Nonetheless, consumer protection laws in most states include "lemon laws" and a federal "lemon law" specifies statutory remedies for used-car buyers in the event that a dealer fails to honor its warranty.

Pooling equilibrium
The outcome when only one message is available and an uninformed person cannot determine quality.

Separating equilibrium
The outcome when signaling provides full information to a previously uninformed person.

MyEconLab Study Plan 12.1
Key Terms Quiz
Solutions Video

 # CHECKPOINT 12.1

Describe the lemons problem and explain how the used-car market solves it.

Practice Problems

An earthquake damaged car factories and decreased the production of popular Japanese cars. The demand for good late-model used cars soared and car dealers scrambled to get their hands on used vehicles.

1. Explain the effect of the eathquake on the price of a good used car and the price of a lemon.

2. If you have a late-model car that you know isn't a lemon, will you sell it privately or sell it to a dealer? Explain your answer.

In the News

Choosing the right college
Connie Pollack, a college admissions consultant, says that the challenge for the student is to find the college that pushes the right academic, financial, and social buttons to deliver four happy years without having to make a new choice after the first year.

Source: *Pittsburgh Post-Gazette*, February 12, 2016

Do the applicants or the colleges have private information? Give an example of such private information. Does this market have an adverse selection problem?

Solutions to Practice Problems

1. The increase in demand for good used cars shifts the demand curve rightward. With no change in supply, the price of a good car rises. At the higher price, the *quantity supplied* of good cars increases. The higher price for good cars gives dealers an incentive to fix problems with lemons and offer them for sale with a warranty as good cars, so the supply of lemons decreases (lemons and good cars are substitutes in production—see Chapter 4, pp. 95–96). The decrease in the supply of lemons raises their price.

2. If you sell your used car privately, you offer it without a warranty. Assuming the potential buyer doesn't know you, your car without a warranty would be perceived as a lemon. You would not be able to sell it for the price of the good car that it is. You would sell it to a dealer if he offered you more than the price of a lemon.

Solution to In the News

Colleges and students know the grades and test scores, so these are not private information. Students know how dedicated they are to studying, how they will finance four years at college, and what social activities they want to experience. The student's true "academic, financial, and social buttons" are private information. Colleges try to draw more applicants by looking like comfortable, friendly, safe, and relaxed places with engaged and helpful faculty and staff. The true quality of the college and its faculty is the college's private information. With both colleges and potential students having private information, adverse selection occurs in the market for college places and the best match isn't always achieved.

12.2 INFORMATION PROBLEMS IN INSURANCE MARKETS

MyEconLab Concept Video

Just as buyers and sellers gain from trading goods and services, so they can also gain by trading risk. But risk is a "bad," not a good. The good that is traded is *risk avoidance*. A buyer of risk avoidance can gain because the value of avoiding a risk is greater than the price that must be paid to others to get them to bear shares of the risk. And a seller of risk avoidance faces a lower cost of risk than the price that people are willing to pay to avoid it.

People trade risk in financial markets and insurance markets. Here, we'll focus on insurance markets.

■ Insurance Markets

You can see in *Eye on the U.S. Economy* below that insurance plays a huge role in our economic lives.

Insurance reduces the risk that each person faces by sharing or *pooling* the risks. When you buy insurance against the risk of an unwanted event, you pay an insurance company a *premium*. If the unwanted event occurs, the insurance company pays you the amount of the insured loss.

EYE on the U.S. ECONOMY
Insurance in the United States

We spend 11 percent of our income on insurance. That's more than we spend on cars or food. In addition, we buy Social Security and unemployment insurance through our taxes.

Auto insurance reduces the risk of financial loss in the event of an auto accident or theft. We spent $112 billion on this insurance in 2014 (see the figure).

Property and casualty insurance reduces the risk of financial loss in the event of an accident involving damage to property or persons. It includes workers' compensation and fire insurance. In 2014, we spent $390 billion on this insurance.

Life insurance reduces the risk of financial loss in the event of death. Almost 80 percent of households in the United States have life insurance,

and the amount paid in premiums in 2014 was $487 billion.

Health insurance reduces the risk of financial loss in the event of illness.

It can provide funds to cover both lost earnings and the cost of medical care. We spent $991 billion on this type of insurance in 2014.

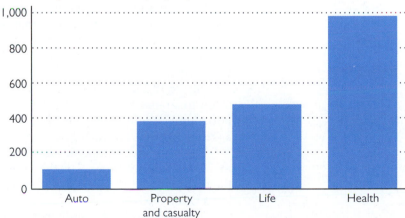

SOURCES OF DATA: Insurance Information Institute (www.iii.org) and Centers for Medicare and Medicaid Services (www.cms.gov).

Think about auto collision insurance. You know that there is a chance that you will be involved in an auto accident. The chance is small but always present. If you do have an accident and your car gets seriously damaged, you face the cost and inconvenience of getting it fixed. Worse, if you suffer serious personal injury, you also face a loss of income and the cost of medical care. For you, the cost of an auto accident is large and if you had to bear such cost, you'd like some help.

Because the chance that you will have a serious and costly auto accident is small, you can get that help by making a deal with an auto insurance company that is beneficial to both you and the insurer: You pay an annual premium to the insurance company and the company pays you a sum of money based on an agreed formula if you have an accident and incur a loss.

Insurance companies can get information from statistics on past accidents and costs that enable them to determine the premiums and payout conditions they can offer and still earn a profit. None of the company's policyholders knows whether they'll have an accident and the insurance company doesn't know *who* will have an accident, but it knows *how many* accidents there will be and what they will cost. An insurance company can *pool* the risks of a large population and enable everyone to share the costs.

People are risk averse—they don't like risk—so they are happy to buy insurance at prices that enable insurance companies to make a profit. By spreading the risk, insurance companies lower the risk for everyone.

But insurance companies do have a problem and it is a general problem that affects all types of insurance: Their customers have private information about their own behavior and its effects on the likelihood that they will make an insurance claim. There is asymmetric information in the insurance market.

◼ Asymmetric Information in Insurance

Although asymmetric information is present in all types of insurance, we'll stick with auto collision insurance. Some drivers are careful and some are aggressive. A careful driver is less likely to have an accident than an aggressive driver. Each driver knows which type he or she is, but the insurance company doesn't know. Yet it would benefit the insurance company to know, for it could then charge the higher-risk aggressive driver a higher premium and the lower-risk careful driver a lower premium.

Without knowledge about driver types, all insured drivers get the same deal. There is a *pooling equilibrium* like that in the used-car market without dealer warranties. Careful drivers and aggressive drivers pay the same premium, but the insurance companies incur losses on aggressive drivers and make profits on careful drivers.

Figure 12.5 illustrates this pooling equilibrium outcome. The demand for collision insurance by careful drivers is D_C and the demand by all drivers is D. The horizontal distance between the curves D_C and D is the quantity demanded by aggressive drivers at each price.

The insurance companies don't know the driver type to which they are selling, so the supply curve, S, is the same for all drivers. It is based on an average of the marginal cost of insuring an aggressive driver and the marginal cost of insuring a careful driver.

In this example, the equilibrium premium is $1,000 a year and 60 million careful drivers and 60 million aggressive drivers are insured.

You're now going to see that this outcome is inefficient for two reasons: it creates moral hazard and adverse selection.

FIGURE 12.5

Inefficient Pooling Equilibrium in an Auto Insurance Market

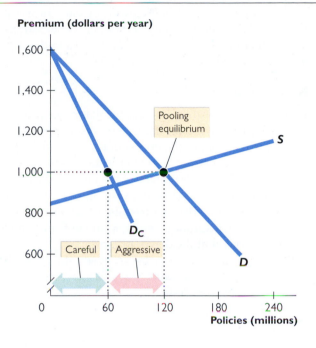

With no information on driver type, insurance companies offer all drivers the same deal. The insurance supply curve is S.

The demand curve D_C is the demand for auto insurance by careful drivers. The demand curve $D = D_C + D_A$ is the demand for auto insurance by all drivers. The horizontal distance between the two demand curves is the quantity demanded by aggressive drivers at each premium level.

A pooling equilibrium occurs at the intersection of S and D at a premium of $1,000 a year with 120 million insured drivers divided equally between careful and aggressive.

In this equilibrium, moral hazard and adverse selection make insurance companies look for ways of separating the two driver types.

Moral Hazard

Moral hazard is the tendency for a person with private information to use it in ways that impose costs on an uninformed party with whom they have made an agreement.

Moral hazard arises in many settings. For example, big banks face moral hazard. They know they are too big for governments to let them fail so they make loans that are too risky. Insurance companies face moral hazard because an insured person is less likely than an uninsured person to behave in ways that avoid the insured loss. For example, fire insurance lessens the incentive to install smoke detectors, fire alarms, and a sprinkler system.

In the case of auto insurance, a driver with full collision coverage has less incentive than a driver with little or no collision coverage to drive carefully. Once a person has bought insurance, her or his incentives change and the change adversely affects the interest of the insurance company.

Moral hazard
The tendency for a person with private information to use it in ways that impose costs on an uninformed party with whom they have made an agreement.

Adverse Selection

Adverse selection arises because people at greater risk are more likely to buy insurance than those for whom a risk is very small. For example, a person with a family history of serious illness is more likely to buy health insurance than a person with a family history of good health. Similarly, an aggressive driver is more likely than a careful driver to take the fullest possible coverage. So more of the insured risks arise from the activities of the riskiest people.

Insurance companies have an incentive to find ways around the moral hazard and adverse selection problems. By doing so, they can lower premiums for low-risk people and raise premiums for high-risk people.

MyEconLab Concept Video

Screening
When an uninformed person creates an incentive for an informed person to reveal relevant private information.

Insurance companies try to make a careless driver or an aggressive driver pay a higher premium…

… than a careful driver.

■ Screening in Insurance Markets

Screening occurs when an uninformed person creates an incentive for an informed person to reveal relevant private information. Insurance companies use the "no-claim" bonus and the deductible as *screens* to separate high-risk aggressive drivers and low-risk careful drivers and set premiums in line with the risk arising from the two types of drivers.

No-Claim Bonus

A *no-claim bonus* is a discount in the insurance premium for drivers who don't make claims. A driver accumulates a no-claim bonus by driving safely and avoiding accidents. The longer the period of no-claim, the greater is the no-claim bonus. And the greater the bonus, the greater is the incentive to drive carefully.

The no-claim bonus enables the informed driver to reveal her or his type to the uninformed insurance company and get insurance at a lower price, in line with the lower risk that the driver presents. A driver who makes claims also reveals her or his type to the insurance company and gets insurance at a higher price, in line with the higher risk that the driver presents.

The no-claim bonus helps to lessen the moral hazard problem. With a bonus at stake for making a claim, a driver has a stronger incentive to be careful and try harder to avoid accidents.

Deductible

Insurance companies also use a deductible. A *deductible* is the amount of a loss that the insured person agrees to bear personally. The larger the deductible, the lower is the premium, and the decrease in the premium is more than proportionate to the increase in the deductible. By offering insurance with full coverage—no deductible—on terms that are attractive only to aggressive high-risk drivers and by offering coverage with a deductible on more favorable terms that are attractive to careful low-risk drivers, insurance companies can do profitable business with everyone. Aggressive high-risk drivers choose policies with a low deductible and a high premium; careful low-risk drivers choose policies with a high deductible and a low premium.

The size of the deductible chosen reveals to the insurance company whether the driver is aggressive or careful.

■ Separating Equilibrium with Screening

With screening that indicates driver types, insurance companies can supply insurance on different terms to the different groups. With only two groups, aggressive and careful, it can offer premiums at two different levels: a higher premium for aggressive drivers and a lower premium for careful drivers. The higher premium is an incentive for aggressive drivers to behave as if they were careful, so the number of aggressive drivers decreases and the number of careful drivers increases. The outcome is a separating equilibrium.

Figure 12.6 illustrates this outcome and contrasts it with the pooling equilibrium that arises without screening.

Figure 12.6(a) shows the situation for careful drivers and 12.6(b) for aggressive drivers. We're assuming that the two groups are of equal size in the sense that they have identical demand curves, D_C and D_A (as before in Figure 12.5). But as you're about to see, the two groups don't end up of equal size when they have responded to the incentives they face.

■ **FIGURE 12.6**

Two Outcomes in Auto Insurance Compared

MyEconLab Animation

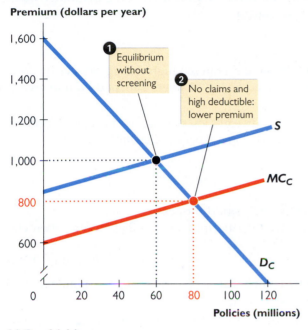

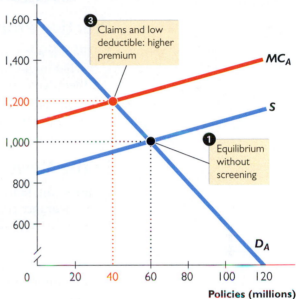

(a) Careful drivers

(b) Aggressive and careless drivers

Careful drivers in part (a) have demand curve D_C and aggressive and careless drivers in part (b) have demand curve D_A. With no screening, the supply curve of insurance is S in both parts.

❶ Without screening the equilibrium premium is $1,000 and 60 million drivers are careful and 60 million are aggressive and careless.

With screening, the supply of insurance to careful drivers is MC_C in part (a) and to aggressive and careless drivers is MC_A in part (b).

In part (a), ❷ equilibrium occurs at a premium of $800 and 80 million drivers reveal that they are careful.

In part (b), ❸ equilibrium occurs at a premium of $1,200 and 40 million drivers reveal that they are aggressive and careless.

In a separating equilibrium, 20 million drivers switch from being aggressive to being careful.

Without screening provided by a no-claim bonus and deductible, insurance companies offer the same supply of insurance to all drivers. The equilibrium without screening is the same as in Figure 12.5: Everyone pays $1,000 a year and there are 60 million of each type of driver.

With screening, the insurance companies base their supply to each group on the marginal cost (*MC*) of serving them. For careful drivers in part (a), the supply curve is MC_C. The equilibrium insurance premium is $800 a year and the number of drivers who are, or who behave as if they are, careful increases to 80 million. Without screening, the market *under*provides insurance to this group and is inefficient. With screening, the market is efficient.

For the aggressive drivers in part (b), the marginal cost of serving them is MC_A and this marginal cost determines the supply to this group. The equilibrium insurance premium is $1,200 a year and the number of drivers who remain aggressive decreases to 40 million. Without screening, the market *over*provides insurance to this group and is inefficient. Again, with screening, the market is efficient.

You've now seen two examples of markets with asymmetric information in which creative signaling and screening overcome what would be market failure and achieve an efficient outcome.

MyEconLab Study Plan 12.2
Key Terms Quiz
Solutions Video

CHECKPOINT 12.2

Describe the asymmetric information problems in the insurance market and explain how they are solved.

Practice Problems

1. Pam is a low-risk careful driver and Fran is a high-risk aggressive driver. What might an auto-insurance company do to get Pam and Fran to reveal their driver type?

2. Using Figure 12.6, show the deadweight losses that arise in an equilibrium without screening that are avoided in a separating equilibrium with screening.

In the News

Insurers aim to track drivers through smartphones

Auto-insurance companies are testing smartphone apps that monitor their customers' driving habits.

Source: Forbes, August 5, 2014

1. How could auto-insurance companies use information on driving habits? Is that information private and asymmetric?

2. How might smartphone monitoring of driving habits influence adverse selection and moral hazard?

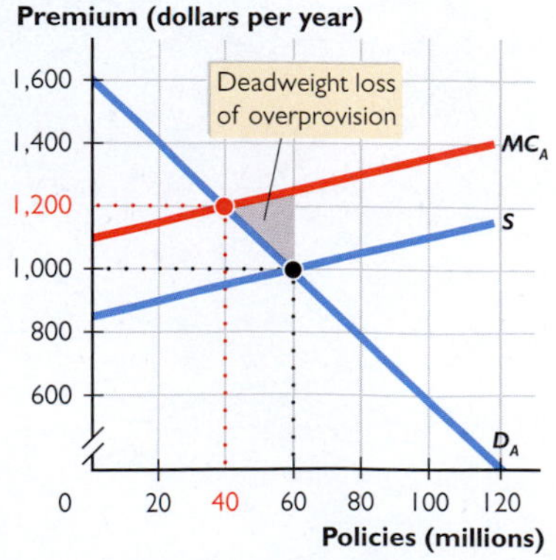

Solutions to Practice Problems

1. The insurance company will offer policies with deductibles that enable drivers to reveal their private information. Pam reveals that she is a low-risk driver by taking a high deductible and low premium. Fran reveals that she is a high-risk driver by taking a low deductible and high premium.

2. For low-risk careful drivers, by taking a high deductible and low premium, 80 million get insurance for $800 a year compared to 60 million paying $1,000 a year without screening. The gray triangle in Figure 1 shows the deadweight loss from underprovision without screening. This deadweight loss is avoided by screening.

    For high-risk aggressive drivers, by taking a low deductible and high premium, 40 million get insurance for $1,200 a year compared to 60 million paying $1,000 a year without screening. The gray triangle in Figure 2 shows the deadweight loss from overprovision without screening. This deadweight loss is avoided by screening.

Solutions to In the News

1. Auto-insurance companies can use information about driving habits obtained from smartphone apps to separate the market by known risk differences and this information makes driving habits neither private nor asymmetric.

2. Adverse selection: With information on driving habits available to auto-insurance companies, adverse selection is reduced. Moral hazard: Knowing that their driving is being monitored, driving carelessly is more costly, so some careless drivers become less careless.

FIGURE 1

Premium (dollars per year)

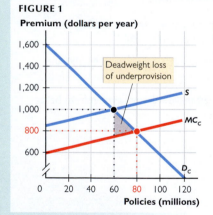

FIGURE 2

Premium (dollars per year)

12.3 THE ECONOMICS OF HEALTHCARE

MyEconLab Concept Video

Governments in the United States spend more on healthcare than on any other item, and by a big margin. The key reason is that if left to the market alone healthcare would be underprovided and unfairly distributed.

You are now going to see how governments influence the provision of healthcare, how healthcare markets in the United States compare with those in some other countries, and how it might be possible to improve on our current healthcare programs.

We begin by seeing why an unregulated market without government intervention would underprovide and unfairly distribute healthcare—why there would be a healthcare market failure.

■ Healthcare Market Failure

Healthcare consists of healthcare services (the services of physicians, specialists, nurses, other professionals, and hospitals) and health insurance. Both of these components of healthcare would be underprovided and unfairly distributed without some government action.

Four features of healthcare make it a special good:

- Asymmetric information
- Underestimation of benefit
- Underestimation of future needs
- Inequality in the ability to pay

Asymmetric Information

Asymmetric information is present in both the market for health insurance and the market for healthcare services. In the insurance market, the buyers—potential patients—have private information and in the care market the sellers—physicians and hospitals—have private information. These information asymmetries lead to adverse selection and moral hazard.

Adverse Selection and Moral Hazard in Health Insurance   Some people exercise, eat healthy diets, watch their weight, and rarely get sick. Others are couch potatoes who don't exercise, eat high-fat and high-sugar diets, are overweight, and not only get sick more often but also are at long-term risk for diabetes and heart disease.

Information about whether a person has a healthy or unhealthy lifestyle is private information not available to the insurance companies.

Adverse selection arises because some of the healthiest people choose to not buy insurance. Moral hazard arises because once insured, a person has less incentive to adopt a healthy lifestyle and some will yield to the temptation to drift into unhealthy habits.

Faced with a lack of information about individual lifestyle choices, providers of health insurance (like auto-insurance suppliers) offer lower premiums with high deductibles so that buyers can reveal information about their lifestyle. The fittest and healthiest choose a high deductible and low premium and the least fit and unhealthiest choose a low deductible and high premium. The market tries to find a separating equilibrium. But the other problems that we examine below make an efficient outcome unlikely.

Moral Hazard in Healthcare Services High-quality providers of healthcare services diagnose and prescribe treatments reliably and at the lowest possible cost. Low-quality providers make diagnosis errors and over-prescribe expensive drugs and other treatments. But the information about the quality and reliability of the healthcare provider is private. The buyers (patients and insurance companies) don't know the quality of the providers. In this regard, the market for healthcare services is like the market for used cars.

Moral hazard arises that increases the cost of healthcare services. Providers have an incentive to play it safe and overtreat a patient. Neither the patient nor the insurance company has information with which to prevent this inefficiency.

Health Maintenance Organizations partly address this moral hazard problem. By working with a limited number of service providers, an insurance company can monitor the quality of the service and control costs. But even with this arrangement, the service provider has more information than the insurer so the problem is lessened but not completely overcome.

Underestimation of Benefit

People don't have enough information to value the benefit of healthcare correctly. Most people lack the medical knowledge to determine their treatment needs. And many (especially healthy and young people) optimistically underestimate the health risks that they face. So they undervalue the insurance policies that can help them pay for healthcare; and they undervalue the healthcare resources that stand ready to help them when needed.

EYE on the U.S. ECONOMY
Healthcare in the United States: A Snapshot

Expenditure on healthcare takes 17.5 percent of U.S. incomes. Forty-one percent of this expenditure is private—spending on health insurance and out-of-pocket payments for healthcare services. The rest is financed by taxes—spending by federal and state governments on Medicare, Medicaid, and other public programs.

Figure 1 shows the distribution of the healthcare dollar across these types of expenditures.

Of the 318 million people in the United States in 2014, 190 million had private health insurance.

More than one half of all employed people—about 70 million—buy health insurance through their employer.

Tax breaks are available on health-insurance payments, the largest being for the self-employed who can deduct the entire payment.

About 75 million people limit their healthcare cost by using a Health Maintenance Organization (HMO).

The federal and state Medicare and Medicaid programs cover almost 119 million people.

An estimated 36 million have no health insurance, and a further 25 million are reckoned to be underinsured—have some insurance but not enough for a big emergency.

Some of the uninsured are healthy and *choose* not to insure. Others can't afford insurance and don't qualify for Medicare or Medicaid.

Per person covered, government programs are more costly than private insurance because they serve the aged, the disabled, and the chronically sick.

Figure 2 shows expenditure per person. With almost 119 million people covered by Medicare and Medicaid at a total cost of $1,115 billion, governments spend $9,389 per person per year on public programs.

The cost of private insurance per person covered is 56 percent of the cost of the government programs at $5,219 per person per year.

Out-of-pocket expenditure, which includes spending by the uninsured, is $1,037 per person per year.

Underestimation of Future Needs

People take too short a view of the benefits of healthcare. The young and healthy know that they will become old and less healthy and will likely become big consumers of healthcare. But the time horizon over which they plan doesn't stretch that far into the future. The end result is that many people perceive too small a marginal benefit from health insurance, and they are not willing to pay what it is actually worth to them.

Inequality in the Ability to Pay

For many people, the price of health insurance is beyond their ability to pay for it. Two groups of people are unable to afford adequate health insurance: those with a long-term health problem and the aged. But these people are the ones with the greatest need for healthcare.

Most people want to live in a society that treats these less healthy, older, and poorer people with compassion and ensure that they are provided with access to affordable healthcare. So there is an additional social benefit from healthcare for less healthy, older, and poorer people.

Because asymmetric information brings adverse selection and moral hazard, and because the marginal social benefit of healthcare exceeds the marginal benefit perceived by its consumers, a competitive market in healthcare would underprovide it. And the underprovision of the competitive market has two dimensions. It is inefficient, and it is unfair.

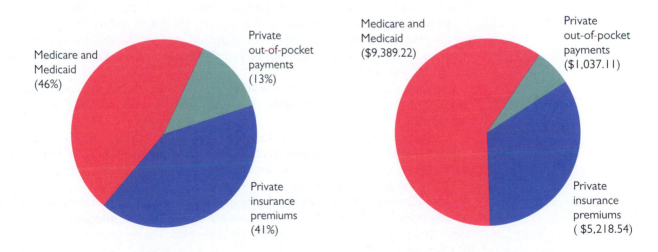

Figure 1 Private and Public Expenditures on Healthcare

Figure 2 Private and Public Expenditures per Person

Source of data: Centers for Medicare and Medicaid Services, Data Tables 1, 2, and 22.

Because the market would deliver an inefficient and unfair outcome, health-care is provided by the public choices of governments. But with alternative methods and scales of public provision available, governments must consider the effects of the alternatives in making their choices.

■ Alternative Public Choice Solutions

We're now going to examine the public choices that deliver healthcare services. You can see in *Eye on the Global Economy* on p. 311 that there is a wide range of levels of expenditure on healthcare. Public expenditures pay 83 percent of the healthcare bills in the United Kingdom, 70 percent in Canada, and 46 percent in the United States. But among these three countries, public expenditure per person is highest in the United States.

Different political priorities lead to this variety in healthcare expenditures. And the differences have implications for both the efficiency and the cost of healthcare.

We'll look at three approaches to supplementing or replacing the market: one used in Canada and the United Kingdom and two used in the United States. The three approaches are

- Universal coverage, single payer
- Private and government insurance
- Subsidized private insurance: Obamacare

Universal Coverage, Single Payer

In Canada and the United Kingdom, healthcare is provided by a system with two key features: universal coverage and a single payer.

Universal coverage means that everyone is covered by health insurance, with no exceptions and no excluded preconditions.

Single payer means that the government alone pays the healthcare bills. The government pays the doctors, nurses, and hospitals. In the United Kingdom, though not in Canada, the government also pays for prescription drugs.

In the United Kingdom, most of the doctors are employed by the government and most of the hospitals are government owned. In Canada, the doctors and hospitals are independent private agents, but they may not sell their services other than to the government.

Because the government is the sole buyer of healthcare services, it chooses the quantity of care to supply. A public choice, not a market equilibrium, determines the quantity of healthcare service.

Patients access healthcare services at a zero (or low) price, so the quantity demanded is that at which the marginal benefit is zero (or low). But the demand for healthcare has no direct effect on the quantity actually available, which is determined by the government's supply decision.

The quantity demanded exceeds the quantity supplied and in the absence of a market price to allocate the scarce resources, services are allocated on a first-come, first-served basis (see Chapter 6, pp. 141–142). The result is a long wait time for treatment.

Defenders of this system say that inefficiencies are small and worth accepting because the outcome is fair as everyone has equal access to services. But it isn't exactly true that everyone has equal access. Some people are better at playing the system than others and are able to jump the line.

EYE on the GLOBAL ECONOMY
Healthcare Expenditures and Health Outcomes

The best U.S. healthcare is the best in the world, but it is costly. And U.S. healthcare expenditure is projected to rise as the "baby boom" generation ages.

Figure 1 compares U.S. healthcare expenditure with that of seven other rich countries. The data are average dollars spent on healthcare per person in each country. (The data here are measured on a different basis to those on p. 308.) The figure shows that the United States spends twice as much per person as Canada, Germany, France, and Australia; 2.5 times that of the United Kingdom and Japan; and three times that of Italy.

Another feature of U.S. healthcare expenditure that you can see in Figure 1 is its very large public component (the blue bars in the figure).

Government expenditure per person on healthcare in the United States is higher than in any of the other countries in the figure. It exceeds that in Canada, where selling private health insurance is illegal, and in Germany and France, where there is a greater acceptance of high taxes and big government than in the United States.

A further feature of U.S. healthcare is that health outcomes, measured by life expectancy and quality of health, are as good or better in the other rich countries than those in the United States.

The World Health Organization has constructed an index of the efficiency of healthcare based on life expectancy, health quality, and the fairness of financing care. Figure 2 shows the efficiency index for the same countries

as those in Figure 1. Despite its high expenditure, the United States is at the bottom of this efficiency table.

Comparing the data in the two figures makes U.S. healthcare look the costliest and least efficient. But the comparison is not unbiased. It ignores the effects of international trade in healthcare services. Tens of thousands of Canadians as well as people from farther away come to the United States to get high-quality healthcare. Expenditure on these foreigners raises U.S expenditure in Figure 1 and the greater healthiness of these foreigners raises the efficiency indexes of other countries in Figure 2. It also gives a low weight to wait times for treatment, which are greater in other countries than in the United States. Also, these data are pre-Obamacare.

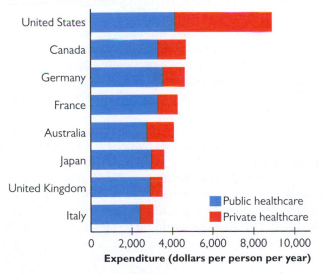

Figure 1 Healthcare Expenditure

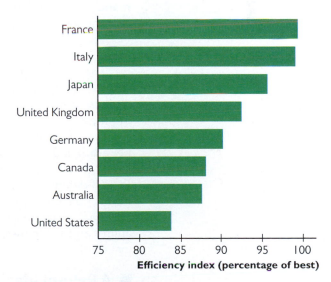

Figure 2 Healthcare Efficiency

Sources of data: World Development Indicators, World Bank, and the World Health Organization.

Private and Government Insurance

In the United States, most healthcare services are provided by private doctors and hospitals that receive their incomes from three sources: private health insurance, governments, and patients. Private health insurance pays 41 percent of the bills; government Medicare, Medicaid, and other programs pay 46 percent; and the remaining 13 percent comes from patients. Patients' out-of-pocket payments arise because some people are uninsured, and those who are insured face deductibles in their private insurance policies or co-payments for services provided under Medicare and Medicaid.

The scale of out-of-pocket costs combined with conditions set out in insurance plans and the demand for healthcare service determine the quantity of healthcare service provided. Measured by visits to a physician's office, that quantity is 1 billion patients per year. (The average number of physician visits is 3 per person per year.)

Inefficient Overproduction? We don't know whether private insurance together with Medicare and Medicaid provides the efficient quantity of healthcare. But the scale of expenditure on these programs relative to what is spent in other rich countries, suggests that they do overprovide.

Uncontrolled Expenditure Government healthcare expenditure is determined by the quantity of care demanded, not by a fixed budget. Without changes in the Medicare and Medicaid programs, this expenditure will grow as the aged population grows.

Obamacare

The *Patient Protection and Affordable Care Act, 2010* (Obamacare) has created a Health Insurance Marketplace to provide subsidized insurance.

On the supply side of the new marketplace are private insurers. On the demand side are the uninsured and those who want to find a better plan than their current one.

To qualify for subsidies, plans offered through the marketplace must cover pre-existing conditions, preventive services, and 10 essential health benefits.

The premium paid for one of these plans depends on family size and income. An example: A couple both aged 31 with two children and earning close to the median family income of $55,000 receive a subsidy (as a tax credit) of $3,636 leaving them to pay $3,984 for a $7,620 policy.

Families with no health insurance are required to pay an annual fee of $695 per adult and $347.50 per child or 2.5 percent of income, whichever is higher, with a maximum family fee of $2,085 a year.

To determine whether the outcome of the Obamacare subsidy achieves an efficient outcome, we would need to have an estimate of the extent to which the marginal social benefit of health insurance for the affected families exceeds their ability and willingness to pay for it. The subsidy might be too large, too small, or just right.

■ A Reform Idea?

The power of the market leads economists to seek a market solution to all resource allocation problems, and healthcare is no exception.

The Medicare and Medicaid programs are in effect an open-ended commitment of public funds to the healthcare of the aged and those too poor to buy private healthcare. Healthcare in the United States faces two problems: Too many people are uninsured and healthcare costs too much. These problems are going to get worse if nothing major is done to reverse a trend.

The Patient Protection and Affordable Care Act (Obamacare) addresses the first of these problems by requiring everyone to be insured and by creating a new Pre-Existing Condition Insurance Plan, financed partly by the government. But the Act does little to address the problem of overexpenditure, and this problem is extremely serious. It is so serious that without massive change, the present open-ended healthcare programs will bankrupt the United States.

A solution to both the problem of coverage and access and the problem of overexpenditure has been suggested by Laurence Kotlikoff, an economics professor at Boston University.

He proposes a universal private health insurance Basic Plan that creates incentives to improve health and deliver healthcare services efficiently. Each year, each American gets a voucher to buy health insurance from a company of their choice. The voucher's value equals the expected cost of covering the person, which is determined by health indicators. (Example: An 80-year-old diabetic might get a $70,000 voucher while a healthy 14-year-old girl might get a $3,000 voucher.) The total value of vouchers does not exceed 10 percent of total U.S. income. Public expenditure on healthcare grows as income grows, and an Independent Panel adds procedures and technologies covered by the Basic Plan but at a slower pace than in the current system.

Healthcare vouchers would work like the education vouchers that we explain in Chapter 10 (see p. 261). They would provide the cost discipline of the British and Canadian systems with the choice that is so important and valued by Americans.

Professor Laurence J. Kotlikoff of Boston University; author of The Healthcare Fix *and creator of* Medicare Part C for All.

EYE on YOUR LIFE

MyEconLab Critical Thinking Exercise

Signaling Your Ability

You've seen how used-car dealers signal with warranties. You, too, send signals.

You know how smart you are and how hard you're willing to work. But this information is private. It is known to you but not to your potential employers.

How can you signal your ability to potential employers? The answer is by your choice of education.

Michael Spence, an economist at Stanford University and joint winner of the 2001 Nobel Prize with George Akerlof and Joseph Stiglitz, explained how education choices send signals.

Think of people as having just two possible levels of ability: either high or low. Each person knows her or his own ability, but potential employers don't have this information.

People send signals to potential employers by their choice of education. For a person with low ability, the opportunity cost of a university education is high—not just the tuition and cost of books, but the cost in time and effort to get passing grades.

For a person with high ability, the opportunity cost of a college or university education is lower. For these

people, good grades take hard work but they can be attained with reasonable effort. So only people with high ability choose a college or university education.

Employers know each person's education (and grades), so they can offer a high wage for high ability and a low wage for low ability. There is a separating equilibrium in the market for workers of differing ability.

Even if your education contributed nothing to improve your ability, your eductaion choice would still signal your ability.

MyEconLab Study Plan 12.3
Solutions Video

 CHECKPOINT 12.3

Explain the information problems and other economic problems in healthcare markets.

Practice Problems

1. Describe the asymmetric information problem in the market for healthcare services and explain how the problem is dealt with.
2. What are the sources of inefficiency in the U.S. health-insurance market?

In the News

Are out-of-pocket medical costs too high?
Health-insurance premiums have increased and been accompanied by higher deductibles, which means that out-of-pocket costs have increased. Some say higher out-of-pocket costs lower prices and send buyers to efficient healthcare providers. Others say higher out-of-pocket costs puts quality healthcare out of reach for those with lower incomes.

Source: *The Wall Street Journal*, April 10, 2016

1. How do larger deductibles and larger out-of-pocket costs change the incentives that people face in the market for health insurance?
2. How do larger deductibles and larger out-of-pocket costs influence adverse selection and moral hazard in the market for health insurance?

Solutions to Practice Problems

1. In the market for healthcare services, the suppliers are physicians, specialists, other healthcare professionals, and hospitals. The demanders are patients and the insurance companies that pay most of the patients' bills. Asymmetric information arises because medical workers have private information about a patient's condition, the treatments available, and the cost-effectiveness of the treatment they prescribe. Healthcare providers face moral hazard. HMOs, with insurance companies selecting and monitoring service providers, lessen the moral hazard.
2. Two sources of inefficiency in the U.S. market for health insurance are pre-existing conditions and other serious health risks that are uninsurable and the underprovision that arises from 46 million Americans having no health insurance and millions more being underinsured.

Solutions to In the News

1. Larger deductibles and larger out-of-pocket costs strengthen the incentives for: (1) Healthy families to buy healthcare insurance; (2) People not to visit the doctor with minor health problems; (3) People with unhealthy lifestyles to try to reform.
2. Larger deductibles and larger out-of-pocket costs decrease adverse selection as healthier people choose to buy insurance with lower premiums; and decrease moral hazard as insured people, faced with higher deductibles, have a strengthened incentive to adopt a healthy lifestyle.

CHAPTER SUMMARY

Key Points

1. Describe the lemons problem and explain how the used-car market solves it.

- In some markets, one side of a market has private information—asymmetric information.
- In the market for used cars, the seller knows and the buyer doesn't know if a car is a lemon.
- Adverse selection results in a pooling equilibrium with too many lemons and too few good cars being traded.
- Dealers' warranties act as signals and enable the market to achieve a separating equilibrium that is efficient.

2. Describe the asymmetric information problems in the insurance market and explain how they are solved.

- In insurance markets, buyers are better informed than sellers about the risk being insured.
- Without screening, too few low-risk people would be insured.
- Moral hazard arises in insurance: An insured person has less incentive than an uninsured person to avoid the insured loss.
- The no-claim bonus and deductible reveal risk and enable insurance markets to reach an efficient separating equilibrium.

3. Explain the information problems and other economic problems in healthcare markets.

- Governments provide healthcare because asymmetric information, underestimation of its value, failure to look far enough into the future, and the inability of many to pay for it bring healthcare market failure.
- A free market would underprovide healthcare and distribute it unfairly.
- In some countries, governments provide healthcare at a zero or low price and ration with wait times.
- U.S. private insurance, Medicare, and Medicaid possibly overprovide for those covered.
- Obamacare provides subsidized insurance and compels everyone to make a minimum contribution for health coverage.
- Healthcare vouchers could cut cost, increase coverage, and retain choice.

Key Terms

MyEconLab Key Terms Quiz

Adverse selection, 297
Asymmetric information, 294
Lemons problem, 294

Moral hazard, 303
Pooling equilibrium, 299
Private information, 294

Screening, 304
Separating equilibrium, 299
Signaling, 298

MyEconLab Chapter 12 Study Plan

 CHAPTER CHECKPOINT

Study Plan Problems and Applications

1. Judy knows that her car is a lemon and offers it for sale. If the used-car market is working efficiently, will buyers know whether her car is a lemon? Why or why not?

2. Some car dealers offer used cars for sale with warranties and some offer them without warranties. Describe the equilibrium in the market for used cars. Is the market efficient?

3. **Stalling complaints about fixed GM cars**
In 2014, GM recalled 2.6 million vehicles to repair a safety defect in their ignition switches. Some of the recalled vehicles stalled and locked up, but a concerned GM said the problem with the recalled part did not appear to be the source of vehicles stalling.

Source: NBC News, January 17, 2016

Did GM sell some lemons? If GM did, what was the private information that it had that buyers did not know? If GM didn't sell lemons, explain why not.

Use the following information to work Problems **4** and **5**.

Mary is an 18-year-old student, who recently bought a used car. Mary is looking to buy car insurance. Insurance companies compete for her business.

4. Is there a moral hazard problem in a transaction between Mary and an insurance company? Explain why or why not.

5. Is there an adverse selection problem in a transaction between Mary and an insurance company? Explain why or why not.

6. If you have private information that you are a more aggressive driver than your driving record indicates, would you buy collision insurance? If the insurance company offers you a large deductible or a no-claim bonus are you likely to take the offer? Why or why not?

Use the following information to work Problems **7** to **9**.

President Obama campaigned on a healthcare reform plan that did not include mandatory health insurance. Hillary Clinton wanted mandatory health insurance with no opting out. In 2009, the President said he would support making health insurance mandatory with the cost covered by employers, but those who could not afford to pay and small businesses would be exempt.

7. If health insurance were optional, would healthy people be more likely or less likely to buy insurance?

8. What obstacles to efficiency does optional health insurance create?

9. U.S. healthcare per person costs twice that of other rich countries. Does the United States overprovide? Do other countries underprovide? What economic concepts do you need to answer? What data might be relevant?

10. If U.S. healthcare were delivered like basic education is, how would the healthcare system compare to that in Canada? Would it be efficient?

 11. Read *Eye on the Market For Used Cars* on p. 298 and then explain how a warranty signals that a car isn't a lemon and why it is in a used-car dealer's self-interest to offer a warranty.

Instructor Assignable Problems and Applications

MyEconLab Homework, Quiz, or Test if assigned by instructor

1. Describe the used-car market in the United States. How many used cars get traded per year and at what average price? How does the market enable buyers to avoid lemons? What role, if any, do governments play in the used-car market?

2. Zaneb is a high-school teacher and is well known in her community for her honesty, integrity, and sense of social responsibility. She is shopping for a used car. She plans to buy the car from a local car dealer and auto insurance from a major insurance company. What asymmetric information problems is Zaneb likely to encounter and what arrangements are likely to help cope with those problems? Explain your answers.

3. Suppose that there are two national football leagues: The Time League and The Bonus for Win League. The players have private information about their effort. In The Time League, players receive a fixed wage based on the time they spend practicing and playing matches. In The Bonus for Win League, the players are paid one wage for a loss, a higher wage for a tie, and the highest wage of all for a win. Describe the moral hazard and adverse selection problems in these two leagues. Which league best addresses these problems?

4. **Oilers, Jets top NHLers' no-trade lists**
   ESPN asked 10 player agents to name their top three most frequent no-trade teams. The top three, in order, were the Edmonton Oilers, the Winnipeg Jets, and the New York Islanders.

   Source: *Sportsnet*, March 25, 2016

   Provide an example of private information that a hockey player who wants a no-trade clause possesses. Does a hockey player with a long-term contract that includes a no-trade clause present a moral hazard to his team? Does a hockey player with a long-term contract that includes a no-trade clause present adverse selection problems to his team?

5. What are the key economic problems in providing an efficient quantity and distribution of healthcare insurance and service? Explain how the U.S. healthcare system addresses these problems.

6. What are the three alternative approaches for supplementing or replacing the market in healthcare services and how does each address the sources of healthcare market failure?

7. What are the problems that Medicare and Medicaid address and what problems do they cause?

8. What is the cost of healthcare in the United States compared to that in Canada and the United Kingdom? Do health outcomes correlate with healthcare costs? Can you think of explanations for the facts you've just provided?

9. What is Laurence Kotlikoff's proposal for fixing healthcare in the United States? Draw a graph to illustrate how his proposal would work and show whether it could be efficient.

MyEconLab Chapter 12 Study Plan

Multiple Choice Quiz

1. A market with asymmetric information is one in which _____.

A. sellers offer a product for sale at a low price and buyers are pleased to get a bargain
B. sellers know how reliable the product is and they share that information with buyers
C. only the buyers or the sellers have information about the quality of the product
D. buyers are willing to pay less for the product than the price at which sellers are offering it for sale

2. The lemons problem arises in markets in which _____.

A. sellers are better informed than buyers about which products are reliable
B. buyers are better informed than sellers about which products are reliable
C. there is a shortage of lemons
D. buyers have private information

3. In the market for used cars with no warranties, _____ lemons are bought and the equilibrium is a _____ equilibrium.

A. too few; separating
B. too many; separating
C. only; pooling
D. no; pooling

4. In a used-car market in which dealers offer cars with warranties, _____.

A. there is private information
B. a separating equilibrium does not occur
C. a lemons problem does not arise
D. the market is inefficient

5. Moral hazard arises in the insurance market because _____.

A. buyers of insurance have private information that they can use
B. insurance companies can offer a range of premiums to buyers
C. buyers can opt to take a deductible or a no-claim bonus
D. insurance companies can match premiums to customer risk

6. The private market delivers *too little* healthcare because _____.

A. insurance companies cannot avoid the problems of moral hazard and adverse selection
B. too many young healthy people buy insurance
C. insurance companies cannot monitor healthcare providers
D. insurance companies profits are too large

7. The healthcare system in the United States costs per person _____ what it costs in other rich countries and U.S. health outcomes rank _____.

A. double; lower
B. half; higher
C. double; higher
D. half; lower

How much would you
pay for a song?

Consumer Choice
and Demand

13

**When you have completed your study of this chapter,
you will be able to**

1 Calculate and graph a budget line that shows the limits to a person's
consumption possibilities.

2 Explain marginal utility theory and use it to derive a consumer's demand
curve.

3 Use marginal utility theory to explain the paradox of value: why water
is vital but cheap while diamonds are relatively useless but expensive.

MyEconLab Big Picture Video

13.1 CONSUMPTION POSSIBILITIES

How much you are willing to pay for a song depends on your income and on how much you want the song. We begin our study of consumption choices by looking at how income and prices limit what a person can afford. We describe the limit on buying plans by using a budget line. Let's look at the budget line of Tina—a student like you.

■ The Budget Line

Budget line
A line that describes the limits to consumption possibilities and that depends on a consumer's budget and the prices of goods and services.

A **budget line** describes the limits to consumption possibilities. Tina has already committed most of her income to renting an apartment, buying textbooks, paying her campus meal plan, and saving a few dollars each month. Having made these decisions, Tina has a remaining budget of $4 a day, which she spends on two goods: bottled water and chewing gum. The price of water is $1 a bottle, and the price of gum is 50¢ a pack. If Tina spends all of her available budget, she reaches the limits of her consumption of bottled water and gum.

Figure 13.1 illustrates Tina's budget line. Rows *A* through *E* in the table show five possible ways of spending $4 on these two goods. If Tina spends all of her $4 on gum, she can buy 8 packs a day. In this case, she has nothing available to spend on bottled water. Row *A* shows this possibility. At the other extreme, if Tina spends her entire $4 on bottled water, she can buy 4 bottles a day and no gum. Row *E* shows this possibility. Rows *B*, *C*, and *D* show three other possible combinations that Tina can afford.

■ **FIGURE 13.1**

Consumption Possibilities   MyEconLab Animation

Tina's budget line shows the boundary between what she can and cannot afford. The rows of the table list Tina's affordable combinations of bottled water and chewing gum when her budget is $4 a day, the price of water is $1 a bottle, and the price of chewing gum is 50¢ a pack. For example, row *A* tells us that Tina exhausts her $4 budget when she buys 8 packs of gum and no water.

The figure graphs Tina's budget line. Points *A* through *E* on the graph represent the rows of the table.

Possibility	Water (bottles per day)	Chewing gum (packs per day)
A	0	8
B	1	6
C	2	4
D	3	2
E	4	0

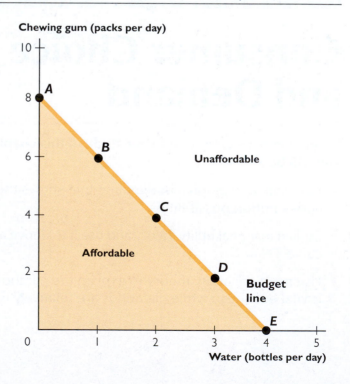

Points *A* through *E* in Figure 13.1 graph the possibilities in the table. The line passing through these points is Tina's budget line, which marks the boundary between what she can and cannot afford. She can afford any combination on the budget line and inside it (in the orange area). She cannot afford any combination outside the budget line (in the white area).

The budget line in Figure 13.1 is similar to the *production possibilities frontier,* or *PPF,* in Chapter 3 (pp. 60–61). Both curves show a limit to what is feasible. The *PPF* is a technological limit, so it changes only when technology changes. The budget line depends on the consumer's budget and on prices, so it changes when the budget or prices change.

■ A Change in the Budget

Figure 13.2 shows the effect of a change in Tina's budget on her consumption possibilities. When Tina's budget increases, her consumption possibilities expand, and her budget line shifts outward. When her budget decreases, her consumption possibilities shrink and her budget line shifts inward.

On the initial budget line (the same as in Figure 13.1), Tina's budget is $4. On a day when Tina loses her wallet with $2 in it, she has only $2 to spend. Her new budget line in Figure 13.2 shows how much she can consume with a budget of $2. She can buy any of the combinations on the $2 budget line.

On a day when Tina sells an old CD for $2, she has $6 available and her budget line shifts rightward. She can now buy any of the combinations on the $6 budget line.

■ **FIGURE 13.2**

Changes in a Consumer's Budget   MyEconLab Animation

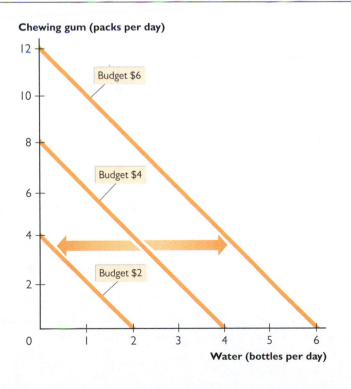

A decrease in the budget shifts the budget line leftward, and an increase in the budget shifts the budget line rightward.

Lower prices in a sale expand consumption possibilities.

■ Changes in Prices

If the price of one good rises when the prices of other goods and the budget remain the same, consumption possibilities shrink. If the price of one good falls when the prices of other goods and the budget remain the same, consumption possibilities expand. To see these changes in consumption possibilities, let's see what happens to Tina's budget line when the price of a bottle of water changes.

A Fall in the Price of Water

Figure 13.3 shows the effect on Tina's budget line of a fall in the price of a bottle of water from $1 to 50¢ when the price of gum and her budget remain unchanged. If Tina spends all of her budget on bottled water, she can now afford 8 bottles a day. Her consumption possibilities have expanded. Because the price of gum is unchanged, if she spends all her budget on gum, she can still afford only 8 packs of gum a day. Her budget line has rotated outward.

A Rise in the Price of Water

Figure 13.4 shows the effect on Tina's budget line of a rise in the price of a bottle of water from $1 to $2 when the price of gum and her budget remain unchanged. If Tina spends all of her budget on bottled water, she can now afford only 2 bottles a day. Tina's consumption possibilities have shrunk. Again, because the price of gum is unchanged, if Tina spends all her budget on gum, she can still afford only 8 packs of gum a day. Her budget line has rotated inward.

■ FIGURE 13.3

A Fall in the Price of Water   MyEconLab Animation

When the price of water falls from $1 a bottle to 50¢ a bottle, the budget line rotates outward and becomes less steep.

Possibility	Water (bottles per day)		Chewing gum (packs per day)
	$1 a bottle	50¢ a bottle	
A	0	0	8
B	1	2	6
C	2	4	4
D	3	6	2
E	4	8	0

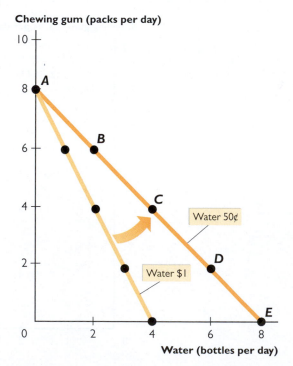

■ Prices and the Slope of the Budget Line

Notice that when the price of bottled water changes and the price of gum remains unchanged, the slope of the budget line changes. In Figure 13.3, when the price of bottled water falls, the budget line becomes less steep. In Figure 13.4, when the price of a bottle of water rises, the budget line becomes steeper.

Recall that "slope equals rise over run." The rise is an *increase* in the quantity of gum, and the run is a *decrease* in the quantity of bottled water. The slope of the budget line is negative, which means that there is a tradeoff between the two goods. Along the budget line, consuming more of one good implies consuming less of the other good. The slope of the budget line is an *opportunity cost*. It tells us what the consumer must give up to get one more unit of a good.

Let's calculate the slopes of the three budget lines in Figures 13.3 and 13.4:

- When the price of water is $1 a bottle, the slope of the budget line is 8 packs of gum divided by 4 bottles of water, which equals 2 packs of gum per bottle.
- When the price of water is 50¢ a bottle, the slope of the budget line is 8 packs of gum divided by 8 bottles of water, which equals 1 pack of gum per bottle.
- When the price of water is $2 a bottle, the slope of the budget line is 8 packs of gum divided by 2 bottles of water, which equals 4 packs of gum per bottle.

■ FIGURE 13.4

A Rise in the Price of Water

MyEconLab Animation

Possibility	Water (bottles per day) $2 a bottle	Water (bottles per day) $1 a bottle	Chewing gum (packs per day)
A	0	0	8
	1	1	6
B	1	2	4
		3	2
C	2	4	0

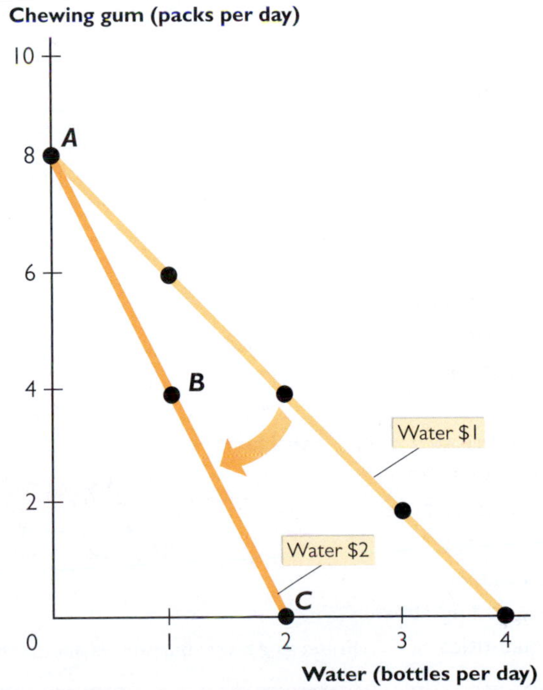

When the price of water rises from $1 a bottle to $2 a bottle, the budget line rotates inward and becomes steeper.

Think about what these slopes mean as opportunity costs. When the price of water is $1 a bottle and the price of gum is 50¢ a pack, it costs 2 packs of gum to buy a bottle of water. When the price of water is 50¢ a bottle and the price of gum is 50¢ a pack, it costs 1 pack of gum to buy a bottle of water. And when the price of water is $2 a bottle and the price of gum is 50¢ a pack, it costs 4 packs of gum to buy a bottle of water.

Another name for an opportunity cost is a relative price. A **relative price** is the price of one good in terms of another good. If the price of gum is 50¢ a pack and the price of water is $1 a bottle, the relative price of water is 2 packs of gum per bottle. It is calculated as the price of water divided by the price of gum ($1 a bottle ÷ 50¢ a pack = 2 packs per bottle).

When the price of the good plotted on the *x*-axis falls, other things remaining the same, the budget line becomes less steep, and the opportunity cost and relative price of the good on the *x*-axis fall.

Relative price
The price of one good in terms of another good—an opportunity cost. It equals the price of one good divided by the price of another good.

EYE on the U.S. ECONOMY
Relative Prices on the Move

Over a number of years, relative prices change a great deal and the figure shows some of these changes between 2005 and 2015 for 15 items that feature in most students' budgets.

These relative prices are measured as the price of the item in terms of a basket of other goods—as the price of the item divided by the average price of all goods and services.

Eggs, textbooks, and beef had the largest relative price increases. Air travel, chicken, apples, electricity, coffee, bread, gasoline, and oranges also had higher relative prices.

The largest relative price decrease is that of a computer, which has fallen by 92 percent. The relative prices of smartphone plans, tomatoes, and bananas have also fallen.

These changes in relative prices change consumption possibilities and change peoples' choices. Lower relative prices provide an incentive to buy greater quantities; higher relative prices provide an incentive to find substitutes and buy smaller quantities.

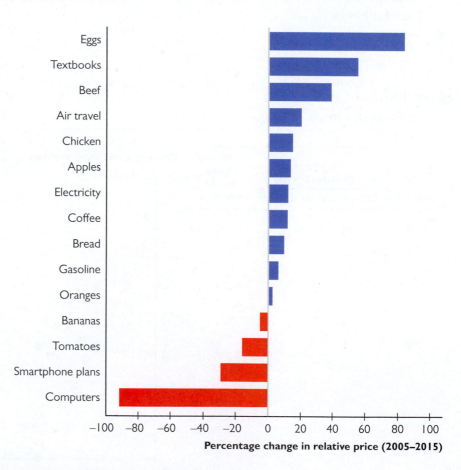

SOURCE OF DATA: Bureau of Labor Statistics.

CHECKPOINT 13.1

MyEconLab Study Plan 13.1
Key Terms Quiz
Solutions Video

Calculate and graph a budget line that shows the limits to a person's consumption possibilities.

Practice Problems

Jerry's burger and magazine budget is $12 a week. The price of a burger is $2, and the price of a magazine is $4.

1. List the combinations of burgers and magazines that Jerry can afford.

2. What is the relative price of a magazine? Explain your answer.

3. Draw a graph of Jerry's budget line with the quantity of magazines plotted on the x-axis. Describe how his budget line changes if, other things remaining the same, the following changes occur one at a time:
   • The price of a magazine falls.
   • Jerry's budget for burgers and magazines increases.

In the News

Gas price could fall below $2 a gallon
The price of gasoline keeps falling. It was close to $3.50 a gallon a year ago, is $2.59 a gallon now, and is expected to fall below $2 a gallon by year's end.
Source: CNBC, August 11, 2015

Donna buys only two goods: gasoline and pasta. Explain how the events in the news clip change Donna's consumption possibilities, the relative price of pasta, and her budget in terms of pasta.

Solutions to Practice Problems

1. Jerry can afford 3 magazines and no burgers; 2 magazines and 2 burgers; 1 magazine and 4 burgers; no magazines and 6 burgers.

2. The relative price of a magazine is the number of burgers that Jerry must forgo to get 1 magazine, which equals the price of a magazine divided by the price of a burger, or 2 burgers per magazine.

3. The budget line is a straight line from 6 burgers on the y-axis to 3 magazines on the x-axis (Figure 1). With a fall in the price of a magazine, Jerry can buy more magazines. His budget line rotates outward (Figure 2). With a bigger budget, Jerry can buy more of both goods. His budget line shifts outward (Figure 3).

Solution to In the News

When the price of gas falls, Donna's consumption possibilities expand—her budget line rotates outward. The relative price of pasta is its price divided by the price of gas. A fall in the price of gas raises the relative price of pasta. Donna's budget in terms of pasta is the maximum quantity of pasta that she can buy. This quantity does not change when the price of gas falls.

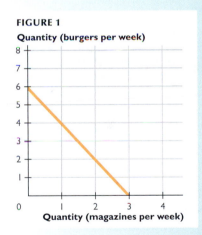

FIGURE 1
Quantity (burgers per week)

FIGURE 2
Quantity (burgers per week)

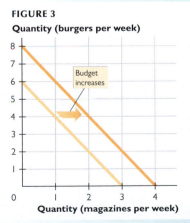

FIGURE 3
Quantity (burgers per week)

Utility
The benefit or satisfaction that a person gets from the consumption of a good or service.

Total utility
The total benefit that a person gets from the consumption of a good or service. Total utility generally increases as the quantity consumed of a good increases.

Marginal utility
The change in total utility that results from a one-unit increase in the quantity of a good consumed.

Diminishing marginal utility
The general tendency for marginal utility to decrease as the quantity of a good consumed increases.

13.2   MARGINAL UTILITY THEORY

The budget line tells us about consumption *possibilities*, but it doesn't tell us a person's consumption *choice*. Choices depend on *possibilities* and *preferences*. To describe preferences, economists use the concept of utility.* **Utility** is the benefit or satisfaction that a person gets from the consumption of a good or service. To understand how we use utility to explain people's choices, we distinguish between two concepts:

- Total utility
- Marginal utility

■ Total Utility

Total utility is the total benefit that a person gets from the consumption of a good or service. Total utility depends on the quantity of the good consumed *in a given period*—more consumption generally gives more total utility. Table 13.1 shows Tina's total utility from bottled water and chewing gum. If she consumes no bottled water and no gum, she gets no utility. If she consumes 1 bottle of water a day, she gets 15 units of utility. If she consumes 1 pack of gum a day, it provides her with 32 units of utility. As Tina increases the quantity of bottled water or the packs of gum she consumes, her total utility increases.

■ Marginal Utility

Marginal utility is the change in total utility that results from a one-unit increase in the quantity of a good consumed. Table 13.1 shows the calculation of Tina's marginal utility from bottled water and chewing gum. Let's find Tina's marginal utility from a 3rd bottle of water a day (highlighted in the table). Her total utility from 3 bottles is 36 units, and her total utility from 2 bottles is 27 units. So for Tina, the marginal utility from drinking a 3rd bottle of water each day is

Marginal utility from the 3rd bottle of water = 36 units − 27 units = 9 units.

In the table, marginal utility appears midway between the quantities because the *change* in consumption produces the *marginal* utility. The table displays the marginal utility from each quantity of water and gum consumed.

Notice that Tina's marginal utility decreases as her daily consumption of water and gum increases. For example, her marginal utility from bottled water decreases from 15 units from the first bottle per day to 12 units from the second and 9 units from the third. Similarly, her marginal utility from chewing gum decreases from 32 units from the first pack per day to 16 units from the second and 8 units from the third. This decrease in marginal utility as the quantity of a good consumed increases is called the principle of **diminishing marginal utility**.

To see why marginal utility diminishes, think about the following situations: In one, you've been studying all day and have had nothing to drink. Someone offers you a bottle of water. The marginal utility you get from that water is large. In the other, you've been drinking all day and you've drunk 7 bottles. Now someone offers you another bottle of water, and you say thanks very much and sip it slowly. You enjoy the 8th bottle of the day, but the marginal utility from it is tiny.

*Economists also use an alternative method of describing preferences called *indifference curves*, which are described in the optional appendix to this chapter.

EYE on the PAST

Jeremy Bentham, William Stanley Jevons, and the Birth of Utility

The concept of utility was revolutionary when Jeremy Bentham (1748–1832) proposed it in the early 1800s. He used the idea to advance his then radical support for free education, free medical care, and social security. It was another fifty years before William Stanley Jevons (1835–1882) developed the concept of *marginal* utility and used it to predict people's consumption choices. For the first time, economists could distinguish between cost and value and a basic theory of demand was born.

Jeremy Bentham

William Stanley Jevons

TABLE 13.1

Tina's Total Utility and Marginal Utility

Bottled water			Chewing gum		
Quantity (bottles per day)	Total utility	Marginal utility	Quantity (packs per day)	Total utility	Marginal utility
0	0		0	0	
		15			32
1	15		1	32	
		12			16
2	27		2	48	
		9			8
3	36		3	56	
		6			6
4	42		4	62	
		5			4
5	47		5	66	
		4			2
6	51		6	68	
		3			1
7	54		7	69	
		2			0
8	56		8	69	

The table shows Tina's total utility and marginal utility from bottled water and chewing gum.

Marginal utility is the change in total utility when the quantity consumed increases by one unit. When Tina's consumption of bottled water increases from 2 bottles a day to 3 bottles a day, her total utility from bottled water increases from 27 units to 36 units. So Tina's marginal utility from the 3rd bottle of water is 9 units.

Total utility increases and marginal utility diminishes as the quantity of a good consumed increases.

Similarly, suppose you've been out of gum for more than a day. A friend offers you a pack. Relief! You chew and receive a lot of utility. On another day, you've gone through 7 packs and chewed until your jaw aches. You're offered an 8th pack, and this time you say thanks, no thanks! The 8th pack of gum would bring you no marginal utility.

■ Graphing Tina's Utility Schedules

We illustrate a consumer's preferences with a total utility curve and a marginal utility curve like those in Figure 13.5. Part (a) shows that as Tina drinks more bottled water, her total utility from water increases. It also shows that total utility increases at a decreasing rate—diminishing marginal utility. Part (b) graphs Tina's marginal utility from water. The steps in part (a) are placed side by side in part (b). The curve that passes through the midpoints of the bars in part (b) is Tina's marginal utility curve.

The numbers in Table 13.1 and the graphs in Figure 13.5 describe Tina's preferences and, along with her budget line, enable us to predict the choices that she makes. That is our next task.

MyEconLab Concept Video

■ Maximizing Total Utility

The consumer's goal is to allocate the available budget in the way that maximizes total utility. The consumer achieves this goal by choosing the affordable combination of goods at which the *sum* of the utilities obtained from all goods consumed is as large as possible.

We can find a consumer's best budget allocation by using a two-step **utility-maximizing rule**:

1. Allocate the entire available budget.
2. Make the marginal utility per dollar equal for all goods.

Utility-maximizing rule
The rule that leads to the greatest total utility from all the goods and services consumed. The rule is
1. Allocate the entire available budget.
2. Make the marginal utility per dollar equal for all goods.

Allocate the Available Budget

If a consumer can buy more of one good without buying less of another good, then total utility can be increased. When utility is maximized, it isn't possible to buy more of one good without decreasing the quantity of another good. In this situation, the consumer has allocated the entire available budget.

With a budget of $4, the price of water at $1 per bottle, and the price of gum at 50¢ a pack, Tina allocates her budget to bottled water and gum at a point *on* her budget line in Figure 13.1 (p. 320). If she was at a point *inside* her budget line, she could buy more water or more gum without giving up any of the other good and she would not be maximizing utility.

Equalize the Marginal Utility Per Dollar

The second step to maximizing utility is to find the affordable combination that makes the marginal utility per dollar from both goods equal. The **marginal utility per dollar** from a good is the marginal utility from the good relative to the price paid for the good.

Marginal utility per dollar
The marginal utility from a good relative to the price paid for the good.

Calculating the Marginal Utility Per Dollar   The marginal utility per dollar from a good equals the marginal utility (MU) from the good divided by the price (P) paid for the good. For example, if Tina buys 2 packs of gum, her marginal utility from gum (MU_G) is 16 units. At a price (P_G) of 50¢ a pack, her marginal utility *per dollar* from gum (MU_G/P_G) is 16 units ÷ 50¢, which equals 32 units per dollar.

Tina's Utility-Maximizing Choice   If Tina spends $1 more on water and $1 less on gum, her total utility from water increases, her total utility from gum decreases, and her total utility from both water and gum might increase, decrease, or not

FIGURE 13.5

Total Utility and Marginal Utility   MyEconLab Animation

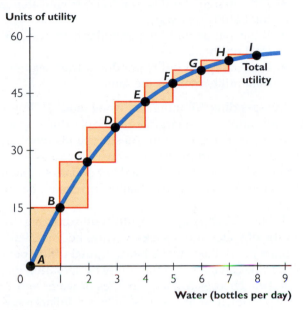

Units of utility

(a) Total utility

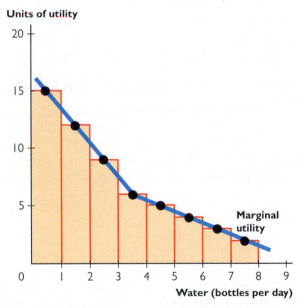

Units of utility

(b) Marginal utility

The table shows Tina's total utility from bottled water and calculates her marginal utility.

Part (a) graphs Tina's total utility from bottled water. It also shows the extra total utility she gains from each additional bottle of water—her marginal utility—as the steps along the total utility curve.

Part (b) shows how Tina's marginal utility from bottled water diminishes by placing the bars shown in part (a) side by side as a series of declining steps.

Water (bottles per day)	0	1	2	3	4	5	6	7	8
Total utility	0	15	27	36	42	47	51	54	56
Marginal utility		15	12	9	6	5	4	3	2
	A	*B*	*C*	*D*	*E*	*F*	*G*	*H*	*I*

change. What happens to her total utility from both goods depends on the marginal utility per dollar for each good.

- If the marginal utility per dollar from water *exceeds* that from gum, total utility increases.
- If the marginal utility per dollar from water *is less than* that from gum, total utility decreases.
- If the marginal utility per dollar from water *equals* that from gum, total utility remains the same.

By spending $1 more on water and $1 less on gum, Tina's total utility increases only if the marginal utility per dollar from water exceeds the marginal utility per dollar from gum. As she spends more on water and less on gum, the marginal utility from water decreases and the marginal utility from gum increases. When Tina has allocated her dollars so that the marginal utility per dollar is the same for both goods, total utility cannot be increased any further: Utility is maximized.

Table 13.2 shows Tina's utility-maximizing choice. If Tina chooses row *B* (1 bottle of water and 6 packs of gum) her marginal utility per dollar from water (15 units per dollar) *exceeds* her marginal utility per dollar from gum (4 units per dollar). She can increase total utility by spending more on water and less on gum.

If Tina chooses row *D* (3 bottles of water and 2 packs of gum) her marginal utility per dollar from water (9 units per dollar) *is less than* her marginal utility per dollar from gum (32 units per dollar). She can increase total utility by spending more on gum and less on water.

If Tina chooses row *C* (2 bottles of water and 4 packs of gum) her marginal utility per dollar from water (12 units per dollar) *equals* her marginal utility per dollar from gum. This combination maximizes Tina's total utility.

■ Finding an Individual Demand Curve

We can use marginal utility theory to find a person's demand schedule and demand curve. In fact, we've just found one entry in Tina's demand schedule and one point on her demand curve for bottled water: When the price of bottled water is $1 and other things remain the same (the price of gum is 50¢ and her budget is $4 a day), the quantity of water that Tina buys is 2 bottles a day (row *C* in Table 13.2).

Which one has the highest marginal utility per dollar?

■ TABLE 13.2

Tina's Marginal Utilities per Dollar: Water $1 a Bottle and Gum 50¢ a Pack

The rows of the table show Tina's marginal utility per dollar from water and gum for the affordable combinations when the price of water is $1 a bottle, the price of gum is 50¢ a pack, and her budget is $4.

By equalizing the marginal utilities per dollar from water and gum, Tina maximizes her total utility. Her utility-maximizing choice is to buy 2 bottles of water and 4 packs of gum.

	Bottled water			Chewing gum		
	Quantity (bottles per day)	Marginal utility	Marginal utility per dollar	Quantity (packs per day)	Marginal utility	Marginal utility per dollar
A	0			8	0	0
				7	1	2
B	1	15	15	6	2	4
				5	4	8
C	2	12	12	4	6	12
				3	8	16
D	3	9	9	2	16	32
				1	32	64

■ **TABLE 13.3**

Tina's Marginal Utilities per Dollar: Water 50¢ a Bottle and Gum 50¢ a Pack

	Bottled water			Chewing gum		
	Quantity (bottles per day)	Marginal utility	Marginal utility per dollar	Quantity (packs per day)	Marginal utility	Marginal utility per dollar
D	3	9	18	5	4	8
E	4	6	12	4	6	12
F	5	5	10	3	8	16

The rows of the table show Tina's marginal utility per dollar from water and gum for the affordable combinations when the price of water is 50¢ a bottle, the price of gum is 50¢ a pack, and her budget is $4. By equalizing the marginal utilities per dollar from water and gum, Tina maximizes her total utility. Her utility-maximizing choice is to buy 4 bottles of water and 4 packs of gum.

To find another point on Tina's demand curve for bottled water, let's see what Tina buys when the price of water falls to 50¢ a bottle. If Tina continued to buy 2 bottles of water and 4 packs of gum, her marginal utility per dollar from water would increase from 12 to 24 and be twice the marginal utility per dollar from gum (row *C* in Table 13.2). Also, Tina would spend only $3, so she would have another $1 available.

Row *E* of Table 13.3 shows Tina's new utility-maximizing choice, and this choice is a second point on her demand curve for bottled water: When the price of bottled water is 50¢ (other things remaining the same), Tina buys 4 bottles of water a day. Figure 13.6 shows Tina's demand curve that we've just derived.

■ **FIGURE 13.6**

Tina's Demand for Bottled Water   MyEconLab Animation

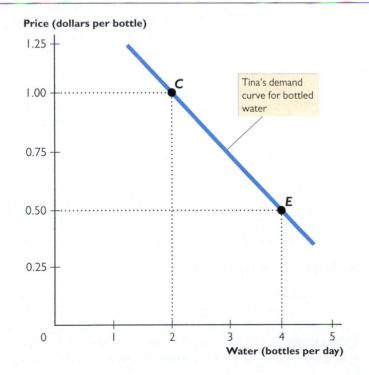

When the price of water is $1 a bottle (and Tina's budget is $4 and the price of a pack of gum is 50¢), she buys 2 bottles of water and 4 packs of gum a day. Tina is at point *C* on her demand curve for water.

When the price of water falls to 50¢ a bottle and other things remain the same, Tina buys 4 bottles of water and 4 packs of gum a day and moves to point *E* on her demand curve for bottled water.

MyEconLab Study Plan 13.2
Key Terms Quiz
Solutions Video

 CHECKPOINT 13.2

Explain marginal utility theory and use it to derive a consumer's demand curve.

Practice Problems

TABLE 1

Burgers		Magazines	
Quantity per week	Total utility	Quantity per week	Total utility
0	0	0	0
1	14	1	100
2	24	2	120
3	32	3	134
4	38	4	144

Table 1 shows Jerry's total utility from burgers and magazines. The price of a burger is $2, the price of a magazine is $4, and Jerry has $12 a week to spend.

1. Calculate Jerry's marginal utility and marginal utility per dollar from burgers when he buys 4 burgers a week. Calculate Jerry's marginal utility per dollar from magazines when he buys 1 magazine a week.

2. If Jerry buys 4 burgers and 1 magazine a week, does he maximize his total utility? To maximize total utility will he buy more or fewer burgers? Explain.

3. What quantities of burgers and magazines maximize Jerry's utility?

In the News

Bird flu spikes egg prices; some hit $3 a dozen

Egg prices have tripled at some supermarkets as buyers scramble for solutions.

Source: *USAToday*, June 9, 2015

How does the event described in the news clip change the budget line and the quantity of eggs that Americans buy?

Solutions to Practice Problems

1. The marginal utility from the 4th burger equals the total utility from 4 burgers minus the total utility from 3 burgers, which is 6 units. Jerry's marginal utility per dollar from burgers (MU_B/P_B) equals his marginal utility of 6 units divided by the price of a burger, $2, which equals 3 units per dollar. The marginal utility from the first magazine is 100 units. Jerry's marginal utility per dollar from magazines (MU_M/P_M) equals his marginal utility, 100 units, divided by the price of a magazine, $4, which is 25 units per dollar.

2. If Jerry buys 4 burgers for $8 and 1 magazine for $4, he spends his $12 budget. Marginal utility per dollar from burgers (MU_B/P_B) = 3 (Solution **1**) is *less* than his marginal utility per dollar from magazines (MU_M/P_M) = 25 (Solution **1**), so Jerry does *not* maximize total utility. To do so, he must buy fewer burgers and more magazines.

3. Jerry maximizes utility if he buys 2 burgers and 2 magazines a week. He spends $4 on burgers, $8 on magazines, his $12 budget. His marginal utility from burgers (24 − 14) is 10. Dividing 10 by $2 gives ($MU_B/P_B$) = 5 units per dollar. His marginal utility from magazines (120 − 100) is 20. Dividing 20 by $4 gives ($MU_M/P_M$) = 5 units per dollar. Jerry's marginal utility per dollar from each good is 5 units per dollar, so his utility is maximized.

Solution to In the News

The budget line rotates inward. Consumers allocate their budget between eggs (E) and other items (X) such that (MU_E/P_E) = (MU_X/P_X). As the price of eggs (P_E) rises, (MU_E/P_E) falls. So with (MU_E/P_E) < (MU_X/P_X), consumers will reallocate their income to make (MU_E/P_E) rise and equal (MU_X/P_X). To make (MU_E/P_E) rise, (MU_E) must rise, which will occur as the quantity of eggs bought decreases.

13.3 EFFICIENCY, PRICE, AND VALUE

MyEconLab Concept Video

Marginal utility theory helps us to deepen our understanding of the concept of efficiency and to see more clearly the distinction between *value* and *price*. Let's see how.

■ Consumer Efficiency

When Tina allocates her limited budget to maximize her total utility, she is using her resources efficiently. Any other allocation of her budget would leave her able to attain a higher level of total utility.

But when Tina has allocated her budget to maximize her total utility, she is *on* her demand curve for each good. A demand curve describes the quantity demanded at each price *when total utility is maximized*. When we studied efficiency in Chapter 6, we learned that a demand curve is also a willingness-to-pay curve. It tells us a consumer's *marginal benefit*—the benefit from consuming an additional unit of a good. You can now give the idea of marginal benefit a deeper meaning.

> **Marginal benefit is the maximum price a consumer is willing to pay for an extra unit of a good or service when total utility is maximized.**

■ The Paradox of Value

For centuries, philosophers were puzzled by the paradox of value. Water is more valuable than a diamond because water is essential to life itself. Yet water is much cheaper than a diamond. Why? Adam Smith tried to solve this paradox, but it was not until marginal utility theory had been developed that anyone could give a satisfactory answer.

You can solve this puzzle by distinguishing between *total* utility and *marginal* utility. Total utility tells us about relative value; marginal utility tells us about relative price. The total utility from water is enormous, but remember, the more we consume of something, the smaller is its marginal utility. We use so much water that its marginal utility—the benefit we get from one more glass of water—diminishes to a small value. Diamonds, on the other hand, have a small total utility relative to water, but because we buy few diamonds, they have a large marginal utility. When a household has maximized its total utility, it has allocated its budget so that the marginal utility per dollar is equal for all goods. Diamonds have a high price and a high marginal utility. Water has a low price and a low marginal utility. When the high marginal utility of diamonds is divided by the high price of a diamond, the result is a marginal utility per dollar that equals the low marginal utility of water divided by the low price of water. The marginal utility per dollar is the same for diamonds as for water.

Consumer Surplus

Consumer surplus measures value in excess of the amount paid. In Figure 13.7, the demand for and supply of water in part (a) determine the price of water P_W and the quantity of water consumed Q_W. The demand for and supply of diamonds in part (b) determine the price of a diamond P_D and the quantity of diamonds Q_D. Water is cheap but provides a large consumer surplus, while diamonds are expensive but provide a small consumer surplus.

■ FIGURE 13.7

The Paradox of Value

Part (a) shows the demand for water, *D*, and the supply of water, *S*. Demand and supply determine the price of water at P_W and the quantity at Q_W. The consumer surplus from water is the large green triangle.

Part (b) shows the demand for diamonds, *D*, and the supply of diamonds, *S*. Demand and supply determine the price of a diamond at P_D and the quantity at Q_D. The consumer surplus from diamonds is the small green triangle.

Water is valuable—has a large consumer surplus—but cheap. Diamonds are less valuable than water—have a smaller consumer surplus—but are expensive.

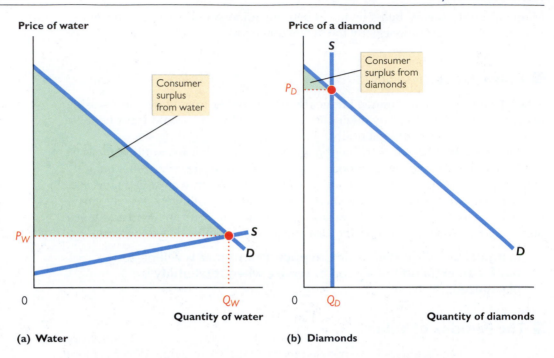

Consumer surplus from water

(a) Water

Consumer surplus from diamonds

(b) Diamonds

EYE on SONG DOWNLOADS AND STREAMING

How Much Would You Pay for a Song?

We can work out the willingness to pay for a song by finding the demand curve for songs and then finding the consumer surplus. To find the demand curve, we need to look at the expenditures, quantities, and prices in the market for songs.

In 2015, Americans spent $6.3 billion on all forms of recorded music, down from $14 billion in 2000. But the combined quantity bought *increased* from 1 billion in 2000 to 1.5 billion in 2015 and the average price of a unit of recorded music fell from $14 to $4.28.

The average price fell because the mix of formats changed dramatically. In 2000, we bought almost 1 billion CDs, but in 2015 we bought only 98 million. Instead of buying CDs, we downloaded 1.3 billion music files and paid for 16 million streaming subscriptions.

Figure 1 shows the longer history of the changing formats of recorded music.

The music that we buy is several different goods. We'll distinguish singles from albums and focus on the demand for singles.

In 2000, we bought 100 million singles at an average price of $5.00. In 2015, we downloaded 1,200 million singles at an average price of $1.20.

Figure 2 shows the demand curve in the market for singles. One point on the demand curve is the 2000 price and quantity—100 million at $5.00 per single. Another point on the demand curve is that for 2015—1,200 million singles downloaded at $1.20 each.

If the demand curve has not shifted and is linear (assumed here), we can calculate the change in consumer

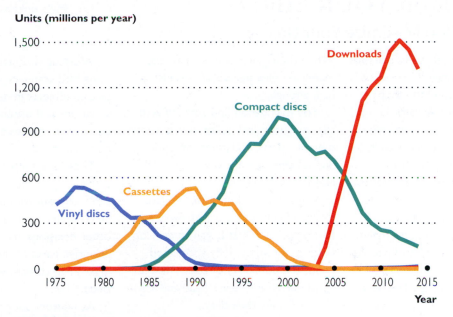

Figure 1 Changing Formats of Recorded Music

SOURCE OF DATA: Recording Industry Association of America.

surplus generated by the fall in the price and the increase in the quantity demanded. In Figure 2, the area shaded green shows this change in consumer surplus. That increase in consumer surplus is 2.47 billion, which is $2.06 per single.

The increase in consumer surplus of $2.06 per song is an estimate of how much more an average buyer would be willing to pay for an average song.

Paid subscriptions for streaming increase consumer surplus even more. A streaming subscription is a fixed cost per month, so the price of a song—an average price—is the monthly subscription divided by the number of different songs played. But the price of the marginal song is zero, and consumer surplus becomes the entire area under the demand curve at a zero price minus the fixed subscription cost.

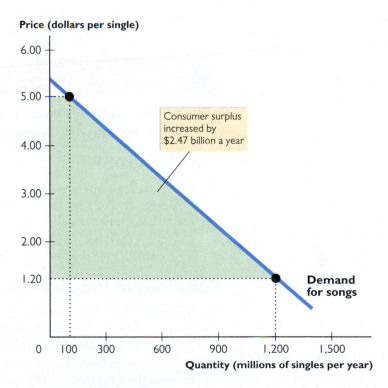

Figure 2 The Market for Singles

EYE on YOUR LIFE
Do You Maximize Your Utility?

MyEconLab Critical Thinking Exercise

You might be thinking that this marginal utility stuff is pretty unreal! You know that you don't go around the shops with a marginal utility calculator in hand. You just buy what you can afford and want, and that's all there is to it.

Well, marginal utility theory isn't about how people make their choices. It's about what choices people make. It's a tool that enables economists to explain the choices that people make.

You see lots of examples of people juggling their purchases to equalize marginal utilities per dollar. The next time you're in a checkout line, note the items that someone had second thoughts about and stuffed into the magazine rack alongside the tabloids.

When the crunch came to pay, the marginal utility per dollar was just not high enough.

You might even find yourself actually using marginal utility to make your own decisions. It clarifies the options, and it helps to make the value of the alternatives explicit.

When Jeremy Bentham, and later William Stanley Jevons (see *Eye on the Past* on p. 327), first began to develop ideas about utility, they speculated about the possibility of attaching a utility meter to a person's head and actually measuring the utility.

Today, a new branch of economics called *neuroeconomics* is moving toward achieving that nineteenth-century dream.

Working with neuroscientists and using MRI scanners, economists are placing subjects in decision-making situations and observing how the brain behaves as choices are made and outcomes learned.

These are early days, but results so far suggest that while some decisions are rational (and can be seen to be computed in the frontal cortex), other decisions are made using primitive parts of the brain that make snap choices without careful calculation.

As neuroeconomics advances, it will illuminate the way choices are made and might improve our ability to predict the choices that people make.

MyEconLab Study Plan 13.3
Solutions Video

 CHECKPOINT 13.3

Use marginal utility theory to explain the paradox of value: why water is vital but cheap while diamonds are relatively useless but expensive.

Practice Problems

1. In a year, Tony streams 50 movies at $3 each and pays $50 for 10,000 gallons of tap water. Tony is maximizing total utility. If Tony's marginal utility from water is 0.5 unit per gallon, what is his marginal utility from a movie?

2. Over the years, Americans have spent a smaller percentage of income on food and a larger percentage on cars. Explain the paradox of value.

Solutions to Practice Problems

1. Marginal utility from a movie ÷ $3 = Marginal utility from a gallon of tap water ÷ 0.5¢. So the marginal utility from a movie is 600 times the marginal utility from a gallon of water: 600 × 0.5 or 300 units.

2. The average person has one car and the marginal utility from driving the car exceeds the marginal utility from food. While food is cheap and cars are expensive, consumers allocate their income to make the marginal utility per dollar from food and cars equal. There is no paradox of value.

CHAPTER SUMMARY

Key Points

1. **Calculate and graph a budget line that shows the limits to a person's consumption possibilities.**

   - Consumption possibilities are constrained by the budget and prices. Some combinations of goods are affordable, and some are not affordable.
   - The budget line is the boundary between what a person can and cannot afford with a given budget and given prices.
   - The slope of the budget line determines the relative price of the good measured on the *x*-axis in terms of the good measured on the *y*-axis.
   - A change in one price changes the slope of the budget line. A change in the budget shifts the budget line but does not change its slope.

2. **Explain marginal utility theory and use it to derive a consumer's demand curve.**

   - Consumption possibilities and preferences determine consumption choices.
   - Total utility is maximized when the entire budget is spent and marginal utility per dollar is equal for all goods.
   - If the marginal utility per dollar from good *A* exceeds that from good *B*, total utility increases if the quantity purchased of good *A* increases and the quantity purchased of good *B* decreases.
   - Marginal utility theory implies the law of demand. That is, other things remaining the same, the higher the price of a good, the smaller is the quantity demanded of that good.

3. **Use marginal utility theory to explain the paradox of value: why water is vital but cheap while diamonds are relatively useless but expensive.**

   - When consumers maximize total utility, they use resources efficiently.
   - Marginal utility theory resolves the paradox of value.
   - When we talk loosely about value, we are thinking of *total* utility or consumer surplus, but price is related to *marginal* utility.
   - Water, which we consume in large amounts, has a high total utility and a large consumer surplus but a low price and low marginal utility.
   - Diamonds, which we consume in small amounts, have a low total utility and a small consumer surplus but a high price and a high marginal utility.

Key Terms

Budget line, 320
Diminishing marginal utility, 326
Marginal utility, 326

Marginal utility per dollar, 328
Relative price, 324
Total utility, 326

Utility, 326
Utility-maximizing rule, 328

CHAPTER CHECKPOINT

Study Plan Problems and Applications

Amy has $12 a week to spend on coffee and soda. The price of coffee is $2 a cup, and soda is $1 a can. Use this information to work Problems **1** and **2**.

1. Draw a graph of Amy's budget line. Can Amy buy 7 cans of soda and 2 cups of coffee a week? Can she buy 7 cups of coffee and 2 cans of soda a week? What is the relative price of a cup of coffee?

2. Suppose that the price of soda remains at $1 a can but the price of coffee rises to $3 a cup. Draw Amy's new budget line. If she buys 6 cans of soda, what is the maximum number of cups of coffee she can buy in a week? Has the relative price of coffee changed?

Use Table 1, which shows Ben's utility, to work Problems **3** and **4**.

3. Calculate the values of *A*, *B*, *C*, and *D* in the table. Does the principle of diminishing marginal utility apply to Ben's consumption of orange juice? Why or why not?

4. Would Ben ever want to buy more than one carton of orange juice a day or no orange juice? Explain your answer.

5. Every day, Josie buys 2 cups of coffee and 1 sandwich for lunch. The price of coffee is $2 a cup and the price of a sandwich is $5. Josie's choice of lunch maximizes her total utility, and she spends only $9 on lunch. Compare Josie's marginal utility from coffee with her marginal utility from the sandwich.

6. Susie spends $28 a week on sundaes and magazines. The price of a sundae is $4 and the price of a magazine is $4. Table 2 shows Susie's marginal utility from sundaes and magazines. How many sundaes does she buy? If the price of a sundae doubles to $8 and other things remain the same, how many sundaes will she buy? What are two points on her demand curve for sundaes?

7. When Erin has $25 to spend, she sees 2 movies at $10 a movie ticket and buys 1 six-pack of soda. Calculate the price of soda. If her budget for soda and movies increases to $50, what is the change in the relative price of a movie ticket? How does her marginal utility per dollar from movies change?

8. **Watch video without dinging data caps**
   Verizon, the biggest wireless company, will let its customers watch ad-sponsored video free from data caps.
   Source: Associated Press, December 15, 2015
   Explain the effect of exempting video from data caps on a person's budget line and the quantities of video and other data used.

9. **Compared to other liquids, gasoline is cheap**
   In 2008, when gasoline hit $4 a gallon, motorists complained, but they didn't complain about $18 for 16 ml of HP ink ($4,294.58 per gallon).
   Source: *The New York Times*, May 27, 2008
   Explain why the prices of printer ink and gasoline might provide an example of the paradox of value.

10. Read *Eye on Song Downloads and Streaming* on pp. 334–335, then draw a student's budget lines for single songs versus other goods and services in 2000 and 2015. Explain why the budget line changed between 2000 and 2015.

TABLE 1

Orange juice (cartons per day)	Total utility	Marginal utility
0	0	
		7
1	7	
		5
2	A	
		B
3	15	
		2
4	C	
		D
5	18	

TABLE 2

Sundaes		Magazines	
Quantity per week	Marginal utility	Quantity per week	Marginal utility
1	60	1	40
2	56	2	32
3	50	3	28
4	42	4	25
5	32	5	23
6	20	6	22

Instructor Assignable Problems and Applications

MyEconLab Homework, Quiz, or Test if assigned by instructor

1. In 2015, Americans downloaded 1,200 million singles at $1.20 each and 100 million albums at $10 each. They also bought 1 million singles on vinyl at $11 each and 100 million albums on CDs at $12.50 each. What does marginal utility theory tell you about the ratio of the marginal utility from singles on vinyl to the marginal utility from singles downloads? What does it tell you about the ratio of the marginal utility from albums on CDs to the marginal utility from album downloads?

2. Tim buys 2 smoothies and sees 1 movie a week when he has $16 to spend, the price of a movie ticket is $8, and the price of a smoothie is $4. What is the relative price of a movie ticket? If the price of a movie ticket falls to $4, how will Tim's consumption possibilities change? Explain.

3. Jim spends all his income on apartment rent, food, clothing, and vacations. He gets a pay raise from $3,000 a month to $4,000 a month. At the same time, airfares and other vacation-related expenses increase by 50 percent. How has Jim's budget in terms of airfares and other vacation-related expenses changed? Is Jim better off or worse off in his new situation?

Use Table 1, which shows Martha's total utility from burgers and pasta, to work Problems **4** to **6**.

4. When Martha buys 3 burgers and 2 dishes of pasta a week, what is her total utility and her marginal utility from the third burger? If the price of a burger is $4, what is her marginal utility per dollar from burgers?

5. When the price of a burger is $4, the price of pasta is $8 a dish, and Martha has $24 a week to spend, she buys 2 burgers and 2 dishes of pasta. Does she maximize her total utility? Explain your answer.

6. When the price of a burger is $4, Martha has $24 to spend, and the price of pasta falls from $8 to $4 a dish, how many burgers and dishes of pasta does Martha buy? What are two points on Martha's demand curve for pasta?

Use the following information to work Problems **7** and **8**.

Table 2 shows the marginal utility that Ali gets from smoothies and movies. Ali has $30 a week to spend. The price of a movie ticket is $6, and the price of a smoothie is $3.

7. If Ali buys 4 smoothies a week and sees 3 movies, does he spend all $30? What is his utility from smoothies and his utility from movies? Does he maximize his utility? If not, which good must he buy more of?

8. When Ali allocates his budget so as to maximize his utility, what does he buy and what is the marginal utility per dollar?

Use the following information to work Problems **9** and **10**.

Apple Music could match Spotify subscribers by 2016
Apple Music is expected to have 16 million paid subscribers by the end of 2016. Spotify has 20 million paid subscribers.

Source: *Newsweek*, December 18, 2015

9. Compare the budget line for a streaming subscription with that for song downloads at $1 per song.

10. Compare the marginal utility of a downloaded song with that of a streamed song.

TABLE 1

Burgers		Pasta	
Quantity per week	Total utility	Dishes per week	Total utility
0	0	0	0
1	10	1	20
2	18	2	36
3	25	3	48
4	31	4	56
5	36	5	60
6	40	6	62

TABLE 2

Quantity per week	Marginal utility from	
	Smoothies	Movies
1	7	30
2	6	24
3	5	18
4	4	12
5	3	6
6	2	0

Multiple Choice Quiz

1. A consumer's consumption possibilities depend on all of the following items *except* _____.

   A. the prices of the goods that the consumer wants to buy
   B. the consumer's budget
   C. the quantities of the goods that the consumer can afford
   D. the consumer's preferences

2. Jane's budget line _____.

   A. shifts outward with no change in its slope if her budget increases and prices don't change
   B. rotates inward if the prices of both goods double and her budget doesn't change
   C. shifts inward with no change in its slope if the price of one good rises and her budget doesn't change
   D. rotates outward if her budget increases and prices don't change

3. Total utility _____ and marginal utility _____ as more of a good is consumed.

   A. increases; increases
   B. diminishes; diminishes
   C. increases; diminishes
   D. diminishes; increases

4. Tom will maximize his total utility if he buys the quantities of pasta and milk at which _____.

   A. the marginal utility from pasta equals the marginal utility from milk
   B. he spends all of his budget and marginal utility from each good is equal
   C. the marginal utility from the more expensive good is less than the marginal utility from the cheaper good
   D. he spends all his budget and the marginal utility per dollar from pasta and milk are equal

5. Sara buys bread and bananas and is maximizing her total utility. If the price of bananas rises, Sara will maximize her total utility by _____.

   A. increasing her budget so that she can buy the same quantities
   B. buying more bananas and less bread
   C. buying fewer bananas and possibly more bread
   D. buying less bread and possibly more bananas

6. When Joe's budget increases, he will spend the increase in his budget on _____.

   A. normal goods
   B. inferior goods
   C. more of all the goods he usually buys
   D. essential goods

7. The paradox of value arises when people _____.

   A. prefer to buy cheap goods rather than expensive goods
   B. spend more on expensive useless goods than on cheap useful goods
   C. buy so much of a useful good that its price falls
   D. get the same marginal utility per dollar from cheap useful goods and useless expensive goods

APPENDIX: INDIFFERENCE CURVES

You are going to discover a neat idea—that of drawing a map of a person's preferences. A preference map is based on the intuitively appealing assumption that people can sort all the possible combinations of goods into three groups: preferred, not preferred, and indifferent. To make this idea concrete, let's ask Tina to tell us how she ranks combinations of bottled water and chewing gum.

■ An Indifference Curve

Figure A13.1(a) shows part of Tina's answer. She tells us that she currently consumes 2 bottles of water and 4 packs of gum a day at point C. She then lists all the combinations of bottled water and chewing gum that she says are as acceptable to her as her current consumption. When we plot these combinations of water and gum, we get the green curve. This curve is the key element in a map of preferences and is called an indifference curve.

An **indifference curve** is a line that shows combinations of goods among which a consumer is *indifferent*. The indifference curve in Figure A13.1(a) tells us that Tina is just as happy to consume 2 bottles of water and 4 packs of gum a day at point C as to consume the combination of water and gum at any other point along the indifference curve. Tina also says that she prefers all the combinations of bottled water and gum above the indifference curve—the yellow area—to those on the indifference curve. These combinations contain more water, more gum, or

Indifference curve

A line that shows combinations of goods among which a consumer is *indifferent*.

■ FIGURE A13.1

A Preference Map

MyEconLab Animation

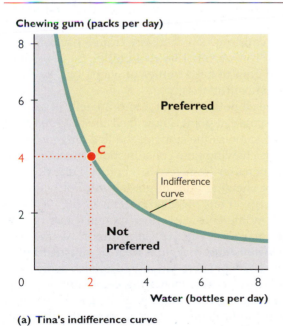

(a) Tina's indifference curve

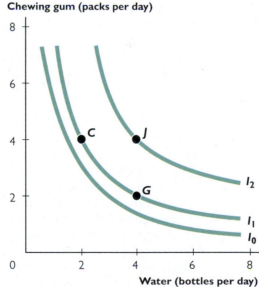

(b) Tina's preference map

In part (a), Tina consumes 2 bottles of water and 4 packs of chewing gum a day at point C. She is indifferent between all the points on the green indifference curve. She prefers any point above the indifference curve (yellow area) to any point on it, and she prefers any point on the indifference curve to any point below it (gray area).

Part (b) shows three indifference curves of Tina's preference map. She prefers point J to point C or G, so she prefers any point on I_2 to any point on I_1.

more of both. She also prefers any combination on the indifference curve to any combination in the gray area below the indifference curve. These combinations contain less water, less gum, or less of both.

The indifference curve in Figure A13.1(a) is just one of a whole family of such curves. This indifference curve appears again in Figure A13.1(b) labeled I_1. The curves labeled I_0 and I_2 are two other indifference curves. Tina prefers any point on indifference curve I_2, such as point J, to any point on indifference curve I_1, such as points C or G. She prefers any point on I_1 to any point on I_0. We refer to I_2 as being a higher indifference curve than I_1 and to I_1 as being higher than I_0.

A preference map is a series of indifference curves that resemble the contour lines on a map. By looking at the shape of the contour lines on a map, we can draw conclusions about the terrain. Similarly, by looking at the shape of the indifference curves, we can draw conclusions about a person's preferences.

■ Marginal Rate of Substitution

Marginal rate of substitution

The rate at which a person will give up good Y (the good measured on the y-axis) to get more of good X (the good measured on the x-axis) and at the same time remain on the same indifference curve.

The concept of the marginal rate of substitution is the key to "reading" a preference map. The **marginal rate of substitution** (MRS) is the rate at which a person will give up good Y (the good measured on the y-axis) to get more of good X (the good measured on the x-axis) and at the same time remain indifferent (remain on the same indifference curve). The marginal rate of substitution is measured by the magnitude of the slope of an indifference curve.

If the indifference curve is *steep*, the marginal rate of substitution is *high*. The person is willing to give up a large quantity of good Y to get a small quantity of good X while remaining indifferent. If the indifference curve is *flat*, the marginal rate of substitution is *low*. The person is willing to give up only a small amount of good Y to get a large amount of good X and remain indifferent.

Figure A13.2 shows you how to calculate the marginal rate of substitution. Suppose that Tina consumes 2 bottles of water and 4 packs of gum at point C on indifference curve I_1. We calculate her marginal rate of substitution by measuring the magnitude of the slope of the indifference curve at point C. To measure this magnitude, place a straight line against, or tangent to, the indifference curve at point C. Along that red line, as gum consumption decreases from 8 packs to zero packs, water consumption increases from zero bottles to 4 bottles. So at point C, Tina is willing to give up 8 packs of gum to get 4 bottles of water, or 2 packs of gum per bottle. Her marginal rate of substitution is 2.

Now suppose that Tina consumes 4 bottles of water and 2 packs of gum at point G. The slope of the indifference curve at point G now measures her marginal rate of substitution. That slope is the same as the slope of the line tangent to the indifference curve at point G. Here, as chewing gum consumption decreases from 4 packs to zero, water consumption increases from zero to 8 bottles. So at point G, Tina is willing to give up 4 packs of chewing gum to get 8 bottles of water, or 1/2 a pack of gum per bottle. Her marginal rate of substitution is 1/2.

Diminishing marginal rate of substitution

The general tendency for the marginal rate of substitution to decrease as the consumer moves down along the indifference curve, increasing consumption of the good measured on the x-axis and decreasing consumption of the good measured on the y-axis.

As Tina moves down along her indifference curve, her marginal rate of substitution diminishes. Diminishing marginal rate of substitution is the key assumption of consumer theory. **Diminishing marginal rate of substitution** is the general tendency for the marginal rate of substitution to diminish as the consumer moves down along an indifference curve, increasing consumption of the good measured on the x-axis and decreasing consumption of the good measured on the y-axis. The shape of a person's indifference curves incorporates the principle of the diminishing marginal rate of substitution because the curves are bowed toward the origin.

FIGURE A13.2

The Marginal Rate of Substitution

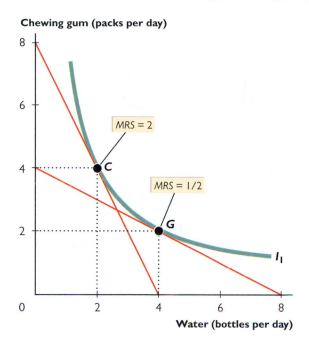

The magnitude of the slope of an indifference curve is called the marginal rate of substitution (*MRS*).

The red line at point *C* tells us that Tina is willing to give up 8 packs of gum to get 4 bottles of water. Her marginal rate of substitution at point *C* is 8 divided by 4, which equals 2.

The red line at point *G* tells us that Tina is willing to give up 4 packs of gum to get 8 bottles of water. Her marginal rate of substitution at point *G* is 4 divided by 8, which equals 1/2.

■ Consumer Equilibrium

The consumer's goal is to buy the affordable quantities of goods that make her or him as well off as possible. The indifference curves describe the consumer's preferences, and they tell us that the higher the indifference curve, the better off is the consumer. So the consumer's goal can be restated as: to allocate his or her budget in such a way as to get onto the highest attainable indifference curve.

The consumer's budget and the prices of the goods limit the consumer's choices. The budget line illustrated in Figure 13.1 (p. 320) summarizes the limits on the consumer's choice. We combine the indifference curves of Figure A13.1(b) with the budget line of Figure 13.1 to work out the consumer's choice and find the consumer equilibrium.

Figure A13.3 shows Tina's budget line from Figure 13.1 and her indifference curves from Figure A13.1(b). Tina's *best affordable point* is 2 bottles of water and 4 packs of gum—at point C. Here, Tina

- Is on her budget line.
- Is on her highest attainable indifference curve.
- Has a marginal rate of substitution between water and gum equal to the relative price of water in terms of gum.

For every point inside the budget line, such as point *L*, there are points *on* the budget line that Tina prefers. For example, she prefers any point on the budget line between *F* and *H* to point *L*. So she chooses a point on the budget line.

■ **FIGURE A13.3**

Consumer Equilibrium

Tina's best affordable point is *C*. At that point, she is on her budget line and also on the highest attainable indifference curve.

At a point such as *H*, Tina is willing to give up more bottled water in exchange for chewing gum than she has to. She can move to point *L*, which is just as good as point *H*, and have some unspent budget. She can spend that budget and move to *C*, a point that she prefers to point *L*.

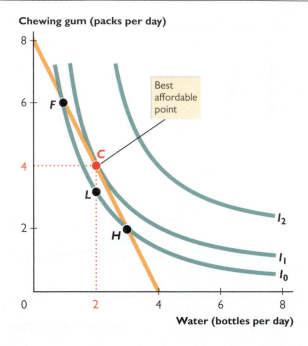

Checked out at the best affordable point.

Every point on the budget line lies on an indifference curve. For example, point *F* lies on the indifference curve I_0. At point *F*, Tina's marginal rate of substitution (the magnitude of the slope of the indifference curve I_0) is greater than the relative price (the magnitude of the slope of the budget line). Tina is willing to give up more chewing gum to get an additional bottle of water than the budget line says she must. So she moves along her budget line from *F* toward *C*. As she does so, she passes through a number of indifference curves (not shown in the figure) located between indifference curves I_0 and I_1. All of these indifference curves are higher than I_0 so Tina prefers any point on them to point *F*. When Tina gets to point *C*, she is on the highest attainable indifference curve. If she keeps moving along the budget line, she starts to encounter indifference curves that are lower than I_1. So Tina chooses point *C*—her best affordable point.

At the chosen point, the marginal rate of substitution (the magnitude of the slope of the indifference curve) equals the relative price (the magnitude of the slope of the budget line).

We can now use this model of consumer choice to predict the effect of a change in the price of water on the quantity of water demanded. That is, we can use this model to generate the demand curve for bottled water.

■ **Deriving the Demand Curve**

To derive Tina's demand curve for bottled water, we change the price of water, shift the budget line, and work out the new best affordable point. Figure A13.4(a) shows the change in the budget line and the change in consumer equilibrium when the price of water falls from $1 a bottle to 50¢ a bottle.

Initially, when the price of water is $1 a bottle, Tina consumes at point C in part (a). When the price of a bottle of water falls from $1 to 50¢, her budget line rotates outward and she can now get onto a higher indifference curve. Her best affordable point is now point K. Tina increases the quantity of water she buys from 2 to 4 bottles a day. She continues to buy 4 packs of gum a day.

Figure A13.4(b) shows Tina's demand curve for bottled water. When the price of water is $1 a bottle, she buys 2 bottles a day, at point A. When the price of water falls to 50¢ a bottle, she buys 4 bottles a day, at point B. Tina's demand curve traces out her best affordable quantity of water as the price of a bottle of water varies.

■ **FIGURE A13.4**

Deriving Tina's Demand Curve   My EconLab Animation

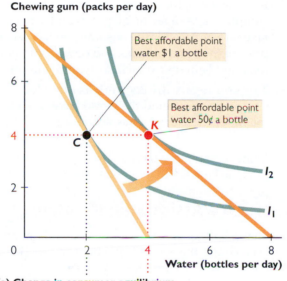

(a) Change in consumer equilibrium

In part (a), when the price of water is $1 a bottle, Tina consumes at point C. When the price of water falls from $1 to 50¢ a bottle, she consumes at point K.

In part (b), when the price of water is $1 a bottle, Tina is at point A. When the price of water falls from $1 to 50¢ a bottle, Tina moves along her demand curve for bottled water from point A to point B.

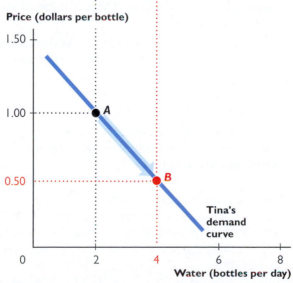

(b) Demand curve

APPENDIX CHECKPOINT

Study Plan Problems and Applications

Sara has $12 to spend on popcorn and nuts. Popcorn is $3 a bag, and nuts is $3 a bag. Figure 1 illustrates Sara's preferences. Use Figure 1 to work Problems **1** to **3**.

1. What is the relative price of nuts and what is the opportunity cost of a bag of nuts? Draw a graph of Sara's budget line with nuts on the *x*-axis.

2. What quantities of popcorn and nuts does Sara buy and what is her marginal rate of substitution of popcorn for nuts at her consumption point?

3. Suppose that the price of nuts falls to $1.50 a bag and the price of popcorn and Sara's budget remain unchanged. What quantities of popcorn and nuts does Sara buy now? What are two points on Sara's demand curve for nuts?

4. In most states, there is no sales tax on food. Some people say that a consumption tax—a tax on all goods and services—would be better. If all sales taxes are replaced by a consumption tax, what would happen to the relative price of food and haircuts and how would you change your purchases of food and haircuts? Which tax would you prefer?

5. **Taxes on sugary drinks work as intended**
Governments around the world have put a tax on sugary drinks, and the demand for these drinks has decreased.

Source: *The Economist*, November 28, 2015

Draw a graph to illustrate how a tax on sugary drinks changes the budget line, the best affordable point, and the demand for sugary drinks.

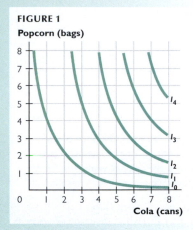

FIGURE 1
Popcorn (bags)

Instructor Assignable Problems and Applications

Marc has a budget of $20 a month to spend on lattes and e-books. The price of a latte is $5, and the price of an e-book is $10. Figure 2 illustrates his preferences. Use Figure 2 to work Problems **1** to **3**.

1. What is the relative price of a latte in terms of e-books and what is the opportunity cost of a latte? Draw a graph of Marc's budget line with e-books on the *x*-axis.

2. What quantities of lattes and e-books does Marc buy? At his consumption point, calculate his marginal rate of substitution of e-books for lattes.

3. If the price of an e-book falls to $5 but the price of a latte and Marc's budget remain unchanged, what quantities of lattes and e-books does Marc now buy? What are two points on Marc's demand curve for e-books?

4. **The Beatles set to stream on Christmas Eve**
The Beatles are set to join the streaming revolution as its revenue generation overtakes that from downloads.

Source: *Billboard*, December 18, 2015

Draw a graph to illustrate a Beatle fan's preferences, and budget lines for streaming versus other goods and for downloads versus others goods. On your graph, show the best affordable point before and after Christmas 2015.

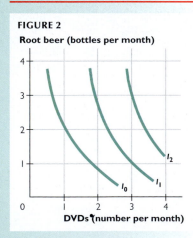

FIGURE 2
Root beer (bottles per month)

Key Terms

Diminishing marginal rate of substitution, 342	Indifference curve, 341	Marginal rate of substitution, 342

Which store has the lower costs:
Walmart or 7-Eleven?

Production and Cost

When you have completed your study of this chapter, you will be able to

1 Explain and distinguish between the economic and accounting measures of a firm's cost of production and profit.

2 Explain the relationship between a firm's output and labor employed in the short run.

3 Explain the relationship between a firm's output and costs in the short run.

4 Derive and explain a firm's long-run average cost curve.

 Big Picture Video

14.1 ECONOMIC COST AND PROFIT

A Walmart store is much larger than a 7-Eleven and clearly costs more to operate. But which store has the lower cost per customer served? Now the answer is not so obvious. You'll find the answer at the end of this chapter.

Like a Walmart store and a 7-Eleven, the 20 million firms in the United States differ in size. They also differ in what they produce. But all firms perform the same basic economic function: They hire factors of production and organize them to produce and sell goods and services. To understand the behavior of a firm, we need to know its goals.

■ The Firm's Goal

If you asked a group of entrepreneurs what they are trying to achieve, you would get many different answers. Some would talk about making a high-quality product, others about business growth, others about market share, and others about job satisfaction of the work force. All of these goals might be pursued, but they are not the fundamental goal. They are a means to a deeper goal.

The firm's goal is to *maximize profit*. A firm that does not seek to maximize profit is either eliminated or bought by firms that *do* seek to achieve that goal. To calculate a firm's profit, we must determine its total revenue and total cost. Economists have a special way of defining and measuring cost and profit, which we'll explain and illustrate by looking at Sam's Smoothies, a firm that is owned and operated by Samantha.

■ Accounting Cost and Profit

In 2016, Sam's Smoothies' total revenue from the sale of smoothies was $150,000. The firm paid $20,000 for fruit, yogurt, and honey; $22,000 in wages for the labor it hired; and $3,000 in interest to the bank. These items totaled $45,000.

Sam's accountant said that the depreciation of the firm's blenders, refrigerators, and shop during 2016 was $10,000. Depreciation is the fall in the value of the firm's capital, and accountants calculate it by using the Internal Revenue Service's rules, which are based on standards set by the Financial Accounting Standards Board. So the accountant reported the firm's total cost for 2016 as $55,000 and the firm's profit as $95,000—$150,000 of total revenue minus $55,000 of total costs.

Sam's accountant measures cost and profit to ensure that the firm pays the correct amount of income tax and to show the bank how Sam's has used its bank loan. Economists have a different purpose: to predict the firm's decisions. These decisions respond to *opportunity cost* and *economic profit*.

■ Opportunity Cost

To produce its output, a firm employs factors of production: land, labor, capital, and entrepreneurship. Another firm could have used these same resources to produce other goods or services. In Chapter 3 (pp. 66–67), resources can be used to produce either smartphones or bikes, so the opportunity cost of producing a smartphone is the number of bikes forgone. Pilots who fly passengers for Southwest Airlines can't at the same time fly freight for FedEx. Construction workers who are building an office high-rise can't simultaneously build apartments. A journalist writing for the *New York Times* can't at the same time create

Web news reports for CNN. And Samantha can't simultaneously run her smoothies business and a flower shop.

The highest-valued alternative forgone is the opportunity cost of a firm's production. From the viewpoint of the firm, this opportunity cost is the amount that the firm must pay the owners of the factors of production it employs to attract them from their best alternative use. So a firm's opportunity cost of production is the cost of the factors of production it employs.

To determine these costs, let's return to Sam's and look at the opportunity cost of producing smoothies.

Explicit Costs and Implicit Costs

The amount that a firm pays to attract resources from their best alternative use is either an explicit cost or an implicit cost. A cost paid in money is an **explicit cost**. Because the amount spent could have been spent on something else, an explicit cost is an opportunity cost. The wages that Samantha pays labor, the interest she pays the bank, and her expenditure on fruit, yogurt, and honey are explicit costs.

A firm incurs an **implicit cost** when it uses a factor of production but does not make a direct money payment for its use. The two categories of implicit cost are economic depreciation and the cost of the resources of the firm's owner.

Economic depreciation is the opportunity cost of the firm using capital that it owns. It is measured as the change in the *market value* of capital—the market price of the capital at the beginning of the period minus its market price at the end of the period. Suppose that Samantha could have sold her blenders, refrigerators, and shop on December 31, 2015, for $250,000. If she can sell the same capital on December 31, 2016, for $246,000, her economic depreciation during 2016 is $4,000. This is the opportunity cost of using her capital during 2016, not the $10,000 depreciation calculated by Sam's accountant.

Interest is another cost of capital. When the firm's owner provides the funds used to buy capital, the opportunity cost of those funds is the interest income forgone by not using them in the best alternative way. If Sam loaned her firm funds that could have earned her $1,000 in interest, this amount is an implicit cost of producing smoothies.

When a firm's owner supplies labor, the opportunity cost of the owner's time spent working for the firm is the wage income forgone by not working in the best alternative job. For example, instead of working at her next best job that pays $34,000 a year, Sam supplies labor to her smoothies business. This implicit cost of $34,000 is part of the opportunity cost of producing smoothies.

Finally, a firm's owner often supplies entrepreneurship, the factor of production that organizes the business and bears the risk of running it. The return to entrepreneurship is **normal profit**. Normal profit is part of a firm's opportunity cost because it is the cost of a forgone alternative—running another firm. Instead of running Sam's Smoothies, Sam could earn $16,000 a year running a flower shop. This amount is an implicit cost of production at Sam's Smoothies.

■ Economic Profit

A firm's **economic profit** equals total revenue minus total cost. Total revenue is the amount received from the sale of the product. It is the price of the output multiplied by the quantity sold. Total cost is the sum of the explicit costs and implicit costs and is the opportunity cost of production.

Explicit cost
A cost paid in money.

Implicit cost
An opportunity cost incurred by a firm when it uses a factor of production for which it does not make a direct money payment.

Economic depreciation
An opportunity cost of a firm using capital that it owns—measured as the change in the *market value* of capital over a given period.

Normal profit
The return to entrepreneurship. Normal profit is part of a firm's opportunity cost because it is the cost of not running another firm.

Economic profit
A firm's total revenue minus total cost.

■ **TABLE 14.1**

Economic Accounting

Item		
Total Revenue		**$150,000**
Explicit Costs		
Cost of fruit, yogurt, and honey	$20,000	
Wages	$22,000	
Interest	$3,000	
Implicit Costs		
Samantha's forgone wages	$34,000	
Samantha's forgone interest	$1,000	
Economic depreciation	$4,000	
Normal profit	$16,000	
Opportunity Cost		**$100,000**
Economic Profit		**$50,000**

Because one of the firm's implicit costs is *normal profit*, the return to the entrepreneur equals normal profit plus economic profit. If a firm incurs an economic loss, the entrepreneur receives less than normal profit.

Table 14.1 summarizes the economic cost concepts, and Figure 14.1 compares the economic view and the accounting view of cost and profit. Sam's total revenue (price multiplied by quantity sold) is $150,000; the opportunity cost of the resources that Sam uses is $100,000; and Sam's economic profit is $50,000.

■ **FIGURE 14.1**

Two Views of Cost and Profit   MyEconLab Animation

Both economists and accountants measure a firm's total revenue the same way. It equals the price multiplied by the quantity sold of each item.

Economists measure economic profit as total revenue minus opportunity cost. Opportunity cost includes explicit costs and implicit costs. Normal profit is an implicit cost.

Accountants measure profit as total revenue minus explicit costs—costs paid in money—and depreciation.

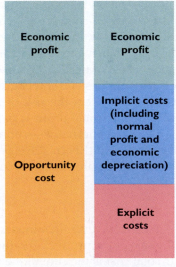

The economic view   The accounting view

CHECKPOINT 14.1

MyEconLab Study Plan 14.1
Key Terms Quiz
Solutions Video

Explain and distinguish between the economic and accounting measures of a firm's cost of production and profit.

Practice Problems

Lee, a programmer, earned $35,000 in 2015, but in 2016, he began to manufacture body boards. After one year, he submitted the following data to his accountant.

- He stopped renting out his cottage for $3,500 a year and used it as his factory. The market value of the cottage increased from $70,000 to $71,000.
- He spent $50,000 on materials, phone, utilities, etc.
- He leased machines for $10,000 a year.
- He paid $15,000 in wages.
- He used $10,000 from his savings account, which pays 5 percent a year interest.
- He borrowed $40,000 at 10 percent a year from the bank.
- He sold $160,000 worth of body boards.
- Normal profit is $25,000 a year.

1. Calculate Lee's explicit costs, implicit costs, and economic profit in 2016.

2. Lee's accountant recorded the depreciation on Lee's cottage during 2016 as $7,000. What did the accountant say Lee's profit or loss was in 2016?

In the News

What does it cost to make 100 pairs of running shoes?
An Asian manufacturer of running shoes pays its workers $275 to make 100 pairs an hour. Workers use company-owned equipment that costs $300 an hour in forgone interest and economic depreciation. Materials cost $900.

Source: washpost.com

Which costs are explicit costs? Which are implicit costs? With total revenue from the sale of 100 pairs of shoes of $1,650, calculate economic profit.

Solutions to Practice Problems

1. Lee's explicit costs are costs paid with money: $50,000 on materials, phone, utilities, etc; $10,000 on leased machines; $15,000 in wages; and $4,000 in bank interest. These items total $79,000.
   Lee's implicit costs are $35,000 in forgone wages; $3,500 in forgone rent; the $1,000 increase in the value of his cottage is economic depreciation of −$1,000; $500 in forgone interest; and $25,000 in normal profit. These items total $63,000.
   Economic profit equals total revenue ($160,000) minus total cost, which equals $79,000 + $63,000, or $142,000. So economic profit in 2016 was $160,000 − $142,000, or $18,000.

2. The accountant measures Lee's profit as total revenue minus explicit costs minus depreciation: $160,000−$79,000−$7,000, or $74,000.

Solution to In the News

Explicit costs are wages ($275) and materials ($900). Implicit costs are the forgone interest and economic depreciation ($300). Economic profit equals total revenue ($1,650) minus total cost ($1,475), which is $175.

MyEconLab Concept Video

SHORT RUN AND LONG RUN

The main goal of this chapter is to explore the influences on a firm's costs. The key influence on cost is the quantity of output that the firm produces per period. The greater the output rate, the higher is the total cost of production. But the effect of a change in production on cost depends on how soon the firm wants to act. A firm that plans to change its output rate tomorrow has fewer options than a firm that plans ahead and intends to change its production six months from now.

To study the relationship between a firm's output decision and its costs, we distinguish between two decision time frames:

- The short run
- The long run

The Short Run: Fixed Plant

Short run

The time frame in which the quantities of some resources are fixed. In the short run, a firm can usually change the quantity of labor it uses but not its technology and quantity of capital.

The **short run** is the time frame in which the quantities of some resources are fixed. For most firms, the fixed resources are the firm's technology and capital—its equipment and buildings. The management organization is also fixed in the short run. The fixed resources that a firm uses are its *fixed factors of production* and the resources that it can vary are its *variable factors of production*. The collection of fixed resources is the firm's *plant*. So in the short run, a firm's plant is fixed.

Sam's Smoothies' plant is its blenders, refrigerators, and shop. Sam's cannot change these inputs in the short run. An electric power utility can't change the number of generators it uses in the short run. An airport can't change the number of runways, terminal buildings, and traffic-control facilities in the short run.

To increase output in the short run, a firm must increase the quantity of variable factors it uses. Labor is usually the variable factor of production. To produce more smoothies, Sam must hire more labor. Similarly, to increase the production of electricity, a utility must hire more engineers and run its generators for longer hours. To increase the volume of traffic it handles, an airport must hire more check-in clerks, cargo handlers, and air-traffic controllers.

Short-run decisions are easily reversed. A firm can increase or decrease output in the short run by increasing or decreasing the number of labor hours it hires.

The Long Run: Variable Plant

Long run

The time frame in which the quantities of *all* resources can be varied.

The **long run** is the time frame in which the quantities of *all* resources can be varied. That is, the long run is a period in which the firm can change its *plant*.

To increase output in the long run, a firm can increase the size of its plant. Sam's Smoothies can install more blenders and refrigerators and increase the size of its shop. An electric power utility can install more generators. And an airport can build more runways, terminals, and traffic-control facilities.

Long-run decisions are not easily reversed. Once a firm buys a new plant, its resale value is usually much less than the amount the firm paid for it. The fall in value is economic depreciation. It is called a *sunk cost* to emphasize that it is irrelevant to the firm's decisions. Only the short-run cost of changing its labor inputs and the long-run cost of changing its plant size are relevant to a firm's decisions.

We're going to study costs in the short run and the long run. We begin with the short run and describe the limits to the firm's production possibilities.

14.2 · SHORT-RUN PRODUCTION

MyEconLab Concept Video

To increase the output of a fixed plant, a firm must increase the quantity of labor it employs. We describe the relationship between output and the quantity of labor employed by using three related concepts:

- Total product
- Marginal product
- Average product

■ Total Product

Total product (*TP*) is the total quantity of a good produced in a given period. Total product is an output *rate*—the number of units produced per unit of time (for example, per hour, day, or week). Total product changes as the quantity of labor employed increases and we illustrate this relationship as a total product schedule and total product curve like those in Figure 14.2. The total product schedule (the table below the graph) lists the maximum quantity of smoothies per hour that Sam can produce with her existing plant at each quantity of labor. Points *A* through *H* on the *TP* curve correspond to the columns in the table.

Total product
The total quantity of a good produced in a given period.

■ **FIGURE 14.2**

Total Product Schedule and Total Product Curve

MyEconLab Animation

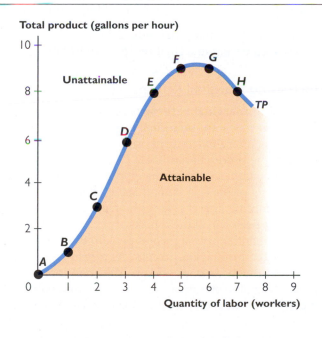

Quantity of labor (workers)	0	1	2	3	4	5	6	7
Total product (gallons per hour)	0	1	3	6	8	9	9	8
	A	*B*	*C*	*D*	*E*	*F*	*G*	*H*

The total product schedule shows how the quantity of smoothies that Sam's can produce changes as the quantity of labor employed changes. In column *C*, Sam's employs 2 workers and can produce 3 gallons of smoothies an hour.

The total product curve, *TP*, graphs the data in the table. Points *A* through *H* on the curve correspond to the columns of the table. The total product curve separates attainable outputs from unattainable outputs. Points below the *TP* curve are inefficient. Points on the *TP* curve are efficient.

Like the *production possibilities frontier* (see Chapter 3, p. 62), the total product curve separates attainable outputs from unattainable outputs. All the points that lie above the curve are unattainable. Points that lie below the curve, in the orange area, are attainable, but they are inefficient: They use more labor than is necessary to produce a given output. Only the points *on* the total product curve are efficient.

■ Marginal Product

Marginal product
The change in total product that results from a one-unit increase in the quantity of labor employed.

Marginal product (*MP*) is the change in total product that results from a one-unit increase in the quantity of labor employed. It tells us the contribution to total product of adding one additional worker. When the quantity of labor increases by more than one worker, we calculate marginal product as

Marginal product = Change in total product ÷ Change in quantity of labor.

Figure 14.3 shows Sam's Smoothies' marginal product curve, *MP*, and its relationship with the total product curve. You can see that as the quantity of labor increases from 1 to 3 workers, marginal product increases. But as more than 3 workers are employed, marginal product decreases. When the seventh worker is employed, marginal product is negative.

Notice that the steeper the slope of the total product curve in part (a), the greater is marginal product in part (b). And when the total product curve turns downward in part (a), marginal product is negative in part (b).

The total product curve and marginal product curve in Figure 14.3 incorporate a feature that is shared by all production processes in firms as different as the Ford Motor Company, Jim's Barber Shop, and Sam's Smoothies:

- Increasing marginal returns initially
- Decreasing marginal returns eventually

Increasing Marginal Returns

Increasing marginal returns
When the marginal product of an additional worker exceeds the marginal product of the previous worker.

Increasing marginal returns occur when the marginal product of an additional worker exceeds the marginal product of the previous worker. The source of increasing marginal returns is increased specialization and greater division of labor in the production process.

For example, if Samantha employs just one worker, that person must learn all the aspects of making smoothies: running the blender, cleaning it, fixing breakdowns, buying and checking the fruit, and serving the customers. That one person must perform all these tasks.

If Samantha hires a second person, the two workers can specialize in different parts of the production process. As a result, two workers can produce more than twice as much as one worker. The marginal product of the second worker is greater than the marginal product of the first worker. Marginal returns are increasing. Most production processes experience increasing marginal returns initially.

Decreasing Marginal Returns

Decreasing marginal returns
When the marginal product of an additional worker is less than the marginal product of the previous worker.

All production processes eventually reach a point of *decreasing* marginal returns. **Decreasing marginal returns** occur when the marginal product of an additional worker is less than the marginal product of the previous worker. Decreasing marginal returns arise from the fact that more and more workers use the same equipment and work space. As more workers are employed, there is less and less that is productive for the additional worker to do. For example, if Samantha hires a

FIGURE 14.3

Total Product and Marginal Product

MyEconLab Animation

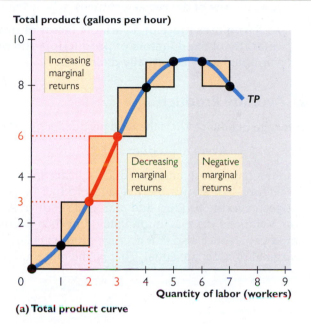

(a) Total product curve

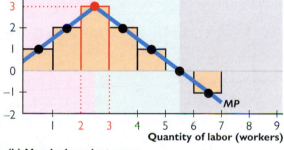

(b) Marginal product curve

The table calculates marginal product, and the orange bars illustrate it. When labor increases from 2 to 3 workers, total product increases from 3 gallons to 6 gallons of smoothies an hour. So marginal product is the orange bar whose height is 3 gallons (in both parts of the figure).

In part (b), marginal product is graphed midway between the labor inputs to emphasize that marginal product is the result of *changing* the labor input. Marginal product increases to a maximum (when 3 workers are employed in this example) and then declines—diminishing marginal product.

Quantity of labor (workers)	0		1		2		3		4		5		6		7
Total product (gallons per hour)	0		1		3		6		8		9		9		8
Marginal product (gallons per worker)		1		2		3		2		1		0		−1	

fourth worker, output increases but not by as much as it did when she hired the third worker. In this case, three workers exhaust all the possible gains from specialization and the division of labor. By hiring a fourth worker, Sam's produces more smoothies per hour, but the equipment is being operated closer to its limits. Sometimes the fourth worker has nothing to do because the machines are running without the need for further attention.

Hiring yet more workers continues to increase output but by successively smaller amounts until Samantha hires the sixth worker, at which point total product stops rising. Add a seventh worker, and the workplace is so congested that the workers get in each other's way and total product falls.

Decreasing marginal returns are so pervasive that they qualify for the status of a law: the **law of decreasing returns**, which states that

Law of decreasing returns
As a firm uses more of a variable factor of production, with a given quantity of fixed factors, the marginal product of the variable factor eventually decreases.

> **As a firm uses more of a variable factor of production, with a given quantity of fixed factors of production, the marginal product of the variable factor eventually decreases.**

■ Average Product

Average product *(AP)* is the total product per worker employed. It is calculated as

$$\text{Average product} = \text{Total product} \div \text{Quantity of labor}.$$

Average product
Total product divided by the quantity of a factor of production. The average product of labor is total product divided by the quantity of labor employed.

Another name for average product is *productivity*.

Figure 14.4 shows the average product of labor, *AP*, and the relationship between average product and marginal product. Average product increases from 1 to 3 workers (its maximum value) but then decreases as yet more workers are employed. Notice also that average product is largest when average product and marginal product are equal. That is, the marginal product curve cuts the average

---

■ **FIGURE 14.4**

Average Product and Marginal Product

MyEconLab Animation

The table calculates average product. For example, when the quantity of labor is 3 workers, total product is 6 gallons an hour, so average product is 6 gallons ÷ 3 workers, which equals 2 gallons per worker.

The average product curve is *AP*.

For the quantity of labor at which marginal product *exceeds* average product, average product is *increasing* and the *AP* curve is upward sloping.

For the quantity of labor at which marginal product is *less than* average product, average product is *decreasing* and the *AP* curve is downward sloping.

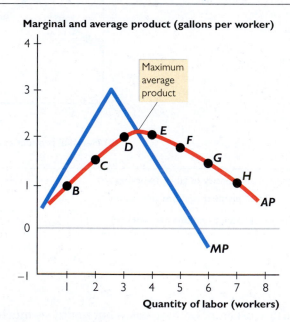

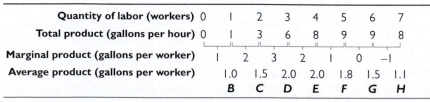

Quantity of labor (workers)	0		1		2		3		4		5		6		7
Total product (gallons per hour)	0		1		3		6		8		9		9		8
Marginal product (gallons per worker)		1		2		3		2		1		0		−1	
Average product (gallons per worker)			1.0		1.5		2.0		2.0		1.8		1.5		1.1	
			B		*C*		*D*		*E*		*F*		*G*		*H*

product curve at the point of maximum average product. For employment levels at which marginal product exceeds average product, the average product curve slopes upward and average product increases as more labor is employed. For employment levels at which marginal product is less than average product, the average product curve slopes downward and average product decreases as more labor is employed.

The relationship between average product and marginal product is a general feature of the relationship between the average value and the marginal value of any variable. *Eye on Your Life* looks at a familiar example.

EYE on YOUR LIFE

MyEconLab Critical Thinking Exercise

Your Average and Marginal Grades

Jen, a part-time student, takes one course each semester over five semesters. In the first semester, she takes calculus and her grade is a C (2). This grade is her marginal grade. It is also her average grade—her GPA.

In the next semester, Jen takes French and gets a B (3)—her new marginal grade. When the marginal value exceeds the average value, the average rises. Because Jen's marginal grade exceeds her average grade, the marginal grade pulls her average up. Her GPA rises to 2.5.

In the third semester, Jen takes economics and gets an A (4). Again her marginal grade exceeds her average, so the marginal grade pulls her average up. Jen's GPA is now 3—the average of 2, 3, and 4.

In the fourth semester, she takes history and gets a B (3). Now her marginal grade equals her average. When the marginal value equals the average value, the average doesn't change. So Jen's average remains at 3.

In the fifth semester, Jen takes English and gets a C (2). When the marginal value is below the average

value, the average falls. Because Jen's marginal grade, 2, is below her average of 3, the marginal grade pulls the average down. Her GPA falls.

This relationship between Jen's ❶ marginal grade and ❷ average grade is similar to the relationship between marginal product and average product.

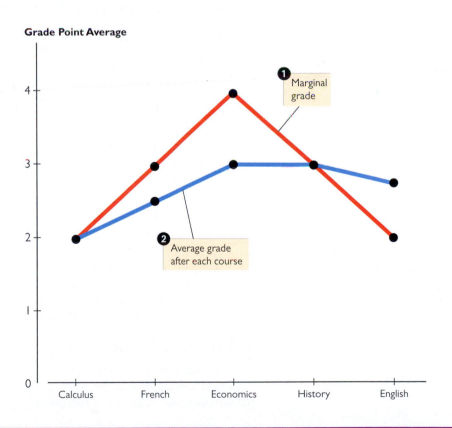

MyEconLab Study Plan 14.2

Key Terms Quiz

Solutions Video

CHECKPOINT 14.2

Explain the relationship between a firm's output and labor employed in the short run.

Practice Problems

Tom leases a farmer's field and grows pineapples. Tom hires students to pick and pack the pineapples. Table 1 sets out Tom's total product schedule.

1. Calculate the marginal product of the third student and the average product of three students.

2. Over what range of numbers of students does marginal product increase?

3. When marginal product increases, is average product greater than, less than, or equal to marginal product?

In the News

Deere, struggling with sales, to lay off 220

Deere & Co. plans to lay off 220 workers and decrease its output of farm equipment.

Source: *The Wall Street Journal*, November 30, 2015

If Deere & Co. is operating at maximum total product before it cuts its workforce, how will the marginal product of a worker change in the short run?

Solutions to Practice Problems

1. The marginal product of the third student is the change in total product that results from hiring the third student. When Tom hires 2 students, total product is 220 pineapples a day. When Tom hires 3 students, total product is 300 pineapples a day. Marginal product of the third student is the total product of 3 students minus the total product of 2 students, which is 300 pineapples − 220 pineapples or 80 pineapples a day.

   Average product equals total product divided by the number of students. When Tom hires 3 students, total product is 300 pineapples a day, so average product is 300 pineapples ÷ 3 students, which equals 100 pineapples per student.

2. Marginal product of the first student is 100 pineapples a day, of the second student is 120 pineapples a day, and of the third is 80 pineapples a day. So marginal product increases when Tom hires the first and second students.

3. When Tom hires 1 student, marginal product is 100 pineapples and average product is 100 pineapples per student. When Tom hires 2 students, marginal product is 120 pineapples and average product is 110 pineapples per student. When Tom hires the second student, marginal product is increasing and average product is less than marginal product.

Solution to In the News

As Deere cuts its workforce, output at the plant will decrease as Deere slides back down along its total product curve. At the same time, Deere's marginal product will increase in the short run (see Fig 14.3 on p. 355).

TABLE 1

Labor (students)	Total product (pineapples per day)
0	0
1	100
2	220
3	300
4	360
5	400
6	420
7	430

14.3   SHORT-RUN COST

MyEconLab Concept Video

To produce more output (total product) in the short run, a firm must employ more labor, which means that it must increase its costs. We describe the relationship between output and cost using three cost concepts:

- Total cost
- Marginal cost
- Average cost

■ Total Cost

A firm's **total cost** (*TC*) is the cost of all the factors of production used by the firm. Total cost divides into two parts: total fixed cost and total variable cost. **Total fixed cost** (*TFC*) is the cost of a firm's fixed factors of production: land, capital, and entrepreneurship. In the short run, the quantities of these inputs don't change as output changes, so total fixed cost doesn't change as output changes. **Total variable cost** (*TVC*) is the cost of a firm's variable factor of production—labor. To change its output in the short run, a firm must change the quantity of labor it employs, so total variable cost changes as output changes.

Total cost is the sum of total fixed cost and total variable cost. That is,

$$TC = TFC + TVC.$$

Table 14.2 shows Sam's Smoothies' total costs. Sam's fixed costs are $20 an hour regardless of whether it operates or not—*TFC* is $20 an hour. To produce smoothies, Samantha hires labor, which costs $12 an hour. *TVC* equals the number of workers multiplied by $12 per hour. For example, to produce 6 gallons an hour, Samantha hires 3 workers, so *TVC* is $36. *TVC* increases as output increases. *TC* is the sum of *TFC* and *TVC*. So to produce 6 gallons an hour, *TC* is $56 an hour. Check the calculation in each row and note that to produce some outputs—2 gallons an hour, for example—Sam hires a worker for only part of an hour.

Total cost
The cost of all the factors of production used by a firm.

Total fixed cost
The cost of the firm's fixed factors of production—the cost of land, capital, and entrepreneurship.

Total variable cost
The cost of the firm's variable factor of production—the cost of labor.

■ TABLE 14.2

Sam's Smoothies' Total Costs

Labor (workers per hour)	Output (gallons per hour)	Total fixed cost	Total variable cost	Total cost
			(dollars per hour)	
0	0	20	0	20.00
1.00	1	20	12.00	32.00
1.60	2	20	19.20	39.20
2.00	3	20	24.00	44.00
2.35	4	20	28.20	48.20
2.65	5	20	31.80	51.80
3.00	6	20	36.00	56.00
3.40	7	20	40.80	60.80
4.00	8	20	48.00	68.00
5.00	9	20	60.00	80.00

Sam's fixed factors of production are land, capital, and entrepreneurship. Total fixed cost is constant regardless of the quantity produced. Sam's variable factor of production is labor. Total variable cost is the cost of labor. Total cost is the sum of total fixed cost and total variable cost.

The highlighted row shows that to produce 6 gallons of smoothies, Sam's hires 3 workers. Total fixed cost is $20 an hour. Total variable cost is the cost of the 3 workers. At $12 an hour, 3 workers cost $36. Sam's total cost of producing 6 gallons an hour is $20 plus $36, which equals $56.

Figure 14.5 illustrates Sam's total cost curves. The green total fixed cost curve (*TFC*) is horizontal because total fixed cost does not change when output changes. It is a constant $20 an hour. The purple total variable cost curve (*TVC*) and the blue total cost curve (*TC*) both slope upward because variable cost increases as output increases. The arrows highlight total fixed cost as the vertical distance between the *TVC* and *TC* curves.

Let's now look at Sam's Smoothies' marginal cost.

■ Marginal Cost

Marginal cost

The change in total cost that results from a one-unit increase in output.

In Figure 14.5, total variable cost and total cost increase at a decreasing rate at small levels of output and then begin to increase at an increasing rate as output increases. To understand these patterns in the changes in total cost, we need to use the concept of *marginal cost*.

A firm's **marginal cost** is the change in total cost that results from a one-unit increase in output. Table 14.3 on p. 361 calculates the marginal cost for Sam's Smoothies. When, for example, output increases from 5 gallons to 6 gallons an hour, total cost increases from $51.80 to $56. So the marginal cost of this gallon of smoothies is ($56 − $51.80), or $4.20. Notice that marginal cost is located midway between the total costs to emphasize that it is the result of *changing* outputs.

Marginal cost tells us how total cost changes as output changes. The final cost concept tells us what it costs, on average, to produce a unit of output. Let's now look at Sam's average costs.

■ **FIGURE 14.5**

Total Cost Curves at Sam's Smoothies

MyEconLab Animation

Total fixed cost (*TFC*) is constant—it graphs as a horizontal line—and total variable cost (*TVC*) increases as output increases. Total cost (*TC*) also increases as output increases.

The vertical distance between the total cost curve and the total variable cost curve is total fixed cost, as illustrated by the two arrows.

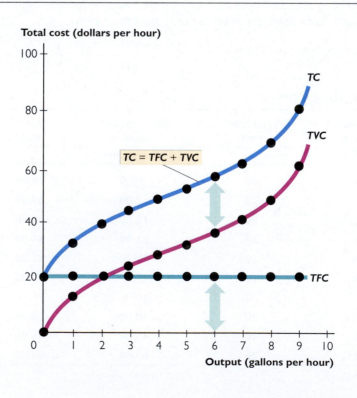

■ Average Cost

There are three average cost concepts:

- Average fixed cost
- Average variable cost
- Average total cost

Average fixed cost (*AFC*) is total fixed cost per unit of output. **Average variable cost** (*AVC*) is total variable cost per unit of output. **Average total cost** (*ATC*) is total cost per unit of output. The average cost concepts are calculated from the total cost concepts as follows:

$$TC = TFC + TVC.$$

Divide each total cost term by the quantity produced, *Q*, to give

$$\frac{TC}{Q} = \frac{TFC}{Q} + \frac{TVC}{Q}.$$

or

$$ATC = AFC + AVC$$

Table 14.3 shows these average costs. For example, when output is 6 gallons an hour, *AFC* is ($20 ÷ 6), which equals $3.33; *AVC* is ($36 ÷ 6), which equals $6.00; and *ATC* is ($56 ÷ 6), which equals $9.33. Note that *ATC* ($9.33) equals *AFC* ($3.33) plus *AVC* ($6.00).

Average fixed cost
Total fixed cost per unit of output.

Average variable cost
Total variable cost per unit of output.

Average total cost
Total cost per unit of output, which equals average fixed cost plus average variable cost.

■ **TABLE 14.3**

Sam's Smoothies' Marginal Cost and Average Cost

Output (gallons per hour)	Total cost (dollars per hour)	Marginal cost (dollars per gallon)	Average fixed cost	Average variable cost	Average total cost
				(dollars per gallon)	
0	20.00		–	–	–
		12.00			
1	32.00		20.00	12.00	32.00
		7.20			
2	39.20		10.00	9.60	19.60
		4.80			
3	44.00		6.67	8.00	14.67
		4.20			
4	48.20		5.00	7.05	12.05
		3.60			
5	51.80		4.00	6.36	10.36
		4.20			
6	56.00		3.33	6.00	9.33
		4.80			
7	60.80		2.86	5.83	8.69
		7.20			
8	68.00		2.50	6.00	8.50
		12.00			
9	80.00		2.22	6.67	8.89

To produce 6 gallons of smoothies an hour, Sam's total cost is $56. Table 14.2 shows that this total cost is the sum of total fixed cost ($20) and total variable cost ($36).

Marginal cost is the increase in total cost that results from a one-unit increase in output. When Sam's increases output from 5 gallons to 6 gallons an hour, total cost increases from $51.80 to $56.00, an increase of $4.20 a gallon. The marginal cost of the sixth gallon an hour is $4.20. Marginal cost is located midway between the total costs to emphasize that it is the result of *changing* output.

When Sam's produces 6 gallons an hour, average fixed cost ($20 ÷ 6 gallons) is $3.33 a gallon; average variable cost ($36 ÷ 6 gallons) is $6.00 a gallon; average total cost ($56 ÷ 6 gallons) is $9.33 a gallon.

Figure 14.6 graphs the marginal cost and average cost data in Table 14.3. The red marginal cost curve (*MC*) is U-shaped because of the way in which marginal product changes. Recall that when Samantha hires a second or a third worker, marginal product increases and output increases to 6 gallons an hour (Figure 14.3 on p. 355). Over this output range, marginal cost decreases as output increases. When Samantha hires a fourth or a fifth worker, marginal product decreases but output increases up to 9 gallons an hour (Figure 14.3). Over this output range, marginal cost increases as output increases.

The green average fixed cost curve (*AFC*) slopes downward. As output increases, the same constant total fixed cost is spread over a larger output. The blue average total cost curve (*ATC*) and the purple average variable cost curve (*AVC*) are U-shaped. The vertical distance between the average total cost and average variable cost curves is equal to average fixed cost—as indicated by the two arrows. That distance shrinks as output increases because average fixed cost decreases with increasing output.

The marginal cost curve intersects the average variable cost curve and the average total cost curve at their minimum points. That is, when marginal cost is less than average cost, average cost is decreasing; and when marginal cost exceeds average cost, average cost is increasing. This relationship holds for both the *ATC* curve and the *AVC* curve and is another example of the relationship you saw in Figure 14.4 for average product and marginal product.

FIGURE 14.6

Average Cost Curves and Marginal Cost Curve at Sam's Smoothies   MyEconLab Animation

Average fixed cost decreases as output increases. The average fixed cost curve (*AFC*) slopes downward.

The average total cost curve (*ATC*) and average variable cost curve (*AVC*) are U-shaped. The vertical distance between these two curves is equal to average fixed cost, as illustrated by the two arrows.

Marginal cost is the change in total cost when output increases by one unit. The marginal cost curve (*MC*) is U-shaped and intersects the average variable cost curve (*AVC*) and the average total cost curve (*ATC*) at their minimum points.

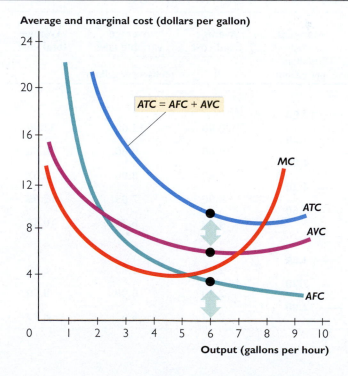

■ Why the Average Total Cost Curve Is U-Shaped

MyEconLab Concept Video

Average total cost, *ATC*, is the sum of average fixed cost, *AFC*, and average variable cost, *AVC*. So the shape of the *ATC* curve combines the shapes of the *AFC* and *AVC* curves. The U shape of the average total cost curve arises from the influence of two opposing forces:

- Spreading total fixed cost over a larger output
- Decreasing marginal returns

When output increases, the firm spreads its total fixed costs over a larger output and its average fixed cost decreases—its average fixed cost curve slopes downward.

Decreasing marginal returns means that as output increases, ever larger amounts of labor are needed to produce an additional unit of output. So average variable cost eventually increases, and the *AVC* curve eventually slopes upward.

The shape of the average total cost curve combines these two effects. Initially, as output increases, both average fixed cost and average variable cost decrease, so average total cost decreases and the *ATC* curve slopes downward. But as output increases further and decreasing marginal returns sets in, average variable cost begins to increase. Eventually, average variable cost increases more quickly than average fixed cost decreases, so average total cost increases and the *ATC* curve slopes upward.

All the short-run cost concepts that you've met are summarized in Table 14.4.

■ **TABLE 14.4**

A Compact Glossary of Costs

Term	Symbol	Definition	Equation
Fixed cost		The cost of a fixed factor of production that is independent of the quantity produced	
Variable cost		The cost of a variable factor of production that varies with the quantity produced	
Total fixed cost	*TFC*	Cost of the fixed factors of production	
Total variable cost	*TVC*	Cost of the variable factor of production	
Total cost	*TC*	Cost of all factors of production	$TC = TFC + TVC$
Marginal cost	*MC*	Change in total cost resulting from a one-unit increase in output (*Q*)	$MC = \Delta TC \div \Delta Q^*$
Average fixed cost	*AFC*	Total fixed cost per unit of output	$AFC = TFC \div Q$
Average variable cost	*AVC*	Total variable cost per unit of output	$AVC = TVC \div Q$
Average total cost	*ATC*	Total cost per unit of output	$ATC = AFC + AVC$

*In this equation, the Greek letter delta (Δ) stands for "change in."

■ Cost Curves and Product Curves

A firm's cost curves and product curves are linked, and Figure 14.7 shows how. The upper graph shows the average product curve, *AP*, and the marginal product curve, *MP*. The lower graph shows the average variable cost curve, *AVC*, and the marginal cost curve, *MC*.

As labor increases up to 2.5 workers a day (upper graph), output increases to 4 units a day (lower graph). Marginal product and average product rise and marginal cost and average variable cost fall. At the point of maximum marginal product, marginal cost is at a minimum.

As labor increases to 3.5 workers a day (upper graph), output increases to 7 units a day (lower graph). Marginal product falls and marginal cost rises, but average product continues to rise and average variable cost continues to fall. At the point of maximum average product, average variable cost is at a minimum. As labor increases further, output increases. Average product diminishes and average variable cost increases.

■ Shifts in the Cost Curves

The position of a firm's short-run cost curves, in Figures 14.5 and 14.6, depends on two factors:

- Technology
- Prices of factors of production

Technology

A technological change that increases productivity shifts the total product curve upward. It also shifts the marginal product curve and the average product curve upward. With a better technology that increases productivity, the same factors of production can produce more output, so an advance in technology lowers the average and marginal costs and shifts the short-run cost curves downward.

For example, advances in robotic technology have increased productivity in the automobile industry. As a result, the product curves of Chrysler, Ford, and GM have shifted upward, and their average and marginal cost curves have shifted downward. But the relationships between their product curves and cost curves have not changed. The curves are still linked, as in Figure 14.7.

Often a technological advance results in a firm using more capital, a fixed factor of production, and less labor, a variable factor of production. For example, today telephone companies use computers to connect long-distance calls instead of the human operators they used in the 1980s. When a telephone company makes this change, total variable cost decreases and total cost decreases, but total fixed cost increases. This change in the mix of fixed cost and variable cost means that at small output levels, average total cost might increase, but at large output levels, average total cost decreases.

Prices of Factors of Production

An increase in the price of a factor of production increases costs and shifts the cost curves. But how the curves shift depends on which resource price changes. An increase in rent or some other component of *fixed* cost shifts the fixed cost curves (*TFC* and *AFC*) upward and shifts the total cost curve (*TC*) upward but leaves the variable cost curves (*AVC* and *TVC*) and the marginal cost curve (*MC*) unchanged.

FIGURE 14.7

Product Curves and Cost Curves

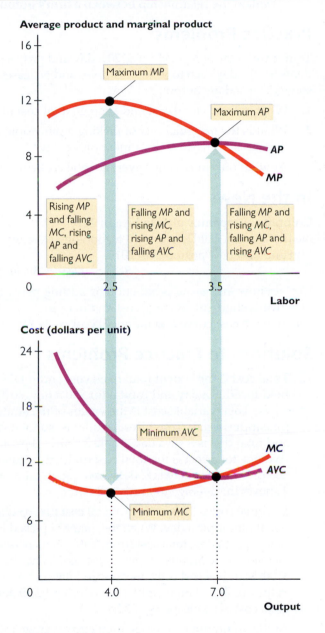

Average product and marginal product

Maximum MP

Maximum AP

AP

MP

Rising MP and falling MC, rising AP and falling AVC

Falling MP and rising MC, rising AP and falling AVC

Falling MP and rising MC, falling AP and rising AVC

Labor

Cost (dollars per unit)

Minimum AVC

MC

AVC

Minimum MC

Output

A firm's *MC* curve is linked to its *MP* curve. If, as the firm hires more labor up to 2.5 workers a day, the firm's marginal product rises, its marginal cost falls. If marginal product is at a maximum, marginal cost is at a minimum. If, as the firm hires more labor, its marginal product diminishes, its marginal cost rises.

A firm's *AVC* curve is linked to its *AP* curve. If, as the firm hires more labor up to 3.5 workers a day, its average product rises, its average variable cost falls. If average product is at a maximum, average variable cost is at a minimum. If as the firm hires more labor its average product diminishes, its average variable cost rises.

An increase in wage rates or some other component of *variable* cost shifts the variable cost curves (*TVC* and *AVC*) and the marginal cost curve (*MC*) upward but leaves the fixed cost curves (*AFC* and *TFC*) unchanged. So, for example, if the interest expense paid by a trucking company increases, the fixed cost of transportation services increases, but if the wage rate paid to truck drivers increases, the variable cost and marginal cost of transportation services increase.

MyEconLab Study Plan 14.3
Key Terms Quiz
Solutions Video

■ # CHECKPOINT 14.3

Explain the relationship between a firm's output and costs in the short run.

Practice Problems

Tom leases a farmer's field for $120 a day and grows pineapples. He pays students $100 a day each to pick pineapples and he leases capital at $80 a day. Table 1 shows Tom's daily output.

1. What is Tom's total cost and average total cost of 300 pineapples a day?

2. What is the marginal cost of picking a pineapple when the quantity increases from 360 to 400 pineapples a day?

3. At what output is Tom's average total cost a minimum?

In the News

Colorado companies plan to hire in 2016
Nearly a quarter of Denver-area technology executives plan to increase production and add new positions in 2016.

Source: *Denver Business Journal*, December 21, 2015

Explain how increasing production by adding new positions changes a Denver-area firm's short-run average cost and marginal cost. How will the firm's short-run average cost curve and marginal cost curve change if the wage rate rises?

Solutions to Practice Problems

1. Total cost is the sum of total fixed cost and total variable cost. Tom leases the field for $120 a day and capital for $80 a day, so Tom's total fixed cost is $200 a day. Total variable cost is the wages of the students. To produce 300 pineapples a day, Tom hires 3 students, so total variable cost is $300 a day and total cost is $500 a day. Table 2 shows the total cost (*TC*) schedule. Average total cost is the total cost divided by total product. The total cost of 300 pineapples a day is $500, so average total cost is $1.67 a pineapple. Table 2 shows the average total cost schedule.

2. Marginal cost is the increase in total cost that results from picking one additional pineapple a day. When the quantity picked increases from 360 to 400 pineapples a day, total cost (from Table 2) increases from $600 to $700. The increase in the number of pineapples is 40, and the increase in total cost is $100. Marginal cost is the increase in total cost ($100) divided by the increase in the number of pineapples (40), which is $2.50 per pineapple. So the marginal cost of a pineapple is $2.50.

3. At the minimum of average total cost, average total cost equals marginal cost. Minimum average total cost of a pineapple between 300 and 360 pineapples is $1.67. Table 2 shows that the marginal cost of increasing output from 300 to 360 pineapples a day is $1.67 a pineapple.

Solution to In the News

An increase in output and employment increases the firm's short-run average cost and marginal cost as the firm moves along its *ATC* and *MC* curves. If the wage rate rises, average cost and marginal cost increase at *all* output levels and the *MC*, *AVC*, and *ATC* curves shift upward.

TABLE 1

Labor (students)	Output (pineapples per day)
0	0
1	100
2	220
3	300
4	360
5	400
6	420
7	430

TABLE 2

Labor	TP	TC	MC	ATC
0	0	200		–
			1.00	
1	100	300		3.00
			0.83	
2	220	400		1.82
			1.25	
3	300	500		1.67
			1.67	
4	360	600		1.67
			2.50	
5	400	700		1.75
			5.00	
6	420	800		1.90
			10.00	
7	430	900		2.09

14.4 LONG-RUN COST

In the long run, a firm can vary both the quantity of labor and the quantity of capital. A small firm, such as Sam's Smoothies, can increase its plant size by moving into a larger building and installing more machines. A big firm such as General Motors can decrease its plant size by closing down some production lines.

We are now going to see how costs vary in the long run when a firm varies its plant—the quantity of capital it uses—along with the quantity of labor it uses.

The first thing that happens is that the distinction between fixed cost and variable cost disappears. All costs are variable in the long run.

■ Plant Size and Cost

When a firm changes its plant size, its cost of producing a given output changes. In Table 14.3 on p. 361 and Figure 14.6 on p. 362, the lowest average total cost that Samantha can achieve is $8.50 a gallon, which occurs when she produces 8 gallons of smoothies an hour. Samantha wonders what would happen to her average total cost if she increased the size of her plant by renting a bigger building and installing a larger number of blenders and refrigerators. Will the average total cost of producing a gallon of smoothies fall, rise, or remain the same?

Each of these three outcomes is possible, and they arise because when a firm changes the size of its plant, it might experience

- Economies of scale
- Diseconomies of scale
- Constant returns to scale

Economies of Scale

Economies of scale are features of a firm's technology that make average total cost *fall* as the output rate increases. The main source of economies of scale is greater specialization of both labor and capital.

Specialization of Labor If Ford produced 100 cars a week, each production line worker would have to perform many different tasks. But if Ford produces 10,000 cars a week, each worker can specialize in a small number of tasks and become highly proficient at them. The result is that the average product of labor increases and the average total cost of producing a car falls.

Specialization also occurs off the production line. For example, a small firm usually does not have a specialist sales manager, personnel manager, and production manager. One person covers all these activities. But when a firm is large enough, specialists perform these activities. Average product increases, and the average total cost falls.

Specialization of Capital At a small output rate, firms often must employ general-purpose machines and tools. For example, with an output of a few gallons an hour, Sam's Smoothies uses regular blenders like the one in your kitchen. But if Sam's produces hundreds of gallons an hour, it uses commercial blenders that fill, empty, and clean themselves. The result is that the output rate is larger and the average total cost of producing a gallon of smoothies is lower.

Economies of scale
Features of a firm's technology that make average total cost *fall* as output increases.

Specialization of both labor and capital on an auto-assembly line.

Diseconomies of scale
Features of a firm's technology that make average total cost *rise* as output increases.

Diseconomies of Scale

Diseconomies of scale are features of a firm's technology that make average total cost *rise* as output increases. Diseconomies of scale arise from the difficulty of coordinating and controlling a large enterprise. The larger the firm, the greater is the cost of communicating both up and down the management hierarchy and among managers. Eventually, management complexity brings rising average total cost. Diseconomies of scale occur in all production processes but in some perhaps only at a very large output rate.

Constant Returns to Scale

Constant returns to scale Features of a firm's technology that keep average total cost constant as output increases.

Constant returns to scale are features of a firm's technology that keep average total cost *constant* as output increases. Constant returns to scale occur when a firm is able to replicate its existing production facility including its management system. For example, Ford might double its production of Fusion cars by doubling its production facility for those cars. It can build an identical production line and hire an identical number of workers. With the two identical production lines, Ford produces exactly twice as many cars. The average total cost of producing a Fusion is identical in the two plants. Ford's average total cost remains constant as it increases production.

■ The Long-Run Average Cost Curve

Long-run average cost curve
A curve that shows the lowest average total cost at which it is possible to produce each output when the firm has had sufficient time to change both its plant size and labor employed.

The **long-run average cost curve** shows the lowest average total cost at which it is possible to produce each output when the firm has had sufficient time to change both its plant size and its labor force.

Figure 14.8 shows Sam's Smoothies' long-run average cost curve *LRAC*. This long-run average cost curve is derived from the short-run average total cost curves for different possible plant sizes.

With its current small plant, Sam's Smoothies operates on the average total cost curve ATC_1 in Figure 14.8. The other three average total cost curves are for

---

■ **FIGURE 14.8**

Long-Run Average Cost Curve

MyEconLab Animation

In the long run, Samantha can vary both the plant size and the quantity of labor she employs. The long-run average cost curve traces the lowest attainable average total cost of producing each output. The dark blue curve is the long-run average cost curve *LRAC*.

Sam's experiences economies of scale as output increases up to 14 gallons an hour, constant returns to scale for outputs between 14 gallons and 19 gallons an hour, and diseconomies of scale for outputs that exceed 19 gallons an hour.

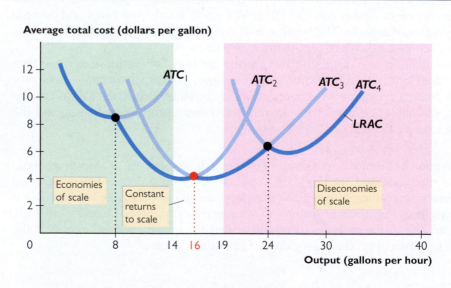

successively bigger plants. In this example, for outputs up to 8 gallons an hour, the existing plant with average total cost curve ATC_1 produces smoothies at the lowest attainable average cost. For outputs between 8 and 16 gallons an hour, average total cost is lowest on ATC_2. For outputs between 16 and 24 gallons an hour, average total cost is lowest on ATC_3. And for outputs in excess of 24 gallons an hour, average total cost is lowest on ATC_4.

The segment of each of the four average total cost curves for which that plant has the lowest average total cost is highlighted in dark blue in Figure 14.8. The scallop-shaped curve made up of these four segments is Sam's Smoothies' long-run average cost curve.

Economies and Diseconomies of Scale

When economies of scale are present, the *LRAC* curve slopes downward. The *LRAC* curve in Figure 14.8 shows that Sam's Smoothies experiences economies of scale for output rates up to 14 gallons an hour. At output rates between 14 and 19 gallons an hour, the firm experiences constant returns to scale. And at output rates that exceed 19 gallons an hour, the firm experiences diseconomies of scale.

EYE on RETAILERS' COSTS   MyEconLab Critical Thinking Exercise

Which Store Has the Lower Costs: Walmart or 7-Eleven?

Walmart's "small" supercenters measure 99,000 square feet and serve an average of 30,000 customers a week. The average 7-Eleven store, most of which today are attached to gas stations, measures 2,000 square feet and serves 5,000 customers a week.

Which retailing technology has the lower operating cost? The answer depends on the scale of operation.

At a small number of customers per week, it costs less per customer to operate a store of 2,000 square feet than one of 99,000 square feet.

In the figure, the average total cost curve of operating a 7-Eleven store of 2,000 square feet is $ATC_{7\text{-}Eleven}$ and the average total cost curve of a store of 99,000 square feet is $ATC_{Walmart}$. The dark blue curve is a retailer's long-run average cost curve *LRAC*.

If the number of customers is Q a week, the average total cost per transaction is the same for both stores.

For a store that serves more than Q customers a week, the least-cost

method is the big store.

For fewer than Q customers a week, the least-cost method is the small store. The least-cost store is not always the biggest store.

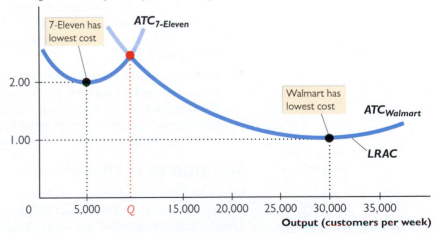

CHECKPOINT 14.4

Derive and explain a firm's long-run average cost curve.

Practice Problems

To grow pineapples, Tom leases 1 field for $120 a day and capital for $80 a day and hires students at $100 a day each. Suppose that Tom now leases 2 fields for $240 a day and twice as much capital for $160 a day. Table 1 shows his outputs.

1. What is Tom's average total cost of a pinapple when he farms 2 fields and produces 220 pineapples a day?

2. Make a graph of Tom's average total cost curves using 1 field and 2 fields. Show on the graph Tom's long-run average cost curve. Over what output range will Tom use 1 field? 2 fields?

3. Does Tom experience constant returns to scale, economies of scale, or diseconomies of scale?

In the News

Hiring spree at Tesla Motors

Bay Area-based electric car maker Tesla is looking to hire 1,648 workers to expand its model lineup, build a battery factory, and develop self-driving cars.

Source: *CBS San Francisco*, December 8, 2015

Explain the effects of the expansion plan on Tesla's total fixed cost, total variable cost, short-run *ATC* curve, and *LRAC* curve.

Solutions to Practice Problems

1. Total cost equals fixed cost ($400 a day) plus $100 a day for each student. Tom can produce 220 pineapples with 2 fields and 1 student, so total cost is $500 a day. Average total cost is the total cost divided by output, which at 220 pineapples a day is $500 divided by 220, or $2.27. The "*ATC* (2 fields)" column of Table 2 shows Tom's average total cost schedule for 2 fields.

2. Figure 1 shows Tom's average total cost curve using 1 field as ATC_1. This curve graphs the data on *ATC* (1 field) and *TP* (1 field) in Table 2, which was calculated in Table 2 on p. 366. Using 2 fields, the average total cost curve is ATC_2. Tom's long-run average cost curve is the lower segments of the two *ATC* curves, highlighted in Figure 1. If Tom produces up to 300 pineapples a day, he will use 1 field. If he produces more than 300 pineapples a day, he will use 2 fields.

3. Tom experiences economies of scale up to an output of 740 pineapples a day because as he increases his plant and produces up to 740 pineapples a day, the average total cost of picking a pineapple decreases. (We don't have enough information to know what happens to Tom's average total cost if he uses three fields and three units of capital.)

Solution to In the News

Expanding the model lineup, building a battery factory, and developing a self-driving car will raise Tesla's total fixed cost; hiring 1,648 workers will raise Tesla's total variable cost. As Tesla increases output, it will move along its *ATC* curve. With a larger capacity, Tesla will move rightward along its *LRAC* curve.

TABLE 1

Labor (students per day)	Output 1 field	Output 2 fields
	(pineapples per day)	
0	0	0
1	100	220
2	220	460
3	300	620
4	360	740
5	400	820
6	420	860
7	430	880

TABLE 2

TP (1 field)	ATC (1 field)	TP (2 fields)	ATC (2 fields)
100	3.00	220	2.27
220	1.82	460	1.30
300	1.67	620	1.13
360	1.67	740	1.08
400	1.75	820	1.10
420	1.90	860	1.16
430	2.09	880	1.25

FIGURE 1

Average total cost (dollars per pineapple)

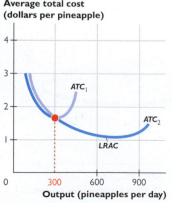

CHAPTER SUMMARY

Key Points

1. Explain and distinguish between the economic and accounting measures of a firm's cost of production and profit.

- Firms seek to maximize economic profit, which is total revenue minus total cost.
- Total cost equals opportunity cost—the sum of explicit costs and implicit costs, which include normal profit.

2. Explain the relationship between a firm's output and labor employed in the short run.

- In the short run, the firm can change the output it produces by changing only the quantity of labor it employs.
- A total product curve shows the limits to the output that the firm can produce with a given quantity of capital and different quantities of labor.
- As the quantity of labor increases, the marginal product of labor increases initially but eventually decreases—the law of decreasing returns.

3. Explain the relationship between a firm's output and costs in the short run.

- As total product increases, total fixed cost is constant, and total variable cost and total cost increase.
- As total product increases, average fixed cost decreases; average variable cost, average total cost, and marginal cost decrease at small outputs and increase at large outputs so their curves are U-shaped.

4. Derive and explain a firm's long-run average cost curve.

- In the long run, the firm can change the size of its plant.
- Long-run cost is the cost of production when all inputs have been adjusted to produce at the lowest attainable cost.
- The long-run average cost curve traces out the lowest attainable average total cost at each output when both the plant size and labor can be varied.
- The long-run average cost curve slopes downward with economies of scale and upward with diseconomies of scale.

Key Terms

MyEconLab Key Terms Quiz

Average fixed cost, 361
Average product, 356
Average total cost, 361
Average variable cost, 361
Constant returns to scale, 368
Decreasing marginal returns, 354
Diseconomies of scale, 368
Economic depreciation, 349

Economic profit, 349
Economies of scale, 367
Explicit cost, 349
Implicit cost, 349
Increasing marginal returns, 354
Law of decreasing returns, 356
Long run, 352
Long-run average cost curve, 368

Marginal cost, 360
Marginal product, 354
Normal profit, 349
Short run, 352
Total cost, 359
Total fixed cost, 359
Total product, 353
Total variable cost, 359

CHAPTER CHECKPOINT

Study Plan Problems and Applications

1. Joe runs a shoe shine stand at the airport. Joe has no skills, no job experience, and no alternative job. Entrepreneurs in the shoe shine business earn $10,000 a year. Joe pays the rent of $2,000 a year, and his total revenue is $15,000 a year. He borrowed $1,000 at 20 percent a year to buy equipment. At the end of one year, Joe was offered $500 for his business and all its equipment. Calculate Joe's annual explicit costs, implicit costs, and economic profit.

2. Len's body board factory rents equipment for shaping boards and hires students. Table 1 sets out Len's total product schedule. Construct Len's marginal product and average product schedules. Over what range of workers do marginal returns increase?

Use the following information to work Problems **3** to **6**.

Len's body board factory pays $60 a day for equipment and $200 a day to each student it hires. Table 1 sets out Len's total product schedule.

3. Construct Len's total variable cost and total cost schedules. What does the difference between total cost and total variable cost at each output equal?

4. Construct the average fixed cost, average variable cost, and average total cost schedules and the marginal cost schedule.

5. At what output is Len's average total cost at a minimum? At what output is Len's average variable cost at a minimum?

6. Explain why the output at which average variable cost is at a minimum is smaller than the output at which average total cost is at a minimum.

7. Table 2 shows the costs incurred at Pete's peanut farm. Complete the table.

TABLE 1

Labor (workers per day)	Total product (body boards per day)
0	0
1	20
2	44
3	60
4	72

TABLE 2

Labor	TP	TVC	TC	AFC	AVC	ATC	MC
0	0	0	100				
1	10	35					
2	24	70					
3	38	105					
4	44	140					

8. **Gap to close 175 stores in North America**
   Gap announced that it will close 175 (nearly 26 percent) of its North American stores. It will terminate an unknown number of workers and cut 250 headquarters jobs.

   Source: *The Washington Post*, June 15, 2015

   Thinking of a Gap store as a unit of capital, explain why Gap is reducing the number of stores and workers. Is Gap making a long-run decision or a short-run decision? Is Gap taking advantage of economies of scale?

 9. Read *Eye on Retailers' Costs* on p. 369 and draw a graph to show how the retailers' cost curves would change if they introduced cost-saving self-checkouts.

Instructor Assignable Problems and Applications

MyEconLab Homework, Quiz, or
Test if assigned by instructor

1. If the *ATC* curves of a Walmart store and a 7-Eleven are like those in *Eye on Retailers' Costs* on p. 369, and if each type of store operates at its minimum *ATC*, which store has the lower total cost? How can you be sure? Which has the lower marginal cost? How can you be sure? Sketch each firm's marginal cost curve.

2. Sonya used to earn $25,000 a year selling real estate, but she now sells greeting cards. The return to entrepreneurship in the greeting cards industry is $14,000 a year. Over the year, Sonya bought $10,000 worth of cards from manufacturers and sold them for $58,000. Sonya rents a shop for $5,000 a year and spends $1,000 on utilities and office expenses. Sonya owns a cash register, which she bought for $2,000 with funds from her savings account. Her bank pays 3 percent a year on savings accounts. At the end of the year, Sonya was offered $1,600 for her cash register.
Calculate Sonya's explicit costs, implicit costs, and economic profit for the year.

Use the following information to work Problems **3** to **5**.

Yolanda runs a bullfrog farm. When she employs 1 person, she produces 1,000 bullfrogs a week. When she hires a second worker, her total product doubles. Her total product doubles again when she hires a third worker. When she hires a fourth worker, her total product increases but by only 1,000 bullfrogs. Yolanda pays $1,000 a week for equipment and $500 a week to each worker she hires.

3. Construct Yolanda's marginal product and average product schedules. Over what range of workers does Yolanda's experience increasing marginal returns?

4. Construct Yolanda's total variable cost and total cost schedules. Calculate Yolanda's total fixed cost.

5. At what output is Yolanda's average total cost at a minimum?

6. Table 1 shows some of the costs incurred at Bill's Bakery. Calculate the values of *A, B, C, D*, and *E*. Show your work.

TABLE 1

Labor	TP	TVC	TC	AFC	AVC	ATC	MC
1	100	350	850	*C*	3.50	*D*	
							2.50
2	240	700	*B*	2.08	2.92	5.00	
							E
3	380	*A*	1,550	1.32	2.76	4.08	
							5.83
4	440	1,400	1,900	1.14	3.18	4.32	
							11.67
5	470	1,750	2,250	1.06	3.72	4.79	

7. **Solar and wind got so cheap, so fast**
Solar panels and wind turbines are more efficient than they used to be and they cost less to produce.
Source: *The Atlantic*, December 2, 2015

Explain how the facts reported in the news clip affect the short-run and long-run average total cost of producing electricity. How do the facts affect the marginal cost of producing electricity?

MyEconLab Chapter 14 Study Plan ## Multiple Choice Quiz

1. A firm's cost of production equals _____.
   A. all the costs paid with money, called explicit costs
   B. the implicit costs of using all the firm's own resources
   C. all explicit costs and implicit costs, excluding normal profit
   D. the costs of all resources used by the firm whether bought in the market-place or owned by the firm

2. The average product of labor increases as output increases if _____.
   A. marginal product exceeds average product
   B. average product exceeds marginal product
   C. total product increases
   D. marginal product increases

3. Marginal returns start to decrease when more and more workers _____.
   A. have to share the same equipment and workspace
   B. produce less and less total output
   C. require jobs to be too specialized
   D. produce less and less average product

4. Average variable cost is at a minimum when _____.
   A. marginal cost equals average variable cost
   B. average total cost is at a minimum
   C. marginal cost exceeds average fixed cost
   D. average total cost exceeds average variable cost

5. An increase in the rent that a firm pays for its factory does not increase _____.
   A. total cost
   B. fixed cost
   C. marginal cost
   D. average fixed cost

6. An increase in the wage rate _____.
   A. shifts the average total cost curve and the marginal cost curve upward
   B. shifts the average fixed cost and average variable cost curve upward
   C. increases average variable cost but does not change marginal cost
   D. does not change average variable cost but increases average total cost

7. When average variable cost is at its minimum level, marginal product _____.
   A. equals average product
   B. exceeds average product
   C. is less than average product
   D. is at its maximum level

8. In the long run, with an increase in the plant size, _____.
   A. the short-run average total cost curve shifts downward
   B. the long-run average cost curve slopes downward
   C. the short-run average total cost curve shifts downward if economies of scale exist
   D. the average total cost of production rises

Where have all the record stores gone?

Perfect Competition

15

When you have completed your study of this chapter, you will be able to

1 Explain a perfectly competitive firm's profit-maximizing choices and derive its supply curve.

2 Explain how output, price, and profit are determined in the short run.

3 Explain how output, price, and profit are determined in the long run and explain why perfect competition is efficient.

MyEconLab Big Picture Video

375

MyEconLab Concept Video

MARKET TYPES

The four market types are

- Perfect competition
- Monopoly
- Monopolistic competition
- Oligopoly

■ Perfect Competition

Perfect competition
A market in which there are many firms, each selling an identical product; many buyers; no barriers to the entry of new firms into the industry; no advantage to established firms; and buyers and sellers are well informed about prices.

Perfect competition exists when

- Many firms sell an identical product to many buyers.
- There are no barriers to entry into (or exit from) the market.
- Established firms have no advantage over new firms.
- Sellers and buyers are well informed about prices.

These conditions that define perfect competition arise when the market demand for the product is large relative to the output of a single producer. This situation arises when economies of scale are absent so the efficient scale of each firm is small. But a large market and the absence of economies of scale are not sufficient to create perfect competition. In addition, each firm must produce a good or service that has no characteristics that are unique to that firm so that consumers don't care from which firm they buy. Firms in perfect competition all look the same to the buyer.

Wheat farming, fishing, wood pulping and paper milling, the manufacture of paper cups and plastic shopping bags, lawn service, dry cleaning, and the provision of laundry services are all examples of highly competitive industries.

■ Other Market Types

Monopoly
A market in which one firm sells a good or service that has no close substitutes and a barrier blocks the entry of new firms.

Monopoly arises when one firm sells a good or service that has no close substitutes and a barrier blocks the entry of new firms. In some places, the phone, gas, electricity, and water suppliers are local monopolies—monopolies that are restricted to a given location. For many years, a global firm called DeBeers had a near international monopoly in diamonds. Microsoft has a near monopoly in producing the operating system for a personal computer.

Monopolistic competition
A market in which a large number of firms compete by making similar but slightly different products.

Monopolistic competition arises when a large number of firms compete by making similar but slightly different products. Each firm is the sole producer of the particular version of the good in question. For example, in the market for running shoes, Nike, Reebok, Fila, Asics, New Balance, and many others make their own versions of the perfect shoe. The term "monopolistic competition" reminds us that each firm has a monopoly on a particular brand of shoe but the firms compete with each other.

Oligopoly
A market in which a small number of interdependent firms compete.

Oligopoly arises when a small number of *interdependent* firms compete. Airplane manufacture is an example of oligopoly. Oligopolies might produce almost identical products, such as Duracell and Energizer batteries; or they might produce differentiated products, such as the colas produced by Coke and Pepsi.

We study perfect competition in this chapter, monopoly in Chapter 16, monopolistic competition in Chapter 17, and oligopoly in Chapter 18.

15.1 A FIRM'S PROFIT-MAXIMIZING CHOICES

MyEconLab Concept Video

A firm's objective is to maximize its *economic profit*, which is equal to *total revenue* minus the *total cost* of production. *Normal profit*, the return that the firm's entrepreneur can obtain on average, is part of the firm's cost.

In the short run, a firm achieves its objective by deciding the quantity to produce. This quantity influences the firm's total revenue, total cost, and economic profit. In the long run, a firm achieves its objective by deciding whether to enter or exit a market.

These are the key decisions that a firm in perfect competition makes. Such a firm does *not* choose the price at which to sell its output. The firm in perfect competition is a **price taker**—it cannot influence the price of its product.

■ Price Taker

To see why a firm in perfect competition is a price taker, imagine that you are a wheat farmer in Kansas. You have a thousand acres under cultivation—which sounds like a lot. But then you go on a drive through Colorado, Oklahoma, Texas, and back up to Nebraska and the Dakotas. You find unbroken stretches of wheat covering millions of acres. And you know that there are similar vistas in Canada, Argentina, Australia, and Ukraine. Your thousand acres are a drop in the ocean. Nothing makes your wheat any better than any other farmer's, and all the buyers of wheat know the price they must pay. If the going price of wheat is $4 a bushel, you are stuck with that price. You can't get a higher price than $4, and you have no incentive to offer it for less than $4 because you can sell your entire output at that price.

The producers of most agricultural products are price takers. We'll illustrate perfect competition with another agriculture example: the market for maple syrup. The next time you pour syrup on your pancakes, think about the competitive market that gets this product from the sap of the maple tree to your table!

Dave's Maple Syrup is one of more than 11,000 similar firms in the maple syrup market of North America. Dave is a price taker. Like the Kansas wheat farmer, he can sell any quantity he chooses at the going price but none above that price. Dave faces a *perfectly elastic* demand. The demand for Dave's syrup is perfectly elastic because syrup from Don Harlow, Casper Sugar Shack, and all the other maple farms in North America are *perfect substitutes* for Dave's syrup.

We'll explore Dave's decisions and their implications for the way a competitive market works. We begin by defining some revenue concepts.

■ Revenue Concepts

In perfect competition, market demand and market supply determine the price. A firm's *total revenue* equals this given price multiplied by the quantity sold. A firm's **marginal revenue** is the change in total revenue that results from a one-unit increase in the quantity sold.

In perfect competition, marginal revenue equals price.

The reason is that the firm can sell any quantity it chooses at the going market price. So if the firm sells one more unit, it sells it for the market price and total revenue increases by that amount. This increase in total revenue is marginal revenue.

The table in Figure 15.1 illustrates the equality of marginal revenue and price. The price of syrup is $8 a can. Total revenue is equal to the price multiplied by the

Price taker
A firm that cannot influence the price of the good or service that it produces.

Wheat farmers and maple syrup farmers are price takers.

Marginal revenue
The change in total revenue that results from a one-unit increase in the quantity sold.

quantity sold. So if Dave sells 10 cans, his total revenue is $8 × 10, which equals $80. If the quantity sold increases from 10 cans to 11 cans, total revenue increases from $80 to $88, so marginal revenue is $8 a can, the same as the price.

Figure 15.1 illustrates price determination and revenue in the perfectly competitive market. Market demand and market supply in part (a) determine the market price. Dave is a price taker, so he sells his syrup for the market price. The demand curve for Dave's syrup is the horizontal line at the market price in part (b). Because price equals marginal revenue, the demand curve for Dave's syrup is Dave's marginal revenue curve (*MR*). The total revenue curve (*TR*), in part (c), shows the total revenue at each quantity sold. Because he sells each can for the market price, the total revenue curve is an upward-sloping straight line.

■ Profit-Maximizing Output

As output increases, total revenue increases, but total cost also increases. Because of *decreasing marginal returns* (see Chapter 14, pp. 354–356), total cost eventually increases faster than total revenue. There is one output level that maximizes economic profit, and a perfectly competitive firm chooses this output level.

■ **FIGURE 15.1**

Demand, Price, and Revenue in Perfect Competition

MyEconLab Animation

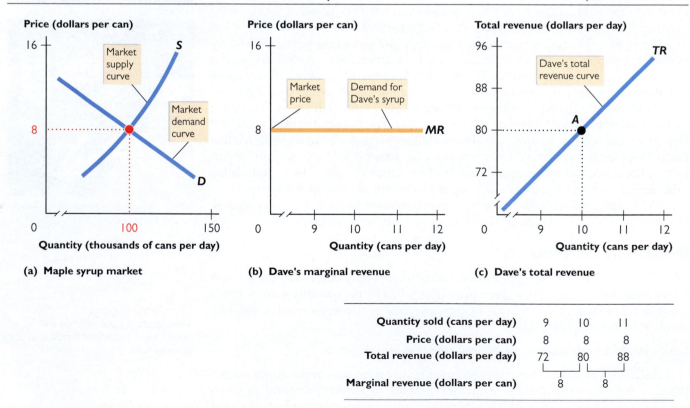

Quantity sold (cans per day)	9	10	11
Price (dollars per can)	8	8	8
Total revenue (dollars per day)	72	80	88
Marginal revenue (dollars per can)		8	8

Part (a) shows the market for maple syrup. The market price is $8 a can. The table calculates total revenue and marginal revenue.

Part (b) shows Dave's marginal revenue curve (*MR*), which is also the demand curve for Dave's syrup.

Part (c) shows Dave's total revenue curve (*TR*). Point *A* corresponds to the second column of the table.

One way to find the profit-maximizing output is to use a firm's total revenue and total cost curves. Profit is maximized at the output level at which total revenue exceeds total cost by the largest amount. Figure 15.2 shows how to do this for Dave's Maple Syrup.

The table lists Dave's total revenue, total cost, and economic profit at different output levels. Figure 15.2(a) shows the total revenue and total cost curves. These curves are graphs of the numbers shown in the first three columns of the table. The total revenue curve (TR) is the same as that in Figure 15.1(c). The total cost curve (TC) is similar to the one that you met in Chapter 14 (p. 360). Figure 15.2(b) is an economic profit curve.

Dave makes an economic profit on outputs between 4 and 13 cans of syrup a day. At outputs of fewer than 4 cans a day and more than 13 cans a day, he incurs an economic loss. Outputs of 4 cans and 13 cans of syrup a day are *break-even points*—points at which total cost equals total revenue and economic profit is zero.

The profit curve is at its highest when the vertical distance between the *TR* and *TC* curves is greatest. In this example, profit maximization occurs at an output of 10 cans of syrup a day. At this output, Dave's economic profit is $29 a day.

FIGURE 15.2

Total Revenue, Total Cost, and Economic Profit

MyEconLab Animation

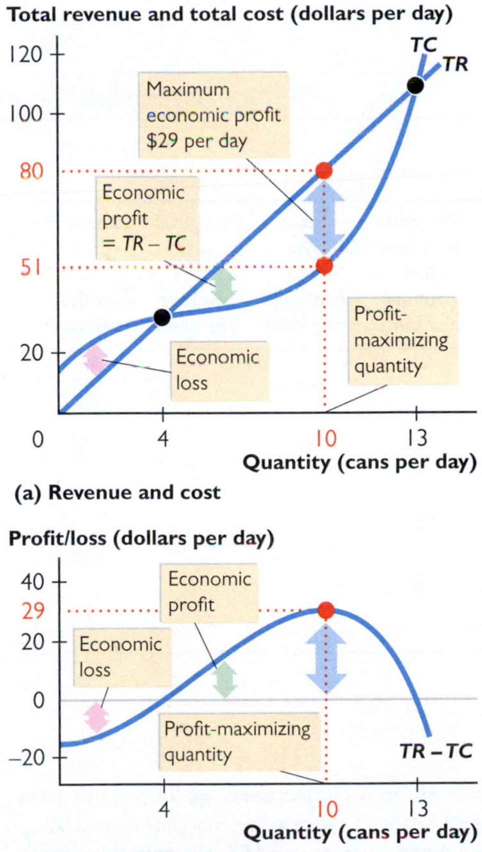

(a) Revenue and cost

(b) Economic profit and loss

Quantity (Q) (cans per day)	Total revenue (TR)	Total cost (TC)	Economic profit (TR – TC)
	(dollars per day)		
0	0	15	–15
1	8	22	–14
2	16	27	–11
3	24	30	–6
4	**32**	**32**	**0**
5	40	33	7
6	48	34	14
7	56	36	20
8	64	40	24
9	72	44	28
10	**80**	**51**	**29**
11	88	60	28
12	96	76	20
13	**104**	**104**	**0**
14	112	144	–32

The table calculates Dave's economic profit at each quantity of syrup produced.

In part (a), economic profit (total revenue minus total cost) is the vertical distance between the total revenue (TR) and total cost (TC) curves.

In part (b), economic profit is the height of the profit curve, TR – TC.

If Dave produces less than 4 cans of syrup a day, he incurs an economic loss.

If Dave produces between 4 and 13 cans of syrup a day, he makes an economic profit. Dave's maximum economic profit is $29 a day when he produces 10 cans of syrup a day.

■ Marginal Analysis and the Supply Decision

Another way to find the profit-maximizing output is to use *marginal analysis,* which compares marginal revenue, *MR*, with marginal cost, *MC*. As output increases, marginal revenue is constant but marginal cost eventually increases.

If marginal revenue exceeds marginal cost ($MR > MC$), then the revenue from selling one more unit exceeds the cost of producing that unit and an *increase* in output increases economic profit. If marginal revenue is less than marginal cost ($MR < MC$), then the revenue from selling one more unit is less than the cost of producing that unit and a *decrease* in output increases economic profit. If marginal revenue equals marginal cost ($MR = MC$), then the revenue from selling one more unit equals the cost incurred to produce that unit. Economic profit is maximized and either an increase or a decrease in output *decreases* economic profit. The rule ($MR = MC$) is a prime example of marginal analysis.

Figure 15.3 illustrates these propositions. If Dave increases output from 9 to 10 cans of syrup a day, marginal revenue ($8) exceeds marginal cost ($7), so by producing the 10th can economic profit increases. The last column of the table shows that economic profit increases from $28 to $29. The blue area in the figure shows the increase in economic profit when Dave produces the 10th can per day.

If Dave increases production from 10 to 11 cans of syrup a day, marginal revenue ($8) is less than marginal cost ($9), so by producing the 11th can, economic profit decreases. The last column of the table shows that economic profit decreases from $29 to $28. The red area in the figure shows the economic loss that arises when Dave increases production from 10 to 11 cans of syrup per day.

■ **FIGURE 15.3**

Profit-Maximizing Output

MyEconLab Animation

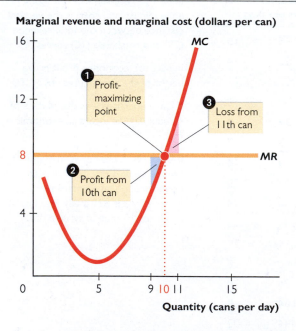

Quantity (Q) (cans per day)	Total revenue (TR) (dollars per day)	Marginal revenue (MR) (dollars per can)	Total cost (TC) (dollars per day)	Marginal cost (MC) (dollars per can)	Economic profit (TR – TC) (dollars per day)
8	64		40		24
		8		4	
9	72		44		28
		8		7	
10	80		51		29
		8		9	
11	88		60		28
		8		16	
12	96		76		20

❶ Profit is maximized when marginal revenue equals marginal cost at 10 cans of syrup a day. ❷ If Dave increases output from 9 to 10 cans of syrup a day, marginal cost is $7, which is less than the marginal revenue of $8, so profit increases. ❸ If Dave increases output from 10 to 11 cans of syrup a day, marginal cost is $9, which exceeds the marginal revenue of $8, so profit decreases.

Dave maximizes economic profit by producing 10 cans of syrup a day, the quantity at which marginal revenue equals marginal cost.

A firm's profit-maximizing output is its *quantity supplied*. Dave's *quantity supplied* at a price of $8 a can is 10 cans a day. If the price were higher than $8 a can, he would increase production. If the price were lower than $8 a can, he would decrease production. These profit-maximizing responses to different prices are the foundation of the law of supply:

Other things remaining the same, the higher the price of a good, the greater is the quantity supplied of that good.

■ Temporary Shutdown Decision

MyEconLab Concept Video

Sometimes, the price falls so low that a firm cannot cover its costs. What does the firm do in such a situation? The answer depends on whether the firm expects the low price to be permanent or temporary.

If a firm incurs an economic loss that it believes is permanent and sees no prospect of ending, the firm exits the market. We'll study this action later in this chapter when we look at the firm's decisions in the long run (pp. 390–393).

If a firm incurs an economic loss that it believes is temporary, it remains in the market, but it might temporarily shut down. To decide whether to produce or to shut down, the firm compares the loss it would incur in the two situations.

Loss When Shut Down

If the firm shuts down temporarily, it receives no revenue and incurs no variable costs. The firm still incurs fixed costs. So, if a firm shuts down, it incurs an economic loss equal to total fixed cost. This loss is the largest that a firm need incur.

Loss When Producing

A firm that produces an output receives revenue and incurs both fixed costs and variable costs. The firm incurs an economic loss equal to total fixed cost *plus* total variable cost *minus* total revenue. If total revenue exceeds total variable cost, the firm's economic loss is less than total fixed cost. But if total revenue is less than total variable cost, the firm's economic loss will exceed total fixed cost.

The Shutdown Point

If total revenue is less than total variable cost, a firm shuts down temporarily and limits its loss to an amount equal to total fixed cost. If total revenue just equals total variable cost, a firm is indifferent between producing and shutting down. This situation arises when price equals minimum average variable cost and the firm produces the quantity at which average variable cost is a minimum—called the **shutdown point**.

Figure 15.4 illustrates the firm's shutdown decision and the shutdown point that we've just described for Dave's maple syrup farm. Dave's average variable cost curve is *AVC* and his marginal cost curve is *MC*. Average variable cost has a minimum of $3 a can when output is 7 cans of syrup a day. The *MC* curve intersects the *AVC* curve at its minimum. (We explained this relationship between the marginal and average values of a variable in Chapter 14; see pp. 356–357 and pp. 360–362.) The figure shows the marginal revenue curve *MR* when the price is $3 a can, a *price equal to minimum average variable cost*.

Shutdown point
The point at which price equals minimum average variable cost and the quantity produced is that at which average variable cost is at its minimum.

■ **FIGURE 15.4**

The Shutdown Decision

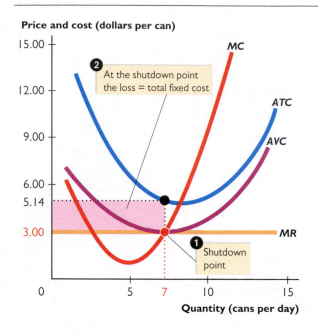

Quantity (Q) (cans per day)	Total revenue (TR)	Total variable cost (TVC)	Total fixed cost (TFC)	Total cost (TC)	Economic profit (TR – TC)
		(dollars per day)			
6	18	19	15	34	−16
7	21	21	15	36	−15
8	24	25	15	40	−16

❶ The shutdown point is at minimum average variable cost. At a price below minimum average variable cost, the firm shuts down and produces no output. At a price equal to minimum average variable cost, the firm is indifferent between shutting down and producing no output or producing the output at minimum average variable cost. Either way, ❷ the firm minimizes its economic loss and incurs a loss equal to total fixed cost.

If Dave produces at the shutdown point, he produces 7 cans of syrup a day and sells them for $3 a can. He incurs an economic loss equal to $2.14 a can and a total economic loss of $15 a day. Dave's loss equals total fixed cost. If Dave shuts down, he also incurs an economic loss equal to total fixed cost.

The table lists Dave's total revenue, total variable cost, total fixed cost, total cost, and economic profit at three output levels. The middle output, 7 cans of syrup a day, is that at which Dave's average variable cost is at its minimum—$3 a can. The numbers in the table show that when the price is $3 a can and Dave produces 7 cans of syrup a day, he incurs a loss, and that loss equals total fixed cost.

■ The Firm's Short-Run Supply Curve

A perfectly competitive firm's short-run supply curve shows how the firm's profit-maximizing output varies as the price varies, other things remaining the same. This supply curve is based on the marginal analysis and shutdown decision that we've just explored.

Figure 15.5 derives Dave's supply curve. Part (a) shows the marginal cost and average variable cost curves, and part (b) shows the supply curve. There is a direct link between the marginal cost and average variable cost curves and the firm's supply curve. Let's see what that link is.

In Figure 15.5(a), if the price is above minimum average variable cost, Dave maximizes profit by producing the output at which marginal cost equals marginal revenue, which also equals price. We determine the quantity produced at each price from the marginal cost curve. At a price of $8 a can, the marginal revenue curve is MR_1 and Dave maximizes profit by producing 10 cans a day. If the price rises to $12 a can, the marginal revenue curve is MR_2 and Dave increases production to 11 cans a day.

If price equals minimum average variable cost, Dave maximizes profit (minimizes loss) by either producing the quantity at the shutdown point or shutting down and producing no output. But if the price is below minimum average variable cost, Dave shuts down and produces no output.

Figure 15.5(b) shows Dave's short-run supply curve. At prices that exceed minimum average variable cost, the supply curve is the same as the marginal cost curve. At prices below minimum average variable cost, Dave shuts down and produces nothing. His supply curve runs along the vertical axis. At a price of $3 a can, Dave is indifferent between shutting down and producing 7 cans of syrup a day at the shutdown point (T). Either way, he incurs a loss equal to total fixed cost.

So far, we have studied one firm in isolation. We have seen that the firm's profit-maximizing actions depend on the price, which the firm takes as given. In the next section, you'll learn how market supply is determined.

■ **FIGURE 15.5**

A Perfectly Competitive Firm's Supply Curve

MyEconLab Animation

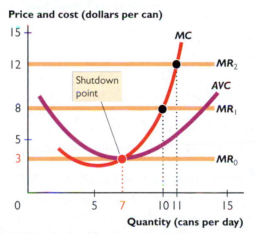

(a) Marginal cost and average variable cost

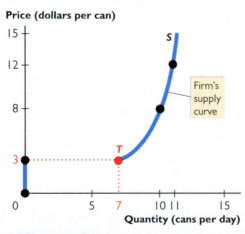

(b) Firm's supply curve

Part (a) shows Dave's profit-maximizing output at various prices. At $12 a can, Dave produces 11 cans of syrup a day; at $8 a can, he produces 10 cans of syrup a day; and at $3 a can, he produces either 7 cans of syrup a day or nothing.

At any price below $3 a can, Dave produces nothing. The minimum average variable cost is the shutdown point.

Part (b) shows Dave's supply curve. At $3 a can, Dave is indifferent between producing the quantity at the shutdown point T and not producing.

At all prices above $3 a can, Dave's supply curve is made up of the marginal cost curve, in part (a), *above* minimum average variable cost.

At all prices below $3 a can, Dave produces nothing and his supply curve runs along the vertical axis.

MyEconLab Study Plan 15.1
Key Terms Quiz
Solutions Video

CHECKPOINT 15.1

Explain a perfectly competitive firm's profit-maximizing choices and derive its supply curve.

Practice Problems

1. Sarah's Salmon Farm produced 1,000 fish last week. The marginal cost was $30 a fish, average variable cost was $20 a fish, and the market price was $25 a fish. Did Sarah maximize profit? If Sarah did not maximize profit and if nothing has changed will she increase or decrease the number of fish she produces to maximize her profit this week?

Use the following information to work Problems **2** to **4**.

Trout farming is a perfectly competitive industry and all trout farms have the same cost curves. When the market price of a fish is $25, farms maximize profit by producing 200 fish a week. At this output, average total cost is $20 a fish, and average variable cost is $15 a fish. Minimum average variable cost is $12 a fish.

2. If the price of a fish falls to $20, will a farm produce 200 fish a week?

3. If the price of a fish falls to $12, what will the trout farmer do?

4. What are two points on a trout farm's supply curve?

In the News

U.S. Steel lays off 756
With a drop in the demand for steel pipe and tube, U.S. Steel Corporation will idle plants in Ohio and Texas and lay off 756 workers.
Source: *The Wall Street Journal*, January 6, 2015

As U.S. Steel responded to the fall in demand, how did its marginal cost change? What can you say about minimum *AVC* in the plants that closed?

Solutions to Practice Problems

1. Profit is maximized when marginal cost equals marginal revenue. In perfect competition, marginal revenue equals the market price, which was $25 a fish last week. Because marginal cost exceeded marginal revenue, Sarah did not maximize profit. To maximize profit, Sarah will decrease her output until marginal cost falls to $25 a fish (Figure 1).

2. The farm will produce fewer than 200 fish a week. The marginal cost curve slopes upward, so to lower marginal cost to $20, the farm cuts production.

3. If the price of a fish falls to $12, farms cut output until marginal cost equals $12. Because $12 a fish is also minimum average variable cost, farms are at the shutdown point—some farms produce the profit-maximizing output and others produce nothing.

4. One point on a farmer's supply curve is 200 fish at $25 a fish. Another point is the shutdown point (Solution **3**) or zero at a price below $12 a fish.

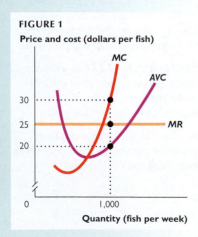

FIGURE 1

Price and cost (dollars per fish)

Solution to In the News

The fall in demand for steel pipe and tube lowered the price of steel pipe and tube. U.S. Steel cut production. Marginal cost decreased to equal the lower price. At the plants that closed temporarily, the firm's minimum *AVC* exceeded price.

| 15.2 OUTPUT, PRICE, AND PROFIT IN THE SHORT RUN | MyEconLab Concept Video |

Demand and supply determine the price and quantity in a perfectly competitive market. We first study short-run supply when the number of firms is fixed.

■ Market Supply in the Short Run

The market supply curve in the short run shows the quantity supplied at each price by a fixed number of firms. The quantity supplied at a given price is the sum of the quantities supplied by all firms at that price.

Figure 15.6 shows the supply curve for the competitive syrup market. In this example, the market consists of 10,000 firms exactly like Dave's Maple Syrup. The table shows how the market supply schedule is constructed. The shutdown point occurs at a price of $3 a can. At prices below $3 a can, every firm in the market shuts down; the quantity supplied is zero. At a price of $3 a can, each firm is indifferent between shutting down (producing nothing) or operating and producing 7 cans of syrup a day. The quantity supplied by each firm is *either* 0 or 7 cans of syrup a day, and the quantity supplied in the market is *between* 0 (all firms shut down) and 70,000 cans (all firms produce 7 cans a day each). At prices above $3 a can, we sum the quantities supplied by the 10,000 firms, so the quantity supplied in the market is 10,000 times the quantity supplied by one firm.

At prices below $3 a can, the market supply curve runs along the vertical axis. Supply is perfectly inelastic. At $3 a can, the market supply curve is horizontal. Supply is perfectly elastic. Above $3 a can, the supply curve is upward sloping.

■ FIGURE 15.6

The Market Supply Curve — MyEconLab Animation

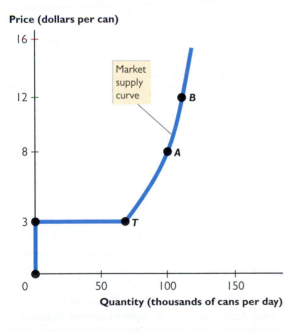

	Price	Dave's quantity supplied	Market quantity supplied
	(dollars per can)	(cans per day)	
B	12	11	110,000
A	8	10	100,000
T	3	0 or 7	0 to 70,000

A market with 10,000 identical firms has a supply schedule like that of an individual firm, but the quantity supplied is 10,000 times greater. Market supply is perfectly elastic at the price at which the shutdown point occurs.

■ Short-Run Equilibrium in Normal Times

Market demand and market supply determine the price and quantity bought and sold. Figure 15.7(a) shows a short-run equilibrium in the syrup market. The market supply curve S is the same as that in Figure 15.6.

If the demand curve D_1 shows market demand, the equilibrium price is $5 a can. Although market demand and market supply determine this price, each firm takes the price as given and produces its profit-maximizing output, which is 9 cans of syrup a day. With 10,000 identical firms, market output is 90,000 cans a day.

Figure 15.7(b) shows the situation that Dave faces. The price is $5 a can, so Dave's marginal revenue is constant at $5 a can. Dave maximizes profit by producing 9 cans of syrup a day.

Figure 15.7(b) also shows Dave's average total cost curve (ATC). Recall that average total cost is the cost per unit produced. It equals total cost divided by the quantity of output produced.

Here, when Dave produces 9 cans of syrup a day, his average total cost is $5 a can, exactly the same as the market price. So Dave sells syrup for exactly the same price as his average cost of production and economic profit is zero.

Making zero economic profit means that Dave earns *normal profit* from running his business.

The short-run equilibrium in which a firm makes zero economic profit is just one of three possible situations. A competitive market might also deliver a positive economic profit or an economic loss. Let's look at these other two cases.

■ **FIGURE 15.7**

Zero Economic Profit in the Short Run   MyEconLab Animation

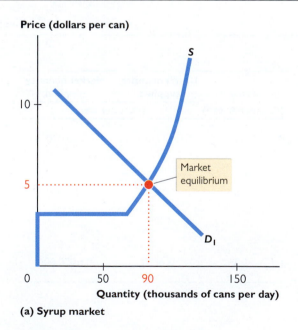

(a) Syrup market

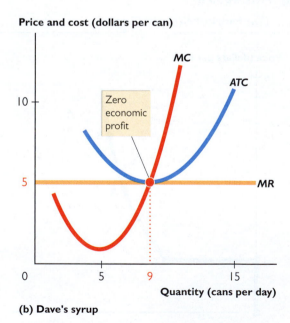

(b) Dave's syrup

In part (a), with the market demand curve D_1 and the market supply curve S, the equilibrium market price of syrup is $5 a can.

In part (b), marginal revenue is $5 a can, so Dave produces 9 cans a day. At this quantity, the price ($5) equals average total cost, so Dave makes zero economic profit.

■ Short-Run Equilibrium in Good Times

Market demand might be greater or less than D_1 in Figure 15.7 and the price might be higher or lower than $5 a can. Figure 15.8(a) shows another short-run equilibrium in the syrup market. The supply curve S is the same as that in Figure 15.6.

If the demand curve D_2 shows market demand, the equilibrium price is $8 a can. Although market demand and market supply determine this price, each firm takes the price as given and produces its profit-maximizing output, which is 10 cans of syrup a day. Because the market has 10,000 identical firms, market output is 100,000 cans of syrup a day.

Figure 15.8(b) shows the situation that Dave faces. The price is $8 a can, so Dave's marginal revenue is constant at $8 a can. Dave maximizes profit by producing 10 cans of syrup a day.

Figure 15.8(b) also shows Dave's average total cost curve (*ATC*). Recall that average total cost is the cost per unit produced. It equals total cost divided by the quantity of output produced. Here, when Dave produces 10 cans of syrup a day, his average total cost is $5.10 a can. So the price of $8 a can exceeds average total cost by $2.90 a can. This amount is Dave's economic profit per can.

If we multiply the economic profit per can of $2.90 by the quantity of syrup produced, 10 cans a day, we arrive at Dave's economic profit, which is $29 a day. The blue rectangle shows this economic profit. The height of that rectangle is the profit per can, $2.90, and the length is the 10 cans of syrup a day, so the area of the rectangle (height × length) measures Dave's economic profit of $29 a day.

■ FIGURE 15.8

Positive Economic Profit in the Short Run

MyEconLab Animation

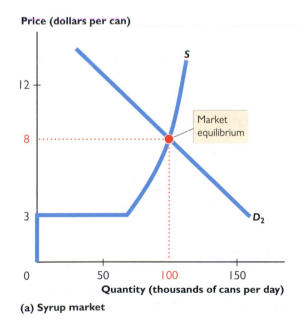

(a) Syrup market

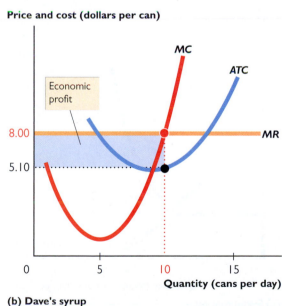

(b) Dave's syrup

In part (a), with the market demand curve D_2 and the market supply curve S, the equilibrium market price of syrup is $8 a can.

In part (b), marginal revenue is $8 a can. Dave produces 10 cans a day. Because price ($8) exceeds average total cost ($5.10), Dave makes a positive economic profit.

■ Short-Run Equilibrium in Bad Times

Figure 15.9 shows the syrup market in a loss-incurring situation. The market demand curve is now D_3. The market still has 10,000 firms and their costs are the same as before, so the market supply curve, S, is also the same as before.

With the demand and supply curves shown in Figure 15.9(a), the equilibrium price of syrup is $3 a can and the equilibrium quantity is 70,000 cans a day.

Figure 15.9(b) shows the situation that Dave faces. The price is $3 a can, so Dave's marginal revenue is constant at $3 a can. Dave maximizes profit by producing 7 cans of syrup a day.

Figure 15.9(b) also shows Dave's average total cost curve (ATC), and you can see that when Dave produces 7 cans of syrup a day, his average total cost is $5.14 a can. Now the price of $3 a can is less than average total cost by $2.14 a can. This amount is Dave's economic loss per can. If we multiply the economic loss per can of $2.14 by the quantity of syrup produced, 7 cans a day, we arrive at Dave's economic loss, which is shown by the red rectangle.

Figure 15.9(b) also shows Dave's average variable cost curve (AVC). Notice that Dave is operating at the shutdown point. Dave might equally well produce no output. Either way, his economic loss would be equal to his total fixed cost. If the price were a bit higher than $3 a can, Dave would still incur an economic loss, but a smaller one. And if the price were lower than $3 a can, Dave would shut down and incur an economic loss equal to total fixed cost.

■ FIGURE 15.9

Economic Loss in the Short Run   MyEconLab Animation

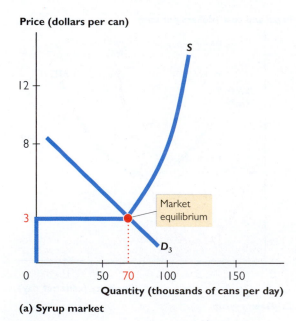

(a) Syrup market

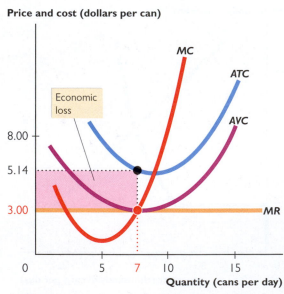

(b) Dave's syrup

In part (a), with the market demand curve D_3 and the market supply curve S, the equilibrium market price of syrup is $3 a can.

In part (b), Dave's marginal revenue is $3 a can, so he produces 7 cans of syrup a day. At this quantity, the price ($3) is less than average total cost ($5.14), so Dave incurs an economic loss shown by the red rectangle.

CHECKPOINT 15.2

MyEconLab Study Plan 15.2
Solutions Video

Explain how output, price, and profit are determined in the short run.

Practice Problems

Tulip growing is perfectly competitive and all growers have the same costs. The market price is $25 a bunch, and each grower maximizes profit by producing 2,000 bunches a week. Average total cost is $20 a bunch, and average variable cost is $15 a bunch. Minimum average variable cost is $12 a bunch.

1. What is the economic profit that each grower is making in the short run?

2. What is the price at the grower's shutdown point?

3. What is each grower's economic profit at the shutdown point?

In the News

Airfares will drop to record lows this fall
With a fall in the price of jet fuel, the price of an average round-trip airline ticket will slip to $244 next month, about 5% lower than the same time last year.
Source: *Fortune*, July 27, 2015

Explain how a fall in the price of jet fuel changes the marginal cost of producing air trips and changes the equilibrium price and quantity of air trips in the short run.

Solutions to Practice Problems

1. The market price ($25) exceeds the average total cost ($20), so growers make an economic profit of $5 a bunch. Each grower produces 2,000 bunches a week, so a grower's economic profit is $10,000 a week.
   Figure 1 illustrates the situation. The grower's marginal revenue equals the market price ($25 a bunch). The grower maximizes profit by producing 2,000 bunches, so at 2,000 bunches the marginal cost curve (*MC*) cuts the marginal revenue curve (*MR*). The average total cost of producing 2,000 bunches is $20, so the *ATC* curve passes through this point. Economic profit equals the area of the blue rectangle.

2. The price at which a grower will shut down temporarily is equal to minimum average variable cost—$12 a bunch (Figure 1).

3. At the shutdown point, the grower incurs an economic loss equal to total fixed cost. Figure 2 shows the data to calculate *TFC*. When 2,000 bunches a week are grown, *ATC* is $20 a bunch and *AVC* is $15 a bunch.
   $ATC = AFC + AVC$, so $AFC = ATC - AVC$. *AFC* is $5 a bunch. Total fixed cost equals $10,000 a week— $TFC = AFC \times Q$, $5 a bunch $\times$ 2,000 bunches a week. At the shutdown point, the grower incurs an economic loss of $10,000 a week.

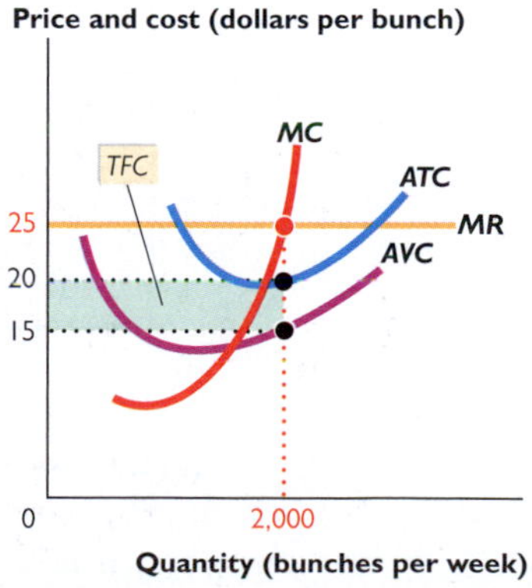

Solution to In the News

A fall in the price of jet fuel decreases an airline's marginal cost of producing air trips. The airline's marginal cost curve shifts downward. With lower marginal cost of an air trip, the market supply of air trips increases and the market supply curve shifts rightward. The increase in supply lowers the equilibrium price of an air trip and increases the equilibrium quantity of air trips in the short run.

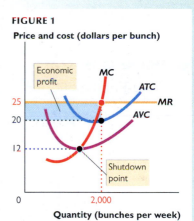

FIGURE 1
Price and cost (dollars per bunch)

FIGURE 2
Price and cost (dollars per bunch)

15.3 OUTPUT, PRICE, AND PROFIT IN THE LONG RUN

Competitive markets are in a constant state of change. Price, quantity, and economic profit fluctuate as demand and supply change. None of the three situations that we described on the previous pages—normal times, good times, or bad times—last forever in perfect competition. Market forces operate to compete away economic profits and eliminate economic losses to move the price toward the lowest possible price. That price equals minimum average total cost. In the long run, a firm in perfect competition produces at minimum average total cost and makes zero economic profit. (The firm's entrepreneur earns normal profit—part of the firm's total costs.)

Figure 15.10 illustrates a perfectly competitive market in long-run equilibrium and highlights the forces that bring the market to this situation. In Figure 15.10(a), the firm's average total cost curve is *ATC*, and the firm produces at the point of minimum average total cost—9 cans a day at an average total cost of $5 a can. If the price rises above or falls below $5 a can, market forces operate to move the price back toward $5 a can. The arrows pointing toward $5 represent these forces.

In Figure 15.10(b) the market demand curve is *D*. With this market demand, the price equals minimum average total cost only if the market supply curve is *S*. If supply is less than *S* (the supply curve is to the left of *S*), the price is above $5 a can; if supply exceeds *S* (the supply curve is to the right of *S*), the price is below $5 a can. Market forces operate to shift the supply curve back to *S*, and the arrows pointing toward *S* represent these forces.

■ **FIGURE 15.10**

Long-Run Equilibrium

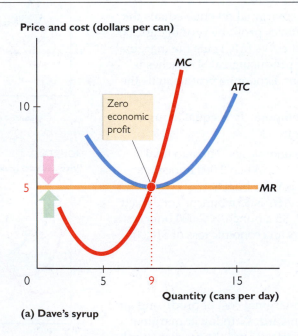

(a) Dave's syrup

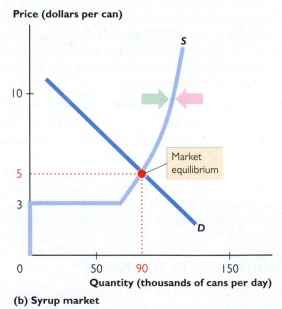

(b) Syrup market

In part (a), minimum average total cost is $5 a can. In long-run equilibrium, the price and marginal revenue are pulled to this level. The firm makes zero economic profit.

In part (b), if the price is above $5 a can, above minimum *ATC* in part (a), supply increases and the price falls. If the price is below $5, supply decreases and the price rises.

■ Entry and Exit

Entry and exit are the market forces that shift the supply curve and move the price to minimum average total cost in the long run. In the short run, firms might make a positive economic profit (as in Figure 15.8) or incur an economic loss (as in Figure 15.9). But in the long run, firms makes zero economic profit.

In the long run, firms respond to economic profit and economic loss by either entering or exiting a market. New firms enter a market in which the existing firms are making economic profits, and some existing firms exit a market in which firms are incurring economic losses. Temporary economic profit or temporary economic loss, like a win or loss at a casino, does not trigger entry and exit. But the prospect of persistent economic profit or economic loss does.

Entry and exit influence the market price, the quantity produced, and economic profit. The immediate effect of the decision to enter or exit a market is to shift the market supply curve. If more firms enter a market, supply increases and the market supply curve shifts rightward. If some firms exit a market, supply decreases and the market supply curve shifts leftward.

Let's see what happens when new firms enter a market.

The Effects of Entry

Figure 15.11 shows the effects of entry. Initially, the market is in long-run equilibrium. Demand is D_0, supply is S_0, the price is $5 a can, and the quantity is 90,000 cans of syrup a day. A surge in the popularity of syrup increases market demand, and the demand curve shifts to D_1. The price rises to $8 a can, and firms in the syrup market increase output to 100,000 cans a day and make an economic profit.

Times are good for syrup producers like Dave, so other potential syrup producers want some of the action. New firms begin to enter the market. As they enter,

With the prospect of economic profit, a new business opens.

■ FIGURE 15.11

The Effects of Entry

MyEconLab Animation

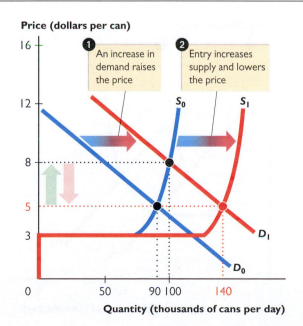

Starting in long-run equilibrium,

① Market demand increases and the market demand curve shifts from D_0 to D_1. The price of syrup rises from $5 to $8 a can.

Economic profit brings entry.

② As firms enter the market, the market supply curve shifts rightward, from S_0 to S_1. The equilibrium price falls from $8 to $5 a can, and the quantity produced increases from 100,000 to 140,000 cans of syrup a day.

supply increases and the market supply curve shifts rightward to S_1. With the greater market supply and unchanged market demand, the market price falls from $8 to $5 a can and the equilibrium quantity increases to 140,000 cans a day.

Market output increases, but because the price falls, Dave and the other producers decrease output. As the price falls, each firm's output gradually returns to its original level. Because the number of firms in the market increases, the market as a whole produces more.

As the price falls, each firm's economic profit decreases. When the price falls to $5 a can, economic profit disappears and each firm makes zero economic profit. The entry process stops, and the market is again in long-run equilibrium.

You have just discovered a key proposition:

Economic profit is an incentive for new firms to enter a market, but as they do so, the price falls and the economic profit of each existing firm decreases.

■ The Effects of Exit

Economic loss brings exit.

Figure 15.12 shows the effects of exit. Again we begin on demand curve D_0 and supply curve S_0 in long-run equilibrium. A new high-nutrition breakfast food decreases the demand for maple syrup. The market demand curve shifts from D_0 to D_2. Firms' costs are the same as before, so the market supply curve is S_0.

With demand at D_2 and supply at S_0, the price falls to $3 a can and 70,000 cans a day are produced. The firms in the syrup market incur economic losses.

Times are tough for syrup producers, and Dave must seriously think about leaving his dream business and finding some other way of making a living. But other producers are in the same situation as Dave, and some start to exit the market while Dave is still thinking through his options.

■ **FIGURE 15.12**

The Effects of Exit

MyEconLab Animation

Starting in long-run equilibrium,

❶ Market demand decreases and the market demand curve shifts from D_0 to D_2. The price of syrup falls from $5 to $3 a can.

Economic loss brings exit.

❷ As some firms exit the market, the market supply curve shifts leftward, from S_0 to S_2. The equilibrium price rises from $3 to $5 a can, and the quantity produced decreases from 70,000 to 50,000 cans of syrup a day.

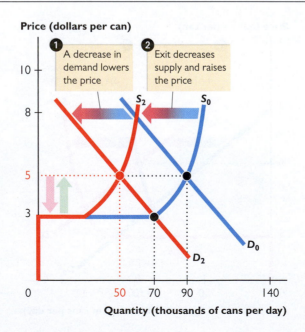

As some firms exit, the market supply curve shifts leftward to S_2, output decreases from 70,000 to 50,000 cans of syrup a day and the market price rises from $3 to $5 a can.

As the price rises, Dave and each other firm that remains in the market move up along their supply curves and increase output. That is, for each firm that remains in the market, the profit-maximizing output *increases*. As the price rises and each firm sells more, economic loss decreases. When the price rises to $5 a can, each firm makes zero economic profit. Dave earns normal profit (part of the firm's total cost) and he is happy that he can still make a living producing syrup.

You have just discovered a second key proposition:

Economic loss is an incentive for firms to exit a market, but as they do so, the price rises and the economic loss of each remaining firm decreases.

Change in Demand

Initially, a competitive market is in long-run equilibrium and the firms are making zero economic profit (and entrepreneurs are earning normal profit). Now market demand increases. The market price rises, firms increase production to keep marginal cost equal to price, and firms make an economic profit. The market is now in short-run equilibrium but not in long-run equilibrium.

Economic profit is an incentive for new firms to enter the market. As firms enter, market supply increases and the market price falls. With a lower price, firms decrease output to keep marginal cost equal to price. Notice that as firms enter the market, market output increases, but each firm's output decreases. Eventually, enough firms enter to eliminate economic profit and the market returns to long-run equilibrium.

The key difference between the initial long-run equilibrium and the new long-run equilibrium is the number of firms. A permanent increase in demand increases the number of firms. Each firm produces the same output in the new long-run equilibrium as initially and makes zero economic profit. In the process of moving from the initial equilibrium to the new one, firms make economic profit.

The demand for airline travel in the world economy increased during the 1990s, and the deregulation of the airlines freed up firms to seek profit opportunities. The result was a massive rate of entry of new airlines. The process of competition and change in the airline market were similar to what we have just studied.

A decrease in demand triggers a similar response, except in the opposite direction. The decrease in demand brings a lower price, economic loss, and exit. Exit decreases market supply, raises the price, and eliminates the economic loss.

Technological Change

New technologies lower cost, so as firms adopt a new technology, their cost curves shift downward. With lower costs, market supply increases and the price falls. Firms that use the new technology make an economic profit and firms that stick with the old technology incur economic losses. New-technology firms enter and old-technology firms exit. The price keeps falling until all the firms are using the new technology and economic profit is zero. The lower prices and better products that technological advances bring are permanent gains for consumers. *Eye on Record Stores* (on pp. 394–395) looks at the effects of technological change in the retail market for recorded music.

EYE on RECORD STORES

MyEconLab Critical Thinking Exercise

Where Have All the Record Stores Gone?

Beecker Street Records in New York City (see p. 375) describes its inventory as vintage and out-of-print LPs and CDs. No longer do record stores sell the latest singles and albums.

The world was very different in 1995, when more than 8,000 record stores traded in an almost perfectly competitive market.

Figure 1 illustrates the average total cost curve, ATC, marginal cost curve, MC, and marginal revenue curve, MR_0, for one of these 8,000 stores.

Competition was fierce in the record retail business and economic profit was hard to find. In Figure 1, the record store is earning zero economic

profit and the market is in long-run equilibrium.

Although competition was fierce, it was about to notch up a gear. The dot-com boom had started.

The expansion of the Internet during the 1990s laid the foundation for many new ways of doing business. One of these was a new way of delivering recorded music.

Amazon was one of the first firms to take advantage of the technological advance made possible by the Internet when Amazon.com started trading in 1995.

At first, Amazon was an online bookstore. But entrepreneur Jeff

An Amazon server farm replaces hundreds of traditional record stores.

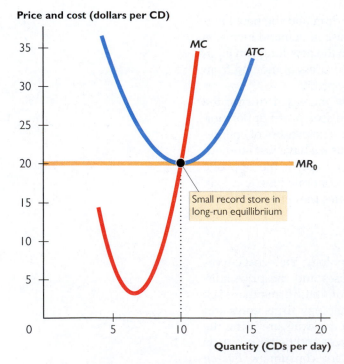

Figure 1 Small Independent Record Store Before Internet

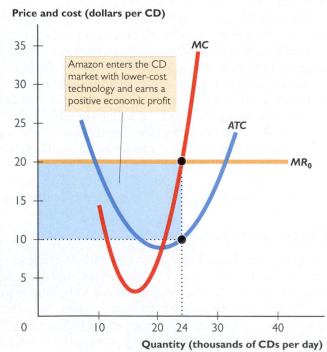

Figure 2 Amazon Enters CD Retail Market

Bezos quickly saw that the technologies being laid down for selling books could also be used to sell CDs (and just about anything).

This new technology also had much lower costs than traditional "bricks and mortar" retailing.

Figure 2 shows the average total cost curve and marginal cost curve using Amazon's lower-cost technology. The numbers are just examples, but first look carefully at the axes of Figures 1 and 2. Amazon can produce a larger output at a lower cost than the traditional record store can.

Online retailing wasn't profitable at first, but with its superior low-cost technology economic profit eventually rolled in. Figure 2 shows the economic profit available at the prices charged by traditional record stores applied to a store using the new technology.

Positive economic profit attracts new entry. And that's what happened in the online music business. The technology also kept advancing, with MP3 files replacing physical CDs. As Amazon, Apple's iTunes store, and others entered the market for MP3 downloads, the price of recorded music fell and firms' profits were trimmed.

Figure 3 shows where perfect competition among online music download stores drives the price and quantity. Price falls to make marginal revenue MR_1, a level at which economic profit has vanished in a new long-run equilibrium.

This lower price means hard times for small independent record stores. The fall in price is too big for these small stores to cover even their average variable cost, AVC, and with no

prospect of prices rising again, the independent stores avoid the economic losses by exiting.

Figure 4 illustrates the economic loss incurred by a traditional independent record store facing competition from online retailers when marginal revenue has fallen to MR_1.

Faced with this loss, the store exits. That's where the record stores have gone. They've exited to avoid the losses created by online competition.

Sundance, in San Marcos, Texas, is one of 4,000 traditional record stores that exited.

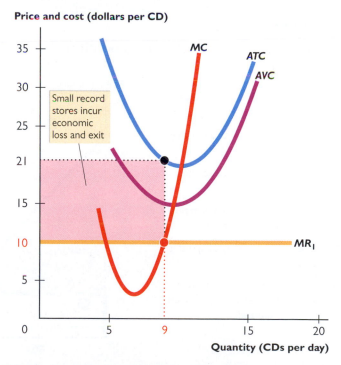

Figure 3 More Large Online Music Stores Enter and Compete   **Figure 4 Small Independent Record Store Exits**

■ Is Perfect Competition Efficient?

An efficient outcome is one in which scarce resources are allocated to their highest-value use. Perfect competition achieves such an outcome. It is efficient.

To see why, first recall the conditions for an efficient allocation of resources. Resources are used efficiently when it is not possible to get more of one good without giving up something that is valued more highly. When this outcome is achieved, marginal benefit equals marginal cost and total surplus (consumer surplus plus producer surplus) is maximized. That is the outcome achieved in perfect competition.

We derive a firm's supply curve in perfect competition from its marginal cost curve. The supply curve is the marginal cost curve at all points above the minimum of average variable cost (the shutdown price). Because the market supply curve is found by summing the quantities supplied by all the firms at each price, the market supply curve is the entire market's marginal cost curve.

The market demand curve is the marginal benefit curve. Because the market supply curve and market demand curve intersect at the equilibrium price, that price equals both marginal cost and marginal benefit.

Figure 15.13 illustrates the efficiency of perfect competition. We've labeled the market demand curve $D = MB$ and the market supply curve $S = MC$ to remind you that these curves are also the marginal benefit (MB) and marginal cost (MC) curves.

These demand and supply curves intersect at the equilibrium price and equilibrium quantity. The price equals marginal benefit and marginal cost, total surplus is maximized, and the equilibrium quantity is efficient. Any departure from this outcome is inferior to it and brings an avoidable deadweight loss.

FIGURE 15.13

The Efficiency of Perfect Competition

MyEconLab Animation

❶ Market equilibrium occurs at a price of $5 a can and a quantity of 90,000 cans of syrup a day.

❷ The supply curve is also the marginal cost curve.

❸ The demand curve is also the marginal benefit curve.

At the market equilibrium, marginal benefit equals marginal cost.

❹ The efficient quantity of syrup is produced.

❺ Total surplus, the sum of consumer surplus and producer surplus, is maximized.

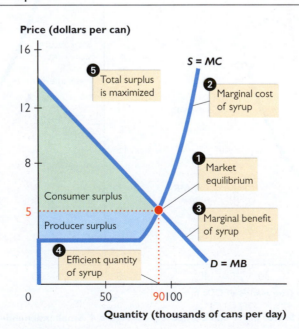

■ Is Perfect Competition Fair?

You've seen many situations in which perfect competition brings gains and losses. When the demand for an item decreases, most producers incur at least a temporary loss and some of them go out of business. When a technological change lowers costs, entrepreneurs who are quick to adopt the technology gain and others who respond slowly lose. Is it fair that some entrepreneurs gain and others lose?

When a natural disaster such as extreme weather or an earthquake strikes, the prices of essential items sold in competitive markets shoot upward, bringing gains for sellers and pain for buyers. Is that type of outcome fair?

You studied the fairness of markets in Chapter 6 (pp. 161–163) and saw two views of what is fair: fair rules and a fair result. According to the fair-rules view, an outcome is fair if property rights are enforced and people acquire resources, goods, and services through voluntary exchange. According to the fair-result view, an outcome is fair if the poorest aren't too poor and the richest aren't too rich. Are the competitive market outcomes we've just described fair on these two views of fairness?

The situations we've described appear to be fair on both views. Perfect competition places no restrictions on anyone's actions, all trade is voluntary, consumers pay the lowest possible prices, and entrepreneurs earn only normal profit. But price hikes arising from shortages following a natural disaster might be exceptions. In such situations, large windfall gains for a few and high prices for essential items for many might be regarded as an unfair result. If it is considered unfair, it must be compared with the fairness of an alternative mechanism for allocating scarce resources.

EYE on YOUR LIFE
The Perfect Competition That You Encounter

MyEconLab Critical Thinking Exercise

Many of the markets that you encounter every day are highly competitive and almost perfectly competitive. While you don't run into perfect competition on a daily basis, you do have dealings in some perfectly competitive markets. Two of those markets are the Internet auctions organized by eBay and one of its subsidiaries, StubHub.

If you have a ticket for a game between the Giants and the Braves but can't use it, you can sell it on StubHub for the going market price (minus a commission). And if you're desperate to see the game but missed out on getting a ticket, you can buy one for the going price (plus a commission) on the same Web site.

StubHub takes a commission and makes a profit. But competition between StubHub, Ticketmaster, and other ticket brokers ensure that profits are competed away in the long run, with entrepreneurs earning normal profit.

Just about every good or service that you buy and take for granted, no matter where you buy it, is available because of the forces of competition. Your home, your food, your clothing, your books, your DVDs, your MP3 files, your computer, your bike, your car,…; the list is endless. No one organizes all the magic that enables

you to buy this vast array of products. Competitive markets and entrepreneurs striving to make the largest possible profit make it happen.

When either demand or technology changes and makes the current allocation of resources the wrong one, the market swiftly and silently acts. It sends signals to entrepreneurs that bring entry and exit and a new and efficient use of scarce resources.

It is no exaggeration or hype to say that your entire life is influenced by and benefits immeasurably from the forces of competition. Adam Smith's invisible hand might be hidden from view, but it is enormously powerful.

MyEconLab Study Plan 15.3
Solutions Video

CHECKPOINT 15.3

Explain how output, price, and profit are determined in the long run and explain why perfect competition is efficient.

Practice Problems

Tulip growing is a perfectly competitive industry, and all tulip growers have the same cost curves. The market price of tulips is $15 a bunch, and each grower maximizes profit by producing 1,500 bunches a week. The average total cost of producing tulips is $21 a bunch. Minimum average variable cost is $12 a bunch, and the minimum average total cost is $18 a bunch.

1. What is a tulip grower's economic profit in the short run and how does the number of tulip growers change in the long run?
2. In the long run, what is the price and the tulip grower's economic profit?

In the News

California's commercial drone industry is taking off
Customers are finding ever more creative ways to use drones, and 3D Robotics Inc., America's largest producer of consumer drones, expects sales to soar.
Source: *Los Angeles Times*, June 13, 2015

Explain what is happening in the market for commercial drones. How would you expect the price of a drone to change in the short run and the long run? How would you expect the economic profit of a drone producer such as 3D Robotics to change in the short run and in the long run?

Solutions to Practice Problems

1. The price is less than average total cost, so the tulip grower is incurring an economic loss in the short run. Because the price exceeds minimum average variable cost, the tulip grower continues to produce. The economic loss equals the loss per bunch ($21 minus $15) multiplied by the number of bunches (1,500 per week), which equals $9,000 per week (Figure 1). Because tulip growers are incurring economic losses, some growers will exit in the long run. The number of tulip growers will decrease.
2. In the long run, the price will be such that economic profit is zero. That is, as growers exit, the price will rise until it equals minimum average total cost. In the long run, the price will be $18 a bunch (Figure 2) and a tulip grower will make zero economic profit because average total cost equals price.

Solution to In the News

With customers finding ever more creative ways to use drones, the demand for drones is increasing. In the short run, an increase in demand brings a rise in the price of a drone and an increase in the quantity of drones supplied. The higher price increases the economic profit of drone producers in the short run. Economic profit is an incentive for new firms to enter the market. In the long run, entry increases supply, which lowers the price and increases the quantity of drones demanded. As the price of a drone falls, economic profit decreases. In the new long-run equilibrium, the price of a drone is lower and drone producers make zero economic profit.

FIGURE 1

Price and cost (dollars per bunch)

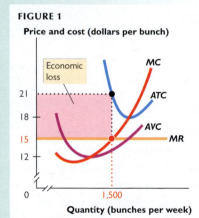

Quantity (bunches per week)

FIGURE 2

Price and cost (dollars per bunch)

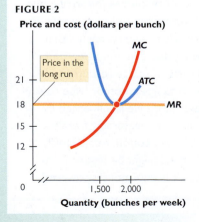

Quantity (bunches per week)

CHAPTER SUMMARY

Key Points

1. **Explain a perfectly competitive firm's profit-maximizing choices and derive its supply curve.**

   - A perfectly competitive firm is a price taker.
   - Marginal revenue equals price.
   - The firm produces the output at which price equals marginal cost.
   - If price is less than minimum average variable cost, the firm temporarily shuts down.
   - A firm's supply curve is the upward-sloping part of its marginal cost curve at all prices at or above minimum average variable cost (the shutdown point) and the vertical axis at all prices below minimum average variable cost.

2. **Explain how output, price, and profit are determined in the short run.**

   - Market demand and market supply determine price.
   - Firms choose the quantity to produce that maximizes profit, which is the quantity at which marginal cost equals price.
   - In short-run equilibrium, a firm can make a positive economic profit, make zero economic profit, or incur an economic loss.

3. **Explain how output, price, and profit are determined in the long run and explain why perfect competition is efficient.**

   - Economic profit induces entry, which increases market supply and lowers price and profit. Economic loss induces exit, which decreases market supply, raises price, and lowers the losses.
   - In the long run, economic profit is zero and there is no entry or exit.
   - An increase in demand increases the number of firms and increases the equilibrium quantity.
   - An advance in technology that lowers the cost of producing a good increases market supply, lowers the price, and increases the quantity.
   - Perfect competition is efficient because it makes marginal benefit equal marginal cost, and it is fair because trade is voluntary, consumers pay the lowest possible prices, and entrepreneurs earn normal profit.

Key Terms

MyEconLab Key Terms Quiz

Marginal revenue, 377
Monopolistic competition, 376
Monopoly, 376

Oligopoly, 376
Perfect competition, 376

Price taker, 377
Shutdown point, 381

CHAPTER CHECKPOINT

MyEconLab Chapter 15 Study Plan

Study Plan Problems and Applications

1. Look at the list to the left. In what type of market is each good or service in the list sold? Explain your answers.

2. Explain why in a perfectly competitive market, the firm is a price taker. Why can't the firm choose the price at which it sells its good?

3. Table 1 shows the demand schedule for Lin's Fortune Cookies. Calculate Lin's marginal revenue for each quantity demanded. Compare Lin's marginal revenue and price. In what type of market does Lin's Fortune Cookies operate?

Table 1 shows the demand schedule for Lin's Fortune Cookies. Table 2 shows some cost data for Lin's. Use this information to work Problems **4** to **7**. (Hint: Make a sketch of Lin's short-run cost curves.)

4. At a market price of $50 a batch, what quantity does Lin's produce and what is the firm's economic profit in the short run?

5. At a market price of $35.20 a batch, what quantity does Lin's produce and what is the firm's economic profit in the short run?

6. Create Lin's short-run supply schedule and make a graph of Lin's short-run supply curve. Explain why only part of Lin's short-run supply curve is the same as its marginal cost curve.

7. At a market price of $83 a batch, what quantity does Lin's produce and what is the firm's economic profit in the short run? Do firms enter or exit the market and what is Lin's economic profit in the long run?

LIST

- Wheat
- Jeans
- Printer cartridges
- Toothpaste
- Gym membership in a town with one gym

TABLE 1

Price (dollars per batch)	Quantity demanded (batches per day)
50	0
50	1
50	2
50	3
50	4
50	5
50	6

TABLE 2

Quantity (batches per day)	AFC	AVC	ATC	MC
	(dollars per batch)			
1	84.0	51.0	135	
				37
2	42.0	44.0	86	
				29
3	28.0	39.0	67	
				27
4	21.0	36.0	57	
				32
5	16.8	35.2	52	
				40
6	14.0	36.0	50	
				57
7	12.0	39.0	51	
				83
8	10.5	44.5	55	

Use the following information to work Problems **8** to **10**.

Quebec losing hold over maple syrup industry to U.S. competition

The Federation of Quebec Maple Syrup Producers tries to limit production and stockpiles a "strategic reserve" to keep the price of syrup high. But Quebec producers are feeling increased competition from Vermont, New York, and Maine, where market share has increased and is expected to increase further in 2017 and 2018.

Source: *The Globe and Mail*, April 6, 2015

8. Draw a graph to describe the maple syrup market and the cost and revenue of one maple syrup producer in 2016, assuming that all producers are making a positive economic profit because of the actions of the Federation of Quebec Maple Syrup Producers.

9. Starting with the industry making a positive economic profit, explain how the maple syrup market and the profit of an individual producer will change in the long run.

10. If the demand for maple syrup increases, what will happen to price, quantity, and the economic profit of a producer in the short run and in the long run?

11. Read *Eye on Record Stores* on pp. 394–395 and explain how Internet retailing of recorded music changed the constraints faced by small traditional record stores. Why did many record stores exit rather than shut down temporarily?

Instructor Assignable Problems and Applications

MyEconLab Homework, Quiz, or Test if assigned by instructor

1. Why did Amazon enter the market for recorded music and why did independent record stores exit?

2. How does competition among online music retailers influence economic profit?

3. Look at the list to the right. In what type of market is each of the goods and services in the list sold? Explain your answers.

4. Suppose that the restaurant industry is perfectly competitive. Joe's Diner is always packed in the evening but rarely has a customer at lunchtime. Why doesn't Joe's Diner close—temporarily shut down—at lunchtime?

Use the following information to work Problems **5** to **7**.

Figure 1 shows the short-run cost curves of a toy producer. The market has 1,000 identical producers and Table 1 shows the market demand schedule for toys.

5. At a market price of $21 a toy, what quantity does the firm produce in the short run and does the firm make a positive economic profit, a zero economic profit, or an economic loss?

6. At a market price of $12 a toy, how many toys does the firm produce and what is its economic profit in the short run? How will the number of firms in the market change in the long run?

7. At what market prices would the firm shut down temporarily? What is the market price of a toy in long-run equilibrium? How many firms will be in the toy market in the long run? Explain your answer.

Use the following information to work Problems **8** and **9**.

California plans to crack down on the use of fumigants by growers of strawberries. The biggest burden will fall on Ventura County's growers, who produce about 90 percent of the nation's crop.

8. Draw graphs of the U.S. strawberry market in long-run equilibrium before the pollution crackdown: one of the U.S. market and one of a California grower. Now show the short-run effects of the pollution crackdown.

9. On the graph, show the long-run effects of the pollution crackdown.

Use the following information to work Problems **10** and **11**.

Grain, soybean prices fall

Grain and soybean prices tumbled on news that production would be greater than previously expected. The bigger-than-expected production forecasts come as grain farmers are wrestling with a decrease in overseas demand for grain.

Source: *The Wall Street Journal*, November 10, 2015

10. Why did soybean prices fall in 2015? Draw graphs to show the soybean market and the cost and revenue curves of a soybean farmer at the start and end of 2015. Show the change in the soybean farmer's economic profit.

11. Why did grain prices fall in 2015? Draw graphs to show the grain market and the cost and revenue curves of an individual grain farmer at the start and end of 2015. Show the change in the grain farmer's economic profit.

LIST

- Breakfast cereals
- Smartphones
- The only restaurant in a small town
- Oranges
- Air travel in a town serviced by one airline

FIGURE 1

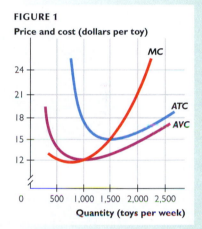

Price and cost (dollars per toy)

TABLE 1

Price (dollars per toy)	Quantity demanded (thousands of toys per week)
24	1,000
21	1,500
18	2,000
15	2,500
12	3,000

MyEconLab Chapter 15 Study Plan

Multiple Choice Quiz

1. In perfect competition, all the following situations arise *except* _____.

   A. firms produce an identical good or service
   B. each firm chooses the price at which to sell the good it produces
   C. firms can sell any quantity they choose to produce at the market price
   D. buyers know each seller's price

2. A firm that is producing the quantity at which marginal cost exceeds both average total cost and the market price will increase its economic profit by _____.

   A. producing a larger quantity
   B. raising the price to equal marginal cost
   C. producing a smaller quantity
   D. producing the quantity that minimizes average total cost

3. A firm will shut down in the short run if at the profit-maximizing quantity, _____.

   A. total revenue is less than total cost
   B. marginal revenue is less than average fixed cost
   C. average total cost exceeds the market price
   D. marginal revenue is less than average variable cost

4. At the shutdown point, the firm _____.

   A. incurs an economic loss equal to total variable cost
   B. makes zero economic profit
   C. incurs a loss equal to total fixed cost
   D. stops production to decrease its economic loss

5. In the short run, the profit-maximizing firm will _____.

   A. break even if marginal revenue equals marginal cost
   B. make an economic profit if marginal cost is less than average total cost
   C. incur an economic loss if average fixed cost exceeds marginal revenue
   D. incur an economic loss if average total cost exceeds marginal revenue

6. A firm's short-run supply curve is the same as _____ if it produces the good.

   A. its marginal revenue curve
   B. the upward-sloping part of its marginal cost curve
   C. its marginal cost curve above minimum average variable cost
   D. its marginal cost curve above minimum average total cost

7. A permanent increase in demand _____ economic profit in the short run and some firms will _____ in the long run.

   A. does not change; exit the market
   B. increases; enter the market
   C. increases; raise their price
   D. does not change; advertise their good

8. Perfect competition is efficient because all the following conditions hold *except* _____.

   A. total product is maximized
   B. firms maximize profit and produce on their supply curves
   C. consumers get a real bargain and pay a price below the value of the good
   D. firms minimize their average total cost of producing the good

Are Microsoft's prices too high?

Monopoly

When you have completed your study of this chapter, you will be able to

1 Explain how monopoly arises and distinguish between single-price monopoly and price-discriminating monopoly.

2 Explain how a single-price monopoly determines its output and price.

3 Compare the performance of a single-price monopoly with that of perfect competition.

4 Explain how price discrimination increases profit.

5 Explain why natural monopoly is regulated and the effects of regulation.

16

CHAPTER CHECKLIST

MyEconLab Big Picture Video

403

Monopoly
A market in which one firm sells a good or service that has no close substitutes and a barrier blocks the entry of new firms.

Barrier to entry
Any constraint that protects a firm from competitors.

Natural monopoly
A monopoly that arises because one firm can meet the entire market demand at a lower average total cost than two or more firms could.

16.1 MONOPOLY AND HOW IT ARISES

Microsoft faces almost no competition in the market for PC operating systems. Does the absence of competition result in buyers paying too high a price for Windows? You will find the answer in this chapter.

The market for PC operating systems is an example of **monopoly**, a market in which one firm sells a good or service that has no close substitutes and in which a barrier to entry prevents competition from new firms.

■ No Close Substitute

If a good has a close substitute, even though only one firm produces it, that firm effectively faces competition from the producers of substitutes. An example of a good that does not have close substitutes is water supplied by a local public utility. While it does have a close substitute for drinking—bottled spring water—it has no substitutes for doing the laundry, taking a shower, or washing a car.

Technological change can create substitutes and weaken a monopoly. For example, Fedex, UPS, and e-mail are close substitutes for the services provided by the U.S. Postal Service and have weakened its monopoly.

The arrival of a new product can also create a monopoly. For example, the technologies of the information age have provided opportunities for Google and Microsoft to become near monopolies in their markets (See *Eye on the U.S. Economy* on p. 406).

■ Barrier to Entry

Any constraint that protects a firm from facing new competitors is a **barrier to entry**. There are three types of barrier to entry:

- Natural
- Legal
- Ownership

Natural Barrier to Entry

When economies of scale enable a single firm to meet the entire market demand at a lower average total cost than two or more firms could, a natural barrier to entry creates a **natural monopoly**.

Figure 16.1 illustrates a natural monopoly in the distribution of electric power. Here, the demand curve for electric power is *D*, and the long-run average cost curve is *LRAC*. Economies of scale prevail over the entire length of this *LRAC* curve, indicated by the fact that the curve slopes downward. One firm can produce 4 million kilowatt-hours at 5¢ a kilowatt-hour. At this price, the quantity demanded is 4 million kilowatt-hours. So if the price was 5¢ a kilowatt-hour, one firm could supply the entire market. If two or more firms shared the market, average total cost would be higher.

To see why the situation shown in Figure 16.1 creates a barrier to entry, think about what would happen if a second firm tried to enter the market. Such a firm would find it impossible to make a profit. If it produced less than the original firm, it would have to charge a higher price and it would have no customers. If it produced the same quantity as the original firm, the price would fall below average total cost for both firms and one of them would be forced out of business. There is room for only one firm in this market.

◼ FIGURE 16.1

Natural Monopoly

MyEconLab Animation

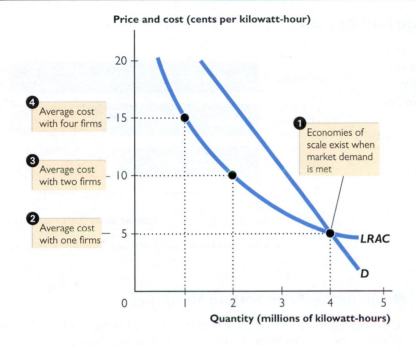

The demand curve for electric power is *D*, and the long-run average cost curve is *LRAC*.

1 Economies of scale exist over the entire *LRAC* curve.

One firm can distribute 4 million kilo-watt-hours at a **2** cost of 5¢ a kilo-watt-hour.

Two firms can distribute this same total output at a **3** cost of 10¢ a kilowatt-hour.

Four firms can distribute this same total output at a **4** cost of 15¢ a kilowatt-hour.

One firm can meet the market demand at a lower cost than two or more firms can, and the market is a natural monopoly.

Legal Barrier to Entry

A legal barrier to entry creates a legal monopoly. A **legal monopoly** is a market in which competition and entry are restricted by the granting of a public franchise, government license, patent, or copyright.

A *public franchise* is an exclusive right granted to a firm to supply a good or service, an example of which is the U.S. Postal Service's exclusive right to deliver first-class mail. A *government license* controls entry into particular occupations, professions, and industries. An example is Michael's Texaco in Charleston, Rhode Island, which is the only firm in the area licensed to test for vehicle emissions.

A *patent* is an exclusive right granted to the inventor of a product or service. A *copyright* is an exclusive right granted to the author or composer of a literary, musical, dramatic, or artistic work. Patents and copyrights are valid for a limited time period that varies from country to country. In the United States, a patent is valid for 20 years. Patents are designed to encourage the *invention* of new products and production methods. They also stimulate *innovation*—the use of new inventions—by encouraging inventors to publicize their discoveries and offer them for use under license. Patents have stimulated innovations in areas as diverse as soybean seeds, pharmaceuticals, memory chips, and video games.

Ownership Barrier to Entry

A monopoly can arise in a market in which competition and entry are restricted by a concentration of ownership. An example is the global wholesale market in sunglasses, which is controlled by Luxottica, an Italian firm, that almost certainly made your glasses, regardless of the brand and where you bought them.

Legal monopoly
A market in which competition and entry are restricted by the granting of a public franchise, government license, patent, or copyright.

The global wholesale market for designer sunglasses is close to being a monopoly.

EYE on the U.S. ECONOMY
Information-Age Monopolies

Information-age technologies have created three big natural monopolies—firms with large fixed plant costs but almost zero marginal cost that experience economies of scale.

The operating system of 92 percent of personal computers is some version of Microsoft's Windows. Google performs 66 percent of all Internet searches. And Facebook gets 50 percent of all visits to social media sites.

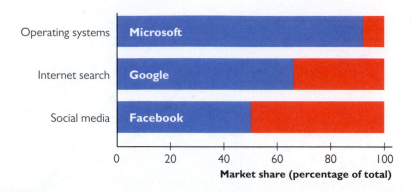

■ Monopoly Price-Setting Strategies

A monopoly faces a tradeoff between price and the quantity sold. To sell a larger quantity, the monopoly must set a lower price. But there are two price-setting possibilities that create different tradeoffs:

- Single price
- Price discrimination

Single Price

Single-price monopoly
A monopoly that must sell each unit of its output for the same price to all its customers.

A **single-price monopoly** is a firm that must sell each unit of its output for the same price to all its customers. Luxottica sells sunglasses (of a given type and quality) for the same price to all its customers. Luxottica is a *single-price* monopoly because if it tried to sell at a higher price to some customers than to others, only the low-price customers would buy from Luxottica. The others would buy from Luxottica's low-price customers.

Price Discrimination

Price-discriminating monopoly
A monopoly that sells different units of a good or service for different prices not related to cost differences.

A **price-discriminating monopoly** is a firm that sells different units for different prices not related to cost differences. Many firms price discriminate. Airlines offer a dizzying array of different prices for the same trip. Pizza producers charge one price for a single pizza and almost give away a second one. Different customers might pay different prices (like airfares), or one customer might pay different prices for different quantities bought (like the bargain price for a second pizza).

When a firm price discriminates, it appears to be doing its customers a favor. In fact, the firm is charging each group of customers the highest price that it can get them to pay and it is increasing its profit.

Not all monopolies can price discriminate. The main obstacle to the practice of price discrimination is resale by the customers who buy for a low price. Because of resale possibilities, price discrimination is limited to monopolies that sell goods and services that cannot be resold.

CHECKPOINT 16.1

Explain how monopoly arises and distinguish between single-price monopoly and price-discriminating monopoly.

Practice Problems

Use the information about the firms listed below to work Problems **1** and **2**.

    a. Coca-Cola cuts its price below that of Pepsi-Cola to increase profit.

    b. A single firm, protected by a barrier to entry, produces a personal service that has no close substitutes.

    c. A barrier to entry exists, but the good has some close substitutes.

    d. A museum offers discounts to students and seniors.

    e. A firm can sell any quantity it chooses at the going price.

    f. A firm experiences economies of scale even when it produces the quantity that meets the entire market demand.

1. Which of the six cases are monopolies or might give rise to monopoly?

2. Which are natural monopolies and which are legal monopolies? Can any of them price discriminate? If so, why?

In the News

Allegiant Air nonstop flights from Tulsa to Washington, D.C./Baltimore
From May 19 to August 16, Allegiant Air will enable Tulsa-area travelers to fly nonstop to Washington, D.C./Baltimore. The airline says the seasonal destination could become year-round if demand is sufficiently large.

                           Source: *Tulsa World*, January 13, 2016

Allegiant Air is the only airline flying nonstop on this route. What type of monopoly is Allegiant? What would be the barrier to entry?

Solutions to Practice Problems

1. Monopoly arises when a single firm produces a good or service that has no close substitutes and a barrier to entry exists. Monopoly arises in **b** and **f**. In **a**, there is more than one firm. In **c**, the good has close substitutes. In **d**, a monopoly might be able to price discriminate, but other types of firms (for example, pizza producers) price discriminate and they are not monopolies. In **e**, the demand for the firm's output is perfectly elastic and there is no limit to what it can sell. This firm operates in a perfectly competitive market.

2. Natural monopoly exists when one firm can meet the entire market demand at a lower price than two or more firms could: **f** is a natural monopoly, but **b** could be. Legal monopoly exists when the granting of a right creates a barrier to entry: **b** might be a legal monopoly. Because a personal service cannot be resold, **b** could price discriminate.

Solution to In the News

Allegiant Air is a natural monopoly on this nonstop route. Before Allegiant entered the market, demand on this route nonstop was too small for any firm to operate. Allegiant is exploring whether demand is large enough for one firm to be profitable. The barrier to entry is a natural barrier that arises from demand and cost.

16.2 SINGLE-PRICE MONOPOLY

To understand how a single-price monopoly makes its output and price decisions, we must first study the link between price and marginal revenue.

■ Price and Marginal Revenue

Because in a monopoly there is only one firm, the demand for the firm's output is the market demand. Let's look at Bobbie's Barbershop, the sole supplier of haircuts in Cairo, Nebraska. The table in Figure 16.2 shows the demand schedule for Bobbie's haircuts. For example, at $12, consumers demand 4 haircuts an hour (row *E*).

Total revenue is the price multiplied by the quantity sold. For example, in row *D*, Bobbie sells 3 haircuts at $14 each, so total revenue is $42. *Marginal revenue* is the change in total revenue resulting from a one-unit increase in the quantity sold. For example, if the price falls from $16 (row *C*) to $14 (row *D*), the quantity sold increases from 2 to 3 haircuts. Total revenue rises from $32 to $42, so the change in total revenue is $10. Because the quantity sold increases by 1 haircut, marginal revenue equals the change in total revenue and is $10. We place marginal revenue between the two rows to emphasize that marginal revenue relates to the *change* in the quantity sold.

Figure 16.2 shows the market demand curve and Bobbie's marginal revenue curve (*MR*) and also illustrates the calculation that we've just made. At each output, marginal revenue is less than price—the marginal revenue curve lies below the demand curve because a lower price is received on *all* units sold, not just on the marginal unit. For example, at a price of $16, Bobbie sells 2 haircuts (point *C*). If she lowers the price to $14 a haircut, she sells 3 haircuts and has a revenue gain

FIGURE 16.2

Demand and Marginal Revenue

The table shows the market demand schedule for haircuts and Bobbie's total revenue and marginal revenue schedules.

If the price of a haircut falls from $16 to $14, the quantity sold increases from 2 to 3 haircuts.

❶ Total revenue lost on the first 2 haircuts is $4; ❷ total revenue gained on the third haircut is $14; so ❸ marginal revenue is $10.

	Price (dollars per haircut)	Quantity demanded (haircuts per hour)	Total revenue (dollars per hour)	Marginal revenue (dollars per haircut)
A	20	0	0	
				18
B	18	1	18	
				14
C	16	2	32	
				10
D	14	3	42	
				6
E	12	4	48	
				2
F	10	5	50	

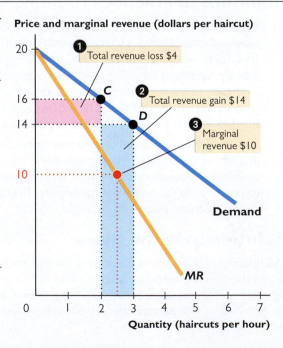

of $14 on the third haircut. But she now receives only $14 a haircut on the first two—$2 a haircut less than before. So she loses $4 of revenue on the first 2 haircuts. To calculate marginal revenue, she must deduct this amount from the revenue gain of $14. So her marginal revenue is $10, which is less than the price $14.

Notice that the marginal revenue curve has *twice the slope* of the demand curve. A fall in price of $10 increases the quantity demanded by 5, but marginal revenue falls by $10 when the quantity increases by 2.5.

■ Marginal Revenue and Elasticity

In Chapter 5 (pp. 122–123), you learned about the *total revenue test* for the price elasticity of demand. If a *fall* in price *increases* total revenue, demand is elastic; and if a *fall* in price *decreases* total revenue, demand is inelastic.

The total revenue test implies that when demand is elastic, marginal revenue is positive and when demand is inelastic, marginal revenue is negative. Figure 16.3 illustrates this relationship between elasticity and marginal revenue.

In part (a) as the price *falls* from $20 to $10, marginal revenue (shown by the blue bars) is *positive* and total revenue in part (b) *increases*, so demand is elastic. In part (a) as the price *falls* from $10 to zero, marginal revenue (the red bars) is *negative* and total revenue in part (b) *decreases*, so demand is *inelastic*. At a price of $10, total revenue is at a maximum, demand is unit elastic, and marginal revenue is zero.

■ FIGURE 16.3

Marginal Revenue and Elasticity   MyEconLab Animation

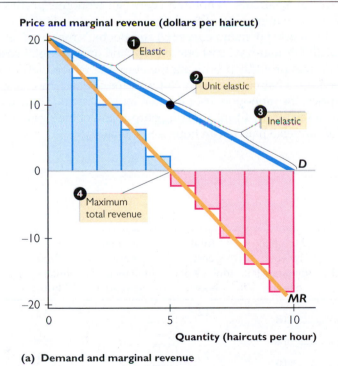

(a) Demand and marginal revenue

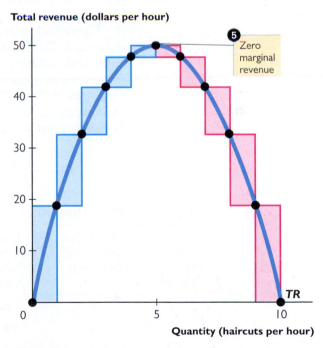

(b) Total revenue

As the price falls, if marginal revenue is positive (the blue bars), ❶ demand is elastic; if marginal revenue is zero, ❷ demand is unit elastic; if marginal revenue is negative (the red bars), ❸ demand is inelastic. At zero marginal revenue in part (a), ❹ total revenue is maximized. And at maximum total revenue in part (b), ❺ marginal revenue is zero.

The relationship between marginal revenue and elasticity implies that a monopoly never profitably produces along the inelastic range of its demand curve. If a monopoly did produce along the inelastic range of its demand curve, it could increase total revenue by raising its price and selling a smaller quantity. Also, by producing less, the firm's total cost would fall and the firm's profit would increase. Let's look at a monopoly's output and price decision.

■ Output and Price Decision

To determine the output level and price that maximize a monopoly's profit, we study the behavior of both revenue and costs as output varies.

Table 16.1 summarizes the information we need about Bobbie's revenue, costs, and economic profit. Economic profit, which equals total revenue minus total cost, is maximized at $12 an hour when Bobbie sells 3 haircuts an hour for $14 each. If she sold 2 haircuts for $16 each, her economic profit would be only $9. And if she sold 4 haircuts for $12 each, her economic profit would be only $8.

You can see why 3 haircuts is Bobbie's profit-maximizing output by looking at the marginal revenue and marginal cost. When Bobbie increases output from 2 to 3 haircuts, her marginal revenue is $10 and her marginal cost is $7. Profit increases by the difference, $3 an hour. If Bobbie increases output yet further, from 3 to 4 haircuts, her marginal revenue is $6 and her marginal cost is $10. In this case, marginal cost exceeds marginal revenue by $4, so profit decreases by $4 an hour.

Figure 16.4 illustrates the information contained in Table 16.1. Part (a) shows Bobbie's total revenue curve (*TR*) and her total cost curve (*TC*). It also shows Bobbie's economic profit as the vertical distance between the *TR* and *TC* curves. Bobbie maximizes her profit at 3 haircuts an hour and earns an economic profit of $12 an hour ($42 of total revenue minus $30 of total cost).

Figure 16.4(b) shows the market demand curve (*D*) and Bobbie's marginal revenue curve (*MR*) along with her marginal cost curve (*MC*) and average total cost curve (*ATC*). Bobbie maximizes profit by producing the output at which marginal cost equals marginal revenue—3 haircuts an hour. But what price does she charge for a haircut? To set the price, the monopoly uses the demand curve and finds the highest price at which it can sell the profit-maximizing output. In Bobbie's case, the highest price at which she can sell 3 haircuts an hour is $14 a haircut.

■ **TABLE 16.1**

A Monopoly's Output and Price Decision

	Price (dollars per haircut)	Quantity demanded (haircuts per hour)	Total revenue (dollars per hour)	Marginal revenue (dollars per haircut)	Total cost (dollars per hour)	Marginal cost (dollars per haircut)	Profit (dollars per hour)
A	20	0	0		12		−12
				18		5	
B	18	1	18		17		1
				14		6	
C	16	2	32		23		9
				10		7	
D	14	3	42		30		12
				6		10	
E	12	4	48		40		8
				2		15	
F	10	5	50		55		−5

When Bobbie produces 3 haircuts an hour, her average total cost is $10 (read from the *ATC* curve at the quantity 3 haircuts) and her price is $14 (read from the *D* curve). Her profit per haircut is $4 ($14 minus $10). Bobbie's economic profit is shown by the blue rectangle, which equals the profit per haircut ($4) multiplied by the number of haircuts (3 an hour), for a total of $12 an hour.

A positive economic profit is an incentive for firms to enter a market. But barriers to entry prevent that from happening in a monopoly. So in a monopoly, the firm can make a positive economic profit and continue to do so indefinitely.

A monopoly charges a price that exceeds marginal cost, but does it always make an economic profit? The answer is no. Bobbie makes a positive economic profit in Figure 16.4. But suppose that Bobbie's landlord increases the rent on her barbershop. If Bobbie pays an additional $12 an hour in shop rent, her fixed cost increases by that amount. Her marginal cost and marginal revenue don't change, so her profit-maximizing output remains at 3 haircuts an hour. Her profit decreases by the additional rent of $12 an hour to zero. If Bobbie pays more than an additional $12 an hour for rent, she incurs an economic loss. If this situation were permanent, Bobbie would go out of business. But monopoly entrepreneurs are creative, and Bobbie might find another shop at a lower rent.

FIGURE 16.4

A Monopoly's Profit-Maximizing Output and Price

MyEconLab Animation

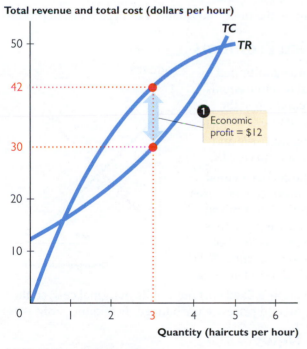

(a) Total revenue and total cost

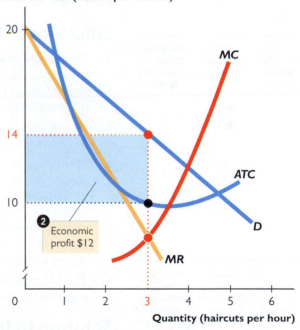

(b) Demand, marginal revenue, and marginal cost

In part (a), economic profit is maximized when total revenue (*TR*) minus total cost (*TC*) is greatest. ❶ Economic profit is the vertical distance between the *TR* and *TC* curves. The profit-maximizing output is 3 haircuts an hour and economic profit is $12 an hour.

In part (b), economic profit is maximized when marginal cost (*MC*) equals marginal revenue (*MR*). The price is determined by the demand curve (*D*) and is $14. ❷ Economic profit, the blue rectangle, is $12—the profit per haircut ($4) multiplied by 3 haircuts.

MyEconLab Study Plan 16.2

Solutions Video

CHECKPOINT 16.2

Explain how a single-price monopoly determines its output and price.

Practice Problems

Minnie's Mineral Springs is a single-price monopoly. Table 1 shows the demand schedule for Minnie's spring water (columns 1 and 2) and the firm's total cost schedule (columns 2 and 3).

1. Calculate Minnie's total revenue and marginal revenue schedules.

2. Draw the demand curve and Minnie's marginal revenue curve.

3. Calculate Minnie's profit-maximizing output, price, and economic profit.

4. If Minnie's is hit with a conservation tax of $14 an hour, what are Minnie's new profit-maximizing output, price, and economic profit?

TABLE 1

Price (dollars per bottle)	Quantity (bottles per hour)	Total cost (dollars per hour)
10	0	1
9	1	2
8	2	4
7	3	7
6	4	12
5	5	18

In the News

Macy's and Luxottica sign exclusive agreement

Macy's and Luxottica will add 500 LensCrafters locations to their current 670 locations of Sunglass Hut. Together, Macy's and Sunglass Hut have more than tripled the size of the sunglass business at Macy's in the past six years. Luxottica makes most of the eyewear sold in North America.

Source: *Business Wire*, November 11, 2015

How does Luxottica determine the price and quantity of eyeglasses to produce?

Solutions to Practice Problems

TABLE 2

Quantity (bottles per hour)	Total revenue (dollars per hour)	Marginal revenue (dollars per bottle)
0	0	
1	9	9
2	16	7
3	21	5
4	24	3
5	25	1

1. Total revenue equals price multiplied by quantity sold. Marginal revenue equals the change in total revenue when the quantity increases by one unit (Table 2).

2. Figure 1 shows the demand curve and Minnie's marginal revenue curve, *MR*.

3. Marginal cost, *MC*, is the change in total cost when the quantity produced increases by 1 bottle (Table 3). Profit is maximized when $MR = MC$ by producing 3 bottles an hour (Figure 1). The price is $7 a bottle. Economic profit equals total revenue ($21) minus total cost ($7), which is $14 an hour.

4. The $14 tax increases Minnie's fixed cost but not its marginal cost, so the profit-maximizing output and price are unchanged. Economic profit is zero.

FIGURE 1

Price and cost (dollars per bottle)

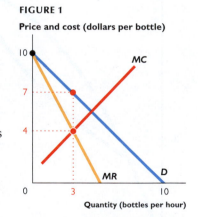

TABLE 3

Quantity (bottles per hour)	Total cost (dollars per hour)	Marginal cost (dollars per bottle)
0	1	
1	2	1
2	4	2
3	7	3
4	12	5
5	18	6

Solution to In the News

Luxottica is (almost) a monopoly and it sets the price of eyeglasses to maximize economic profit. Luxottica knows its total costs, so it calculates the marginal cost of a pair of glasses. The firm uses its market experience to estimate the demand for glasses and calculates marginal revenue. The firm produces the number of pairs of glasses that makes marginal revenue equal to marginal cost and sets the highest price that its customers are willing to pay for the profit-maximizing quantity.

16.3 MONOPOLY AND COMPETITION COMPARED

MyEconLab Concept Video

Imagine a market in which many small firms operate in perfect competition. Then suppose that a single firm buys out all these small firms and creates a monopoly. What happens in this market to the quantity produced, the price, and efficiency?

■ Output and Price

Figure 16.5 shows the market that we'll study. The market demand curve is D. Initially, with many small firms in the market, the market supply curve is S, which is the sum of the supply curves—and marginal cost curves—of the firms. The equilibrium price is P_C, which makes the quantity demanded equal the quantity supplied. The equilibrium quantity is Q_C. Each firm takes the price P_C and maximizes its profit by producing the output at which its own marginal cost equals the price.

A single firm now buys all the firms in this market. Consumers don't change, so the demand curve doesn't change. But the monopoly recognizes this demand curve as a constraint on its sales and knows that its marginal revenue curve is MR.

The market supply curve in perfect competition is the sum of the marginal cost curves of the firms in the industry. So the monopoly's marginal cost curve is the market supply curve of perfect competition—labeled $S = MC$. The monopoly maximizes profit by producing the quantity at which marginal revenue equals marginal cost, which is Q_M. This output is smaller than the competitive output, Q_C. The monopoly charges the price P_M, which is higher than P_C.

Compared to perfect competition, a single-price monopoly produces a smaller output and charges a higher price.

■ FIGURE 16.5

Monopoly's Smaller Output and Higher Price

MyEconLab Animation

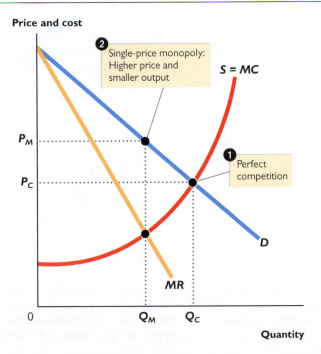

❶ A competitive industry produces the quantity Q_C at price P_C.

❷ A single-price monopoly produces the quantity Q_M at which marginal revenue equals marginal cost and sells that quantity for the price P_M. Compared to perfect competition, a single-price monopoly produces a smaller output and raises the price.

■ Is Monopoly Efficient?

You learned in Chapter 6 that resources are used efficiently when marginal benefit equals marginal cost. Figure 16.6(a) shows that perfect competition achieves this efficient use of resources. The demand curve ($D = MB$) shows the marginal benefit to consumers. The supply curve ($S = MC$) shows the marginal cost (opportunity cost) to producers. At the competitive equilibrium, the price is P_C and the quantity is Q_C. Marginal benefit equals marginal cost, and resource use is efficient. Total surplus (Chapter 6, p. 155), the sum of *consumer surplus,* the green triangle, and *producer surplus,* the blue area, is maximized.

Figure 16.6(b) shows that monopoly is inefficient. Monopoly output is Q_M and price is P_M. Price (marginal benefit) exceeds marginal cost and the underproduction creates a *deadweight loss* (Chapter 6, p. 157), which is shown by the gray area. Consumers lose partly by getting less of the good, shown by the gray triangle above P_C, and partly by paying more for the good. Consumer surplus shrinks to the smaller green triangle. Producers lose by selling less of the good, shown by the part of the gray area below P_C, but gain by selling their output for a higher price, shown by the dark blue rectangle. Producer surplus expands and is larger in monopoly than in perfect competition.

■ **FIGURE 16.6**

The Inefficiency of Monopoly
MyEconLab Animation

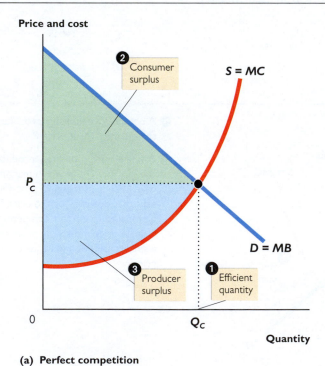

(a) Perfect competition

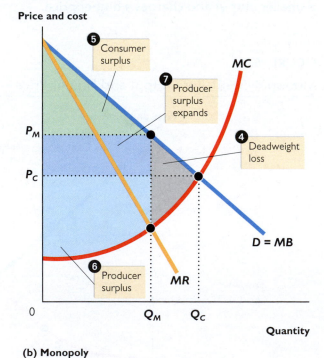

(b) Monopoly

In perfect competition, ❶ the equilibrium quantity is the efficient quantity, Q_C, because at that quantity the price, P_C, equals marginal benefit and marginal cost. The sum of ❷ consumer surplus and ❸ producer surplus is maximized.

In a single-price monopoly, the equilibrium quantity, Q_M, is inefficient because the price, P_M, which equals marginal benefit, exceeds marginal cost. ❹ A deadweight loss arises. ❺ Consumer surplus shrinks, and ❻ producer surplus expands by the area ❼.

Is Monopoly Fair?

Monopoly is inefficient because it creates a deadweight loss. But monopoly also *redistributes* consumer surplus. The producer gains, and the consumers lose.

Figure 16.6 shows this redistribution. The monopoly gets the difference between the higher price, P_M, and the competitive price, P_C, on the quantity sold, Q_M. So the dark blue rectangle shows the part of the consumer surplus taken by the monopoly. This portion of the loss of consumer surplus is not a loss to society. It is redistribution from consumers to the monopoly producer.

Are the gain for the monopoly and the loss for consumers fair? You learned about two standards of fairness in Chapter 6: fair *rules* and a fair *result*. Redistribution from the rich to the poor is consistent with the fair-result view. So on this view of fairness, whether monopoly redistribution is fair or unfair depends on who is richer: the monopoly or the consumers of its product. It might be either. Whether the *rules* are fair depends on whether the monopoly has benefited from a protected position that is not available to anyone else. If everyone is free to acquire the monopoly, then the rules are fair. So monopoly is inefficient and it might be, but is not always, unfair.

The pursuit of monopoly profit leads to an additional costly activity that we'll now describe: rent seeking.

Rent Seeking

Rent seeking is the lobbying for special treatment from the government to create economic profit or to divert consumer surplus or producer surplus away from others. ("Rent" is a general term in economics that includes all forms of surplus such as consumer surplus, producer surplus, and economic profit.) Rent seeking does not always create a monopoly, but it always restricts competition and often creates a monopoly.

Scarce resources can be used to produce the goods and services that people value or they can be used in rent seeking. Rent seeking is potentially profitable for the rent seeker but costly to society because it uses scarce resources purely to transfer wealth from one person or group to another person or group rather than to produce the things that people value.

To see why rent seeking occurs, think about the two ways in which a person might become the owner of a monopoly:

- Buy a monopoly.
- Create a monopoly.

Buy a Monopoly

A person might try to make a monopoly profit by buying a firm (or a right) that is protected by a barrier to entry. Buying a taxicab medallion in New York City is an example. The number of medallions is restricted, so their owners are protected from unlimited entry into the industry. A person who wants to operate a taxi must buy a medallion from someone who already has one.

But anyone is free to enter the bidding for a medallion. So competition among buyers drives the price up to the point at which they make only zero economic profit. For example, competition for the right to operate a taxi in New York City has led to a price of $600,000 for a taxi medallion, which is sufficiently high to eliminate economic profit for taxi operators and leave entrepreneurs with only normal profit.

Rent seeking

The lobbying for special treatment from the government to create economic profit or to divert consumer surplus or producer surplus away from others.

Create a Monopoly

Because buying a monopoly means paying a price that soaks up the economic profit, creating a monopoly by rent seeking is an attractive alternative to buying one. Rent seeking is a political activity. It takes the form of lobbying and trying to influence the political process to get laws that create legal barriers to entry. Such influence might be sought by making campaign contributions in exchange for legislative support or by indirectly seeking to influence political outcomes through publicity in the media or by direct contact with politicians and bureaucrats. An example of a rent created in this way is the law that restricts the quantities of textiles that can be imported into the United States. Another is a law that limits the quantity of tomatoes that can be imported into the United States. These laws restrict competition, which decreases the quantity for sale and increases prices.

Rent-Seeking Equilibrium

Rent seeking is a competitive activity. If an economic profit is available, a rent seeker will try to get some of it. Competition among rent seekers pushes up the cost of rent seeking until it leaves the monopoly earning only a zero economic profit after paying the rent-seeking costs.

Figure 16.7 shows a rent-seeking equilibrium. The cost of rent seeking is a fixed cost that must be added to a monopoly's other costs. The average total cost curve, which includes the fixed cost of rent seeking, shifts upward until it just touches the demand curve. Consumer surplus is unaffected. But the deadweight loss of monopoly now includes the original deadweight loss plus the economic profit consumed by rent seeking, which the enlarged gray area shows.

■ **FIGURE 16.7**

Rent-Seeking Equilibrium   MyEconLab Animation

❶ Rent-seeking costs exhaust economic profit. The firm's rent-seeking costs are fixed costs. They increase total fixed cost and average total cost. The *ATC* curve shifts upward until, at the profit-maximizing price, the firm breaks even.

❷ Monopoly profit-maximization shrinks consumer surplus relative to its maximum level in perfect competition, but rent-seeking doesn't shrink consumer surplus any further.

❸ The deadweight loss increases and now includes the original deadweight loss plus the economic profit consumed by rent seeking.

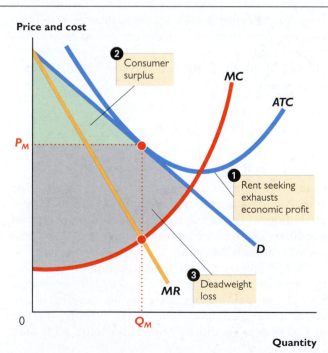

CHECKPOINT 16.3

MyEconLab Study Plan 16.3
Key Terms Quiz
Solutions Video

Compare the performance of a single-price monopoly with that of perfect competition.

Practice Problems

Township is a small isolated community served by one newspaper that can meet the market demand at a lower cost than two or more newspapers could. The *Township Gazette* is the only source of news. Figure 1 shows the marginal cost of printing the *Township Gazette* and the market demand for it. The *Township Gazette* is a profit-maximizing, single-price monopoly.

1. How many copies of the *Township Gazette* are printed each day and what is the price of the *Township Gazette*?

2. What is the efficient number of copies of the *Township Gazette* and what is the price at which the efficient number of copies could be sold?

3. Is the number of copies printed the efficient quantity? Explain your answer.

4. On the graph, show the consumer surplus that is redistributed from consumers to the *Township Gazette* and the deadweight loss that arises because the *Township Gazette* is a monopoly.

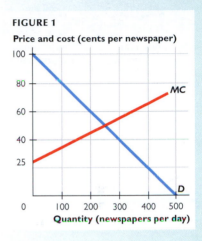

FIGURE 1

Price and cost (cents per newspaper)

In the News

Ticketmaster's near monopoly challenged as technology changes
In the 1990s, to see Michael Jordan or Garth Brooks live you had to buy the ticket through Ticketmaster, or from a scalper. Today, Ticketmaster has merged with concert promoter Live Nation and now controls the sale of tickets to sports and music events. Competitors have entered the market, and event tickets are now sold through Internet auction markets.

How will the increased competition in the sale of tickets affect the service fee component of the price and the efficiency of the market? Will scalpers survive?

Solutions to Practice Problems

1. The profit-maximizing quantity of the *Township Gazette* is 150 a day, where marginal revenue equals marginal cost. The price is 70¢ a copy (Figure 2).

2. The efficient quantity is 250 copies, where quantity demanded (marginal benefit) equals marginal cost and the price would be 50¢ a copy (Figure 2).

3. The number of copies printed is not efficient because the marginal benefit of the 150th copy (70¢) exceeds its marginal cost (40¢) (Figure 2).

4. In Figure 2, the blue rectangle ❶ shows the consumer surplus transferred from the consumers to the *Township Gazette* and the gray triangle ❷ shows the deadweight loss created.

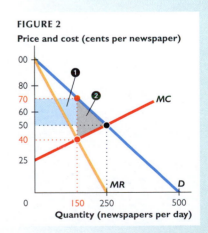

FIGURE 2

Price and cost (cents per newspaper)

Solution to In the News

The price you pay for an event ticket is the sum of the price of the event plus a service fee. As a monopoly, Ticketmaster charges the profit-maximizing fee. The monopoly has weakened and competition has increased, but sellers still charge the profit-maximizing fee, although a lower fee. The ticket-selling market is more efficient, but scalpers now compete with resale auctions and appear to survive.

Why does a hairdresser charge seniors, veterans, and kids $3 less than other customers?

16.4   PRICE DISCRIMINATION

Price discrimination—selling a good or service at a number of different prices—is widespread. You encounter it when you travel, go to the movies, get your hair cut, buy pizza, or visit an art museum. At first sight, it appears that price discrimination contradicts the assumption of profit maximization. Why would a movie operator allow children to see movies at half price? Why would a hairdresser charge students and senior citizens less? Aren't these firms losing profit by being nice to their customers?

Deeper investigation shows that far from lowering profit, price discriminators make a bigger profit than they would otherwise. So a monopoly has an incentive to find ways of discriminating and charging each buyer the highest possible price. Some people pay less with price discrimination, but others pay more.

Most price discriminators are *not* monopolies, but monopolies do price discriminate when they can. To be able to price discriminate, a firm must

- Identify and separate different types of buyers.
- Sell a product that cannot be resold.

Price discrimination is charging different prices for a single good or service because the willingness to pay varies across buyers. Not all price *differences* are price *discrimination*. Some goods that are similar but not identical have different prices because they have different production costs. For example, the cost of producing electricity depends on time of day. If an electric power company charges a higher price for consumption between 7:00 and 9:00 in the morning and between 4:00 and 7:00 in the evening than it does at other times of the day, the company is not price discriminating.

■ Price Discrimination and Consumer Surplus

The key idea behind price discrimination is to convert consumer surplus into economic profit. To extract every dollar of consumer surplus from every buyer, the monopoly would have to offer each individual customer a separate price schedule based on that customer's own willingness to pay. Such price discrimination cannot be carried out in practice because a firm does not have enough information about each consumer's demand curve. But firms try to extract as much consumer surplus as possible, and to do so, they discriminate in two broad ways:

- Among groups of buyers
- Among units of a good

Discriminating Among Groups of Buyers

To price discriminate among groups of buyers, the firm offers different prices to different types of buyers, based on things such as age, employment status, or some other easily distinguished characteristic. This type of price discrimination works when each group has a different average willingness to pay for the good or service.

For example, a face-to-face sales meeting with a customer might bring a large and profitable order. For salespeople and other business travelers, the marginal benefit from an airplane trip is large and the price that such a traveler will pay for a trip is high. In contrast, for a vacation traveler, any of several different trips or even no vacation trip are options. So for vacation travelers, the marginal benefit of a trip is small and the price that such a traveler will pay for a trip is low. Because business travelers are willing to pay more than vacation travelers are, it is possible for an airline to profit by price discriminating between these two groups.

Discriminating Among Units of a Good

To price discriminate among units of a good, the firm charges the same prices to all its customers but offers a lower price per unit for a larger number of units bought. When Pizza Hut charges $10 for one home-delivered pizza and $14 for two, it is using this type of price discrimination. In this example, the price of the second pizza is only $4.

Let's see how an airline exploits the differences in demand by business and vacation travelers and increases its profit by price discriminating.

◼ Profiting by Price Discriminating

Global Air has a monopoly on an exotic route. Figure 16.8 shows the demand curve (*D*) for travel on this route and Global Air's marginal revenue curve (*MR*). It also shows Global Air's marginal cost (*MC*) and average total cost (*ATC*) curves.

Initially, Global is a single-price monopoly and maximizes its profit by producing 8,000 trips a year (the quantity at which *MR* equals *MC*). The price is $1,200 a trip. The average total cost of a trip is $600, so economic profit is $600 a trip. On 8,000 trips, Global's economic profit is $4.8 million a year, shown by the blue rectangle. Global's customers enjoy a consumer surplus shown by the green triangle.

◼ **FIGURE 16.8**

A Single-Price Monopoly's Price and Economic Profit

MyEconLab Animation

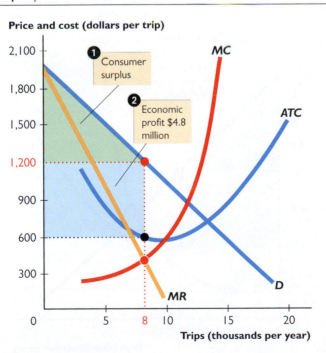

Global Air has a monopoly on an air route. The demand curve for travel on this route is *D*, and Global's marginal revenue curve is *MR*. Its marginal cost curve is *MC*, and its average total cost curve is *ATC*.

As a single-price monopoly, Global maximizes profit by selling 8,000 trips a year at $1,200 a trip.

❶ Global's customers enjoy a consumer surplus—the green triangle.

❷ Global makes an economic profit of $4.8 million a year—the blue rectangle.

Global is struck by the fact that many of its customers are business travelers, and Global suspects that they are willing to pay more than $1,200 a trip. So Global does some market research, which tells Global that some business travelers are willing to pay as much as $1,800 a trip. Also, these customers almost always make their travel plans at the last moment. Another group of business travelers is willing to pay $1,600. These customers know a week ahead when they will travel, and prefer a flexible ticket. Yet another group is willing to pay up to $1,400. These travelers know two weeks ahead when they will travel, and they are happy to buy a restricted ticket.

So Global announces a new fare schedule: No restrictions, $1,800; 7-day advance purchase, flexible, $1,600; 14-day advance purchase, flexible, $1,400; 14-day advance purchase, must stay at least 7 days, $1,200.

Figure 16.9 shows the outcome with this new fare structure and also shows why Global is pleased with its new fares. It sells 2,000 trips at each of its four prices. Global's economic profit increases by the area of the blue steps in the figure. Its economic profit is now its original $4.8 million a year plus an additional $2.4 million from its new higher fares. Consumer surplus has shrunk to the sum of the smaller green triangles.

■ Perfect Price Discrimination

Perfect price discrimination
Price discrimination that extracts the entire consumer surplus by charging the highest price that consumers are willing to pay for each unit.

But Global thinks that it can do even better. It plans to achieve **perfect price discrimination**, which extracts the entire consumer surplus by charging the highest price that consumers are willing to pay for each unit. To do so, Global must get creative and come up with a host of additional business fares ranging between $2,000 and $1,200, each one of which appeals to a small segment of the business market.

■ FIGURE 16.9

Price Discrimination

MyEconLab Animation

Global revises its fare structure. It now offers no restrictions at $1,800; 7-day advance purchase, flexible at $1,600; 14-day advance purchase, flexible at $1,400; and 14-day advance purchase, must stay at least 7 days, at $1,200.

Global sells 2,000 units at each of its four new fares. Its economic profit increases by $2.4 million a year to $7.2 million a year, which is shown by the original profit (light blue rectangle) plus the blue steps. Global's customers' consumer surplus shrinks to the sum of the green areas.

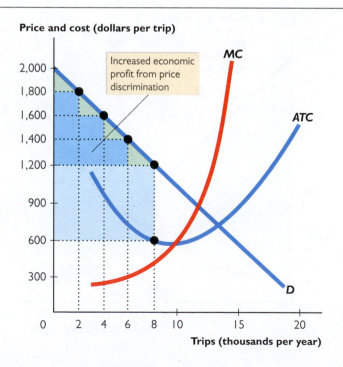

Once Global is discriminating finely between different customers and getting from each customer the maximum he or she is willing to pay, something special happens to marginal revenue. Recall that for the single-price monopoly, marginal revenue is less than price. The reason is that when the price is cut to sell a larger quantity, the price is lower on all units sold. But with perfect price discrimination, Global sells only the marginal seat at the lower price. All the other customers continue to buy the trip at the highest price they are willing to pay. So for the perfect price discriminator, marginal revenue equals price and the demand curve becomes the marginal revenue curve.

With marginal revenue equal to price, Global can obtain yet greater profit by increasing output up to the point at which price (and marginal revenue) is equal to marginal cost.

So Global now seeks additional travelers who will not pay as much as $1,200 a trip but who will pay more than marginal cost. More creative pricing comes up with vacation specials and other fares that have combinations of advance reservation, minimum stay, and other restrictions that make these fares unattractive to Global's existing customers but attractive to a further group of travelers. With all these fares and specials, Global extracts the entire consumer surplus and maximizes economic profit.

Figure 16.10 shows the outcome with perfect price discrimination. The dozens of fares paid by the original travelers who are willing to pay between $1,200 and $2,000 have extracted the entire consumer surplus from this group and converted it into economic profit for Global. The new fares between $900 and $1,200 have attracted 3,000 additional travelers but have taken their entire consumer surplus also. Global is making an economic profit of more than $9 million a year.

FIGURE 16.10

Perfect Price Discrimination

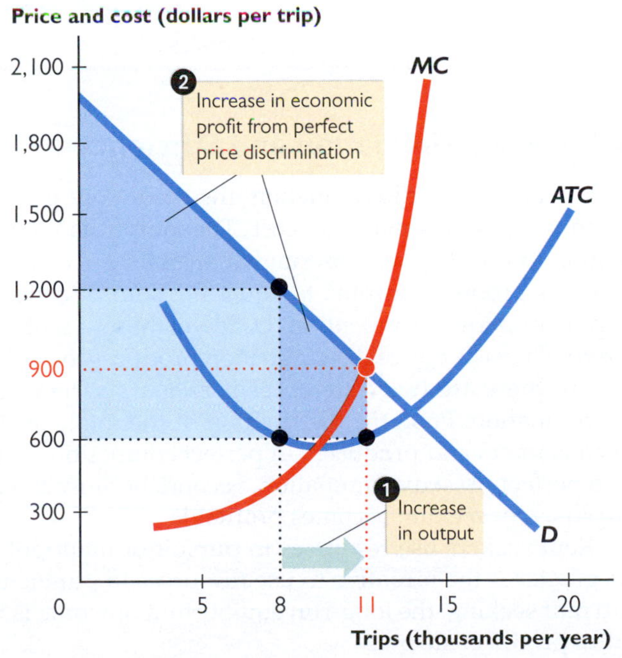

With perfect price discrimination, the demand curve becomes Global's marginal revenue curve. Economic profit is maximized when the lowest price equals marginal cost.

❶ Global increases output to 11,000 trips a year.

❷ Global's economic profit increases to $9.35 million a year.

EYE on the U.S. ECONOMY
Airline Price Discrimination

United Airlines' normal flexible economy fare from San Francisco to Washington, D.C., is $897, but it has a range of cheaper fares with its lowest-price ticket at $239. On a typical flight, passengers might be paying as many as 20 different fares.

The airlines sort their customers according to their willingness to pay by offering a variety of options that attract price-sensitive leisure travelers but don't get bought by business travelers.

Despite the sophistication of the airlines' pricing schemes, almost 15 percent of seats fly empty. The marginal cost of filling an empty seat is close to zero, so a ticket sold at a few dollars would be profitable.

The airlines compete with online booking sites. Low fares are now feasible, thanks to dozens of online travel agents. Shopping around the airlines with bids from travelers, these travel agents broker thousands of tickets a day and obtain the lowest possible fares for their customers.

Would it bother you to hear how little I paid for this flight?

Credit: William Hamilton

■ Price Discrimination and Efficiency

With perfect price discrimination, the monopoly increases output to the point at which price equals marginal cost. This output is identical to that of perfect competition. Perfect price discrimination pushes consumer surplus to zero but increases producer surplus to equal the sum of consumer surplus and producer surplus in perfect competition. Deadweight loss with perfect price discrimination is zero. So perfect price discrimination produces the efficient quantity.

But there are two differences between perfect competition and perfect price discrimination. First, the distribution of the total surplus is different. It is shared by consumers and producers in perfect competition while the producer gets it all with perfect price discrimination. Second, because the producer grabs all the total surplus, rent seeking becomes profitable.

Rent seekers use resources in pursuit of monopoly, and the bigger the rents, the greater is the incentive to use resources to pursue those rents. With free entry into rent seeking, the long-run equilibrium outcome is that rent seekers use up the entire producer surplus.

CHECKPOINT 16.4

Explain how price discrimination increases profit.

Practice Problems

Village, a small isolated town, has one doctor. For a 30-minute consultation, the doctor charges a rich person twice as much as a poor person.

1. Does the doctor practice price discrimination? Is the doctor using resources efficiently? Does the doctor's pricing scheme redistribute consumer surplus? If so, explain how.

2. If the doctor decided to charge everyone the maximum price that he or she would be willing to pay, what would be the consumer surplus? Would the market for medical service in Village be efficient?

In the News

Where to find the best travel deals
Travel discounts as high as 50 percent are available if you know where to look for them. Examples are companion and two-for-one sales on airlines and Amtrak, and second-, third-, fourth-, or fifth-night-free deals offered by hotels. A Southwest Airlines' senior fare can be up to 40 percent less than other discounted fares.

Source: USA Today, December 10, 2015

How do airlines, railroads, and hotels increase profit by price discriminating?

Solutions to Practice Problems

1. The doctor practices price discrimination because rich people and poor people pay a different price for the same service: a 30-minute consultation. The doctor provides the profit-maximizing number of consultations and charges rich people more than poor people. As a monopoly, the total number of consultations is less than that at which marginal benefit equals the marginal cost of providing the medical service. Because marginal benefit does not equal marginal cost, the doctor is not using resources efficiently. With price discrimination, some consumer surplus is redistributed to the doctor as profit.

2. The doctor decides to practice perfect price discrimination. If successful, with perfect price discrimination, marginal revenue equals price. To maximize economic profit, the doctor increases the number of consultations to make the lowest price charged equal to the marginal cost of providing the service. The doctor takes the entire consumer surplus, so consumer surplus is zero.
   Marginal benefit equals price, so resources are being used efficiently.

Solution to In the News

A trip by air or rail or a night in a hotel cannot be resold, so price discrimination is possible. Offering a discount is price discrimination. Price discrimination is profitable because marginal cost is lower than the single-price monopoly's profit-maximizing price. Selling additional units for a discountd price that is greater than marginal cost increases economic profit.

16.5 MONOPOLY REGULATION

Natural monopoly presents a dilemma. With economies of scale, a natural monopoly produces at the lowest possible cost. But with market power, the monopoly has an incentive to raise the price above the competitive price and produce too little—to operate in the self-interest of the monopoly and not in the social interest.

Regulation—rules administered by a government agency to influence prices, quantities, entry, and other aspects of economic activity in a firm or industry—is a possible solution to this dilemma.

To implement regulation, the government establishes agencies to oversee and enforce the rules. For example, the Surface Transportation Board regulates prices on interstate railroads and some trucking and bus lines, and water and oil pipelines. By the 1970s, almost a quarter of the nation's output was produced by regulated industries (far more than just natural monopolies) and a process of deregulation began.

Deregulation is the process of removing regulation of prices, quantities, entry, and other aspects of economic activity in a firm or industry. During the past 30 years, deregulation has occurred in domestic air transportation, telephone service, interstate trucking, and banking and financial services. Cable TV was deregulated in 1984, re-regulated in 1992, and deregulated again in 1996.

Regulation is a *possible* solution to the dilemma presented by monopoly but not a sure-bet solution. There are two theories about how regulation actually works: the *social interest theory* and the *capture theory*.

The **social interest theory** is that the political and regulatory process relentlessly seeks out inefficiency and introduces regulation that eliminates deadweight loss and allocates resources efficiently.

The **capture theory** is that the political and regulatory process gets captured by the regulated firm and ends up serving its self-interest, with maximum economic profit, underproduction, and deadweight loss. The regulator gets captured because the producer's gain is large and visible while each individual consumer's gain is small and invisible. No individual consumer has an incentive to oppose the regulation, but the producer has a big incentive to lobby for it.

Which theory of regulation best explains real-world regulations? Does regulation serve the social interest or the self-interest of monopoly producers?

■ Efficient Regulation of a Natural Monopoly

A cable TV company is a *natural monopoly* (pp. 404–405)—it can supply the entire market at a lower price than two or more competing firms can. Cox Communications, based in Atlanta, supplies cable TV to households in 16 states. It has invested heavily in satellite receiving dishes, cables, and control equipment and so has large fixed costs. These fixed costs are part of the company's average total cost. Its average total cost decreases as the number of households served increases because the fixed cost is spread over a larger number of households. Unregulated, Cox Communications serves the number of households that maximizes profit. Like all single-price monopolies, the profit-maximizing quantity is less than the efficient quantity and underproduction results in a deadweight loss (see Figure 16.6, p. 414).

How can Cox be regulated to produce the efficient quantity of cable TV service? The answer is by being regulated to set its price equal to marginal cost, known as the **marginal cost pricing rule**. The quantity demanded at a price equal

---

Regulation
Rules administered by a government agency to influence prices, quantities, entry, and other aspects of economic activity in a firm or industry.

Deregulation
The process of removing regulation of prices, quantities, entry, and other aspects of economic activity in a firm or industry.

Social interest theory
The theory that regulation achieves an efficient allocation of resources.

Capture theory
The theory that the regulation serves the self-interest of the producer and results in maximum profit, underproduction, and deadweight loss.

Marginal cost pricing rule
A rule that sets price equal to marginal cost to achieve an efficient output.

to marginal cost is the efficient quantity—the quantity at which marginal benefit equals marginal cost.

Figure 16.11 illustrates the marginal cost pricing rule. The demand curve for cable TV is *D*. Cox's marginal cost curve is *MC*. That marginal cost curve is (assumed to be) horizontal at $10 per household per month—that is, the cost of providing each additional household with a month of cable programming is $10. The efficient outcome occurs if the price is regulated at $10 per household per month with 8 million households served.

But there is a problem: Because average total cost exceeds marginal cost, a firm that follows the marginal cost pricing rule incurs an economic loss. So a cable TV company that is required to use a marginal cost pricing rule will not stay in business for long. How can the firm cover its costs and, at the same time, obey a marginal cost pricing rule?

One possibility is price discrimination (see pp. 418–422). Another possibility is to use a two-part price (called a *two-part tariff*). For example, local telephone companies charge consumers a monthly fee for being connected to the telephone system and then charge a price equal to marginal cost (zero) for each local call. A cable TV operator can charge a one-time connection fee that covers its fixed cost and then charge a monthly fee equal to marginal cost.

■ Second-Best Regulation of a Natural Monopoly

Regulation of a natural monopoly cannot always achieve an efficient outcome. Two possible ways of enabling a regulated monopoly to avoid an economic loss are

- Average cost pricing
- Government subsidy

■ FIGURE 16.11

Natural Monopoly: Marginal Cost Pricing   MyEconLab Animation

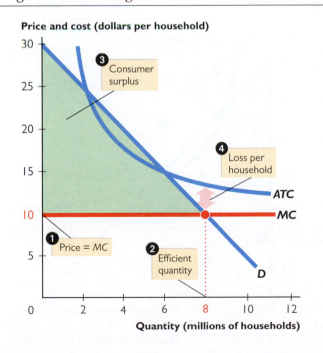

The market demand curve for cable TV is *D*. A cable TV operator's marginal cost *MC* is a constant $10 per household per month. Its fixed cost is large, and the average total cost curve, which includes average fixed cost, is *ATC*.

❶ Price is set equal to marginal cost at $10 a month.

❷ At this price, the efficient quantity (8 million households) is served.

❸ Consumer surplus is maximized as shown by the green triangle.

❹ The firm incurs a loss on each household served, shown by the red arrow.

Average Cost Pricing

Average cost pricing rule
A rule that sets price equal to average total cost to enable a regulated firm to avoid economic loss.

The **average cost pricing rule** sets price equal to average total cost. With this rule the firm produces the quantity at which the average total cost curve cuts the demand curve. This rule results in the firm making zero economic profit—breaking even. But because for a natural monopoly average total cost exceeds marginal cost, the quantity produced is less than the efficient quantity and a deadweight loss arises. Figure 16.12 illustrates the average cost pricing rule. The price is $15 a month and 6 million households buy cable TV. The gray triangle shows the deadweight loss.

Government Subsidy

A government subsidy is a direct payment to the firm equal to its economic loss. But to pay a subsidy, the government must raise the revenue by taxing some other activity. You saw in Chapter 8 that taxes themselves generate deadweight loss.

And the Second-Best Is...

Which is the better option, average cost pricing or marginal cost pricing with a government subsidy? The answer turns on the relative magnitudes of the two deadweight losses. Average cost pricing generates a deadweight loss in the market served by the natural monopoly. A subsidy generates deadweight losses in the markets for the items that are taxed to pay the subsidy. The smaller deadweight loss is the second-best solution to regulating a natural monopoly. Making this calculation in practice is too difficult and average cost pricing is generally preferred to a subsidy.

▮ **FIGURE 16.12**

Natural Monopoly: Average Cost Pricing

MyEconLab Animation

❶ Price is set equal to average total cost at $15 a month.

At this price, ❷ the quantity of households served (6 million) is less than the efficient quantity (8 million households).

❸ Consumer surplus shrinks to the smaller green triangle.

❹ A producer surplus enables the firm to pay its total fixed cost and break even.

❺ A deadweight loss, shown by the gray triangle, arises.

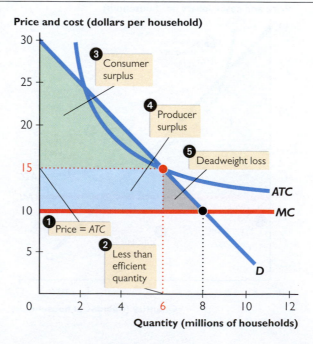

EYE on MICROSOFT

MyEconLab Critical Thinking Exercise

Are Microsoft's Prices Too High?

Microsoft's prices are too high in the sense that they exceed marginal cost and result in fewer copies sold of the Windows operating system and Office application than the efficient quantities.

Profit Maximization

The figure illustrates how Microsoft prices its products to maximize profit. The demand for copies of the Windows operating system is D. The marginal revenue curve is MR. The marginal cost of an additional copy is very small and we assume it to be zero, with marginal cost curve MC.

Profit is maximized by producing the quantity at which marginal revenue equals marginal cost. In the figure, that quantity is 4 million copies of Windows per month. The price is $300 per copy and Microsoft receives a producer surplus shown by the area of the blue rectangle.

Inefficiency

The efficient quantity is 8 million copies per month, where price and marginal benefit equal marginal cost. Because the actual quantity is smaller than the efficient quantity, a deadweight loss arises and the area of the gray triangle shows its magnitude. The area of the green triangle shows the consumer surplus.

Fixed Cost

The marginal cost of a copy of Windows might be close to zero, but the fixed cost of developing the software is large. Microsoft must earn at least enough revenue to pay these fixed costs.

Earning enough to pay the firm's fixed costs does not inevitably lead to inefficiency. Some firms with zero marginal cost and the market power to charge a high price do choose to provide the efficient quantity of their services at a zero price.

The Google Solution

Google is one such firm. The price of an Internet search on Google is zero. The quantity of searches is that at which the marginal benefit of a search equals the zero marginal cost, so the quantity of searches is the efficient quantity.

Google earns revenue, and a very large revenue, by selling advertising that

more than pays its fixed operating costs.

Efficiency

Advertising on Google is more effective than a TV or poster advertisement because it is targeted at potential buyers of products based on the topics of their searches.

The Google solution delivers the efficient quantity of zero-marginal-cost Internet search activity.

The Google solution might also deliver the efficient quantity of advertising. It will do so if Google is able to achieve perfect price discrimination in the market for advertising.

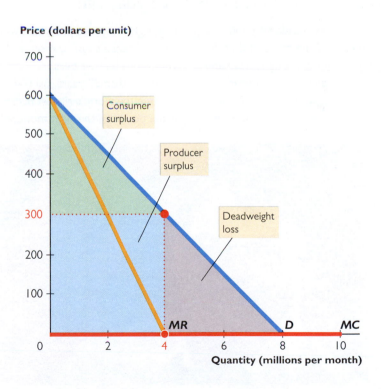

Implementing average cost pricing presents the regulator with a challenge because it is not possible to be sure of a firm's costs. So regulators use one of two practical rules:

- Rate of return regulation
- Price cap regulation

Rate of Return Regulation

Rate of return regulation

A regulation that sets the price at a level that enables a firm to earn a specified target rate of return on its capital.

Under **rate of return regulation**, the price is set at a level that enables the firm to earn a specified target rate of return on its capital. This type of regulation can end up serving the self-interest of the firm rather than the social interest. The firm's managers have an incentive to inflate costs by spending on items such as private jets, free baseball tickets (disguised as public relations expenses), and lavish entertainment. Managers also have an incentive to use more capital than the efficient amount. The *rate* of return on capital is regulated but not the *total* return on capital, and the greater the amount of capital, the greater is the total return.

EYE on YOUR LIFE
Monopoly in Your Everyday Life

MyEconLab Critical Thinking Exercise

When Bill Gates decided to quit Harvard in 1975, he realized that PCs would need an operating system and applications programs to interact with the computer's hardware. He also knew that whoever owned the copyright on these programs would have a license to print money. And he wanted to be that person.

In less than 30 years, Bill Gates became the world's richest person. Such is the power of the right monopoly.

You, along with millions of other PC users, have willingly paid the monopoly price for Windows and Microsoft Office. Sure, the marginal cost of a copy of these programs is close to zero, so the quantity sold is way too few. There is a big deadweight loss.

Compared with the alternative of no Windows, you're better off. But are you better off than you would be if there were many alternatives to Windows competing for your attention? To answer this question, think about the applications—spreadsheets, word processing, and so on—that you need to make your computer useful. With lots of operating systems, what would happen to the cost of developing applications? Would you have more or less choice?

Price Cap Regulation

For the reason that we've just examined, rate of return regulation is increasingly being replaced by price cap regulation. A **price cap regulation** is a price ceiling—a rule that specifies the highest price the firm is permitted to set. This type of regulation lowers the price and gives the firm an incentive to minimize its costs. But what happens to the quantity produced?

Recall that in a competitive market, a price ceiling set below the equilibrium price decreases output and creates a shortage (see Chapter 7, pp. 171–172). In contrast, in natural monopoly a price ceiling increases output. The reason is that at the regulated price, the firm can sell any quantity it chooses up to the quantity demanded. So each additional unit sold brings in the same additional revenue: marginal revenue equals price. The regulated price exceeds marginal cost, so the profit-maximizing quantity becomes the quantity demanded at the price ceiling.

Figure 16.13 illustrates this outcome. Unregulated, a cable TV operator maximizes profit by serving 4 million households at a price of $20 a month. With a price cap set at $15 a month, the firm is permitted to sell any quantity it chooses at that price or at a lower price. The profit-maximizing quantity now increases to 6 million households. Serving fewer than 6 million households, the firm incurs a loss—average total cost exceeds the price cap. Serving more than 6 million households is possible but only by lowering the price along the demand curve. Again, average total cost exceeds price and the firm incurs a loss.

In Figure 16.13, the price cap delivers average cost pricing. In practice, the regulator might set the cap too high. For this reason, price cap regulation is often combined with *earnings sharing regulation*—a regulation that requires firms to make refunds to customers when profits rise above a target level.

Price cap regulation
A rule that specifies the highest price that a firm is permitted to set—a price ceiling.

FIGURE 16.13

Natural Monopoly: Price Cap Regulation

MyEconLab Animation

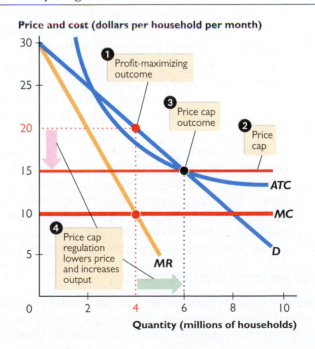

❶ With no regulation, a cable TV operator serves 4 million households at a price of $20 a month.

❷ A price cap regulation sets the maximum price at $15 a month.

❸ Only when 6 million households are served can the firm break even. (When fewer than 6 million households are served or more than 6 million households are served, the firm incurs an economic loss.) The firm has an incentive to keep costs as low as possible and to produce the quantity demanded at the price cap.

❹ The price cap regulation lowers the price and increases the number of households served.

MyEconLab Study Plan 16.5
Key Terms Quiz
Solutions Video

CHECKPOINT 16.5

Explain why natural monopoly is regulated and the effects of regulation.

Practice Problems

An unregulated natural monopoly bottles Elixir, a unique health product that has no substitutes. The monopoly's total fixed cost is $150,000, and its marginal cost is 10¢ a bottle. Figure 1 illustrates the demand for Elixir.

1. How many bottles of Elixir does the monopoly sell and what is the price of a bottle of Elixir? Is the monopoly's use of resources efficient?

2. Suppose that the government introduces a marginal cost pricing rule. What is the price of Elixir, the quantity sold, and the monopoly's economic profit?

3. Suppose that the government introduces an average cost pricing rule. What is the price of Elixir, the quantity sold, and the monopoly's economic profit?

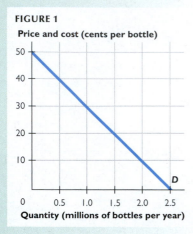

FIGURE 1

In the News

Michigan's oversight of cable TV firms shuts off

Michigan's cable TV subscribers have had to live with soaring monopoly fees, and on January 1, 2016, they became even more vulnerable as funds that regulators had used for cable TV oversight were cut off.

Source: *Detroit Free Press*, December 31, 2015

How could the Michigan regulators have protected cable TV subscribers from rising fees and why, most likely, didn't they?

Solutions to Practice Problems

1. The monopoly will produce 1 million bottles a year—the quantity at which marginal revenue equals marginal cost. The price is 30¢ a bottle—the highest price at which the monopoly can sell the 1 million bottles a year (Figure 2). The monopoly's use of resources is inefficient. If resource use were efficient, the monopoly would produce the quantity at which marginal benefit (price) equals marginal cost: 2 million bottles a year.

2. With a marginal cost pricing rule, the price is 10¢ a bottle and the monopoly produces 2 million bottles a year. The monopoly incurs an economic loss equal to its total fixed costs of $150,000 a year. The monopoly would need a subsidy from the government to keep it in business.

3. With an average cost pricing rule, the firm produces the quantity at which price equals average total cost. Average total cost equals average variable cost plus average fixed cost. Average variable cost equals marginal cost and is 10¢ a bottle. Average fixed cost is $150,000 divided by the quantity produced. For example, at 1 million bottles, average fixed cost is 15¢ and at 1.5 million bottles, average fixed cost is 10¢ a bottle. The average total cost of producing 1.5 million bottles is 20¢ a bottle and they can be sold for 20¢ a bottle. So the monopoly produces 1.5 million bottles a year and breaks even.

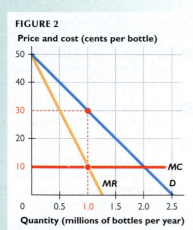

FIGURE 2

Solution to In the News

Rate of return regulation or price cap regulation might have been used to keep cable TV rates close to marginal cost or average total cost. Most likely cable TV prices are not regulated because the cable TV firms have captured the regulator.

CHAPTER SUMMARY

Key Points

1. **Explain how monopoly arises and distinguish between single-price monopoly and price-discriminating monopoly.**

   - In monopoly, a single producer of a good or service that has no close substitutes operates behind a natural, legal, or ownership barrier to entry.
   - A monopoly can price discriminate when there is no resale possibility.
   - Where resale is possible, a firm charges a single price.

2. **Explain how a single-price monopoly determines its output and price.**

   - The demand for a monopoly's output is the market demand, and a single-price monopoly's marginal revenue is less than price.
   - A monopoly maximizes profit by producing the quantity at which marginal revenue equals marginal cost and by charging the maximum price that consumers are willing to pay for that quantity.

3. **Compare the performance of a single-price monopoly with that of perfect competition.**

   - A single-price monopoly price is higher and quantity produced is smaller than in a perfectly competitive market and a deadweight loss arises.
   - Monopoly imposes a loss on society that equals its deadweight loss plus the cost of the resources devoted to rent seeking.

4. **Explain how price discrimination increases profit.**

   - Perfect price discrimination captures the entire consumer surplus. Prices are the highest that each consumer is willing to pay for each unit.
   - With perfect price discrimination, the monopoly is efficient but rent seeking uses some or all of the producer surplus.

5. **Explain why natural monopoly is regulated and the effects of regulation.**

   - Regulation might achieve an efficient use of resources or help the monopoly to maximize economic profit.
   - A natural monopoly is efficient if its price equals marginal cost, but a second-best outcome is for price to equal average total cost.
   - A price cap supported by earnings sharing regulation is the most effective practical method of regulating a natural monopoly.

Key Terms

MyEconLab Key Terms Quiz

Average cost pricing rule, 426
Barrier to entry, 404
Capture theory, 424
Deregulation, 424
Legal monopoly, 405
Marginal cost pricing rule, 424

Monopoly, 404
Natural monopoly, 404
Perfect price discrimination, 420
Price cap regulation, 429
Price-discriminating monopoly, 406
Rate of return regulation, 428

Regulation, 424
Rent seeking, 415
Single-price monopoly, 406
Social interest theory, 424

CHAPTER CHECKPOINT

Study Plan Problems and Applications

Use the following information to work Problems **1** to **3**.

Elixir Spring produces a unique and highly prized mineral water. The firm's total fixed cost is $5,000 a day, and its marginal cost is zero. Table 1 shows the demand schedule for Elixir Spring water.

TABLE 1

Price (dollars per bottle)	Quantity (bottles per day)
10	0
8	2,000
6	4,000
4	6,000
2	8,000
0	10,000

1. On a graph, show the demand curve for Elixir water and Elixir Spring's marginal revenue curve. What are Elixir's profit-maximizing price, output, and economic profit?

2. Compare Elixir's profit-maximizing price with the marginal cost of producing the profit-maximizing output. At the profit-maximizing price, is the demand for Elixir Spring water inelastic or elastic?

3. Suppose that there are 1,000 springs, all able to produce this water at zero marginal cost and with zero fixed costs. Compare the equilibrium price and quantity produced with Elixir Spring's price and quantity produced.

4. Blue Rose Inc. is the only flower grower to have cracked the secret of making a blue rose. Figure 1 shows the demand for blue roses and the marginal cost of producing a blue rose. What is Blue Rose's profit-maximizing output? What price does Blue Rose Inc. charge and is it efficient?

FIGURE 1

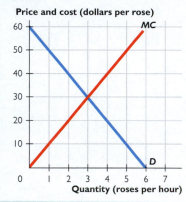

Hawaii Cable Television is a natural monopoly. Sketch a market demand curve and the firm's cost curves. Use your graph to work Problems **5** to **8**.

5. If Hawaii Cable is unregulated and maximizes profit, show in your graph the price, quantity, economic profit, consumer surplus, and deadweight loss.

6. If Hawaii Cable is unregulated and it gives householders a 50 percent discount for second and third connections, describe how its economic profit, consumer surplus, and deadweight loss would change.

7. If Hawaii Cable is regulated in the social interest, show in your graph the price, quantity, economic profit, consumer surplus, and deadweight loss.

8. If Hawaii Cable is subject to a price cap regulation that enables it to break even, show in your graph the price, quantity, economic profit, consumer surplus, and deadweight loss.

Use the following information to work Problems **9** and **10**.

Unfair postal competition

With the rise of e-mail, the volume of snail mail has fallen precipitously, and the U.S. Postal Service has been losing billions of dollars. It is an unjustified legal monopoly that is heavily subsidized and Congress should end it.

Source: The Cato Institute, January 8, 2016

9. Why is the U.S. Postal Service not a natural monopoly? Explain why it could be efficient to keep it in operation with a subsidy.

10. Draw a graph to illustrate the U.S. Postal Service's price, quantity produced, consumer surplus, producer surplus, and deadweight loss.

11. Read *Eye on Microsoft* on p. 427 and explain how Windows' price, quantity bought, consumer surplus, producer surplus, and deadweight loss would change if Microsoft were able to sell ads that appear every time a user opens a program. Illustrate your answer with a graph.

Instructor Assignable Problems and Applications

MyEconLab Homework, Quiz, or Test if assigned by instructor

Use the following information to work Problems **1** and **2**.

Microsoft: We're not gouging Europe on Windows 7 pricing

Regulators in the European Union have charged Microsoft with illegally tying Internet Explorer (IE) to Windows and mandated that a version of Windows be offered stripped of IE. A news report suggested that when Microsoft launches Windows 7, it will charge a higher price for the IE-stripped version than the price for a full version that includes IE. Microsoft denied this report but announced that it would offer the full version of Windows 7 at a lower upgrade price.

Source: computerworld.com

1. How does Microsoft set the price of Windows and would it be in the firm's self-interest to set a different price for a version stripped of IE?

2. Why might Microsoft offer the full version of Windows 7 to European customers at a lower upgrade price?

Use the following information to work Problems **3** and **4**.

Bobbie's Hair Care is a natural monopoly. Table 1 shows the demand schedule (the first two columns) and Bobbie's marginal cost schedule (the middle and third columns). Bobbie has done a survey and discovered that she has four types of customers each hour: one woman who is willing to pay $18, one senior who is willing to pay $16, one student who is willing to pay $14, and one boy who is willing to pay $12. Suppose that Bobbie's fixed costs are $20 an hour and Bobbie's price discriminates.

3. What is the price each type of customer is charged and how many haircuts an hour does Bobbie's sell? What is the increase in Bobbie's economic profit that results from price discrimination?

4. Who benefits from Bobbie's price discrimination? Is the quantity of haircuts efficient?

TABLE 1

Price (dollars per haircut)	Quantity (haircuts per hour)	Marginal cost (dollars per hour)
20	0	—
18	1	1
16	2	4
14	3	8
12	4	12
10	5	18

Use the following information to work Problems **5** to **10**.

Big Top is the only circus in the nation. Table 2 sets out the demand schedule for circus tickets and the cost schedule for producing the circus.

5. Calculate Big Top's profit-maximizing price, output, and economic profit if it charges a single price for all tickets.

6. When Big Top maximizes profit, what is the consumer surplus and producer surplus and is the circus efficient? Explain why or why not.

7. At the market equilibrium price, no children under 10 years old attend the circus. Big Top offers children under 10 a discount of 50 percent. How will this discount change the consumer surplus and producer surplus? Will Big Top be more efficient by offering the discount to children?

8. If Big Top is regulated to produce the efficient output, what is the quantity of tickets sold, what is the price of a ticket, and what would be the consumer surplus?

9. If Big Top is regulated to charge a price equal to average total cost, what is the quantity of tickets sold, the price of a ticket, and economic profit?

10. Draw a graph to illustrate the circus market if regulators set a price cap that enables Big Top to break even. Show the deadweight loss in your graph.

TABLE 2

Price (dollars per ticket)	Quantity (tickets per show)	Total cost (dollars per show)
20	0	1,000
18	100	1,600
16	200	2,200
14	300	2,800
12	400	3,400
10	500	4,000
8	600	4,600
6	700	5,200
4	800	5,800

MyEconLab Chapter 16 Study Plan

Multiple Choice Quiz

1. A firm is a natural monopoly if _____.

   A. it can produce the good at a price below its competitor's price

   B. it can produce a larger quantity of the good than other firms

   C. the government grants it a public franchise or patent

   D. it can satisfy the market demand at a lower average total cost than other firms

2. A monopoly _____.

   A. can choose its price and output and always has the option of price discriminating

   B. is a price taker and by offering a range of discounts can price discriminate

   C. that produces a good that cannot be resold might choose to price discriminate

   D. book store that offers a discount on Tuesdays is price discriminating

3. A single-price monopoly maximizes profit by producing the quantity at which _____.

   A. its total revenue will be as large as possible

   B. marginal revenue equals marginal cost and setting the price equal to marginal revenue

   C. marginal revenue equals marginal cost and setting the price equal to marginal cost

   D. marginal revenue equals marginal cost and setting the price equal to the most people are willing to pay for that quantity

4. A monopoly sets its price such that demand for the good produced is _____.

   A. unit elastic

   B. inelastic

   C. elastic

   D. either elastic or inelastic, but never unit elastic

5. A single-price monopoly is _____.

   A. inefficient because it converts consumer surplus to producer surplus

   B. inefficient because it produces too small an output and creates a dead-weight loss

   C. efficient because buyers are paying a price equal to their willingness to pay

   D. efficient because it is the only producer of the good

6. A monopoly that price discriminates _____.

   A. benefits buyers because it offers the good at a variety of prices

   B. gains because it converts consumer surplus to economic profit

   C. uses resources more efficiently than would a competitive market

   D. enables buyers to maximize their consumer surplus

7. Governments regulate natural monopoly by capping the price at _____.

   A. marginal revenue and allowing the monopoly to maximize profit

   B. marginal cost so that the monopoly is efficient and makes zero economic profit

   C. average total cost, which allows the monopoly to be inefficient but make zero economic profit

   D. the buyers' willingness to pay, which makes the monopoly operate efficiently

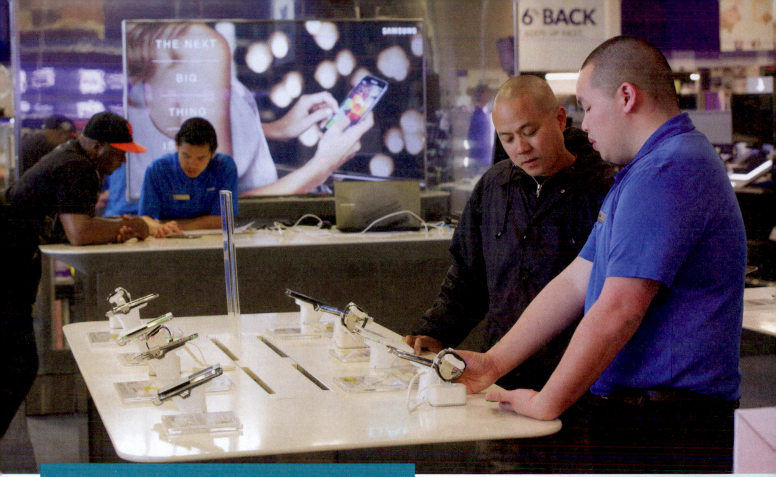

Monopolistic Competition

17

When you have completed your study of this chapter, you will be able to

1 Describe and identify monopolistic competition.

2 Explain how a firm in monopolistic competition determines its output and price in the short run and the long run.

3 Explain why firms develop new and improved products and incur large advertising costs.

MyEconLab Big Picture Video

17.1 WHAT IS MONOPOLISTIC COMPETITION?

Samsung, HTC, Apple: Which smartphone will you choose? Smartphones are sold in a market that is neither perfect competition nor monopoly. Smartphone producers possess some power to set their prices as monopolies do. But unlike monopoly, they face competition from the entry of new firms as the firms in perfect competition do. We call a market like the one in which smartphone producers operate *monopolistic competition*.

■ Describing Monopolistic Competition

Monopolistic competition is a market structure in which

- A large number of firms compete.
- Each firm produces a differentiated product.
- Firms compete on price, quality, and features.
- Firms advertise.
- Firms are free to enter and exit.

Large Number of Firms

In monopolistic competition, as in perfect competition, the industry consists of a large number of firms. The presence of a large number of firms has three implications for the firms in the industry.

Small Market Share   Each firm has a small share of the market so, while each firm can influence the price of its own product, it has little power to influence the average market price.

No Market Dominance   Each firm must be sensitive to the average market price of the product, but it does not pay attention to any one individual competitor. Because all the firms are relatively small, no single firm can dictate market conditions, so no one firm's actions directly affect the actions of the other firms.

Collusion Impossible   Firms sometimes try to profit from illegal agreements—collusion—with other firms to fix prices and not undercut each other. Collusion is impossible when the market has a large number of firms, as it does in monopolistic competition.

Product Differentiation

Product differentiation is making a product that is slightly different from the products of competing firms. A differentiated product has close substitutes but it does not have perfect substitutes. Some people will pay more for one variety so when its price rises, the quantity demanded decreases but it does not (necessarily) decrease to zero. For example, Adidas, Asics, Diadora, Etonic, Fila, New Balance, Nike, Puma, Under Armour, and Reebok all make differentiated running shoes. Other things remaining the same, if the price of Adidas running shoes rises and the prices of the other shoes remain constant, Adidas sells fewer shoes.

Competing on Price, Quality, and Features

Product differentiation enables a firm to compete with other firms in three areas: price, quality, and features.

About 20 firms, each with a small market share, produce a wide variety of treadmills.

Product differentiation
Making a product that is slightly different from the products of competing firms.

Price Because its product is differentiated, a firm in monopolistic competition faces a downward-sloping demand curve, and like a monopoly, the firm can set both its price and its output.

Quality The quality of a product includes its design and reliability, and its ease of use. Go to the J.D. Power Consumer Center at jdpower.com, and you'll see the many dimensions on which this rating agency rates the quality of autos, boats, financial services, travel and accommodation services, telecommunication services, and new homes—all examples of products that have a large range of quality variety. There is a tradeoff between the product's quality and its price. A higher-quality product usully costs more to produce and sells for a higher price.

Features The features of a product include its physical characteristics, the way it works, and things it can do. Differences in features are a key source of product differentiation. Think about the features of a car that make one brand or model different from another. Aside from the shape of its body, its engine design and size, transmission system, and safety features such as audio sensors and rear-view camera are all examples of features that differentiate cars. Just about every product and service that you can think of has differentiating features. Features and quality are related, and as with quality, there is a tradeoff between features and price. More elaborate features cost more to produce and raise the price.

Advertising

Because of product differentiation, a firm in monopolistic competition must advertise its product. A firm that produces a high-quality product wants to sell it for a suitably high price. To be able to do so, it must advertise its product in a way that convinces buyers that they are getting the higher quality for which they are paying. For example, drug companies advertise their brand-name drugs to persuade buyers that they are superior to the lower-priced generic alternatives. A low-quality producer uses advertising to persuade buyers that although the quality is low, the low price more than compensates for this fact.

Entry and Exit

In monopolistic competition, there are no barriers to entry. Consequently, a firm cannot make an economic profit in the long run. When firms make economic profits, new firms enter the industry. This entry lowers prices and eventually eliminates economic profits. When economic losses are incurred, some firms leave the industry. This exit increases prices and profits of the remaining firms and eventually eliminates the economic losses. In long-run equilibrium, firms neither enter nor leave the industry and the firms in the industry make zero economic profit.

■ Identifying Monopolistic Competition

To identify monopolistic competition and distinguish it from perfect competition on the one side and oligopoly and monopoly on the other side, we must determine whether a market has many competing firms or is dominated by a small number of firms. To measure this feature of markets, economists use two indexes called measures of concentration. These indexes are

- The four-firm concentration ratio
- The Herfindahl-Hirschman Index

The Four-Firm Concentration Ratio

Four-firm concentration ratio
The percentage of the total revenue in an industry accounted for by the four largest firms in the industry.

The **four-firm concentration ratio** is the percentage of the total revenue of the industry accounted for by the four largest firms in the industry. The range of the concentration ratio is from almost zero for perfect competition to 100 percent for monopoly. This ratio is the main measure used to assess market structure.

Table 17.1 shows two calculations of the four-firm concentration ratio: one for tire makers and one for printers. In this example, 14 firms produce tires. The four largest firms have 80 percent of the industry's total revenue, so the four-firm concentration ratio is 80 percent. In the printing industry, with 1,004 firms, the four largest firms have only 0.5 percent of the industry's total revenue, so the four-firm concentration ratio is 0.5 percent.

A low concentration ratio indicates a high degree of competition, and a high concentration ratio indicates an absence of competition. A monopoly has a concentration ratio of 100 percent—the largest (and only) firm has 100 percent of the total revenue. A four-firm concentration ratio that exceeds 60 percent is regarded as an indication of a market that is highly concentrated and dominated by a few firms—oligopoly. A ratio of less than 40 percent is regarded as an indication of a competitive market—monopolistic competition.

■ **TABLE 17.1**

Concentration Ratio Calculations

(a) Firms' total revenue

Tire makers		Printers	
Firm	(millions of dollars)	Firm	(millions of dollars)
Top, Inc.	200	Fran's	4
ABC, Inc.	250	Ned's	3
Big, Inc.	150	Tom's	2
XYZ, Inc.	100	Jill's	1
4 largest firms	700	4 largest firms	10
Other 10 firms	175	Other 1,000 firms	1,990
Industry	875	Industry	2,000

(b) Four-firm concentration ratios

Tire makers	$ million	Printers	$ million
Total revenue of 4 largest firms	700	Total revenue of 4 largest firms	10
Industry's total revenue	875	Industry's total revenue	2,000

Four-firm concentration ratio

$$\frac{700}{875} \times 100 = 80 \text{ percent}$$

Four-firm concentration ratio

$$\frac{10}{2,000} \times 100 = 0.5 \text{ percent}$$

The Herfindahl-Hirschman Index

The **Herfindahl-Hirschman Index**—also called the HHI—is the square of the percentage market share of each firm summed over the 50 largest firms (or summed over all the firms if there are fewer than 50) in a market. For example, if there are four firms in a market and the market shares of the firms are 50 percent, 25 percent, 15 percent, and 10 percent, the Herfindahl-Hirschman Index is

$$HHI = 50^2 + 25^2 + 15^2 + 10^2 = 3,450$$

In perfect competition, the HHI is small. For example, if each of the 50 largest firms in an industry has a market share of 0.1 percent, the HHI is ($0.1^2 \times 50$), which equals 0.5. In a monopoly, the HHI is 10,000—the firm has 100 percent of the market: $100^2 = 10,000$.

The HHI is one of the measures of the degree of competition used by the U.S. Department of Justice to classify markets and guide decisions on mergers. A market in which the HHI is less than 1,500 is regarded as being competitive and an example of monopolistic competition. A market in which the HHI lies between 1,500 and 2,500 is regarded as being moderately competitive. It is also an example of monopolistic competition. But a market in which the HHI exceeds 2,500 is regarded as being uncompetitive. The Justice Department scrutinizes any merger of firms in a market in which the HHI exceeds 2,500 that is likely to increase the HHI by more than 100 points.

Concentration measures are a useful indicator of the degree of competition in a market, but they must be supplemented by other information to determine a market's structure. Table 17.2 summarizes the range of other information, along with the measures of concentration that determine which market structure describes a particular real-world market.

Herfindahl-Hirschman Index
The square of the percentage market share of each firm summed over the 50 largest firms (or summed over all the firms if there are fewer than 50) in a market.

TABLE 17.2

Market Structure

Characteristics	Perfect competition	Monopolistic competition	Oligopoly	Monopoly
Number of firms in industry	Many	Many	Few	One
Product	Identical	Differentiated	Identical or differentiated	No close substitutes or regulated
Barriers to entry	None	None	Moderate	High
Firm's control over price	None	Some	Considerable	Considerable
Concentration ratio	0	Low	High	100
HHI	Close to 0	Less than 2,500	More than 2,500	10,000
Examples	Wheat, corn	Food, clothing	Computer chips	Local water supply

EYE on the U.S. ECONOMY
Examples of Monopolistic Competition

These ten industries operate in monopolistic competition. They have a large number of firms, shown in parentheses after the industry's name.

The red bars show the percentage of industry total revenue received by the 4 largest firms. The green bars show the percentage of industry total revenue received by the next 4 largest firms. The entire red, green, and blue bars show the percentage of industry total revenue received by the 20 largest firms.

The Herfindahl-Hirschman Index is shown on the right.

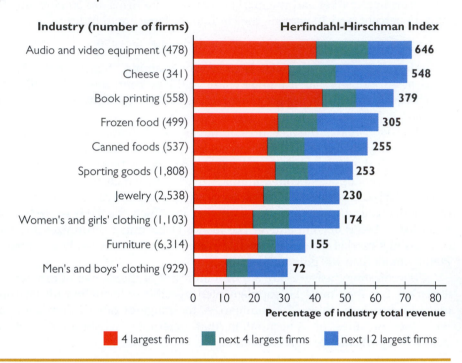

Industry (number of firms) — **Herfindahl-Hirschman Index**

Industry	HHI
Audio and video equipment (478)	646
Cheese (341)	548
Book printing (558)	379
Frozen food (499)	305
Canned foods (537)	255
Sporting goods (1,808)	253
Jewelry (2,538)	230
Women's and girls' clothing (1,103)	174
Furniture (6,314)	155
Men's and boys' clothing (929)	72

Percentage of industry total revenue

■ 4 largest firms   ■ next 4 largest firms   ■ next 12 largest firms

SOURCE OF DATA: U.S. Census Bureau.

Limitations of Concentration Measures

The two main limitations of concentration measures alone as determinants of market structure are their failure to take proper account of:

- The geographical scope of the market
- Barriers to entry and firm turnover

Geographical Scope of the Market   Concentration measures take a national view of the market, but some goods and services are sold in a *regional* market and some in a *global* one. The ready-mix concrete industry consists of highly concentrated regional markets, but the national concentration numbers suggest a market that is close to perfect competition. The four-firm concentration ratio for automobiles is 87, and the HHI is 2,725. Competition from imports give the market in new automobiles the features of monopolistic competition, but the concentration measures suggest a highly concentrated market.

Barriers to Entry and Firm Turnover   A market with a high concentration measure might nonetheless be competitive because low barriers to entry create *potential competition* and a lot of firm turnover. The few firms in a market face competition from many firms that can easily enter the market and will do so if economic profits are available. For example, many small communities have only a small number of restaurants, but there are no restrictions on opening a restaurant and many firms attempt to do so.

CHECKPOINT 17.1

MyEconLab Study Plan 17.1

Key Terms Quiz

Solutions Video

Describe and identify monopolistic competition.

Practice Problems

Table 1 shows the total revenue of the 50 firms in the tattoo industry.

1. Calculate the four-firm concentration ratio and the HHI. What is the market structure of the tattoo industry?

2. What would the market structure of the tattoo industry be if each firm operated in a different city and the cities were spread across the nation?

3. What additional information would you need about the tattoo industry to be sure that it is an example of monopolistic competition?

4. Suppose that a new tattoo technology makes it easier for anyone to enter the tattoo market. How might the market structure change?

TABLE 1

Firm	Total revenue (dollars)
Bright Spots	450
Freckles	325
Love Galore	250
Native Birds	200
Next 16 firms (each)	50
Next 30 firms (each)	20
Industry	**2,625**

In the News

Gloria Jean's hosts "Free Coffee for a Year" sweepstakes
Selling its own-roast light to dark varieties and its signature chillers, mochas, lattes, and hot cocoas, Gloria Jean's Coffees is offering "Free Coffee for a Year" to one sweepstakes winner at each of its 60 locations.
Source: *QSR Magazine*, January 15, 2016

In what type of market does Gloria Jean's compete? Explain your answer.

Solutions to Practice Problems

1. The four-firm concentration ratio is 46.7. Revenue of the four largest firms is $450 + 325 + 250 + 200 = 1,225$, which is 46.7 percent of the total revenue of $2,625. The HHI is 671.14. The market shares from largest to smallest are 17.1, 12.4, 9.5, 7.6, 1.9, and 0.8 percent. Square these numbers to get: $\text{HHI} = 292.41 + 153.76 + 90.25 + 57.76 + (3.61 \times 16) + (0.64 \times 30) = 671.14$. The four-firm concentration ratio and the HHI suggest that the tattoo industry is an example of monopolistic competition unless there are other reasons that would make the concentration measures unreliable guides.

2. If the 50 firms in the tattoo industry operate in different cities spread across the nation, each firm is effectively without competition. The market might be a series of monopolies.

3. The additional information needed is information about product differentiation; competition on price, quality, and advertising; and evidence of low barriers to the entry of new firms.

4. This new tattoo technology would most likely lead to the entry of more firms, greater product differentiation, and more competition.

Solution to In the News

The market type in which Gloria Jean's Coffees and the other coffee shops compete is monopolistic competition. The number of coffee shops is large, and they offer differentiated coffees and other drinks and food. No single firm completely dominates the market and the firms compete on quality, price, and advertising. New coffee shops are free to enter the market with their own varieties.

17.2 OUTPUT AND PRICE DECISIONS

Think about the decisions that Lucky Brand must make about the jeans it produces. First, Lucky Brand must decide on the design and quality of its jeans and on its advertising program. We'll suppose that the firm has already made these decisions so that we can concentrate on the firm's output and pricing decisions. Then we'll study design, quality, and advertising decisions in the next section.

Because Lucky Brand has chosen the design and quality of its jeans and the amount of advertising, it faces given costs and market demand. How, with these costs and market demand for its jeans, does the firm decide the *quantity* of jeans to produce and the *price* at which to sell them?

■ The Firm's Profit-Maximizing Decision

A firm in monopolistic competition makes its output and price decision just as a monopoly firm does. Lucky Brand maximizes profit by producing the quantity at which marginal revenue equals marginal cost and by charging the highest price that buyers are willing to pay for this quantity.

Figure 17.1 illustrates this decision for Lucky Brand. The demand curve is *D*. The *MR* curve shows the marginal revenue curve associated with this demand curve and the *MR* curve is derived just like the marginal revenue curve of a single-price monopoly in Chapter 16. The *ATC* curve shows the average total cost of producing Lucky jeans, and *MC* is the marginal cost curve. Profit is maximized by producing 125 pairs of jeans a day and selling them at a price of $100 a pair. When the firm produces 125 pairs of jeans a day, average total cost is $50 a pair and economic profit is $6,250 a day ($50 a pair multiplied by 125 pairs a day). The blue rectangle shows Lucky Brand's economic profit.

■ **FIGURE 17.1**

Output and Price in Monopolistic Competition   MyEconLab Animation

❶ Profit is maximized where marginal revenue equals marginal cost.

❷ Lucky Brand's profit-maximizing quantity is 125 pairs of jeans a day.

❸ The profit-maximizing price is $100 a pair, which exceeds the average total cost of $50 a pair, so Lucky Brand makes an economic profit of $50 a pair.

❹ The blue rectangle illustrates economic profit and its area, which equals $6,250 a day ($50 a pair multiplied by 125 pairs), measures economic profit.

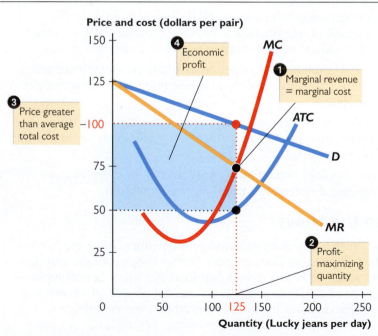

■ Profit Maximizing Might Be Loss Minimizing

Lucky Brand in Figure 17.1 is making a healthy economic profit, but such an outcome is not inevitable. The demand for a firm's product might be too low for it to make an economic profit. Excite@Home was such a firm. Offering high-speed Internet service over the same cable that provides television, Excite@Home hoped to capture a large share of the Internet portal market in competition with AOL, MSN, and a host of other providers.

Figure 17.2 illustrates the situation facing Excite@Home in 2001. The demand curve for its portal service is *D*, the marginal revenue curve is *MR*, the average total cost curve is *ATC*, and the marginal cost curve is *MC*. Excite@Home maximizes profit—equivalently, it minimizes its loss—by producing the output at which marginal revenue equals marginal cost. In Figure 17.2, this output is 40,000 customers connected. Excite@Home charges the highest price that 40,000 buyers are willing to pay for its service, which from the demand curve is $40 a month. With 40,000 customers, Excite@Home's average total cost is $50 a customer, so Excite@Home incurs an economic loss of $400,000 a month ($10 a customer multiplied by 40,000 customers). The red rectangle shows the economic loss.

The largest economic loss that a firm will incur is equal to total fixed cost. The reason is that if the profit-maximizing (loss-minimizing) price is less than average variable cost, the firm will shut down temporarily and produce nothing (just like a firm in perfect competition—see pp. 381–382).

So far, the firm in monopolistic competition looks like a single-price monopoly. It produces the quantity at which marginal revenue equals marginal cost and then charges the highest price that buyers are willing to pay for that quantity. The difference between monopoly and monopolistic competition lies in what happens when firms either make an economic profit or incur an economic loss.

■ FIGURE 17.2

Economic Loss in the Short Run

MyEconLab Animation

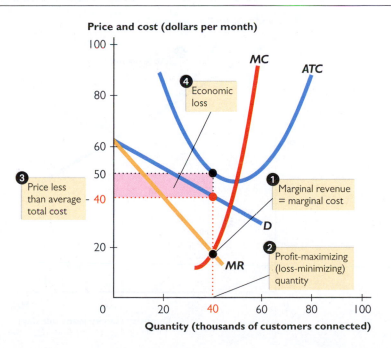

❶ Profit is maximized and loss is minimized where marginal revenue equals marginal cost.

❷ The loss-minimizing quantity is 40,000 customers connected.

❸ The price of $40 a month is less than average total cost of $50 a month, so the firm incurs an economic loss of $10 a customer.

❹ The red rectangle illustrates economic loss and its area, which equals $400,000 a month ($10 a customer multiplied by 40,000 customers), measures the economic loss.

■ Long Run: Zero Economic Profit

A firm like Excite@Home is not going to incur an economic loss for long. Eventually, it exits the market. So in the long run, no firm in the market will be incurring an economic loss. Also, there is no restriction on entry in monopolistic competition, so if firms in an industry are making economic profits, other firms have an incentive to enter that industry and each firm's economic profit falls. So in the long run, firms will enter until all firms are making zero economic profit.

Lucky Brand is making an economic profit, which is an incentive for Calvin Klein and other firms to start producing jeans similar to Lucky jeans. As new firms enter the jeans market, the demand for Lucky jeans decreases. At each point in time, the firm maximizes its profit by producing the quantity at which marginal revenue equals marginal cost and by charging the highest price that buyers are willing to pay for this quantity. But as demand decreases, marginal revenue decreases, so the profit-maximizing quantity and price fall.

Figure 17.3 shows Lucky Brand's long-run equilibrium. The demand curve for Lucky jeans and the marginal revenue curve have shifted leftward. The firm produces 75 pairs of jeans a day and sells them for $70 each. At this output level, average total cost is also $70 a pair, so Lucky Brand is making zero economic profit on its jeans. When all the firms in the industry are making zero economic profit, there is no incentive for new firms to enter.

If demand is so low relative to costs that firms incur economic losses, exit will occur. As firms leave an industry, the demand for the products of the remaining firms increases and their demand curves shift rightward. The exit process ends when all the firms in the industry are making zero economic profit.

■ FIGURE 17.3

Output and Price in the Long Run

MyEconLab Animation

Economic profit encourages entry, which decreases the demand for each firm's product. Economic loss encourages exit, which increases the demand for each remaining firm's product.

When the demand curve touches the average total cost curve at the quantity at which marginal revenue equals marginal cost, the market is in long-run equilibrium.

❶ The output that maximizes Lucky Brand's profit is 75 pairs of jeans a day.

❷ The price, $70 a pair, equals average total cost.

❸ Economic profit is zero.

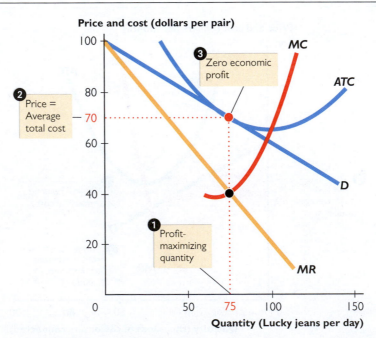

■ Monopolistic Competition and Perfect Competition

MyEconLab Concept Video

Figure 17.4 compares monopolistic competition and perfect competition in the long run and highlights two key differences: excess capacity and markup.

Excess Capacity

A firm's **efficient scale** is the quantity at which average total cost is a minimum—the quantity at the bottom of the U-shaped *ATC* curve. A firm's **excess capacity** is the amount by which its efficient scale exceeds the quantity it produces. Figure 17.4(a) shows that in the long run Lucky Brand has *excess capacity*. Because the demand curve for Lucky jeans is downward sloping, zero economic profit occurs where the *ATC* curve is downward sloping. Figure 17.4(b) shows a firm in perfect competition in the long run. The firm has no excess capacity because its demand curve is horizontal. Zero economic profit occurs at minimum average total cost.

Efficient scale
The quantity at which average total cost is a minimum.

Excess capacity
The amount by which the efficient scale exceeds the quantity that the firm produces.

Markup

A firm's **markup** is the amount by which its price exceeds its marginal cost. Figure 17.4(a) shows Lucky Brand's markup. Figure 17.4(b) shows the zero markup of a firm in perfect competition. Buyers pay a higher price in monopolistic competition than in perfect competition and pay more than marginal cost.

Markup
The amount by which price exceeds marginal cost.

■ FIGURE 17.4

Excess Capacity and Markup in the Long Run

MyEconLab Animation

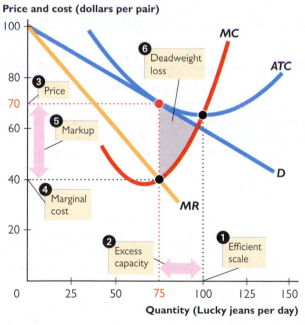

(a) Monopolistic competition

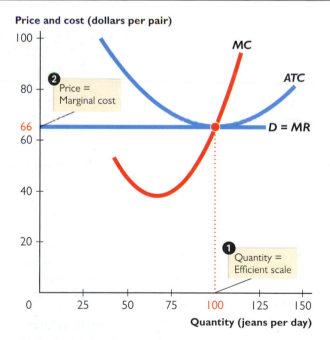

(b) Perfect competition

❶ The efficient scale (at minimum *ATC*) is 100 pairs a day. In the long run in monopolistic competition, the firm produces 75 pairs of jeans a day and has ❷ excess capacity. ❸ Price exceeds ❹ marginal cost by ❺ the markup and ❻ creates a deadweight loss.

In contrast, the firm in perfect competition has no excess capacity and no markup because the demand for the firm's output is perfectly elastic. ❶ The quantity produced equals the efficient scale and ❷ price equals marginal cost.

■ Is Monopolistic Competition Efficient?

You've learned that resources are used efficiently when marginal benefit equals marginal cost. You've also learned that price measures marginal benefit. So if the price of a pair of Lucky jeans exceeds the marginal cost of producing them, then the quantity of Lucky jeans produced is less than the efficient quantity. And you've just seen that in long-run equilibrium in monopolistic competition, that price *does* exceed marginal cost.

Deadweight Loss

Because price exceeds marginal cost, monopolistic competition creates deadweight loss, just like monopoly. Figure 17.4(a) shows this deadweight loss. But is monopolistic competition less efficient than perfect competition?

Making the Relevant Comparison

Two economists meet in the street, and one asks the other, "How is your husband?" "Compared to what?" is the quick reply. This bit of economic wit illustrates a key point: Before we can make an effective comparison, we must check out the available alternatives.

The markup that drives a gap between price and marginal cost in monopolistic competition arises from product differentiation. Lucky Brand jeans are not quite the same as jeans from Banana Republic, CK, Diesel, DKNY, Earl Jeans, Levi, Ralph Lauren, or any of the other dozens of producers of jeans, so the demand for Lucky jeans is not perfectly elastic. The only way in which the demand for jeans from Lucky Brand might be perfectly elastic is if there were only one kind of jeans and Lucky Brand, along with every other firm, made them. In this situation, Lucky jeans would be indistinguishable from all other jeans. They wouldn't even have identifying labels.

If there were only one kind of jeans, the marginal benefit from a pair of jeans would almost certainly be less than it is with variety. People value variety. And people value variety not only because it enables each person to select what he or she likes best but also because it provides an external benefit. Most of us enjoy seeing variety in the choices of others. Contrast a scene from the China of the 1960s when everyone wore a Mao tunic with the China of today, when everyone wears the clothes of their own choosing. Or contrast a scene from the Germany of the 1930s when almost everyone who could afford a car owned a first-generation Volkswagen Beetle with the world of today, with its variety of styles and types of automobiles.

If people value variety, why don't we see infinite variety? The answer is that variety is costly. Each different variety of any product must be designed, and then customers must be informed about it. These initial costs of design and advertising—called setup costs—mean that some varieties that are too close to others already available are just not worth creating.

The Bottom Line

Product variety is both valued and costly. The efficient degree of product variety is the one for which the buyer's willingness to pay equals the marginal cost of product variety. The loss that arises because the willingness to pay for one more unit of a given variety exceeds its marginal cost is offset by the gain that arises from having more product variety. So compared to the alternative—complete product uniformity—monopolistic competition is efficient.

CHECKPOINT 17.2

MyEconLab Study Plan 17.2
Key Terms Quiz
Solutions Video

Explain how a firm in monopolistic competition determines its output and price in the short run and the long run.

Practice Problems

Natti is a dot-com entrepreneur who has established a Web site at which people can design and buy incredible sunglasses. Natti pays $4,000 a month for her Web server and Internet connection. The sunglasses that her customers design are made to order by another firm, and Natti pays this firm $50 a pair. Natti has no other costs. Table 1 shows the demand schedule for Natti's sunglasses.

1. Calculate Natti's profit-maximizing output, price, and economic profit.

2. Do you expect other firms to enter the market and compete with Natti?

3. What happens to the demand for Natti's sunglasses in the long run? What happens to Natti's economic profit in the long run?

TABLE 1

Price (dollars per pair)	Quantity (pairs per month)
250	0
200	50
150	100
100	150
50	200
0	250

In the News

Blockbuster retail stores gone

In 2000, Blockbuster was at the top of the video rental market with solid profits, thousands of retail locations, and millions of customers eager to rent their movies and videogames. Unable to compete with Internet-based services, the last Blockbuster retail store closed in 2014.

Source: *Fortune*, November 9, 2014

Explain why the switch to Internet-based services brought economic loss to Blockbuster and led to its exit.

Solutions to Practice Problems

1. Marginal cost is $50 a pair—the price that Natti pays her supplier of sunglasses. To find marginal revenue, calculate the change in total revenue when the quantity increases by 1 pair of sunglasses. Figure 1 shows the demand curve, marginal revenue curve, and marginal cost curve. Profit is maximized when Natti produces 100 pairs a month at which marginal cost equals marginal revenue and sells them at $150 a pair. Average total cost is $90—the sum of $50 marginal (and average variable) cost and $40 average fixed cost. Economic profit is $60 a pair on 100 pairs a month, or $6,000 a month.

2. Natti is making an economic profit, so firms have an incentive to enter the Web sunglasses market and will do so.

3. As firms enter the market, the demand for Natti's sunglasses decreases. The *D* and *MR* curves in Figure 1 shift leftward. The quantity decreases, the price falls, and Natti's economic profit decreases. In the long run, Natti makes zero economic profit.

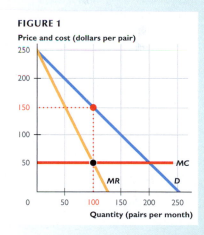

FIGURE 1

Price and cost (dollars per pair)

Solution to In the News

As people switched to Internet-based services, the demand for video rental decreased. Blockbuster's marginal revenue decreased and its *MR* curve shifted leftward. Eventually, with Blockbuster's average total cost exceeding price, the firm was incurring an economic loss. To limit the loss, Blockbuster retail stores were closed, and by 2014 they were all gone.

MyEconLab Concept Video

17.3 INNOVATION AND ADVERTISING

You've seen how a firm makes its output and price decisions for a product that is already designed and advertised. We're now going to study a firm's product design and quality and advertising decisions.

■ Design and Quality Decision

Economic profit attracts entry, and entry erodes profit. To enjoy ongoing economic profit, a firm in monopolistic competition must continually innovate.

The decision to allocate resources to product innovation is made using the same profit-maximizing calculation that you've already studied. At a low level of innovation activity, the marginal revenue it brings in exceeds the marginal cost. At a high level of innovation activity, its marginal cost exceeds marginal revenue. When the marginal cost of innovation activity equals its marginal revenue, the firm is doing the profit-maximizing amount of innovation.

Think about Electronic Arts, which releases a new version of Madden NFL once a year. It could do so twice a year or every two years. Also, the firm could employ more coders and designers to make the game even better than it is, or employ fewer and make an inferior version of the game. For EA, the marginal revenue from a new version equals its marginal cost on a one-year revision cycle.

It is easy to list new designs and new products that transform the quality of life. Kitchen and other household appliances, computers, cars, smartphones, and apps are examples of products that keep getting better. But do we get enough innovation and product improvement? Do consumers get all the features and quality that they are willing to pay for?

The answer is perhaps not. The value to the consumer of a product improvement is its marginal benefit, which equals the amount the consumer is willing to pay. In other words, the value of a product improvement is the increase in price that the consumer is willing to pay. The marginal benefit to the producer is marginal revenue, which, when profit is maximized, equals marginal cost. Because price exceeds marginal cost in monopolistic competition, product improvement is not pushed to its efficient level.

A new version of a game is released at an interval and with the features that generate a marginal revenue equal to marginal cost so that profit is maximized.

■ Advertising

Firms that differentiate their products need to ensure that their customers and potential customers know the features, quality, and price of their products. Advertising is the means firms use to achieve this end. Advertising is itself a product—a service—that is traded in a monopolistic competition market. That is, the firms that produce advertising services are large in number, differentiate their advertising products, and compete on price, design, and quality.

You already know a lot about the advertising industry. You view its products every day. Some of the biggest producers of advertising services are Google, Facebook, Pinterest, and YouTube, with Snapchat and other specialized social media websites snapping at their heels. In 2016, expenditure on advertising exceeded $200 billion, with a third each spent on Internet advertising, TV commercials, and print (magazines and newspapers). This enormous scale of advertising occurs because it increases advertisers' profits and is profitable for its suppliers.

We'll first look at the demand for advertising and see how it increases the profits of advertisers and at the same time might benefit the buyers of advertised products. Then we'll take a look at the supply side of the advertising market.

■ The Demand for Advertising

The demand for advertising arises from its effects on a firm's cost, revenue, and economic profit. We'll look first at its effects on a firm's costs, and then at its effects on demand and revenue.

Advertising and Cost

The cost of advertising is a fixed cost: It does not vary with output. Expenditure on advertising increases a firm's average cost, but it also increases the quantity sold. If advertising increases the quantity sold by a large enough amount, average total cost can fall, profit increase, and the consumer enjoy a lower price.

Figure 17.5 shows how advertising expenditures change a firm's average total cost. The blue curve shows the average total cost of production. The red curve shows the firm's average total cost of production plus the average cost of advertising. The height of the shaded area between the two curves shows the average fixed cost of advertising. The total cost of advertising is fixed. But the average cost of advertising decreases as output increases.

In this example, if the quantity sold increases from 25 pairs of jeans a day with no advertising to 100 pairs of jeans a day with advertising, average total cost falls from $60 a pair to $40 a pair. The reason is that although the total fixed cost has increased, the greater fixed cost is spread over a greater output, so average total cost falls.

To know whether the lower cost and greater quantity increase a firm's profit, we need to see how advertising changes the demand for the firm's product.

■ FIGURE 17.5

Advertising Cost and Total Cost

MyEconLab Animation

Advertising costs are fixed costs.

❶ When advertising costs are added to ❷ the average total cost of production, ❸ average total cost increases by more at small outputs than at large outputs.

❹ If advertising enables the quantity sold to increase from 25 pairs of jeans a day to 100 pairs a day, the firm's average total cost *falls* from $60 a pair to $40 a pair.

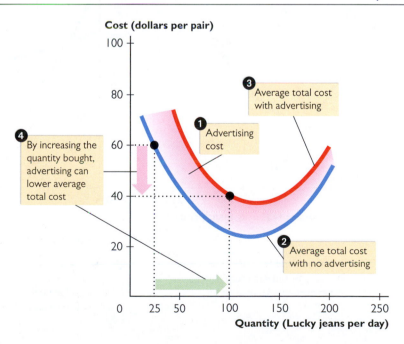

Advertising and Demand

Advertising changes the demand for a firm's product. But how? Does demand increase or does it decrease? The most natural answer is that advertising increases demand. By informing people about the quality of its products or by persuading people to switch from the products of other firms, a firm might expect to increase the demand for its own products.

But all firms in monopolistic competition advertise. And all seek to persuade customers that they have the best deal. If advertising enables a firm to survive, it might increase the number of firms in the market. And to the extent that it increases the number of firms, it decreases the demand for any one firm's product. With all firms advertising, the demand for any one firm's product might become more elastic. So advertising can end up not only lowering average total cost but also lowering the price and decreasing the markup.

Figure 17.6 illustrates this possible effect of advertising. In part (a), with no advertising, the demand for Lucky jeans is not very elastic. Profit is maximized at 75 pairs of jeans a day, and the markup is large. In part (b), advertising, which is a fixed cost, increases average total cost and shifts the average total cost curve upward from ATC_0 to ATC_1, but leaves the marginal cost curve unchanged at MC. The demand for Lucky jeans becomes much more elastic, the profit-maximizing quantity increases, and the firm's markup shrinks.

FIGURE 17.6

Advertising and the Markup

MyEconLab Animation

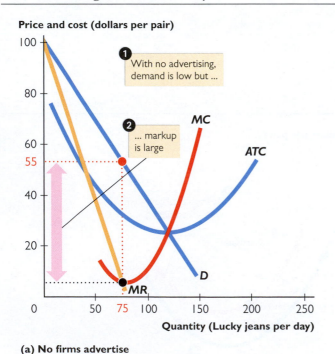

(a) No firms advertise

❶ With no firms advertising, the demand for Lucky jeans is low and not very elastic, so ❷ Lucky Brand's markup is large.

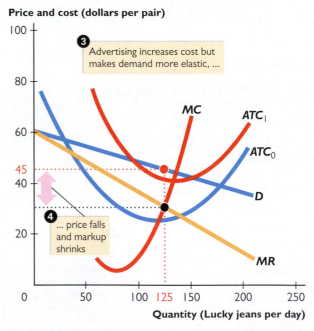

(b) All firms advertise

❸ Lucky Brand's advertising shifts its average total cost curve upward from ATC_0 to ATC_1. If, with all firms advertising, the demand for Lucky jeans becomes more elastic, ❹ the price of Lucky jeans falls and Lucky Brand's markup shrinks.

EYE on SMARTPHONES

Which Smartphone?

There is a lot of product differentiation in smartphones: Samsung makes more than 60 varieties; so does HTC; LG makes 26; and Apple makes 13. In the three months from April through June 2016, dozens of new varieties of smartphones were introduced by the top 20 firms in this market. Why is there so much variety in smartphones?

The answer is that preferences are diverse and the cost of matching the diversity of preference is low.

Think about the ways in which smartphones differ: just a few of them are their dimensions, weight, navigation tools, talk time, standby time, screen, camera features, audio features, memory, connectivity, processor speed, storage, and network capability.

Each one of these features comes in dozens of varieties. If we combine only 10 of these features, each having 6 varieties, there are 1 million different possible smartphone designs.

Firms produce variety only when the marginal cost of doing so is less than the marginal benefit. The marginal cost of some smartphone variety is not large. Adding a feature to a camera, making the memory a bit bigger, and using a more economical battery are all relatively low-cost adjustments that phone designers can make.

But a technology exists for adding variety at almost zero cost that increases product differentiation to make each smartphone unique to the preferences of each individual. This technology is the app.

Apple has only 13 versions of the iPhone, but with the growing number of apps, each owner can load their iPhone with all the apps they want.

In long-run equilibrium, entry and innovation will drive economic profit toward zero. Each smartphone maker will offer a degree of product differentiation that equates the marginal cost of variety with its marginal revenue. But the pursuit of economic profit will spur ever more innovation and consumers will be confronted with ever wider choice.

Using Advertising to Signal Quality

In 2014, Budweiser spent $12 million for 90 seconds of Super Bowl TV time to advertise Bud Light. The ad showed a night of partying with Minka Kelly, Arnold Schwarzenegger, Don Cheadle, and a llama in a hotel elevator. No information about Bud Light. So why did Budweiser spend all this money? The answer is to signal a high-quality product.

A **signal** is an action taken by an informed person (or firm) to send a message to less-informed people. Think about two beers: Bud and Dud.

Dud knows that its beer is low quality. So Dud knows that while it could get a lot of people to try Dud by advertising, they would all quickly discover its poor quality and switch back to the beer they bought before. Dud's cost of advertising would exceed the revenue it generated.

Bud, in contrast, knows that its product has a high-quality consistent taste and that once someone has tried it, there is a good chance that they'll never drink anything but Bud. If Bud ran a costly advertising campaign, more people would try Bud and many would stick with it. The revenue earned would exceed the cost of the advertising campaign.

So Bud spends a lot of money to make a big splash. Beer drinkers who see Bud's splashy ads believe that the firm would not spend so much money advertising if its product were not truly good. So the beer drinker reasons that Bud is indeed a really good product. The flashy expensive ad has signaled that Bud is really good without saying anything about Bud.

Signal
An action taken by an informed person (or firm) to send a message to less-informed people.

EYE on YOUR LIFE
Some Selling Costs You Pay

MyEconLab Critical Thinking Exercise

When you buy a new pair of running shoes, you're buying materials that cost $9, paying the producer in Asia and the shipping company for production and transportation costs of $8, paying the U.S. government an import duty of $3, and paying advertisers, retailers, and others who provide sales and distribution services $50.

The table provides a breakdown of the cost of a pair of shoes. Notice the huge gap between the retailer's cost and the price that you pay. The retail markup is about 100 percent.

Running shoes are not unusual. Almost everything that you buy includes a selling cost component that exceeds one half of the total cost. Your clothing, food, electronic items, airline travel, magazines, and even your textbooks cost more to sell than they cost to produce.

| Raw materials $9 | Production costs $8 | Import duty $3 | Selling costs $50 |

Manufacturer (Asia)		Nike (Beaverton, Oregon)		Retailer (your town)	
Materials	$9.00				
Cost of labor	$2.75	Cost of shoe to Nike	$20.00	Cost of shoe to retailer	$35.50
Cost of capital	$3.00	Sales, distribution, and administration	$5.00	Sales clerk's wages	$9.50
Profit	$1.75	Advertising	$4.00	Shop rent	$9.00
Shipping	$0.50	Research & development	$0.25	Retailer's other costs	$7.00
Import duty	$3.00	Nike's profit	$6.25	Retailer's profit	$9.00
Nike's cost	**$20.00**	**Retailer's cost**	**$35.50**	**Price paid by you**	**$70.00**

Brand Names

Many firms, and Budweiser is one of them, create a brand name and spend a lot of advertising dollars promoting it. Why? What benefit does a brand name bring to justify the sometimes high cost of establishing it? The answer is that a brand name provides consumers with information about the quality of a product and it provides the producer with an incentive to achieve a consistent quality standard.

To see how a brand name helps the consumer, think about how you use one. You're on a road trip, and it is time to find a bed. You see roadside ads for Holiday Inn and for Annie's Driver's Stop. You know about Holiday Inn: You've stayed in one, and you've seen its ads. You know what to expect from it. You have no information at all about Annie's. It might be better than Holiday Inn, but without that knowledge, you're not going to chance it. You use the brand name as information and stay at Holiday Inn.

This same story explains why a brand name provides an incentive to the producer to achieve a consistent quality. Because no one knows whether Annie's is offering a good standard of service, it has no incentive to do so. But equally, because everyone expects a given standard of service from Holiday Inn, a failure to meet a customer's expectation would almost surely lose that customer to a competitor. So Holiday Inn has an incentive to deliver what it promises in the advertising that creates its brand name.

■ The Supply of Advertising

The firms that supply advertising do so jointly with the supply of some other service or good: TV stations with programming, Google with Internet search, Facebook with social media, and *Sports Illustrated* with news and feature articles.

Two-Sided Market

Because firms produce advertising jointly with something else, these firms trade in what has been called a "two-sided market." One side is for advertising and the other side is for the firm's product.

Competition for advertising among TV, social media, and print (magazines and newspapers) is fierce but entry into the market is difficult for TV and social media because startup costs are high and economies of scale reward large players with the lowest average cost. Entry is easier for print producers and a wide variety of niche magazines supply advertising.

When operating in a two-sided market, suppliers of advertising face two interdependent demand curves. The greater the number of users of the firm's product, the greater is the demand for its advertising services. For example, the more people who visit Facebook, the greater is the demand for Facebook advertising.

Profit-Maximizing Decisions

The profit-maximizing decision of Facebook and the other Internet firms is to offer their main product at a zero price to maximize the quantity demanded—maximize the number of users—to make the demand for its advertising services as large as possible. For the same reason, print suppliers of advertising sell the magazines and newspapers for a price close to marginal cost and below average cost. These firms then sell the profit-maximizing quantity of space for advertising. They choose this quantity in the same way as all firms: the quantity that makes marginal revenue equal to marginal cost. They sell the space for the highest price that advertisers are willing to pay determined by the advertisers' demand curve.

■ Equilibrium and Efficiency in the Advertising Market

The quantity and quality of advertising is determined by the interaction of the demand by advertisers and the price and output decisions of the suppliers of advertising. Whether the advertising market does a good job and produces the efficient quantity and quality is not well understood. To the extent that advertising and brand names provide consumers with information about the precise nature of product differences and product quality, they benefit the consumer and enable a better product choice to be made. And to the extent that signalling and brand names provide firms with the incentive to deliver consistent quality, they further benefit the consumer. But the opportunity cost of advertising must be weighed against the gain to the consumer.

The final verdict on the efficiency of monopolistic competition is ambiguous. In some cases, the gains from extra product variety and innovation more than offset the advertising costs and the deadweight loss arising from excess capacity. The smartphone, laptop and tablet computers, streaming video services, games and apps all make our lives easier and more fun. You can book a substitute for your snow-cancelled flight while standing in the checkout line at Target. In a few years from now, you will be able to ride in your driverless vehicle and use travel time for other activities. It seems obvious that gains like these more than offset a bit of deadweight loss from excess capacity and price exceeding marginal cost.

MyEconLab Study Plan 17.3
Key Terms Quiz
Solutions Video

 # CHECKPOINT 17.3

Explain why firms develop new and improved products and incur large advertising costs.

Practice Problems

Bianca bakes delicious cookies. Her total fixed cost is $40 a day, and her average variable cost is $1 a bag. Few people know about Bianca's Cookies, and she maximizes her profit by selling 10 bags a day for $5 a bag. Bianca thinks that if she spends $50 a day on advertising, she will sell 25 bags a day for $5 a bag.

1. If Bianca's belief about the effect of advertising is correct, can she increase her economic profit by advertising?

2. If Bianca advertises, will her average total cost increase or decrease at the quantity produced?

3. If Bianca advertises, will she continue to sell her cookies for $5 a bag or will she raise her price or lower her price?

In the News

Snapchat's daily mobile video views said to rival Facebook's
Snapchat is turning into a mobile-video juggernaut that delivers more than 7 billion video clips each day to rival the amount watched on Facebook, which has 15 times as many users. A stronghold in mobile video is good news for Snapchat's advertising dollars.

Source: Bloomberg, January 12, 2016

How does Snapchat help firms in monopolistic competition to maximize profit?

Solutions to Practice Problems

1. With no advertising, Bianca's total revenue is $50 (10 bags at $5 a bag) and her total cost is $50 ($40 total fixed cost plus $10 total variable cost). Bianca's economic profit is zero. With $50 a day advertising expenditure, total revenue is $125 (25 bags at $5 a bag) and total cost is $115 ($90 total fixed cost plus $25 total variable cost). Bianca's economic profit with no price change is $10 a day, so Bianca can increase her economic profit by advertising.

2. If Bianca advertises, her average *total* cost will decrease. With no advertising, her average total cost is $5 a bag (total cost of $50 ÷ 10 bags). With advertising, her average total cost is $4.60 a bag (total cost of $115 ÷ 25 bags).

3. We can't say if Bianca will sell her cookies for $5 a bag. Advertising changes the demand for her cookies. Although it increases fixed cost, marginal cost remains at $1 a bag. Bianca will sell the profit-maximizing quantity at the highest price she can charge for that quantity.

Solution to In the News

In monopolistic competition, entry keeps driving economic profit to zero. Innovation— the development of a new differentiated product—is necessary to boost economic profit. And advertising is necessary to bring new differentiated products to the attention of potential buyers. Snapchat enables advertising to reach a well-defined market of young smartphone users.

CHAPTER SUMMARY

Key Points

1. **Describe and identify monopolistic competition.**

   - Monopolistic competition is a market structure in which a large number of firms compete; each firm produces a product that is slightly different from the products of its competitors; firms compete on price, quality, and advertising; and new firms are free to enter the industry.

   - Monopolistic competition is identified by a low degree of concentration measured by either the four-firm concentration ratio or the HHI.

2. **Explain how a firm in monopolistic competition determines its output and price in the short run and the long run.**

   - The firm in monopolistic competition faces a downward-sloping demand curve and produces the quantity at which marginal revenue equals marginal cost and price exceeds marginal cost.

   - Entry and exit result in zero economic profit and excess capacity in long-run equilibrium.

   - In monopolistic competition, price exceeds marginal cost but buyers benefit from product variety.

3. **Explain why firms develop new and improved products and incur large advertising costs.**

   - Firms in monopolistic competition innovate and develop new products to maintain economic profit.

   - Firms create a brand name to signal quality and to provide the incentive to maintain quality.

   - Advertising expenditures can lower average total cost and can increase competition and lower price.

   - Product development, a brand name, and advertising increase profit but can also benefit buyers.

Key Terms

Efficient scale, 445

Excess capacity, 445

Four-firm concentration ratio, 438

Herfindahl-Hirschman Index, 439

Markup, 445

Product differentiation, 436

Signal, 451

CHAPTER CHECKPOINT

Study Plan Problems and Applications

1. Think about the markets for cable television service, wheat, athletic shoes, soda, toothbrushes, and ready-mix concrete. Which of these markets are examples of monopolistic competition? Explain your selections.

2. The four-firm concentration ratio for audio equipment makers is 30 and for electric lamp makers is 89. The HHI for audio equipment makers is 464 and for electric lamp makers is 2,850. Which of these markets is an example of monopolistic competition?

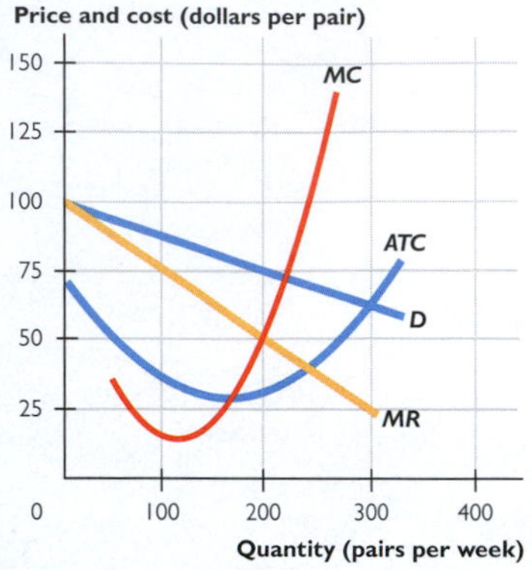

Use Figure 1, which shows the demand curve, marginal revenue curve, and cost curves of Lite and Kool, Inc., a producer of running shoes in monopolistic competition, to work Problems 3 to 5.

3. In the short run, what quantity does Lite and Kool produce, what price does it charge, and does it make an economic profit?

4. In the short run, does Lite and Kool have excess capacity and what is its markup?

5. Do you expect firms to enter the running shoes market or exit from that market in the long run? Explain your answer.

Use Figure 2, which shows the demand curve, marginal revenue curve, and cost curves of Stiff Shirt, Inc., a producer of shirts in monopolistic competition, to work Problems 6 and 7.

6. In the short run, what is the quantity that Stiff Shirt produces, the price it charges, its economic profit, markup, and excess capacity?

7. In the long run, will new firms enter the shirt market or will firms exit from that market and will the price of a shirt rise or fall? Explain your answer.

8. Mike's, a firm in monopolistic competition, produces bikes. With no advertising, Mike's profit-maximizing output is 500 bikes a day and the price is $100 a bike. Now all firms begin to advertise. With advertising, Mike's maximizes profit by producing 1,000 bikes a day and charging $50 a bike. How does advertising change Mike's markup and excess capacity?

9. **Netflix profits slide**
   Netflix has hit a bump in the road on its quest to reach 60 million to 90 million subscribers in the United States and, by the end of 2016, become fully global. Netflix faces fierce competition from streaming rivals like Amazon, HBO, and Hulu and also competes against cable, satellite, YouTube, and DVDs.
   Source: *The New York Times*, October 14, 2015

   Explain why more firms have entered the streaming-video market and how the economic profit of firms in the market will likely change. What will economic profit be in the long run? Explain your answer.

10. Read *Eye on Smartphones* on p. 451 and explain why smartphone producers offer such a large variety of their products. Draw a graph of a firm's cost and revenue curves if all smartphones are identical. Use your graph to illustrate the effects of the firm introducing a new, differentiated smartphone.

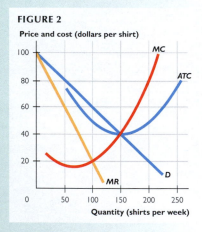

FIGURE 1

Price and cost (dollars per pair)

FIGURE 2

Price and cost (dollars per shirt)

Instructor Assignable Problems and Applications

1. Washtenaw Dairy in Ann Arbor, Michigan, sells 63 flavors of Strohs Mooney's ice cream, and Ben and Jerry's Web site also lists 63 different flavors of ice cream. These numbers are similar to the varieties of smartphones sold by Samsung, Nokia, and Motorola. Toyota makes only 16 varieties of vehicles and Boeing makes 16 varieties of airplanes. Why is there more variety in smartphones and ice cream than in automobiles and airplanes?

2. The HHI for automobiles is 2,350, for sporting goods is 253, for batteries is 2,883, and for jewelry is 230. Which of these markets is an example of monopolistic competition?

Use Figure 1 to work Problems **3** and **4**.

Figure 1 shows the demand curve, marginal revenue curve, and cost curves of La Bella Pizza, a firm in monopolistic competition.

3. What is the quantity that La Bella Pizza produces, the price it charges, its markup, and its excess capacity? Is the market in short-run or long-run equilibrium? Explain your answer.

4. If La Bella advertises its pizza online and demand increases, how will the number of pizzas sold change? How will the price of a pizza and La Bella's excess capacity change? Explain your answer.

Use the following information to work Problems **5** and **6**.

Sony announces Smart Tennis Sensor
Tennis racket maker Babolat introduced its smart racket Play Pure Drive in 2013. Smash and Shot Stats soon followed. Now Sony is partnering with Wilson to make Smart Tennis Sensor, a device that sits at the bottom of a racket's handle and tracks every metric and statistic that a tennis player or coach could need.

Source: *Gizmag*, August 22, 2014

5. How are Babolat, Sony, and other smart racket producers attempting to maximize economic profit? Draw a graph to illustrate Babolat's short-run economic profit in the market for smart tennis rackets.

6. Explain why the economic profit that Babolat and Sony make in this market is likely to be temporary. Draw a graph to illustrate the outcome in the long run. Show the excess capacity and markup in the long run.

7. Some people happily pay more for Coke or Pepsi than they are willing to pay for a nonbranded cola. And some people happily pay more for Tylenol than they are willing to pay for generic acetaminophen. How do brand names help consumers? How do brand names change the behavior of producers? Why would it not be efficient to make brand names illegal?

Use the following information to work Problems **8** and **9**.

Suppose that Tommy Hilfiger's marginal cost of a jacket is a constant $100 and at one of the firm's shops, total fixed cost is $2,000 a day. The profit-maximizing number of jackets sold in this shop is 20 a day. When the shops nearby start to advertise their jackets, this Tommy Hilfiger shop spends $2,000 a day advertising its jackets, and its profit-maximizing output jumps to 50 jackets a day.

8. What is this shop's average total cost of a jacket sold before it starts to advertise? What is its average total cost of a jacket with advertising?

9. What happens to Tommy's markup and its economic profit? Why?

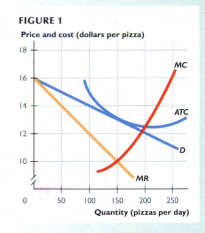

FIGURE 1

Multiple Choice Quiz

1. Monopolistic competition differs from _____.

   A. monopoly because firms cannot set their own price

   B. oligopoly because firms produce differentiated goods or services

   C. perfect competition because the goods or services produced are differentiated

   D. monopoly because the good produced by each firm has no close substitute

2. The four largest firms in a market have the following market shares of total revenue: 20 percent, 15 percent, 10 percent, and 5 percent. The _____ in this industry is _____.

   A. four-firm concentration ratio; 50 percent

   B. four-firm concentration ratio; 750 percent

   C. Herfindahl-Hirschman Index; 50

   D. Herfindahl-Hirschman Index; 2,500

3. A firm in monopolistic competition maximizes its profit by _____.

   A. differentiating its good and producing the quantity at which price equals marginal revenue

   B. producing the quantity at which marginal revenue equals marginal cost and then adding a markup

   C. raising its price and producing so that it always has excess capacity

   D. producing the quantity at which marginal cost equals marginal revenue and charging the highest price at which it can sell that quantity

4. A firm in monopolistic competition that is maximizing profit _____.

   A. always makes a positive economic profit in the short run

   B. never needs to shut down because its price always exceeds minimum average variable cost

   C. might, in the short run, sell at a price that is less than average total cost

   D. shuts down temporarily if it incurs a loss equal to total variable cost

5. In the long run, each firm in monopolistic competition _____.

   A. makes zero economic profit

   B. makes as much economic profit as it would if it were a monopoly

   C. has the same markup and excess capacity as it would if the market were perfectly competitive

   D. creates the same deadweight loss as it would if it were a monopoly

6. If one firm advertises and other firms in the market don't, then _____.

   A. the demand for the advertised good becomes more elastic

   B. the profit-maximizing quantity of the advertised good decreases because total fixed costs increase

   C. the average cost of producing a small quantity of the advertised good rises but the average total cost of producing a large quantity might fall

   D. the economic profit made from the advertised good increases

7. Each firm in monopolistic competition uses a brand name and advertising to achieve all of the following *except* to _____.

   A. differentiate its good from its competitors' goods

   B. signal quality and reliability of its good

   C. signal its market share

   D. influence the demand for its good

Is four too few?

Oligopoly

When you have completed your study of this chapter, you will be able to

1 Describe and identify oligopoly and explain how it arises.

2 Explain the dilemma faced by firms in oligopoly.

3 Use game theory to explain how output and price are determined in oligopoly.

4 Describe the antitrust laws that regulate oligopoly.

18

MyEconLab Big Picture Video

18.1 WHAT IS OLIGOPOLY?

You have lots of choice when you get a smartphone, but much less choice about your wireless plan provider. Four firms share the U.S. market for wireless service, which is an *oligopoly*. Whether four firms is too few depends on whether they behave like firms in competition or like a monopoly, either of which is possible.

The distinguishing features of oligopoly are that

- A small number of firms compete.
- Natural or legal barriers prevent the entry of new firms.

■ Small Number of Firms

In contrast to monopolistic competition and perfect competition, an oligopoly consists of a small number of firms. Each firm has a large share of the market, the firms are interdependent, and they face a temptation to collude.

Interdependence

Energizer and Duracell dominate the market for batteries.

With a small number of firms in a market, each firm's actions influence the profits of the other firms. To see how, suppose you run one of the three gas stations in a small town. If you cut your price, your market share increases, and your profits might increase too. But the market share and profits of the other two firms fall. In this situation, the other firms will most likely cut their prices too. If they do cut their prices, your market share and profit take a tumble. So before deciding to cut your price, you must predict how the other firms will react and take into account the effects of their reactions on your own profit. Your profit depends on the actions of the other firms, and their profit depends on your actions. You and the other two firms are interdependent.

Temptation to Collude

Cartel
A group of firms acting together to limit output, raise price, and increase economic profit.

When a small number of firms share a market, they can increase their profits by forming a cartel and acting like a monopoly. A **cartel** is a group of firms acting together—colluding—to limit output, raise price, and increase economic profit. Cartels are illegal in the United States (and most other countries), although international cartels can operate legally (see *Eye on the Global Economy* on p. 467). But even when there is no formal cartel, firms might try to operate like a cartel.

For reasons that you'll discover in this chapter, cartels tend to be unstable and eventually break down.

■ Barriers to Entry

Either natural or legal barriers to entry can create oligopoly. You saw in Chapter 16 how economies of scale and market demand form a natural barrier to entry that can create a *natural monopoly*. These same factors can also create a natural oligopoly.

Like natural monopoly, a natural oligopoly arises from the interaction of the market demand for a good or service and the extent of economies of scale in its production. Figure 18.1 illustrates two natural oligopolies.

The demand curve, D (in both parts of the figure), shows the market demand for taxi rides in a town. If the average total cost curve of a taxi company is ATC_1

FIGURE 18.1

Natural Oligopoly

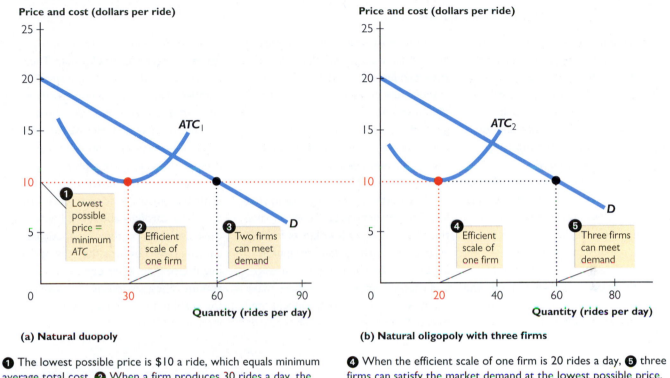

(a) Natural duopoly

(b) Natural oligopoly with three firms

❶ The lowest possible price is $10 a ride, which equals minimum average total cost. ❷ When a firm produces 30 rides a day, the efficient scale, ❸ two firms can satisfy the market demand. This natural oligopoly has two firms—a natural duopoly.

❹ When the efficient scale of one firm is 20 rides a day, ❺ three firms can satisfy the market demand at the lowest possible price. This natural oligopoly has three firms.

in part (a), the market is a natural **duopoly**—a market with only two firms. You can probably see some examples of duopoly where you live. Some cities have only two suppliers of milk, two local newspapers, two taxi companies, two car rental firms, two copy centers, or two college bookstores.

Notice in part (a) that the efficient scale of one firm is 30 rides a day. The lowest price at which the firm would remain in business is $10 a ride. At that price, the quantity of rides demanded is 60 a day, the quantity that can be provided by just two firms. There is no room in this market for three firms. To sell more than 60 rides a day, the price would have to fall below $10 a ride. But then the firms would incur an economic loss, and one of them would exit. If the market has only one firm, it would make an economic profit and a second firm would enter to take some of the business and economic profit.

If the average total cost curve of a taxi company is ATC_2 in part (b), the efficient scale of one firm is 20 rides a day. This market is large enough for three firms, but it is not large enough for a fourth firm. Economies of scale limit the market to three firms because each firm would incur an economic loss if there were four of them. And this market will not operate with two firms because with only two, economic profit would encourage the entry of a third firm.

Duopoly

A market with only two firms.

EYE on the U.S. ECONOMY
Examples of Oligopoly

You're familiar with a few of the industries shown in the figure. You probably know, for example, that Kellogg's makes most of the breakfast cereals consumed in the United States. It is said that Kellogg's does more business before eight o'clock in the morning than most firms do all day!

You probably also know that Airbus and Boeing make most of the airplanes that fly our skies and that Ford and GM make most of the trucks on America's roads and highways.

Less visible for good health reasons, you might know that Phillip Morris and RJ Reynolds make most of the cigarettes sold in the United States.

Some of the industries in the figure are less familiar, but you use a lot of their products. One of them is the manufacture of glass bottles and jars. When you buy anything that comes in glass, there's a good chance that the container was made in Toledo, Ohio, by Owens-Illinois, the world's largest glass packaging manufacturer.

Three others play a big role in your life. The petrochemical industry makes the plastic in everyday objects from your toothbrush to your computer keyboard. And the computer storage and recording devices industries make the hard drive in your laptop and the microphone in your smartphone.

All of the industries shown in the figure are examples of oligopoly: They are industries dominated by a small number of firms, have a high four-firm concentration ratio, and, with three exceptions, have an HHI that exceeds 2,500. One exception, breakfast cereals, is unquestionably an oligopoly.

In all of these industries, the largest firms pay close attention to each other and think carefully about the impact of their decisions on their competitors and the repercussions they themselves might face from their competitors' reactions. They are industries in which the small number of large firms are interdependent.

A legal oligopoly arises when a legal barrier to entry protects the small number of firms in a market. A city might license two taxi firms or two bus companies, for example, even though the combination of market demand and economies of scale leaves room for more than two firms.

When barriers to entry create an oligopoly, firms can make an economic profit in the long run without fear of triggering the entry of additional firms.

■ Identifying Oligopoly

Identifying oligopoly is the flip side of identifying monopolistic competition. But the borderline between the two market types is hard to pin down. We need to know whether a market is an oligopoly or monopolistic competition for two reasons. First, we want to be able to make predictions about how the market operates and how output and price will respond to such factors as a change in demand or a change in costs. Second, we want to know whether the firms in a market are delivering an efficient outcome that serves the social interest.

The key features of a market that we need to identify are whether the firms are so few that they recognize the interdependencies among them and whether they are acting in a similar way to a monopoly.

As a practical matter, we try to identify oligopoly by looking at the four-firm concentration ratio and the Herfindahl-Hirschman Index, qualified with other information about the geographical scope of the market and barriers to entry.

As we noted in Chapter 17, a market in which the HHI lies between 1,000 and 2,500 is usually an example of monopolistic competition, and a market in which the HHI exceeds 2,500 is usually an example of oligopoly.

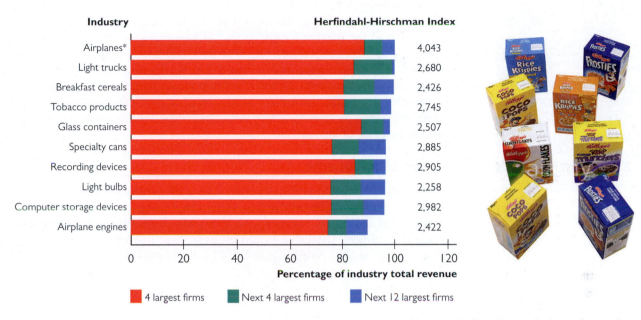

Industry   **Herfindahl-Hirschman Index**

Industry	HHI
Airplanes*	4,043
Light trucks	2,680
Breakfast cereals	2,426
Tobacco products	2,745
Glass containers	2,507
Specialty cans	2,885
Recording devices	2,905
Light bulbs	2,258
Computer storage devices	2,982
Airplane engines	2,422

0   20   40   60   80   100   120

Percentage of industry total revenue

■ 4 largest firms   ■ Next 4 largest firms   ■ Next 12 largest firms

SOURCES OF DATA: U.S. Census Bureau and item marked * authors calculation from industry report.

CHECKPOINT 18.1

Describe and identify oligopoly and explain how it arises.

Practice Problems

1. What are the distinguishing features of oligopoly?

2. Why are breakfast cereals made by firms in oligopoly? Why isn't there monopolistic competition in that industry?

3. Duracell's share of revenue in the market for batteries is 45 percent. Energizer's share is 35 percent. A few smaller firms share the rest of the market. In what type of market are batteries sold? Explain your answer.

Solutions to Practice Problems

1. The distinguishing features of oligopoly are a small number of interdependent firms competing behind natural or legal barriers to entry.

2. Breakfast cereals are made by firms in oligopoly because economies of scale and the size of the market limit the number of firms that can make a profit.

3. The market for batteries is an oligopoly, and with two dominant firms it is a duopoly. The number of firms is small, their actions are interdependent, and economies of scale and the market demand create a natural barrier to entry.

Boeing and Airbus share the market for big passenger airplanes.

18.2 THE OLIGOPOLISTS' DILEMMA

Oligopoly might operate like monopoly, like perfect competition, or somewhere between these two extremes. To see these alternative possible outcomes, we'll study duopoly in the market for airplanes. Airbus and Boeing are the only makers of large commercial jet aircraft. Suppose that they have identical costs. To keep the numbers simple, assume that total fixed cost is zero and that regardless of the rate of production, the marginal cost of producing an airplane is $1 million.

Figure 18.2 shows the market demand curve for airplanes. Airbus and Boeing share this market. The total quantity sold and the quantities sold by each firm depend on the price of an airplane.

■ Monopoly Outcome

If this industry had only one firm operating as a single-price monopoly, its marginal revenue curve would be the one shown in Figure 18.2. Marginal revenue equals marginal cost when 6 airplanes a week are produced and the price of an airplane is $13 million. Total cost would be $6 million and total revenue would be $78 million, so economic profit would be $72 million a week.

■ **FIGURE 18.2**

A Market for Airplanes

❶ With market demand curve, *D*, marginal revenue curve, *MR*, and marginal cost curve, *MC*, a monopoly airplane maker maximizes profit by producing 6 airplanes a week and selling them at a price of $13 million an airplane.

❷ With perfect competition among airplane makers, the market equilibrium quantity is 12 airplanes a week and the equilibrium price is $1 million an airplane.

❸ A cartel might achieve the monopoly equilibrium, break down and result in the perfect competition equilibrium, or operate somewhere between these two extreme outcomes.

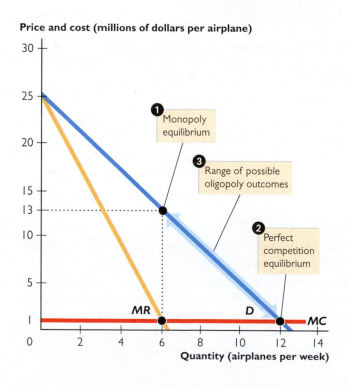

Cartel to Achieve Monopoly Outcome

Can the two firms achieve the monopoly outcome that we've just found and maximize their joint profit? They can attempt to do so by forming a cartel.

Suppose that Airbus and Boeing agreed to limit the total production of airplanes to 6 a week. The market demand curve tells us that the price of an airplane would be $13 million and economic profit would be $72 million a week. Suppose that the two firms also agree to split the market evenly and each produce 3 airplanes a week. They would each make an economic profit of $36 million a week—see Table 18.1.

Would it be in the self-interest of Airbus and Boeing to stick to their agreement and limit production to 3 airplanes a week each?

To begin answering this question, notice that with the price of an airplane exceeding marginal cost, if one firm increased production, it would increase its profit. But if both firms increased output whenever price exceeded marginal cost, the end of the process would be the same as perfect competition.

■ Perfect Competition Outcome

You can see the perfect competition outcome in Figure 18.2. The equilibrium is where the market supply curve, which is the marginal cost curve, intersects the market demand curve. The quantity is 12 airplanes a week, and the price is the same as marginal cost—$1 million per airplane.

■ Other Possible Cartel Breakdowns

Because price exceeds marginal cost, a cartel is likely to break down. But a cartel might not unravel all the way to perfect competition. In *Eye on the Global Economy* on p. 467, you can see the brief history of a sometimes successful and sometimes unsuccessful cartel in the global market for oil. You can see why a cartel breaks down, but not all the way to perfect competition, by looking at some alternative outcomes in the airplane industry example.

Boeing Increases Output to 4 Airplanes a Week

Suppose that starting from a cartel that achieves the monopoly outcome, Boeing increases output by 1 airplane a week. Table 18.2 keeps track of the data. With Boeing producing 4 airplanes a week and Airbus producing 3 airplanes a week, total output is 7 airplanes a week. To sell 7 airplanes a week, the price must fall. The market demand curve in Figure 18.2 tells us that the quantity demanded is 7 airplanes a week when the price is $11 million an airplane.

The market total revenue would now be $77 million, total cost would be $7 million, and economic profit would fall to $70 million. But the distribution of this economic profit is now unequal. Boeing would gain, and Airbus would lose.

Boeing would now receive $44 million a week in total revenue, have a total cost of $4 million, and make an economic profit of $40 million. Airbus would receive $33 million a week in total revenue, incur a total cost of $3 million, and make an economic profit of $30 million.

So by increasing its output by 1 airplane a week, Boeing can increase its economic profit by $4 million and cause the economic profit of Airbus to fall by $6 million.

Because the two firms in this example are identical, we could rerun the above story with Airbus increasing production by 1 airplane a week and Boeing holding

TABLE 18.1   MONOPOLY OUTCOME

	Boeing	Airbus	Market total
Quantity (airplanes a week)	3	3	6
Price ($ million per airplane)	13	13	13
Total revenue ($ million)	39	39	78
Total cost ($ million)	3	3	6
Economic profit ($ million)	36	36	72

TABLE 18.2   BOEING INCREASES OUTPUT TO 4 AIRPLANES PER WEEK

	Boeing	Airbus	Market total
Quantity (airplanes a week)	4	3	7
Price ($ million per airplane)	11	11	11
Total revenue ($ million)	44	33	77
Total cost ($ million)	4	3	7
Economic profit ($ million)	40	30	70

output at 3 airplanes a week. In this case, Airbus would make $40 million a week and Boeing would make $30 million a week.

Boeing is better off producing 4 airplanes a week if Airbus sticks with 3 a week. But is it in Airbus's interest to hold its output at 3 airplanes a week? To answer this question, we need to compare the economic profit Airbus makes if it maintains its output at 3 airplanes a week with the profit it makes if it produces 4 airplanes a week. What is Airbus' economic profit if it produces 4 airplanes a week with Boeing also producing 4 airplanes a week?

Airbus Increases Output to 4 Airplanes a Week

With both firms producing 4 airplanes a week, total output is 8 airplanes a week. To sell 8 airplanes a week, the price must fall further. The market demand curve in Figure 18.2 tells us that the quantity demanded is 8 airplanes a week when the price is $9 million an airplane.

Table 18.3 keeps track of the data. The market total revenue would now be $72 million, total cost would be $8 million, and economic profit would fall to $64 million. With both firms producing the same output, the distribution of this economic profit is now equal.

Each firm would now receive $36 million a week in total revenue, have a total cost of $4 million, and make an economic profit of $32 million. For Airbus, this outcome is an improvement on the previous one by $2 million a week. For Boeing, this outcome is worse than the previous one by $8 million.

This outcome is better for Airbus, but would Boeing go along with it? You know that Boeing would be worse off if it decreased its output to 3 airplanes a week because it would get the outcome that Airbus has in Table 18.2—an economic profit of only $30 million a week. But would Boeing be better off if it increased output to 5 airplanes a week?

Boeing Increases Output to 5 Airplanes a Week

Suppose now that Airbus maintains its output at 4 airplanes a week and Boeing increases output to 5 a week. Table 18.4 keeps track of the data. Total output is now 9 airplanes a week. To sell this quantity, the price must fall to $7 million an airplane. Market total revenue is $63 million and total cost is $9 million, so economic profit for the two firms is $54 million. The distribution of this economic profit is again unequal. But now both firms would lose.

Boeing would now receive $35 million a week in total revenue, have a total cost of $5 million, and make an economic profit of $30 million—$2 million less than it would make if it maintained its output at 4 airplanes a week. Airbus would receive $28 million a week in total revenue, incur a total cost of $4 million, and make an economic profit of $24 million—$8 million less than before. So neither firm gains by increasing total output beyond 8 airplanes a week.

■ The Oligopoly Cartel Dilemma

With a cartel, both firms make the maximum available economic profit. If both firms increase production, both see their profit fall. If only one firm increases production, that firm makes a larger economic profit while the other makes a lower economic profit. So what will the firms do? We can speculate about what they will do, but to work out the answer, we need some game theory.

TABLE 18.3   AIRBUS INCREASES OUTPUT TO 4 AIRPLANES PER WEEK

	Boeing	Airbus	Market total
Quantity (airplanes a week)	4	4	8
Price ($ million per airplane)	9	9	9
Total revenue ($ million)	36	36	72
Total cost ($ million)	4	4	8
Economic profit ($ million)	32	32	64

TABLE 18.4   BOEING INCREASES OUTPUT TO 5 AIRPLANES PER WEEK

	Boeing	Airbus	Market total
Quantity (airplanes a week)	5	4	9
Price ($ million per airplane)	7	7	7
Total revenue ($ million)	35	28	63
Total cost ($ million)	5	4	9
Economic profit ($ million)	30	24	54

EYE on the GLOBAL ECONOMY
The OPEC Global Oil Cartel

The Organization of the Petroleum Exporting Countries (OPEC) is an international cartel of oil-producing nations that was created in 1960.

OPEC describes its objective as being "to co-ordinate and unify petroleum policies among member countries in order to secure fair and stable prices …" These words can be interpreted as "restricting the production of oil to keep its price high."

During the 1960s, the cartel quietly built its organization and prepared the ground for its push to dominate the global oil market. OPEC's first opportunity came in 1973 when, with an Arab-Israeli war raging, it organized an embargo on oil shipments to the United States and Europe. The price of oil rose to four times its previous level. OPEC's second opportunity came with the Iranian revolution in 1979 when it more than doubled the price of oil.

The figure shows both these price hikes. The price rose from about $8 a barrel in 1970 to more than $86 a barrel by 1980. (To compare prices over a number of years, we express them in terms of the value of the dollar in 2015.)

During the 1980s, many new sources of oil supply opened up and the OPEC cartel lost control of the global market. The cartel broke down, and the price of oil fell.

The price of oil remained remarkably stable during the 1990s, and the power of OPEC was countered by a large supply of oil from other sources.

From 2003 to 2008, Asian demand for oil grew dramatically and OPEC

OPEC ministers meeting at the organization's headquarters in Vienna

again dominated the global market, restricted its production, and pushed the world price to a new high in 2008.

But OPEC lost power again during the global recession of 2009 and the years that followed. A slowing of growth in China decreased the

demand for oil. And the development of fracking technology in the United States increased the supply of oil and natural gas. In 2015, the United States joined the ranks of oil exporters, which contributed to a steep fall in the oil price.

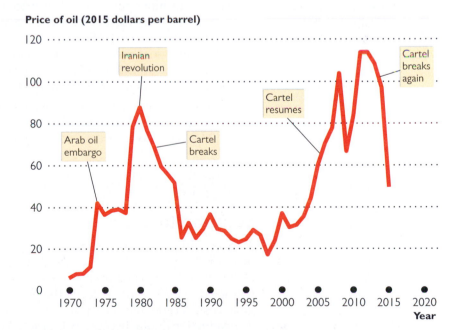

Sources of data: OPEC and Bureau of Economic Analysis.

MyEconLab Study Plan 18.2

Solutions Video

CHECKPOINT 18.2

Explain the dilemma faced by firms in oligopoly.

Practice Problems

Isolated Island has two natural gas wells, one owned by Tom and the other owned by Jerry. Each well has a valve that controls the flow of gas. The marginal cost of producing gas is zero. Table 1 gives the demand schedule for the gas.

1. If Tom and Jerry form a cartel and maximize their joint profit, what will be the price of gas and the quantity produced?

2. If Tom and Jerry are forced to sell at the perfectly competitive price, what will be the price of gas and the total quantity produced?

3. If Tom and Jerry compete as duopolists, what will be the price of gas?

In the News

OPEC calls for co-operation to stem price collapse

OPEC has asked the world's largest oil producers to help stop a price collapse. But OPEC member Saudi Arabia, the world's biggest oil exporter, wants to keep output high.

Source: *Financial Times*, January 25, 2016

For information about OPEC, see p. 467. Explain how an effective profit-maximizing oil producers' cartel would influence the global market for oil and the world price of oil. Why does Saudi Arabia want to keep output high?

Solutions to Practice Problems

1. If Tom and Jerry form a cartel and maximize their joint profit, they will charge the monopoly price. This price is the highest price the market will bear when together they produce the quantity at which marginal revenue equals marginal cost. Marginal cost is zero, so we need to find the price at which marginal revenue is zero. Marginal revenue is zero when total revenue is a maximum, which occurs when output is 6 units a day (Table 2) and price is $6 a unit (see the demand schedule in Table 1).

2. If Tom and Jerry are forced to sell at the perfectly competitive price, the price will equal marginal cost. Marginal cost is zero, so in this case, the price will be zero and the total quantity produced will be 12 units a day.

3. If Tom and Jerry compete as duopolists, they will increase production to more than the monopoly quantity. The price will fall, but they will not drive the price down to zero.

Solution to In the News

A successful profit-maximizing oil cartel would operate as a monopoly. It would produce the quantity at which marginal revenue equals marginal cost and agree on production levels for each member of the cartel. With the quantity produced restricted to the monopoly level, the price would be high and would exceed marginal cost. A cartel fails because there is no incentive for each member to stick to its production quota. Because price exceeds marginal cost, each member of the cartel has an incentive to overproduce, like Saudi Arabia in the news clip.

TABLE 1

Price (dollars per unit)	Quantity demanded (units per day)
12	0
11	1
10	2
9	3
8	4
7	5
6	6
5	7
4	8
3	9
2	10
1	11
0	12

TABLE 2

Quantity (units per day)	Total revenue (dollars per day)	Marginal revenue (dollars per unit)
0	0	
		11
1	11	
		9
2	20	
		7
3	27	
		5
4	32	
		3
5	35	
		1
6	36	
		−1
7	35	
		−3
8	32	
		−5
9	27	
		−7
10	20	
		−9
11	11	
		−11
12	0	

18.3 GAME THEORY

MyEconLab Concept Video

Game theory is the tool that economists use to analyze *strategic behavior*—behavior that recognizes mutual interdependence and takes account of the expected behavior of others. John von Neumann invented game theory in 1937, and today it is a major research field in economics.

Game theory helps us to understand oligopoly and many other forms of economic, political, social, and even biological rivalries. We will begin our study of game theory and its application to the behavior of firms by thinking about familiar games that we play for fun.

■ What Is a Game?

What is a game? At first thought, the question seems silly. After all, there are many different games. There are ball games and parlor games, games of chance and games of skill. But what is it about all these different activities that make them games? What do all these games have in common? All games share three features:

- Rules
- Strategies
- Payoffs

Let's see how these common features of games apply to a game called "the prisoners' dilemma." The **prisoners' dilemma** is a game between two prisoners that shows why it is hard to cooperate even when it would be beneficial to both players to do so. This game captures the essential feature of the duopolists' dilemma that we've just been studying. The prisoners' dilemma also provides a good illustration of how game theory works and how it generates predictions.

■ The Prisoners' Dilemma

Art and Bob have been caught red-handed, stealing a car. During the district attorney's interviews with the prisoners, he begins to suspect that he has stumbled on the two people who committed a multimillion-dollar bank robbery some months earlier. But this is just a suspicion. The district attorney has no evidence on which he can convict them of the greater crime unless he can get them to confess. He makes the prisoners play a game with the following rules.

Rules

Each prisoner (player) is placed in a separate room and cannot communicate with the other player. Each is told that he is suspected of having carried out the bank robbery and that

- If both of them confess to the larger crime, each will receive a reduced sentence of 3 years for both crimes.
- If he alone confesses and his accomplice does not, he will receive an even shorter sentence of 1 year, while his accomplice will receive a 10-year sentence.
- If neither of them confesses to the larger crime, each will receive a 2-year sentence for car theft.

Game theory

The tool that economists use to analyze *strategic behavior*—behavior that recognizes mutual interdependence and takes account of the expected behavior of others.

Prisoners' dilemma

A game between two prisoners that shows why it is hard to cooperate even when it would be beneficial to both players to do so.

Strategies

All the possible actions of each player in a game.

Payoff matrix

A table that shows the payoffs for each player for every possible combination of actions by the players.

TABLE 18.5 PRISONERS' DILEMMA
PAYOFF MATRIX

Each square shows the payoffs for the two players, Art and Bob, for each possible pair of actions. In each square, the red triangle shows Art's payoff and the blue triangle shows Bob's. For example, if both confess, the payoffs are in the top left square.

Nash equilibrium

An equilibrium in which each player takes the best possible action given the action of the other player.

Strategies

In game theory, **strategies** are all the possible actions of each player. Art and Bob each have two possible strategies:

- Confess to the bank robbery.
- Deny having committed the bank robbery.

Payoffs

Because there are two players, each with two strategies, there are four possible outcomes:

- Both confess.
- Both deny.
- Art confesses and Bob denies.
- Bob confesses and Art denies.

Each prisoner can work out exactly what happens to him—his *payoff*—in each of these four situations. We can tabulate the four possible payoffs for each of the prisoners in what is called a payoff matrix for the game. A **payoff matrix** is a table that shows the payoffs for every possible action by each player given every possible action by the other player.

Table 18.5 shows a payoff matrix for Art and Bob. The squares show the payoffs for the two prisoners—the red triangle in each square shows Art's, and the blue triangle shows Bob's. If both prisoners confess (top left), each gets a prison term of 3 years. If Bob confesses but Art denies (top right), Art gets a 10-year sentence and Bob gets a 1-year sentence. If Art confesses and Bob denies (bottom left), Art gets a 1-year sentence and Bob gets a 10-year sentence. Finally, if both of them deny (bottom right), neither can be convicted of the bank robbery charge but both are sentenced for the car theft—a 2-year sentence.

Equilibrium

The equilibrium of a game occurs when each player takes the best possible action given the action of the other player. This equilibrium concept is called **Nash equilibrium**. It is so named because John Nash of Princeton University, who received the Nobel Prize for Economic Science in 1994, proposed it. (The same John Nash was portrayed by Russell Crowe in *A Beautiful Mind*.)

In the case of the prisoners' dilemma, equilibrium occurs when Art makes his best choice given Bob's choice and when Bob makes his best choice given Art's choice. Let's find the equilibrium.

First, look at the situation from Art's point of view. If Bob confesses, it pays Art to confess because in that case, he is sentenced to 3 years rather than 10 years. If Bob does not confess, it still pays Art to confess because in that case, he receives 1 year rather than 2 years. So no matter what Bob does, Art's best action is to confess.

Second, look at the situation from Bob's point of view. If Art confesses, it pays Bob to confess because in that case, he is sentenced to 3 years rather than 10 years. If Art does not confess, it still pays Bob to confess because in that case, he receives 1 year rather than 2 years. So no matter what Art does, Bob's best action is to confess.

Because each player's best action is to confess, each does confess and each gets a 3-year prison term. The district attorney has solved the bank robbery. This is the equilibrium of the game.

Not the Best Outcome

The equilibrium of the prisoners' dilemma game is not the best outcome for the prisoners. Isn't there some way in which they can cooperate and get the shorter 2-year prison term? There is not, because the players cannot communicate with each other. Each player can put himself in the other player's place and can figure out what the other will do. The prisoners are in a dilemma. Each knows that he can serve only 2 years if he can trust the other to deny. But each also knows that it is not in the best interest of the other to deny. So each prisoner knows that he must confess, thereby delivering a bad outcome for both.

Let's now see how we can use the ideas we've just developed to understand the behavior of firms in oligopoly. We'll start by returning to the duopolists' dilemma.

◼ The Duopolists' Dilemma

The dilemma of Airbus and Boeing is similar to that of Art and Bob. Each firm has two strategies. It can produce airplanes at the rate of

- 3 airplanes a week
- 4 airplanes a week

Because each firm has two strategies, there are four possible combinations of actions for the two firms:

- Both firms produce 3 airplanes a week (monopoly outcome).
- Both firms produce 4 airplanes a week.
- Airbus produces 3 airplanes and Boeing produces 4 airplanes a week.
- Boeing produces 3 airplanes and Airbus produces 4 airplanes a week.

◼ The Payoff Matrix

Table 18.6 sets out the payoff matrix for this game. It is constructed in exactly the same way as the payoff matrix for the prisoners' dilemma in Table 18.5. The squares show the payoffs for Airbus and Boeing. In this case, the payoffs are economic profits. (In the case of the prisoners' dilemma, the payoffs were losses.)

The table shows that if both firms produce 4 airplanes a week (top left), each firm makes an economic profit of $32 million. If both firms produce 3 airplanes a week (bottom right), they make the monopoly profit, and each firm makes an economic profit of $36 million. The top right and bottom left squares show what happens if one firm produces 4 airplanes a week while the other produces 3 airplanes a week. The firm that increases production makes an economic profit of $40 million, and the one that keeps production at the monopoly quantity makes an economic profit of $30 million.

Equilibrium of the Duopolists' Dilemma

What do the firms do? To answer this question, we must find the equilibrium of the duopoly game.

TABLE 18.6   DUOPOLISTS' DILEMMA PAYOFF MATRIX

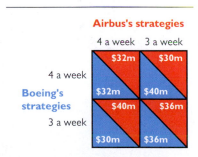

Each square shows the payoffs from a pair of actions. For example, if both firms produce 3 airplanes a week, the payoffs are recorded in the bottom right square. The red triangle shows Airbus's payoff, and the blue triangle shows Boeing's.

TABLE 18.7 THE NASH EQUILIBRIUM

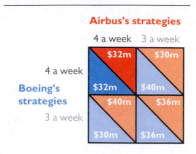

The Nash equilibrium is for each firm to produce 4 airplanes a week.

Using the information in Table 18.7, look at things from Airbus's point of view. Airbus reasons as follows: Suppose that Boeing produces 4 airplanes a week. If I, Airbus, produce 3 a week, I will make an economic profit of $30 million. If I also produce 4 a week, I will make an economic profit of $32 million. So I'm better off producing 4 airplanes a week. Airbus continues to reason: Now suppose Boeing produces 3 a week. If I produce 4 a week, I will make an economic profit of $40 million, and if I produce 3 a week, I will make an economic profit of $36 million. Economic profit of $40 million is better than economic profit of $36 million, so I'm better off if I produce 4 airplanes a week. So regardless of whether Boeing produces 3 a week or 4 a week, it pays Airbus to produce 4 airplanes a week.

Because the two firms face identical situations, Boeing comes to the same conclusion as Airbus, so both firms produce 4 a week. The equilibrium of the duopoly game is that both firms produce 4 airplanes a week.

Collusion Is Profitable but Difficult to Achieve

In the duopolists' dilemma that you've just studied, Airbus and Boeing end up in a situation that is similar to that of the prisoners in the prisoners' dilemma game. They don't achieve the best joint outcome. Because each produces 4 airplanes a week, each makes an economic profit of $32 million a week.

If firms were able to collude, they would agree to limit their production to 3 airplanes a week each and they would each make the monopoly profit of $36 million a week.

The outcome of the duopolists' dilemma shows why it is difficult for firms to collude. Even if collusion were a legal activity, firms in duopoly would find it difficult to implement an agreement to restrict output. Like the players of the prisoners' dilemma game, the duopolists would reach a Nash equilibrium in which they produce more than the joint profit-maximizing quantity.

If two firms have difficulty maintaining a collusive agreement, oligopolies with more than two firms have an even harder time. The operation of OPEC (see *Eye on the Global Economy* on p. 467) illustrates this difficulty. To raise the price of oil, OPEC must limit global oil production. The members of this cartel meet from time to time and set a production limit for each member nation. Almost always, within a few months of a decision to restrict production, some (usually smaller) members of the cartel break their quotas, production increases, and the price sags below the cartel's desired target. The OPEC cartel plays an oligopoly dilemma game similar to the prisoners' dilemma. Only in 1973, 1979–1980, and 2005–2007 did OPEC manage to keep its members' production under control and raise the price of oil.

MyEconLab *Concept Video*

■ Advertising and Research Games in Oligopoly

Every month, Coke and Pepsi, Nike and Adidas, Procter & Gamble and Kimberly-Clark, Nokia and Motorola, and hundreds of other pairs of big firms locked in fierce competition spend millions of dollars on advertising campaigns and on research and development (R&D). They make decisions about whether to increase or cut the advertising budget or whether to undertake a large R&D effort aimed at lowering production costs or at making the product more reliable. (Usually, the more reliable a product, the more expensive it is to produce, but the more people are willing to pay for it.) These choices can be analyzed as games. Let's look at some examples of these types of games.

Advertising Game

A key to success in the soft drink industry is to run huge advertising campaigns. These campaigns affect market share but are costly to run. Table 18.8 shows some hypothetical numbers for the advertising game that Pepsi and Coke play. Each firm has two strategies: Advertise or don't advertise. If neither firm advertises, they each make $50 million (bottom right of the payoff matrix). If each firm advertises, each firm's profit is lower by the amount spent on advertising (top left square of the payoff matrix). If Pepsi advertises but Coke does not, Pepsi gains and Coke loses (top right square of the payoff matrix). Finally, if Coke advertises and Pepsi does not, Coke gains and Pepsi loses (bottom left square).

Pepsi reasons as follows: Regardless of whether Coke advertises, we're better off advertising. Coke reasons similarly: Regardless of whether Pepsi advertises, we're better off advertising. Because advertising is the best strategy for both players, it is the Nash equilibrium. The outcome of this game is that both firms advertise and make less profit than they would if they could collude to achieve the cooperative outcome of no advertising.

Research and Development Game

A key to success in the facial tissue market is to design a product that people value highly relative to the cost of producing it. The firm that develops the most highly valued product and the least-cost technology for producing it gains a competitive edge. It can undercut the rest of the market, increase its market share, and increase its economic profit. But it is costly to undertake the R&D that can ultimately result in an improved product and increased profit. So the cost of R&D must be deducted from the increased profit. If no firm does R&D, every firm can be better off, but if one firm initiates the R&D activity, all firms must follow.

Table 18.9 illustrates the dilemma (with hypothetical numbers) for the R&D game that Kimberly-Clark (Kleenex) and Procter & Gamble (Puffs) play. Each firm has two strategies: Do R&D or do no R&D. If neither firm does R&D, Kimberly-Clark makes $30 million and Procter & Gamble makes $70 million (bottom right of the payoff matrix). If each firm does R&D, each firm's profit is lower by the amount spent on R&D (top left square of the payoff matrix). If Kimberly-Clark does R&D but Procter & Gamble does not, Kimberly-Clark gains and Procter & Gamble loses (top right square of the payoff matrix). Finally, if Procter & Gamble conducts R&D and Kimberly-Clark does not, Procter & Gamble gains and Kimberly-Clark loses (bottom left square).

Kimberly-Clark reasons as follows: Regardless of whether Procter & Gamble undertakes R&D, we're better off doing R&D. Procter & Gamble reasons similarly: Regardless of whether Kimberly-Clark does R&D, we're better off doing R&D.

Because R&D is the best strategy for both players, it is the Nash equilibrium. The outcome of this game is that both firms conduct R&D. They make less profit than they would if they could collude to achieve the cooperative outcome of no R&D.

The real-world situation has more players than Kimberly-Clark and Procter & Gamble. A large number of other firms, especially producers of store brands, strive to capture market share from Procter & Gamble and Kimberly-Clark. So the R&D effort by these two firms not only serves the purpose of maintaining shares in their own battle but also helps to keep barriers to entry high enough to preserve their joint market share.

TABLE 18.8   THE ADVERTISING GAME PAYOFF MATRIX

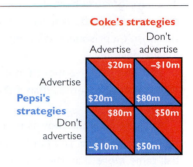

For each pair of strategies, the red triangle shows Coke's payoff, and the blue triangle shows Pepsi's. If both firms advertise, they make less than if neither firm advertises. But each firm is better off advertising if the other doesn't advertise. The Nash equilibrium for this prisoners' dilemma advertising game is for both firms to advertise.

TABLE 18.9   THE R&D GAME PAYOFF MATRIX

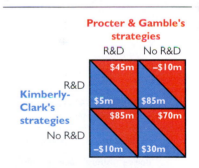

For each pair of strategies, the red triangle shows Procter & Gamble's payoff, and the blue triangle shows Kimberly-Clark's. If both firms do R&D, they make less than if neither firm undertakes R&D. But each firm is better off doing R&D if the other does no R&D. The Nash equilibrium for this prisoners' dilemma R&D game is for both firms to do R&D.

EYE on YOUR LIFE
A Game You Might Play

MyEconLab Critical Thinking Exercise

The payoff matrix here describes a game that might be familiar to you. But it isn't a prisoners' dilemma. It's a lovers' dilemma.

Jane and Jim have more fun if they do something together than if they do things alone.

But Jane likes the movies more than the ball game, and Jim likes the ball game more than the movies.

The payoff matrix describes how much they like the various outcomes (measured in units of utility).

What do they do?

By comparing the utility numbers for different strategies, you can figure out that Jim never goes to the movies alone and Jane never goes to the ball game alone.

You can also figure out that Jim doesn't go to the ball game alone and Jane doesn't go to the movies alone.

They always go out together. But do they go to the movies or the ball game?

The answer is that we can't tell. This game has no unique equilibrium. The payoffs tell you that Jane and Jim might go to either the game or the movies.

In a repeated game, they'll probably alternate between the two and might even toss a coin to decide which to go to on any given evening.

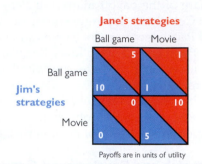

Payoffs are in units of utility

■ Repeated Games

The games that we've studied are played just once. In contrast, most real-world games get played repeatedly. This fact suggests that real-world duopolists might find some way of learning to cooperate so that they can enjoy a monopoly profit. If a game is played repeatedly, one player has the opportunity to penalize the other player for previous "bad" behavior. If Airbus produces 4 airplanes this week, perhaps Boeing will produce 4 next week. Before Airbus produces 4 this week, won't it take account of the possibility of Boeing producing 4 next week? What is the equilibrium of this more complicated dilemma game when it is repeated indefinitely?

The monopoly equilibrium might occur if each firm knows that the other will punish overproduction with overproduction, "tit for tat." Let's see why.

Table 18.10 keeps track of the numbers. Suppose that Boeing contemplates producing 4 airplanes in week 1. This move will bring it an economic profit of $40 million and will cut the economic profit of Airbus to $30 million. In week 2, Airbus will punish Boeing and produce 4 airplanes. But Boeing must go back to 3 airplanes to induce Airbus to cooperate again in week 3. So in week 2, Airbus makes an economic profit of $40 million, and Boeing makes an economic profit of $30 million. Adding up the profits over these two weeks of play, Boeing would have made $72 million by cooperating (2 × $36 million) compared with $70 million from producing 4 airplanes in week 1 and generating Airbus's tit-for-tat response.

What is true for Boeing is also true for Airbus. Because each firm makes a larger profit by sticking to the monopoly output, both firms do so and the monopoly price, quantity, and profit prevail.

In reality, whether a duopoly (or more generally an oligopoly) works like a one-play game or a repeated game depends primarily on the number of players and the ease of detecting and punishing overproduction. The larger the number of players, the harder it is to maintain the monopoly outcome.

TABLE 18.10 PAYOFFS WITH PUNISHMENT

Period of play	Cooperate		Overproduce	
	Boeing profit	Airbus profit	Boeing profit	Airbus profit
	(millions of dollars)			
1	36	36	40	30
2	36	36	30	40

EYE on the WIRELESS OLIGOPOLY

Is Four Too Few?

Your smartphone plan is almost certainly with one of four firms: Verizon, AT&T, Sprint, or T-Mobile. The pie chart in Figure 1 shows the four firms' market shares along with that of a token fifth firm, U.S. Cellular.

With a third of the market each, Verizon and AT&T are the dominant players, but sharing almost equally the other third, Sprint and T-Mobile are also significant participants in what is a wireless service oligopoly.

Does this market have enough firms? Is four too few? Would consumers be better served if more firms entered the market?

The number of firms that a market can support depends on the extent of its economies of scale and the market demand. We don't have data on the firms' long-run average cost curves that would tell us about the economies of scale, but we do have information about the firms' profits. We can use

that profit information to get an indirect look at economies of scale.

The pie chart in Figure 2 shows the gross earnings of the four wireless firms. (Gross means before deducting depreciation.)

Because of economies of scale, the two larger firms have much bigger gross profits than the two smaller firms. But the two smaller firms are large enough to earn a profit. With the two smaller firms being profitable, and with each having about a one-sixth market share, it seems likely that demand in the U.S. wireless market is large enough for more than four firms to profitably survive.

If more firms could operate profitably in this market, we should expect to see entry. And that is exactly what is happening. Google, in collaboration with Dish Network, is entering with a virtual wireless service. There might be room for even more firms.

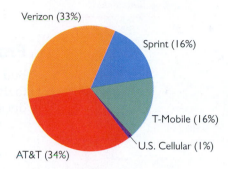

Figure 1 Wireless Subscriber Shares

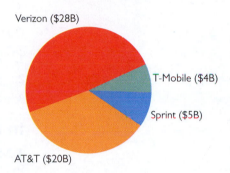

Figure 2 Wireless Gross Profit

Sources of data: Statista.com and Forbes.com.

■ Is Oligopoly Efficient?

The quantity produced of any good or service is the efficient quantity if the price (which measures marginal benefit) equals marginal cost. Does oligopoly produce efficient quantities of goods and services?

You've seen that if firms in oligopoly play a repeated prisoners' dilemma game, they can end up restricting output to the monopoly level and making the same economic profit as a monopoly would make. You've also seen that even when the firms don't cooperate, they don't necessarily drive the price down to marginal cost. So generally, oligopoly is not efficient. It suffers from the same source of inefficiency as monopoly.

Also, firms in oligopoly might end up operating at a higher average total cost than the lowest attainable cost because their advertising and research budgets are higher than the socially efficient level.

Because oligopoly creates inefficiency and firms in oligopoly have an incentive to try to behave like a monopoly, the United States has established antitrust laws that seek to reduce market power and move the oligopoly outcome closer to the efficient competitive outcome. In the next section, we study U.S. antitrust law.

MyEconLab Study Plan 18.3
Key Terms Quiz
Solutions Video

CHECKPOINT 18.3

Use game theory to explain how output and price are determined in oligopoly.

Practice Problems

Bud and Wise are the only two producers of New Age beer, which is designed to displace root beer. Bud and Wise are trying to work out the quantity to produce. They know that if

- Both limit production to 10,000 gallons a day, they will make the maximum attainable joint profit of $200,000 a day—$100,000 a day each.
- One produces 20,000 gallons a day while the other produces 10,000 a day, the one that produces 20,000 gallons will make an economic profit of $150,000 and the one that sticks with 10,000 gallons will incur an economic loss of $50,000.
- Both produce 20,000 gallons a day, each will make zero economic profit.

1. Construct a payoff matrix for the game that Bud and Wise must play.
2. Find the Nash equilibrium of the game that Bud and Wise play.
3. What is the equilibrium of the game if Bud and Wise play it repeatedly?

In the News

T-Mobile launches campaign against 'dark duopoly' of AT&T, Verizon
In a social media campaign, T-Mobile CEO John Legere urges wireless users to join him to defeat "the dark force" of AT&T and Verizon. He says they already control too much of the frequency bands used for wireless and that if they get more at the upcoming auction, wireless service will become a duopoly.

Source: *The Dallas Morning News*, June 23, 2015

What is the game that T-Mobile, AT&T, and Verizon are playing?

Solutions to Practice Problems

1. Table 1 shows the payoff matrix for the game that Bud and Wise must play.
2. The Nash equilibrium is for both to produce 20,000 gallons of New Age beer a day. To see why, notice that regardless of the quantity that Bud produces, Wise makes more profit by producing 20,000 gallons of New Age beer a day. The same is true for Bud. So Bud and Wise each produce 20,000 gallons of New Age beer a day.
3. If Bud and Wise play this game repeatedly, each produces 10,000 gallons of New Age beer a day and makes maximum economic profit. They can achieve this outcome by playing a tit-for-tat strategy.

Solution to In the News

T-Mobile, AT&T, and Verizon are playing a prisoners' dilemma game for control of a large share of the frequency bands used by smartphones. Each firm could bid a low price for the share that minimizes its cost, or bid a high price for more than it currently plans to use. The Nash equilibrium is for all three to bid too high a price for too much bandwidth. It is possible that AT&T and Verizon might outbid T-Mobile and become a duopoly.

TABLE 1

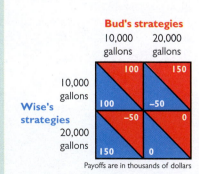

Payoffs are in thousands of dollars

18.4 ANTITRUST LAW

Antitrust law is the body of law that regulates oligopolies and prohibits them from becoming monopolies or behaving like monopolies.

■ The Antitrust Laws

Congress passed the first antitrust law, the Sherman Act, in 1890 in an atmosphere of outrage and disgust at the actions and practices of J. P. Morgan, John D. Rockefeller, and W. H. Vanderbilt—the so-called "robber barons."

A wave of mergers at the turn of the twentieth century produced stronger antitrust laws. The Clayton Act of 1914 supplemented the Sherman Act, and Congress created the Federal Trade Commission to enforce the antitrust laws.

Table 18.11 summarizes the two main provisions of the Sherman Act. Section 1 of the act is precise. Conspiring with others to restrict competition is illegal. But section 2 is general and imprecise. Just what is an "attempt to monopolize"? The Clayton Act and its two amendments, the Robinson-Patman Act of 1936, and the Celler-Kefauver Act of 1950, which outlaw specific practices, answer this question. Table 18.11 describes these practices and summarizes the main provisions of these three acts.

■ Three Antitrust Policy Debates

Price fixing is *always* a violation of the antitrust law. If the Justice Department can prove the existence of price fixing, a defendant can offer no acceptable excuse. But other practices are more controversial and generate debate among antitrust lawyers and economists. We'll examine three of these practices:

- Resale price maintenance
- Predatory pricing
- Tying arrangements

Resale Price Maintenance

Most manufacturers sell their products to the final consumer indirectly through a wholesale and retail distribution system. **Resale price maintenance** occurs when a manufacturer agrees with a distributor on the price at which the product will be resold.

Resale price maintenance (also called vertical price fixing) *agreements* are illegal under the Sherman Act. But it isn't illegal for a manufacturer to refuse to supply a retailer who doesn't accept the manufacturer's guidance on what the price should be.

Attorneys general in 41 states alleged that Universal, Sony, Warner, Bertelsmann, and EMI kept CD prices artificially high between 1995 and 2000 with a practice called "minimum-advertised pricing." The companies denied the allegation but made a large payment to settle the case.

Does resale price maintenance create an inefficient or efficient use of resources? Economists can be found on both sides of this question.

Inefficient Resale Price Maintenance   Resale price maintenance is inefficient if it enables dealers to charge the monopoly price. By setting and enforcing the resale price, the manufacturer might be able to achieve the monopoly price.

Antitrust law
A body of law that regulates oligopolies and prohibits them from becoming monopolies or behaving like monopolies.

Resale price maintenance
An agreement between a manufacturer and a distributor on the price at which a product will be resold.

■ **TABLE 18.11**

The Antitrust Laws: A Summary

The Sherman Act, 1890

Section 1:

Every contract, combination in the form of trust or otherwise, or conspiracy, in restraint of trade or commerce among the several States, or with foreign nations, is hereby declared to be illegal.

Section 2:

Every person who shall monopolize, or attempt to monopolize, or combine or conspire with any other person or persons, to monopolize any part of the trade or commerce among the several States, or with foreign nations, shall be deemed guilty of a felony.

Clayton Act, 1914

Robinson-Patman Act, 1936

Celler-Kefauver Act, 1950

These acts prohibit the following practices only if they substantially lessen competition or create monopoly:

1. Price discrimination.
2. Contracts that require other goods to be bought from the same firm (called tying arrangements).
3. Contracts that require a firm to buy all its requirements of a particular item from a single firm (called requirements contracts).
4. Contracts that prevent a firm from selling competing items (called exclusive dealing).
5. Contracts that prevent a buyer from reselling a product outside a specified area (called territorial confinement).
6. Acquiring a competitor's shares or assets.
7. Becoming a director of a competing firm.

Efficient Resale Price Maintenance Resale price maintenance might be efficient if it enables a manufacturer to induce dealers to provide the efficient standard of service. Suppose that SilkySkin wants shops to demonstrate the use of its new unbelievable moisturizing cream in an inviting space. With resale price maintenance, SilkySkin can offer all the retailers the same incentive and compensation. Without resale price maintenance, a discount drug store might offer SilkySkin products at a low price. Buyers would then have an incentive to visit a high-price shop and get the product demonstrated and then buy from the low-price shop. The low-price shop would be a free rider (like the consumer of a public good in Chapter 11, p. 271), and an inefficient level of service would be provided.

SilkySkin could pay a fee to retailers that provide good service and leave the resale price to be determined by the competitive forces of supply and demand. But it might be too costly for SilkySkin to monitor shops and ensure that they provided the desired level of service.

Predatory Pricing

Predatory pricing is setting a low price to drive competitors out of business with the intention of setting a monopoly price when the competition has gone. John D. Rockefeller's Standard Oil Company was the first to be accused of this practice in the 1890s, and it has been claimed often in antitrust cases since then. Predatory pricing is an attempt to create a monopoly and as such it is illegal under Section 2 of the Sherman Act.

It is easy to see that predatory pricing is an idea, not a reality. Economists are skeptical that predatory pricing occurs. They point out that a firm that cuts its price below the profit-maximizing level forgoes profit during the low-price period. Even if the firm succeeds in driving its competitors out of business, new competitors will enter when the firm raises its price above average total cost and makes an economic profit. So any potential gain from a monopoly position is temporary. A high and certain loss is a poor exchange for a temporary and uncertain gain. No case of predatory pricing has been definitively found.

Predatory pricing
Setting a low price to drive competitors out of business with the intention of setting a monopoly price when the competition has gone.

Tying Arrangements

A **tying arrangement** is an agreement to sell one product only if the buyer agrees to buy another, different product. With tying, the only way the buyer can get the one product is to buy the other product at the same time. Microsoft has been accused of tying Internet Explorer and Windows. Textbook publishers sometimes tie a Web site and a textbook and force students to buy both. (You can't buy the book you're now reading, new, without the Web site. But you can buy the Web site access without the book, so these products are not tied.)

Could publishers of textbooks make more money by tying a book and access to a Web site? The answer is sometimes but not always. Think about what you are willing to pay for a book and access to a Web site. To keep the numbers simple, suppose that you and other students are willing to pay $40 for a book and $10 for access to a Web site. The publisher can sell these items separately for these prices or bundled for $50. There is no gain to the publisher from bundling.

But now suppose that you and only half of the students are willing to pay $40 for a book and $10 for a Web site. And suppose that the other half of the students are willing to pay $40 for a Web site and $10 for a book. Now if the two items are sold separately, the publisher can charge $40 for the book and $40 for the Web site. Half the students buy the book but not the Web site, and the other half buy the Web site but not the book. But if the book and Web site are bundled for $50, everyone buys the bundle and the publisher makes an extra $10 per student. In this case, bundling has enabled the publisher to price discriminate.

There is no simple, clear-cut test of whether a firm is engaging in tying or whether, by doing so, it has increased its market power and profit and created inefficiency.

Tying arrangement
An agreement to sell one product only if the buyer agrees to buy another, different product.

■ Recent Antitrust Showcase: The United States Versus Microsoft

In 1998, the U.S. Department of Justice, along with a number of states, charged Microsoft, the world's largest producer of software for personal computers, with violations of both sections of the Sherman Act. A 78-day trial followed that pitched two prominent MIT economics professors against each other (Franklin Fisher for the government and Richard Schmalensee for Microsoft).

The Case Against Microsoft

The claims against Microsoft were that it

- Possessed monopoly power in the market for PC operating systems.
- Used *predatory pricing* and *tying arrangements* to achieve a monopoly in the market for Web browsers.
- Used other anticompetitive practices to strengthen its monopoly in these two markets.

It was claimed that with 80 percent of the market for PC operating systems, Microsoft had excessive monopoly power. This monopoly power arose from two barriers to entry: economies of scale and network economies. Microsoft's average total cost falls as production increases (economies of scale) because the fixed cost of developing an operating system like Windows is large while the marginal cost of producing one copy of Windows is small. Further, as the number of Windows users increases, the range of Windows applications expands (network economies), so a potential competitor would need to produce not only a competing operating system but also an entire range of supporting applications.

When Microsoft entered the Web browser market with its Internet Explorer (IE), it offered the browser for a zero price. This price was viewed as *predatory pricing*. Microsoft integrated IE with Windows so that anyone who uses this operating system would not need a separate browser such as Netscape Communicator. Microsoft's competitors claimed that this practice was an illegal *tying arrangement*.

Microsoft's Response

Microsoft challenged all these claims. It said that although Windows was the dominant operating system, it was vulnerable to competition from other operating systems such as Linux and Apple's Mac OS and that there was a permanent threat of competition from new entrants.

Microsoft claimed that integrating Internet Explorer with Windows provided a single, unified product of greater consumer value. Instead of tying, Microsoft said, the browser and operating system constituted a single product. It was like a refrigerator with a chilled water dispenser or an automobile with a stereo player.

The Outcome

The court agreed that Microsoft was in violation of the Sherman Act and ordered that it be broken into two firms: an operating systems producer and an applications producer. Microsoft successfully appealed this order. But in the final judgment, Microsoft was ordered to disclose details about how its operating system works to other software developers so that they could compete effectively against Microsoft. In the summer of 2002, Microsoft began to comply with this order.

◼ Merger Rules

You've now seen how the antitrust laws can be used to prevent an oligopoly from becoming a monopoly or trying to behave like one. We end by examining another way of trying to gain monopoly power—two or more oligopoly firms merging to increase their ability to control the market price. Mergers are subject to rules that are designed to limit monopoly power from arising and we close our explanation of the antitrust laws by seeing how they are used to review and sometimes to block a merger.

Mergers are often in the headlines. United Airlines and Continental Airlines merged to form United Continental in 2010 and American Airlines and US Airways merged in 2015. Firms can benefit from a merger in two ways: They can lower costs and they can increase market power. Lower costs are not a threat to the social interest but increased market power is. For this reason, the Federal Trade Commission (FTC) challenges proposed mergers that will substantially lessen competition and not bring lower costs.

To determine the effects of a merger on competitiveness, the FTC uses guidelines based on the Herfindahl-Hirschman Index (HHI), which is explained in Chapter 17 (p. 439). *Eye on the U.S. Economy*, below, describes the FTC guidelines and looks at a high-profile merger of smartphone service providers that was blocked by applying the guidelines.

EYE on the U.S. ECONOMY
No Wireless Service Merger

The figure (part a) summarizes the Federal Trade Commission's (FTC) guidelines on mergers. In a market in which the Herfindahl-Hirschman Index (HHI) is less than 1,500, a proposed merger is not challenged. But if the HHI is above 1,500, the FTC considers a challenge. If the HHI is between 1,500 and 2,500, a merger is challenged if it would increase the HHI by more than 100 points. And if the HHI exceeds 2,500, the market is already so concentrated that a merger is challenged if it increases the index by 100 points and normally is blocked if the index rises by more than 200 points.

In 2011, AT&T wanted to buy T-Mobile from the German firm Deutsche Telekom. But the market for wireless service is highly concentrated. Verizon, the largest service provider, had close to 40 percent of the market share. AT&T had a 30 percent share and Sprint and T-Mobile had about 12 percent each. Another 14 small firms shared the remaining market. So the four largest firms in this market

had a 94 percent market share. The HHI was around 2,800.

Part (b) of the figure shows how the HHI would have changed with the merger of AT&T and T-Mobile. It would have increased the HHI by around 700 points.

With an HHI of 2,800 and an increase of 700, there was a presumption that the merger would give AT&T too much market power. The FTC was presented with no evidence to challenge this conclusion, so it decided to block the merger.

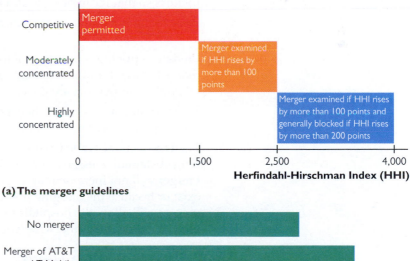

(a) The merger guidelines

(b) Merger of wireless service providers

MyEconLab Study Plan 18.4
Key Terms Quiz
Solutions Video

CHECKPOINT 18.4

Describe the antitrust laws that regulate oligopoly.

Practice Problems

1. Explain each of the following terms:
   - Attempt to monopolize
   - Price fixing
   - Predatory pricing
   - Tying arrangements

2. Since 1987, hundreds of hospital mergers have taken place and rarely has the U.S. Federal Trade Commission challenged a hospital merger. What can you infer about the structure of the market in hospital services?

In the News

Merger of beer giants faces obstacles

Mega-brand beers have lost market share to wine and craft beer. In response, Anheuser-Busch InBev and SABMiller, the two biggest brewers in the world, are discussing a merger that would be scrutinized by antitrust regulators.

Source: *The New York Times*, September 16, 2015

How would a merger benefit the two big brewers? Under what circumstances would the Federal Trade Commission (FTC) challenge the merger?

Solutions to Practice Problems

1. An attempt to monopolize is an attempt by a company to drive out its competitors so that it can operate as a monopoly.

   Price fixing is making an agreement with competitors to set a specified price and not to vary it.

   Predatory pricing is the attempt to drive out competitors by setting a price that is too low for others to make a profit, then setting the monopoly price when the competitors are gone.

   Tying arrangements exist when a company does not offer a buyer the opportunity to buy one item without at the same time buying another item.

2. The U.S. Federal Trade Commission will challenge a hospital merger only if it substantially lessens competition. Such a situation will not arise if (1) the merger will not increase market power either because strong competitors exist or because the merging hospitals are sufficiently differentiated; (2) the merger will allow the hospitals to reduce cost; or (3) the merger will eliminate a hospital that otherwise would have failed and exited the market.

Solution to In the News

A merger of the two big beer producers would make the new giant producer more profitable and more likely to set prices too high. The FTC will look at the beer market HHI. If it is between 1,500 and 2,500, the FTC will challenge the merger if it increases the HHI by more than 100 points. If the HHI exceeds 2,500, the FTC will challenge the merger if it increases the HHI by 100 points and normally will block the merger if it raises the index by more than 200 points.

CHAPTER SUMMARY

Key Points

1. Describe and identify oligopoly and explain how it arises.

- Oligopoly is a market type in which a small number of interdependent firms compete behind a barrier to entry.
- Both natural (economies of scale and market demand) and legal barriers to entry create oligopoly.

2. Explain the dilemma faced by firms in oligopoly.

- If firms in oligopoly act together to restrict output, they make the same economic profit as a monopoly, but each firm can make a larger profit by increasing production.
- The oligopoly dilemma is whether to restrict or expand output.

3. Use game theory to explain how output and price are determined in oligopoly.

- In the prisoners' dilemma game, two players acting in their own interests harm their joint interest. Oligopoly is a prisoners' dilemma game.
- If firms cooperated, they could earn the monopoly profit, but in a one-play game, they overproduce and can drive the price and economic profit to the levels of perfect competition.
- Advertising and research and development create a prisoners' dilemma for firms in oligopoly.
- In a repeated game, a punishment strategy can lead to monopoly output, price, and economic profit.
- Oligopoly is usually inefficient because the price (marginal benefit) exceeds marginal cost and cost might not be the lowest attainable.

4. Describe the antitrust laws that regulate oligopoly.

- The Sherman Act (1890) and the Clayton Act (1914) make price-fixing agreements among firms illegal.
- Resale price maintenance might be efficient if it enables a producer to ensure the efficient level of service by distributors.
- Predatory pricing might bring temporary gains.
- Tying arrangements can facilitate price discrimination.
- The Federal Trade Commission examines and possibly blocks mergers if they would restrict competition too much.

Key Terms

MyEconLab Key Terms Quiz

Antitrust law, 477
Cartel, 460
Duopoly, 461
Game theory, 469

Nash equilibrium, 470
Payoff matrix, 470
Predatory pricing, 479
Prisoners' dilemma, 469

Resale price maintenance, 477
Strategies, 470
Tying arrangement, 479

CHAPTER CHECKPOINT

Study Plan Problems and Applications

Use the following information to work Problems **1** and **2**.

When the first automobiles were built in 1901, they were made by skilled workers using hand tools. Later, in 1913, Henry Ford introduced the moving assembly line, which lowered costs and speeded production. Over the years, the production line has become ever more mechanized, and today robots replace people in many tasks.

1. Sketch the average total cost curve and the demand curve for automobiles in 1901 and in 2016.

2. Describe the changing barriers to entry in the automobile industry and explain how the combination of market demand and economies of scale has changed the structure of the industry over the past 100 years.

Use the following information to work Problems **3** to **5**.

Isolated Island has two taxi companies, one owned by Ann and the other owned by Zack. Figure 1 shows the market demand curve for taxi rides, *D*, and the average total cost curve of one of the firms, *ATC*.

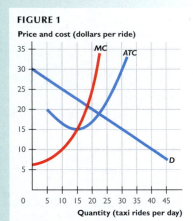

FIGURE 1

3. If Ann and Zack produce the same quantity of rides as would be produced in perfect competition, what are the quantity of rides, the price of a ride, and the economic profit of Ann and Zack? Would Ann and Zack have an incentive to collude and raise their price? Explain why or why not.

4. If Ann and Zack form a cartel and produce the same quantity of rides as would be produced in monopoly, what are the quantity of rides, the price of a ride, and the economic profit of Ann and Zack? Would Ann and Zack have an incentive to break the cartel agreement and cut their price? Explain why or why not.

5. Suppose that Ann and Zack have two strategies: collude, fix the monopoly price, and limit the number of rides or break the collusion, cut the price, and produce more rides. Create a payoff matrix for the game that Ann and Zack play, and find the Nash equilibrium for this game if it is played just once. Do the people of Isolated Island get the efficient quantity of taxi rides?

Use the following information to work Problems **6** and **7**.

Coke, Pepsi and the new front in the cola wars
The cola wars between Coca-Cola and PepsiCo may become even tougher as consumers seek out healthier alternatives to sugary soft drinks. But both Coke and Pepsi are getting higher prices for soda, thanks to new 8-ounce cans replacing the standard 12-ounce size.

Source: CBC News, February 12, 2015

6. Describe the cola wars that Coca-Cola and PepsiCo play as a game. What type of game is it? What are some of the strategies in the game?

7. With two strategies—8-ounce can and 12-ounce can—and with assumed payoffs, create a payoff matrix for the game if the equilibrium outcome is for both firms to choose 8-ounce cans.

8. Read *Eye On the Wireless Oligopoly* on p. 475 and then explain the effects of economies of scale and demand on the market for smartphone plans and illustrate it with a graph based on Figure 18.1.

Instructor Assignable Problems and Applications

MyEconLab Homework, Quiz, or Test if assigned by instructor

1. AT&T and Verizon have two pricing strategies: Set a high (monopoly) price or set a low (competitive) price. Suppose that if they both set a competitive price, economic profit for both is zero. If they both set a monopoly price, AT&T makes an economic profit of $100 million and Verizon makes an economic profit of $200 million. If AT&T sets a low price and Verizon sets a high price, AT&T makes an economic profit of $200 million and Verizon incurs an economic loss of $100 million; if AT&T sets a high price and Verizon sets a low price, AT&T incurs an economic loss of $50 million and Verizon makes an economic profit of $250 million.

   - Create the payoff matrix for this game.
   - What is the equilibrium of this game?
   - Is the equilibrium efficient?
   - Is this game a prisoners' dilemma?

Use the following information to work Problems **2** and **3**.

The United States claims that Canada subsidizes the production of softwood lumber and that U.S. imports of Canadian lumber damage the interests of U.S. producers. The United States has imposed a tariff on Canadian imports to counter the subsidy. Canada is thinking of retaliating by refusing to export water to California. Table 1 shows a payoff matrix for the game that the United States and Canada are playing.

2. What is the United States' best strategy? What is Canada's best strategy? What is the outcome of this game? Explain.

3. Is this game like a prisoners' dilemma or different in some crucial way? Explain. Which country would benefit more from a free trade agreement?

4. Agile Airlines is making $10 million a year economic profit on a route on which it has a monopoly. Wanabe Airlines is considering entering the market and operating on this route. Agile warns Wanabe to stay out and threatens to cut the price to the point at which Wanabe will make no profit if it enters. Wanabe does some research and determines that the payoff matrix for the game in which it is engaged with Agile is that shown in Table 2. Does Wanabe believe Agile's assertion? Does Wanabe enter or not? Explain.

Use this information to work Problems **5** to **7**.

DOJ investigation prompts lawsuits alleging that airlines are fixing airfares
It is alleged that Southwest Airlines, American Airlines, Delta Air Lines, and United Airlines have been colluding to limit the increases in their capacity with the intent of increasing airfares. The airlines say the allegations are without merit and that the airline industry is highly competitive with more people flying than ever before.

Source: *The Dallas Morning News*, July 8, 2015

5. Explain how limiting the increase in capacity could lead to higher airfares.

6. Explain how limiting the increase in capacity could lead to greater profit for the airlines, smaller consumer surplus, and deadweight loss. Illustrate your explanation with a graph.

7. Describe the fare-fixing scheme as the equilibrium outcome of an oligopoly cartel game played by the airlines. Explain why the cartel survived.

TABLE 1

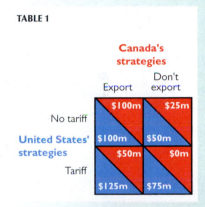

TABLE 2

MyEconLab Chapter 18 Study Plan

Multiple Choice Quiz

1. Which of the following statements is *incorrect*. In oligopoly, _____.

A. barriers to entry prevent new firms entering
B. each firm's profit is influenced by each other firms' advertising
C. each firm's action is influenced by the actions and reactions of each other firm
D. each firm is a price taker and the price is the monopoly profit-maximizing price

2. If firms in oligopoly form a cartel, it will likely break down because _____.

A. firms cannot agree on how to share the economic profit
B. the price set by the cartel is too low
C. with price exceeding marginal cost, a firm might expand production to increase its profit
D. firms realize that their allocation of resources is inefficient

3. The oligopoly dilemma is whether to _____.

A. act together to restrict output and raise the price
B. raise the price to the monopoly profit-maximizing price
C. cheat on others in the cartel to take advantage of profit opportunities
D. lower the price to the perfectly competitive price

4. In the prisoners' dilemma game, each player _____.

A. consults the other player to determine his best action
B. chooses the best outcome for the other player
C. chooses the best outcome for himself
D. chooses the best outcome for both players together

5. A Nash equilibrium _____.

A. is the outcome that delivers maximum economic profit
B. is the outcome in which each player takes the best action given the other player's action
C. changes each time the game is played
D. is the best possible outcome for the two players

6. In an advertising prisoners' dilemma game, _____.

A. both firms will advertise and end up with lower profits than if neither advertises
B. only one firm will advertise because the other firm sees the advertising expenditure as a waste
C. the two firms agree on the total advertising budget and split it equally
D. neither firm will advertise because both realize that it lowers profit

7. Each of the following practices violates U.S. antitrust law *except* _____.

A. an agreement to sell one good only if the buyer purchases another good
B. an agreement between the manufacturer and the seller to charge a given price for the good
C. starting a price war with other sellers of a similar good
D. cutting the price to increase market share to 100 percent, then raising the price

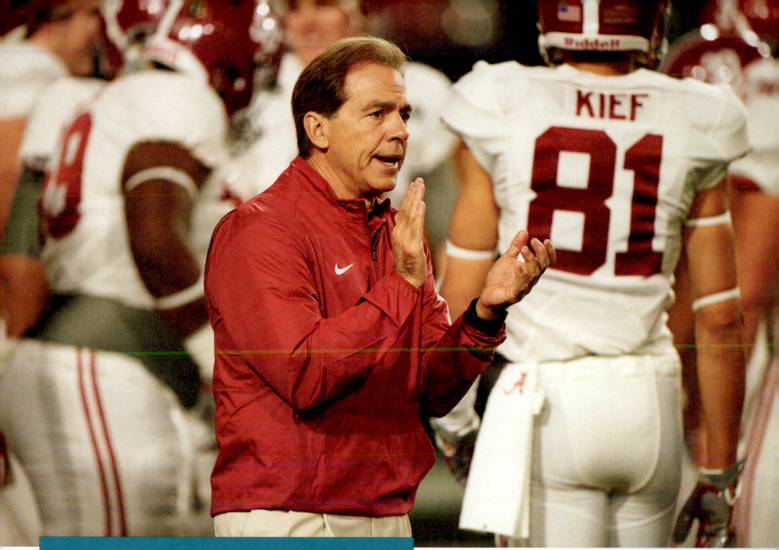

Markets for Factors of Production

19

When you have completed your study of this chapter, you will be able to

1 Explain how the value of marginal product determines the demand for a factor of production.

2 Explain how wage rates and employment are determined and how labor unions influence labor markets.

3 Explain how capital and land rental rates and natural resource prices are determined.

MyEconLab Big Picture Video

MyEconLab Concept Video

THE ANATOMY OF FACTOR MARKETS

The four factors of production are

- Labor
- Capital
- Land (natural resources)
- Entrepreneurship

Factor markets
The markets in which the services of the factors of production are traded.

Factor prices
The prices of the services of the factors of production.

The *services* of labor, capital, and land are traded in **factor markets**, which determine their **factor prices**. Entrepreneurial services are not traded in markets and entrepreneurs receive the profit or bear the loss that results from their decisions. Let's take a brief look at the anatomy of the factor markets.

Markets for Labor Services

Labor services are the physical and mental work effort that people supply to produce goods and services. A *labor market* is a collection of people and firms who trade *labor services*. Some labor services are traded day by day, called casual labor. People who pick fruit and vegetables often just show up at a farm and take whatever work is available that day. But most labor services, like those of a football coach, are traded on a contract. The price of labor services is a wage rate.

Most labor markets have many buyers and sellers and are competitive. But in some labor markets a labor union organizes labor and introduces an element of monopoly into the market. We'll study both competitive labor markets and labor unions in this chapter.

Markets for Capital Services

Capital consists of the tools, instruments, machines, buildings, and other constructions that have been produced in the past and that businesses now use to produce goods and services. These physical objects are themselves goods—*capital goods*—and are traded in goods markets, just as bottled water and toothpaste are.

A market for *capital services* is a *rental market*—a market in which the services of capital are hired. An example of a market for capital services is the vehicle rental market in which Avis, Budget, Hertz, U-Haul, and many other firms offer automobiles and trucks for hire. The price of capital services is a rental rate.

Most capital services are not traded in a market. Instead, a firm buys capital equipment and uses it itself. But the services of the capital that a firm owns and operates itself have an *implicit* price that arises from depreciation and interest costs (see Chapter 14, p. 349). Think of this price as the *implicit rental rate* of the capital that a firm owns.

Markets for Land Services and Natural Resources

Land consists of all the gifts of nature—natural resources. The market for land as a factor of production is the market for the *services of land*—the *use* of land. The price of the services of land is a rental rate.

Most natural resources, such as farm land and rivers, can be used repeatedly. But a few natural resources are nonrenewable. **Nonrenewable natural resources** are resources that can be used only once and cannot be replaced once they have been used. Examples are oil, natural gas, and coal. The prices of natural resources are determined in global *commodity markets* and are called *commodity prices*.

Nonrenewable natural resources
Natural resources that can be used only once and cannot be replaced once they have been used.

19.1 THE DEMAND FOR A FACTOR OF PRODUCTION

MyEconLab Concept Video

We begin our study of factor markets by learning about the demand for factors of production, and we use labor as the example. The demand for a factor of production is a **derived demand**—it is derived from the demand for the goods and services that it is used to produce. You've seen, in Chapters 15 through 18, how a firm determines its profit-maximizing output. The quantities of factors of production demanded are a direct consequence of firms' output decisions. Firms hire the quantities of factors of production that maximize profit.

To decide the quantity of a factor of production to hire, a firm compares the cost of hiring an additional unit of the factor with its value to the firm. The cost of hiring an additional unit of a factor of production is called the *factor price*. The value to the firm of hiring one more unit of a factor of production is called the factor's **value of marginal product**, which equals the price of a unit of output multiplied by the marginal product of the factor of production. To study the demand for a factor of production, we'll examine the demand for labor.

Derived demand
The demand for a factor of production, which is derived from the demand for the goods and services that it is used to produce.

Value of marginal product
The value to a firm of hiring one more unit of a factor of production, which equals the price of a unit of output multiplied by the marginal product of the factor of production.

■ Value of Marginal Product

Table 19.1 shows you how to calculate the value of marginal product of labor at Max's Wash 'n' Wax car wash service. The first two columns show Max's *total product* schedule—the number of car washes per hour that each quantity of labor can produce. The third column shows the *marginal product* of labor—the change in total product that results from a one-unit increase in the quantity of labor employed. (See Chapter 14, pp. 353–357, for a refresher on product schedules.) Max can sell car washes at the going market price of $6 a wash. Given this information, we can calculate the value of marginal product (fourth column). It equals price multiplied by marginal product. For example, the marginal product of hiring the second worker is 4 car washes an hour. Each wash brings in $6, so the value of marginal product of the second worker is $24 (4 washes at $6 each).

TABLE 19.1

Calculating the Value of Marginal Product

	Quantity of labor (workers)	Total product (car washes per hour)	Marginal product (washes per additional worker)	Value of marginal product (dollars per additional worker)
A	0	0		
			5	30
B	1	5		
			4	24
C	2	9		
			3	18
D	3	12		
			2	12
E	4	14		
			1	6
F	5	15		

The value of marginal product of labor equals the price of the product multiplied by the marginal product of labor.

The price of a car wash is $6.

The marginal product of the second worker (in column 3) is 4 washes, so the value of marginal product of the second worker (in column 4) is $6 a wash multiplied by 4 washes, which equals $24.

The Value of Marginal Product Curve

Figure 19.1 graphs the value of marginal product of labor at Max's Wash 'n' Wax as the number of workers that Max hires changes. The blue bars that show the value of marginal product of labor correspond to the numbers in Table 19.1. The curve labeled *VMP* is Max's value of marginal product curve.

■ A Firm's Demand for Labor

The value of marginal product of labor and the wage rate determine the quantity of labor demanded by a firm. The value of marginal product of labor tells us the additional revenue the firm earns by hiring one more worker. The wage rate tells us the additional cost the firm incurs by hiring one more worker.

Because the value of marginal product decreases as the quantity of labor employed increases, there is a simple rule for maximizing profit: Hire labor up to the point at which the value of marginal product equals the wage rate. If the value of marginal product of labor exceeds the wage rate, a firm can increase its profit by employing one more worker. If the wage rate exceeds the value of marginal product of labor, a firm can increase its profit by employing one less worker. But if the wage rate equals the value of marginal product of labor, the firm cannot increase its profit by changing the number of workers it employs. The firm is making the maximum possible profit.

So the quantity of labor demanded by a firm is the quantity at which the wage rate equals the value of marginal product of labor.

■ FIGURE 19.1

The Value of Marginal Product at Max's Wash 'n' Wax   MyEconLab Animation

The blue bars show the value of marginal product of the labor that Max hires based on the numbers in Table 19.1.

The orange line labeled *VMP* is the firm's value of marginal product of labor curve.

	Quantity of labor (workers)	Value of marginal product (dollars per additional worker)
A	1	30
B	2	24
C	3	18
D	4	12
E	5	6

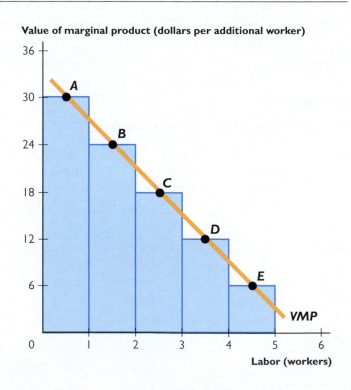

■ A Firm's Demand for Labor Curve

A firm's demand for labor curve is also its value of marginal product curve. Figure 19.2 shows Max's value of marginal product curve in part (a) and Max's demand for labor curve in part (b). The *x*-axis measures the number of workers hired in both parts. The *y*-axis measures the value of marginal product in part (a) and the wage rate—dollars per hour—in part (b).

Suppose the wage rate is $15 an hour. You can see in part (a) that if Max hires 1 worker, the value of marginal product of labor is $30 an hour. Because the worker costs only $15 an hour, Max makes a profit of $15 an hour. If Max hires a second worker, the value of marginal product of this worker is $24 an hour, so on the second worker, Max makes a profit of $9 an hour. If Max hires a third worker, the value of marginal product of this worker is $18 an hour, so on this worker, Max makes a profit of $3 an hour. Max's profit on these three workers is $27 an hour—$15 on the first, $9 on the second, and $3 on the third worker.

If Max hired a fourth worker, his profit would fall. The fourth worker generates a value of marginal product of only $12 an hour but costs $15 an hour, so Max does not hire a fourth worker. The quantity of labor demanded by Max when the

■ FIGURE 19.2

The Demand for Labor at Max's Wash 'n' Wax

MyEconLab Animation

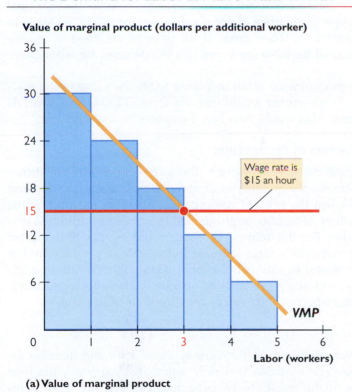

(a) Value of marginal product

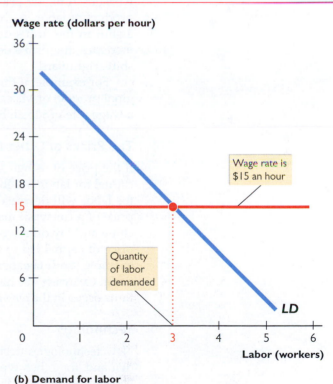

(b) Demand for labor

At a wage rate of $15 an hour, Max makes a profit on the first 3 workers hired but would incur a loss on the fourth worker in part (a), so the quantity of labor demanded is 3 workers in part (b).

Max's demand for labor curve in part (b) is the same as the value of marginal product curve in part (a). The demand for labor curve slopes downward because the value of marginal product of labor diminishes as the quantity of labor employed increases.

wage rate is $15 an hour is 3 workers, which is a point on Max's demand for labor curve, *LD*, in Figure 19.2(b).

If the wage rate rose to $21 an hour, Max would decrease the quantity of labor demanded to 2 workers. If the wage rate fell to $9 an hour, Max would increase the quantity of labor demanded to 4 workers.

A change in the wage rate brings a change in the quantity of labor demanded and a movement along the demand for labor curve. A change in any other influence on the firm's labor-hiring plans changes the demand for labor and shifts the demand for labor curve.

■ Changes in the Demand for Labor

The demand for labor depends on

- The price of the firm's output
- The prices of other factors of production
- Technology

The Price of the Firm's Output

The higher the price of the good or service produced by the firm, the greater is the firm's demand for labor. The price of the firm's good affects the firm's demand for labor through its influence on the value of marginal product of the firm's workers. A higher price of the good or service increases the value of the marginal product of labor. A change in the price of the good or service produced leads to a shift in the firm's demand for labor curve. If the price of the good or service increases, the firm's demand for labor increases and the demand for labor curve shifts rightward.

For example, if the price of a car wash increased to $8, the value of the marginal product of Max's fourth worker would increase from $12 to $16 an hour. At a wage rate of $15 an hour, Max would now hire 4 workers instead of 3.

The Prices of Other Factors of Production

If the price of using capital decreases relative to the wage rate, a firm substitutes capital for labor and increases the quantity of capital it uses. Usually, the demand for labor will decrease when the price of using capital falls. For example, if the price of a car wash machine falls, Max might decide to install an additional machine and lay off a worker. But the demand for labor could increase if the lower price of capital led to a sufficiently large increase in the scale of production. For example, with cheaper capital equipment available, Max might install an additional car wash machine and hire more labor to operate it. These factor substitutions occur in the *long run* when the firm can change the scale of its plant.

Technology

New technologies decrease the demand for some types of labor and increase the demand for other types. For example, if a new automated car wash machine becomes available, Max might install one of these machines and fire most of his workers—a decrease in the demand for car wash workers. But the firms that manufacture and service automatic car wash machines hire more labor—the demand for these types of labor increases. During the 1980s and 1990s, electronic telephone exchanges decreased the demand for telephone operators and increased the demand for computer programmers and electronics engineers.

CHECKPOINT 19.1

Explain how the value of marginal product determines the demand for a factor of production.

MyEconLab Study Plan 19.1
Key Terms Quiz
Solutions Video

Practice Problems

Kaiser's produces smoothies. The market for smoothies is perfectly competitive, and the price of a smoothie is $4. The labor market is competitive, and the wage rate is $40 a day. Table 1 shows Kaiser's total product schedule.

1. Calculate the marginal product and the value of marginal product of the fourth worker.

2. How many workers will Kaiser's hire to maximize its profit? How many smoothies a day will Kaiser's produce?

3. If the price of a smoothie rises to $5, how many workers will Kaiser's hire?

4. Kaiser's installs a machine that increases the marginal product of labor by 50 percent. If the price of a smoothie remains at $4 and the wage rate rises to $48 a day, how many workers does Kaiser's hire?

TABLE 1

Workers	Smoothies per day
1	7
2	21
3	33
4	43
5	51
6	55

In the News

U.S. economy gained jobs in hiring slowdown
The Labor Department reported a slowdown in hiring but not all the news about jobs is gloomy. McDonald's plans to raise wages in a strengthening labor market. And Walmart plans to raise wages to a minimum of $9 an hour.
Source: The New York Times, April 4, 2015

Explain why jobs growth is slow in some parts of the economy and strong in others. Why would McDonald's and Walmart raise the wage rates of their workers?

Solutions to Practice Problems

1. The *MP* of the 4th worker equals the *TP* of 4 workers (43 smoothies) minus the *TP* of 3 workers (33 smoothies), which is 10 smoothies. The *VMP* of the 4th worker equals the *MP* of the 4th worker (10 smoothies) multiplied by the price of a smoothie ($4), which is $40 a day.

2. Kaiser's maximizes profit by hiring the number of workers that makes the *VMP* of labor equal to the wage rate ($40 a day). Kaiser's hires 4 workers. The marginal product of the 4th worker is 10 smoothies and the price of a smoothie is $4, so the *VMP* of labor is $40 a day, which equals the wage rate. Kaiser's produces 43 smoothies a day.

3. Kaiser's maximizes profit by hiring 5 workers. The *MP* is 8 smoothies and the price is $5, so the *VMP* of labor is $40 a day—equal to the wage rate.

4. When Kaiser's hires 5 workers, the *MP* is 12 smoothies. The price of a smoothie is $4, so the *VMP* of labor is $48 a day— equal to the wage rate.

Solution to In the News

Firms hire the quantity of labor at which the *VMP* of labor equals the wage rate. Jobs growth is slow if the *VMP* of labor grows slowly and is strong if the *VMP* of labor grows quickly. McDonald's and Walmart would raise the wage rates they pay when the *VMP* of their workers increases and the market wage rate increases.

MyEconLab Concept Video

19.2 LABOR MARKETS

For most of us, a labor market is our only source of income. We work and earn a wage. What determines the amount of labor that we supply?

■ The Supply of Labor

People supply labor to earn an income. Many factors influence the quantity of labor that a person plans to provide, but a key factor is the wage rate.

To see how the wage rate influences the quantity of labor supplied, think about Larry's labor supply decision, which Figure 19.3 illustrates. Larry enjoys his leisure time, and he would be pleased if he didn't have to spend his evenings and weekends working at Max's Wash 'n' Wax. But Max pays him $15 an hour, and at that wage rate, Larry chooses to work 30 hours a week. The reason is that he is offered a wage rate that is high enough to make him regard this use of his time as the best available to him. If he were offered a lower wage rate, Larry would not be willing to give up so much leisure. If he were offered a higher wage rate, Larry would want to work even longer hours, but only up to a point. Offer Larry $25 an hour, and he would be willing to work a 40-hour week (and earn $1,000). With the goods and services that Larry can buy for $1,000, his priority would be a bit more leisure time if the wage rate increased further. If the wage rate increased above $25 an hour, Larry would cut back on his work hours and take more leisure. Larry's labor supply curve eventually bends backward.

Larry works as a car washer, but he enjoys his leisure time.

■ FIGURE 19.3

An Individual's Labor Supply Curve

MyEconLab Animation

❶ At a wage rate of $15 an hour,

❷ Larry is willing to supply 30 hours a week of labor.

❸ Larry's quantity of labor supplied ❹ increases as the wage rate increases up to ❺ a maximum, and then further increases in the wage rate ❻ bring a decrease in the quantity of labor supplied.

Larry's labor supply curve is upward sloping but eventually it bends backward.

	Wage rate (dollars per hour)	Quantity of labor (hours per week)
A	40	30
B	35	35
C	30	39
D	25	40
E	20	37
F	15	30
G	10	17
H	5	0

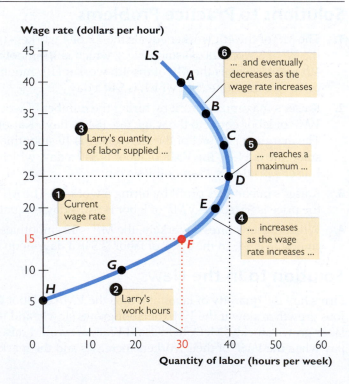

Market Supply Curve

Larry's supply curve shows the quantity of labor supplied by one person as that person's wage rate changes. Most people behave like Larry, but people have different wage rates at which they are willing to work and at which their labor supply curve bends backward. A market supply curve shows the quantity of labor supplied by all households in a particular job. It is found by adding together the quantities supplied by all households at each wage rate. Also, along a market supply curve, the wage rates available in other jobs remain the same. For example, along the supply curve of car wash workers, we hold constant the wage rates of car salespeople, mechanics, and all other types of labor.

Offer Larry more for car washing than for oil changing, and he will supply more of his labor to car washing. The market supply curve in a given job slopes upward like the one in Figure 19.4, which shows the market supply curve of car wash workers in a large city.

■ Influences on the Supply of Labor

The supply of labor changes when influences other than the wage rate change. The key factors that change the supply of labor are

- Adult population
- Preferences
- Time in school and training

■ FIGURE 19.4

The Supply of Car Wash Workers

MyEconLab Animation

	Wage rate (dollars per hour)	Quantity of labor (workers)
A	25	400
B	20	370
C	15	300
D	10	170
E	5	0

The supply curve of car wash workers shows how the quantity of labor supplied changes when the wage rate changes, other things remaining the same.

In a market for a specific type of labor, the quantity supplied increases as the wage rate increases, other things remaining the same.

Adult Population

An increase in the adult population, caused either by a birth rate that exceeds the death rate or by immigration, increases the supply of labor. Historically, the population of the United States has been strongly influenced by immigration.

Preferences

In 2015, 54 percent of women had jobs, up from 36 percent in 1960. In contrast, in 2015, 65 percent of men had jobs, down from 79 percent in 1960. Many factors contributed to these changes, which economists classify as *changes in preferences*. These changes occur slowly but accumulate to make a large difference in the supply of labor. The result has been a large increase in the supply of female labor and a decrease in the supply of male labor.

Time in School and Training

The more people who remain in school for full-time education and training, the smaller is the supply of low-skilled labor. Today in the United States, almost everyone completes high school and more than 50 percent of high-school graduates enroll in college or university. Although many students work part time, the supply of labor by students is less than it would be if they were full-time workers. So when more people pursue higher education, other things remaining the same, the supply of low-skilled labor decreases. But time spent in school and training converts low-skilled labor into high-skilled labor. The greater the proportion of people who receive a higher education, the greater is the supply of high-skilled labor.

When the amount of work that people want to do at a given wage rate changes, the supply of labor changes. An increase in the adult population or an increase in the percentage of women with jobs increases the supply of labor. An increase in college enrollment decreases the supply of low-skilled labor. Later, it increases the supply of high-skilled labor. Changes in the supply of labor shift the supply of labor curve, just like the shifts of the supply curve that you studied in Chapter 4 (p. 95).

■ Competitive Labor Market Equilibrium

Labor market equilibrium determines the wage rate and employment. In Figure 19.5, the market demand curve for car wash workers is *LD*. Here, if the wage rate is $15 an hour, the quantity of labor demanded is 300 workers. If the wage rate rises to $20 an hour, the quantity demanded decreases to 200 workers. And if the wage rate falls to $13 an hour, the quantity demanded increases to 350 workers. The supply curve of car wash workers is *LS*—the same curve as in Figure 19.4.

Figure 19.5 shows the equilibrium in the labor market. The equilibrium wage rate is $15 an hour, and the equilibrium number of car wash workers is 300. If the wage rate exceeded $15 an hour, there would be a surplus of car wash workers. More people would be looking for car wash jobs than firms were willing to hire. In such a situation, the wage rate would fall as firms found it easy to hire people at a lower wage rate. If the wage rate were less than $15 an hour, there would be a shortage of car wash workers. Firms would not be able to fill all the jobs they had available. In this situation, the wage rate would rise as firms found it necessary to offer a higher wage rate to attract workers. Only at a wage rate of $15 an hour are there no market forces operating to change the wage rate.

EYE on the COACH

Why Is a Coach Worth $7 Million?

Nick Saban, head coach of the Alabama Crimson Tide, earns $7 million a year, more than 70 times what the University of Alabama pays an average professor. Why does the University of Alabama pay a football coach the same amount that it pays 70 professors?

Nick Saban is worth 70 professors because his value of marginal product (*VMP*) to the University of Alabama is at least 70 times that of a professor.

Few people have the talent and willingness to work hard and take the stress of being head coach of a top college football program. Mr. Saban is one of these few people and possibly the best of them. The consequence is that the supply of coaches like Nick Saban is small and inelastic.

To hire a top coach, the University of Alabama must pay the market price and that price is determined by the small supply and a high *VMP*.

The *VMP* of a football coach is high, much higher than that of a professor, because of the revenue that a successful football team generates. Some of that revenue comes directly from the game and includes the football gear and theme clothing licensed by the University. But most of the revenue comes from increased donations by alumni and wealthy local and national patrons. The better the coach, the better is the team's performance and the greater is the revenue from these sources. Nick Saban brings in at least $7 million a year to the University of Alabama.

In contrast, a professor, even an outstanding one, generates a modest revenue for the University. He or she attracts a few students and obtains some research grant funds from the National Science Foundation or other private foundation. But the *VMP* of a professor is modest—around a 70th of the *VMP* of Nick Saban.

FIGURE 19.5

Labor Market Equilibrium

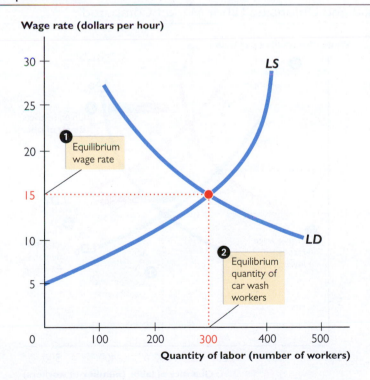

Labor market equilibrium determines the wage rate and employment. The wage rate adjusts to make the quantity of labor demanded equal the quantity of labor supplied.

❶ The equilibrium wage rate is $15 an hour.

❷ The equilibrium quantity of labor is 300 workers.

If the wage rate exceeds $15 an hour, the quantity supplied exceeds the quantity demanded. With a surplus of labor, the wage rate falls.

If the wage rate is below $15 an hour, the quantity demanded exceeds the quantity supplied. With a shortage of labor, the wage rate rises.

■ Labor Unions

Labor union
An organized group of workers that aims to increase the wage rate and influence other job conditions of its members.

A **labor union** is an organized group of workers that aims to increase the wage rate and influence other job conditions of its members. In some labor markets, labor unions have a powerful effect on the wage rate and employment. To see the effects of a labor union, let's see what happens if a union enters a competitive labor market.

A Union Enters a Competitive Labor Market

A labor union that enters a competitive labor market can try to restrict the supply of labor or it can try to increase the demand for labor. If the union restricts the supply of labor below its competitive level, the wage rate rises. If that is all the union is able to do, the wage rate rises, but the number of jobs decreases. There is a tradeoff between the wage rate and the number of jobs.

Figure 19.6 illustrates a labor market before and after a union enters it. Before the union enters the market, the demand curve is LD_0, the supply curve is LS_0, the wage rate is $15 an hour, and 300 workers are employed.

When a labor union enters this market, it restricts the supply of labor and the supply of labor curve shifts leftward to LS_1. The wage rate rises to $20 an hour and employment decreases to 200 workers. The union simply picks its preferred position along the demand curve that defines the tradeoff it faces between employment and the wage rate.

Because restricting the supply of labor brings a higher wage rate at the cost of jobs, unions also try to increase the demand for labor.

■ **FIGURE 19.6**

A Competitive Labor Market and Unionized Labor Market Compared   MyEconLab Animation

❶ In a competitive labor market, the demand for labor is LD_0, the supply of labor is LS_0, the equilibrium wage rate is $15 an hour, and the equilibrium quantity of labor is 300 workers.

❷ A labor union restricts the supply of labor and the supply of labor curve shifts leftward to LS_1.

❸ The wage rate rises to $20 an hour, but employment decreases to 200 workers—jobs are traded off for a higher wage rate.

❹ If the union action increases labor productivity and increases the demand for union labor, the demand for labor curve shifts rightward to LD_1.

❺ With supply at LS_1, the increase in demand raises the wage rate to $25 an hour and employment increases to 250 workers.

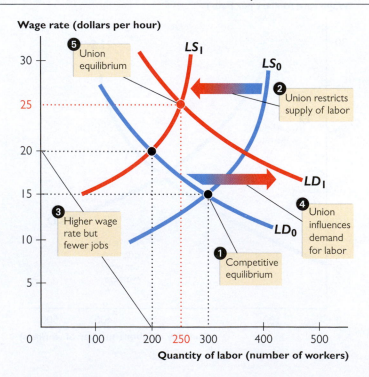

How Labor Unions Try to Increase the Demand for Labor

Labor unions try to increase the demand for union labor by increasing their value of marginal product and by supporting minimum wage laws and import restrictions.

The value of marginal product of union workers might be increased (and the demand for union labor increased) by union-sponsored job training programs, apprenticeship, and other on-the-job training activities.

A minimum wage law might increase the demand for union labor by increasing the cost of employing low-skilled nonunion labor. An increase in the wage rate of low-skilled labor leads to a decrease in the quantity demanded of low-skilled labor and to an increase in the demand for high-skilled union labor, a substitute for low-skilled labor.

By supporting import restrictions, labor unions try to increase the demand for the goods and services produced by union workers.

Figure 19.6 shows the effects of a labor union that is able to increase the demand for the labor of its members. The demand curve shifts rightward to LD_1. With the supply of labor curve LS_1, the wage rate rises to $25 an hour and employment increases from 200 to 250 workers.

How much of a difference to wage rates do unions make? To answer this question, we must look at the wages of unionized and nonunionized workers who do similar work. The evidence suggests that after allowing for skill differences, the union–nonunion wage gap lies between 10 percent and 25 percent. For example, unionized airline pilots earn about 25 percent more than nonunion pilots with the same level of skill.

EYE on YOUR LIFE

MyEconLab Critical Thinking Exercise

Job Choice and Income Prospects

Your job choice will have a big impact on your income. To provide you with some guidance on this impact, the figure shows wage rates for 16 occupations (or groups of occupations) reported by the Bureau of Labor Statistics.

You can see that economists are highly paid but not the highest. John Maynard Keynes, one of the leading economists of the last century, expressed the hope that economists would one day be as useful as dentists. If wage rates measure usefulness, you can see that the average economist isn't as useful as the average dentist. Nor is a university teacher of economics as useful as a dentist!

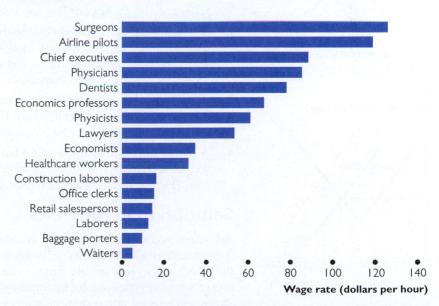

SOURCE OF DATA: National Compensation Survey, Bureau of Labor Statistics.

MyEconLab Study Plan 19.2
Key Terms Quiz
Solutions Video

CHECKPOINT 19.2

Explain how wage rates and employment are determined and how labor unions influence labor markets.

Practice Problems

In Greenville, where fast-food outlets hire teenagers and seniors, the following events occur one at a time and other things remain the same. Explain the influence of each event on the market for fast-food workers.

1. Seniors flock to Greenville and make it their home.

2. Greenville becomes a major tourist center attracting thousands of additional visitors every day.

3. The price of fast food falls.

4. Fast-food workers join a union and it gets a law passed that raises the minimum age and lowers the maximum age of a fast-food worker.

In the News

25 million new jobs coming to America, thanks to technology
Oxford researchers say that half of the jobs in America will be computerized over the next 20 years. Robert Cohen, a senior fellow at the Economic Strategy Institute, says "cloud computing, Big Data, and the Internet of Things will employ millions of people in new types of jobs."

Source: *Fortune*, January 15, 2016

Explain how advances in computer technology destroy and create jobs.

Solutions to Practice Problems

1. An increase in the number of seniors increases the supply of fast-food labor. The supply curve shifts rightward from S_0 to S_2 (Figure 1). The wage rate falls, and the number of fast-food workers employed increases.

2. A boost in visitor numbers increases the demand for fast food, which in turn increases the demand for fast-food workers. The demand curve shifts rightward from D_0 to D_1 (Figure 2). The wage rate rises, and the number of fast-food workers employed increases.

3. A fall in the price of fast food decreases the demand for fast-food workers. The demand curve shifts leftward from D_0 to D_2 (Figure 2). The wage rate falls, and the number of fast-food workers employed decreases.

4. A rise in the minimum age and a fall in the maximum age of a fast-food worker decreases the supply of labor. The supply curve shifts leftward from S_0 to S_1 (Figure 1). The wage rate rises, and the number employed decreases.

Solution to In the News

Advances in computer technology enable computers to replace some types of jobs. An example is self-checkouts replacing grocery store cashiers. Advances in computer technology also enable things to be done that were previously impossible and create new types of jobs. Examples are jobs for salespeople in smartphone stores and jobs for app coders. Advances in computer technology lower the *VMP* of labor in the jobs it destroys and increase the *VMP* of labor in the jobs it creates.

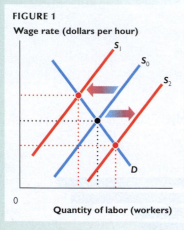

FIGURE 1

Wage rate (dollars per hour)

Quantity of labor (workers)

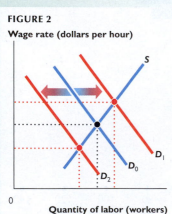

FIGURE 2

Wage rate (dollars per hour)

Quantity of labor (workers)

19.3   CAPITAL AND NATURAL RESOURCE MARKETS

MyEconLab Concept Video

The markets for capital and land can be understood by using the same basic ideas that you've seen when studying markets for labor. But markets for nonrenewable natural resources are different. We'll now examine three groups of factor markets:

* Capital markets
* Land markets
* Nonrenewable natural resource markets

■ Capital Markets

The demand for capital is based on the *value of marginal product of capital*. Profit-maximizing firms hire the quantity of capital at which the value of marginal product of capital equals the *rental rate of capital*. The *lower* the rental rate, other things remaining the same, the *greater* is the quantity of capital *demanded*. The supply of capital responds in the opposite way to the rental rate. The *higher* the rental rate, other things remaining the same, the *greater* is the quantity of capital *supplied*. The equilibrium rental rate makes the quantity of capital demanded equal to the quantity supplied.

Figure 19.7 illustrates the market for the rental of tower cranes, capital used to construct high-rise buildings. With the demand curve *D* and supply curve *S*, the equilibrium rental rate is $1,000 per day and 100 tower cranes are rented.

■ **FIGURE 19.7**

A Market for Capital Services

MyEconLab Animation

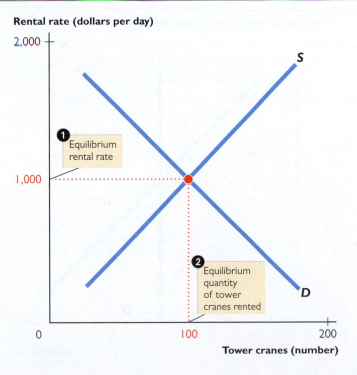

The demand curve for tower crane rentals is *D* and the supply curve is *S*.

❶ The equilibrium rental rate is $1,000 per day.

❷ The equilibrium quantity of cranes rented is 100.

■ Land Markets

The demand for land is a derived demand and is based on the *value of marginal product of land*. The quantity of land demanded for rent is that at which the value of marginal product of land equals the *rental rate of land*. The *lower* the rental rate, other things remaining the same, the *greater* is the quantity of land *demanded*.

But the supply of land is special: The quantity of land is fixed, so the supply of each block of land is *perfectly inelastic*.

The equilibrium rental rate of land makes the quantity of land demanded equal to the quantity available. Figure 19.8 illustrates the market for a 10-acre block in Manhattan. The quantity supplied is 10 acres regardless of the rental rate. The demand curve is *D* and the equilibrium rental rate is $1,000 an acre per day.

The *VMP* of a block of land depends on the prices of the things that the land produces. The *VMP* of farmland in Iowa depends on the price of grain; the *VMP* of land on Fifth Avenue rented by McDonald's depends on the price of a Big Mac.

Notice that the prices of things produced by land influence the rental rate of land and not the reverse. The rental rate of land in Manhattan is high because the high prices of a Big Mac and most other things in Manhattan make the *VMP* of land in Manhattan high. Similarly, relative to Manhattan, the rental rate of land in Des Moines is low because the low prices of a Big Mac and most other things in Des Moines make the *VMP* of land in Des Moines low.

Changes in the prices of the things produced by land change its *VMP*, which changes the rental rate. But for land on a long-term lease, the rental rate equals the *VMP* not in a single year but the *VMP* expected on average over the lease. For this reason, the rental rate of land fluctuates less than the prices of its products.

■ **FIGURE 19.8**

A Market for Land

MyEconLab Animation

The demand curve for a 10-acre block of land is *D*, and the supply curve is *S*.

Market equilibrium occurs at a rental rate of $1,000 an acre per day.

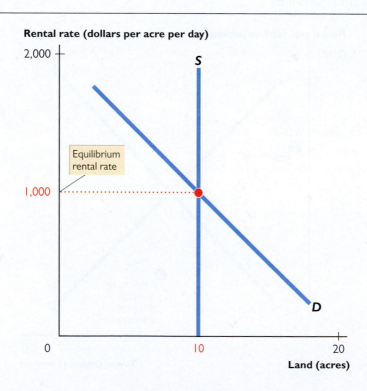

■ Nonrenewable Natural Resource Markets

Nonrenewable natural resources are those that we use to produce energy. Burning one of these fuels converts it to energy and other by-products, and once used the resource cannot be re-used. The natural resources that we use to make metals are also nonrenewable, but they can be used again, at some cost, by recycling them.

The value of marginal product of oil, gas, and coal determine the demand for these nonrenewable natural resources. The demand side of the markets for these resources is just like the demand side of all factor markets.

It is the supply side of a nonrenewable natural resource market that is special.

The Quantity of a Nonrenewable Natural Resource

The *stock* of a nonrenewable natural resource is the quantity in existence at a given time. This quantity is fixed by nature and past use and is independent of the price of the resource. The *proven reserves* of a nonrenewable natural resource is the quantity that has been discovered and that can be accessed at prices close to the current price. This quantity increases over time because advances in technology enable ever less accessible sources to be discovered.

Both of these quantity concepts of a nonrenewable natural resource influence its price, but the influence is indirect. The direct influence on price is the rate at which the resource is supplied for use in production—the *supply of the resource*.

The Supply of a Nonrenewable Natural Resource

The owner of a nonrenewable natural resource is willing to supply any quantity for the right price. But what *is* the right price? It is the price that gives the same expected profit as holding the resource in inventory and selling it next year. This price is lower than the price expected next year by an amount determined by the interest rate.

To see why, think about the choices of Saudi Arabia, a country with a large inventory of oil. Saudi Arabia can sell oil now and use the revenue to buy U.S. government bonds, or it can keep the oil in the ground and sell it next year.

If Saudi Arabia sells the oil and buys bonds, it earns the interest rate on the bonds. If it keeps its oil in the ground this year and sells it next year, it makes a profit equal to the price increase (or incurs a loss equal to the price decrease) between now and next year. If Saudi Arabia expects the percentage rise in the price of oil to exceed the interest rate on bonds, it will hold oil off the market this year. If it expects the percentage rise in the price of oil to be less than the interest rate on bonds, it will want to sell oil today.

Saudi Arabia will be equally happy to sell or hold oil at the price that makes next year's expected price higher than today's price by the same percentage as the interest rate on bonds. For example, if next year's expected price is $84 a barrel and the interest rate is 5 percent (0.05), Saudi Arabia will be willing to sell oil now for $80 a barrel. It will sell none for less than $80 a barrel and will sell as much as possible at more than $80 a barrel.

With the price expected to rise to $84 a barrel next year, Saudi Arabia is indifferent between selling oil now for $80 a barrel and not selling it now but waiting until next year and selling it for $84 a barrel. Saudi Arabia expects to make the same profit either way. So at $80 a barrel, Saudi Arabia will sell whatever quantity is demanded. Saudi Arabia's supply is *perfectly elastic* at $80 a barrel.

Equilibrium in a Nonrenewable Natural Resource Market

In a nonrenewable natural resource market, the equilibrium price is the one that gives suppliers an expected profit equal to the interest rate. The equilibrium quantity is the quantity demanded at that price.

Over time, the equilibrium quantity of natural resources used changes as the demand for them changes. The price also changes over time, for two reasons.

First, expectations change. The forces that influence expectations are not well understood. The expected future price of a natural resource depends on the expected future rate of use and rate of discovery of new sources of supply. But one person's expectation about a future price also depends on guesses about other people's expectations. These guesses can change abruptly and become

EYE on the GLOBAL ECONOMY
Oil and Metal Prices

The price of oil hit a high of $114 a barrel in 2011 and then crashed to less than $30 a barrel in 2016.

Figure 1 shows the history of the real price of oil (measured in terms of the value of money in 2015). It also shows the path that the price would have followed if, starting in 1970, it had risen at a rate equal to the interest rate (the Hotelling Principle). The actual price of oil has fluctuated mostly above the Hotelling price path.

The reason that the price of oil has fluctuated above the level predicted by the Hotelling Principle is that the market has been influenced by the fluctuating strength of a global cartel.

If a nonrenewable natural resource has a small number of producers, it is in the self-interest of these producers to create a cartel, restrict production, and raise the price to the monopoly profit-maximizing level. Established in 1960, the Organization of the Petroleum Exporting Countries (OPEC) had this aim, but it had to wait until 1973 for its first

success. In that year, OPEC had 12 members (Iran, Iraq, Kuwait, Saudi Arabia, Venezuela, Qatar, Indonesia, Libya, United Arab Emirates, Algeria, Nigeria, and Ecuador), and when a group of Arab states led by Egypt and Syria launched an attack against Israel, the predominantly Arab OPEC imposed an oil embargo against the

United States. The price of oil shot up from $10 to $40 a barrel. The Iranian Revolution of 1979 saw a further strenthening of the OPEC cartel, when the price climbed to more than $80 a barrel.

At $80 a barrel, many countries can produce oil at a profit, and advances in production technology made

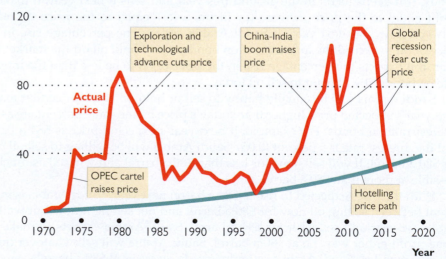

Figure 1 The Price of Oil

self-reinforcing. When the expected future price of a natural resource changes for whatever reason, its supply changes to reflect that expectation.

Second, suppliers of a natural resource expect the price to rise by the same percentage as the interest rate. If expectations are correct on average and nothing happens to change expectations, the price *does* rise by the same percentage as the interest rate. The proposition that the price of a nonrenewable natural resource is expected to rise at a rate equal to the interest rate is called the *Hotelling Principle*. It was first realized by Harold Hotelling, an economist at Columbia University.

Eye on the Global Economy below explains why the prices of some natural resources have not followed the path predicted by the Hotelling Principle, and in the case of oil, have mostly been higher than the Hotelling path.

even more new sources of supply profitable. The United States, Canada, Norway, and the United Kingdom ramped up production and delivered a serious blow to OPEC. No longer able to control global production, OPEC lost control of the price, and competitive forces drove it down to $25 a barrel by the late 1990s.

Driven by rapid economic growth in China and India, the demand for oil increased much faster than supply, and during the 10 years from 1998 to 2008 the price rose to $100 a barrel. This price increase was delivered by the working of a competitive market and was only temporary. As China's economic growth slowed and

the world economy grew more slowly, the price of oil fell. By early 2016, oil was under $30 a barrel.

The prices of metal ores in Figure 2 follow similar swings to those in the price of oil during the 2000s. But in earlier years, these prices tell a very different story from that of the price of oil.

Back in 1980, ecologist Paul Ehrlich said that with rapid population growth, the world would run out of natural resources. Arguing that human ingenuity would overcome pressure on resources, economist Julian Simon bet Ehrlich that the prices of five metals would fall during the 1980s.

Figure 2 shows that Simon won the bet, and that metals prices continued to fall through 2002.

But metals prices began to rise in 2003 and they rose more steeply as demand from China and India grew. Then when Asia slowed, metal prices fell again.

SOURCE OF DATA: International Monetary Fund, World Economic Outlook Database, October 2015.

Figure 2 The Price of Metals

MyEconLab Study Plan 19.3
Solutions Video

CHECKPOINT 19.3

Explain how capital and land rental rates and natural resource prices are determined.

Practice Problems

1. Which of the items in List 1 are nonrenewable natural resources, which are renewable natural resources, and which are not natural resources? Explain your answers.

2. In the market for a nonrenewable natural resource, explain what determines the equilibrium price and the equilibrium quantity.

LIST 1

- Beaches in Florida
- Lake Powell
- Empire State Building
- Silver mines in Arizona
- The Great Lakes
- National parks
- Redwood forests
- The Statue of Liberty

In the News

Farmland rents soften with grain prices, but still high
Millions of acres of U.S. farmland that grow corn, soybean, and wheat are rented, and land rent is the biggest cost of growing these crops. With rising crop prices, rents doubled during the past six years. Today, with falling crop prices, rents are falling, but they are still high.

Source: Reuters, December 23, 2014

1. Explain how the price of grain affects the rent in the market for farmland.

2. Why might rents remain high when grain prices fall?

Solutions to Practice Problems

1. Natural resources include all the gifts of nature. A nonrenewable natural resource is one that once used cannot be used again. A renewable natural resource is one that can be used repeatedly.

   Nonrenewable natural resources include silver mines in Arizona.

   Renewable natural resources include beaches in Florida, Lake Powell, the Great Lakes, national parks, and redwood forests.

   The Empire State Building and the Statue of Liberty are national landmarks, but they are not natural resources. Labor and capital were used to build the Empire State Building. The Statue of Liberty was a gift from France and not a gift of nature.

2. In a nonrenewable natural resource market, the equilibrium price is the price that gives suppliers an expected profit equal to the interest rate. The equilibrium quantity is the quantity demanded at that price.

Solutions to In the News

1. Farmland is a renewable resource—a factor of production. The demand for farmland is a derived demand, which is determined by the value of marginal product (*VMP*) of farmland. A rise in the price of grain increases the *VMP* of farmland, increases the demand for farmland, and raises the equilibrium rental rate of land. A fall in the price of grain decreases the *VMP* of farmland, decreases the demand for farmland, and lowers the equilibrium rental rate.

2. Most farmland is rented on a long-term lease. The rental rate equals the *VMP* of farmland not in a single year but on average over the years of a lease. For this reason, the rental rate of farmland fluctuates less than the price of grain.

CHAPTER SUMMARY

Key Points

1. **Explain how the value of marginal product determines the demand for a factor of production.**

   - The demand for a factor of production is a derived demand—it is derived from the demand for the goods and services that the factor of production is used to produce.
   - The quantity of a factor of production that is demanded depends on its price and the value of its marginal product, which equals the price of the product multiplied by marginal product.
   - Changes in technology bring changes in the demand for labor.

2. **Explain how wage rates and employment are determined and how labor unions influence labor markets.**

   - An individual's quantity of labor supplied is influenced by the wage rate: At low wage rates, the quantity of labor supplied increases as the wage rate rises; at high wage rates, the quantity of labor supplied *decreases* as the wage rate rises—the individual's supply of labor curve eventually bends backward.
   - The quantity of labor supplied by all households increases as the wage rate rises—the market supply of labor curve is upward sloping.
   - Wage rates are determined by demand and supply in labor markets.
   - A labor union can raise the wage rate by restricting the supply of labor or by increasing the demand for labor.

3. **Explain how capital and land rental rates and natural resource prices are determined.**

   - Capital and land rental rates are determined by demand and supply in capital and land markets; natural resource prices are determined by demand and supply in commodity markets.
   - The demand for capital, land, and nonrenewable natural resources is determined by the value of their marginal products.
   - The supply of land is perfectly inelastic and the demand for land determines the rental rate.
   - The supply of a nonrenewable natural resource is perfectly elastic at a price that makes its expected price rise at a rate equal to the interest rate. Expectations fluctuate and so do natural resource prices.

Key Terms

MyEconLab Key Terms Quiz

Derived demand, 489
Factor markets, 488
Factor prices, 488

Labor union, 498
Nonrenewable natural resources, 488
Value of marginal product, 489

CHAPTER CHECKPOINT

Study Plan Problems and Applications

1. A California asparagus farmer is maximizing profit. The price of asparagus is $2 a bunch, a farm worker's wage rate is $12 an hour, and the asparagus farm employs six workers. What is the marginal product of the sixth farm worker? If, when the price of asparagus rises to $3 a bunch, the farm hires eight workers, what is the marginal product of the eighth worker?

2. Through the 1990s, the percentage of high school students who decided to go to college increased. Draw a demand-supply graph to illustrate the effect of this increase on the market for college graduates. Explain its effect on the market for college professors.

3. If your college switched to online delivery of its courses, what changes do you predict would occur in the factor markets in the town where your college is located?

4. If soccer becomes more popular in the United States and basketball becomes less popular, is it true that professional basketball players will earn more than they earn today? Use the laws of demand and supply in factor markets to explain your answer.

5. Suppose that Palm Island, the world's largest grower of coconuts, plans to build its first airport on 100 acres of productive farm land. Palm Islanders expect the world price of coconuts to rise by 200 percent next year and remain high for the next decade. Explain the influence of these events on Palm Island's labor market and land market.

6. Is it true that the opening of a new diamond mine in the Yukon in Canada will lower the world price of diamonds and lower the wage rate paid to diamond workers in South Africa? Use a graph to illustrate your answer.

Use the following information to work Problems **7** to **9**.

USDA to grant $3 million for robots to roam farmlands
The USDA's National Robotics Initiative (NRI) will give $3 million in grants to farm robotics researchers. Already robots herd sheep, sort grapes, and distinguish good lettuce leaves from bad ones. Research funded by the NRI will develop harvesting systems for orchards; robots that pick, fertilize, and plant apple trees; and new ways to use drones to collect and analyze farm data.

Source: *Modern Farmer*, December 31, 2015

7. Explain the effects of new farm robotic technologies on the value of marginal product of farm capital, farm labor, and farm land.

8. Explain how the widespread use of farm robots will change the rental rate of farm land.

9. Explain how the widespread use of farm robots will create better paying farm jobs.

10. Read *Eye on the Coach* on p. 497 and then draw demand-supply graphs to illustrate the markets for football coaches and economics professors. Explain the differences in the equilibrium wage rates and the quantities employed.

Instructor Assignable Problems and Applications

MyEconLab Homework, Quiz, or Test if assigned by instructor

1. Is the market for college football coaches competitive? If it is, why don't they all earn the same wage rate? Is the market for Nick Saban competitive? How is his compensation determined?

2. In the years after World War II, the birth rate increased and the so-called baby boom generation was created. That generation is now beginning to retire. Draw a demand-supply graph to illustrate the effects of this increase in the number of seniors on the market for medical services.

Use the following information to work Problems **3** and **4**.

A new coffee shop opens and to maximize profit it hires 5 workers at the competitive wage rate. The price of a cup of coffee is $4 and the value of marginal product of workers in the coffee shop is $12 an hour.

3. What is the marginal product of the coffee shop workers? How much does a coffee shop worker earn?

4. If the price of a cup of coffee rises from $4 to $5 and the coffee shop continues to hire workers at the competitive wage rate, explain how the value of marginal product and the number of workers hired will change.

Use the following information to work Problems **5** to **7**.

An ex-Google coder makes twice as much freelancing
James Knight quit a well-paid job writing software for Google to go freelance and is now earning about double his Google pay as a freelancer. In a war for talent, companies are paying as much as $1,000 per hour for freelancers with the right skills. The demand for coders soared with the arrival of the iPhone in 2007. More recently, coders started working on software for fridges, watches, and clothing. The Bureau of Labor Statistics says the demand for coders will grow at more than twice the average jobs growth rate.

Source: Bloomberg, January 19, 2016

5. Explain what happened to the value of marginal product of coders after 2007 and explain why it happened.

6. Explain what happened in the market for coders after 2007 to demand, supply, and the quantities demanded and supplied and draw a graph to show the changes that occurred in the market for coders.

7. Explain how the Bureau of Labor Statistics expects the market for coders to change in the future and draw a graph to show the expected changes.

8. Suppose that Bananaland is the world's largest grower of bananas. Bananaland plans to double its population in 3 years by hiring well-educated people from the United States. To increase the number of entrepreneurs, Bananaland encourages anyone with $1 million to immigrate. Explain the influence of these events on Bananaland's labor market and land market.

9. Hong Kong is much more densely populated than is the United States. Compare the rental rate on land in Hong Kong with that in Chicago. Explain why the percentage of commercial buildings that are new is lower in downtown Chicago than in Hong Kong.

MyEconLab Chapter 19 Study Plan

Multiple Choice Quiz

1. A firm's demand for labor is determined by _____.

    A. the market wage rate

    B. the price of the good that the firm produces and the wage rate it pays

    C. the marginal product of labor and the market wage rate

    D. the price of the good that the firm produces and the marginal product of labor

2. The value of marginal product of labor increases if _____.

    A. more labor is hired

    B. more of the good is produced

    C. the market price of the good produced rises

    D. using a new technology reduces the demand for labor

3. An individual's supply of labor curve is _____.

    A. horizontal at the market wage rate

    B. upward sloping as the wage rate rises

    C. upward sloping at low wage rates but becomes downward sloping at high wage rates

    D. vertical at the standard number of hours a person works per day

4. In a competitive labor market for bakers, the equilibrium wage rate _____.

    A. rises if bakers become more productive

    B. falls if the supply of bakers decreases

    C. rises if the market price of bakery items falls

    D. rises if new technology makes it easier for anyone to be a baker

5. A union will _____ if it can _____.

    A. raise the wage rate of its members; decrease the marginal product of its union members

    B. raise the wage rate of its members; introduce minimum qualifications, which will restrict membership of the union

    C. increase the number of union jobs; restrict membership of the union

    D. increase the number of union jobs; increase the union wage rate

6. To maximize profit, a firm _____.

    A. uses the quantity of land at which the rental rate equals the value of marginal product of land

    B. balances the rental rate of capital against the wage rate of labor

    C. uses the quantity of capital at which the marginal revenue equals the value of marginal product of capital

    D. uses the quantity of capital at which the suppliers' expected profit equals the value of marginal product of capital

7. Which of the following statements about a nonrenewable natural resource market is *incorrect*?

    A. The demand for the resource is determined by its value of marginal product.

    B. The supply of the resource is perfectly elastic at the market price.

    C. The price of the resource is expected to rise over time at a rate equal to the interest rate.

    D. The supply of the resource is perfectly inelastic.

Economic Inequality

20

When you have completed your study of this chapter, you will be able to

1 Describe the economic inequality in the United States.

2 Explain how economic inequality arises.

3 Explain how governments redistribute income and describe the effects of redistribution on economic inequality.

MyEconLab Big Picture Video

MyEconLab Concept Video

20.1 MEASURING ECONOMIC INEQUALITY

Market income
A household's wages, interest, rent, and profit earned in factor markets before paying income taxes.

Money income
Market income plus cash payments to households by the government.

To measure economic inequality, we look at the distributions of income and wealth. A household's *income* is the amount that it *receives in a given period*. A household's **market income** equals the wages, interest, rent, and profit that the household earns in factor markets before paying income taxes. The Census Bureau defines another income concept, **money income**, which equals *market income* plus cash payments to households by the government. We will use the *money income* concept to describe the distribution of income in the United States.

A household's *wealth* is the value of the things it *owns at a point in time*. Wealth is measured as the market value of a household's home, the stocks and bonds that it owns, and the money in its bank accounts minus its debts such as outstanding credit card balances.

To describe the *distribution of income*, imagine the population of the United States lined up from the lowest to the highest income earner. Now divide the line into five equal-sized groups, each with 20 percent of the population. These groups are called *quintiles*.

Next, share out the total money income among these groups so that the shares represent the U.S. income distribution. Table 20.1(a) lists the percentages received by each group.

Share out the pie of total wealth in a similar way. Table 20.1(b) shows the percentages owned by each of *seven* groups. The two poorest quintiles are added together and have negative wealth, while the richest quintile is broken into smaller groups to show the wealth distribution inside that quintile.

■ **TABLE 20.1**

The Distributions of Money Income and Wealth in the United States

In part (a), the 20 percent of households with the lowest incomes receive 3.3 percent of total money income, while the 20 percent of households with the highest incomes receive 50 percent of total income.

In part (b), the poorest 40 percent of households have negative wealth, while the richest 1 percent own 36.7 percent.

SOURCES OF DATA: Part (a): Carmen DeNavas-Walt and Bernadette D. Proctor, U.S. Census Bureau, Current Population Reports, P60-252, *Income and Poverty in the United States: 2014*, U.S. Government Printing Office, Washington, DC, 2015.
Part (b): Edward N. Wolff, "Household Wealth Trends in The United States, 1962-2013: What Happened Over the Great Recession?" National Bureau of Economic Research Working Paper 20733, December 2014.

(a) Income distribution in 2014 (median household income $53,657)

	Percentage of		Cumulative percentage of	
	Households	Income	Households	Income
A	Lowest 20	3.3	20	3.3
B	Second 20	9.0	40	12.3
C	Third 20	14.8	60	27.1
D	Fourth 20	22.9	80	50.0
E	Highest 20	50.0	100	100.0

(b) Wealth distribution in 2013 (median household wealth $63,800)

	Percentage of		Cumulative percentage of	
	Households	Wealth	Households	Wealth
A'	Lowest 40	−0.9	40	−0.9
B'	Next 20	2.7	60	1.8
C'	Next 20	9.3	80	11.1
D'	Next 10	11.8	90	22.9
E'	Next 5	12.2	95	35.1
F'	Next 4	28.2	99	63.3
G'	Highest 1	36.7	100	100.0

■ Lorenz Curves

A **Lorenz curve** graphs the cumulative percentage of income (or wealth) on the *y*-axis against the cumulative percentage of households on the *x*-axis. Figure 20.1 shows the Lorenz curves for income and wealth in the United States. To generate the Lorenz curve for income, we graph the cumulative percentage of income against the cumulative percentage of households. Points *A* to *D* on the graph correspond to the rows identified by those letters in the table. For example, row *B* and point *B* show that the 40 percent of households with the lowest incomes in 2014 received 12.3 percent of total income—3.3 percent plus 9.0 percent from Table 20.1(a).

To generate the Lorenz curve for wealth, we graph the cumulative percentage of wealth against the cumulative percentage of households. Points *A′* to *F′* on the graph correspond to the rows identified by those letters in the table of Figure 20.1. For example, row *C′* and point *C′* show that the poorest 80 percent of households owned 11.1 percent of total wealth——0.9 percent plus 2.7 percent plus 9.3 percent from Table 20.1(b).

If income (or wealth) were distributed equally, each 20 percent of households would receive 20 percent of total income (or own 20 percent of total wealth), and the Lorenz curve would be the straight line labeled "Line of equality." The Lorenz curves based on the actual distributions of income and wealth are always below the line of equality. The closer the Lorenz curve is to the line of equality, the more equal is the distribution. You can see that the Lorenz curve for wealth is much farther away from the line of equality than is the Lorenz curve for income. The distribution of wealth is much more unequal than the distribution of income.

Lorenz curve

A curve that graphs the cumulative percentage of income (or wealth) against the cumulative percentage of households.

■ FIGURE 20.1

Lorenz Curves for Income and Wealth in the United States

MyEconLab Animation

Cumulative percentage of		
Households	Income	Wealth
20	A 3.3	
40	B 12.3	A′ −0.9
60	C 27.1	B′ 1.8
80	D 50.0	C′ 11.1
90		D′ 22.9
95		E′ 35.1
99		F′ 63.3

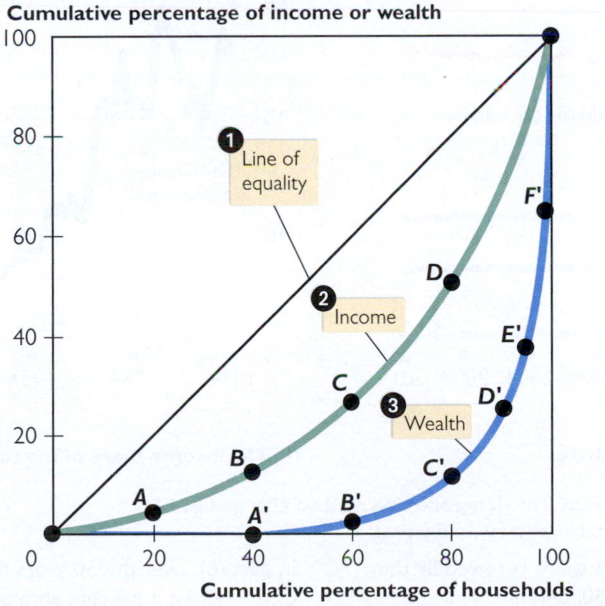

SOURCES OF DATA: See Table 20.1.

❶ If income or wealth were distributed equally, the Lorenz curve would lie along the straight line labeled "Line of equality."

❷ The income Lorenz curve shows the cumulative percentage of income graphed against the cumulative percentage of households. The 20 percent of households with the lowest incomes received 3.3 percent of total income (*A*), and the 80 percent of households with the lowest incomes received 50 percent of total income (*D*).

❸ The wealth Lorenz curve shows the cumulative percentage of wealth graphed against the cumulative percentage of households. The poorest 40 percent of households have no wealth (*A′*), and 99 percent of households own 63.3 percent (*F′*). The richest 1 percent own 36.7 percent.

■ Inequality over Time

Incomes have been getting more unequal. In 2014, 67 percent of Americans told the Gallup poll that they thought incomes were too unequal. Twenty-three years earlier, in 1991, only 21 percent of Americans thought that the rich were too rich and the poor too poor.

Since the mid-1970s, the highest incomes have increased faster than the lower incomes and the gap between the rich and the poor has widened. Figure 20.2(a) shows this widening gap by looking at the income share of each quintile between 1974 and 2014. The data are based on money income. The share received by the highest quintile increased from 44 percent in 1974 to 51 percent in 2014. All of the other quintiles saw their shares of total income fall.

A key feature of rising inequality is the trend in the incomes of the super rich. Emmanuel Saez of the University of California, Berkeley, used tax returns data to get the numbers graphed in Figure 20.2(b).

After decades of a falling share called the "Great Compression," the share of income received by the richest one percent began to climb in 1975. By 2014 (the latest year in the database), the richest one percent were earning 18 percent of the nation's income. The bottom quintile earns 3.3 percent of total income, so an average household in the top one percent receives 109 times the average income of a household in the lowest quintile. Movie stars, sports stars, and the CEOs of large corporations are among these super rich.

■ FIGURE 20.2

Trends in the Distribution of Income   MyEconLab Animation

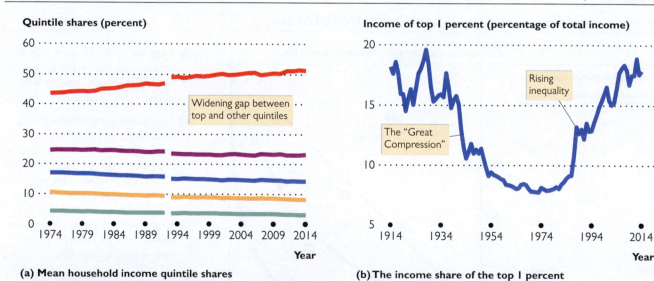

(a) Mean household income quintile shares   **(b) The income share of the top 1 percent**

SOURCES OF DATA: Part (a): See Table 20.1 Note: The data collection method changed in 1993.
Part (b): The World Wealth and Income Database, www.wid.world.

In part (a), from 1974 to 2014 the income share received by the highest quintile rose from 44 percent to 50, percent. The shares received by the other quintiles fell. The lowest quintile share fell from 4 percent to 3.3 percent, the second lowest from 11 percent to 9 percent, and the middle from 17 percent to 14.8 percent.

In part (b), over the 50 years from 1924 to 1974, the income share of the richest 1 percent shrank from 20 percent to 8 percent during the "Great Compression." After 1974, the income share of the top 1 percent increased, and rapidly during the 1980s and 1990s.

■ Poverty

Households with very low incomes are considered to be living in poverty. What is poverty? How do we measure it, how much poverty is there, and is the amount of poverty decreasing or increasing?

Poverty is a state in which a household's income is too low to be able to buy the quantities of food, shelter, and clothing that are deemed necessary. The Census Bureau considers a household to be living in poverty if its income is less than a defined level that varies with household size and that is updated each year to reflect changes in the cost of living. In 2015, the poverty level for a household with 2 adults and 2 children was an income of $24,250.

In 2014, 47 million Americans had incomes below the poverty level. Figure 20.3(a) shows the distribution of poverty by race in 2014. Almost one half (41 percent) of people living in poverty are white.

To measure the *incidence* of poverty, we look at the poverty *rate*—the percentage of families living in poverty. In 2014, the poverty rate was 15 percent. Figure 20.3(b) shows the poverty rates and their trends for white, black, and Hispanic families from 1974 through 2014.

The white poverty rate has fluctuated around 10 percent. For black families, the poverty rate fell from 35 percent in 1983 to 24 percent in 2008, but then increased to 27 percent in 2012. For Hispanic families, the poverty rate increased during the 1980s, then decreased during the 1990s, before increasing again through 2012.

Poverty
A state in which a household's income is too low to be able to buy the quantities of food, shelter, and clothing that are deemed necessary.

■ **FIGURE 20.3**

Poverty Rates in the United States

MyEconLab Animation

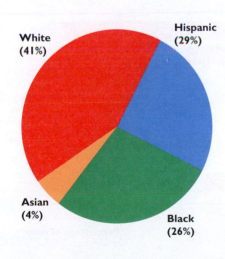

(a) The distribution of poverty in 2014

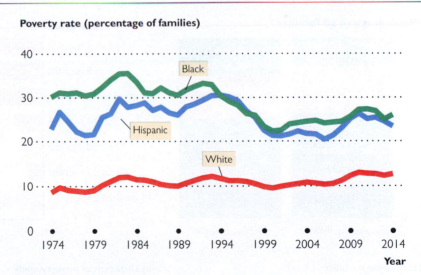

(b) Trends in poverty rates

SOURCE OF DATA: See Table 20.1

Part (a) shows that white families account for 41 percent of the poor. But part (b) shows that the poverty *rates* for blacks and Hispanics are double the rate for whites. The poverty rate of black families fell during the 1980s and the 1990s. The poverty rate of Hispanics also fell during the 1990s, but it had previously increased. The poverty rates of all groups increased in 2009 and 2010.

■ Economic Mobility

Economic mobility is the movement of a family up or down through the income distribution and into and out of poverty. If there were no economic mobility, a family would be stuck at a given point in the income distribution and be persistently rich, middle-class, poor, or in poverty. Also, in such a situation, the data on the *annual* income distribution would be a good indicator of *life-time* inequality. But if there is economic mobility, life-time inequality is not as great as the inequality in a single year. How much economic mobility is there?

Mobility Through the Income Quintiles

One indicator of mobility is the extent to which families move up and down through the income quintiles. Katharine Bradbury, an economist at the Federal Reserve Bank of Boston, has provided information on this mobility. Figure 20.4(a) shows what she found. The figure shows the percentages of families in the poorest and richest quintiles that remained in the same quintile and the percentages of families that moved up or down by one quintile or more than one quintile over a ten-year period.

About 60 percent of families remain in the poorest and richest quintiles, but about 20 percent of families move up or down by more than one quintile. That is, around one in five rich families and one in five poor families become average families over a ten-year period. But because the quintile income shares don't change much, one in five average families become either rich or poor. These data tell us that there is a lot of economic mobility in the United States.

■ **FIGURE 20.4**

Income Mobility and Poverty Duration   MyEconLab Animation

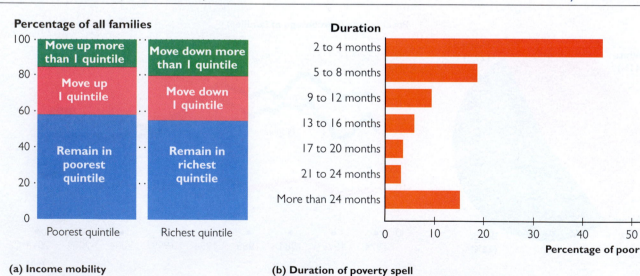

(a) Income mobility   **(b) Duration of poverty spell**

Sources of data: Part (a): Katharine Bradbury, "Trends in U.S. Family Income Mobility, 1969–2006," Federal Reserve Bank of Boston, Working Paper No. 11-10. Part (b): U.S. Census Bureau, Survey of Income and Program Participation.

In part (a), almost 60 percent of families remain in the richest or poorest quintile for a decade or longer and about 20 percent move up or down by more than one quintile during a decade.

In part (b), almost 50 percent of families living in poverty remain in that state for 2 to 4 months. But 15 percent of families living in poverty remain in that state for more than 2 years.

Mobility In and Out of Poverty

Another measure of economic mobility is provided by the duration of poverty. If a household is living in poverty for a few months it faces serious hardship during those months, but it faces a less serious problem than it would if its poverty persisted for several months or, worse yet, for several years, or even generations.

Because the duration of poverty is an additional indicator of the hardship that poverty brings, the Census Bureau provides measures of duration. Figure 20.4(b) shows the data for the period 2009 to 2011, the most recent available.

About 45 percent of poverty lasts for between 2 and 4 months. So for almost a half of poor families, poverty is not persistent. But for 15 percent of poor families, poverty lasts for more than 2 years, so a large number of poor households—about 7 million—experience chronic poverty.

The Sources of Economic Mobility

What are the sources of economic mobility? Some of it arises from fluctuations in job opportunities—from changes in the employment status of families. And some arises from changes over a family's life-cycle. Families experience income growth as their workers become more skilled and experienced. As a family continues to get older and its workers retire, its income falls. So if we look at three households that have identical lifetime incomes—that are economically equal—but one is young, one is middle-aged, and one is old, we will see a great deal of inequality. Inequality of annual incomes overstates the degree of lifetime inequality.

EYE on the GLOBAL ECONOMY
Global Inequality

There is much more income inequality in the global economy than in the United States. The Lorenz curves in this figure provide a comparative picture. You can see that the global Lorenz curve lies much farther from the line of equality than does the U.S. Lorenz curve.

Numbers that highlight the comparison are the percentages of families that get a half (50 percent) of the income. In the United States, the richest 20 percent of families get a half of the income and the remaining 80 percent share the other half. In the global economy the richest 8 percent of families get a half of the income and the remaining 92 percent share the other half.

Global incomes are rising and by some estimates, inequality is decreasing. But other estimates suggest that global inequality, like U.S. inequality, is increasing. Better data are needed to settle this issue.

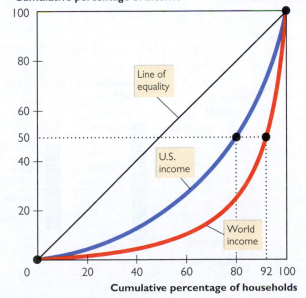

SOURCES OF DATA: U.S. income: See Table 20.1. World income: Branko Milanovic, "Global Income Inequality by the Numbers: in History and Now—An Overview," The World Bank Development Research Group Poverty and Inequality Team, Policy Research Working Paper 6259, November 2012.

EYE on INEQUALITY

MyEconLab Critical Thinking Exercise

Who Are the Rich and the Poor?

In the United States today (excluding the ultra rich sports and entertainment superstars and top corporate executives), the families with the highest incomes are likely to be college-educated Asian married couples between 45 and 54 years of age living together with two children in the Northeast.

At the other extreme, the person with the lowest income is likely to be a black woman over 65 years of age who lives alone somewhere in the South and has fewer than nine years of elementary school education. Another low-income group are young women who have not completed high school,

have a child (or children), and who live without a partner. These snapshot profiles are the extremes in the figure.

The figure illustrates the dominant importance of education in influencing income. People with a post-graduate professional degree (an MBA and a law degree are examples) or a doctorate degree earn, on average, five times the income of someone who has not completed high school.

Household type and size are the next largest influences on income. A married couple with two children have, on average, an income three times that of a single female household.

Race is also a significant factor that influences income. Asian households earn, on average, 75 percent more income than Hispanic origin households.

The age of a householder shows the life-cycle influence on the income distribution. Those aged between 45 and 54 have incomes double those aged 65 and over and aged 15 to 24.

Region of residence has a small influence on income, the Northeast having the highest incomes at almost 20 percent higher than those in the South.

Within these categories, there is enormous individual variation.

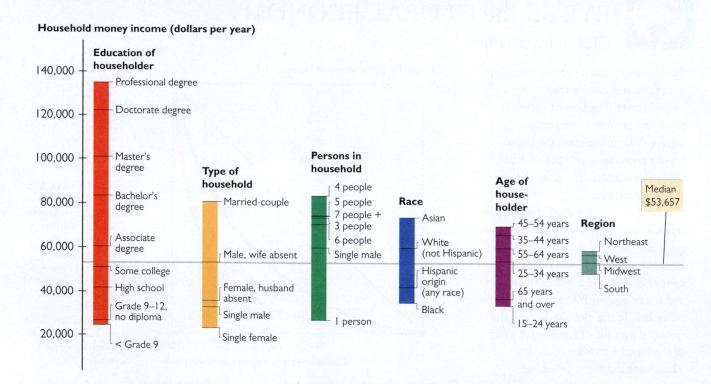

SOURCE OF DATA: Current Population Survey, HINC-01. Selected Characteristics of Households, by Total Money Income in 2014.

CHECKPOINT 20.1

MyEconLab Study Plan 20.1
Key Terms Quiz
Solutions Video

Describe the economic inequality in the United States.

Practice Problems

Table 1 shows the distribution of money income in Canada and Table 20.1(a) on p. 512 shows the distribution of money income in the United States.

1.   Create a table that shows the cumulative percentages of households and income in Canada.

2.   Draw the Lorenz curves for Canada and the United States. Compare the distribution of income in Canada with that in the United States. Which distribution is more unequal?

In the News

Home prices in 20 U.S. cities climb by most since July 2014
Home prices in 20 U.S. cities increased 5.8 percent from a year earlier, the biggest advance since July 2014. Rising property values are increasing household wealth for homeowners and offsetting some of the fall in wealth resulting from the drop in stock prices.

Source: *Bloomberg*, January 27, 2016

If most of the wealth of the wealthiest households consists of stocks and most of the wealth of other households consists of their homes, explain how the information provided in the news clip changed the distribution of wealth. Which wealth quintile would experience a decrease in its share of wealth?

Solutions to Practice Problems

1.   Table 2 shows the cumulative percentages of Canadian households and income: The lowest 20 percent of households receive 4.8 percent of total income and the second lowest 20 percent receive 10.7 percent of total income, so the lowest 40 percent of households receive 15.5 percent of total income. The other rows of the table are calculated in a similar way.

2.   A Lorenz curve plots the cumulative percentage of income against the cumulative percentage of households. The blue curve in Figure 1 plots the Canadian data in Table 2. The green curve is the U.S. Lorenz curve. The line of equality shows an equal distribution. The Canadian Lorenz curve lies closer to the line of equality than does the U.S. Lorenz curve, so the distribution of income in the United States is more unequal than that in Canada.

Solution to In the News

A household's wealth is the value of the things it owns at a point in time. Wealth is measured as the market value of a household's home, the stocks and bonds that it owns, and the money in its bank accounts minus its debts. Because most of the wealth of poorer households is made up of their homes, as home prices increased, the percentage of total wealth of the lower quintiles increased and the percentage of total wealth held by the top wealth quintile decreased. The fact that stock prices fell decreased the wealth of the top quintile and lowered its share of wealth further.

TABLE 1   CANADIAN DATA

Households	Money income (percentage)
Lowest 20 percent	4.8
Second 20 percent	10.7
Third 20 percent	16.5
Fourth 20 percent	24.0
Highest 20 percent	44.0

TABLE 2

Cumulative percentage of	
Households	Income
20	4.8
40	15.5
60	32.0
80	56.0
100	100.0

FIGURE 1

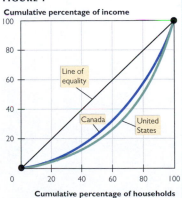

MyEconLab Concept Video

20.2 HOW ECONOMIC INEQUALITY ARISES

Economic inequality arises from a wide variety of factors. The five key ones that we'll examine here are

- Human capital
- Discrimination
- Financial and physical capital
- Entrepreneurial ability
- Personal and family characteristics

■ Human Capital

Human capital is the accumulated skill and knowledge of human beings. To see how human capital differences affect economic inequality, we'll study an economy with two levels of human capital, which we'll call *high-skilled labor* and *low-skilled labor*. Low-skilled labor might be law clerks, hospital orderlies, or bank tellers, and high-skilled labor might be attorneys, surgeons, or bank CEOs.

The Demand for High-Skilled and Low-Skilled Labor

High-skilled workers can perform tasks that low-skilled workers would perform badly or couldn't even perform at all. Imagine an untrained person doing surgery or piloting an airplane. High-skilled workers have a higher value of marginal product (*VMP*) than low-skilled workers do. As we learned in Chapter 19, a firm's demand for labor curve is derived from and is the same as the firm's value of marginal product of labor curve.

Figure 20.5(a) shows the demand curves for high-skilled and low-skilled labor. At any given employment level, firms are willing to pay a higher wage rate to a high-skilled worker than to a low-skilled worker. The gap between the two wage rates measures the value of marginal product of skill. For example, at an employment level of 2,000 hours, firms are willing to pay a high-skilled worker $25 an hour and a low-skilled worker only $10 an hour, a difference of $15 an hour. Thus the value of marginal product of skill is $15 an hour.

The Supply of High-Skilled and Low-Skilled Labor

A skill is costly to acquire and its opportunity cost includes expenditures, such as tuition, and lower earnings while the skill is being acquired. When a person goes to school full time, that cost is the total earnings forgone. When a person acquires a skill through on-the-job training, he or she earns a lower wage rate than someone who is doing a comparable job but not undergoing training. In this case, the cost of acquiring the skill is equal to the wage paid to a person not being trained minus the wage paid to a person being trained.

Because skills are costly to acquire, a high-skilled person is not willing to work for the same wage rate that a low-skilled person is willing to accept. The position of the supply curve of high-skilled workers reflects the cost of acquiring the skill. Figure 20.5(b) shows two supply curves: one of high-skilled workers and the other of low-skilled workers. The supply curve of high-skilled workers is S_H, and that of low-skilled workers is S_L.

The high-skilled worker's supply curve lies above the low-skilled worker's supply curve. The vertical distance between the two supply curves is the

■ **FIGURE 20.5**

Skill Differentials

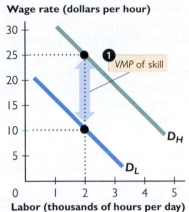

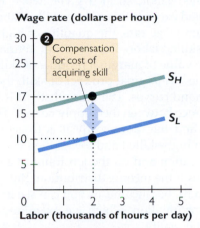

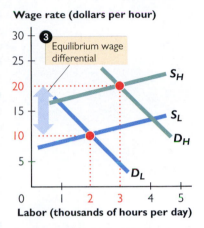

(a) Demand for high-skilled and low-skilled labor

(b) Supply of high-skilled and low-skilled labor

(c) Markets for high-skilled and low-skilled labor

In part (a), D_L is the demand curve for low-skilled labor and D_H is the demand curve for high-skilled labor. ❶ The vertical distance between these two curves is the value of marginal product of skill.

In part (b), S_L is the supply curve of low-skilled workers and S_H is the supply curve of high-skilled workers. ❷ The vertical distance

between these two curves is the required compensation for the cost of acquiring a skill.

In part (c), low-skilled workers earn a wage rate of $10 an hour and high-skilled workers earn a wage rate of $20 an hour. ❸ The $10 equilibrium wage differential is the effect of acquiring skill.

compensation that high-skilled workers require for the cost of acquiring the skill. For example, suppose that the quantity of low-skilled labor supplied is 2,000 hours at a wage rate of $10 an hour. This wage rate compensates the low-skilled workers mainly for their time on the job. Consider next the supply of high-skilled workers. To induce high-skilled labor to supply 2,000 hours, firms must pay a wage rate of $17 an hour. This wage rate for high-skilled labor is higher than that for low-skilled labor because high-skilled labor must be compensated not only for the time on the job but also for the time and other costs of acquiring the skill.

Wage Rates of High-Skilled and Low-Skilled Labor

To work out the wage rates of high-skilled and low-skilled labor, we have to bring together the effects of skill on the demand for and supply of labor.

Figure 20.5(c) shows the demand curves and the supply curves for high-skilled and low-skilled labor. These curves are the same as those plotted in parts (a) and (b). Equilibrium occurs in the market for low-skilled labor where the supply and demand curves for low-skilled labor intersect. The equilibrium wage rate is $10 an hour, and the quantity of low-skilled labor employed is 2,000 hours. Equilibrium in the market for high-skilled workers occurs where the supply and demand curves for high-skilled workers intersect. The equilibrium wage rate is $20 an hour, and the quantity of high-skilled labor employed is 3,000 hours.

As you can see in Figure 20.5(c), the equilibrium wage rate of high-skilled labor is higher than that of low-skilled labor. There are two reasons why this occurs: First, high-skilled labor has a higher value of marginal product than does low-skilled labor, so at a given wage rate, the quantity of high-skilled labor demanded exceeds that of low-skilled labor. Second, skills are costly to acquire, so at a given wage rate, the quantity of high-skilled labor supplied is less than that of low-skilled labor. The wage differential (in this case, $10 an hour) depends on both the value of marginal product of skill and the cost of acquiring it. The higher the value of marginal product of skill, the larger is the vertical distance between the demand curves. The more costly it is to acquire a skill, the larger is the vertical distance between the supply curves. The higher the value of marginal product of skill and the more costly it is to acquire, the larger is the wage differential between high-skilled and low-skilled workers.

Education and on-the-job training enable people to acquire skills and move up through the income distribution. But education is the most important contributor to a higher income, as you can see in *Eye on the U.S. Economy* below.

Discrimination, which we examine next, is another possible source of economic inequality.

EYE on the U.S. ECONOMY
Does Education Pay?

The figure shows that there are large differences in earnings based on the degree of education.

Rates of return on high school and college education have been estimated to be in the range of 5 to 10 percent a year after allowing for inflation, which suggests that a college degree is a better investment than almost any other that a person can undertake.

Based on average income data, the gain from graduating from high school is $17,400 a year. But the gain from going to college or university and getting a bachelor's degree is greater and brings in an additional $50,000 a year.

Remaining at the university to complete a master's degree (usually one more year of study) brings in an extra $15,000 a year, and working for a professional degree increases income by another $62,000 a year.

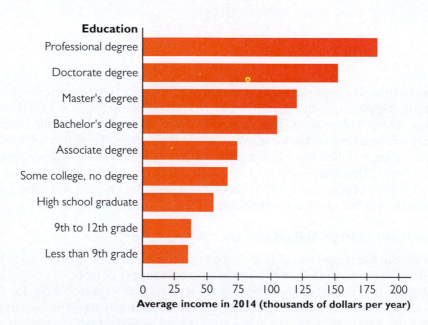

Average income in 2014 (thousands of dollars per year)

SOURCE OF DATA: Current Population Survey, HINC-01. Selected Characteristics of Households, by Total Money Income in 2014.

■ Discrimination

Persistent earnings differences exist between women and men and among the races. You can see them in *Eye on the U.S. Economy* below. Does discrimination contribute to these differences? It might, but economists can't isolate and measure the effect of discrimination, so we can't say by how much, or even whether, earnings differences arise from this source.

To see the difficulty in isolating the effects of discrimination, consider the market for investment advisors. Suppose that black women and white men are equally good at providing investment advice. If there is no race and sex discrimination, average wage rates are the same for both groups.

But if some people are willing to pay more for investment advice from a white man than they are willing to pay for the same advice from a black woman, the market-determined value of marginal product of black women is lower than that of white men, and the demand for investment advice from black women is lower than that from white men. The result is a lower equilibrium wage rate (and fewer high-paying jobs) for black women than for white men.

For discrimination to work in this way and bring *persistent* wage differences, people must be *persistently* willing to pay more than necessary for investment advice. People will begin to notice that they can get a better deal if they buy investment advice from black women. Substitution away from high-cost white men toward lower-cost black women will shift demand and eventually eliminate the wage difference.

EYE on the U.S. ECONOMY
Sex and Race Earnings Differences

The figure shows the earnings of different race and sex groups expressed as a percentage of the earnings of white men.

In 2015, white women earned, on average, 81 percent of what white men earned. Black men earned 74 percent, and black women earned 67 percent. Men and women of Hispanic origin earned only 69 percent and 62 percent, respectively, of white men's wages.

These earnings differentials have persisted since 2009, and only those of white women have begun to narrow in a significant way.

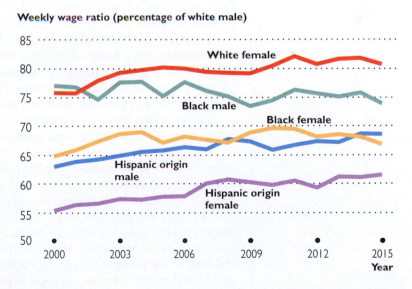

SOURCE OF DATA: Bureau of Labor Statistics.

■ Financial and Physical Capital

The people with the highest incomes are usually those who own large amounts of financial capital and physical capital. These people receive incomes in the form of interest and dividend payments and from capital gains—increases in the stock market value.

Families with a large amount of capital tend to become even more wealthy across generations for two reasons. First, they bequeath wealth to their children and second, rich people marry rich partners (on average).

Saving, and the wealth accumulation that it brings, is not inevitably a source of increased inequality and can even be a source of increased equality. When a household saves to redistribute an uneven income over the life cycle, it enjoys more equal consumption. Also, if a lucky generation that has a high income saves a large amount and makes a bequest to a generation that is unlucky, this act of saving also decreases the degree of inequality.

■ Entrepreneurial Ability

Some of the most spectacularly rich people have benefited from unusual entrepreneurial talent. Household names such as Bill Gates (Microsoft), Sergey Brin and Larry Page (Google), and Mark Zuckerberg (Facebook) are examples of people who began life with modest amounts of wealth and modest incomes and through a combination of hard work, good luck, and outstanding entrepreneurship have become extremely rich.

But some very poor people, and some who fall below the poverty level, have also tried their hands at being entrepreneurs. We don't hear much about these people. They are not in the headlines. But they have put together a business plan, borrowed heavily, and through a combination of hard work, bad luck, and in some cases poor decisions have become extremely poor.

■ Personal and Family Characteristics

Each individual's personal and family characteristics play a crucial role, for either good or ill, in influencing economic well-being.

People who are exceptionally good looking and talented with stable and creative families enjoy huge advantages over the average person. Many movie stars, entertainers, and extraordinarily talented athletes are in this category. These people enjoy some of the highest incomes because their personal or family characteristics make the value of marginal product of their labor very large.

Success often breeds yet further success. A large income can generate a large amount of saving, which in turn generates yet more interest income.

Adverse personal circumstances, such as chronic physical or mental illness, drug abuse, or an unstable home life possibly arising from the absence of a parent or from an abusive or negligent parent, place a huge burden on many people and result in low incomes and even poverty.

A tough life, just like its opposite, can be self-reinforcing. Weak physical or mental health makes it difficult to study and obtain a skill and results in a low labor income or no income because a job is just too hard to hold down. And the children of the poorest people find it hard to get into college and university, and so find it difficult to break the cycle of poverty.

CHECKPOINT 20.2

MyEconLab Study Plan 20.2
Solutions Video

Explain how economic inequality arises.

Practice Problems

In the United States in 2010, 30 million people had full-time managerial jobs that paid an average of $1,200 a week and 10 million people had full-time sales jobs that paid an average of $600 a week.

1. Explain why managers are paid more than salespeople.

2. Explain why, despite the higher weekly wage, more people are employed as managers than as salespeople.

3. As more firms offer their goods and services for sale online, how does the market for salespeople change?

In the News

As Ttech booms, workers turn to coding for career change
Paul Minton, a 26-year-old math major, made $20,000 a year as a waiter. After completing a three-month course at Galvanize, a coding school in San Francisco, his starting salary at a web start-up was more than $100,000 a year. Coding schools can't keep up with the demand for workers like Paul Minton.

Source: *The New York Times*, July 28, 2015

Why are graduates who work as waiters going to coding school?

Solutions to Practice Problems

1. A typical manager has incurred a higher cost of education and on-the-job training than has the typical salesperson. The supply curve of managers, S_H, lies above that of salespeople, S_L (Figure 1). With better education and on-the-job training, managers have more human capital and a higher value of marginal product than do salespeople. The demand curve for managers, D_H, is greater than the demand for salespeople, D_L. Figure 1 illustrates why managers are paid more than salespeople.

2. Figure 1 shows that the demand and supply for each type of labor leads to a greater employment for managers than for salespeople despite the higher wage rate for managers.

3. As more people shop online, firms will hire fewer salespeople. The demand for salespeople will decrease and fewer people will work in sales. How their wage rate and employment will change depends on how the supply of salespeople changes.

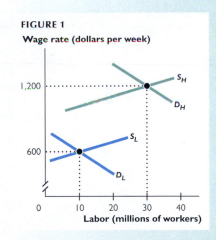

FIGURE 1

Solution to In the News

College graduates have accumulated general human capital but do not have the specific skills that many employers seek and that have a high value of marginal product. Even as a math major, Paul Minton's best-paying job was as a $20,000 a year waiter. By going to coding school, Paul invested in new human capital and obtained skills that are in high demand. The value of marginal product of a skilled coder is greater than that of a waiter, so Paul's wage rate as a coder is higher than as a waiter.

MyEconLab Concept Video

20.3 INCOME REDISTRIBUTION

We've described the distribution of income and wealth in the United States and examined the five main sources of economic inequality. Our task in this final section is to study the *redistribution* of income by government.

How do governments redistribute income? What is the scale of redistribution? Why do we vote for policies that redistribute income? What are the challenges in designing policies that achieve a fair and efficient distribution of income and reduction of poverty?

■ How Governments Redistribute Income

The three main ways in which governments in the United States redistribute income are

- Income taxes
- Income maintenance programs
- Subsidized services

Income Taxes

Income taxes may be progressive, regressive, or proportional (see Chapter 8, p. 207). A *progressive income tax* is one that taxes income at an average rate that increases with the level of income. A *regressive income tax* is one that taxes income at an average rate that decreases with the level of income. A *proportional income tax* (also called a *flat-rate income tax*) is one that taxes income at a constant rate, regardless of the level of income.

The federal government, most state governments, and some city governments impose income taxes. The detailed tax arrangements vary across the individual states, but the income tax system overall is progressive. The poorest working households receive money from the government through an earned income tax credit. The federal income tax rate starts at 10 percent of each additional dollar earned on the lowest taxed incomes and rises through 15 percent, 25 percent, 28 percent, 33 percent, and 35 percent of each additional dollar earned on successively higher incomes.

Income Maintenance Programs

Three main types of programs redistribute income by making direct payments (in cash, services, or vouchers) to people in the lower part of the income distribution. They are

- Social Security programs
- Unemployment compensation
- Welfare programs

Social Security Programs Social Security is a public insurance system paid for by compulsory payroll taxes on employers and employees. Social Security has two main components: Old Age, Survivors, Disability, and Health Insurance (OASDHI), which provides monthly cash payments to retired or disabled workers or their surviving spouses and children; and Medicare, which provides hospital and health insurance for the elderly and disabled. In 2015, Social Security supported 65 million people, who received average monthly checks of $1,340.

Unemployment Compensation   To provide an income to unemployed workers, every state has established an unemployment compensation program. Under these programs, a tax is paid that is based on the income of each covered worker and such a worker receives a benefit when he or she becomes unemployed. The details of the benefits vary from state to state.

Welfare Programs   The purpose of welfare programs is to provide incomes for people who do not qualify for Social Security or unemployment compensation. The programs are

1. Supplementary Security Income (SSI) program, which is designed to help the neediest elderly, disabled, and blind people

2. Temporary Assistance for Needy Families (TANF) program, which is designed to help families that have inadequate financial resources

3. Supplemental Nutrition Assistance Program (SNAP), which is designed to help the poorest households obtain a basic diet

4. Medicaid, which is designed to cover the costs of medical care for households that receive help under the SSI and TANF programs

Subsidized Services

A great deal of redistribution takes place in the United States through the provision of subsidized services—services provided by the government at prices far below the cost of production. The taxpayers who consume these goods and services receive a transfer in kind from the taxpayers who do not consume them. The two most important areas in which this form of redistribution takes place are education—both kindergarten through grade 12 and college and university—and healthcare. But neither necessarily redistributes from the rich to the poor.

In 2015–2016, a student enrolled at the University of California, Berkeley, who is not a resident of California, paid a tuition of $48,240. This amount is probably close to the cost of providing a year's education at Berkeley. But a California resident paid tuition of only $13,432. So California households with a member enrolled at Berkeley received a benefit from the government of $34,808 a year. Many of these households have above-average incomes.

Government provision of healthcare services has grown to equal the scale of private provision. Medicaid provides high-quality and high-cost healthcare to millions of people who earn too little to buy such services themselves. Medicaid redistributes from the rich to the poor. Medicare, which is available to all over 65 years of age, is not targeted at the poor.

◼ The Scale of Income Redistribution

A household's income in the absence of government redistribution is its *market income*. We can measure the scale of income redistribution by calculating the percentage of market income paid in taxes minus the percentage received in benefits at each income level. The available data include redistribution through taxes and cash and noncash benefits to welfare recipients. The data do not include the value of subsidized services such as a college education, which might decrease the total scale of redistribution from the rich to the poor.

Figure 20.6 shows how government actions change the distribution of income. Part (a) shows two Lorenz curves and compares them with the line of equality.

Disposable income
Market income plus cash benefits paid by the government minus taxes.

The blue Lorenz curve describes the distribution of *market income*. The red Lorenz curve shows the distribution of **disposable income**, which is income after all taxes and benefits, including Medicaid and Medicare benefits. The Lorenz curve for *disposable income* is closer to the line of equality than that for *market income*, which tells us that the distribution of disposable income is more equal than the distribution of market income.

Figure 20.6(b) shows that redistribution increases the share received by the lowest four quintiles and decreases the share received by the highest quintile.

The sources of income at different income levels provide another measure of the scale of redistribution. The poorest quintile receives 80 percent of its income from the government. The second quintile receives 32 percent of its income from the government. In contrast, the richest quintile receives almost nothing from the government and receives a third of its income from capital—interest, dividends, and capital gains on financial assets.

■ **FIGURE 20.6**

The Scale of Income Redistribution   MyEconLab Animation

Taxes and income maintenance programs reduce the degree of inequality that the market generates. In part (a), the Lorenz curve moves closer to the line of equality.

Part (b) shows the redistribution in 2011. The quintile with the lowest incomes received net benefits that increased their share of total income by 2.3 percentage points. The middle two quintiles received bigger shares from redistribution. Even the fourth quintile received more in benefits than it paid in taxes. The quintile with the highest incomes paid taxes that decreased their share of total income by 9.3 percentage points.

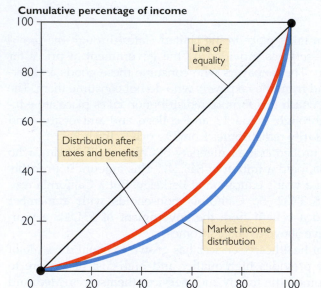

(a) Before and after redistribution

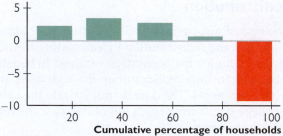

(b) Redistribution

SOURCE OF DATA: The Distribution of Household Income and Federal Taxes, 2011, Congressional Budget Office, November 2014.

■ Why We Redistribute Income

Why do we vote for government policies that redistribute income? Why don't we leave everyone to make voluntary contributions to charities that help the poor?

There are two ways of approaching these questions: normative and positive. The normative approach discusses why we *should* compel everyone to help the poor and looks for principles to guide the appropriate scale of redistribution. The positive approach seeks reasons why we *do* compel everyone to help the poor and tries to explain the actual scale of redistribution.

Normative Theories of Income Redistribution

Philosophy and politics, not economics, are the subjects that consider the normative theories of redistribution. Not surprisingly, there are several different points of view on whether income should be redistributed and, if so, on what scale.

Utilitarianism points to the ideal distribution being one of equality. But efficiency is also desirable. And greater equality can be achieved only at the cost of greater inefficiency—the *big tradeoff* (defined in Chapter 6, p. 161). The redistribution of income creates the big tradeoff because it uses scarce resources and weakens incentives, which decreases the total size of the economic pie to be shared.

A dollar collected from a rich person does not translate into a dollar received by a poor person. Some of it gets used up in the process of redistribution. Tax-collecting agencies such as the Internal Revenue Service and welfare-administering agencies (as well as tax accountants and lawyers) use skilled labor, computers, and other scarce resources to do their work. The bigger the scale of redistribution, the greater is the opportunity cost of administering it.

But the cost of collecting taxes and making welfare payments is a small part of the total cost of redistribution. A bigger cost arises from the inefficiency—*excess burden*—of taxes and benefits (see Chapter 8, p. 194). Greater equality can be achieved only by taxing productive activities such as work and saving. Taxing people's income from their work and saving lowers the after-tax income they receive. This lower income makes them work and save less, which in turn results in smaller output and less consumption not only for the rich who pay the taxes but also for the poor who receive the benefits.

Benefit recipients as well as taxpayers face weaker incentives. In fact, under the welfare arrangements that prevailed before the 1996 reforms, the weakest incentives to work were those faced by households that benefited from welfare. When a welfare recipient got a job, benefits were withdrawn and eligibility for programs such as Medicaid ended, so the household in effect paid a tax of more than 100 percent on its earnings. This arrangement locked poor households in a welfare trap.

Recognizing the tension between equality and efficiency, philosopher John Rawls proposed the principle that income should be redistributed to the point at which it maximizes the size of the slice of the economic pie received by the person with the smallest slice.

Libertarian philosophers such as Robert Nozick (see Chapter 6, p. 161) say that any redistribution is wrong because it violates the sanctity of private property and voluntary exchange.

Modern political parties stand in the center of the extremes that we've just described. Some favor a bit more redistribution than others, but the major political parties are broadly happy with the prevailing scale of redistribution.

Median voter theory
The theory that governments pursue policies that make the median voter as well off as possible.

Positive Theories of Income Redistribution

A good positive theory of income redistribution would explain why some countries have more redistribution than others and why redistribution has increased over the past 200 years. We don't have such a theory, but economists have proposed a promising idea called the median voter theory. The **median voter theory** is that the policies that governments pursue are those that make the median voter as well off as possible. If a proposal can be made that improves the well-being of the median voter, a political party that makes the proposal can improve its standing in an election.

The median voter theory arises from thinking about how a democratic political system such as that of the United States works. In this system, governments must propose policies that appeal to enough voters to get them elected. And in a majority voting system, the voter whose views carry the most weight is the one in the middle—the median voter.

The median voter wants income to be redistributed to the point at which her or his own after-tax income is as large as possible. Taxing the rich by too much would weaken their incentives to create businesses and jobs and lower the median voter's after-tax income. But taxing the rich by too little would leave some money on the table that could be transferred to the median voter.

The median voter might be concerned about the poor and want to reduce poverty. Unselfishly, the median voter might simply be concerned about the plight of the poor and want to help them. Self-interestedly, the median voter might believe that if there is too much poverty, there will be too much crime and some of it will touch her or his life.

If for either reason the median voter wants to help the poor, the political process will deliver a greater scale of redistribution to reflect this voter preference.

■ The Major Welfare Challenge

Among the poorest people in the United States (see p. 518) are young women who have not completed high school, have a child (or children), live without a partner, and are more likely to be black or Hispanic than white. These young women and their children present the major welfare challenge.

There are about 10 million single mothers, and a quarter of them receive no support from their children's fathers. The long-term solution to the problem of these women is education and job training—acquiring human capital. The short-term solution is welfare. But welfare must be designed in ways that strengthen the incentive to pursue the long-term solution. And a change in the U.S. welfare programs introduced during the 1990s pursues this approach.

The Current Approach: TANF

Passed in 1996, the Personal Responsibility and Work Opportunities Reconciliation Act created the Temporary Assistance for Needy Families (TANF) program. TANF is a block grant that is paid to the states, which administer payments to individuals. It is not an open-ended entitlement program. An adult member of a household receiving assistance must either work or perform community service, and there is a five-year limit for assistance.

These measures go a long way toward removing one of the most serious poverty problems while being sensitive to the potential inefficiency of welfare. But some economists want to go further and introduce a negative income tax.

Negative Income Tax

The negative income tax is not on the political agenda, but it is popular among economists, and it is the subject of several real-world experiments. A **negative income tax** provides every household with a guaranteed minimum annual income and taxes all earned income at a fixed rate. Suppose the guaranteed minimum annual income is $10,000 and the tax rate is 25 percent. A household with no earned income receives the $10,000 guaranteed minimum income from the government. This household "pays" income tax of *minus* $10,000, hence the name "negative income tax."

A household that earns $40,000 a year pays $10,000—25 percent of its earned income—to the government. But this household also receives from the government the $10,000 guaranteed minimum income, so it pays no net income tax. It has the break-even income. Households that earn between zero and $40,000 a year receive more from the government than they pay to the government. They "pay" a negative income tax.

A household that earns $60,000 a year pays $15,000—25 percent of its earned income—to the government. But this household receives from the government the $10,000 guaranteed minimum income, so it pays a net income tax of $5,000. All households that earn more than $40,000 a year pay more to the government than they receive from it. They pay a positive amount of income tax.

A negative income tax doesn't eliminate the excess burden of taxation, but it does improve the incentives to work and save at all levels of income.

Negative income tax

A tax and redistribution scheme that provides every household with a guaranteed minimum annual income and taxes all earned income at a fixed rate.

EYE on YOUR LIFE

MyEconLab Critical Thinking Exercise

What You Pay and Gain Through Redistribution

You are on both sides of the redistribution equation, but what's your bottom line? Are you a net receiver or a net payer? Try to work out which one.

Your Tax Payments

You might pay some income tax and you certainly pay sales taxes and taxes on gasoline and other items.

If you have a job, your payslip shows the amount of income tax you're paying.

You can calculate the sales taxes you pay by keeping track for a week every time you buy something.

You can work out how much tax you pay on gas and other items by

checking the scale of these taxes in your state at www.taxadmin.org.

Your Benefits

Now for the benefits. If you're receiving any direct cash payments such as unemployment benefits, these are easy to identify. But most likely, you don't receive any money from the government.

You do, though, receive the benefits of services provided by government. The biggest of these is most likely the cost of your education.

It costs much more than the tuition you're paying to provide your education. One estimate of the value of

your education is the tuition paid by an out-of-state student minus the tuition paid by a state resident. Work out that number.

Now think about all the other benefits you receive from government. Try to estimate what all the government-provided services are worth to you.

Your Bottom Line

Now work out your bottom line—the benefits you receive minus the taxes you pay. Most likely, you have a net benefit, but that situation will change when you graduate. As your income rises, you will move to the other side of the redistribution equation.

MyEconLab Study Plan 20.3
Key Terms Quiz
Solutions Video

CHECKPOINT 20.3

Explain how governments redistribute income and describe the effects of redistribution on economic inequality.

Practice Problems

Table 1 shows the distribution of market income in an economy and Table 2 shows how the government taxes and redistributes income.

1. Calculate the income shares of each quintile after taxes and benefits.
2. Draw this economy's Lorenz curves before and after taxes and benefits.

In the News

Free college and healthcare for all–how would Bernie Sanders pay for it?
Bernie Sanders wants free tuition at public colleges and universities, free healthcare, and a transportation infrastructure program that creates 1 million jobs for disadvantaged youth. Without spelling out the details, he would tax wealthy individuals and corporations and Wall Street stock trades to pay the bill.

Source: *CNN*, January 14, 2016

What features of Bernie's plan make the distribution of income more unequal?

Solutions to Practice Problems

1. Table 3 shows that to obtain the income after taxes and benefits, multiply each quintile's market income by the tax rate, subtract the taxes paid, and add the benefits received. Then calculate each quintile's share of total income.

TABLE 1   MARKET INCOME

Households	Income (millions of dollars per year)
Lowest quintile	5
Second quintile	10
Third quintile	18
Fourth quintile	28
Highest quintile	39

TABLE 2   TAXES AND BENEFITS

Households	Income tax rate	Benefits (millions of dollars)
Lowest quintile	0	10
Second quintile	10%	8
Third quintile	18%	3
Fourth quintile	28%	0
Highest quintile	39%	0

TABLE 3

Households	Market income (millions of dollars)	Tax paid (millions of dollars)	Benefits received (millions of dollars)	Income after tax and benefits (millions of dollars)	Income after tax and benefits (percentage of total income)
Lowest quintile	5	0.0	10	15.0	16.0
Second quintile	10	1.0	8	17.0	18.1
Third quintile	18	3.2	3	17.8	19.0
Fourth quintile	28	7.8	0	20.2	21.5
Highest quintile	39	15.2	0	23.8	25.4

2. To draw the Lorenz curves, calculate the cumulative shares of total income. For example, before taxes and benefits, the lowest quintile has 5 percent and the two lowest quintiles have 15 percent (5 + 10). After taxes and benefits, the lowest quintile has 16 percent and the two lowest quintiles have 34.1 percent (16.0 + 18.1). Figure 1 plots the Lorenz curves.

Solution to In the News

It is not possible to predict the effects of such a revolutionary economic change on the distribution of income, but two features push against less inequality. First, most of the winners from free tuition would be wealthier families because they have a higher college attendance rate. Second, some of the losers from higher corporate taxes would be older families who rely on income from capital.

FIGURE 1

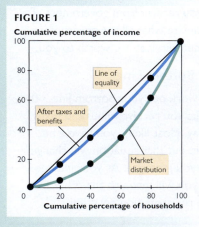

Cumulative percentage of income

CHAPTER SUMMARY

Key Points

1. **Describe the economic inequality in the United States.**

   - The distributions of income and wealth describe economic inequality.
   - The 20 percent of households with the lowest incomes receive about 3 percent of total money income and the 1 percent of households with the highest wealth own about one third of total wealth.
   - The distribution of income has become more unequal over the past few decades.
   - During a decade, almost 20 percent of families move up or down by a quintile or more.
   - About 47 million Americans have incomes below the poverty level and for 15 percent of these families, poverty lasts for more than two years.

2. **Explain how economic inequality arises.**

   - Economic inequality arises from inequality of labor market outcomes, ownership of capital, entrepreneurial ability, and personal and family characteristics.
   - In labor markets, skill differences result in earnings differences. Discrimination might also contribute to earnings differences.
   - Inherited capital, unusual entrepreneurial talent, and personal or family good fortune or misfortune widen the gap between rich and poor.

3. **Explain how governments redistribute income and describe the effects of redistribution on economic inequality.**

   - Governments redistribute income through progressive income taxes, income maintenance programs, and provision of subsidized services.
   - Normative theories of redistribution recognize the tension between equality and efficiency—the big tradeoff—and seek principles to guide the political debate.
   - The main positive theory of redistribution is the median voter theory.
   - The negative income tax is a proposal for addressing the big tradeoff.

Key Terms

MyEconLab Key Terms Quiz

Disposable income, 528
Lorenz curve, 513
Market income, 512
Median voter theory, 530

Money income, 512
Negative income tax, 531
Poverty, 515

MyEconLab Chapter 20 Study Plan

CHAPTER CHECKPOINT

Study Plan Problems and Applications

TABLE 1

Households	Money income (percentage)
Lowest quintile	8
Second quintile	13
Third quintile	18
Fourth quintile	23
Highest quintile	38

FIGURE 1

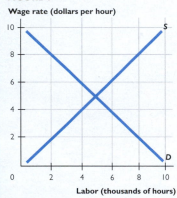

Wage rate (dollars per hour)

Labor (thousands of hours)

TABLE 2

Households	Market income (percentage)
Lowest quintile	5
Second quintile	9
Third quintile	20
Fourth quintile	30
Highest quintile	36

1. Table 1 shows the distribution of money income in Australia. Calculate the cumulative distribution of income for Australia and draw the Lorenz curve for Australian income. In which country is the income distribution more unequal: Australia or the United States?

2. **China inequality among world's worst**
China has one of the world's highest levels of inequality. A Peking University report says the richest 1 percent own a third of the country's wealth, and the poorest 25 percent own 1 percent of the country's wealth.
Source: *The Financial Times*, January 14, 2016
Where is wealth more unequally distributed: China or the United States?

3. Figure 1 shows the market for low-skilled workers. With on-the-job training, low-skilled workers can become high-skilled workers. The value of marginal product of high-skilled workers at each employment level is twice the value of marginal product of low-skilled workers, but the cost of acquiring skill adds $2 an hour to the wage rate that will attract high-skilled labor. What is the equilibrium wage rate of low-skilled labor and the number of low-skilled workers employed? What is the equilibrium wage rate of high-skilled labor and the number of high-skilled workers employed?

4. Why do economists think that discrimination in the labor market is an unlikely explanation for the persistent inequality in earnings between women and men and among the races?

Use Table 2 and the following information to work Problems **5** to **7**.

Suppose that the government redistributes income by taxing the 60 percent of households with the highest market incomes 10 percent, then distributing the tax collected as an equal benefit to the 40 percent with the lowest market income.

5. Calculate the distribution of income after taxes and benefits and draw the Lorenz curve (i) before taxes and benefits and (ii) after taxes and benefits.

6. If the cost of administering the redistribution scheme takes 50 percent of the taxes collected, what is the distribution of income after taxes and benefits?

7. If the people whose market incomes are taxed cut their work hours and their market incomes fall by 10 percent, what is the distribution of income after taxes and benefits?

8. **The $1.4 billion trick to make us accept income inequality**
Lotteries take money from the poor and redistribute it unequally. The poor, the uneducated, and minorities play the lottery the most, and it takes a big chunk of their income.
Source: *The Huffington Post*, January 12, 2016
If the news clip is correct, how does a lottery change the distribution of income? Draw two Lorenz curves to illustrate your answer.

9. Read *Eye on Inequality* on p. 518, then rank the influences on the degree of income inequality—education, household type, household size, age of householder, race, and region of residence—in order of importance.

Instructor Assignable Problems and Applications

MyEconLab Homework, Quiz, or Test if assigned by instructor

1. Which influence adds more, on average, to a household's income: getting a professional degree, getting married, getting older, or moving to California? Which of these influences, on average, adds least?

2. Table 1 shows the income share for each household quintile and the cumulative shares. Provide the values for **A, B, C, D**, and **E**.

3. Table 2 shows the distribution of prize money among the top 20 professional golfers. Calculate the cumulative distribution of income of these golfers and draw the prize money Lorenz curve of these golfers. Which distribution is more unequal: the distribution of income of these golfers or that of the United States as a whole?

4. Suppose the cost of acquiring a skill increases and the value of marginal product of skill increases. Draw demand-supply graphs of the labor markets for high-skilled and low-skilled labor to explain what happens to the equilibrium wage rate of low-skilled labor, the equilibrium wage rate of high-skilled labor, and the number of high-skilled workers employed.

TABLE 1

Households	Income	
(quintile)	(%)	(cumulative %)
First	7.4	7.4
Second	13.2	**A**
Third	**B**	38.7
Fourth	25.0	**C**
Fifth	**D**	**E**

TABLE 2

Professional golfers	Income (percentage)
Lowest 20 percent	15
Second 20 percent	16
Third 20 percent	18
Fourth 20 percent	20
Highest 20 percent	31

Use the following information to work Problems **5** and **6**.

In a year, 130,000 aircraft mechanics and service technicians earned an average of $20 an hour whereas 30,000 elevator installers and repairers earned an average of $25 an hour. The skill and training for these two jobs are very similar.

5. Draw the demand and supply curves for these two types of labor. What feature of your graph accounts for the differences in the two wage rates and what feature accounts for the differences in the quantities employed of these two types of labor?

6. Suppose that a government law required both groups of workers to be paid $22.50 an hour. Draw a graph to illustrate what would happen to the quantities employed of the two types of labor.

Use the following information to work Problems **7** to **11**.

California: The nation's most unequal state
In California, researchers found, it really matters where you live. Residents of Silicon Valley live more than four years longer than the average American, earn nearly double the income, and have nearly triple the number of graduate degrees. Residents of Central Valley live nearly a year less than the average American, earn barely more than a poverty-line income, and nearly four in ten failed to graduate from high school.

Source: *CNN*, May 6, 2015

7. Explain why the first sentence of the news clip is not correct.

8. Explain how the news clip confuses cause and effect in its account of economic inequality in California.

9. What is the main source of inequality in California and what are its effects on inequality?

10. Explain how the labor markets of California translate education differences into earnings differences.

11. Illustrate the labor markets for college graduates in Silicon Valley and high school graduates in Central Valley with a graph.

MyEconLab Chapter 20 Study Plan

Multiple Choice Quiz

1. A Lorenz curve plots the _____.

   A. trend in the cumulative percentage of income received by each quintile against the trend in the number of households
   B. average income received by each quintile against the number of households in the quintile
   C. percentage of total income received by each quintile against the percentage of households in the quintile
   D. cumulative percentage of income against the cumulative percentage of households

2. Which of the following statements is correct?

   A. The closer the Lorenz curve is to the line of equality, the more unequal is the distribution of income.
   B. The farther the Lorenz curve is from the line of equality, the more unequal is the distribution of income.
   C. If the Lorenz curve crosses the line of equality the distribution of income is more unequal at high income levels than at low income levels.
   D. The Lorenz curve for wealth is closer to the line of equality than the Lorenz curve for income.

3. In recent years, as the gap between the rich and the poor has increased, the Lorenz curve has _____.

   A. shifted away from the line of equality
   B. not changed, but there has been a movement down along it
   C. shifted closer to the line of equality
   D. not changed, but there has been a movement up along it

4. Of all the Americans who live in poverty, most are _____ families, while the highest poverty rate is among _____ families.

   A. black; Hispanic
   B. black; white
   C. white; black and Hispanic
   D. Hispanic; white

5. Economic inequality arises from all of the following *except* _____.

   A. inequality of human capital
   B. inequality of education attainment
   C. a shortage of high-skilled labor
   D. discrimination

6. Income redistribution in the United States results in the income share of the _____ rising and the income share of the _____ falling.

   A. lowest quintile; other four quintiles
   B. two lowest quintiles; other three quintiles
   C. three lowest quintiles; other two quintiles
   D. four lowest quintiles; highest quintile

7. When governments redistribute income, they _____.

   A. give every dollar collected in taxes to poor people
   B. are influenced by how people vote in elections
   C. improve economic efficiency
   D. set the tax and benefit rates that make everyone work and save more

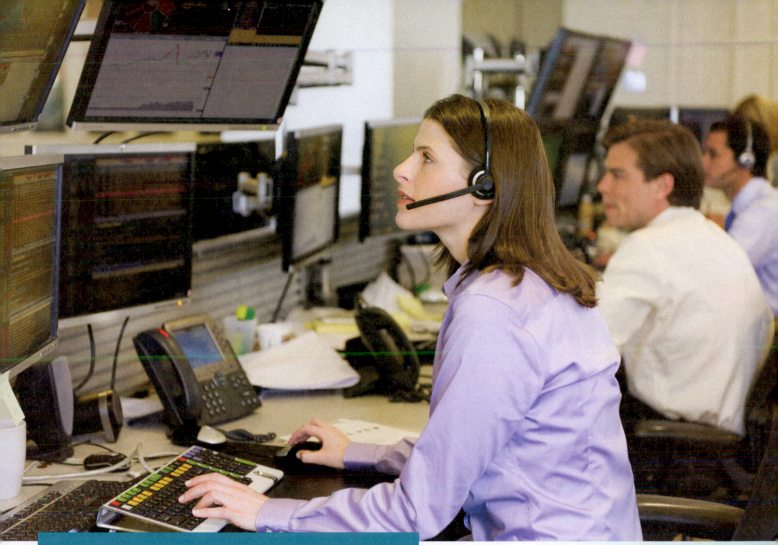

GDP: A Measure of Total Production and Income

21

When you have completed your study of this chapter, you will be able to

1 Define GDP and explain why the value of production, income, and expenditure are the same for an economy.

2 Describe how economic statisticians measure GDP and distinguish between nominal GDP and real GDP.

3 Describe the uses of real GDP and explain its limitations as a measure of the standard of living.

MyEconLab **Big Picture Video**

MyEconLab Concept Video

21.1 GDP, INCOME, AND EXPENDITURE

Where is the U.S. economy heading? Will it remain weak, begin to expand more rapidly, or sink into a recession?

Everyone wants to know the answers to these questions. The people who make business decisions—homebuilders, auto producers, wireless service providers, airlines, oil producers, airplane makers, farmers, and retailers—want to know the answers so they can plan their production to align with demand. Governments want the answers because the amount of tax revenue that they collect depends on how much people earn and spend, which in turn depends on the state of the economy. Governments and the Federal Reserve want to know because they might be able to take actions that avoid excessive bust or boom. Ordinary citizens want the answers to plan their big decisions such as how long to remain in school, whether to rent or buy a new home, and how much to save toward retirement.

To assess the state of the economy we measure gross domestic product, or GDP. You're about to discover that GDP measures the value of total production, total income, and total expenditure.

■ GDP Defined

Gross domestic product (GDP)

The market value of all the final goods and services produced within a country in a given time period.

We measure total production as **gross domestic product**, or **GDP**, which is the market value of all the final goods and services produced within a country in a given time period. This definition has four parts, which we'll examine in turn.

Value Produced

To measure total production, we must add together the production of apples and oranges, bats and balls. Just counting the items doesn't get us very far. Which is the greater total production: 100 apples and 50 oranges or 50 apples and 100 oranges?

GDP answers this question by valuing items at their *market value*—at the prices at which the items are traded in markets. If the price of an apple is 10 cents and the price of an orange is 20 cents, the market value of 100 apples plus 50 oranges is $20 and the market value of 50 apples and 100 oranges is $25. By using market prices to value production, we can add the apples and oranges together.

What Produced

Final good or service

A good or service that is produced for its final user and not as a component of another good or service.

Intermediate good or service

A good or service that is used as a component of a final good or service.

A **final good or service** is something that is produced for its final user and not as a component of another good or service. A final good or service contrasts with an **intermediate good or service**, which is used as a component of a final good or service. For example, a Ford car is a final good, but a Firestone tire that Ford buys and installs on the car is an intermediate good. In contrast, if you buy a replacement Firestone tire for your car, then that tire is a final good. The same good can be either final or intermediate depending on how it is used.

GDP does not count the value of everything that is produced. With one exception, it includes only those items that are traded in markets and does not include the value of goods and services that people produce for their own use. For example, if you buy a car wash, the value produced is included in GDP. But if you wash your own car, your production is not counted as part of GDP. The exception is the market value of homes that people own. GDP puts a rental value on these homes and pretends that the owners rent their homes to themselves.

Where Produced

Only goods and services that are produced *within a country* count as part of that country's GDP. Nike Corporation, a U.S. firm, produces sneakers in Vietnam, and the market value of those shoes is part of Vietnam's GDP, not part of U.S. GDP. Toyota, a Japanese firm, produces automobiles in Georgetown, Kentucky, and the value of this production is part of U.S. GDP, not part of Japan's GDP.

When Produced

GDP measures the value of production *during a given time period.* This time period is either a quarter of a year—called the quarterly GDP data—or a year—called the annual GDP data. The Federal Reserve and others use the quarterly GDP data to keep track of the short-term evolution of the economy, and economists use the annual GDP data to examine long-term trends.

GDP measures not only the value of total production but also total income and total expenditure. The circular flow model that you studied in Chapter 2 explains why.

◼ Circular Flows in the U.S. Economy

Four groups buy the final goods and services produced: households, firms, governments, and the rest of the world. Four types of expenditure correspond to these groups:

- Consumption expenditure
- Investment
- Government expenditure on goods and services
- Net exports of goods and services

Consumption Expenditure

Consumption expenditure is the expenditure by households on consumption goods and services. It includes expenditures on *nondurable goods* such as orange juice and pizza, *durable goods* such as televisions and smartphones, and *services* such as rock concerts and haircuts. Consumption expenditure also includes house and apartment rents, including the rental value of owner-occupied housing.

Consumption expenditure
The expenditure by households on consumption goods and services.

Investment

Investment is the purchase of new *capital goods* (tools, instruments, machines, and buildings) and additions to inventories. Capital goods are *durable goods* produced by one firm and bought by another. Examples are PCs produced by HP and bought by Ford Motor Company, and airplanes produced by Boeing and bought by United Airlines. Investment also includes the purchase of new homes by households.

At the end of a year, some of a firm's output might remain unsold. For example, if Ford produces 4 million cars and sells 3.9 million of them, the other 0.1 million (100,000) cars remain unsold. In this case, Ford's inventory of cars increases by 100,000. When a firm adds unsold output to inventory, we count those items as part of investment.

It is important to note that investment does *not* include the purchase of stocks and bonds. In macroeconomics, we reserve the term "investment" for the purchase of new capital goods and the additions to inventories.

Investment
The purchase of new *capital goods* (tools, instruments, machines, buildings) and additions to inventories.

Government Expenditure on Goods and Services

Government expenditure on goods and services is expenditure by all levels of government on goods and services. For example, the U.S. Defense Department buys missiles and other weapons systems, the State Department buys travel services, the White House buys Internet services, and state and local governments buy cruisers for law enforcement officers.

Net Exports of Goods and Services

Net exports of goods and services is the value of exports of goods and services minus the value of imports of goods and services. **Exports of goods and services** are items that firms in the United States produce and sell to the rest of the world. **Imports of goods and services** are items that households, firms, and governments in the United States buy from the rest of the world. Imports are produced in other countries, so expenditure on imports is not included in expenditure on U.S.-produced goods and services. If exports exceed imports, net exports are positive and expenditure on U.S.-produced goods and services increases. If imports exceed exports, net exports are negative and expenditure on U.S.-produced goods and services decreases.

Total Expenditure

Total expenditure on goods and services produced in the United States is the sum of the four items that you've just examined. We call consumption expenditure C, investment I, government expenditure on goods and services G, and net exports of goods and services NX. So total expenditure, which is also the total amount received by the producers of final goods and services, is

$$\text{Total expenditure} = C + I + G + NX.$$

Income

Labor earns wages, capital earns interest, land earns rent, and entrepreneurship earns profits. Households receive these incomes. Some part of total income, called *undistributed profit,* is a combination of interest and profit that firms retain and do not pay to households. But from an economic viewpoint, undistributed profit is income paid to households and then loaned to firms.

■ Expenditure Equals Income

Figure 21.1 shows the circular flows of income and expenditure that we've just described. The figure is based on Figures 2.4 and 2.5 (on p. 49 and p. 51), but it includes some more details and additional flows.

We call total income Y and show it by the blue flow from firms to households. When households receive their incomes, they pay some in taxes and save some. Some households receive benefits from governments. **Net taxes** equal taxes paid minus cash benefits received and are the green flow from households to governments labeled NT. **Saving** is the amount of income that is not paid in net taxes or spent on consumption goods and services. Saving flows from households to financial markets and is the green flow labeled S. These two green flows are not expenditures on goods and services. They are just flows of money. Because households allocate all their incomes after paying net taxes to consumption and saving,

$$Y = C + S + NT.$$

Government expenditure on goods and services
The expenditure by all levels of government on goods and services.

Net exports of goods and services
The value of exports of goods and services minus the value of imports of goods and services.

Exports of goods and services
Items that firms in the United States produce and sell to the rest of the world.

Imports of goods and services
Items that households, firms, and governments in the United States buy from the rest of the world.

Net taxes
Taxes paid minus cash benefits received from governments.

Saving
The amount of income that is not paid in net taxes or spent on consumption goods and services.

The red flows show the four expenditure flows: consumption expenditure from households to firms, government expenditure from governments to firms, and net exports from the rest of the world to firms. Investment flows from the financial markets, where firms borrow, to the firms that produce capital goods.

Because firms pay out everything they receive as incomes to the factors of production, total expenditure equals total income. That is,

$$Y = C + I + G + NX.$$

From the viewpoint of firms, the value of production is the cost of production, which equals income. From the viewpoint of purchasers of goods and services, the value of production is the cost of buying it, which equals expenditure. So

The value of production equals income equals expenditure.

The circular flow and the equality of income and expenditure provide two approaches to measuring GDP that we'll study in the next section.

■ **FIGURE 21.1**

The Circular Flow of Income and Expenditure   MyEconLab Animation

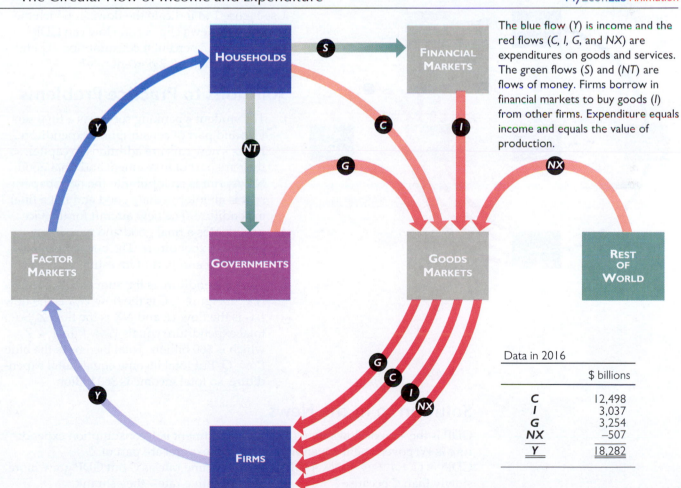

The blue flow (Y) is income and the red flows (C, I, G, and NX) are expenditures on goods and services. The green flows (S) and (NT) are flows of money. Firms borrow in financial markets to buy goods (I) from other firms. Expenditure equals income and equals the value of production.

Data in 2016

	$ billions
C	12,498
I	3,037
G	3,254
NX	−507
Y	18,282

CHECKPOINT 21.1

Define GDP and explain why the value of production, income, and expenditure are the same for an economy.

Practice Problems

1. Classify each of the items in List 1 as a final good or service or as an intermediate good or service and identify which is a component of consumption expenditure, investment, or government expenditure on goods and services.

2. Figure 1 shows the flows of expenditure and income on Lotus Island. In 2016, R was $10 billion; W was $30 billion; U was $12 billion; J was $15 billion; and Z was $3 billion. Calculate total expenditure and total income.

In the News

U.S. economy ended 2015 with slow growth

GDP increased at an annual rate of 0.7 percent in the final quarter of 2015. Government expenditure grew at the same 0.7 percent rate, but consumption expenditure grew at a rate of 2.2 percent. Investment and net exports shrank.

Source: BEA News Release, January 29, 2016

Use Figure 1 to indicate the flows in which the items in the news clip occur. How can GDP increase by 0.7 percent if consumption expenditure increased at a 2.2 percent rate?

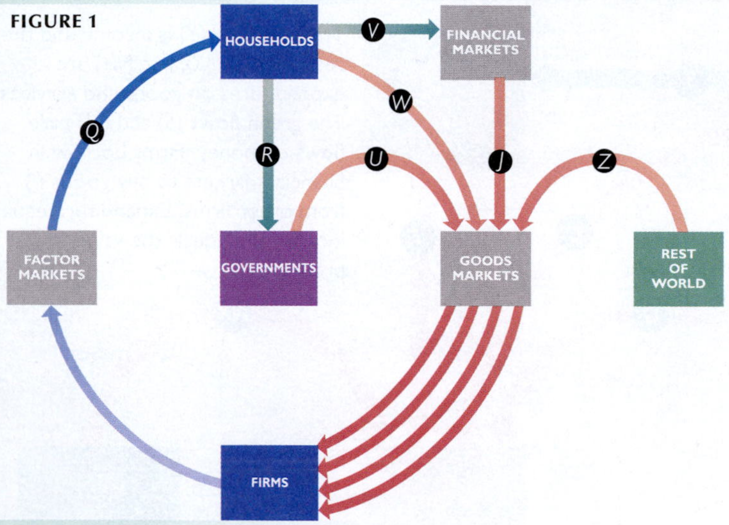

Solutions to Practice Problems

1. The student's banking service is a final service and part of consumption expenditure. Hertz's new cars are additions to capital, so they are part of investment and final goods. Newsprint is an input into the newspaper, so it is an intermediate good and not a final expenditure. The new aircraft for the vice president is a final good and part of government expenditure. The new house is a final good and part of investment.

2. Total expenditure is the sum of C, I, G, and NX. In Figure 1, C is the flow W; I is the flow J; G is the flow U; and NX is the flow Z. So total expenditure equals W + J + U + Z, which is $60 billion. Total income is the blue flow, Q. But total income equals total expenditure, so total income is $60 billion.

LIST 1

- Banking services bought by a student
- New cars bought by Hertz, the car rental firm
- Newsprint bought by *USA Today* from International Paper
- The purchase of a new aircraft for the vice president
- New house bought by Beyoncé

FIGURE 1

HOUSEHOLDS
V
FINANCIAL MARKETS
W
Q
R
U
J
Z
FACTOR MARKETS
GOVERNMENTS
GOODS MARKETS
REST OF WORLD
FIRMS

Solution to In the News

GDP is the sum of flows W, J, U, and Z. Investment is J; consumption expenditure is W; government expenditure is U; and exports are part of Z.
GDP = C + I + G + NX. GDP grew at the same rate as G but GDP grew more slowly than C because I + NX grew at a negative rate—they shrank.

21.2   MEASURING U.S. GDP

MyEconLab Concept Video

U.S. GDP is the market value of all the final goods and services produced within the United States during a year. In 2016, U.S. GDP was $18.3 trillion. The Bureau of Economic Analysis in the U.S. Department of Commerce measures GDP by using two approaches:

- Expenditure approach
- Income approach

■ The Expenditure Approach

The expenditure approach measures GDP by using data on consumption expenditure, investment, government expenditure on goods and services, and net exports. This approach is like attaching a meter to the circular flow diagram on all the flows running through the goods markets to firms and measuring the magnitudes of those flows. Table 21.1 shows this approach. The first column gives the terms used in the U.S. National Income and Product Accounts. The next column gives the symbols we used in the previous section.

Using the expenditure approach, GDP is the sum of consumption expenditure on goods and services (C), investment (I), government expenditure on goods and services (G), and net exports of goods and services (NX). The third column gives the expenditures in 2016. GDP measured by the expenditure approach was $18,282 billion in the first quarter of 2016, expressed at an annual rate.

Net exports were negative in 2016 because imports exceeded exports. Imports were $2,686 billion and exports were $2,179 billion, so net exports—exports minus imports—were –$507 billion as shown in the table.

The fourth column in Table 21.1 shows the relative magnitudes of the expenditures. Consumption expenditure is by far the largest component of total expenditure; investment and government expenditure are the next largest and they are a similar size; and net exports is the smallest component. In 2016, consumption expenditure was 68.4 percent, investment was 16.6 percent, government expenditure was 17.8 percent, and net exports were a negative 2.8 percent of GDP.

■ TABLE 21.1

GDP: The Expenditure Approach

MyEconLab Real-time data

Item	Symbol	Amount in 2016 (first quarter) (billions of dollars)	Percentage of GDP
Consumption expenditure	C	12,498	68.4
Investment	I	3,037	16.6
Government expenditure	G	3,254	17.8
Net exports	NX	−507	−2.8
GDP	Y	18,282	100.0

SOURCE OF DATA: U.S. Department of Commerce, Bureau of Economic Analysis.

The expenditure approach measures GDP by adding together consumption expenditure (C), investment (I), government expenditure (G), and net exports (NX).

In 2016, GDP measured by the expenditure approach was $18,282 billion.

Expenditures Not in GDP

Total expenditure (and GDP) does not include all the things that people and businesses buy. GDP is the value of *final goods and services*, so spending that is *not* on final goods and services is not part of GDP. Spending on intermediate goods and services is not part of GDP, although it is not always obvious whether an item is an intermediate good or a final good (see *Eye on the U.S. Economy* below). Also, we do not count as part of GDP spending on

- Used goods
- Financial assets

Used Goods   Expenditure on used goods is not part of GDP because these goods were part of GDP in the period in which they were produced and during which time they were new goods. For example, a 2015 automobile was part of GDP in 2015. If the car is traded on the used car market in 2017, the amount paid for the car is not part of GDP in 2017.

Financial Assets   When households buy financial assets such as bonds and stocks, they are making loans, not buying goods and services. The expenditure on newly produced capital goods is part of GDP, but the purchase of financial assets is not.

 # EYE on the U.S. ECONOMY
Is a Computer Program an Intermediate Good or a Final Good?

When American Airlines buys a new reservations software package, is that like General Motors buying tires? If it is, then software is an *intermediate good* and it is not counted as part of GDP. Airline ticket sales, like GM cars, are part of GDP, but the intermediate goods that are used to produce air transportation or cars are *not* part of GDP.

Or is American Airlines' purchase of new software like General Motors' purchase of a new assembly-line robot? If it is, then the software is a capital good and its purchase is the purchase of a final good. In this case, the software purchase is an *investment* and it *is* counted as part of GDP.

Brent Moulton worked as a government economist in the Bureau of Economic Analysis (BEA). Moulton's job was to oversee periodic adjustments to the GDP estimates to incorporate new data and new ideas about the economy.

The biggest change made was in how the purchase of computer software by firms is classified. Before 1999, it was regarded as an *intermediate good*. But since 1999, it has been treated as an *investment*.

How big a deal is this? When the BEA recalculated the 1996 GDP, the change increased the estimate of the 1996 GDP by $115 billion. That is a lot of money. To put it in perspective: GDP

in 1996 was $7,662 billion. So the adjustment was 1.5 percent of GDP.

This change is a good example of the ongoing effort by the BEA to keep the GDP measure as accurate as possible.

■ The Income Approach

To measure GDP using the income approach, the Bureau of Economic Analysis uses income data collected by the Internal Revenue Service and other agencies. The BEA takes the incomes that firms pay households for the services of the factors of production they hire—wages for labor services, interest for the use of capital, rent for the use of land, and profits for entrepreneurship—and sums those incomes. This approach is like attaching a meter to the circular flow diagram on all the flows running through factor markets from firms to households and measuring the magnitudes of those flows. Let's see how the income approach works.

The U.S. National Income and Product Accounts divide incomes into two big categories:

- Wage income
- Interest, rent, and profit income

Wage Income

Wage income, called *compensation of employees* in the national accounts, is the total payment for labor services. It includes net wages and salaries plus fringe benefits paid by employers such as healthcare insurance, Social Security contributions, and pension fund contributions.

Interest, Rent, and Profit Income

Interest, rent, and profit income, called *net operating surplus* in the national accounts, is the total income earned by capital, land, and entrepreneurship.

Interest income is the interest that households receive on capital. A household's capital is equal to its net worth—its assets minus its borrowing.

Rent includes payments for the use of land and other rented factors of production. It includes payments for rented housing and imputed rent for owner-occupied housing. (Imputed rent is an estimate of what homeowners would pay to rent the housing they own and use themselves. By including this item in the national accounts, we measure the total value of housing services, whether they are owned or rented.)

Profit includes the profits of corporations and the incomes of proprietors who run their own businesses. These incomes are a mixture of interest and profit.

Table 21.2 shows the relative magnitudes of these components of incomes.

Net Domestic Product at Factor Cost

The sum of wages, interest, rent, and profit is *net domestic product at factor cost*. Net domestic product at factor cost is not GDP, and we must make two further adjustments to get to GDP: one from factor cost to market prices and another from net product to gross product.

From Factor Cost to Market Price

The expenditure approach values goods and services at market prices, and the income approach values them at factor cost—the cost of the factors of production used to produce them. Indirect taxes (such as sales taxes) and subsidies (payments by government to firms) make these two values differ. Sales taxes make market prices exceed factor cost, and subsidies make factor cost exceed market prices. To convert the value at factor cost to the value at market prices, we must add indirect taxes and subtract subsidies.

TABLE 21.2

GDP: The Income Approach

The sum of all incomes equals net domestic product at factor cost. The income approach measure of GDP equals net domestic product at factor cost plus indirect taxes less subsidies plus depreciation (capital consumption).

In 2016, GDP measured by the income approach was $18,550 billion. This amount is $268 billion more than GDP measured by the expenditure approach—a statistical discrepancy of –$268 billion.

Wages are by far the largest part of total income.

Item	Amount in 2016 (first quarter) (billions of dollars)	Percentage of GDP
Wages (compensation of employees)	9,908	54.2
Interest, rent, and profit (net operating surplus)	4,576	25.0
Net domestic product at factor cost	14,484	79.2
Indirect taxes less subsidies	1,192	6.5
Depreciation (capital consumption)	2,874	15.7
GDP (income approach)	18,550	101.4
Statistical discrepancy	−268	−1.4
GDP (expenditure approach)	18,282	100.0

SOURCE OF DATA: U.S. Department of Commerce, Bureau of Economic Analysis.

Depreciation
The decrease in the value of capital that results from its use and from obsolescence.

From Net Product to Gross Product

The income approach measures *net* product and the expenditure approach measures *gross* product. The difference is **depreciation**, which is the decrease in the value of capital that results from its use and from obsolescence. Firms' profits, which are included in the income approach, are net of depreciation, so the income approach gives a *net* measure. Investment, which is included in the expenditure approach, includes the purchase of capital to replace worn out or obsolete capital, so the expenditure approach gives a *gross* measure. To get *gross* domestic product from the income approach, we must *add* depreciation to total income.

Statistical Discrepancy

The expenditure approach and income approach do not deliver exactly the same estimate of GDP. If a taxi driver doesn't report all his tips, they get missed in the income approach, but they get caught by the expenditure approach when he spends his income. So the sum of expenditures might exceed the sum of incomes. But most income gets reported to the Internal Revenue Service on tax returns while many items of expenditure are not recorded and must be estimated. So the sum of incomes might exceed the sum of estimated expenditures.

The discrepancy between the expenditure approach and the income approach estimates of GDP is called the *statistical discrepancy*, and it is calculated as the GDP expenditure total minus the GDP income total.

The two measures of GDP provide a check on the accuracy of the numbers. If the two are wildly different, we will want to know what mistakes we've made. Have we omitted some item? Have we counted something twice? The fact that the two estimates are close gives some confidence that they are reasonably accurate. But the expenditure total is regarded as the more reliable estimate of GDP, so the discrepancy is added to or subtracted from income to reconcile the two estimates.

Table 21.2 summarizes the calculation of GDP using the income approach and its reconciliation with GDP using the expenditure approach. The table also shows the relative magnitudes of the components of the income measure.

■ GDP and Related Measures of Production and Income

Although GDP is the main measure of total production, you will sometimes encounter another: gross *national* product or GNP.

Gross National Product

A country's *gross national product*, or *GNP*, is the market value of all the final goods and services produced anywhere in the world in a given time period by the factors of production supplied by the residents of that country. For example, Nike's income from the capital that it supplies to its Vietnam shoe factory is part of U.S. GNP but not part of U.S. GDP. It is part of Vietnam's GDP. Similarly, Toyota's income on the capital it supplies to its Kentucky auto plant is part of U.S. GDP but not part of U.S. GNP. It is part of Japan's GNP.

GNP equals GDP plus net factor income received from or paid to other countries. The difference between U.S. GDP and GNP is small. But in an oil-rich Middle Eastern country such as Bahrain, where a large amount of capital is owned by foreigners, GNP is much smaller than GDP; and in a poor country such as Bangladesh, whose people work abroad and send income home, GNP is much larger than GDP.

Disposable Personal Income

You've seen that consumption expenditure is the largest component of aggregate expenditure. The main influence on consumption expenditure is *disposable personal income*, which is the income received by households minus personal income taxes paid. Because disposable personal income plays an important role in influencing spending, the national accounts measure this item along with a number of intermediate totals that you can see in Figure 21.2. This figure shows how disposable personal income is calculated and how it relates to GDP and GNP.

■ FIGURE 21.2

GDP and Related Product and Income Measures   MyEconLab Animation

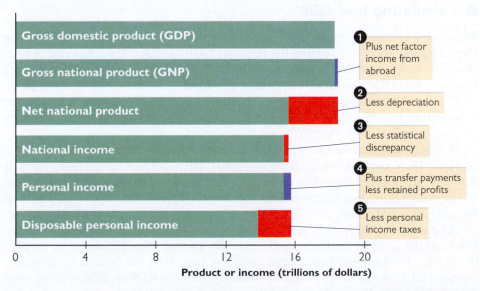

Product or income (trillions of dollars)

SOURCE OF DATA: U.S. Department of Commerce, Bureau of Economic Analysis.

The bars show six related product and income measures and the relationship among them.

1 Add net factor income from abroad to GDP to get GNP.

2 Subtract depreciation from GNP to get net national product.

3 Subtract the statistical discrepancy between the expenditure and income measures to get national income.

4 Add transfer payments by governments less profits retained by firms to get personal income.

5 Finally, subtract personal income taxes to get disposable personal income.

■ Real GDP and Nominal GDP

You've seen that GDP measures total expenditure on final goods and services in a given period. Suppose that we want to compare GDP in two periods, say 2009 and 2016. In 2009, GDP was $14,418 billion and by 2016, it was $18,282 billion—27 percent higher than in 2009. What does this 27 percent increase mean?

The answer is a combination of two things:

- We produced more goods and services.
- We paid higher prices for our goods and services.

Producing more goods and services contributes to an improvement in our standard of living. Paying higher prices means that our *cost of living* has increased but our standard of living has not. So it matters a great deal why GDP has increased. If the 27 percent increase is accounted for mainly by higher prices, our standard of living hasn't changed much. But if the 27 percent increase is accounted for mainly by the production of more goods and services, our standard of living might have increased a lot.

You're now going to see how economists at the Bureau of Economic Analysis isolate the effects on GDP of an increase in production. Their first step is to distinguish between two GDP concepts: real GDP and nominal GDP.

Real GDP is the value of the final goods and services produced in a given year expressed in terms of the prices in a *reference base year*. The *reference base year* is the year we choose against which to compare all other years. In the United States today, the *reference base year* is 2009.

Real GDP contrasts with **nominal GDP**, which is the value of the final goods and services produced in a given year expressed in terms of the prices of that same year. Nominal GDP is just a more precise name for GDP.

The method used to calculate real GDP has changed in recent years and is now a bit technical, but the essence of the calculation hasn't changed. Here, we describe the essence of the calculation. An appendix to this chapter describes the technical details of the method used by the Bureau of Economic Analysis.

■ Calculating Real GDP

The goal of calculating *real GDP* is to measure the extent to which total production has increased and remove from the nominal GDP numbers the influence of price changes. To focus on the principles and keep the numbers easy to work with, we'll calculate real GDP for an economy that produces only one good in each of the GDP categories: consumption expenditure (*C*), investment (*I*), and government expenditure (*G*). We'll ignore exports and imports by assuming that net exports (exports minus imports) is zero.

Table 21.3 shows the quantities produced and the prices in 2009 (the *base year*) and in 2016. In part (a), we calculate nominal GDP in 2009. For each item, we multiply the quantity produced by its price to find the total expenditure on the item. We then sum the expenditures to find nominal GDP, which in 2009 is $100 million. Because 2009 is the base year, real GDP and nominal GDP are equal in 2009.

In part (b) of Table 21.3, we calculate nominal GDP in 2016. Again, we calculate nominal GDP by multiplying the quantity of each item produced by its price to find the total expenditure on the item. We then sum the expenditures to find nominal GDP, which in 2016 is $300 million. Nominal GDP in 2016 is three times its value in 2009. But by how much has the quantity of final goods and services produced increased? That's what real GDP will tell us.

Real GDP
The value of the final goods and services produced in a given year expressed in terms of the prices in a *reference base year*.

Nominal GDP
The value of the final goods and services produced in a given year expressed in terms of the prices of that same year.

■ **TABLE 21.3**

Calculating Nominal GDP and Real GDP in 2009 and 2016

Item		Quantity (millions of units)	Price (dollars per unit)	Expenditure (millions of dollars)
(a) In 2009				
C	T-shirts	10	5	50
I	Computer chips	3	10	30
G	Security services	1	20	20
Y	Real GDP and Nominal GDP in 2009			100
(b) In 2016				
C	T-shirts	4	5	20
I	Computer chips	2	20	40
G	Security services	6	40	240
Y	Nominal GDP in 2016			300
(c) Quantities of 2016 valued at prices of 2009				
C	T-shirts	4	5	20
I	Computer chips	2	10	20
G	Security services	6	20	120
Y	Real GDP in 2016			160

The base year is 2009, so real GDP and nominal GDP are equal in that year.

Between 2009 and 2016, the production of security services (G) increased, but the production of T-shirts (C) and computer chips (I) decreased. In the same period, the price of a T-shirt remained constant, but the other two prices doubled.

Nominal GDP increased from $100 million in 2009 in part (a) to $300 million in 2016 in part (b).

Real GDP in part (c), which is calculated by using the quantities of 2016 in part (b) and the prices of 2009 in part (a), increased from $100 million in 2009 to $160 million in 2016, a 60 percent increase.

In part (c) of Table 21.3, we calculate real GDP in 2016. You can see that the quantity of each good and service produced in part (c) is the same as that in part (b). They are the quantities of 2016. You can also see that the prices in part (c) are the same as those in part (a). They are the prices of the base year—2009.

For each item, we now multiply the quantity produced in 2016 by its price in 2009 to find what the total expenditure would have been in 2016 if prices had remained the same as they were in 2009. We then sum these expenditures to find real GDP in 2016, which is $160 million.

Nominal GDP in 2016 is three times its value in 2009, but real GDP in 2016 is only 1.6 times its 2009 value—a 60 percent increase in *real* GDP.

■ Using the Real GDP Numbers

In the example that we've just worked through, we found the value of real GDP in 2016 based on the prices of 2009. This number alone enables us to compare production in two years only. By repeating the calculation that we have done for 2016 using the data for each year between 2009 and 2016, we can calculate the *annual* percentage change of real GDP—the annual growth rate of real GDP. This is the most common use of the real GDP numbers. Also, by calculating real GDP every three months—known as *quarterly real GDP*—the Bureau of Economic Analysis is able to provide valuable information that is used to interpret the current state of the economy. This information is used to guide both government macroeconomic policy and business production and investment decisions.

MyEconLab Study Plan 21.2

Key Terms Quiz

Solutions Video

CHECKPOINT 21.2

Describe how economic statisticians measure GDP and distinguish between nominal GDP and real GDP.

Practice Problems

Table 1 shows some of the items in the U.S. National Income and Product Accounts in 2015. Use Table 1 to work Problems **1** to **3**.

TABLE 1

Item	Amount (trillions of dollars)
Consumption expenditure	12.1
Government expenditure	3.2
Indirect taxes less subsidies	1.2
Depreciation	2.8
Net factor income from abroad	0.2
Investment	3.0
Net exports	−0.5
Statistical discrepancy	−0.3

1. Use the expenditure approach to calculate U.S. GDP in 2015.
2. What was U.S. GDP as measured by the income approach in 2015? What was net domestic product at factor cost in 2015?
3. Calculate U.S. GNP and U.S. national income in 2015.
4. Table 2 shows some data for an economy. If the base year is 2015, calculate the economy's nominal GDP and real GDP in 2016.

In the News

Facebook is the reason for the productivity slowdown, no, really
Facebook's WhatsApp is free and it sells no advertising. So WhatsApp's value of production in GDP is zero. Assume that WhatsApp's services are produced by 300 people all of whom earn $100,000 a year. By this measure, WhatsApp's value of production in GDP is $30 million.

Source: *Forbes*, February 13, 2016

What are the two approaches to measuring GDP described in the news clip? Why is one of these measures of the contribution of WhatsApp to GDP wrong?

TABLE 2

(a) In 2015:

Item	Quantity	Price
Apples	60	$0.50
Oranges	80	$0.25

(b) In 2016:

Item	Quantity	Price
Apples	160	$1.00
Oranges	220	$2.00

Solutions to Practice Problems

1. GDP was $17.8 trillion. The expenditure approach sums the expenditure on final goods and services. That is, $Y = C + I + G + NX$.
   In 2015, U.S. GDP = $(12.1 + 3.0 + 3.2 − 0.5) trillion = $17.8 trillion.

2. GDP as measured by the income approach was $18.1 trillion. GDP (income approach) = GDP (expenditure approach) *minus* Statistical discrepancy. In 2015, GDP (income approach) = $17.8 trillion − (−$0.3 trillion), or $18.1 trillion. Net domestic product at factor cost plus indirect taxes less subsidies plus depreciation equals GDP (income approach), so net domestic product at factor cost equals $(18.1 − 1.2 − 2.8) trillion, or $14.1 trillion.

3. GNP = GDP + Net factor income from abroad. In 2015, GNP was $18.0 trillion ($17.8 trillion + $0.2 trillion). National income = GNP − Depreciation, which equals $18.0 trillion − $2.8 trillion, or $15.2 trillion.

4. In 2016, nominal GDP equals (160 apples × $1) + (220 oranges × $2), or $600. Real GDP equals (160 apples × $0.50) + (220 oranges × $0.25), or $135.

Solution to In the News

The two approaches to measuring GDP are the expenditure approach and the income approach. One of the measures in the news clip is wrong because the two approaches arrive at the same estimate of GDP. The news clip's income approach measure of $30 million is incorrect. The income approach measure is zero because Facebook incurs a a loss of $30 million when it pays its workers.

21.3   THE USES AND LIMITATIONS OF REAL GDP

MyEconLab Concept Video

We use estimates of real GDP for three main purposes:

- To compare the standard of living over time
- To track the course of the business cycle
- To compare the standard of living among countries

■ The Standard of Living Over Time

A nation's *standard of living* is measured by the value of goods and services that its people enjoy, *on average*. Income per person determines what people can afford to buy and real GDP is a measure of real income. So *real GDP per person*—real GDP divided by the population—is a commonly used measure for comparing the standard of living over time.

Real GDP per person tells us the value of goods and services that the average person can enjoy. By using *real* GDP, we remove any influence that rising prices and a rising cost of living might have had on our comparison.

A handy way of comparing real GDP per person over time is to express it as a ratio of its value in some reference year. Table 21.4 provides the numbers for the United States that compare 2016 with 56 years earlier, 1960. In 1960, real GDP per person was $17,217 and in 2016 it was $56,200, or 3.3 times its 1960 level. To the extent that real GDP per person measures the standard of living, people in 2016 were 3.3 times as well off as their grandparents had been in 1960.

Figure 21.3 shows the entire 56 years of real GDP per person from 1960 to 2016 and displays two features of our changing standard of living:

1. The growth of potential GDP per person

2. Fluctuations of real GDP per person around potential GDP

Potential GDP is the level of real GDP when all the economy's factors of production—labor, capital, land, and entrepreneurial ability—are fully employed. When some factors of production are *unemployed*, real GDP is *below* potential GDP. And when some factors of production are *overemployed* and working harder and for longer hours than can be maintained in the long run, real GDP *exceeds* potential GDP.

You've seen that real GDP per person in 2016 was 3.3 times that of 1960. But in 2016, some labor and other factors of production were unemployed and the economy was producing less than potential GDP. To measure the trend in the standard of living, we must remove the influence of short-term fluctuations and focus on the path of potential GDP.

The growth rate of potential GDP fluctuates less than the growth rate of real GDP. During the 1960s, potential GDP per person grew at an average rate of 2.9 percent a year, but after 1970, its growth rate slowed to 2.1 percent a year. Then, after 2007, it slowed to 0.5 percent a year. This growth slowdown means that potential GDP is lower today (and lower by a large amount) than it would have been if the 1960s growth rate could have been maintained. If potential GDP had kept growing at the 1960s pace, potential GDP per person in 2016 would have been $36,000 more than it actually was. The cumulatively lost income from the growth slowdown of the 1970s is a staggering $509,000 per person (see Chapter 24, p. 616). Understanding the reasons for the growth slowdown is one of the major tasks of macroeconomists.

TABLE 21.4   REAL GDP PER PERSON IN 1960 AND 2016

Year	1960	2016
Real GDP (billions)	$3,106	$18,282
Population (millions)	180.4	325.3
Real GDP per person	$17,217	$56,200

Potential GDP
The value of real GDP when all the economy's factors of production—labor, capital, land, and entrepreneurial ability—are fully employed.

■ **FIGURE 21.3**

Real GDP and Potential GDP per Person in the United States: 1960–2016

MyEconLab Animation

Real GDP grows and fluctuates around the growth path of potential GDP. Potential GDP per person grew at an annual rate of 2.9 percent during the 1960s and slowed to 2.1 percent after 1970 and slowed again to 0.5 percent after 2007.

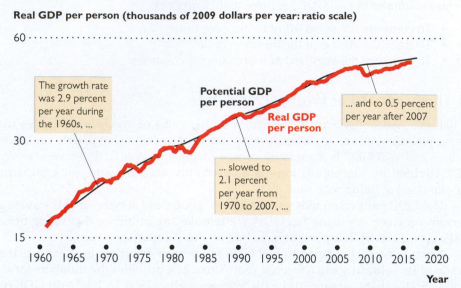

Real GDP per person (thousands of 2009 dollars per year: ratio scale)

The growth rate was 2.9 percent per year during the 1960s, ...

Potential GDP per person

Real GDP per person

... and to 0.5 percent per year after 2007

... slowed to 2.1 percent per year from 1970 to 2007, ...

SOURCES OF DATA: Bureau of Economic Analysis and the Congressional Budget Office.

Business cycle

A periodic but irregular up-and-down movement of total production and other measures of economic activity.

Recession

A period during which real GDP decreases for at least two successive quarters; or defined by the NBER as "a period of significant decline in total output, income, employment, and trade, usually lasting from six months to a year, and marked by contractions in many sectors of the economy."

■ Tracking the Course of the Business Cycle

We call the fluctuations in the pace of economic activity the business cycle. A **business cycle** is a periodic but irregular up-and-down movement of total production and other measures of economic activity such as employment and income. The business cycle isn't a regular, predictable, and repeating cycle like the phases of the moon. The timing and the intensity of the business cycle vary a lot, but every cycle has two phases:

1. Expansion
2. Recession

and two turning points:

1. Peak
2. Trough

Figure 21.4 shows these features of the most recent U.S. business cycle using real GDP as the measure of economic activity. An *expansion* is a period during which real GDP increases. In the early stage of an expansion, real GDP remains below potential GDP and as the expansion progresses, real GDP eventually exceeds potential GDP.

A common definition of **recession** is a period during which real GDP decreases—its growth rate is negative—for at least two successive quarters. The National Bureau of Economic Research (NBER), which dates the U.S. business cycle phases and turning points, defines a recession more broadly as a significant decline in economic activity spread across the economy, lasting more than a few months,

FIGURE 21.4

The Most Recent U.S. Business Cycle

MyEconLab Real-time data

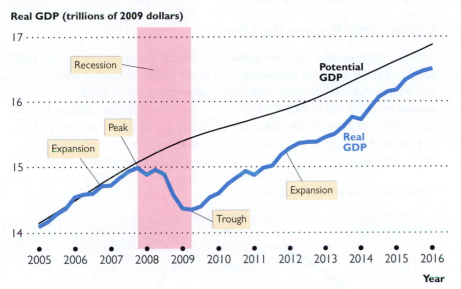

SOURCES OF DATA: Bureau of Economic Analysis, the Congressional Budget Office, and the National Bureau of Economic Research.

The most recent business cycle peak was in the fourth quarter of 2007 and the trough was in the second quarter of 2009 after which a new expansion began. Between the peak and the trough, the economy was in a recession. The recession was extremely deep and the expansion that followed was extremely weak—real GDP has remained a long way below potential GDP.

normally visible in real GDP, real income, employment, industrial production, and wholesale-retail sales. This definition means that sometimes the NBER declares a recession even though real GDP has not decreased for two successive quarters. A recession in 2001 was such a recession. An expansion ends and a recession begins at a business cycle peak. A peak is the highest level of real GDP that has been attained up to that time. A recession ends at a trough when real GDP reaches a low point and from which a new expansion begins.

The shaded bar in Figure 21.4 highlights the 2008–2009 recession. This recession was unusually severe. It lowered real GDP to its 2005 level. The end of a recession isn't the end of pain. When an expansion begins, real GDP is below potential GDP. And even after two years into the expansion that followed the 2008–2009 recession, real GDP had not returned to its previous peak level and the gap between real GDP and potential GDP was wide.

The period that began in 1991 following a severe recession and that ended with the global financial crisis of 2008 was so free from serious downturns in real GDP and other indicators of economic activity that it was called the *Great Moderation*, a name that contrasts it with the Great Depression. Some starry-eyed optimists even began to declare that the business cycle was dead. This long period of expansion also turned the attention of macroeconomists away from the business cycle and toward a focus on economic growth and the possibility of achieving faster growth.

But the 2008–2009 recession put the business cycle back on the agenda. Economists were criticized for not predicting it, and old divisions among economists that many thought were healed erupted in the pages of *The Economist* and *The New York Times* and online on a host of blogs.

We'll be examining the causes of recession and the alternative views among economists in greater detail as you progress through the rest of your study of macroeconomics.

EYE on BOOMS AND BUSTS

MyEconLab Critical Thinking Exercise

How Do We Track Economic Booms and Busts?

The National Bureau of Economic Research (NBER) Business Cycle Dating Committee determines the dates of U.S. business cycle turning points.

To identify the date of a business cycle peak, the NBER committee looks at data on industrial production, total employment, real GDP, and wholesale and retail sales.

Of these variables, real GDP is the most reliable measure of aggregate domestic production.

But when the NBER committee met in November 2008 to determine when the economy went into recession, the two measures of real GDP—the expenditure approach and the income approach—told conflicting stories.

For a few quarters in 2007 and 2008, because of the statistical discrepancy, the two estimates of real GDP did "not speak clearly about the date of a peak in activity."

So the NBER committee looked closely at the data on real personal income, real manufacturing, wholesale and retail sales, industrial production, and employment. All of these data peaked between November 2007 and June 2008. Weighing all the evidence, the committee decided that November 2007 was the peak.

But as the figure shows, real GDP didn't begin a sustained fall until the second quarter of 2008.

In contrast to the difficult task of dating the business cycle peak, the trough was clear. It occurred in the second quarter of 2009.

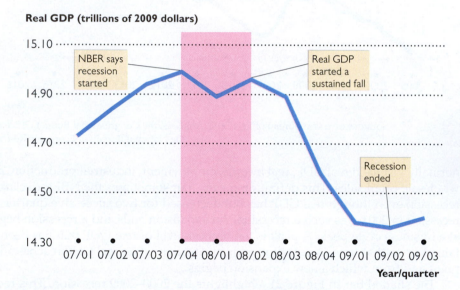

SOURCES OF DATA: Bureau of Economic Analysis and the National Bureau of Economic Research.

Let's now leave comparisons of the standard of living over time and business cycles and briefly see how we compare the standard of living among countries.

■ The Standard of Living Among Countries

To use real GDP per person to compare the standard of living among countries, we must convert the numbers for other countries into U.S. dollars. To calculate real GDP, we must also use a common set of prices—called *purchasing power parity prices*—for all countries. The International Monetary Fund performs these calculations and if you turn back to Figure 2.3 on p. 46 you can see some comparisons based on these data. They tell, for example, that an average American has a standard of living (income per person) almost 6 times that of an average person in China.

Real GDP provides an easy way of comparing living standards. But real GDP doesn't include *all* the goods and services produced. Also, real GDP has nothing to say about factors other than the goods and services that affect the standard of living. Let's explore these limitations of real GDP.

■ Goods and Services Omitted from GDP

GDP measures the value of goods and services that are bought in markets. GDP excludes

- Household production
- Underground production
- Leisure time
- Environment quality

Household Production

Household production is the production of goods and services (mainly services) in the home. Examples of this production are preparing meals, changing a light bulb, cutting grass, washing a car, and helping a student with homework. Because we don't buy these services in markets, they are not counted as part of GDP. The result is that GDP *underestimates* the value of the production.

Many items that were traditionally produced at home are now bought in the market. For example, more families now eat in fast-food restaurants—one of the fastest-growing industries in the United States—and use day-care services. These trends mean that food preparation and child-care services that were once part of household production are now measured as part of GDP. So real GDP grows more rapidly than does real GDP plus home production.

Underground Production

Underground production is the production of goods and services hidden from the view of government because people want to avoid taxes and regulations or their actions are illegal. Because underground production is unreported, it is omitted from GDP.

Examples of underground production are the distribution of illegal drugs, farm work that uses illegal workers who are paid less than the minimum wage, and jobs that are done for cash to avoid paying income taxes. This last category might be quite large and includes tips earned by cab drivers, hairdressers, and hotel and restaurant workers.

Edgar L. Feige, an economist at the University of Wisconsin, estimates that U.S. underground production was about 16 percent of GDP during the early 1990s. Underground production in many countries, especially in most developing countries, is estimated to be larger than that in the United States.

Leisure Time

Leisure time is an economic good that is not valued as part of GDP. Yet the marginal hour of leisure time must be at least as valuable to us as the wage we earn for working. If it were not, we would work instead. Over the years, leisure time has steadily increased as the workweek gets shorter, more people take early retirement, and the number of vacation days increases. These improvements in our standard of living are not measured in real GDP.

Environment Quality

Pollution is an economic *bad* (the opposite of a *good*). The more we pollute our environment, other things remaining the same, the lower is our standard of living. This lowering of our standard of living is not measured by real GDP.

■ Other Influences on the Standard of Living

The quantity of goods and services consumed is a major influence on the standard of living. But other influences are

- Health and life expectancy
- Political freedom and social justice

Health and Life Expectancy

Good health and a long life—the hopes of everyone—do not show up directly in real GDP. A higher real GDP enables us to spend more on medical research, healthcare, a good diet, and exercise equipment. As real GDP has increased, our life expectancy has lengthened. But we face new health and life expectancy problems every year. Drug abuse is taking young lives at a rate that causes serious concern. When we take these negative influences into account, real GDP growth might overstate the improvements in the standard of living.

Political Freedom and Social Justice

A country might have a very large real GDP per person but have limited political freedom and social justice. For example, a small elite might enjoy political liberty and extreme wealth while the majority of people have limited freedom and live in poverty. Such an economy would generally be regarded as having a lower standard of living than one that had the same amount of real GDP but in which everyone enjoyed political freedom.

EYE on YOUR LIFE
Making GDP Personal

MyEconLab Critical Thinking Exercise

As you read a newspaper or business magazine, watch a TV news show, or browse a news Web site, you often come across reports about GDP.

What do these reports mean for you? Where in the National Income and Product Accounts do *your* transactions appear? How can you use information about GDP in your life?

Your Contribution to GDP

Your own economic transactions show up in the National Income and Product Accounts on both the expenditure side and the income side—as part of the expenditure approach and part of the income approach to measuring GDP.

Most of your expenditure is part of Consumption Expenditure. If you were to buy a new home, that item would appear as part of Investment. Because much of what you buy is produced in another country, expenditure on these goods shows up as part of Imports.

If you have a job, your income appears in Compensation of Employees.

Because the GDP measure of the value of production includes only market transactions, some of your own production of goods and services is most likely not counted in GDP.

What are the nonmarket goods and services that you produce? How would you go about valuing them?

Making Sense of the Numbers

To use the GDP numbers in a news report, you must first check whether the reporter is referring to *nominal* GDP or *real* GDP.

Using U.S. real GDP per person, check how your income compares with the average income in the United States. When you see GDP numbers for other countries, compare your income with that of a person in France, or Canada, or China.

EYE on the GLOBAL ECONOMY
Which Country Has the Highest Standard of Living?

You've seen that as a measure of the standard of living, GDP has limitations. To compare the standard of living across countries, we must consider other factors in addition to GDP.

GDP measures only the market value of all the final goods and services produced and bought in markets. GDP omits some goods and services (those produced in the home and in the hidden economy). It omits the value of leisure time, of good health and long life expectancy, as well as of political freedom and social justice. It also omits the damage (negative value) that pollution does to the environment.

These limitations of GDP as a measure of the standard of living apply in every country. So to make international comparisons of the standard of living, we must look at real GDP and other indicators. Nonetheless, real GDP per person is a major component of international comparisons.

Many alternatives to GDP have been proposed. One, called Green GDP, subtracts from GDP an estimate of the cost of greenhouse gas emissions and other negative influences on the environment. Another measure, called the Happy Planet Index, or HPI, goes further and subtracts from GDP an estimate of the cost of depleting nonrenewable resources.

Neither the Green GDP nor the HPI are reliable measures because they rely on guesses about the costs of pollution and resource depletion that are subjective and unreliable.

Taking an approach that focuses on the quality of life factors, the United Nations (UN) has constructed a Human Development Index (HDI), which combines income (GDP), life expectancy and health, and education.

The figure shows the relationship between the HDI and income per person in 2014. (In the figure, each dot represents a country.) These two measures of the standard of living tell a similar but not identical story.

The United States has a high HDI and a high income per person, but it doesn't have the highest of either.

Qatar is an example of a handful of countries with a higher income per person.

Australia and Norway are two of the countries with a higher HDI. In these countries, people live longer than do people in the United States and have universal access to healthcare.

The HDI doesn't include political freedom and social justice. If it did, the United States would score highly on that component of the index.

The bottom line is that we don't know which country has the highest standard of living, but we do know that GDP per person alone does not provide the complete answer.

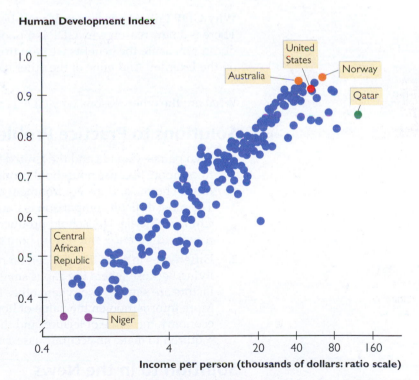

SOURCE OF DATA: *United Nations Human Development Report*, 2014.

MyEconLab Study Plan 21.3
Key Terms Quiz
Solutions Video

 CHECKPOINT 21.3

Describe the uses of real GDP and explain its limitations as a measure of the standard of living.

Practice Problems

The United Nations Human Development Report gives the data for 2014 in Table 1. Other information suggests that household production is similar in Canada and the United States and smaller than in China and Russia. The underground economy is larger in Russia and China and a similar proportion of each of these economies. Canadians and Americans enjoy more leisure hours than do the Chinese and Russians. Canada and the United States spend significantly more on the environment than do China and Russia. Use this information and ignore any other influences to work Problems **1** and **2**.

1. In which pair (or pairs) of countries is it easiest to compare the standard of living? And in which pair (or pairs) is it most difficult? Explain why.

2. Do the differences in real GDP per person correctly rank the standard of living in these four countries? What additional information would we need to be able to make an accurate assessment of the relative standard of living in these four countries?

TABLE 1

Country	Real GDP per person
China	$12,547
Russia	$22,352
United States	$52,947
Canada	$42,155

In the News

Why GDP fails as a measure of well-being

There is a new reason why GDP is a poor measure of economic well-being: It doesn't measure the benefits we gain from free apps and lots of other free stuff on the Internet. And none of the other indexes deal with this problem.

Source: *CBS News*, January 27, 2016

What are the other reasons why GDP is a poor measure of economic well-being?

Solutions to Practice Problems

1. Two pairs—Canada and the United States, and China and Russia—are easy to compare because household production, the underground economy, leisure hours, and the environment are similar in the countries in each pair. The most difficult comparison is Canada and the United States with either China or Russia. Household production and the underground economy narrow the differences but leisure hours and the environment widen them.

2. Differences in real GDP per person probably correctly rank the standard of living because where the gap is small (Canada and the United States), other factors are similar, and where other factors differ, the gaps are huge. More information on the value of household production, the underground economy, the value of leisure, and the value of environmental differences is required to make an accurate assessment of relative living standards.

Solution to In the News

Because GDP measures production that is traded in markets, it does not include household production, leisure time, health and life expectancy, political freedom, and social justice. These contributors to economic well-being are what other indexes such as green GDP and the HDI are designed to deal with.

CHAPTER SUMMARY

Key Points

1. Define GDP and explain why the value of production, income, and expenditure are the same for an economy.

- GDP is the market value of all final goods and services produced within a country in a given time period.
- We can value goods and services either by what they cost to produce (incomes) or by what people are willing to pay (expenditures).
- The value of production equals income equals expenditure.

2. Describe how economic statisticians measure GDP and distinguish between nominal GDP and real GDP.

- BEA measures GDP by summing expenditures and by summing incomes. With no errors of measurement the two totals are the same, but in practice, a small statistical discrepancy arises.
- A country's GNP is similar to its GDP, but GNP is the value of production by factors of production supplied by the residents of a country.
- Nominal GDP is the value of production using the prices of the current year and the quantities produced in the current year.
- Real GDP is the value of production using the prices of a base year and the quantities produced in the current year.

3. Describe the uses of real GDP and explain its limitations as a measure of the standard of living.

- We use real GDP per person to compare the standard of living over time.
- We use real GDP to determine when the economy has reached a business cycle peak or trough.
- We use real GDP per person expressed in purchasing power parity dollars to compare the standard of living among countries.
- Real GDP omits some goods and services and ignores some factors that influence the standard of living.
- The Human Development Index takes some other factors into account.

Key Terms

MyEconLab Key Terms Quiz

Business cycle, 552
Consumption expenditure, 539
Depreciation, 546
Exports of goods and services, 540
Final good or service, 538
Government expenditure on goods and services, 540

Gross domestic product (GDP), 538
Imports of goods and services, 540
Intermediate good or service, 538
Investment, 539
Net exports of goods and services, 540
Net taxes, 540

Nominal GDP, 548
Potential GDP, 551
Real GDP, 548
Recession, 552
Saving, 540

CHAPTER CHECKPOINT

Study Plan Problems and Applications

1. Figure 1 shows the flows of income and expenditure in an economy. In 2013, *U* was $2 trillion, *V* was $1.5 trillion, *W* was $7 trillion, *J* was $1.5 trillion, and *Z* was zero. Calculate total income, net taxes, and GDP.

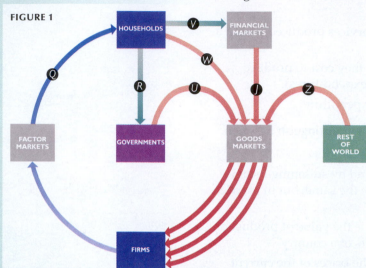

FIGURE 1

Use the following data to work Problems **2** and **3**.

The national accounts of Parchment Paradise are kept on (you guessed it) parchment. A fire in the statistics office destroys some accounts, leaving only the following data:

- GDP (income approach) $2,900
- Consumption expenditure $2,000
- Indirect taxes less subsidies $100
- Interest, rent, and profit $500
- Investment $800
- Government expenditure $400
- Wages $2,000
- Net factor income from abroad $50
- Net exports −$200

2. Calculate GDP (expenditure approach) and depreciation.

3. Calculate net domestic product at factor cost, the statistical discrepancy, and GNP.

Use the following information to work Problems **4** to **6**.

An economy produces only fun and food. Table 1 shows the prices and the quantities of fun and food produced in 2016 and 2017. The base year is 2016.

4. Calculate nominal GDP in 2016 and 2017.

5. Calculate the percentage increase in real GDP in 2017.

6. If potential GDP was $270 in 2016 and it grew by 1 percent in 2017, in which phase of the business cycle is the economy? Explain.

TABLE 1

(a) In 2016:

Item	Quantity	Price
Fun	40	$2
Food	60	$3

(b) In 2017:

Item	Quantity	Price
Fun	35	$3
Food	65	$2

Use the following information to work Problems **7** to **9**.

Uncertain outlook

The Commerce Department reported that in December 2015, retail sales rose by 0.2, net exports decreased, inventories held by businesses rose by 0.1 percent, and total sales by businesses fell by 0.6 percent.

Source: Commerce Department, February 2016

7. Which component of GDP changed because retail sales increased? Which component of GDP changed because business inventories increased?

8. Explain the effect of the fall in net exports on GDP.

9. Does the statement that total sales by businesses fell by 0.6 percent mean that GDP decreased by 0.6 percent? Explain your answer.

 10. Read *Eye on Booms and Busts* on p. 554 and explain why the NBER reported that the 2008 recession began before real GDP had fallen for two successive quarters.

Instructor Assignable Problems and Applications

MyEconLab Homework, Quiz, or Test if assigned by instructor

1. In France, real GDP was the same in 2012 as it had been in 2011, but in the last quarter of 2012 and the first quarter of 2013, France's real GDP decreased. In the United States, real GDP increased in 2012, and in the first quarter of 2013, it was higher than in the last quarter of 2012.

   Based on this information, which country was in a recession at the beginning of 2013? What features of the information provided led you to your conclusion?

2. Classify each of the items in List 1 as a final good or service or an intermediate good or service and identify it as a component of consumption expenditure, investment, or government expenditure on goods and services.

Use the following information to work Problems **3** and **4**.

Mitsubishi Heavy Industries makes the wings of the new Boeing 787 Dreamliner in Japan. Toyota assembles cars for the U.S. market in Kentucky.

3. Explain where these activities appear in the National Income and Product Accounts of the United States.

4. Explain where these activities appear in the National Income and Product Accounts of Japan.

Use the data on the economy of Iberia in Table 1 to work Problems **5** and **6**.

5. Calculate Iberia's GDP.

6. Calculate Iberia's imports of goods and services.

Use Table 2, which shows an economy's total production and the prices of the final goods it produced in 2016 and 2017, to work Problems **7** to **9**.

7. Calculate nominal GDP in 2016 and 2017.

8. The base year is 2016. Calculate real GDP in 2016 and 2017.

9. Calculate the percentage increase in real GDP in 2017.

Use the following information to work Problems **10** and **11**.

New U.S. home sales surged

Purchases of new U.S. homes surged in December and 2015 was the best year for housing since 2007. Existing-home sales also increased in the best year since 2006. The inventory of existing homes on the market was smaller than demand.

Source: *Bloomberg*, January 28, 2016

10. Where do new-home sales appear in the circular flow of expenditure and income? Explain how a surge in new home sales affects real GDP.

11. Where do sales and inventories of existing homes appear in the circular flow of expenditure and income? Explain how an increase in sales of existing homes and a low inventory of existing homes affects real GDP.

12. **Worries about China's slowing growth**

    China reported that its real GDP grew by 6.9 percent in 2015, down from 7.3 percent in 2014. Experts think that China has overstated its true growth rate and many fear that its growth will slow further.

    Source: *The Economist*, January 19, 2016

    How does China's real GDP growth compare with that of the United States? If China's growth slows further, would that mean it was in a recession?

LIST 1

- Banking services bought by Target
- Security system bought by the White House
- Coffee beans bought by Starbucks
- New coffee machines bought by Starbucks
- Starbucks grande mocha frappuccino bought by a student
- New battle ship bought by the U.S. navy

TABLE 1

Item	Amount
Net taxes	$18 billion
Government expenditure	$20 billion
Saving	$15 billion
Consumption expenditure	$67 billion
Investment	$21 billion
Exports	$30 billion.

TABLE 2

(a) In 2016:

Item	Quantity	Price
Fish	100	$2
Berries	50	$6

(b) In 2017:

Item	Quantity	Price
Fish	75	$5
Berries	65	$10

MyEconLab Chapter 21 Study Plan

Multiple Choice Quiz

1. Gross domestic product is the market value of all the _____ in a given time period.

   A. goods and services bought by Americans
   B. goods and services produced by American companies in all countries
   C. final goods and services produced by all firms located in the United States
   D. U.S.-produced goods and services bought in the United States

2. A _____ is a final good and _____ is an intermediate good.

   A. new car bought by a student; a used SUV bought by a dealer
   B. new textbook; a used textbook
   C. new iPhone bought by a student; a new computer bought by Walmart
   D. tank of gasoline bought by you; jet fuel bought by Southwest Airlines

3. Saving equals _____.

   A. income minus consumption expenditure minus net taxes
   B. income minus net taxes
   C. total income minus total expenditure
   D. net taxes minus government expenditure

4. The expenditure approach to measuring U.S. GDP equals _____.

   A. the sum of U.S. consumption expenditure and U.S. investment
   B. U.S. government expenditure minus taxes paid by Americans
   C. all expenditure on final goods and services produced in the United States in a given time period
   D. all expenditure by Americans on goods and services produced in the United States in a given time period

5. When using the income approach to measure GDP at market prices, in addition to summing all factor incomes it is necessary to _____.

   A. subtract depreciation because profit is not reported as net profit
   B. add depreciation because capital depreciates when goods are manufactured
   C. add indirect taxes less subsidies to convert aggregate income from factor cost to market prices
   D. add a statistical discrepancy which is the sum of depreciation and indirect taxes less subsidies

6. The following statements about the business cycle are correct *except* _____.

   A. it is a regular predictable cycle in real GDP around potential GDP
   B. from the peak to the trough, the economy is in a recession
   C. from the trough to the peak, the economy is in an expansion
   D. it is a periodic movement in economic activity including employment

7. Real GDP per person is not an accurate measure of the standard of living because it _____.

   A. includes the goods and services that governments buy
   B. omits the goods and services that people produce for themselves
   C. includes goods and services bought by firms
   D. omits the goods and services imported from other countries

APPENDIX: MEASURING REAL GDP

This appendix explains the method used by the Bureau of Economic Analysis (BEA) to calculate real GDP using a measure called **chained-dollar real GDP**. We begin by explaining the problem that arises from using the prices of the base year (the method on pp. 548–549) and how the problem can be overcome.

Chained-dollar real GDP
The measure of real GDP calculated by the Bureau of Economic Analysis.

■ The Problem With Base Year Prices

When we calculated real GDP on pp. 548–549, we found that real GDP in 2016 was 60 percent greater than it was in 2009. But instead of using the prices of 2009 as the constant prices, we could have used the prices of 2016. In this case, we would have valued the quantities produced in 2009 at the prices of 2016. By comparing the values of real GDP in 2009 and 2016 at the constant prices of 2016, we get a different number for the percentage increase in production. If you use the numbers in Table 21.3 on p. 549 to value 2009 production at 2016 prices, you will get a real GDP in 2009 of $150 million (2016 dollars). Real GDP in 2016 at 2016 prices is $300 million. So by using the prices of 2016, production doubled—a 100 percent increase—from 2009 to 2016. Did production in fact increase by 60 percent or 100 percent?

The problem arises because to calculate real GDP, we weight the quantity of each item produced by its price. If all prices change by the same percentage, then the *relative* weight on each good or service doesn't change and the percentage change in real GDP from the first year to the second is the same regardless of which year's prices we use. But if prices change by different percentages, then the *relative* weight on each good or service *does* change and the percentage change in real GDP from the first year to the second depends on which prices we use. So which year's prices should we use: those of the first year or those of the second?

The answer given by the BEA method is to use the prices of both years. If we calculate the percentage change in real GDP twice, once using the prices of the first year and again using the prices of the second year, and then take the average of those two percentage changes, we get a unique measure of the change in real GDP and one that gives equal importance to the *relative* prices of both years.

To illustrate the calculation of the BEA measure of real GDP, we'll work through an example. The method has three steps:

- Value production in the prices of adjacent years.
- Find the average of two percentage changes.
- Link (chain) to the base year.

■ Value Production in the Prices of Adjacent Years

The first step is to value production in *adjacent* years at the prices of both years. We'll make these calculations for 2016, and its preceding year, 2015.

Table A21.1 shows the quantities produced and prices in the two years. Part (a) shows the nominal GDP calculation for 2015—the quantities produced in 2015 valued at the prices of 2015. Nominal GDP in 2015 is $145 million. Part (b) shows the nominal GDP calculation for 2016—the quantities produced in 2016 valued at the prices of 2016. Nominal GDP in 2016 is $172 million. Part (c) shows the value of the quantities produced in 2016 at the prices of 2015. This total is $160 million. Finally, part (d) shows the value of the quantities produced in 2015 at the prices of 2016. This total is $158 million.

■ **TABLE A21.1**

Real GDP Calculation Step 1: Value Production in Adjacent Years at Prices of Both Years

Step 1 is to value the production of adjacent years at the prices of both years.

Here, we value the production of 2015 and 2016 at the prices of both 2015 and 2016.

The value of 2015 production at 2015 prices, in part (a), is nominal GDP in 2015.

The value of 2016 production at 2016 prices, in part (b), is nominal GDP in 2016.

Part (c) calculates the value of 2016 production at 2015 prices, and part (d) calculates the value of 2015 production at 2016 prices.

We use these numbers in Step 2.

Item		Quantity (millions of units)	Price (dollars per unit)	Expenditure (millions of dollars)
(a) In 2015				
C	T-shirts	3	5	15
I	Computer chips	3	10	30
G	Security services	5	20	100
Y	Nominal GDP in 2015			145
(b) In 2016				
C	T-shirts	4	4	16
I	Computer chips	2	12	24
G	Security services	6	22	132
Y	Nominal GDP in 2016			172
(c) Quantities of 2016 valued at prices of 2015				
C	T-shirts	4	5	20
I	Computer chips	2	10	20
G	Security services	6	20	120
Y	2016 production at 2015 prices			160
(d) Quantities of 2015 valued at prices of 2016				
C	T-shirts	3	4	12
I	Computer chips	3	12	36
G	Security services	5	22	110
Y	2015 production at 2016 prices			158

Find the Average of Two Percentage Changes

The second step is to find the percentage change in the value of production based on the prices in the two adjacent years. Table A21.2 summarizes these calculations.

Valued at the prices of 2015, production increased from $145 million in 2015 to $160 million in 2016, an increase of 10.3 percent. Valued at the prices of 2016, production increased from $158 million in 2015 to $172 million in 2016, an increase of 8.9 percent. The average of these two percentage changes in the value of production is 9.6. That is, (10.3 + 8.9) ÷ 2 = 9.6.

We've now found the *growth rate* of real GDP in 2016. But we also want to calculate the *level* of real GDP. This level depends on the *reference base year*. The simplest example is when the previous year (2015 in this case) is the base year. In 2015, real GDP equals nominal GDP, which is $145 million. Real GDP in 2016, valued in 2015 dollars is 9.6 percent higher than in 2015 and equals $159 million.

Although the real GDP of $159 million is expressed in 2015 dollars, the calculation uses the average of the *relative prices* of the final goods and services that make up GDP in 2015 and 2016.

When the base year is not the previous year, we need to link or chain the current year to the base year. Let's see how we do this linking.

■ TABLE A21.2

Real GDP Calculation Step 2: Find Average of Two Percentage Changes

Value of Production in Adjacent Years		Millions of dollars
2015 production at 2015 prices		145
2016 production at 2015 prices		160
Percentage change in production at 2015 prices	10.3	
2015 production at 2016 prices		158
2016 production at 2016 prices		172
Percentage change in production at 2016 prices	8.9	
Average of two percentage changes in production	**9.6**	

Using the numbers calculated in Step 1, we find the percentage change in production from 2015 to 2016 valued at 2015 prices, which is 10.3 percent.

We also find the percentage change in production from 2015 to 2016 valued at 2016 prices, which is 8.9 percent.

We then find the average of these two percentage changes, which is 9.6 percent.

Link (Chain) to the Base Year

To link to the base year, we repeat the calculation that we've just described to obtain the real GDP growth rate each year. Real GDP equals nominal GDP in the base year, which currently is 2009. By applying the calculated growth rates to each successive year, we can obtain *chained-dollar real GDP* in 2009 dollars.

Figure A21.1 shows an example with real GDP equal to nominal GDP at $62 million in the base year, 2009, and assumed growth rates of real GDP for each year between 2008 and 2016. The 2016 growth rate is the 9.6 percent that we calculated in Table A21.2 above.

Starting with real GDP in the base year, we apply the calculated percentage change of 4.6 percent, so real GDP in 2010 was 4.6 percent higher than $62 million, which is $65 million. Repeating the calculation, real GDP in 2011 is 7.1 percent higher, which is $69 million, and in 2012, real GDP is 8.2 percent higher, which is $75 million. By 2015, real GDP has grown to $83 million. In 2016, real GDP is 9.6 percent higher than $83 million, which is $91 million.

The same method is used to chain-link the years before the base year. For example, real GDP in 2008 is 3.2 percent lower than in 2009 at $60 million.

■ FIGURE A21.1

Real GDP Calculation Step 3: Link (Chain) to the Base Year   MyEconLab Animation

Year	2008	**2009**	2010	2011	2012	2013	2014	2015	**2016**
Growth Rate (percent per year)		3.2	4.6	7.1	8.2	2.7	3.5	4.6	**9.6**
Chained-Dollar Real GDP (millions of 2009 dollars)	60	**62**	65	69	75	77	80	83	**91**

The growth rate of real GDP from one year to the next is calculated for every pair of years and then linked to the base year. Suppose that real GDP was $62 million in the base year, 2009. By applying the growth rate between each pair of years, we find the chained-dollar real GDP for each year, expressed in terms of the value of the dollar in the base year. Here, the percentages for 2008 through to 2016 are assumed. By 2016, the chained-dollar real GDP has increased to $91 million in 2009 dollars.

TABLE 1

(a) In 2015:

Item	Quantity	Price
Bananas	100	$10
Coconuts	50	$12

(b) In 2016:

Item	Quantity	Price
Bananas	110	$15
Coconuts	60	$10

TABLE 2

(a) In 2015:

Item	Quantity	Price
Food	100	$2
Fun	50	$6

(b) In 2016:

Item	Quantity	Price
Food	75	$5
Fun	65	$10

APPENDIX CHECKPOINT

Study Plan Problems

An island economy produces only bananas and coconuts. Table 1 gives the quantities produced and prices in 2015 and in 2016. The base year is 2015.

1. Calculate nominal GDP in 2015 and nominal GDP in 2016.
2. Calculate the value of 2016 production in 2015 prices and the percentage increase in production when valued at 2015 prices.
3. Calculate the value of 2015 production in 2016 prices and the percentage increase in production when valued at 2016 prices.
4. Use the chained-dollar method to calculate real GDP in 2015 and 2016. In terms of what dollars is each of these two real GDPs measured?
5. Using the chained-dollar method, compare the growth rates of nominal GDP and real GDP in 2016.
6. If the base year is 2016, use the chained-dollar method to calculate real GDP in 2015 and 2016. In terms of what dollars is each of these two real GDPs measured?
7. If the base year is 2016, compare the growth rates of nominal GDP and real GDP in 2016.

Instructor Assignable Problems

An economy produces only food and fun. Table 2 shows the quantities produced and prices in 2015 and 2016. The base year is 2016.

1. Calculate nominal GDP in 2015 and nominal GDP in 2016.
2. Calculate the value of 2016 production in 2015 prices and the percentage increase in production when valued at 2015 prices.
3. Calculate the value of 2015 production in 2016 prices and the percentage increase in production when valued at 2016 prices.
4. Using the chained-dollar method, calculate real GDP in 2015 and 2016. In terms of what dollars is each of these two real GDPs measured?
5. Using the chained-dollar method, compare the growth rates of nominal GDP and real GDP in 2016.
6. If the base year is 2015, use the chained-dollar method to calculate real GDP in 2015 and 2016. In terms of what dollars is each of these two real GDPs measured?
7. If the base year is 2015, compare the growth rates of nominal GDP and real GDP in 2016.

Key Term

Chained-dollar real GDP, 563

Are we back at full employment?

Jobs and Unemployment

22

CHAPTER CHECKLIST

When you have completed your study of this chapter, you will be able to

1 Define the unemployment rate and other labor market indicators.

2 Describe the trends and fluctuations in the indicators of the state of the U.S. labor market.

3 Describe the types of unemployment, define full employment, and explain the link between unemployment and real GDP.

MyEconLab Big Picture Video

MyEconLab Concept Video

22.1 LABOR MARKET INDICATORS

Every month, 1,600 field interviewers and supervisors working on a joint project between the Bureau of Labor Statistics (or BLS) and the Bureau of the Census survey 60,000 households and ask a series of questions about the age and labor market status of their members. This survey is called the *Current Population Survey*. Let's look at the types of data collected by this survey.

■ Current Population Survey

Figure 22.1 shows the categories into which the BLS divides the population. It also shows the relationships among the categories. The first category divides the population into two groups: the working-age population and others. The **working-age population** is the total number of people aged 16 years and over who are not in jail, hospital, or some other form of institutional care or in the U.S. Armed Forces. In May 2016, the estimated population of the United States was 322.3 million, the working-age population was 252.9 million, and 69.4 million people were under 16 years of age, in the military, or living in institutions.

The second category divides the working-age population into two groups: those in the labor force and those not in the labor force. The **labor force** is the number of people employed plus the number unemployed. In May 2016, the U.S. labor force was 158.4 million and 94.5 million people were not in the labor force. Most of those not in the labor force were in school full time or had retired from work.

The third category divides the labor force into two groups: the employed and the unemployed. In May 2016 in the United States, 151.0 million people were employed and 7.4 million people were unemployed.

■ Population Survey Criteria

The survey counts as *employed* all persons who, during the week before the survey, either

1. Worked at least 1 hour as paid employees or worked 15 hours or more as unpaid workers in their family business or
2. Were not working but had jobs or businesses from which they were temporarily absent.

The survey counts as *unemployed* all persons who, during the week before the survey,

1. Had no employment,
2. Were available for work,

and either

1. Had made specific efforts to find employment during the previous four weeks or
2. Were waiting to be recalled to a job from which they had been laid off.

People in the working-age population who by the above criteria are neither employed nor unemployed are classified as not in the labor force.

Working-age population
The total number of people aged 16 years and over who are not in jail, hospital, or some other form of institutional care or in the U.S. Armed Forces.

Labor force
The number of people employed plus the number unemployed.

To be counted as unemployed, a person must not only want a job but also have tried to find one.

■ **FIGURE 22.1**

Population Labor Force Categories

MyEconLab Real-time data

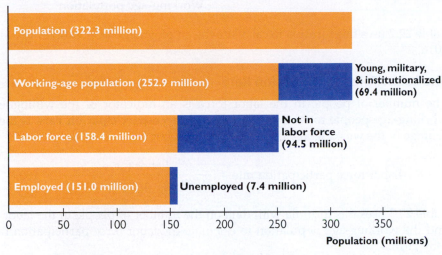

The U.S. population is divided into the working-age population and the young, military, and institutionalized. The working-age population is divided into the labor force and those not in the labor force. The labor force is divided into those employed and those unemployed. The figure shows the data for May 2016.

SOURCE OF DATA: Bureau of Labor Statistics.

■ Three Labor Market Indicators

Using the numbers from the Current Population Survey, the BLS calculates several indicators of the state of the labor market. The three main labor market indicators are

- The unemployment rate
- The employment–population ratio
- The labor force participation rate

The Unemployment Rate

The amount of unemployment—the number of people who want jobs but can't find them—is an indicator of unused labor resources. The BLS reports the absolute number of people unemployed and the **unemployment rate**, which is the percentage of the people in the labor force who are unemployed. That is,

$$\text{Unemployment rate} = \frac{\text{Number of people unemployed}}{\text{Labor force}} \times 100.$$

Table 22.1 shows the number of people unemployed and the number in the labor force in May 2016 and uses the formula above to calculate the unemployment rate in that month.

The Employment–Population Ratio

The number of people of working age who have jobs is an indicator of both the availability of jobs and the degree of match between people's skills and the skills that employers demand. The BLS calculates the **employment–population ratio** as the percentage of the people of working age who are employed.

Unemployment rate
The percentage of the people in the labor force who are unemployed.

TABLE 22.1 UNEMPLOYMENT RATE: MAY 2016

Unemployed	7.4 million
Labor force	158.4 million
Calculation	$\frac{7.4}{158.4} \times 100$
Unemployment rate	4.7 percent

Employment–population ratio
The percentage of the people of working age who are employed.

TABLE 22.2 EMPLOYMENT–POPULATION RATIO: MAY 2016

Employed	151.0 million
Working-age population	252.9 million
Calculation	$\frac{151.0}{252.9} \times 100$
Employment–population ratio	59.7 percent

Labor force participation rate
The percentage of the working-age population in the labor force.

TABLE 22.3 LABOR FORCE PARTICIPATION RATE: MAY 2016

Labor force	158.4 million
Working-age population	252.9 million
Calculation	$\frac{158.4}{252.9} \times 100$
Labor force participation rate	62.6 percent

Marginally attached worker
A person who does not have a job, is available and willing to work, has not made specific efforts to find a job within the previous four weeks, but has looked for work sometime in the recent past.

Discouraged worker
A marginally attached worker who has not made specific efforts to find a job within the past four weeks because previous unsuccessful attempts to find a job were discouraging.

The BLS calculates the employment–population ratio using the formula:

$$\text{Employment–population ratio} = \frac{\text{Number of people employed}}{\text{Working-age population}} \times 100.$$

Table 22.2 uses this formula to calculate the employment–population ratio in May 2016.

The Labor Force Participation Rate

The number of people in the labor force is an indicator of the willingness of working-age people to take jobs. The **labor force participation rate** is the percentage of the working-age population in the labor force. That is,

$$\text{Labor force participation rate} = \frac{\text{Labor force}}{\text{Working–age population}} \times 100.$$

Table 22.3 uses this formula with data on the number of people in the labor force and the working-age population to calculate the labor force participation rate in May 2016.

■ Alternative Measures of Unemployment

The official definition of unemployment omits two types of underused labor:

- Marginally attached workers
- Part-time workers who want full-time work

Marginally Attached Workers

A **marginally attached worker** is a person who does not have a job, is available and willing to work, has not made specific efforts to find a job within the previous four weeks, but has looked for work sometime in the recent past. Marginally attached workers think of themselves as being in the labor force and unemployed. A **discouraged worker** is a person who is similar to an unemployed worker, but who has not made specific efforts to find a job within the previous four weeks because previous unsuccessful attempts were discouraging.

Other marginally attached workers differ from discouraged workers only in their reasons for not having looked for a job during the previous four weeks. For example, Martin doesn't have a job and is available for work, but he has not looked for work in the past four weeks because he was busy cleaning his home after a flood. He is a marginally attached worker but not a discouraged worker. Lena, Martin's wife, doesn't have a job and is available for work, but she hasn't looked for work in the past four weeks because she's been looking for six months and hasn't had a single job offer. She is a discouraged worker.

Neither the unemployment rate nor the labor force participation rate includes marginally attached workers. In May 2016, 538,000 people were discouraged workers. If we add them to both the number of people counted as unemployed and the labor force, the unemployment rate becomes 5.0 percent—a bit higher than the standard definition of the unemployment rate. Also in May 2016, 1,713,000 people were marginally attached workers. If we add them and the discouraged workers to both the number counted as unemployed and the labor force, the unemployment rate becomes 6.0 percent—1.3 percentage points higher than the standard definition.

EYE on the U.S. ECONOMY
The Current Population Survey

The Bureau of Labor Statistics and the Bureau of the Census go to great lengths to collect accurate labor force data. They constantly train and retrain around 1,600 field interviewers and supervisors. Each month, each field interviewer contacts 37 households and asks basic demographic questions about everyone living at the address and detailed labor force questions about those aged 16 or over.

Once a household has been selected for the survey, it is questioned for four consecutive months and then again for the same four months a year later. Each month, the addresses that have been in the panel eight times are removed and 6,250 new addresses are added. The rotation and overlap of households provide very reliable information about month-to-month and year-to-year changes in the labor market.

The first time that a household is in the panel, an interviewer, armed with a hand-held computer, visits it. If the household has a telephone, most of the subsequent interviews are conducted by phone, many of them from one of the three telephone interviewing centers in Hagerstown, Maryland; Jeffersonville, Indiana; and Tucson, Arizona.

For more information about the Current Population Survey, visit www.bls.gov/cps/cps_faq.htm.

Part-Time Workers Who Want Full-Time Work

The Current Population Survey measures the number of full-time workers and part-time workers. **Full-time workers** are those who usually work 35 hours or more a week. **Part-time workers** are those who usually work less than 35 hours a week. Part-time workers are divided into two groups: part time for economic reasons and part time for noneconomic reasons.

People who work **part time for economic reasons** (also called *involuntary part-time workers)* are people who work 1 to 34 hours but are looking for full-time work. These people are unable to find full-time work because of unfavorable business conditions or seasonal decreases in the availability of full-time work.

People who work part time for noneconomic reasons do not want full-time work and are not available for such work. This group includes people with health problems, family or personal responsibilities, or education commitments that limit their availability for work.

The Bureau of Labor Statistics uses the data on full-time and part-time status to measure the slack in the labor market that results from people being underemployed—employed but not able to find as much employment as they would like.

In May 2016, when employment was 151.0 million, full-time employment was 123.1 million and part-time employment was 27.9 million. An estimated 6.4 million people worked part time for economic reasons. When this number, along with marginally attached workers, is added to the number unemployed, the unemployment rate becomes 9.6 percent.

Full-time workers
People who usually work 35 hours or more a week.

Part-time workers
People who usually work less than 35 hours a week.

Part time for economic reasons
People who work 1 to 34 hours per week but are looking for full-time work and cannot find it because of unfavorable business conditions.

MyEconLab Study Plan 22.1
       Key Terms Quiz
       Solutions Video
       Real-Time Data

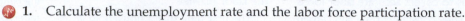
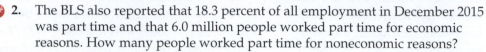

CHECKPOINT 22.1

Define the unemployment rate and other labor market indicators.

Practice Problems

The BLS reported that in December 2015, the labor force was 157.8 million, employment was 149.9 million, and the working-age population was 252.0 million.

1. Calculate the unemployment rate and the labor force participation rate.

2. The BLS also reported that 18.3 percent of all employment in December 2015 was part time and that 6.0 million people worked part time for economic reasons. How many people worked part time for noneconomic reasons?

In the News

Summer 2015 youth labor market
From April to July 2015, the number of employed youth 16 to 24 years old rose by 2.1 million to 20.3 million and youth unemployment increased from 2.1 million to 2.8 million. In July, the youth labor force grew by 2.8 million to a total of 23.1 million and the youth population was 38.5 million.

Source: BLS Press Release, August 18, 2015

How did the youth unemployment rate change from April to July? Calculate the youth labor force participation rate in July.

Solutions to Practice Problems

1. The unemployment rate is 5.0 percent. The labor force equals employment plus unemployment. So unemployment equals the labor force minus employment, which equals (157.8 million − 149.9 million), or 7.9 million. The unemployment rate equals unemployment as a percentage of the labor force. Unemployment rate = (7.9 ÷ 157.8) × 100 or 5 percent. The labor force participation rate is 65.5 percent. The labor force participation rate equals the labor force as a percentage of the working-age population. Labor force participation rate = (157.8 ÷ 252.0) × 100, or 62.6 percent.

2. 21.4 million people worked part time for noneconomic reasons. Employment was 149.9 million. Part-time employment was 18.3 percent of 149.9 million, which equals 27.4 million. Given that 6.0 million worked part time for economic reasons, then 27.4 million minus 6.0 million, or 21.4 million, worked part time for noneconomic reasons.

Solution to In the News

The unemployment rate is the number unemployed as a percentage of the labor force. The April employment equals the July employment (20.3 million) minus the increase of 2.1 million from April to July, or 18.2 million. The labor force equals employed plus unemployed. The April labor force was (18.2 million + 2.1 million), or 20.3 million. In April, 2.1 million were unemployed, so the April unemployment rate was (2.1 ÷ 20.3) × 100, or 10.3 percent. In July, 2.8 million were unemployed and the labor force was 23.1 million, so the unemployment rate was 12.1 percent. From April to July, the unemployment rate rose from 10.3 percent to 12.1 percent. The July labor force participation rate equals the labor force (23.1 million) as a percentage of the youth population (38.5 million), or 60 percent.

22.2   LABOR MARKET TRENDS AND FLUCTUATIONS

MyEconLab Concept Video

What do we learn about the U.S. labor market from changes in the unemployment rate, the labor force participation rate, and the alternative measures of unemployment? Let's explore the trends and fluctuations in these indicators.

■ Unemployment Rate

Figure 22.2 shows the U.S. unemployment rate over the 88 years from 1929 to 2016. The most striking event visible in this figure is the **Great Depression**, a period of high unemployment, low incomes, and extreme economic hardship that lasted from 1929 to 1939. By 1933, the worst of the Great Depression years, real GDP had fallen by a huge 30 percent and as the figure shows, one in four of the people who wanted jobs couldn't find them. The horrors of the Great Depression led to the New Deal and shaped political attitudes that persist today.

During the 1960s, the unemployment rate gradually fell to 3.5 percent. These years saw a rapid rate of job creation, partly from the demands placed on the economy by the growth of defense production during the Vietnam War and partly from an expansion of consumer spending encouraged by an expansion of social programs. Another burst of rapid job creation driven by the "new economy"— the high-technology sector driven by the expansion of the Internet—lowered the unemployment rate to below average from 1995 through the early 2000s.

During the recessions of 1973–1975, 1981–1982, 1990–1991, and 2008–2009, the unemployment rate increased. While the popular representation of the 2008–2009 recession compares it with the Great Depression, you can see in Figure 22.2 that 2010 is strikingly different from 1933, the year in which the unemployment rate peaked during the Great Depression.

Great Depression
A period of high unemployment, low incomes, and extreme economic hardship that lasted from 1929 to 1939.

■ FIGURE 22.2

The U.S. Unemployment Rate: 1929–2016

MyEconLab Real-time data

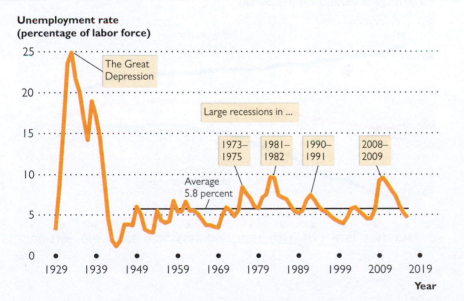

The average unemployment rate from 1948 to 2016 was 5.8 percent. The unemployment rate increases in recessions and decreases in expansions. Unemployment was at its lowest during World War II and the expansions of the 1950s, 1960s, and the 1990s and at its highest during the Great Depression and the recessions of 1981–1982 and 2008–2009.

SOURCE OF DATA: Bureau of Labor Statistics.

■ The Participation Rate

Figure 22.3 shows the labor force participation rate, which increased from 59 percent in 1960 to 67 percent at its peak in 1999. Why did the labor force participation rate increase? The main reason is an increase in the number of women who have entered the labor force.

Figure 22.3 shows that from 1960 to 1999, the participation rate of women increased from 37 percent to 60 percent. This increase is spread across women of all age groups and occurred for four main reasons. First, more women pursued a college education and so increased their earning power. Second, technological change in the workplace created a large number of white-collar jobs with flexible work hours that many women found attractive. Third, technological change in the home increased the time available for paid employment. And fourth, families looked increasingly to a second income to balance tight budgets.

Figure 22.3 also shows another remarkable trend in the U.S. labor force: The participation rate of men *decreased* from 83 percent in 1960 to 70 percent in 2016. Some of the decrease occurred as older men chose to retire earlier. But some arose from job loss at an age at which finding a new job is difficult. Decreased labor force participation of younger men occurred because more remained in school.

Downward Trend Since 2000

The downward trend in the labor force participation rate that began in 2000 might arise in part from a mismeasurement of unemployment. Recall that the labor force is the sum of the employed and the unemployed. If we don't count all the people who are unemployed, then we don't count all the people in the labor force. Some new measures provide a broader view of unemployment.

FIGURE 22.3

The Changing Face of the Labor Market: 1960–2016   MyEconLab Real-time data

The labor force participation rate increased from 1960 to 1999 but then decreased slightly.

The labor force participation rate of women has driven these trends, increasing strongly from 37 percent in 1960 to 60 percent in 1999.

The labor force participation rate of men has decreased steadily.

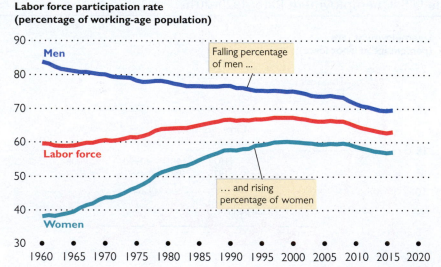

Source of data: Bureau of Labor Statistics.

EYE on the GLOBAL ECONOMY
Unemployment and Labor Force Participation

Unemployment

U.S. unemployment falls inside the range experienced by other countries. The highest unemployment rates have been in the United Kingdom, Canada, and the Eurozone; and the lowest have been in Japan and the newly industrializing Asian economies.

Differences in unemployment rates were large during the early1980s, narrowed through the 1990s and early 2000s, and widened after the 2008–2009 recession.

The Eurozone, with a higher average unemployment rate than the United States, also has higher unemployment benefits and more regulated labor markets.

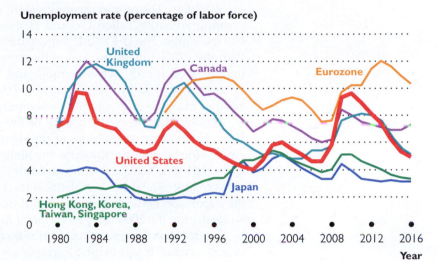

Figure I Unemployment

Source of data: International Monetary Fund, *World Economic Outlook,* April 2016.

Labor Force Participation

The labor force participation rate of women has increased in most advanced nations. But the participation rate of women in the labor force varies a great deal around the world. The figure compares eight other countries with the United States.

The U.S. rank is surprisingly low. Economists Francine D. Blau and Lawrence M. Kahn who have studied these data say that other countries have more "family-friendly" labor market policies. But they say these labor market policies encourage part-time work and U.S. women are more likely than women in other countries to have good full-time jobs as managers or professionals.

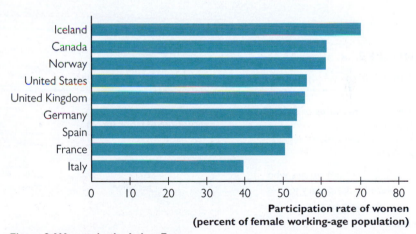

Figure 2 Women in the Labor Force

Source of data: OECD

Cultural factors play a central role in influencing national differences in women's work choices. But education, and particularly the percentage of women with a college degree, is the dominant source of international differences in women's and men's job market prospects.

■ Alternative Measures of Unemployment

You've seen that the official measure of unemployment does not include marginally attached workers and people who work part time for economic reasons. The Bureau of Labor Statistics (BLS) now provides three broader measures of the unemployment rate, known as U-4, U-5, and U-6, that include these wider groups of the jobless. The official unemployment rate (based on the standard definition of unemployment) is called U-3 and as these names imply, there are also U-1 and U-2 measures. The U-1 and U-2 measures of the unemployment rate are narrower than the official measure. U-1 is the percentage of the labor force that has been unemployed for 15 weeks or more and is a measure of long-term involuntary unemployment. U-2 is the percentage of the labor force that has been laid off and is another measure of involuntary unemployment.

Figure 22.4 shows the history of these six measures of unemployment since 1996. The relative magnitudes of the six measures are explained by what they include—the broader the measure, the higher the average. The gap between U-5 and U-6—part-time workers who want full-time work— is the largest. The six measures follow similar but not identical tracks: rising during recessions and falling in the expansion between recessions. But during the 2001 recession, U-1 barely rose while during the 2008–2009 recession, it more than doubled in less than a year.

Notice that the unemployment rate, on all six measures, keeps rising after a recession ends: It lags behind the business cycle. When an expansion begins, firms start hiring slowly. Some unemployed workers get jobs, but the labor force increases as marginally attached workers start to look for jobs. In the early stages of an expansion, the number of marginally attached workers looking for jobs exceeds the number of people hired and the unemployment rate increases.

■ FIGURE 22.4

Alternative Measures of Unemployment: 1996–2016

MyEconLab Real-time data

The alternative measures of unemployment are

U-1 People unemployed 15 weeks or longer

U-2 People laid off and others who completed a temporary job

U-3 Total unemployed (official measure)

U-4 Total unemployed plus discouraged workers

U-5 U-4 plus other marginally attached workers

U-6 U-5 plus employed part time for economic reasons

U-1, U-2, and U-3 are percentages of the labor force.

U-4, U-5, and U-6 are percentages of the labor force plus the unemployed in the added category.

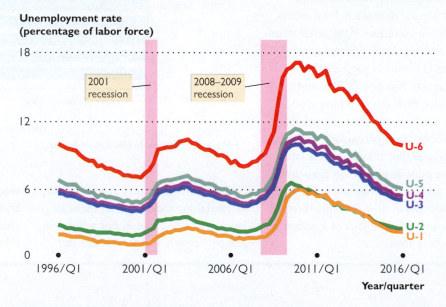

SOURCE OF DATA: Bureau of Labor Statistics.

CHECKPOINT 22.2

Describe the trends and fluctuations in the indicators of the state of the U.S. labor market.

MyEconLab Study Plan 22.2
Key Terms Quiz
Solutions Video

Practice Problems

1. Figure 1 shows the unemployment rate in the United States from 1960 to 2016. In which decade—the 1960s, 1970s, 1980s, 1990s, or 2000s—was the average unemployment rate the lowest and what brought low unemployment in that decade? In which decade was the average unemployment rate the highest and what brought high unemployment in that decade?

2. Describe the trends in the labor force participation rates of men, women, and all working-age people.

In the News

Blue in red states
Unemployment is 4.9 percent—less than half of the Great Recession peak—but Bernie Sanders got a big cheer when he dismissed the official unemployment rate as not reflecting those who are involuntarily working part time, or those who have become so discouraged they have given up looking for employment.
Source: *U.S. News & World Report*, February 12, 2016

1. Which of the alternative measures of unemployment does Bernie Sanders think is more relevant than the official unemployment rate and what was its level at the start of 2016?

2. By how much did the broadest measure of unemployment change from its 2008–2009 "Great Recession" peak?

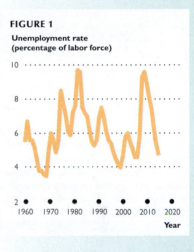

FIGURE 1

**Unemployment rate
(percentage of labor force)**

Solutions to Practice Problems

1. Figure 1 shows that the unemployment rate was lowest during the 1960s when defense spending on the Vietnam War and expansion of social programs brought rapid expansions and lowered the unemployment rate.

   Figure 1 shows that the unemployment rate was highest during the 1980s. During the 1981–1982 recession it increased to almost 10 percent.

2. The labor force participation rate of women increased because (1) better-educated women earn more, (2) more white-collar jobs with flexible work hours were created, (3) people have more time for paid employment, and (4) families increasingly needed two incomes to balance their budgets. The labor force participation rate of men decreased because more men remained in school and some men took early retirement. The overall labor force participation rate increased.

Solutions to In the News

1. Bernie Sanders prefers the U-6 measure of unemployment, which includes discouraged workers, other marginally attached workers, and part-time workers for economic reasons. At the start of 2016, U-6 was 10 percent.

2. The broadest measure of unemployment, U-6, peaked at about 17 percent during the 2008–2009 recession, so at the start of 2016, it was about 60 percent of its peak.

22.3 UNEMPLOYMENT AND FULL EMPLOYMENT

There is always someone without a job who is searching for one, so there is always some unemployment. The key reason is that the labor market is constantly churning. New jobs are created and old jobs die; and some people move into the labor force and some move out of it. This churning creates unemployment.

We distinguish among three types of unemployment:

- Frictional unemployment
- Structural unemployment
- Cyclical unemployment

■ Frictional Unemployment

Frictional unemployment is the unemployment that arises from people entering and leaving the labor force, from quitting jobs to find better ones, and from the ongoing creation and destruction of jobs—from normal labor turnover. Frictional unemployment is a permanent and healthy phenomenon in a dynamic, growing economy.

There is an unending flow of people into and out of the labor force as people move through the stages of life—from being in school to finding a job, to working, perhaps to becoming unhappy with a job and looking for a new one, and finally, to retiring from full-time work.

There is also an unending process of job creation and job destruction as new firms are born, firms expand or contract, and some firms fail and go out of business.

The flows into and out of the labor force and the processes of job creation and job destruction create the need for people to search for jobs and for businesses to search for workers. Businesses don't usually hire the first person who applies for a job, and unemployed people don't usually take the first job that comes their way. Instead, both firms and workers spend time searching for what they believe will be the best available match. By this process of search, people can match their own skills and interests with the available jobs and find a satisfying job and a good income.

Frictional unemployment
The unemployment that arises from people entering and leaving the labor force, from quitting jobs to find better ones, and from the ongoing creation and destruction of jobs—from normal labor turnover.

A new graduate interviews for a job.

■ Structural Unemployment

Structural unemployment is the unemployment that arises when changes in technology or international competition change the skills needed to perform jobs or change the locations of jobs. Structural unemployment usually lasts longer than frictional unemployment because workers must retrain and possibly relocate to find a job. For example, when banks introduced the automatic teller machine in the 1970s, many bank-teller jobs were destroyed. Meanwhile, new jobs for life-insurance salespeople and retail clerks were created. The former bank tellers remained unemployed for several months until they moved, retrained, and got one of these new jobs. Structural unemployment is painful, especially for older workers for whom the best available option might be to retire early but with a lower income than they had expected.

Sometimes, the amount of structural unemployment is small. At other times, it is large, and at such times, structural unemployment can become a serious long-term problem. It was especially large during the late 1970s and early 1980s.

Structural unemployment
The unemployment that arises when changes in technology or international competition change the skills needed to perform jobs or change the locations of jobs.

Bank tellers lost jobs to computer technology.

■ Cyclical Unemployment

The fluctuating unemployment over the business cycle—the higher than normal unemployment at a business cycle trough and the lower than normal unemployment at a business cycle peak—is called **cyclical unemployment**. A worker who is laid off because the economy is in a recession and who gets rehired some months later when the expansion begins has experienced cyclical unemployment.

■ "Natural" Unemployment

Natural unemployment is the unemployment that arises from frictions and structural change—when all the unemployment is frictional and structural and there is no cyclical unemployment. Natural unemployment as a percentage of the labor force is called the **natural unemployment rate**.

Full employment is defined as a situation in which the unemployment rate equals the natural unemployment rate.

What determines the natural unemployment rate? Is it constant or does it change over time?

The natural unemployment rate is influenced by many factors, but the most important ones are

- The age distribution of the population
- The pace of structural change
- The real wage rate
- Unemployment benefits

Cyclical unemployment
The fluctuating unemployment over the business cycle that increases during a recession and decreases during an expansion.

Natural unemployment rate
The unemployment rate when all the unemployment is frictional and structural and there is no cyclical unemployment.

Full employment
When the unemployment rate equals the natural unemployment rate.

EYE on the U.S. ECONOMY
How Long Does it Take to Find a Job?

The duration of unemployment spells varies over the business cycle. In 2000 at the business cycle peak, the median time to find a job was 6 weeks; in 2011 at the start of a weak expansion, it was 21 weeks; and in 2016 after a long but weak expansion, it was 11 weeks.

The figure provides more information: It shows the percentage of the unemployed at four unemployment durations. You can see that long-term unemployment (27 weeks and over) was much greater in 2011 than it was at the business cycle peak in 2000. The 2016 data lie between the extremes of 2000 and 2011.

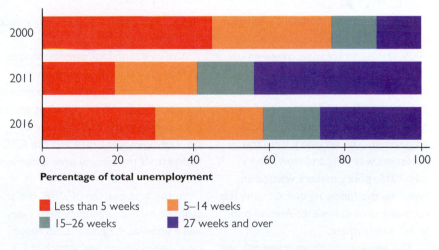

Percentage of total unemployment

■ Less than 5 weeks   ■ 5–14 weeks
■ 15–26 weeks   ■ 27 weeks and over

SOURCE OF DATA: Bureau of Labor Statistics.

The Age Distribution of the Population

An economy with a young population has lots of new job seekers every year and a high level of frictional unemployment. An economy with an aging population has fewer new job seekers and less frictional unemployment.

The Pace of Structural Change

The pace of structural change is sometimes slow, so the same jobs using the same machines remain in place for many years. But sometimes a technological upheaval sweeps aside the old ways, wipes out millions of jobs, and makes the skills once used to perform these jobs obsolete. The amount of structural unemployment fluctuates with the pace of technological change. The change is driven by fierce international competition, especially from fast-changing Asian economies. A high level of structural unemployment is present in some parts of the United States today.

The Real Wage Rate

The natural unemployment rate is influenced by the real wage rate. Anything that raises the real wage above the market equilibrium creates a surplus of labor and increases the natural unemployment rate. The real wage might exceed the market equilibrium for two reasons: a minimum wage and an efficiency wage. The federal minimum wage creates unemployment because it is set above the equilibrium wage of low-skilled young workers. An efficiency wage is a wage set by firms above the going market wage to attract the most productive workers, get them to work hard, and discourage them from quitting. When firms set efficiency wages, some workers would like to work for these firms but can't get jobs.

EYE on FULL EMPLOYMENT

MyEconLab Critical Thinking Exercise

Are We Back at Full Employment?

The U.S. economy has spent a long time away from full employment. In 2009, during a recession triggered by the Global Financial Crisis, the unemployment rate soared to 10 percent and the broader U-6 measure of underutilized labor hovered at almost 18 percent. The recovery from this recession was long and slow. And in mid-2016, policy makers wanted answers to the following questions: Is the recovery now complete? Are we back at full employment?

The answers to these questions are a major input into the decisions of the Federal Reserve on the pace at which to raise interest rates. (You will learn about these decisions and their effects in Chapters 27, 28, and 33.)

We've defined full employment as a state in which the unemployment rate equals the natural unemployment rate. So the first way to find an answer is to compare the BLS measure of the unemployment rate and the CBO estimate of the natural unemployment rate.

In the first quarter of 2016, the actual and natural unemployment rates were equal at 4.9 percent. So based on these numbers, we're back at full employment.

But the natural unemployment rate is only an estimate. It varies over time and is influenced by many factors. Also, the employment–population ratio and the labor force participation rate data point to a different answer to the full-employment question. Both of these measures fell by 3 percentage points between 2007 and 2016. Three percent of the working-age population had disappeared from the labor force. Where did these people go? Did they represent hidden unemployment?

A way of answering this question has been suggested by economists at the Federal Reserve Bank of Atlanta. Their idea is to use an indicator they call the Z-Pop ratio, which is the percentage of the working-age population

Unemployment Benefits

Unemployment benefits increase the natural unemployment rate by lowering the opportunity cost of job search. European countries have more generous unemployment benefits and higher natural unemployment rates than the United States. Extending unemployment benefits raises the natural unemployment rate.

There is no controversy about the existence of a natural unemployment rate. Nor is there disagreement that the natural unemployment rate changes. But economists don't know its exact size or the extent to which it fluctuates. The Congressional Budget Office estimates the natural unemployment rate and its estimate for 2016 was 4.9 percent—equal to the actual unemployment rate in that year.

■ Unemployment and Real GDP

Cyclical unemployment is the fluctuating unemployment over the business cycle—unemployment that increases during a recession and decreases during an expansion. At full employment, there is *no* cyclical unemployment. At a business cycle trough, cyclical unemployment is *positive* and at a business cycle peak, cyclical unemployment is *negative*.

Figure 22.5(a) shows the unemployment rate in the United States between 1980 and 2016. It also shows the natural unemployment rate and cyclical unemployment. The natural unemployment rate in this figure was estimated by the Congressional Budget Office (CBO).

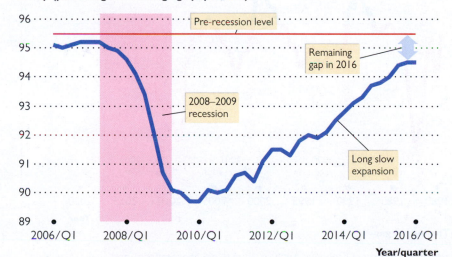

SOURCE OF DATA: Bureau of Labor Statistics, formula proposed by the Federal Reserve Bank of Atlanta, and authors' calculations.

that is fully utilized. The people counted as fully utilized are those working full-time, those working part-time for a noneconomic reason, and those who say they don't want a job.

The figure shows the Z-Pop ratio. Before the 2008–2009 recession, 95.2 percent of the population was fully utilized by this definition. The number fell to 89.7 percent and then slowly climbed. In 2016, 94.5 percent of the population was fully utilized.

So the Z-Pop ratio gives almost the same answer as that by comparing the unemployment rate with the natural unemployment rate, but not quite. It shows a small amount of underused labor remaining in 2016.

■ **FIGURE 22.5**

The Relationship Between Unemployment and the Output Gap

As the unemployment rate fluctuates around the natural unemployment rate in part (a), the output gap—real GDP minus potential GDP expressed as a percentage of potential GDP—fluctuates around a zero output gap in part (b).

When the unemployment rate *exceeds* the natural unemployment rate, real GDP is below potential GDP and the output gap is negative (the red sections in both parts).

When the unemployment rate is *below* the natural unemployment rate, real GDP is above potential GDP and the output gap is positive (the blue sections in both parts).

The natural unemployment rate shown in the graph is the Congressional Budget Office's estimate. It might turn out to be an underestimate for the years since 2008.

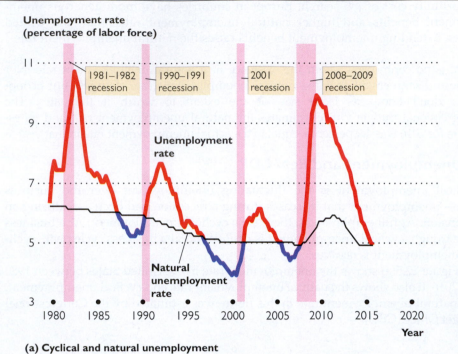

(a) Cyclical and natural unemployment

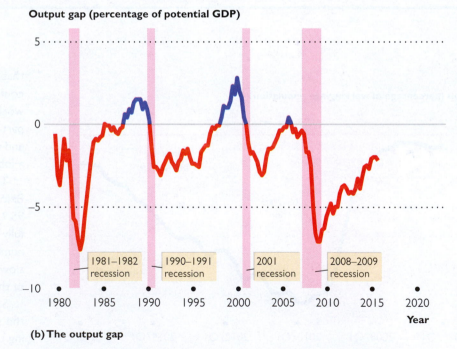

(b) The output gap

Sources of data: Bureau of Economic Analysis, Bureau of Labor Statistics, and Congressional Budget Office.

In Figure 22.5(a), you can see that during most of the 1980s, the early 1990s, early 2000s, and during 2008–2009, the unemployment rate was above the natural unemployment rate, so cyclical unemployment was positive (the red sections of the line). You can also see that during the late 1980s, from 1997 to 2001, and during 2005–2008 the unemployment rate was below the natural unemployment rate, so cyclical unemployment was negative (the blue sections of the line).

As the unemployment rate fluctuates around the natural unemployment rate, real GDP fluctuates around potential GDP. **Potential GDP** is the value of real GDP when the economy is at full employment—all the economy's factors of production (labor, capital, land, and entrepreneurial ability) are employed. Real GDP equals potential GDP when the economy is at full employment. Real GDP minus potential GDP expressed as a percentage of potential GDP is called the **output gap**.

Figure 22.5(b) shows the U.S. *output gap* from 1980 to 2016. You can see that as the unemployment rate fluctuates around the natural unemployment rate, the output gap also fluctuates. Most of the time, when the unemployment rate is above the natural unemployment rate, in part (a), the output gap is negative (real GDP is below potential GDP), in part (b); when the unemployment rate is below the natural unemployment rate, the output gap is positive (real GDP is above potential GDP); and when the unemployment rate equals the natural unemployment rate, the output gap is zero (real GDP equals potential GDP).

The general tendency for unemployment to be above the natural rate when real GDP is below potential GDP did not describe the situation in 2016. In that year, the unemployment rate had fallen to equal the natural rate but the output gap was about 2 percent below potential GDP. This discrepancy might arise from errors in estimating the natural unemployment rate and potential GDP.

Potential GDP
The value of real GDP when the economy is at full employment—all the economy's factors of production (labor, capital, land, and entrepreneurial ability) are employed.

Output gap
Real GDP minus potential GDP expressed as a percentage of potential GDP.

EYE on YOUR LIFE

MyEconLab Critical Thinking Exercise

Your Labor Market Status and Activity

You are going to spend a lot of your life in the labor market. Most of the time, you'll be supplying labor services. But first, you must find a job. Most likely, one job will not last your entire working life. You will want to find a new job when you decide to quit or when changing economic conditions destroy your current job.

As you look for a job, get a job, quit a job, or get laid off and look for a new job, you will pass through many and possibly all of the population categories used in the Current Population Survey that you've learned about in this chapter.

Think about your current labor market status while you are studying economics.

- Are you in the labor force or not?
- If you are in the labor force, are you employed or unemployed?
- If you are employed, are you a part-time or a full-time worker?

Now think about someone you know who is unemployed or has been unemployed. Classify the unemployment experienced by this person as

- frictional,
- structural, or
- cyclical.

How can you tell the type of unemployment experienced by this person?

The labor market conditions that you face today or when you graduate and look for a job depend partly on general national economic conditions—on whether the economy is in recession or booming.

Labor market conditions also depend on where you live. Visit the Bureau of Labor Statistics' Web site at www.bls.gov. There you can find information on employment and unemployment for your state and metropolitan area or county. By comparing the labor market conditions in your own region with those in other areas, you can figure out where it might be easier to find work.

MyEconLab Study Plan 22.3
Key Terms Quiz
Solutions Video

CHECKPOINT 22.3

Describe the types of unemployment, define full employment, and explain the link between unemployment and real GDP.

Practice Problems

Recovery won't improve unemployment

Despite some optimism about the seeds of recovery, the Congressional Budget Office (CBO) sees joblessness rising. The CBO sees unemployment peaking at 10.4% next year from an average of 9.3% this year, before it falls to 9.1% in 2011.

Source: *Fortune*, August 25, 2009

Before the recession began, the U.S. unemployment rate was about 6 percent.

1. As a recession begins, firms quickly make layoffs. Is this rise in unemployment mostly a rise in frictional, structural, or cyclical unemployment?

2. Why does unemployment continue to rise as an expansion begins?

In the News

The small but serious threat of a U.S. recession

The unemployment rate is 4.9 percent, its level in 2008 before the recession. While it is unlikely that the United States will slip into recession this year, below-trend real GDP growth cannot be ruled out and some Wall Street economists say there is a 20 percent chance of recession in 2016.

Source: *The Financial Times*, February 5, 2016

1. Using the information in the news clip along with that in Figure 22.5 (p. 582), how would you describe the state of the U.S. economy through 2014 and 2015 and at the beginning of 2016?

2. How would "below-trend real GDP growth" change the unemployment rate and what type of unemployment would change?

Solutions to Practice Problems

1. When a recession starts, firms are quick to lay off workers. Most of the rise in unemployment is cyclical—related to the state of the economy. The unemployment rate rises quickly as the number of layoffs increases.

2. The unemployment rate lags behind the business cycle. When an expansion begins, firms start hiring slowly. Some unemployed workers get jobs, but the labor force increases as marginally attached workers start to look for jobs. In the early stages of an expansion, the number of marginally attached workers looking for jobs exceeds the number of people hired and unemployment increases.

Solutions to In the News

1. In 2014 and 2015, the U.S. economy was recovering from the 2008–2009 recession. The unemployment rate was falling and the output gap was shrinking slowly. At the start of 2016, the unemployment rate was below its long-term average and the economy was close to full employment

2. Below-trend real GDP growth would increase the unemployment rate and cyclical unemployment would increase.

CHAPTER SUMMARY

Key Points

1. **Define the unemployment rate and other labor market indicators.**

- The unemployment rate is the number of people unemployed as a percentage of the labor force, and the labor force is the sum of the number of people employed and the number unemployed.
- The labor force participation rate is the labor force as a percentage of the working-age population.

2. **Describe the trends and fluctuations in the indicators of the state of the U.S. labor market.**

- The unemployment rate fluctuates with the business cycle, increasing in recessions and decreasing in expansions.
- The labor force participation rate of women has increased, and the labor force participation rate of men has decreased.

3. **Describe the types of unemployment, define full employment, and explain the link between unemployment and real GDP.**

- Unemployment can be frictional, structural, or cyclical.
- Full employment occurs when there is no cyclical unemployment and at full employment, the unemployment rate equals the natural unemployment rate.
- Potential GDP is the real GDP produced when the economy is at full employment.
- As the unemployment rate fluctuates around the natural unemployment rate, real GDP fluctuates around potential GDP and the output gap fluctuates between negative and positive values.

Key Terms

MyEconLab Key Terms Quiz

Cyclical unemployment, 579
Discouraged worker, 570
Employment–population ratio, 569
Frictional unemployment, 578
Full employment, 579
Full-time workers, 571

Great Depression, 573
Labor force, 568
Labor force participation rate, 570
Marginally attached worker, 570
Natural unemployment rate, 579
Output gap, 583

Part time for economic reasons, 571
Part-time workers, 571
Potential GDP, 583
Structural unemployment, 578
Unemployment rate, 569
Working-age population, 568

MyEconLab Chapter 22 Study Plan

CHAPTER CHECKPOINT

Study Plan Problems and Applications

Use the following information gathered by a BLS labor market survey of four households to work Problems **1** and **2**.

- Household 1: Candy worked 20 hours last week setting up her Internet shopping business. The rest of the week, she completed application forms and attended two job interviews. Husband Jerry worked 40 hours at his job at GM. Daughter Meg, a student, worked 10 hours at her weekend job at Starbucks.
- Household 2: Joey, a full-time bank clerk, was on vacation. Wife, Serena, who wants a full-time job, worked 10 hours as a part-time checkout clerk.
- Household 3: Ari had no work last week but was going to be recalled to his regular job in two weeks. Partner Kosta, after months of searching for a job and not being able to find one, has stopped looking and will go back to school.
- Household 4: Mimi and Henry are retired. Son Hank is a professional artist, who painted for 12 hours last week and sold one picture.

1. Classify each of the 10 people into the labor market category used by the BLS. Who are part-time workers and who are full-time workers? Of the part-time workers, who works part time for economic reasons?

2. Calculate the unemployment rate and the labor force participation rate, and compare these rates with those in the United States in 2016.

3. Describe two examples of people who work part time for economic reasons and two examples of people who work part time for noneconomic reasons.

4. Explain the relationship between the percentage of employed workers who have part-time jobs and the business cycle.

5. Distinguish among the three types of unemployment: frictional, structural, and cyclical. Provide an example of each type of unemployment in the United States today.

6. Describe the relationship between the unemployment rate and the natural unemployment rate as the output gap fluctuates between being positive and being negative.

Use the following information to work Problems **7** and **8**.

Unemployment falls to 4.9 percent, lowest in 8 years
U.S. unemployment of 4.9 percent is full employment. Only 151,000 jobs were created in January, down from 262,000 in December. With falling oil prices, 7,000 energy jobs were lost in January but 29,000 manufacturing jobs were added.
Source: CNN Money, February 5, 2016

7. Using the information provided in the news clip, which types of unemployment were present in the U.S. economy in January 2016?

8. How would you expect a shrinking energy sector and an expanding manufacturing sector to influence the actual and natural unemployment rates?

9. Read *Eye on Full Employment* on pp. 580–581. In which year, 2000 or 2016, was real GDP below potential GDP? How can you tell from the graph on p. 582?

Instructor Assignable Problems and Applications

MyEconLab Homework, Quiz, or
Test if assigned by instructor
Real-Time Data

1. In the United States,
   - Compare the duration of unemployment in 2016 with that in 2000 and explain whether the difference was most likely the result of frictions, structural change, or the business cycle.
   - How does the unemployment of marginally attached workers influence the duration of unemployment in 2016 compared with that in 2000?

2. The Bureau of Labor Statistics reported that in the second quarter of 2008 the working-age population was 233,410,000, the labor force was 154,294,000, and employment was 146,089,000. Calculate for that quarter the labor force participation rate and the unemployment rate.

3. In July 2016, in the economy of Sandy Island, 10,000 people were employed and 1,000 were unemployed. During August 2016, 80 people lost their jobs and didn't look for new ones, 20 people quit their jobs and retired, 150 people who had looked for work were hired, 50 people became discouraged workers, and 40 new graduates looked for work. Calculate the change in the unemployment rate from July 2016 to August 2016.

4. The BLS survey reported the following data in a community of 320 people: 200 worked at least 1 hour as paid employees; 20 did not work but were temporarily absent from their jobs; 40 did not have jobs and didn't want to work; 10 were available for work and last week they had looked for work; and 6 were available for work and were waiting to be recalled to their previous job. Calculate the unemployment rate and the labor force participation rate.

5. Describe the trends and fluctuations in the unemployment rate in the United States from 1949 through 2016. In which periods was the unemployment rate above average and in which periods was it below average?

6. Describe how the labor force participation rate in the United States changed between 1960 and 2016. Contrast and explain the different trends in the labor force participation rates of women and men.

7. Explain why the natural unemployment rate is not zero and why the unemployment rate fluctuates around the natural unemployment rate.

Use the following information to work Problems **8** and **9**.

The metro areas with the lowest and highest unemployment
In December 2015, Ames, Iowa, had the lowest unemployment in the United States at 2.2 percent of the workforce. At the other end of the scale was El Centro, California, with 19.6 percent of its workforce unemployed.
                                                            Source: *Forbes*, February 9, 2016
In the depth of the 2008–2009 recession, the unemployment rate in Ames peaked at 5.7 percent. In El Centro, it peaked at 30.3 percent.

8. Use the information provided to estimate how much of the unemployment in Ames and El Centro in 2009 was cyclical and how much was natural. Explain your assumptions in arriving at your estimates.

9. How would you explain the difference in the unemployment rates in Ames and El Centro in December 2015? Why is the difference almost certainly not explained by different cyclical unemployment rates?

MyEconLab Chapter 22 Study Plan

Multiple Choice Quiz

1. The BLS counts Jody as being unemployed if she _____.

  A. had a job last month but not this month
  B. doesn't have a job because the U.S. factory where she worked cannot compete with cheap Chinese imports
  C. wants a job and looked for a job last year but has now stopped looking
  D. wants a job and is willing to take a job but after searching last week cannot find a job

2. A marginally attached worker is a person who _____.

  A. works part time for economic reasons
  B. works part time for noneconomic reasons
  C. doesn't work, is available and willing to work, but hasn't looked for a job recently
  D. has no job but would like one and has gone back to school to retrain

3. If the BLS included all marginally attached workers as being unemployed, the _____ would be _____.

  A. unemployment rate; higher
  B. labor force; unchanged
  C. labor force participation rate; lower
  D. unemployment rate; lower

4. When the economy goes into recession, the biggest increase in unemployment is _____.

  A. structural because jobs are lost in most states
  B. cyclical because jobs are lost in many industries as they cut production
  C. frictional because the creation of jobs slows
  D. the combination of structural and frictional as few new jobs are created

5. The economy is at full employment when all unemployment is _____.

  A. structural
  B. cyclical
  C. structural and cyclical
  D. structural and frictional

6. Potential GDP is the value of real GDP when _____.

  A. the unemployment rate equals the natural unemployment rate
  B. there is no frictional unemployment
  C. there is no structural unemployment
  D. the unemployment rate is zero

7. When the unemployment rate_____ the natural unemployment rate, real GDP is _____ potential GDP and the output gap is _____.

  A. exceeds; below; negative
  B. is below; below; negative
  C. exceeds; above; positive
  D. is below; above; negative

Which movie *really* was
the biggest box office hit?

The CPI and the Cost of Living

23

When you have completed your study of this chapter, you will be able to

1 Explain what the Consumer Price Index (CPI) is and how it is calculated.

2 Explain the limitations of the CPI and describe other measures of the price level.

3 Adjust money values for inflation and calculate real wage rates and real interest rates.

MyEconLab Big Picture Video

MyEconLab Concept Video

Consumer Price Index
A measure of the average of the prices paid by urban consumers for a fixed market basket of consumption goods and services.

Reference base period
A period for which the CPI is defined to equal 100. Currently, the reference base period is 1982–1984.

23.1   THE CONSUMER PRICE INDEX

To see which movie was the biggest box office hit, we need a way of comparing prices in different periods. That's what the Consumer Price Index or CPI enables us to do. The **Consumer Price Index** is a measure of the average of the prices paid by urban consumers for a fixed market basket of consumption goods and services. The Bureau of Labor Statistics (BLS) calculates the CPI every month, and we can use these numbers to compare what the fixed market basket costs this month with what it cost in some previous month or other period.

■ Reading the CPI Numbers

The CPI is defined to equal 100 for a period called the **reference base period**. Currently, the reference base period is 1982–1984. That is, the CPI equals 100 on the average over the 36 months from January 1982 through December 1984.

In May 2016, the CPI was 240.2. This number tells us that the average of the prices paid by urban consumers for a fixed market basket of consumption goods and services was 140.2 percent higher in May 2016 than it was on the average during 1982–1984.

In April 2016, the CPI was 239.3. Comparing the CPI in May 2016 with the CPI in April 2016 tells us that the average of the prices paid by urban consumers for a fixed market basket of consumption goods and services *increased* by 0.9 percentage points in May 2016.

■ Constructing the CPI

Constructing the CPI is a huge operation that costs millions of dollars and involves three stages:

- Selecting the CPI market basket
- Conducting the monthly price survey
- Calculating the CPI

■ The CPI Market Basket

The first stage in constructing the CPI is to determine the *CPI market basket*. This "basket" contains the goods and services represented in the index and the relative importance, or weight, attached to each of them. The idea is to make the weight of the items in the CPI basket the same as in the budget of an average urban household. For example, if the average household spends 2 percent of its income on public transportation, then the CPI places a weight of 2 percent on the prices of bus, subway, and other transit system rides.

Although the CPI is calculated every month, the CPI market basket isn't updated every month. The information used to determine the CPI market basket comes from a survey, called the *Consumer Expenditure Survey*, that discovers what people actually buy. This survey is an ongoing activity, and the CPI market basket is being refreshed with increasing frequency. An astonishing 88,000 individuals and families contribute information.

The reference base period for the CPI has been fixed at 1982–1984 for more than 20 years and doesn't change when a new Consumer Expenditure Survey is used to update the market basket.

Figure 23.1 shows the CPI market basket in May 2016. The basket contains around 80,000 goods and services arranged in the eight large groups shown in the figure. The most important item in a household's budget is housing, which accounts for 42.1 percent of total expenditure. Transportation comes next at 15.4 percent. Third in relative importance is food and beverages at 14.8 percent. These three groups account for almost three quarters of the average household budget. Medical care takes 8.4 percent, education and communication takes 7.1 percent, recreation takes 5.8 percent, and apparel (clothing and footwear) takes 3.2 percent. Another 3.2 percent is spent on other goods and services.

The BLS breaks down each of these categories into smaller ones. For example, education and communication breaks down into textbooks and supplies, tuition, telephone services, and personal computer services.

As you look at these numbers, remember that they apply to the average household. Each individual household is spread around the average. Think about your own expenditure and compare it with the average.

■ The Monthly Price Survey

Each month, BLS employees check the prices of the 80,000 goods and services in the CPI market basket in 30 metropolitan areas. Because the CPI aims to measure price changes, it is important that the prices recorded each month refer to exactly the same items. For example, suppose the price of a box of jelly beans has increased but a box now contains more beans. Has the price of a jelly bean increased? The BLS employee must record the details of changes in quality, size, weight, or packaging so that price changes can be isolated from other changes.

Once the raw price data are in hand, the next task is to calculate the CPI.

■ **FIGURE 23.1**

The CPI Market Basket

MyEconLab Animation

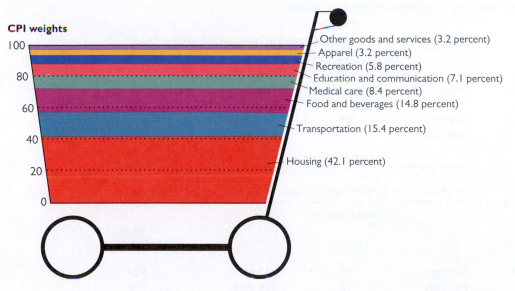

This shopping cart is filled with the items that an average urban household buys. Housing (42.1 percent), transportation (15.4 percent), and food and beverages (14.8 percent) take almost three quarters of household income.

SOURCE OF DATA: Bureau of Labor Statistics.

■ Calculating the CPI

The CPI calculation has three steps:

- Find the cost of the CPI market basket at reference base period prices.
- Find the cost of the CPI market basket at current period prices.
- Calculate the CPI for the reference base period and the current period.

We'll work through these three steps for a simple example. Suppose the CPI market basket contains only two goods and services: oranges and haircuts. We'll construct an annual CPI rather than a monthly CPI with the reference base period 2010 and the current period 2016.

Table 23.1 shows the quantities in the CPI market basket and the prices in the base period and the current period. Part (a) contains the data for the base period. In that period, consumers bought 10 oranges at $1 each and 5 haircuts at $8 each. To find the cost of the CPI market basket in the base period prices, multiply the quantities in the CPI market basket by the base period prices. The cost of oranges is $10 (10 at $1 each), and the cost of haircuts is $40 (5 at $8 each). So total expenditure in the base period on the CPI market basket is $50 ($10 + $40).

Part (b) contains the price data for the current period. The price of an orange increased from $1 to $2, which is a 100 percent increase ($1 ÷ $1 × 100 = 100 percent). The price of a haircut increased from $8 to $10, which is a 25 percent increase ($2 ÷ $8 × 100 = 25 percent).

The CPI provides a way of averaging these price increases by comparing the cost of the basket rather than the price of each item. To find the cost of the CPI market basket in the current period, 2016, multiply the quantities in the basket by their 2016 prices. The cost of oranges is $20 (10 at $2 each), and the cost of haircuts is $50 (5 at $10 each). So total expenditure on the fixed CPI market basket at current period prices is $70 ($20 + $50).

■ **TABLE 23.1**

The Consumer Price Index: A Simplified CPI Calculation

(a) The cost of the CPI market basket at base period prices: 2010

Item	CPI market basket Quantity	Price	Cost of CPI basket
Oranges	10	$1 each	$10
Haircuts	5	$8 each	$40
		Cost of CPI market basket at base period prices	$50

(b) The cost of the CPI market basket at current period prices: 2016

Item	CPI market basket Quantity	Price	Cost of CPI basket
Oranges	10	$2 each	$20
Haircuts	5	$10 each	$50
		Cost of CPI market basket at current period prices	$70

You've now taken the first two steps toward calculating the CPI. The third step uses the numbers you've just calculated to find the CPI for 2010 and 2016. The formula for the CPI is

$$CPI = \frac{\text{Cost of CPI basket at current period prices}}{\text{Cost of CPI basket at base period prices}} \times 100.$$

In Table 23.1, you established that the cost of the CPI market basket was $50 in 2010 and $70 in 2016. If we use these numbers in the CPI formula, we can find the CPI for 2010 and 2016. The base period is 2010, so

$$CPI \text{ in } 2010 = \frac{\$50}{\$50} \times 100 = 100.$$

$$CPI \text{ in } 2016 = \frac{\$70}{\$50} \times 100 = 140.$$

The principles that you've applied in this simplified CPI calculation apply to the more complex calculations performed every month by the BLS.

◼ Measuring Inflation and Deflation

The CPI is a measure of the **price level**, an average of the *level* of prices during a given period. The **inflation rate** is a measure of the percentage *change* in the price level from one period to the next. To calculate the annual inflation rate using the CPI measure of the price level, we use the formula

$$\text{Inflation rate} = \frac{(\text{CPI in current year} - \text{CPI in previous year})}{\text{CPI in previous year}} \times 100.$$

Suppose that the current year is 2016 and the CPI for 2016 was 140. And suppose that in the previous year, 2015, the CPI was 120. Then in 2016,

$$\text{Inflation rate} = \frac{(140 - 120)}{120} \times 100 = 16.7 \text{ percent.}$$

If the inflation rate is *negative*, the CPI is *falling* and we have **deflation**. The United States has rarely experienced deflation, but 2009 was one of those rare years. You can check the latest data by visiting the BLS Web site. In July 2009, the CPI was 215.4, and in July 2008, it was 220.0. So during the year to July 2009,

$$\text{Inflation rate} = \frac{(215.4 - 220.0)}{220.0} \times 100 = -2.1 \text{ percent.}$$

Price level
An average of the *level* of prices during a given period.

Inflation rate
The percentage *change* in the price level from one period to the next.

Deflation
A situation in which the CPI is *falling* and the inflation rate is *negative*.

◼ The Price Level, Inflation, and Deflation in the United States

Figure 23.2(a) on p. 594 shows the U.S. price level measured by the CPI between 1976 and 2016. The price level increased every year during this period until 2009 when it fell slightly. During the late 1970s and in 1980, the price level was increasing rapidly, but since the early 1980s, the rate of increase has slowed.

Figure 23.2(b) shows the U.S. inflation rate. When the price level rises rapidly, the inflation rate is high; when the price level rises slowly, the inflation rate is low; and when the price level is falling, the inflation rate is negative.

EYE on the PAST

700 Years of Inflation and Deflation

These extraordinary data show that inflation became a persistent problem only after 1900. During the preceding 600 years, inflation was almost unknown. Inflation increased slightly during the sixteenth century after Europeans discovered gold in America. But this inflation barely reached 2 percent a year—less than we have today—and eventually subsided. The Industrial Revolution saw a temporary burst of inflation followed by a period of deflation.

SOURCES OF DATA: E.H. Phelps Brown and Sheila V. Hopkins, *Economica*, 1955, and Robert Sahr, http://oregonstate.edu/dept/pol_sci/fac/sahr/sahr.htm.

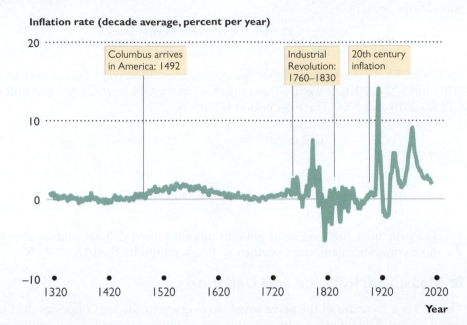

Inflation rate (decade average, percent per year)

Columbus arrives in America: 1492

Industrial Revolution: 1760–1830

20th century inflation

MyEconLab Real-time data

FIGURE 23.2

The CPI and the Inflation Rate: 1976–2016

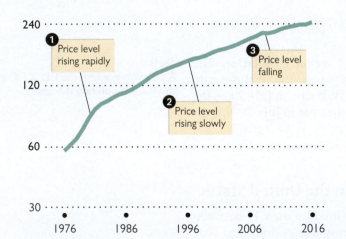

CPI (1982–1984 = 100; ratio scale)

❶ Price level rising rapidly

❷ Price level rising slowly

❸ Price level falling

(a) CPI: 1976–2016

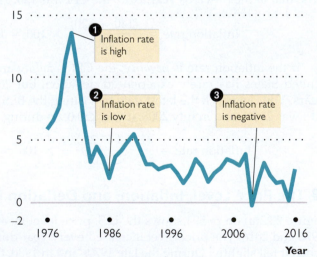

Inflation rate (percent per year)

❶ Inflation rate is high

❷ Inflation rate is low

❸ Inflation rate is negative

(b) CPI inflation rate: 1976–2016

SOURCE OF DATA: Bureau of Labor Statistics.

❶ The price level in part (a) was rising rapidly during the 1970s and 1980s and the inflation rate in part (b) was high.

❷ The price level was rising slowly during the 1990s and 2000s and the inflation rate was low.

❸ In 2009, the price level fell and the inflation rate was negative.

594

CHECKPOINT 23.1

MyEconLab Study Plan 23.1
Key Terms Quiz
Solutions Video

Explain what the Consumer Price Index (CPI) is and how it is calculated.

Practice Problems

A Consumer Expenditure Survey in Sparta shows that people buy only juice and cloth. In 2015, the year of the Consumer Expenditure Survey and also the reference base year, the average household spent $40 on juice and $25 on cloth. Table 1 sets out the prices of juice and cloth in 2015 and 2016.

1. Calculate the CPI market basket and the percentage of the average household budget spent on juice in the reference base year.

2. Calculate the CPI in 2016 and the inflation rate between 2015 and 2016.

3. Table 2 shows the CPI in Sparta. Calculate the inflation rates in 2015 and 2016. Did the CPI rise in 2016? Did the inflation rate increase in 2016?

TABLE 1 PRICES

	2015	2016
Juice	$4 a bottle	$4 a bottle
Cloth	$5 a yard	$6 a yard

In the News

U.S. Consumer Price Index down 0.1 percent
The U.S. CPI fell 0.1 percent in December 2015. The price of gasoline fell by 3.9 percent. Rents increased 0.2 percent, and medical care costs increased 0.1 percent.
Source: CNBC, Wednesday, January 20, 2016

Did the United States experience inflation or deflation in December 2015? Which of the items mentioned in the news clip has the highest weight in the CPI and which has the lowest weight?

TABLE 2

Year	CPI
2014	200
2015	219
2016	237

Solutions to Practice Problems

1. The CPI market basket is the quantities bought during the Consumer Expenditure Survey year, 2015. The average household spent $40 on juice at $4 a bottle, so it bought 10 bottles of juice. The average household spent $25 on cloth at $5 a yard, so it bought 5 yards of cloth. The CPI market basket is made up of 10 bottles of juice and 5 yards of cloth.
   In the reference base year, the average household spent $40 on juice and $25 on cloth, so the household budget was $65. Expenditure on juice was 61.5 percent of the household budget: ($40 ÷ $65) × 100 = 61.5 percent.

2. To calculate the CPI in 2016, find the cost of the CPI market basket in 2015 and 2016. In 2015, the CPI basket costs $65 ($40 for juice + $25 for cloth). In 2016, the CPI market basket costs $70 (10 bottles of juice at $4 a bottle + 5 yards of cloth at $6 a yard). The CPI in 2016 is ($70 ÷ $65) × 100 = 107.7. The inflation rate is [(107.7 − 100) ÷ 100] × 100 = 7.7 percent.

3. The inflation rate in 2015 is [(219 − 200) ÷ 200] × 100 = 9.5 percent. The inflation rate in 2016 is [(237 − 219) ÷ 219] × 100 = 8.2 percent. In 2016, the CPI increased, but the inflation rate decreased.

Solution to In the News

Deflation occurs when the CPI falls. The CPI fell by 0.1 percent in December 2015 so the United States experienced deflation. The weight in the CPI is highest on rents, which are part of housing (42.1 percent of CPI market basket). The weight on gasoline is part of transportation, the second largest category in the CPI market basket (15.4 percent). The smallest weight is on medical care (8.4 percent).

MyEconLab Concept Video

Cost of living index
A measure of the change in the amount of money that people need to spend to achieve a given standard of living.

23.2 THE CPI AND OTHER PRICE LEVEL MEASURES

The CPI is one of several alternative *price level* measures. Its purpose is to measure the cost of living or what amounts to the same thing, the *value of money*. The CPI is sometimes called a **cost of living index** —a measure of the change in the amount of money that people need to spend to achieve a given standard of living. The CPI is not a perfect measure of the cost of living (value of money) for two broad reasons.

First, the CPI does not try to measure all the changes in the cost of living. For example, the cost of living rises in a severe winter as people buy more natural gas and electricity to heat their homes. A rise in the prices of these items increases the CPI. But the increased quantities of natural gas and electricity bought don't change the CPI because the CPI market basket is fixed. So part of this increase in spending—the increase in the cost of maintaining a given standard of living—doesn't show up as an increase in the CPI.

Second, even those components of the cost of living that are measured by the CPI are not always measured accurately. The result is that the CPI is possibly a biased measure of changes in the cost of living.

Let's look at some of the sources of bias in the CPI and the ways the BLS tries to overcome them.

■ Sources of Bias in the CPI

The potential sources of bias in the CPI are

- New goods bias
- Quality change bias
- Commodity substitution bias
- Outlet substitution bias

New Goods Bias

Every year, some new goods become available and some old goods disappear. Make a short list of items that you take for granted today that were not available 10 or 20 years ago. This list includes smartphones; tablet computers; and flat-panel, large-screen television sets. A list of items no longer available or rarely bought includes audiocassette players, vinyl records, photographic film, and typewriters.

When we want to compare the cost of living in 2016 with that in 2006, 1996, or 1986, we must do so by comparing the prices of different baskets of goods. We can't compare the same baskets because today's basket wasn't available 10 years ago and the basket of 10 years ago isn't available today.

To make comparisons, the BLS tries to measure the price of the service performed by yesterday's goods and today's goods. It tries to compare, for example, the price of listening to recorded music, regardless of the technology that delivers that service. But the comparison is hard to make. Today's smartphone delivers an improved quality of sound and level of convenience compared to yesterday's Walkman and Discman.

How much of a new product represents an increase in quantity and quality and how much represents a higher price? The BLS does its best to answer this question, but there is no sure way of making the necessary adjustment. It is believed that the arrival of new goods puts an upward bias into the CPI and its measure of the inflation rate.

To measure the CPI, the BLS must compare the price of today's smartphone with that of the 1970s Walkman and 1980s Discman.

Quality Change Bias

Cars, smartphones, laptops, and many other items get better every year. For example, central locking, airbags, and antilock braking systems all add to the quality of a car. But they also add to the cost. Is the improvement in quality greater than the increase in cost? Or do car prices rise by more than can be accounted for by quality improvements? To the extent that a price rise is a payment for improved quality, it is not inflation. Again, the BLS does the best job it can to estimate the effects of quality improvements on price changes. But the CPI probably counts too much of any price rise as inflation and so overstates inflation.

To compare the price of today's cars with those of earlier years, the BLS must value the improvements in features and quality.

Commodity Substitution Bias

Changes in relative prices lead consumers to change the items they buy. People cut back on items that become relatively more costly and increase their consumption of items that become relatively less costly. For example, suppose the price of carrots rises while the price of broccoli remains constant. Now that carrots are more costly relative to broccoli, you might decide to buy more broccoli and fewer carrots. Suppose that you switch from carrots to broccoli, spend the same amount on vegetables as before, and get the same enjoyment as before. Your cost of vegetables has not changed. The CPI says that the price of vegetables has increased because it ignores your substitution between goods in the CPI market basket.

When consumers substitute lower priced broccoli for higher priced carrots, the CPI overstates the rise in the price of vegetables.

Outlet Substitution Bias

When confronted with higher prices, people use discount stores more frequently and convenience stores less frequently. This phenomenon is called *outlet substitution*. Suppose, for example, that gas prices rise by 10¢ a gallon. Instead of buying from your nearby gas station for $4.599 a gallon, you now drive farther to a gas station that charges $4.499 a gallon. Your cost of gas has increased because you must factor in the cost of your time and the gas that you use driving several blocks down the road. But your cost has not increased by as much as the 10¢ a gallon increase in the pump price. However, the CPI says that the price of gas has increased by 10¢ a gallon because the CPI does not measure outlet substitution.

The growth of online shopping in recent years has provided an alternative to discount stores that makes outlet substitution even easier and potentially makes this source of bias more serious.

As consumers shop around for the lowest prices, outlet substitution occurs and the CPI overstates the rise in prices actually paid.

■ The Magnitude of the Bias

You have reviewed the sources of bias in the CPI. But how big is the bias? When this question was tackled in 1996 by a Congressional Advisory Commission chaired by Michael Boskin, an economics professor at Stanford University, the answer was that the CPI overstated inflation by 1.1 percentage points a year. That is, if the CPI reports that inflation is 3.1 percent a year, most likely inflation is actually 2 percent a year.

In the period since the Boskin Commission reported, the BLS has taken steps to reduce the CPI bias. The more frequent Consumer Expenditure Survey that we described earlier in this chapter is one of these steps. Beyond that, the BLS uses ever more sophisticated models and methods to try to eliminate the sources of bias and make the CPI as accurate as possible.

■ Two Consequences of the CPI Bias

A bias in the CPI has two main undesirable consequences: It leads to

- Distortion of private contracts
- Increases in government outlays and decreases in taxes

Distortion of Private Contracts

Suppose the United Automobile Workers union (UAW) and Ford Motor Company agree to a three-year wage deal to pay $30 an hour in the first year with increases equal to the percentage change in the CPI in the following years. If the CPI increases by 5 percent each year, the wage rate will increase to $31.50 in the second year and $33.08 in the third year.

Now suppose that the CPI is biased and the true increase in the cost of living is 3 percent a year. In the second year, $30.90 rather than $31.50, and in the third year, $31.83, not $33.08, compensates workers for the higher cost of living. So in the second year, the workers gain 60¢ an hour, or $21 for a 35-hour workweek. And in the third year, they gain $1.25 an hour, or $43.75 for a 35-hour workweek.

The workers' gain is Ford's loss. With a work force of a few thousand, the loss amounts to several thousand dollars a week and a few million dollars over the life of a 3-year wage contract.

Increases in Government Outlays and Decreases in Taxes

The CPI is used to adjust the incomes of the 54 million Social Security beneficiaries, 47 million food stamp recipients, and 4 million retired former military personnel and federal civil servants (and their surviving spouses), and the budget for 3 million school lunches. Close to a third of federal government outlays are linked directly to the CPI. A bias in the CPI would increase all of these expenditures by more than required to compensate for the fall in the buying power of the dollar. Even a 1 percent bias would accumulate over a decade to almost a trillion dollars.

The CPI is also used to adjust the income levels at which higher tax rates apply. The tax rates on large incomes are higher than those on small incomes so, as incomes rise, if these adjustments were not made, the burden of taxes would rise relentlessly. To the extent that the CPI is biased upward, the tax adjustments over-compensate for rising prices and decrease the amount paid in taxes.

■ Alternative Consumer Price Indexes

Three alternative measures of the price level that we'll describe here aim to improve on the CPI. These measures are the

- Chained Consumer Price Index (C-CPI)
- Personal Consumption Expenditures Price Index (PCEPI)
- PCEPI Excluding Food and Energy

Chained Consumer Price Index (C-CPI)

Chained Consumer Price Index
A measure of the price level calculated using current month and previous month prices and expenditures.

The **Chained Consumer Price Index (C-CPI)** is measure of the price level calculated using current month and previous month prices and expenditures. It is called a "chained" CPI because the inflation rate calculated for the current month is linked back, like the links in a chain, to a reference base month. (See pp. 563–565 for a description of chain linking). Because it uses current period expenditures that are updated every month, the C-CPI avoids the bias in the CPI. It takes account of new goods, quality change, and substitution effects. The only weakness of the C-CPI is that it gets revised several times as the data on recent expenditures get revised.

Personal Consumption Expenditures Price Index (PCEPI)

The **Personal Consumption Expenditures Price Index (PCEPI)** is an average of the current prices of the goods and services included in the consumption expenditure component of GDP expressed as a percentage of base year prices. The PCEPI uses current quantities so, like the C-CPI, it avoids the sources of bias in the CPI.

PCEPI Excluding Food and Energy

Food and energy prices fluctuate much more than other prices and their changes can obscure the underlying trend in the price level. By excluding these highly variable items, the underlying price level and inflation rate can be seen more clearly. The percentage change in the PCEPI excluding food and energy is called the **core inflation rate**.

Figure 23.3 shows the three alternative measures of the price level alongside the CPI since 2000. The two measures that use current period expenditures, the C-CPI and the PCEPI, are similar. They imply that the price level in 2015 was 132 percent higher than in 2000, which represents an annual inflation rate of 1.9 percent. The CPI rises above these two measures at an average annual inflation rate of 2.2 percent, which is an upward bias of 0.3 percentage points. The PCEPI excluding food and energy, the index used to calculate the core inflation rate, rises more slowly than the other measures. It is biased downward because, on average, food and energy prices rise faster than other prices. *Eye on the U.S. Economy* (on p. 600) looks at another way of identifying the underlying inflation rate.

PCEPI

An average of the current prices of the goods and services included in the consumption expenditure component of GDP expressed as a percentage of base year prices.

Core inflation rate

The annual percentage change in the PCEPI excluding the prices of food and energy.

■ **FIGURE 23.3**

Four Measures of Consumer Prices   MyEconLab Real-time data

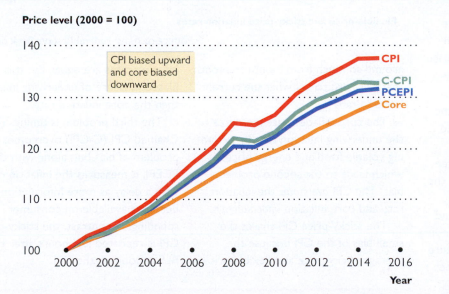

These four measures of the *price level* rise together.

The Chained Consumer Price Index, C-CPI, and the Personal Consumption Expenditures Price Index, PCEPI, provide the most accurate measure of the price level and inflation rate.

The CPI rises fastest reflecting its upward bias and the PCEPI excluding food and energy, the core inflation measure, rises the slowest reflecting its downward bias.

Sources of data: Bureau of Labor Statistics and Bureau of Economic Analysis.

EYE on the U.S. ECONOMY
Measuring and Forecasting Inflation: The Sticky-Price CPI

The *sticky-price CPI* is a price index constructed from the items in the CPI whose prices change infrequently—whose prices are "sticky." These items contrast with the ones whose prices change frequently—whose prices are "flexible."

The table provides some examples. Among the 30 percent of the items in the CPI with flexible prices, the price of motor fuel changes most frequently—on average every 3 weeks. At the other extreme, among the 70 percent of items with sticky prices, the price of medical care services changes least frequently. It remains fixed for more than one year.

The figure shows the CPI inflation rate broken into its sticky-price and flexible-price components. The sticky prices respond to expectations about future market conditions and have small fluctuations. The flexible prices respond to current market conditions and fluctuate a lot.

The sticky-price inflation rate provides information about how expectations of future inflation are changing. Over the five years from 2011 to 2016, when the flexible-price inflation rate was falling, the sticky-price rate was rising. And in 2016, when flexible prices were *falling*, the sticky-price inflation rate exceeded 2 percent per year.

The sticky-price CPI solves three problems with other measures of the price level and inflation rate.

The first problem is volatility and the challenge of probing the underlying inflation rate and predicting its future level. The CPI inflation rate bounces

Examples of Flexible-Price and Sticky-Price Items

Flexible-price items (30 percent of total)	Frequency of adjustment (weeks)	Sticky-price items (70 percent of total)	Frequency of adjustment (weeks)
Motor fuel	3	Recreation	34
Meats, poultry, fish, and eggs	8	Communication	36
New vehicles	9	Public transportation	41
Used cars and trucks	9	Rent of primary residence	48
Women's and girls' apparel	10	Education	48
Cereals and bakery products	14	Medical care services	61

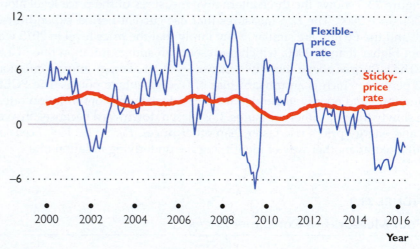

Flexible-price and sticky-price inflation rates

SOURCE OF DATA: Federal Reserve Bank of Atlanta.

around so much from month to month that it is hard to say what the current inflation rate is.

The core inflation rate measures the underlying inflation rate by excluding volatile food and energy prices, which leads to the second problem, bias. The CPI *overstates* the inflation rate and core inflation *understates* it.

The sticky-price CPI shares the small bias of the CPI because the average sticky-price and flexible-price

inflation rates are equal. But it is a less biased measure of underlying inflation than the core inflation rate.

The third problem is timing. The Chained CPI (C-CPI) overcomes the problem of bias but, along with the PCEPI, it measures the inflation rate with a delay as more information becomes available on consumer spending. In contrast, the sticky-price CPI is reported just hours after the BLS announces the CPI.

CHECKPOINT 23.2

MyEconLab Study Plan 23.2
Key Terms Quiz
Solutions Video

Explain the limitations of the CPI and describe other measures of the price level.

Practice Problems

Economists in the Statistics Bureau decide to check the CPI substitution bias. To do so, they conduct a Consumer Expenditure Survey in both 2015 and 2016. Table 1 shows the results of the survey. It shows the items that consumers buy and their prices. The Statistics Bureau fixes the reference base year as 2015.

1. Calculate the CPI in 2016 if the CPI basket contains the 2015 quantities.
2. Calculate the CPI in 2016 if the CPI basket contains the 2016 quantities.
3. Is there any substitution bias in the CPI that uses the 2015 basket? Explain.

TABLE 1

	2015		2016	
Item	Quantity	Price	Quantity	Price
Broccoli	10	$3.00	15	$3.00
Carrots	15	$2.00	10	$4.00

In the News

News releases
In 2015, the CPI increased by 0.7 percent, the C-CPI increased by 0.3 percent, and the PCEPI increased by 0.4 percent.

Sources: Bureau of Economic Analysis and
Bureau of Labor Statistics, February, 2016

Why do these three measures of the price level give different inflation rates?

Solutions to Practice Problems

1. Table 2 shows the calculation of the CPI in 2016 when the CPI basket is made of the 2015 quantities. The cost of the 2015 basket at 2015 prices is $60 and the cost of the 2015 basket at 2016 prices is $90. So the CPI in 2016 using the 2015 basket is ($90 ÷ $60) × 100 = 150.

2. Table 3 shows the calculation of the CPI in 2016 when the CPI basket is made of the 2016 quantities. The cost of the 2016 basket at 2015 prices is $65, and the cost of the 2016 basket at 2016 prices is $85. So the CPI in 2016 using the 2016 basket is ($85 ÷ $65) × 100 = 131.

3. The CPI that uses the 2015 basket displays some bias. With the price of broccoli constant and the price of carrots rising, consumers buy fewer carrots and more broccoli and they spend $85 on vegetables. But they would have spent $90 if they had not substituted broccoli for some carrots. The price of vegetables does not rise by 50 percent as shown by the CPI. Because of substitution, the price of vegetables rises by only 42 percent ($85 is 42 percent greater than $60). Using the 2016 basket, the price of vegetables rises by only 31 percent ($85 compared with $65). A CPI substitution bias exists.

TABLE 2

Item	2015 basket at 2015 prices	2015 basket at 2016 prices
Broccoli	$30	$30
Carrots	$30	$60
Total	$60	$90

TABLE 3

Item	2016 basket at 2015 prices	2016 basket at 2016 prices
Broccoli	$45	$45
Carrots	$20	$40
Total	$65	$85

Solution to In the News

These three measures of the price level are based on the prices of different baskets of goods and services. The CPI basket contains only the goods and services that urban consumers buy in the year of the most recent consumer expenditure survey. The basket of the C-CPI contains the goods and services that urban consumers buy in the two most recent years. The basket of the PCEPI contains the goods and services in GDP that households buy in the two most recent years.

Which postage stamp has the higher real price: the 2¢ stamp of 1916 or today's 47¢ stamp?

23.3 NOMINAL AND REAL VALUES

In 2016, it cost 47 cents to mail a first-class letter. One hundred years earlier, in 1916, that same letter would have cost 2 cents to mail. Does it *really* cost you 23.5 times the amount that it cost your great-great-grandmother to mail a letter?

You know that it does not. You know that a dollar today buys less than what a dollar bought in 1916, so the cost of a stamp has not really increased to 23.5 times its 1916 level. But has it increased at all? Did it really cost you any more to mail a letter in 2016 than it cost your great-great-grandmother in 1916?

The CPI can be used to answer questions like these. In fact, that is one of the main reasons for constructing a price index. Let's see how we can compare the price of a stamp in 1916 and the price of a stamp in 2016.

■ Dollars and Cents at Different Dates

To compare dollar amounts at different dates, we need to know the CPI at those dates. Currently, the CPI equals 100 for reference base period 1982–1984. That is, the average of the CPI in 1982, 1983, and 1984 is 100. (The numbers for the three years are 96.4, 99.6, and 103.9, respectively. Calculate the average of these numbers and check that it is indeed 100.)

In 2016, the CPI was 240.2, and in 1916, it was 10.9. By using these two numbers, we can calculate the relative value of the dollar in 1916 and 2016. To do so, we divide the 2016 CPI by the 1916 CPI. That ratio is 240.2 divided by 10.9, or 22. That is, prices on average were 22 times higher in 2016 than in 1916.

We can use this ratio to convert the price of a 2-cent stamp in 1916 into its 2016 equivalent. The formula for this calculation is

$$\text{Price of stamp in 2016 dollars} = \text{Price of stamp in 1916 dollars} \times \frac{\text{CPI in 2016}}{\text{CPI in 1916}}$$

$$= 2 \text{ cents} \times \frac{240.2}{10.9} = 44 \text{ cents}.$$

So your great-great-grandmother did pay less than you pay! It really cost her 3 cents less to mail that first-class letter than it cost you in 2016. She paid the equivalent of 44 cents in 2016 money, and you paid 47 cents.

We've just converted the 1916 price of a stamp to its 2016 equivalent. We can do a similar calculation the other way around—converting the 2016 price to its 1916 equivalent. The formula for this alternative calculation is

$$\text{Price of stamp in 1916 dollars} = \text{Price of stamp in 2016 dollars} \times \frac{\text{CPI in 1916}}{\text{CPI in 2016}}$$

$$= 47 \text{ cents} \times \frac{10.9}{240.2} = 2.13 \text{ cents}.$$

The interpretation of this number is that you pay the *equivalent* of 2.13 cents in 1916 dollars. Your *real* price of a stamp is 2.13 cents expressed in 1916 dollars.

The calculations that we've just done are examples of converting a *nominal* value into a *real* value. A nominal value is one that is expressed in current dollars. A real value is one that is expressed in the dollars of a given year. We're now going to see how we convert other nominal macroeconomic variables into real variables using a similar method.

■ Nominal and Real Values in Macroeconomics

Macroeconomics makes a big issue of the distinction between the nominal value and the real value of a variable. Three nominal and real variables occupy a central position in macroeconomics. They are

- Nominal GDP and real GDP
- The nominal wage rate and the real wage rate
- The nominal interest rate and the real interest rate

We begin our examination of real and nominal variables in macroeconomics by reviewing what you've already learned about the distinction between nominal GDP and real GDP and interpreting that distinction in a new way.

■ Nominal GDP and Real GDP

When we calculated real GDP in 2016 in terms of 2009 dollars in Chapter 21 (pp. 548–549), we expressed the values of the goods and services produced in 2016 in terms of the prices that prevailed in 2009. We calculated real GDP directly. We didn't multiply nominal GDP in 2016 by the ratio of a price index in the two years.

But we can *interpret* real GDP in 2016 as nominal GDP in 2016 multiplied by the ratio of a price index in 2009 to its value in 2016. The price index that we would use is the **GDP price index**, which is an average of the current prices of all the goods and services included in GDP expressed as a percentage of the base year prices.

The GDP price index in 2009 (the base year) is defined to be 100, so we can interpret real GDP in any year as nominal GDP divided by the GDP price index in

GDP price index
An average of the current prices of all the goods and services included in GDP expressed as a percentage of base year prices.

EYE on the U.S. ECONOMY
Deflating the GDP Balloon

Nominal GDP increased every year between 1980 and 2016 except for 2009. Part of the increase reflects increased production, and part of it reflects rising prices.

You can think of GDP as a balloon that is blown up by growing production and rising prices. In the figure, the GDP price index or *GDP deflator* lets the inflation air—the contribution of rising prices—out of the nominal GDP balloon so that we can see what has happened to real GDP.

The small red balloon for 1980 shows real GDP in that year. The green balloon shows nominal GDP in 2016, and the red balloon for 2016 shows real GDP for that year.

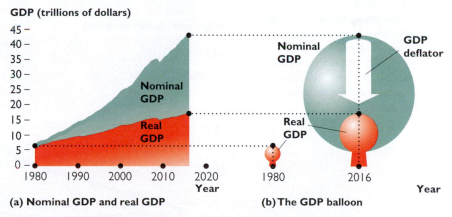

(a) Nominal GDP and real GDP

(b) The GDP balloon

SOURCE OF DATA: Bureau of Economic Analysis.

To see real GDP in 2016, we use the GDP price index to deflate nominal GDP. With the inflation air removed, we can see by how much real GDP grew from 1980 to 2016.

that year multiplied by 100. We don't calculate real GDP this way, but we can interpret it this way.

The GDP price index, or the CPI, or another price index might be used to convert a nominal variable to a real variable.

■ Nominal Wage Rate and Real Wage Rate

Nominal wage rate
The average hourly wage rate measured in current dollars.

Real wage rate
The average hourly wage rate measured in the dollars of a given reference base year.

The price of labor services is the wage rate—the income that an hour of labor earns. In macroeconomics, we are interested in economy-wide performance, so we focus on the *average* hourly wage rate. The **nominal wage rate** is the average hourly wage rate measured in *current* dollars. The **real wage rate** is the average hourly wage rate measured in the dollars of a given reference base year.

To calculate the real wage rate relevant to a consumer, we divide the nominal wage rate by the CPI and multiply by 100. That is,

$$\text{Real wage rate in 2015} = \frac{\text{Nominal wage rate in 2015}}{\text{CPI in 2015}} \times 100.$$

In 2015, the nominal wage rate (average hourly wage rate) of production workers was \$21.04 and the CPI was 237, so

$$\text{Real wage rate in 2015} = \frac{\$21.04}{237} \times 100 = \$8.88.$$

Because we measure the real wage rate in constant base period dollars, a change in the real wage rate measures the change in the quantity of goods and

■ **FIGURE 23.4**

Nominal and Real Wage Rates: 1980–2015

MyEconLab Real-time data

The nominal wage rate has increased every year since 1980. The real wage rate decreased slightly from 1985 through the mid-1990s, after which it increased slightly. Over the entire 35-year period, the real wage rate remained steady.

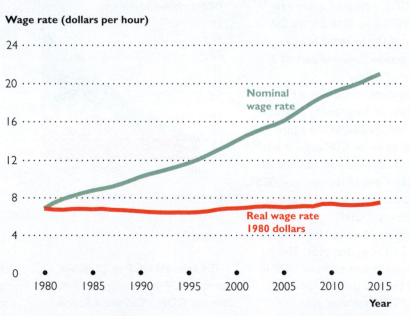

SOURCE OF DATA: Bureau of Labor Statistics.

services that an hour's work can buy. In contrast, a change in the nominal wage rate measures a combination of a change in the quantity of goods and services that an hour's work can buy and a change in the price level. So the real wage rate removes the effects of inflation from the changes in the nominal wage rate.

The real wage rate is a significant economic variable because it measures the real reward for labor services, which is a major determinant of the standard of living. The real wage rate is also significant because it measures the real cost of labor services, which influences the quantity of labor that firms are willing to hire.

Figure 23.4 shows what has happened to the nominal wage rate and the real wage rate in the United States between 1980 and 2015. The nominal wage rate is the average hourly earnings of production workers. This measure is just one of several different measures of average hourly earnings that we might have used.

The nominal wage rate increased from $6.85 an hour in 1980 to $21.04 an hour in 2015, but the real wage rate barely changed. In 1980 dollars, the real wage rate in 2015 was only $8.88 an hour.

The real wage rate barely changed as the nominal wage rate increased because the nominal wage rate grew at a rate almost equal to the inflation rate. When the effects of inflation are removed from the nominal wage rate, we can see what is happening to the buying power of the average wage rate.

You can also see that the real wage rate has fluctuated a little. It decreased slightly until the mid-1990s, after which it increased slightly.

EYE on the PAST
The Nominal and Real Wage Rates of Presidents of the United States

Who earned more, Barack Obama in 2016, or George Washington in 1788? George Washington's pay was $25,000 (on the green line), but in 2016 dollars it was $619,000 (on the red line). Barack Obama was paid $400,000 in 2016.

But presidential accommodations are more comfortable today, and presidential travel arrangements are a breeze compared to earlier times. So adding in the perks of the job, Barack Obama didn't get such a raw deal.

SOURCE OF DATA:
Robert Sahr, Oregon State University, http://oregonstate.edu/cla/polisci/sahr/sahr.

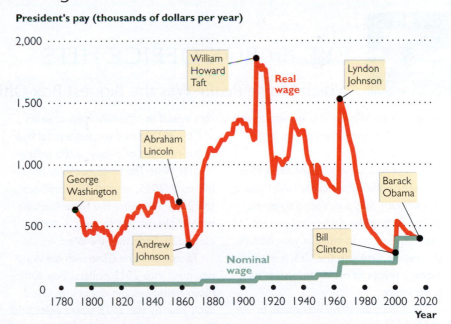

Nominal interest rate

The dollar amount of interest expressed as a percentage of the amount loaned.

Real interest rate

The goods and services forgone in interest expressed as a percentage of the amount loaned and calculated as the nominal interest rate minus the inflation rate.

■ Nominal Interest Rate and Real Interest Rate

You've just seen that we can calculate real values from nominal values by deflating them using the CPI. And you've seen that to make this calculation, we *divide* the nominal value by a price index. Converting a nominal interest rate to a real interest rate is a bit different. To see why, we'll start with their definitions.

A **nominal interest rate** is the dollar amount of interest expressed as a percentage of the amount loaned. For example, suppose that you have $1,000 in a bank deposit—a loan by you to a bank—on which you receive interest of $50 a year. The nominal interest rate is $50 as a percentage of $1,000, which is 5 percent a year.

A **real interest rate** is the goods and services forgone in interest expressed as a percentage of the amount loaned. Continuing with the above example, at the end of one year your bank deposit has increased to $1,050—the original $1,000 plus the $50 interest. Suppose that during the year prices increased by 3 percent, so now you need $1,030 to buy what $1,000 would have bought a year earlier. How much interest did you *really* receive? The answer is $20, or a real interest rate of 2 percent a year.

To convert a nominal interest rate to a real interest rate, we *subtract* the *inflation rate*. That is,

Real interest rate = Nominal interest rate − Inflation rate.

Put your numbers into this formula. Your nominal interest rate is 5 percent a year, and the inflation rate is 3 percent a year, so your real interest rate is 5 percent minus 3 percent, which equals 2 percent a year.

Figure 23.5 shows the nominal and the real interest rates in the United States between 1976 and 2016. When the inflation rate is high, the gap between the real interest rate and nominal interest rate is large. Sometimes, the real interest rate is negative (as it was during the late 1970s) and the lender pays the borrower!

EYE on BOX OFFICE HITS

MyEconLab Critical Thinking Exercise

Which Movie *Really* Was the Biggest Box Office Hit?

Gone with the Wind is the answer to the question that we posed at the beginning of this chapter.

To get this answer, Box Office Mojo (www.boxofficemojo.com) calculates the amount that a movie *really* earns by converting the dollars earned to their equivalent in current year dollars. But rather than use the CPI, it uses the average prices of movie tickets as its price index.

Gone with the Wind was made in 1939. Looking only at its performance in the United States, the movie was

rereleased in nine subsequent years and by 2015 it had earned a total box office revenue of almost $200 million.

Star Wars: The Force Awakens, released in 2015, earned $937 million. So the 2015 *Star Wars: The Force Awakens* earned almost five times the dollars earned by *Gone with the Wind*.

To convert the *Gone with the Wind* revenues into 2015 dollars, Box Office Mojo multiplies the dollars received each year by the 2015 ticket price and divides by the ticket price for the year in which the dollars were earned.

Valuing the tickets for *Gone with the Wind* at 2015 movie-ticket prices, it has earned $1,733 million, almost double *Star Wars: The Force Awakens* revenue.

Because Box Office Mojo uses average ticket prices, the real variable that it compares is the number of tickets sold. The average ticket price in 2015 was $8.43, which means 206 million have seen *Gone with the Wind* and 111 million have seen *Star Wars: The Force Awakens*. *Gone with the Wind* was the biggest hit because it was seen by the greatest number of people.

FIGURE 23.5

Nominal and Real Interest Rates: 1976–2016

MyEconLab Real-time data

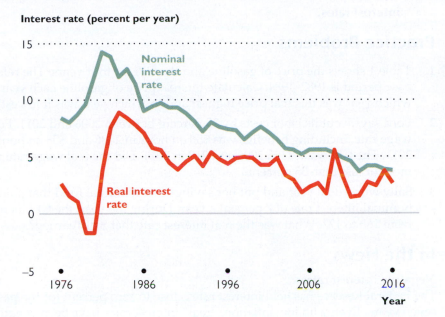

The interest rate shown here is that paid by the safest large corporations on long-term bonds (known as Moody's AAA).

The real interest rate equals the nominal interest rate minus the inflation rate, so the vertical gap between the nominal interest rate and the real interest rate is the inflation rate. The real interest rate is usually positive, but during the late 1970s, it became negative.

SOURCES OF DATA: Federal Reserve and Bureau of Labor Statistics.

EYE on YOUR LIFE
A Student's CPI

MyEconLab Critical Thinking Exercise

The CPI measures the percentage change in the average prices paid for the basket of goods and services bought by a typical urban household.

A student is not a typical household. How have the prices of a student's basket of goods and services changed? The answer is by a lot more than those of an average household.

Suppose that a student spends 25 percent of her income on rent, 25 percent on tuition, 25 percent on books and study supplies, 10 percent on food, 10 percent on transportation, and 5 percent on clothing.

We can use these weights and the data collected by the BLS on individual price categories to find the student's

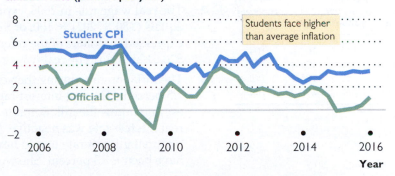

SOURCE OF DATA: Bureau of Labor Statistics.

CPI and the inflation rate that it implies.

The graph shows this student's inflation rate compared to that of the official CPI. Between 2006 and 2016,

the student's CPI rose 34 percent above the official CPI. Rent, textbooks, and tuition are the main items whose prices rose faster than average.

MyEconLab Study Plan 23.3
Key Terms Quiz
Solutions Video

CHECKPOINT 23.3

Adjust money values for inflation and calculate real wage rates and real interest rates.

Practice Problems

TABLE 1

Year	Price of gasoline (cents per gallon)	CPI
1985	112	107.6
1995	115	152.4
2005	230	195.3
2015	245	237.0

1. Table 1 shows the price of gasoline and the CPI for four years. The reference base period is 1982–1984. Calculate the real price of gasoline each year. In which year was this real price highest and in which year was it lowest?

2. Ford says it cut its labor costs by 35 percent between 2006 and 2011. Ford's wage rate, including benefits, was $80 an hour in 2006 and $58 an hour in 2011. The CPI was 202 in 2006 and 218 in 2011. Did the real wage rate fall by more or less than 35 percent?

3. Sally worked all year and put her savings into a mutual fund that paid a nominal interest rate of 7 percent a year. During the year, the CPI increased from 165 to 177. What was the real interest rate that Sally earned?

In the News

Negative interest rates

The Federal Reserve has held interest rates close to zero percent for the past seven years. Even with low inflation, "real" interest rates have been negative.
Source: *San Diego Union Tribune*, February 5, 2016

Explain why with a zero interest rate, even low inflation makes the real interest rate negative. Can the real interest rate exceed the nominal interest rate?

Solutions to Practice Problems

TABLE 2

Year	Price of gasoline (cents per gallon)	CPI	Price of gasoline (1982–1984 cents per gallon)
1985	112	107.6	104
1995	115	152.4	75
2005	230	195.3	118
2015	245	237.0	103

1. To calculate the real price, divide the nominal price by the CPI and multiply by 100. Table 2 shows the calculations. The real price was highest in 2005, when it was 118 cents (1982–1984 cents) per gallon. The real price was lowest in 1995, when it was 75 cents (1982–1984 cents) per gallon.

2. The real wage rate in 2006, expressed in dollars of the reference base year, equals ($80 ÷ 202) × 100, or $39.60 an hour. The real wage rate in 2011, expressed in dollars of the reference base year, equals ($58 ÷ 218) × 100, or $26.61 an hour. The real wage rate of these workers fell by 32.8 percent.

3. The inflation rate during the year equals [(177 − 165) ÷ 165] × 100, which is 7.3 percent. The real interest rate that Sally earned equals the nominal interest rate minus the inflation rate, which is 7.0 − 7.3, or −0.3 percent. Sally's real interest rate was negative. (If Sally had kept her savings in cash, her nominal interest rate would have been zero, and her real interest rate would have been −7.3 percent. She would have been worse off.)

Solution to In the News

The real interest rate equals the nominal interest rate minus the inflation rate. So if the nominal interest rate equals zero, the real interest rate equals the negative of the inflation rate. If the inflation rate is 1 percent, the real interest rate is *minus* 1 percent, a negative number. The real interest rate exceeds the nominal interest rate if the inflation rate is negative (if there is deflation).

CHAPTER SUMMARY

Key Points

1. Explain what the Consumer Price Index (CPI) is and how it is calculated.

- The Consumer Price Index (CPI) is a measure of the average of the prices of the goods and services that an average urban household buys.
- The CPI is calculated by dividing the cost of the CPI market basket in the current period by its cost in the base period and then multiplying by 100.

2. Explain the limitations of the CPI and describe other measures of the price level.

- The CPI does not include all the items that contribute to the cost of living.
- The CPI cannot provide an accurate measure of price changes because of new goods, quality improvements, and substitutions that consumers make when relative prices change.
- Other measures of the price level include the Chained Consumer Price Index (C-CPI), the Personal Consumption Expenditures Price Index (PCEPI), and the PCEPI Excluding Food and Energy.
- Both the C-CPI and the PCEPI use current information on quantities and to some degree overcome the sources of bias in the CPI.
- The PCEPI excluding food and energy is used to calculate the core inflation rate, which shows the inflation trend.

3. Adjust money values for inflation and calculate real wage rates and real interest rates.

- To adjust a money value (also called a nominal value) for inflation, we express the value in terms of the dollars of a given year.
- To convert a dollar value of year B to the dollars of year A, multiply the value in year B by the price level in year A and divide by the price level in year B.
- The real wage rate equals the nominal wage rate divided by the CPI and multiplied by 100.
- The real interest rate equals the nominal interest rate minus the inflation rate.

Key Terms

MyEconLab Key Terms Quiz

Chained Consumer Price Index, 598
Consumer Price Index, 590
Core inflation rate, 599
Cost of living index, 596
Deflation, 593

GDP price index, 603
Inflation rate, 593
Nominal interest rate, 606
Nominal wage rate, 604
PCEPI, 599

Price level, 593
Real interest rate, 606
Real wage rate, 604
Reference base period, 590

CHAPTER CHECKPOINT

Study Plan Problems and Applications

1. In Canada, the reference base period for the CPI is 2002. By 2014, prices had risen by 25.2 percent since the base period. The inflation rate in Canada in 2015 was 1.1 percent. Calculate the CPI in Canada in 2015.

2. In Brazil, the reference base period for the CPI is 2000. By 2005, prices had risen by 51 percent since the base period. The inflation rate in Brazil in 2006 was 10 percent, and in 2007, the inflation rate was 9 percent. Calculate the CPI in Brazil in 2006 and 2007. Brazil's CPI in 2008 was 173. Did Brazil's cost of living increase or decrease in 2008?

3. Tables 1 and 2 show the quantities of the goods that Suzie bought and the prices she paid during two consecutive weeks. Suzie's CPI market basket contains the goods she bought in Week 1. Calculate the cost of Suzie's CPI market basket in Week 1 and in Week 2. What percentage of the CPI market basket is gasoline? Calculate the value of Suzie's CPI in Week 2 and her inflation rate in Week 2.

Use the following information to work Problems **4** and **5**.

The GDP price index in the United States in 2008 was about 99, and real GDP in 2008 was $14.8 trillion (2009 dollars). The GDP price index in 2013 was about 107, and real GDP in 2013 was $15.5 trillion (2009 dollars).

4. Calculate nominal GDP in 2008 and in 2013 and the percentage increase in nominal GDP between 2008 and 2013.

5. What was the percentage increase in production between 2008 and 2013, and by what percentage did the price level rise between 2008 and 2013?

6. Table 3 shows the prices that Terry paid for some of his expenditures in June and July 2016. Explain and discuss why these prices might have led to commodity substitution or outlet substitution.

7. In 2015, Annie, an 80-year-old, is telling her granddaughter Mary about the good old days. Annie says that in 1935, you could buy a nice house for $15,000 and a jacket for $5. Mary says that in 2015 such a house cost $220,000 and such a jacket cost $70. The CPI in 1935 was 16.7 and in 2015 it was 218.1. Which house has the lower real price? Which jacket has the lower real price?

Use the following information to work Problems **8** and **9**.

Consumer prices drop as falling oil costs push inflation lower
Falling oil prices pushed the CPI down 0.1 percent in December 2015. Energy prices fell 2.4 percent and the price of gasoline fell by 3.9 percent.
Source: Los Angeles Times, January 20, 2016

8. Given the further information that the weight on energy prices in the CPI is 8 percent, by how much would the CPI have changed in December 2015 if energy prices had not changed?

9. By what percentage did the prices of other items in the CPI basket change?

10. Read *Eye on Box Office Hits* on p. 606 and using BLS data for the CPI in 1982 and 1997, determine which movie had the greater *real* box office revenues, *E.T.: The Extra-Terrestrial*, which earned $435 million in 1982 or *Titanic*, which earned $601 million in 1997.

TABLE 1 DATA FOR WEEK 1

Item	Quantity	Price (per unit)
Coffee	11 cups	$3.25
DVDs	1	$25.00
Gasoline	15 gallons	$2.50

TABLE 2 DATA FOR WEEK 2

Item	Quantity	Price (per unit)
Coffee	11 cups	$3.25
DVDs	3	$12.50
Gasoline	5 gallons	$3.00
Concert	1 ticket	$95.00

TABLE 3

Item	Price in June	Price in July
	(dollars per unit)	
Steak	4.11	4.01
Bread	3.25	3.12
Bacon	3.62	3.64
Milk	2.62	2.62
Tomatoes	1.60	1.62
Apples	1.18	1.19
Bananas	0.62	0.66
Chicken	1.28	1.26
Lettuce	1.64	1.68

Instructor Assignable Problems and Applications

MyEconLab Homework, Quiz, or Test if assigned by instructor

1. Compare the method used by Box Office Mojo on p. 606 to calculate real box office receipts with the method used on p. 602 to calculate the real price of a postage stamp. Compare and contrast the real variables that each method calculates.

2. Pete is a student who spends 10 percent of his expenditure on books and supplies, 30 percent on tuition, 30 percent on rent, 10 percent on food and drink, 10 percent on transportation, and the rest on clothing. The price index for each item was 100 in 2006. Table 1 shows the prices in 2016. What is Pete's CPI in 2016? (Hint: The contribution of each item to the CPI is its price weighted by its share of total expenditure.) Did Pete experience a higher or lower inflation rate between 2006 and 2016 than the student whose CPI is shown on p. 607?

3. The people on Coral Island buy only juice and cloth. The CPI market basket contains the quantities bought in 2016. The average household spent $60 on juice and $30 on cloth in 2016 when the price of juice was $2 a bottle and the price of cloth was $5 a yard. In the current year, 2017, juice is $4 a bottle and cloth is $6 a yard. Calculate the CPI and the inflation rate in 2017.

4. Tables 2 and 3 show the quantities of the goods that Harry bought and the prices he paid during two consecutive weeks. Harry's CPI market basket contains the goods he bought in Week 1. Calculate Harry's CPI in Week 2. What was his inflation rate in Week 2?

Use the following information to work Problems **5** and **6**.

The base year is 2012. Real GDP in 2012 was $15 trillion. The GDP price index in 2012 was 105, and real GDP in 2015 was $16 trillion.

5. Calculate nominal GDP in 2012 and in 2015 and the percentage increase in nominal GDP from 2012 to 2015.

6. What was the percentage increase in production from 2012 to 2015, and by what percentage did the price level rise from 2012 to 2015?

7. In 1988, the average wage rate was $9.45 an hour and in 2008 the average wage rate was $18.00 an hour. The CPI in 1988 was 118.3 and in 2008 it was 215.3. In which year was the real wage rate higher?

8. Imagine that you are given $1,000 to spend and told that you must spend it all buying items from a Sears catalog. But you do have a choice of catalog. You may select from the 1903 catalog or from Sears.com today. You will pay the prices quoted in the catalog that you choose.

   Which catalog will you choose and why? Refer to any biases in the CPI that might be relevant to your choice.

Use the following information to work Problems **9** and **10**.

Brazil keeps interest rates on hold
Brazil's inflation rate climbed to 10.7 percent at the end of 2015 and the country's Monetary Policy Committee kept its benchmark interest rate at 14.25 percent.
Source: *The Financial Times*, January 20, 2016

9. Calculate the real interest rate in Brazil.

10. To maintain this real interest rate, how must the nominal interest rate change if the inflation rate falls to 4.5 percent a year?

TABLE 1

Item	Price in 2016
Books and supplies	172.6
Tuition	169.0
Rent	159.0
Food and drink	129.8
Transportation	115.4
Clothing	92.9

TABLE 2   DATA FOR WEEK 1

Item	Quantity	Price (per unit)
Coffee	5 cups	$3.00
iTunes songs	5	$1.00
Gasoline	10 gallons	$2.00

TABLE 3   DATA FOR WEEK 2

Item	Quantity	Price (per unit)
Coffee	4 cups	$3.25
iTunes songs	10	$1.00
Gasoline	10 gallons	$3.00

MyEconLab Chapter 23 Study Plan

Multiple Choice Quiz

1. The CPI measures the average prices paid by _____ for _____.

   A. urban consumers; a fixed basket of consumption goods and services
   B. urban consumers; the average basket of goods and services they buy
   C. all consumers; housing, transportation, and food
   D. everyone who earns an income; the necessities of life

2. The BLS reported that the CPI in July 2010 was 226. This news tells you that _____.

   A. consumer prices during July were 226 percent higher than they were during the base year
   B. the CPI inflation rate in July was 26 percent a year
   C. consumer prices rose by 26 percent during the month of July
   D. the prices of consumption goods and services have risen, on average, by 126 percent since the base year

3. When the price level _____ the inflation rate _____.

   A. rises rapidly; increases
   B. rises rapidly; is high
   C. falls; is zero
   D. rises slowly; falls

4. The CPI bias arises from all of the following items *except* _____.

   A. the introduction of new goods and services
   B. the improved quality of goods
   C. the goods and services bought by poor people
   D. consumers' responses to price changes

5. Of the alternative measures of the price level, the _____ overcomes the bias of the CPI and is a better measure of the inflation rate because it _____.

   A. GDP price index; uses a current basket
   B. PCEPI; uses a current basket of all consumption goods
   C. PCEPI excluding food and energy; is less volatile
   D. GDP price index; includes all goods and services bought by Americans

6. If nominal GDP increases by 5 percent a year and the GDP price index rises by 2 percent a year, then real GDP increases by _____.

   A. 7 percent a year
   B. 3 percent a year
   C. 2.5 percent a year
   D. 10 percent a year

7. When the CPI increases from 200 in 2016 to 210 in 2017 and the nominal wage rate is constant at $10 an hour, the real wage rate _____.

   A. increases by 10 percent
   B. increases to $15 an hour
   C. decreases by 5 percent
   D. is $10 an hour

8. When the price level is rising at _____ and the real interest rate is 1 percent a year, the nominal interest rate is 3 percent a year.

   A. 4 percent a year
   B. 3 percent a year
   C. 2 percent a year
   D. 1 percent a year

Why do Americans earn more and produce more than Europeans?

Potential GDP and the Natural Unemployment Rate

24

When you have completed your study of this chapter, you will be able to

1 Explain what determines potential GDP.

2 Explain what determines the natural unemployment rate.

 MyEconLab **Big Picture Video**

MyEconLab Concept Video

MACROECONOMIC APPROACHES AND PATHWAYS

In the three previous chapters, you learned how economists define and measure real GDP, employment and unemployment, the price level, and the inflation rate—the key variables that *describe* macroeconomic performance. Your task in this chapter and those that follow is to learn the *macroeconomic theory* that *explains* macroeconomic performance and provides the basis for *policies* that might improve it.

The macroeconomic theory that we present is today's consensus view on how the economy works. But it isn't the view of all macroeconomists. Today's consensus is a merger of three earlier schools of thought that have contrasting views about the causes of recessions and the best policies for dealing with them. Some economists continue to identify with these schools of thought, and the severity of the 2008–2009 recession and slow recovery intensified debate and gave economists of all shades of opinion a platform from which to present their views.

We begin with an overview of the three schools of thought from which today's consensus has emerged.

■ The Three Main Schools of Thought

The three main schools of macroeconomic thought are

- Classical macroeconomics
- Keynesian macroeconomics
- Monetarist macroeconomics

Classical Macroeconomics

Classical macroeconomics
The view that the market economy works well, that aggregate fluctuations are a natural consequence of an expanding economy, and that government intervention cannot improve the efficiency of the market economy.

According to **classical macroeconomics,** markets work well and deliver the best available macroeconomic performance. Aggregate fluctuations are a natural consequence of an expanding economy with rising living standards, and government intervention can only hinder the ability of the market to allocate resources efficiently. The first classical macroeconomists included Adam Smith, David Ricardo, and John Stuart Mill, all of whom worked in the 18th and 19th centuries. Modern day classical economists include the 2004 Nobel Laureates Edward C. Prescott of the University of Arizona and Finn E. Kydland of Carnegie-Mellon University and the University of California at Santa Barbara.

Classical macroeconomics fell into disrepute during the Great Depression of the 1930s, a time when many people believed that *capitalism*, the political system of private ownership, free markets, and democratic political institutions, could not survive and began to advocate *socialism*, a political system based on state ownership of capital and central economic planning.

Classical macroeconomics predicted that the Great Depression would eventually end but offered no method for ending it more quickly.

Keynesian Macroeconomics

Keynesian macroeconomics
The view that the market economy is inherently unstable and needs active government intervention to achieve full employment and sustained economic growth.

According to **Keynesian macroeconomics,** the market economy is inherently unstable and requires active government intervention to achieve full employment and sustained economic growth. One person, John Maynard Keynes, and his book *The General Theory of Employment, Interest, and Money*, published in 1936, began this school of thought. Keynes' theory was that depression and high unemployment occur when households don't spend enough on consumption goods and services and businesses don't spend enough investing in new capital. That is, too little *private* spending is the cause of depression (and recession). To counter the problem of too little private spending, *government* spending must rise.

This Keynesian view picked up many followers and by the 1950s it was the mainstream, but it lost popularity during the inflationary 1970s when it seemed ever more remote from the problems of that decade. The global recession of 2008–2009 and the fear of another great depression revived interest in Keynesian ideas and brought a new wave of attacks on classical macroeconomics with Nobel Laureate Paul Krugman leading the charge in the columns of the *New York Times*.

Monetarist Macroeconomics

According to **monetarist macroeconomics,** the *classical* view of the world is broadly correct but in addition to fluctuations that arise from the normal functioning of an expanding economy, fluctuations in the quantity of money generate the business cycle. A slowdown in the growth rate of money brings recession and a large decrease in the quantity of money brought the Great Depression.

Milton Friedman, intellectual leader of the Chicago School of economists during the 1960s and 1970s, was the most prominent monetarist. The view that monetary contractions are the sole source of recessions and depressions is held by few economists today. But the view that the quantity of money plays a role in economic fluctuations is accepted by all economists and is part of today's consensus.

Monetarist macroeconomics
The view that the market economy works well, that aggregate fluctuations are a natural consequence of an expanding economy, but that fluctuations in the quantity of money generate the business cycle.

■ Today's Consensus

Each of the earlier schools provides insights and ingredients that survive in today's consensus. *Classical* macroeconomics provides the story of the economy at or close to full employment. But the classical approach doesn't explain how the economy performs in the face of a major slump in spending.

Keynesian macroeconomics takes up the story in a recession or depression. When spending is cut and the demand for most goods and services and the demand for labor all decrease, prices and wage rates don't fall but the quantity of goods and services sold and the quantity of labor employed do fall and the economy goes into recession. In a recession, an increase in spending by governments, or a tax cut that leaves people with more of their earnings to spend, can help to restore full employment.

Monetarist macroeconomics elaborates the Keynesian story by emphasizing that a contraction in the quantity of money brings higher interest rates and borrowing costs, which are a major source of cuts in spending that bring recession. Increasing the quantity of money and lowering the interest rate in a recession can help to restore full employment. And keeping the quantity of money growing steadily in line with the expansion of the economy's production possibilities can help to keep inflation in check and can also help to moderate the severity of a recession.

Another component of today's consensus is the view that the *long-term* problem of economic growth is more important than the *short-term* problem of recessions. Take a look at *Eye on the U.S. Economy,* on p. 616, and you will see why. Even a small slowdown in economic growth brings a huge cost in terms of a permanently lower level of income per person. This cost is much larger than that arising from the income lost during recessions. But the costs of recessions are serious because they are concentrated on those who are unemployed.

EYE on the U.S. ECONOMY
The Lucas Wedge and the Okun Gap

During the 1960s, U.S. real GDP per person grew at a rate of 2.9 percent a year. The black line in part (a) shows the path that would have been followed if this growth rate had been maintained. After 1970, growth slowed to 2.0 percent per year and the blue line shows the path that real GDP per person followed. University of Chicago economist Robert E. Lucas, Jr. pointed out the large output loss that resulted from this growth slowdown. Part (a) shows this loss as the *Lucas wedge*, which is equivalent to a staggering $509,000 per person or 10 years' income.

Real GDP fluctuates around potential GDP and when the output gap is negative, output is lost. Brookings Institution economist Arthur B. Okun drew attention to this loss. Part (b) shows this loss as the *Okun gap*, which is equivalent to $34,000 per person or about 8 months' income.

Smoothing the business cycle and eliminating the Okun gap has a big payoff. But finding ways of restoring real GDP growth to its 1960s rate has a vastly bigger payoff.

SOURCES OF DATA: Bureau of Economic Analysis, the Congressional Budget Office, and authors' assumptions and calculations.

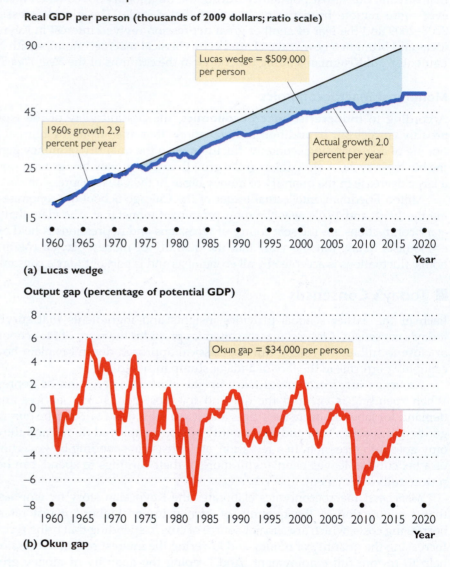

Real GDP per person (thousands of 2009 dollars; ratio scale)

> Lucas wedge = $509,000 per person

> 1960s growth 2.9 percent per year

> Actual growth 2.0 percent per year

(a) Lucas wedge

Output gap (percentage of potential GDP)

> Okun gap = $34,000 per person

(b) Okun gap

■ The Road Ahead

This book bases your tour of macroeconomics on the new consensus. We begin in this chapter and the two that follow by explaining what determines potential GDP and the pace at which it grows. We then study money and explain what brings inflation. Finally, we explain how real and monetary forces interact to bring about the business cycle. We also explain the policy tools available to governments and central banks to improve macroeconomic performance.

24.1   POTENTIAL GDP

MyEconLab Concept Video

Potential GDP is the value of real GDP when all the economy's factors of production—labor, capital, land, and entrepreneurial ability—are fully employed. It is vital to understand the forces that determine potential GDP for three reasons. First, when the economy is *at* full employment, real GDP equals potential GDP; so actual real GDP is determined by the same factors that determine potential GDP. Second, real GDP can exceed potential GDP only temporarily as it approaches and then recedes from a business cycle peak. So potential GDP is the *sustainable* upper limit of production. Third, real GDP fluctuates around potential GDP, which means that on the average over the business cycle, real GDP equals potential GDP.

We produce the goods and services that make up real GDP by using the *factors of production:* labor and human capital, physical capital, land (and natural resources), and entrepreneurship. At any given time, the quantities of capital, land, and entrepreneurship and the state of technology are fixed. But the quantity of labor is not fixed. It depends on the choices that people make about the allocation of time between work and leisure. So with fixed quantities of capital, land, and entrepreneurship and fixed technology, real GDP depends on the quantity of labor employed. To describe this relationship between real GDP and the quantity of labor employed, we use a relationship that is similar to the production possibilities frontier, which is called the production function.

Potential GDP
The value of real GDP when all the economy's factors of production—labor, capital, land, and entrepreneurial ability—are fully employed.

EYE on the GLOBAL ECONOMY
Potential GDP in the United States and the European Union

In 2015, real GDP in the United States was $65 per hour worked. In the 28 countries of the European Union, real GDP averaged only $50 per hour worked—a gap of 25 percent. (Both numbers are measured in 2015 U.S. dollars.) Part (a) of the figure shows this difference.

Not only do Americans produce more per hour than Europeans, they work longer hours too. In 2015, Americans worked an average of almost 40 hours per week while Europeans worked an average of only 35 hours per week—a difference of 12.5 percent. Part (b) of the figure shows this difference.

Europeans achieve their shorter work hours by taking longer vacations and having more sick days than Americans.

The combination of greater production per hour and longer work hours translates into a substantially larger real GDP per worker in the United States than in Europe.

In 2015, real GDP per worker in the United States was $120,000 while in Europe it was only $75,000—a gap of almost 40 percent.

This chapter enables you to understand the sources of these differences in wage rates, work hours, and production.

SOURCE OF DATA: Organization for Economic Cooperation and Development.

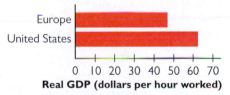

(a) Real GDP per hour worked

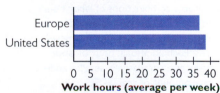

(b) Average weekly hours

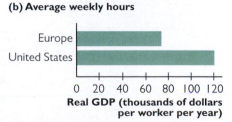

(c) Real GDP per worker

■ The Production Function

Production function

A relationship that shows the maximum quantity of real GDP that can be produced as the quantity of labor employed changes and all other influences on production remain the same.

The **production function** is a relationship that shows the maximum quantity of real GDP that can be produced as the quantity of labor employed changes and all other influences on production remain the same. Figure 24.1 shows a production function, which is the curve labeled *PF*.

In Figure 24.1, 100 billion labor hours can produce a real GDP of $11 trillion (at point *A*); 200 billion hours can produce a real GDP of $16 trillion (at point *B*); and 300 billion hours can produce a real GDP of $20 trillion (at point *C*).

The production function shares a feature of the *production possibilities frontier* that you studied in Chapter 3 (p. 62). Like the *PPF*, the production function is a boundary between the attainable and the unattainable. It is possible to produce at any point along the production function and beneath it in the shaded area. But it is not possible to produce at points above the production function. Those points are unattainable.

Diminishing returns

The tendency for each additional hour of labor employed to produce a successively smaller additional amount of real GDP.

The production function displays **diminishing returns**—each additional hour of labor employed produces a successively smaller additional amount of real GDP. The first 100 billion hours of labor produces $11 trillion of real GDP. The second 100 billion hours of labor increases real GDP from $11 trillion to $16 trillion, so the

■ **FIGURE 24.1**

The Production Function

MyEconLab Animation

The production function shows the maximum quantity of real GDP that can be produced as the quantity of labor employed changes and all other influences on production remain the same. In this example, 100 billion hours of labor can produce $11 trillion of real GDP at point A, 200 billion hours of labor can produce $16 trillion of real GDP at point B, and 300 billion hours of labor can produce $20 trillion of real GDP at point C.

The production function separates attainable combinations of labor hours and real GDP from unattainable combinations and displays diminishing returns: Each additional hour of labor produces a successively smaller additional amount of real GDP.

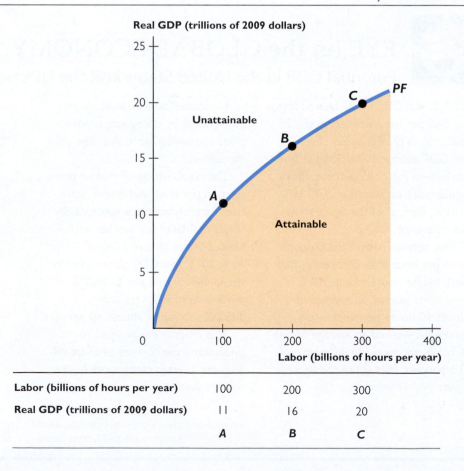

Labor (billions of hours per year)	100	200	300
Real GDP (trillions of 2009 dollars)	11	16	20
	A	*B*	*C*

second 100 billion hours produces only an additional $5 trillion of real GDP. The third 100 billion hours of labor increases real GDP from $16 trillion to $20 trillion, so the third 100 billion hours produces only an additional $4 trillion of real GDP.

Diminishing returns arise because the quantity of capital (and other factors of production) is fixed. As more labor is hired, the additional output produced decreases because the extra workers have less capital with which to work. For example, a forest service has three chain saws and an axe and hires three workers to clear roads and trails of fallen trees and debris during the spring thaw. Hiring a fourth worker will contribute less to the amount cleared than the amount that the third worker added, and hiring a fifth worker will add even less.

Because real GDP depends on the quantity of labor employed, potential GDP depends on the production function and the quantity of labor employed. To find potential GDP, we must understand what determines the quantity of labor employed.

■ The Labor Market

You've already studied the tool that we use to determine the quantity of labor employed: demand and supply. In macroeconomics, we apply the concepts of demand, supply, and market equilibrium to the economy-wide labor market.

The quantity of labor employed depends on firms' decisions about how much labor to hire (the demand for labor). It also depends on households' decisions about how to allocate time between employment and other activities (the supply of labor). And it depends on how the labor market coordinates the decisions of firms and households (labor market equilibrium). So we will study

- The demand for labor
- The supply of labor
- Labor market equilibrium

The Demand for Labor

The **quantity of labor demanded** is the total labor hours that all the firms in the economy plan to hire during a given time period at a given real wage rate. The **demand for labor** is the relationship between the quantity of labor demanded and the real wage rate when all other influences on firms' hiring plans remain the same. The lower the real wage rate, the greater is the quantity of labor demanded.

The real wage rate is the *nominal wage rate* (the dollars per hour that people earn on average) divided by the price level (see Chapter 23, p. 604). We express the real wage rate in constant dollars—today in 2009 dollars. Think of the real wage rate as the quantity of real GDP that an hour of labor earns.

The lower the real wage rate, the greater is the quantity of labor that firms find it profitable to hire. The real wage rate influences the quantity of labor demanded because what matters to firms is not the number of dollars they pay for an hour of labor (the nominal wage rate) but how much output they must sell to earn those dollars. So firms compare the extra output that an hour of labor can produce with the real wage rate.

If an additional hour of labor produces at least as much additional output as the real wage rate, a firm hires that labor. At a small quantity of labor, an extra hour of labor produces more output than the real wage rate. But each additional hour of labor produces less additional output than the previous hour. As a firm hires more labor, eventually the extra output from an extra hour of labor equals the real wage rate. This equality determines the quantity of labor demanded at the real wage rate.

Quantity of labor demanded
The total labor hours that all the firms in the economy plan to hire during a given time period at a given real wage rate.

Demand for labor
The relationship between the quantity of labor demanded and the real wage rate when all other influences on firms' hiring plans remain the same.

The Demand for Labor in a Soda Factory   You might understand the demand for labor better by thinking about a single firm rather than the economy as a whole. Suppose that the money wage rate is $15 an hour and that the price of a bottle of soda is $1.50. For the soda factory, the real wage rate is a number of bottles of soda. To find the soda factory's real wage rate, divide the money wage rate by the price of its output—$15 an hour ÷ $1.50 a bottle. The real wage rate is 10 bottles of soda an hour. It costs the soda factory 10 bottles of soda to hire an hour of labor. As long as the soda factory can hire labor that produces more than 10 additional bottles of soda an hour, it is profitable to hire more labor. Only when the extra output produced by an extra hour of labor falls to 10 bottles an hour has the factory reached the profit-maximizing quantity of labor.

Labor Demand Schedule and Labor Demand Curve   We can represent the demand for labor as either a demand schedule or a demand curve. The table in Figure 24.2 shows part of a demand for labor schedule. It tells us the quantity of labor demanded at three different real wage rates. For example, if the real wage rate is $50 an hour (row *B*), the quantity of labor demanded is 200 billion hours a year. If the real wage rate rises to $80 an hour (row *A*), the quantity of labor demanded decreases to 100 billion hours a year. And if the real wage rate falls to $25 an hour (row *C*), the quantity of labor demanded increases to 300 billion hours a year.

Figure 24.2 shows the demand for labor curve. Points *A*, *B*, and *C* on the demand curve correspond to rows *A*, *B*, and *C* of the demand schedule.

■ **FIGURE 24.2**

The Demand for Labor

MyEconLab Animation

Firms are willing to hire labor only if the labor produces more than its real wage rate. So the lower the real wage rate, the more labor firms can profitably hire and the greater is the quantity of labor demanded.

At a real wage rate of $50 an hour, the quantity of labor demanded is 200 billion hours at point *B*.

❶ If the real wage rate rises to $80 an hour, the quantity of labor demanded decreases to 100 billion hours at point *A*.

❷ If the real wage rate falls to $25 an hour, the quantity of labor demanded increases to 300 billion hours at point *C*.

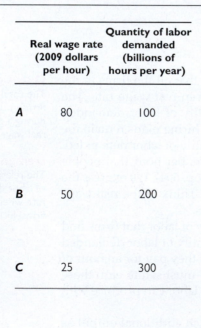

	Real wage rate (2009 dollars per hour)	Quantity of labor demanded (billions of hours per year)
A	80	100
B	50	200
C	25	300

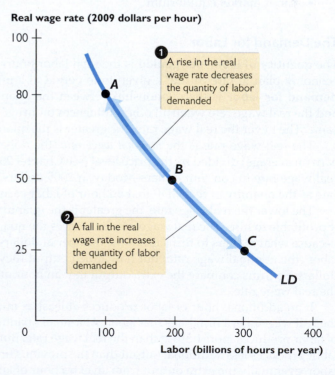

Real wage rate (2009 dollars per hour)

❶ A rise in the real wage rate decreases the quantity of labor demanded

❷ A fall in the real wage rate increases the quantity of labor demanded

Labor (billions of hours per year)

The Supply of Labor

The **quantity of labor supplied** is the number of labor hours that all the households in the economy plan to work during a given time period at a given real wage rate. The **supply of labor** is the relationship between the quantity of labor supplied and the real wage rate when all other influences on work plans remain the same.

We can represent the supply of labor as either a supply schedule or a supply curve. The table in Figure 24.3 shows a supply of labor schedule. It tells us the quantity of labor supplied at three different real wage rates. For example, if the real wage rate is $50 an hour (row *B*), the quantity of labor supplied is 200 billion hours a year. If the real wage rate falls to $25 an hour (row *A*), the quantity of labor supplied decreases to 100 billion hours a year. And if the real wage rate rises to $75 an hour (row *C*), the quantity of labor supplied increases to 300 billion hours a year.

Figure 24.3 shows the supply of labor curve. It corresponds to the supply schedule, and the points *A*, *B*, and *C* on the supply curve correspond to the rows *A*, *B*, and *C* of the supply schedule.

The real wage rate influences the quantity of labor supplied because what matters to people is not the number of dollars they earn but what those dollars will buy. The quantity of labor supplied increases as the real wage rate increases for two reasons:

- Hours per person increase.
- Labor force participation increases.

Quantity of labor supplied
The number of labor hours that all the households in the economy plan to work during a given time period at a given real wage rate.

Supply of labor
The relationship between the quantity of labor supplied and the real wage rate when all other influences on work plans remain the same.

FIGURE 24.3

The Supply of Labor

MyEconLab Animation

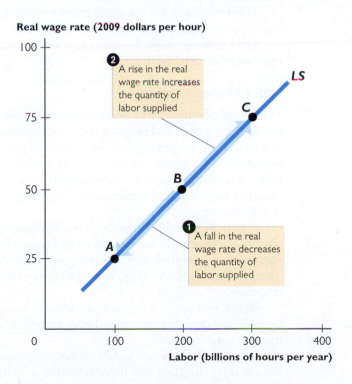

	Real wage rate (2009 dollars per hour)	Quantity of labor supplied (billions of hours per year)
C	75	300
B	50	200
A	25	100

Households are willing to supply labor only if the real wage rate is high enough to attract them from other activities. The higher the real wage rate, the greater is the quantity of labor supplied.

At a real wage rate of $50 an hour, the quantity of labor supplied is 200 billion hours at point *B*.

❶ If the real wage rate falls to $25 an hour, the quantity of labor supplied decreases to 100 billion hours at point *A*.

❷ If the real wage rate rises to $75 an hour, the quantity of labor supplied increases to 300 billion hours at point *C*.

Hours per Person   The real wage rate is the opportunity cost of taking leisure and not working. As the opportunity cost of taking leisure rises, other things remaining the same, households choose to work more. But other things don't remain the same. A higher real wage rate brings a higher income, which increases the demand for leisure and encourages less work.

So a rise in the real wage rate has two opposing effects. But for most households, the opportunity cost effect is stronger than the income effect, so a rise in the real wage rate brings an increase in the quantity of labor supplied.

Labor Force Participation   Most people have productive opportunities outside the labor force and choose to work only if the real wage rate exceeds the value of other productive activities. For example, a parent might spend time caring for her or his child. The alternative is day care. The parent will choose to work only if he or she can earn enough per hour to pay the cost of day care and have enough left to make the work effort worthwhile. The higher the real wage rate, the more likely it is that a parent will choose to work and so the greater is the labor force participation rate.

Other Influences on Labor Supply Decisions   Many factors other than the real wage rate influence labor supply decisions and influence the position of the labor supply curve. Income taxes and unemployment benefits are two of these factors.

The work-leisure decision depends on the *after-tax* wage rate—the wage rate actually received by the household. So, for a given wage rate, the income tax decreases the after-tax wage rate and the quantity of labor supplied decreases. The result is a decrease in the supply of labor. (The income tax rate doesn't change the demand for labor because for the employer, the cost of labor is the before-tax wage rate.)

Unemployment benefits lower the cost of searching for a job and encourage unemployed workers to take longer to find the best job available. The result is a decrease in the supply of labor.

Higher income tax rates and more generous unemployment benefits decrease the supply of labor—the labor supply curve lies farther to the left.

Let's now see how the labor market determines employment, the real wage rate, and potential GDP.

Labor Market Equilibrium

The forces of supply and demand operate in labor markets just as they do in the markets for goods and services. The price of labor services is the real wage rate. A rise in the real wage rate eliminates a shortage of labor by decreasing the quantity demanded and increasing the quantity supplied. A fall in the real wage rate eliminates a surplus of labor by increasing the quantity demanded and decreasing the quantity supplied. If there is neither a shortage nor a surplus, the labor market is in equilibrium.

Figure 24.4(a) shows the labor market equilibrium. The demand curve and the supply curve are the same as those in Figures 24.2 and 24.3. In part (a), if the real wage rate is less than $50 an hour, the quantity of labor demanded exceeds the quantity supplied and there is a shortage of labor. In this situation, the real wage rate rises.

If the real wage rate exceeds $50 an hour, the quantity of labor supplied exceeds the quantity demanded and there is a surplus of labor. In this situation, the real wage rate falls.

If the real wage rate is $50 an hour, the quantity of labor demanded equals the quantity supplied and there is neither a shortage nor a surplus of labor. In this

FIGURE 24.4

Labor Market Equilibrium and Potential GDP

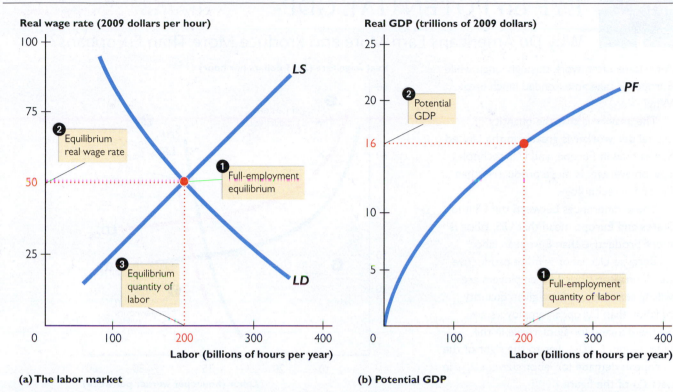

(a) The labor market

(b) Potential GDP

❶ Full employment occurs when the quantity of labor demanded equals the quantity of labor supplied. **❷** The equilibrium real wage rate is $50 an hour, and **❸** the equilibrium quantity of labor employed is 200 billion hours a year.

Potential GDP is the real GDP produced on the production function by the full-employment quantity of labor. **❶** The full-employment quantity of labor, 200 billion hours a year, produces a **❷** potential GDP of $16 trillion.

situation, the labor market is in equilibrium and the real wage rate remains constant. The equilibrium quantity of labor is 200 billion hours a year. When the equilibrium quantity of labor is employed, the economy is at full employment. So the full-employment quantity of labor is 200 billion hours a year.

Full Employment and Potential GDP

When the labor market is in equilibrium, the economy is at full employment and real GDP equals potential GDP.

You've seen that the quantity of real GDP depends on the quantity of labor employed. The production function tells us how much real GDP a given amount of employment can produce. Now that we've determined the full-employment quantity of labor, we can find potential GDP.

Figure 24.4(b) shows the relationship between labor market equilibrium and potential GDP. The equilibrium quantity of labor employed in Figure 24.4(a) is 200 billion hours. The production function in Figure 24.4(b) tells us that 200 billion hours of labor produces $16 trillion of real GDP. This quantity of real GDP is potential GDP.

EYE on POTENTIAL GDP

Why Do Americans Earn More and Produce More Than Europeans?

Americans often work through lunch while Europeans take an extended lunch break. Why?

The answer is that the quantity of capital per worker is greater in the United States than in Europe, and U.S. technology, on average, is more productive than European technology.

These differences between the United States and Europe mean that U.S. labor is more productive than European labor.

Because U.S. labor is more productive than European labor, U.S. employers are willing to pay more for a given quantity of labor than European employers are. So the demand for labor curve in the United States, LD_{US}, lies to the right of the European demand for labor curve, LD_{EU}, in part (a) of the figure.

This difference in the productivity of labor also means that the U.S. production function, PF_{US}, lies above the European production function, PF_{EU}, in part (b) of the figure.

Higher income taxes and unemployment benefits in Europe mean that to induce a person to take a job, a firm in Europe must offer a higher wage rate than a firm in the United States has to offer. So the European labor supply curve, LS_{EU}, lies to the left of the U.S. labor supply curve, LS_{US}.

Equilibrium employment is greater in the United States than in Europe— Americans work longer hours—and the equilibrium real wage rate is higher in the United States than in Europe.

Potential GDP is higher in the United States than in Europe for two reasons: U.S. workers are more productive per hour of work and they work longer hours than Europeans.

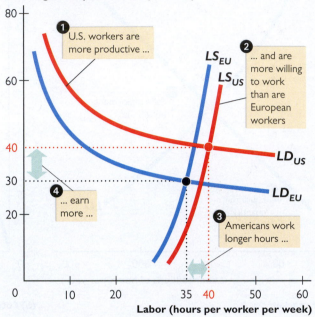

(a) Labor market in Europe and in the United States

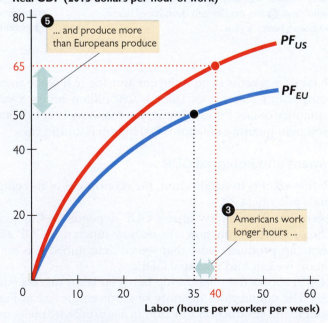

(b) Production function in Europe and in the United States

CHECKPOINT 24.1

MyEconLab Study Plan 24.1
Key Terms Quiz
Solutions Video

Explain what determines potential GDP.

Practice Problem

1. Table 1 describes an economy's production function and demand for labor.

TABLE 1

Quantity of labor demanded (billions of hours per year)	0	1	2	3	4
Real GDP (billions of 2009 dollars)	0	40	70	90	100
Real wage rate (2009 dollars per hour)	50	40	30	20	10

Table 2 describes the supply of labor in this economy.

TABLE 2

Quantity of labor supplied (billions of hours per year)	0	1	2	3	4
Real wage rate (2009 dollars per hour)	10	20	30	40	50

Use the data in Tables 1 and 2 to make graphs of the labor market and production function. What are the equilibrium real wage rate and employment? What is potential GDP?

In the News

Tesla is recruiting

Electric car maker Tesla is recruiting Nevadans with a high school diploma or equivalent to work in the battery gigafactory the company is building.

Source: *Reno Gazette Journal,* July 1, 2016

Explain how Tesla's huge project will influence potential GDP, employment, and the real wage rate in the United States.

Solution to Practice Problem

1. The demand for labor is a graph of the first and last row of Table 1 and the supply of labor is a graph of the data in Table 2 (Figure 1). The production function is a graph of the first two rows of Table 1 (Figure 2).
    Labor market equilibrium occurs when the real wage rate is $30 an hour and 2 billion hours of labor are employed (Figure 1). Potential GDP is the real GDP produced by the equilibrium quantity of labor (2 billion hours in Figure 1). Potential GDP is $70 billion (Figure 2).

Solution to In the News

Potential GDP will increase. With increased capital equipment to manufacture batteries, the U.S. production function will shift upward. With no change in employment, potential GDP would increase. But Tesla's gigafactory project will increase the productivity of labor and increase the demand for labor. The increase in the demand for labor, with no change in the supply of labor, will increase the real wage rate. As the real wage rate rises, the quantity of labor supplied increases. The full-employment quantity of labor increases. Potential GDP, employment, and the real wage rate all increase.

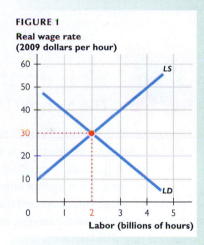

FIGURE 1

Real wage rate
(2009 dollars per hour)

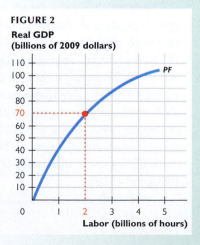

FIGURE 2

Real GDP
(billions of 2009 dollars)

MyEconLab Concept Video

24.2 THE NATURAL UNEMPLOYMENT RATE

So far, we've focused on the forces that determine the real wage rate, the quantity of labor employed, and real GDP at full employment. We're now going to bring unemployment into the picture.

You learned in Chapter 22 that the BLS measures the amount of unemployment by counting the number of people who do not have a job, are willing to work, and have looked for work in the past 4 weeks. And you learned how we classify unemployment as frictional, structural, or cyclical. Finally, you learned that when the economy is at full employment, all the unemployment is frictional or structural and the unemployment rate is called the *natural unemployment rate*.

Measuring, describing, and classifying unemployment tell us a lot about it. But these activities do not *explain* the amount of unemployment that exists or why the unemployment rate changes over time and varies across economies.

Many forces interact to determine the unemployment rate. Understanding these forces is a challenging task. Economists approach this task in two steps. The first step is to understand what determines the natural unemployment rate—the unemployment rate when the economy is at full employment. The second step is to understand what makes unemployment fluctuate around the natural unemployment rate. In this chapter, we take the first of these steps. We take the second step in Chapters 29–31 when we study economic fluctuations.

EYE on the PAST
The Natural Unemployment Rate Over Seven Decades

If we look at the unemployment rate over the decades, we see the ups and downs of the business cycle. Most of the fluctuations are in cyclical unemployment—fluctuations around the natural unemployment rate. But the natural rate also fluctuates.

The figure shows the decade averages of the natural unemployment rate since 1950. During the 1950s and 1960s, the natural rate averaged a bit more than 5 percent. It climbed during the 1970s to more than 6 percent, and it remained high during the 1980s. During the1990s, 2000s, and 2010s, the natural unemployment rate fell to levels slightly lower than those of the 1950s and 1960s.

These changes resulted from the demographic and other influences that we describe in this section.

You will be a member of the labor force of the 2020s and the natural unemployment rate of the third decade of the 2000s will have a big effect on your job market outcome.

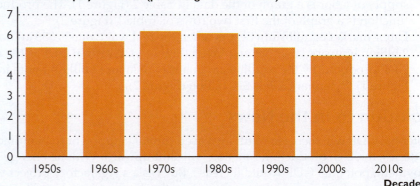

Natural unemployment rate (percentage of labor force)

SOURCE OF DATA: Congressional Budget Office.

To understand the amount of frictional and structural unemployment that exists at the natural unemployment rate, economists focus on two fundamental causes of unemployment that cut across the frictional-structural classification. These two fundamental causes of unemployment are

- Job search
- Job rationing

■ Job Search

Job search is the activity of looking for an acceptable vacant job. Because the labor market is in a constant state of change, there are always some people who have not yet found suitable jobs and who are actively searching. The failure of businesses destroys jobs. The expansion of businesses and the startup of new businesses create jobs. As people pass through different stages of life, some enter or reenter the labor market, others leave their jobs to look for better ones, and others retire. This constant churning in the labor market means that there are always some people looking for jobs, and these people are part of the unemployed.

The amount of job search depends on a number of factors that change over time. The main ones are

- Demographic change
- Unemployment benefits
- Structural change

Job search
The activity of looking for an acceptable vacant job.

Demographic Change

An increase in the proportion of the population that is of working age brings an increase in the entry rate into the labor force and an increase in the unemployment rate. This factor was important in the U.S. labor market during the 1970s. The bulge in the birth rate that occurred in the late 1940s and early 1950s increased the proportion of new entrants into the labor force during the 1970s and brought an increase in the unemployment rate.

As the birth rate declined, the bulge moved into higher age groups and the proportion of new entrants declined during the 1990s. During this period, the unemployment rate decreased.

Another source of demographic change has been an increase in the number of households with two incomes. When unemployment comes to one of these workers, it is possible, with income still flowing in, to take longer to find a new job. This factor might have increased frictional unemployment.

Unemployment Benefits

The opportunity cost of job search influences the length of time that an unemployed person spends searching for a job. With no unemployment benefits, the opportunity cost of job search is high, and a person is likely to accept a job that is found quickly. With generous unemployment benefits, the opportunity cost of job search is low, and a person is likely to spend a considerable time searching for the ideal job.

Generous unemployment benefits are a large part of the story of high unemployment rates in Europe and some other countries such as Canada—see *Eye on the Global Economy* on p. 628.

EYE on the GLOBAL ECONOMY
Unemployment Benefits and the Natural Unemployment Rate

The gap between U.S. and Canadian unemployment rates provides information about the influence of unemployment benefits. The two unemployment rates followed similar cycles, but the Canadian unemployment rate exceeded the U.S. rate, which suggests that the natural unemployment rate was higher in Canada than in the United States.

Why? In 1980, Canadian unemployment benefits increased and are available to all the unemployed. In the United States only 38 percent of the unemployed receive benefits.

U.S. unemployment benefits were extended to provide a further 20 weeks of income to the unemployed during the 2008–2009 recession and this change contributed to narrowing

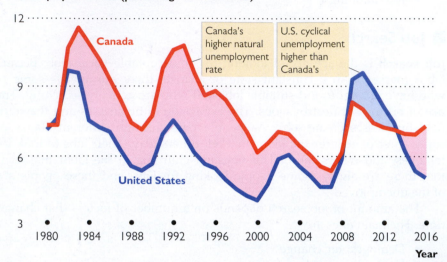

Unemployment rate (percentage of labor force)

Canada

Canada's higher natural unemployment rate

U.S. cyclical unemployment higher than Canada's

United States

SOURCE OF DATA: Bureau of Labor Statistics and Statistics Canada.

the Canada–U.S. unemployment gap. But cyclical unemployment increased in the United States by more than in

Canada and was the main source of the reversal of the gap between the two unemployment rates.

Structural Change

Technological change influences unemployment. Sometimes it brings a structural slump, a condition in which some industries and even regions contract while other industries and regions flourish. When these events occur, labor turnover is high, job search increases, and the natural unemployment rate rises.

At other times, technological change brings a structural boom. It creates new jobs that are a good match for the people who are losing their jobs. When these events occur, labor turnover might be high, but job search decreases because new jobs are found quickly, and the natural unemployment rate falls. The Internet economy of the 1990s is an example of a structural boom. Lots of new jobs were created in every major population center, and those jobs were a good match for the skills available, so the natural unemployment rate decreased.

■ Job Rationing

Job rationing
A situation that arises when the real wage rate is above the full-employment equilibrium level.

Job rationing occurs when the real wage rate is above the full-employment equilibrium level. You have learned that markets allocate scarce resources by adjusting the market price to bring buying plans and selling plans into balance. You can think of the market as *rationing* scarce resources. In the labor market, the real wage rate rations employment and therefore rations jobs. Changes in the real wage rate keep the number of people seeking work and the number of jobs available in balance. But the real wage rate is not the only possible instrument for rationing jobs.

In some industries, the real wage rate is set above the full-employment equilibrium level, which brings a surplus of labor. In these labor markets, jobs are rationed by some other means.

The real wage rate might be set above the full-employment equilibrium level for three reasons:

- Efficiency wage
- Minimum wage
- Union wage

Efficiency Wage

An **efficiency wage** is a real wage rate that is set above the full-employment equilibrium wage rate to induce a greater work effort. The idea is that if a firm pays only the going market average wage, employees have no incentive to work hard because they know that even if they are fired for slacking off, they can find a job with another firm at a similar wage rate. But if a firm pays *more* than the going market average wage, employees have an incentive to work hard because they know that if they are fired, they *cannot* expect to find a job with another firm at a similar wage rate.

Further, by paying an efficiency wage, a firm can attract the most productive workers. Also, its workers are less likely to quit their jobs, so the firm faces a lower rate of labor turnover and lower training costs. Finally, the firm's recruiting costs are lower because it always faces a steady stream of available new workers.

Paying an efficiency wage is costly, so only those firms that can't directly monitor the work effort of their employees use this device. For example, truck drivers and plant maintenance workers might receive efficiency wages. If enough firms pay an efficiency wage, the average real wage rate will exceed the full-employment equilibrium level.

Efficiency wage
A real wage rate that is set above the full-employment equilibrium wage rate to induce greater work effort.

The Minimum Wage

A **minimum wage law** is a government regulation that makes hiring labor for less than a specified wage illegal. If the minimum wage is set below the equilibrium wage, the minimum wage has no effect. The minimum wage law and market forces are not in conflict. But if a minimum wage is set above the equilibrium wage, the minimum wage is in conflict with market forces and unemployment arises.

The current federal minimum wage is $7.25 an hour, and the minimum wage has a major effect in the markets for low-skilled labor. Because skill grows with work experience, teenage labor is particularly affected by the minimum wage.

Minimum wage law
A government regulation that makes hiring labor for less than a specified wage illegal.

Union Wage

A **union wage** is a wage rate that results from collective bargaining between a labor union and a firm. Because a union represents a group of workers, it can usually achieve a wage rate that exceeds the level that would prevail in a competitive labor market.

For the United States, it is estimated that, on average, union wage rates are 30 percent higher than nonunion wage rates. But this estimate probably overstates the true effects of labor unions on the wage rate. In some industries, union wages are higher than nonunion wages because union members do jobs that require greater skill than nonunion jobs. In these cases, even without a union, those workers would earn a higher wage.

One way to calculate the effects of unions is to examine the wages of union and nonunion workers who do nearly identical work. For workers with similar

Union wage
A wage rate that results from collective bargaining between a labor union and a firm.

skill levels, the union-nonunion wage difference is between 10 and 25 percent. For example, pilots who are members of the Air Line Pilots Association earn about 25 percent more than nonunion pilots with the same level of skill.

Labor unions are much more influential in Europe than in the United States. In Europe, unions not only achieve wage rates above those of a competitive market but also have broad political influence on labor market conditions.

Job Rationing and Unemployment

Whether because of efficiency wages, a minimum wage law, or the actions of labor unions, if the real wage rate is above the full-employment equilibrium level, the natural unemployment rate increases. The above-equilibrium real wage rate decreases the quantity of labor demanded and increases the quantity of labor supplied.

Figure 24.5 illustrates job rationing and the frictional and structural unemployment it creates. The full-employment equilibrium real wage rate is $50 an hour, and the equilibrium quantity of labor is 200 billion hours a year. The existence of efficiency wages, the minimum wage, and union wages raises the economy's average real wage rate to $60 an hour. At this wage rate, the quantity of labor demanded decreases to 175 billion hours and the quantity of labor supplied increases to 240 billion hours. Firms ration jobs and choose the workers to hire on the basis of criteria such as education and previous job experience. The labor market is like a game of musical chairs in which a large number of chairs have been removed. So the quantity of labor supplied persistently exceeds the quantity demanded, and additional unemployment arises from job rationing.

■ **FIGURE 24.5**

Job Rationing Increases the Natural Unemployment Rate　　　　　　MyEconLab Animation

The full-employment equilibrium real wage rate is $50 an hour. Efficiency wages, the minimum wage, and union wages put the average real wage rate above the full-employment equilibrium level—at $60 an hour.

❶ The quantity of labor demanded decreases to 175 billion hours.

❷ The quantity of labor supplied increases to 240 billion hours.

❸ A surplus of labor arises and increases the natural unemployment rate.

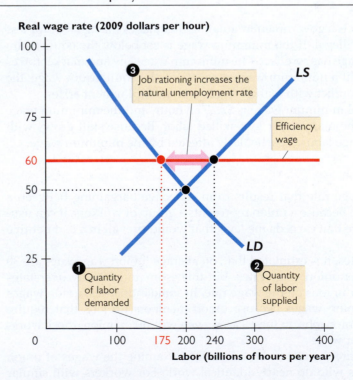

EYE on the U.S. ECONOMY
The Federal Minimum Wage

The *Fair Labor Standards Act* of 1938 set the federal minimum wage in the United States at 25¢ an hour. Over the years, the minimum wage has increased, and in 2016 it was $7.25 an hour. Although the minimum wage has increased, it hasn't kept up with the rising cost of living.

The figure shows the real minimum wage rate in 2009 dollars. You can see that during the late 1960s, the real minimum wage in 2009 dollars was $9 an hour. It decreased during the 1970s and 1980s and has fluctuated around an average of just under $6 an hour since the mid-1980s.

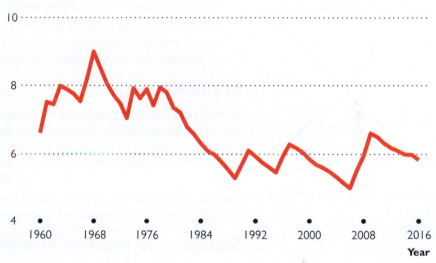

SOURCE OF DATA: Bureau of Labor Statistics.

EYE on YOUR LIFE
Natural Unemployment

MyEconLab Critical Thinking Exercise

You will encounter natural unemployment at many points in your life.

If you now have a job, you probably went through a spell of natural unemployment as you searched for the job.

When you graduate and look for a full-time job, you will most likely spend some more time searching for the best match for your skills and location preferences.

In today's world of rapid technological change, most of us must retool and change our jobs at least once and for many of us, more than once.

You might know an older worker who has recently lost a job and is going through the agony of figuring out what to do next.

Although natural unemployment can be painful for people who experience it, from a social perspective, it is productive. It enables scarce labor resources to be re-allocated to their most valuable uses.

MyEconLab Study Plan 24.2
Key Terms Quiz
Solutions Video

CHECKPOINT 24.2

Explain what determines the natural unemployment rate.

Practice Problems

During the past 50 years, Singapore has seen huge changes: rapid population growth and the introduction of newer and newer technologies. Singapore has modest unemployment benefits, no minimum wage, and weak labor unions.

1. Does Singapore's unemployment arise mainly from job search or job rationing?

2. Which of the factors listed above suggest that Singapore has a higher natural unemployment rate than the United States and which suggest that Singapore has a lower natural unemployment rate?

3. Figure 1 illustrates the labor market in an economy in which at full employment, 1,000 people a day job search. What is the equilibrium real wage rate and employment? Calculate the natural unemployment rate.

FIGURE 1

Real wage rate (2009 dollars per hour)

Labor (thousands of workers per day)

In the News

A mid-year burst of minimum-wage increases starts on July 1

On July 1, the minimum wage will rise in Washington D.C., Los Angeles County, Chicago, and in cities in California, Kentucky, Maryland, and Oregon. San Francisco's minimum wage will rise to $13.00 an hour and Chicago's to $10.50.

Source: *The Wall Street Journal*, July 1, 2016

Explain why some part-time workers, low-skilled workers, and youth workers will gain and why unemployed teenagers will find it hard to get jobs.

Solutions to Practice Problems

1. Singapore's unemployment arises mainly from job search. Of the sources of job rationing (efficiency wages, minimum wages, and union wages) only efficiency wages applies.

2. Singapore's rapid population growth and the introduction of new technologies increase the amount of job search —factors that increase the natural unemployment rate.

   Singapore has modest unemployment benefits, which limit the amount of job search, and no minimum wage and weak labor unions, which limit the amount of job rationing—factors that lower the natural unemployment rate

3. Labor market equilibrium determines the equilibrium real wage rate at $3 an hour and full employment at 3,000 workers. Unemployment is 1,000, so the labor force is 4,000 and the natural unemployment rate equals $(1,000 \div 4,000) \times 100$, or 25 percent.

Solution to In the News

When the minimum wage rises, firms will retain those workers who produce at least as much output per hour as the minimum wage rate. Job experience helps part-time and low-skilled employees retain their jobs, but teenagers with no experience will find it hard to get jobs.

CHAPTER SUMMARY

Key Points

1. **Explain what determines potential GDP.**

   - Potential GDP is the quantity of real GDP that the full-employment quantity of labor produces.
   - The production function describes the relationship between real GDP and the quantity of labor employed when all other influences on production remain the same. As the quantity of labor increases, real GDP increases.
   - The quantity of labor demanded increases as the real wage rate falls, other things remaining the same.
   - The quantity of labor supplied increases as the real wage rate rises, other things remaining the same.
   - At full-employment equilibrium, the real wage rate makes the quantity of labor demanded equal the quantity of labor supplied.

2. **Explain what determines the natural unemployment rate.**

   - The unemployment rate at full employment is the natural unemployment rate.
   - Unemployment is always present because of job search and job rationing.
   - Job search is influenced by demographic change, unemployment benefits, and structural change.
   - Job rationing arises from an efficiency wage, the minimum wage, and a union wage.

Key Terms

MyEconLab Key Terms Quiz

Classical macroeconomics, 614
Demand for labor, 619
Diminishing returns, 618
Efficiency wage, 629
Job rationing, 628

Job search, 627
Keynesian macroeconomics, 614
Minimum wage law, 629
Monetarist macroeconomics, 615
Potential GDP, 617

Production function, 618
Quantity of labor demanded, 619
Quantity of labor supplied, 621
Supply of labor, 621
Union wage, 629

CHAPTER CHECKPOINT

Study Plan Problems and Applications

Use the events in List 1, which occur in the United States one at a time, to work Problems **1** to **4**.

LIST 1

- Dell introduces a new supercomputer that everyone can afford.
- A major hurricane hits Florida.
- More high school graduates go to college.
- The CPI rises.
- An economic slump in the rest of the world decreases U.S. exports.

1. Sort the items into four groups: those that change the production function, those that change the demand for labor, those that change the supply of labor, and those that do not change the production function, the demand for labor, or the supply of labor. Say in which direction any changes occur.

2. Which of the events increase the equilibrium quantity of labor and which decrease it?

3. Which of the events raise the real wage rate and which lower it?

4. Which of the events increase potential GDP and which decrease it?

Use the information set out in Table 1 and Table 2 about the economy of Athabasca to work Problems **5** and **6**.

5. Calculate the quantity of labor employed, the real wage rate, and potential GDP.

6. If the labor force participation increases, explain how employment, the real wage rate, and potential GDP change.

Use the following information to work Problems **7** and **8**.

Suppose that the United States cracks down on illegal immigrants and returns millions of workers to their home countries.

7. Explain how the U.S. real wage rate, U.S. employment, and U.S. potential GDP would change.

8. In the countries to which the immigrants return, explain how employment, the real wage rate, and potential GDP would change.

TABLE 1   PRODUCTION FUNCTION

Labor hours (millions)	Real GDP (millions of 2009 dollars)
0	0
1	10
2	19
3	27
4	34
5	40

9. Two island economies, Cocoa Island and Plantation Island, are identical in every respect except one. A survey tells us that at full employment, people on Cocoa Island spend 1,000 hours a day on job search, while the people on Plantation Island spend 2,000 hours a day on job search. Which economy has the greater potential GDP? Which has the higher real wage rate? And which has the higher natural unemployment rate?

TABLE 2   LABOR MARKET

Real wage rate (2009 dollars per hour)	Quantity of labor demanded	Quantity of labor supplied
	(millions of hours per year)	
10	1	5
9	2	4
8	3	3
7	4	2
6	5	1

10. **Where are all the workers?**
The baby boomers—people born between 1946 and 1964—are retiring and the percentage of adult Americans working or actively looking for a job is at its lowest level in nearly forty years.

Source: *U.S. News & World Report*, July 16, 2015

How would you expect the change in the labor force described in the news clip to affect potential GDP and the natural unemployment rate?

11. Read *Eye on Potential GDP* on p. 624 and then explain why potential GDP per worker per week is greater in the United States than in Europe. What could induce Europeans to work the same hours as Americans and would that close the gap between potential GDP per worker in the two economies?

Instructor Assignable Problems and Applications

MyEconLab Homework, Quiz, or Test if assigned by instructor

Use the following information to work Problems **1** and **2**.

In South Korea, real GDP per hour of labor is $22, the real wage rate is $15 per hour, and people work an average of 46 hours per week.

1. Draw a graph of the demand for and supply of labor in South Korea and the United States. Mark a point at the equilibrium quantity of labor per person per week and the real wage rate in each economy. Explain the difference in the two labor markets.

2. Draw a graph of the production functions in South Korea and the United States. Mark a point on each production function that shows potential GDP per hour of work in each economy. Explain the difference in the two production functions.

Use the following list of events that occur one at a time to work Problems **3** to **6**.

- The Middle East cuts supplies of oil to the United States.
- The New York Yankees win the World Series.
- U.S. labor unions negotiate wage hikes that affect all workers.
- A huge scientific breakthrough doubles the output that an additional hour of U.S. labor can produce.
- Migration to the United States increases the working-age population.

3. Sort the items into four groups: those that change the production function, those that change the demand for labor, those that change the supply of labor, and those that do not change the production function, the demand for labor, or the supply of labor. Say in which direction each change occurs.

4. Which of the events increase the equilibrium quantity of labor and which decrease the equilibrium quantity of labor?

5. Which of the events raise the real wage rate and which of the events lower the real wage rate?

6. Which of the events increase potential GDP and which decrease potential GDP?

Use the information set out in Table 1 and Table 2 about the economy of Nautica to work Problems **7** and **8**.

7. What is the quantity of labor employed, potential GDP, the real wage rate, and total labor income?

8. Suppose that the government introduces a minimum wage of $0.80 an hour. What is the real wage rate, the quantity of labor employed, potential GDP, and unemployment? Does the unemployment arise from job search or job rationing? Is the unemployment cyclical? Explain.

9. Blizzard of 2016 ranks 4th among worst winter storms of past 100 years
Millions of Americans were digging out after the Blizzard of 2016 blanketed 434,000 square miles of the mid-Atlantic and parts of the Northeast with several feet of snow. The storm, which disrupted the lives of 103 million people, ranks as the fourth worst winter storm to impact the Northeast.

Source: AccuWeather.com, January 31, 2016

Explain the effect of the Blizzard of 2016 on the economy of the mid-Atlantic and Northeast states. How did it impact the production function, the labor market, and potential GDP?

TABLE 1 PRODUCTION FUNCTION

Labor (hours per day)	Real GDP (2009 dollars per year)
0	0
10	100
20	180
30	240
40	280

TABLE 2 LABOR MARKET

Real wage rate (2009 dollars per hour)	Quantity of labor demanded	Quantity of labor supplied
	(hours per day)	
1.00	10	50
0.80	20	40
0.60	30	30
0.40	40	20

MyEconLab Chapter 24 Study Plan

Multiple Choice Quiz

1. U.S. potential GDP is the value of the goods and services produced in the United States _____.

   A. in the reference base year
   B. when the U.S. unemployment rate is zero
   C. when the U.S. economy is at full employment
   D. when the U.S. inflation rate is zero

2. The demand for labor curve shows the relationship between _____.

   A. the quantity of labor employed and firms' profits
   B. all households' willingness to work and the real wage rate
   C. the quantity of labor businesses are willing to hire and the real wage rate
   D. the labor force and the real wage rate

3. The supply of labor is the relationship between _____.

   A. the quantity of labor supplied and leisure time forgone
   B. the real wage rate and the quantity of labor supplied
   C. firms' willingness to supply jobs and the real wage rate
   D. the labor force participation rate and the real wage rate

4. Households' labor supply decisions are influenced by all of the following *except* _____.

   A. the opportunity cost of taking leisure and not working
   B. the after-tax wage rate
   C. unemployment benefits
   D. the number of full-time jobs available

5. The full-employment quantity of labor _____.

   A. increases if labor becomes more productive
   B. cannot increase because everyone who wants a job has one
   C. increases as the economy moves along its production function
   D. decreases if the income tax rate decreases

6. The natural unemployment rate _____.

   A. increases if unemployment benefits become more generous
   B. increases in a recession
   C. increases as the average age of the labor force rises
   D. decreases as firms outsource manufacturing jobs

7. Job rationing _____.

   A. increases the natural unemployment rate
   B. has no effect on the natural unemployment rate
   C. increases labor turnover as firms compete for high-quality labor
   D. decreases the demand for labor, which lowers the real wage rate

8. An efficiency wage results in all of the following *except* _____.

   A. a decrease in the rate of labor turnover
   B. an increase in the full-employment quantity of labor
   C. greater work effort
   D. an increase in the cost of monitoring work effort

Economic Growth

25

When you have completed your study of this chapter, you will be able to

CHAPTER CHECKLIST

1 Define and calculate the economic growth rate, and explain the implications of sustained growth.

2 Explain the sources of labor productivity growth.

3 Review theories of the causes and effects of economic growth.

4 Describe policies that speed economic growth.

MyEconLab **Big Picture Video**

MyEconLab *Concept Video*

Economic growth
A sustained expansion of production possibilities.

Economic growth rate
The annual percentage change of real GDP.

25.1 THE BASICS OF ECONOMIC GROWTH

Some nations are rich and others poor because they have enjoyed or missed out on **economic growth**—a sustained expansion of production possibilities. Maintained over decades, rapid economic growth transforms a poor nation into a rich one. Such has been the experience of Hong Kong, South Korea, Taiwan, and some other Asian economies. Slow economic growth or the absence of growth can condemn a nation to devastating poverty. Such has been the fate of Sierra Leone, Somalia, Zambia, and much of the rest of Africa.

Economic growth is different from the rise in incomes that occurs during the recovery from a recession. Economic growth is a sustained trend, not a temporary cyclical expansion.

■ Calculating Growth Rates

We express the **economic growth rate** as the annual percentage change of real GDP. To calculate this growth rate, we use the formula:

$$\text{Growth rate of real GDP} = \frac{\text{Real GDP in current year} - \text{Real GDP in previous year}}{\text{Real GDP in previous year}} \times 100.$$

For example, if real GDP in the current year is \$8.4 trillion and if real GDP in the previous year was \$8.0 trillion, then

$$\text{Growth rate of real GDP} = \frac{\$8.4 \text{ trillion} - \$8.0 \text{ trillion}}{\$8.0 \text{ trillion}} \times 100 = 5 \text{ percent.}$$

The growth rate of real GDP tells us how rapidly the total economy is expanding. This measure is useful for telling us about potential changes in the balance of economic power among nations, but it does not tell us about changes in the standard of living.

The standard of living depends on real GDP per person (also called *per capita real GDP*), which is real GDP divided by the population. So the contribution of real GDP growth to the change in the *standard of living* depends on the growth rate of real GDP per person. We use the above formula to calculate this growth rate, replacing real GDP with real GDP per person.

Suppose, for example, that in the current year, when real GDP is \$8.4 trillion, the population is 202 million. Then real GDP per person in the current year is \$8.4 trillion divided by 202 million, which equals \$41,584. And suppose that in the previous year, when real GDP was \$8.0 trillion, the population was 200 million. Then real GDP per person in that year was \$8.0 trillion divided by 200 million, which equals \$40,000.

Use these two values of real GDP per person with the growth formula to calculate the growth rate of real GDP per person. That is,

$$\text{Growth rate of real GDP per person} = \frac{\$41,584 - \$40,000}{\$40,000} \times 100 = 4 \text{ percent.}$$

EYE on the PAST
How Fast Has Real GDP per Person Grown?

If you're a middle-class American, you know what life is like in a household that spends (at least) $150 a day. Try to imagine life with only $1 a day to spend. That is the amount that a billion people in today's world struggle to live on. It is also the amount that our ancestors lived on for the first million years of human existence.

The figure shows estimates of incomes (real GDP per person) over more than a million years expressed in the value of the dollar in 2015. Real GDP per person averaged $330 a year—a bit less than $1 a day—until 1620! It rose to $400 a year when Aristotle and Plato were teaching in Athens, but slipped back during the next thousand years to $275 as the Roman Empire collapsed. When the Black Death gripped Europe in the 1340s, incomes fell to a 1-million-year low, and even when the Pilgrim Fathers began to arrive in America in

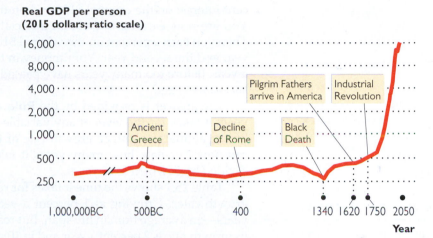

Real GDP per person
(2015 dollars; ratio scale)

SOURCE OF DATA: J. Bradford DeLong, "*Estimating World GDP, One Million B.C.–Present*" updated and converted to 2015 dollars.

the 1620s, incomes were still the same as those of Ancient Greece.

Beginning around 1750, first in England and then in Europe and the United States, an astonishing change known as the Industrial Revolution occurred. Real GDP per person

exploded. By 1850, it was twice its 1650 level. By 1950, it was more than five times its 1850 level, and by 2015, it was more than three times its 1950 level. This chapter explores the story of economic growth—of its causes and its effects.

We can also calculate the growth rate of real GDP per person by using the formula:

$$\text{Growth rate of real GDP per person} = \text{Growth rate of real GDP} - \text{Growth rate of population.}$$

In the example you've just worked through, the growth rate of real GDP is 5 percent. The population changes from 200 million to 202 million, so

$$\text{Growth rate of population} = \frac{202 \text{ million} - 200 \text{ million}}{200 \text{ million}} \times 100 = 1 \text{ percent.}$$

and

$$\text{Growth rate of real GDP per person} = 5 \text{ percent} - 1 \text{ percent} = 4 \text{ percent.}$$

This formula makes it clear that real GDP per person grows only if real GDP grows faster than the population. If the growth rate of the population exceeds the growth of real GDP, then real GDP per person falls.

■ The Magic of Sustained Growth

Sustained growth of real GDP per person can transform a poor society into a wealthy one. The reason is that economic growth is like compound interest. If you put $100 in the bank and earn 5 percent a year interest on it, after one year, you have $105. If you leave that money in the bank for another year, you earn 5 percent interest on the original $100 and on the $5 interest that you earned last year. You are now earning interest on interest! The next year, things get even better. Then you earn 5 percent on the original $100 and on the interest earned in the first year and the second year. Your money in the bank is *growing* at a rate of 5 percent a year. Before too many years have passed, you'll have $200 in the bank. But after *how many* years?

The answer is provided by the **Rule of 70**, which states that the number of years it takes for the level of any variable to double is approximately 70 divided by the annual percentage growth rate of the variable. Using the Rule of 70, you can now calculate how many years it takes your $100 to become $200. It is 70 divided by 5, which is 14 years.

Table 25.1 shows the time it takes for real GDP per person to double at various growth rates. Growing at 1 percent a year, real GDP per person doubles in 70 years—an average human life span. But real GDP per person doubles in 35 years if its growth rate is 2 percent a year and in 10 years if its growth rate is 7 percent a year.

We can use the Rule of 70 to answer other questions about economic growth. For example, in 2015, U.S. real GDP per person was approximately 4 times that of China. China's recent growth rate of real GDP per person was 7 percent a year. If this growth rate were maintained, how long would it take China's real GDP per person to reach that of the United States in 2015? The answer, provided by the Rule of 70, is 20 years. China's real GDP per person doubles in 10 years and doubles again to 4 times its current level in another 10 years.

Rule of 70
The number of years it takes for the level of any variable to double is approximately 70 divided by the annual percentage growth rate of the variable.

TABLE 25.1   GROWTH RATES

Growth rate (percent per year)	Years for level to double
1	70
2	35
5	14
7	10
10	7

EYE on the U.S. ECONOMY
U.S. Growth Is Slowing

To achieve its transformative effects on the standard of living, the economic growth rate must be high and maintained over many years. You can see in the graph that the U.S. growth has not been maintained at a high rate.

The growth rate of potential GDP per person has slowed every decade since the 1960s with the consequence that the doubling period has blown out from 24 years in the 1960s to 125 years in the 2010s.

Why U.S. growth has slowed is not fully understood, but we will explore possible reasons in this chapter.

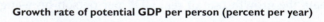

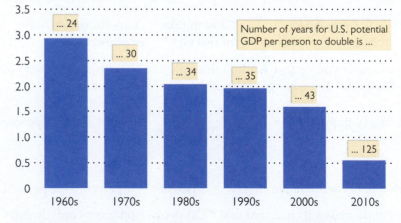

Growth rate of potential GDP per person (percent per year)

Number of years for U.S. potential GDP per person to double is …

1960s … 24
1970s … 30
1980s … 34
1990s … 35
2000s … 43
2010s … 125

SOURCES OF DATA: Congressional Budget Office and authors' calculations.

CHECKPOINT 25.1

MyEconLab Study Plan 25.1
Key Terms Quiz
Solutions Video

Define and calculate the economic growth rate, and explain the implications of sustained growth.

Practice Problems

1. Mexico's real GDP was 13,769 billion pesos in 2014 and 14,120 billion pesos in 2015. Mexico's population growth rate in 2015 was 1.2 percent. Calculate Mexico's economic growth rate in 2015 and the growth rate of real GDP per person in Mexico in 2015.

2. Calculate the approximate number of years it will take for real GDP per person to double if an economy maintains an economic growth rate of 12 percent a year and a population growth rate of 2 percent a year.

3. Calculate the change in the number of years it will take for real GDP per person in India to double if the growth rate of real GDP per person increases from 8 percent a year to 10 percent a year.

In the News

China's economic growth in 2015 is slowest in 25 years
China's growth rate slowed to an annual rate of 6.8 percent in the fourth quarter of 2015, down from 7.3 percent in 2014.
Source: *The Wall Street Journal*, January 19, 2016
If China's growth rate has slowed from 9 percent a year and remains at 6.8 percent a year, how many additional years will it take for China's real GDP to double?

Solutions to Practice Problems

1. Mexico's economic growth rate in 2015 was 2.5 percent. The economic growth rate equals the percentage change in real GDP:
[(Real GDP in 2015 − Real GDP in 2014) ÷ Real GDP in 2014] × 100, which is
[(14,120 billion − 13,769 billion) ÷ 13,769 billion] × 100, or 2.5 percent.
The growth rate of real GDP per person equals 1.3 percent.
Growth rate of real GDP per person equals (Growth rate of real GDP − Population growth rate), which is (2.5 percent − 1.2 percent), or 1.3 percent.

2. It will take 7 years for real GDP per person to double. The growth rate of real GDP per person equals the economic growth rate minus the population growth rate. Real GDP per person grows at 12 percent minus 2 percent, which is 10 percent a year. The Rule of 70 tells us that the level of a variable that grows at 10 percent a year will double in 70 ÷ 10 years, or 7 years.

3. Two years. The Rule of 70 tells us that a variable that grows at 8 percent a year will double in 70 ÷ 8 years, which is approximately 9 years. By increasing its growth rate to 10 percent a year, the variable will double in 7 years.

Solution to In the News

With a growth rate of 9 percent a year, real GDP per person will double in 8 years (70 ÷ 9). If the growth rate is maintained at 6.8 percent a year, real GDP per person will double in 10 years (70 ÷ 6.8)—taking an additional 2 years.

25.2 LABOR PRODUCTIVITY GROWTH

Real GDP grows when the quantities of the factors of production grow or when persistent advances in technology make them increasingly productive. To understand what determines the growth rate of real GDP, we must understand what determines the growth rates of the factors of production and the rate of increase in their productivity. You're going to see how saving and investment determine the growth rate of physical capital and how the growth of physical capital and human capital and advances in technology interact to determine the economic growth rate.

We are interested in real GDP growth because it contributes to improvements in our standard of living. But our standard of living improves only if we produce more goods and services with each hour of labor. So our main concern is to understand the forces that make our labor more productive. Let's start by defining labor productivity.

■ Labor Productivity

Labor productivity
The quantity of real GDP produced by one hour of labor.

Labor productivity is the quantity of real GDP produced by one hour of labor. It is calculated by using the formula:

$$\text{Labor productivity} = \frac{\text{Real GDP}}{\text{Aggregate hours}}.$$

For example, if real GDP is $8,000 billion and if aggregate hours are 200 billion, then we can calculate labor productivity as

$$\text{Labor productivity} = \frac{\$8,000\ \text{billion}}{200\ \text{billion hours}} = \$40\ \text{per hour}.$$

When labor productivity grows, real GDP per person grows. So the growth in labor productivity is the basis of the rising standard of living. What makes labor productivity grow? We'll answer this question by considering the influences on labor productivity growth under two broad headings:

- Saving and investment in physical capital
- Expansion of human capital and discovery of new technologies

These two broad influences on labor productivity growth interact and are the sources of the extraordinary growth in productivity during the past 200 years. Although they interact, we'll begin by looking at each on its own.

■ Saving and Investment in Physical Capital

Saving and investment in physical capital increase the amount of capital per worker and increase labor productivity. Labor productivity took a dramatic upturn when the amount of capital per worker increased during the Industrial Revolution. Production processes that use hand tools can create beautiful objects, but production methods that use large amounts of capital per worker, such as auto plant assembly lines, enable workers to be much more productive. The accumulation of capital on farms and building sites; in textile factories, iron foundries and steel mills, coal mines, chemical plants, and auto plants; and at banks and insurance companies added incredibly to the productivity of our labor.

A strong and experienced farm worker of 1830, using a scythe, could harvest 3 acres of wheat a day. A farm worker of 1831, using a mechanical reaper, could harvest 15 acres a day. And a farm worker of today, using a combine harvester, can harvest and thresh hundreds of acres a day.

The next time you see a movie set in the old West, look carefully at how little capital there is. Try to imagine how productive you would be in such circumstances compared with your productivity today.

Capital Accumulation and Diminishing Marginal Returns

Although saving and investment in additional capital is a source of labor productivity growth, without the expansion of human capital and technological change, it would not bring sustained economic growth. Eventually growth would slow and most likely stop. The reason is a fundamental fact about capital known as the **law of diminishing marginal returns**, which states

> **If the quantity of capital is small, an increase in capital brings a large increase in production; and if the quantity of capital is large, an increase in capital brings a small increase in production.**

This law applies to all factors of production, not only to capital, and is the reason why the demand for labor curve slopes downward (see Chapter 24, p. 620).

You can see why the law of diminishing marginal returns applies to capital by thinking about how your own productivity is influenced by the capital you own. When you got your first computer your small quantity of capital increased and your productivity increased enormously. You most likely don't have two computers, but if you do, the productivity boost from your second computer was much smaller than that from the first. If you don't have two computers, one of the reasons is that you doubt it would be worth the expense because it would contribute such a small amount to your labor productivity.

Farm labor productivity increased from harvesting 3 acres per day in 1830…

to harvesting hundreds of acres per day in the twenty-first century.

Productivity curve
The relationship that shows how real GDP per hour of labor changes as the quantity of capital per hour of labor changes.

Illustrating the Law of Diminishing Marginal Returns

Figure 25.1 illustrates the relationship between capital and productivity. The curve *PC* is a **productivity curve**, which shows how real GDP per hour of labor changes as the quantity of capital per hour of labor changes.

In Figure 25.1, when the quantity of capital (measured in real dollars) increases from $40 to $80 per hour of labor, real GDP per hour of labor increases from $30 to $50, a $20 or 67 percent increase. But when the quantity of capital increases from $180 to $220 per hour of labor, the same $40 increase as before, real GDP per hour of labor increases from $80 to $84, only a $4 or 5 percent increase. If capital per hour of labor keeps increasing, labor productivity increases by ever smaller amounts and eventually stops rising.

■ Expansion of Human Capital and Discovery of New Technologies

The expansion of human capital and the discovery of new technologies have a profoundly different effect on labor productivity than capital accumulation has. They don't display diminishing marginal returns.

Expansion of Human Capital Human capital—the accumulated skill and knowledge of people—comes from three sources:

1. Education and training
2. Job experience
3. Health and diet

■ FIGURE 25.1

The Effects of an Increase in Capital

MyEconLab Animation

When workers are equipped with more capital, they become more productive. The productivity curve *PC* shows how an increase in capital per hour of labor increases real GDP per hour of labor.

❶ When the quantity of capital per hour of labor increases from a low $40 to $80, real GDP per hour of labor increases by $20.

❷ When the quantity of capital per hour of labor increases from a high $180 to $220, real GDP per hour of labor increases by $4.

An equal-size increase in capital per hour of labor brings a diminishing increase in output, the greater is the quantity of capital.

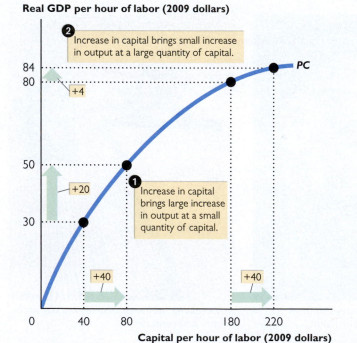

Real GDP per hour of labor (2009 dollars)

❷ Increase in capital brings small increase in output at a large quantity of capital.

+4

+20

❶ Increase in capital brings large increase in output at a small quantity of capital.

+40   +40

Capital per hour of labor (2009 dollars)

A hundred years ago, most people attended school for around eight years. A hundred years before that, most people had no formal education at all. Today, 90 percent of Americans complete high school and more than 60 percent go to college or university. Our ability to read, write, and communicate effectively contributes enormously to our productivity.

The education of thousands of scientists, engineers, mathematicians, biologists, computer programmers, and people equipped with a host of other specialist skills has made huge contributions to labor productivity and to the advance in technology.

While formal education is productive, school is not the only place where people acquire human capital. We also learn from on-the-job experience—from *learning by doing*. One carefully studied example illustrates the importance of learning by doing. Between 1941 and 1944 (during World War II), U.S. shipyards produced 2,500 Liberty Ships—cargo ships built to a standardized design. In 1941, it took 1.2 million person-hours to build a ship. By 1942, it took 600,000, and by 1943, it took only 500,000. Not much change occurred in the physical capital employed during these years, but an enormous amount of human capital was accumulated. Thousands of workers and managers learned from experience and their productivity more than doubled in two years.

Strong, healthy, well-nourished workers are much more productive than those who lack good nutrition, healthcare, and opportunities to exercise. This fact creates a virtuous circle. Improved healthcare, diet, and exercise increase labor productivity; and increased labor productivity brings the increased incomes that make these health improvements possible.

The expansion of human capital is the most fundamental source of economic growth because it directly increases labor productivity and is the source of the discovery of new technologies.

Discovery of New Technologies   The growth of physical capital and the expansion of human capital have made large contributions to economic growth, but the discovery of new technologies has made an even greater contribution.

The development of writing, one of the most basic human skills, was the source of some of the earliest productivity gains. The ability to keep written records made it possible to reap ever-larger gains from specialization and trade. Imagine how hard it would be to do any kind of business if all the accounts, invoices, and agreements existed only in people's memories.

Production using 1950s technology.

Later, the development of mathematics laid the foundation for the eventual extension of knowledge in physics, chemistry, and biology. This base of scientific knowledge was the foundation for the technological advances of the Industrial Revolution 200 years ago and of today's Information Revolution.

Since the Industrial Revolution, technological change has become a part of everyday life. Firms routinely conduct research to develop technologies that are more productive, and partnerships between business and the universities are commonplace in fields such as biotechnology and electronics.

Illustrating the Effects of Human Capital and Technological Change

Figure 25.2 illustrates the effects of the expansion of human capital and the discovery of new technologies and labor productivity: They shift the *productivity curve* upward. In the figure, these influences shift the productivity curve from PC_0 to PC_1. Imagine that PC_0 is the productivity curve in 1960 and PC_1 is the productivity curve for 2015. With capital of $180 per hour of labor, workers could

Production using 2015 technology.

■ **FIGURE 25.2**

The Effects of Human Capital and Technological Change

MyEconLab Animation

When human capital expands or technology advances, labor becomes more productive—a given amount of capital per hour of labor can produce more real GDP per hour of labor.

Here, with the technology of 1960 on PC_0, $180 of capital per hour of labor can produce $40 of goods and services—real GDP per hour of labor.

With the technology of 2015 on PC_1, the same $180 of capital per hour of labor can produce $80 of goods and services—real GDP per hour of labor.

The expansion of human capital and the discovery of new technologies shift the productivity curve upward and are not subject to diminishing marginal returns.

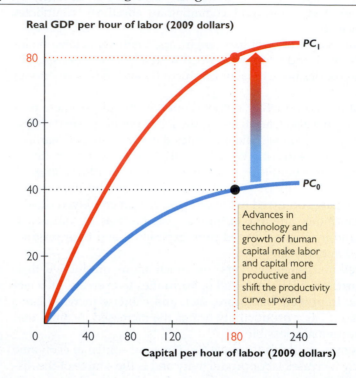

produce $80 of real GDP per hour of labor in 2015. If workers had been equipped with the same amount of capital but with the technology of 1960, they would have produced only $40 of real GDP per hour of labor. The upward shift of the productivity curve illustrates the fact that labor and capital become more productive at each quantity of capital per hour of labor. Capital is still subject to diminishing marginal returns but the overall level of productivity is higher with expanded human capital and more productive technologies.

■ Combined Influences Bring Labor Productivity Growth

To reap the benefits of technological change—to use new technologies to make labor productivity grow—capital must increase. Some of the most powerful and far-reaching technologies are embodied in human capital—for example, language, writing, mathematics, physics, biology, and engineering. But most technologies are embodied in physical capital. For example, to increase the productivity of transportation workers by using the discovery of the internal combustion engine, millions of horse-drawn carriages had to be replaced by automobiles and trucks; more recently, to increase the labor productivity of office workers by using the discovery of computerized word processing, millions of typewriters had to be replaced by computers and printers.

Figure 25.3 shows how the combined effects of capital accumulation, the expansion of human capital, and the discovery of new technologies bring labor productivity growth. In 1960, the productivity curve is PC_0, workers have $80 of capital per hour and produce $25 of real GDP per hour. By 2015, capital has increased to $180 per hour. With no expansion of human capital or technological

FIGURE 25.3

How Labor Productivity Grows

MyEconLab Animation

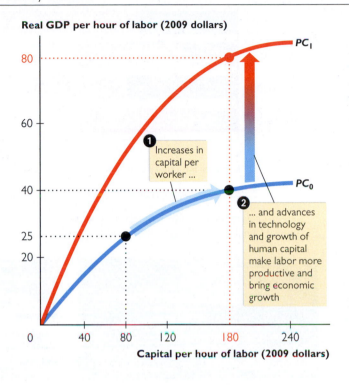

In 1960, workers had $80 of capital per hour of labor and produced real GDP per hour of $25 on PC_0.

❶ When the quantity of capital increased from $80 per hour of labor in 1960 to $180 per hour of labor in 2015, real GDP per hour of labor increased from $25 to $40 along PC_0.

❷ The expansion of human capital and discovery of new technologies shifted the productivity curve upward and increased real GDP per hour of labor from $40 to $80.

advance, real GDP per hour of labor would have increased to $40. But with the human capital and technology of 2015, output per hour increases to $80.

You've now seen what makes labor productivity grow. *Eye on the U.S. Economy* on p. 648 looks at the quantitative importance of the sources of growth since 1960. Real GDP grows because labor becomes more productive and also because the *quantity of labor* increases. Figure 25.4 summarizes the sources of economic growth and shows how the growth in labor productivity together with the growth in the quantity of labor bring real GDP growth.

FIGURE 25.4

The Sources of Economic Growth

MyEconLab Animation

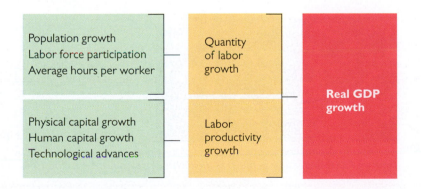

Real GDP depends on the quantity of labor and labor productivity.

The quantity of labor depends on the population, the labor force participation rate, and the average hours per worker.

Labor productivity depends on the amounts of physical capital and human capital and the state of technology.

Growth in the quantity of labor and growth in labor productivity bring real GDP growth.

EYE on the U.S. ECONOMY
U.S. Labor Productivity Growth Since 1960

The figure shows how labor productivity has grown since 1960. It also shows the contributions to productivity growth of advances in technology (the blue bars) and increases in physical capital and human capital (the red bars).

You can see that labor productivity growth during the 1960s was around double its later rate. Growth picked up a bit in the 1980s and 1990s and slowed again after 2007.

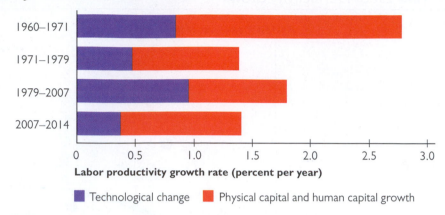

Labor productivity growth rate (percent per year)

■ Technological change   ■ Physical capital and human capital growth

Source of data: Penn World Table 8.1 by Robert C. Feenstra, Robert Inklaar and Marcel P. Timmer, Congressional Budget Office, and authors' calculations.

The Booming Sixties

Plastics, the laser, the computer, the transistor, the space race, the interstate highway system, the shopping mall, and passenger jet were among the technological advances that brought extraordinary labor productivity growth during the 1960s.

Passenger jets and the construction of thousands of miles of interstate highways were among the technological advances that increased labor productivity during the 1960s.

The Stagnant Seventies

An oil price hike and oil embargo as well as higher taxes and expanded regulation slowed productivity growth during the 1970s and the higher cost of energy diverted the focus of technological change toward saving energy rather than increasing labor productivity.

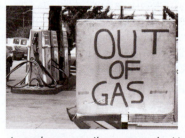

An embargo on oil exports to the United States and a higher cost of energy as well as tax hikes contributed to the productivity growth slowdown of the 1970s.

The Information Age

The Internet has transformed our lives and unlocking the human genome has opened the possibility of dramatic advances in healthcare. But the information age increase in labor productivity is lower than that of the 1960s; and after 2007, global financial turmoil lowered its rate to that of the stagnant 1970s.

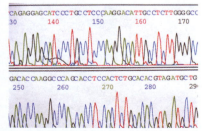

Advances in information technologies and biotechnologies increased productivity during the 1990s and 2000s but not by as much as the technological advances of the 1960s did.

CHECKPOINT 25.2

Explain the sources of labor productivity growth.

Practice Problems

Use the data in Table 1 to work Problems **1** and **2**.

TABLE 1

Item	2015	2016
Aggregate labor hours (billions)	25.0	25.6
Real GDP (billions of 2009 dollars)	1,000	1,050

1. Calculate the growth rate of real GDP in 2016.
2. Calculate labor productivity in 2015 and 2016, and the growth rate of labor productivity in 2016.

In the News

Labor productivity mixed
The BLS reported the following data for the first quarter of 2016: In the nonfarm sector, output increased 0.9 percent as aggregate hours increased by 1.5 percent; in the manufacturing sector, output increased 0.6 percent as aggregate hours decreased by 0.7 percent.

Source: Productivity and Costs, Bureau of Labor Statistics, June 7, 2016

As aggregate hours and output changed, how did labor productivity in each sector change? In which sector was growth in labor productivity greater?

Solutions to Practice Problems

1. The growth rate of real GDP in 2016 was 5 percent. The growth rate equals [($1,050 billion − $1,000 billion) ÷ $1,000 billion] × 100 = 5 percent.
2. Labor productivity is $40.00 an hour in 2015 and $41.02 an hour in 2016.

   Labor productivity equals real GDP divided by aggregate labor hours.

   In 2015, labor productivity was ($1,000 billion ÷ 25 billion) or $40.00 per hour of labor. In 2016, labor productivity was ($1,050 billion ÷ 25.6 billion) or $41.02 per hour of labor.

   The growth rate of labor productivity in 2016 was 2.55 percent.

   Labor productivity growth rate was [($41.02 − $40.00) ÷ $40.00] × 100 or 2.55 percent.

Solution to In the News

In the nonfarm sector, output increased by less than the increase in aggregate hours, so labor productivity decreased. Output growth in manufacturing was less than that in the nonfarm sector, but aggregate hours decreased in manufacturing, so labor productivity increased. Because labor productivity increased in manufacturing and decreased in the nonfarm sector, labor productivity growth was greater in manufacturing.

MyEconLab Concept Video

25.3 CAUSES AND EFFECTS OF ECONOMIC GROWTH

You've seen that real GDP grows when labor productivity and the quantity of labor grow. You've also seen that labor productivity grows when saving and investment increase physical capital, when education and on-the-job training expand human capital, and when research leads to the discovery of new technologies. But what *causes* saving and investment in new capital, the expansion of human capital, the discovery of new technologies, and population growth? Economists have been trying to answer this question and understand why and how poor countries become rich and rich countries become richer since the time of Adam Smith in the eighteenth century. We'll look at two sets of ideas: old and new.

■ Old Growth Theory

Classical growth theory
The theory that the clash between an exploding population and limited resources will eventually bring economic growth to an end.

An old growth theory remains relevant today because some people believe that it might turn out to be correct. It is called **classical growth theory**, and it predicts that a clash between an exploding population and limited resources will eventually bring economic growth to an end. According to classical growth theory, labor productivity growth is temporary. When labor productivity rises and lifts real GDP per person above the subsistence level, which is the minimum real income needed to maintain life, a population explosion occurs. Eventually, the population grows so large that capital per worker and labor productivity fall and real GDP per person returns to the subsistence level.

Adam Smith, Thomas Robert Malthus, and David Ricardo, the leading economists of the late eighteenth and early nineteenth centuries, proposed this theory, but the view is most closely associated with Malthus and is sometimes called the *Malthusian theory*. It is also sometimes called the Doomsday theory.

Many people today are Malthusians. They say that if today's global population of 7 billion explodes to 11 billion by 2200, we will run out of many natural resources and the population will grow faster than the quantity of capital so labor productivity will fall and we will return to the primitive standard of living that was experienced before the Industrial Revolution. (You can see in *Eye on the Past* on p. 639 that for most of human history, people did live on the brink of subsistence.) We must act, say the Malthusians, to contain the population growth. This dismal implication led to economics being called the *dismal science*.

■ New Growth Theory

New growth theory
The theory that our unlimited wants will lead us to ever greater productivity and perpetual economic growth.

New growth theory predicts that our unlimited wants will lead us to ever greater productivity and perpetual economic growth. According to new growth theory, real GDP per person grows because of the choices people make in the pursuit of profit. Paul Romer of Stanford University developed this theory during the 1980s, building on ideas developed by Joseph Schumpeter during the 1930s and 1940s.

Choices and Innovation

The new growth theory emphasizes three facts about market economies:

- Human capital expands because of choices.
- Discoveries result from choices.
- Discoveries bring profit, and competition destroys profit.

Human Capital Expansion and Choices People decide how long to remain in school, what to study, and how hard to study. And when they graduate from school, people make more choices about job training and on-the-job learning. All these choices govern the speed at which human capital expands.

Discoveries and Choices When people discover a new product or technique, they consider themselves lucky. They are right, but chance does not determine the pace at which new discoveries are made—and at which technology advances. It depends on how many people are looking for a new technology and how intensively they are looking.

Discoveries and Profits Profit is the spur to technological change. The forces of competition squeeze profits, so to increase profit, people constantly seek either lower-cost methods of production or new and better products for which people are willing to pay a higher price. Inventors can maintain a profit for several years by taking out a patent or copyright, but eventually a new discovery is copied and profits disappear.

Two other facts play a key role in the new growth theory:

- Many people can use discoveries at the same time.
- Physical activities can be replicated.

Discoveries Used by All Once a profitable new discovery has been made, everyone can use it. For example, when Marc Andreeson created Mosaic, the Web browser that led to the creation of Netscape Navigator and Microsoft's Internet Explorer, everyone who was interested in navigating the Internet had access to a new and more efficient tool. One person's use of a Web browser does not prevent others from using it. This fact means that as the benefits of a new discovery spread, free resources become available. These resources are free because nothing is given up when an additional person uses them. They have a zero opportunity cost.

Replicating Activities Production activities can be replicated. For example, there might be 2, 3, or 53 identical firms making fiber-optic cable by using an identical assembly line and production technique. If one firm increases its capital and output, that *firm* experiences diminishing returns. But the economy can increase its capital and output by adding another identical fiber cable factory, and the *economy* does not experience diminishing returns.

The assumption that capital does not experience diminishing returns is the central novel proposition of the new growth theory. The implication of this simple and appealing idea is astonishing. As capital accumulates, labor productivity grows indefinitely as long as people devote resources to expanding human capital and introducing new technologies.

Perpetual Motion

Economic growth is like the perpetual motion machine in Figure 25.5. Growth is driven by insatiable wants that lead us to pursue profit and innovate. New and better products result from this process; new firms start up, and old firms go out of business. As firms start up and die, jobs are created and destroyed. New and better jobs lead to more leisure and more consumption. But our insatiable wants are still there, so the process continues—wants, profit incentives, innovation, and new products. The economic growth rate depends on the ability and the incentive to innovate.

FIGURE 25.5

A Perpetual Motion Machine

MyEconLab Animation

❶ People want a higher standard of living and are spurred by ❷ profit incentives to make the ❸ innovations that lead to ❹ new and better techniques and new and better products, which in turn lead to ❺ the birth of new firms and the death of some old firms, ❻ new and better jobs, and ❼ more leisure and more consumption goods and services. The result is ❽ a higher standard of living. But people want a yet higher standard of living, and the growth process continues.

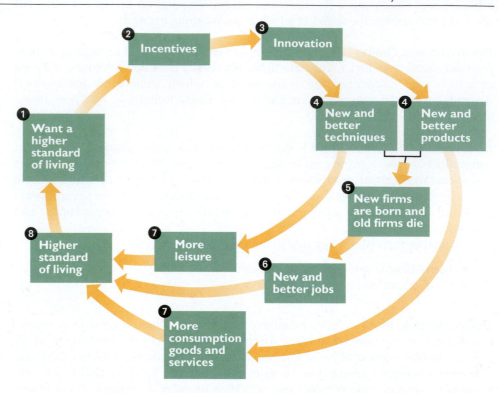

Based on a similar figure in *These Are the Good Old Days: A Report on U.S. Living Standards,* Federal Reserve Bank of Dallas 1993 Annual Report.

■ Economic Growth and the Distribution of Income

Does the gap between high and low incomes widen or narrow as real GDP grows? And what determines the long-term level and trends of income inequality? Economist Simon Kuznets posed these questions in the 1950s. He remarked that getting the answers was hampered by a scarcity of data and strongly held opinions. Over the years since the 1950s, more data have become available, but strongly held opinions continue to get in the way of clear thinking.

The Data

Starting in the early 1980s, income inequality increased in a process that has been called the Great Divergence. The share of total income received by the top 1 percent of Americans moved up from 8 percent in 1980 to 18 percent in 2014. A similar trend is found in many other developed economies. Correspondingly, the income shares of lower income groups decreased.

The Great Divergence is the reverse of the Great Compression that preceded it. From 1913 to 1980, the income share of the top 1 percent *decreased* from 18 percent to 8 percent. Falling income inequality was the only trend known to Kuznets. His data showed that between 1880 and 1950, the share of total income going to the top 5 percent shrank from 31 percent to 20 percent in America and from 46 percent to 24 percent in Britain.

Eye on the U.S. Economy on p. 653 provides a striking perspective on these two contrasting episodes.

EYE on the U.S. ECONOMY
The Changing Shares in the Gains from Economic Growth

A common cry in recent years is that the economy is failing middle-class America. The rich are getting richer and the rest are standing still. Is this description accurate? If it is, the gains from economic growth have gone mainly to the rich.

To check this claim, we need to look at the incomes of the richest and poorest people and see how they have changed over the years. That's what the two figures do. They show the levels of income (per person) in different income groups as a percentage of incomes in 1970 (Figure 1) and 1929 (Figure 2).

Starting the story in 1970, Figure 1 shows that for about 10 years, the incomes of the rich (the top 1 percent) grew at a similar rate to those of other groups (the next top 19 percent and the bottom 20 percent).

Then, in 1983, the incomes of the top 1 percent started to outpace those of others. By 2007, the incomes of the top 1 percent were 5 times their 1970 level, of the next top 19 percent were double, and of the bottom 20 percent were only 1.8 times higher. And the bottom 20 percent made no progress at all from 1999 through 2014. It seems that there was indeed a Great Divergence.

Figure 2 tells a different story. From 1929 to 1970, while the incomes of 99 percent of people were rising to 3 times their 1929 level, those of the top 1 percent stagnated. When the incomes of the top 1 percent increased in the Great Divergence of Figure 1, they increased in a Great Convergence in Figure 2.

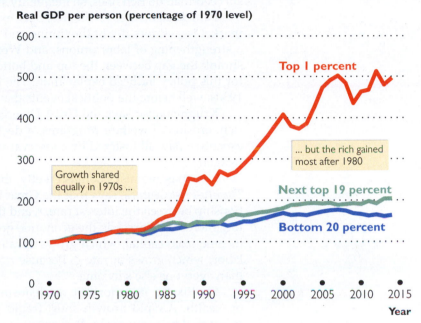

Figure 1 The Unequal Shares Since 1980

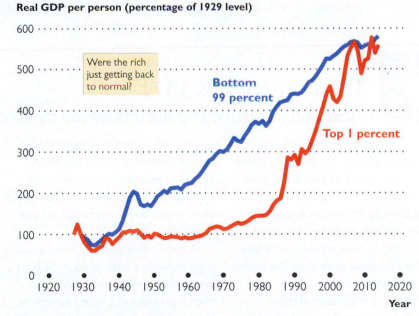

Figure 2 The Rich Climb Back

SOURCES OF DATA: Bureau of Economic Analysis, U.S. Census Bureau, World Wealth and Income Database, and authors' calculations.

The Explanations

Kuznets explained the decrease in inequality as incomes grow as resulting from market forces in a dynamic economy. Everyone is free to create a business. Some succeed and some fail. A greater number of hungry low-income entrepreneurs succeed than do rich ones, so inequality shrinks.

Paul Krugman says the Kuznets explanation of a compression driven by market forces does not fit the timing and that it was progressive income taxation, a strengthening of labor unions, and World War II wage and price controls that shrank the gap between the top and bottom earners. But timing poses a problem for this policy-induced explanation. The largest convergence occurred in the late 1930s, well before the political events that are claimed to have caused it.

Krugman also says the Great Divergence was caused by lower taxes on the rich, erosion of welfare programs, a decline in union membership, and soaring executive pay, all fostered by conservative economic policies initiated by Ronald Reagan.

French economist Thomas Piketty, the author of the best selling *Capital in the Twenty-First Century*, says that the Great Divergence is a consequence of the relationship between the interest rate, r, and the economic growth rate, g. He says that the interest rate exceeds the economic growth rate—$r > g$. The wealthy get their income from capital, which grows at rate r. The rest of us get our incomes from labor, which grows at rate g. Because $r > g$, the incomes of the rich grow faster than everyone else's income.

For Piketty, no automatic mechanism works against the steady concentration of wealth. A rapid growth spurt (rapid technological change) counters the rise in inequality temporarily. But only government redistribution can avoid rising inequality.

Economists do not yet have sound answers to the questions Simon Kuznets posed 60 years ago. We don't know enough to say where inequality is heading.

EYE on YOUR LIFE

MyEconLab Critical Thinking Exercise

How You Influence and Are Influenced by Economic Growth

Many of the choices that you make affect your personal economic growth rate—the pace of expansion of your own standard of living. And these same choices, in combination with similar choices made by millions of other people, have a profound effect on the economic growth of the nation and the world.

The most important of these choices right now is your choice to increase your human capital. By being in school, you have decided to expand your human capital.

You will continue to expand your human capital long after you finish school as your earning power rises with on-the-job experience. You might even decide to return to school at a later stage in your life.

A choice that will become increasingly important later in your life is to accumulate a retirement fund. This choice provides not only a source of income for you when you eventually retire but also financial resources that firms can use to finance the expansion of physical capital.

Not only do your choices influence economic growth; economic growth also has a big influence on you—on how you earn your income and on the standard of living that your income makes possible.

Because of economic growth, the jobs available today are more interesting and less dangerous and strenuous than those of 100 years ago; and jobs are hugely better paid. But for many of us, economic growth means that we must accept change and be ready to learn new skills and get new jobs.

CHECKPOINT 25.3

Review theories of the causes and effects of economic growth.

Practice Problems

1. What is the classical growth theory and why does it predict that economic growth will eventually end?

2. What is the driving force of economic growth according to new growth theory? Why does it predict that economic growth will never end?

In the News

Graphene batteries may slash your phone recharge time to 15 minutes
The world's first graphene battery pack puts more power in a smartphone and recharges in 13 to 15 minutes. Graphene also makes flexible screens possible, improves heart rate and fingerprint sensors, and holds the promise to revolutionize batteries for electric cars.

Source: *Digital Trends*, July 11, 2016

Graphene is a new material that can be 1 atom thick. Which of the growth theories that you've studied in this chapter is best supported by this news clip?

Solutions to Practice Problems

1. The classical growth theory predicts that labor productivity growth is temporary: When labor productivity increases, real GDP per person increases and because it exceeds the real income needed to maintain life, a population explosion occurs. The population becomes so large that capital per worker and labor productivity decrease and real GDP per person returns to its subsistence level.

2. The driving force of economic growth according to new growth theory is a persistent pursuit of profit that is the incentive to innovate along with an absence of diminishing returns. New growth theory predicts that economic growth will never end because our unlimited wants will lead us to make choices that will bring ever-greater productivity and perpetual economic growth.

Solution to In the News

The news clip describes an event that supports the new growth theory. According to this theory, real GDP per person grows because of the choices people make in the pursuit of profit. The perpetual pursuit of profit leads to innovations (graphene and its application to battery technology) that increase labor productivity and increase profit. The perpetual pursuit of profit through innovation will bring persistent economic growth.

25.4 ACHIEVING FASTER GROWTH

Why did it take more than a million years of human life before economic growth began? Why are some countries even today still barely growing? Why don't all societies save and invest in new capital, expand human capital, and discover and apply new technologies on a scale that brings rapid economic growth? What actions can governments take to encourage growth?

■ Preconditions for Economic Growth

The main reason economic growth is either absent or slow is that some societies lack the incentive system that encourages growth-producing activities. One of the fundamental preconditions for creating the incentives that lead to economic growth is economic freedom.

Economic Freedom

Economic freedom is present when people are able to make personal choices, their private property is protected by the rule of law, and they are free to buy and sell in markets. The rule of law, an efficient legal system, and the ability to enforce contracts are essential foundations for creating economic freedom. Impediments to economic freedom are corruption in the courts and government bureaucracy; barriers to trade, such as import bans; high tax rates; stringent regulations on business, such as health, safety, and environmental regulation; restrictions on banks; labor market regulations that limit a firm's ability to hire and lay off workers; and illegal markets, such as those that violate intellectual property rights.

No unique political system is necessary to deliver economic freedom. Democratic systems do a good job, but the rule of law, not democracy, is the key requirement for creating economic freedom. Nondemocratic political systems that respect the rule of law can also work well. Hong Kong is the best example of a place with little democracy but a lot of economic freedom—and a lot of economic growth. No country with a high level of economic freedom is economically poor, but many countries with low levels of economic freedom stagnate.

Property Rights

Economic freedom requires the protection of private property—the factors of production and goods that people own. The social arrangements that govern the protection of private property are called **property rights**. They include the rights to physical property (land, buildings, and capital equipment), to financial property (claims by one person against another), and to intellectual property (such as inventions). Clearly established and enforced property rights provide people with the incentive to work and save. If someone attempts to steal their property, a legal system will protect them. Such property rights also assure people that government itself will not confiscate their income or savings.

Markets

Economic freedom also requires free markets. Buyers and sellers get information and do business with each other in *markets*. Market prices send signals to buyers and sellers that create incentives to increase or decrease the quantities demanded and supplied. Markets enable people to trade and to save and invest. But markets cannot operate without property rights.

Economic freedom
A condition in which people are able to make personal choices, their private property is protected by the rule of law, and they are free to buy and sell in markets.

Property rights
The social arrangements that govern the protection of private property.

Property rights and markets create incentives for people to specialize and trade, to save and invest, to expand their human capital, and to discover and apply new technologies. Early human societies based on hunting and gathering did not experience economic growth because they lacked property rights and markets. Economic growth began when societies evolved the institutions that create incentives. But the presence of an incentive system and the institutions that create it do not guarantee that economic growth will occur. They permit economic growth but do not make it inevitable.

Growth begins when the appropriate incentive system exists because people can specialize in the activities at which they have a comparative advantage and trade with each other. You saw in Chapter 3 how everyone gains from such activity. By specializing and trading, everyone can acquire goods and services at the lowest possible cost. Consequently, people can obtain a greater volume of goods and services from their labor.

As an economy moves from one with little specialization to one that reaps the gains from specialization and trade, its production and consumption grow. Real GDP per person increases, and the standard of living rises.

But for growth to be persistent, people must face incentives that encourage them to pursue the three activities that generate *ongoing* economic growth: saving and investment, expansion of human capital, and the discovery and application of new technologies.

■ Policies to Achieve Faster Growth

To achieve faster economic growth, we must increase the growth rate of capital per hour of labor, increase the growth rate of human capital, or increase the pace of technological advance. The main actions that governments can take to achieve these objectives are

- Create incentive mechanisms.
- Encourage saving.
- Encourage research and development.
- Encourage international trade.
- Improve the quality of education.

Create Incentive Mechanisms

Economic growth occurs when the incentives to save, invest, and innovate are strong enough. These incentives require property rights enforced by a well-functioning legal system. Property rights and a legal system are the key ingredients that are missing in many societies. For example, they are absent throughout much of Africa. The first priority for growth policy is to establish these institutions so that incentives to save, invest, and innovate exist. Post-communist Russia is an example of a country that has attempted to take this step toward establishing the conditions in which economic growth can occur.

Encourage Saving

Saving finances investment, which brings capital accumulation. So encouraging saving can increase the growth of capital and stimulate economic growth. The East Asian economies have the highest saving rates and the highest growth rates. Some African economies have the lowest saving rates and the lowest growth rates.

Tax incentives can increase saving. Individual Retirement Accounts (IRAs) are an example of a tax incentive to save. Economists claim that a tax on consumption rather than on income provides the best incentive to save.

Encourage Research and Development

Everyone can use the fruits of basic research and development efforts. For example, all biotechnology firms can use advances in gene-splicing technology. Because basic inventions can be copied, the inventor's profit is limited and so the market allocates too few resources to this activity.

Governments can direct public funds toward financing basic research, but this solution is not foolproof. It requires a mechanism for allocating public funds to their highest-valued use. The National Science Foundation is one possibly efficient channel for allocating public funds to universities and public research facilities to finance and encourage basic research. Government programs such as national defense and space exploration also lead to innovations that have wide use. Laptop computers and nonstick coatings are two prominent examples of innovations that came from the U.S. space program.

Encourage International Trade

Free international trade stimulates economic growth by extracting all the available gains from specialization and trade. The fastest-growing nations today are those with the fastest-growing exports and imports. The creation of the North American Free Trade Agreement and the integration of the economies of Europe through the formation of the European Union are examples of successful actions that governments have taken to stimulate economic growth through trade.

Improve the Quality of Education

The free market would produce too little education because it brings social benefits beyond the benefits to the people who receive the education. By funding basic education and by ensuring high standards in skills such as language, mathematics, and science, governments can contribute enormously to a nation's growth potential. Education can also be expanded and improved by using tax incentives to encourage improved private provision. Singapore's Information Technology in Education program is one of the best examples of a successful attempt to stimulate growth through education.

■ How Much Difference Can Policy Make?

It is easy to make a list of policy actions that could increase a nation's economic growth rate. It is hard to convert that list into acceptable actions that make a big difference.

Political equilibrium arises from the balance of the interests of one group against the interests of another group. Change brings gains for some and losses for others, so change is slow. And even when change occurs, if the economic growth rate can be increased by even as much as half a percentage point, it takes many years for the full benefits to accrue.

A well-intentioned government cannot dial up a big increase in the economic growth rate, but it can pursue policies that will nudge the economic growth rate upward. Over time, the benefits from these policies will be large.

EYE on RICH AND POOR NATIONS

Why Are Some Nations Rich and Others Poor?

Political stability, property rights protected by the rule of law, and limited government intervention in markets: These are key features of the economies that enjoy high or rapidly rising incomes and they are the features missing in economies that remain poor. All the rich nations have possessed these growth-inducing characteristics for the many decades during which their labor productivity and standard of living have been rising.

The United States started to grow rapidly 150 years ago and overtook Europe in the early 20th century. In the past 50 years, the gaps between these countries haven't changed much. (See part (a) of the figure.)

In a transition from Communism to a market economy, Eastern Europe is now growing faster.

Tribal conflict in Africa and bureaucratic overload in Central and South America have kept growth slow and the gap between the United States and these regions has widened.

Real GDP per person in three Asian economies, in part (b), has converged toward that in the United States. These economies are like fast trains running on the same track at similar speeds with roughly constant gaps between them. Hong Kong is the lead train, and it runs about 15 years in front of Taiwan and almost 40 years in front of the People's Republic of China.

Between 1960 and 2015, Hong Kong and some other smaller countries of Asia transformed themselves from poor developing economies to take their places among the world's richest economies.

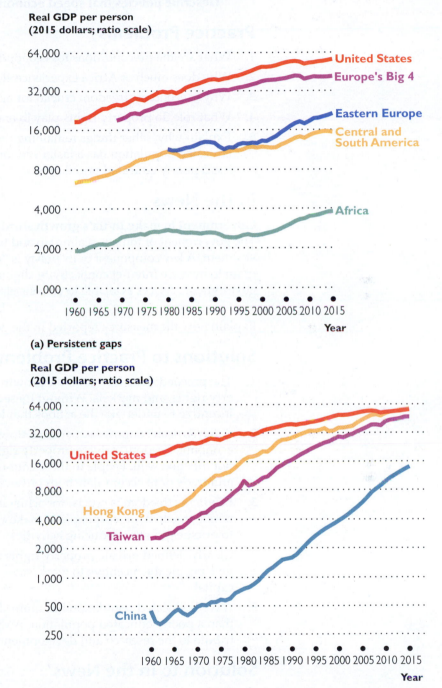

Real GDP per person
(2015 dollars; ratio scale)

(a) Persistent gaps

Real GDP per person
(2015 dollars; ratio scale)

(b) Convergence

SOURCES OF DATA: Penn World Table 8.1 by Robert C. Feenstra, Robert Inklaar and Marcel P. Timmer and International Monetary Fund, *World Economic Outlook Database.*

MyEconLab Study Plan 25.4
         Key Terms Quiz
         Solutions Video

 CHECKPOINT 25.4

Describe policies that speed economic growth.

Practice Problems

1. What are the preconditions for economic growth?

2. Why does much of Africa experience slow economic growth?

3. Why is economic freedom crucial for achieving economic growth?

4. What role do property rights play in encouraging economic growth?

5. Explain why, other things remaining the same, a country with a well-educated population has a faster economic growth rate than a country that has a poorly educated population.

In the News

Government to make India's growth sturdy
The government of India is scaling up and better targeting its infrastructure investment. A key component of its policy is "digitalisation": an infrastructure program to increase Internet connectivity, digitally empower the country, and make government services available to citizens electronically.

                                                            Source: *Business Standard*, July 11, 2016

Explain how the measures reported in the news clip could lead to faster growth.

Solutions to Practice Problems

1. The preconditions for economic growth are economic freedom, private property rights, and markets. Without these preconditions, people have little incentive to undertake the actions that lead to economic growth.

2. Some African countries experience slow economic growth because they lack economic freedom, private property rights are not enforced, and markets do not function well. People in these countries have little incentive to specialize and trade or to accumulate both physical and human capital.

3. Economic freedom is crucial for achieving economic growth because economic freedom allows people to make choices and gives them the incentives to pursue growth-producing activities.

4. Clearly defined private property rights and a legal system to enforce them give people the incentive to work, save, invest, and accumulate human capital.

5. A well-educated population has more skills and greater labor productivity than a poorly educated population. A well-educated population can contribute to the research and development that create new technology.

Solution to In the News

Investment in infrastructure and Internet technology would increase India's stock of physical capital, which would increase labor productivity. Better electronic communication would increase human capital and again increase labor productivity. These measures could lead to faster growth in labor productivity and faster growth in real GDP per person in India.

CHAPTER SUMMARY

Key Points

1. Define and calculate the economic growth rate, and explain the implications of sustained growth.

*   Economic growth is the sustained expansion of production possibilities. The annual percentage change in real GDP measures the economic growth rate.
*   Real GDP per person must grow if the standard of living is to rise.
*   Sustained economic growth transforms poor nations into rich ones.
*   The Rule of 70 tells us the number of years in which real GDP doubles—70 divided by the percentage growth rate of real GDP.

2. Explain the sources of labor productivity growth.

*   Real GDP grows when aggregate hours and labor productivity grow.
*   Real GDP per person grows when labor productivity grows.
*   The interaction of saving and investment in physical capital, expansion of human capital, and technological advances bring labor productivity growth.
*   Saving and investment in physical capital alone cannot bring sustained steady growth because of diminishing marginal returns to capital.

3. Review theories of the causes and effects of economic growth.

*   Classical growth theory predicts that economic growth will end because a population explosion will lower real GDP per person to its subsistence level.
*   New growth theory predicts that capital accumulation, human capital growth, and technological change respond to incentives and can bring persistent growth in labor productivity.
*   Theories about the effect of economic growth on the distribution of income are speculative and make no clear prediction about future trends.

4. Describe policies that speed economic growth.

*   Economic growth requires an incentive system created by economic freedom, property rights, and markets.
*   It might be possible to achieve faster growth by encouraging saving, subsidizing research and education, and encouraging international trade.

Key Terms

MyEconLab Key Terms Quiz

Classical growth theory, 650
Economic freedom, 656
Economic growth, 638
Economic growth rate, 638

Labor productivity, 642
Law of diminishing marginal
  returns, 643
New growth theory, 650

Productivity curve, 644
Property rights, 656
Rule of 70, 640

CHAPTER CHECKPOINT

Study Plan Problems and Applications

1. Explain why sustained growth of real GDP per person can transform a poor country into a wealthy one.

2. In 2015, India's real GDP grew by 7.3 percent a year and its population grew by 1.3 percent a year. If these growth rates are sustained, in what years would
   - Real GDP be twice what it was in 2015?
   - Real GDP per person be twice what it was in 2015?

3. Describe how U.S. potential GDP per person has grown since 1960.

4. Explain the link between labor hours, labor productivity, and real GDP.

5. Explain how saving and investment in capital change labor productivity. Why do diminishing returns arise? Provide an example of diminishing returns. Use a graph of the productivity curve to illustrate your answer.

6. Explain how advances in technology change labor productivity. Do diminishing returns arise? Provide an example of an advance in technology. Use a graph of the productivity curve to illustrate your answer.

7. Explain how an increase in human capital changes labor productivity. Do diminishing returns arise? Provide an example of an increase in human capital. Use a graph of the productivity curve to illustrate your answer.

8. What were the sources of labor productivity growth in the U.S. economy during the fifty years since 1960? How did the 1960s differ from the more recent decades?

9. Draw productivity curves to illustrate the changes in labor productivity that occurred in the U.S. economy in the 1960s and contrast the change with that after 2007. What were the new technologies that arrived in the 1960s?

10. What can governments in Africa do to encourage economic growth and raise the standard of living in their countries?

11. **As China's growth slows, income inequality speeds up**
    China's real GDP growth rate has fallen from 10 percent a year to 6.8 percent a year. At the same time, the distribution of income has become more un-equal. Suggestions for dealing with these problems include encouraging the growth of small firms, expanding the services sector, and investing more in human capital and research.

    Source: Economywatch.com, June 16, 2016
    Compare China's growth slowdown and increased inequality with that of the United States. Would the suggestions for dealing with these problems work?

12. Read *Eye on Rich and Poor Nations* on p. 659. Which nations are the richest and which are growing the fastest? What are the conditions that lead to higher incomes and faster-growing incomes?

Instructor Assignable Problems and Applications

MyEconLab Homework, Quiz, or Test if assigned by instructor

1. Distinguish between low and high incomes and low and high economic growth rates. What are the key features of an economy that are present when incomes are high or fast growing and absent when incomes are low and stagnating or growing slowly? Provide an example of an economy with
   - Low income and slow growth rate.
   - Low income and rapid growth rate.
   - High income with sustained growth over many decades.

Use the following information to work Problems **2** and **3**.

China's growth rate of real GDP in 2005 and 2006 was 10.5 percent a year and its population growth rate was 0.5 percent a year.

2. If these growth rates continue, in what year would real GDP be twice what it was in 2006?

3. If these growth rates continue, in what year would real GDP per person be twice what it was in 2006?

4. Explain how an increase in physical capital and an increase in human capital change labor productivity. Use a graph to illustrate your answer.

5. Table 1 describes labor productivity in an economy. What must have occurred in this economy during year 1?

6. Describe and illustrate in a graph what happened in the economy in Table 1 if in year 1, capital per hour of labor was 30 and in year 2 it was 40.

7. China invests almost 50 percent of its annual production in new capital compared to 15 percent in the United States. Capital per hour of labor in China is about 25 percent of that in the United States. Explain which economy has the higher real GDP per hour of labor, has the faster growth rate of labor productivity, and experiences the more severe diminishing returns.

TABLE 1   LABOR PRODUCTIVITY

Capital per hour of labor	Real GDP per hour of labor	
	in year 1	in year 2
10	7	9
20	13	17
30	18	24
40	22	30
50	25	35
60	27	39
70	28	42

Use the following information to work Problems **8**, **9**, and **10**.

Dear Silicon Valley: Forget flying cars, give us economic growth

We have made enormous advances in computing technology. In Silicon Valley at Alphabet's X labs, people are working on transformative technologies that include driverless cars, high-altitude balloons that deliver the Internet to remote regions of the world, self-navigating drones, and flying wind turbines tethered to a ground station. But despite today's advances in technology, our economic growth rate has slowed.

Source: *MIT Technology Review*, June 21, 2016

8. How would you explain the disconnect between the advances in technology described in the news clip and the pace of real GDP growth?

9. Thinking about the perpetual motion machine of economic growth (Figure 25.5 on p. 652), what are the missing ingredients that make some of today's amazing technologies fail to deliver faster economic growth?

10. Of the preconditions for economic growth and the policies that might achieve faster growth, which are already present in Silicon Valley (and the rest of the U.S. economy), and which, if any, might need to be strengthened?

MyEconLab Chapter 25 Study Plan

Multiple Choice Quiz

1. If real GDP increases from $5 billion to $5.25 billion and the population increases from 2 million to 2.02 million, real GDP per person increases by _____ percent.

  A. 5.0
  B. 1.0
  C. 2.5
  D. 4.0

2. If the population growth rate is 2 percent, real GDP per person will double in 7 years if real GDP grows by _____ percent per year.

  A. 7
  B. 10
  C. 12
  D. 14

3. All of the following increase labor productivity *except* _____.

  A. the accumulation of skill and knowledge
  B. an increase in capital per hour of labor
  C. an increase in consumption
  D. the employment of a new technology

4. The increase in real GDP per hour of labor that results from an increase in capital per hour of labor _____.

  A. is constant and independent of the quantity of capital
  B. is larger at a small quantity of capital than at a large quantity of capital
  C. is smaller at a small quantity of capital than at a large quantity of capital
  D. decreases as technology advances

5. The increase in real GDP per hour of labor that results from an advance in technology makes labor _____ productive _____.

  A. more; at all quantities of capital
  B. less; and capital more productive
  C. more; only at a large quantity of capital
  D. more; and capital less productive

6. The classical growth theory is that real GDP per person _____.

  A. only temporarily rises and then returns to the subsistence level
  B. grows forever
  C. is constant and does not change
  D. increases as the population grows

7. In new growth theory, the source of economic growth is _____.

  A. more leisure
  B. new and better jobs
  C. the persistent want for a higher standard of living
  D. an ever increasing growth rate of capital per hour of labor

8. An economy can achieve faster economic growth *without* _____.

  A. markets and property rights
  B. people being willing to save and invest
  C. incentives to encourage the research for new technologies
  D. an increase in the population growth rate

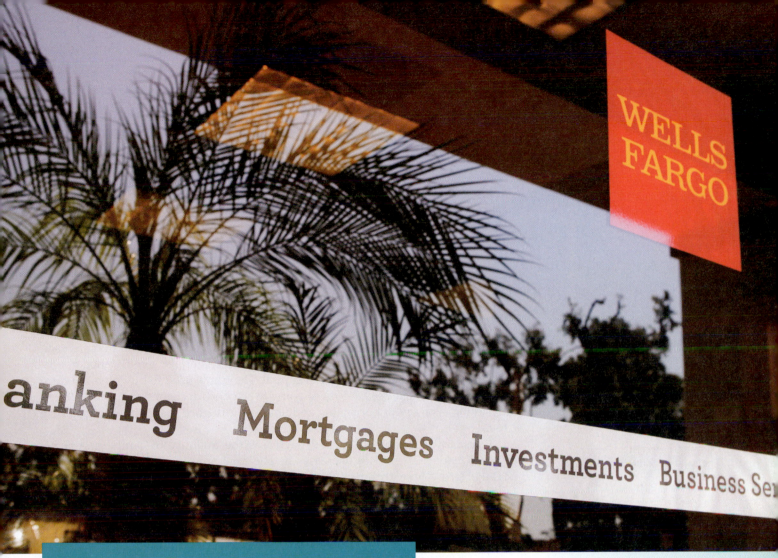

Why have interest rates been so low?

Finance, Saving, and Investment

When you have completed your study of this chapter, you will be able to

1 Describe the financial markets and the key financial institutions.

2 Explain how borrowing and lending decisions are made and how these decisions interact in the loanable funds market.

3 Explain how a government budget surplus or deficit influences the real interest rate, investment, and saving.

26

MyEconLab Big Picture Video

26.1 FINANCIAL INSTITUTIONS AND FINANCIAL MARKETS

To see what determines interest rates and why they have been so low, we need to understand how financial institutions function and financial markets work. The health of these institutions and markets affect saving and investment and the performance of every other market—of the labor market and the markets for goods and services—and the pace of economic growth.

■ Some Finance Definitions

First, we need to distinguish between two forms of capital: physical and financial. We also need to distinguish among investment, capital, wealth, and saving.

Capital—also called **physical capital**—is the tools, instruments, machines, buildings, and other items that have been produced in the past and that are used to produce goods and services. Inventories of raw materials, semifinished goods, and components are part of physical capital. The funds used to buy physical capital are called *financial capital*. You're going to see how decisions about investment and saving, along with borrowing and lending, influence the quantity of physical capital.

Investment (Chapter 21, p. 539) increases the quantity of capital and *depreciation* (Chapter 21, p. 546) decreases it. The total amount spent on new capital is called **gross investment**. The change in the quantity of capital is called **net investment**. Net investment equals gross investment minus depreciation. Figure 26.1 illustrates these concepts. Tom's end-of-year capital of $45,000 equals his initial capital of $30,000 plus net investment of $15,000; and net investment equals gross investment of $35,000 minus depreciation of $20,000.

Capital or physical capital
The tools, instruments, machines, buildings, and other items that have been produced in the past and that are used to produce goods and services.

Gross investment
The total amount spent on new capital.

Net investment
The change in the quantity of capital—equals gross investment minus depreciation.

■ **FIGURE 26.1**

Capital and Investment

MyEconLab Animation

On January 1, 2016, Tom's DVD Burning, Inc. had DVD-recording machines valued at $30,000.

During 2016, the value of Tom's machines fell by $20,000—depreciation—and he spent $35,000 on new machines—gross investment. Tom's net investment was $15,000, so at the end of 2016, Tom had capital valued at $45,000.

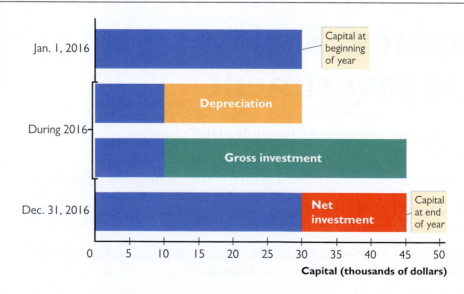

Wealth is the value of all the things that people own. What people own is related to what they earn, but it is not the same thing. People earn an income, which is the amount they receive during a given time period from supplying the services of the resources they own. *Saving* (Chapter 21, p. 540), the amount of income that is not paid in taxes or spent on consumption, adds to wealth. Wealth also increases when the market value of assets rises—called *capital gains*.

If at the end of the school year, you have $250 in the bank and textbooks worth $300 and that's all that you own, your wealth is $550. If during the summer, you earn $5,000 (after-tax income) and spend $1,000 on consumption, your bank account increases to $4,250 and your wealth becomes $4,550. Your wealth has increased by $4,000, which equals your saving—your income of $5,000 minus your consumption expenditure of $1,000.

National wealth and national saving work like this personal example. The wealth of a nation at the end of a year equals its wealth at the start of the year plus its saving during the year, which equals income minus consumption expenditure.

To make real GDP grow, saving and wealth must be transformed into investment and capital. This transformation takes place in the markets for financial capital and through the activities of financial institutions that we now describe.

Wealth
The value of all the things that people own.

■ Markets for Financial Capital

Saving is the source of the funds that are used to finance investment, and these funds are supplied and demanded in three types of financial markets:

- Loan markets
- Bond markets
- Stock markets

Loan Markets

Businesses often want short-term loans to buy inventories or to extend credit to their customers. Sometimes they get these funds in the form of a loan from a bank. Households often want funds to purchase big-ticket items, such as automobiles or household furnishings and appliances. They get these funds as bank loans, often in the form of outstanding credit card balances.

Households also get funds to buy new homes. (Expenditure on new homes is counted as part of investment.) These funds are usually obtained as a loan that is secured by a *mortgage*—a legal contract that gives ownership of a home to the lender in the event that the borrower fails to meet the agreed payment schedule (of loan repayments and interest). Mortgages were at the center of the U.S. credit crisis of 2007–2008.

All of these types of financing take place in loan markets.

Bond Markets

When Walmart expands its business and opens new stores, it gets the funds it needs by selling bonds. Governments—federal, state, and municipal—also get the funds they need to finance a budget deficit by issuing bonds.

A **bond** is a promise to make specified payments on specified dates. For example, you can buy a Western Union bond that promises to pay $6.20 every year until 2035 and then to make a final payment of $100 in October 2036. Bonds issued by firms and governments are traded in the *bond market*.

Bond
A promise to pay specified sums of money on specified dates.

The term of a bond might be long (decades) or short (just a month or two). The U.S. Treasury issues very short-term bonds called *Treasury bills*.

The interest rate on a bond varies with its term to maturity. Usually, the longer the term, the higher is the interest rate. The relationship between the term of a bond and the interest rate is called the *yield curve*.

The interest rate on a bond also varies with its default risk—the risk that the bond issuer will not make the promised payments. The riskier the bond, the higher is its interest rate. Bonds are graded like students' tests on a scale from Aaa to Ccc. (See *Eye on the U.S. Economy* below.)

A special type of bond is a *mortgage-backed security*, which entitles its holder to the income from a package of mortgages. Mortgage lenders create mortgage-backed securities. They make mortgage loans to home buyers and then create securities that they sell to obtain more funds to make more mortgage loans. The holder of a mortgage-backed security is entitled to receive payments that derive from the payments received by the mortgage lender from the homebuyer–borrower. Mortgage-backed securities were at the center of a storm in the financial markets in 2007–2008.

Stock Markets

Stock

A certificate of ownership and claim to the profits that a firm makes.

When Boeing wants to raise funds to expand its airplane-building business, it issues stock. A **stock** is a certificate of ownership and claim to a firm's profits. Boeing has issued about 900 million shares of its stock. If you owned 900 Boeing shares, you would own one millionth of Boeing and be entitled to receive one millionth of its profits.

A *stock market* is a financial market in which shares in corporations' stocks are traded. The New York Stock Exchange, the London Stock Exchange (in England), the Frankfurt Stock Exchange (in Germany), and the Tokyo Stock Exchange are all examples of stock markets.

EYE on the U.S. ECONOMY
Interest Rate Patterns

The *yield curve* shows that in 2016, the U.S. government could borrow by issuing 3-month Treasury Bills at 0.1 percent per year. But on 30-year bonds, it paid almost 2.5 percent. The higher *nominal* interest rate on longer-term bonds reflects inflation expectations.

The government is the least risky borrower and pays the lowest interest rate. The riskiest firms (Ccc) pay higher interest rates than the safest ones (Aaa).

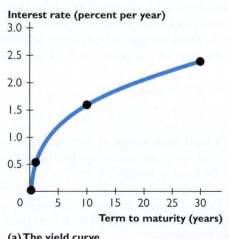

(a) The yield curve

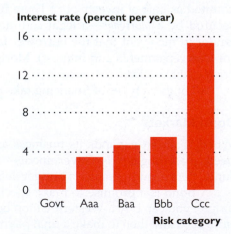

(b) The risk premiums

■ Financial Institutions

Financial markets are highly competitive because of the role played by financial institutions in those markets. A **financial institution** is a firm that operates on both sides of the markets for financial capital: It borrows in one market and lends in another. The key financial institutions are

Financial institution
A firm that operates on both sides of the markets for financial capital: It borrows in one market and lends in another.

- Investment banks
- Commercial banks
- Government-sponsored mortgage lenders
- Pension funds
- Insurance companies

Investment Banks

Investment banks are firms that help other financial institutions and governments raise funds by issuing and selling bonds and stocks, as well as providing advice on transactions such as mergers and acquisitions. Until the late 1980s, the United States maintained a sharp separation between investment banking and commercial banking—a separation that was imposed by the Glass-Steagall Act of 1933. Until 2008, four big Wall Street firms—Goldman Sachs, Lehman Brothers, Merrill Lynch, and Morgan Stanley—provided investment banking services. But in the financial meltdown of 2008, Lehman disappeared and Merrill Lynch was taken over by the Bank of America, a commercial bank.

Commercial Banks

The bank that you use for your own banking services and that issues your credit card is a commercial bank. We'll explain their role in Chapter 27 where we study the role of money in our economy.

Government-Sponsored Mortgage Lenders

Two large financial institutions, the Federal National Mortgage Association, or Fannie Mae, and the Federal Home Loan Mortgage Corporation, or Freddie Mac, are government-sponsored enterprises that buy mortgages from banks, package them into *mortgage-backed securities*, and sell them. In September 2008, Fannie Mae and Freddie Mac owned or guaranteed $6 trillion worth of mortgages (half of the U.S. total of $12 trillion) and were taken over by the federal government.

Pension Funds

Pension funds are financial institutions that use the pension contributions of firms and workers to buy bonds and stocks. The mortgage-backed securities of Fannie Mae and Freddie Mac are among the assets of pension funds. Some pension funds are very large and play an active role in the firms whose stock they hold.

Insurance Companies

Insurance companies enter into agreements with households and firms to provide compensation in the event of accident, theft, fire, ill health, and a host of other misfortunes. Some companies, for example, provide insurance that pays out if a firm fails and cannot meet its bond obligations; and some insure other insurers in a complex network of reinsurance.

Insurance companies receive premiums from their customers, make payments against claims, and use the funds they have received but not paid out as claims to buy bonds and stocks on which they earn interest.

In normal times, insurance companies have a steady flow of funds coming in from premiums and interest on the financial assets they hold and a steady, but smaller, flow of funds paying claims. Their profit is the gap between the two flows. But in unusual times, when large and widespread losses are being incurred, insurance companies can run into difficulty in meeting their obligations. Such a situation arose in 2008 for one of the biggest insurers, AIG, and the firm was taken into public ownership.

■ Insolvency and Illiquidity

Net worth

The total market value of what a financial institution has lent minus the market value of what it has borrowed.

A financial institution's **net worth** is the total market value of what it has lent minus the market value of what it has borrowed. If net worth is positive, the institution is *solvent* and can remain in business. But if its net worth is negative, the institution is *insolvent* and must stop trading. The owners of an insolvent financial institution—usually its stockholders—bear the loss when the assets are sold and debts paid.

A financial institution both borrows and lends, so it is exposed to the risk that its net worth might become negative. To limit that risk, institutions are regulated and a minimum amount of their lending must be backed by their net worth.

Sometimes, a financial institution is solvent but illiquid. A firm is *illiquid* if it has made long-term loans with borrowed funds and is faced with a sudden demand to repay more of what it has borrowed than it has in available cash. In normal times, a financial institution that is illiquid can borrow from another institution. But if all financial institutions are short of cash, the market for loans among financial institutions dries up.

■ Interest Rates and Asset Prices

Stocks, bonds, short-term securities, and loans are collectively called *financial assets*. The *interest rate* on a financial asset is a percentage of the price of the asset.

Because the interest rate is a percentage of the price of an asset, if the asset price rises, other things remaining the same, the interest rate falls. And conversely, if the asset price falls, other things remaining the same, the interest rate rises.

To see this *inverse relationship* between an asset price and interest rate, look at the example of a Microsoft share. In September 2009, the price of a Microsoft share was $25 and each share entitled its owner to 50 cents of Microsoft profit. The interest rate on a Microsoft share as a percentage was

$$\text{Interest rate} = (\$0.50 \div \$25) \times 100 = 2 \text{ percent.}$$

If the price of a Microsoft share increased to $50 and each share still entitled its owner to 50 cents of Microsoft profit, the interest rate on a Microsoft share as a percentage would become

$$\text{Interest rate} = (\$0.50 \div \$50) \times 100 = 1 \text{ percent.}$$

This relationship means that an asset price and interest rate are determined simultaneously—one implies the other. In the next part of this chapter, we learn how asset prices and interest rates are determined in the financial markets.

CHECKPOINT 26.1

MyEconLab Study Plan 26.1
Key Terms Quiz
Solutions Video

Describe the financial markets and the key financial institutions.

Practice Problems

1. Michael is an Internet service provider. On December 31, 2015, he bought an existing business with servers and a building worth $400,000. During 2016, he bought new servers for $500,000. The market value of his older servers fell by $100,000. What was Michael's gross investment, depreciation, and net investment during 2016? What is Michael's capital at the end of 2016?

2. Lori is a student who teaches golf on the weekend and in a year earns $20,000 after paying her taxes. At the beginning of 2016, Lori owned $1,000 worth of books, DVDs, and golf clubs and she had $5,000 in a savings account at the bank. During 2016, the interest on her savings account was $300 and she spent a total of $15,300 on consumption goods and services. The market value of her books, DVDs, and golf clubs did not change. How much did Lori save in 2016? What was her wealth at the end of 2016?

In the News

Banks face increased capital requirements under new rule
Regulators say that some of the world's biggest banks should not be permitted to rely on their own assessment of risk and must hold 40 percent more capital.
Source: Financial Times, March 4, 2016

What are the financial institutions that are required to raise more capital? What exactly is the "capital" referred to in the news clip? How might raising more capital make financial institutions safer?

Solutions to Practice Problems

1. Michael's gross investment during 2016 was $500,000—the market value of the new servers he bought.

    Michael's depreciation during 2016 was $100,000—the fall in the market value of his older servers.

    Michael's net investment during 2016 was $400,000. Net investment equals gross investment minus depreciation, which is ($500,000 − $100,000).

    At the end of 2016, Michael's capital was $800,000. The capital grew during 2016 by the amount of net investment, so at the end of 2016 capital was $400,000 + $400,000, which equals $800,000.

2. Lori saved $5,000. Saving equals income (after tax) minus the amount spent. That is, Lori's saving was $20,300 minus $15,300, or $5,000.
    Lori's wealth at the end of 2016 was $11,000—the sum of her wealth at the start of 2016 ($6,000) plus her saving during 2016 ($5,000).

Solution to In the News

The institutions are some of the world's biggest banks. "Capital" in the news clip is the banks' own funds. By using more of its own funds and less borrowed funds, a financial institution decreases its risk of insolvency in the event that its assets lose value.

MyEconLab Concept Video

Loanable funds market
The aggregate of all the individual financial markets.

26.2 THE LOANABLE FUNDS MARKET

In macroeconomics, we group all the individual financial markets into a single loanable funds market. The **loanable funds market** is the aggregate of the markets for loans, bonds, and stocks. In the loanable funds market, there is just one average interest rate that we refer to as *the* interest rate.

Thinking about financial markets as a single loanable funds market makes sense because the individual markets are highly interconnected with many common influences that move the interest rates on individual assets up and down together.

■ Flows in the Loanable Funds Market

The circular flow model (see Chapter 21, pp. 539–541) provides the accounting framework that describes the flows in the loanable funds market.

Loanable funds are used for three purposes:

1. Business investment
2. Government budget deficit
3. International investment or lending

And loanable funds come from three sources:

1. Private saving
2. Government budget surplus
3. International borrowing

Firms often use *retained earnings*—profits not distributed to stockholders—to finance business investment. These earnings belong to the firm's stockholders and are borrowed from the stockholders rather than being paid to them as dividends. To keep the accounts in the clearest possible way, we think of these retained earnings as being both a use and a source of loanable funds. They are part of business investment on the uses side and part of private saving on the sources side.

We measure all the flows of loanable funds in real terms—in constant 2009 dollars.

You're now going to see how these real flows and the real interest rate are determined in the loanable funds market by studying

- The demand for loanable funds
- The supply of loanable funds
- Equilibrium in the loanable funds market

■ The Demand for Loanable Funds

The *quantity of loanable funds demanded* is the total quantity of funds demanded to finance investment, the government budget deficit, and international investment or lending during a given period. Investment is the major item and the focus of our explanation of the forces that influence the demand side of the loanable funds market. The other two items—the government budget deficit and international investment and lending—can be thought of as amounts to be added to investment. (We study the effects of the government budget later in this chapter on pp. 682–685 and international borrowing and lending in Chapter 34.)

What determines investment and the demand for loanable funds? How does Amazon.com decide how much to borrow to build some new warehouses? Many details influence such a decision, but we can summarize them in two factors:

1. The real interest rate
2. Expected profit

The real interest rate is the opportunity cost of the funds used to finance the purchase of capital, and firms compare the real interest rate with the rate of profit they expect to earn on their new capital. Firms invest only when they expect to earn a rate of profit that exceeds the real interest rate. Fewer projects are profitable at a high real interest rate than at a low real interest rate, so:

Other things remaining the same, the higher the real interest rate, the smaller is the quantity of loanable funds demanded; and the lower the real interest rate, the greater is the quantity of loanable funds demanded.

Demand for Loanable Funds Curve

The **demand for loanable funds** is the relationship between the quantity of loanable funds demanded and the real interest rate when all other influences on borrowing plans remain the same. Figure 26.2 illustrates the demand for loanable funds as a schedule and as a curve.

Demand for loanable funds
The relationship between the quantity of loanable funds demanded and the real interest rate when all other influences on borrowing plans remain the same.

FIGURE 26.2

The Demand for Loanable Funds

MyEconLab Animation

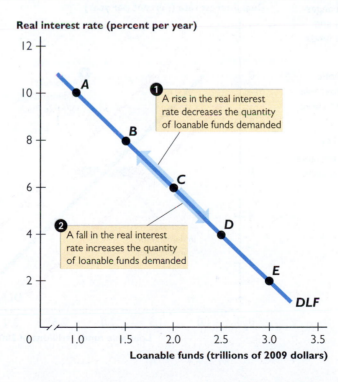

	Real interest rate (percent per year)	Loanable funds demanded (trillions of 2009 dollars)
A	10	1.0
B	8	1.5
C	6	2.0
D	4	2.5
E	2	3.0

❶ A rise in the real interest rate decreases the quantity of loanable funds demanded

❷ A fall in the real interest rate increases the quantity of loanable funds demanded

The table shows the quantity of loanable funds demanded at five real interest rates. The graph shows the demand for loanable funds curve, *DLF*. Points *A* through *E* correspond to the rows of the table.

❶ If the real interest rate rises, the quantity of loanable funds demanded decreases.

❷ If the real interest rate falls, the quantity of loanable funds demanded increases.

To understand the demand for loanable funds, think about Amazon.com's decision to borrow $100 million to build some new warehouses. Suppose that Amazon expects to get a return of $5 million a year from this investment before paying interest costs. If the interest rate is less than 5 percent a year, Amazon expects to make a profit, so it builds the warehouses. If the interest rate is more than 5 percent a year, Amazon expects to incur a loss, so it doesn't build the warehouses. The quantity of loanable funds demanded is greater, the lower is the interest rate.

Changes in the Demand for Loanable Funds

When the expected profit changes, the demand for loanable funds changes. Other things remaining the same, the greater the expected profit from new capital, the greater is the amount of investment and the greater is the demand for loanable funds.

The expected profit rises during a business cycle expansion and falls during a recession; rises when technological change creates profitable new products; rises as a growing population brings increased demand; and fluctuates with contagious swings of optimism and pessimism, called "animal spirits" by Keynes and "irrational exuberance" by Alan Greenspan.

Figure 26.3 shows how the demand for loanable funds curve shifts when the expected profit changes. With average profit expectations, the demand for loanable funds curve is DLF_0. A rise in expected profit shifts the demand curve rightward to DLF_1; a fall in expected profit shifts the demand curve leftward to DLF_2.

■ **FIGURE 26.3**

Changes in the Demand for Loanable Funds   MyEconLab Animation

A change in expected profit changes the demand for loanable funds and shifts the demand for loanable funds curve.

❶ An increase in expected profit increases the demand for loanable funds and shifts the demand curve rightward to DLF_1.

❷ A decrease in expected profit decreases the demand for loanable funds and shifts the demand curve leftward to DLF_2.

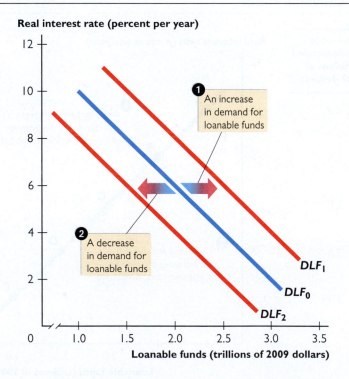

■ The Supply of Loanable Funds

The *quantity of loanable funds supplied* is the total funds available from private saving, the government budget surplus, and international borrowing during a given period. Saving is the main source of supply of loanable funds. A government budget surplus and international borrowing are other sources.

Saving and the supply of loanable funds are determined by decisions by people like you. Suppose that you've graduated and landed a great job that pays you $50,000 a year. How do you decide how much of your income to spend on consumption goods and how much to save and supply in the loanable funds market? Your decision will be influenced by many factors, but chief among them are

1. The real interest rate
2. Disposable income
3. Wealth
4. Expected future income
5. Default risk

We begin by focusing on the real interest rate.

> **Other things remaining the same, the higher the real interest rate, the greater is the quantity of loanable funds supplied; and the lower the real interest rate, the smaller is the quantity of loanable funds supplied.**

The Supply of Loanable Funds Curve

The **supply of loanable funds** is the relationship between the quantity of loanable funds supplied and the real interest rate when all other influences on lending plans remain the same. Figure 26.4 illustrates the supply of loanable funds.

Supply of loanable funds
The relationship between the quantity of loanable funds supplied and the real interest rate when all other influences on lending plans remain the same.

The key reason the supply of loanable funds curve slopes upward is that the real interest rate is the *opportunity cost* of consumption expenditure. A dollar spent is a dollar not saved, so the interest that could have been earned on that saving is forgone. Forgone interest is the opportunity cost of consumption regardless of whether a person is a lender or a borrower. For a lender, saving less means receiving less interest. For a borrower, saving less means paying less off a loan (or increasing a loan) and paying more interest.

By thinking about student loans, you can see why the real interest rate influences saving and the supply of loanable funds. If the real interest rate on student loans jumped to 20 percent a year, graduates would save more (buying cheaper food and finding lower-rent accommodations) to pay off their loans as quickly as possible and avoid, as much as possible, paying the higher interest cost of their loan. If the real interest rate on student loans fell to 1 percent a year, graduates would save less and take longer to pay off their loans because the interest burden would be easier to bear.

Changes in the Supply of Loanable Funds

A change in any influence on saving, other than the real interest rate, changes the supply of loanable funds. The other four factors listed above—disposable income, wealth, expected future income, and default risk—are the main things that change the supply of loanable funds.

■ **FIGURE 26.4**

The Supply of Loanable Funds

The table shows the quantity of loanable funds supplied at five real interest rates. The graph shows the supply of loanable funds curve, *SLF*. Points *A* through *E* correspond to the rows of the table.

❶ If the real interest rate rises, the quantity of loanable funds supplied increases.

❷ If the real interest rate falls, the quantity of loanable funds supplied decreases.

	Real interest rate (percent per year)	Loanable funds supplied (trillions of 2009 dollars)
A	10	3.0
B	8	2.5
C	6	2.0
D	4	1.5
E	2	1.0

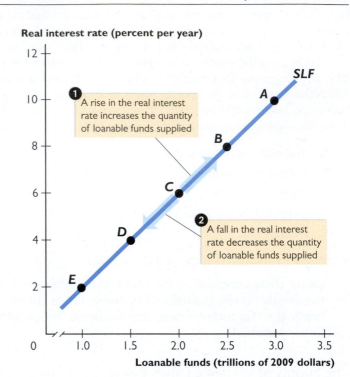

Disposable Income A household's *disposable income* is the income earned minus net taxes. The greater a household's disposable income, other things remaining the same, the greater is its saving. For example, a student whose disposable income is $10,000 a year spends the entire $10,000 and saves nothing. An economics graduate whose disposable income is $50,000 a year spends $40,000 and saves $10,000.

Wealth A household's wealth is what it owns. The greater a household's wealth, other things remaining the same, the less it will save.

Patty is a department store executive who has $15,000 in the bank and no debts: She decides to spend $5,000 on a vacation and save nothing this year. Tony, another department store executive, has nothing in the bank and owes $10,000 on his credit card: He decides to cut consumption and start saving.

Expected Future Income The higher a household's expected future income, other things remaining the same, the smaller is its saving today: If two households have the same current disposable income, the household with the larger expected future disposable income will spend a larger portion of its current disposable income on consumption goods and services and so save less today.

Look at Patty and Tony again. Patty has just been promoted and will receive a $10,000 pay raise next year. Tony has just been told that he will be laid off at the end of the year. On receiving this news, Patty buys a new car—increases her consumption expenditure and cuts her saving—and Tony sells his car and takes the bus—decreases his consumption expenditure and increases his saving.

Most young households expect to have a higher future income for some years and then to have a lower income during retirement. Because of this pattern of income over the life cycle, young people save a small amount, middle-aged people save a lot, and retired people gradually spend their accumulated savings.

Default Risk Default risk is the risk that a loan will not be repaid, or not repaid in full. The greater that risk, the higher is the interest rate needed to induce a person to lend and the smaller is the supply of loanable funds. In normal times, default risk is low but in times of financial crisis when asset prices tumble, default can become widespread as financial institutions become *illiquid* or *insolvent*.

Shifts of the Supply of Loanable Funds Curve

When any of the four influences we've just described changes, the supply of loanable funds changes and the supply of loanable funds curve shifts. An increase in disposable income, or a decrease in wealth, expected future income, or default risk increases the supply of loanable funds.

Figure 26.5 shows how the supply of loanable funds curve shifts. Initially, the supply of loanable funds curve is SLF_0. Then disposable income increases or wealth, expected future income, or default risk decreases. The supply of loanable funds curve shifts rightward from SLF_0 to SLF_1. Changes in these factors in the opposite direction shift the supply curve leftward from SLF_0 to SLF_2.

FIGURE 26.5

Changes in the Supply of Loanable Funds   MyEconLab Animation

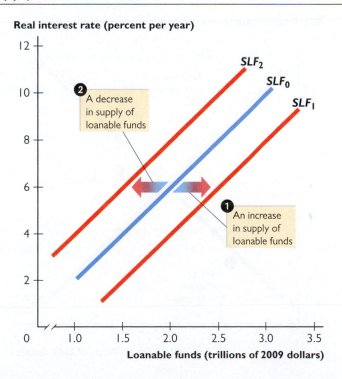

Real interest rate (percent per year)

A decrease in supply of loanable funds

An increase in supply of loanable funds

Loanable funds (trillions of 2009 dollars)

❶ An increase in disposable income or a decrease in wealth, expected future income, or default risk increases the supply of loanable funds and shifts the supply of loanable funds curve rightward from SLF_0 to SLF_1.

❷ A decrease in disposable income or an increase in wealth, expected future income, or default risk decreases the supply of loanable funds and shifts the supply of loanable funds curve leftward from SLF_0 to SLF_2.

■ Equilibrium in the Loanable Funds Market

You've seen that, other things remaining the same, the quantities of loanable funds demanded and supplied depend on the real interest rate. The higher the real interest rate, the greater is the amount of saving and the larger is the quantity of loanable funds supplied. But the higher the real interest rate, the smaller is the amount of investment and the smaller is the quantity of loanable funds demanded. There is one interest rate at which the quantities of loanable funds demanded and supplied are equal, and that interest rate is the equilibrium real interest rate.

Figure 26.6 shows how the demand for and supply of loanable funds determine the real interest rate. The *DLF* curve is the demand curve and the *SLF* curve is the supply curve. When the real interest rate exceeds 6 percent a year, the quantity of loanable funds supplied exceeds the quantity demanded. Borrowers have an easy time finding the funds they want, but lenders are unable to lend all the funds they have available. The real interest rate falls and continues to fall until the quantity of funds supplied equals the quantity of funds demanded.

Alternatively, when the interest rate is less than 6 percent a year, the quantity of loanable funds supplied is less than the quantity demanded. Borrowers can't find the funds they want, but lenders are able to lend all the funds they have available. So the real interest rate rises and continues to rise until the quantity of funds supplied equals the quantity demanded.

Regardless of whether there is a surplus or a shortage of loanable funds, the real interest rate changes and is pulled toward an equilibrium level. In Figure 26.6,

---

FIGURE 26.6

Equilibrium in the Loanable Funds Market

MyEconLab Animation

❶ If the real interest rate is 8 percent a year, the quantity of loanable funds demanded is less than the quantity supplied. There is a surplus of funds, and the real interest rate falls.

❷ If the real interest rate is 4 percent a year, the quantity of loanable funds demanded exceeds the quantity supplied. There is a shortage of funds, and the real interest rate rises.

❸ When the real interest rate is 6 percent a year, the quantity of loanable funds demanded equals the quantity supplied. There is neither a shortage nor a surplus of funds, and the real interest rate is at its equilibrium level.

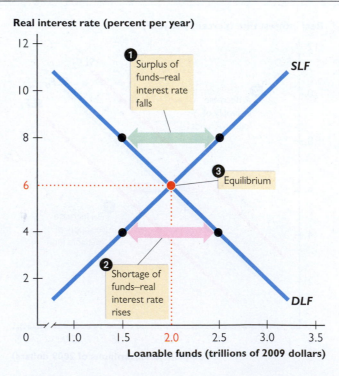

the equilibrium real interest rate is 6 percent a year. At this interest rate, there is neither a surplus nor a shortage of funds. Borrowers can get the funds they want, and lenders can lend all the funds they have available. The plans of borrowers (investors) and lenders (savers) are consistent with each other.

Changes in Demand and Supply

Fluctuations in either the demand for loanable funds or the supply of loanable funds bring fluctuations in the real interest rate and in the equilibrium quantity of funds lent and borrowed. Here we'll illustrate the effects of an increase in each.

An increase in expected profit increases the demand for loanable funds. With no change in supply, there is a shortage of funds and the interest rate rises until the equilibrium is restored. In Figure 26.7(a), the increase in the demand for loanable funds shifts the demand for loanable funds curve rightward from DLF_0 to DLF_1. At a real interest rate of 6 percent a year, there is a shortage of funds. The real interest rate rises to 8 percent a year, and the equilibrium quantity of funds increases.

If one of the influences on saving plans changes and increases saving, the supply of loanable funds increases. With no change in demand, there is a surplus of funds and the interest rate falls until the equilibrium is restored. In Figure 26.7(b), the increase in the supply of loanable funds shifts the supply of loanable funds curve rightward from SLF_0 to SLF_1. At a real interest rate of 6 percent a year, there is a surplus of funds. The real interest rate falls to 4 percent a year, and the equilibrium quantity of funds increases.

Over time, both demand and supply in the loanable funds market fluctuate and the real interest rate rises and falls. Both the supply of loanable funds and the demand for loanable funds tend to increase over time. On the average, they increase at a similar pace, so although demand and supply trend upward, the real interest rate has no trend. It fluctuates around a constant average level.

FIGURE 26.7

Changes in Demand and Supply in the Loanable Funds Market   MyEconLab Animation

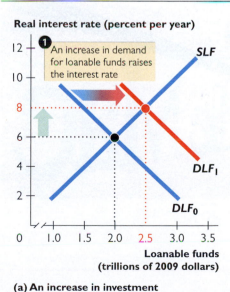

(a) An increase in investment

(b) An increase in saving

❶ If the demand for loanable funds increases and the supply of loanable funds remains the same, the real interest rate rises and the equilibrium quantity of funds increases.

❷ If the supply of loanable funds increases and the demand for loanable funds remains the same, the real interest rate falls and the equilibrium quantity of funds increases.

EYE on the U.S. ECONOMY
The Loanable Funds Market in a Financial Crisis

Financial markets can be turbulent and in 2007 and 2008, events in the loanable funds market created a financial crisis, the effects of which are still with us today.

An increase in default risk decreased supply; and the disappearance of some major Wall Street institutions and lowered profit expectations decreased demand.

Bear Stearns was absorbed by JP Morgan with help from the Federal Reserve; Lehman Brothers' assets were taken over by Barclays; Fannie Mae and Freddie Mac went into government oversight with U.S. taxpayer guarantees; Merrill Lynch became part of the Bank of America; AIG received an $85 billion lifeline from the Federal Reserve and sold off parcels of its business to financial institutions around the world; Wachovia was taken over by Wells Fargo and Washington Mutual by JP Morgan Chase.

But what caused the increase in default risk and the failure of so many financial institutions?

Between 2002 and 2005, interest rates were low. There were plenty of willing borrowers and plenty of willing lenders. Fueled by easy loans, home prices rose rapidly. Lenders bundled their loans into mortgage-backed securities and sold them to eager buyers around the world.

Then, in 2006, interest rates began to rise and home prices began to fall. People defaulted on mortgages; banks took losses and some became insolvent. A downward spiral of lending was under way.

CHECKPOINT 26.2

MyEconLab Study Plan 26.2
Key Terms Quiz
Solutions Video

Explain how borrowing and lending decisions are made and how these decisions interact in the loanable funds market.

Practice Problem

First Call, Inc. is a wireless service provider. It plans to build an assembly plant that costs $10 million if the real interest rate is 6 percent a year. If the real interest rate is 5 percent a year, First Call will build a larger plant that costs $12 million. And if the real interest rate is 7 percent a year, First Call will build a smaller plant that costs $8 million. Use this information to work Problems **1** and **2**.

1. Draw a graph of First Call's demand for loanable funds curve.

2. First Call expects its profit to double next year. If other things remain the same, explain how this increase in expected profit influences First Call's demand for loanable funds.

3. Draw graphs that illustrate how an increase in the supply of loanable funds and a decrease in the demand for loanable funds can lower the real interest rate and leave the equilibrium quantity of loanable funds unchanged.

In the News

The stock market is acting like everything is great
Stock prices measured by the S&P 500 and Dow Jones Industrial Average set new highs this week. Company profits remain low, but investors are betting that higher profits are just around the corner.

Source: *The Washington Post*, July 14, 2016

Are the people who buy stocks suppliers or demanders of loanable funds? If stock prices rise, what happens to the interest rate on stocks? How would you explain the rise in stock prices in the news clip?

Solutions to Practice Problems

1. The demand for loanable funds curve is the downward-sloping curve DLF_0 and passes through the points highlighted in Figure 1.

2. An increase in the expected profit increases investment today, which increases the quantity of loanable funds demanded at each real interest rate. The demand for loanable funds curve shifts rightward to DLF_1 (Figure 1).

3. The increase in the supply of loanable funds shifts the supply curve rightward. The decrease in the demand for loanable funds shifts the demand curve leftward. The real interest rate falls. If the shifts are of the same magnitude, the equilibrium quantity of funds remains unchanged (Figure 2). If the shift of the supply curve is greater (less) than that of the demand curve, then the equilibrium quantity of funds increases (decreases).

Solution to In the News

The buyers of stocks are suppliers of loanable funds. When the price of a financial asset rises, the interest rate on that asset falls. In July 2016, the supply of loanable funds increased as more people bought stocks. The increase in supply lowered the interest rate and raised the prices of stocks.

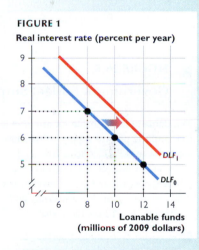

FIGURE 1

Real interest rate (percent per year)

Loanable funds
(millions of 2009 dollars)

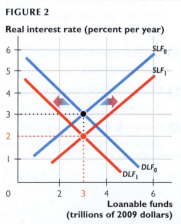

FIGURE 2

Real interest rate (percent per year)

Loanable funds
(trillions of 2009 dollars)

26.3 GOVERNMENT IN LOANABLE FUNDS MARKET

The government enters the loanable funds market when it has a budget surplus or budget deficit. So actions that change the government's budget balance influence the loanable funds market and the real interest rate. A change in the real interest rate influences both saving and investment. To complete our study of the forces that determine the quantity of investment and the real interest rate, we investigate the role played by the government's budget balance.

■ A Government Budget Surplus

A government budget surplus increases the supply of loanable funds. The real interest rate falls, which decreases private saving and decreases the quantity of private funds supplied. The lower real interest rate increases the quantity of loanable funds demanded and increases investment.

Figure 26.8 shows these effects of a government budget surplus. The private supply of loanable funds curve is *PSLF*. The supply of loanable funds curve, *SLF*, shows the sum of the private supply and the government budget surplus. Here, the government budget surplus is $1 trillion, so at each real interest rate the *SLF* curve lies $1 trillion to the right of the *PSLF* curve. That is, the horizontal distance between the *PSLF* curve and the *SLF* curve is the government budget surplus.

■ **FIGURE 26.8**

Government Budget Surplus

The demand for loanable funds curve is *DLF*, and the private supply of loanable funds curve is *PSLF*. With a balanced government budget, the real interest rate is 6 percent a year and investment is $2 trillion a year. Private saving and investment are $2 trillion a year.

❶ A government budget surplus of $1 trillion is added to private saving to determine the supply of loanable funds curve *SLF*.

❷ The real interest rate falls to 4 percent a year.

❸ The quantity of private saving decreases to $1.5 trillion.

❹ The quantity of loanable funds demanded and investment increase to $2.5 trillion.

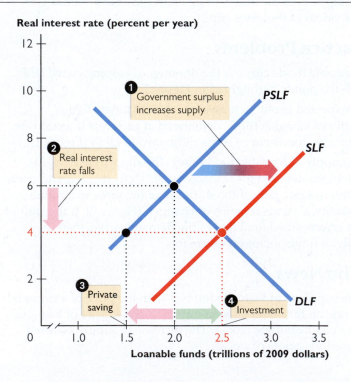

With no government budget surplus, the real interest rate is 6 percent a year, the quantity of loanable funds is $2 trillion a year and investment is $2 trillion a year. But with the government budget surplus of $1 trillion a year, the equilibrium real interest rate falls to 4 percent a year and the quantity of loanable funds increases to $2.5 trillion a year.

The fall in the real interest rate decreases private saving to $1.5 trillion, but investment increases to $2.5 trillion, which is financed by private saving and the government budget surplus (government saving).

◼ A Government Budget Deficit

A government budget deficit increases the demand for loanable funds. The real interest rate rises, which increases private saving and increases the quantity of private funds supplied. But the higher real interest rate decreases investment and the quantity of loanable funds demanded by firms to finance investment.

Figure 26.9 shows these effects of a government budget deficit. The private demand for loanable funds curve is *PDLF*. The demand for loanable funds curve, *DLF*, shows the sum of the private demand and the government budget deficit. Here, the government budget deficit is $1 trillion, so at each real interest rate the *DLF* curve lies $1 trillion to the right of the *PDLF* curve. That is, the horizontal distance between the *PDLF* curve and the *DLF* curve equals the government budget deficit.

With no government budget deficit, the real interest rate is 6 percent a year, the quantity of loanable funds is $2 trillion a year and investment is $2 trillion a

◼ **FIGURE 26.9**

Government Budget Deficit   MyEconLab Animation

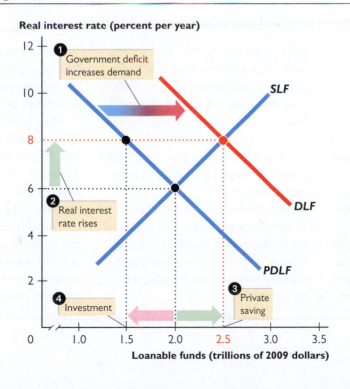

The supply of loanable funds curve is *SLF* and the private demand for loanable funds curve is *PDLF*. With a balanced government budget, the real interest rate is 6 percent a year and the quantity of loanable funds is $2 trillion a year. Private saving and investment are $2 trillion a year.

❶ A government budget deficit of $1 trillion is added to the private demand for funds to determine the demand for loanable funds curve *DLF*.

❷ The real interest rate rises to 8 percent a year.

❸ Private saving and the quantity of loanable funds increase to $2.5 trillion.

❹ Investment decreases to $1.5 trillion. Investment is crowded out.

year. But with the government budget deficit of $1 trillion, the real interest rate rises from 6 percent a year to 8 percent a year and the quantity of loanable funds increases from $2 trillion to $2.5 trillion.

The rise in the real interest rate increases private saving to $2.5 trillion, but investment decreases to $1.5 trillion. The tendency for a government budget deficit to raise the real interest rate and decrease investment is called the **crowding-out effect**. Investment does not decrease by the full amount of the government budget deficit because private saving increases. In this example, private saving increases by $0.5 trillion to $2.5 trillion.

Crowding-out effect
The tendency for a government budget deficit to raise the real interest rate and decrease investment.

The Ricardo-Barro Effect

First suggested by the English economist David Ricardo in the eighteenth century and refined by Robert J. Barro of Harvard University during the 1980s, the Ricardo-Barro effect holds that the effects we've just shown are wrong and that the government budget deficit has no effect on the real interest rate or investment. Barro says that rational taxpayers can see that a deficit today means that future taxes will be higher and future disposable incomes will be smaller. With smaller expected future disposable incomes, saving increases. The increase in saving increases the supply of loanable funds—shifts the *SLF* curve rightward—by an amount equal to the government budget deficit. The supply of loanable funds might increase and lessen the influence of the government budget deficit on the real interest rate and investment, but most economists regard the full Ricardo-Barro effect as unlikely.

EYE on YOUR LIFE
Your Participation in the Loanable Funds Market

MyEconLab Critical Thinking Exercise

Think about the amount of saving that you do. How much of your disposable income do you save? Is it a positive amount or a negative amount?

If you save a positive amount, what do you do with your savings? Do you put them in a bank, in the stock market, in bonds, or just keep money at home? What is the interest rate you earn on your savings?

If you save a negative amount, just what does that mean? It means that you have a deficit (like a government deficit). You're spending more than

your disposable income. In this case, how do you finance your deficit? Do you get a student loan? Do you run up an outstanding credit card balance? How much do you pay to finance your negative saving (your *dissaving*)?

How do you think your saving will change when you graduate and get a better-paying job?

Also think about the amount of investment that you do. You are investing in your human capital by being in school. What is this investment costing you? How are you financing this investment?

When you graduate and start a well-paying job, you will need to decide whether to buy an apartment or a house or to rent your home.

How would you make a decision whether to buy or rent a home? Would it be smart to borrow $300,000 to finance the purchase of a home? How would the interest rate influence your decision?

These examples show just some of the many decisions and transactions you will make in the loanable funds market—the link between your saving and your investment.

EYE on FINANCIAL MARKETS

MyEconLab Critical Thinking Exercise

Why Have Interest Rates Been So Low?

Interest rates were at record low levels from 2008 through 2013 and with what you have learned in this chapter, you can explain why.

The most recent normal year in the U.S. economy was 2007, the eve of the onset of a global financial crisis.

In 2007, the total amount borrowed in the U.S. loanable funds market was $51 trillion, and the real interest rate was 2 percent a year.

The figure illustrates this situation. The supply of loanable funds curve was SLF_{07} and the demand for loanable funds curve was DLF_{07}. Both the demand curve and the supply curve include borrowing and lending decisions by households, firms, governments, the rest of the world, and financial institutions,

including the Federal Reserve (or the Fed). Loanable funds market equilibrium occurred at a real interest rate of 2 percent a year and a total quantity of loanable funds of $51 trillion.

Interest rates fell to a record low because the demand for loanable funds decreased and the supply increased.

On the demand side of the market, by mid-2009, expected profit had fallen, which decreased investment from $2.2 trillion in 2007 to $1.5 trillion and the demand for loanable funds by households and businesses had decreased sharply. But the federal government launched a massive rescue plan that increased its outlays and its demand for loanable funds.

Despite the large increase in government demand, the overall demand for loanable funds decreased: The demand by households, businesses, and financial institutions decreased by more than the demand by the federal government increased.

By 2013, the demand for loanable funds had decreased to DLF_{13}.

On the supply side of the market, the Fed continued to supply large quantities of funds. The Fed's goal was to lower the interest rate and stimulate investment. (You will study the actions that enable the Fed to increase the supply of loanable funds in Chapter 27.)

By 2013, the supply of loanable funds had increased to SLF_{13}.

The equilibrium real interest rate was 0.5 percent per year, and the equilibrium quantity of loanable funds was $55 trillion.

Even without the increase in supply, the real interest rate would have fallen, but the equilibrium quantity of loanable funds would also have fallen.

The increase in the supply of loanable funds limited the decrease in investment and lessened the severity of the recession triggered by the financial crisis.

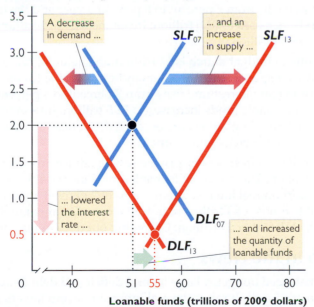

SOURCES OF DATA: Bureau of Economic Analysis and Federal Reserve. The interest rate is the average of the yield on Aaa equities, government bonds, mortgages, and federal funds, adjusted for inflation measured by the consumer price index.

MyEconLab Study Plan 26.3
        Key Terms Quiz
        Solutions Video

CHECKPOINT 26.3

Explain how a government budget surplus or deficit influences the real interest rate, investment, and saving.

Practice Problems

Table 1 shows the demand for loanable funds schedule and the supply of loanable funds schedule when the government budget is balanced.

1. If the government budget surplus is $1 trillion, what are the real interest rate, the quantity of investment, and the quantity of private saving?

2. If the government budget deficit is $1 trillion, what are the real interest rate, the quantity of investment, and the quantity of private saving? Is there any crowding out in this situation?

3. If the government budget deficit is $1 trillion and the Ricardo-Barro effect occurs, what are the real interest rate and the quantity of investment?

In the News

U.S. budget deficit expanded in April
In the year to April 2016, the U.S. budget deficit increased to $511 billion, up from $460 billion a year earlier.

Source: *The Wall Street Journal*, May 11, 2016

Explain the effect of a large federal deficit and debt on economic growth.

Solutions to Practice Problems

1. If the government budget surplus is $1 trillion, the supply of loanable funds increases. Figure 1 shows the supply of loanable funds *SLF*. The equilibrium real interest rate falls from 7 percent to 6 percent a year and the quantity of loanable funds increases to $2.5 trillion. Investment is $2.5 trillion and private saving is $1.5 trillion.

2. If the government budget deficit is $1 trillion, the demand for loanable funds increases. Figure 2 shows the demand for loanable funds curve *DLF*. The equilibrium real interest rate rises from 7 percent to 8 percent a year and the quantity of loanable funds increases to $2.5 trillion. Investment decreases to $1.5 trillion. Crowding out occurs because the deficit increases the real interest rate, which decreases investment.

3. If the Ricardo-Barro effect occurs, private saving adjusts to offset the budget deficit of $1 trillion. The supply of loanable funds increases by $1 trillion and the equilibrium real interest rate remains at 7 percent a year. The quantity of loanable funds is $3 trillion and it finances investment of $2 trillion and the budget deficit of $1 trillion. Crowding out does not occur.

Solution to In the News

Compared to a balanced budget, a large federal deficit and debt increases the demand for loanable funds. It raises the real interest rate and lowers private investment. Investment increases the capital stock, which increases labor productivity and real GDP. The higher real interest rate slows the growth of the capital stock, slows labor productivity growth, and slows real GDP growth.

TABLE 1

Real interest rate (percent per year)	Loanable funds demanded	Loanable funds supplied
	(trillions of 2009 dollars per year)	
4	3.5	0.5
5	3.0	1.0
6	2.5	1.5
7	2.0	2.0
8	1.5	2.5
9	1.0	3.0
10	0.5	3.5

FIGURE 1

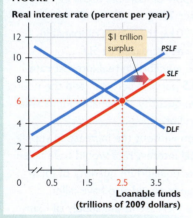

FIGURE 2

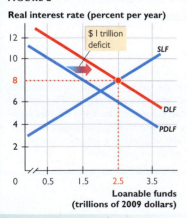

CHAPTER SUMMARY

Key Points

1. **Describe the financial markets and the key financial institutions.**

   • Firms use financial capital to buy and operate physical capital.
   • Gross investment is the total amount spent on physical capital in a given period. Net investment equals gross investment minus depreciation.
   • Wealth is the value of what people own; saving is the amount of disposable income that is not spent, and it adds to wealth.
   • The market for financial capital is a market made up of the markets for loans, bonds, and stocks.

2. **Explain how borrowing and lending decisions are made and how these decisions interact in the loanable funds market.**

   • Other things remaining the same, the lower the real interest rate or the higher the expected profit rate, the greater is the quantity of loanable funds demanded.
   • The demand for loanable funds changes when the expected profit rate changes.
   • Other things remaining the same, the higher the real interest rate, the greater is the quantity of loanable funds supplied.
   • The supply of loanable funds changes when disposable income, wealth, expected future income, or default risk changes.
   • Equilibrium in the loanable funds market determines the real interest rate.
   • At the equilibrium real interest rate, the quantity of loanable funds demanded equals the quantity of loanable funds supplied.

3. **Explain how a government budget surplus or deficit influences the real interest rate, investment, and saving.**

   • A government budget surplus increases the supply of loanable funds and a government budget deficit increases the demand for loanable funds.
   • With no change in private saving, an increase in the government budget deficit raises the real interest rate and crowds out investment.
   • A government budget deficit might increase private saving because it decreases expected future disposable income.

Key Terms

MyEconLab Key Terms Quiz

Bond, 667
Capital or physical capital, 666
Crowding-out effect, 684
Demand for loanable funds, 673
Financial institution, 669
Gross investment, 666
Loanable funds market, 672
Net investment, 666
Net worth, 670
Stock, 668
Supply of loanable funds, 675
Wealth, 667

CHAPTER CHECKPOINT

Study Plan Problems and Applications

1. On January 1, 2016, Terry's Towing Service owned 4 tow trucks valued at $300,000. During 2016, Terry's bought 2 new trucks for a total of $180,000. At the end of 2016, the market value of all the firm's trucks was $400,000. What was Terry's gross investment? Calculate Terry's depreciation and net investment.

Use the following information to work Problems **2** and **3**.

The Bureau of Economic Analysis reported that the U.S. capital stock was $49.6 trillion at the end of 2012, $51.2 trillion at the end of 2013, and $53.6 trillion at the end of 2014. Depreciation in 2013 was $1.6 trillion, and gross investment during 2014 was $3.4 trillion.

2. Calculate U.S. net investment and gross investment during 2013.

3. Calculate U.S. depreciation and net investment during 2014.

4. Mike takes a summer job washing cars. During the summer, he earns an after-tax income of $3,000 and he spends $1,000 on goods and services. What was Mike's saving during the summer and the change, if any, in his wealth?

5. What is the market for financial capital? What is financial capital? Explain why, when the real interest rate rises, the demand for loanable funds does not change but the quantity of funds demanded decreases.

6. With an increase in political tension, many governments increased defense spending, which decreased government budget surpluses. Show, on a graph, the effects of a decrease in government budget surpluses if there is no Ricardo-Barro effect. Explain how the effects differ if there is a partial Ricardo-Barro effect.

7. Rio declares financial emergency ahead of Olympics, requests federal funding
Rio de Janeiro requested federal funding to help pay for public services during the Olympics, at a time when Brazil's federal government revenue has fallen and created a large deficit.
Source: *International Business Times*, July 15, 2016
Draw a graph of the loanable funds market in Brazil. Suppose that the Brazilian government borrows the required funds in the loanable funds market. How will this borrowing change the real interest rate and the quantity of saving in Brazil?

8. German government achieves budget surplus
The German government's budget was balanced in 2014 and moved into a surplus of $13 billion in 2015. Helped by higher tax revenues, the budget surplus was twice as high as expected.
Source: *The Wall Street Journal*, January 13, 2016
Explain the effect of Germany's budget surplus on the loanable funds market in Germany. How will the budget surplus influence economic growth?

9. Read *Eye on Financial Markets* on p. 685. What would the real interest rate and quantity of loanable funds have been in 2013 if the supply of loanable funds had been at its 2007 level? Explain your answer.

Instructor Assignable Problems and Applications

MyEconLab Homework, Quiz, or Test if assigned by instructor

1. Explain why the supply of loanable funds and the demand for loanable funds decreased during the global financial crisis of 2007–2008. Draw a graph of the loanable funds market before the crisis and use your graph to illustrate the source and effects of the crisis on saving, investment, and the real interest rate.

2. On January 1, 2016, Sophie's Internet Cafe owned 10 computer terminals valued at $8,000. During 2016, Sophie's bought 5 new computer terminals at a cost of $1,000 each, and at the end of the year, the market value of all of Sophie's computer terminals was $11,000. What was Sophie's gross investment, depreciation, and net investment?

3. The numbers in the second column of Table 1 are the Federal Reserve's estimates of personal wealth at the end of each year. The numbers in the third column are the Bureau of Economic Analysis's estimates of personal saving each year. In which years did the change in wealth exceed saving? In which years did saving exceed the change in wealth? Given the definitions of saving and wealth, how can the change in wealth differ from saving?

4. Cindy takes a summer job and earns an after-tax income of $8,000. Her living expenses during the summer were $2,000. What was Cindy's saving during the summer and the change, if any, in her wealth?

5. A stock market boom of 2002–2007 increased wealth by trillions of dollars. Explain the effect of this increase in wealth on the equilibrium real interest rate, investment, and saving.

TABLE 1

Year	Wealth	Saving
	(billions of dollars)	
2011	63,544	785
2012	69,598	1,000
2013	79,383	662
2014	84,201	690

Use the following information to work Problems **6** and **7**.

The U.S. saving rate increased from −0.1 percent in 2011 to 2.0 percent in 2012, to 2.4 percent in 2013, to 2.9 percent in 2014, and to 3.0 percent in 2015.

6. How can the saving rate be negative? Why might a negative saving rate be something to worry about? How might U.S. saving be increased?

7. Explain why the U.S. saving rate might have increased and its effect on the supply of loanable funds.

Use the following information to work Problems **8** to **10**.

IMF says it battled crisis well

The International Monetary Fund (IMF) reported that it acted effectively in combating the global recession, especially in Eastern Europe. The IMF made $163 billion available to developing countries. The IMF required countries with large deficits to cut spending or not increase it, but it urged the United States, Western European countries, and China to run deficits to stimulate their economies.

Source: *The Wall Street Journal*, September 29, 2009

8. Explain how an increase in government expenditure will change the government's budget balance and the loanable funds market.

9. Why do you think the IMF required countries with large deficits, like those in Eastern Europe, to cut spending rather than increase it?

10. The Center for Economic and Policy Research in Washington, D.C., claims that the IMF didn't allow developing countries that were looking for loans to expand their deficits sufficiently. Would these countries have weathered the global recession better if they had obtained larger loans from the IMF?

Multiple Choice Quiz

1. Financial capital is the _____.

   A. money used to buy stocks and bonds
   B. money used to buy physical capital
   C. funds that savers supply and buyers of physical capital borrow
   D. money in the bank

2. If the price of a U.S. government bond is $50 and the owner of the bond is entitled to $2.50 income each year, then the interest rate on the bond is _____.

   A. 0.2 percent
   B. 5 percent
   C. 10 percent
   D. 20 percent

3. In the loanable funds market, an increase in _____.

   A. the real interest rate increases the demand for loanable funds
   B. expected profit increases the demand for loanable funds
   C. expected profit doesn't change the demand for loanable funds, but the quantity of loanable funds demanded increases
   D. the real interest rate doesn't change the demand for loanable funds, but the quantity of loanable funds demanded increases

4. The supply of loanable funds increases _____.

   A. when the demand for loanable funds increases
   B. when people increase saving as the real interest rate rises
   C. when disposable income increases or wealth decreases
   D. if net taxes decrease or expected future income increases

5. An increase in expected profit _____ the real interest rate and _____ the quantity of loanable funds.

   A. decreases; decreases
   B. increases; decreases
   C. decreases; increases
   D. increases; increases

6. A government budget surplus _____.

   A. increases the supply of loanable funds
   B. raises the real interest rate
   C. decreases the demand for loanable funds and lowers the real interest rate
   D. decreases net taxes, increases disposable income, and increases saving

7. Crowding out occurs when _____.

   A. households' budgets are in deficit and saving decreases
   B. the government budget is in surplus, so people have paid too much tax
   C. the government budget is in deficit and the real interest rate rises
   D. the government budget is in deficit but taxpayers are rational and the Ricardo-Barro effect operates

8. An increase in the government budget deficit _____.

   A. increases private saving and investment
   B. increases private saving and decreases investment
   C. increases the supply of private saving and decreases investment
   D. decreases private saving and investment

How does the Fed create money
and regulate its quantity?

The Monetary System

CHAPTER CHECKLIST

When you have completed your study of this chapter, you will be able to

1 Define money and describe its functions.

2 Describe the functions of banks.

3 Describe the functions of the Federal Reserve System (the Fed).

4 Explain how the banking system creates money and how the Fed controls the quantity of money.

MyEconLab Big Picture Video

27.1   WHAT IS MONEY?

Money, like fire and the wheel, has been around for a very long time. An incredible array of items has served as money. North American Indians used wampum (beads made from shells), Fijians used whales' teeth, and early American colonists used tobacco. Cakes of salt served as money in Ethiopia and Tibet. What do wampum, whales' teeth, tobacco, and salt have in common? Why are they examples of money? Today, when we want to buy something, we use coins or notes (dollar bills), write a check, send an e-check, present a credit or debit card, or use a smartphone app. Are all these things that we use today money? To answer these questions, we need a definition of money.

■ Definition of Money

Money is any commodity or token that is generally accepted as a *means of payment*. This definition has three parts that we'll examine in turn.

A Commodity or Token

Money is always something that can be recognized and that can be divided up into small parts. So money might be an actual commodity, such as a bar of silver or gold. But it might also be a token, such as a quarter or a $10 bill. Money might also be a virtual token, such as an electronic record in a bank's database (more about this type of money later).

Generally Accepted

Money is *generally* accepted, which means that it can be used to buy *anything and everything*. Some tokens can be used to buy some things but not others. For example, a bus pass is accepted as payment for a bus ride, but you can't use your bus pass to buy toothpaste. So a bus pass is not money. In contrast, you can use a $5 bill to buy either a bus ride or toothpaste—or anything else that costs $5 or less. So a $5 bill is money.

Means of Payment

A **means of payment** is a method of settling a debt. When a payment has been made, the deal is complete. Suppose that Gus buys a car from his friend Ann. Gus doesn't have enough money to pay for the car right now, but he will have enough three months from now, when he gets paid. Ann agrees that Gus may pay for the car in three months' time. Gus buys the car with a loan from Ann and then pays off the loan. The loan isn't money. Money is what Gus uses to pay off the loan.

So what wampum, whales' teeth, tobacco, and salt have in common is that they have served as a generally accepted means of payment, and that is why they are examples of money.

■ The Functions of Money

Money performs three vital functions. It serves as a

- Medium of exchange
- Unit of account
- Store of value

Money
Any commodity or token that is generally accepted as a *means of payment*.

Means of payment
A method of settling a debt.

Medium of Exchange

A **medium of exchange** is an object that is generally accepted in return for goods and services. Money is a medium of exchange. Without money, you would have to exchange goods and services directly for other goods and services—an exchange called **barter**. Barter requires a *double coincidence of wants*. For example, if you want a soda and have only a paperback novel to offer in exchange for it, you must find someone who is selling soda and who also wants your paperback novel. Money guarantees that there is a double coincidence of wants because people with something to sell will always accept money in exchange for it. Money acts as a lubricant that smoothes the mechanism of exchange. Money enables you to specialize in the activity in which you have a comparative advantage (see Chapter 3, pp. 73–75) instead of searching for a double coincidence of wants.

Medium of exchange
An object that is generally accepted in return for goods and services.

Barter
The direct exchange of goods and services for other goods and services, which requires a double coincidence of wants.

Unit of Account

An agreed-upon measure for stating the prices of goods and services is called a *unit of account*. To get the most out of your budget, you have to figure out whether going to a rock concert is worth its opportunity cost. But that cost is not dollars and cents. It is the number of movies, cappuccinos, ice-cream cones, or sticks of gum that you must give up to attend the concert. It's easy to do such calculations when all these goods have prices in terms of dollars and cents (see Table 27.1). If a rock concert costs $64 and a movie costs $8, you know right away that going to the concert costs you 8 movies. If a cappuccino costs $4, going to the concert costs 16 cappuccinos. You need only one calculation to figure out the opportunity cost of any pair of goods and services. For example, the opportunity cost of the rock concert is 128 sticks of gum ($64 ÷ 50¢ = 128 sticks of gum).

Now imagine how troublesome it would be if the rock concert ticket agent posted its price as 8 movies, and if the movie theater posted its price as 2 cappuccinos, and if the coffee shop posted the price of a cappuccino as 2 ice-cream cones, and if the ice-cream shop posted its price as 4 sticks of gum! Now how much running around and calculating do you have to do to figure out how much that rock concert is going to cost you in terms of the movies, cappuccino, ice cream, or sticks of gum that you must give up to attend it? You get the answer for movies right away from the sign posted by the ticket agent. For all the other goods, you're going to have to visit many different places to establish the price of each commodity in terms of another and then calculate prices in units that are relevant for your own decision. Cover up the column labeled "price in money units" in Table 27.1 and see how hard it is to figure out the number of sticks of gum it costs to attend a rock concert. It's enough to make a person swear off rock! How much simpler it is using dollars and cents.

TABLE 27.1 A UNIT OF ACCOUNT SIMPLIFIES PRICE COMPARISONS

Good	Price in money units	Price in units of another good
Rock concert	$64.00	8 movies
Movie	$8.00	2 cappuccinos
Cappuccino	$4.00	2 ice-cream cones
Ice-cream cone	$2.00	4 sticks of gum
Stick of gum	$0.50	

Store of Value

Any commodity or token that can be held and exchanged later for goods and services is called a *store of value*. Money acts as a store of value. If it did not, it would not be accepted in exchange for goods and services. The more stable the value of a commodity or token, the better it can act as a store of value and the more useful it is as money. No store of value is completely stable. The value of a physical object, such as a house, a car, or a work of art, fluctuates over time. The value of the commodities and tokens that we use as money also fluctuates, and when there is inflation, money persistently falls in value.

Fiat money
Objects that are money because the law decrees or orders them to be money.

Currency
Notes (dollar bills) and coins.

M1
Currency held by individuals and businesses, traveler's checks, and checkable deposits owned by individuals and businesses.

M2
M1 plus savings deposits and small time deposits, money market funds, and other deposits.

■ Money Today

Money in the world today is called **fiat money**. *Fiat* is a Latin word that means decree or order. Fiat money is money because the law decrees it to be so. The objects used as money have value only because of their legal status as money.

Today's fiat money consists of

- Currency
- Deposits at banks and other financial institutions

Currency

The notes (dollar bills) and coins that we use in the United States today are known as **currency**. The government declares notes to be money with the words printed on every dollar bill, "This note is legal tender for all debts, public and private."

Deposits

Deposits at banks, credit unions, savings banks, and savings and loan associations are also money. Deposits are money because they can be used to make payments. You don't need to go to the bank to get currency to make a payment. You can write a check or use your debit card to tell your bank to move some money from your account to someone else's.

Currency Inside the Banks Is Not Money

Although currency and bank deposits are money, currency *inside the banks* is *not money*. The reason is while currency is inside a bank, it isn't available as a means of payment. When you get some cash from the ATM, you convert your bank deposit into currency. You change the form of your money, but there is no change in the quantity of money that you own. Your bank deposit decreases, and your currency holding increases.

If we counted bank deposits and currency inside the banks as money, think about what would happen to the quantity of money when you get cash from the ATM. The quantity of money would appear to decrease. Your currency would increase, but both bank deposits and currency inside the banks would decrease.

You can see that counting both bank deposits and currency inside the banks as money would be double counting.

■ Official Measures of Money: M1 and M2

Figure 27.1 shows the items that make up two official measures of money. **M1** consists of currency held by individuals and businesses, traveler's checks, and checkable deposits owned by individuals and businesses. **M2** consists of M1 plus savings deposits and time deposits (less than $100,000), money market funds, and other deposits. Time deposits are deposits that can be withdrawn only after a fixed term. Money market funds are deposits that are invested in short-term securities.

Are M1 and M2 Means of Payment?

The test of whether something is money is whether it is a generally accepted means of payment. Currency passes the test. Checkable deposits also pass the test because they can be transferred from one person to another by using a debit card or writing a check. So all the components of M1 serve as means of payment.

■ **FIGURE 27.1**

Two Measures of Money: June 2016

MyEconLab Real-time data

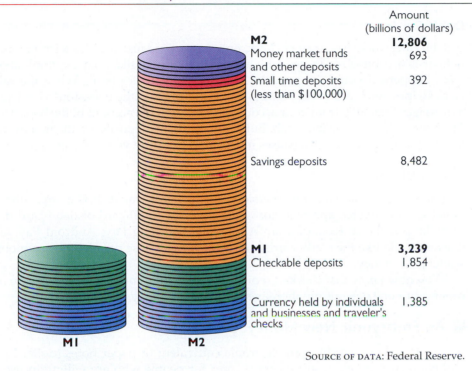

	Amount (billions of dollars)
M2	**12,806**
Money market funds and other deposits	693
Small time deposits (less than $100,000)	392
Savings deposits	8,482
M1	**3,239**
Checkable deposits	1,854
Currency held by individuals and businesses and traveler's checks	1,385

In June 2016, M1 was $3,239 billion—the sum of $1,385 billion currency and traveler's checks and $1,854 billion checkable deposits.

M2 was $12,806 billion—the sum of M1, $8,482 billion savings deposits, $392 billion time deposits, and $693 billion money market funds and other deposits.

SOURCE OF DATA: Federal Reserve.

Some of the savings deposits in M2 are also instantly convertible into a means of payment. You can use the ATM to get currency to pay for your groceries or gas. But other savings deposits, time deposits, and money market funds are not instantly convertible and are *not* a means of payment.

■ Checks, Credit Cards, Debit Cards, and Mobile Wallets

In defining money and describing the things that serve as money today, we have not included checks, credit cards and debit cards, or mobile wallets. Aren't these things that we use when we buy something also money?

Checks

A check is not money. It is an instruction to a bank to make a payment. The easiest way to see why a check is not money is to think about how the quantity of money you own changes if you write a check. You don't suddenly have more money because you've written a check to pay a bill. Your money is your bank deposit, not the value of the checks you've written.

Credit Cards

A credit card is not money. It is a special type of ID card that gets you an instant loan. Suppose that you use your credit card to buy a textbook. You sign or enter your PIN and leave the store with your book. The book may be in your possession, but you've not yet paid for it. You've taken a loan from the bank that issued your credit card. Your credit card issuer pays the bookstore and you eventually get your credit card bill, which you pay using money.

Debit Cards

A debit card works like a paper check, only faster. And just as a check isn't money, neither is a debit card. To see why a debit card works like a check, think about what happens if you use your debit card to buy your textbook. When the sales clerk swipes your card in the bookstore, the computer in the bookstore's bank gets a message: Take $100 from your account and put it in the account of the bookstore. The transaction is done in a flash. But again, the bank deposits are the money and the debit card is the tool that causes money to move from you to the bookstore.

Mobile Wallets

A *mobile wallet* is an electronic version of a physical wallet. It is a smartphone, tablet, or smartwatch app that stores and accesses credit card or debit card data to make purchases. Examples are Apple Pay, Samsung Pay, Android Pay, and Current C. So like the credit cards and debit cards whose data it stores, a mobile wallet isn't money.

You now know that checks, credit and debit cards, and mobile wallets are not money, but one new information-age money is gradually emerging—e-cash.

■ An Embryonic New Money: E-Cash

Electronic cash (or *e-cash*) is an electronic equivalent of paper notes (dollar bills) and coins. It is an electronic currency, and for people who are willing to use it, e-cash works like other forms of money. But for e-cash to become a widely used form of money, it must evolve some of the characteristics of physical currency.

People use physical currency because it is portable, recognizable, transferable, untraceable, and anonymous and can be used to make change. The designers of e-cash aim to reproduce all of these features of notes and coins. Today's e-cash is portable, untraceable, and anonymous, but it has not yet reached the level of recognition that makes it *universally* accepted as a means of payment. E-cash doesn't yet meet the definition of money.

Like notes and coins, e-cash can be used in shops. It can also be used over the Internet. To use e-cash in a shop, the buyer uses a smart card that stores some e-cash and the shop uses a smart card reader. When a transaction is made, e-cash is transferred from the smart card directly to the shop's bank account. Users of smart cards receive their e-cash by withdrawing it from a bank account by using a special ATM or a smartphone.

Several versions of e-cash in U.S. dollars, euros, and other currencies are available on the Internet. The most popular and widely used e-cash system is PayPal, which is owned by eBay. The most sophisticated and secure e-cash is a currency called Bitcoin, which can be used to settle debts and be traded for dollars and other currencies on the Internet.

A handy advantage of e-cash over paper notes arises when you lose your wallet. If it is stuffed with dollar bills, you're out of luck. If it contains e-cash recorded on your smart card, your bank can cancel the e-cash stored on the card and issue you replacement e-cash.

Although e-cash is not yet universally accepted, it is likely that its use will grow and that it will gradually replace physical forms of currency.

CHECKPOINT 27.1

Define money and describe its functions.

Practice Problems

1. In the United States today, which of the items in List 1 are money?

2. In January 2016, currency held by individuals and businesses and traveler's checks were $1,347 billion; checkable deposits owned by individuals and businesses were $1,764 billion; savings deposits were $8,189 billion; small time deposits were $400 billion; and money market funds and other deposits were $709 billion. Calculate M1 and M2 in January 2016.

3. In May 2016, M1 was $3,239 billion; M2 was $12,731 billion; checkable deposits owned by individuals and businesses were $1,861 billion; small time deposits were $393 billion; and money market funds and other deposits were $706 billion. Calculate currency held by individuals and businesses and traveler's checks. Calculate savings deposits.

LIST 1

- Your Visa card
- The quarters inside vending machines
- U.S. dollar bills in your wallet
- The check that you have just written to pay for your rent
- The loan you took out last August to pay for your tuition

In the News

Android Pay adds support for 115 new U.S. banks
Android Pay now operates in the United States and the Uinted Kingdom and is expanding around the world. It supports CITI bank and AMEX and from today, 115 more banks and credit unions are joining the service.

Source: androidheadlines.com, June 30, 2016

As people use mobile wallets to make purchases, will currency disappear? How will the components of M1 change? Will credit cards and debit cards disappear?

Solutions to Practice Problems

1. Money is defined as a means of payment. Only the quarters inside vending machines and U.S. dollar bills in your wallet are money.

2. M1 is $3,111 billion. M1 is the sum of currency held by individuals and businesses and traveler's checks ($1,347 billion) and checkable deposits owned by individuals and businesses ($1,764 billion).
M2 is $12,409 billion. M2 is the sum of M1 ($3,111 billion), savings deposits ($8,189 billion), small time deposits ($400 billion), and money market funds and other deposits ($709 billion).

3. Currency held by individuals and businesses and traveler's checks were $1,378 billion. Currency held by individuals and businesses and traveler's checks equals M1 ($3,239 billion) minus checkable deposits owned by individuals and businesses ($1,861 billion).
Savings deposits are $8,393 billion. Savings deposits equals M2 ($12,731 billion) minus M1 ($3,239 billion) minus small time deposits ($393 billion) minus money market funds and other deposits ($706 billion)

Solution to In the News

Most people will probably carry less currency, but it won't disappear because currency is used in the underground economy. Most of M1 will be checkable deposits. Mobile wallets are digitized credit cards and debit cards, so these cards will not disappear.

MyEconLab Concept Video

27.2   THE BANKING SYSTEM

The banking system consists of the Federal Reserve and the banks and other institutions that accept deposits and that provide the services that enable people and businesses to make and receive payments. Sitting at the top of the system (see Figure 27.2), the Federal Reserve (or the Fed) sets the rules and regulates and influences the activities of banks and other institutions. Three types of financial institutions accept the deposits that are part of the nation's money:

- Commercial banks
- Thrift institutions
- Money market funds

Here, we describe the functions of these institutions, and in the next section, we describe the structure and functions of the Federal Reserve.

■ Commercial Banks

A *commercial bank* is a firm that is chartered by the Comptroller of the Currency in the U.S. Treasury (or by a state agency) to accept deposits and make loans. In 2016, about 5,260 commercial banks operated in the United States, down from 15,000 in the 1980s. The number of banks has shrunk because in 1997 the rules under which banks operate were changed, permitting them to open branches in every state. A wave of mergers followed this change of rules. Also, more than 130 banks failed during the financial crisis of 2008–2009.

Bank Deposits

A commercial bank accepts three broad types of deposits: checkable deposits, savings deposits, and time deposits. A bank pays a low interest rate (sometimes zero) on checkable deposits, and it pays the highest interest rate on time deposits.

■ FIGURE 27.2

The Institutions of the Banking System

MyEconLab Animation

The Federal Reserve regulates and influences the activities of the commercial banks, thrift institutions, and money market funds, whose deposits make up the nation's money.

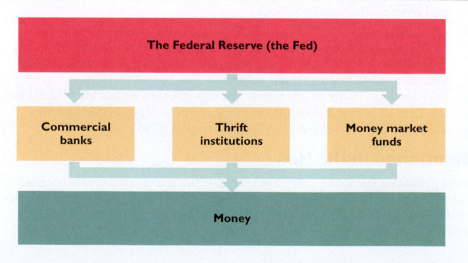

EYE on the PAST
The "Invention" of Banking

It is the sixteenth century somewhere in Europe: Because gold is valuable and easy to steal, goldsmiths have well-guarded safes in which people "deposit" their gold. The goldsmiths issue gold receipts entitling owners to reclaim their "deposits" on demand.

Isabella, who has a receipt for 100 ounces of gold deposited with Samuel Goldsmith, buys some land from Henry. She can pay for the land in one of two ways: She can visit Samuel, collect her gold, and hand the gold to Henry. Or she can give Henry her gold receipt, which enables Henry to claim the 100 ounces of gold.

It is a simpler and safer transaction to use the receipt. When Henry wants to buy something, he too can pass the receipt on to someone else.

So Samuel Goldsmith's gold receipt is circulating as a means of payment. It is money!

Because the receipts circulate while the gold remains in his safe, Samuel realizes that he can lend gold receipts and charge interest for doing so. Samuel writes receipts for gold that he doesn't own, but has on deposit, and lends these receipts. Samuel is one of the first bankers.

Profit and Risk: A Balancing Act

Commercial banks try to maximize their stockholders' wealth by lending for long terms at high interest rates and borrowing from depositors and others. But lending is risky. Risky loans sometimes don't get repaid and the prices of risky securities sometimes fall. In either of these events, a bank incurs a loss that could even wipe out the stockholders' wealth. Also, when depositors see their bank incurring losses, mass withdrawals—called a run on the bank—might create a crisis. So a bank must perform a balancing act. It must be careful in the way it uses the depositors' funds and balance security for depositors and stockholders against high but risky returns. To trade off between risk and profit a bank divides its assets into four parts: reserves, liquid assets, securities, and loans.

Reserves

A bank's **reserves** consist of currency in its vaults plus the balance on its reserve account at the Federal Reserve.

The currency in a bank's vaults is a reserve to meet its depositors' withdrawals. Your bank must replenish currency in its ATM every time you and your friends have raided it for cash for a midnight pizza.

A commercial bank's deposit at the Federal Reserve is similar to your own deposit at a bank. The bank uses its reserve account at the Fed to receive and make payments to other banks and to obtain currency. The Fed requires banks to hold a minimum percentage of deposits as reserves, called the *required reserve ratio*. Banks' *desired* reserves might exceed the required reserves, especially when the cost of borrowing reserves is high.

Reserves
The currency in the bank's vaults plus the balance on its reserve account at the Federal Reserve.

Liquid Assets

Banks' *liquid assets* are short-term Treasury bills and overnight loans to other banks. The interest rates on liquid assets are low but they are low-risk assets. The interest rate on interbank loans, called the **federal funds rate**, is the central target of the Fed's monetary policy actions.

Federal funds rate
The interest rate on interbank loans (loans made in the federal funds market).

Securities and Loans

Securities are bonds issued by the U.S. government and by other organizations. Some bonds have low interest rates and are safe. Some bonds have high interest rates and are risky. Mortgage-backed securities are examples of risky securities.

Loans are the provision of funds to businesses and individuals. Loans earn the bank a high interest rate, but they are risky and, even when not very risky, cannot be called in before the agreed date. Banks earn the highest interest rate on unpaid credit card balances, which are loans to credit card holders.

Bank Assets and Liabilities: The Relative Magnitudes

Figure 27.3 shows the relative magnitudes of the banks' assets and liabilities—deposits and other borrowing—in 2016. After performing their profit-versus-risk balancing acts, the banks kept 17 percent of total assets in reserves (and liquid assets), 22 percent in securities, and 61 percent in loans. Checkable deposits (part of M1) and savings deposits and small time deposits (part of M2) were 75 percent of total funds. Another 13 percent of total funds were borrowed and the banks' own capital—net worth of its stock holders—was 12 percent of total funds.

The commercial banks' asset allocation in 2016 is a new normal and is a consequence of a financial crisis in 2008 and 2009. *Eye on the U.S. Economy* on p. 701 contrasts pre-crisis normal times with the depth of the crisis.

■ **FIGURE 27.3**

Commercial Banks' Assets, Liabilities, and Net Worth   MyEconLab Animation

In 2016, commercial bank loans were 61 percent of total assets, securities were 22 percent, and reserves were 17 percent.

The banks obtained the funds allocated to these assets from three sources: 75 percent from checkable deposits (part of M1) and savings deposits and small time deposits (part of M2); 13 percent borrowed from bond holders; and 12 percent from the banks' stock holders—the banks' net worth.

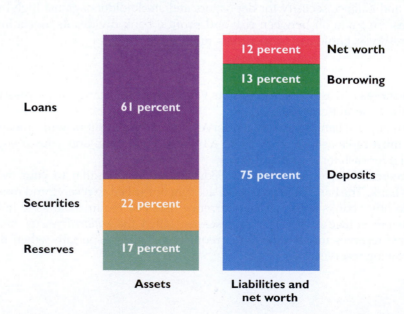

SOURCE OF DATA: Federal Reserve.

EYE on the U.S. ECONOMY
Commercial Banks Under Stress in the Financial Crisis

In normal times, bank reserves are less than 1 percent of total assets and liquid assets are less than 4 percent. Loans are 68 percent and securities 28 percent. July 2007 was such a normal time (the orange bars).

During the financial crisis that started in 2007 and intensified in September 2008, the banks took big hits as the value of their securities and loans fell.

Faced with a riskier world, the banks increased their liquid assets and reserves. In September 2009 (the blue bars), liquid assets were almost 10 percent of total assets and reserves were 8 percent.

The balancing act tipped away from risk-taking and toward security.

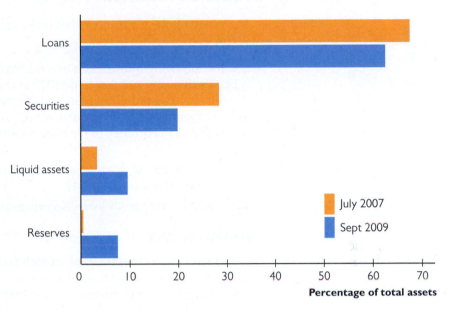

SOURCE OF DATA: Federal Reserve.

■ Thrift Institutions

The three types of thrift institutions are savings and loan associations, savings banks, and credit unions. A *savings and loan association (S&L)* is a financial institution that accepts checkable deposits and savings deposits and that makes personal, commercial, and home-purchase loans. A *savings bank* is a financial institution that accepts savings deposits and makes mostly consumer and home-purchase loans. The depositors own some savings banks (called mutual savings banks). A *credit union* is a financial institution owned by a social or economic group, such as a firm's employees, that accepts savings deposits and makes mostly consumer loans.

Like commercial banks, the thrift institutions hold reserves and must meet minimum reserve ratios set by the Fed.

■ Money Market Funds

A *money market fund* is a financial institution that obtains funds by selling shares and uses these funds to buy assets such as U.S. Treasury bills. Money market fund shares act like bank deposits. Shareholders can write checks on their money market fund accounts, but there are restrictions on most of these accounts. For example, the minimum deposit accepted might be $2,500 and the smallest check a depositor is permitted to write might be $500.

MyEconLab Study Plan 27.2
Key Terms Quiz
Solutions Video

 # CHECKPOINT 27.2

Describe the functions of banks.

Practice Problems

1. What are the institutions that make up the banking system?

2. What is a bank's balancing act?

Use the following information to work Problems **3** and **4**.
A bank's deposits and assets are $320 in checkable deposits and $896 in savings deposits held by individuals and businesses; $840 in small time deposits; $990 in loans to businesses; $400 in outstanding credit card balances; $634 in government securities; $2 in currency in the bank's vault; and $30 in its reserve account at the Fed.

3. Calculate the bank's total deposits, deposits that are part of M1, and deposits that are part of M2.

4. Calculate the bank's loans, securities, and reserves.

In the News

Regulators close Georgia bank in 95th failure for the year
Regulators shut down Atlanta-based Georgian Bank. On July 24, 2009, Georgian Bank had $2 billion in assets and $2 billion in deposits. By September 29, 2009, Georgian Bank had lost about $2 billion in home loans and other assets.
Source: *USA Today*, September 30, 2009
Explain how Georgian Bank's balancing act failed.

Solutions to Practice Problems

1. The institutions that make up the banking system are the Fed, commercial banks, thrift institutions, and money market funds.

2. A bank makes a profit by borrowing from depositors at a low interest rate and lending at a higher interest rate. The bank must hold enough reserves to meet depositors' withdrawals. The bank's balancing act is to balance the risk of loans (profits for stockholders) against the security for depositors.

3. Total deposits are $320 + $896 + $840 = $2,056.
    Deposits that are part of M1 are checkable deposits, $320.
    Deposits that are part of M2 include all deposits, $2,056.

4. Loans are $990 + $400 = $1,390. Securities are $634.
    Reserves are $30 + $2 = $32.

Solution to In the News

In July, Georgian Bank's $2 billion of assets (home loans and securities) balanced its deposits of $2 billion. The bank expected to make a profit on its assets that exceeded the interest it paid to depositors. The financial crisis increased the risk on all financial assets. The bank was now holding assets that were more risky than it had planned. As people defaulted on their home loans and the value of securities fell, the value of Georgian Bank's assets crashed to zero. With fewer assets than deposits, regulators had no choice other than to close the bank and sell its assets and deposits. The bank failed to balance risk against profit.

27.3 THE FEDERAL RESERVE SYSTEM

MyEconLab Concept Video

The **Federal Reserve System (the Fed)** is the central bank of the United States. A central bank is a public authority that provides banking services to banks and governments and regulates financial institutions and markets. A central bank does not provide banking services to businesses and individual citizens. Its only customers are banks such as Bank of America and Citibank and the U.S. government. The Fed is organized into 12 Federal Reserve districts shown in Figure 27.4.

The Fed's main task is to regulate the interest rate and quantity of money to achieve low and predictable inflation and sustained economic expansion.

Federal Reserve System (the Fed)
The central bank of the United States.

■ The Structure of the Federal Reserve

The key elements in the structure of the Federal Reserve are

- The Chair of the Board of Governors
- The Board of Governors
- The regional Federal Reserve Banks
- The Federal Open Market Committee

The Chair of the Board of Governors

The Chair of the Board of Governors is the Fed's chief executive, public face, and center of power and responsibility. When things go right, the Chair gets the credit; when they go wrong, the Chair gets the blame. Janet Yellen, a former University of California, Berkeley, economics professor, is the Fed's current Chair.

Fed Chair Janet Yellen

■ FIGURE 27.4

The Federal Reserve Districts

MyEconLab Animation

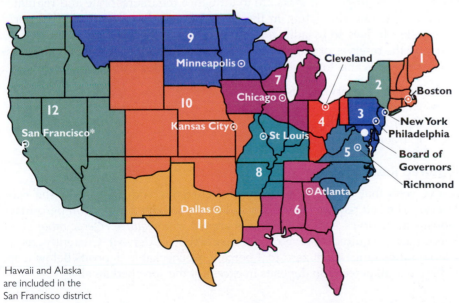

* Hawaii and Alaska
  are included in the
  San Francisco district

The nation is divided into 12 Federal Reserve districts, each having a Federal Reserve Bank. (Some of the larger districts also have branch banks.) The Board of Governors of the Federal Reserve System is located in Washington, D.C.

SOURCE: *Federal Reserve Bulletin.*

The Board of Governors

The Board of Governors has seven members (including the Chair), who are appointed by the President of the United States and confirmed by the Senate, each for a 14-year term. The terms are staggered so that one seat on the board becomes vacant every two years. The President appoints one of the board members as the Chair for a term of four years, which is renewable.

The Regional Federal Reserve Banks

There are 12 regional Federal Reserve Banks, one for each of the 12 Federal Reserve districts shown in Figure 27.4. Each regional Federal Reserve Bank has nine directors, three of whom are appointed by the Board of Governors and six of whom are elected by the commercial banks in the Federal Reserve district. The directors of each regional Federal Reserve Bank appoint that Bank's president, and the Board of Governors approves this appointment.

The Federal Reserve Bank of New York (known as the New York Fed) occupies a special place because it implements some of the Fed's most important policy decisions.

The Federal Open Market Committee

Federal Open Market Committee
The Fed's main policy-making committee.

The **Federal Open Market Committee** (FOMC) is the Fed's main policy-making committee. The FOMC consists of the following twelve members:

- The Chair and the other six members of the Board of Governors
- The president of the Federal Reserve Bank of New York
- Four presidents of the other regional Federal Reserve Banks (on a yearly rotating basis)

The FOMC meets approximately every six weeks to review the state of the economy and to decide the actions to be carried out by the New York Fed.

■ The Fed's Policy Tools

The Fed's most important tasks are to influence the interest rate and regulate the amount of money circulating in the United States. How does the Fed perform these tasks? It does so by adjusting the reserves of the banking system. Also, by adjusting the reserves of the banking system and standing ready to make loans to banks, the Fed is able to prevent bank failures. The Fed's policy tools are

- Required reserve ratios
- Discount rate
- Open market operations
- Extraordinary crisis measures

Required Reserve Ratios

You've seen that banks hold reserves of currency and deposits at the Federal Reserve. The Fed requires the banks and thrifts to hold a minimum percentage of deposits as reserves. This minimum is known as a *required reserve ratio*. The Fed determines a required reserve ratio for each type of deposit. Currently, required reserve ratios range from zero to 3 percent on checkable deposits below a specified level to 10 percent on deposits in excess of the specified level.

Discount Rate

The discount rate is the interest rate at which the Fed stands ready to lend reserves to commercial banks. A change in the discount rate begins with a proposal to the FOMC by at least one of the 12 Federal Reserve Banks. If the FOMC agrees that a change is required, it proposes the change to the Board of Governors for its approval.

Open Market Operations

An **open market operation** is the purchase or sale of government securities—U.S. Treasury bills and bonds—by the Federal Reserve in the open market. When the Fed conducts an open market operation, it makes a transaction with a bank or some other business but it does not transact with the federal government. The New York Fed conducts the Fed's open market operations.

Open market operation
The purchase or sale of government securities—U.S. Treasury bills and bonds—by the New York Fed in the open market.

Extraordinary Crisis Measures

The financial crisis of 2008, the slow recovery, and ongoing financial stress have brought three more tools into play. They are

- Quantitative easing (or QE)
- Credit easing
- Operation Twist

Quantitative Easing (QE)   When the Fed creates bank reserves by conducting a large-scale open market purchase at a low or possibly zero federal funds rate, the action is called *quantitative easing*. There have been three episodes of quantitative easing: QE1, QE2, and QE3—see *Eye on Creating Money* on pp. 714–715.

Credit Easing   When the Fed buys private securities or makes loans to financial institutions to stimulate their lending, the action is called *credit easing*.

Operation Twist   When the Fed buys long-term government securities and sells short-term government securities, the action is called *Operation Twist*. The idea is to lower long-term interest rates and stimulate long-term borrowing and investment expenditure. An Operation Twist was conducted in September 2011.

■ How the Fed's Policy Tools Work

The Fed's normal policy tools work by changing either the demand for or the supply of the monetary base, which in turn changes the interest rate. The **monetary base** is the sum of coins, Federal Reserve notes, and banks' reserves at the Fed.

Monetary base
The sum of coins, Federal Reserve notes, and banks' reserves at the Fed.

By increasing the required reserve ratio, the Fed can force the banks to hold a larger quantity of monetary base. By raising the discount rate, the Fed can make it more costly for the banks to borrow reserves—borrow monetary base. And by selling securities in the open market, the Fed can decrease the monetary base. All of these actions lead to a rise in the interest rate.

Similarly, by decreasing the required reserve ratio, the Fed can permit the banks to hold a smaller quantity of monetary base. By lowering the discount rate, the Fed can make it less costly for the banks to borrow monetary base. And by buying securities in the open market, the Fed can increase the monetary base. All of these actions lead to a decrease in the interest rate.

Open market operations are the Fed's main tool and in the next section you will learn in more detail how they work.

MyEconLab Study Plan 27.3
Key Terms Quiz
Solutions Video

CHECKPOINT 27.3

Describe the functions of the Federal Reserve System (the Fed).

Practice Problems

1. What is the Fed and what is the FOMC?
2. Who is the Fed's chief executive, and what are the Fed's main policy tools?
3. What is the monetary base?
4. Suppose that at the end of December 2009, the monetary base in the United States was $700 billion, Federal Reserve notes were $650 billion, and banks' reserves at the Fed were $20 billion. Calculate the quantity of coins.

In the News

Helicopter Money Primer: The possible next frontier in quantitative easing
Central banks—the Fed, the Bank of Japan, the European Central Bank, the People's Bank of China, and others—have bought trillions of dollars of bonds. The Fed alone has bought $4 trillion worth.

Source: DailyFX, July 15, 2016

What are the Fed's policy tools and which policy tool did the Fed use to increase its assets to $4 trillion?

Solutions to Practice Problems

1. The Federal Reserve System (the Fed) is the U.S. central bank—a public authority that provides banking services to banks and the U.S. government and that regulates the quantity of money and the banking system. The FOMC is the Federal Open Market Committee—the Fed's main policy-making committee.
2. The Fed's chief executive is the Chair of the Board of Governors, currently Janet Yellen. The Fed's main policy tools are required reserve ratios, the discount rate, and open market operations. In unusual times, extraordinary crisis measures are an additional tool.
3. The monetary base is the sum of coins, Federal Reserve notes (dollar bills), and banks' reserves at the Fed.
4. To calculate the quantity of coins, we use the definition of the monetary base: coins plus Federal Reserve notes plus banks' reserves at the Fed.
    Quantity of coins = Monetary base − Federal Reserve notes − Banks' reserves at the Fed.
    So at the end of December 2009,
    Quantity of coins = $700 billion − $650 billion − $20 billion
    = $30 billion.

Solution to In the News

The Fed's policy tools are the required reserve ratio, discount rate, open market operations, and extraordinary crisis measures called *quantitative easing* and *credit easing*. The policy tool used by the Fed to increase its assets to $4 trillion were large-scale open market operations called quantitative easing. These operations were conducted in three bursts known as QE1, QE2, and QE3.

27.4 REGULATING THE QUANTITY OF MONEY

MyEconLab Concept Video

Banks create money, but this doesn't mean that they have smoke-filled back rooms in which counterfeiters are busily working. Remember, most money is deposits, not currency. What banks create is deposits, and they do so by making loans.

■ Creating Deposits by Making Loans

The easiest way to see that banks create deposits is to think about what happens when Andy, who has a Visa card issued by Citibank, uses his card to buy a tank of gas from Chevron. When Andy signs the card sales slip, he takes a loan from Citibank and obligates himself to repay the loan at a later date. At the end of the business day, a Chevron clerk takes a pile of signed credit card sales slips, including Andy's, to Chevron's bank. For now, let's assume that Chevron also banks at Citibank. The bank immediately credits Chevron's account with the value of the slips (minus the bank's commission).

You can see that these transactions have created a bank deposit and a loan. Andy has increased the size of his loan (his credit card balance), and Chevron has increased the size of its bank deposit. And because deposits are money, Citibank has created money.

If, as we've just assumed, Andy and Chevron use the same bank, no further transactions take place. But the outcome is essentially the same when two banks are involved. If Chevron's bank is the Bank of America, then Citibank uses its reserves to pay the Bank of America. Citibank has an increase in loans and a decrease in reserves; the Bank of America has an increase in reserves and an increase in deposits. The banking system as a whole has an increase in loans, an increase in deposits, and no change in reserves.

EYE on YOUR LIFE
Money and Your Role in Its Creation

MyEconLab Critical Thinking Exercise

Imagine a world without money in which you must barter for everything you buy. What kinds of items would you have available for these trades? Would you keep some stocks of items that you know lots of people are willing to accept? Would you really be bartering, or would you be using a commodity as money? How much longer would it take you to conduct all the transactions of a normal day?

Now think about your own holdings of money today. How much money do you have in your pocket or wallet? How much do you have in the bank? How does the money you hold change over the course of a month?

Of the money you're holding, which items are part of M1 and which are part of M2? Are all the items in M2 means of payment?

Now think about the role that *you* play in creating money. Every time you charge something to your credit card, you help the bank that issued it to create money. The increase in your credit card balance is a loan from the bank to you. The bank pays the seller right away. So the seller's bank deposit and your outstanding balance increase together. Money is created.

You contribute to the currency drain that limits the ability of your bank to create money when you visit the ATM and get some cash to pay for your late-night pizza.

Of course, your transactions are a tiny part of the total. But together, you and a few million other students like you play a big role in the money creation process.

If Andy had swiped his card at an automatic payment pump, all these transactions would have occurred at the time he filled his tank, and the quantity of money would have increased by the amount of his purchase (minus the bank's commission for conducting the transactions).

Three factors limit the quantity of deposits that the banking system can create:

- The monetary base
- Desired reserves
- Desired currency holding

The Monetary Base

You've seen that the monetary base is the sum of coins, Federal Reserve notes, and banks' deposits at the Fed. The size of the monetary base limits the total quantity of money that the banking system can create because banks have a desired level of reserves and households and firms have a desired level of currency holding and both of these desired holdings of the monetary base depend on the quantity of money.

Desired Reserves

A bank's *desired* reserves are the reserves that the bank chooses to hold. The *desired reserve ratio* is the ratio of reserves to deposits that a bank wants to hold. This ratio exceeds the *required reserve ratio* by an amount that the banks determine to be prudent on the basis of their daily business requirements.

A bank's *actual reserve ratio* changes when its customers make a deposit or a withdrawal. If a bank's customer makes a deposit, reserves and deposits increase by the same amount, so the bank's reserve ratio increases. Similarly, if a bank's customer makes a withdrawal, reserves and deposits decrease by the same amount, so the bank's reserve ratio decreases.

A bank's **excess reserves** are its actual reserves minus its desired reserves. When the banking system as a whole has excess reserves, banks can create money by making new loans. When the banking system as a whole is short of reserves, banks must destroy money by decreasing the quantity of loans.

Excess reserves
A bank's actual reserves minus its desired reserves.

Desired Currency Holding

We hold our money in the form of currency and bank deposits. The proportion of money held as currency isn't constant but at any given time, people have a definite view as to how much they want to hold in each form of money.

Because households and firms want to hold some proportion of their money in the form of currency, when the total quantity of bank deposits increases, so does the quantity of currency that they want to hold.

Because desired currency holding increases when deposits increase, currency leaves the banks when loans are made and deposits increase. We call the leakage of currency from the banking system the *currency drain*. And we call the ratio of currency to deposits the *currency drain ratio*.

The greater the currency drain ratio, the smaller is the quantity of deposits and money that the banking system can create from a given amount of monetary base. The reason is that as currency drains from the banks, they are left with fewer reserves (and less excess reserves), so they make fewer loans.

■ How Open Market Operations Change the Monetary Base

When the Fed buys securities in an open market operation, it pays for them with newly created bank reserves and money. With more reserves in the banking system, the supply of interbank loans increases, the demand for interbank loans decreases, and the federal funds rate—the interest rate in the interbank loans market—falls.

Similarly, when the Fed sells securities in an open market operation, buyers pay for the securities with bank reserves and money. With smaller reserves in the banking system, the supply of interbank loans decreases, the demand for interbank loans increases, and the federal funds rate rises. The Fed sets a target for the federal funds rate and conducts open market operations on the scale needed to hit its target.

A change in the federal funds rate is only the first stage in an adjustment process that follows an open market operation. If banks' reserves increase, the banks can increase their lending and create even more money. If banks' reserves decrease, the banks must decrease their lending, which decreases the quantity of money. We'll study the effects of open market operations in some detail, beginning with an open market purchase.

The Fed Buys Securities

Suppose the Fed buys $100 million of U.S. government securities in the open market. There are two cases to consider, depending on who sells the securities. A bank might sell some of its securities, or a person or business that is not a commercial bank—the general public—might sell. The outcome is essentially the same in the two cases. To convince you of this fact, we'll study the two cases, starting with the simpler case in which a commercial bank sells securities. (The seller will be someone who thinks the Fed is offering a good price for securities and it is profitable to make the sale.)

FOMC meeting.

A Commercial Bank Sells   When the Fed buys $100 million of securities from the Manhattan Commercial Bank, two things happen:

1. The Manhattan Commercial Bank has $100 million less in securities, and the Fed has $100 million more in securities.
2. To pay for the securities, the Fed increases the Manhattan Commercial Bank's reserve account at the New York Fed by $100 million.

Figure 27.5 shows the effects of these actions on the balance sheets of the Fed and the Manhattan Commercial Bank. Ownership of the securities passes from the commercial bank to the Fed, so the bank's securities decrease by $100 million and the Fed's securities increase by $100 million, as shown by the red-to-blue arrow running from the Manhattan Commercial Bank to the Fed.

The Fed increases the Manhattan Commercial Bank's reserves by $100 million, as shown by the green arrow running from the Fed to the Manhattan Commercial Bank. This action increases the reserves of the banking system.

The commercial bank's total assets remain constant, but their composition changes. Its holdings of government securities decrease by $100 million, and its reserves increase by $100 million. The bank can use these additional reserves to make loans. When the bank makes loans, it creates deposits and the quantity of money increases.

We've just seen that when the Fed buys government securities from a bank, the bank's reserves increase. What happens if the Fed buys government securities from the public—say, from AIG, an insurance company?

■ **FIGURE 27.5**

The Fed Buys Securities from a Commercial Bank   MyEconLab Animation

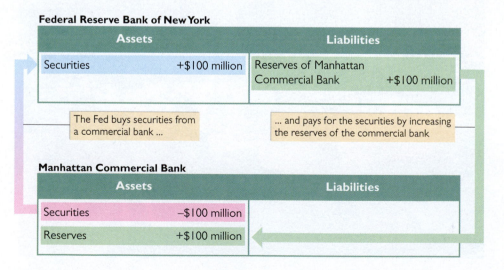

The Nonbank Public Sells   When the Fed buys $100 million of securities from AIG, three things happen:

1. AIG has $100 million less in securities, and the Fed has $100 million more in securities.

2. The Fed pays for the securities with a check for $100 million drawn on itself, which AIG deposits in its account at the Manhattan Commercial Bank.

3. The Manhattan Commercial Bank collects payment of this check from the Fed, and the Manhattan Commercial Bank's reserves increase by $100 million.

Figure 27.6 shows the effects of these actions on the balance sheets of the Fed, AIG, and the Manhattan Commercial Bank. Ownership of the securities passes from AIG to the Fed, so AIG's securities decrease by $100 million and the Fed's securities increase by $100 million (red-to-blue arrow). The Fed pays for the securities with a check payable to AIG, which AIG deposits in the Manhattan Commercial Bank. This payment increases Manhattan's reserves by $100 million (green arrow). It also increases AIG's deposit at the Manhattan Commercial Bank by $100 million (blue arrow). This action increases the reserves of the banking system.

■ **FIGURE 27.6**

The Fed Buys Securities from the Public   MyEconLab Animation

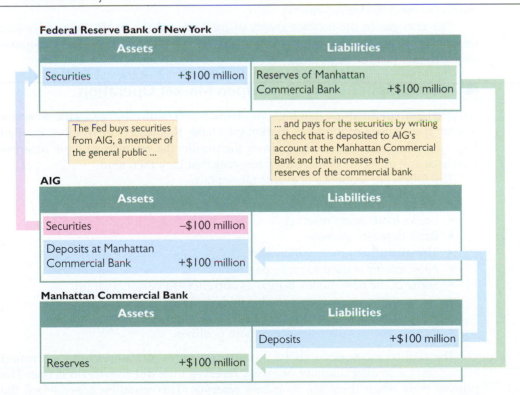

AIG has the same total assets as before, but their composition has changed. It now has more money and fewer securities. The Manhattan Commercial Bank's reserves increase, and so do its deposits—both by $100 million. Because bank reserves and deposits have increased by the same amount, the bank has excess reserves, which it can use to make loans. When it makes loans, the quantity of money increases.

We've worked through what happens when the Fed buys government securities from either a bank or the public. When the Fed sells securities, the transactions that we've just traced operate in reverse.

The Fed Sells Securities

If the Fed sells $100 million of U.S. government securities in the open market, most likely a person or business other than a bank buys them. (A bank would buy them only if it had excess reserves and couldn't find a better use for its funds.)

When the Fed sells $100 million of securities to AIG, three things happen:

1. AIG has $100 million more in securities, and the Fed has $100 million less in securities.

2. AIG pays for the securities with a check for $100 million drawn on its deposit account at the Manhattan Commercial Bank.

3. The Fed collects payment of this check from the Manhattan Commercial Bank by decreasing its reserves by $100 million.

These actions decrease the reserves of the banking system. The Manhattan Commercial Bank is now short of reserves and must borrow in the federal funds market to meet its desired reserve ratio.

The changes in the balance sheets of the Fed and the banks that we've just described are not the end of the story about the effects of an open market operation; they are just the beginning.

■ The Multiplier Effect of an Open Market Operation

An open market purchase that increases bank reserves also increases the *monetary base* by the amount of the open market purchase. Regardless of whether the Fed buys securities from the banks or from the public, the quantity of bank reserves increases and gives the banks excess reserves that they then lend.

The following sequence of events takes place:

- An open market purchase creates excess reserves.
- Banks lend excess reserves.
- Bank deposits increase.
- The quantity of money increases.
- New money is used to make payments.
- Some of the new money is held as currency—a currency drain.
- Some of the new money remains in deposits in banks.
- Banks' desired reserves increase.
- Excess reserves decrease but remain positive.

The sequence described above repeats in a series of rounds, but each round begins with a smaller quantity of excess reserves than did the previous one. The process ends when there are no excess reserves. This situation arises when the increase in the monetary base resulting from the open market operation is willingly held—when the increase in desired reserves plus the increase in desired currency holding equals the increase in the monetary base. Figure 27.7 illustrates and summarizes the sequence of events in one round of the multiplier process.

An open market *sale* works similarly to an open market *purchase*, but the sale *decreases* the monetary base and sets off a multiplier process similar to that described in Figure 27.7. At the end of the process the quantity of money has decreased by an amount that lowers desired reserves and desired currency holding by an amount equal to the decrease in the monetary base resulting from the open market sale. (Make your own version of Figure 27.7 to trace the multiplier process when the Fed *sells* and the banks or public *buys* securities.)

The magnitude of the change in the quantity of money brought about by an open market operation is determined by the money multiplier that we now explain.

■ The Money Multiplier

The **money multiplier** is the number by which a change in the monetary base is multiplied to find the resulting change in the quantity of money. It is also the ratio of the change in the quantity of money to the change in the monetary base.

The magnitude of the money multiplier depends on the desired reserve ratio and the currency drain ratio. The smaller are these two ratios, the larger is the money multiplier. Let's explore the money multiplier in more detail.

Money multiplier

The number by which a change in the monetary base is multiplied to find the resulting change in the quantity of money.

■ FIGURE 27.7

A Round in the Multiplier Process Following an Open Market Operation   MyEconLab Animation

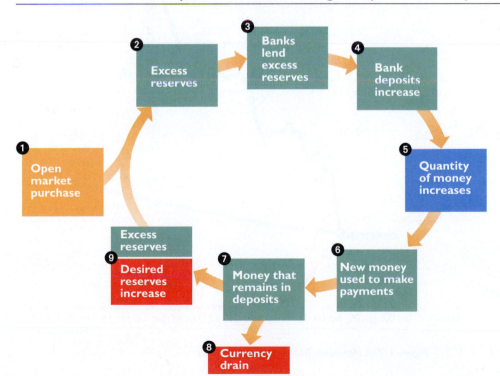

❶ An open market purchase increases bank reserves and ❷ creates excess reserves.

❸ Banks lend the excess reserves, ❹ new deposits are created, and ❺ the quantity of money increases.

❻ New money is used to make payments.

❼ Households and firms receiving payments keep some on deposit in banks and ❽ some in the form of currency—a currency drain.

❾ The increase in bank deposits increases banks' reserves but also increases banks' desired reserves.

Desired reserves increase by less than actual reserves, so the banks still have some excess reserves, but less than before. The process repeats until excess reserves have been eliminated.

To see how the desired reserve ratio and the currency drain ratio determine the size of the money multiplier, begin with two facts:

The quantity of money, M, is the sum of deposits, D, and currency, C, or $M = D + C$, and

The monetary base, MB, is the sum of desired reserves, R, and currency, C, or $MB = R + C$.

The money multiplier is equal to the quantity of money, M, divided by the monetary base, MB, that is,

$$\text{Money multiplier} = M/MB.$$

EYE on CREATING MONEY

MyEconLab Critical Thinking Exercise

How Does the Fed Create Money and Regulate Its Quantity?

During the Great Depression, many banks failed, bank deposits were destroyed, and the quantity of money crashed by 25 percent. Most economists believe that it was these events that turned an ordinary recession in 1929 into a deep and decade-long depression.

Former Fed Chair Ben Bernanke is one of the economists who has studied this tragic episode in U.S. economic history, and he had no intention of witnessing a similar event on his watch.

Figure 1 shows what the Fed did to pump reserves into the banking system. In the fall of 2008 in an episode called QE1 (see p. 705), the Fed doubled the monetary base. In 2010 and 2011, a more gradual but sustained QE2 took the monetary base to more than three times its pre-crisis level. And in 2012 and 2013, a further gradual QE3 raised the monetary base to four times its normal level.

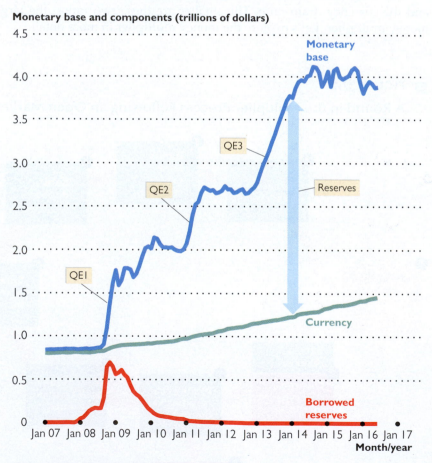

Figure 1 The Monetary Base in Financial Crisis

Because $M = D + C$ and $MB = R + C$,

$$\text{Money multiplier} = (D + C)/(R + C).$$

Now divide each item on the right-hand side of this equation by deposits, D, to get

$$\text{Money multiplier} = (1 + C/D)/(R/D + C/D).$$

Notice that C/D is the currency drain ratio and R/D is the desired reserve ratio. If the currency drain ratio is 50 percent, $C/D = 0.5$; and if the desired reserve ratio is 10 percent, $R/D = 0.1$, then the money multiplier is $1.5/0.6 = 2.5$.

The larger the desired reserve ratio and the larger the currency drain ratio, the smaller is the money multiplier.

The desired reserve ratio and the currency drain ratio that determine the magnitude of the money multiplier are not constant, so neither is the money multiplier constant. You can see in *Eye on Creating Money* below (Figure 2) that the desired reserve ratio and money multiplier changed dramatically in 2008.

(a) Currency drain and reserve ratios

(b) Money multiplier

Figure 2 The Changing Money Multiplier

This extraordinary increase in the monetary base did not bring a similar increase in the quantity of money. Figure 2 shows the reason.

In 2008, the banks' desired reserve ratio, in part (a), increased tenfold from its normal level of 1.2 percent to 12 percent. This increase brought a crash in the money multiplier, in part (b), from a normal value of 9 to an unusually low value of 5.

The surge in the desired reserve ratio is the sole reason for the collapse in the money multiplier. You can see, in part (a), that the other influence on the multiplier, the currency drain ratio, barely changed.

The banks face an unusually high level of risk and this is the main source of the increase in the desired reserve ratio. As the risk faced by banks returns to normal, the desired reserve ratio will fall, and when this happens the Fed will decrease the monetary base or create an explosion in the quantity of money.

Sources of data: Federal Reserve and Bureau of Economic Analysis.

MyEconLab Study Plan 27.4
Key Terms Quiz
Solutions Video

 CHECKPOINT 27.4

Explain how the banking system creates money and how the Fed controls the quantity of money.

Practice Problems

1. How do banks create new deposits by making loans, and what factors limit the amount of deposits and loans that they can create?

2. If the Fed makes an open market sale of $1 million of securities, who can buy the securities? What initial changes occur if the Fed sells to a bank?

3. If the Fed makes an open market sale of $1 million of securities, what is the process by which the quantity of money changes? What factors determine the change in the quantity of money?

In the News

Fed doubles monetary base
During the fourth quarter of 2008, the Fed doubled the monetary base but the quantity of money (M2) increased by only 5 percent.

Source: Federal Reserve

Why did M2 not increase by much more than 5 percent? What would have happened to the quantity of M2 if the Fed had kept the monetary base constant?

Solutions to Practice Problems

1. Banks can make loans when they have excess reserves. When a bank makes a loan, it creates a new deposit for the person who receives the loan. The amount of deposits created (loans made) is limited by the banks' excess reserves, its desired reserve ratio, and the currency drain ratio.

2. The Fed sells securities to banks or the public, but not the government. The initial change is a decrease in the monetary base of $1 million. Ownership of the securities passes from the Fed to the bank, and the Fed's assets decrease by $1 million. The bank pays for the securities by decreasing its reserves at the Fed by $1 million. The Fed's liabilities decrease by $1 million. The bank's total assets are unchanged, but it has $1 million less in reserves and $1 million more in securities.

3. When the Fed sells securities to a bank, the bank's reserves decrease by $1 million. The bank's deposits do not change, so the bank is short of reserves. The bank calls in loans and deposits decrease by the same amount. The desired reserve ratio and the currency drain ratio determine the decrease in the quantity of money. The larger the desired reserve ratio or the currency drain ratio, the smaller is the decrease in the quantity of money.

Solution to In the News

When the Fed increases the monetary base, M2 increases and the increase is determined by the money multiplier, $(1 + C/D)/(R/D + C/D)$, where R/D is the banks' desired reserve ratio and C/D is the currency drain ratio. M2 didn't increase by more than 5 percent because the banks increased their desired reserve ratio, which decreased the money multiplier. If the Fed had kept the monetary base unchanged, M2 would have decreased because the money multiplier decreased.

CHAPTER SUMMARY

Key Points

1. Define money and describe its functions.

- Money is anything that serves as a generally accepted means of payment.
- Money functions as a medium of exchange, unit of account, and store of value.
- M1 consists of currency held by individuals and businesses, traveler's checks, and checkable deposits owned by individuals and businesses.
- M2 consists of M1 plus savings deposits, small time deposits, and money market funds.

2. Describe the functions of banks.

- The deposits of commercial banks and thrift institutions are money.
- Banks borrow short term and lend long term and make a profit on the spread between the interest rates that they pay and receive.

3. Describe the functions of the Federal Reserve System (the Fed).

- The Federal Reserve is the central bank of the United States.
- The Fed influences the economy by setting the required reserve ratio for banks, by setting the discount rate, by open market operations, and by taking extraordinary measures in a financial crisis.

4. Explain how the banking system creates money and how the Fed controls the quantity of money.

- Banks create money by making loans.
- The maximum quantity of deposits the banks can create is limited by the monetary base, the banks' desired reserves, and desired currency holding.
- When the Fed buys securities in an open market operation, it creates bank reserves. When the Fed sells securities in an open market operation, it destroys bank reserves.
- An open market operation has a multiplier effect on the quantity of money.

Key Terms

MyEconLab Key Terms Quiz

Barter, 693

Currency, 694

Excess reserves, 708

Federal funds rate, 700

Federal Open Market
  Committee, 704

Federal Reserve System (the
  Fed), 703

Fiat money, 694

M1, 694

M2, 694

Means of payment, 692

Medium of exchange, 693

Monetary base, 705

Money, 692

Money multiplier, 713

Open market operation, 705

Reserves, 699

MyEconLab Chapter 27 Study Plan

CHAPTER CHECKPOINT

Study Plan Problems and Applications

1. What is money? Would you classify any of the items in List 1 as money?

2. What are the three functions that money performs? Which of the following items perform some but not all of these functions, and which perform all of these functions? Which of the items are money?

   - A checking account at the Bank of America
   - A dime
   - A debit card

3. Monica transfers $10,000 from her savings account at the Bank of Alaska to her money market fund. What is the immediate change in M1 and M2?

4. Terry takes $100 from his checking account and deposits the $100 in his savings account. What is the immediate change in M1 and M2?

5. Suppose that banks had deposits of $500 billion, a desired reserve ratio of 4 percent and no excess reserves. The banks had $15 billion in notes and coins. Calculate the banks' reserves at the central bank.

6. Explain the Fed's policy tools and briefly describe how each works.

7. Table 1 shows a bank's balance sheet. The bank has no excess reserves and there is no currency drain. Calculate the bank's desired reserve ratio.

8. The Fed buys $2 million of securities from AIG. If AIG's bank has a desired reserve ratio of 0.1 and there is no currency drain, calculate the bank's excess reserves as soon as the open market purchase is made, the maximum amount of loans that the banking system can make, and the maximum amount of new money that the banking system can create.

Use the following information to work Problems **9** and **10**.

If the desired reserve ratio is 5 percent, the currency drain ratio is 20 percent of deposits, and the central bank makes an open market purchase of $1 million of securities, calculate the change in

9. The monetary base and the change in its components.

10. The quantity of money, and how much of the new money is currency and how much is bank deposits.

Use the following information to work Problems **11** and **12**.

China conducts open market operations
The People's Bank of China (the central bank of China) indicated it would lower interest rates and inject 685 billion yuan ($105 billion) into the banking system through open market operations.

Source: *Bloomberg News*, February 29, 2016

11. In the open market operation described in the news clip, explain whether the People's Bank of China buys or sells securities. Illustrate the effects of the open market operation on the balance sheets of the banks and the central bank.

12. Explain how the open market operation described in the news clip will change the quantity of money in China.

13. Read *Eye on Creating Money* on pp. 714–715. By how much did the monetary base increase and why didn't M2 increase by the same percentage?

LIST 1

- Store coupons for noodles
- A $100 Amazon.com gift certificate
- Frequent flier miles
- Credit available on your Visa card
- The dollar coins that a coin collector owns

TABLE 1

Assets		Liabilities	
(millions of dollars)			
Reserves at the Fed	20	Checkable deposits	80
Cash in vault	5	Savings deposits	120
Securities	75		
Loans	100		

Instructor Assignable Problems and Applications

1. When the Fed increased the monetary base between 2008 and 2014, which component of the monetary base increased most: banks' reserves or currency? How did the banks' borrowed reserves change?

2. What happened to the money multiplier between 2008 and 2014? What would the money multiplier have been if the currency drain ratio had increased? What would the money multiplier have been if the banks' desired reserve ratio had not changed?

3. What are the three functions that money performs? Which of the items in List 1 perform some but not all of these functions and which of the items are money?

4. Naomi buys $1,000 worth of American Express traveler's checks and charges the purchase to her American Express card. What is the immediate change in M1 and M2?

5. A bank has $500 million in checkable deposits, $600 million in savings deposits, $400 million in small time deposits, $950 million in loans to businesses, $500 million in government securities, $20 million in currency, and $30 million in its reserve account at the Fed. Calculate the bank's deposits that are part of M1, deposits that are part of M2, and the bank's loans, securities, and reserves.

6. What can the Fed do to increase the quantity of money and keep the monetary base constant? Explain why the Fed would or would not

   • Change the currency drain ratio.
   • Change the required reserve ratio.
   • Change the discount rate.
   • Conduct an open market operation.

Use Table 1, which shows the balance sheet of the banking system (aggregated over all the banks), to work Problems **7** and **8**. The desired reserve ratio on all deposits is 5 percent and there is no currency drain.

7. Calculate the banking system's excess reserves. If the banks use all of these excess reserves to make loans, what is the quantity of loans and the quantity of total deposits immediately after the banks have made these loans?

8. If there is no currency drain, what is the quantity of loans and the quantity of total deposits when the banks have no excess reserves?

Use the following information to work Problems **9**, **10**, and **11**.

China lowers reserve requirements
The People's Bank of China lowered the required reserve ratio from 17.5 percent to 17 percent, noting that it remained much higher than in other countries.
Source: *Bloomberg News*, February 29, 2016

9. Compare the required reserve ratio in China and the required reserve ratio on checkable deposits in the United States today.

10. If the currency drain ratio in China is 10 percent of deposits and the desired reserve ratio equals the required reserve ratio, calculate the money multipliers in China and compare it with the U.S. money multiplier.

11. If the currency drain ratio in China is 10 percent of deposits, by how much did the money multiplier change when the required reserve ratio changed as described in the news clip?

LIST 1

- An antique clock
- An S&L savings deposit
- Your credit card
- The coins in the Fed's museum
- Government securities

TABLE 1

Assets		Liabilities	
(millions of dollars)			
Reserves at		Checkable	
the Fed	25	deposits	90
Cash in vault	15	Savings	
Securities	60	deposits	110
Loans	100		

Multiple Choice Quiz

1. A commodity or token is money if it is _____.

   A. generally accepted as a means of payment
   B. a store of value
   C. used in a barter transaction
   D. completely safe as a store of value

2. Money in the United States today includes _____.

   A. currency and deposits at both banks and the Fed
   B. the currency in people's wallets, stores' tills, and the bank deposits that people and businesses own
   C. currency in ATMs and people's bank deposits
   D. the banks' reserves and bank deposits owned by individuals and businesses

3. Rick withdraws $500 from his savings account, keeps $100 as currency, and deposits $400 in his checking account.

   A. M1 increases by $400 and M2 decreases by $500.
   B. M1 does not change, but M2 decreases by $500.
   C. M1 does not change, but M2 decreases by $400.
   D. M1 increases by $500 and M2 does not change.

4. Commercial banks' assets include _____.

   A. bank deposits of individuals and businesses and bank reserves
   B. loans to individuals and businesses and government securities
   C. bank reserves and the deposits in M2
   D. government securities and borrowed funds

5. The Fed's policy tools include all the following *except* _____.

   A. required reserve ratio and open market operations
   B. quantitative easing
   C. discount rate
   D. taxing banks' deposits at the Fed

6. A commercial bank creates money when it does all the following *except* _____.

   A. decreases its excess reserves
   B. makes loans
   C. creates deposits
   D. puts cash in its ATMs

7. An open market _____ of $100 million of securities _____.

   A. purchase; increases bank reserves
   B. sale; increases bank reserves
   C. purchase; decreases the Fed's liabilities
   D. sale; increases the Fed's liabilities

8. The money multiplier _____.

   A. increases if banks increase their desired reserve ratio
   B. increases if the currency drain ratio increases
   C. is 1 if the desired reserve ratio equals the currency drain ratio
   D. decreases if banks increase their desired reserve ratio

What causes inflation?

Money, Interest, and Inflation

28

When you have completed your study of this chapter,
you will be able to

CHAPTER CHECKLIST

1 Explain what determines the demand for money and how the
demand for money and the supply of money determine the *nominal*
interest rate.

2 Explain how in the long run, the quantity of money determines the
price level and money growth brings inflation.

3 Identify the costs of inflation and the benefits of a stable value of
money.

MyEconLab **Big Picture Video**

721

MyEconLab Concept Video

WHERE WE ARE AND WHERE WE'RE HEADING

Before we explore the effects of money on the interest rate and the inflation rate, let's take stock of what we've learned and preview where we are heading.

■ The Real Economy

Real factors that are independent of the price level determine potential GDP and the natural unemployment rate (Chapter 24). The demand for labor and supply of labor determine the quantity of labor employed and the real wage rate at full employment. The full-employment equilibrium quantity of labor and the production function determine potential GDP. At full employment, real GDP equals potential GDP and the unemployment rate equals the natural unemployment rate.

Investment and saving along with population growth, human capital growth, and technological change determine the growth rate of real GDP (Chapter 25).

Investment and saving plans influence the demand for and supply of loanable funds, which in turn determine the real interest rate and the equilibrium amount of investment and saving (Chapter 26).

■ The Money Economy

Money consists of currency and bank deposits. Banks create deposits by making loans, and the Fed influences the quantity of money through its open market operations, which determine the monetary base and the federal funds rate—the interest rate on interbank loans (Chapter 27).

The effects of the Fed's actions and of changes in the quantity of money are complex. In the current chapter (Chapter 28), we focus on the immediate effects and on the long-run or ultimate effects of the Fed's actions.

The immediate effects are on the short-term nominal interest rate. If the Fed increases (or decreases) the quantity of money, the short-term nominal interest rate falls (or rises).

The long-run effects of the Fed's actions are on the price level and the inflation rate. In the long run, the loanable funds market determines the real interest rate and the Fed's actions determine only the price level and the inflation rate. If the Fed increases (or decreases) the quantity of money, the price level rises (or falls). And if the Fed speeds up (or slows down) the rate at which the quantity of money grows, the inflation rate increases (or decreases).

■ Real and Money Interactions and Policy

When the Fed changes the short-term nominal interest rate, other changes ripple through the economy. Expenditure plans change and real GDP, employment, unemployment, and the price level (and inflation rate) all change. In the long run, the real effects fade, leaving changes in only the price level and inflation rate. We lay the foundation for studying the ripple effects of the Fed's actions in Chapters 29–31. These chapters explain how the real and monetary factors interact and describe the short-run constraint on the Fed's choices.

Chapters 32 and 33 build on the foundation of all the preceding chapters. Chapter 32 explains how the government uses fiscal policy to sustain economic growth and stabilize output and employment. Chapter 33 explains how the Fed uses monetary policy to achieve those same goals and to control inflation.

28.1 MONEY AND THE INTEREST RATE

MyEconLab Concept Video

To understand the Fed's influence on the interest rate, we study the demand for money, the supply of money, and the forces that bring equilibrium in the market for money. We'll begin with the demand for money.

■ The Demand for Money

The amount of money that households and firms choose to hold is the **quantity of money demanded**. What determines the quantity of money demanded? The answer is the "price" of money. But what is that "price"?

Two possible answers, both correct, are the value of money and the opportunity cost of holding money. The value of money is the quantity of goods and services that a dollar will buy, which is related to the *price level*. We'll explore this "price" of money when we study the long-run effects of money in the next part of this chapter. The opportunity cost of holding money is the goods and services forgone by holding money rather than some other asset.

To determine the quantity of money to hold, households and firms compare the benefit from holding money to its opportunity cost. They choose to hold the quantity that balances the benefit of holding an *additional* dollar of money against its opportunity cost. What are the benefit and opportunity cost of holding money?

Quantity of money demanded
The amount of money that households and firms choose to hold.

Benefit of Holding Money

You've seen that money is the means of payment (Chapter 27, p. 692). The more money you hold, the easier it is for you to make payments. By holding enough money you can settle your bills at the end of each month without having to spend time and effort raising a loan or selling some other financial asset.

The marginal benefit of holding money is the change in total benefit that results from holding one more dollar as money. The marginal benefit of holding money diminishes as the quantity of money held increases. If you hold only a few dollars in money, then holding a few more dollars brings large benefits—you can buy a coffee or take a bus ride. If you hold enough money to make your normal weekly payments, then holding more dollars brings only a small benefit because you're not very likely to want to spend those extra dollars. Holding even more money brings only a small additional benefit. You barely notice the difference in the benefit of having $1,000 versus $1,001 in your bank account.

To get the most out of your assets, you hold money only up to the point at which its marginal benefit equals its opportunity cost.

Opportunity Cost of Holding Money

The opportunity cost of holding money is the interest rate forgone on an alternative asset. If you can earn 8 percent a year on a mutual fund account, then holding an additional $100 in money costs you $8 a year. Your opportunity cost of holding $100 in money is the goods and services worth $8 that you must forgo.

A fundamental principle of economics is that if the opportunity cost of something increases, people seek substitutes for it. Money is no exception. Other assets such as a mutual fund account are substitutes for money. The higher the opportunity cost of holding money—the higher the interest income forgone by not holding other assets—the smaller is the quantity of money demanded.

Opportunity Cost: *Nominal* Interest Is a *Real* Cost

The opportunity cost of holding money is the nominal interest rate. In Chapter 23 (p. 606), you learned the distinction between the *nominal* interest rate and the *real* interest rate and that

$$\text{Real interest rate} = \text{Nominal interest rate} - \text{Inflation rate}.$$

We can use this equation to find the real interest rate for a given nominal interest rate and inflation rate. For example, if the nominal interest rate on a mutual fund account is 8 percent a year and the inflation rate is 2 percent a year, the real interest rate is 6 percent a year. Why isn't the real interest rate of 6 percent a year the opportunity cost of holding money? That is, why isn't the opportunity cost of holding $100 in money only $6 worth of goods and services forgone?

The answer is that if you hold $100 in money rather than in a mutual fund, your buying power decreases by $8, not by $6. With inflation running at 2 percent a year, on each $100 that you hold as money and that earns no interest, you lose $2 worth of buying power a year. On each $100 that you put into your mutual fund account, you gain $6 worth of buying power a year. So if you hold money rather than a mutual fund, you lose the buying power of $6 plus $2, or $8—equivalent to the nominal interest rate on the mutual fund, not the real interest rate.

Because the opportunity cost of holding money is the nominal interest rate on an alternative asset,

Other things remaining the same, the higher the nominal interest rate, the smaller is the quantity of money demanded.

This relationship describes the decision made by an individual or a firm about how much money to hold. It also describes money-holding decisions for the economy—the sum of the decisions of every individual and firm.

We summarize the influence of the nominal interest rate on money-holding decisions in a demand for money schedule and curve.

The Demand for Money Schedule and Curve

Demand for money
The relationship between the quantity of money demanded and the nominal interest rate, when all other influences on the amount of money that people wish to hold remain the same.

The **demand for money** is the relationship between the quantity of money demanded and the nominal interest rate, when all other influences on the amount of money that people wish to hold remain the same. We illustrate the demand for money with a demand for money schedule and a demand for money curve, such as those in Figure 28.1. If the interest rate is 5 percent a year, the quantity of money demanded is $1 trillion. The quantity of money demanded decreases to $0.98 trillion if the interest rate rises to 6 percent a year and increases to $1.02 trillion if the interest rate falls to 4 percent a year.

The demand for money curve is *MD*. When the interest rate rises, everything else remaining the same, the opportunity cost of holding money rises and the quantity of money demanded decreases—there is a movement up along the demand for money curve. When the interest rate falls, the opportunity cost of holding money falls and the quantity of money demanded increases—there is a movement down along the demand for money curve.

FIGURE 28.1

The Demand for Money   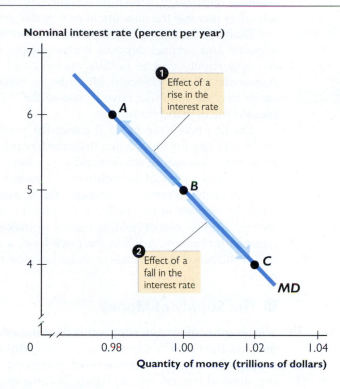MyEconLab Animation

	Nominal interest rate (percent per year)	Quantity of money demanded (trillions of dollars)
A	6	0.98
B	5	1.00
C	4	1.02

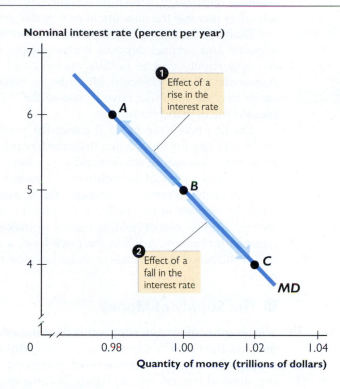

The demand for money schedule is graphed as the demand for money curve, *MD*. Rows A, B, and C in the table correspond to points A, B, and C on the curve. The nominal interest rate is the opportunity cost of holding money.

Other things remaining the same, ❶ an increase in the nominal interest rate decreases the quantity of money demanded, and ❷ a decrease in the nominal interest rate increases the quantity of money demanded.

■ Changes in the Demand for Money

A change in the nominal interest rate brings a change in the quantity of money demanded and a movement along the demand for money curve. A change in any other influence on money holding changes the demand for money. The three main influences on the demand for money are

- The price level
- Real GDP
- Financial technology

The Price Level

The demand for money is proportional to the price level—an *x* percent rise in the price level brings an *x* percent increase in the quantity of money demanded at each nominal interest rate. The reason is that we hold money to make payments: If the price level changes, the quantity of dollars that we need to make payments changes in the same proportion.

Real GDP

The demand for money increases as real GDP increases. The reason is that when real GDP increases, expenditures and incomes increase. To make the increased expenditures and income payments, households and firms must hold larger average amounts of money.

Financial Technology

Changes in financial technology change the demand for money. Most changes in financial technology come from advances in computing and record keeping. Some advances increase the quantity of money demanded, and some decrease it.

Daily interest checking deposits and automatic transfers between checkable deposits and savings deposits enable people to earn interest on money, lower the opportunity cost of holding money, and increase the demand for money. Automatic teller machines, debit cards, and smart cards, which have made money easier to obtain and use, have increased the marginal benefit from money and increased the demand for money.

Credit cards have made it easier for people to buy goods and services on credit and pay for them when their credit card account becomes due. This development has decreased the demand for money.

A change in any of the influences on money holdings that we've just reviewed other than the interest rate changes the demand for money. A rise in the price level, an increase in real GDP, or an advance in financial technology that lowers the opportunity cost of holding money or makes money more useful increases the demand for money. A fall in the price level, a decrease in real GDP, or a technological advance that creates a substitute for money decreases the demand for money.

■ The Supply of Money

Supply of money
The relationship between the quantity of money supplied and the nominal interest rate.

The quantity of money supplied is determined by the actions of the banking system and the Fed. On any given day, the quantity of money supplied is fixed. The **supply of money** is the relationship between the quantity of money supplied and the nominal interest rate. In Figure 28.2, the quantity of money supplied is $1 trillion regardless of the nominal interest rate, so the supply of money curve is the vertical line *MS*.

■ The Nominal Interest Rate

People hold some of their financial wealth as money and some in the form of other financial assets. You have seen that the amount of wealth that people hold as money depends on the nominal interest rate that they can earn on other financial assets. Demand and supply determine the nominal interest rate. We can study the forces of demand and supply in either the market for financial assets or the market for money. Because the Fed influences the quantity of money, we focus on the market for money.

On a given day, the price level, real GDP, and the state of financial technology are fixed. Because these influences on the demand for money are fixed, the demand for money curve is given.

The interest rate is the only influence on the quantity of money demanded that is free to fluctuate. Every day, the interest rate adjusts to make the quantity of money demanded equal the quantity of money supplied—to achieve money market equilibrium.

In Figure 28.2, the demand for money curve is *MD*. The equilibrium interest rate is 5 percent a year. At any interest rate above 5 percent a year, the quantity of money demanded is less than the quantity of money supplied. At any interest rate below 5 percent a year, the quantity of money demanded exceeds the quantity of money supplied.

■ **FIGURE 28.2**

Money Market Equilibrium   MyEconLab Animation

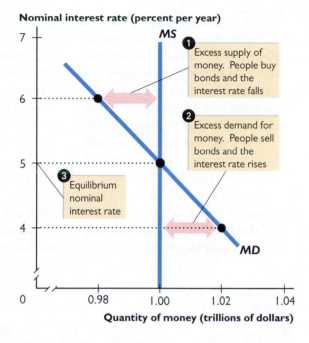

Nominal interest rate (percent per year)

The supply of money curve is *MS*, and the demand for money curve is *MD*.

❶ If the interest rate is 6 percent a year, the quantity of money held exceeds the quantity demanded. People buy bonds, the price of a bond rises, and the interest rate falls.

❷ If the interest rate is 4 percent a year, the quantity of money held falls short of the quantity demanded. People sell bonds, the price of a bond falls, and the interest rate rises.

❸ If the interest rate is 5 percent a year, the quantity of money held equals the quantity demanded. The money market is in equilibrium.

The Interest Rate and Bond Price Move in Opposite Directions   When the government issues a bond, it specifies the dollar amount of interest that it will pay each year on the bond. Suppose that the government issues a bond that pays $100 of interest a year. The interest *rate* that you receive on this bond depends on the price that you pay for it. If the price is $1,000, the interest rate is 10 percent a year—$100 is 10 percent of $1,000.

If the price of the bond *falls* to $500, the interest rate *rises* to 20 percent a year. The reason is that you still receive an interest payment of $100, but this amount is 20 percent of the $500 price of the bond. If the price of the bond *rises* to $2,000, the interest rate *falls* to 5 percent a year. Again, you still receive an interest payment of $100, but this amount is 5 percent of the $2,000 price of the bond.

Interest Rate Adjustment   If the interest rate is above its equilibrium level, people would like to hold less money than they are actually holding. They try to get rid of some money by buying other financial assets such as bonds. The demand for financial assets increases, the prices of these assets rise, and the interest rate falls. The interest rate keeps falling until the quantity of money that people want to hold increases to equal the quantity of money supplied.

Conversely, when the interest rate is below its equilibrium level, people are holding less money than they would like to hold. They try to get more money by selling other financial assets. The demand for these financial assets decreases, the prices of these assets fall, and the interest rate rises. The interest rate keeps rising until the quantity of money that people want to hold decreases to equal the quantity of money supplied.

EYE on the U.S. ECONOMY
Credit Cards and Money

Today, 70 percent of U.S. households own a credit card. That's down a bit from a peak of 83 percent in 2002.

By using a credit card account to buy goods and services, it is possible to economize on money holding. Instead of holding and using money, a card holder buys with a card and then pays off the card account balance (or part of it) on her or his own pay day.

Back in 1970, only 18 percent of U.S. households had a credit card. How has the spread of credit cards affected the quantity of money that we hold?

The answer is that the quantity of M1 money has decreased as a percentage of GDP. Part (a) of the figure shows that as the ownership of credit cards expanded from 18 percent in 1970 to 80 percent in 2007, the quantity of M1 (currency and checkable deposits held by individuals and businesses) fell from 20 percent of GDP to 10 percent.

The expansion of credit card ownership is a change in financial technology that has led to a steady decrease in the demand for M1 money.

Part (b) of the figure shows the effects on the demand for money. Here, we graph the quantity of M1 as a percentage of GDP against the interest rate. As credit card use increased between 1970 and 2007, the demand for money decreased and the demand for money curve shifted leftward from MD_0 to MD_1.

As the interest rate fell between 2007 and 2014, the quantity of money demanded increased along the demand for money curve MD_1.

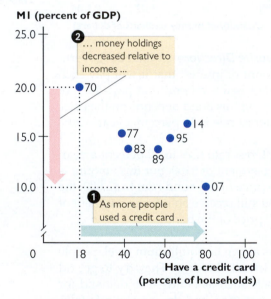

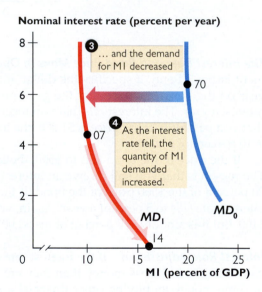

SOURCE OF DATA: Federal Reserve.

(a) Changes in the use of credit cards and money

(b) Changes in the demand for M1

■ Changing the Interest Rate

To change the interest rate, the Fed changes the quantity of money. Figure 28.3 illustrates two changes. The demand for money curve is *MD*. If the Fed increases the quantity of money to $1.02 trillion, the supply of money curve shifts rightward from MS_0 to MS_1 and the interest rate falls to 4 percent a year. If the Fed decreases the quantity of money to $0.98 trillion, the supply of money curve shifts leftward from MS_0 to MS_2 and the interest rate rises to 6 percent a year.

FIGURE 28.3

Interest Rate Changes

MyEconLab Animation

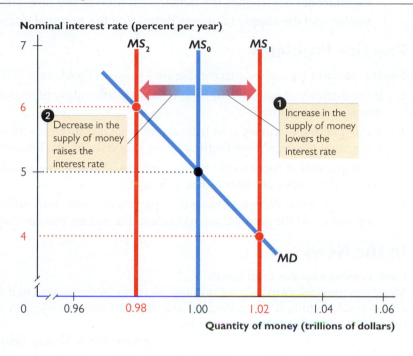

The demand for money is MD, and initially, the supply of money is MS_0. The interest rate is 5 percent a year.

❶ If the Fed increases the quantity of money and the supply of money curve shifts rightward to MS_1, the interest rate falls to 4 percent a year.

❷ If the Fed decreases the quantity of money and the supply of money curve shifts leftward to MS_2, the interest rate rises to 6 percent a year.

EYE on YOUR LIFE
Money Holding and Fed Watching

MyEconLab Critical Thinking Exercise

How much currency (cash) do you have in your wallet, on average? How much money do you keep in your bank account, on average?

Why don't you hold a larger average bank balance by paying off a smaller part of your credit card balance than you can afford to pay?

Wouldn't it be better to keep a bit more money in the bank?

Almost certainly, that would not be a smart idea. Why? Because the opportunity cost of holding that money would be too high.

If you have an outstanding credit card balance, the interest rate on that balance is the opportunity cost of holding money.

By paying off as much of your credit card balance as you can afford, you avoid a high interest rate on the outstanding balance.

Your demand for money is sensitive to this opportunity cost.

Do you watch the Fed? Probably not, but you can learn to become an effective Fed watcher. In the process, you will become much better informed about the state of the U.S. economy and the state of the economy in your region.

To become a Fed watcher, try to get into the habit of visiting the Fed's Web site at www.federalreserve.gov. Type "Beige Book" in the Search tool and look at the latest Beige Book to see what is happening in your region.

Also, keep an eye on the FOMC calendar for the dates of interest rate announcements. On these dates, check the media for opinions on what the Fed's interest rate decision will be. After the decision is made and announced, check the Fed's explanation as to why it made its decision.

MyEconLab Study Plan 28.1
Key Terms Quiz
Solutions Video

CHECKPOINT 28.1

Explain what determines the demand for money and how the demand for money and the supply of money determine the *nominal* interest rate.

Practice Problems

Use the demand for money curve in Figure 1 to work Problems **1** to **3**.

1. If the quantity of money is $4 trillion, what is the supply of money and the nominal interest rate?

2. If the quantity of money is $4 trillion and real GDP increases, how will the interest rate change? Explain the process that changes the interest rate.

3. If the quantity of money is $4 trillion and the Fed decreases it to $3.9 trillion, how will the price of a bond change? Why?

4. If banks increase the interest rate they pay on deposits, how will the demand for money and the nominal interest rate in the money market change?

In the News

Cash is more popular than bonds

Money in the bank earns almost nothing. Even so, in the second half of 2015 an additional $208 billion was added to bank deposits and money market funds and billions of dollars were moved from bonds.

Source: CNN Money, February 5, 2016

What is the opportunity cost of holding money? If people move out of bonds and into money, how will the demand for money and the interest rate change?

Solutions to Practice Problems

1. The supply of money is the curve *MS*. The interest rate is 4 percent a year, at the intersection of MD_1 and *MS* (Figure 2).

2. The demand for money increases, and the demand for money curve shifts from MD_1 to MD_2 (Figure 2). At an interest rate of 4 percent a year, people want to hold more money, so they sell bonds. The price of a bond falls, and the interest rate rises.

3. At 4 percent a year, people would like to hold $4 trillion. With only $3.9 trillion of money available, they sell bonds to get more money. The price of a bond falls, and the interest rate rises. The price will fall and the interest rate will rise until the quantity of money that people want to hold equals the $3.9 trillion available. The interest rate rises to 6 percent a year (Figure 3).

4. A higher interest rate on bank deposits lowers the opportunity cost of holding money, so the demand for money increases. As the demand for money increases, with no change in the supply of money, the nominal interest rate in the money market rises (as Figure 2 shows).

Solution to In the News

The opportunity cost of holding money is the interest rate forgone by not holding bonds. If people sell bonds, the demand for money increases. The increase in the demand for money with no change in the supply of money raises the interest rate on bonds. (People sell bonds, so the price of a bond falls).

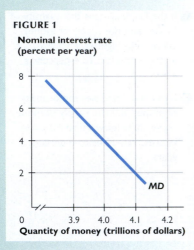

FIGURE 1

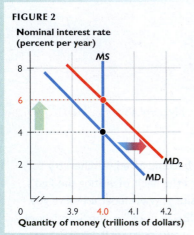

FIGURE 2

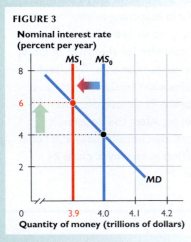

FIGURE 3

28.2   MONEY, THE PRICE LEVEL, AND INFLATION

MyEconLab Concept Video

A change in the nominal interest rate is the initial effect of a change in the quantity of money, but it is not the ultimate or long-run effect. When the interest rate changes, borrowing and lending and investment and consumption spending also change, which in turn change production and prices—change real GDP and the price level.

The details of this adjustment process are complex, and we explore them in the next two chapters. But the place where the process comes to rest—the *long-run outcome*—is easier to describe. It is crucial to understand the long-run outcome because that is where the economy is heading. We're now going to examine the long-run equilibrium in the money market.

■ The Money Market in the Long Run

The *long run* refers to the economy at full employment when real GDP equals potential GDP (Chapter 24, p. 617). Over the business cycle, real GDP fluctuates around potential GDP. But averaging over an expansion and recession and a peak and trough, real GDP equals potential GDP. That is, real GDP equals potential GDP *on average*. So another way to think about the *long run* is as a description of the economy *on average* over the business cycle.

The Long-Run Demand for Money

In the long run, equilibrium in the loanable funds market determines the real interest rate (Chapter 26, pp. 672–679). The nominal interest rate that influences money holding plans equals the real interest rate plus the inflation rate. For now, we'll consider an economy that has no inflation, so the real interest rate equals the nominal interest rate. (We'll consider inflation later in this chapter.)

With the interest rate determined by real forces in the long run, what is the variable that adjusts to make the quantity of money that people plan to hold equal the quantity of money supplied? The answer is the "price" of money. The law of demand applies to money just as it does to any other object. The lower the "price" of money, the greater is the quantity of money that people are willing to hold. What is the "price" of money? It is the *value* of money.

The Value of Money

The *value of money* is the quantity of goods and services that a unit of money will buy. It is the inverse of the *price level, P,* which equals the GDP price index divided by 100. That is,

$$\text{Value of money } = \ 1/P.$$

To see why, suppose that you have \$100 in your wallet. If you spend that money, you can buy goods and services valued at \$100. Now suppose that the price level rises by 10 percent. After the price rise, the quantity of goods and services that \$100 can buy has fallen. Your \$100 can now buy only \$100 divided by 1.1 or \$91 of goods and services. Yesterday's \$100 is worth \$91 today. The price level has risen and the value of money has fallen and each percentage change is the same. The higher the value of money, the smaller is the quantity of money that people plan to hold. If it seems strange that a higher value of money makes people want to hold less money, think about how much money you would plan to hold if the price of a restaurant meal was 20 cents and the price of a movie ticket was 10 cents. You would be happy to hold (say) $1 on average. But if the price of a meal is $20 and the price of a movie ticket is $10, you would want to hold $100 on average. The price level is lower and the value of money higher in the first case than in the second; and the amount of money you would plan to hold is lower in the first case than in the second.

Money Market Equilibrium in the Long Run

In the long run, money market equilibrium determines the value of money. If the quantity of money supplied exceeds the long-run quantity demanded, people go out and spend their surplus money. The quantity of goods and services available is fixed equal to potential GDP, so the extra spending forces prices upward. As the price level rises, the value of money falls.

If the quantity of money supplied is less than the long-run quantity demanded, people lower their spending to build up the quantity of money they hold. The shortage of money translates into a surplus of goods and services, so the spending cut-back forces prices downward. The price level falls and the value of money rises. When the quantity of money supplied equals the long-run quantity demanded, the price level and the value of money are at their equilibrium levels.

Figure 28.4 illustrates long-run money market equilibrium. The long-run demand for money curve is *LRMD*. Its position depends on potential GDP and the equilibrium interest rate. The supply of money is *MS*. Equilibrium occurs when the value of money is 1.

■ **FIGURE 28.4**

Long-Run Money Market Equilibrium

MyEconLab Animation

The long-run demand for money is determined by potential GDP and the equilibrium interest rate.

The *LRMD* curve shows how the quantity of money that households and firms plan to hold, in the long run, depends on the value of money (or 1/*P*, the inverse of the price level).

The *MS* curve shows the quantity of money supplied, which is $1 trillion.

The price level adjusts to make the value of money equal 1 and achieve long-run money market equilibrium.

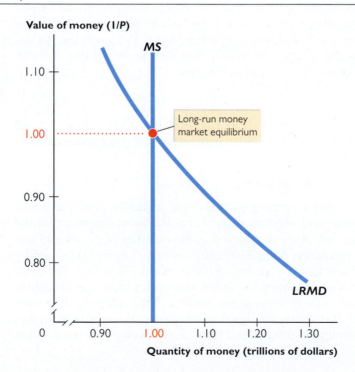

◼ A Change in the Quantity of Money

Suppose that starting from a long-run equilibrium, the Fed increases the quantity of money by 10 percent. In the short run, the greater quantity of money lowers the nominal interest rate. With a lower interest rate, people and businesses borrow more and spend more. But with real GDP equal to potential GDP, there are no more goods and services to buy, so when people go out and spend, prices start to rise. Eventually, a new long-run equilibrium is reached at which the price level has increased in proportion to the increase in the quantity of money. Because the quantity of money increased by 10 percent, the price level has also risen by 10 percent from 1.0 to 1.1.

Figure 28.5 illustrates this outcome. Initially, the supply of money is MS_0 and the quantity of money is $1 trillion. The Fed increases the supply of money to MS_1 and the quantity of money is now $1.1 trillion—a 10 percent increase. There is now a surplus of money and people go out and spend it. The increased spending on the same unchanged quantity of goods and services raises the price level and lowers the value of money. Eventually, the price level has increased by 10 percent from 1.0 to 1.1 and the value of money has decreased by 10 percent from 1.00 to 0.91.

You've just seen a key proposition about the quantity of money and the price level.

In the long run and other things remaining the same, a given percentage change in the quantity of money brings an equal percentage change in the price level.

◼ **FIGURE 28.5**

The Long-Run Effect of a Change in the Quantity of Money

MyEconLab Animation

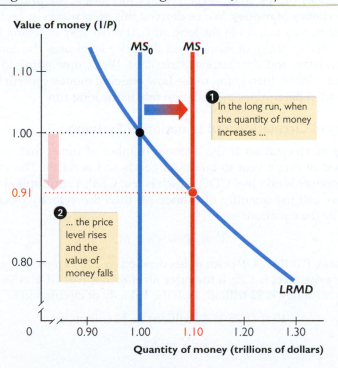

❶ The Fed increases the supply of money from MS_0 to MS_1 and the quantity of money increases from $1 trillion to $1.1 trillion, a 10 percent increase.

❷ The price level rises by 10 percent and the value of money falls by 10 percent to restore long-run money market equilibrium.

The Price Level in a Baby-Sitting Club

It is hard to visualize a long-run equilibrium and even harder to visualize and compare two long-run equilibrium situations like those that we've just described. An example of a simpler situation might help.

In an isolated neighborhood, there are no teenagers but lots of young children, and parents can't find any babysitters. So they form a club and sit for each other. The deal is that each time a parent sits for someone else, he or she receives a token that can be used to buy one babysitting session from another member of the club. The organizer notices that the club is inactive. Every member has a few unspent tokens, but they spend them infrequently. To make the club more active, the organizer decides to issue every member one token for each token that is currently held, so the supply of tokens doubles.

With more tokens to spend, parents start to plan more evenings out. Suddenly, the phones are ringing as parents seek babysitters. Every member of the club wants a sitter, but there are no more sitters than before. After making a few calls and finding no sitters available, anxious parents who really do need a sitter start to offer a higher price: two tokens per session. That does the trick. At the higher price, the quantity of baby-sitting services demanded decreases and the quantity supplied increases. Equilibrium is restored. Nothing real has changed, but the quantity of tokens and the price level have doubled.

Think of the equilibrium quantity of baby-sitting services as potential GDP, the quantity of tokens as the quantity of money, and the price of a baby-sitting session as the price level. You can then see how a given percentage change in the quantity of money at full employment brings an equal percentage change in the price level.

The Quantity Theory of Money

The proposition that when real GDP equals potential GDP, an increase in the quantity of money brings an equal percentage increase in the price level is called the **quantity theory of money**. We've derived this proposition by looking at equilibrium in the money market in the long run. Another way of seeing the relationship between the quantity of money and the price level uses the concepts of *the velocity of circulation* and *the equation of exchange*. We're now going to explore the quantity theory. We're then going to see how ongoing money growth brings inflation and see what determines the inflation rate in the long run.

Quantity theory of money
The proposition that when real GDP equals potential GDP, an increase in the quantity of money brings an equal percentage increase in the price level.

The Velocity of Circulation and Equation of Exchange

The **velocity of circulation** is the average number of times that each dollar of money is used during a year to buy final goods and services. The value of final goods and services is nominal GDP, which is real GDP, Y, multiplied by the price level, P. If we call the quantity of money M, then the velocity of circulation is determined by the equation:

$$V = (P \times Y) \div M.$$

In this equation, P is the GDP price index divided by 100. If the GDP price index is 125, then the price level is 1.25. If the price level is 1.25, real GDP is $8 trillion, and the quantity of money is $2 trillion, then the velocity of circulation is

$$V = (1.25 \times \$8\,\text{trillion}) \div \$2\,\text{trillion, or}$$

$$V = 5.$$

Velocity of circulation
The average number of times that each dollar of money is used during a year to buy final goods and services.

That is, with \$2 trillion of money, each dollar is used an average of 5 times during the year, so \$2 trillion × 5 equals \$10 trillion of goods and services bought.

The **equation of exchange** states that the quantity of money, M, multiplied by the velocity of circulation, V, equals the price level P, multiplied by real GDP, Y. That is,

$$M \times V = P \times Y.$$

The equation of exchange is *always* true because it is implied by the definition of the velocity of circulation. That is, if you multiply both sides of the equation on p. 734 that defines the velocity of circulation by M, you get the equation of exchange.

Using the above numbers—a price level of 1.25, real GDP of \$8 trillion, the quantity of money of \$2 trillion, and the velocity of circulation of 5—you can see that

$$M \times V = \$2\,\text{trillion} \times 5 = \$10\,\text{trillion},$$

and

$$P \times Y = 1.25 \times \$8\,\text{trillion} = \$10\,\text{trillion}.$$

So,

$$M \times V = P \times Y = \$10\,\text{trillion}.$$

The Quantity Theory Prediction

We can rearrange the equation of exchange to isolate the price level on the left side. To do so, divide both sides of the equation of exchange by real GDP to obtain

$$P = (M \times V) \div Y.$$

On the left side is the price level, and on the right side are all the things that influence the price level. But this equation is still just an implication of the definition of the velocity of circulation. To turn the equation into a theory of what determines the price level, we use two other facts: (1) At full employment, real GDP equals potential GDP, which is determined only by real factors and not by the quantity of money; and (2) the velocity of circulation is relatively stable and does not change when the quantity of money changes.

So with V and Y constant, if M increases P must increase, and the percentage increase in P must equal the percentage increase in M.

We can use the above numbers to illustrate this prediction. Real GDP is \$8 trillion, the quantity of money is \$2 trillion, and the velocity of circulation is 5. Put these values into the equation:

$$P = (M \times V) \div Y.$$

to obtain

$$P = (\$2\,\text{trillion} \times 5) \div \$8\,\text{trillion} = 1.25.$$

Now increase the quantity of money from \$2 trillion to \$2.4 trillion. The percentage increase in the quantity of money is

$$(\$2.4\,\text{trillion} - \$2\,\text{trillion}) \div \$2\,\text{trillion} \times 100 = 20\,\text{percent}.$$

Equation of exchange
An equation that states that the quantity of money multiplied by the velocity of circulation equals the price level multiplied by real GDP.

Now find the new price level. It is

$$P = (\$2.4 \text{ trillion} \times 5) \div \$8 \text{ trillion} = 1.50.$$

The price level rises from 1.25 to 1.50, and the percentage increase in the price level is

$$(1.50 - 1.25) \div 1.25 \times 100 = 20 \text{ percent}.$$

When the economy is at full employment (real GDP equals potential GDP) and the velocity of circulation is stable, the price level and the quantity of money increase by the same 20 percent.

◼ Inflation and the Quantity Theory of Money

The equation of exchange tells us about the price *level*, the quantity of money, the quantity of real GDP, and the velocity of circulation. We can turn the equation into one that tells us about *rates of change* or *growth rates* of these variables. We want to make this conversion because we want to know what determines the inflation rate—the rate of change of the price level.

In rates of change or growth rates,

Money growth + Velocity growth = Inflation rate + Real GDP growth,

which means that

Inflation rate = Money growth + Velocity growth − Real GDP growth.

Constant Inflation

Figure 28.6 illustrates three cases in which the inflation rate is constant—at zero, at a low or moderate rate, and at a high or rapid rate. In each case, the velocity growth rate is 1 percent a year and the real GDP growth rate is 3 percent a year. The money growth rate is the only thing that is different across the three cases, and it is this difference that brings the different inflation rates.

If the quantity of money grows at 2 percent a year, there is no inflation. That is,

Inflation rate = 2 percent + 1 percent − 3 percent = 0 percent a year.

With the quantity of money growing at 4 percent a year, the inflation rate is 2 percent a year. That is,

Inflation rate = 4 percent + 1 percent − 3 percent = 2 percent a year.

And with the quantity of money growing at 10 percent a year, the inflation rate is 8 percent a year. That is,

Inflation rate = 10 percent + 1 percent − 3 percent = 8 percent a year.

A Change in the Inflation Rate

We've looked at three different inflation rates—zero, moderate, and rapid—with given growth rates of real GDP and velocity of circulation. We're now going to see what happens when the growth rate of money *changes*. We'll start with an increase in the money growth rate.

■ **FIGURE 28.6**

Money Growth and Inflation   MyEconLab Animation

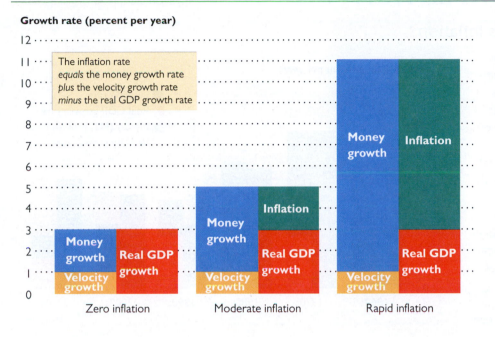

The velocity of circulation grows at 1 percent a year (the orange block), and real GDP grows at 3 percent a year (the red block). The inflation rate (green block) is determined by money growth (blue block).

If the quantity of money grows at 2 percent a year, the inflation rate is zero.

If the quantity of money grows at 4 percent a year, the inflation rate is a moderate 2 percent a year.

But if the quantity of money grows at 10 percent a year, the inflation rate is a rapid 8 percent a year.

Increase in Money Growth Rate When the money growth rate increases, the inflation rate increases slowly and there is a temporary (short-run) increase in the real GDP growth rate. The velocity of circulation increases as the inflation rate speeds up but this increase does not persist. Once the velocity has increased in response to a higher inflation rate, it remains constant at its new level. (You can see in *Eye on Inflation* on p. 738 that velocity growth has been zero for most of the past 40 years. It increased during the 1990s but decreased again during the 2000s.)

A faster inflation reduces potential GDP and slows real GDP growth (for reasons that we explore in the final section of this chapter) but for low inflation rates, these effects are small and are dominated by the main direct effect of money growth on the inflation rate. Eventually, real GDP growth slows to that of potential GDP, velocity growth returns to its long-run rate, and the inflation rate changes by the full amount of the change in the money growth rate.

Decrease in Money Growth Rate When the money growth rate decreases, the effects that we've just described work in the opposite direction.

You can see in *Eye on Inflation* (p. 738) that changes in the growth rate of real GDP and changes in velocity growth have been small in comparison to the changes in the growth rate of money and the inflation rate. So,

> **In the long run and other things remaining the same, a change in the *growth rate* of the quantity of money brings an equal change in the inflation rate.**

The relationship between the money growth rate and the inflation rate is at its clearest when inflation is rapid in *hyperinflation*.

EYE on INFLATION

What Causes Inflation?

According to the quantity theory of money, whether we face a future with inflation, deflation, or a stable price level depends entirely on the rate at which the Fed permits the quantity of money to grow.

But is the quantity theory correct? Does it explain our past inflation with enough accuracy to be a guide to future inflation?

The figure shows how the quantity theory performs in explaining decade-average inflation rates since the 1960s.

The 1960s and 1970s

The 1960s had low inflation (the green bars) and in the 1970s, inflation increased to become a serious problem. The quantity theory does a perfect job of explaining inflation in these two decades. The inflation rate equaled the growth rate of M2 (the blue bars) minus the growth rate of real GDP (the red bars). The velocity of circulation (of M2) was constant.

During the 1970s, an increase in the growth rate of M2 accompanied by a slowdown in the growth rate of real GDP increased the inflation rate—exactly as predicted by the quantity theory of money.

The 1980s and 1990s

The inflation rate fell in 1980s and again in 1990s. And again, the quantity theory does a good job of explaining why. During the 19680s, the M2 growth rate slowed and it slowed again in the 1990s. With the real GDP growth rate unchanged, the inflation

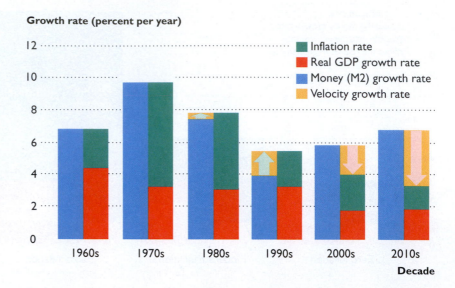

Growth rate (percent per year)

- ■ Inflation rate
- ■ Real GDP growth rate
- ■ Money (M2) growth rate
- ■ Velocity growth rate

SOURCE OF DATA: Federal Reserve and Bureau of Economic Analysis.

rate fell as predicted by the quantity theory. But the inflation rate didn't fall by as much as the theory predicts. Why?

The answer is that the velocity of circulation was increasing (the yellow bars and up-arrows). Financial innovation enabled a given quantity of money to circulate more quickly.

The 2000s and 2010s

During the 2000s and 2010s, the M2 growth rate increased but the inflation rate decreased. The changes in inflation in these two decades are the opposite of what the quantity theory predicts. The reason is that the velocity of circulation decreased (the yellow bars and down-arrows).

Velocity of circulation decreased because interest rates were lowered by the Fed to unprecedented levels.

At very low interest rates, the opportunity cost of holding money is low, so the quantity of money held increases and the velocity decreases.

The Future

To predict future inflation rates, we must predict the future growth rate of M2 and the future real GDP and velocity growth. In the long run, real GDP growth doesn't stray far from 2 to 3 percent and velocity is constant. So the M2 growth rate is the source of possible changes in the inflation rate.

The Fed is able to influence the inflation rate and the money growth rate and, absent any pressures that the Fed finds impossible to resist, we can expect the Fed to do a good job of keeping inflation in check. That doesn't mean zero inflation. It means an inflation rate running at around 2 percent per year.

■ Hyperinflation

When the inflation rate exceeds 50 percent *a month,* it is called **hyperinflation**. An inflation rate of 50 percent per month translates to an inflation rate of 12,875 percent per year. Hyperinflation occurs when the quantity of money grows at a rapid pace. The reason money growth sometimes becomes rapid is that government expenditure gets out of control and exceeds what the government can collect in tax revenue or borrow. In such a situation, the government prints money to finance its spending and the quantity of money increases at an extraordinarily rapid and increasing rate.

Hyperinflation is rare but not unknown (see *Eye on the Past* below). The highest inflation in the world in recent times was in the African nation of Zimbabwe, where the inflation rate peaked at 231,150,888.87 percent a year in July 2008.

Hyperinflation

Inflation at a rate that exceeds 50 percent *a month* (which translates to 12,875 percent per year).

EYE on the PAST
Hyperinflation in Germany in the 1920s

An international treaty signed in 1919 required Germany to pay large amounts as compensation for war damage to other countries in Europe. To meet its obligations, Germany started to print money. The quantity of money increased by 24 percent in 1921, by 220 percent in 1922, and by 43 *billion* percent in 1923!

Not surprisingly, the price level increased rapidly. The figure shows you how rapidly.

In November 1923 when the hyperinflation reached its peak, the price level was more than doubling every day. Wages were paid twice a day, and people spent their morning's wages at lunchtime to avoid the loss in

the value of money that the afternoon would bring.

Hyperinflation made bank notes more valuable as fire kindling than as money. The sight of people burning Reichmarks (the name of Germany's money at that time) was a common one, as the photo shows.

SOURCE OF DATA: Phillip Cagan, "The Monetary Dynamics of Hyperinflation," in Milton Friedman (editor), *Studies in the Quantity Theory of Money*, University of Chicago Press, 1956.

MyEconLab Study Plan 28.2
Key Terms Quiz
Solutions Video

CHECKPOINT 28.2

Explain how in the long run, the quantity of money determines the price level and money growth brings inflation.

Practice Problems

In 2016, the economy of Singapore was at full employment. In Singapore dollars, S$, real GDP was 400 billion. The nominal interest rate was 1.8 percent a year, the inflation rate was −1.6 percent a year (deflation), the price level was 1.02, and the velocity of circulation was 0.76. Use this data to work Problems **1** and **2**.

1. Calculate the real interest rate. If the real interest rate remains unchanged and the inflation rate increases to 2 percent a year and then remains constant, explain how the nominal interest rate will change in the long run.

2. What was the quantity of money in Singapore?

3. If the quantity of money grows at 8 percent a year, velocity of circulation is constant, and potential GDP grows at 6 percent a year, what is the inflation rate in the long run?

In the News

Argentina says consumer prices rose 3.1 percent in June
Argentina's consumer prices increased by 3.1 percent in June and the government forecasts that the 2016 inflation rate will be 40 to 42 percent.
Source: Reuters, July 13, 2016

The quantity of money in Argentina is growing at a rate of 30 percent a year. How can the inflation rate exceed the money growth rate?

Solutions to Practice Problems

1. The real interest rate equals the nominal interest rate minus the inflation rate. That is, the real interest rate equals 1.8 percent a year minus −1.6 percent a year, which equals 3.4 percent a year. If inflation increases to 2 percent a year and remains at 2 percent, then the nominal interest rate will rise from 1.8 percent a year to 5.4 percent a year, which equals the real interest rate (3.4 percent) plus the inflation rate (2 percent).

2. The quantity of money was S$536.8 billion.
    Velocity of circulation (V) = Nominal GDP ($P \times Y$) ÷ Quantity of money (M). Rewrite this equation as: $M = (P \times Y) \div V$
    ($P \times Y$) = 1.02 × S$400 billion, or S$408 billion, so M = S$408 billion ÷ 0.76, or S$536.8 billion.

3. With velocity constant, velocity growth is zero. So the inflation rate in the long run equals the money growth rate minus the real GDP growth rate, which is 8 percent a year minus 6 percent a year, or 2 percent a year.

Solution to In the News

The inflation rate equals the money growth rate plus the velocity growth rate minus the real GDP growth rate. If the inflation rate is 40 percent per year and the money growth rate is 30 percent per year, then the velocity growth rate minus the real GDP growth rate equals 10 percent per year.

28.3   THE COST OF INFLATION

MyEconLab Concept Video

Inflation decreases potential GDP, slows economic growth, and consumes leisure time. These outcomes occur for four reasons that we classify as the four costs of inflation:

- Tax costs
- Shoe-leather costs
- Confusion costs
- Uncertainty costs

■ Tax Costs

We've seen that inflation occurs when the quantity of money grows more rapidly than real GDP. But why would we ever want to make this happen? Why don't we keep the quantity of money growing at the same pace as real GDP grows? One part of the answer is that the government gets revenue from inflation.

Inflation Is a Tax

A government can pay its expenses with newly created money. But the things a government buys with this money aren't free. They are paid for by people and businesses in proportion to the amount of money they hold—by a tax on money holding that we call the inflation tax.

When the government spends newly created money, the quantity of money increases and, as predicted by the quantity theory, the price level rises. The inflation rate equals the growth rate of the quantity of money (other things remaining the same).

To see how the inflation tax gets paid, suppose that the Coca-Cola Company is holding $110,000 in money. The annual inflation rate is 10 percent, and the price level rises from 1.0 to 1.1. At the end of the year, Coca-Cola's money will buy only $100,000 of goods and services ($110,000 ÷ 1.1 = $100,000). The firm has lost $10,000—it has "paid" an inflation tax of $10,000.

Governments in today's world don't create new money by printing it. Money gets created when the central bank buys government bonds. In the United States, the Fed doesn't buy bonds directly from the government: it buys them in open market operations. When the Fed buys bonds, the monetary base increases and the quantity of money increases. The Fed pays the interest it receives on the bonds to the government, so the government ends up paying no interest on its bonds held by the Fed. By this process, the government "prints" money.

Inflation, Saving, and Investment

The income tax on interest income drives a wedge between the before-tax interest rate paid by borrowers and the after-tax interest rate received by lenders. A rise in the income tax rate increases the before-tax interest rate and decreases the after-tax interest rate. The increase in the before-tax interest rate decreases borrowing and investment, and the decrease in the after-tax interest rate decreases lending and saving.

An increase in the inflation rate increases the true tax rate on interest income, and strengthens the effect that we have just described. To see why, let's consider an example.

Suppose that the real interest rate is 4 percent a year and the income tax rate is 50 percent. With no inflation, the nominal interest rate is also 4 percent a year and the real after-tax interest rate is 2 percent a year (50 percent of 4 percent).

Now suppose the inflation rate rises to 4 percent a year, so the nominal interest rate rises to 8 percent a year. The after-tax nominal interest rate rises to 4 percent a year (50 percent of 8 percent). Subtract the 4 percent inflation rate from this amount, and you see that the after-tax real interest rate is zero! The true income tax rate has increased to 100 percent.

The fall in the after-tax real interest rate weakens the incentive to lend and save and the rise in the before-tax interest rate weakens the incentive to borrow and invest. With a fall in saving and investment, the rates of capital accumulation and real GDP growth slow down.

■ Shoe-Leather Costs

The "shoe-leather costs" of inflation are costs that arise from an increase in the velocity of circulation of money and an increase in the amount of running around that people do to try to avoid incurring losses from the falling value of money.

When money loses value at a rapid anticipated rate, it does not function well as a store of value and people try to avoid holding it. They spend their incomes as soon as they receive them, and firms pay out incomes—wages and dividends—as soon as they receive revenue from their sales. The velocity of circulation increases.

During the 1990s when inflation in Brazil was around 80 percent a year, people would end a taxi ride at the ATM closest to their destination, get some cash, pay the driver, and finish their journey on foot. The driver would deposit the cash in his bank account before looking for the next customer.

During the 1920s when inflation in Germany exceeded 50 percent a month—hyperinflation—wages were paid and spent twice in a single day!

Imagine the inconvenience of spending most of your time figuring out how to keep your money holdings close to zero.

One way of keeping money holdings low is to find other means of payment such as tokens, commodities, or even barter. All of these are less efficient than money as a means of payment. For example, in Israel during the 1980s, when inflation reached 1,000 percent a year, the U.S. dollar started to replace the increasingly worthless shekel. Consequently, people had to keep track of the exchange rate between the shekel and the dollar hour by hour and had to engage in many additional and costly transactions in the foreign exchange market.

■ Confusion Costs

We make economic decisions by comparing marginal cost and marginal benefit. Marginal cost is a real cost—an opportunity forgone. Marginal benefit is a real benefit—a willingness to forgo an opportunity. Although costs and benefits are real, we use money as our unit of account and standard of value to calculate them. Money is our measuring rod of value. Borrowers and lenders, workers and employers, all make agreements in terms of money. Inflation makes the value of money change, so it changes the units on our measuring rod.

Does it matter that our units of value keep changing? Some economists think it matters a lot. Others think it matters only a little.

Economists who think it matters a lot point to the obvious benefits of stable units of measurement in other areas of life. For example, suppose that we had not invented an accurate time-keeping technology and clocks and watches gained 5 to

15 minutes a day. Imagine the hassle you would have arriving at class on time or catching the start of the ball game. For another example, suppose that a tailor used an elastic tape measure. You would end up with a jacket that was either too tight or too loose, depending on how tightly the tape was stretched.

For a third example, recall the crash of the Mars Climate Orbiter.

> Mars Climate Orbiter...failed to achieve Mars orbit because of a navigation error....Spacecraft operating data needed for navigation were provided...in English units rather than the specified metric units. This was the direct cause of the failure. (Mars Program Independent Assessment Team Summary Report, March 14, 2000)

If rocket scientists can't make correct calculations that use just two units of measurement, what chance do ordinary people and business decision makers have of making correct calculations that involve money when its value keeps changing?

These examples of confusion and error that can arise from units of measurement don't automatically mean that a changing value of money is a big problem. But they raise the possibility that it might be.

■ Uncertainty Costs

A high inflation rate brings increased uncertainty about the long-term inflation rate. Will inflation remain high for a long time or will price stability be restored? This increased uncertainty makes long-term planning difficult and gives people a shorter-term focus. Investment falls, and so the economic growth rate slows.

But this increased uncertainty also misallocates resources. Instead of concentrating on the activities at which they have a comparative advantage, people find it more profitable to search for ways of avoiding the losses that inflation inflicts. As a result, inventive talent that might otherwise work on productive innovations works on finding ways of profiting from the inflation instead.

Uncertainty about inflation makes the economy behave a bit like a casino in which some people gain and some lose and no one can predict where the gains and losses will fall. Gains and losses occur because of unpredictable changes in the value of money. In a period of rapid, unpredictable inflation, resources get diverted from productive activities to forecasting inflation. It becomes more profitable to forecast the inflation rate correctly than to invent a new product. Doctors, lawyers, accountants, farmers—just about everyone—can make themselves better off, not by specializing in the profession for which they have been trained but by spending more of their time dabbling as amateur economists and inflation forecasters and managing their investment portfolios.

From a social perspective, this diversion of talent resulting from uncertainty about inflation is like throwing scarce resources onto the garbage heap. This waste of resources is a cost of inflation.

■ How Big Is the Cost of Inflation?

The cost of inflation depends on its rate and its predictability. The higher the inflation rate, the greater is the cost. And the more unpredictable the inflation rate, the greater is the cost. Peter Howitt of Brown University, building on work by Robert Barro of Harvard University, has estimated that if inflation is lowered from 3 percent a year to zero, the growth rate of real GDP will rise by between 0.06 and 0.09 percentage points a year. These numbers might seem small, but they are growth rates. After 30 years, real GDP would be 2.3 percent higher and the accumulated value of all the additional future output would be worth 85 percent of current GDP, or $15.5 trillion!

In hyperinflation, the costs are much greater. Hyperinflation is rare, but there have been some spectacular examples of it. Several European countries experienced hyperinflation during the 1920s after World War I and again during the 1940s after World War II. In these examples the costs of inflation were enormous.

Hyperinflation is more than just a historical curiosity. It has occurred in the recent past. In 1994, Brazil almost reached the hyperinflation stratosphere with a monthly inflation rate of 40 percent. A cup of coffee that cost 15 cruzeiros in 1980 cost 22 billion cruzeiros in 1994. Between 1989 and 1994, Russia experienced a near hyperinflation. In 2016, the inflation rate in Venezuela soared past 1,000 percent per year—not quite hyperinflation but a ripping 21 percent per month.

The most spectacular recent hyperinflation was in Zimbabwe, which peaked at 231,150,888.87 percent per year. At that point, the monetary system collapsed, the Zimbabwe dollar was taken out of circulation and replaced by the U.S. dollar, and economic life was at a near standstill.

MyEconLab Study Plan 28.3
Solutions Video

 # CHECKPOINT 28.3

Identify the costs of inflation and the benefits of a stable value of money.

Practice Problems

1. Ben has $1,000 in his savings account and the bank pays an interest rate of 5 percent a year. The inflation rate is 3 percent a year. The government taxes the interest that Ben earns on his deposit at 20 percent. Calculate the after-tax nominal interest rate and the after-tax real interest rate that Ben earns.

2. Economy A has a stable price level—no inflation. Economy B is in a hyper-inflation—prices are rising at a rate of 50 percent per month. Describe and explain the differences between these two economies in the money growth rate, the velocity of circulation, the nominal interest rate, and the frequency of wage payments.

Solutions to Practice Problems

1. Ben's interest income equals 5 percent of $1,000, which is $50. The government takes $10 of his $50 of interest in tax, so the interest income Ben earns after tax is $40. The after-tax nominal interest rate is ($40 ÷ $1,000) × 100, which equals 4 percent a year.
   The after-tax real interest rate equals the after-tax nominal interest rate minus the inflation rate. The after-tax nominal interest rate is 4 percent a year. So the after-tax real interest rate equals 4 percent a year minus the inflation rate of 3 percent a year, which is 1 percent a year.

2. The equation of exchange tells us that economy B has a higher money growth rate than economy A. With hyperinflation, the opportunity cost of holding money is higher in economy B, so economy B also has a higher velocity of circulation and more frequent wage payments than economy A. The nominal interest rate equals the real interest rate plus the expected inflation rate, so economy B has the higher nominal interest rate.

CHAPTER SUMMARY

Key Points

1. **Explain what determines the demand for money and how the demand for money and the supply of money determine the *nominal* interest rate.**

   - The demand for money is the relationship between the quantity of money demanded and the nominal interest rate, other things remaining the same. The higher the nominal interest rate, other things remaining the same, the smaller is the quantity of money demanded.
   - Increases in real GDP increase the demand for money. Some advances in financial technology increase the demand for money, and some advances decrease it.
   - Each day, the price level, real GDP, and financial technology are given and money market equilibrium determines the nominal interest rate.
   - To lower the interest rate, the Fed increases the supply of money. To raise the interest rate, the Fed decreases the supply of money.

2. **Explain how in the long run, the quantity of money determines the price level and money growth brings inflation.**

   - In the long run, real GDP equals potential GDP and the real interest rate is the level that makes the quantity of loanable funds demanded equal the quantity of loanable funds supplied in the global financial market.
   - The nominal interest rate in the long run equals the equilibrium real interest rate plus the inflation rate.
   - Money market equilibrium in the long run determines the price level.
   - An increase in the quantity of money, other things remaining the same, increases the price level by the same percentage.
   - The inflation rate in the long run equals the growth rate of the quantity of money minus the growth rate of potential GDP.
   - The equation of exchange and the velocity of circulation provide an alternative way of viewing the relationship between the quantity of money and the price level (and money growth and inflation).

3. **Identify the costs of inflation and the benefits of a stable value of money.**

   - Inflation has four costs: tax costs, shoe-leather costs, confusion costs, and uncertainty costs.
   - The higher the inflation rate, the greater are these four costs.

Key Terms

MyEconLab Key Terms Quiz

Demand for money, 724	Quantity of money demanded, 723	Velocity of circulation, 734
Equation of exchange, 735	Quantity theory of money, 734	
Hyperinflation, 739	Supply of money, 726	

CHAPTER CHECKPOINT

Study Plan Problems and Applications

1. Draw a graph to illustrate the demand for money. On the graph show the effect of an increase in real GDP and the effect of an increase in the number of families that have a credit card.

2. If the Fed makes a decision to cut the quantity of money, explain the short-run effects on the quantity of money demanded and the nominal interest rate.

3. The Fed conducts an open market purchase of securities. Explain the effects of this action on the nominal interest rate in the short run and the value of money in the long run.

In 2007, the United States was at full employment. The quantity of money was growing at 6.4 percent a year, the nominal interest rate was 4.4 percent a year, real GDP grew at 1.9 percent a year, and the inflation rate was 2.9 percent a year. Use this information to work Problems **4** and **5**.

4. Calculate the real interest rate.

5. Was the velocity of circulation constant? (Hint: Use the quantity theory of money.) If the velocity of circulation was not constant, how did it change and why might it have changed?

6. If the quantity of money is $3 trillion, real GDP is $10 trillion, the price level is 0.9, the real interest rate is 2 percent a year, and the nominal interest rate is 7 percent a year, calculate the velocity of circulation, the value of $M \times V$, and nominal GDP.

7. If the velocity of circulation is growing at 1 percent a year, the real interest rate is 2 percent a year, the nominal interest rate is 7 percent a year, and the growth rate of real GDP is 3 percent a year, calculate the inflation rate, the growth rate of money, and the growth rate of nominal GDP.

8. Suppose that the government passes a new law that sets a limit on the interest rate that credit card companies can charge on overdue balances. As a result, the nominal interest rate charged by credit card companies falls from 15 percent a year to 7 percent a year. If the average income tax rate is 30 percent, explain how the after-tax real interest rate on overdue credit card balances changes.

Annualized inflation in Venezuela soars to 1,000 percent
Inflation in Venezuela hit a monthly rate of 23.3 percent in June and it was feared that it would soon move into unstoppable hyperinflation. The country faced constant looting and social unrest.

Source: *PanAm Post*, July 15, 2016

9. What is hyperinflation? Is Venezuela in a hyperinflation?

10. Compare inflation in Venezuela in 2016 with that in Germany in 1923. Why did Germany print money in 1923 and create hyperinflation? Why is Venezuela printing money today? Why does a high inflation rate bring looting and social unrest?

 11. Read *Eye on Inflation* on p. 738. Why did inflation increase during the 1970s? In which decades did velocity growth break the link between money growth and inflation?

Instructor Assignable Problems and Applications

MyEconLab Homework, Quiz, or Test if assigned by instructor

1. Explain what causes inflation. Why is it easier to predict the decade-average inflation rate than the inflation rate in a single year?

2. If the Fed doubled the quantity of money and nothing else changed, what would happen to the price level in the short run and the long run? What would happen to the inflation rate?

3. Suppose that banks launch an aggressive marketing campaign to get everyone to use debit cards for every conceivable transaction. They offer prizes to new debit card holders and introduce a charge on using a credit card. How would the demand for money and the nominal interest rate change?

4. Draw a graph of the money market to illustrate equilibrium in the short run. If the growth rate of the quantity of money increases, explain what happens to the real interest rate and the nominal interest rate in the short run.

5. The Fed conducts an open market sale of securities. Explain the effects of this action in the short run on the nominal interest rate and in the long run on the value of money and the price level.

6. What is the quantity theory of money? Define the velocity of circulation and explain how it is measured.

7. If the velocity of circulation is constant, real GDP is growing at 3 percent a year, the real interest rate is 2 percent a year, and the nominal interest rate is 7 percent a year, calculate the inflation rate, the growth rate of money, and the growth rate of nominal GDP.

8. Sara has $200 in currency and $2,000 in a bank account on which the bank pays no interest. The inflation rate is 2 percent a year. Calculate the amount of inflation tax that Sara pays in a year.

Use the following information to work Problems **9** to **12**.

Fed's easy money can't control price level

Robert F. Stauffer, Emeritus Professor of Economics at Roanoke College, Salem, Virginia, argues that the Fed's monetary policy cannot closely control the price level, and an inflation target can be achieved only by chance. He takes issue with Harvard economist Martin Feldstein, who argues that the Fed's easy money policy will eventually raise the inflation rate to more than 3 percent.

Source: *The Wall Street Journal*, July 14, 2016

9. Why might Robert Stauffer be right? If he is right, what is he implying about the equation of exchange and the quantity theory of money?

10. Why might Martin Feldstein be right? If he is right, what is he implying about the equation of exchange and the quantity theory of money?

11. When Martin Feldstein describes the Fed's monetary policy as "easy," he means that the Fed has created a lot of money, has made money grow at a fast rate, and has pushed interest rates down. Looking at the graph in *Eye on Inflation* (p. 738), has money been "easy" during the 2010s? In which decade was it most "easy"?

12. If the money growth rate and real GDP growth rate of the 2010s are maintained and if the velocity growth rate is zero, will the inflation rate rise to 3 percent as predicted by Martin Feldstein?

MyEconLab Chapter 28 Study Plan

Multiple Choice Quiz

1. Holding money provides a benefit _____.

   A. because it is a means of payment
   B. because its opportunity cost is low
   C. which is constant no matter how much money is held
   D. because most money is in bank deposits

2. The opportunity cost of holding money _____.

   A. is determined by the inflation rate
   B. is zero because money earns no interest
   C. equals the nominal interest rate on bonds
   D. equals the real interest rate on bonds

3. The quantity of money demanded increases if _____.

   A. the supply of money increases
   B. the nominal interest rate falls
   C. banks increase the interest rate on deposits
   D. the price of a bond falls

4. If the Fed increases the quantity of money, people will be holding _____.

   A. too much money, so they buy bonds and the interest rate rises
   B. too much money, so they buy bonds and the interest rate falls
   C. the quantity of money they demand and banks will hold more money
   D. more money and will increase their demand for money

5. In the long run, money market equilibrium determines the _____.

   A. real interest rate
   B. price level
   C. nominal interest rate
   D. economic growth rate

6. If the quantity theory of money is correct and other things remain the same, an increase in the quantity of money increases _____.

   A. nominal GDP and the velocity of circulation
   B. the price level and potential GDP
   C. real GDP
   D. nominal GDP and the price level

7. In the long run with a constant velocity of circulation, the inflation rate _____.

   A. is constant and equals the money growth rate
   B. equals the money growth rate minus the growth rate of real GDP
   C. equals the growth rate of real GDP minus the growth rate of money
   D. is positive if the economic growth rate is positive

8. The costs of inflation do *not* include _____.

   A. the cost of running around to compare prices at different outlets
   B. the increased opportunity cost of holding money
   C. the tax on money held by individuals and businesses
   D. an increase in saving and investment

Why did the U.S. economy
go into recession in 2008?

Aggregate Supply and Aggregate Demand

29

**When you have completed your study of this chapter,
you will be able to**

1 Define and explain the influences on aggregate supply.

2 Define and explain the influences on aggregate demand.

3 Explain how trends and fluctuations in aggregate demand and
aggregate supply bring economic growth, inflation, and the
business cycle.

MyEconLab Big Picture Video

MyEconLab Concept Video

29.1 AGGREGATE SUPPLY

The purpose of the aggregate supply–aggregate demand model is to explain how real GDP and the price level are determined. The model uses similar ideas to those that you encountered in Chapter 4 where you learned how the quantity and price are determined in a competitive market. But the *aggregate* supply–*aggregate* demand model (*AS-AD* model) isn't just an application of the competitive market model. Some differences arise because the *AS-AD* model is a model of an imaginary market for the total of all the final goods and services that make up real GDP. The quantity in this "market" is real GDP and the price is the price level measured by the GDP price index.

The *quantity of real GDP supplied* is the total amount of final goods and services that firms in the United States plan to produce and it depends on the quantities of

- Labor employed
- Capital, human capital, and the state of technology
- Land and natural resources
- Entrepreneurial talent

You saw in Chapter 24 that at full employment, real GDP equals *potential GDP*. The quantities of land, capital and human capital, the state of technology, and the amount of entrepreneurial talent are fixed. Labor market equilibrium determines the quantity of labor employed, which is equal to the quantity of labor demanded and the quantity of labor supplied at the equilibrium real wage rate.

Over the business cycle, real GDP fluctuates around potential GDP because the quantity of labor employed fluctuates around its full employment level. The aggregate supply–aggregate demand model explains these fluctuations.

We begin on the supply side with the basics of aggregate supply.

■ Aggregate Supply Basics

Aggregate supply
The relationship between the quantity of real GDP supplied and the price level when all other influences on production plans remain the same.

Aggregate supply is the relationship between the quantity of real GDP supplied and the price level when all other influences on production plans remain the same. This relationship can be described as follows:

Other things remaining the same, the higher the price level, the greater is the quantity of real GDP supplied, and the lower the price level, the smaller is the quantity of real GDP supplied.

Figure 29.1 illustrates aggregate supply as an aggregate supply schedule and aggregate supply curve. The aggregate supply schedule lists the quantities of real GDP supplied at each price level, and the upward-sloping *AS* curve graphs these points.

The figure also shows potential GDP: $16 trillion in the figure. When the price level is 105, the quantity of real GDP supplied is $16 trillion, which equals potential GDP (at point *C* on the *AS* curve).

Along the aggregate supply curve, the price level is the only influence on production plans that changes. A rise in the price level brings an increase in the quantity of real GDP supplied and a movement up along the aggregate supply curve; a fall in the price level brings a decrease in the quantity of real GDP supplied and a movement down along the aggregate supply curve.

Aggregate Supply Schedule and Aggregate Supply Curve   MyEconLab Animation

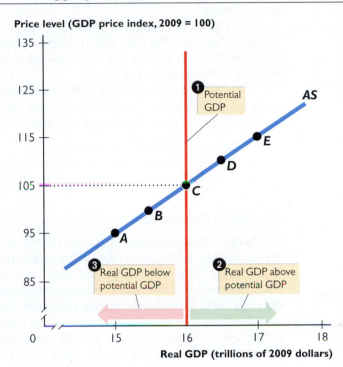

Price level (GDP price index, 2009 = 100)	Quantity of real GDP supplied (trillions of 2009 dollars)
E 115	17.0
D 110	16.5
C 105	16.0
B 100	15.5
A 95	15.0

The aggregate supply schedule and aggregate supply curve, *AS*, show the relationship between the quantity of real GDP supplied and the price level when all other influences on production plans remain the same. Each point *A* through *E* on the *AS* curve corresponds to the row identified by the same letter in the schedule.

① Potential GDP is $16 trillion, and when the price level is 105, real GDP equals potential GDP.

② If the price level is above 105, real GDP exceeds potential GDP.

③ If the price level is below 105, real GDP is less than potential GDP.

Among the other influences on production plans that remain constant along the *AS* curve are

- The money wage rate
- The money prices of other resources

In contrast, along the potential GDP line, when the price level changes, the money wage rate and the money prices of other resources change by the same percentage as the change in the price level to keep the real wage rate (and other real prices) at the full-employment equilibrium level.

Why the *AS* Curve Slopes Upward

Why does the quantity of real GDP supplied increase when the price level rises and decrease when the price level falls? The answer is that a movement along the *AS* curve brings a change in the real wage rate (and changes in the real cost of other resources whose money prices are fixed). If the price level rises, the real wage rate falls, and if the price level falls, the real wage rate rises. When the real wage rate changes, firms change the quantity of labor employed and the level of production.

Think about a concrete example. A ketchup producer has a contract with its workers to pay them $20 an hour. The firm sells ketchup for $1 a bottle. The real wage rate of a ketchup bottling worker is 20 bottles of ketchup. That is, the firm must sell 20 bottles of ketchup to buy one hour of labor. Now suppose the price of ketchup falls to 50 cents a bottle. The real wage rate of a bottling worker has increased to 40 bottles—the firm must now sell 40 bottles of ketchup to buy one hour of labor.

If the price of a bottle of ketchup increased, the real wage rate of a bottling worker would fall. For example, if the price increased to $2 a bottle, the real wage rate would be 10 bottles per worker—the firm needs to sell only 10 bottles of ketchup to buy one hour of labor.

Firms respond to a change in the real wage rate by changing the quantity of labor employed and the quantity produced. For the economy as a whole, employment and real GDP change. There are three ways in which these changes occur:

- Firms change their output rate.
- Firms shut down temporarily or restart production.
- Firms go out of business or start up in business.

Change in Output Rate

To change its output rate, a firm must change the quantity of labor that it employs. It is profitable to hire more labor if the additional labor costs less than the revenue it generates. If the price level rises and the money wage rate doesn't change, an extra hour of labor that was previously unprofitable becomes profitable. So when the price level rises and the money wage rate doesn't change, the quantity of labor demanded and production increase. If the price level falls and the money wage rate doesn't change, an hour of labor that was previously profitable becomes unprofitable. So when the price level falls and the money wage rate doesn't change, the quantity of labor demanded and production decrease.

Temporary Shutdowns and Restarts

A firm that is incurring a loss might foresee a profit in the future. Such a firm might decide to shut down temporarily and lay off its workers.

The price level relative to the money wage rate influences temporary shutdown decisions. If the price level rises relative to wages, fewer firms decide to shut down temporarily; so more firms operate and the quantity of real GDP supplied increases. If the price level falls relative to wages, a larger number of firms find that they cannot earn enough revenue to pay the wage bill and so temporarily shut down. The quantity of real GDP supplied decreases.

Business Failure and Startup

People create businesses in the hope of earning a profit. When profits are squeezed or when losses arise, more firms fail, fewer new firms start up, and the number of firms decreases. When profits are generally high, fewer firms fail, more firms start up, and the number of firms increases.

The price level relative to the money wage rate influences the number of firms in business. If the price level rises relative to wages, profits increase, the number of firms in business increases, and the quantity of real GDP supplied increases. If the price level falls relative to wages, profits fall, the number of firms in business decreases, and the quantity of real GDP supplied decreases.

In a severe recession, business failure can be contagious. The failure of one firm puts pressure on both its suppliers and its customers and can bring a flood of failures and a large decrease in the quantity of real GDP supplied.

■ Changes in Aggregate Supply

Aggregate supply changes when any influence on production plans other than the price level changes. In particular, aggregate supply changes when

- Potential GDP changes.
- The money wage rate changes.
- The money prices of other resources change.

Change in Potential GDP

Anything that changes potential GDP changes aggregate supply and shifts the aggregate supply curve. Figure 29.2 illustrates such a shift. You can think of point C as an anchor point. The AS curve and potential GDP line are anchored at this point, and when potential GDP changes, aggregate supply changes along with it. When potential GDP increases from $16 trillion to $17 trillion, point C shifts to point C', and the AS curve and potential GDP line shift rightward together. The AS curve shifts from AS_0 to AS_1.

Change in Money Wage Rate

A change in the money wage rate changes aggregate supply because it changes firms' costs. The higher the money wage rate, the higher are firms' costs and the smaller is the quantity that firms are willing to supply at each price level. So an increase in the money wage rate decreases aggregate supply.

■ FIGURE 29.2

An Increase in Potential GDP

MyEconLab Animation

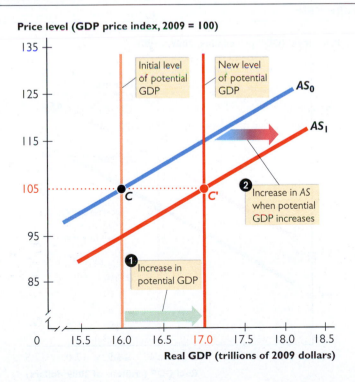

❶ An increase in potential GDP increases aggregate supply.

❷ When potential GDP increases from $16 trillion to $17 trillion, the aggregate supply curve shifts rightward from AS_0 to AS_1.

Suppose that the money wage rate is $52.50 an hour and the price level is 105. Then the real wage rate is $50 an hour ($52.50 × 100 ÷ 105 = $50)—see Chapter 23, p. 604. If the full-employment equilibrium real wage rate is $50 an hour, the economy is at full employment and real GDP equals potential GDP. In Figure 29.3, the economy is at point C on the aggregate supply curve AS_0. The money wage rate is $52.50 an hour at all points on AS_0.

Now suppose the money wage rate rises to $57.50 an hour but the full-employment equilibrium real wage rate remains at $50 an hour. Real GDP now equals potential GDP when the price level is 115, at point D on the aggregate supply curve AS_2. (If the money wage rate is $57.50 an hour and the price level is 115, the real wage rate is $57.50 × 100 ÷ 115 = $50 an hour.) The money wage rate is $57.50 an hour at all points on AS_2. The rise in the money wage rate *decreases* aggregate supply and shifts the aggregate supply curve leftward from AS_0 to AS_2.

A change in the money wage rate does not change potential GDP. The reason is that potential GDP depends only on the economy's real ability to produce and on the full-employment quantity of labor, which occurs at the equilibrium *real* wage rate. The equilibrium real wage rate can occur at any money wage rate.

Change in Money Prices of Other Resources

A change in the money prices of other resources has a similar effect on firms' production plans to a change in the money wage rate. It changes firms' costs. At each price level, firms' real costs change and the quantity that firms are willing to supply changes so aggregate supply changes.

■ **FIGURE 29.3**

A Change in the Money Wage Rate   MyEconLab Animation

A rise in the money wage rate decreases aggregate supply. The aggregate supply curve shifts leftward from AS_0 to AS_2. A rise in the money wage rate does not change potential GDP.

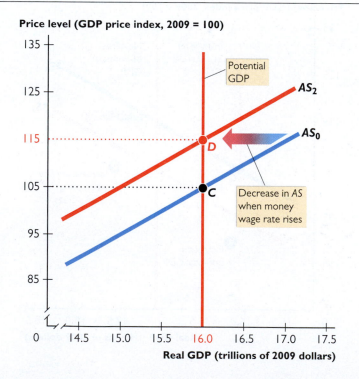

CHECKPOINT 29.1

MyEconLab Study Plan 29.1
Key Terms Quiz
Solutions Video

Define and explain the influences on aggregate supply.

Practice Problem

1. Explain the influence of each of the events in List 1 on the quantity of real GDP supplied and aggregate supply in India and use a graph to illustrate.

In the News

A midyear burst of minimum-wage increases starts on July 1
On July 1, 2016, the minimum wage will increase in 14 U.S. cities, states, and counties, and in the District of Columbia. In San Francisco, the minimum wage will rise to $13.00 by 2018.

Source: The Wall Street Journal, July 1, 2016

Explain how the widespread rise in the minimum wage will influence aggregate supply.

> **LIST 1**
> - Fuel prices rise.
> - U.S. firms move their IT and data functions to India.
> - Walmart and Starbucks open in India.
> - Universities in India increase the number of engineering graduates.
> - The money wage rate in India rises.
> - The price level in India rises.

Solution to Practice Problem

1. As fuel prices rise, the quantity of real GDP supplied at the current price level decreases. The *AS* curve shifts leftward (Figure 1).

   As U.S. firms move their IT and data functions to India, real GDP supplied at the current price level increases. The *AS* curve shifts rightward (Figure 2).

   As Walmart and Starbucks open, the quantity of real GDP supplied at the current price level increases. The *AS* curve shifts rightward (Figure 2).

   With more graduates, the number of skilled workers increases, and production increases at the current price level. The *AS* curve shifts rightward (Figure 2).

   As the money wage rate rises, firms' costs increase and the quantity of real GDP supplied at the current price level decreases. The *AS* curve shifts leftward (Figure 1).

   As the price level increases, other things remaining the same, businesses become more profitable and increase the quantity of real GDP supplied along the *AS* curve (Figure 3). The *AS* curve does not shift.

FIGURE 1

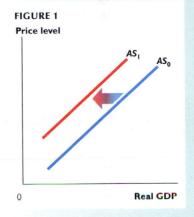

Solution to In the News

The widespread rise in the minimum wage will increase the money wage rate. At the current price level, a rise in the money wage rate increases the real wage rate and decreases aggregate supply. If the rise in the minimum wage increases the natural unemployment rate, potential GDP decreases and aggregate supply decreases further.

FIGURE 2

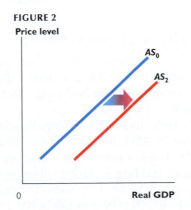

FIGURE 3

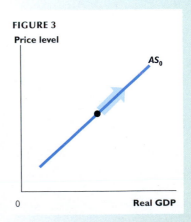

29.2   AGGREGATE DEMAND

The *quantity of real GDP demanded* (*Y*) is the total amount of final goods and services produced in the United States that people, businesses, governments, and foreigners plan to buy. This quantity is the sum of the real consumption expenditure (*C*), investment (*I*), government expenditure on goods and services (*G*), and exports (*X*) minus imports (*M*). That is,

$$Y = C + I + G + X - M.$$

Many factors influence expenditure plans. To study aggregate demand, we divide those factors into two parts: the price level and everything else. We'll first consider the influence of the price level on expenditure plans and then consider the other influences.

■ Aggregate Demand Basics

Aggregate demand
The relationship between the quantity of real GDP demanded and the price level when all other influences on expenditure plans remain the same.

Aggregate demand is the relationship between the quantity of real GDP demanded and the price level when all other influences on expenditure plans remain the same. This relationship can be described as follows:

Other things remaining the same, the higher the price level, the smaller is the quantity of real GDP demanded; and the lower the price level, the greater is the quantity of real GDP demanded.

Figure 29.4 illustrates aggregate demand by using an aggregate demand schedule and aggregate demand curve. The aggregate demand schedule lists the quantities of real GDP demanded at each price level, and the downward-sloping *AD* curve graphs these points.

Along the aggregate demand curve, the only influence on expenditure plans that changes is the price level. A rise in the price level decreases the quantity of real GDP demanded and brings a movement up along the aggregate demand curve; a fall in the price level increases the quantity of real GDP demanded and brings a movement down along the aggregate demand curve.

The price level influences the quantity of real GDP demanded because a change in the price level brings a change in

- The buying power of money
- The real interest rate
- The real prices of exports and imports

The Buying Power of Money

A rise in the price level lowers the buying power of money and decreases the quantity of real GDP demanded. To see why, think about the buying plans in two economies—Russia and Japan—where the price level has changed a lot in recent years.

Anna lives in Moscow, Russia. She has worked hard all summer and has saved 20,000 rubles (the ruble is the currency of Russia), which she plans to spend attending graduate school after she has earned her economics degree. So Anna's money holding is 20,000 rubles. Anna has a part-time job, and her income from this job pays her expenses. The price level in Russia rises by 100 percent. Anna needs 40,000 rubles to buy what 20,000 rubles once bought. To make up some of the fall in the buying power of her money, Anna slashes her spending.

■ **FIGURE 29.4**

Aggregate Demand Schedule and Aggregate Demand Curve

MyEconLab Animation

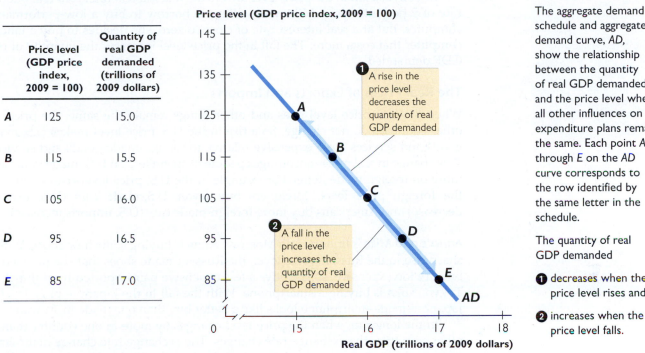

	Price level (GDP price index, 2009 = 100)	Quantity of real GDP demanded (trillions of 2009 dollars)
A	125	15.0
B	115	15.5
C	105	16.0
D	95	16.5
E	85	17.0

The aggregate demand schedule and aggregate demand curve, AD, show the relationship between the quantity of real GDP demanded and the price level when all other influences on expenditure plans remain the same. Each point A through E on the AD curve corresponds to the row identified by the same letter in the schedule.

The quantity of real GDP demanded

❶ decreases when the price level rises and

❷ increases when the price level falls.

Similarly, a fall in the price level, other things remaining the same, brings an increase in the quantity of real GDP demanded. To see why, think about the buying plans of Mika, who lives in Tokyo, Japan. She too has worked hard all summer and has saved 200,000 yen (the yen is the currency of Japan), which she plans to spend attending school next year. The price level in Japan falls by 10 percent; now Mika needs only 180,000 yen to buy what 200,000 yen once bought. With a rise in what her money buys, Mika decides to buy a smartphone.

The Real Interest Rate

When the price level rises, the real interest rate rises. You saw in Chapter 28 (p. 725) that an increase in the price level increases the amount of money that people want to hold—increases the demand for money. When the demand for money increases, the nominal interest rate rises. In the short run, the inflation rate does not change, so a rise in the nominal interest rate brings a rise in the real interest rate. Faced with a higher real interest rate, businesses and people delay plans to buy new capital and consumer durable goods and they cut back on spending. As the price level rises, the quantity of real GDP demanded decreases.

Anna and Mika Again Think about Anna and Mika again. Both of them want to buy a computer. In Moscow, a rise in the price level increases the demand for money and raises the real interest rate. At a real interest rate of 5 percent a year,

Anna was willing to borrow to buy the new computer. But at a real interest rate of 10 percent a year, she decides that the payments would be too high, so she delays buying it. The rise in the price level decreases the quantity of real GDP demanded.

In Tokyo, a fall in the price level lowers the real interest rate. At a real interest rate of 5 percent a year, Mika was willing to borrow to buy a low-performance computer. But at a real interest rate of close to zero, she decides to buy a fancier computer that costs more: The fall in the price level increases the quantity of real GDP demanded.

The Real Prices of Exports and Imports

When the U.S. price level rises and other things remain the same, the prices in other countries do not change. So a rise in the U.S. price level makes U.S.-made goods and services more expensive relative to foreign-made goods and services. This change in real prices encourages people to spend less on U.S.-made items and more on foreign-made items. For example, if the U.S. price level rises relative to the foreign price level, foreigners buy fewer U.S.-made cars (U.S. exports decrease) and Americans buy more foreign-made cars (U.S. imports increase).

Anna's and Mika's Imports   In Moscow, Anna is buying some new shoes. With a sharp rise in the Russian price level, the Russian-made shoes that she planned to buy are too expensive, so she buys a less expensive pair imported from Brazil. In Tokyo, Mika is buying a smartphone. With the fall in the Japanese price level, a Japanese-made smartphone looks like a better buy than one made in Taiwan.

In the long run, when the price level changes by more in one country than in other countries, the exchange rate changes. The exchange rate change neutralizes the price level change, so this international price effect on buying plans is a short-run effect only. But in the short run, it is a powerful effect.

■ Changes in Aggregate Demand

A change in any factor that influences expenditure plans other than the price level brings a change in aggregate demand. When aggregate demand increases, the aggregate demand curve shifts rightward, which Figure 29.5 illustrates as the rightward shift of the AD curve from AD_0 to AD_1. When aggregate demand decreases, the aggregate demand curve shifts leftward, which Figure 29.5 illustrates as the leftward shift of the AD curve from AD_0 to AD_2. The factors that change aggregate demand are

- Expectations about the future
- Fiscal policy and monetary policy
- The state of the world economy

Expectations

An increase in expected future income increases the amount of consumption goods (especially big-ticket items such as cars) that people plan to buy now. Aggregate demand increases. An increase in expected future inflation increases aggregate demand because people decide to buy more goods and services now before their prices rise. An increase in expected future profit increases the investment that firms plan to undertake now. Aggregate demand increases.

A decrease in expected future income, future inflation, or future profit has the opposite effect and decreases aggregate demand.

■ **FIGURE 29.5**

Change in Aggregate Demand

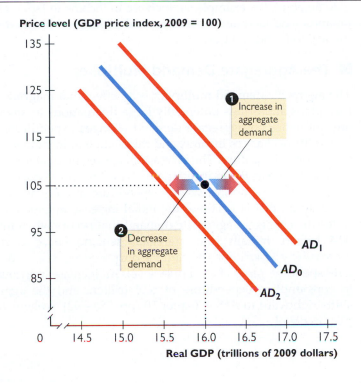

Price level (GDP price index, 2009 = 100)

❶ Increase in aggregate demand

❷ Decrease in aggregate demand

AD₁

AD₀

AD₂

Real GDP (trillions of 2009 dollars)

❶ Aggregate demand *increases if*

• Expected future income, inflation, or profits increase.
• The government or the Federal Reserve takes steps that increase planned expenditure.
• The exchange rate falls or the global economy expands.

❷ Aggregate demand *decreases if*

• Expected future income, inflation, or profits decrease.
• The government or the Federal Reserve takes steps that decrease planned expenditure.
• The exchange rate rises or the global economy contracts.

Fiscal Policy and Monetary Policy

We study the effects of policy actions on aggregate demand in Chapters 32 and 33. Here, we'll just briefly note that the government can use **fiscal policy**—changing taxes, transfer payments, and government expenditure on goods and services—to influence aggregate demand. The Federal Reserve can use **monetary policy**—changing the quantity of money and the interest rate—to influence aggregate demand. A tax cut or an increase in either transfer payments or government expenditure on goods and services increases aggregate demand. A cut in the interest rate or an increase in the quantity of money increases aggregate demand.

Fiscal policy
Changing taxes, transfer payments, and government expenditure on goods and services.

Monetary policy
Changing the quantity of money and the interest rate.

The World Economy

Two main influences that the world economy has on aggregate demand are the foreign exchange rate and foreign income. The foreign exchange rate is the amount of a foreign currency that you can buy with a U.S. dollar. Other things remaining the same, a rise in the foreign exchange rate decreases aggregate demand.

To see how the foreign exchange rate influences aggregate demand, suppose that $1 exchanges for 100 Japanese yen. A Fujitsu phone made in Japan costs 12,500 yen, and an equivalent Motorola phone made in the United States costs $110. In U.S. dollars, the Fujitsu phone costs $125, so people around the world buy the cheaper U.S. phone. Now suppose the exchange rate rises to 125 yen per dollar. At 125 yen per dollar, the Fujitsu phone costs $100 and is now cheaper than the Motorola phone. People will switch from the U.S. phone to the Japanese phone.

U.S. exports will decrease and U.S. imports will increase, so U.S. aggregate demand will decrease.

An increase in foreign income increases U.S. exports and increases U.S. aggregate demand. For example, an increase in income in Japan and Germany increases Japanese and German consumers' and producers' planned expenditures on U.S.-made goods and services.

■ The Aggregate Demand Multiplier

The aggregate demand multiplier is an effect that magnifies changes in expenditure plans and brings potentially large fluctuations in aggregate demand. When any influence on aggregate demand changes expenditure plans, the change in expenditure changes income; and the change in income induces a change in consumption expenditure. The increase in aggregate demand is the initial increase in expenditure plus the induced increase in consumption expenditure.

Suppose that an increase in expenditure induces an increase in consumption expenditure that is 1.5 times the initial increase in expenditure. Figure 29.6 illustrates the change in aggregate demand that occurs when investment increases by $0.4 trillion. Initially, the aggregate demand curve is AD_0. Investment then increases by $0.4 trillion ($\Delta I$) and the purple curve $AD_0 + \Delta I$ now describes aggregate spending plans at each price level. An increase in income induces an increase in consumption expenditure of $0.6 trillion, and the aggregate demand curve shifts rightward to AD_1. Chapter 30 (pp. 788–792) explains the expenditure multiplier in detail.

■ **FIGURE 29.6**

The Aggregate Demand Multiplier

MyEconLab Animation

❶ An increase in investment ❷ increases aggregate demand and increases income.

❸ A multiplier effect induces an increase in consumption expenditure, which ❹ increases aggregate demand by more than the initial increase in investment.

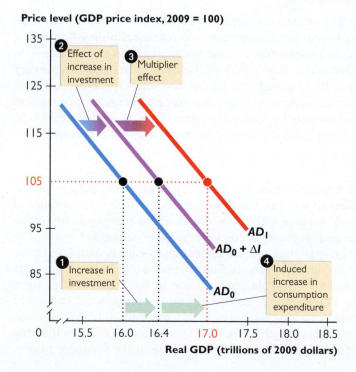

CHECKPOINT 29.2

MyEconLab Study Plan 29.2
Key Terms Quiz
Solutions Video

Define and explain the influences on aggregate demand.

Practice Problems

1. Mexico trades with the United States. Explain the effect of each of the following events on Mexico's aggregate demand.
   - The government of Mexico cuts income taxes.
   - The United States experiences strong economic growth.
   - Mexico sets new environmental standards that require factories to upgrade their production facilities.

2. Explain the effect of each of the following events on the quantity of real GDP demanded and aggregate demand in Mexico.
   - Europe trades with Mexico and goes into a recession.
   - The price level in Mexico rises.
   - Mexico increases the quantity of money.

In the News

Investment and government expenditure down and exports up

The BEA announced that nonresidential investment and federal government spending decreased in the first quarter of 2016 while U.S. exports increased and U.S. imports decreased.

Source: Bureau of Economic Analysis, June 28, 2016

Explain how the items in the news clip influenced U.S. aggregate demand.

FIGURE 1
Price level

AD₁
AD₀

0   Real GDP

Solutions to Practice Problems

1. A tax cut increases disposable income, which increases consumption expenditure, which increases aggregate demand. Strong U.S. growth increases the demand for Mexican-produced goods, which increases Mexico's aggregate demand. As factories upgrade their facilities, investment increases. Aggregate demand increases. In each case, the *AD* curve shifts rightward (Figure 1).

2. A recession in Europe decreases the demand for Mexico's exports, so aggregate demand decreases. The *AD* curve shifts leftward (Figure 2). A rise in the price level decreases the quantity of real GDP demanded along the *AD* curve, but the *AD* curve does not shift (Figure 3). An increase in the quantity of money increases aggregate demand, and the *AD* curve shifts rightward (Figure 1).

Solution to In the News

The decrease in nonresidential investment and federal government expenditure decreased aggregate demand. The fall in U.S. imports and rise in U.S. exports increased the demand for U.S.-produced goods and services and increased U.S. aggregate demand.

FIGURE 2
Price level

AD₀
AD₂

0   Real GDP

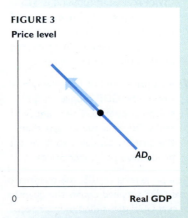

FIGURE 3
Price level

AD₀

0   Real GDP

29.3 EXPLAINING ECONOMIC TRENDS AND FLUCTUATIONS

The main purpose of the *AS-AD* model is to explain business cycle fluctuations in real GDP and the price level. But the model also helps our understanding of economic growth and inflation trends that we've studied in earlier chapters. The first step toward explaining economic trends and fluctuations is to combine aggregate supply and aggregate demand and determine macroeconomic equilibrium.

■ Macroeconomic Equilibrium

Macroeconomic equilibrium
When the quantity of real GDP demanded equals the quantity of real GDP supplied at the point of intersection of the *AD* curve and the *AS* curve.

Aggregate supply and aggregate demand determine real GDP and the price level. **Macroeconomic equilibrium** occurs when the quantity of real GDP demanded equals the quantity of real GDP supplied at the point of intersection of the *AD* curve and the *AS* curve. Figure 29.7 shows such an equilibrium at a price level of 105 and real GDP of $16 trillion.

To see why this position is the equilibrium, think about what happens if the price level is something other than 105. Suppose the price level is 95 and real GDP is $15 trillion (point *A* on the *AS* curve). The quantity of real GDP demanded exceeds $15 trillion, so firms are unable to meet the demand for their output. Inventories decrease, and customers clamor for goods and services. In this situation, firms increase production and raise prices. Eventually they can meet demand when real GDP is $16 trillion and the price level is 105.

Now suppose that the price level is 115 and that real GDP is $17 trillion (point *B* on the *AS* curve). The quantity of real GDP demanded is less than $17 trillion, so firms are unable to sell all their output. Unwanted inventories pile up. Firms cut production and lower prices until they can sell all their output, which occurs when real GDP is $16 trillion and the price level is 105.

■ **FIGURE 29.7**

Macroeconomic Equilibrium

Macroeconomic equilibrium occurs when the quantity of real GDP supplied on the *AS* curve equals the quantity of real GDP demanded on the *AD* curve.

❶ At a price level of 95, the quantity of real GDP supplied is $15 trillion at point *A*. The quantity of real GDP demanded exceeds the quantity supplied, so firms increase production and raise prices.

❷ At a price level of 115, the quantity of real GDP supplied is $17 trillion at point *B*. The quantity of real GDP demanded is less than the quantity supplied, so firms cut production and lower prices.

At a price level of 105, the quantity of real GDP supplied equals the quantity of real GDP demanded in macroeconomic equilibrium.

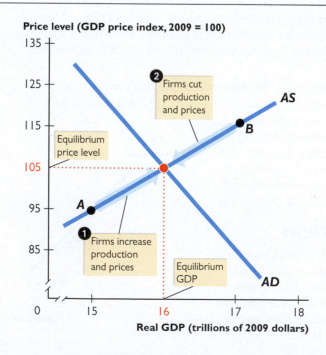

■ Three Types of Macroeconomic Equilibrium

In macroeconomic equilibrium, the economy might be at full employment or above or below full employment. Figure 29.8(a) shows these three possibilities. **Full-employment equilibrium**—when equilibrium real GDP equals potential GDP—occurs where the *AD* curve intersects the aggregate supply curve *AS**.

At a higher money wage rate, aggregate supply is AS_1. Real GDP is \$15.5 trillion and is less than potential GDP. The economy is *below full employment* and there is a **recessionary gap**. At a lower money wage rate, aggregate supply is AS_2. In this situation, real GDP is \$16.5 trillion and is greater than potential GDP. The economy is *above full employment* and there is an **inflationary gap**.

Adjustment toward Full Employment

When real GDP is below or above potential GDP, the money wage rate gradually changes to restore full employment. Figure 29.8(b) illustrates this adjustment.

In a *recessionary gap*, there is a surplus of labor and firms can hire new workers at a lower wage rate. As the money wage rate falls, the *AS* curve shifts from AS_1 toward *AS** and the price level falls and real GDP rises. The money wage continues to fall until real GDP equals potential GDP—full-employment equilibrium.

In an *inflationary gap*, there is a shortage of labor and firms must offer a higher wage rate to hire the labor they demand. As the money wage rate rises, the *AS* curve shifts from AS_2 toward *AS** and the price level rises and real GDP falls. The money wage rate continues to rise until real GDP equals potential GDP.

Full-employment equilibrium
When equilibrium real GDP equals potential GDP.

Recessionary gap
A gap that exists when potential GDP exceeds real GDP and that brings a falling price level.

Inflationary gap
A gap that exists when real GDP exceeds potential GDP and that brings a rising price level.

■ **FIGURE 29.8**

Output Gaps and Full-Employment Equilibrium   MyEconLab Animation

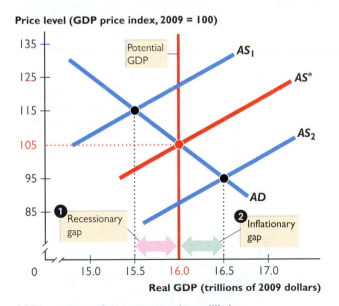

(a) Three types of macroeconomic equilibrium

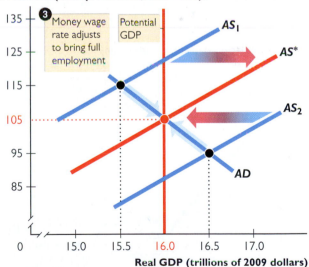

(b) Adjustment to full employment

In part (a), when equilibrium real GDP is less than potential GDP, ❶ there is a recessionary gap; when equilibrium real GDP is greater than potential GDP, ❷ there is an inflationary gap; and when equilibrium real GDP equals potential GDP, the economy is at full employment.

In part (b), when an output gap exists ❸ the money wage rate adjusts to move the economy toward full employment. With a recessionary gap, the money wage rate falls and the *AS* curve shifts rightward from AS_1 to *AS**. With an inflationary gap, the money wage rate rises and the *AS* curve shifts leftward from AS_2 to *AS**.

■ Economic Growth and Inflation Trends

Economic growth results from a growing labor force and increasing labor productivity, which together make potential GDP grow (Chapter 25, pp. 642–647). Inflation results from a growing quantity of money that outpaces the growth of potential GDP (Chapter 28, pp. 734–738).

The *AS-AD* model can be used to understand economic growth and inflation trends. In the *AS-AD* model, economic growth is increasing potential GDP—a persistent rightward shift in the potential GDP line. Inflation arises from a persistent increase in aggregate demand at a faster pace than that of the increase in potential GDP—a persistent rightward shift of the *AD* curve at a faster pace than the growth of potential GDP. *Eye on the U.S. Economy* below shows how the *AS-AD* model explains U.S. economic growth and inflation trends.

EYE on the U.S. ECONOMY
U.S. Economic Growth, Inflation, and the Business Cycle

U.S. economic growth, inflation, and the business cycle result from changes in aggregate supply and aggregate demand.

A rightward movement in the U.S. potential GDP line brings economic growth and a greater rightward movement of the U.S. *AD* curve brings inflation. Part (a) shows the shifting curves that generate growth and inflation.

Part (b) shows the history of U.S. real GDP growth and inflation from 1970 to 2015. Each dot represents the real GDP and price level in a year—the black dot 1970 and the red dot 2015. The rightward movement of the dots is economic growth and the upward movement is a rising price level—inflation.

When the dots follow a path that is gently rising, as during the 1990s, the inflation rate is low and real GDP growth is quite rapid. When the dots follow a path that is steep, as during the 1970s, inflation is rapid and economic growth is slow.

Notice that the dots move rightward and upward in waves and occasionally

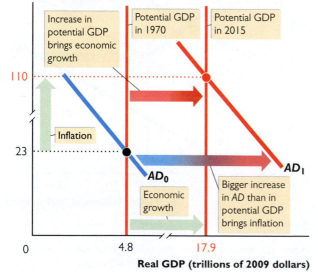

(a) Economic growth and inflation

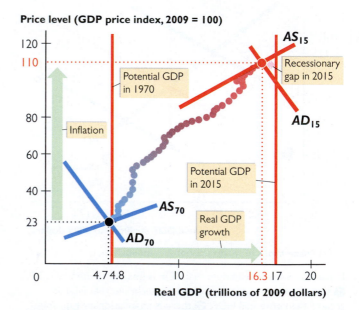

(b) U.S. economic growth and inflation

■ The Business Cycle

The business cycle results from fluctuations in aggregate supply and aggregate demand. Aggregate supply fluctuates because labor productivity grows at a variable pace, which brings fluctuations in the growth rate of potential GDP. The resulting cycle is called a **real business cycle**. But aggregate demand fluctuations are the main source of the business cycle. The key reason is that the swings in aggregate demand occur more quickly than changes in the money wage rate that change aggregate supply. The result is that the economy swings from inflationary gap to full employment to recessionary gap and back again.

Eye on the U.S. Economy below shows the most recent cycle interpreted as driven by aggregate demand fluctuations. But in the 2008–2009 recession, both aggregate demand and aggregate supply were at work as you can see on p. 769.

Real business cycle
A cycle that results from fluctuations in the pace of growth of labor productivity and potential GDP.

---

leftward. The pattern shows the business cycle expansions and recessions.

By comparing the dots with potential GDP, we can see that the economy was at full employment in 1970 and had a recessionary gap in 2015.

Part (c) shows how changes in aggregate demand create the business cycle, and part (d) shows the most recent cycle from 2000 to 2015.

When the AD curve is AD_0 in part (c), the economy is at point A and there is an inflationary gap. Part (d) identifies the actual gap in 2000 as A.

A decrease in aggregate demand to AD_1 lowers real GDP to potential GDP and the economy moves to point B in parts (c) and (d).

A further decrease in aggregate demand to AD_2 lowers real GDP to

below potential GDP and opens up a recessionary gap at point C in both parts (c) and (d).

In reality, AD rarely decreases. It increases at a slower pace than the increase in potential GDP. Also, in reality, AS fluctuates. But the relative positions of the AS and AD curves and the potential GDP line are like those shown in part (c).

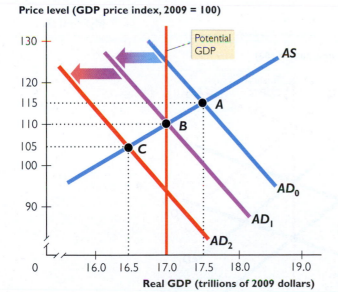

(c) Aggregate demand fluctuations

(d) The U.S. output gap

SOURCES OF DATA: Bureau of Labor Statistics, Bureau of Economic Analysis, and Congressional Budget Office.

■ Inflation Cycles

You've seen that inflation occurs if aggregate demand grows faster than potential GDP. But just as there are cycles in real GDP, there are also cycles in the inflation rate. And the two cycles are related. To study the interaction of real GDP and inflation cycles, we distinguish between two sources of inflation:

- Demand-pull inflation
- Cost-push inflation

Demand-Pull Inflation

Demand-pull inflation

Inflation that starts because aggregate demand increases.

Inflation that starts because aggregate demand increases is called **demand-pull inflation**. Demand-pull inflation can be kicked off by any of the factors that change aggregate demand but the only thing that can sustain it is growth in the quantity of money.

Figure 29.9 illustrates the process of demand-pull inflation. Potential GDP is $16 trillion. Initially, the aggregate demand curve is AD_0, the aggregate supply curve is AS_0, and real GDP equals potential GDP. Aggregate demand increases, shifting the aggregate demand curve to AD_1. Real GDP increases and the price level rises. There is now an *inflationary gap*. A shortage of labor brings a rise in the money wage rate, which shifts the aggregate supply curve to AS_1. The price level rises further and real GDP returns to potential GDP.

The quantity of money increases again, and the aggregate demand curve shifts rightward to AD_2. The price level rises further, and real GDP again exceeds potential GDP. Yet again, the money wage rate rises and decreases aggregate supply. The AS curve shifts to AS_2, and the price level rises further. As the quantity of money continues to grow, aggregate demand increases and the price level rises in an ongoing demand-pull inflation spiral.

■ FIGURE 29.9

A Demand-Pull Inflation

MyEconLab Animation

Each time the quantity of money increases, aggregate demand increases and the aggregate demand curve shifts rightward from AD_0 to AD_1 to AD_2, and so on.

Each time real GDP increases above potential GDP, the money wage rate rises and the aggregate supply curve shifts leftward from AS_0 to AS_1 to AS_2, and so on.

The price level rises from 105 to 108, 116, 120, 128, and so on.

A demand-pull inflation spiral results with real GDP fluctuating between $16 trillion and $16.5 trillion.

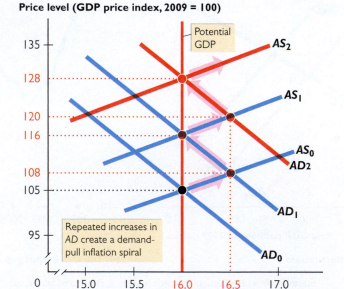

Cost-Push Inflation

Inflation that begins with an increase in cost is called **cost-push inflation**. The two main sources of cost increases are increases in the money wage rate and increases in the money prices of raw materials such as oil.

Cost-push inflation can be kicked off by an increase in costs but the only thing that can sustain it is growth in the quantity of money.

Figure 29.10 illustrates cost-push inflation. The aggregate demand curve is AD_0, the aggregate supply curve is AS_0, and real GDP equals potential GDP. The world price of oil rises, which decreases aggregate supply. The aggregate supply curve shifts leftward to AS_1, the price level rises, and real GDP decreases so there is a *recessionary gap*.

When real GDP decreases, unemployment rises above its natural rate and the Fed increases the quantity of money to restore full employment. Aggregate demand increases and the AD curve shifts rightward to AD_1. Real GDP returns to potential GDP but the price level rises further.

Oil producers now see the prices of everything they buy rising so they raise the price of oil again to restore its new higher relative price. The AS curve now shifts to AS_2, the price level rises again, and real GDP decreases again.

If the Fed responds yet again with an increase in the quantity of money, aggregate demand increases and the AD curve shifts to AD_2. The price level rises even higher and full employment is again restored. A cost-push inflation spiral results.

The combination of a decreasing real GDP and a rising price level is called **stagflation**. You can see that stagflation poses a dilemma for the Fed. If the Fed does not respond when producers raise the oil price, the economy remains below full employment. If the Fed increases the quantity of money to restore full employment, it invites another oil price hike that will call forth yet a further increase in the quantity of money.

Cost-push inflation
An inflation that begins with an increase in cost.

Stagflation
The combination of recession (decreasing real GDP) and inflation (rising price level).

FIGURE 29.10

A Cost-Push Inflation

MyEconLab Animation

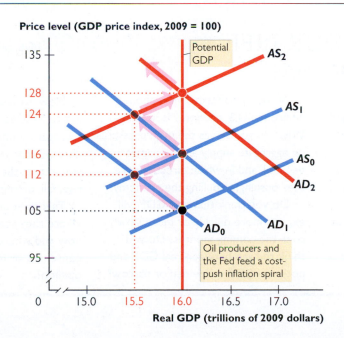

Each time a cost increase occurs, the aggregate supply curve shifts leftward from AS_0 to AS_1 to AS_2, and so on.

Each time real GDP decreases below potential GDP, the Fed increases the quantity of money and the aggregate demand curve shifts rightward from AD_0 to AD_1 to AD_2, and so on.

The price level rises from 105 to 112, 116, 124, 128, and so on.

A cost-push inflation spiral results with real GDP fluctuating between $16 trillion and $15.5 trillion.

■ Deflation and the Great Depression

When a financial crisis hit the United States in October 2008, many people feared a repeat of the dreadful events of the 1930s. From 1929 through 1933, the United States and most of the world experienced deflation and depression—the *Great Depression*. The price level fell by 22 percent and real GDP fell by 31 percent.

The recession of 2008–2009 turned out to be much less severe than the Great Depression. Real GDP fell by less than 4 percent and the price level continued to rise, although at a slower pace. Why was the Great Depression so bad and why was 2008–2009 so mild in comparison? You can answer these questions with what you've learned in this chapter.

During the Great Depression, banks failed and the quantity of money contracted by 25 percent. The Fed stood by and took no action to counteract the collapse of buying power, so aggregate demand also collapsed. Because the money wage rate didn't fall immediately, the decrease in aggregate demand brought a large fall in real GDP. The money wage rate and price level fell eventually, but not until employment and real GDP had shrunk to 75 percent of their 1929 levels.

In contrast, during the 2008 financial crisis, the Fed bailed out troubled financial institutions and doubled the monetary base. The quantity of money kept growing. Also, the government increased its own expenditures, which added to aggregate demand. The combined effects of continued growth in the quantity of money and increased government expenditure limited the fall in aggregate demand and prevented a large decrease in real GDP.

The challenge that now lies ahead is to unwind the monetary and fiscal stimulus as the components of private expenditure—consumption expenditure, investment, and exports—begin to increase and return to more normal levels and so bring an increase in aggregate demand. Too much stimulus will bring an inflationary gap and faster inflation. Too little stimulus will leave a recessionary gap.

You will explore these monetary and fiscal policy actions and their effects in Chapters 32 and 33.

EYE on YOUR LIFE
Using the *AS-AD* Model

MyEconLab Critical Thinking Exercise

Using all the knowledge that you have accumulated over the term, and by watching or reading the current news, try to figure out where the U.S. economy is in its business cycle right now.

First, can you determine if real GDP is currently above, below, or at potential GDP? Second, can you determine if real GDP is expanding or contracting in a recession?

Next, try to form a view about where the U.S. economy is heading. What do you see as the main pressures on aggregate supply and aggregate demand, and in which directions are they pushing or pulling the economy?

Do you think that real GDP will expand more quickly or more slowly over the coming months? Do you think the gap between real GDP and potential GDP will widen or narrow?

How do you expect the labor market to be affected by the changes in aggregate supply and aggregate demand that you are expecting? Do you expect the unemployment rate to rise, fall, or remain constant?

Talk to your friends in class about where they see the U.S. economy right now and where it is heading. Is there a consensus or is there a wide range of opinion?

EYE on the BUSINESS CYCLE

MyEconLab Critical Thinking Exercise

Why Did the U.S. Economy Go into Recession in 2008?

What causes the business cycle and what caused the 2008–2009 recession?

Business Cycle Theory

The mainstream business cycle theory is that potential GDP grows at a steady rate while aggregate demand grows at a fluctuating rate.

Because the money wage rate is slow to change, if aggregate demand grows more quickly than potential GDP, real GDP moves above potential GDP and an inflationary gap emerges. The inflation rate rises and real GDP is pulled back toward potential GDP.

If aggregate demand grows more slowly than potential GDP, real GDP moves below potential GDP and a recessionary gap emerges. The inflation rate slows. Because the money wage rate responds very slowly to the recessionary gap, real GDP does not return to potential GDP until another increase in aggregate demand occurs.

Fluctuations in investment are the main source of fluctuations in aggregate demand. Consumption expenditure responds to changes in income.

A recession can also occur if aggregate supply decreases to bring stagflation. And a recession might occur because both aggregate demand and aggregate supply decrease.

The 2008–2009 Recession

The 2008–2009 recession is an example of a recession caused by a decrease in both aggregate demand and aggregate supply. The figure illustrates these two contributing forces.

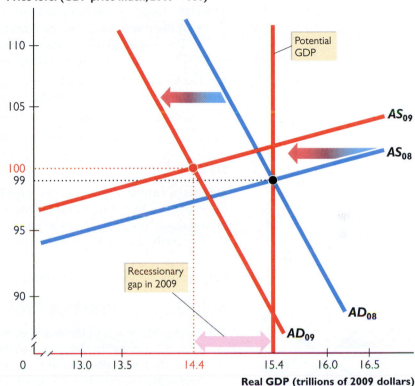

SOURCES OF DATA: Bureau of Economic Analysis and Congressional Budget Office.

At the peak in 2008, real GDP was $15.4 trillion and the price level was 99. In the second quarter of 2009, real GDP had fallen to $14.4 trillion and the price level had risen to 100.

The financial crisis that began in 2007 and intensified in 2008 decreased the supply of loanable funds and investment fell. In particular, construction investment collapsed.

Recession in the global economy decreased the demand for U.S. exports, so this component of aggregate demand also decreased.

The decrease in aggregate demand was moderated by a large injection of spending by the U.S. government, but this move was not enough to stop aggregate demand from decreasing.

We cannot account for the combination of a rise in the price level and a decrease in real GDP with a decrease in aggregate demand alone. Aggregate supply must also have decreased. The rise in oil prices in 2007 and a rise in the money wage rate were the two factors that brought about the decrease in aggregate supply.

MyEconLab Study Plan 29.3
Key Terms Quiz
Solutions Video

 CHECKPOINT 29.3

Explain how trends and fluctuations in aggregate demand and aggregate supply bring economic growth, inflation, and the business cycle.

Practice Problems

The U.S. economy is at full employment when the following events occur:
- A deep recession hits the world economy.
- The world oil price rises by a large amount.
- U.S. businesses expect future profits to fall.

1. Explain the effect of each event separately on aggregate demand and aggregate supply. How will real GDP and the price level change in the short run?

2. Explain the combined effect of these events on real GDP and the price level.

3. Which event, if any, brings stagflation?

In the News

U.S. risks future of low growth, says IMF

International Monetary Fund managing director Christine Lagarde says that a falling labor force participation rate and falling productivity will slow U.S. real GDP growth. IMF economists say business investment will also slow.

Source: *Financial Times*, June 22, 2016

Explain this news report in terms of the *AS-AD* model.

Solutions to Practice Problems

1. A deep recession in the world economy decreases U.S. aggregate demand. The *AD* curve shifts leftward. In the short run, U.S. real GDP decreases and the price level falls (Figure 1). A rise in the world oil price decreases U.S. aggregate supply. The *AS* curve shifts leftward. In the short run, U.S. real GDP decreases and the price level rises (Figure 2). A fall in expected future profits decreases U.S. aggregate demand. The *AD* curve shifts leftward. In the short run, U.S. real GDP decreases and the price level falls (Figure 1).

2. All three events decrease U.S. real GDP (Figures 1 and 2). The deep world recession and the fall in expected future profits decrease the price level (Figure 1). The rise in the world oil price increases the price level (Figure 2). So the combined effect on the price level is ambiguous.

3. Stagflation is a rising price level and a decreasing real GDP together. The rise in the world oil price brings stagflation because it decreases aggregate supply, decreases real GDP, and raises the price level (Figure 2).

Solution to In the News

The news report contains information about likely future developments in U.S. aggregate supply and aggregate demand. A falling labor force participation rate and falling productivity will slow the growth rate of U.S. potential GDP and aggregate supply. A slowdown in business investment will slow the growth rate of aggregate demand. The combination of these changes will slow the growth rate of real GDP. Their effects on the price level depend on whether aggregate supply or aggregate demand slows most.

FIGURE 1

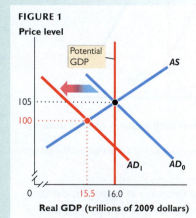

Real GDP (trillions of 2009 dollars)

FIGURE 2

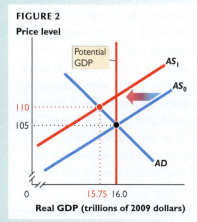

Real GDP (trillions of 2009 dollars)

CHAPTER SUMMARY

Key Points

1. Define and explain the influences on aggregate supply.

- Aggregate supply is the relationship between the quantity of real GDP supplied and the price level when all other influences on production plans remain the same.

- The *AS* curve slopes upward because with a given money wage rate, a rise in the price level lowers the real wage rate, increases the quantity of labor demanded, and increases the quantity of real GDP supplied.

- A change in potential GDP, a change in the money wage rate, or a change in the money price of other resources changes aggregate supply.

2. Define and explain the influences on aggregate demand.

- Aggregate demand is the relationship between the quantity of real GDP demanded and the price level when all other influences on expenditure plans remain the same.

- The *AD* curve slopes downward because a rise in the price level decreases the buying power of money, raises the real interest rate, raises the real price of domestic goods compared with foreign goods, and decreases the quantity of real GDP demanded.

- A change in expected future income, inflation, and profits; a change in fiscal policy and monetary policy; and a change in the foreign exchange rate and foreign real GDP all change aggregate demand—the aggregate demand curve shifts.

3. Explain how trends and fluctuations in aggregate demand and aggregate supply bring economic growth, inflation, and the business cycle.

- Aggregate demand and aggregate supply determine real GDP and the price level in macroeconomic equilibrium, which can occur at full employment or above or below full employment.

- Away from full employment, gradual changes in the money wage rate move real GDP toward potential GDP.

- Economic growth is a persistent increase in potential GDP, and inflation occurs when aggregate demand grows at a faster rate than potential GDP.

- Business cycles occur because aggregate demand and aggregate supply fluctuate.

- Demand-pull and cost-push forces bring inflation and real GDP cycles.

Key Terms

MyEconLab Key Terms Quiz

Aggregate demand, 756
Aggregate supply, 750
Cost-push inflation, 767
Demand-pull inflation, 766

Fiscal policy, 759
Full-employment equilibrium, 763
Inflationary gap, 763
Macroeconomic equilibrium, 762

Monetary policy, 759
Real business cycle, 765
Recessionary gap, 763
Stagflation, 767

CHAPTER CHECKPOINT

Study Plan Problems and Applications

1. As more people in India have access to higher education, explain how potential GDP and aggregate supply will change in the long run.

2. Explain the effect of each of the following events on the quantity of U.S. real GDP demanded and the demand for U.S. real GDP:
   • The world economy goes into a strong expansion.
   • The U.S. price level rises.
   • Congress raises income taxes.

3. The United States is at full employment when the Fed cuts the quantity of money, other things remaining the same. Explain the effect of the cut in the quantity of money on aggregate demand in the short run.

TABLE 1

Price level (GDP price index)	Real GDP demanded	Real GDP supplied
	(billions of 2009 dollars)	
90	900	600
100	850	700
110	800	800
120	750	900
130	700	1,000

4. Table 1 sets out an economy's aggregate demand and aggregate supply schedules. What is the macroeconomic equilibrium? If potential GDP is $600 billion, what is the type of macroeconomic equilibrium? Explain how real GDP and the price level will adjust in the long run.

5. Suppose that the U.S. economy has a recessionary gap and the world economy goes into an expansion. Explain the effect of the expansion on U.S. real GDP and unemployment in the short run.

6. Explain the effect of the Fed's action that increases the quantity of money on the macroeconomic equilibrium in the short run. Explain the adjustment process that returns the economy to full employment.

Use Figure 1 to work Problems **7** to **9**. Initially, the economy is at point B.

7. Some events change aggregate demand from AD_0 to AD_1. Describe two possible events.What is the new equilibrium point? If potential GDP is $1 trillion, describe the type of macroeconomic equilibrium.

FIGURE 1

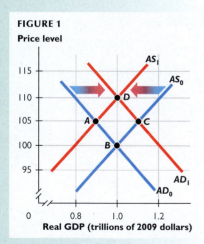

8. Some events change aggregate supply from AS_0 to AS_1. Describe two possible events. What is the new equilibrium point? If potential GDP is $1 trillion, does the economy have an inflationary gap, a recessionary gap, or no gap?

9. Some events change aggregate demand from AD_0 to AD_1 and aggregate supply from AS_0 to AS_1. What is the new macroeconomic equilibrium?

10. **"Brexit" expected to rattle U.S. economy**
    The United Kingdom vote to leave the European Union (known as Brexit) is expected to affect the U.S. economy by driving up the value of the dollar. But it is not thought that Brexit alone will shrink the U.S. economy.
    Source: *The Wall Street Journal*, June 24, 2016

    Explain how a high value of the dollar affects U.S. real GDP and on an *AS-AD* graph show the macroeconomic equilibrium in the U.S. economy with and without the effects of Brexit.

11. Read *Eye on the Business Cycle* on p. 769. What caused the 2008–2009 recession and how do we know that a decrease in aggregate supply played a role?

Instructor Assignable Problems and Applications

MyEconLab Homework, Quiz, or Test if assigned by instructor

1. What, according to the mainstream theory of the business cycle, is the most common source of recession: a decrease in aggregate demand, a decrease in aggregate supply, or both? Which is the most likely component of aggregate demand to start a recession? How does the aggregate demand multiplier influence a recession?

2. Suppose that the United States is at full employment. Explain the effect of each of the following events on aggregate supply:
   - Union wage settlements push the money wage rate up by 10 percent.
   - The price level increases.
   - Potential GDP increases.

3. Suppose that the United States is at full employment. Then the federal government cuts taxes, and all other influences on aggregate demand remain the same. Explain the effect of the tax cut on aggregate demand in the short run.

Use the following information to work Problems **4** and **5**.

Because fluctuations in the world oil price make the U.S. short-run macroeconomic equilibrium fluctuate, someone suggests that the government should vary the tax rate on oil, lowering the tax when the world oil price rises and increasing the tax when the world oil price falls, to stabilize the oil price in the U.S. market.

4. How would such an action influence aggregate demand?

5. How would such an action influence aggregate supply?

6. Table 1 sets out the aggregate demand and aggregate supply schedules in Japan. Potential GDP is 600 trillion yen. What is the short-run macroeconomic equilibrium? Does Japan have an inflationary gap or a recessionary gap and what is its magnitude?

7. Suppose that the world price of oil rises. On an *AS-AD* graph, show the effect of the world oil price rise on U.S. macroeconomic equilibrium in the short run. Explain the adjustment process that restores the economy to full employment.

8. Explain the effects of a global recession on the U.S. macroeconomic equilibrium in the short run. Explain the adjustment process that restores the economy to full employment.

TABLE 1

Price level (GDP price index)	Real GDP demanded	Real GDP supplied
	(trillions of 2005 yen)	
75	600	400
85	550	450
95	500	500
105	450	550
115	400	600
125	350	650
135	300	700

Use the following information to work Problems **9** and **10**.

Brexit means a bumpy road ahead for the U.K. economy
The decision by the U.K. people to leave the European Union has already brought a sharp fall in the value of the pound and is expected to lower business and household spending.

Source: *Financial Times*, June 24, 2016

9. Explain the effects of a fall in the value of the U.K. pound and lower spending by businesses and households on U.K. aggregate demand and aggregate supply.

10. The U.K. economy in 2016 was close to full employment. Use the *AS-AD* model to show the effect on U.K. real GDP of the effects of Brexit described in the news clip.

MyEconLab Chapter 29 Study Plan

Multiple Choice Quiz

1. Aggregate supply increases when _____.

   A. the price level rises
   B. the money wage rate falls
   C. consumption increases
   D. the money price of oil increases

2. When potential GDP increases, _____.

   A. aggregate demand increases
   B. aggregate supply increases
   C. both aggregate demand and aggregate supply increase
   D. the price level rises

3. The quantity of real GDP demanded increases if _____.

   A. the buying power of money increases
   B. the money wage rate rises
   C. the price level falls
   D. the nominal interest rate falls

4. An increase in expected future income increases _____.

   A. consumption expenditure, which increases current aggregate demand
   B. investment, which increases current aggregate supply
   C. the demand for money, which decreases current aggregate demand
   D. future consumption expenditure and has no effect on current aggregate demand

5. Macroeconomic equilibrium occurs when the quantity of real GDP _____ equals the quantity of _____.

   A. demanded; real GDP supplied
   B. demanded; potential GDP
   C. supplied; potential GDP
   D. demanded; real GDP supplied and potential GDP

6. If the economy is at full employment and the Fed increases the quantity of money, _____.

   A. aggregate demand increases, a recessionary gap appears, and the money wage rate starts to rise
   B. aggregate supply increases, the price level starts to fall, and an expansion begins
   C. aggregate demand increases, an inflationary gap appears, and the money wage rate starts to rise
   D. potential GDP and aggregate supply increase together and the price level does not change

7. Over the past decade, the demand for goods produced in China has brought a sustained increase in the demand for China's exports that has outstripped the growth of supply. As a result, China has experienced a _____.

   A. period of stable prices and sustained economic growth
   B. rising price level and demand-pull inflation
   C. rising price level and cost-push inflation
   D. rising price level and a falling real wage rate

Aggregate Expenditure Multiplier

30

When you have completed your study of this chapter, you will be able to

1 Explain how real GDP influences expenditure plans.

2 Explain how real GDP adjusts to achieve equilibrium expenditure.

3 Explain the expenditure multiplier.

4 Derive the *AD* curve from equilibrium expenditure.

MyEconLab Big Picture Video

MyEconLab Concept Video

30.1 EXPENDITURE PLANS AND REAL GDP

When the government spends $1 million on a highway construction project, does that expenditure stimulate consumption expenditure in a multiplier effect? This question lies at the core of this chapter.

To answer the question, we use the *aggregate expenditure model*, a model that explains what determines the quantity of real GDP demanded and changes in that quantity *at a given price level.*

The aggregate expenditure model—also known as the *Keynesian model*—was originally designed to explain what happens in an economy in deep recession when firms can't cut their prices any further but can increase production without raising their prices, so the price level is actually fixed. The severity of the global recession of 2008–2009 gave the model a rebirth and the question of the size of the government expenditure multiplier became a hot issue.

You learned in Chapter 21 (pp. 539–541) that aggregate expenditure equals the sum of consumption expenditure, *C*, investment, *I,* government expenditure on goods and services, *G*, and net exports, *NX*. **Aggregate planned expenditure** is the sum of the spending plans of households, firms, and governments. We divide expenditure plans into autonomous expenditure and induced expenditure. *Autonomous expenditure* does not respond to changes in real GDP and *induced expenditure* does respond to changes in real GDP. We start by looking at induced expenditure and its main component, consumption expenditure.

■ The Consumption Function

The **consumption function** is the relationship between consumption expenditure and disposable income, other things remaining the same. *Disposable income* is aggregate income—GDP—minus net taxes. (Net taxes are taxes paid to the government minus transfer payments received from the government.)

Households must either spend their disposable income on consumption or save it. A decision to spend a dollar on consumption is a decision not to save a dollar. The consumption decision and the saving decision is one decision.

Consumption Plans

For households and the economy as a whole, as disposable income increases, planned consumption expenditure increases. But the increase in planned consumption is less than the increase in disposable income. The table in Figure 30.1 shows a consumption schedule. It lists the consumption expenditure that people plan to undertake at each level of disposable income.

Figure 30.1 shows a consumption function based on the consumption schedule. Along the consumption function, the points labeled *A* through *E* correspond to the columns of the table. For example, when disposable income is $9 trillion at point *D*, consumption expenditure is $8 trillion. Along the consumption function, as disposable income increases, consumption expenditure increases.

At point *A* on the consumption function, consumption expenditure is $2 trillion even though disposable income is zero. This consumption expenditure is called *autonomous consumption,* and it is the amount of consumption expenditure that would take place in the short run even if people had no current income. This consumption expenditure would be financed either by spending past savings or by borrowing.

Aggregate planned expenditure

Planned consumption expenditure plus planned investment, plus planned government expenditure, plus planned exports minus planned imports.

Consumption function

The relationship between consumption expenditure and disposable income, other things remaining the same.

◼ FIGURE 30.1

The Consumption Function   MyEconLab Animation

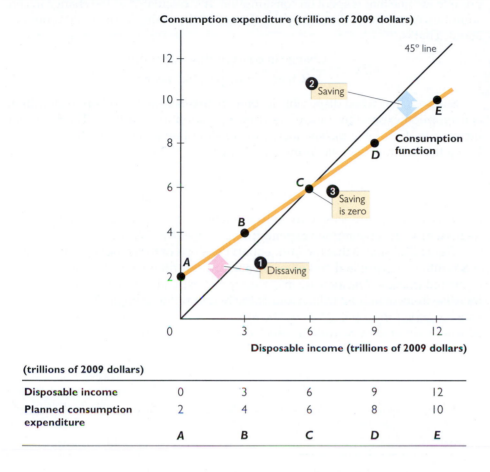

The table shows consumption expenditure (and saving) plans at various levels of disposable income. The figure graphs these data as the consumption function. The figure also shows a 45° line along which consumption expenditure equals disposable income.

❶ When the consumption function is above the 45° line, saving is negative (dissaving occurs).

❷ When the consumption function is below the 45° line, saving is positive.

❸ At the point where the consumption function intersects the 45° line, all disposable income is consumed and saving is zero.

(trillions of 2009 dollars)					
Disposable income	0	3	6	9	12
Planned consumption expenditure	2	4	6	8	10
	A	B	C	D	E

Figure 30.1 also shows a 45° line. Because the scale on the *x*-axis measures disposable income and the scale on the *y*-axis measures consumption expenditure, and because the two scales are equal, along the 45° line consumption expenditure equals disposable income. So the 45° line serves as a reference line for comparing consumption expenditure and disposable income. Between *A* and *C*, consumption expenditure exceeds disposable income; between *C* and *E*, disposable income exceeds consumption expenditure; and at point *C*, consumption expenditure equals disposable income.

You can see saving in Figure 30.1. When consumption expenditure exceeds disposable income (and the consumption function is above the 45° line), saving is negative—called *dissaving*. When consumption expenditure is less than disposable income (the consumption function is below the 45° line), saving is positive. And when consumption expenditure equals disposable income (the consumption function intersects the 45° line), saving is zero.

When consumption expenditure exceeds disposable income, past savings are used to pay for current consumption. Such a situation cannot last forever, but it can and does occur if disposable income falls temporarily.

Marginal Propensity to Consume

Marginal propensity to consume

The fraction of a change in disposable income that is spent on consumption—the change in consumption expenditure divided by the change in disposable income that brought it about.

The **marginal propensity to consume** (*MPC*) is the fraction of a change in disposable income that is spent on consumption. It is calculated as the change in consumption expenditure divided by the change in disposable income that brought it about. That is,

$$MPC = \frac{\text{Change in consumption expenditure}}{\text{Change in disposable income}}.$$

Suppose that when disposable income increases from $6 trillion to $9 trillion, consumption expenditure increases from $6 trillion to $8 trillion. The $3 trillion increase in disposable income increases consumption expenditure by $2 trillion. Using these numbers in the formula to calculate the *MPC*,

$$MPC = \frac{\$2 \text{ trillion}}{\$3 \text{ trillion}} = 0.67.$$

The marginal propensity to consume tells us that when disposable income increases by $1, consumption expenditure increases by 67¢.

Figure 30.2 shows that the *MPC* equals the slope of the consumption function. A $3 trillion increase in disposable income from $6 trillion to $9 trillion is the base of the red triangle. The increase in consumption expenditure that results from this increase in income is $2 trillion and is the height of the triangle. The slope of the consumption function is given by the formula "slope equals rise over run" and is $2 trillion divided by $3 trillion, which equals 0.67—the *MPC*.

■ **FIGURE 30.2**

Marginal Propensity to Consume

The marginal propensity to consume, *MPC*, is equal to the change in consumption expenditure divided by the change in disposable income, other things remaining the same.

The slope of the consumption function measures the *MPC*.

In the figure:

❶ A $3 trillion change in disposable income brings

❷ a $2 trillion change in consumption expenditure, so

❸ the *MPC* equals $2 trillion ÷ $3 trillion = 0.67.

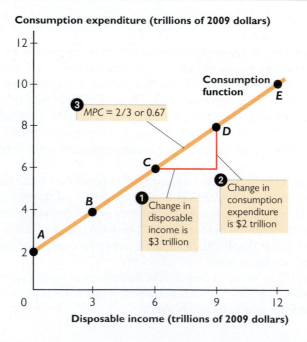

Other Influences on Consumption Expenditure

Consumption plans are influenced by many factors other than disposable income. The more important influences are

- Real interest rate
- Wealth
- Expected future income

Real Interest Rate When the real interest rate falls, consumption expenditure increases (and saving decreases) and when the real interest rate rises, consumption expenditure decreases (and saving increases).

Wealth and Expected Future Income When either wealth or expected future income decreases, consumption expenditure also decreases and when wealth or expected future income increases, consumption expenditure also increases.

Figure 30.3 shows the effects of these influences on the consumption function. When the real interest rate falls or when wealth or expected future income increases, the consumption function shifts upward from CF_0 to CF_1. Such a shift occurs during the expansion phase of the business cycle if a stock market boom increases wealth and expected future income increases.

When the real interest rate rises, or when wealth or expected future income decreases, the consumption function shifts downward from CF_0 to CF_2. Such a shift occurs during a recession if a stock market crash decreases wealth and expected future income decreases.

■ **FIGURE 30.3**

Shifts in the Consumption Function   MyEconLab Animation

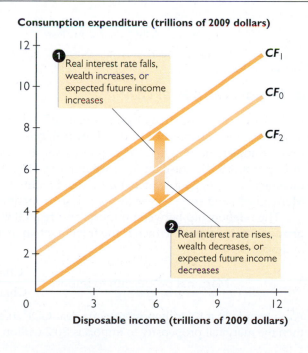

1. A fall in the real interest rate or an increase in either wealth or expected future income increases consumption expenditure and shifts the consumption function upward from CF_0 to CF_1.

2. A rise in the real interest rate or a decrease in either wealth or expected future income decreases consumption expenditure and shifts the consumption function downward from CF_0 to CF_2.

EYE on the U.S. ECONOMY
The U.S. Consumption Function

Each dot in the figure represents consumption expenditure and disposable income in the United States for a year between 1960 and 2015 (some labeled).

The lines labeled CF_{60} and CF_{15} are estimates of the U.S. consumption function in 1960 and 2015, respectively.

The slope of these consumption functions—the marginal propensity to consume—is 0.87, which means that a $1 increase in disposable income brings an 87¢ increase in consumption expenditure.

The consumption function shifted upward from 1960 to 2015—autonomous consumption increased—because as economic growth brought higher expected future income and greater wealth, people chose to increase consumption expenditure from a given disposable income.

During the recession of 2009, the consumption function temporarily shifted downward as a fall in house prices lowered wealth and encouraged people to save more.

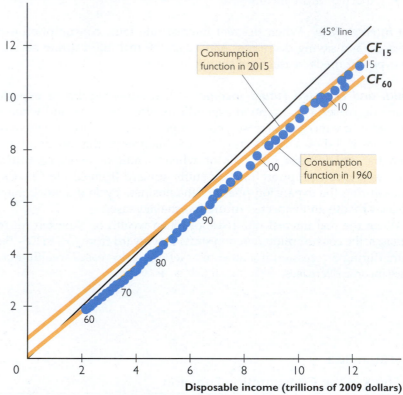

SOURCE OF DATA: Bureau of Economic Analysis.

■ Imports and Real GDP

Imports are the other major component of induced expenditure. Many factors influence U.S. imports, but in the short run, one factor dominates: U.S. real GDP. Other things remaining the same, an increase in U.S. real GDP brings an increase in U.S. imports. Because an increase in real GDP is also an increase in income, as incomes increase, people increase their expenditures on most goods and services. Many goods and services are imported, so as incomes increase imports increase.

The relationship between imports and real GDP is described by the **marginal propensity to import**, which is the fraction of an increase in real GDP that is spent on imports.

Marginal propensity to import
The fraction of an increase in real GDP that is spent on imports—the change in imports divided by the change in real GDP.

$$\text{Marginal propensity to import} = \frac{\text{Change in imports}}{\text{Change in real GDP}}.$$

For example, if a $1 trillion increase in real GDP increases imports by $0.2 trillion, then the marginal propensity to import is $0.2 trillion ÷ $1 trillion, which is 0.2.

CHECKPOINT 30.1

MyEconLab Study Plan 30.1
Key Terms Quiz
Solutions Video

Explain how real GDP influences expenditure plans.

Practice Problems

1. Suppose that the marginal propensity to consume is 0.8. If disposable income increases by $0.5 trillion, by how much will consumption expenditure change?

2. Explain how each of the following events influences the U.S. consumption function:
   • The marginal propensity to consume decreases.
   • U.S. autonomous consumption decreases.
   • Americans expect an increase in future income.

3. Figure 1 shows the consumption function. What is the marginal propensity to consume, and what is autonomous consumption?

In the News

Spending rises by more than personal income
Personal disposable income increased $68.6 billion in April and $33.9 billion in May. Personal consumption expenditures increased $141.2 in April and $53.5 billion in May.

Source: Bureau of Economic Analysis News Release, June 29, 2016

How can consumers increase spending by more than the increase in personal income?

Solutions to Practice Problems

1. Consumption expenditure will increase by $0.4 trillion, which is 0.8 multiplied by the change in disposable income of $0.5 trillion.

2. The marginal propensity to consume equals the slope of the consumption function. So when the marginal propensity to consume decreases, the consumption function becomes flatter.
   Autonomous consumption is the y-axis intercept of the consumption function. So when autonomous expenditure decreases, the consumption function shifts downward.
   When expected future income increases, current consumption expenditure increases and the consumption function shifts upward.

3. When disposable income increases by $100 billion, consumption expenditure increases by $80 billion. The *MPC* is $80 billion ÷ $100 billion = 0.8.
   Autonomous consumption (consumption expenditure that is independent of disposable income) equals the y-axis intercept and is $80 billion (Figure 2).

Solution to In the News

Other things remaining the same, a rise in personal income brings a smaller rise in consumption expenditure in a movement along the consumption function. When consumption expenditure rises by more than the rise in personal income, the consumption function has shifted upward. Autonomous consumption expenditure increased as households spent part of their past savings or increased their debt and spent part of their expected future income.

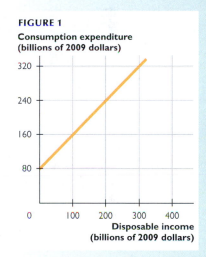

FIGURE 1
Consumption expenditure
(billions of 2009 dollars)

Disposable income
(billions of 2009 dollars)

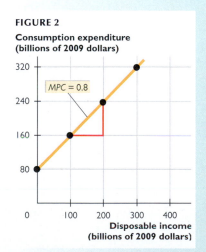

FIGURE 2
Consumption expenditure
(billions of 2009 dollars)

MPC = 0.8

Disposable income
(billions of 2009 dollars)

MyEconLab Concept Video

30.2 EQUILIBRIUM EXPENDITURE

You are now going to discover how, with a fixed price level, aggregate expenditure plans interact to determine real GDP. We will study the relationship between aggregate planned expenditure and real GDP; and we'll study the forces that make aggregate planned expenditure and actual expenditure equal.

But first we'll return to the distinction between *induced* expenditure and *autonomous* expenditure.

■ Induced Expenditure and Autonomous Expenditure

Aggregate planned expenditure is the sum of *induced* expenditure and *autonomous* expenditure. *Induced* expenditure equals consumption expenditure minus imports. You've seen that consumption expenditure increases when disposable income increases. But disposable income equals aggregate income—real GDP—minus net taxes. So disposable income and consumption expenditure increase when real GDP increases. You've also seen that imports increase when real GDP increases. An increase in real GDP brings a larger increase in consumption expenditure than in imports, so induced expenditure—consumption expenditure minus imports—increases as real GDP increases.

Autonomous expenditure—expenditure that does not respond directly to changes in real GDP—consists of investment, government expenditure on goods and services, exports, and autonomous consumption expenditure. These items of aggregate expenditure do change but in response to influences other than real GDP. For example, investment responds to the real interest rate and expected profit. Government expenditure on goods and services depends on the government's policy priorities. And exports depend on global demand for U.S.-produced goods and services.

We combine induced expenditure plans and autonomous expenditure to determine aggregate planned expenditure and equilibrium real GDP.

■ Aggregate Planned Expenditure and Real GDP

An aggregate expenditure schedule and an aggregate expenditure curve describe the relationship between aggregate planned expenditure and real GDP. The table in Figure 30.4 sets out an aggregate expenditure schedule. The columns are the components of aggregate expenditure, *C*, *I*, *G*, *X*, and *M*, and aggregate planned expenditure, *AE*, equals $C + I + G + X - M$.

Figure 30.4 plots an aggregate expenditure curve. The aggregate expenditure curve is the red line *AE*. Points *A* through *F* on that curve correspond to the rows of the table. The *AE* curve is a graph of aggregate planned expenditure (the last column) plotted against real GDP (the first column).

The horizontal lines in Figure 30.4 show the components of autonomous expenditure *I*, *G*, and *X*. The line labeled $C + I + G + X$ adds consumption expenditure to these components of autonomous expenditure. Aggregate expenditure is expenditure on U.S.-produced goods and services, but the line $C + I + G + X$ includes expenditure on imports. So the *AE* curve is the $C + I + G + X$ line minus imports. For example, if a student buys a Honda motorbike made in Japan, the student's expenditure is part of *C*, but it is not an expenditure on a U.S.-produced good. To find the expenditure on U.S.-produced goods, we subtract the value of the imported motorbike.

■ **FIGURE 30.4**

Aggregate Expenditure

MyEconLab Animation

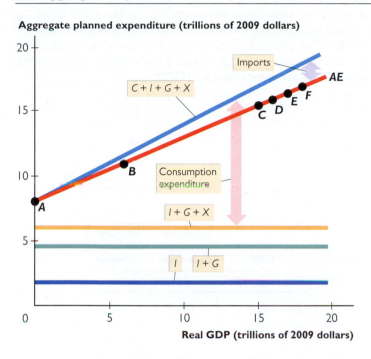

The aggregate expenditure schedule shows the relationship between aggregate planned expenditure and real GDP. For example, in row *B* of the table, when real GDP is $6 trillion, aggregate planned expenditure is $11.0 trillion ($5.60 + $1.75 + $2.75 + $1.50 − $0.60). As real GDP increases, aggregate planned expenditure increases.

This relationship is graphed as the aggregate expenditure curve *AE*. The components of aggregate expenditure that increase with real GDP are consumption expenditure and imports.

The other components—investment, government expenditure, and exports—do not vary with real GDP.

	Real GDP (Y)	Consumption expenditure (C)	Investment (I)	Government expenditure (G)	Exports (X)	Imports (M)	Aggregate planned expenditure (AE = C + I + G + X − M)
				(trillions of 2009 dollars)			
A	0	2.00	1.75	2.75	1.50	0	8.00
B	6.00	5.60	1.75	2.75	1.50	0.60	11.00
C	15.00	11.00	1.75	2.75	1.50	1.50	15.50
D	16.00	11.60	1.75	2.75	1.50	1.60	16.00
E	17.00	12.20	1.75	2.75	1.50	1.70	16.50
F	18.00	12.80	1.75	2.75	1.50	1.80	17.00

Figure 30.4 shows that aggregate planned expenditure increases as real GDP increases. But notice that for each $1 increase in real GDP, aggregate planned expenditure increases by less than $1. For example, when real GDP increases by $1 trillion, from $15 trillion in row *C* to $16 trillion in row *D* of the table, aggregate planned expenditure increases by $0.5 trillion, from $15.5 trillion to $16.0 trillion. This feature of the *AE* curve is important and plays a big role in determining equilibrium expenditure and the effect of a change in autonomous expenditure.

The *AE* curve summarizes the relationship between aggregate planned expenditure and real GDP. But what determines the point on the *AE* curve at which the economy operates? What determines actual aggregate expenditure?

■ Equilibrium Expenditure

Equilibrium expenditure
The level of aggregate expenditure that occurs when aggregate *planned* expenditure equals real GDP.

Equilibrium expenditure occurs when aggregate *planned* expenditure equals real GDP. In Figure 30.5(a) aggregate planned expenditure equals real GDP at all the points on the 45° line. Equilibrium occurs where the *AE* curve intersects the 45° line at point *D* with real GDP at $16 trillion. If real GDP is less than $16 trillion, aggregate planned expenditure exceeds real GDP; and if real GDP exceeds $16 trillion, aggregate planned expenditure is less than real GDP.

■ **FIGURE 30.5**

Equilibrium Expenditure

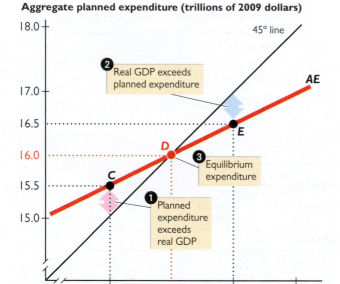

(a) Equilibrium expenditure

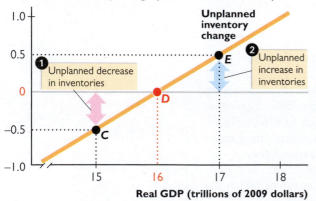

(b) Unplanned inventory change

MyEconLab Animation

	Real GDP	Aggregate planned expenditure	Unplanned inventory change
		(trillions of 2009 dollars)	
C	15.0	15.5	−0.5
D	**16.0**	**16.0**	**0.0**
E	17.0	16.5	0.5

The table shows expenditure plans and unplanned changes in inventories at different levels of real GDP. Part (a) of the figure illustrates equilibrium expenditure, and part (b) shows the unplanned inventory changes that bring changes in real GDP.

❶ When aggregate planned expenditure exceeds real GDP, an unplanned decrease in inventories occurs. Firms increase production, and real GDP increases.

❷ When real GDP exceeds aggregate planned expenditure, an unplanned increase in inventories occurs. Firms decrease production, and real GDP decreases.

❸ When aggregate planned expenditure equals real GDP, there are no unplanned inventory changes and real GDP remains at its equilibrium level.

■ Convergence to Equilibrium

At equilibrium expenditure, production plans and spending plans agree, and there is no reason for production or spending to change. But when aggregate planned expenditure and actual aggregate expenditure are unequal, production plans and spending plans are misaligned, and a process of convergence toward equilibrium expenditure occurs. Throughout this convergence process, real GDP adjusts.

What are the forces that move aggregate expenditure toward equilibrium? To answer this question, we look at a situation in which aggregate expenditure is away from equilibrium.

Convergence from Below Equilibrium

Suppose that in Figure 30.5, real GDP is $15 trillion. At this level of real GDP, actual aggregate expenditure is also $15 trillion, but aggregate planned expenditure is $15.5 trillion—point C in Figure 30.5(a). Aggregate planned expenditure exceeds actual expenditure. When people spend $15.5 trillion and firms produce goods and services worth $15 trillion, firms' inventories decrease by $0.5 trillion—point C in Figure 30.5(b). This change in inventories is *unplanned*. Because the change in inventories is part of investment, the decrease in inventories decreases actual investment. So actual investment is $0.5 trillion less than planned investment.

Real GDP doesn't remain at $15 trillion for long. Firms have inventory targets based on their sales, and when inventories fall below target, firms increase production. Firms keep increasing production as long as unplanned decreases in inventories occur.

Eventually firms will have increased production by $1 trillion, so real GDP will have increased to $16 trillion. At this real GDP, aggregate planned expenditure rises to $16 trillion—point D in Figure 30.5(a). With aggregate planned expenditure equal to actual expenditure, the unplanned change in inventories is zero and firms hold production constant. The economy has converged on equilibrium expenditure.

Convergence from Above Equilibrium

Now suppose that in Figure 30.5, real GDP is $17 trillion. Actual aggregate expenditure is also $17 trillion, but aggregate planned expenditure is $16.5 trillion—point E in Figure 30.5(a). Actual expenditure exceeds planned expenditure and firms' inventories pile up by an unwanted $0.5 trillion—point E in Figure 30.5(b).

Real GDP doesn't remain at $17 trillion. Firms now want to lower their inventories, so they decrease production.

Eventually firms will have decreased production by $1 trillion, so real GDP will have decreased to $16 trillion. At this real GDP, aggregate planned expenditure falls to $16 trillion—point D in Figure 30.5(a). With aggregate planned expenditure equal to actual expenditure, the unplanned change in inventories is zero and firms hold production constant. The economy has converged on equilibrium expenditure.

Starting from below equilibrium, unplanned decreases in inventories induce firms to increase production; starting from above equilibrium, unplanned increases in inventories induce firms to decrease production. In both cases, production is pulled toward the equilibrium level at which there are no unplanned inventory changes.

EYE on the PAST

Say's Law and Keynes' Principle of Effective Demand

During the Industrial Revolution, which began around 1760 and lasted for 70 years, technological change was rapid. People have talked about the "new economy" of the 1990s, but the 1990s was just another phase of a process that began in the truly new economy of the late 1700s. The pace of change in economic life during those years was unprecedented. Never before had old jobs been destroyed and new jobs created on such a scale. In this environment of rapid economic change, people began to wonder whether the economy could create enough jobs and a high enough level of demand to ensure that people would buy all the things that the new industrial economy could produce.

A French economist, Jean-Baptiste Say, provided the assurance that people were looking for. Born in 1767 (he was 9 years old when Adam Smith's *Wealth of Nations* was published—see Chapter 1, p. 18), Say suffered the wrath of Napoleon for his conservative call for smaller and leaner government and was the most famous economist of his era. His book *A Treatise on Political Economy (Traité d'économie politique),* published in 1803, became the best-selling university economics textbook in both Europe and America.

In this book, Say reasoned that *supply creates its own demand*—an idea that came to be called *Say's Law.*

You've seen Say's Law at work in the full-employment economy. The real wage rate adjusts to ensure that the quantity of labor demanded equals the quantity of labor supplied and real

GDP equals potential GDP. The real interest rate adjusts to ensure that the quantity of investment that firms plan equals the quantity of saving. Because saving equals income minus consumption expenditure, the equilibrium real interest rate ensures that consumption expenditure plus investment exactly equals potential GDP.

Say's Law came under attack at various times during the nineteenth century. But it came under an onslaught during the Great Depression of the 1930s. With a quarter of the labor force unemployed and real GDP at around three quarters of potential GDP, it seemed like a stretch to argue that supply creates its own demand. But there was no simple principle or slogan with which to replace Say's Law.

In the midst of the Great Depression, in 1936, a British economist, John Maynard Keynes, provided the catch phrase that the world was looking for: *effective demand.*

Born in England in 1883, Keynes was one of the outstanding people of the twentieth century. He was a prolific writer on economic issues, represented Britain at the Versailles peace conference at the end of World War I, and played a prominent role in creating the International Monetary Fund, which monitors the global macroeconomy today.

Keynes revolutionized macroeconomic thinking by turning Say's Law on its head. In Keynes' view, supply does *not* create its own demand, and *effective demand* determines real GDP. If businesses spend less on new capital than the amount that people save,

equilibrium expenditure will be less than potential GDP. Prices and wages are sticky, and resources can become unemployed and remain unemployed indefinitely.

The aggregate expenditure model in this chapter is the modern distillation of Keynes' idea.

Jean-Baptiste Say

John Maynard Keynes

CHECKPOINT 30.2

Explain how real GDP adjusts to achieve equilibrium expenditure.

Practice Problems

Table 1 gives real GDP (*Y*) and its components in billions of dollars.

1. Calculate aggregate planned expenditure when real GDP is $200 billion and when real GDP is $600 billion.

2. Calculate equilibrium expenditure.

3. If real GDP is $200 billion, explain the process that moves the economy toward equilibrium expenditure.

4. If real GDP is $600 billion, explain the process that moves the economy toward equilibrium expenditure.

TABLE 1

	A	B	C	D	E	F	G
1		Y	C	I	G	X	M
2	A	100	110	50	60	60	15
3	B	200	170	50	60	60	30
4	C	300	230	50	60	60	45
5	D	400	290	50	60	60	60
6	E	500	350	50	60	60	75
7	F	600	410	50	60	60	90

In the News

Retailers scale back after inventory buildups

Big retailers are lowering inventories built up earlier this year. Economists say the buildup of inventories increased economic growth and a pullback by retailers and manufacturers may slow economic growth for the rest of the year.

Source: *The Wall Street Journal*, September 25, 2015

Explain why a fall in inventories might slow economic growth and a buildup of inventories might boost economic growth.

Solutions to Practice Problems

1. Aggregate planned expenditure equals $C + I + G + X - M$. When real GDP is $200 billion (row *B* of Table 1), aggregate planned expenditure is $310 billion. When real GDP is $600 billion (row *F*), aggregate planned expenditure is $490 billion.

2. Equilibrium expenditure occurs when aggregate planned expenditure equals real GDP. Equilibrium expenditure is $400 billion (row *D* of Table 1).

3. If real GDP is $200 billion, aggregate planned expenditure is $310 billion, which exceeds real GDP. Firms' inventories decrease by $110 billion. Firms' expenditure plans are not fulfilled, so they increase production to restore their inventories. Real GDP increases. As long as aggregate planned expenditure exceeds real GDP, firms increase production and real GDP increases.

4. If real GDP is $600 billion, aggregate planned expenditure is $490 billion, which is less than real GDP. Firms' inventories increase by $110 billion. Firms cut production and try to reduce their inventories. Real GDP decreases. As long as aggregate planned expenditure is less than real GDP, firms' inventories will increase. Firms will cut production as they try to reduce their inventories to their target level. Real GDP decreases.

Solution to In the News

When firms reduce their target level of inventories, planned investment falls and equilibrium expenditure and real GDP decrease. Economic growth will slow. When firms plan to build up their inventories, the reverse occurs. Equilibrium expenditure and real GDP increase and economic growth might pick up.

Multiplier
The amount by which a change in any component of autonomous expenditure is magnified or multiplied to determine the change in equilibrium expenditure and real GDP that it generates.

30.3 EXPENDITURE MULTIPLIERS

When autonomous expenditure (investment, government expenditure, or exports) increases, aggregate expenditure and real GDP also increase. A **multiplier** determines the amount by which a change in any component of autonomous expenditure is magnified or multiplied to determine the change in equilibrium expenditure and real GDP that it generates.

■ The Basic Idea of the Multiplier

An increase in investment increases real GDP, which increases disposable income and consumption expenditure. The increase in consumption expenditure adds to the increase in investment and a multiplier determines the magnitude of the resulting increase in aggregate expenditure.

Figure 30.6 illustrates the multiplier. The initial aggregate expenditure schedule graphs as AE_0. Equilibrium expenditure and real GDP are $16 trillion. You can see this equilibrium in row B of the table and where the curve AE_0 intersects the 45° line at point B in the figure.

Suppose that investment increases by $0.5 trillion. This increase in investment increases aggregate planned expenditure by $0.5 trillion at each level of real GDP. The new AE curve is AE_1. The new equilibrium expenditure (row D') occurs where AE_1 intersects the 45° line and is $18 trillion (point D'). At this real GDP, aggregate planned expenditure equals real GDP. The increase in equilibrium expenditure ($2 trillion) is *larger* than the increase in investment ($0.5 trillion).

■ FIGURE 30.6

The Multiplier

Real GDP (Y)	Aggregate planned expenditure				
	Original (AE₀)		New (AE₁)		
	(trillions of 2009 dollars)				
15.00	A	15.25	A'	15.75
16.00	**B**	**16.00**	**B'**	16.50
17.00	C	16.75	C'	17.25
18.00	**D**	17.50	**D'**	**18.00**
19.00	E	18.25	E'	18.75

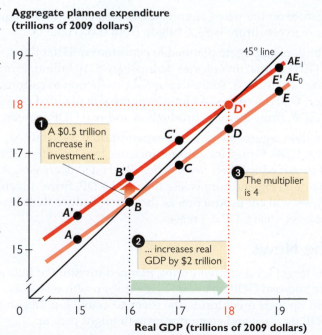

① A $0.5 trillion increase in investment shifts the AE curve upward by $0.5 trillion from AE_0 to AE_1.

② Equilibrium expenditure increases by $2 trillion, from $16 trillion to $18 trillion.

③ The increase in equilibrium expenditure is 4 times the increase in autonomous expenditure, so the multiplier is 4.

■ The Size of the Multiplier

The multiplier is the amount by which a change in autonomous expenditure is multiplied to determine the change in equilibrium expenditure that it generates. To calculate the multiplier, we divide the change in equilibrium expenditure by the change in autonomous expenditure that generated it. That is,

$$\text{Multiplier} = \frac{\text{Change in equilibrium expenditure}}{\text{Change in autonomous expenditure}}.$$

The change in equilibrium expenditure also equals the change in real GDP, which we'll call ΔY. In Figure 30.6, the change in autonomous expenditure is a change in investment, which we'll call ΔI. The multiplier is

$$\text{Multiplier} = \frac{\Delta Y}{\Delta I}.$$

In Figure 30.6, equilibrium expenditure increases by \$2 trillion ($\Delta Y = \$2$ trillion) and investment increases by \$0.5 trillion ($\Delta I = \$0.5$ trillion), so

$$\text{Multiplier} = \frac{\Delta Y}{\Delta I} = \frac{\$2 \text{ trillion}}{\$0.5 \text{ trillion}} = 4.$$

The multiplier is 4—real GDP changes by 4 times the change in investment.

Why is the multiplier greater than 1? It is because an increase in autonomous expenditure induces further increases in aggregate expenditure—induced expenditure increases. If the State of California spends \$10 million on a new highway, aggregate expenditure and real GDP immediately increase by \$10 million. Highway construction workers now have more income, and they spend part of it on cars, vacations, and other goods and services. Real GDP now increases by the initial \$10 million plus the extra consumption expenditure. The producers of cars, vacations, and other goods now have increased incomes, and they in turn spend part of the increase on consumption goods and services. Additional income induces additional expenditure, which creates additional income.

■ The Multiplier and the *MPC*

Ignoring imports and income taxes, the magnitude of the multiplier depends only on the marginal propensity to consume. To see why, let's do a calculation. The change in real GDP (ΔY) equals the change in consumption expenditure (ΔC) plus the change in investment. (ΔI) That is,

$$\Delta Y = \Delta C + \Delta I.$$

But with no income taxes, the change in consumption expenditure is determined by the change in real GDP and the marginal propensity to consume. It is

$$\Delta C = MPC \times \Delta Y.$$

Now substitute $MPC \times \Delta Y$ for ΔC in the previous equation:

$$\Delta Y = MPC \times \Delta Y + \Delta I.$$

Now solve for ΔY as

$$(1 - MPC) \times \Delta Y = \Delta I,$$

and rearrange the equation:

$$\Delta Y = \frac{1}{(1 - MPC)} \Delta I.$$

Finally, divide both sides of the equation by ΔI to give

$$\text{Multiplier} = \frac{\Delta Y}{\Delta I} = \frac{1}{(1 - MPC)}.$$

In Figure 30.6, the MPC is 0.75. So if we use this value of MPC,

$$\text{Multiplier} = \frac{\Delta Y}{\Delta I} = \frac{1}{(1 - 0.75)} = \frac{1}{0.25} = 4.$$

The greater the marginal propensity to consume, the larger is the multiplier. For example, with a marginal propensity to consume of 0.9, the multiplier would be 10. Let's now look at the influence of imports and income taxes.

■ The Multiplier, Imports, and Income Taxes

The size of the multiplier depends on imports and income taxes, both of which make the multiplier smaller.

When an increase in investment increases real GDP and consumption expenditure, part of the increase in expenditure is on imports, not U.S.-produced goods and services. Only expenditure on U.S.-produced goods and services increases U.S. real GDP. The larger the marginal propensity to import, the smaller is the multiplier.

When an increase in investment increases real GDP, income tax payments increase, so disposable income increases by less than the increase in real GDP and consumption expenditure increases by less than it would if income tax payments had not changed. The marginal tax rate determines the extent to which income tax payments change when real GDP changes. The **marginal tax rate** is the fraction of a change in real GDP that is paid in income taxes. The larger the marginal tax rate, the smaller are the changes in disposable income and real GDP that result from a given change in autonomous expenditure.

Marginal tax rate
The fraction of a change in real GDP that is paid in income taxes—the change in tax payments divided by the change in real GDP.

The marginal propensity to import and the marginal tax rate together with the marginal propensity to consume determine the multiplier, and their combined influence determines the slope of the AE curve. The general formula for the multiplier is

$$\text{Multiplier} = \frac{\Delta Y}{\Delta I} = \frac{1}{(1 - \text{Slope of } AE \text{ curve})}.$$

Figure 30.7 compares two situations. In Figure 30.7(a), there are no imports and no income taxes. The slope of the AE curve equals MPC, which is 0.75, so the multiplier is 4 (as we calculated above). In Figure 30.7(b), imports and income taxes decrease the slope of the AE curve to 0.5. In this case,

$$\text{Multiplier} = \frac{\Delta Y}{\Delta I} = \frac{1}{(1 - 0.5)} = 2.$$

Over time, the value of the multiplier changes as the marginal tax rate, the marginal propensity to consume, and the marginal propensity to import change. These ongoing changes make the multiplier hard to predict.

MyEconLab Animation

FIGURE 30.7

The Multiplier and the Slope of the *AE* Curve

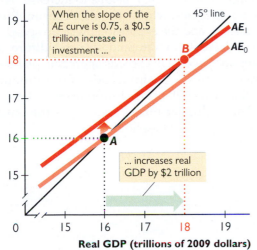

Aggregate planned expenditure
(trillions of 2009 dollars)

When the slope of the *AE* curve is 0.75, a $0.5 trillion increase in investment …

… increases real GDP by $2 trillion

(a) Multiplier is 4

Real GDP (trillions of 2009 dollars)

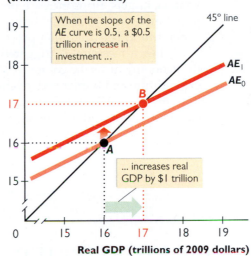

Aggregate planned expenditure
(trillions of 2009 dollars)

When the slope of the *AE* curve is 0.5, a $0.5 trillion increase in investment …

… increases real GDP by $1 trillion

(b) Multiplier is 2

Real GDP (trillions of 2009 dollars)

In part (a), with no imports and no income taxes, the slope of the *AE* curve equals the marginal propensity to consume, which in this example is 0.75. The multiplier is 4.

In part (b), with imports and income taxes, the slope of the *AE* curve is less than the marginal propensity to consume. In this example, the slope of the *AE* curve is 0.5 and the multiplier is 2.

EYE on YOUR LIFE

Looking for Multipliers

MyEconLab Critical Thinking Exercise

You can see multipliers in your daily life if you look in the right places and in the right way.

Look for an event in your home city or state that brings new economic activity. It might be a major construction project that is going on near your home or school. It might be a major sporting event that occurs infrequently and brings a large number of people to a city. Or it might be a major new business that moves into an area or expands its activity level.

What supplies do you see being delivered to the site, event, or new business? How many people do you estimate have jobs at this new activity? Where do the supplies and the workers come from?

This new economic activity sets off a multiplier process. What are the first round multiplier effects? Whose incomes are higher because of the purchase of these supplies and the expenditure of the workers hired by the project?

Where do the workers buy their coffee and lunch? Do their purchases create new jobs for students and others in local coffee shops and fast-food outlets?

Where do the workers and suppliers spend the rest of their incomes?

Now think about the second round and subsequent round effects. Where do the students hired by coffee shops spend their incomes and what additional jobs do those expenditures create?

The process goes on and on.

■ Business-Cycle Turning Points

When an expansion is triggered by an increase in autonomous expenditure, as the economy turns the corner into expansion, aggregate planned expenditure exceeds real GDP. Firms see their inventories taking an unplanned dive. To meet their inventory targets, firms increase production, and real GDP begins to increase. This initial increase in real GDP brings higher incomes, which stimulate consumption expenditure. The multiplier process kicks in, and the expansion picks up speed.

When a recession is triggered by a decrease in autonomous expenditure, as the economy turns the corner into recession, real GDP exceeds aggregate planned expenditure and unplanned inventories pile up. To cut inventories, firms produce less, and real GDP falls. This initial fall in real GDP brings lower incomes. People cut their consumption expenditure. The multiplier process reinforces the initial cut in autonomous expenditure, and the recession takes hold.

EYE on the MULTIPLIER

MyEconLab Critical Thinking Exercise

How Big Is the Government Expenditure Multiplier?

Christina Romer, former Chair of the President's Council of Economic Advisers, has estimated the government expenditure multiplier to be 1.6. This number led administration economists to predict that the stimulus plan that increased government expenditure would prevent the unemployment rate from rising much above 8 percent. This prediction turned out to be optimistic and one reason might be that the multiplier assumption is also too optimistic.

Robert Barro, a leading macroeconomist at Harvard University, has studied the effects of very large increases in government expenditure during wars. He finds that the multiplier is only 0.8, which means that real GDP increases by *less than* the increase in government expenditure. The reason is that some private expenditure, mainly investment, gets "crowded out" and real GDP falls.

John Taylor of Stanford University, another leading macroeconomist, agrees with Barro that the government expenditure multiplier is less than 1. He says that crowding out gets more severe as time passes, so the multiplier gets smaller after two years and smaller still after three years.

A big multiplier can occur only if there is substantial slack in the economy—when the recessionary gap is large.

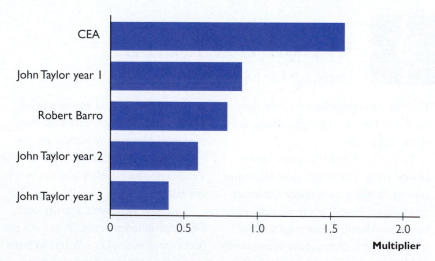

SOURCES OF DATA: Council of Economic Advisers (CEA), Christina Romer and Jared Bernstein, "The Job Impact of the American Recovery and Reinvestment Plan," January 2009; Robert J. Barro, "Government Spending Is No Free Lunch," *The Wall Street Journal*, January 22, 2009; John F. Cogan, Tobias Cwik, John B. Taylor, Volker Wieland, "New Keynesian versus Old Keynesian Government Spending Multipliers," February 2009.

CHECKPOINT 30.3

MyEconLab Study Plan 30.3
Key Terms Quiz
Solutions Video

Explain the expenditure multiplier.

Practice Problems

An economy has no imports and no income taxes, *MPC* is 0.80, and real GDP is $150 billion. Businesses increase investment by $5 billion. Use this information to answer Problems **1** and **2**.

1. Calculate the multiplier and the change in real GDP.

2. Calculate the new level of real GDP and explain why real GDP increases by more than $5 billion.

3. In an economy with no imports and no income taxes, an increase in autonomous expenditure of $2 trillion increases equilibrium expenditure by $8 trillion. Calculate the multiplier and the marginal propensity to consume. What happens to the multiplier if an income tax is introduced?

In the News

Infrastructure spending as a catalyst of growth
Government infrastructure spending has a large multiplier. Expenditure on construction projects goes directly back into the economy through wages. And improved infrastructure boosts productivity and economic growth.
Source: European Bank for Reconstruction and Development, August 5, 2015

Explain what determines the size of the multiplier effect of infrastructure spending.

Solutions to Practice Problems

1. The multiplier equals $1/(1 - MPC)$. *MPC* is 0.8, so the multiplier is 5.
    Real GDP increases by $25 billion. The increase in investment increases real GDP by the multiplier (5) times the change in investment ($5 billion).

2. Real GDP increases from $150 billion to $175 billion. Real GDP increases by more than $5 billion because the increase in investment induces an increase in consumption expenditure.

3. The multiplier is the increase in equilibrium expenditure ($8 trillion) divided by the increase in autonomous expenditure ($2 trillion). The multiplier is 4.

    The marginal propensity to consume is 0.75.
    The multiplier is $1/(1 - MPC)$. So $4 = 1/(1 - MPC)$, and *MPC* is 0.75.

    If the government introduces an income tax, the slope of the *AE* curve becomes smaller and the multiplier becomes smaller.

Solution to In the News

Expenditure on infrastructure projects of $1 billion will increase real GDP by more than $1 billion—a multiplier effect—because when a new project begins, jobs are created and wage payments increase. Workers spend part of the higher incomes on consumption, which creates more jobs. These workers earn an income and spend part of it on consumption. The size of the expenditure multiplier depends on the slope of the *AE* curve, which in turn depends on the *MPC*, the marginal propensity to import, and the marginal tax rate.

30.4 THE *AD* CURVE AND EQUILIBRIUM EXPENDITURE

In this chapter, we've studied the aggregate expenditure model, in which firms change production when sales and inventories change but they don't change their prices. The aggregate expenditure model determines equilibrium expenditure and real GDP at a given price level. In Chapter 29, we studied the simultaneous determination of real GDP and the price level using the *AS-AD* model. The aggregate demand curve and equilibrium expenditure are related, and this section shows you how.

■ Deriving the *AD* Curve from Equilibrium Expenditure

The *AE* curve is the relationship between aggregate planned expenditure and real GDP when all other influences on expenditure plans remain the same. A movement along the *AE* curve arises from a change in real GDP.

The *AD* curve is the relationship between the quantity of real GDP demanded and the price level when all other influences on expenditure plans remain the same. A movement along the *AD* curve arises from a change in the price level.

Equilibrium expenditure depends on the price level. When the price level rises, other things remaining the same, aggregate planned expenditure decreases and equilibrium expenditure decreases. And when the price level falls, other things remaining the same, aggregate planned expenditure increases and equilibrium expenditure increases. The reason is that a change in the price level changes the buying power of money, the real interest rate, and the real prices of exports and imports (see Chapter 29, pp. 756–758).

When the price level rises, each of these effects decreases aggregate planned expenditure at each level of real GDP, so the *AE* curve shifts downward. A fall in the price level has the opposite effect. When the price level falls, the *AE* curve shifts upward.

Figure 30.8(a) shows the effects of a change in the price level on the *AE* curve and equilibrium expenditure. When the price level is 105, the *AE* curve is AE_0, and it intersects the 45° line at point *B*. Equilibrium expenditure is $16 trillion. If the price level rises to 125, aggregate planned expenditure decreases and the *AE* curve shifts downward to AE_1. Equilibrium expenditure decreases to $15 trillion at point *A*. If the price level falls to 85, aggregate planned expenditure increases and the *AE* curve shifts upward to AE_2. Equilibrium expenditure increases to $17 trillion at point *C*.

The changes in the price level that shift the *AE* curve and change equilibrium expenditure bring movements along the *AD* curve. Figure 30.8(b) shows these movements. At a price level of 105, the quantity of real GDP demanded is $16 trillion—point *B* on the *AD* curve. If the price level rises to 125, the quantity of real GDP demanded decreases along the *AD* curve to $15 trillion at point *A*. If the price level falls to 85, the quantity of real GDP demanded increases along the *AD* curve to $17 trillion at point *C*.

The two parts of Figure 30.8 are connected and illustrate the relationship between the *AE* curve and the *AD* curve. Each point of equilibrium expenditure corresponds to a point on the *AD* curve. The equilibrium expenditure points *A*, *B*, and *C* (part a) correspond to the points *A*, *B*, and *C* on the *AD* curve (part b).

FIGURE 30.8

Equilibrium Expenditure and Aggregate Demand

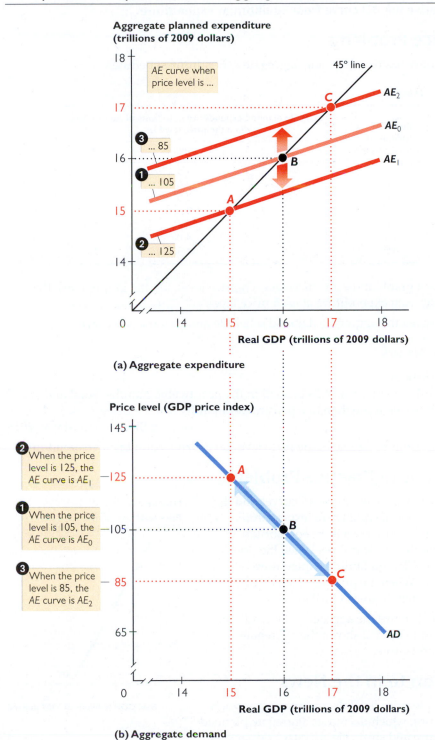

(a) Aggregate expenditure

(b) Aggregate demand

A change in the price level shifts the *AE* curve and results in a movement along the *AD* curve.

❶ When the price level is 105, equilibrium expenditure is $16 trillion at point *B* on the *AE* curve AE_0 and the quantity of real GDP demanded is $16 trillion at point *B* on the *AD* curve.

❷ When the price level rises to 125, the *AE* curve shifts downward to AE_1 and equilibrium expenditure decreases to $15 trillion at point *A*. The quantity of real GDP demanded decreases along the *AD* curve to point *A*.

❸ When the price level falls to 85, the *AE* curve shifts upward to AE_2 and equilibrium expenditure increases to $17 trillion at point *C*. The quantity of real GDP demanded increases along the *AD* curve to point *C*.

Points *A*, *B*, and *C* on the *AD* curve in part (b) correspond to the equilibrium expenditure points *A*, *B*, and *C* in part (a).

MyEconLab Study Plan 30.4

Solutions Video

CHECKPOINT 30.4

Derive the *AD* curve from equilibrium expenditure.

Practice Problems

An economy has the following aggregate expenditure schedules:

TABLE 1

Real GDP (trillions of 2009 dollars)	Aggregate planned expenditure in trillions of 2009 dollars when the price level is		
	115	105	95
0	1.0	1.5	2.0
1.0	1.5	2.0	2.5
2.0	2.0	2.5	3.0
3.0	2.5	3.0	3.5
4.0	3.0	3.5	4.0
5.0	3.5	4.0	4.5
6.0	4.0	4.5	5.0

1. Make a graph of the *AE* curve at each price level. On the graph, mark the equilibrium expenditure at each price level.
2. Construct the aggregate demand schedule and plot the *AD* curve.

In the News

Brazil's inflation

Brazil's inflation rate was 9.28 percent in the past twelve months. Food and beverage prices rose more than one percent per month.

Source: Bloomberg, May 6, 2016

Explain the effect of a rise in the price level on Brazil's equilibrium expenditure.

Solutions to Practice Problems

1. Figure 1 shows the three *AE* curves and the three levels of equilibrium expenditure. When the price level is 95, equilibrium expenditure is $4 trillion. When the price level is 105, equilibrium expenditure is $3 trillion. When the price level is 115, equilibrium expenditure is $2 trillion.

2. Table 2 shows the aggregate demand schedule, and Figure 2 shows the aggregate demand curve.

Solution to In the News

A rise in the price level decreases consumption expenditure, which decreases aggregate planned expenditure and shifts the *AE* curve downward. Brazil's equilibrium expenditure decreases.

FIGURE 1

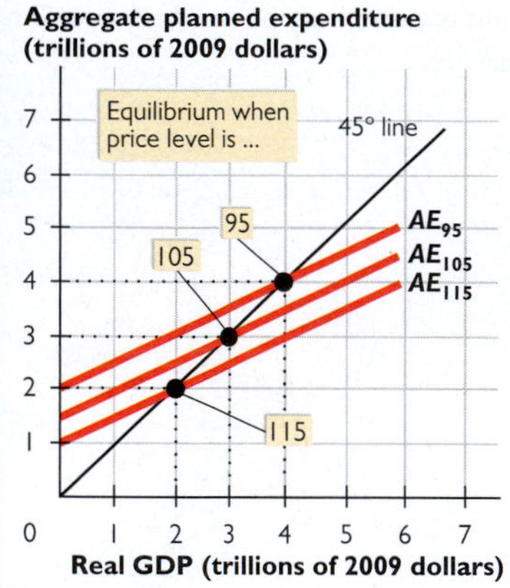

Aggregate planned expenditure (trillions of 2009 dollars)

TABLE 2

Price level	Real GDP demanded (trillions of 2009 dollars)
95	4
105	3
115	2

FIGURE 2

Price level (GDP price index, 2009 = 100)

CHAPTER SUMMARY

Key Points

1. Explain how real GDP influences expenditure plans.

- Autonomous expenditure is the sum of the components of aggregate expenditure that real GDP does not influence directly.
- Induced expenditure is the sum of the components of aggregate expenditure that real GDP influences.
- Consumption expenditure varies with disposable income and real GDP and depends on the marginal propensity to consume.
- Imports vary with real GDP and depend on the marginal propensity to import.

2. Explain how real GDP adjusts to achieve equilibrium expenditure.

- Actual aggregate expenditure equals real GDP, but when aggregate planned expenditure differs from real GDP, firms have unplanned inventory changes.
- If aggregate planned expenditure exceeds real GDP, firms increase production and real GDP increases. If real GDP exceeds aggregate planned expenditure, firms decrease production and real GDP decreases.
- Real GDP changes until aggregate planned expenditure equals real GDP.

3. Explain the expenditure multiplier.

- When autonomous expenditure changes, equilibrium expenditure changes by a larger amount: There is a multiplier.
- The multiplier is greater than 1 because a change in autonomous expenditure changes induced expenditure.
- The larger the marginal propensity to consume, the larger is the multiplier.
- Income taxes and imports make the multiplier smaller.

4. Derive the *AD* curve from equilibrium expenditure.

- The *AD* curve is the relationship between the quantity of real GDP demanded and the price level when all other influences on expenditure plans remain the same.
- The quantity of real GDP demanded on the *AD* curve is the equilibrium real GDP when aggregate planned expenditure equals real GDP.

Key Terms

MyEconLab **Key Terms Quiz**

Aggregate planned expenditure, 776
Consumption function, 776
Equilibrium expenditure, 784
Marginal propensity to consume, 778

Marginal propensity to import, 780
Marginal tax rate, 790
Multiplier, 788

CHAPTER CHECKPOINT

Study Plan Problems and Applications

Table 1 shows disposable income and saving in an economy. Use Table 1 to answer Problems **1** and **2**.

TABLE 1

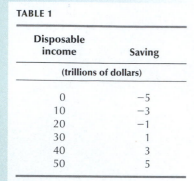

Disposable income	Saving
(trillions of dollars)	
0	−5
10	−3
20	−1
30	1
40	3
50	5

1. Calculate consumption expenditure at each level of disposable income. Over what range of disposable income is there dissaving? Estimate the level of disposable income at which saving is zero.

2. Calculate the marginal propensity to consume. If wealth increases by $10 trillion, in which direction will the consumption function change?

Use Table 2 to work Problems **3**, **4**, and **5**. Table 2 shows real GDP, *Y*, the components of planned expenditure, and aggregate planned expenditure (in millions of dollars) in an economy in which taxes are constant.

TABLE 2

Y	\multicolumn{6}{c}{Planned expenditure}
	C	*I*	*G*	*X*	*M*	*AE*
0	2.0	1.75	1.0	1.25	0	6.0
2	**Q**	1.75	1.0	1.25	0.4	6.8
4	4.4	**R**	1.0	1.25	0.8	7.6
6	5.6	1.75	**S**	1.25	1.2	8.4
8	6.8	1.75	1.0	**T**	1.6	9.2
10	8.0	1.75	1.0	1.25	**U**	10.0
12	9.2	1.75	1.0	1.25	2.4	**V**

3. Find the value of Q, R, S, T, U, and V.

4. Calculate the marginal propensity to consume and the marginal propensity to import. What is equilibrium expenditure?

5. If investment crashes to $0.55 million but nothing else changes, what is equilibrium expenditure and what is the multiplier?

6. Figure 1 shows aggregate planned expenditure when the price level is 100. When the price level increases to 110, aggregate planned expenditure changes by $0.5 trillion. What is the quantity of real GDP demanded when the price level is 100 and 110?

FIGURE 1

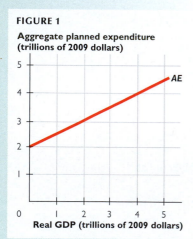

Aggregate planned expenditure (trillions of 2009 dollars)

Real GDP (trillions of 2009 dollars)

Use this information to work Problems **7** and **8**.

U.S. durable goods orders rebound strongly

The Commerce Department reported that orders for durable goods increased 4.9 percent in January. Civilian aircraft orders surged 54.2 percent.

Source: Reuters, February 25, 2016

7. Explain the process by which an increase in durable goods orders at a constant price level changes equilibrium expenditure and real GDP.

8. What determines the increase in aggregate demand resulting from an increase in durable goods orders?

9. Read *Eye on the Multiplier* on p. 792. Why do multiplier estimates differ? What conditions would be consistent with a large multiplier?

Instructor Assignable Problems and Applications

MyEconLab Homework, Quiz, or Test if assigned by instructor

1. The output gap in the second quarter of 2009 was $0.8 trillion. How much fiscal stimulus would be required to close the output gap if the multiplier was as large as the Obama team believes? How much fiscal stimulus would be required if the multiplier was as large as Robert Barro believes?

Table 1 shows disposable income and consumption expenditure in an economy. Use Table 1 to work Problems **2** and **3**.

2. Calculate saving at each level of disposable income. Over what range of disposable income does consumption expenditure exceed disposable income? Calculate autonomous consumption expenditure.

3. Calculate the marginal propensity to consume. At what level of disposable income will saving be zero? If expected future income increases, in which direction will the consumption function change?

TABLE 1

Disposable income	Consumption expenditure
(billions of dollars)	
200	350
400	500
600	650
800	800
1,000	950

Use the following information to work Problems **4** to **6**.

In an economy with no exports and no imports, autonomous consumption is $1 trillion, the marginal propensity to consume is 0.8, investment is $5 trillion, and government expenditure on goods and services is $4 trillion. Taxes are $4 trillion and do not vary with real GDP.

4. If real GDP is $30 trillion, calculate disposable income, consumption expenditure, and aggregate planned expenditure. What is equilibrium expenditure?

5. If real GDP is $30 trillion, explain the process that takes the economy to equilibrium expenditure. If real GDP is $40 trillion, explain the process that takes the economy to equilibrium expenditure.

6. If investment increases by $0.5 trillion, calculate the change in equilibrium expenditure and the multiplier.

Use the following information to work Problems **7** and **8**.

Figure 1 shows the aggregate demand curve in an economy. Suppose that aggregate planned expenditure increases by $0.75 trillion for each $1 trillion increase in real GDP.

7. If investment increases by $1 trillion, calculate the change in the quantity of real GDP demanded if the price level is constant at 105.

8. Compare the shift of the *AD* curve with the $1 trillion increase in investment. Explain the magnitude of the shift of the *AD* curve.

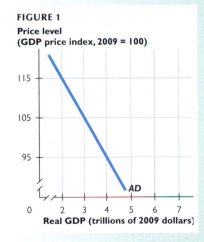

FIGURE 1

Price level
(GDP price index, 2009 = 100)

Use the following information to work Problems **9** and **10**.

U.S. durable goods orders slump most in three years
The Commerce Department reported that orders for U.S. durable goods fell in January by the most in three years. Orders for commercial aircraft and business equipment fell most. Machinery orders dropped 10.4 percent.
Source: Bloomberg, February 29, 2012

9. Explain the process by which a decrease in durable goods orders at a constant price level changes equilibrium expenditure and real GDP.

10. What determines the decrease in aggregate demand resulting from a decrease in durable goods orders?

MyEconLab Chapter 30 Study Plan

Multiple Choice Quiz

1. The consumption function shows how an increase in _____ influences _____.

   A. income; households' aggregate planned expenditure
   B. nominal GDP; consumption expenditure
   C. disposable income; consumption expenditure
   D. consumption as a fraction of income; real GDP

2. The marginal propensity to consume tells us by how much _____ changes when _____ changes.

   A. consumption expenditure; wealth
   B. the real interest rate; planned consumption
   C. expected future income; the percentage of income spent
   D. consumption expenditure; disposable income

3. Induced expenditure includes _____.

   A. consumption expenditure, government expenditure, and exports
   B. investment, exports, and imports
   C. consumption expenditure and imports
   D. consumption expenditure, investment, and government expenditure

4. The aggregate planned expenditure curve _____ increases.

   A. slopes upward because induced expenditure increases as income
   B. is horizontal because autonomous expenditure is constant when income
   C. shifts upward if induced expenditure increases as income
   D. slopes upward because autonomous expenditure

5. If real GDP _____ planned expenditure, the economy converges to equilibrium expenditure because inventories _____ and firms increase production.

   A. exceeds; pile up
   B. exceeds; are run down
   C. is less than; are run down
   D. is less than; pile up

6. The multiplier equals _____ divided by _____.

   A. the marginal propensity to consume; autonomous expenditure
   B. 1; (1 − Slope of the *AE* curve)
   C. 1; Slope of the *AE* curve
   D. Slope of the *AE* curve; the marginal propensity to consume

7. The multiplier will increase if the marginal propensity to consume _____ or the marginal tax rate _____.

   A. increases; decreases
   B. increases; increases
   C. decreases; increases
   D. decreases; decreases

8. A rise in the price level shifts the *AE* curve _____.

   A. upward and creates a movement up along the *AD* curve
   B. downward and creates a movement up along the *AD* curve
   C. upward and shifts the *AD* curve rightward
   D. downward and shifts the *AD* curve leftward

Can we have low unemployment *and* low inflation?

The Short-Run Policy Tradeoff

31

When you have completed your study of this chapter, you will be able to

1 Describe the short-run tradeoff between inflation and unemployment.

2 Distinguish between the short-run and the long-run Phillips curves and describe the shifting tradeoff between inflation and unemployment.

3 Explain how the Fed can influence the inflation rate and the unemployment rate.

MyEconLab Big Picture Video

MyEconLab Concept Video

Short-run Phillips curve

The relationship between the inflation rate and the unemployment rate when the natural unemployment rate and the expected inflation rate remain constant.

31.1 THE SHORT-RUN PHILLIPS CURVE

We *can* have low inflation and low unemployment. To see why, you need to understand the long-run Phillips curve and a temporary tradeoff called the short-run Phillips curve. The **short-run Phillips curve** shows the relationship between the inflation rate and the unemployment rate when the natural unemployment rate and the expected inflation rate remain constant.

Figure 31.1 illustrates the short-run Phillips curve. Here, the natural unemployment rate is 6 percent and the expected inflation rate is 3 percent a year. At full employment, the unemployment rate equals the natural unemployment rate and the inflation rate equals the expected inflation rate at point *B*. This point is the anchor point for the short-run Phillips curve.

In an expansion, the unemployment rate decreases and the inflation rate rises. For example, the economy might move to a point such as *A*, where the unemployment rate is 5 percent and the inflation rate is 4 percent a year.

In a recession, the unemployment rate increases and the inflation rate falls. For example, the economy might move to a point such as *C*, where the unemployment rate is 7 percent and the inflation rate is 2 percent a year.

The short-run Phillips curve presents a *tradeoff* between inflation and unemployment. A lower unemployment rate can be achieved only by paying the cost of a higher inflation rate, and a lower inflation rate can be achieved only by paying the cost of a higher unemployment rate. For example, in Figure 31.1, a decrease in the unemployment rate from 6 percent to 5 percent costs a 1-percentage-point increase in the inflation rate from 3 percent a year to 4 percent a year.

■ **FIGURE 31.1**

A Short-Run Phillips Curve

MyEconLab Animation

❶ If the natural unemployment rate is 6 percent, and ❷ the expected inflation rate is 3 percent a year, then ❸ point *B* is at full employment on a short-run Phillips curve.

❹ The short-run Phillips curve (*SRPC*) shows the tradeoff between inflation and unemployment at the given natural unemployment rate and expected inflation rate.

A higher unemployment rate brings a lower inflation rate, and a lower unemployment rate brings a higher inflation rate.

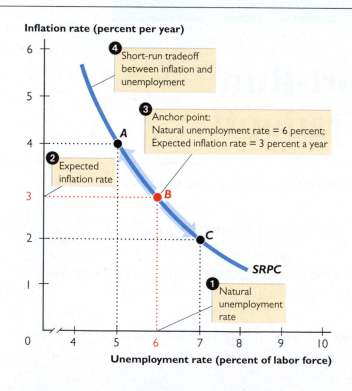

■ Aggregate Supply and the Short-Run Phillips Curve

The short-run Phillips curve is another way of looking at the upward-sloping aggregate supply curve that you learned about in Chapter 29—see pp. 750–754.

Both the short-run Phillips curve and the aggregate supply curve arise because the money wage rate is fixed in the short run.

Along an aggregate supply curve, the money wage rate is fixed. So when the price level rises, the *real wage rate* falls, and a fall in the real wage rate increases the quantity of labor employed and increases the quantity of real GDP supplied.

The events that we've just described also play out along a short-run Phillips curve. The rise in the price level means that the inflation rate has (perhaps temporarily) increased. The increase in the quantity of labor employed means a decrease in the number unemployed and a fall in the unemployment rate.

So a movement along an aggregate supply curve is equivalent to a movement along a short-run Phillips curve. Let's explore these connections between the aggregate supply curve and the short-run Phillips curve a bit more closely.

Unemployment and Real GDP

In a given period, with a fixed amount of capital and a given state of technology, real GDP depends on the quantity of labor employed. At full employment, the quantity of real GDP is *potential GDP* and the unemployment rate is the natural unemployment rate. If real GDP exceeds potential GDP, employment exceeds its full-employment level and the unemployment rate falls below the natural unemployment rate. Similarly, if real GDP is less than potential GDP, employment is less than its full-employment level and the unemployment rate rises above the natural unemployment rate.

The quantitative relationship between the unemployment rate and real GDP was first estimated by economist Arthur M. Okun and is called **Okun's Law**. Okun's Law states that for each percentage point that the unemployment rate is above (below) the natural unemployment rate, real GDP is 2 percent below (above) potential GDP. For example, if the natural unemployment rate is 6 percent and potential GDP is $10 trillion, then when the actual unemployment rate is 7 percent, real GDP is $9.8 trillion—98 percent of potential GDP, or 2 percent below potential GDP. And when the actual unemployment rate is 5 percent, real GDP is $10.2 trillion—102 percent of potential GDP, or 2 percent above potential GDP. Table 31.1 summarizes this relationship.

Inflation and the Price Level

The inflation rate is the percentage change in the price level. So starting from last period's price level, the higher the inflation rate, the higher is the current period's price level. Suppose that last year, the price level was 100. If the inflation rate is 2 percent, the price level rises to 102; if the inflation rate is 3 percent, the price level rises to 103; and if the inflation rate is 4 percent, the price level rises to 104.

With these relationships between the unemployment rate and real GDP (in Table 31.1) and between the inflation rate and the price level, we can establish the connection between the short-run Phillips curve and the aggregate supply curve. Figure 31.2 shows this connection.

First suppose that in the current year, real GDP equals potential GDP and the unemployment rate equals the natural unemployment rate. In Figure 31.2, real

Okun's Law
For each percentage point that the unemployment rate is above (below) the natural unemployment rate, real GDP is 2 percent below (above) potential GDP.

TABLE 31.1

	Unemployment rate (percent)	Real GDP (trillions of 2009 dollars)
A	5	10.2
B	6	10.0
C	7	9.8

GDP is $10 trillion and the unemployment rate is 6 percent. The economy is at point *B* on the short-run Phillips curve in part (a) and point *B* on the aggregate supply curve in part (b). The inflation rate is 3 percent a year (its expected rate) in part (a), and the price level is 103 (also its expected level) in part (b).

Next suppose that instead of being at full employment, the economy is above full employment with real GDP of $10.2 trillion at point *A* on the aggregate supply curve in Figure 31.2(b). In this case, the unemployment rate is 5 percent in Table 31.1 and the economy is at point *A* on the short-run Phillips curve in Figure 31.2(a). The inflation rate is 4 percent a year (higher than expected) in part (a), and the price level is 104 (also higher than expected) in part (b).

Finally, suppose that the economy is below full employment with real GDP of $9.8 trillion at point *C* on the aggregate supply curve in Figure 31.2(b). In this case, the unemployment rate is 7 percent in Table 31.1 and the economy is at point *C* on the short-run Phillips curve in Figure 31.2(a). The inflation rate is 2 percent a year (lower than expected) in part (a), and the price level is 102 (also lower than expected) in part (b).

■ **FIGURE 31.2**

The Short-Run Phillips Curve and the Aggregate Supply Curve

MyEconLab Animation

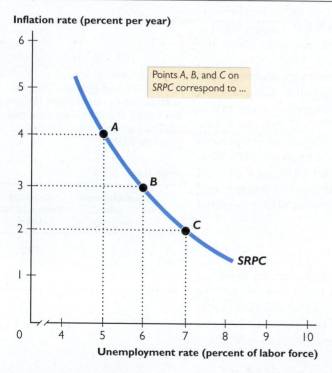

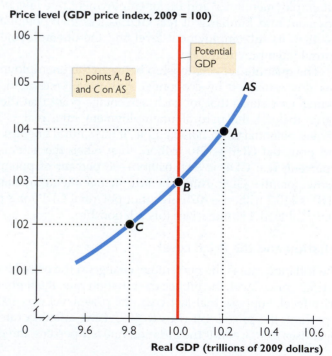

(a) The short-run Phillips curve

(b) The aggregate supply curve

Point *A* on the Phillips curve corresponds to point *A* on the aggregate supply curve: The unemployment rate is 5 percent and the inflation rate is 4 percent a year in part (a), and real GDP is $10.2 trillion and the price level is 104 in part (b).

Point *B* on the Phillips curve corresponds to point *B* on the aggregate supply curve: The unemployment rate is 6 percent and the inflation rate is 3 percent a year in part (a), and real GDP is $10 trillion and the price level is 103 in part (b).

Point *C* on the Phillips curve corresponds to point *C* on the aggregate supply curve: The unemployment rate is 7 percent and the inflation rate is 2 percent a year in part (a), and real GDP is $9.8 trillion and the price level is 102 in part (b).

■ Aggregate Demand Fluctuations

A decrease in aggregate demand that brings a movement down along the aggregate supply curve from point *B* to point *C* lowers the price level and decreases real GDP. That same decrease in aggregate demand brings a movement down along the Phillips curve from point *B* to point *C*.

Similarly, an increase in aggregate demand that brings a movement up along the aggregate supply curve from point *B* to point *A* raises the price level and increases real GDP relative to what they would have been. That same increase in aggregate demand brings a movement up along the Phillips curve from point *B* to point *A*.

EYE on the GLOBAL ECONOMY
Inflation and Unemployment

The Phillips curve is so named because New Zealand economist A. W. (Bill) Phillips discovered the relationship in about 100 years of unemployment and wage inflation data for the United Kingdom.

The figure shows data on inflation and unemployment in the United Kingdom over most of the twentieth century—1900 to 1997. The data reveal no neat, tight tradeoff. The short-run tradeoff shifts around a great deal.

The highest inflation rate in 1975 did not occur at the lowest unemployment rate, and the lowest inflation rate in 1922 did not occur at the highest unemployment rate. But the lowest unemployment rate in 1917 did bring a high inflation rate. And the highest unemployment rate during the Great Depression of the 1930s brought a gently falling price level.

A.W. (Bill) Phillips

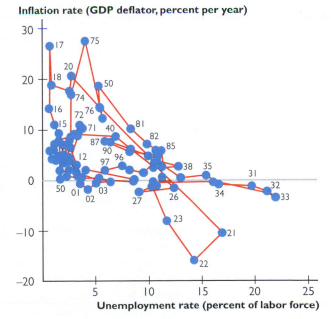

SOURCE: Michael Parkin, "Unemployment, Inflation, and Monetary Policy," *Canadian Journal of Economics*, November 1998.

EYE on the PAST
The U.S. Phillips Curve

Phillips made his discovery in 1958, two years before the election of John F. Kennedy as President of the United States. Very soon thereafter, two young American economists, Paul A. Samuelson and Robert M. Solow, both at MIT and eager to help the new Kennedy administration to pursue a low-unemployment strategy, looked for a Phillips curve in the U.S. data. The figure shows what they found: The red line joining the blue dots shows no recognizable relationship between inflation and unemployment for the 20 or so years that they studied.

Giving more weight to the 1950s experience, Samuelson and Solow proposed the Phillips curve shown in the figure. They believed that the U.S. Phillips curve provided support for the then growing view that the new Kennedy administration could pursue a low unemployment policy with only a moderate rise in the inflation rate.

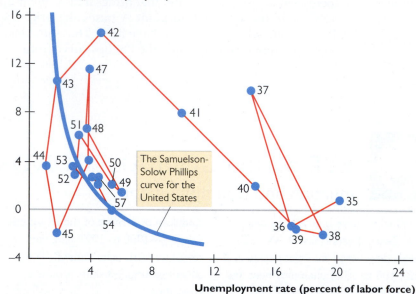

SOURCE OF DATA: Paul A. Samuelson and Robert M. Solow, "Problem of Achieving and Maintaining a Stable Price Level, Analytical Aspects of Anti-Inflation Policy." *American Economic Review*, 50(2), May 1960.

As the 1960s unfolded, the Samuelson-Solow version of the Phillips curve began to look like a permanent tradeoff between inflation and unemployment. But in the late 1960s and early 1970s, the relationship disappeared in the face of rising inflation expectations.

■ Why Bother with the Phillips Curve?

You've seen that the short-run Phillips curve is another way of looking at the aggregate supply curve. And you might be wondering, why bother with the short-run Phillips curve? Isn't the aggregate supply curve adequate for describing the short-run tradeoff?

The Phillips curve is useful for two reasons. First, it focuses directly on two policy targets: the inflation rate and the unemployment rate. Second, the aggregate supply curve shifts whenever the money wage rate or potential GDP changes. Such changes occur every day, so the aggregate supply curve is not a stable tradeoff. The short-run Phillips curve isn't a stable tradeoff either, but it is more stable than the aggregate supply curve. The short-run Phillips curve shifts only when the natural unemployment rate changes or when the expected inflation rate changes.

CHECKPOINT 31.1

MyEconLab Study Plan 31.1
Key Terms Quiz
Solutions Video

Describe the short-run tradeoff between inflation and unemployment.

Practice Problems

Table 1 describes five possible outcomes in a country for 2017, depending on the level of aggregate demand in that year. Potential GDP is $10 trillion, and the natural unemployment rate is 5 percent.

1. Calculate the inflation rate for each possible outcome.

2. Use Okun's Law to find real GDP at each unemployment rate in Table 1.

3. What are the expected price level and the expected inflation rate in 2017?

4. Plot the short-run Phillips curve for 2017. Mark the points A, B, C, D, and E that correspond to the data in Table 1 and that you have calculated.

5. Plot the aggregate supply curve for 2017. Mark the points A, B, C, D, and E that correspond to the data in Table 1.

TABLE 1

	Price level (2016 = 100)	Unemployment rate (percentage)
A	102.5	9
B	105.0	6
C	106.0	5
D	107.5	4
E	110.0	3

In the News

U.K. unemployment rate hit lowest since 2005
The unemployment rate in the United Kingdom fell to 4.9 percent in the three months to May, its lowest level since 2005. In the same three months, wages rose by 2.3 percent, their biggest increase since October 2015.

Source: Reuters, July 20, 2016

With the expected inflation rate steady, did the U.K. economy move along its short-run Phillips curve? If so, in which direction? Or did the economy move off its short-run Phillips curve?

Solutions to Practice Problems

1. The inflation rate in 2017 equals the price level in 2017 minus the price level in 2016. So for A, the inflation rate is $102.5 - 100$, which equals 2.5 percent per year. Calculate the inflation rate at the other points in the same way.

2. Okun's Law: For each 1 percentage point the unemployment rate U exceeds the natural unemployment rate U^* (5 percent), real GDP is below potential GDP by 2 percent. So for A, U exceeds U^* by 4 percentage points, so real GDP is 8 percent below potential GDP, equal to $9.2 trillion. Calculate real GDP at the other points in the same way.

3. The expected price level is the price level at full employment—row C. The expected price level is 106, and the expected inflation rate is 6 percent.

4. Plot the inflation rate (Solution 1) against the unemployment rate (Table 1) to get the short-run Phillips curve (Figure 1).

5. Plot the price level (Table 1) against real GDP (Solution 2) to get the aggregate supply curve (Figure 2).

Solution to In the News

With the expected inflation rate steady, the increase in wage inflation and decrease in unemployment imply that the U.K. economy remained on its short-run Phillips curve and moved leftward up along it as the wage inflation rate rose and the unemployment rate fell.

FIGURE 1

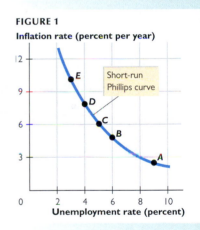

Inflation rate (percent per year)

Short-run Phillips curve

Unemployment rate (percent)

FIGURE 2

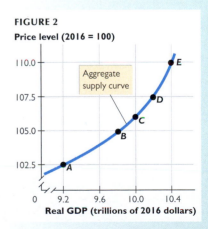

Price level (2016 = 100)

Aggregate supply curve

Real GDP (trillions of 2016 dollars)

MyEconLab Concept Video

31.2 SHORT-RUN AND LONG-RUN PHILLIPS CURVES

The short-run Phillips curve shows the *tradeoff* between inflation and unemployment when the natural unemployment rate and expected inflation rate remain the same. Changes in the natural unemployment rate and the expected inflation rate change the short-run tradeoff and changes in the expected inflation rate give rise to a *long-run* Phillips curve that we'll now examine.

■ The Long-Run Phillips Curve

Long-run Phillips curve
The relationship between inflation and unemployment when the economy is at full employment. The long-run Phillips curve is a vertical line at the natural unemployment rate.

The **long-run Phillips curve** shows the relationship between inflation and unemployment when the economy is at full employment. At full employment, the unemployment rate is the *natural unemployment rate,* so on the long-run Phillips curve, there is only one possible unemployment rate: the natural unemployment rate.

In contrast, the inflation rate can take on any value at full employment. You learned in Chapter 28 (pp. 734–737) that at full employment, for a given real GDP growth rate, the greater the money growth rate, the greater is the inflation rate.

This description of the economy at full employment tells us the properties of the long-run Phillips curve: It is a vertical line located at the natural unemployment rate. In Figure 31.3, the long-run Phillips curve is *LRPC* along which the unemployment rate equals the natural unemployment rate and any inflation rate is possible.

■ **FIGURE 31.3**

The Long-Run Phillips Curve

MyEconLab Animation

The long-run Phillips curve is a vertical line at the natural unemployment rate. In the long run, there is no unemployment–inflation tradeoff.

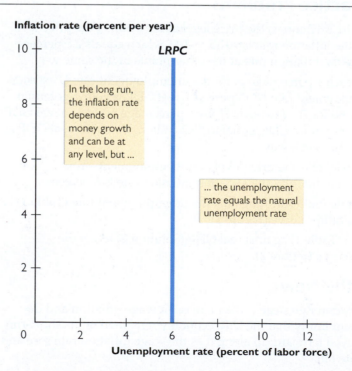

■ Expected Inflation

The **expected inflation rate** is the inflation rate that people forecast and use to set the money wage rate and other money prices. Suppose there is full employment and McDonald's servers earn $10 an hour. With no inflation, a money wage rate of $10 an hour keeps the market for servers in equilibrium. But with 10 percent inflation, a constant money wage rate means a falling real wage rate and a shortage of servers. Now, a 10 percent rise in the money wage rate to $11 is needed to keep the market for servers in equilibrium. If McDonald's and everyone else expect 10 percent inflation, the money wage rate will rise by 10 percent to prevent a labor shortage from arising.

If expectations about the inflation rate turn out to be correct, the price level rises by the 10 percent expected and the real wage rate remains constant at its full-employment equilibrium level and unemployment remains at the natural unemployment rate.

Because the actual inflation rate equals the expected inflation rate at full employment, we can interpret the long-run Phillips curve as the relationship between inflation and unemployment when the inflation rate equals the expected inflation rate.

Figure 31.4 shows short-run Phillips curves for two expected inflation rates. A short-run Phillips curve shows the tradeoff between inflation and unemployment at *a particular expected inflation rate*. When the expected inflation rate changes, the short-run Phillips curve shifts to intersect the long-run Phillips curve at the new expected inflation rate.

Expected inflation rate
The inflation rate that people forecast and use to set the money wage rate and other money prices.

■ FIGURE 31.4

Short-Run and Long-Run Phillips Curves

MyEconLab Animation

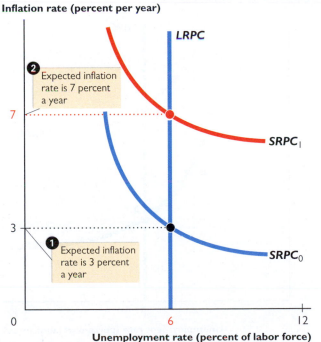

If the natural unemployment rate is 6 percent, the long-run Phillips curve is *LRPC*.

1 If the expected inflation rate is 3 percent a year, the short-run Phillips curve is $SRPC_0$.

2 If the expected inflation rate is 7 percent a year, the short-run Phillips curve is $SRPC_1$.

In Figure 31.4, when the expected inflation rate is 3 percent a year, the short-run Phillips curve is $SRPC_0$ and when the expected inflation rate is 7 percent a year, the short-run Phillips curve is $SRPC_1$.

■ The Natural Rate Hypothesis

Natural rate hypothesis
The proposition that when the inflation rate changes, the unemployment rate changes *temporarily* and eventually returns to the natural unemployment rate.

The **natural rate hypothesis** is the proposition that when the inflation rate changes, the unemployment rate changes *temporarily* and eventually returns to the natural unemployment rate. The temporary change in the unemployment rate occurs because the real wage rate changes, which leads to a change in the quantity of labor demanded. The unemployment rate returns to the natural rate because eventually, the money wage rate changes to catch up with the change in the price level and return the real wage rate to its full-employment level.

Figure 31.5 illustrates the natural rate hypothesis. Initially, the inflation rate is 3 percent a year and the economy is at full employment, at point A. Then the quantity of money grows more rapidly, at a rate that will generate inflation at 7 percent a year in the long run. In the short run, with a fixed money wage rate, the real wage rate falls, the quantity of labor employed increases and the unemployment rate falls. The inflation rate rises to 5 percent a year, and the economy moves from point A to point B. When the higher inflation rate is expected, the money wage rate increases. As the expected inflation rate increases from 3 percent to 7 percent a year, the short-run Phillips curve shifts upward from $SRPC_0$ to $SRPC_1$. Inflation speeds up and the unemployment rate returns to the natural unemployment rate. In Figure 31.5, the economy moves from point B to point C.

■ **FIGURE 31.5**

The Natural Rate Hypothesis

MyEconLab Animation

The inflation rate is 3 percent a year, and the economy is at full employment, at point A. Then the inflation rate increases.

In the short run, the money wage rate is fixed and the increase in the inflation rate brings a decrease in the unemployment rate—a movement along $SRPC_0$ to point B.

Eventually, the higher inflation rate is expected, the money wage rate rises, and the short-run Phillips curve shifts upward gradually to $SRPC_1$. At the higher expected inflation rate, unemployment returns to the natural unemployment rate—the natural rate hypothesis. The economy is at point C.

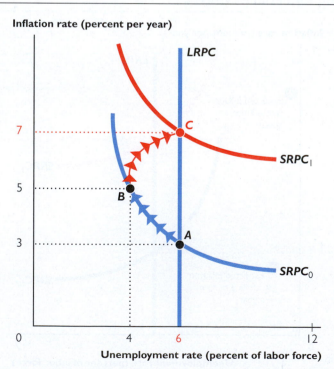

EYE on the PAST
A Live Test of the Natural Rate Hypothesis

The figure describes the U.S. economy from 1960 to 1971 and shows that the natural rate hypothesis describes these years well.

The natural unemployment rate was around 6 percent, so the long-run Phillips curve, *LRPC*, was located at that unemployment rate.

In 1960, the inflation rate and the expected inflation rate were around 1 percent a year. The short-run Phillips curve was $SRPC_0$.

Through 1966, the expected inflation rate remained at 1 percent a year but the actual inflation rate edged up and the unemployment rate decreased below the natural unemployment rate. The economy moved up along $SRPC_0$ from point *A* to point *B*.

Then, from 1967 to 1969, the inflation rate increased and so did the expected inflation rate. As the expected inflation rate rose. the short-run Phillips curve shifted upward. By 1969, the economy had moved to point *C*.

By 1970, the expected inflation rate was around 5 percent a year. As the higher inflation rate came to be expected, the unemployment rate increased.

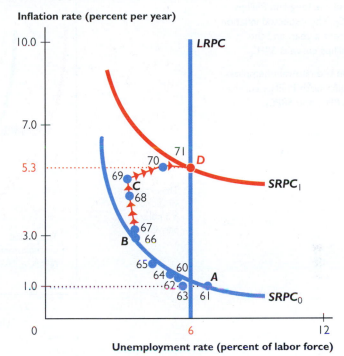

SOURCE OF DATA: Bureau of Labor Statistics and Bureau of Economic Analysis.

By 1971, the unemployment rate had returned to the natural unemployment rate, the short-run Phillips curve had shifted upward to $SRPC_1$, and the economy had moved to point *D*.

Notice the similarity between the actual events during this period and

the natural rate hypothesis, which Figure 31.5 illustrates.

Edmund S. Phelps of Columbia University and Milton Friedman of the University of Chicago proposed the natural rate hypothesis and predicted these events *before* they occurred.

■ Changes in the Natural Unemployment Rate

If the natural unemployment rate changes, both the long-run Phillips curve and the short-run Phillips curve shift. When the natural unemployment rate increases, both the long-run Phillips curve and the short-run Phillips curve shift rightward; and when the natural unemployment rate decreases, both the long-run Phillips curve and the short-run Phillips curve shift leftward.

Figure 31.6 illustrates these changes. When the natural unemployment rate is 6 percent, the long-run Phillips curve is $LRPC_0$. If the expected inflation rate is 3 percent a year, the short-run Phillips curve is $SRPC_0$. A decrease in the natural

■ **FIGURE 31.6**

Changes in the Natural Unemployment Rate

MyEconLab Animation

The natural unemployment rate is 6 percent, and the long-run Phillips curve is $LRPC_0$. The expected inflation rate is 3 percent a year, and the short-run Phillips curve is $SRPC_0$.

A decrease in the natural unemployment rate shifts both Phillips curves leftward to $LRPC_1$ and $SRPC_1$.

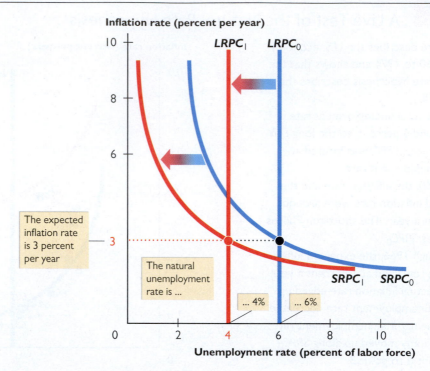

unemployment rate, with no change in the expected inflation rate, shifts both Phillips curves leftward to $LRPC_1$ and $SRPC_1$.

■ Have Changes in the Natural Unemployment Rate Changed the Tradeoff?

Changes in the natural unemployment rate have changed the tradeoff. According to the Congressional Budget Office, the natural unemployment rate increased from about 5 percent in 1950 to more than 6 percent in the mid-1970s and then decreased to 4.8 percent by 2000. It has been constant at this level through 2009.

You learned about the factors that influence the natural unemployment rate in Chapter 24 (pp. 627–630). Those factors divide into two groups: influences on job search and influences on job rationing. Job search is influenced by demographic change, unemployment compensation, and structural change. Job rationing arises from efficiency wages, the minimum wage, and union wages.

A bulge in the birth rate (known as the "baby boom") that occurred after World War II in the late 1940s and early 1950s, brought a bulge in the number of young people entering the labor force during the late 1960s and early 1970s. This bulge in the number of new entrants increased the amount of job search and increased the natural unemployment rate.

Structural change during the 1970s and 1980s, much of it a response to massive hikes in the world price of oil, also contributed to the increase in the natural unemployment rate during the 1970s and early 1980s.

EYE on the TRADEOFF

Can We Have Low Unemployment *and* Low Inflation?

In the short run, we can have low unemployment only if we permit the inflation rate to rise. And we can have low inflation only if we permit the unemployment rate to increase. In the long run, we can improve the unemployment–inflation tradeoff.

We can have low unemployment if we can lower the natural unemployment rate, but that is hard to do.

We can have low inflation if we can lower the expected inflation rate. That, too, is hard to do, but it isn't as hard as lowering the natural unemployment rate. The expected inflation rate does change frequently and sometimes by large amounts.

The years 2000–2015 show how changes in the expected inflation rate change the short-run tradeoff.

During these years, the natural unemployment rate was constant at 5 percent, so the long-run Phillips curve remained fixed at *LRPC*.

The expected inflation rate was 2.5 percent a year in 2000–2002 and the short-run Phillips curve was $SRPC_0$. The expected inflation rate then increased to 3.5 percent a year, where

it remained until 2005, and the short-run Phillips curve shifted to $SRPC_1$.

In 2006, the expected inflation rate decreased to 2.5 percent a year and the short-run Phillips curve shifted back from $SRPC_1$ to $SRPC_0$. The tradeoff improved.

In 2015, the expected inflation rate decreased again to zero percent a year and the short-run Phillips curve shifted downward from $SRPC_0$ to $SRPC_2$. The tradeoff improved still further. The 2015 data show that we can have low inflation and low unemployment.

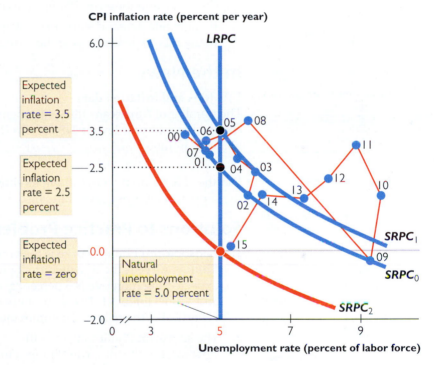

SOURCE OF DATA: Bureau of Labor Statistics and Congressional Budget Office.

As the baby boom generation approached middle age during the 1980s and 1990s, the number of new labor market entrants decreased and the natural unemployment rate decreased too. Also, during the 1990s, rapid technological change brought an increase in productivity and an increase in the demand for labor that shortened the time people spent on job search and lowered the natural unemployment rate yet further. During the 2000s, the natural unemployment rate remained steady.

The changes in the natural unemployment rate that we've just described shifted the short-run and long-run Phillips curves rightward during the 1960s and 1970s and shifted them leftward during the 1980s and 1990s.

MyEconLab Study Plan 31.2
Key Terms Quiz
Solutions Video

CHECKPOINT 31.2

Distinguish between the short-run and the long-run Phillips curves and describe the shifting tradeoff between inflation and unemployment.

Practice Problems

Figure 1 shows a short-run Phillips curve and a long-run Phillips curve.

1. Identify the curves and label them. What is the expected inflation rate and what is the natural unemployment rate?

2. If the expected inflation rate increases to 7.5 percent a year, show the new short-run and long-run Phillips curves.

3. If the natural unemployment rate increases to 8 percent, show the new short-run and long-run Phillips curves.

4. If aggregate demand starts to grow more rapidly and the inflation rate eventually hits 10 percent a year, how do unemployment and inflation change?

In the News

U.S. jobs and inflation data

The number of Americans filing for unemployment benefits in June was unchanged at a 43-year low of 248,000. Producer prices recorded their biggest gain in a year in June.

Source: Reuters, July 14, 2016

Did the U.S. economy move along its short-run Phillips curve? If so, how? Or did the short-run Phillips curve shift? If so, how?

Solutions to Practice Problems

1. The long-run Phillips curve is the vertical curve, *LRPC,* and the short-run Phillips curve is the downward-sloping curve, $SRPC_0$ (Figure 2). The expected inflation rate is 5 percent a year—the inflation rate at which *LRPC* and $SRPC_0$ intersect. The natural unemployment rate is 6 percent. The *LRPC* is vertical at the natural unemployment rate.

2. The short-run Phillips curve shifts upward, but the long-run Phillips curve does not change (Figure 2).

3. Both the short-run and long-run Phillips curves shift rightward (Figure 3).

4. Figure 4 shows that as expectations change, the inflation rate rises to 10 percent a year and unemployment falls and then gradually returns to its natural rate.

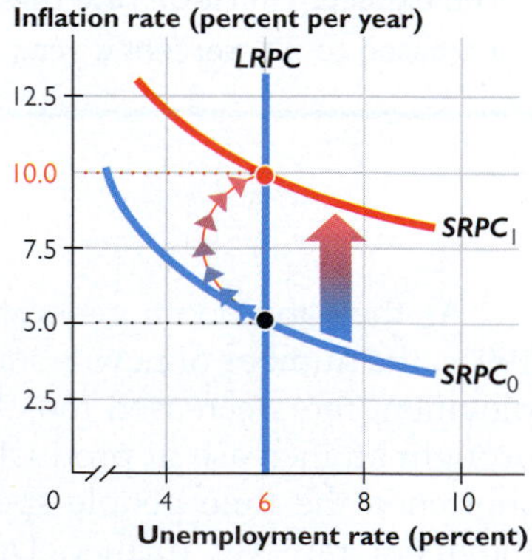

Solution to In the News

The facts about unemployment and inflation in the news clip are consistent with an increase in the expected inflation rate and an upward shift in the short-run Phillips curve. With the number of Americans unemployed unchanged, the economy did not move along a short-run Phillips curve.

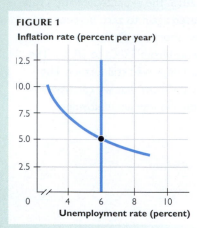

FIGURE 1

Inflation rate (percent per year)

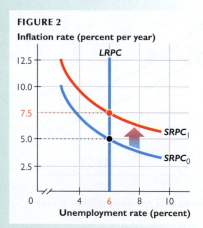

FIGURE 2

Inflation rate (percent per year)

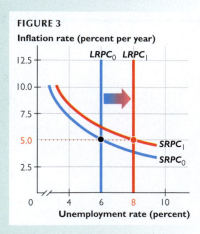

FIGURE 3

Inflation rate (percent per year)

FIGURE 4

Inflation rate (percent per year)

31.3 INFLUENCING INFLATION AND UNEMPLOYMENT

MyEconLab Concept Video

How can the Fed influence the inflation rate and the unemployment rate and achieve low levels of both? The basic answer is that the Fed can try to lower the expected inflation rate. When the expected inflation rate is low, as it was in 2000, the tradeoff is more favorable than when the expected inflation rate is high, as it was in 1980.

■ Influencing the Expected Inflation Rate

The *expected inflation rate* is the inflation rate that people forecast and use to set the money wage rate and other money prices. To forecast the inflation rate, people use the same basic method that they use to forecast other variables that affect their lives.

Data make up the first ingredient in forecasting—data about the past behavior of the phenomenon that we want to forecast. When people lay heavy bets that the Detroit Lions will win a game, they base their forecast on the performance of the Lions and the other teams in recent games.

Science is the second ingredient in forecasting—the specific science that seeks to understand the phenomenon that we wish to forecast. If we want to know whether it is likely to rain tomorrow, we turn to the science of meteorology. Science tells people how to interpret data.

So to forecast inflation, people use data about past inflation and other relevant variables and the science of economics, which seeks to understand the forces that cause inflation.

You already know the relevant economics: the *AS-AD* model. You know that the money growth rate determines the growth of aggregate demand in the long run. And you know that the trend growth rate of real GDP is the growth rate of aggregate supply in the long run. So the trend money growth rate minus the trend real GDP growth rate determines the trend inflation rate.

The inflation rate fluctuates around its trend as the demand-pull and cost-push forces generate the business cycle. In an expansion, the inflation rate rises above trend, and in a recession, the inflation rate falls below trend as aggregate demand fluctuates to bring movements along the aggregate supply curve. And you know that the money growth rate is one of the influences on these aggregate demand fluctuations.

The Fed determines the money growth rate, so the major ingredient in a forecast of inflation is a forecast of the Fed's actions. Professional Fed watchers and economic forecasters use these ideas along with a lot of data and elaborate statistical models of the economy to forecast the inflation rate.

When all the relevant data and economic science are used to forecast inflation, the resulting forecast is called a **rational expectation**. The rational expectation of the inflation rate is a forecast based on the Fed's forecasted monetary policy along with forecasts of the other forces that influence aggregate demand and aggregate supply. But the dominant factor is the Fed's monetary policy.

To lower the expected inflation rate, the Fed must conduct its monetary policy in a manner that creates confidence about future inflation. Chapter 33 explores some of the strategies that might achieve such an outcome. If the Fed can lower inflation expectations, it might achieve lower inflation but not a lower unemployment rate. That is constrained by the natural unemployment rate. If the Fed targets the unemployment rate, trouble lies ahead as you're now about to see.

Rational expectation
The forecast that results from the use of all the relevant data and economic science.

■ Targeting the Unemployment Rate

Suppose the Fed decides that it wants to lower the unemployment rate. To do so, it speeds up the growth rate of aggregate demand by speeding up the growth rate of money and lowering interest rates. With the expected inflation rate anchored at a low level, the first effect of this action is a lower unemployment rate and a slightly higher inflation rate. But if the Fed drives the unemployment rate below the natural unemployment rate, the inflation rate will continue to rise.

As a higher inflation rate becomes expected, wages and prices start to rise more rapidly, so the actual inflation rate rises further. If the Fed keeps aggregate demand (and the quantity of money) growing fast enough, the inflation rate will keep rising and the unemployment rate will remain below the natural unemployment rate. But eventually, both inflation and unemployment will rise in a return to full employment and the natural rate of unemployment.

Figure 31.7 illustrates the sequence of changes that we've just described. The economy is below full employment with low inflation. Inflation expectations are well anchored at 3 percent per year. Unemployment is above the natural unemployment rate of 6 percent. The economy is on its short-run Phillips curve, $SRPC_0$ at point A, to the right of its long-run Phillips curve, $LRPC$.

Now the Fed speeds up the money growth rate and lowers interest rates. Aggregate demand begins to increase at a faster pace. With no change in expected inflation, money wage rates continue to rise by the same amount as before. As the unemployment rate falls and the inflation rate rises, the economy moves up along

---

Targeting the Unemployment Rate   MyEconLab Animation

The economy starts out at point A.

The Fed wants to lower the unemployment rate, so it makes aggregate demand grow faster and the economy slides leftward and upward along $SRPC_0$. The unemployment rate falls but the inflation rate rises.

If the Fed makes aggregate demand keep growing after the unemployment rate has fallen below the natural unemployment rate, the inflation rate keeps rising and the higher inflation becomes expected.

A rising expected inflation rate shifts the short-run Phillips curve upward toward $SRPC_1$ (red arrows). The unemployment rate remains below the natural unemployment rate throughout the adjustment to point B.

The unemployment rate has fallen but only temporarily, and the cost is permanently higher inflation.

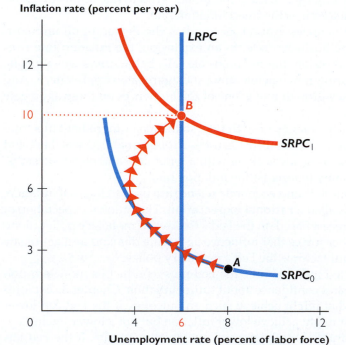

$SRPC_0$. When the expected inflation rate rises, the short-run Phillips curve shifts upward toward $SRPC_1$. The Fed's action lowers the unemployment rate but only temporarily and at the cost of permanently higher inflation. The economy follows the path of the red arrows—and unemployment remains below its natural unemployment rate until, eventually, the economy arrives at point B.

Reversing the Policy to Lower Inflation

If the inflation that results from targeting unemployment becomes unacceptably high, the only way in which low inflation can be restored is to reverse the sequence of events just described. By lowering the growth rate of aggregate demand by slowing money growth and raising interest rates, the Fed can induce a recession. The unemployment rate moves above the natural unemployment rate but inflation eventually subsides and full employment returns.

Inflation Reduction in Practice

It was back in 1981 that the Fed was last faced with a high inflation rate, and to slow it, we paid a high price. The Fed's policy action was unexpected. Money wage rates had been set too high for the path that the Fed followed. The consequence was recession—a decrease in real GDP and increased unemployment. Because it is difficult to lower the inflation rate without bringing on a recession, it is dangerous to use monetary policy to directly target unemployment. Keeping inflation low and stable is the best that monetary policy can do to keep unemployment low.

EYE on YOUR LIFE
The Short-Run Tradeoff in Your Life

MyEconLab Critical Thinking Exercise

The short-run tradeoff enters your life in three distinct ways:

1) It helps you to interpret and understand the current state of the U.S. economy.
2) It helps you to understand the policy decisions taken by the Fed.
3) It encourages you to take a stand on the relative weight that should be given to unemployment or inflation.

The State of the Economy

Consider the change in the U.S. unemployment rate and inflation rate over the past year. Did they change in the same direction or in opposite directions? Can you interpret the change as a movement along a short-run Phillips curve or as a shifting short-run Phillips curve? Can you think of reasons why the short-run Phillips curve might have shifted? Did the natural unemployment rate change? Did the expected inflation rate change?

Was your expected inflation rate the same as what people on the average expected?

The Fed's Recent Decisions

What has the Fed been doing to the interest rate over the past year? How do you think the changes in unemployment and inflation affected the Fed's policy decisions?

Unemployment or Inflation

You've seen that in the long run, there is no tradeoff between unemployment and inflation. But in the short run, there is a tradeoff. If the inflation rate is high, how much unemployment is worth putting up with, and for how long, to lower the inflation rate?

Economists don't agree on the answer to this question. Some say that if inflation is too high, it must be lowered quickly. Some even say that no unemployment is worth enduring to lower inflation.

What is your view? Which is worse, too much inflation or too much unemployment?

MyEconLab Study Plan 31.3
Key Terms Quiz
Solutions Video

CHECKPOINT 31.3

Explain how the Fed can influence the inflation rate and the unemployment rate.

Practice Problems

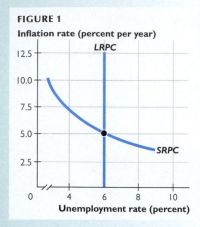

FIGURE 1

Inflation rate (percent per year)

LRPC

SRPC

Unemployment rate (percent)

Figure 1 shows the Phillips curves. Suppose that the current inflation rate is 5 percent a year and the Fed announces that it will slow the money growth rate so that inflation will fall to 2.5 percent a year.

1. If no one believes the Fed and inflation is expected to be 5 percent a year, explain how the Fed's action will affect inflation and unemployment next year.

2. If everyone believes the Fed, explain the effect of the Fed's action on inflation and unemployment next year.

3. If no one believes the Fed but the Fed keeps inflation at 2.5 percent for many years, explain the effect of the Fed's action on inflation and unemployment.

In the News

FOMC press release, June 15, 2016
The FOMC expects inflation to remain low in the near term, but to rise to 2 percent over the medium term.

Source: Board of Governors of the Federal Reserve System

Where on the short-run Phillips curve does the Fed believe the economy to be? What is the Fed anticipating will happen to the short-run Phillips curve?

Solutions to Practice Problems

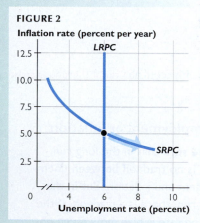

FIGURE 2

Inflation rate (percent per year)

LRPC

SRPC

Unemployment rate (percent)

1. The inflation rate falls and the unemployment rate rises as the economy moves down along its short-run Phillips curve (see Figure 2).

2. The inflation rate falls to 2.5 percent a year, and unemployment remains at 6 percent. People believe the Fed so expected inflation falls to 2.5 percent a year. The short-run Phillips curve shifts downward to $SRPC_1$ (Figure 3).

3. Initially, inflation falls below 5 percent a year and unemployment rises above 6 percent. The longer the Fed maintains this policy, the lower the expected inflation will be and the short-run Phillips curve will shift downward. The unemployment rate will decrease. Eventually, inflation will be 2.5 percent a year when the unemployment rate returns to 6 percent (Figure 4).

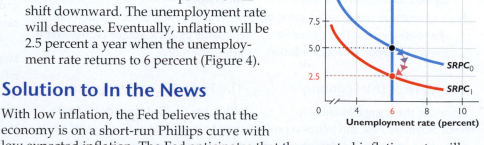

FIGURE 4

Inflation rate (percent per year)

LRPC

SRPC₀

SRPC₁

Unemployment rate (percent)

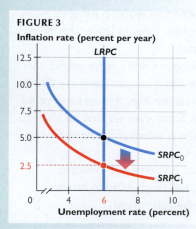

FIGURE 3

Inflation rate (percent per year)

LRPC

SRPC₀

SRPC₁

Unemployment rate (percent)

Solution to In the News

With low inflation, the Fed believes that the economy is on a short-run Phillips curve with low expected inflation. The Fed anticipates that the expected inflation rate will rise, so the *SRPC* will shift upward and the actual inflation rate will rise. This forecast implies that the unemployment rate is slightly below the natural rate.

CHAPTER SUMMARY

Key Points

1. Describe the short-run tradeoff between inflation and unemployment.

- The short-run Phillips curve is the downward-sloping relationship between the inflation rate and the unemployment rate when all other influences on these two variables remain the same.
- The short-run Phillips curve presents a *tradeoff* between inflation and unemployment.
- The short-run Phillips curve is another way of looking at the aggregate supply curve.

2. Distinguish between the short-run and the long-run Phillips curves and describe the shifting tradeoff between inflation and unemployment.

- The long-run Phillips curve shows the relationship between inflation and unemployment when the unemployment rate equals the natural unemployment rate and the inflation rate equals the expected inflation rate.
- The long-run Phillips curve is vertical at the *natural unemployment rate,* and there is no long-run tradeoff between unemployment and inflation.
- When the expected inflation rate changes, the short-run Phillips curve shifts to intersect the long-run Phillips curve at the new expected inflation rate.
- When the money growth rate changes, the unemployment rate changes temporarily and eventually returns to the natural unemployment rate—the natural rate hypothesis.
- Changes in the natural unemployment rate shift both the *SRPC* and the *LRPC.*

3. Explain how the Fed can influence the inflation rate and the unemployment rate.

- The rational expectation of the inflation rate is based on forecasts of the Fed's monetary policy and its influence on aggregate demand growth.
- A fall in the expected inflation rate improves the short-run tradeoff.
- Targeting the unemployment rate can only bring temporarily lower unemployment and at the cost of permanently higher inflation.

Key Terms

MyEconLab Key Terms Quiz

Expected inflation rate, 809
Long-run Phillips curve, 808
Natural rate hypothesis, 810

Okun's Law, 803
Rational expectation, 815
Short-run Phillips curve, 802

CHAPTER CHECKPOINT

Study Plan Problems and Applications

Table 1 describes four situations that might arise in 2018, depending on the level of aggregate demand. Table 2 describes four situations that might arise in 2019. Use Tables 1 and 2 to work Problems **1** to **4**.

TABLE 1   DATA 2018

Price level (2017 = 100)	Real GDP (trillions of 2017 dollars)	Unemployment rate (percent)
A 102	11.0	9
B 104	11.1	7
C 106	11.2	5
D 110	11.4	3

TABLE 2   DATA 2019

Price level (2017 = 100)	Real GDP (trillions of 2017 dollars)	Unemployment rate (percent)
A 108	11.1	9
B 110	11.2	7
C 112	11.3	5
D 116	11.5	3

1. Plot the short-run Phillips curve and aggregate supply curve for 2018 and mark the points *A*, *B*, *C*, and *D* on each curve that correspond to the data in Table 1.

2. In 2019, the outcome turned out to be row *C* of Table 1. Plot the short-run Phillips curve for 2019 and mark the points *A*, *B*, *C*, and *D* that correspond to the data in Table 2.

3. Compare the short-run Phillips curve of 2019 with that of 2018.

4. What is Okun's Law? If the natural unemployment rate is 6 percent, does this economy behave in accordance with Okun's Law?

5. Suppose that the natural unemployment rate is 7 percent in 2016 and it decreases to 6 percent in 2017 with no change in expected inflation. Explain how the short-run and long-run tradeoffs change.

6. Suppose that the natural unemployment rate is 7 percent and the expected inflation rate in 2017 is 3 percent a year. If the inflation rate is expected to rise to 5 percent a year in 2018, explain how the short-run and the long-run Phillips curves will change.

7. The inflation rate is 2 percent a year, and the quantity of money is growing at a pace that will maintain that inflation rate. The natural unemployment rate is 7 percent, and the current unemployment rate is 9 percent. In what direction will the unemployment rate change? How will the short-run Phillips curve and the long-run Phillips curve shift?

8. From 1991 until 2013, the average inflation rate in Russia was 151.48 percent per year. Explain how a history of rapid inflation might influence the short-run and long-run Phillips curves in Russia.

Use the following information to work Problems **9** and **10**.

India seeks more reserved central bank

There is a conflict in India between politicians who want faster growth and lower unemployment, and the central bank governor who wants price stability. The government is replacing the central bank governor and possibly increasing its inflation target.

Source: *The Wall Street Journal*, July 5, 2016

9. Sketch India's short-run and long-run Phillips curves if the expected inflation rate rises from 5 percent per year to 7 percent per year and the natural unemployment rate is constant at 8 percent.

10. If the government replaces the central bank governer and pursues faster growth by increasing aggregate demand, how will inflation and unemployment change? How will India's Phillips curves change?

11. Read *Eye on the Tradeoff* on p. 813. How can the Phillips curve account for the combination of inflation and unemployment in 2015? Do the data for that year mean that there is no tradeoff?

Instructor Assignable Problems and Applications

1. Suppose that the U.S. economy fully recovers from the 2008–2009 recession, but the natural unemployment rate has risen to 8 percent and the expected inflation rate is zero. How would the short-run and long-run Phillips curves change? Would the tradeoff be more favorable or less favorable than that of 2015? Draw a graph to illustrate your answer.

2. In an economy, the natural unemployment rate is 4 percent and the expected inflation rate is 3 percent a year. Draw a graph of the short-run and long-run Phillips curves that display this information. Label each curve.

Table 1 describes four possible situations that might arise in 2017, depending on the level of aggregate demand in 2017. Table 2 describes four possible situations that might arise in 2018. Use Tables 1 and 2 to work Problems **3** and **4**.

3. Plot the short-run Phillips curve and aggregate supply curve for 2017 and mark the points *A*, *B*, *C*, and *D* on each curve that correspond to the data in Table 1.

4. In 2017, the outcome turned out to be row *D* of Table 1. Plot the short-run Phillips curve for 2018 and mark the points *A*, *B*, *C*, and *D* that correspond to the data in Table 2.

5. Explain the relationship between the long-run Phillips curve and potential GDP and the short-run Phillips curve and the aggregate supply curve.

6. The inflation rate is 3 percent a year, and the quantity of money is growing at a pace that will maintain the inflation rate at 3 percent a year. The natural unemployment rate is 4 percent, and the current unemployment rate is 3 percent. In what direction will the unemployment rate change? How will the short-run Phillips curve and the long-run Phillips curve shift?

7. The inflation rate is 6 percent a year, the unemployment rate is 4 percent, and the economy is at full employment. The Fed announces that it intends to slow the money growth rate to keep the inflation rate at 3 percent a year for the foreseeable future. People believe the Fed. Explain how unemployment and inflation change in the short run and in the long run.

Use the following information to work Problems **8** to **10**.

Brazilian inflation and growth get worse

Brazil's central bank has increased its inflation forecast to 9 percent and cut its forecast for real GDP growth, which it now says will be minus 1.1 percent.

Source: *The Wall Street Journal*, June 24, 2015

8. According to Okun's Law, how would you expect Brazil's fall in real GDP (negative growth rate) to change the unemployment rate?

9. Draw two short-run Phillips curves and a long-run Phillips curve for Brazil. On your graph, place two points, one for Brazil in 2014 and one for the central bank's expectations about the outcome in 2015. Explain any assumptions you make.

10. Explain and illustrate with a graph the effects of the central bank of Brazil trying to lower the inflation rate by unexpectedly slowing the money growth rate. Explain how the unemployment rate will change in the short run and in the long run if the central bank persists with a lower money growth rate. Contrast the outcome with that for an expected slowing of money growth.

TABLE 1   DATA 2017

	Price level (2016 = 100)	Real GDP (trillions of 2016 dollars)	Unemployment rate (percent)
A	102	10.0	8
B	104	10.1	6
C	106	10.2	4
D	110	10.4	2

TABLE 2   DATA 2018

	Price level (2016 = 100)	Real GDP (trillions of 2016 dollars)	Unemployment rate (percent)
A	108	10.3	8
B	110	10.4	6
C	112	10.5	4
D	116	10.7	2

Multiple Choice Quiz

1. The short-run Phillips curve shows that, other things remaining the same, _____.

   A. an increase in expected inflation will lower the unemployment rate
   B. a fall in unemployment will lower the inflation rate
   C. the inflation rate rises by 1 percent when unemployment falls by 1 percent
   D. a rise in the inflation rate and a fall in the unemployment rate occur together

2. The long-run Phillips curve _____.

   A. is a horizontal curve at the expected inflation rate
   B. is a vertical curve at the natural unemployment rate
   C. slopes downward as the inflation rate falls
   D. slopes upward as the unemployment rate falls

3. The short-run Phillips curve intersects the long-run Phillips curve at _____.

   A. the expected inflation rate and the current unemployment rate
   B. the current inflation rate and the natural unemployment rate
   C. the expected inflation rate and the natural unemployment rate
   D. the current inflation rate and the current unemployment rate

4. An increase in the expected inflation rate, other things remaining the same, _____.

   A. shifts the short-run Phillips curve upward
   B. creates a movement up along the short-run Phillips curve
   C. decreases the natural unemployment rate and shifts the long-run Phillips curve leftward
   D. creates a movement up along the long-run Phillips curve with no change in the short-run Phillips curve

5. A decrease in the natural unemployment rate _____.

   A. shifts both the short-run and the long-run Phillips curves leftward
   B. shifts the short-run Phillips curve leftward but the long-run Phillips curve does not change
   C. creates a movement along the short-run Phillips curve
   D. increases the expected inflation rate and shifts the short-run Phillips curve upward

6. Suppose that the unemployment rate exceeds the natural unemployment rate and the Fed increases the money growth rate. If the Fed's action is _____.

   A. unexpected, the unemployment rate falls but the inflation rate rises
   B. unexpected, the inflation rate doesn't change but the unemployment rate falls
   C. expected, the inflation rate rises but the unemployment rate doesn't change
   D. expected, the unemployment rate doesn't change and the inflation rate equals the expected inflation rate

Can fiscal stimulus end
a recession?

Fiscal Policy

32

**When you have completed your study of this chapter,
you will be able to**

1 Describe the federal budget, the process that creates it, and a challenge that it faces.

2 Explain how fiscal stimulus is used to fight a recession.

3 Explain the supply-side effects of fiscal policy on employment, potential GDP, and the economic growth rate.

MyEconLab Big Picture Video

MyEconLab Concept Video

32.1 THE FEDERAL BUDGET

The federal budget is an annual statement of the tax revenues, outlays, and surplus or deficit of the government of the United States, together with the laws and regulations that authorize these revenues and outlays.

The federal budget has two purposes: to finance the activities of the federal government and to achieve macroeconomic objectives. The first purpose of the federal budget was its only purpose before the Great Depression years of the 1930s. The second purpose evolved as a response to the Great Depression and was initially based on the ideas of *Keynesian macroeconomics* (described in Chapter 24, pp. 614–615). **Fiscal policy** is the use of the federal budget to achieve the macroeconomic objectives of high and sustained economic growth and full employment.

Fiscal policy
The use of the federal budget to achieve the macroeconomic objectives of high and sustained economic growth and full employment.

■ The Institutions and Laws

The President and Congress make the budget and develop fiscal policy on a fixed annual time line and fiscal year. The U.S. fiscal year runs from October 1 this year to September 30 in the next calendar year. Fiscal 2018 is the fiscal year that begins on October 1, 2017.

The Roles of the President and Congress

The President *proposes* a budget to Congress each February. After Congress has passed the budget acts in September, the President either signs those acts into law or vetoes the entire budget bill. The President does not have the veto power to eliminate specific items in a budget bill and approve others—known as a line-item veto. Although the President proposes and ultimately approves the budget, the task of making the tough decisions on spending and taxes rests with Congress.

Congress begins its work on the budget with the President's proposal. The House of Representatives and the Senate develop their own budget ideas in their respective House and Senate Budget Committees. Formal conferences between the two houses eventually resolve differences of view, and a series of spending acts and an overall budget act are usually passed by both houses before the start of the fiscal year.

Figure 32.1 summarizes the budget time line and the roles of the President and Congress in the budget process.

■ Budget Balance and Debt

Budget balance
Tax revenues minus outlays.

The government's **budget balance** is equal to tax revenues minus outlays. That is,

$$\text{Budget balance} = \text{Tax revenues} - \text{Outlays}$$

If tax revenues equal outlays, the government has a *balanced budget*. The government has a *budget surplus* if tax revenues exceed outlays. The government has a *budget deficit* if outlays exceed tax revenues.

The budget projections for the 2017 fiscal year were tax revenues of $3,477 billion, outlays of $4,089 billion, and a budget deficit of $612 billion. You can see that $3,477 − $4,089 = −$612.

The government budget balance is equal to government saving, which might be zero (balanced budget), positive (budget surplus), or negative (budget deficit). When the government has a budget deficit, it incurs debt. That is, the government

■ **FIGURE 32.1**

The Federal Budget Time Line for Fiscal 2018   MyEconLab Animation

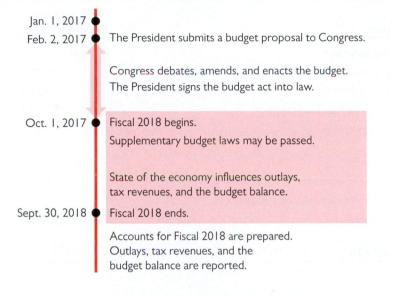

The federal budget process begins with the President's proposals in February.

Congress debates and amends the President's proposals and enacts a budget before the start of the fiscal year on October 1.

The President signs the budget act into law.

Throughout the fiscal year, Congress might pass supplementary budget laws. The budget outcome is calculated after the end of the fiscal year.

borrows to finance its budget deficit. When the government has a budget surplus, it repays some of its debt. The amount of government debt outstanding—debt that has arisen from past budget deficits—is called **national debt**.

The national debt at the end of a fiscal year equals the national debt at the end of the previous fiscal year plus the budget deficit or minus the budget surplus. For example,

Debt at the end of 2017 = Debt at the end of 2016 + Budget deficit in 2017.

At the end of the 2016 fiscal year, national debt was $19,433 billion. With a budget deficit of $612 billion in 2017, national debt at the end of the 2017 fiscal year becomes $20,045 billion. That is, $20,045 = $19,433 + $612.

National debt
The amount of government debt outstanding—debt that has arisen from past budget deficits.

A Personal Analogy

The government's budget and debt are like your budget and debt, only bigger. If you take a student loan each year to go to school, you have a budget deficit and a growing debt. After graduating, if you have a job and repay some of your loan each year, you have a budget surplus each year and a shrinking debt.

■ The Federal Budget in Fiscal 2017

Table 32.1 (on p. 826) shows the magnitudes of the main items in the federal budget in 2017. Personal income taxes and Social Security taxes are the major sources of revenue. **Transfer payments**—Social Security benefits, Medicare and Medicaid benefits, unemployment benefits, and other cash benefits paid to individuals and firms—take the largest share of the government's financial resources. Expenditure on goods and services, which includes the government's defense and homeland security budgets, is also large.

Eye on the Global Economy and *Eye on the Past* put the government's revenues, outlays, and deficit in a global and historical perspective.

Transfer payments
Social Security benefits, Medicare and Medicaid benefits, unemployment benefits, and other cash benefits.

■ **TABLE 32.1**

The Federal Budget in Fiscal 2017   MyEconLab Real-time data

The federal budget for 2017 was expected to be in a deficit. Tax revenues of $3,477 billion were expected to be $612 billion less than outlays of $4,089 billion.

Personal income taxes are the largest revenue source and transfer payments are the largest outlay.

Item	Projections (billions of dollars)
Tax Revenues	**3,477**
Personal income taxes	1,724
Social Security taxes	1,185
Corporate income taxes	343
Indirect taxes	225
Outlays	**4,089**
Transfer payments	2,574
Expenditure on goods and services	1,211
Debt interest	304
Balance	**−612**

SOURCE OF DATA: *Budget of the United States Government, Fiscal Year 2017.*

EYE on the GLOBAL ECONOMY
The U.S. Budget in Global Perspective

The United States is not alone in having a government budget deficit. All the major countries share this experience. But the United States has one of the largest budget deficits as a percentage of GDP.

To compare the budget deficits across countries, we use the concept of the "general government" deficit, which combines all levels of government: federal, state, and local.

Japan, the United Kingdom, and the United States have large deficits while Australia, Canada, the newly industrialized Asian economies, and even the Euro area have smaller deficits. New Zealand has a small budget surplus.

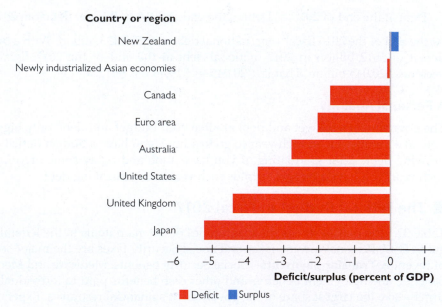

SOURCE OF DATA: International Monetary Fund, *World Economic Outlook*, April 2016.

EYE on the PAST
Federal Tax Revenues, Outlays, Deficits, and Debt

Except for a few years at the end of the 1990s, the U.S. federal government has had a budget deficit every year since 1970. You can see this fact in Figure 1, which shows the budget balance along with tax revenues and outlays from 1950 to 2015 all measured as percentages of GDP.

Figure 2 shows national debt as a percentage of GDP—the debt-to-GDP ratio. Gross debt equals Net debt held by the public plus debt held in federal government accounts.

Enormous deficits during World War II had left a legacy of debt equal to more than a year's GDP.

During the 1950s and 1960s, the government's debt-to-GDP ratio tumbled as balanced budgets combined with rapid real GDP growth. By 1974, the debt-to-GDP ratio had fallen to a low of 23 percent.

Budget deficits returned during the 1970s and swelled in the 1980s as the defense budget increased and some tax rates were cut. The result was a growing debt-to-GDP ratio that climbed to almost 50 percent by 1995.

Expenditure restraint combined with sustained real GDP growth lowered the debt-to-GDP ratio during the 1990s, but a surge in expenditures on defense and homeland security, further tax cuts, and a spending surge in 2009 and 2010 to fight the global financial crisis and recession, all combined to raise the debt-to-GDP ratio again.

Since 2010, the government has striven to keep spending under control and gradually shrink the deficit.

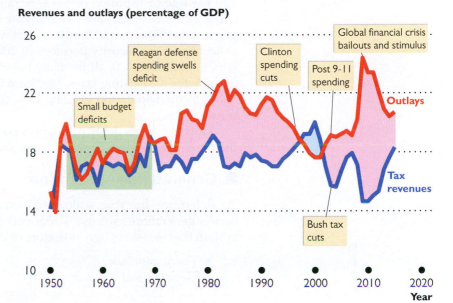

Figure 1 Tax Revenues, Outlays, and Deficits

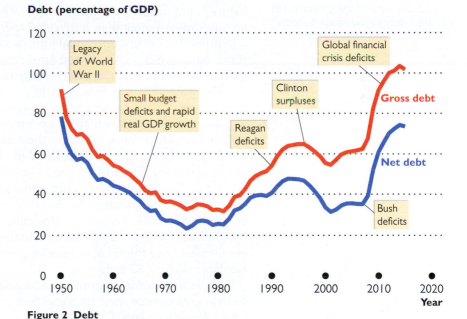

Figure 2 Debt

SOURCE OF DATA: *Budget of the U.S. Government, Fiscal Year 2017*, Historical Tables, Tables 7.1 and 14.1.

■ A Fiscal Policy Challenge

You've seen that the U.S. government has run a budget deficit and piled up debt for most of the past 40 years. That debt is going to keep growing as deficits become harder to avoid.

The age distribution of the U.S. population is the source of the problem. A surge in the birth rate after World War II created what is called the "baby boom generation." There are 77 million "baby boomers" and the first of them started collecting Social Security pensions in 2008 and became eligible for Medicare benefits in 2011. By 2030, all the baby boomers will be supported by Social Security and, under the existing laws, Medicare benefit payments will have doubled. The aging of the population is going to keep the government's debt rising for many future years.

How big is this debt? And who's going to bear its burden? Will it be borne by the current generation or will it be passed on for a future generation to bear?

■ Generational Accounting

To determine the true scale of government obligations and their distribution across generations, we use a tool called *generational accounting*—an accounting system that measures two indicators of the true state of the government's budget::

- Fiscal imbalance
- Generational imbalance

Fiscal Imbalance

Fiscal imbalance
The *present value* of the government's commitments to pay future benefits minus the *present value* of its future tax revenues..

Fiscal imbalance is the *present value* of the government's commitments to pay future benefits minus the *present value* of its future tax revenues. A *present value* is an amount of money that, if invested today, will earn interest and grow to equal a required future amount. Fiscal imbalance measures the government's true debt. It measures today's value of the future cost of the programs to which the government is committed minus today's value of the future taxes it will collect.

The government's obligation to pay Social Security pensions and Medicare benefits on an already declared scale are a debt owed by the government and are just as real as the bonds that the government issues to finance its current budget deficit. Fiscal imbalance measures the dollar value of this obligation.

Economist Jagadeesh Gokhale of the Cato Institute has reported an estimate of U.S. fiscal imbalance in his book *The Government Debt Iceberg* (see *Eye on the U.S. Economy*). The government's debt is like an iceberg because most of it is hidden.

Gokhale estimates that the Social Security and Medicare fiscal imbalance was $68 trillion in 2014. To put the $68 trillion in perspective, note that U.S. GDP in 2014 was $17 trillion. So the fiscal imbalance was 4 times the value of one year's production. And the fiscal imbalance grows every year by an amount that in 2014 was approaching $2 trillion.

These are enormous numbers and point to a catastrophic future. How can the federal government meet its Social Security and Medicare obligations? There are four alternative ways:

1. Raise income taxes
2. Raise Social Security taxes
3. Cut Social Security benefits
4. Cut other federal government spending

Because the fiscal imbalance grows every year, delaying a start on tackling the problem increases the scale of the changes needed. If we had started addressing the fiscal imbalance in 2003 and made only one of the four possible changes, income taxes would need to be raised by 69 percent, or Social Security taxes raised by 95 percent, or Social Security benefits cut by 56 percent. Cutting other government spending turns out not to be an effective alternative. Even if the government stopped *all* its other spending, including that on national defense, the saving would not eliminate the imbalance. By combining the four measures, the pain from each could be lessened, but the pain would still be severe.

Why isn't there a fifth option: keep borrowing by selling government bonds? At the current scale of deficit and debt, that option is viable. But at some point, bond holders would see that the government's debt was so large that the government would not be able to pay the interest on it. If that point were reached, the U.S. and global economies would collapse and go into deep recession or even depression.

Generational Imbalance

A fiscal imbalance must eventually be corrected and when it is, people either pay higher taxes or receive lower benefits. The concept of generational imbalance tells us who will pay. **Generational imbalance** is the division of the fiscal imbalance between the current and future generations.

In the estimates of generational imbalance, the current generation is people born before 1988, and the future generation those born in or after 1988. With division of the population, the current generation will bear most of the cost but the next generation will pick up a big chunk of the Medicare tab.

Eye on the U.S. Economy shows an estimate of the scale of fiscal imbalance and how it is distributed across the current and next generation.

Generational imbalance
The division of the fiscal imbalance between the current and future generations.

EYE on the U.S. ECONOMY
Fiscal and Generational Imbalances

The figure shows how the fiscal imbalance is divided between Social Security benefits and Medicare, and how it is distributed across the current and the next (your) generation.

Medicare is by far the major source of the imbalance.

The current generation will pay for almost all its Social Security but it will not pay for all its Medicare, and much will fall on future generations. If we sum both items, the current generation will pay 83 percent and future generations will pay 17 percent of the fiscal imbalance.

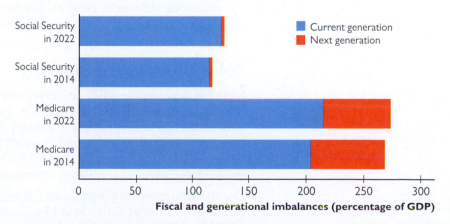

SOURCE OF DATA: Jagadeesh Gokhale, *The Government Debt Iceberg*, The Institute of Economic Affairs, London, 2014.

MyEconLab Study Plan 32.1
Key Terms Quiz
Solutions Video

CHECKPOINT 32.1

Describe the federal budget, the process that creates it, and a challenge that it faces.

Practice Problems

1. What are the tax revenues and outlays in the federal budget, and what was the projected budget balance for Fiscal 2017?

2. At the end of Fiscal 2016 national debt was $19.4 trillion. If the budget deficit remains at its Fiscal 2017 level for two years, what will the national debt be at the end of Fiscal 2018?

3. What are the three ways in which the U.S. fiscal imbalance might be successfully addressed?

In the News

U.S. budget deficit widens to near two-year high
Over the year to June 2016, the U.S. federal government deficit totaled $523 billion, which is 20.6 percent higher than a year earlier.

Source: *The Wall Street Journal*, July 13, 2016

Given the information in the news clip, by how much did U.S. national debt change between June 2014 and June 2016?

Solutions to Practice Problems

1. The tax revenues are personal income taxes, Social Security taxes, corporate income taxes, and indirect taxes; the outlays are transfer payments, expenditure on goods and services, and debt interest. The projected budget balance for Fiscal 2017 was a deficit of $612 billion.

2. At the end of 2016, national debt was $19.4 trillion. The budget deficit in 2017 was $612 billion or $0.6 trillion. Adding $0.6 trillion per year to the 2016 national debt for two years takes the debt to $20.6 trillion at the end of 2018.

3. The three ways in which the U.S. fiscal imbalance might be successfully addressed are 1) a rise in income taxes, 2) a rise in Social Security taxes, and 3) a cut in Social Security benefits. The fourth way of cutting the deficit—cutting other spending—would not be successful because there isn't enough other spending to cut.

Solution to In the News

National debt in June 2016 = National debt in June 2014 + Budget deficit in 2015 + Budget deficit in 2016. So the change in the national debt from June 2014 to June 2016 = Budget deficit in 2015 + Budget deficit in 2016. The budget deficit in 2016 was $523 billion. The budget deficit in 2015 was 20.6 percent lower than $523 billion, which is $523 billion divided by 1.206 and equals $434 billion. (Check by calculating the percentage difference between $523 and $434.)

Use these numbers in the formula: Change in the national debt from June 2014 to June 2016 = Budget deficit in 2015 + Budget deficit in 2016 = $434 billion + $523 billion = $957 billion.

32.2 FISCAL STIMULUS

MyEconLab Concept Video

We've described the federal budget and the institutions that make fiscal policy, and now we're going to study the *effects* of fiscal policy. We begin by exploring its effects on aggregate demand.

■ Fiscal Policy and Aggregate Demand

A number of different fiscal policy actions might be used in an attempt to stimulate aggregate demand. Government expenditure on goods and services or government transfer payments might be increased and taxes might be cut. And these changes might occur as an automatic response to the state of the economy or as a result of new spending or tax decisions by Congress.

A fiscal policy action that is triggered by the state of the economy is called an **automatic fiscal policy**. For example, an increase in unemployment induces an increase in transfer payments, and a fall in incomes induces a decrease in tax revenues.

A fiscal policy action that is initiated by an act of Congress is called a **discretionary fiscal policy**. A discretionary fiscal policy action requires a change in a spending program or in a tax law. Increases in defense spending or cuts in the income tax rates are examples of discretionary fiscal policy.

Automatic fiscal policy
A fiscal policy action that is triggered by the state of the economy.

Discretionary fiscal policy
A fiscal policy action that is initiated by an act of Congress.

■ Automatic Fiscal Policy

Automatic fiscal policy is a consequence of tax revenues and outlays that fluctuate with real GDP. These features of fiscal policy are called **automatic stabilizers** because they work to stabilize real GDP without explicit action by the government.

Automatic stabilizers
Features of fiscal policy that stabilize real GDP without explicit action by the government.

Induced Taxes

On the revenue side of the budget, tax laws define tax *rates*, not tax *dollars*. Tax dollars paid depend on tax rates and incomes. But incomes vary with real GDP, so tax revenues depend on real GDP. Taxes that vary with real GDP are called **induced taxes**. When real GDP increases in an expansion, wages and profits rise, so the taxes paid on these incomes—induced taxes—rise. When real GDP decreases in a recession, wages and profits fall, so the induced taxes on these incomes fall.

Induced taxes
Taxes that vary with real GDP.

Needs-Tested Spending

On the expenditure side of the budget, the government creates programs that entitle suitably qualified people and businesses to receive benefits. The spending on such programs is called *needs-tested spending*, and it results in transfer payments that depend on the economic state of individual citizens and businesses. In a recession, as the unemployment rate increases, needs-tested spending on unemployment benefits and food stamps increases. In an expansion, the unemployment rate falls and needs-tested spending decreases.

Automatic Stimulus

Because government tax revenues fall and outlays increase in a recession, automatic stabilizers provide stimulus that helps to shrink the recessionary gap. Similarly, because tax revenues rise and outlays decrease in a boom, automatic stabilizers shrink an inflationary gap.

Structural surplus or deficit
The budget balance that would occur if the economy were at full employment.

Cyclical surplus or deficit
The budget balance that arises because tax revenues and outlays are not at their full-employment levels.

■ Cyclical and Structural Budget Balances

To identify the government budget deficit that arises from the business cycle, we distinguish between the budget's structural balance and its cyclical balance. The **structural surplus or deficit** is the budget balance that would occur if the economy were at full employment. That is, the structural balance is the balance that the full-employment level of real GDP would generate given the spending programs and tax laws that Congress has created. The **cyclical surplus or deficit** is the budget balance that arises purely because tax revenues and outlays are not at their full-employment levels. That is, the cyclical balance is the balance that arises because tax revenues rise and outlays fall in an inflationary gap and tax revenues fall and outlays rise in a recessionary gap.

The *actual* budget balance equals the sum of the structural balance and cyclical balance. A cyclical deficit corrects itself when full employment returns, but a structural deficit requires action by Congress. *Eye on the U.S. Economy* below looks at the recent history of the U.S. structural and cyclical balances.

EYE on the U.S. ECONOMY
The U.S. Structural and Cyclical Budget Balances

The U.S. federal budget balance in 2015 was a deficit of $1 trillion and the recessionary gap was close to $1 trillion. With such a large recessionary gap, you would expect some of the deficit to be cyclical. But how much of the 2015 deficit was cyclical? How much was structural?

According to the Congressional Budget Office (CBO), a quarter of the 2015 deficit was cyclical. The figure shows the actual and cyclical balances as percentages of GDP from 1990 through 2015.

The structural balance equals the actual balance minus the cyclical balance. You can see that the structural deficit was small in 2007, increased in 2008, and exploded in 2009. The 2009 fiscal stimulus package created most of this structural deficit.

When full employment returns, which the CBO says will be in 2018, the cyclical deficit will vanish, but the structural deficit must be addressed by further acts of Congress. No one knows the discretionary measures that will be taken to reduce the structural deficit and this situation creates uncertainty.

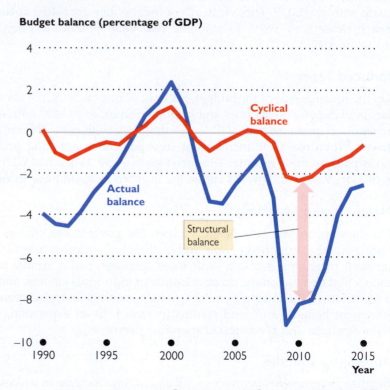

SOURCE OF DATA: Congressional Budget Office.

■ Discretionary Fiscal Policy

Discretionary fiscal policy can take the form of a change in government outlays or a change in tax revenues. And a change in government outlays can take the form of a change in expenditure on goods and services or a change in transfer payments. *Other things remaining the same*, a change in any of the items in the government budget changes aggregate demand and has a multiplier effect—aggregate demand changes by a greater amount than the initial change in the item in the government budget. These multiplier effects are similar to the ones that you studied in Chapters 29 and 30. (Other things might not remain the same, and we'll look at some possible offsetting factors after we've explained the basic Keynesian idea.)

The Government Expenditure Multiplier

The **government expenditure multiplier** is the effect of a change in government expenditure on goods and services on aggregate demand. Government expenditure is a component of aggregate expenditure, so when government expenditure increases, aggregate demand increases. Real GDP increases and induces an increase in consumption expenditure, which brings a further increase in aggregate expenditure. A multiplier process like the one described in Chapter 30 (pp. 788–792) ensues.

> **Government expenditure multiplier**
> The effect of a change in government expenditure on goods and services on aggregate demand.

The Tax Multiplier

The **tax multiplier** is the magnification effect of a change in taxes on aggregate demand. A *decrease* in taxes *increases* disposable income, which increases consumption expenditure. A decrease in taxes works like an increase in government expenditure. But the magnitude of the tax multiplier is smaller than the government expenditure multiplier because a $1 tax cut generates *less than* $1 of additional expenditure. The marginal propensity to consume determines the initial increase in expenditure induced by a tax cut and the magnitude of the tax multiplier. For example, if the marginal propensity to consume is 0.75, then the initial increase in consumption expenditure induced by a $1 tax cut is only 75 cents. In this case, the tax multiplier is 0.75 times the magnitude of the government expenditure multiplier.

> **Tax multiplier**
> The effect of a change in taxes on aggregate demand.

The Transfer Payments Multiplier

The **transfer payments multiplier** is the effect of a change in transfer payments on aggregate demand. This multiplier works like the tax multiplier but in the opposite direction. An *increase* in transfer payments *increases* disposable income, which *increases* consumption expenditure. The magnitude of the transfer payments multiplier is similar to that of the tax multiplier. Just as a $1 tax cut generates *less than* $1 of additional expenditure, so also does a $1 increase in transfer payments. Again, it is the marginal propensity to consume that determines the increase in expenditure induced by an increase in transfer payments.

> **Transfer payments multiplier**
> The effect of a change in transfer payments on aggregate demand.

The Balanced Budget Multiplier

The **balanced budget multiplier** is the magnification effect on aggregate demand of a *simultaneous* change in government expenditure and taxes that leaves the budget balance unchanged. The balanced budget multiplier is not zero. It is greater than zero because a $1 increase in government expenditure injects a dollar more into aggregate demand while a $1 tax rise (or decrease in transfer payments) takes less than $1 from aggregate demand. So when both government expenditure and taxes increase by $1, aggregate demand increases.

> **Balanced budget multiplier**
> The effect on aggregate demand of a *simultaneous* change in government expenditure and taxes that leaves the budget balance unchanged.

■ A Successful Fiscal Stimulus

If real GDP is below potential GDP, the government might pursue a fiscal stimulus by increasing its expenditure on goods and services, increasing transfer payments, cutting taxes, or doing some combination of all three. Figure 32.2 shows us how these actions increase aggregate demand for a successful stimulus package.

In Figure 32.2(a), potential GDP is $16 trillion but real GDP is only $15 trillion. The economy is at point A and there is a *recessionary gap* (see Chapter 29, p. 763).

To eliminate the recessionary gap and restore full employment, the government introduces a fiscal stimulus. An increase in government expenditure or a tax cut increases aggregate expenditure by ΔE. If this were the only change in spending plans, the AD curve would become $AD_0 + \Delta E$ in Figure 32.2(b). But the initial increase in government expenditure sets off a multiplier process, which increases consumption expenditure. As the multiplier process plays out, aggregate demand increases and the AD curve shifts rightward to AD_1.

With no change in the price level, the economy would move from the initial point A to point B on AD_1. But the increase in aggregate demand combined with the upward-sloping aggregate supply curve brings a rise in the price level, and the economy moves to a new equilibrium at point C. The price level rises to 105, real GDP increases to $16 trillion, and the economy returns to full employment.

The "Cash for Clunkers" program stimulated aggregate demand.

■ **FIGURE 32.2**

Fiscal Stimulus in the *AS-AD* Model

MyEconLab Animation

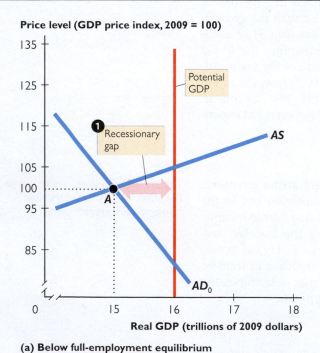

(a) Below full-employment equilibrium

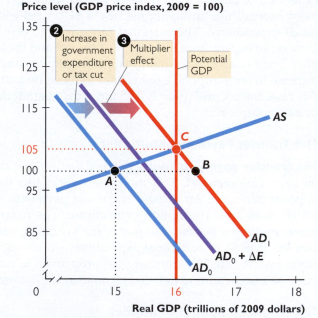

(b) Potential GDP

Potential GDP is $16 trillion. At point A, real GDP is $15 trillion, and ❶ there is a $1 trillion recessionary gap. ❷ An increase in government expenditure or a tax cut increases expenditure by ΔE.

❸ The multiplier increases induced expenditure. The AD curve shifts rightward to AD_1, the price level rises to 105, real GDP increases to $16 trillion, and the recessionary gap is eliminated.

EYE on FISCAL STIMULUS

MyEconLab Critical Thinking Exercise

Can Fiscal Stimulus End a Recession?

In February 2009, in the depths of the 2008–2009 recession, Congress passed the American Recovery and Reinvestment Act, a $787 billion fiscal stimulus package that the President signed at an economic forum in Denver.

This act of Congress is an example of discretionary fiscal policy. Did this action by Congress contribute to ending the 2008–2009 recession and making the recession less severe than it might have been?

The Obama Administration economists are confident that the answer is yes: The stimulus package made a significant contribution to easing and ending the recession.

But many, and perhaps most, economists think that the stimulus package played a small role and that the truly big story is not discretionary fiscal policy but the role played by automatic stabilizers.

Let's take a closer look at the fiscal policy actions and their likely effects.

Discretionary Fiscal Policy

In a number of speeches, President Obama promised that fiscal stimulus would save or create 650,000 jobs by the end of the 2009 summer. In October 2009, the Administration economists declared the promise fulfilled. Fiscal stimulus had saved or created the promised 650,000 jobs.

This claim of success might be correct but it isn't startling and it isn't a huge claim. To see why, start by asking how much GDP 650,000 people would produce. In 2009, each employed person produced $100,000 of real GDP on average. So 650,000 people would produce $65 billion of GDP.

Although the fiscal stimulus passed by Congress totalled $787 billion, by October 2009 only 20 percent of the stimulus had been spent (or taken in tax breaks). So the stimulus was about $160 billion.

If government outlays of $160 billion created $65 billion of GDP, the multiplier was 0.4 (65/160 = 0.4).

This multiplier is much smaller than the 1.6 that the Obama economists say will eventually occur. They believe, like Keynes, that the multiplier starts out small and gets larger over time as spending plans respond to rising incomes. An initial increase in expenditure increases aggregate expenditure. But the increase in aggregate expenditure generates higher incomes, which in turn induces greater consumption expenditure.

Automatic Fiscal Policy

Government revenue is sensitive to the state of the economy. When personal incomes and corporate profits fall, income tax revenues fall too. When unemployment increases, outlays on unemployment benefits and other social welfare benefits increase. These fiscal policy changes are automatic. They occur with speed and without help from Congress.

The scale of automatic fiscal policy changes depends on the depth of recession. In 2009, real GDP sank to 6 percent below potential GDP—a recessionary gap of $800 billion.

Responding to this deep recession, tax revenues crashed and transfer payments skyrocketed. The figure below shows the magnitudes as percentages of GDP. You can see that the automatic stabilizers were much bigger than the discretionary actions—six times as large. This automatic action, not the stimulus package, played the major role in limiting job losses.

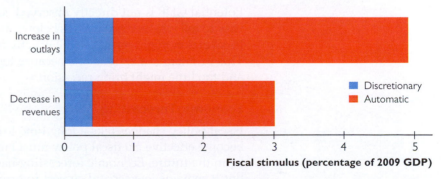

Fiscal stimulus (percentage of 2009 GDP)

SOURCES OF DATA: Budget of the United States, 2010, Bureau of Economic Analysis, and White House press releases.

■ Limitations of Discretionary Fiscal Policy

Discretionary fiscal stabilization policy looks easy. Calculate the output gap and the multiplier, and determine the direction and size of the change in government expenditure or taxes that will eliminate the gap. In reality, discretionary fiscal policy is seriously hampered by many factors, four of which are

- Lawmaking time lag
- Shrinking area of lawmaker discretion
- Estimating potential GDP
- Economic forecasting

Lawmaking Time Lag

The lawmaking time lag is the amount of time it takes Congress to pass the laws needed to change taxes or spending. This process takes time because each member of Congress has a different idea about what is the best tax or spending program to change, so long debates and committee meetings are needed to reconcile conflicting views. The economy might benefit from fiscal stimulation today, but by the time Congress acts, a different fiscal medicine might be needed.

Shrinking Area of Lawmaker Discretion

During the 2000s, federal spending increased faster than in any other peacetime period. This growth in spending was driven by two forces: increased security threats and an aging population.

The increased security threat resulted in a large increase in expenditure on the military and homeland security. The aging population brought a very large increase in expenditure on entitlement programs such as Medicare.

The growth of this spending has reduced the areas in which Congress can act to change either taxes or outlays. Around 80 percent of the federal budget is effectively off limits for discretionary policy action, and the remaining 20 percent of items are very hard to cut.

So even if the state of the economy calls for a change in fiscal policy, Congress's room to maneuver is severely limited.

Estimating Potential GDP

Potential GDP is not directly observed, so it must be estimated. Because it is not easy to tell whether real GDP is below, above, or at potential GDP, a discretionary fiscal action might move real GDP *away* from potential GDP instead of toward it. This problem is a serious one because too large a fiscal stimulus brings inflation and too little might bring recession.

Economic Forecasting

Fiscal policy changes take a long time to enact in Congress and yet more time to become effective. So fiscal policy must target forecasts of where the economy will be in the future. Economic forecasting has improved enormously in recent years, but it remains inexact and subject to error. So for a second reason, discretionary fiscal action might move real GDP *away* from potential GDP and create the very problems that it seeks to correct.

Further problems with discretionary fiscal policy actions arise from their supply-side effects that we will examine in the next section.

CHECKPOINT 32.2

MyEconLab Study Plan 32.2
Key Terms Quiz
Solutions Video

Explain how fiscal stimulus is used to fight a recession.

Practice Problems

1. Classify the following items as automatic fiscal policy, discretionary fiscal policy, or not part of fiscal policy.
   - A decrease in tax revenues in a recession
   - Additional government expenditure to upgrade highways
   - An increase in the public education budget
   - A cut in infrastructure expenditure during a boom

2. Explain how aggregate demand changes when government expenditure on national defense increases by $100 billion.

3. Explain how aggregate demand changes when the government increases taxes by $100 billion.

4. Explain how aggregate demand changes when the government increases both expenditure on goods and services and taxes by $100 billion.

In the News

Clinton and Trump on fiscal policy
In the 2016 Presidential election campaign, both Hillary Clinton and Donald Trump committed to big government infrastructure spending and tax cuts.
Source: The Wall Street Journal, July 27, 2016

What policy will change aggregate demand the most: an increase in infrastructure spending or a cut in taxes?

Solutions to Practice Problems

1. A decrease in tax revenues in a recession is an automatic fiscal policy.
   Expenditure to upgrade highways is a discretionary fiscal policy.
   An increase in the public education budget is a discretionary fiscal policy.
   A cut in infrastructure expenditure is a discretionary fiscal policy.

2. Aggregate demand increases by more than $100 billion because government expenditure increases induced expenditure.

3. Aggregate demand decreases but by less than $100 billion because the tax increase decreases disposable income, which decreases induced expenditure.

4. An increase in government expenditure of $100 billion increases aggregate demand by more than $100 billion. An increase in taxes of $100 billion decreases aggregate demand by less than $100 billion. The increase is greater than the decrease, so together aggregate demand increases. The balanced budget multiplier is positive.

Solution to In the News

Infrastructure spending is expenditure on goods and services and its effect on aggregate demand is determined by the *government expenditure multiplier*. The effect of a decrease in taxes on aggregate demand is determined by the *tax multiplier*. The magnitude of the government expenditure multiplier exceeds the tax multiplier, so infrastructure spending will increase aggregate demand by more than a tax cut of the same magnitude.

MyEconLab Concept Video

32.3 THE SUPPLY SIDE: POTENTIAL GDP AND GROWTH

Supply-side effects
The effects of fiscal policy on potential GDP and the economic growth rate.

You've seen how fiscal policy can influence the output gap by changing aggregate demand and real GDP relative to potential GDP. But fiscal policy also influences potential GDP and the growth rate of potential GDP. These influences on potential GDP and economic growth arise because the government provides public goods and services that increase productivity and because taxes change the incentives that people face. These influences, called **supply-side effects**, operate more slowly than the demand-side effects emphasized by Keynesians. Supply-side effects are often ignored in times of recession when the focus is on fiscal stimulus and restoring full employment. But in the long run, the supply-side effects of fiscal policy dominate and determine potential GDP.

We'll begin an account of the supply side with a brief explanation of how full employment and potential GDP are determined in the absence of government services and taxes. Then we'll see how government services and taxes change employment and potential GDP.

■ Full Employment and Potential GDP

The quantity of labor demanded and the quantity of labor supplied depend on the real wage rate. The higher the real wage rate, other things remaining the same, the smaller is the quantity of labor demanded and the greater is the quantity of labor supplied. When the real wage rate has adjusted to make the quantity of labor demanded equal to the quantity of labor supplied, there is full employment. And when the quantity of labor is the full-employment quantity, real GDP equals potential GDP.

This brief description of how potential GDP and the full-employment quantity of labor are determined is a summary of the more detailed account in Chapter 24 (pp. 617–623).

How do taxes and the provision of government services—the elements of fiscal policy—influence employment and potential GDP?

■ Fiscal Policy, Employment, and Potential GDP

Both sides of the government budget influence potential GDP. The expenditure side provides public goods and services that enhance productivity and make labor more productive. The revenue side levies taxes that modify incentives that change the full-employment quantities of labor, as well as the amount of saving and investment.

Public Goods and Productivity

Governments provide a legal system and other infrastructure services such as roads and highways, fire-fighting and policing services, and national security, all of which increase the nation's productive potential. Today's world provides a vivid demonstration of the role that good government plays in enhancing productivity. Compare the chaos and absence of productivity in parts of the Middle East and Africa with the order and calm and the productivity they permit in the United States and other industrialized countries.

Public goods and services, financed by the government budget, increase the real GDP that a given amount of labor can produce. So the provision of public goods and services increases potential GDP.

Taxes and Incentives

A tax drives a wedge—called the **tax wedge**—between the price paid by a buyer and the price received by a seller. In the labor market, the income tax drives a wedge between the cost of labor to employers and the take-home pay of workers and decreases the equilibrium quantity of labor employed. A smaller quantity of labor produces a smaller amount of real GDP, so taxes lower potential GDP.

The income tax wedge is only a part of the tax wedge that affects decisions to supply labor. Taxes on expenditure also create a tax wedge that affects employment and potential GDP.

Taxes on consumption expenditure add to the tax wedge that lowers potential GDP. The reason is that a tax on consumption expenditure raises the prices paid for consumption goods and services and is equivalent to a cut in the real wage rate. The incentive to supply labor depends on the goods and services that an hour of labor can buy. The higher the tax on consumption expenditure, the smaller is the quantity of goods and services that an hour of labor buys and the weaker is the incentive to supply labor.

The expenditure tax rate must be added to the income tax rate to find the total tax wedge. If the income tax rate is 25 percent and the tax rate on consumption expenditure is 10 percent, a dollar earned buys only 65 cents worth of goods and services. The tax wedge is 35 percent.

Tax wedge
The gap created by a tax between what a buyer pays and what a seller receives. In the labor market, it is the gap between the before-tax wage rate and the after-tax wage rate.

EYE on the GLOBAL ECONOMY
Some Real-World Tax Wedges

Edward C. Prescott of the Arizona State University, who shared the 2004 Nobel Prize for Economic Science, has estimated the tax wedges for a number of countries. The U.S. tax wedge is a combination of consumption taxes, income taxes, and Social Security taxes.

Among the industrial countries, the U.S. tax wedge is relatively small. Prescott estimates that in France, (marginal) taxes on consumption are 33 percent and taxes on incomes are 49 percent. The estimates for the United Kingdom fall between those for France and the United States. The figure shows these components of the tax wedges in the three countries.

According to Prescott's estimates, the tax wedge has a powerful effect on

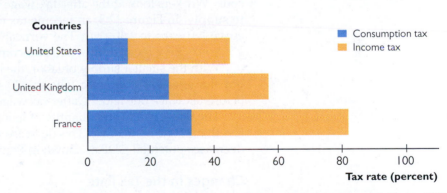

SOURCE OF DATA: Edward C. Prescott, *American Economic Review*, 2003.

employment and potential GDP. Potential GDP per person in France is lower than that of the United States, and the entire difference can be attributed to the difference in the tax wedge in the two countries.

Potential GDP per person in the United Kingdom is lower than that of the United States, and about a third of the difference arises from the different tax wedges. (The rest is due to different productivities.)

■ Fiscal Policy and Potential GDP: A Graphical Analysis

Figure 32.3 illustrates the effects of fiscal policy on potential GDP. It begins with the economy at full employment and with no income tax.

Full Employment With No Income Tax

In part (a), the demand for labor curve is *LD*, and the supply of labor curve is *LS*. The equilibrium real wage rate is $30 an hour, and 250 billion hours of labor a year are employed. The economy is at full employment. In Figure 32.3(b), the production function is *PF*. (This production function incorporates the productivity of an efficient provision of public services.) When 250 billion hours of labor are employed, real GDP—which is also potential GDP—is $18 trillion.

Let's now see how an income tax changes potential GDP.

The Effects of the Income Tax

The tax on labor income influences potential GDP by changing the full-employment quantity of labor. The income tax weakens the incentive to work and drives a wedge between the take-home wage of workers and the cost of labor to firms. The result is a smaller quantity of labor employed and a smaller potential GDP. Figure 32.3 shows this outcome.

In the labor market in part (a), the income tax has no effect on the demand for labor because the quantity of labor that firms plan to hire depends only on how productive labor is and what labor costs—the real wage rate. The demand for labor curve remains at *LD*.

But the income tax changes the supply of labor. With no income tax, the real wage rate is $30 an hour and 250 billion hours of labor a year are employed. An income tax weakens the incentive to work. Workers must pay the government part of each dollar of the before-tax wage rate, as determined by the income tax code. Workers look at the after-tax wage rate when they decide how much labor to supply. In Figure 32.3, an income tax of $15 an hour shifts the supply of labor curve leftward to *LS + tax*. The vertical distance between the *LS* curve and the *LS + tax* curve measures the $15 of income tax.

With the smaller supply of labor, the before-tax wage rate rises to $35 an hour but the after-tax wage rate falls to $20 an hour. The gap created between the before-tax wage rate and the after-tax wage rate is the *tax wedge*.

The new equilibrium quantity of labor employed is 200 billion hours a year—less than in the no-tax case. This decrease in the full-employment quantity of labor decreases potential GDP as shown in Figure 32.3(b).

Changes in the Tax Rate

A change in the income tax rate changes equilibrium employment and potential GDP. In the example that you've just worked through, the tax rate is about 43 percent—a $15 tax on a $35 wage rate. If the income tax rate is increased, the supply of labor decreases yet more and the *LS + tax* curve shifts farther leftward. Equilibrium employment and potential GDP decrease.

If the income tax rate is decreased, the supply of labor increases and the *LS + tax* curve shifts rightward. Equilibrium employment and potential GDP increase.

You can now see that a tax cut has two effects: It increases aggregate demand by boosting consumption expenditure and it increases potential GDP.

FIGURE 32.3

Fiscal Policy and Potential GDP

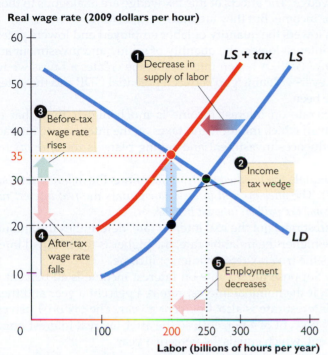

(a) Income tax in the labor market

(b) Income tax and potential GDP

In part (a), the demand for labor is *LD* and the supply of labor is *LS*. With no income tax, the equilibrium real wage rate is $30 an hour and employment is 250 billion hours. In part (b), the production function, *PF*, tells us that 250 billion hours of labor (full employment of labor) produces a potential GDP of $18 trillion.

An income tax ❶ decreases the supply of labor and creates ❷ an income tax wedge between the wage that firms pay and the wage that workers receive. ❸ The before-tax wage rate paid by employers rises and ❹ the after-tax wage rate received by workers falls. ❺ Employment decreases and ❻ potential GDP decreases.

Taxes, Deficits, and Economic Growth

You've just seen how taxes can change incentives in the labor market and influence potential GDP. Taxes also affect the market for financial capital, which influences the amount of saving and investment; and saving and investment in turn affect the pace of capital accumulation and the economic growth rate.

Fiscal policy influences the economic growth rate in two ways:

First, taxes drive a wedge between the interest rate paid by borrowers and the interest rate received by lenders. This wedge lowers the amount of saving and investment and slows the economic growth rate.

Second, if the government has a budget deficit, then government borrowing to finance the deficit competes with firms' borrowing to finance investment and to some degree, government borrowing "crowds out" private investment.

Let's examine these two influences on economic growth a bit more closely.

Interest Rate Tax Wedge

Lenders pay an income tax on the interest they receive from borrowers, which creates an interest rate tax wedge. The effects of this tax wedge are analogous to those of the tax wedge on labor income. But they are more serious for two reasons.

First, a tax on wages lowers the quantity of labor employed and lowers potential GDP, while a tax on interest lowers the quantity of saving and investment and slows the *growth rate of real GDP*. A tax on interest income creates a Lucas wedge (Chapter 24, p. 616)—an ever-widening gap between potential GDP and the potential GDP that might have been.

Second, the true tax rate on interest income is much higher than that on wages because of the way in which inflation and taxes on the interest rate interact. The interest rate that influences investment and saving plans is the *after-tax real interest rate*.

The *real interest rate* equals the *nominal interest rate* minus the *inflation rate* (see Chapter 23, pp. 606–607). The *after-tax real interest rate* equals the *real interest rate* minus the amount of *income tax paid on interest income*.

But the nominal interest rate, not the real interest rate, determines the amount of tax to be paid; and the higher the inflation rate, the higher is the nominal interest rate, and the higher is the true tax rate on interest income.

Here is an example. Suppose the tax rate on interest income is 40 percent of the nominal interest rate. If the nominal interest rate is 4 percent a year and there is no inflation, the real interest rate is also 4 percent a year. The tax on 4 percent interest is 1.6 percent (40 percent of 4 percent), so the after-tax real interest rate is 4 percent minus 1.6 percent, which equals 2.4 percent a year.

Now suppose that the nominal interest rate is 10 percent a year and the inflation rate is 6 percent a year, so the real interest rate is still 4 percent a year. The tax on 10 percent interest is 4 percent (40 percent of 10 percent), so now the after-tax real interest rate is 4 percent minus 4 percent, which equals zero. The true tax rate in this case is not 40 percent but 100 percent!

Even modest inflation makes the true tax rate on interest income extremely high and results in a smaller equilibrium quantity of saving and investment, a slower rate of capital accumulation, and a slower growth rate of real GDP.

Deficits and Crowding Out

With no change in the government's outlays, a tax cut that increases the budget deficit brings an increase in the demand for loanable funds. (You learned about this effect of a government budget deficit in Chapter 26, pp. 683–684.) An increase in the demand for loanable funds raises the real interest rate and crowds out private investment. There is uncertainty about the magnitude of the crowding-out effect but no doubt about its presence.

You can see that this effect of an income tax cut works against the incentive effect. A lower income tax rate shrinks the tax wedge and stimulates employment, saving, and investment, but a higher budget deficit crowds out some investment.

■ The Supply-Side Debate

Before 1980, few economists paid attention to the supply-side effects of taxes on employment and potential GDP. Then, when Ronald Reagan took office as President, a group of supply-siders began to argue the virtues of cutting taxes. Arthur Laffer was one of them. Laffer and his supporters were not held in high esteem among mainstream economists, but they did become influential for a period. They correctly argued that tax cuts would increase employment and increase output. But they incorrectly argued that tax cuts would increase tax revenues by enough to decrease the budget deficit. Given that U.S. tax rates are among the lowest in the industrial world, it is unlikely that tax cuts would increase tax revenues. When the Reagan administration did cut taxes, the budget deficit increased, a fact that reinforces this view.

Supply-side economics became tarnished because of its association with Laffer and came to be called "voodoo economics." But mainstream economists, including Martin Feldstein, a Harvard professor who was Reagan's chief economic adviser, recognized the power of tax cuts as incentives but took the standard view that tax cuts without spending cuts would swell the budget deficit and bring a crowding-out effect. This view is now widely accepted by economists on both sides of the political debate.

■ Long-Run Fiscal Policy Effects

The long-run consequences of fiscal policy are the most profound ones. If investment is crowded out by a large budget deficit, the economic growth rate slows and potential GDP gets ever farther below what it might have been as the Lucas wedge widens. If a large budget deficit persists so that debt increases, confidence in the value of money is eroded and inflation erupts. History provides many examples of this consequence of a fiscal stimulus that gets out of control. It is these long-run effects of fiscal policy that make it vital to keep government outlays and budget deficits under control and to have a plan for restoring a balanced budget at full employment.

EYE on YOUR LIFE
MyEconLab Critical Thinking Exercise
Your Views on Fiscal Policy and How Fiscal Policy Affects You

Consider the U.S. economy right now. Using all the knowledge that you have accumulated during your course and by reading or watching the current news, try to determine the macroeconomic policy issues that face the U.S. economy today.

Do we have a business-cycle problem? Does the economy have a recessionary gap or an inflationary gap, or is the economy back at full employment?

Do we have a productivity problem? Is potential GDP either too low or growing too slowly?

In light of your assessment of the current state of the U.S. economy, what type of fiscal policy would you recommend and vote for?

Are you more concerned about the provision of public services, the size of the budget deficit, or the size of the tax wedge?

If you are more concerned about the provision of public services, would your preferred package include increased spending? If so, on what programs? How would you pay for the expenditure?

If you are more concerned about the size of the budget deficit, how would you propose lowering it?

If you are more concerned about the tax wedge, would your preferred fiscal package include tax cuts? If it would, what public services would you cut to achieve lower taxes?

Consider recent changes in fiscal policy that you have seen reported in the media. What do you think these changes say about the federal government's views of the state of the economy? Do these views agree with yours?

Thinking further about the recent changes in fiscal policy: How do you expect these changes to affect you? How might your spending, saving, and labor supply decisions change?

Using your own responses to fiscal policy changes as an example, are these policy changes influencing aggregate demand, aggregate supply, or both? How do you think they will change real GDP?

MyEconLab Study Plan 32.3
Key Terms Quiz
Solutions Video

CHECKPOINT 32.3

Explain the supply-side effects of fiscal policy on employment, potential GDP, and the economic growth rate.

Practice Problems

1. The government cuts the income tax rate. Explain the effects of this action on the supply of labor, demand for labor, equilibrium employment, the real wage rate, and potential GDP.

2. What is the true income tax rate on interest income if the nominal interest rate is 8 percent a year, the inflation rate is 5 percent a year, and the tax rate on nominal interest is 25 percent?

3. If the government cuts its outlays but tax revenue is unchanged, explain the effects on saving, investment, the real interest rate, and the growth rate of real GDP.

In the News

New Social Security bill raises payroll tax cap
Currently the 12.4 percent Social Security tax applies only on earnings up to $118,500. The House of Representatives wants to expand the tax and make it apply to higher earnings and eventually, by 2021, to apply it to earnings up to $308,750.

Source: *Investopedia*, July 29, 2016

Explain how the expanded payroll tax will influence employment and potential GDP.

Solutions to Practice Problems

1. When the government cuts the income tax rate, the supply of labor increases but the demand for labor does not change. The equilibrium level of employment increases. The real wage rate paid by employers decreases and the real wage rate received by workers increases—the tax wedge shrinks. With increased employment, potential GDP increases.

2. The true tax is 66.67 percent. With a nominal interest rate of 8 percent a year and a tax rate of 25 percent, the tax paid is 25 percent of 8 percent, which is 2 percent. The before-tax real interest rate is 8 percent minus 5 percent, which is 3 percent a year. The true tax paid is 2 percent tax divided by 3 percent before-tax real interest rate, or 66.67 percent.

3. If the government cuts outlays but tax revenue is unchanged, the budget deficit decreases or the budget surplus increases. Either way, in the loanable funds market, the real interest rate falls and private saving decreases, but total saving and investment increase. With greater investment, capital grows more quickly, and so does real GDP.

Solution to In the News

The expanded payroll tax will increase the tax wedge and raise the cost of labor. It will decrease the quantity of labor demanded and decrease the equilibrium employment. With a decrease in employment, potential GDP will decrease.

CHAPTER SUMMARY

Key Points

1. **Describe the federal budget, the process that creates it, and a challenge that it faces.**

   - The federal budget is an annual statement of the outlays, tax revenues, and budget surplus or deficit of the government of the United States.
   - Fiscal policy is the use of the federal budget to finance the federal government and to influence macroeconomic performance.
   - An ever rising national debt and large fiscal imbalance is a major fiscal policy challenge.

2. **Explain how fiscal stimulus is used to fight a recession.**

   - Fiscal policy can be either discretionary or automatic.
   - Changes in government expenditure and changes in taxes have multiplier effects on aggregate demand and can be used to try to keep real GDP at potential GDP.
   - In practice, lawmaking time lags, a shrinking area of lawmaker discretion, the difficulty of estimating potential GDP, and the limitations of economic forecasting seriously hamper discretionary fiscal policy.
   - Automatic stabilizers arise because tax revenues and outlays fluctuate with real GDP.

3. **Explain the supply-side effects of fiscal policy on employment, potential GDP, and the economic growth rate.**

   - The provision of public goods and services increases productivity and increases potential GDP.
   - Income taxes create a wedge between the wage rate paid by firms and received by workers and lower both employment and potential GDP.
   - Income taxes create a wedge between the interest rate paid by firms and received by lenders and lower saving and investment and the growth rate of real GDP.
   - A government budget deficit raises the real interest rate and crowds out some private investment, which slows real GDP growth.

Key Terms

MyEconLab Key Terms Quiz

Automatic fiscal policy, 831
Automatic stabilizers, 831
Balanced budget multiplier, 833
Budget balance, 824
Cyclical surplus or deficit, 832
Discretionary fiscal policy, 831
Fiscal imbalance, 828

Fiscal policy, 824
Generational imbalance, 829
Government expenditure multiplier, 833
Induced taxes, 831
National debt, 825
Structural surplus or deficit, 832

Supply-side effects, 838
Tax multiplier, 833
Tax wedge, 839
Transfer payments, 825
Transfer payments multiplier, 833

CHAPTER CHECKPOINT

Study Plan Problems and Applications

1. Suppose that in an economy, investment is $400 billion, saving is $400 billion, tax revenues are $500 billion, exports are $300 billion, and imports are $200 billion. Calculate government expenditure and the government's budget balance.

2. Classify the following items as automatic fiscal policy actions, discretionary fiscal policy actions, or neither.

   • An increase in expenditure on homeland security
   • An increase in unemployment benefits paid during a recession
   • Decreased expenditures on national defense during peace time
   • An increase in Medicaid expenditure brought about by a flu epidemic
   • A cut in farm subsidies

3. The U.S. economy is in recession and has a large recessionary gap. Describe what automatic fiscal policy might occur. Describe a fiscal stimulus that could be used that would not increase the budget deficit.

OilPatch is a mineral rich economy in which the government gets most of its tax revenue from oil royalties. But OilPatch has an income tax. Table 1 describes the labor market in OilPatch and Table 2 describes the economy's production function. The government introduces an income tax of $2 per hour worked. Use Tables 1 and 2 to work Problems **4** to **6**.

4. What are the levels of employment and potential GDP in OilPatch, what is the real wage rate paid by employers, and what is the after-tax real wage rate received by workers?

5. If OilPatch eliminates its income tax, what then are the levels of employment and potential GDP and what is the real wage rate in OilPatch?

6. If OilPatch doubles its income tax to $4 an hour, what then are the levels of employment and potential GDP? What is the real wage rate paid by employers and the after-tax real wage rate received by workers?

7. The income tax rate on all forms of income is 40 percent and there is a tax of 10 percent on all consumption expenditure. The nominal interest rate is 7 percent a year and the inflation rate is 5 percent a year. What is the size of the tax wedge on wages and what is the true tax rate on interest income?

8. **The global economy is in bad shape and getting worse**
   The world economy is growing slowly and productive public investment that boosts both the demand and supply sides of the economy is not being used, either because debts are high or because governments are misguidedly pursuing austerity.

   Source: *MarketWatch*, May 2, 2016
   Explain the effects of public investment on aggregate demand and supply.

9. The Canadian Prime Minister Stephen Harper warned on November 6, 2008, that if policy makers adopt too strong a fiscal stimulus, then long-term growth might be jeopardized. Explain what he meant.

10. Read *Eye on Fiscal Stimulus* on p. 835. How big was the fiscal stimulus package of 2008–2009, how many jobs was it expected to create, and how large was the multiplier implied by that expectation? Did the stimulus work?

TABLE 1   LABOR MARKET

Real wage rate (dollars per hour)	Quantity of labor demanded	supplied
	(thousands of hours)	
10	6	2
11	5	3
12	4	4
13	3	5
14	2	6
15	1	7

TABLE 2   PRODUCTION FUNCTION

Employment (thousands of hours)	Real GDP (millions of dollars)
2	6
3	11
4	15
5	18
6	20
7	21

Instructor Assignable Problems and Applications

MyEconLab Homework, Quiz, or Test if assigned by instructor

1. From the peak in 1929 to the Great Depression trough in 1933, government tax revenues fell by 1.9 percent of GDP and government expenditure increased by 0.3 percent. Real GDP fell by 25 percent. Compare and contrast this experience with the fiscal policy that accompanied the 2008–2009 recession. What did fiscal policy do to moderate the last recession that was largely absent during the Great Depression?

2. Suppose that the U.S. government increases its expenditure on highways and bridges by $100 billion. Explain the effect that this expenditure would have on aggregate demand and real GDP.

3. Suppose that the U.S. government increases its expenditure on highways and bridges by $100 billion. Explain the effect that this expenditure would have on needs-tested spending and the government's budget balance.

Table 1 describes the labor market in LowTaxLand and Table 2 describes the economy's production function. LowTaxLand introduces an income tax of $1 per hour worked. Use Tables 1 and 2 to work Problems **4** to **6**.

4. What are the levels of employment and potential GDP in LowTaxLand, what is the real wage rate paid by employers, and what is the after-tax real wage rate received by workers?

5. If LowTaxLand eliminates its income tax, what then are the levels of employment and potential GDP and what is the real wage rate in LowTaxLand?

6. If LowTaxLand doubles its income tax to $2 an hour, what then are the levels of employment and potential GDP? What is the real wage rate paid by employers and the after-tax real wage rate received by workers?

7. Describe the supply-side effects of a fiscal stimulus and explain how a tax cut will influence potential GDP.

8. Use an aggregate supply–aggregate demand graph to illustrate the effects on real GDP and the price level of a fiscal stimulus when the economy is in recession.

Use the following information to work Problems **9** to **11**.

CBO expects higher long-term deficits
The Congressional Budget Office (CBO) says the national debt is on an upward path and will hit 122 percent of GDP in 2040. Healthcare programs and Social Security benefits are the large drivers of spending over the coming decades.
Source: *The Wall Street Journal*, July 12, 2016

9. Explain why the national debt does not measure the federal government's true indebtedness. How does the nation's fiscal imbalance provide a more accurate account of government's debt?

10. If the government decided to slow the growth of debt by cutting transfer payments and raising taxes by the same amount, how would this fiscal policy influence the budget deficit and real GDP?

11. How do healthcare programs and Social Security benefits drive spending and the deficit and how do they create fiscal imbalance and generational imbalance?

TABLE 1   LABOR MARKET

Real wage rate (dollars per hour)	Quantity of labor demanded	supplied
	(thousands of hours)	
10.00	18	6
10.50	15	9
11.00	12	12
11.50	9	15
12.00	6	18
12.50	3	21

TABLE 2   PRODUCTION FUNCTION

Employment (thousands of hours)	Real GDP (millions of dollars)
6	7
9	12
12	16
15	19
18	21
21	22

MyEconLab Chapter 32 Study Plan

Multiple Choice Quiz

1. The federal government's major outlay in its budget is _____ and its major source of revenue is _____.

   A. debt interest; sales of government bonds
   B. expenditure on goods and services; taxes on goods and services
   C. Social Security and other benefits; personal income taxes
   D. subsidies to farmers; corporate taxes

2. U.S. national debt _____ when the federal government's _____.

   A. increases; outlays exceed tax revenue
   B. decreases; outlays exceed tax revenue
   C. increases; tax revenue rises faster than outlays
   D. decreases; tax revenue rises faster than outlays

3. Discretionary fiscal policy to stimulate the economy includes _____.

   A. lowering the tax rate paid by households with middle incomes
   B. raising the tax on gasoline
   C. the fall in tax revenue as the economy goes into recession
   D. the rise in tax revenue collected from businesses as their profits increase

4. Automatic fiscal policy _____.

   A. requires an action of the government
   B. is weak unless the government cuts its outlays to reduce the deficit
   C. operates as the economy moves along its business cycle
   D. reduces the deficit as the economy goes into recession

5. Needs-tested spending is _____ fiscal policy because it _____.

   A. automatic; increases in recession and decreases in expansion
   B. discretionary; increases when tax revenue increases
   C. automatic; increases when the government's budget deficit falls
   D. discretionary; is determined by economic hardship

6. A government expenditure multiplier _____.

   A. equals 1
   B. is less than the tax multiplier
   C. exceeds 1
   D. equals the tax multiplier

7. When the government lowers the income tax rate, _____.

   A. employment increases and potential GDP increases
   B. employment does not change but labor productivity falls
   C. labor productivity rises and employment decreases
   D. both labor productivity and potential GDP increase

8. A tax cut increases _____.

   A. aggregate demand but has no effect on aggregate supply
   B. aggregate demand because it increases disposable income and increases aggregate supply because it is an incentive to supply more labor
   C. aggregate demand because it increases consumption expenditure and decreases aggregate supply because labor productivity falls
   D. aggregate supply but has no effect on aggregate demand

Did the Fed save us from
another Great Depression?

Monetary Policy

**When you have completed your study of this chapter,
you will be able to**

1 Describe the objectives of U.S. monetary policy, the framework for
achieving those objectives, and the Fed's monetary policy actions.

2 Explain the transmission channels through which the Fed influences
real GDP and the inflation rate.

3 Explain and compare alternative monetary policy strategies.

33

CHAPTER CHECKLIST

MyEconLab Big Picture Video

MyEconLab Concept Video

33.1 HOW THE FED CONDUCTS MONETARY POLICY

A nation's monetary policy objectives and the framework for setting and achieving those objectives stem from the relationship between the central bank and the government. We'll describe the objectives of U.S. monetary policy and the framework and assignment of responsibility for achieving those objectives.

■ Monetary Policy Objectives

The objectives of monetary policy are ultimately political. In the United States, these objectives are set out in the mandate of the Board of Governors of the Federal Reserve System, which is defined by the Federal Reserve Act of 1913 and its subsequent amendments.

Federal Reserve Act

The Fed's mandate was most recently clarified in an amendment to the Federal Reserve Act passed by Congress in 2000, which states that

> The Board of Governors of the Federal Reserve System and the Federal Open Market Committee shall maintain long-run growth of the monetary and credit aggregates commensurate with the economy's long-run potential to increase production, so as to promote effectively the goals of maximum employment, stable prices, and moderate long-term interest rates.

This description of the Fed's monetary policy objectives has two distinct parts: a statement of goals and a prescription of the means by which to pursue the goals.

Goals: The Dual Mandate

The Fed's goals are often described as a "dual mandate" to achieve stable prices and also maximum employment.

The goal of "stable prices" doesn't mean a constant price level. Rather, it is interpreted to mean keeping the inflation rate low and predictable. Success in achieving this goal also ensures "moderate long-term interest rates."

The goal of "maximum employment" means attaining the maximum sustainable growth rate of potential GDP, keeping real GDP close to potential GDP, and keeping the unemployment rate close to the natural unemployment rate.

In the *long run*, these goals are in harmony and reinforce each other. Price stability is the key goal. It provides the best available environment for households and firms to make the saving and investment decisions that bring economic growth. So price stability encourages the maximum sustainable growth rate of potential GDP.

Price stability delivers moderate long-term interest rates because the nominal interest rate equals the real interest rate plus the inflation rate. With stable prices, the nominal interest rate is close to the real interest rate and, most of the time, this rate is likely to be moderate.

While the Fed's goals are in harmony in the long run, the Fed faces a tradeoff in the short run. For example, by taking an action that is designed to lower the inflation rate and achieve stable prices, the unemployment rate rises in the short run and slows real GDP growth. And using monetary policy to try to lower the unemployment rate and boost real GDP growth brings the risk of a rising inflation rate. (See Chapter 31, pp. 816–817.)

Means for Achieving the Goals

The 2000 law instructs the Fed to pursue its goals by "maintain[ing] long-run growth of the monetary and credit aggregates commensurate with the economy's long-run potential to increase production." You can perhaps recognize this statement as being consistent with the quantity theory of money that you studied in Chapter 28 (see pp. 734–737). The "economy's long-run potential to increase production" is the growth rate of potential GDP. The "monetary and credit aggregates" are the quantities of money and loans. By keeping the growth rate of the quantity of money in line with the growth rate of potential GDP, the Fed is expected to be able to maintain full employment and keep the price level stable.

Prerequisite for Achieving the Goals

The financial crisis that started in the summer of 2007 and intensified in the fall of 2008 brought the problem of financial instability to the top of the Fed's agenda. The focus of policy became the single-minded pursuit of **financial stability**—of enabling financial markets and institutions to resume their normal functions of allocating capital resources and risk.

The pursuit of financial stability by the Fed is not an abandonment of the mandated goals of maximum employment and stable prices. Rather, it is a prerequisite for attaining those goals. Financial instability has the potential to bring severe recession and deflation—falling prices—and undermine the attainment of the mandated goals.

To pursue its mandated monetary policy goals, the Fed must make the general concepts of maximum employment and stable prices precise and operational.

Financial stability
A situation in which financial markets and institutions function normally to allocate capital resources and risk.

■ Operational "Maximum Employment" Goal

The Fed pays close attention to the business cycle and tries to steer a steady course between inflation and recession. To gauge the state of output and employment relative to full employment, the Fed looks at a large number of indicators that include the labor force participation rate, the unemployment rate, measures of capacity utilization, activity in the housing market, the stock market, and regional information gathered by the regional Federal Reserve Banks. All these data are summarized in the Fed's *Beige Book*.

The *output gap*—the percentage deviation of real GDP from potential GDP—summarizes the state of aggregate demand relative to potential GDP. A positive output gap—an *inflationary gap*—brings rising inflation. A negative output gap—a *recessionary gap*—results in lost output and unemployment above the natural unemployment rate. The Fed tries to minimize the output gap.

■ Operational "Stable Prices" Goal

The Fed believes that core inflation provides the best indication of whether price stability is being achieved. The *core inflation rate* is the annual percentage change in the Personal Consumption Expenditure Price Index (PCEPI) *excluding* the prices of food and energy (see Chapter 23, p. 599).

Since January 2012, the Fed has regarded price stability as being achieved when the core inflation rate is 2 percent a year. Before 2012, the Fed avoided a numerical target for the core inflation rate. Former Fed Chair Alan Greenspan said that "price stability is best thought of as an environment in which inflation is so low and stable over time that it does not materially enter into the decisions of households and firms."

■ Responsibility for Monetary Policy

Who is responsible for monetary policy in the United States? What are the roles of the Fed, Congress, and the President?

The Role of the Fed

The Federal Reserve Act makes the Board of Governors of the Federal Reserve System and the Federal Open Market Committee (FOMC) responsible for the conduct of monetary policy. We described the composition of the FOMC in Chapter 27 (see p. 704). The FOMC makes a monetary policy decision at eight scheduled meetings a year and publishes its minutes three weeks after each meeting.

The Role of Congress

Congress plays no role in making monetary policy decisions, but the Federal Reserve Act requires the Board of Governors to report on monetary policy to Congress. The Fed makes two reports each year, one in February and another in July. These reports, along with the Fed Chair's testimony before Congress and the minutes of the FOMC, communicate the Fed's thinking on monetary policy to lawmakers and the public.

The Role of the President

The formal role of the President of the United States is limited to appointing the members and the Chair of the Board of Governors. But some Presidents—Richard Nixon was one—have tried to influence the Fed's decisions.

You now know the objectives of monetary policy and can describe the framework and assignment of responsibility for achieving those objectives. Your next task is to see how the Fed conducts its monetary policy.

■ Policy Instrument

To conduct its monetary policy, the Fed must select a **monetary policy instrument**, a variable that the Fed can directly control or closely target and that influences the economy in desirable ways.

The Federal Funds Rate

The Fed's choice of monetary policy instrument is the **federal funds rate**, which is the interest rate on loans of reserves among banks. These interbank loans are made in what is called the federal funds market.

How does the Fed decide the appropriate level for the federal funds rate? And how, having made that decision, does the Fed move the federal funds rate to its target level?

Interest Rate Decision-Making

The Federal Open Market Committee (FOMC) sets the federal funds rate target at the level that gets its forecasts of inflation and the output gap as close as possible to their desired levels. Before making its decision, the FOMC gathers and processes a large amount of information about the economy, the way it responds to shocks, and the way it responds to policy. The FOMC then processes all these data and comes to a judgment about the best level for the federal funds rate.

The Fed does not pursue formal published targets: It has implicit targets but the economy deviates from these targets most of the time. When it does, the Fed

Monetary policy instrument
A variable that the Fed can directly control or closely target and that influences the economy in desirable ways.

Federal funds rate
The interest rate at which banks can borrow and lend reserves in the federal funds market.

FIGURE 33.1

The Fed's Key Monetary Policy Instrument: The Federal Funds Rate

MyEconLab Real-time data

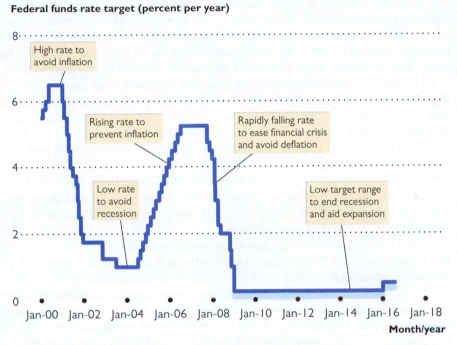

Federal funds rate target (percent per year)

SOURCE OF DATA: Board of Governors of the Federal Reserve System.

The Fed sets a target for the federal funds rate and then takes actions to keep the rate close to the target.

When the Fed wants to slow inflation, it raises the federal funds rate target.

When the inflation rate is below the target and the Fed wants to avoid recession, it lowers the federal funds rate target.

When the Fed focused on restoring financial stability during the global financial crisis, it cut the federal funds rate target aggressively to almost zero. The Fed also set the target as a range, which is shown in light blue.

places relative weights on its two objectives and, constrained by the short-run tradeoff (see Chapter 31), decides how quickly to try to get inflation back on track or the economy back to full employment.

Figure 33.1 shows the federal funds rate since 2000. You can see that the federal funds rate was 5.5 percent at the beginning of 2000, and during 2000 and 2001 the Fed increased the rate to 6.5 percent. The Fed raised the interest rate to this high level to lower the inflation rate.

Between 2002 and 2004, the federal funds rate was set at historically low levels. The reason is that with inflation well anchored at close to 2 percent a year, the Fed was less concerned about inflation than it was about recession, so it wanted to lean in the direction of avoiding recession.

From mid-2004 through early 2006, the Fed was increasingly concerned about the build-up of inflation pressures and it raised the federal funds rate target on 17 occasions to take it to 5.25 percent, a level that was held until September 2007.

When the global financial crisis began, the Fed acted cautiously in cutting the federal funds rate target. But as the crisis intensified, rate cuts became more frequent and larger, ending in December 2008 with an interest rate close to zero. The normal changes of a quarter of a percentage point (also called 25 *basis points*) were abandoned as the Fed slashed the rate, first by an unusual 50 basis points and finally, in December 2008, by an unprecedented 100 basis points. Since the end of 2008, the federal funds rate has been close to zero.

You've now seen how the Fed sets the federal funds rate target and your next task is to see how the Fed makes the federal funds rate hit its target.

■ Hitting the Federal Funds Rate Target

The federal funds rate is the interest rate that banks earn (or pay) when they lend (or borrow) reserves. The federal funds rate is also the opportunity cost of holding reserves. Holding a larger quantity of reserves is the alternative to lending reserves to another bank, and holding a smaller quantity of reserves is the alternative to borrowing reserves from another bank. So the quantity of reserves that banks are willing to hold varies with the federal funds rate: The higher the federal funds rate, the smaller is the quantity of reserves that the banks plan to hold.

The Fed controls the quantity of reserves supplied, and the Fed can change this quantity by conducting an open market operation. You learned in Chapter 27 (pp. 709–712) how an open market purchase increases reserves and an open market sale decreases reserves. To hit the federal funds rate target, the New York Fed conducts open market operations until the supply of reserves is at just the right quantity to hit the target federal funds rate.

Figure 33.2 illustrates this outcome in the market for bank reserves. The *x*-axis measures the quantity of bank reserves on deposit at the Fed, and the *y*-axis measures the federal funds rate. The demand for reserves—the willingness of the banks to hold reserves—is the curve labeled *RD*.

The Fed's open market operations determine the supply of reserves, which is the supply curve *RS*. To decrease reserves, the Fed conducts an open market sale. To increase reserves, the Fed conducts an open market purchase.

Equilibrium in the market for bank reserves determines the federal funds rate where the quantity of reserves demanded by the banks equals the quantity of reserves supplied by the Fed. By using open market operations, the Fed adjusts the quantity of reserves supplied to keep the federal funds rate on target.

■ **FIGURE 33.2**

Equilibrium in the Market for Bank Reserves

MyEconLab Animation

The federal funds rate (on the *y*-axis) is the opportunity cost of holding reserves: The higher the federal funds rate, the smaller is the quantity of reserves that banks want to hold. The demand curve for bank reserves is *RD*.

❶ The FOMC sets the federal funds rate target at 5 percent a year.

❷ The New York Fed conducts open market operations to make the quantity of reserves supplied equal to $50 billion and the supply of reserves curve is *RS*.

❸ Equilibrium in the market for bank reserves occurs at the target federal funds rate.

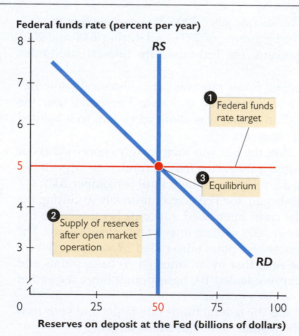

■ Restoring Financial Stability in a Financial Crisis

During the global financial crisis, the Fed took extraordinary steps to restore financial stability. Chapter 27 describes the tools of quantitative easing and credit easing employed by the Fed (p. 705) and *Eye on Creating Money* (pp. 714–715) shows the enormous surge in bank reserves and the monetary base brought about by "quantitative easing"—QE1—in 2008.

Figure 33.3 illustrates the Fed's QE1 action in the market for bank reserves. In normal times, the demand for reserves is RD_0 and the supply of reserves is RS_0. The federal funds rate is 5 percent and bank reserves are $50 billion.

At a time of financial instability and panic, banks' assessment of risk increases and they decide to hold more of their assets in safe, reserve deposits at the Fed. The demand for reserves increases and the demand curve becomes RD_1. If the Fed took no actions, the federal funds rate would rise, bank lending would shrink, the quantity of money would decrease, and a recession would intensify.

To avoid this outcome, the Fed's lending programs pump billions of dollars into the banks. The supply of reserves increases to RS_1, and the federal funds rate falls to zero. The banks don't start lending their increased reserves. They hang on to them. But flush with reserves, banks don't call in loans and deepen the recession. The Fed's action averted a worsening financial crisis.

Although the Fed avoided a more severe financial crisis, we don't know how bad things would have become without the extraordinary action. *Eye on the Fed in a Crisis* on p. 856 compares some features of the 2008–2009 recession with the Great Depression of the early 1930s.

■ **FIGURE 33.3**

The Market for Bank Reserves in a Financial Crisis   MyEconLab Animation

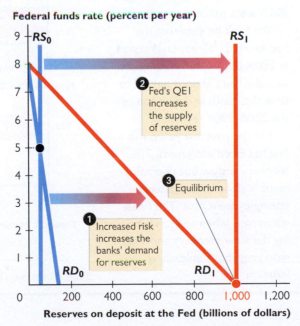

In a normal time, the demand for bank reserves is RD_0 and the supply of reserves is RS_0. The federal funds rate is 5 percent per year.

In a financial crisis:

❶ The banks face increased risk, so they increase their demand for reserves and the demand curve shifts to RD_1.

❷ The Fed's QE1 and other actions increase the supply of reserves and the supply curve shifts to RS_1.

❸ The equilibrium federal funds rate falls to zero and the quantity of reserves explodes to $1,000 billion.

EYE on the FED IN A CRISIS

Did the Fed Save Us From Another Great Depression?

The story of the Great Depression is complex and even today, after almost 80 years of research, economists are not in full agreement on its causes. But one part of the story is clear and it is told by Milton Friedman and Anna J. Schwartz: The Fed got it wrong.

An increase in financial risk drove the banks to increase their holdings of reserves and everyone else to lower their bank deposits and hold more currency.

Between 1929 and 1933, (Figure 1) the banks' desired reserve ratio increased from 8 percent to 12 percent and the currency drain ratio increased from 9 percent to 19 percent.

The money multiplier (Figure 2) fell from 6.5 to 3.8.

The quantity of money (Figure 3) crashed by 35 percent.

This massive contraction in the quantity of money was accompanied by a similar contraction of bank loans and by the failure of many banks.

Friedman and Schwartz say that this contraction of money and bank loans and the failure of banks could (and should) have been avoided by a more alert and wise Fed.

The Fed could have injected reserves into the banks to accommodate their desire for

greater security by holding more reserves and to offset the rise in currency holdings as people switched out of bank deposits.

Ben Bernanke's Fed did almost exactly what Friedman and Schwartz said the Fed needed to do in the Great Depression.

At the end of 2008, when the banks faced increased financial risk, the Fed flooded them with the reserves that they wanted to hold (Figure 1).

The money multiplier fell from 9.1 in 2008 to 3.3 in 2013 (Figure 2)—much more than it had fallen between 1929 and 1933—but there was no contraction of the quantity of money (Figure 3). Rather, the quantity of M2 increased by 37.5 percent in the 5 years to August 2013, a 6.6 percent annual rate.

We can't be sure that the Fed averted a Great Depression in 2009, but we can be confident that the Fed's actions helped to limit the depth and duration of the 2008–2009 recession.

For the past few years, the Fed has faced a dilemma. The recovery is slow but unemployment is close to the natural unemployment rate. The Fed's dilemma is when to stop fighting the slow recovery and start worrying about unleashing inflation.

Milton Friedman and Anna J. Schwartz, authors of A Monetary History of the United States, *who say the Fed turned an ordinary recession into the Great Depression.*

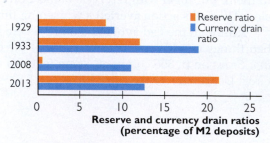

Figure 1 The Flight to Safety: Reserve and Currency Ratios Increase

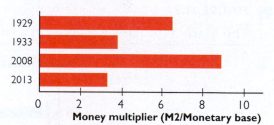

Figure 2 The Collapsing Money Multiplier

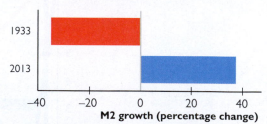

Figure 3 Money Contraction Versus Growth

SOURCE OF DATA: Federal Reserve Board.

CHECKPOINT 33.1

MyEconLab Study Plan 33.1
Key Terms Quiz
Solutions Video

Describe the objectives of U.S. monetary policy, the framework for achieving those objectives, and the Fed's monetary policy actions.

Practice Problems

1. What are the objectives of U.S. monetary policy?

2. What is core inflation and how does it differ from total PCEPI inflation?

3. What is the Fed's monetary policy instrument and what influences the level at which the Fed sets it?

4. Figure 1 shows the demand curve for bank reserves, *RD*. The current quantity of reserves supplied is $20 billion. The Fed wants to set the federal funds rate at 4 percent a year. Illustrate the target on the graph and show the supply of reserves that will achieve the target. Does the Fed conduct an open market operation and if so, does it buy or sell securities?

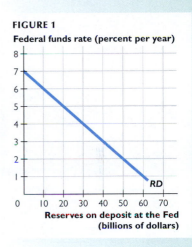

FIGURE 1

In the News

Fed defines price stability

The FOMC announced that it judges a 2 percent inflation rate to be consistent with the Fed's statutory mandate. The committee did not think it appropriate to specify a fixed goal for employment.

> Source: Federal Reserve Monetary Policy Release, January 25, 2012

Explain why the FOMC might be willing to define price stability but not think it appropriate to specify a fixed employment goal.

Solutions to Practice Problems

1. The objectives of U.S. monetary policy are to achieve stable prices (interpreted as a core inflation rate of about 2 percent per year) and maximum employment (interpreted as full employment).

2. Core inflation excludes the changes in the prices of food and fuel. The total PCEPI inflation rate includes the changes in all consumer prices. The core inflation rate fluctuates less than the total PCEPI inflation rate.

3. The federal funds rate is the Fed's monetary policy instrument and the inflation rate and output gap are two of the influences on the level at which the Fed sets the federal funds rate.

4. Figure 2 shows the market for bank reserves. With the initial quantity of reserves of $20 billion, the federal funds rate must have been 5 percent a year at point *A*. To set the federal funds rate at 4 percent a year, the Fed must conduct an open market purchase to increase the supply of reserves to *RS*. With supply *RS*, the federal funds rate equals the 4 percent target rate.

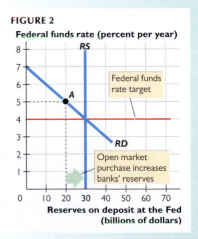

FIGURE 2

Solution to In the News

Many factors influence employment and the FOMC looks at a large number of indicators to judge whether the maximum-employment goal is being achieved. The price level is influenced by monetary policy alone in the long run and is measured by one preferred price index, so the FOMC can give a fixed quantitative definition of the price-stability goal.

33.2 MONETARY POLICY TRANSMISSION

You've seen that the Fed's goal is to keep the inflation rate around 2 percent a year and to keep the output gap close to zero. You've also seen how the Fed uses its market power to set the federal funds rate at the level that is designed to achieve these objectives. We're now going to trace the events that follow a change in the federal funds rate and see how those events lead to the ultimate policy goals. We'll begin with a quick overview of the transmission process and then look a bit more closely at each step.

■ Quick Overview

When the Fed lowers the federal funds rate, other short-term interest rates and the exchange rate also fall. The quantity of money and the supply of loanable funds increase. The long-term real interest rate falls. The lower real interest rate increases consumption expenditure and investment. The lower exchange rate makes U.S. exports cheaper and imports more costly, so net exports increase. Easier bank loans reinforce the effect of lower interest rates on aggregate expenditure. Aggregate demand increases, which increases real GDP and the price level relative to what they would have been. Real GDP growth and inflation speed up.

When the Fed raises the federal funds rate, as the sequence of events that we've just reviewed plays out, the effects are in the opposite directions.

Figure 33.4 provides a schematic summary of these ripple effects for both a cut and a rise in the federal funds rate. These ripple effects stretch out over a period of between one and two years. The interest rate and exchange rate effects are immediate. The effects on money and bank loans follow in a few weeks and run for a few months. Real long-term interest rates change quickly and often in anticipation of the short-term rate changes. Spending plans change and real GDP growth changes after about one year. The inflation rate changes between one year and two years after the change in the federal funds rate. But these time lags are not entirely predictable and can be longer or shorter. We're going to look at each stage in the transmission process, starting with the interest rate effects.

■ Interest Rate Changes

The first effect of a monetary policy decision by the FOMC is a change in the federal funds rate. Other interest rates then change. These interest rate effects occur quickly and relatively predictably.

The interest rate on U.S. government 3-month Treasury bills is immediately affected by a change in the federal funds rate. A powerful *substitution effect* keeps these two rates close to each other. Banks have a choice about how to hold their short-term liquid assets and a loan to another bank is a close substitute for holding Treasury bills. If the interest rate on Treasury bills is higher than the federal funds rate, the banks increase the quantity of Treasury bills held and decrease loans to other banks. The price of a Treasury bill rises and the interest rate falls. Similarly, if the interest rate on Treasury bills is lower than the federal funds rate, the banks decrease the quantity of Treasury bills held and increase loans to other banks. The price of a Treasury bill falls, and the interest rate rises. When the interest rate on Treasury bills is close to the federal funds rate, there is no incentive for a bank to switch between making loans to other banks and holding Treasury bills. Both the Treasury bill market and the federal funds market are in equilibrium.

FIGURE 33.4

Ripple Effects of the Fed's Actions

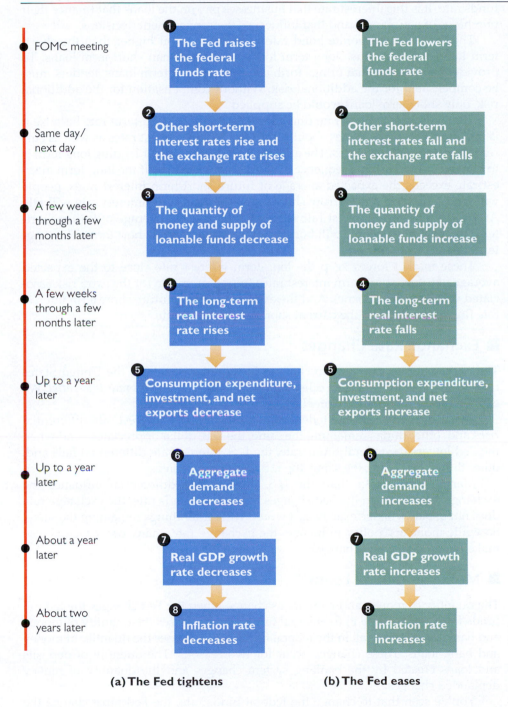

(a) The Fed tightens

(b) The Fed eases

The Fed changes its interest rate target and conducts open market operations to ❶ change the federal funds rate. The same day ❷ other short-term interest rates change and so does the exchange rate. A few weeks through a few months after the FOMC meeting, ❸ the quantity of money and supply of loanable funds change, which ❹ changes the long-term real interest rate.

Up to a year after the FOMC meeting, ❺ consumption expenditure, investment, and net exports change, which ❻ changes aggregate demand.

Eventually, the change in the federal funds rate has ripple effects that ❼ change real GDP and about two years after the FOMC meeting, ❽ the inflation rate changes.

Long-term interest rates also change, but not by as much as short-term rates. The long-term corporate bond rate, the interest rate paid on bonds issued by large corporations, is the most significant interest rate to be influenced by the federal funds rate. It is this interest rate that businesses pay on the loans that finance their purchases of new capital and that influences their investment decisions.

The long-term corporate bond rate is generally a bit higher than the short-term interest rate because long-term loans are riskier than short-term loans. To provide the incentive that brings forth a supply of long-term loans, lenders must be compensated for the additional risk. Without compensation for the additional risk, only short-term loans would be supplied.

The long-term interest rate fluctuates less than the short-term rate because it is influenced by expectations about future short-term interest rates as well as current short-term interest rates. The alternative to borrowing or lending long term is to borrow or lend using a sequence of short-term securities. If the long-term interest rate exceeds the expected average of future short-term interest rates, people will lend long term and borrow short term. The long-term interest rate will fall. And if the long-term interest rate is below the expected average of future short-term interest rates, people will borrow long term and lend short term. The long-term interest rate will rise.

These market forces keep the long-term interest rate close to the expected average of future short-term interest rates (plus a premium for the extra risk associated with long-term loans). And the expected average future short-term interest rate fluctuates less than the current short-term interest rate.

■ Exchange Rate Changes

The exchange rate responds to changes in the interest rate in the United States relative to the interest rates in other countries—the *U.S. interest rate differential*. We explain this influence in Chapter 34 (see pp. 888, 891, 893).

When the Fed raises the federal funds rate, the U.S. interest rate differential rises and, other things remaining the same, the U.S. dollar appreciates. And when the Fed lowers the federal funds rate, the U.S. interest rate differential falls and, other things remaining the same, the U.S. dollar depreciates.

Many factors other than the U.S. interest rate differential influence the exchange rate, so when the Fed changes the federal funds rate, the exchange rate does not usually change exactly as it would with other things remaining the same. So while monetary policy influences the exchange rate, many other factors also make the exchange rate change.

■ Money and Bank Loans

The quantity of money and bank loans change when the Fed changes the federal funds rate target. A rise in the federal funds rate decreases the quantity of money and bank loans; and a fall in the federal funds rate increases the quantity of money and bank loans. These changes occur for two reasons: The quantity of deposits and loans created by the banking system changes and the quantity of money demanded changes.

You've seen that to change the federal funds rate, the Fed must change the quantity of bank reserves. A change in the quantity of bank reserves changes the monetary base, which in turn changes the quantity of deposits and loans that the banking system can create. A rise in the federal funds rate decreases reserves and decreases the quantity of deposits and bank loans created; and a fall in the federal funds rate increases reserves and increases the quantity of deposits and bank loans created.

The quantity of money created by the banking system must be held by households and firms. The change in the interest rate changes the quantity of money demanded. A fall in the interest rate increases the quantity of money demanded and a rise in the interest rate decreases the quantity of money demanded.

A change in the quantity of money and the supply of bank loans directly affects consumption and investment plans. With more money and easier access to loans, consumers and firms spend more. With less money and loans harder to get, consumers and firms spend less.

■ The Long-Term Real Interest Rate

Demand and supply in the market for loanable funds determine the long-term real interest rate, which equals the long-term nominal interest rate minus the expected inflation rate. The long-term real interest rate influences expenditure decisions.

In the long run, demand and supply in the loanable funds market depend only on real forces—on saving and investment decisions. But in the short run, when the price level is not fully flexible, the supply of loanable funds is influenced by the supply of bank loans. Changes in the federal funds rate change the supply of bank loans, which changes the supply of loanable funds and changes the real interest rate in the loanable funds market.

A fall in the federal funds rate that increases the supply of bank loans increases the supply of loanable funds and lowers the equilibrium real interest rate. A rise in the federal funds rate that decreases the supply of bank loans decreases the supply of loanable funds and raises the equilibrium real interest rate.

These changes in the real interest rate, along with the other factors we've just described, change expenditure plans.

■ Expenditure Plans

The ripple effects that follow a change in the federal funds rate change three components of aggregate expenditure:

- Consumption expenditure
- Investment
- Net exports

Other things remaining the same, the lower the real interest rate, the greater is the amount of consumption expenditure and the smaller is the amount of saving.

Again, other things remaining the same, the lower the real interest rate, the greater is the amount of investment.

Finally, and again other things remaining the same, the lower the interest rate, the lower is the exchange rate and the greater are exports and the smaller are imports.

A cut in the federal funds rate increases all the components of aggregate expenditure; a rise in the federal funds rate decreases all the components of aggregate expenditure. These changes in aggregate expenditure plans change aggregate demand, which in turn changes real GDP and the inflation rate.

■ The Fed Fights Recession

We're now going to pull all the steps in the transmission story together. We'll start with inflation below target and real GDP below potential GDP. The Fed takes actions that are designed to restore full employment. Figure 33.5 shows the effects of the Fed's actions, starting in the market for bank reserves and ending in the market for real GDP.

In Figure 33.5(a), which shows the market for bank reserves, the FOMC lowers the target federal funds rate from 5 percent to 4 percent a year. To achieve the new target, the New York Fed buys securities and increases the supply of reserves in the banking system from RS_0 to RS_1.

With increased reserves, the banks create deposits by making loans and the supply of money increases. The short-term interest rate falls and the quantity of money demanded increases. In Figure 33.5(b), the supply of money increases from MS_0 to MS_1, the interest rate falls from 5 percent to 4 percent a year, and the quantity of money increases from $3 trillion to $3.1 trillion. The interest rate in the money market and the federal funds rate are kept close to each other by the powerful substitution effect described on p. 858.

■ **FIGURE 33.5**

The Fed Fights Recession

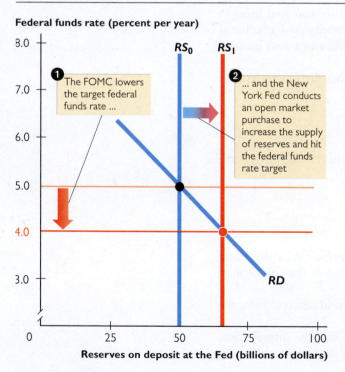

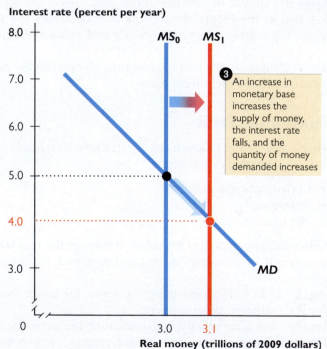

(a) Market for bank reserves

❶ The FOMC lowers the federal funds rate target from 5 percent to 4 percent a year. ❷ The New York Fed buys securities in an open market operation and increases reserves from RS_0 to RS_1 to hit the new federal funds rate target.

(b) Money market

❸ The supply of money increases from MS_0 to MS_1, the short-term interest rate falls, and the quantity of money demanded increases. The short-term interest rate and the federal funds rate change by similar amounts.

Banks create money by making loans. In the long run, an increase in the supply of bank loans is matched by a rise in the price level and the quantity of real loans is unchanged. But in the short run, with a sticky price level, an increase in the supply of bank loans increases the supply of (real) loanable funds. In Figure 33.5(c), the supply of loanable funds curve shifts rightward from SLF_0 to SLF_1. With the demand for loanable funds at DLF, the real interest rate falls from 6 percent to 5.5 percent a year.

Figure 33.5(d) shows aggregate demand and aggregate supply and the recessionary gap that triggered the Fed's action. The increase in money and loans and the decrease in the real interest rate increase aggregate planned expenditure. (Not shown in the figure, a fall in the interest rate lowers the exchange rate, which increases net exports and aggregate planned expenditure.) The increase in aggregate expenditure, ΔE, increases aggregate demand and shifts the aggregate demand curve rightward to $AD_0 + \Delta E$. A multiplier process begins. The increase in expenditure increases income, which induces an increase in consumption expenditure. Aggregate demand increases further, and the aggregate demand curve shifts rightward, eventually to AD_1. The new equilibrium is at full employment but with a higher price level (and faster inflation).

MyEconLab Animation

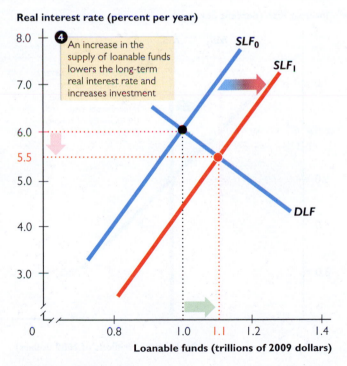

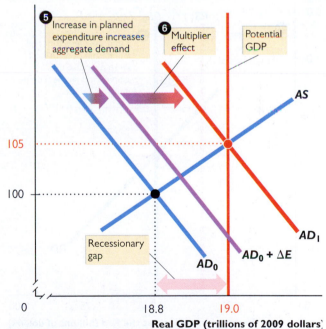

(c) Market for loanable funds

An increase in the quantity of money increases the supply of loans.
4 An increase in the supply of bank loans increases the supply of loanable funds from SLF_0 to SLF_1 and the real interest rate falls. Investment increases.

(d) Real GDP and the price level

5 Aggregate planned expenditure increases and the aggregate demand curve shifts to $AD_0 + \Delta E$. **6** A multiplier effect increases aggregate demand to AD_1. Real GDP increases and the price level rises (inflation speeds up).

■ The Fed Fights Inflation

If the inflation rate is too high and real GDP is above potential GDP, the Fed takes actions that are designed to lower the inflation rate and restore price stability. Figure 33.6 shows the effects of the Fed's actions starting in the market for reserves and ending in the market for real GDP.

In Figure 33.6(a), which shows the market for bank reserves, the FOMC raises the target federal funds rate from 5 percent to 6 percent a year. To achieve the new target, the New York Fed sells securities and decreases the supply of reserves in the banking system from RS_0 to RS_1.

With decreased reserves, the banks shrink deposits by decreasing loans and the supply of money decreases. The short-term interest rate rises and the quantity of money demanded decreases. In Figure 33.6(b), the supply of money decreases from MS_0 to MS_1, the interest rate rises from 5 percent to 6 percent a year, and the quantity of money decreases from $3 trillion to $2.9 trillion.

With a decrease in reserves, banks must decrease the supply of loans. The supply of (real) loanable funds decreases, and the supply of loanable funds curve shifts leftward in Figure 33.6(c) from SLF_0 to SLF_1. With the demand for loanable funds at DLF, the real interest rate rises from 6 percent to 6.5 percent a year.

■ **FIGURE 33.6**

The Fed Fights Inflation

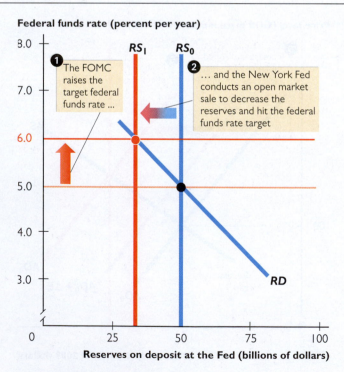

(a) Market for bank reserves

❶ The FOMC raises the federal funds rate target from 5 percent to 6 percent a year. ❷ The New York Fed sells securities in an open market operation and decreases reserves from RS_0 to RS_1 to hit the new federal funds rate target.

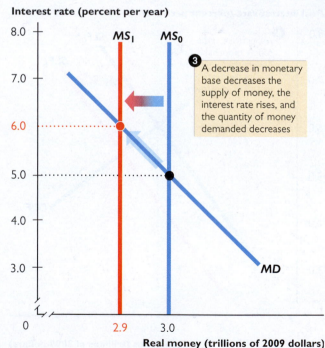

(b) Money market

❸ The supply of money decreases from MS_0 to MS_1, the short-term interest rate rises, and the quantity of money demanded decreases. The short-term interest rate and the federal funds rate change by similar amounts.

Figure 33.6(d) shows aggregate demand and aggregate supply in the market for real GDP and the inflationary gap to which the Fed is reacting. The decrease in the quantity of money and loans and the rise in the real interest rate decrease aggregate planned expenditure. The decrease in aggregate expenditure, ΔE, decreases aggregate demand and shifts the aggregate demand curve leftward to $AD_0 - \Delta E$. A multiplier process begins. The decrease in expenditure decreases income, which induces a decrease in consumption expenditure. Aggregate demand decreases further, and the aggregate demand curve shifts leftward, eventually to AD_1. The economy returns to full employment. Real GDP is equal to potential GDP. The price level falls (the inflation rate slows).

In both of the examples, we have given the Fed a perfect hit at achieving full employment and keeping the price level stable. If the Fed changed aggregate demand by too little and too late, or by too much and too early, the economy would not have returned to full employment. Too little action would leave a recessionary or an inflationary gap. Too much action would overshoot the objective. If the Fed hits the brakes too hard, it pushes the economy from inflation to recession. If it stimulates too much, it turns recession into inflation.

MyEconLab Animation

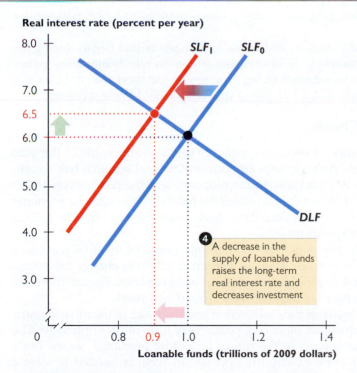

(c) Market for loanable funds

A decrease in the quantity of money decreases the supply of loans. ❹ A decrease in the supply of bank loans decreases the supply of loanable funds from SLF_0 to SLF_1 and the real interest rate rises. Investment decreases.

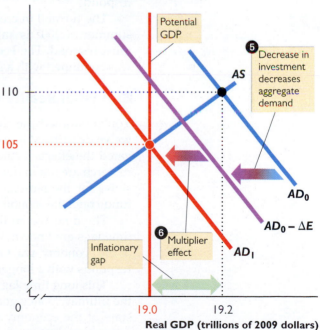

(d) Real GDP and the price level

❺ Aggregate planned expenditure decreases and the aggregate demand curve shifts to $AD_0 - \Delta E$. ❻ A multiplier effect decreases aggregate demand to AD_1. Real GDP decreases and the price level falls (inflation slows down).

■ Loose Links and Long and Variable Lags

The ripple effects of monetary policy that we've just analyzed with the precision of an economic model are, in reality, very hard to predict and influence.

To achieve its goals of price stability and full employment, the Fed needs a combination of good judgment and good luck. Too large an interest rate cut in an underemployed economy can bring inflation, as it did during the 1970s. And too large an interest rate rise in an inflationary economy can create unemployment, as it did in 1981 and 1991.

Loose links in the chain that runs from the federal funds rate to the ultimate policy goals make unwanted policy outcomes inevitable. And time lags that are both long and variable add to the Fed's challenges.

Loose Links from Federal Funds Rate to Spending

The long-term real interest rate that influences spending plans is linked only loosely to the federal funds rate. Also, the response of the long-term real interest rate to a change in the nominal rate depends on how inflation expectations change. The response of expenditure plans to changes in the real interest rate depends on many factors that make the response hard to predict.

Time Lags in the Adjustment Process

The Fed is especially handicapped by the fact that the monetary policy transmission process is long and drawn out. Also, the economy does not always respond in exactly the same way to a given policy change. Further, many factors other than policy are constantly changing and bringing new situations to which policy must respond.

The turmoil in credit markets and home loan markets that began during the summer of 2007 is an example of unexpected events to which monetary policy must respond. The Fed found itself facing an ongoing inflation risk, but that risk was combined with a fear that a collapse of spending would bring recession.

■ A Final Reality Check

You've studied the theory of monetary policy. Does it really work in the way we've described? It does. An enormous amount of statistical research has investigated the effects of the Fed's actions on the economy and the conclusions of this research are not in doubt. When the Fed raises the federal funds rate, the economy slows for the reasons that we've described. And when the Fed cuts the federal funds rate, the economy speeds up.

The time lags in the adjustment process are not predictable, but the average time lags are known. On average, after the Fed takes action to change the course of the economy, real GDP begins to change about one year later. The inflation rate responds with a longer time lag that averages around two years.

This long time-lag between the Fed's action and a change in the inflation rate, the ultimate policy goal, makes monetary policy very difficult to implement. The state of the economy two years in the future cannot be predicted, so the Fed's actions might turn out to be exactly the opposite of what is needed to steer a steady course between recession and inflation.

You've now seen how the Fed operates and studied the effects of its actions. We close this chapter by looking at alternative approaches to monetary policy.

CHECKPOINT 33.2

MyEconLab Study Plan 33.2
Solutions Video

Explain the transmission channels through which the Fed influences real GDP and the inflation rate.

Practice Problems

1. List the sequence of events in the transmission from a rise in the federal funds rate to a change in the inflation rate.

The economy has slipped into recession and the Fed takes actions to lessen its severity. Use this information to work Problems **2** and **3**.

2. What action does the Fed take? Illustrate the effects of the Fed's actions in the money market and the loanable funds market.

3. Explain how the Fed's actions change aggregate demand and real GDP.

In the News

Strong U.S. employment report brightens economic outlook
The U.S. economy added more jobs than expected in both June and July. Wages increased more rapidly and real GDP was expected to grow faster. These developments raise the likelihood of a Fed interest rate increase.
Source: Reuters, August 5, 2016

What are the ripple effects and time lags that the Fed must consider in deciding when to raise the interest rate?

Solutions to Practice Problems

1. When the Fed raises the federal funds rate, other short-term interest rates rise and the exchange rate rises; the quantity of money and supply of loanable funds decrease and the long-term real interest rate rises; consumption, investment, and net exports decrease; aggregate demand decreases; and eventually the real GDP growth rate and the inflation rate decrease.

2. The Fed lowers the federal funds rate, which lowers the short-term interest rate, and increases the supply of money (Figure 1). The supply of loans and the supply of loanable funds increase. The real interest rate falls (Figure 2).

3. A lower real interest rate (and exchange rate) and greater quantity of money and loanable funds increase aggregate expenditure and the *AD* curve shifts to $AD_0 + \Delta E$. A multiplier effect increases aggregate demand and the *AD* curve shifts to AD_1. Real GDP increases and recession is avoided (Figure 3).

Solution to In the News

Following a change in the interest rate: several months later the quantity of money and loans respond; up to a year later, expenditure plans and real GDP respond; and up to two years later the inflation rate responds.

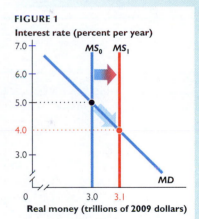

FIGURE 1
Interest rate (percent per year)

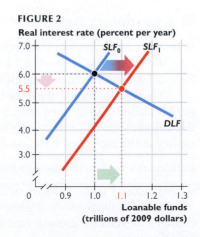

FIGURE 2
Real interest rate (percent per year)

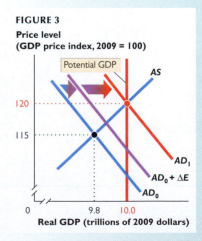

FIGURE 3
Price level
(GDP price index, 2009 = 100)

33.3 ALTERNATIVE MONETARY POLICY STRATEGIES

We're going to end our discussion of monetary policy by examining alternative strategies that the Fed might have chosen, and that some economists believe would improve macroeconomic outcomes. All the possible monetary policy strategies can be placed in two broad categories: *discretionary* and *rule-based*.

The Fed's monetary policy is discretionary. A central bank that pursues a **discretionary monetary policy** sets its policy instrument at the level it believes will best achieve its mandated policy goals. To make its interest rate decision, the FOMC gathers and analyzes a vast amount of data and comes to a judgment about the level that will best achieve price stability and full employment.

The alternative to discretionary monetary policy is rule-based policy. A **rule-based monetary policy** is one based on a rule for setting the policy instrument. Supporters of a rule-based policy say it is more predictable than discretionary policy and it reduces uncertainty about future policy decisions. Less uncertainty boosts business investment and economic growth. And less uncertainty about future inflation promotes the efficient working of capital markets and labor markets where agreements are based on long-term contracts.

Two alternative monetary policy rules have been proposed. They are

- An interest rate rule
- A monetary base rule

Discretionary monetary policy

A monetary policy that sets a central bank's policy instrument at the level it believes will best achieve its mandated policy goals.

Rule-based monetary policy

A monetary policy that is based on a rule for setting the policy instrument.

■ An Interest Rate Rule

John B. Taylor of Stanford University has proposed a rule for setting the federal funds rate—the *Taylor Rule*. The goal of this rule is to achieve 2 percent inflation and full employment. If the inflation rate is at the target of 2 percent and there is no output gap, the Taylor Rule sets the federal funds rate to neutral at 4 percent a year. A 1-percent deviation of the inflation rate from the target and a 1-percent deviation of real GDP from potential GDP moves the federal funds rate up or down by 0.5 percent.

The Taylor Rule was derived by crunching a large amount of U.S. macroeconomic data to construct a statistical model of the economy. The rule was then tested in this model and shown to be more effective than the Fed's decisions at attaining the mandated monetary policy goals.

■ A Monetary Base Rule

Bennett T. McCallum of Carnegie-Mellon University has proposed a rule for setting the monetary base—the *McCallum Rule*—with the same goal as the Taylor Rule: 2 percent inflation and full employment.

The *quantity theory of money* (Chapter 28, p. 734) provides the foundation for the McCallum Rule. The quantity theory links inflation to the money growth rate, the velocity growth rate, and the real GDP growth rate. In the McCallum Rule, money is the monetary base, so the quantity theory equation becomes

Inflation rate = Monetary base growth rate + Velocity growth rate − Real GDP growth rate

where velocity is the velocity of circulation of the monetary base.

The rule determines a growth rate for the monetary base that responds to changes in velocity growth and real GDP growth to deliver the 2 percent target inflation rate.

EYE on the U.S. ECONOMY
The Fed's Decisions Versus Two Rules

The Taylor Rule

Figure 1 shows the Fed's decisions and the federal funds rate that the *Taylor Rule* would have set. If the rule delivers the best path for the federal funds rate, then the Fed kept the interest rate too low for too long in 2004 and 2005 and then raised it too quickly and by too much in 2006. John Taylor says the Fed's deviation from the rule contributed to the global financial crisis of 2007. Over the years since 2009, the Fed has again kept the federal funds rate well below what the Taylor Rule would have set. If the rule is correct, the Fed is stoking inflation.

The McCallum Rule

Figure 2 shows the Fed's decision and the monetary base that the *McCallum Rule* would have delivered. If the rule delivers the best path for the monetary base, then the Fed wandered around too much. It increased the base by too much too quickly in each of the quantitative easing episodes (see Chapter 27, p. 705). The McCallum Rule agrees with the Taylor Rule: If the rules are correct, then the Fed is fuelling a future outbreak of inflation.

Federal funds rate (percent per year)

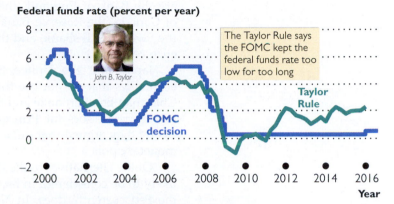

Figure 1 Taylor Rule Versus FOMC

Monetary base (trillions of dollars, ratio scale)

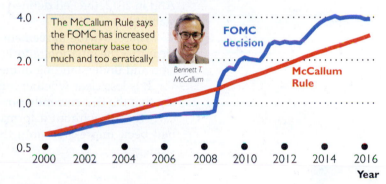

Figure 2 McCallum Rule Versus FOMC

Eye on the U.S. Economy compares the Fed's decisions with the Taylor and McCallum rules. Two other strategies that the Fed might use are discretionary policies that are constrained by tightly defined objectives. They are

- Inflation targeting
- Money growth targeting

■ Inflation Targeting

Inflation targeting is a monetary policy regime in which the central bank makes a public agreement with the government to achieve an explicit inflation target and to explain how its policy actions will achieve that target.

The idea of inflation targeting is to state clearly and publicly the goals of monetary policy, to establish a framework of accountability, and to keep the inflation rate low and stable while maintaining a high and stable level of employment.

Inflation targets are usually specified in terms of a range for the CPI inflation rate. This range is typically between 1 percent and 3 percent a year, with an aim to achieve an average inflation rate of 2 percent a year. Because the lags in the

Inflation targeting
A monetary policy strategy in which the central bank makes a public agreement with the government to achieve an explicit inflation target and to explain how its policy actions will achieve that target.

operation of monetary policy are long, if the inflation rate falls outside the target range, the expectation is that the central bank will move the inflation rate back to the target over the next two years.

Several major central banks practice inflation targeting and have done so since the mid-1990s. The most committed inflation-targeting central banks are the Bank of England (the central bank of the United Kingdom), the Bank of Canada, the Reserve Bank of Australia, the Reserve Bank of New Zealand, the Swedish Riksbank, and the European Central Bank (the central bank of the euro countries).

Japan and the United States are the most prominent major industrial economies that do not use this monetary policy strategy. But when former Fed Chairman Ben Bernanke and former Fed Governor Frederic S. Mishkin were economics professors (at Princeton University and Columbia University, respectively) they argued that inflation targeting is a sensible way in which to conduct monetary policy.

Of the alternatives to the Fed's current strategy, inflation targeting is the most likely to be considered. In fact, some economists see it as a small step from what the Fed currently does. In November 2007, the Fed took a major step toward greater transparency, a central feature of inflation targeting, by publishing FOMC members' detailed forecasts of inflation, real GDP growth, and unemployment. And in 2012, the Fed defined an inflation rate of 2 percent as consistent with price stability.

There is wide agreement that inflation targeting achieves its goals. It's also clear that the inflation reports of inflation targeters have raised the level of discussion and understanding of the monetary policy process.

It is less clear whether inflation targeting does better than the implicit targeting that the Fed currently pursues in achieving low and stable inflation. The Fed's own record, without a formal inflation target agreement with the government, had been impressive until the global financial crisis raised questions about its strategy.

EYE on the GLOBAL ECONOMY
Inflation Targeting Around the World

Five advanced economies and the Eurozone have inflation targets (shown by the green bars) designed to anchor inflation expectations.

In four of the economies, the inflation targets have been achieved (orange lines), and the other two economies achieved near misses.

In all six cases, high-quality central bank inflation reports encourage an enhanced level of public discussion about inflation and awareness of each central bank's views and policy decisions

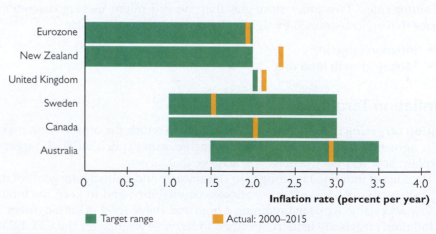

SOURCES OF DATA: National central banks and World Economic Outlook database, April 2016.

■ Money Targeting Rule

As long ago as 1948, Nobel Laureate Milton Friedman proposed a targeting rule for the quantity of money. Friedman's **k-percent rule** makes the quantity of money grow at a rate of k percent a year, where k equals the growth rate of potential GDP. Friedman's k-percent rule relies on a stable demand for money, which translates to a stable velocity of circulation. Friedman had examined data on money and nominal GDP and argued that the velocity of circulation of money was one of the most stable macroeconomic variables and that it could be exploited to deliver a stable price level and small business cycle fluctuations.

Friedman's idea remained just that until the 1970s, when inflation increased to more than 10 percent a year in the United States and to much higher rates in some other major countries.

During the mid-1970s, in a bid to end the inflation, the central banks of most major countries adopted the k-percent rule for the growth rate of the quantity of money. The Fed, too, began to pay close attention to the growth rates of money aggregates, including M1 and M2.

Inflation rates fell during the early 1980s in the countries that had adopted a k-percent rule. But one by one, these countries abandoned the k-percent rule.

Money targeting works when the demand for money curve is stable and predictable—when the velocity of circulation is stable. But in the world of the 1980s, and possibly in the world of today, technological change in the banking system leads to large and unpredictable shifts in the demand for money curve, which make the use of monetary targeting unreliable.

With money targeting, aggregate demand fluctuates because the demand for money fluctuates. With interest rate targeting, aggregate demand is insulated from fluctuations in the demand for money (and the velocity of circulation).

Monetary policy is a work in progress supported by the Fed and other central banks engaging in an ongoing research program and sharing of experience and ideas.

> **k-percent rule**
> A monetary policy rule that makes the quantity of money grow at k percent per year, where k equals the growth rate of potential GDP.

EYE on YOUR LIFE

MyEconLab **Critical Thinking Exercise**

Your Views on Monetary Policy and How Monetary Policy Affects You

Using the knowledge that you have accumulated during your course and by reading or watching the current news, try to determine the monetary policy issues that face the U.S. economy today.

What is the greater monetary policy risk: inflation or recession? If the risk is inflation, what action do you expect the Fed to take? If the risk is recession, what do you expect the Fed to do?

Which of these problems, inflation or recession, do you care most about? Do you want the Fed to be more cautious about inflation and keep the interest rate high, or more cautious about recession and keep the interest rate low?

When Ben Bernanke was an economics professor at Princeton, he studied inflation targeting and found that it works well.

Do you think the United States should join the ranks of inflation targeters? Should the Fed announce an inflation target?

Watch the media for commentary on the Fed's interest rate decisions and evolving monetary policy strategy.

MyEconLab Study Plan 33.3
Key Terms Quiz
Solutions Video

CHECKPOINT 33.3

Explain and compare alternative monetary policy strategies.

Practice Problems

1. What is the Fed's monetary policy strategy and what are the alternative strategies that it could have adopted?
2. Why does the Fed not target the quantity of money?
3. Which countries practice inflation targeting? How does this monetary policy strategy work and does it achieve a lower inflation rate?

In the News

The failed oracles of economic growth

For nearly a decade, central bankers have been promising to raise growth and create jobs. The oracles of monetary policy have failed. We need some new ones. One such alternative is offered by John Taylor, the Stanford University economist who long ago proposed rules to govern central bank strategies.

Source: Terence Corcoran, *Financial Post*, July 21, 2016

What is the rule for monetary policy proposed by John Taylor and why might it do a better job than the monetary policy of the past decade?

Solutions to Practice Problems

1. The Fed's monetary policy has mandated goals but it is free to use its discretion in achieving it goals. The Fed could have adopted four alternative monetary policy strategies. It could use one of two rule-based policies: an interest rate rule or a monetary base rule. It could adopt one of two alternative targeting policies: inflation targeting, or *k*-percent money targeting. The Fed's discretionary policy is only a short step away from inflation targeting.

2. The Fed does not target the quantity of money because it believes that the demand for money is too unstable and fluctuations in demand would bring unwanted fluctuations in interest rates, aggregate demand, real GDP, and the inflation rate.

3. The countries that practice inflation targeting are the United Kingdom, Canada, Australia, New Zealand, Sweden, and the European countries that use the euro. Inflation targeting works by announcing a target inflation rate, setting the overnight interest rate (equivalent to the U.S. federal funds rate) to achieve the target, and publishing reports that explain how and why the central bank believes that its current policy actions will achieve its ultimate policy goals. New Zealand and the United Kingdom have narrowly missed their inflation targets, but the other inflation targeters have achieved their goals.

Solution to In the News

The Taylor Rule is a formula for setting the federal funds rate. The rule makes the interest rate respond to departures from an inflation target and an output gap in a predictable way. Employing a rule brings greater certainty and provides a stronger anchor for inflation expectations, which improves the short-run policy tradeoff. Greater certainty might also stimulate investment to speed economic growth and job creation.

CHAPTER SUMMARY

Key Points

1. **Describe the objectives of U.S. monetary policy, the framework for achieving those objectives, and the Fed's monetary policy actions.**

   - The Federal Reserve Act requires the Fed to use monetary policy to achieve the "dual mandate" of maximum employment and stable prices.
   - The Fed's goals can come into conflict in the short run.
   - The Fed translates the goal of stable prices as a core inflation rate of between 1 and 2 percent a year.
   - The Fed's monetary policy instrument is the federal funds rate.
   - The Fed sets the federal funds rate at the level that makes its forecast of inflation and other goals equal to their targets.
   - The Fed hits its federal funds rate target by using open market operations and in times of financial crisis by quantitative easing and credit easing.

2. **Explain the transmission channels through which the Fed influences real GDP and the inflation rate.**

   - A change in the federal funds rate changes other interest rates, the exchange rate, the quantity of money and loans, aggregate demand, and eventually real GDP and the inflation rate.
   - Changes in the federal funds rate change real GDP about one year later and change the inflation rate with an even longer time lag.

3. **Explain and compare alternative monetary policy strategies.**

   - The main alternatives to the Fed's discretionary policy are an interest rate rule, a monetary base rule, inflation targeting, and money growth targeting.
   - Rules dominate discretion in monetary policy because they bring greater certainty about future policy actions and better enable the central bank to manage inflation expectations.

Key Terms

Discretionary monetary policy, 868
Federal funds rate, 852
Financial stability, 851
Inflation targeting, 869

k-percent rule, 871
Monetary policy instrument, 852
Rule-based monetary policy, 868

CHAPTER CHECKPOINT

Study Plan Problems and Applications

1. **Central bankers warn of QE threat to budget discipline**
   The German and Dutch central bank presidents warn that quantitative easing and low interest rates make discipline in government budgeting more important. Debt and deficits must be cut.

   Source: *Financial Times*, March 13, 2015

   How might a government budget deficit and debt threaten financial stability and make the central bank's job harder?

Use the following information to work Problems **2** to **4**.

Suppose that the U.S. economy is at full employment when strong economic growth in Asia increases the demand for U.S.-produced goods and services.

2. Explain how the U.S. price level and real GDP will change in the short run.

3. Explain how the U.S. price level and real GDP will change in the long run if the Fed takes monetary policy actions that are consistent with its objectives as set out in the Federal Reserve Act of 2000.

4. Explain whether the Fed faces a tradeoff in the short run.

5. What is the Fed's "dual mandate" for the conduct of monetary policy? What are the means to achieving the goals of the dual mandate?

6. What is financial stability? What actions has the Fed taken since 2007 in pursuit of financial stability? Use a graph to illustrate the effects of the Fed's actions.

Use the following information to work Problems **7** to **9**.

Figure 1 shows the aggregate demand curve, *AD*, and the short-run aggregate supply curve, *AS*, in the economy of Artica. Potential GDP is $300 billion.

7. What are the price level and real GDP? Does Artica have an unemployment problem or an inflation problem? Why?

8. What do you predict will happen if the central bank takes no monetary policy actions? What monetary policy action would you advise the central bank to take and what do you predict will be the effect of that action?

9. Suppose that a drought decreases potential GDP in Artica to $250 billion. Explain what happens if the central bank lowers the federal funds rate. Do you recommend that the central bank lower the interest rate? Why?

10. **Premature to rule out an interest rate increase this year**
    Federal Reserve Bank of New York President William Dudley says that in the current state of the economy, it would be worse for the Fed to raise rates too soon than moving slightly too late and adjusting by raising rates more quickly.

    Source: *Wall Street Journal*, August 1, 2016

    What are some of the problems that could arise if the Fed raises interest rates too soon or too late?

11. Read *Eye on the Fed in a Crisis* on p. 856. What are the key differences in monetary policy between the Great Depression and the slow recovery from the 2008–2009 recession?

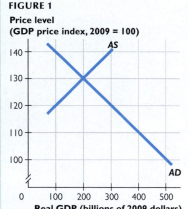

FIGURE 1

Price level
(GDP price index, 2009 = 100)

Instructor Assignable Problems and Applications

MyEconLab Homework, Quiz, or Test if assigned by instructor

1. In which episode, the Great Depression or the 2008–2009 recession, did the banks' desired reserve ratio and the currency drain ratio increase by the larger amount and the money multiplier fall by the larger amount?

2. Compare and contrast the Fed's monetary policy response to the surge in desired reserves and currency holdings in the Great Depression and the 2008–2009 recession.

Use the following information to work Problems **3** to **5**.

The U.S. economy is at full employment when the world price of oil begins to rise sharply. Short-run aggregate supply decreases.

3. Explain how the U.S. price level and real GDP will change in the short run.

4. Explain how the U.S. price level and real GDP will change in the long run if the Fed takes monetary policy actions that are consistent with its objectives as set out in the Federal Reserve Act of 2000.

5. Does the Fed face a tradeoff in the short run? Explain why or why not.

Use the following information to work Problems **6** to **9**.

Figure 1 shows the aggregate demand curve, *AD*, and the short-run aggregate supply curve, *AS*, in the economy of Freezone. Potential GDP is $300 billion.

6. What are the price level and real GDP? Does Freezone have an unemployment problem or an inflation problem? Why?

7. What do you predict will happen in Freezone if the central bank takes no monetary policy actions? What monetary policy action would you advise the central bank to take and what do you predict will be the effect of that action?

8. What happens in Freezone if the central bank lowers the federal funds rate? Do you recommend that the central bank lower the interest rate? Why?

9. What happens in Freezone if the central bank conducts an open market sale of securities? How will the interest rate change? Do you recommend that the central bank conduct an open market sale of securities? Why?

10. Suppose that inflation is rising toward 5 percent a year, and the Fed, Congress, and the White House are discussing ways of containing inflation without damaging employment and output. The President wants to cut aggregate demand but to do so in a way that will give the best chance of keeping investment high to encourage long-term economic growth. Explain the Fed's best action for meeting the President's objectives.

Use the following information to work Problems **11** and **12**.

What the U.S. jobs report means for the Fed
Despite U.S. job creation exceeding forecasts in July, experts believe that with weak output growth, the Fed will not raise the interest rate until after the U.S. presidential election.

Source: *Financial Times*, August 5, 2016

11. Explain why the Fed might be cautious about raising interest rates despite strong jobs growth.

12. What is the problem that might arise if the Fed keeps the interest rate too low for too long?

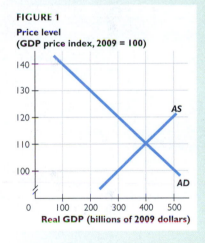

FIGURE 1

Price level
(GDP price index, 2009 = 100)

MyEconLab Chapter 33 Study Plan

Multiple Choice Quiz

1. The Fed's "dual mandate" is to achieve _____.

   A. a government budget surplus and low interest rates
   B. low inflation and maximum employment
   C. a stable quantity of money and stable prices
   D. zero unemployment and a stable means of payment

2. The Fed's operational goals include _____.

   A. a core inflation rate between 1 and 2 percent a year and an output gap as small as possible
   B. an economic growth rate of 3 percent a year and an unemployment rate equal to the natural unemployment rate
   C. a strong U.S. dollar on foreign exchange markets and a positive output gap
   D. maximum growth of stock prices and a low core inflation rate

3. The Fed's monetary policy instrument is the _____.

   A. inflation rate
   B. federal funds rate
   C. long-term interest rate
   D. monetary base

4. The Fed fights inflation by _____.

   A. lowering the federal funds rate, which lowers interest rates and decreases aggregate demand
   B. raising the federal funds rate, which raises interest rates and decreases aggregate demand
   C. decreasing the monetary base, which raises the interest rate and increases saving
   D. lowering the long-term real interest rate, which increases investment and spurs economic growth

5. To fight unemployment and close a recessionary gap, the Fed _____.

   A. stimulates aggregate demand by lowering the federal funds rate, which increases the quantity of money
   B. stimulates aggregate supply by lowering the federal funds rate, which increases potential GDP
   C. increases employment, which increases real GDP
   D. increases bank reserves, which banks use to make new loans to businesses, which increases aggregate supply

6. The Fed's choice of monetary policy strategy is _____.

   A. discretionary monetary policy
   B. the *k*-percent rule for money growth
   C. adjusting the federal funds rate to best fulfill its dual mandate
   D. setting the foreign exchange rate of the dollar

7. A monetary policy rule is _____ to discretionary monetary policy because _____.

   A. superior; discretion limits what the Fed can do in a financial crisis
   B. inferior; a rule makes it harder for people to forecast the inflation rate
   C. superior; a rule keeps inflation expectations anchored
   D. equivalent; the Fed uses its discretion to set the rule

International Finance

34

When you have completed your study of this chapter, you will be able to

1 Describe a country's balance of payments accounts and explain what determines the amount of international borrowing and lending.

2 Explain how the exchange rate is determined and why it fluctuates.

MyEconLab Big Picture Video

MyEconLab Concept Video

34.1 FINANCING INTERNATIONAL TRADE

When Apple, Inc. imports iPods manufactured in Taiwan, it pays for them using Taiwanese dollars. When a French construction company buys an earthmover from Caterpillar, Inc., it uses U.S. dollars. Whenever we buy things from another country, we pay in the currency of that country. It doesn't make any difference what the item being traded is; it might be a consumption good or a service or a capital good, a building, or even a firm.

We're going to study the markets in which different types of currency are bought and sold. But first we're going to look at the scale of international trading and borrowing and lending and at the way in which we keep our records of these transactions. These records are called the balance of payments accounts.

■ Balance of Payments Accounts

A country's **balance of payments accounts** record its international trading, borrowing, and lending. There are in fact three balance of payments accounts:

- Current account
- Capital and financial account
- Official settlements account

The **current account** records receipts from the sale of goods and services to other countries (exports), minus payments for goods and services bought from other countries (imports), plus the net amount of interest and transfers (such as foreign aid payments) received from and paid to other countries. The **capital and financial account** records foreign investment in the United States minus U.S. investment abroad. The **official settlements account** records the change in U.S. official reserves. **U.S. official reserves** are the government's holdings of foreign currency. If U.S. official reserves increase, the official settlements account balance is negative. The reason is that holding foreign money is like investing abroad and U.S. investment abroad is a minus item in the capital and financial account. (And if official reserves decrease, the official settlements account balance is positive.)

The sum of the balances on the three accounts always equals zero. That is, to pay for our current account deficit, we must either borrow more from abroad than we lend abroad or use our official reserves to cover the shortfall.

Table 34.1 shows the U.S. balance of payments accounts in 2015. Items in the current account and capital and financial account that provide foreign currency to the United States have a plus sign; items that cost the United States foreign currency have a minus sign. The table shows that in 2015, U.S. imports exceeded U.S. exports and the current account deficit was $463 billion. To pay for imports that exceeded the value of our exports we borrowed from the rest of the world. The capital and financial account tells us by how much. We borrowed $402 billion (foreign investment in the United States) and made $200 billion of loans to the rest of the world (U.S. investment abroad). With other net foreign borrowing of −$1 billion, the capital and financial account balance would be $201 billion. Omitted items and measurement error create an unusually large statistical discrepancy of $268 billion. Official reserves increased by $6 billion and are shown in Table 34.1 as a negative $6 billion, a convention that makes the three accounts sum to zero.

You might better understand the balance of payments accounts and the way in which they are linked if you think about the income and expenditure, borrowing and lending, and bank account of an individual.

Balance of payments accounts
The accounts in which a nation records its international trading, borrowing, and lending.

Current account
Record of receipts from the sale of goods and services to other countries (exports), minus payments for goods and services bought from other countries (imports), plus the net amount of interest and transfers received from and paid to other countries.

Capital and financial account
Record of foreign investment in the United States minus U.S. investment abroad.

Official settlements account
Record of the change in U.S. official reserves.

U.S. official reserves
The government's holdings of foreign currency.

EYE on the U.S. ECONOMY
The U.S. Balance of Payments

The numbers in Table 34.1 provide a snapshot of the U.S. balance of payments in 2015. This figure puts this snapshot into perspective by showing how the balance of payments evolved from 1980 to 2015.

A current account deficit emerged during the 1980s but briefly disappeared with a near-zero balance in the recession of the early 1990s. As the economy resumed its expansion during the 1990s, the current account deficit increased and kept on increasing until 2006.

As economic growth slowed and the economy went into recession, imports shrank and so did the current account deficit.

The capital and financial account balance is almost a mirror image of the current account balance and the reason is that the official settlements

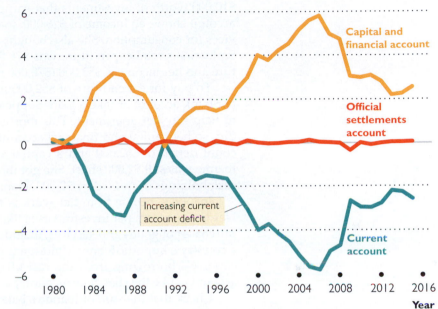

SOURCE OF DATA: Bureau of Economic Analysis.

balance—the change in foreign exchange reserves—is very small in comparison with the balances on the other two accounts.

TABLE 34.1

The U.S. Balance of Payments Accounts in 2015

MyEconLab Real-time data

Current account	(billions of dollars)
Exports of goods and services	+2,261
Imports of goods and services	−2,761
Net interest	+193
Net transfers	−156
Current account balance	**−463**
Capital and financial account	
Foreign investment in the United States	+402
U.S. investment abroad	−200
Other net foreign investment in the United States	−1
Statistical discrepancy	+268
Capital and financial account balance	**+469**
Official settlements account	
Official settlements account balance	**−6**

The three balance of payments accounts are the current account, the capital and financial account, and the official settlements account.

The sum of the balances on the three accounts is always zero. That is, the official settlements account balance always equals the negative of the sum of the current account balance and the capital and financial account balance.

In 2015, the statistical discrepancy was unusually large.

SOURCE OF DATA: Bureau of Economic Analysis.

Personal Analogy

You have a set of personal balance of payments accounts that parallel those of a nation. You have a current account, a capital account, and a settlements account.

Your current account records your income from supplying the services of factors of production and your expenditure on goods and services. Consider, for example, Joanne. She worked in 2015 and earned an income of $25,000. Joanne has $10,000 worth of investments that earned her interest of $1,000. Joanne's current account shows an income of $26,000. Joanne spent $18,000 buying goods and services for consumption. She also bought a new apartment, which cost her $60,000. So Joanne's total expenditure was $78,000. The difference between her expenditure and her income is $52,000 ($78,000 minus $26,000).

To pay for expenditure of $52,000 in excess of her income, Joanne has to use her bank account or take a loan. Suppose that Joanne took a mortgage of $50,000 to help buy her apartment. This mortgage was the only borrowing that Joanne did, so her capital and financial account surplus was $50,000. With a current account deficit of $52,000 and a capital and financial account surplus of $50,000, Joanne was still $2,000 short. She got that $2,000 from her own bank account. Her cash holdings decreased by $2,000. Joanne's settlements balance was $2,000.

Joanne's income from her work is like a country's income from its exports. Her income from her investments is like a country's interest from foreigners. Her purchases of goods and services, including her purchase of an apartment, are like a country's imports. Joanne's mortgage—borrowing from someone else—is like a country's borrowing from the rest of the world. The change in Joanne's bank account is like the change in a country's official reserves.

Check that the sum of Joanne's balances is zero. Her current account balance is −$52,000, her capital and financial account balance is +$50,000, and her settlements account balance is +$2,000, so the sum of the three balances is zero.

■ Borrowers and Lenders, Debtors and Creditors

A country that is borrowing more from the rest of the world than it is lending to the rest of the world is called a **net borrower**. Similarly, a **net lender** is a country that is lending more to the rest of the world than it is borrowing from it.

The United States is a net borrower, but it is a relative newcomer to the ranks of net borrower nations. Throughout the 1960s and most of the 1970s, the United States was a net lender. It had a surplus on its current account and a deficit on its capital and financial account. It was not until 1983 that the United States became a significant net borrower. Between 1983 and 1987, U.S. borrowing increased each year. Then it decreased and was briefly zero in 1991. From 1991 through 2006, U.S. borrowing increased, but after 2006 it decreased. The average net foreign borrowing by the United States between 1983 and 2015 was $313 billion a year.

Most countries are net borrowers like the United States. But a small number of countries, including China and oil-rich Saudi Arabia, are net lenders.

A net borrower might be reducing its net assets held in the rest of the world, or it might be going deeper into debt. A nation's total stock of foreign investment determines whether the nation is a debtor or creditor. A **debtor nation** is a country that during its entire history has borrowed more from the rest of the world than it has lent to the rest of the world. A debtor nation has a stock of outstanding debt to the rest of the world that exceeds the stock of its own claims on the rest of the world. A **creditor nation** is a country that during its entire history has invested more in the rest of the world than other countries have invested in it.

Net borrower
A country that is borrowing more from the rest of the world than it is lending to the rest of the world.

Net lender
A country that is lending more to the rest of the world than it is borrowing from the rest of the world.

Debtor nation
A country that during its entire history has borrowed more from the rest of the world than it has lent to the rest of the world.

Creditor nation
A country that during its entire history has invested more in the rest of the world than other countries have invested in it.

■ Current Account Balance

What determines a country's current account balance and net foreign borrowing? Why has the United States had a deficit every year since 1980 but one?

In popular political commentary, the blame for a long string of deficits is placed on an unfair, unlevel playing field. The suggestion is that successive U.S. governments have negotiated trade deals that have disadvantaged the United States, lost export markets, encouraged imports, and cost American jobs. The implication of this view is that the current account deficit can be turned around by a return to tariffs and other trade restrictions that enable high-cost U.S. producers to compete with low-cost foreign producers.

This line of reasoning is wrong for three reasons: First, it doesn't fit the timing of trade deals. Second, trade deals influence what and how much we trade with other countries, not the balance of that trade. And third, the government budget deficit and private saving deficit is the source of the current account deficit.

Let's explore these three reasons for rejecting the politically popular story.

Timing

The U.S. current account deficit started in 1982, peaked in 1987, shrank to zero in 1991, increased to a new and higher peak in 2006, and then shrank again. (The figure in *Eye on the U.S. Economy* on p. 879 shows the details.) This timing and direction of change in the current account deficit does not align with the timing of U.S. trade agreements shown in Table 34.2. The current account was already in deficit when the first trade deals were signed. Following the start of NAFTA in 1994, the deficit did increase but after 2006, with NAFTA still in place, the deficit decreased. By 2007, with nine major trade deals operating, the deficit started to fall. This lack of alignment of trade deals and current account deficit makes clear that we need to look elsewhere for the cause of the deficit.

Free Trade Agreements and the Quantity of Trade

When trade barriers are removed in a free trade agreement, the quantity of both exports and imports increases. Exports increase because buyers in the other country face lower prices for U.S.-produced goods and services. And U.S. imports increase because Americans get foreign-produced items at lower prices. The data confirm these trade-creating effects. In 1980, before the trade deals in place today, U.S. international trade (the sum of exports and imports) was 12 percent of GDP. Today, as a consequence of the deals in place, U.S. international trade has grown to 29 percent of GDP.

Current Account Deficit, Budget Deficit, and Private Saving Deficit

You are now going to see why the government budget deficit and the gap between private sector saving and investment—the private sector deficit—is the source of the current account deficit.

Begin by recalling that exports of goods and services (X) and imports of goods and services (M) are the largest items in the current account (see Table 34.1). Exports minus imports are net exports (NX) and fluctuations in net exports are the main source of fluctuations in the current account balance.

To see how the government budget along with private saving and investment determine net exports, we need to recall some of the things that we learned about the national income accounts in Chapter 21. Table 34.3 will refresh your memory and summarize some calculations.

TABLE 34.2
U.S. TRADE AGREEMENTS

Start year	Countries
1985	Israel
1988	Canada
1994	NAFTA (Canada and Mexico)
2001	Jordan
2004	Australia, Chile, Singapore
2005	CAFTA (6 Central American countries)
2006	Morroco, Oman
2007	Peru
2012	Panama, Columbia, South Korea

Part (a) of Table 34.3 lists the national income variables with their symbols. Part (b) defines three balances. *Net exports* are exports of goods and services minus imports of goods and services.

Private sector balance
Saving minus investment.

The **private sector balance** is saving minus investment. If saving exceeds investment, a private sector surplus is lent to other sectors. If investment exceeds saving, borrowing from other sectors finances a private sector deficit.

Government sector balance
The sum of the budget balances of the federal, state, and local governments—net taxes minus government expenditure on goods and services.

The **government sector balance** is the sum of the budget balances of the federal, state, and local governments. It is equal to net taxes minus government expenditure on goods and services. If that number is positive, a government sector surplus is lent to other sectors; if that number is negative, borrowing from other sectors must finance a government sector budget deficit.

Part (b) of Table 34.3 shows the values of these balances for the United States in 2015. As you can see, net exports were −$522 billion, a deficit. The private sector saved $3,317 billion and invested $3,057 billion, so it had a surplus of $260 billion. The government sector's revenue from net taxes was $2,436 billion and its expenditure was $3,218 billion, so the government sector balance was −$782 billion, a deficit.

Part (c) of Table 34.3 shows the relationship among the three balances.

■ **TABLE 34.3**

Net Exports, the Government Budget, Saving, and Investment

		Symbols and equations	United States in 2015 (billions of dollars)
Net exports equals exports minus imports.	**(a) Variables**		
	Exports	X	2,264
The private sector balance equals saving minus investment.	Imports	M	2,786
	Investment	I	3,057
	Saving	S	3,317
The government sector balance equals net taxes minus government expenditure on goods and services.	Government expenditure	G	3,218
	Net taxes	NT	2,436
	(b) Balances		
These three balances are related: Net exports equals the sum of the private sector and government sector balances.	Net exports	$X - M$	$2{,}264 - 2{,}786 = -522$
	Private sector balance	$S - I$	$3{,}317 - 3{,}057 = 260$
	Government sector balance	$NT - G$	$2{,}436 - 3{,}218 = -782$
	(c) Relation among balances		
	National accounts	$Y = C + I + G + X - M = C + S + NT$	
	Rearranging:	$(X - M) = (S - I) + (NT - G)$	
	Net exports	$X - M$	−522
	Equals:		
	Private sector balance	$S - I$	260
	Plus:		
	Government sector balance	$NT - G$	−782

Source of data: Bureau of Economic Analysis, 2016. (The *National Income and Product Accounts* measures of exports and imports are slightly different from the Balance of Payments Accounts measures in Table 34.1 on p. 879. The government sector includes state and local governments.)

From the national income accounts, we know that real GDP, Y, is the sum of consumption expenditure, C; investment, I; government expenditure on goods and services, G; and net exports, $(X - M)$. Real GDP also equals the sum of consumption expenditure, C, saving, S, and net taxes, NT. Rearranging these equations tells us that net exports equals $(S - I)$, the private sector balance, plus $(NT - G)$, the government sector balance. That is,

$$\text{Net exports} = (S - I) + (NT - G)$$

Should we be concerned that the United States is a net borrower? The answer is probably not. Our international borrowing finances the purchase of new capital goods. In 2015, businesses spent $3,057 billion on new buildings, plant, and equipment. Governments spent $613 billion on defense equipment and public structures. All these purchases added to the nation's capital, and much of it increased labor productivity. Governments also purchased education and healthcare services, which increased human capital.

Our international borrowing is financing private and public investment, not consumption.

EYE on the GLOBAL ECONOMY
Current Account Balances Around the World

The figure shows a sample of current account balances around the world in 2015. No country or region has a balanced current account with the value of exports and other receipts equal to the value of imports and other payments.

The United States has the largest current account deficit, and other advanced economies, the Euro area, China, and developing Asian economies have large surpluses.

Countries with deficits have government budget deficits and a shortage of saving to finance investment. Surplus countries also mostly have government budget deficits but have high levels of saving that more than covers the cost of business investment.

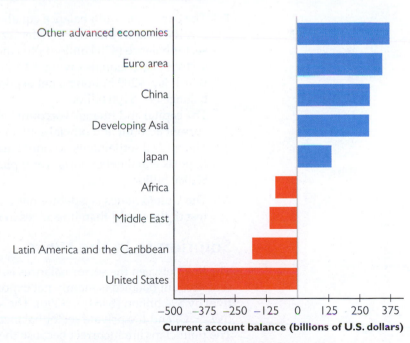

Current account balance (billions of U.S. dollars)

SOURCE OF DATA: International Monetary Fund, *World Economic Outlook*, April 2016

MyEconLab Study Plan 34.1
Key Terms Quiz
Solutions Video

 CHECKPOINT 34.1

Describe a country's balance of payments accounts and explain what determines the amount of international borrowing and lending.

Practice Problems

Use the following information about the United States to work Problems **1** and **2**.

Imports of goods and services: $2,000 billion; interest paid to the rest of the world: $500 billion; interest received from the rest of the world: $400 billion; decrease in U.S. official reserves: $10 billion; government sector balance: $200 billion; saving: $1,800 billion; investment: $2,000 billion; net transfers: zero.

1. Calculate the current account balance, the capital and financial account balance, the official settlements account balance, and exports of goods and services.

2. Is the United States a debtor or a creditor nation?

In the News

U.S. current account deficit highest in 7 years
The U.S. current account deficit in 2015 was $484 billion, up from $390 billion in 2014, and the highest since 2008. Some politicians say the deficit is the result of bad trade deals with nations engaged in unfair trading practices.
Source: U.S. News & World Report, March 17, 2016

Explain how the sum of the government budget balance and the personal sector balance changed in 2015; and explain why the politicians are wrong.

Solutions to Practice Problems

1. The current account balance equals net exports plus net interest from abroad (−$100 billion) plus net transfers (zero). Net exports equal the government sector balance ($200 billion) plus the private sector balance. The private sector balance equals saving ($1,800 billion) minus investment ($2,000 billion), which is −$200 billion So net exports are zero, and the current account balance is −$100 billion.
   The capital and financial account balance is the negative of the sum of the current account and official settlements account balances, which is $90 billion. The official settlements account balance is a *surplus* of $10 billion.
   Exports equal net exports (zero) plus imports ($2,000 billion), which equals $2,000 billion.

2. The United States is a debtor nation because it pays more in interest to the rest of the world than it receives in interest from the rest of the world.

Solution to In the News

The link between the sector balances is: $(X - M) = (S - I) + (NT - G)$. The current account balance is mainly net exports, which decreased (became more negative) by $94 billion ($484 − $390). The sum of the government budget balance $(NT - G)$ and the private sector balance $(S - I)$ also decreased by $94 billion. The politicians are incorrect because the U.S. current account has been in deficit since long before most of the trade deals were negotiated and the budget deficit financed by foreign borrowing is the main source of the current account deficit.

34.2 THE EXCHANGE RATE

MyEconLab Concept Video

When we buy foreign goods or invest in another country, we pay using that country's currency. When foreigners buy U.S.-made goods or invest in the United States, they pay in U.S. dollars. We get foreign currency and foreigners get U.S. dollars in the foreign exchange market. The **foreign exchange market** is the market in which the currency of one country is exchanged for the currency of another. The foreign exchange market is not a place like a downtown flea market or produce market. It is made up of thousands of people: importers and exporters, banks, and specialist traders of foreign exchange, called foreign exchange brokers. The foreign exchange market opens on Monday morning in Hong Kong, which is still Sunday evening in New York. As the day advances, markets open in Singapore, Tokyo, Bahrain, Frankfurt, London, New York, Chicago, and San Francisco. As the U.S. West Coast markets close, Hong Kong is only an hour away from opening for the next business day. Dealers around the world are in continual contact, and on a typical day in 2016, around $5 trillion is traded.

The price at which one currency exchanges for another is called a **foreign exchange rate**. For example, in August 2016, one U.S. dollar bought 90 euro cents. The exchange rate was 0.90 euros per dollar. We can also express the exchange rate in terms of dollars per euro, which in August 2016 was $1.11 per euro. Figure 34.1 shows the history of the U.S. dollar exchange rate against the euro since 2000 in terms of euros per dollar.

Currency appreciation is the rise in the value of one currency in terms of another currency. For example, when the dollar rose from just over 1.00 euros to 1.17 euros in 2000, the dollar appreciated by 17 percent.

Foreign exchange market
The market in which the currency of one country is exchanged for the currency of another.

Foreign exchange rate
The price at which one currency exchanges for another.

Currency appreciation
The rise in the value of one currency in terms of another currency.

■ **FIGURE 34.1**

The U.S. Dollar Exchange Rate Against the Euro

MyEconLab Real-time data

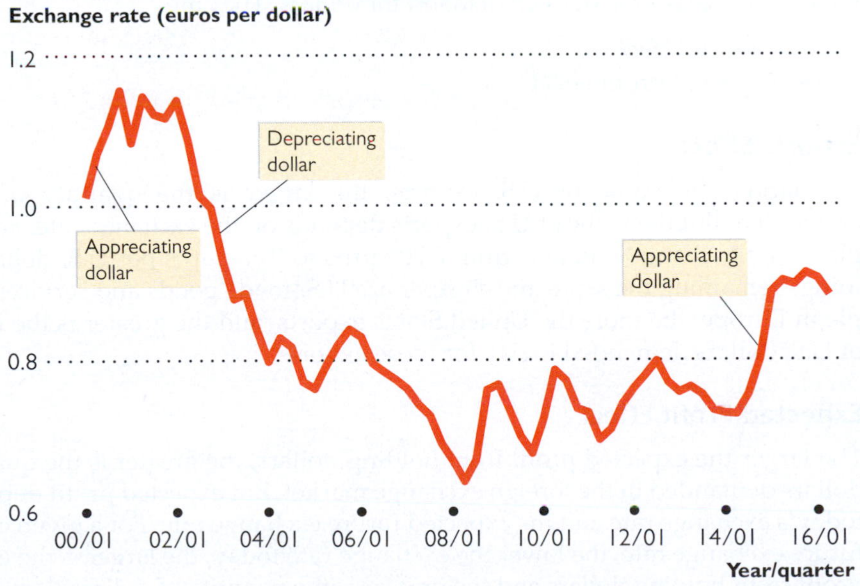

In 2000, and again in 2015, the value of the dollar rose against the euro—the dollar *appreciated*. From 2002 to 2008, the value of the dollar fell against the euro—the dollar *depreciated*. The overall fall was from a high of 1.17 euros per dollar in 2001 to a low of 0.64 euros per dollar in 2008.

From 2008 to 2014, through the turmoil of global financial crisis and repeated financial and political crises in Europe, the value of the dollar against the euro fluctuated between around 0.70 and 0.80 euros per dollar.

SOURCE OF DATA: Board of Governors of the Federal Reserve System.

Currency depreciation
The fall in the value of one currency in terms of another currency.

Currency depreciation is the fall in the value of one currency in terms of another currency. For example, when the dollar fell from 1.17 euros in 2000 to 0.63 euros in 2008, the dollar depreciated by 46 percent. Why does the U.S. dollar fluctuate in value? Why does it sometimes depreciate and sometimes appreciate?

The exchange rate is a price. And like all prices, demand and supply determine the exchange rate. So to understand the forces that determine the exchange rate, we need to study demand and supply in the foreign exchange market. We'll begin by looking at the demand side of the market.

■ Demand in the Foreign Exchange Market

The quantity of U.S. dollars that traders plan to buy in the foreign exchange market in a given period of time depends on many factors, but the main ones are

- The exchange rate
- Interest rates in the United States and other countries
- The expected future exchange rate

Let's look first at the relationship between the quantity of dollars demanded in the foreign exchange market and the exchange rate.

■ The Law of Demand for Foreign Exchange

People do not buy dollars because they enjoy them. The demand for dollars is a *derived demand*. People demand dollars so that they can buy U.S.-made goods and services (U.S. exports). They also demand dollars so that they can buy U.S. assets such as bank accounts, bonds, stocks, businesses, and real estate. Nevertheless, the law of demand applies to dollars just as it does to anything else that people value.

Other things remaining the same, the higher the exchange rate, the smaller is the quantity of dollars demanded. For example, if the price of the U.S. dollar rises from 0.70 euros to 0.80 euros but nothing else changes, the quantity of U.S. dollars that people plan to buy decreases. Why does the exchange rate influence the quantity of dollars demanded? There are two separate reasons, and they are related to the two sources of the derived demand for dollars. They are

- Exports effect
- Expected profit effect

Exports Effect

The larger the value of U.S. exports, the larger is the quantity of dollars demanded. But the value of U.S. exports depends on the exchange rate. For example, if the exchange rate falls from 0.70 euros to 0.60 euros per U.S. dollar, other things remaining the same, the cheaper are U.S.-made goods and services to people in Europe, the more the United States exports, and the greater is the quantity of U.S. dollars demanded to pay for those exports.

Expected Profit Effect

The larger the expected profit from holding dollars, the greater is the quantity of dollars demanded in the foreign exchange market. But expected profit depends on today's exchange rate and the expected future exchange rate. For a given expected future exchange rate, the lower the exchange rate today, the larger is the expected profit from holding dollars and the greater is the quantity of dollars demanded in the foreign exchange market.

■ **FIGURE 34.2**

The Demand for Dollars

MyEconLab Animation

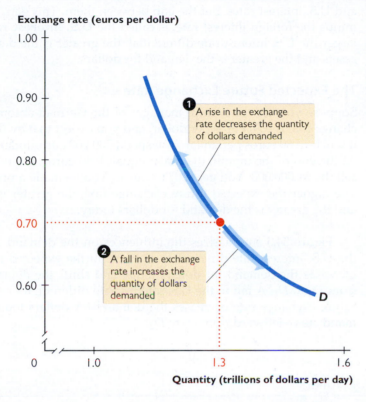

Other things remaining the same, the quantity of dollars that people plan to buy in the foreign exchange market depends on the exchange rate.

❶ If the exchange rate rises, the quantity of dollars demanded decreases and there is a movement up along the demand curve for dollars.

❷ If the exchange rate falls, the quantity of dollars demanded increases and there is a movement down along the demand curve for dollars.

To understand this effect, suppose that you think the dollar will be worth 0.80 euros by the end of the month. If a dollar costs 0.75 euros today, you buy dollars. But a person who thinks that the dollar will be worth 0.75 euros at the end of the month does not buy dollars. Now suppose that today's exchange rate falls to 0.65 euros per dollar. More people think that they can profit from buying dollars, so the quantity of dollars demanded today increases.

Figure 34.2 shows the demand curve for U.S. dollars in the foreign exchange market. For the two reasons we've just reviewed, when the foreign exchange rate rises, other things remaining the same, the quantity of dollars demanded decreases and there is a movement up along the demand curve, as shown by the arrow. When the exchange rate falls, other things remaining the same, the quantity of dollars demanded increases and there is a movement down along the demand curve, as shown by the arrow.

■ Changes in the Demand for Dollars

A change in any other influence on the quantity of U.S. dollars that people plan to buy in the foreign exchange market brings a change in the demand for dollars. These other influences are

- Interest rates in the United States and other countries
- The expected future exchange rate

Interest Rates in the United States and Other Countries

If you can borrow in another country and lend in the United States at a higher interest rate, you will make a profit. What matters is not the values of the foreign and U.S. interest rates, but the gap between them. This gap, the U.S. interest rate minus the foreign interest rate, is called the **U.S. interest rate differential**. The larger the U.S. interest rate differential, the greater is the demand for U.S.-dollar assets and the greater is the demand for dollars.

U.S. interest rate differential
The U.S. interest rate minus the foreign interest rate.

The Expected Future Exchange Rate

Suppose you are the finance manager of the German automaker BMW. The exchange rate is 0.70 euros per dollar, and you expect that by the end of the month, it will be 0.80 euros per dollar. You spend 700,000 euros today and buy $1,000,000. At the end of the month, the dollar equals 0.80 euros, as you predicted, and you sell the $1,000,000. You get 800,000 euros. You've made a profit of 100,000 euros. The higher the expected future exchange rate, the greater is the expected profit and the greater is the demand for dollars today.

Figure 34.3 summarizes the influences on the demand for dollars. A rise in the U.S. interest rate differential or a rise in the expected future exchange rate increases the demand for dollars today and shifts the demand curve rightward from D_0 to D_1. A fall in the U.S. interest rate differential or a fall in the expected future exchange rate decreases the demand for dollars today and shifts the demand curve leftward from D_0 to D_2.

■ FIGURE 34.3

Changes in the Demand for Dollars   MyEconLab Animation

❶ The demand for dollars increases if:

- ■ The U.S. interest rate differential increases.
- ■ The expected future exchange rate rises.

❷ The demand for dollars decreases if:

- ■ The U.S. interest rate differential decreases.
- ■ The expected future exchange rate falls.

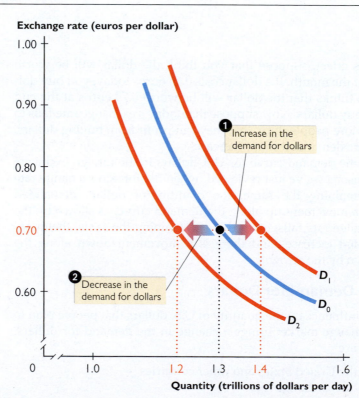

Supply in the Foreign Exchange Market

The quantity of U.S. dollars that traders plan to sell in the foreign exchange market in a given period of time depends on many factors, but the main ones are

- The exchange rate
- Interest rates in the United States and other countries
- The expected future exchange rate

Does this list of factors seem familiar? It should: It is the same list as that for demand. The demand side and the supply side of the foreign exchange market are influenced by all the same factors. But the ways in which these three factors influence supply are the opposite of the ways in which they influence demand.

Let's look first at the relationship between the quantity of dollars supplied in the foreign exchange market and the exchange rate.

The Law of Supply of Foreign Exchange

Traders supply U.S. dollars in the foreign exchange market when people and businesses buy other currencies. They buy other currencies so that they can buy foreign-made goods and services (U.S. imports). Traders also supply dollars and buy foreign currencies so that people and businesses can buy foreign assets such as bank accounts, bonds, stocks, businesses, and real estate. The law of supply applies to dollars just as it does to anything else that people plan to sell.

Other things remaining the same, the higher the exchange rate, the greater is the quantity of dollars supplied in the foreign exchange market. For example, if the price of the U.S. dollar rises from 0.70 euros to 0.80 euros but nothing else changes, the quantity of U.S. dollars that people plan to sell in the foreign exchange market increases. Why does the exchange rate influence the quantity of dollars supplied?

There are two reasons, and they parallel the two reasons on the demand side of the market. They are

- Imports effect
- Expected profit effect

Imports Effect

The larger the value of U.S. imports, the larger is the quantity of foreign currency demanded to pay for these imports. And when people buy foreign currency, they supply dollars. So the larger the value of U.S. imports, the greater is the quantity of dollars supplied in the foreign exchange market. But the value of U.S. imports depends on the exchange rate. The higher the exchange rate, other things remaining the same, the cheaper are foreign-made goods and services to Americans. So the more the United States imports, the greater is the quantity of U.S. dollars supplied in the foreign exchange market to pay for these imports.

Expected Profit Effect

The larger the expected profit from holding a foreign currency, the greater is the quantity of that currency demanded and the greater is the quantity of dollars supplied in the foreign exchange market. But the expected profit depends on today's exchange rate and the expected future exchange rate. For a given expected future exchange rate, the higher the exchange rate today, the larger is the expected profit from selling dollars and the greater is the quantity of dollars supplied in the foreign exchange market.

■ **FIGURE 34.4**

The Supply of Dollars

Other things remaining the same, the quantity of dollars that people plan to sell in the foreign exchange market depends on the exchange rate.

1 If the exchange rate rises, the quantity of dollars supplied increases and there is a movement up along the supply curve of dollars.

2 If the exchange rate falls, the quantity of dollars supplied decreases and there is a movement down along the supply curve of dollars.

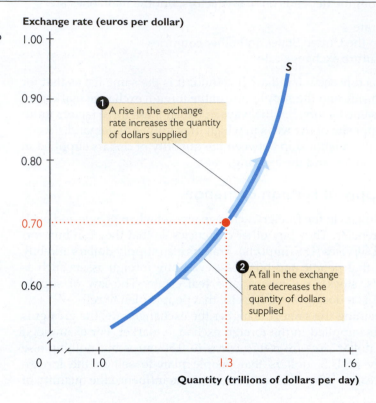

For the two reasons we've just reviewed, other things remaining the same, when the exchange rate rises, the quantity of dollars supplied increases, and when the exchange rate falls, the quantity of dollars supplied decreases. Figure 34.4 shows the supply curve of U.S. dollars in the foreign exchange market. In this figure, when the exchange rate rises, other things remaining the same, there is an increase in the quantity of dollars supplied and a movement up along the supply curve, as shown by the arrow. When the exchange rate falls, other things remaining the same, there is a decrease in the quantity of dollars supplied and a movement down along the supply curve, as shown by the arrow.

■ Changes in the Supply of Dollars

A change in any other influence on the quantity of U.S. dollars that people plan to sell in the foreign exchange market brings a change in the supply of dollars, and the supply curve of dollars shifts. Supply either increases or decreases. These other influences on supply parallel the other influences on demand but have exactly the opposite effects. These influences are

- Interest rates in the United States and other countries
- The expected future exchange rate

Interest Rates in the United States and Other Countries

The larger the U.S. interest rate differential, the smaller is the demand for foreign assets and the smaller is the supply of dollars in the foreign exchange market.

The Expected Future Exchange Rate

Other things remaining the same, the higher the expected future exchange rate, the smaller is the supply of dollars. To see why, suppose that the dollar is trading at 0.70 euros per dollar today and you think that by the end of the month, the dollar will trade at 0.80 euros per dollar. You were planning on selling dollars today, but you decide to hold off and wait until the end of the month. If you supply dollars today, you get only 0.70 euros per dollar. But at the end of the month, if the dollar is worth 0.80 euros as you predict, you'll get 0.80 euros for each dollar you supply. You'll make a profit of 0.10 euros per dollar. So the higher the expected future exchange rate, other things remaining the same, the smaller is the expected profit from selling U.S. dollars and the smaller is the supply of dollars today.

Figure 34.5 summarizes the influences on the supply of dollars. A rise in the U.S. interest rate differential or the expected future exchange rate decreases the supply of dollars today and shifts the supply curve leftward from S_0 to S_1. A fall in the U.S. interest rate differential or the expected future exchange rate increases the supply of dollars today and shifts the supply curve rightward from S_0 to S_2.

■ **FIGURE 34.5**

Changes in the Supply of Dollars   MyEconLab Animation

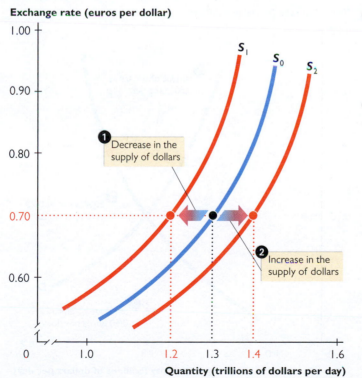

❶ The supply of dollars increases if:

■ The U.S. interest rate differential decreases.
■ The expected future exchange rate falls.

❷ The supply of dollars decreases if:

■ The U.S. interest rate differential increases.
■ The expected future exchange rate rises.

■ Market Equilibrium

Demand and supply in the foreign exchange market determine the exchange rate. Just as in all the other markets you've studied, the price (the exchange rate) acts as a regulator. If the exchange rate is too high, there is a surplus—the quantity supplied exceeds the quantity demanded. If the exchange rate is too low, there is a shortage—the quantity supplied is less than the quantity demanded. At the equilibrium exchange rate, there is neither a shortage nor a surplus. The quantity supplied equals the quantity demanded.

Figure 34.6 illustrates market equilibrium. The demand for dollars is *D*, and the supply of dollars is *S*. The equilibrium exchange rate is 0.70 euros per dollar. At this exchange rate, the quantity demanded equals the quantity supplied and is $1.3 trillion a day. If the exchange rate is above 0.70 euros, for example, 0.80 euros per dollar, there is a surplus of dollars and the exchange rate falls. If the exchange rate is below 0.70 euros, for example, 0.60 euros per dollar, there is a shortage of dollars and the exchange rate rises.

The foreign exchange market is constantly pulled to its equilibrium by the forces of supply and demand. Foreign exchange dealers are constantly looking for the best price they can get. If they are selling, they want the highest price available. If they are buying, they want the lowest price available. Information flows from dealer to dealer through the worldwide computer network, and the price adjusts second by second to keep buying plans and selling plans in balance. That is, price adjusts second by second to keep the market at its equilibrium.

■ FIGURE 34.6

Equilibrium Exchange Rate

MyEconLab Animation

The demand curve for dollars is *D*, and the supply curve is *S*.

❶ If the exchange rate is 0.80 euros per dollar, there is a surplus of dollars and the exchange rate falls.

❷ If the exchange rate is 0.60 euros per dollar, there is a shortage of dollars and the exchange rate rises.

❸ If the exchange rate is 0.70 euros per dollar, there is neither a shortage nor a surplus of dollars and the exchange rate remains constant. The market is in equilibrium.

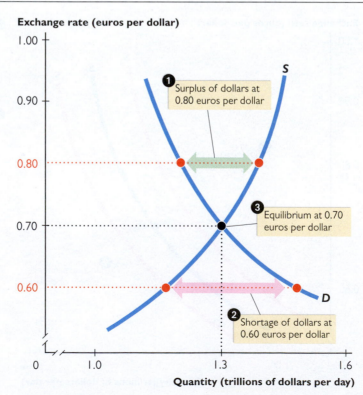

EYE on the DOLLAR

MyEconLab Critical Thinking Exercise

Why Does Our Dollar Fluctuate?

Our dollar fluctuates: Sometimes its value rises and sometimes it falls. Let's see what makes our dollar fluctuate by looking at two episodes in its bouncing life.

A Falling Dollar: 2001–2008

Between 2001 and 2008, the dollar fell from 1.15 euros to 0.64 euros per dollar. Figure 1 explains this fall.

In 2001, the demand and supply curves were those labeled D_{01} and S_{01}. The exchange rate was 1.15 euros per dollar. During the next few years, U.S. economic growth slipped below the European growth rate, European inflation fell, interest rates in Europe exceeded those in the United States, and the U.S. current account deficit continued to increase.

Under these conditions, currency traders expected the exchange rate to fall. The demand for dollars decreased and the supply of dollars increased. The demand curve shifted leftward to D_{08} and the supply curve shifted rightward to S_{08}. The exchange rate fell to 0.64 euros per dollar.

From 2008 to 2014, the dollar fluctuated around a slightly rising trend. Then, in 2015, the dollar appreciated very quickly.

A Rising Dollar: 2014–2015

The dollar appreciated against the euro when it rose from 0.73 euros per dollar in 2014 to 0.90 euros per dollar in 2015. Figure 2 explains why this happened.

In 2014, the demand and supply curves were those labeled D_{14} and S_{14}. The equilibrium exchange rate was 0.73 euros per dollar—where the quantity of dollars supplied equaled the quantity of dollars demanded.

During 2015, the U.S. economy expanded faster than the European economy. In Europe, interest rates were expected to fall as the central bank tried to stimulate a stagnant economy. U.S. interest rates were low, but the Fed's next move was expected to be upward. In this environment, the dollar was expected to appreciate against the euro.

With an expected dollar appreciation, the demand for dollars increased and the supply of dollars decreased. The demand curve shifted from D_{14} to D_{15} and the supply curve shifted from S_{14} to S_{15}. These two reinforcing shifts made the exchange rate rise to 0.90 euros per dollar.

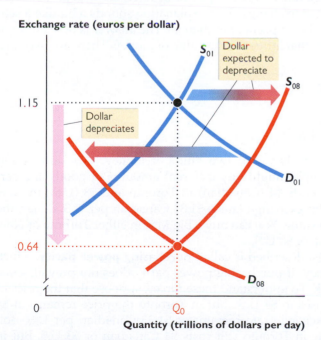

Figure 1 2001 to 2008

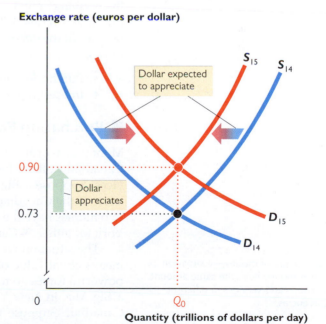

Figure 2 2014 to 2015

Why Exchange Rates Are Volatile

You've seen that sometimes the dollar depreciates and at other times it appreciates. The exchange rates of other currencies are similarly volatile. The Japanese yen, Canadian dollar, and Mexican peso along with most currencies swing between appreciation and depreciation. Yet the quantity of dollars (and other currencies) traded in the foreign exchange market each day barely changes. Why?

A large part of the answer is that everyone in the foreign exchange market is potentially either a buyer or a seller—a demander or a supplier. Each trader has a price above which he or she will sell and below which he or she will buy.

This fact about the participants in the foreign exchange market means that supply and demand are not independent. The same shocks to the foreign exchange market that change the demand for a currency also change its supply. Demand and supply change in *opposite directions*, and the result is large price changes and small quantity changes.

The two key influences that change both demand and supply in the foreign exchange market are the interest rate differential and the expected future exchange rate.

A rise in the U.S. interest rate differential *increases* the *demand* for U.S. dollars in the foreign exchange market and *decreases* the *supply*. A rise in the expected future exchange rate also increases the demand for U.S. dollars and decreases the supply.

These common influences that change demand and supply in *opposite directions* bring changes in the exchange rate and little change in the quantities of currencies traded. They can bring cumulative movements in the exchange rate or frequent changes of direction—volatility.

MyEconLab Concept Video

■ Exchange Rate Expectations

The changes in the exchange rate that we've just considered occur in part because the exchange rate is expected to change. This explanation sounds a bit like a self-fulfilling forecast. What makes expectations change? The answer is new information about the deeper forces that influence the value of money. There are two such forces:

- Purchasing power parity
- Interest rate parity

■ Purchasing Power Parity

Money is worth what it will buy. But two kinds of money, U.S. dollars and Canadian dollars, for example, might buy different amounts of goods and services. Suppose a Big Mac costs $4 (Canadian) in Toronto and $3 (U.S.) in New York. If the Canadian dollar exchange rate is $1.33 Canadian per U.S. dollar, the two monies have the same value. You can buy a Big Mac in either Toronto or New York for either $4 Canadian or $3 U.S.

The situation we've just described is called **purchasing power parity**, which means equal value of money. If purchasing power parity does not prevail, some powerful forces go to work. To understand these forces, suppose that the price of a Big Mac in New York rises to $4 U.S., but in Toronto the price remains at $4 Canadian. Suppose the exchange rate remains at $1.33 Canadian per U.S. dollar. In this case, a Big Mac in Toronto still costs $4 Canadian or $3 U.S. But in

Purchasing power parity
Equal value of money—a situation in which money buys the same amount of goods and services in different currencies.

EYE on the GLOBAL ECONOMY
Purchasing Power Parity

Purchasing power parity (PPP) is a long-run phenomenon. In the short run, deviations from PPP can be large.

The figure shows the large range of deviations from PPP in August 2016, which stretches from 30 percent over-valued to 65 percent undervalued.

The Swiss franc and the Icelandic krona were the most overvalued currencies and according to PPP, they will depreciate at some point in the future.

The most undervalued currencies in August 2016 were the Russian ruble and South African rand. PPP predicts that these currencies will appreciate at some time in the future.

PPP theory predicts that a currency might depreciate or appreciate but the theory does not help to predict *when* it will depreciate or appreciate.

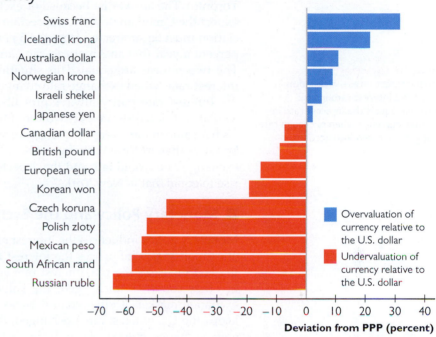

SOURCE OF DATA: PACIFIC FX Service, University of British Columbia.

New York, it costs $4 U.S. or $5.32 Canadian. Money buys more in Canada than in the United States. Money is not of equal value in both countries.

If all (or most) prices have increased in the United States and not increased in Canada, then people will generally expect that the U.S. dollar exchange rate is going to fall. The demand for U.S. dollars decreases, and the supply of U.S. dollars increases. The U.S. dollar exchange rate falls, as expected. If the U.S. dollar falls to $1.00 Canadian and there are no further price changes, purchasing power parity is restored. A Big Mac now costs $4 in either U.S. dollars or Canadian dollars in both New York and Toronto.

If prices increase in Canada and other countries but remain constant in the United States, then people will generally expect that the value of the U.S. dollar in the foreign exchange market is too low and that the U.S. dollar exchange rate will rise. The demand for U.S. dollars increases, and the supply of U.S. dollars decreases. The U.S. dollar exchange rate rises, as expected.

Ultimately, the value of money is determined by prices. So the deeper forces that influence the exchange rate have tentacles that spread throughout the economy. If prices in the United States rise faster than those in other countries, the exchange rate falls. And if prices in the United States rise more slowly than those in other countries, the exchange rate rises.

Interest Rate Parity

Suppose a Canadian dollar bank deposit in a Toronto bank earns 5 percent a year and a U.S. dollar bank deposit in a New York bank earns 3 percent a year. Why does anyone deposit money in New York? Why doesn't all the money flow to Toronto? The answer is: Because of exchange rate expectations. Suppose people expect the Canadian dollar to depreciate by 2 percent a year. This 2 percent depreciation must be subtracted from the 5 percent interest to obtain the net return of 3 percent a year that an American can earn by depositing funds in a Toronto bank. The two returns are equal. This situation is one of **interest rate parity**—equal interest rates when exchange rate changes are taken into account.

Interest rate parity always prevails. Funds move to get the highest return available. If interest rate parity did not hold because the Canadian dollar had too high a value in the foreign exchange market, the expected return in Toronto would be lower than in New York. In seconds, traders would sell the Canadian dollar, its exchange rate would fall, and the expected return from lending in Toronto would rise to equal that in New York.

■ Monetary Policy and the Exchange Rate

Monetary policy influences the interest rate (see Chapter 28, pp. 726–729), so monetary policy also influences the interest rate differential and the exchange rate. If the Fed increases the U.S. interest rate and other central banks keep interest rates in other countries unchanged, the value of the U.S. dollar rises in the foreign exchange market. If other central banks increase their interest rates and the Fed keeps the U.S. interest rate unchanged, the value of the U.S. dollar falls in the foreign exchange market. So exchange rates fluctuate in response to changes and expected changes in monetary policy in the United States and around the world.

■ Pegging the Exchange Rate

Some central banks try to avoid exchange rate fluctuations by pegging the value of their currency against another currency. Suppose the Fed wanted to keep the dollar at 0.70 euros per dollar. If the exchange rate rose above 0.70 euros, the Fed would sell dollars and if it fell below 0.70 euros, the Fed would buy dollars.

Figure 34.7 illustrates foreign exchange market intervention. The supply of dollars is S, and initially, the demand for dollars is D_0. The equilibrium exchange rate is 0.70 euros per dollar, which is also the Fed's target—the horizontal red line.

If the demand for dollars increases to D_1, the Fed increases the supply of dollars—sells dollars—and prevents the exchange rate from rising. If the demand for dollars decreases to D_2, the Fed decreases the supply of dollars—buys dollars—and prevents the exchange rate from falling.

When the Fed buys dollars, it uses its reserves of euros; when the Fed sells dollars, it takes euros in exchange and its reserves of euros increase. As long as the demand for dollars fluctuates around and on average remains at D_0, the Fed's reserves of euros fluctuate but neither run dry nor persistently increase.

But if the demand for dollars decreased permanently to D_2, the Fed would have to buy dollars and sell euros every day to maintain the exchange rate at 0.70 euros per dollar. The Fed would soon run out of euros, and when it did, the dollar would sink. If the demand for dollars increased permanently to D_1, the Fed would have to sell dollars and buy euros every day. The Fed would be piling up unwanted euros and at some point would let the dollar rise.

Interest rate parity
Equal interest rates—a situation in which the interest rate in one currency equals the interest rate in another currency when exchange rate changes are taken into account.

FIGURE 34.7

Foreign Exchange Market Intervention

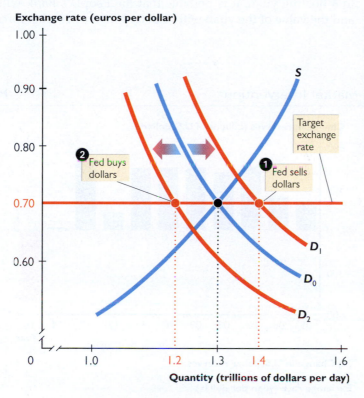

Initially, the demand for dollars is D_0, the supply of dollars is S, and the exchange rate is 0.70 euros per dollar. The Fed can intervene in the foreign exchange market to keep the exchange rate close to its target rate (0.70 euros per dollar in this example).

1 If demand increases from D_0 to D_1, the Fed sells dollars to increase the supply of dollars and maintain the exchange rate.

2 If demand decreases from D_0 to D_2, the Fed buys dollars to decrease the supply of dollars and maintain the exchange rate.

Persistent intervention on one side of the market cannot be sustained.

■ The People's Bank of China in the Foreign Exchange Market

Although the Fed could peg the value of the dollar, it chooses not to do so. But China's central bank, the People's Bank of China, does intervene to peg the value of its currency—the yuan. *Eye on the Global Economy* on p. 899 shows the result of this intervention.

During much of the period that the yuan was pegged to the U.S. dollar, China piled up U.S. dollar reserves. Figure 34.8(a) shows the numbers. During 2007 to 2009, China's reserves increased by more than $1 trillion.

Figure 34.8(b), which shows the market for U.S. dollars priced in terms of the yuan, explains why China's reserves increased. The demand curve D and supply curve S intersect at 5 yuan per dollar. If the People's Bank of China took no actions in the foreign exchange market, this exchange rate would be the equilibrium rate. (This particular value is only an example. No one knows what the yuan-dollar exchange rate would be with no intervention.)

By intervening in the market and buying U.S. dollars, the People's Bank can peg the yuan at 6.10 yuan per dollar. But to do so, it must keep holding the dollars that it buys. In Figure 34.8(b), the People's Bank buys $76 billion (the actual quantity that the People's Bank bought in 2012).

Only by allowing the yuan to appreciate can China stop accumulating dollars. Since July 2005, the People's Bank has permitted the yuan to rise in value.

But China continues to intervene in the foreign exchange market to manage the rate of appreciation of the yuan. The scale of intervention fell sharply in 2012. Eventually, when China's foreign exchange market becomes more accustomed to a floating yuan, it is possible that the People's Bank will end its intervention and the value of the yuan will be determined by market forces.

■ **FIGURE 34.8**

China's Foreign Exchange Market Intervention   MyEconLab Real-time data

China was piling up reserves of U.S. dollars during 2005 through 2013. The build-up of reserves was very large. Part (a) shows the numbers.

Part (b) shows the market for the U.S. dollar in terms of the Chinese yuan. Note that a higher exchange rate (yuan per dollar) means a lower value of the yuan and a higher value of the dollar. The yuan appreciates when the number of yuan per dollar decreases.

❶ With demand curve *D* and supply curve *S*, the equilibrium exchange rate is 5 yuan per dollar. (The actual equilibrium value is not known, and the value assumed is only an example.)

❷ In 2012, the People's Bank of China had a target exchange rate of 6.10 yuan per dollar. At this exchange rate, the yuan is *undervalued*.

❸ To keep the exchange rate pegged at its target level, the People's Bank of China must buy U.S. dollars in exchange for yuan, and China's reserves of U.S. dollars pile up.

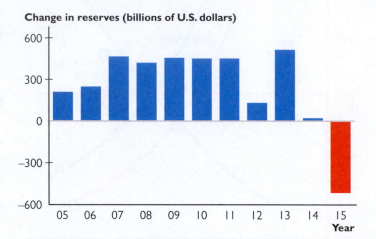

(a) Change in U.S. dollar reserves

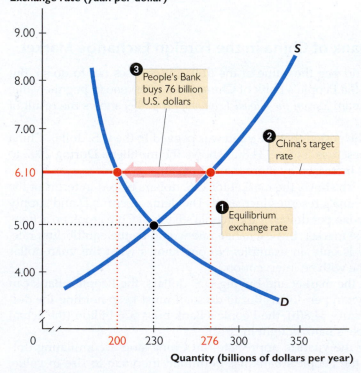

(b) Managing the yuan

Source of data: The People's Bank of China.

EYE on the GLOBAL ECONOMY
The Managed Yuan

The Chinese central bank, the People's Bank of China, pegged the value of the yuan in terms of the U.S. dollar for more than 10 years. The figure shows the value of the yuan (yuan per U.S. dollar) from the early 1990s to 2016.

The yuan was devalued in January 1994. It appreciated a bit during 1994 and 1995. But it was then pegged at 8.28 yuan per U.S. dollar, a value that the People's Bank of China maintained for more than 10 years. In July 2005, the yuan began a managed float—a managed appreciation of the yuan. Then, in July 2008, the exchange rate was again pegged, this time at 6.8 yuan per dollar. Since early 2010, the yuan has again been on a managed float.

SOURCE OF DATA: PACIFIC FX Service, University of British Columbia.

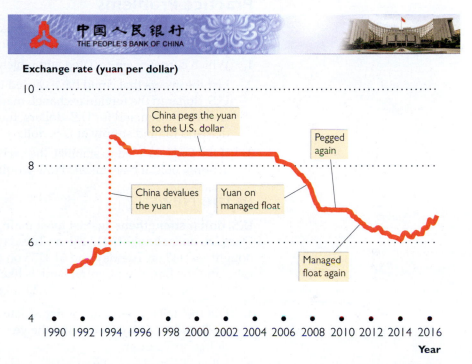

Exchange rate (yuan per dollar)

- China pegs the yuan to the U.S. dollar
- China devalues the yuan
- Yuan on managed float
- Pegged again
- Managed float again

Year

EYE on YOUR LIFE

MyEconLab Critical Thinking Exercise

Your Foreign Exchange Transactions

If you plan to go to Europe for a vacation next summer, you will need some euros. What is the best way to get euros?

You could just take your ATM/debit card or credit card and use an ATM in Europe. You'll get euros from the cash machine, and your bank account in the United States will get charged for the cash you obtain.

When you get euros, the number of euros you request is multiplied by the exchange rate to determine how many dollars to take from your bank account.

You have just made a transaction in the foreign exchange market. You have exchanged dollars for euros.

The exchange rate that you paid was probably costly. Your bank took a commission for helping you get euros. Some banks charge as much as 5 percent. Check in advance. It might be better to buy euros from your bank before you leave on your trip.

Another question has possibly occurred to you: How many euros will your budget buy next summer? Should

you get the euros now at a price that is certain or would it be better to wait until closer to your travel date and take a chance on the value of the dollar then?

No one can answer this question. But you can buy euros today at a fixed price for delivery at a later date. (This transaction is made in a market called the forward exchange market.) Again, though, you'll end up paying a big commission for the service.

MyEconLab Study Plan 34.2
Key Terms Quiz
Solutions Video

CHECKPOINT 34.2

Explain how the exchange rate is determined and why it fluctuates.

Practice Problems

Suppose that yesterday, the U.S. dollar was trading in the foreign exchange market at 100 yen per dollar. Today, the U.S. dollar is trading at 105 yen per dollar.

1. Which currency appreciated and which depreciated today?

2. List the events that could have caused today's change in the value of the U.S. dollar in the foreign exchange market. Did the events on your list change the demand for U.S. dollars, the supply of U.S. dollars, or both the demand for and supply of U.S. dollars?

3. If the Fed had tried to stabilize the exchange rate at 100 yen per dollar, what action would it have taken? How would U.S. official reserves have changed?

In the News

U.S. dollar strengthens against most main rivals
One U.S. dollar bought ¥113.885 on Tuesday and ¥114.600 on Monday. One euro bought $1.1143 on Tuesday and $1.1155 on Monday. The Fed has raised interest rates and the European Central Bank is likely to lower interest rates.
Source: Wall Street Journal, February 16, 2016

1. Did the dollar appreciate or depreciate against the euro and the Japanese yen on Tuesday? Did the euro and the yen appreciate or depreciate against the dollar on Tuesday?

2. What events changed the exchange rate between the euro and the dollar?

Solutions to Practice Problems

1. Because the price of the U.S. dollar is a larger number of yen, the U.S. dollar has appreciated. The yen has depreciated because it buys fewer dollars.

2. The main events might be an increase in the U.S. interest rate, a decrease in the Japanese interest rate, or a rise in the expected future exchange rate of the U.S. dollar.
   The events listed change both the demand for and supply of U.S. dollars. The events increase the demand for and decrease the supply of U.S. dollars.

3. To stabilize the exchange rate, the Fed would have sold U.S. dollars to increase the supply of dollars in the foreign exchange market. When the Fed sells U.S. dollars, it buys foreign currency, so U.S. official reserves would have increased.

Solutions to In the News

1. Because one dollar bought fewer yen on Tuesday, the dollar depreciated against the yen and the yen appreciated against the dollar. Because one euro bought fewer dollars on Tuesday, the euro depreciated against the dollar and the dollar appreciated against the euro.

2. A change and expected future change in the U.S.- Europe interest rate differential increased demand and decreased supply in the market for U.S. dollars and decreased demand and increased supply in the market for euros. These changes depreciated the euro and appreciated the U.S. dollar.

CHAPTER SUMMARY

Key Points

1. **Describe a country's balance of payments accounts and explain what determines the amount of international borrowing and lending.**

   - Foreign currency is used to finance international trade and the purchase of foreign assets.
   - A country's balance of payments accounts record its international transactions.
   - Historically, the United States has been a net lender to the rest of the world, but in 1983 that situation changed and the United States became a net borrower. In 1989 the United States became a debtor nation.
   - Net exports are equal to the private sector balance plus the government sector balance.

2. **Explain how the exchange rate is determined and why it fluctuates.**

   - Foreign currency is obtained in exchange for domestic currency in the foreign exchange market.
   - The exchange rate is determined by demand and supply in the foreign exchange market.
   - The lower the exchange rate, the greater is the quantity of dollars demanded. A change in the exchange rate brings a movement along the demand curve for dollars.
   - Changes in the expected future exchange rate and the U.S. interest rate differential change the demand for dollars and shift the demand curve.
   - The lower the exchange rate, the smaller is the quantity of dollars supplied. A change in the exchange rate brings a movement along the supply curve of dollars.
   - Changes in the expected future exchange rate and the U.S. interest rate differential change the supply of dollars and shift the supply curve.
   - Fluctuations in the exchange rate occur because fluctuations in the demand for and supply of dollars are not independent.
   - A central bank can intervene in the foreign exchange market to smooth fluctuations in the exchange rate.

Key Terms

MyEconLab Key Terms Quiz

Balance of payments accounts, 878
Capital and financial account, 878
Creditor nation, 880
Currency appreciation, 885
Currency depreciation, 886
Current account, 878

Debtor nation, 880
Foreign exchange market, 885
Foreign exchange rate, 885
Government sector balance, 882
Interest rate parity, 896
Net borrower, 880

Net lender, 880
Official settlements account, 878
Private sector balance, 882
Purchasing power parity, 894
U.S. interest rate differential, 888
U.S. official reserves, 878

CHAPTER CHECKPOINT

Study Plan Problems and Applications

Table 1 gives some data that describe the economy of Antarctica in 2050. Use Table 1 to answer Problems **1** and **2**.

TABLE 1

Item	(billions of dollars)
Imports	150
Exports of goods and services	50
Net interest	−10
Net transfers	35
Foreign investment in Antarctica	125
Antarctica's investment abroad	55

1. Calculate Antarctica's current account balance, capital and financial account balance, and the increase in Antarctica's official reserves.

2. Is Antarctica a debtor nation or a creditor nation? Are its international assets increasing or decreasing? Is Antarctica borrowing to finance investment or consumption? Explain.

3. **U.S. trade gap widened in June due to import surge**
   The U.S. trade deficit soared in June to $44.5 billion. Higher oil prices and increased purchases of pharmaceuticals and smartphones swelled imports.
   Source: *Wall Street Journal*, August 5, 2016

   Explain how the United States pays for its international trade deficit.

4. The U.S. dollar depreciates. Explain which of the following events could have caused the depreciation and why.
   - The Fed intervened in the foreign exchange market. Did the Fed buy or sell U.S. dollars?
   - People began to expect that the U.S. dollar would depreciate.
   - The U.S. interest rate differential increased.
   - Foreign investment in the United States increased.

Suppose that the inflation rate is lower in Japan than it is in the United States, and that the difference in the inflation rates persists for some years. Use this information to answer Problems **5** to **7**.

5. Will the U.S. dollar appreciate or depreciate against the yen and will purchasing power parity be violated? Why or why not?

6. Will U.S. interest rates be higher or lower than Japanese interest rates and will interest rate parity hold? Why or why not?

7. Explain how the expected future exchange rate will change.

8. Suppose that the U.K. pound is trading at 1.82 U.S. dollars per U.K. pound and at this exchange rate purchasing power parity holds. The U.S. interest rate is 2 percent a year and the U.K. interest rate is 4 percent a year. Calculate the U.S. interest rate differential. What is the U.K. pound expected to be worth in terms of U.S. dollars one year from now?

9. **Pound plunges on U.K. vote to leave the European Union**
   Britain's vote to leave the European Union lowered the pound from $1.50 to $1.32 in tumultuous hours of foreign exchange trading.
   Source: *Wall Street Journal*, June 24, 2016

   Did the vote to leave the European Union make the British pound appreciate of depreciate against the U.S. dollar? Which of the influences on demand and supply in the foreign exchange market most likey changed to bring this rapid and large change in the dollar-pound exchange rate?

10. Read *Eye on the Dollar* on p. 893. When and why did the dollar rise against the euro and when and why did it fall?

Instructor Assignable Problems and Applications

MyEconLab Homework, Quiz, or Test if assigned by instructor

1. If the European Central Bank starts to raise its policy interest rate before the Fed starts to raise the federal funds rate target, what do you predict will happen to the dollar-euro exchange rate? Illustrate your answer with an appropriate graphical analysis.

2. Table 1 gives some data that describe the economy of Atlantis in 2020. Calculate the current account balance, the capital and financial account balance, the government sector balance, and the private sector balance.

3. The U.S. dollar appreciates, and U.S. official reserves increase. Explain which of the following events might have caused these changes to occur and why.
   - The Fed intervened in the foreign exchange market and sold U.S. dollars.
   - The Fed conducted an open market operation and sold U.S. bonds.
   - People began to expect that the U.S. dollar would appreciate.
   - The U.S. interest rate differential narrowed.

4. Which of the following events might have caused the euro to appreciate and why?
   - The European Central Bank sold euros in the foreign exchange market.
   - The Fed intervened in the foreign exchange market and bought U.S. dollars.
   - The EU interest rate differential increased.
   - Profits increased in Europe, and U.S. investment in Europe surged.

Use the following information to work Problems **5** and **6**.

Suppose that the euro keeps appreciating against the U.S. dollar. The Fed decides to stop the euro from appreciating (stop the U.S. dollar from depreciating) and intervenes in the foreign exchange market.

5. What actions might the Fed take in the foreign exchange market? Could these actions persist in the long run? Would the Fed's actions prevent interest rate parity from being achieved? Why or why not?

6. Are there any other actions that the Fed could take to raise the foreign exchange value of the dollar? Explain your answer.

Use the following information to work Problems **7** and **8**.

In August 2013, the exchange rate between the U.S. dollar and the Brazilian real was 3.125 real per dollar. In the same month, the price of a Big Mac was 23 real in Sao Paulo and $3.99 in New York. Brazil's interest rate was 14.25 percent per year and the U.S. interest rate was 1 percent per year.

Sources: Pacific Exchange Rate Service and *The Economist*

7. Does purchasing power parity (PPP) hold between Brazil and the United States? If not, does PPP predict that the Brazilian real will appreciate or depreciate against the U.S. dollar?

8. Does interest rate parity hold between Brazil and the United States? If interest rate parity does hold, what is the expected rate of appreciation or depreciation of the Brazilian real against the U.S. dollar? If the Fed raised the interest rate while the Brazilian interest rate remained at 14.25 percent a year, how would the expected appreciation or depreciation of the real change?

TABLE 1

Item	(billions of dollars)
Government expenditure	200
Saving	100
Increase in official reserves of Atlantis	5
Net foreign investment in Atlantis	50
Net taxes	150
Investment	125

Multiple Choice Quiz

1. The current account balance equals _____.

   A. exports minus imports plus net interest and net transfers
   B. net exports plus net foreign investment in the United States
   C. the capital and financial account balance minus the official settlements account balance
   D. net exports plus the official settlements balance

2. China's official reserves have ballooned, fueled by strong foreign investment and large trade surpluses. China is a net _____ and a _____ nation.

   A. lender; debtor
   B. borrower; debtor
   C. lender; creditor
   D. borrower; creditor

3. Net exports equal the _____.

   A. private sector balance plus the government sector balance
   B. private sector balance minus the government sector balance
   C. government sector balance minus the private sector balance
   D. private sector balance plus the government's budget deficit

4. A net exports deficit will become a surplus if _____.

   A. the government budget deficit is turned into a surplus and the private sector has a surplus
   B. the private sector surplus adjusts to equal the government sector deficit
   C. private saving and government saving exceed private investment
   D. the country appreciates its currency

5. The quantity of U.S. dollars demanded in the foreign exchange market increases if _____.

   A. the value of U.S. imports increases
   B. traders expect the future exchange rate to rise
   C. the U.S. interest rate rises relative to those in other countries
   D. the U.S. dollar depreciates against other currencies

6. The supply of U.S. dollars in the foreign exchange market increases if _____.

   A. the value of U.S. imports increases
   B. the U.S. interest rate differential decreases
   C. the U.S. dollar depreciates against other currencies
   D. the U.S. dollar is expected to appreciate against other currencies in the future

7. Purchasing power parity _____.

   A. holds if the price of a good is the same number of euros, pounds, or dollars
   B. means that the value of the euro, the pound, and the dollar are equal
   C. always holds because exchange rates adjust automatically
   D. implies that international trade is competitive

8. To keep the yuan–U.S. dollar exchange rate constant, _____.

   A. the Fed agrees not to sell U.S. dollars in the foreign exchange market
   B. the People's Bank of China buys U.S. dollars
   C. the Fed and the People's Bank agree on the value of the exchange rate
   D. the Fed does not buy yuan in the foreign exchange market

Glossary

Abatement technology A production technology that reduces or prevents pollution. (p. 249)

Ability-to-pay principle The proposition that people should pay taxes according to how easily they can bear the burden. (p. 206)

Absolute advantage When one person (or nation) is more productive than another—needs fewer inputs or takes less time to produce a good or perform a production task. (p. 73)

Adverse selection The tendency for people to enter into transactions that bring them benefits from their private information and impose costs on the uninformed party. (p. 297)

Aggregate demand The relationship between the quantity of real GDP demanded and the price level when all other influences on expenditure plans remain the same. (p. 756)

Aggregate planned expenditure Planned consumption expenditure plus planned investment plus planned government expenditure plus planned exports minus planned imports. (p. 776)

Aggregate supply The relationship between the quantity of real GDP supplied and the price level when all other influences on production plans remain the same. (p. 750)

Allocative efficiency A situation in which the quantities of goods and services produced are those that people *value most highly*—it is not possible to produce more of a good or service without giving up some of aother good that people *value more highly*. (p. 143)

Antitrust law A body of law that regulates oligopolies and prohibits them from becoming monopolies or behaving like monopolies. (p. 477)

Asymmetric information A situation in which either the buyer or the seller has private information. (p. 294)

Automatic fiscal policy A fiscal policy action that is triggered by the state of the economy. (p. 831)

Automatic stabilizers Features of fiscal policy that stabilize real GDP without explicit action by the government. (p. 831)

Average cost pricing rule A rule that sets price equal to average total cost to enable a regulated firm to avoid economic loss. (p. 426)

Average fixed cost Total fixed cost per unit of output. (p. 361)

Average product Total product divided by the quantity of a factor of production. The average product of labor is total product divided by the quantity of labor employed. (p. 356)

Average tax rate The percentage of income that is paid in tax. (p. 207)

Average total cost Total cost per unit of output, which equals average fixed cost plus average variable cost. (p. 361)

Average variable cost Total variable cost per unit of output. (p. 361)

Balance of payments accounts The accounts in which a nation records its international trading, borrowing, and lending. (p. 878)

Balanced budget multiplier The effect on aggregate demand of a *simultaneous* change in government expenditure and taxes that leaves the budget balance unchanged. (p. 833)

Barrier to entry Any constraint that protects a firm from competitors. (p. 404)

Barter The direct exchange of goods and services for other goods and services, which requires a double coincidence of wants. (p. 693)

Benefit The benefit of something is the gain or pleasure that it brings, measured by what you are willing to give up to get it. (p. 9)

Benefit-cost analysis An accounting exercise to determine the total benefit, total cost, and net benefit of a proposed project. (p. 276)

Benefits principle The proposition that people should pay taxes equal to the benefits they receive from public goods and services. (p. 206)

Big tradeoff A tradeoff between efficiency and fairness that recognizes the cost of making income transfers. (p. 161)

Black market An illegal market that operates alongside a government-regulated market. (p. 171)

Bond A promise to pay specified sums of money on specified dates. (p. 667)

Budget balance Tax revenues minus outlays. (p. 824)

Budget line A line that describes the limits to consumption possibilities and that depends on a consumer's budget and the prices of goods and services. (p. 320

Business cycle A periodic but irregular up-and-down movement of total production and other measures of economic activity. (p. 552)

Capital Tools, instruments, machines, buildings, and other items that have been produced in the past and that businesses now use to produce goods and services. (pp. 37, 666)

Capital and financial account Record of foreign investment in the United States minus U.S. investment abroad. (p. 878)

Capital goods Goods bought by businesses and governments to increase productive resources to use over future periods to produce other goods. (p. 34)

Capture theory The theory that regulation serves the self-interest of the producer and results in maximum profit, underproduction, and deadweight loss. (p. 424)

Cartel A group of firms acting together to limit output, raise price, and increase economic profit. (p. 460)

Chained Consumer Price Index A measure of the price level calculated using current month and previous month prices and expenditures. (p. 598)

Chained-dollar real GDP The measure of real GDP calculated by the Bureau of Economic Analysis. (p. 563)

Change in demand A change in the quantity that people plan to buy when any influence on buying plans other than the price of the good changes. (p. 88)

Change in the quantity demanded A change in the quantity of a good that people plan to buy that results from a change in the price of the good with all other influences on buying plans remaining the same. (p. 90)

Change in the quantity supplied A change in the quantity of a good that suppliers plan to sell that results from a change in the price of the good with all other influences on selling plans remaining the same. (p. 97)

Change in supply A change in the quantity that suppliers plan to sell when any influence on selling plans other than the price of the good changes. (p. 95)

Circular flow model A model of the economy that shows the circular flow of expenditures and incomes that result from decision makers' choices and the way those choices interact to determine what, how, and for whom goods and services are produced. (p. 48)

Classical growth theory The theory that the clash between an exploding population and limited resources will eventually bring economic growth to an end. (p. 650)

Classical macroeconomics The view that the market economy works well, that aggregate fluctuations are a natural consequence of an expanding economy, and that government intervention cannot improve the efficiency of the market economy. (p. 614)

Coase theorem The proposition that if property rights exist and the costs of enforcing them are low, then the market outcome is efficient and it doesn't matter who has the property rights. (p. 249)

Command system A system that allocates resources by the order of someone in authority. (p. 141)

Command-and-control regulation The direct regulation of what is and is not permitted. (p. 251

Common resource A resource that can be used only once, but no one can be prevented from using what is available. (p. 269)

Comparative advantage The ability of a person to perform an activity or produce a good or service at a lower opportunity cost than anyone else. (p. 73)

Complement A good that is consumed with another good. (p. 88)

Complement in production A good that is produced along with another good. (p. 95)

Constant returns to scale Features of a firm's technology that keep average total cost constant as output increases. (p. 368)

Consumer Price Index A measure of the average of the prices paid by urban consumers for a fixed market basket of consumption goods and services. (p. 590)

Consumer surplus The marginal benefit from a good or service in excess of the price paid for it, summed over the quantity consumed. (p. 149)

Consumption expenditure The expenditure by households on consumption goods and services. (p. 539)

Consumption function The relationship between consumption expenditure and disposable income, other things remaining the same. (p. 776)

Consumption goods and services Goods and services that individuals and governments buy and use in the current period. (p. 34)

Core inflation rate The annual percentage change in the PCEPI excluding the prices of food and energy. (p. 599)

Cost of living index A measure of the change in the amount of money that people need to spend to achieve a given standard of living. (p. 596)

Cost-push inflation An inflation that begins with an increase in costs. (p. 767)

Creditor nation A country that during its entire history has invested more in the rest of the world than other countries have invested in it. (p. 880)

Cross elasticity of demand A measure of the responsiveness of the demand for a good to a change in the price of a substitute or complement when other things remain the same. (p. 131)

Cross-section graph A graph that shows the values of an economic variable for different groups in a population at a point in time. (p. 24)

Crowding-out effect The tendency for a government budget deficit to raise the real interest rate and decrease investment. (p. 684)

Currency Notes (dollar bills) and coins. (p. 694)

Currency appreciation The rise in the value of one currency in terms of another currency. (p. 885)

Currency depreciation The fall in the value of one currency in terms of another currency. (p. 886)

Current account Record of receipts from the sale of goods and services to other countries (exports), minus payments for goods and services bought from other countries (imports), plus the net amount of interest and transfers received from and paid to other countries. (p. 878)

Cyclical surplus or deficit The budget balance that arises because tax revenues and outlays are not at their full-employment levels. (p. 832)

Cyclical unemployment The fluctuating unemployment over the business cycle that increases during a recession and decreases during an expansion. (p. 579)

Deadweight loss The decrease in total surplus that results from an inefficient underproduction or overproduction. (p. 157)

Debtor nation A country that during its entire history has borrowed more from the rest of the world than it has lent to the rest of the world. (p. 880)

Decreasing marginal returns When the marginal product of an additional worker is less than the marginal product of the previous worker. (p. 354)

Deflation A situation in which the price level is *falling* and the inflation rate is *negative*. (p. 593)

Demand The relationship between the quantity demanded and the price of a good when all other influences on buying plans remain the same. (p. 85)

Demand curve A graph of the relationship between the quantity demanded of a good and its price when all the other influences on buying plans remain the same. (p. 86)

Demand for labor The relationship between the quantity of labor demanded and the real wage rate when all other influences on firms' hiring plans remain the same. (p. 619)

Demand for loanable funds The relationship between the quantity of loanable funds demanded and the real interest rate when all other influences on borrowing plans remain the same. (p. 673)

Demand for money The relationship between the quantity of money demanded and the nominal interest rate, when all other influences on the amount of money that people wish to hold remain the same. (p. 724)

Demand schedule A list of the quantities demanded at each different price when all the other influences on buying plans remain the same. (p. 86)

Demand-pull inflation An inflation that starts because aggregate demand increases. (p. 766)

Depreciation The decrease in the value of capital that results from its use and from obsolescence. (p. 546)

Deregulation The process of removing regulation of prices, quantities, entry, and other aspects of economic activity in a firm or an industry. (p. 424)

Derived demand The demand for a factor of production that is derived from the demand for the goods and services that it is used to produce. (p. 489)

Diminishing marginal rate of substitution The general tendency for the marginal rate of substitution to decrease as the consumer moves down along the indifference curve, increasing consumption of the good measured on the *x*-axis and decreasing consumption of the good measured on the *y*-axis. (p. 342)

Diminishing marginal utility The general tendency for marginal utility to decrease as the quantity of a good consumed increases. (p. 326)

Diminishing returns The tendency for each additional hour of labor employed to produce a successively smaller additional amount of real GDP. (p. 618)

Direct relationship A relationship between two variables that move in the same direction. (p. 26)

Discouraged worker A marginally attached worker who has not made specific efforts to find a job within the past four weeks because previous unsuccessful attempts to find a job were discouraging. (p. 570)

Discretionary fiscal policy A fiscal policy action that is initiated by an act of Congress. (p. 824)

Discretionary monetary policy Monetary policy that is based on expert assessment of the current economic situation. (p. 868)

Diseconomies of scale Features of a firm's technology that make average total cost rise as output increases. (p. 368)

Disposable income Market income plus cash benefits paid by the government minus taxes. (p. 528)

Dumping When a foreign firm sells its exports at a lower price than its cost of production. (p. 234)

Duopoly A market with only two firms. (p. 461)

Economic depreciation An opportunity cost of a firm using capital that it owns—measured as the change in the *market value* of capital over a given period. (p. 349)

Economic freedom A condition in which people are able

to make personal choices, their private property is protected by the rule of law, and they are free to buy and sell in markets. (p. 656)

Economic growth The sustained expansion of production possibilities. (pp. 70, 638)

Economic growth rate The annual percentage change of real GDP. (p. 638)

Economic model A description of the economy or part of the economy that includes only those features assumed necessary to explain the observed facts. (p. 15)

Economic profit A firm's total revenue minus total cost. (p. 349)

Economics The social science that studies the choices that individuals, businesses, government, and entire societies make as they cope with *scarcity*, the influences on those choices, and the arrangements that coordinate them. (p. 2)

Economies of scale Features of a firm's technology that make average total cost fall as output increases. (p. 367)

Efficiency wage A real wage rate that is set above the full-employment equilibrium wage rate to induce greater work effort. (p. 629)

Efficient scale The quantity at which average total cost is a minimum. (p. 445)

Elastic demand When the percentage change in the quantity demanded exceeds the percentage change in price. (p. 116)

Elastic supply When the percentage change in the quantity supplied exceeds the percentage change in price. (p. 126)

Employment–population ratio The percentage of the people of working age who are employed. (p. 569)

Entrepreneurship The human resource that organizes labor, land, and capital to produce goods and services. (p. 38)

Equation of exchange An equation that states that the quantity of money multiplied by the velocity of circulation equals the price level multiplied by real GDP. (p. 735)

Equilibrium expenditure The level of aggregate expenditure that occurs when aggregate *planned* expenditure equals real GDP. (p. 784)

Equilibrium price The price at which the quantity demanded equals the quantity supplied. (p. 100)

Equilibrium quantity The quantity bought and sold at the equilibrium price. (p. 100)

Excess burden The amount by which the burden of a tax exceeds the tax revenue received by the government—the deadweight loss from a tax. (p. 194)

Excess capacity The amount by which the efficient scale exceeds the quantity that the firm produces. (p. 445)

Excess reserves A bank's actual reserves minus its desired reserves. (p. 708)

Excludable A good, service, or resource is excludable if it is possible to prevent someone from enjoying its benefits. (p. 268)

Expected inflation rate The inflation rate that people forecast and use to set the money wage rate and other money prices. (p. 809)

Explicit cost A cost paid in money. (p. 349)

Export subsidy A payment by the government to a producer to cover part of the cost of production that is exported. (p. 231)

Exports The goods and services that firms in one country sell to people and firms in other countries. (p. 216)

Exports of goods and services Items that firms in the United States produce and sell to the rest of the world. (p. 540)

Externality A cost or a benefit that arises from production and that falls on someone other than the producer; or a cost or benefit that arises from consumption and that falls on someone other than the consumer. (p. 244)

Factor markets Markets in which the services of factors of production are bought and sold. (pp. 48, 488)

Factor prices The prices of the services of the factors of production. The wage rate is the price of labor, the interest rate is the price of capital, and rent is the price of land. (p. 488)

Factors of production The productive resources that are used to produce goods and services—land, labor, capital, and entrepreneurship. (p. 36)

FairTax A proposal to tax the purchase of consumption goods and services above the poverty level, considered by the United States Congress in 1999. (p. 209)

Federal funds rate The interest rate at which banks can borrow and lend reserves (interbank loans) in the federal funds market. (pp. 700, 852)

Federal Open Market Committee The Fed's main policy-making committee. (p. 704)

Federal Reserve System (the Fed) The central bank of the United States. (p. 703)

Fiat money Objects that are money because the law decrees or orders them to be money. (p. 694)

Final good or service A good or service that is produced for its final user and not as a component of another good or service. (p. 538)

Financial institution A firm that operates on both sides of the market for financial capital: It borrows in one market and lends in another. (p. 669)

Financial stability A situation in which financial markets and institutions function normally to allocate capital resources and risk. (p. 851)

Firms The institutions that organize the production of goods and services. (p. 48

Fiscal imbalance The present value of the government's commitments to pay future benefits minus the present value of its tax revenues. (p. 828)

Fiscal policy Changing taxes, transfer payments, and government expenditure on goods and services. (p. 759) The use of the federal budget to achieve the macroeconomic objectives of high and sustained economic growth and full employment. (p. 824)

Flat tax A tax system with a constant average and marginal tax rate: A proportional tax. (p. 208)

Foreign exchange market The market in which the currency of one country is exchanged for the currency of another. (p. 885)

Foreign exchange rate The price at which one currency exchanges for another. (p. 885)

Four-firm concentration ratio The percentage of the total revenue in an industry accounted for by the four largest firms in the industry. (p. 438)

Free rider A person who enjoys the benefits of a good or service without paying for it. (p. 271)

Frictional unemployment The unemployment that arises from people entering and leaving the labor force, from quitting jobs to find better ones, and from the ongoing creation and destruction of jobs—from normal labor turnover. (p. 578)

Full employment When the unemployment rate equals the natural unemployment rate. (p. 579)

Full-employment equilibrium When equilibrium real GDP equals potential GDP. (p. 763)

Full-time workers People who usually work 35 hours or more a week. (p. 571)

Game theory The tool that economists use to analyze *strategic behavior*—behavior that recognizes mutual interdependence and takes account of the expected behavior of others. (p. 469)

GDP price index An average of the current prices of all the goods and services included in GDP expressed as a percentage of base-year prices. (p. 603)

Generational imbalance The division of the fiscal imbalance between the current and future generations. (p. 829)

Goods and services The objects (goods) and the actions (services) that people value and produce to satisfy human wants. (p. 3)

Goods markets Markets in which goods and services are bought and sold. (p. 48)

Government expenditure multiplier The effect of a change in government expenditure on goods and services on aggregate demand. (p. 833)

Government expenditure on goods and services The expenditure by all levels of government on goods and services. (p. 540)

Government sector balance The sum of the budget balances of the federal, state, and local governments— net taxes minus government expenditure on goods and services. (p. 882)

Great Depression A period of high unemployment, low incomes, and extreme economic hardship that lasted from 1929 to 1939. (p. 573)

Gross domestic product (GDP) The market value of all the final goods and services produced within a country in a given time period. (p. 538)

Gross investment The total amount spent on new capital goods. (p. 666)

Herfindahl-Hirschman Index The square of the percentage market share of each firm summed over the 50 largest firms (or summed over all the firms if there are fewer than 50) in a market. (p. 439)

Horizontal equity The requirement that taxpayers with the same ability to pay should pay the same taxes. (p. 206)

Households Individuals or groups of people living together. (p. 48)

Human capital The knowledge and skill that people obtain from education, on-the-job training, and work experience. (p. 37)

Hyperinflation Inflation at a rate that exceeds 50 percent a *month* (which translate to 12,875 percent a year). (p. 739)

Implicit cost An opportunity cost incurred by a firm when it uses a factor of production for which it does not make a direct money payment. (p. 349)

Import quota A quantitative restriction on the import of a good that limits the maximum quantity of a good that may be imported in a given period. (p. 229)

Imports The goods and services that people and firms in one country buy from firms in other countries. (p. 216)

Imports of goods and services Items that households, firms, and governments in the United States buy from the rest of the world. (p. 540)

Incentive A reward or a penalty— a "carrot" or a "stick"—that encourages or discourages an action. (p. 11)

Income elasticity of demand A measure of the responsiveness of the demand for a good to a change in income when other things remain the same. (p. 132)

Increasing marginal returns When the marginal product of an additional worker exceeds the marginal product of the previous worker. (p. 354)

Indifference curve A line that shows combinations of goods among which a consumer is *indifferent*. (p. 341

Individual transferable quota (ITQ) A production limit that is assigned to an individual, who is free to transfer (sell) the quota to someone else. (p. 286)

Induced taxes Taxes that vary with real GDP. (p. 831)

Inelastic demand When the percentage change in the quantity demanded is less than the percentage change in price. (p. 116)

Inelastic supply When the percentage change in the quantity supplied is less than the percentage change in price. (p. 126)

Infant-industry argument The argument that it is necessary to protect a new industry to enable it to grow into a mature industry that can compete in world markets. (p. 233)

Inferior good A good for which demand decreases when income increases and demand increases when income decreases. (p. 89)

Inflation rate The percentage change in the price level from one year to the next. (p. 593)

Inflation targeting A monetary policy strategy in which the central bank makes a public commitment to achieving an explicit inflation target and to explaining how its policy actions will achieve that target. (p. 869)

Inflationary gap A gap that exists when real GDP exceeds potential GDP and that brings a rising price level. (p. 763)

Interest Income paid for the use of capital. (p. 39)

Interest rate parity Equal interest rates—a situation in which the interest rate in one currency equals the interest rate in another currency when exchange rate changes are taken into account. (p. 896)

Intermediate good or service A good or service that is used as a component of a final good or service. (p. 538)

Inverse relationship A relationship between two variables that move in opposite directions. (p. 27)

Investment The purchase of new *capital goods*—tools, instruments, machines, buildings, and additions to inventories. (p. 539)

Job rationing A situation that arises when the real wage rate is above the full-employment equilibrium level. (p. 628)

Job search The activity of looking for an acceptable vacant job. (p. 627)

Keynesian macroeconomics The view that the market economy is inherently unstable and needs active government intervention to achieve full employment and sustained economic growth. (p. 614)

***k*-percent rule** A monetary policy rule that makes the quantity of money grow at *k* percent per year, where *k* equals the growth rate of potential GDP. (p. 871)

Labor The work time and work effort that people devote to producing goods and services. (p. 37)

Labor force The number of people employed plus the number unemployed. (p. 568)

Labor force participation rate The percentage of the working-age population who are members of the labor force. (p. 570)

Labor productivity The quantity of real GDP produced by one hour of labor. (p. 642)

Labor union An organized group of workers that aims to increase wages and influence other job conditions of its members. (p. 498)

Land The "gifts of nature," or *natural resources*, that we use to produce goods and services. (p. 36)

Law of decreasing returns As a firm uses more of a variable input, with a given quantity of fixed inputs, the marginal product of the variable input eventually decreases. (p. 356)

Law of demand Other things remaining the same, if the price of a good rises, the quantity demanded of that good decreases; and if the price of a good falls, the quantity demanded of that good increases. (p. 85)

Law of diminishing marginal returns If the quantity of capital is small, an increase in capital brings a large increase in production; and if the quantity of capital is large, an increase in capital brings a small increase in production. (p. 643)

Law of market forces When there is a surplus, the price falls; when there is a shortage, the price rises. (p. 100)

Law of supply Other things remaining the same, if the price of a good rises, the quantity supplied of that good increases; and if the price of a good falls, the quantity supplied of that good decreases. (p. 92)

Legal monopoly A market in which competition and entry are restricted by the granting of a public franchise, government license, patent, or copyright. (p. 405)

Lemons problem The problem that when it is not possible to distinguish reliable products from lemons, there are too many lemons and too few reliable products. (p. 294)

Linear relationship A relationship that graphs as a straight line. (p. 26)

Loanable funds market The aggregate of all the individual financial markets. (p. 672)

Long run The time frame in which the quantities of *all* resources can be varied. (p. 352)

Long-run average cost curve A curve that shows the lowest average total cost at which it is possible to produce each output when the firm has had sufficient time to change both its plant size and labor employed. (p. 368)

Long-run Phillips curve The vertical line that shows the relationship between inflation and unemployment when the economy is at full employment. (p. 808)

Lorenz curve A curve that graphs the cumulative percentage of income (or wealth) against the cumulative percentage of households. (p. 513)

Loss Income earned by an entrepreneur for running a business when that income is negative. (p. 39)

M1 Currency held by individuals and firms, traveler's checks, and checkable deposits owned by individuals and businesses. (p. 694)

M2 M1 plus savings deposits and small time deposits, money market funds, and other deposits. (p. 694)

Macroeconomic equilibrium When the quantity of real GDP demanded equals the quantity of real GDP supplied at the point of intersection of the *AD* curve and the *AS* curve. (p. 762)

Macroeconomics The study of the aggregate (or total) effects on the national economy and the global economy of the choices that individuals, businesses, and governments make. (p. 3)

Margin A choice on the margin is a choice that is made by comparing *all* the relevant alternatives systematically and incrementally. (p. 10)

Marginal benefit The benefit that arises from a one-unit increase in an activity. The marginal benefit of something is measured by what you *are willing to* give up to get *one additional* unit of it. (p. 10)

Marginal cost The opportunity cost that arises from a one-unit increase in an activity. The marginal cost of something is what you *must* give up to get one additional unit of it. (p. 10) The marginal cost of producing a good is the change in total cost that results from a one-unit increase in output. (p. 360)

Marginal cost pricing rule A rule that sets price equal to marginal cost to achieve an efficient output. (p. 424)

Marginal external benefit The benefit from an additional unit of a good or service that people other than the consumer of the good or service enjoy. (p. 257)

Marginal external cost The cost of producing an additional unit of a good or service that falls on people other than the producer. (p. 246)

Marginal private benefit The benefit from an additional unit of a good or service that the consumer of that good or service receives. (p. 257)

Marginal private cost The cost of producing an additional unit of a good or service that is borne by the producer of that good or service. (p. 246)

Marginal product The change in total product that results from a one-unit increase in the quantity of labor employed. (p. 354)

Marginal propensity to consume The fraction of a change in disposable income that is spent on consumption—the change in consumption expenditure divided by the change in disposable income that brought it about. (p. 778)

Marginal propensity to import The fraction of an increase in real GDP that is spent on imports—the change in imports divided by the change in real GDP. (p. 780)

Marginal rate of substitution The rate at which a person will give up good Y (the good measured on the y-axis) to get more of good X (the good measured on the x-axis) and at the same time remain on the same indifference curve. (p. 342)

Marginal revenue The change in total revenue that results from a one-unit increase in the quantity sold. (p. 377)

Marginal social benefit The marginal benefit enjoyed by society—by the consumer of a good or service and by everyone else who benefits from it. It is the sum of marginal private benefit and marginal external benefit. (p. 257)

Marginal social cost The marginal cost incurred by the entire society—by the producer and by everyone else on whom the cost

falls. It is the sum of marginal private cost and marginal external cost. (p. 246)

Marginal tax rate The percentage of an additional dollar of income that is paid in tax. (p. 207) The fraction of a change in real GDP that is paid in income taxes—the change in tax payments divided by the change in real GDP. (p. 790)

Marginal utility The change in total utility that results from a one-unit increase in the quantity of a good consumed. (p. 326)

Marginal utility per dollar The marginal utility from a good relative to the price paid for the good. (p. 328)

Marginally attached worker A person who does not have a job, is available and willing to work, has not made specific efforts to find a job within the previous four weeks, but has looked for work sometime in the recent past. (p. 570)

Market Any arrangement that brings buyers and sellers together and enables them to get information and do business with each other. (p. 48)

Market equilibrium When the quantity demanded equals the quantity supplied—buyers' and sellers' plans are in balance. (p. 100)

Market failure A situation in which the market delivers an inefficient outcome. (p. 157)

Market income A household's wages, interest, rent, and profit earned in factor markets before paying income taxes. (p. 512)

Markup The amount by which price exceeds marginal cost. (p. 445)

Means of payment A method of settling a debt. (p. 692)

Median voter theory The theory that governments pursue policies that make the median voter as well off as possible. (p. 530)

Medium of exchange An object that is generally accepted in return for goods and services. (p. 693)

Microeconomics The study of the choices that individuals and businesses make and the way these choices interact and are influenced by governments. (p. 2)

Minimum wage law A government regulation that makes hiring labor services for less than a specified wage illegal. (pp. 177, 629)

Monetarist macroeconomics The view that the market economy works well, that aggregate fluctuations are the natural consequence of an expanding economy, but that fluctuations in the quantity of money generate the business cycle. (p. 615)

Monetary base The sum of coins, Federal Reserve notes, and banks' reserves at the Fed. (p. 705)

Monetary policy Changing the quantity of money and the interest rate. (p. 759)

Monetary policy instrument A variable that the Fed can directly control or closely target and that influences the economy in desirable ways. (p. 852)

Money Any commodity or token that is generally accepted as a means of payment. (p. 692)

Money income Market income plus cash payments to households by the government. (p. 512)

Money multiplier The number by which a change in the monetary base is multiplied to find the resulting change in the quantity of money. (p. 713)

Monopolistic competition A market in which a large number of firms compete by making similar but slightly different products. (p. 376)

Monopoly A market in which one firm sells a good or service that has no close substitutes and a barrier blocks the entry of new firms. (pp. 376, 404)

Moral hazard The tendency for a person with private information to use it in ways that impose costs on an uninformed party with whom they have made an agreement. (p. 303)

Multiplier The amount by which a change in any component of autonomous expenditure is magnified or multiplied to determine the change that it generates in equilibrium expenditure and real GDP. (p. 788)

Nash equilibrium An equilibrium in which each player takes the best possible action given the action of the other player. (p. 470)

National debt The amount of government debt outstanding— the debt that has arisen from past budget deficits. (p. 825)

Natural monopoly A monopoly that arises because one firm can meet the entire market demand at a lower average total cost than two or more firms could. (p. 404)

Natural rate hypothesis The proposition that when the inflation rate changes, the unemployment rate changes *temporarily* and eventually returns to the natural unemployment rate. (p. 810)

Natural unemployment rate The unemployment rate when all the unemployment is frictional and structural and there is no cyclical unemployment. (p. 579)

Negative externality A production or consumption activity that creates an external cost. (p. 244)

Negative income tax A tax and redistribution scheme that provides every household with a guaranteed minimum annual income and taxes all earned income at a fixed rate. (p. 531)

Negative relationship A relationship between two variables that move in opposite directions. (p. 27)

Net borrower A country that is borrowing more from the rest of the world than it is lending to the rest of the world. (p. 880)

Net exports of goods and services The value of exports of goods and services minus the value of imports of goods and services. (p. 540)

Net investment The change in the quantity of capital— equals gross investment minus depreciation. (p. 666)

Net lender A country that is lending more to the rest of the world than it is borrowing from the rest of the world. (p. 880)

Net taxes Taxes paid minus cash benefits received from governments. (p. 540)

Net worth The total market value of what a financial institution has lent minus the market value of what it has borrowed. (p. 670)

New growth theory The theory that our unlimited wants will lead us to ever greater productivity and perpetual economic growth. (p. 650)

Nominal GDP The value of the final goods and services produced in a given year expressed in terms of the prices of that same year. (p. 548)

Nominal interest rate The dollar amount of interest expressed as a percentage of the amount loaned. (p. 606)

Nominal wage rate The average hourly wage rate measured in *current* dollars. (p. 604)

Nonexcludable A good, service, or resource is nonexcludable if it is impossible (or extremely costly) to prevent someone from enjoying its benefits. (p. 268)

Nonrenewable natural resources Natural resources that can be used only once and that cannot be replaced once they have been used. (p. 488)

Nonrival A good, service, or resource is nonrival if its use by one person does not decrease the quantity available to someone else. (p. 268)

Normal good A good for which demand increases when income increases and demand decreases when income decreases. (p. 89)

Normal profit The return to entrepreneurship. Normal profit is part of a firm's opportunity cost because it is the cost of not running another firm. (p. 349)

Official settlements account Record of the change in U.S. official reserves. (p. 878)

Okun's Law For each percentage point that the unemployment rate is above the natural unemployment rate, real GDP is 2 percent below potential GDP. (p. 803)

Oligopoly A market in which a small number of interdependent firms compete. (p. 376)

Open market operation The purchase or sale of government securities—U.S. Treasury bills and bonds—by the New York Fed in the open market. (p. 705)

Opportunity cost The opportunity cost of something is the best thing you *must* give up to get it. (p. 8)

Output gap Real GDP minus potential GDP expressed as a percentage of potential GDP. (p. 583)

Part time for economic reasons People who work 1 to 34 hours per week but are looking for full-time work and cannot find it because of unfavorable business conditions. (p. 571)

Part-time workers People who usually work less than 35 hours a week. (p. 571)

Payoff matrix A table that shows the payoffs for each player for every possible combination of actions by the players. (p. 470)

PCEPI An average of the current prices of the goods and services included in the consumption expenditure component of GDP expressed as a percentage of base-year prices. (p. 599)

Perfect competition A market in which there are many firms, each selling an identical product; many buyers; no barriers to the entry of new firms into the industry; no advantage to established firms; and buyers and sellers are well informed about prices. (p. 376)

Perfect price discrimination Price discrimination that extracts the entire consumer surplus by charging the highest price that

consumers are willing to pay for each unit. (p. 420)

Perfectly elastic demand When the quantity demanded changes by a very large percentage in response to an almost zero percentage change in price. (p. 116)

Perfectly elastic supply When the quantity supplied changes by a very large percentage in response to an almost zero percentage change in price. (p. 126)

Perfectly inelastic demand When the percentage change in the quantity demanded is zero for any percentage change in the price. (p. 116)

Perfectly inelastic supply When the percentage change in the quantity supplied is zero for any percentage change in the price. (p. 126)

Physical capital The tools, instruments, machines, buildings, and other items that have been produced in the past and that are used to produce goods and services. (p. 666)

Pooling equilibrium The outcome when only one message is available and an uninformed person cannot determine quality. (p. 299)

Positive externality A production or consumption activity that creates an external benefit. (p. 244)

Positive relationship A relationship between two variables that move in the same direction. (p. 26)

Potential GDP The value of real GDP when all the economy's factors of production—labor, capital, land, and entrepreneurial ability—are fully employed. (pp. 551, 583, 617)

Poverty A state in which a household's income is too low to be able to buy the quantities of food, shelter, and clothing that are deemed necessary. (p. 515)

Predatory pricing Setting a low price to drive competitors out of business with the intention of setting a monopoly price when the competition has gone. (p. 479)

Price cap A government regulation that places an *upper* limit on the price at which a particular good, service, or factor of production may be traded. (p. 170)

Price cap regulation A rule that specifies the highest price that a firm is permitted to set—a price ceiling. (p. 429)

Price ceiling A government regulation that places an *upper* limit on the price at which a particular good, service, or factor of production may be traded. (p. 170)

Price-discriminating monopoly A monopoly that sells different units of a good or service for different prices not related to cost differences. (p. 406)

Price elasticity of demand A measure of the responsiveness of the quantity demanded of a good to a change in its price when all other influences on buyers' plans remain the same. (p. 114)

Price elasticity of supply A measure of the responsiveness of the quantity supplied of a good to a change in its price when all other influences on sellers' plans remain the same. (p. 126)

Price floor A government regulation that places a *lower* limit on the price at which a particular good, service, or factor of production may be traded. (p. 176)

Price level An average of the level of prices during a given period. (p. 593)

Price taker A firm that cannot influence the price of the good or service that it produces. (p. 377)

Prisoners' dilemma A game between two prisoners that shows why it is hard to cooperate, even when it would be beneficial to both players to do so. (p. 469)

Private good A good or service that can be consumed by only one person at a time and only by the person who has bought it or owns it. (p. 268)

Private information Information relevant to a transaction that is possessed by some market participants but not all. (p. 294)

Private sector balance Saving minus investment. (p. 882)

Producer surplus The price of a good in excess of the marginal cost of producing it, summed over the quantity produced. (p. 152)

Product differentiation Making a product that is slightly different from the products of competing firms. (p. 436)

Production efficiency A situation in which the economy is getting all that it can from its resources and cannot produce more of one good or service without producing less of something else. (p. 62)

Production function A relationship that shows the maximum quantity of real GDP that can be produced as the quantity of labor employed changes and all other influences on production remain the same. (p. 618)

Production possibilities frontier The boundary between the combinations of goods and services that can be produced and the combinations that cannot be produced, given the available factors

of production and the state of technology. (p. 60)

Production quota A government regulation in a market that places an upper limit on the quantity that may be supplied. (p. 183)

Productivity curve The relationship that shows how real GDP per hour of labor changes as the quantity of capital per hour of labor changes. (p. 644)

Profit Income earned by an entrepreneur for running a business. (p. 39)

Progressive tax A tax whose average rate increases as income increases. (p. 207)

Property rights Social arrangements that govern the protection of private property—legally established titles to the ownership, use, and disposal of factors of production and goods and services that are enforceable in the courts. (pp. 249, 656)

Proportional tax A tax whose average rate is constant at all income levels. (p. 207)

Public good A good or service that can be consumed simultaneously by everyone and from which no one can be excluded. (p. 269)

Public provision The production of a good or service by a public authority that receives most of its revenue from the government. (p. 259)

Purchasing power parity Equal value of money—a situation in which money buys the same amount of goods and services in different currencies. (p. 894)

Quantity demanded The amount of any good, service, or resource that people are willing and able to buy during a specified period at a specified price. (p. 85)

Quantity of labor demanded The total labor hours that all the firms in the economy plan to hire during a given time period at a given real wage rate. (p. 619)

Quantity of labor supplied The number of labor hours that all the households in the economy plan to work during a given time period at a given real wage rate. (p. 621)

Quantity of money demanded The amount of money that households and firms choose to hold. (p. 723)

Quantity supplied The amount of any good, service, or resource that people are willing and able to sell during a specified period at a specified price. (p. 92)

Quantity theory of money The proposition that when real GDP equals potential GDP, an increase in the quantity of money brings an equal percentage increase in the price level. (p. 734)

Rate of return regulation A regulation that sets the price at a level that enables a firm to earn a specified target rate of return on its capital. (p. 428)

Rational choice A choice that uses the available resources to best achieve the objective of the person making the choice. (p. 9)

Rational expectation The forecast resulting from use of all the relevant data and economic science. (p. 815)

Rational ignorance The decision not to acquire information because the marginal cost of doing so exceeds the marginal benefit. (p. 277)

Real business cycle A cycle that results from fluctuations in the pace of growth of labor productivity and potential GDP. (p. 765)

Real GDP The value of the final goods and services produced in a given year expressed in terms of the prices in a *base year*. (p. 548)

Real interest rate The goods and services forgone in interest expressed as a percentage of the amount loaned and calculated as the nominal interest rate minus the inflation rate. (p. 606)

Real wage rate The average hourly wage rate measured in the dollars of a given reference base year. (p. 604)

Recession A period during which real GDP decreases for at least two successive quarters; or defined by the NBER as "a period of significant decline in total output, income, employment, and trade, usually lasting from six months to a year, and marked by contractions in many sectors of the economy." (p. 552)

Recessionary gap A gap that exists when potential GDP exceeds real GDP and that brings a falling price level. (p. 763)

Reference base period A period for which the CPI is defined to equal 100. Currently, the reference base period is 1982–1984. (p. 590)

Regressive tax A tax whose average rate decreases as income increases. (p. 207)

Regulation Rules administered by a government agency to influence prices, quantities, entry, and other aspects of economic activity in a firm or an industry. (p. 424)

Relative price The price of one good in terms of another good—an opportunity cost. It equals the price of one good divided by the price of another good. (p. 324)

Rent Income paid for the use of land (p. 39)

Rent ceiling A regulation that makes it illegal to charge more than a specified rent for housing. (p. 170)

Rent seeking Lobbying and other political activity that aims to capture the gains from trade. The act of obtaining special treatment by the government to create economic profit or divert consumer surplus or producer surplus away from others. (pp. 237, 415)

Resale price maintenance An agreement between a manufacturer and a distributor on the price at which a product will be resold. (p. 477)

Reserves The currency in the bank's vaults plus the balance on its reserve account at a Federal Reserve Bank. (p. 699)

Rival A good, service, or resource is rival if its use by one person decreases the quantity available to someone else. (p. 268)

Rule-based monetary policy A monetary policy that is based on a rule for setting the policy instrument. (p. 868)

Rule of 70 The number of years it takes for the level of any variable to double is approximately 70 divided by the annual percentage growth rate of the variable. (p. 640)

Saving The amount of income that is not paid in net taxes or spent on consumption goods and services. (p. 540)

Scarcity The condition that arises because wants exceed the ability of resources to satisfy them. (p. 2)

Scatter diagram A graph of the value of one variable against the value of another variable. (p. 24)

Screening When an uninformed person creates an incentive for an informed person to reveal relevant private information. (p. 304)

Search activity The time spent looking for someone with whom to do business. (p. 172)

Self-interest The choices that are best for the individual who makes them. (p. 4)

Separating equilibrium The outcome when signaling provides full information to a previously uninformed person. (p. 299)

Short run The time frame in which the quantities of some resources are fixed. In the short run, a firm can usually change the quantity of labor it uses but not its technology and quantity of capital. (p. 352)

Short-run Phillips curve The relationship between the inflation rate and the unemployment rate when the natural unemployment rate and the expected inflation rate remain constant. (p. 802)

Shutdown point The point at which price equals minimum average variable cost and the quantity produced is that at which average variable cost is at a minimum. (p. 381)

Signal An action taken by an informed person (or firm) to send a message to less-informed people. (p. 451)

Signaling When an informed person takes an action that sends

information to uninformed persons. (p. 298)

Single-price monopoly A monopoly that must sell each unit of its output for the same price to all its customers. (p. 406)

Slope The change in the value of the variable measured on the y-axis divided by the change in the value of the variable measured on the x-axis. (p. 29)

Social interest The choices that are best for society as a whole. (p. 4)

Social interest theory The theory that regulation achieves an efficient allocation of resources. (p. 424)

Stagflation A combination of recession (falling real GDP) and inflation (rising price level). (p. 767)

Stock A certificate of ownership and claim to the profits that a firm makes. (p. 668)

Strategies All the possible actions of each player in a game. (p. 470)

Structural surplus or deficit The budget balance that would occur if the economy were at full employment. (p. 832)

Structural unemployment The unemployment that arises when changes in technology or international competition change the skills needed to perform jobs or change the locations of jobs. (p. 578)

Subsidy A payment by the government to a producer to cover part of the cost of production. (p. 260)

Substitute A good that can be consumed in place of another good. (p. 88)

Substitute in production A good that can be produced in place of another good. (p. 95)

Supply The relationship between the quantity supplied and the price of a good when all other influences on selling plans remain the same. (p. 92)

Supply curve A graph of the relationship between the quantity supplied of a good and its price when all the other influences on selling plans remain the same. (p. 93)

Supply of labor The relationship between the quantity of labor supplied and the real wage rate when all other influences on work plans remain the same. (p. 621)

Supply of loanable funds The relationship between the quantity of loanable funds supplied and the real interest rate when all other influences on lending plans remain the same. (p. 675)

Supply of money The relationship between the quantity of money supplied and the nominal interest rate. (p. 726)

Supply schedule A list of the quantities supplied at each different price when all the other influences on selling plans remain the same. (p. 93)

Supply-side effects The effects of fiscal policy on potential GDP and the economic growth rate. (p. 838)

Targeting rule A decision rule for monetary policy that sets the policy instrument at a level that makes the central bank's forecast of the ultimate policy goals equal to their targets. (p. 848)

Tariff A tax imposed on a good when it is imported. (p. 225)

Tax incidence The division of the burden of a tax between the buyer and the seller. (p. 192)

Tax multiplier The effect of a change in taxes on aggregate demand. (p. 833)

Tax wedge The gap created by a tax between what a buyer pays and what a seller receives. In the labor market, it is the gap between the before-tax wage rate and the after-tax wage rate. (p. 839)

Taxable income Total income minus a personal exemption and a standard deduction (or other allowable deductions). (p. 196)

Time-series graph A graph that measures time on the x-axis and the variable or variables in which we are interested on the y-axis. (p. 24)

Total cost The cost of all the factors of production used by a firm. (p. 359)

Total fixed cost The cost of the firm's fixed factors of production—the cost of land, capital, and entrepreneurship. (p. 359)

Total product The total quantity of a good produced in a given period. (p. 353)

Total revenue The amount spent on a good and received by the seller and equals the price of the

good multiplied by the quantity of the good sold. (p. 122)

Total revenue test A method of estimating the price elasticity of demand by observing the change in total revenue that results from a price change (with all other influences on the quantity sold remaining unchanged). (p. 123)

Total surplus The sum of consumer surplus and producer surplus. (p. 155)

Total utility The total benefit that a person gets from the consumption of a good or service. Total utility generally increases as the quantity consumed of a good increases. (p. 326)

Total variable cost The cost of the firm's variable factor of production—the cost of labor. (p. 359)

Tradeoff An exchange—giving up one thing to get something else. (pp. 8, 63)

Tragedy of the commons The overuse of a common resource that arises when its users have no incentive to conserve it and use it sustainably. (p. 280)

Transactions costs The opportunity costs of making trades in

a market or conducting a transaction. (p. 159)

Transfer payments Social Security benefits, Medicare and Medicaid benefits, unemployment benefits, and other cash benefits. (p. 825)

Transfer payments multiplier The effect of a change in transfer payments on aggregate demand. (p. 833)

Trend A general tendency for the value of a variable to rise or fall over time. (p. 24)

Tying arrangement An agreement to sell one product only if the buyer agrees to buy another, different product. (p. 479)

Unemployment rate The percentage of the people in the labor force who are unemployed. (p. 569)

Union wage A wage rate that results from collective bargaining between a labor union and a firm. (p. 629)

Unit elastic demand When the percentage change in the quantity demanded equals the percentage change in price. (p. 116)

Unit elastic supply When the percentage change in the quantity supplied equals the percentage change in price. (p. 126)

U.S. interest rate differential The U.S. interest rate minus the foreign interest rate. (p. 888)

U.S. official reserves The government's holdings of foreign currency. (p. 878)

Utility The benefit or satisfaction that a person gets from the consumption of a good or service. (p. 326)

Utility-maximizing rule The rule that leads to the greatest total utility from all the goods and services consumed. The rule is: 1. Allocate the entire available budget. 2. Make the marginal utility per dollar equal for all goods. (p. 328)

Value of marginal product The value to a firm of hiring one more unit of a factor of production, which equals the price of a unit of output multiplied by the marginal product of the factor of production. (p. 489)

Velocity of circulation The average number of times that each dollar of money is used during a year to buy final goods and services. (p. 734)

Vertical equity The requirement that taxpayers with a greater ability to pay bear a greater share of the taxes. (p. 207)

Voucher A token that the government provides to households, which they can use to buy specified goods or services. (p. 261)

Wages Income paid for the services of labor. (p. 39)

Wealth The value of all the things that people own. (p. 667)

Working-age population The total number of people aged 16 years and over who are not in jail, hospital, or some other form of institutional care or in the U.S. Armed Forces. (p. 568)

Index

Abatement technology, 249
Ability-to-pay principle, 206
Absolute advantage, 73, 74–75
Accounting
   cost and profit, 348, 350
   fiscal imbalance, 828–829
   generational, 828–829
   generational imbalance, 829
Addictive substances, 124
Advanced economies, 41–43, 45
Adverse selection, 297, 303, 307
Advertising
   brand name, 452
   demand for, 449–450
   innovation and, 448–453
   market equilibrium in, 453
   markup and, 450
   in monopolistic competition, 437,
      448–452
   oligopoly and, 472–473
   quality signals in, 451
Age distribution, 580
Aggregate demand, 756–760
   AS-AD model and, 750, 768
   changes in, 758–760
   cost-push inflation, 767
   demand-pull inflation and, 766
   equilibrium expenditure and,
      794–795
   fiscal/monetary policy
      influencing, 759
   fiscal policy and, 831
   fluctuations in, 805
   foreign exchange rate influencing,
      759–760, 885
   multiplier in, 760
   price levels and real GDP in,
      756–757
   real business cycle and, 765
   real interest rates and, 757–758
   world economy influencing,
      759–760
Aggregate demand curve, 757
Aggregate demand schedule, 757
Aggregate expenditure
   with consumption expenditure, 861
   decreases in, 865
   equilibrium expenditure and, 784

federal funds rate changing, 861
government expenditure in,
   833, 834
increases in, 789, 863
induced and autonomous
   expenditures in, 782
model, 776, 786
real GDP and, 782–783, 785,
   788, 792
real interest rates and, 863
schedule, 782–783
Aggregate planned expenditure, 776
   multiplier in, 788
   real GDP and, 782–783, 785,
      788, 792
   real interest rates and, 863
Aggregate supply, 750–754
   in *AS-AD* model, 750, 768
   changes in, 753–754
   cost-push inflation, 767
   demand-pull inflation and, 766
   money wage rate in, 753–754, 763
   real business cycle and, 765
   real GDP and, 750–751, 762
   recession from, 769
   short-run Phillips curve and,
      803–804
Aggregate supply curve (*AS* curve),
   751, 767
Aggregate supply schedule, 751
Agriculture
   price elasticity of demand in, 124
   production quotas, 183–185
Airbus, 464–466, 471–472, 474
Airline industry, 219, 419–422,
   464–466, 471–472, 474,
   481, 544
Air pollution, 251–253
Akerlof, George, 294, 313
Allocative efficiency, 143–145
Amazon, 394–395
American Recovery and Reinvest-
   ment Act of 2009, 203, 835
Andreeson, Marc, 651
Antitrust laws, 477
   merger rules and, 480–481
   Microsoft, 479–480
   policy debates in, 477–479

predatory pricing and, 479
tying arrangements in, 479
in United States, 477–478
AS-AD model, 768
   aggregate supply and demand in,
      750, 768
   fiscal stimulus in, 834
   with goods and services, 750
Asset prices, 670
Asymmetric information, 294,
   302–303, 307–308
AT&T, 475, 481
Auto insurance, 304–305
Automatic fiscal policy, 831, 835
Automatic stabilizers, 831
Autonomous consumption, 776
Autonomous expenditure, 776, 782
Average cost, 361–363
Average cost curve, 362
Average cost pricing, 426
Average cost pricing rule, 426
Average fixed cost, 361
Average fixed cost curve, 362
Average income
   education and, 522
   in global economy, 45–46
   United States and, 45–46
Average product, 356–357
Average tax rate, 207
Average total cost, 361
Average total cost curve, 362, 363,
   386, 410–411
Average variable cost, 361

Baby boomers, 828
Balanced budget, 824
Balanced budget multiplier, 833
Balance of payments account, 878
   in international finance, 878–879
   international trading with, 878
   of United States, 878–879
Banking system
   commercial banks in, 698–701
   Europe's creation of, 699
   Federal Reserve System in, 698
   monetary base and, 708
   money market funds and, 698, 701
   thrift institutions in, 698, 701

Bank loans
  federal funds rate and, 861
  households and businesses
    receiving, 667
  interest rates and, 858–860
  money and, 860–861
Bank reserves
  currency drain ratio and, 856
  federal funds rate and, 862–863
  in financial crisis, 855
  market equilibrium in, 854, 855
  of United States, 896
Banks
  deposits of, 698
  excess reserves of, 708
  investment, 669
  liquid assets of, 700
  loans by, 700
  reserves of, 699
Barriers to entry, 404
  business turnover and, 440
  legal, 405
  monopoly caused by, 404–405
  in oligopoly, 460–461
  ownership and, 405
Barro, Robert J., 684, 743, 792
Barter, 693
Base-year prices, 563
Benefit-cost analysis, 276
Benefits, 9. *See also* Marginal benefits
  of education, 12
  external, 257–258
  marginal external/private/social,
    257–258
  private, 257–258
  social, 257–258
  welfare, 50
Benefits principle, 206
Bentham, Jeremy, 327, 336
Bernanke, Ben, 714, 856, 870, 871
Bezos, Jeff, 394–395
Bias
  commodity substitution, 597
  in CPI, 596–597
  CPI consequences of, 598
  magnitude of, 597
  of new goods, 596
  outlet substitution, 597
  quality change, 597
Big tradeoff, 161, 163, 207–209, 529
Bitcoin, 696
Black market, 171–172

Blau, Francine D., 575
Board of Governors, 703–704
Boeing, 43, 464–466, 471–472, 474
Bond markets, 667–668
Bonds, 667
Borrowers, 880, 883
Boskin, Michael, 597
Bradbury, Katharine, 516
Brand names, 453
Break-even income, 379
BRICS nations, 41–42, 43
Brin, Sergey, 524
Budget balance, 824
Budget deficit, 824
  business cycles with, 832
  crowding out and, 842
  demand for loanable funds and, 842
  economic growth and, 842
  of government loanable funds,
    683–684
  government obligations
    influencing, 826
  tax revenues and, 824–825,
    841–842
  of United States, 827
Budget line, 320
  opportunity costs and, 324
  PPF similar to, 321
  prices and slope of, 323–324
Budgets, 320–321
Budget surplus, 682–683, 824–825
Bureaucrats, 277
Bureau of Economic Analysis (BEA),
  544, 545, 563
Bureau of Labor Statistics (BLS), 583
Business cycle, 552
  with budget balances, 832
  phases of, 552–553
  real, 765
  turning points in, 792
  in United States, 553–554
Business cycle theory, 769
Businesses
  bank loans received by, 667
  barriers to entry/turnover of, 440
  in circular flow, 48
  in circular flows, 49, 51
  cost/profit accounting of, 348, 350
  demand for labor curve of,
    491–492
  demand for labor of, 490
  economic loss and, 392–393

  economic policy of, 14
  economic profit incentive of,
    390, 410
  economic profits goal of, 377
  failures of, 752
  market entry of, 391–392
  market exit of, 391–393
  monopolistic competition
    involving, 436–437
  opportunity cost of, 348–349
  output prices of, 492
  profit-maximizing decisions of,
    378–379, 380, 442–443, 619
  profits maximization goal of, 348
  profits squeezed in, 752
  retained earnings of, 672
  short-run supply curve of,
    382–383
  shutdown decisions of, 381–382
Buyers
  change in demand and, 89
  e-cash used by, 696
  exchange rates and, 894
  lemons problem and, 294–295
  markets for sellers and, 656–657
  price discrimination and,
    418–419
Buying power, 756–757

Capacity, excess, 445
Cap-and-trade, 251–252, 255
Cap Executive Officer Pay Act of
  2009, proposed, 181
Capital, 37, 666
  accumulation, 643
  in factors of production, 37
  financial, 37, 524, 666, 841
  human, 37, 44, 520–522,
    644–645, 652
  income, 200, 203
  increasing, 644–646
  interest cost of, 348
  investment and, 667
  markets, 501
  natural resources and, 503–505
  physical, 44, 524, 642–643, 666
  services, 488, 501
  specialization of, 367
  taxes and, 200, 203
Capital and financial account, 878
Capital gains, 667
Capital goods, 34, 539

Capital in the Twenty-First Century
(Piketty), 654
Capture theory, 424
Card, David, 179
Career choices, 47
Cartel, 460
global oil, 467
monopolies and, 465–467
oligopoly and, 460, 466
Celler-Kefauver Act of 1950, 477–478
Central American Free Trade Agreement (CAFTA), 225, 234
Central bank, 703, 870
Ceteris paribus, 30
**Chained Consumer Price Index
(C-CPI), 598–599,** 600
Chained-dollar real GDP, 563, 565
Change in demand, 88
income and, 89
influence of, 88–89, 102, 106–107
perfect competition and, 393
quantity demanded changes
and, 90
**Change in quantity demanded,
90,** 115
Change in supply, 95
influence of, 95–96, 104, 106–107
quantity supplied changes and, 97
Change in the quantity supplied, 97
Checks, 695
Circular flow model, 48
Circular flows, 48–50
with financial market, 541
in global economy, 52–53
government in, 51
households and businesses in, 48
income and expenditure in, 541
in loanable funds market, 672
markets with, 48
model of, 49
money flows and, 48–49
real flows and, 48–49
in United States economy, 539–540
Classical growth theory, 650
Classical macroeconomics, 614, 615
Clayton Act of 1914, 477–478
Clean Air Act of 1970, 251
Clean technologies, 251
Climate change, 6, 246, 254–255
Clinton, Bill, 52
Close substitutes, 376, 404
Coase, Ronald, 249

Coase theorem, 249–250
Collusion, 436, 460, 472
Command-and-control regulation, 251
Command system, 141
Commercial banks
in banking system, 698–701
deposits of, 698
financial crisis stressing, 701
liquid assets of, 700
loans by, 700
net worth of, 700
profit and risk of, 699
reserves of, 699
securities sold by, 710
Commodities, 692
Commodity substitution bias, 597
Common resources, 269
efficient use of, 284–286
external costs and, 282
fishing/overfishing and, 280–283
overuse of, 280–281
public goods and, 158
quotas and, 285–286
tragedy of the commons and,
280–287
unsustainable use of, 280–281
Comparative advantage, 73
absolute advantage compared to,
73, 74–75
in international trade, 216
national, 216
opportunity cost compared to,
73, 74–75
Comparisons, relevant, 446
Competition, 413–416. *See also*
Monopolistic competition;
Perfect competition
Competitive markets, 84, 155,
394–395
Complement, 88
Complement in production, 95–96
Compromise, 163
Computer programs, 544
Concentration measures, 440
Concentration ratios, 438
Confusion costs, 742–743
Congress
federal budget role of, 824
law-making time lag and
discretion of, 836
monetary policy role of, 852
Social Security tax role of, 202–203

Congressional Budget Office (CBO),
579, 832
Constant inflation, 736
Constant returns to scale, 368
Consumer Price Index (CPI), 590
alternative measures of, 598–599
bias consequences in, 598
bias sources in, 596–597
calculating, 592–593
goods and services and, 590–594
inflation rate and, 593, 606–607
market basket and, 590–591
real GDP and, 603–604
real value calculations of, 603–604
sticky-price CPI, 600
student's, 607
Consumers
budget changes of, 321
demand and supply with, 98
equilibrium, 343–344
facing monopolies, 429
Federal Reserve buying securities
from, 711–712
in globalization, 221
income redistribution of, 531
in international trade, 216–217, 237
perfect competition and, 397
price elasticity of demand and, 133
resource allocation and, 163
selling costs encountered by, 452
Consumer surplus, 149
decrease in, 231
demand and marginal benefit, 148
demand curve vs., 335
international trade with, 227–228
measures of, 333
price discrimination and, 418–419
rent ceilings and, 173–174
Consumption
autonomous, 776
of goods and services, 539
negative and positive externalities
in, 245
possibilities, 320–324
taxing, 658
Consumption expenditure, 539
aggregate demand multiplier
and, 760
aggregate expenditure with, 861
autonomous expenditure and, 782
disposable personal income
influencing, 547

Consumption expenditure (*continued*)
government expenditure influencing, 834
income changes and, 769
induced expenditure and, 782
influences on, 779
interest rate changes and, 858–860
multipliers and, 788–792
opportunity cost of, 675
real GDP increases influencing, 792, 833
taxes on, 839, 840
Consumption function, 776
disposable income relationship in, 776–779
slope of, 778
in United States, 780
Consumption goods and services, 34, 590–591, 599
Contests, 141
Copyright laws, 271, 405
Core inflation rate, 599, 851
Correlation, 15
Cost curve, 364
Cost of living index, 596
Cost-push inflation, 767
Costs. *See also* Marginal cost; Opportunity cost; Total cost
average, 361–363, 426
average fixed, 361, 362
average total, 361–363, 386, 410–411
average variable, 361
businesses profit accounting of, 348, 350
capital's interest, 348
confusion, 742–743
of education, 12
explicit, 349
external, 246–247, 252, 282
fixed, 427
glossary of, 363
implicit, 349
interest, 348
long-run, 367–369
marginal external/private/social, 246–247, 252
plant size and long run, 367–368
private, 246–247, 282
profits and, 348, 350
selling, 452
shoe-leather, 742

short-run, 359–365
social, 246–247, 282
total fixed, 359
total variable, 359
transactions, 159
uncertainly, 743
zero marginal, 427
Credit cards, 695–696, 728
Credit easing, 705
Creditor nation, 880
Credit Unions, 701
Cross elasticity of demand, 131–132
Cross-section graphs, 24–25
Crowding-out effect, 684, 842
Cultural factors, 575
Currency, 694
desired holding of, 708
drain, 708
drain ratio, 708, 856
Currency appreciation, 885
Currency depreciation, 886
Current account, 878
Current account balance
free trade agreements and quantity of trade, 881
global economy and, 883
net exports and, 882–883
private sector deficit and, 881–882
timing and, 881
U.S. deficits and, 881
Cyclical surplus or deficit, 832
Cyclical unemployment, 579

Deadweight loss, 157
average cost pricing generating, 426
efficient equilibrium and, 283
import quotas and, 231
monopolies and, 414, 429
monopolistic competition creating, 446
natural monopolies and, 424
overproduction and, 157
political process with, 275
pollution causing, 248
production quota creating, 184
regulations causing, 158
rent ceilings and, 173
rent seeking and, 416
tariffs and, 228
taxes causing, 193
underproduction causing, 157
in used car market, 299

Dealer warranties, 298–299
DeBeers, 376
Debit cards, 696
Debtor nation, 880
Debts, 827
Decreasing marginal returns, 354–355
Deductibles, 304
Default risk, 677, 680
Deflation, 593
Great Depression and, 768
historical, 594
inflation and, 593–594, 738
nominal GDP and, 603–604
Demand, 85. *See also* Aggregate demand; Change in demand; Price elasticity of demand
change in, 88–89, 102, 106–107, 393, 679
consumer surplus and, 148–149
consumers with supply and, 98
cross elasticity of, 131–132
derived, 489, 886
for dollars, 886–888
effective, 786
elastic/inelastic, 116, 194–195
in foreign exchange market, 886
income elasticity of, 132–133
individual, 87, 330–331
in international finance, 886–887
law of, 85, 86, 98, 102–107, 886–887
in loanable funds market, 672–674
marginal product and, 503
marginal revenue and, 408
market, 87, 390
market equilibrium influenced by, 102–107
in markets, 296
nominal interest rates determined by, 726–727
in perfect competition, 377
perfectly elastic/inelastic, 116, 195–196
selling costs and, 452
supply and, 102–107
supply's opposite direction change with, 107
supply's same direction change with, 106
unit elastic, 116
for used cars, 294–295
in your life, 98

Demand curve, 86
  consumer surplus vs., 335
  deriving, 344–345
  elasticity along linear, 120
  elasticity and, 116, 119
  individual's, 330–331
  marginal benefits and, 144–145
Demand for labor, 619
  of businesses, 490
  changes in, 492
  curve, 491–492
  in factor markets, 490
  in labor markets, 619–620
  labor unions increasing, 499
  technology influencing, 492
Demand for labor curve, 491–492
Demand for loanable funds, 673
  budget deficit and, 842
  changes in, 674
Demand for money, 724
  financial technology changing, 726
  in long run, 731
  nominal interest rates and, 724
  opportunity cost and, 724–725
  price levels in, 725
  real GDP in, 725
Demand-pull inflation, 766
Demand schedule, 86
Demand-side effects, 838
Demographic changes, in job
    search, 627
Deposits, 694
  of commercial banks, 698
  loans and, 707–708
Depreciation, 546
Deregulation, 424
Derived demand, 489, 886
Developing economies
  BRICS nations as, 41–42, 43
  emerging markets and, 41–42
  global economy with, 41–44
  human capital in, 44
  physical capital in, 44
  production in, 43
**Diminishing marginal rate of
    substitution**, 342
**Diminishing marginal
    utility**, 326
Diminishing returns, 618–619
Direct relationship, 27
Discount rate, 705
Discouraged worker, 570

Discretionary fiscal policy, 831, 833,
    835–836
Discretionary monetary policy, 868
Discrimination, 523
Diseconomies of scale, 368, 369
Disposable income, 528, 676,
    776–779
Disposable personal income, 547
Dissaving, 777
Diversity, 236
Division of labor, 18, 354–355
Dollars
  demand for, 886–888
  Euro compared to, 885
  exchange rate and, 894
  in foreign exchange market,
    886–887
  interest rates changes and, 888
  marginal utility per, 328–331
  rise and fall of, 894
  supply of, 889–891
  United States foreign exchange,
    886–887
Domestic market, 183
Domestic production, 229
Donovan, Shaun, 203
Dreamliner, 43
Dual mandate, 850
Dumping, 234
Duopolists' dilemma, 471
Duopoly, 460–461
Durable goods, 539

Earnings differences, 523
Earnings sharing regulation, 429
eBay, 156, 397, 696
E-cash, 696
E-checks, 696
E-commerce, 156
Economic depreciation, 349
Economic freedom, 656
Economic growth, 70, 71, 72, **638**
  budget deficit and, 842
  calculating, 638–639
  countries' varying degrees of, 659
  education quality and, 658
  in global economy, 659
  goods and services and, 656–657
  incentive mechanisms
    creating, 657
  income distribution and, 652–654
  inflation trends and, 764

  international trade in, 658
  perpetual motion and, 651–652
  preconditions for, 656–658
  with quantity of labor, 647
  rate of, 638–639
  research and development in, 658
  rule of 70 and, 640
  saving encouraging, 657–658
  sources of, 647
  standard of living influenced
    by, 652
  taxes influencing, 841–842
  theories of, 650–652
  in U.S. economy, 764–765
Economic growth rate, 638–639
Economic inequality
  discrimination and, 523
  family/personal characteristics
    and, 524
  financial capital and, 524
  Great Divergence, 652–654
Economic model, **15**
Economic profit, 349–350
  business' goal of, 377
  business incentive of, 390, 410
  revenue concepts in, 377–378
  in short run, 386–388
  single-price monopoly and,
    419–420
  total revenue/total cost and, 379
  zero, 386, 444
Economic(s), **2**
  accounting, 348, 350
  beginning of, 18
  business loss in, 391–393
  core ideas of, 8–11
  as decision tool, 14
  forecasting in, 836
  health-care problems and, 307–310
  Hong Kong's growth in, 72
  mobility, 516–517
  models, 15, 26–28
  policies in, 26
  production possibility expansion
    in, 70, 71
  rational choices in, 9–10
  real GDP and tracking of, 554
  short run loss in, 388, 443
  Smith, Adam, in, 18
  as social science, 14–15
  voodoo, 843
  zero profits in, 386, 444

Economies of scale, 367–368, 369

Economy. *See also* Eye on the U.S.
  Economy; Global economy;
  United States
  advanced, 41, 43
  developing, 41–43
  economic growth in, 764–765
  education and United States,
    518, 522
  emerging market, 41–42
  fiscal policy influencing, 843
  information age, 5–6, 38, 648
  interest rates in, 685
  money, 722
  post-industrial, 47
  PPF possibilities expanding in,
    70, 71
  production in United States, 34–35
  real, 722
  real GDP tracking of, 554
  recession in, 769
  United States circular flows in,
    539–540
  United States insurance markets
    in, 301
  world, 759–760

Education
  average income and, 522
  costs and benefits of, 12
  economic growth and quality
    of, 658
  employment abilities through, 313
  external benefits of, 257–258
  income influenced by, 518, 522

Effective demand, 786

Efficiency
  allocative, 143
  common resources and, 284–286
  market, 154–159
  of minimum wage, 180–181
  of monopolistic competition, 446
  of monopoly, 414
  of natural monopolies, 424–429
  of oligopoly, 475
  of perfect competition, 396
  of price discrimination, 422
  production, 62–63, 74–75, 143
  of public goods, 274
  of public provision, 259, 275–277
  of rent ceiling, 173–174
  in resource allocation, 143–146
  of taxes, 193

  in used car market, 299
  vouchers achieving, 261
  zero marginal cost and, 427

Efficiency wage, 629

Efficient equilibrium, 283

Efficient scale, 445

Ehrlich, Paul, 505

Elastic demand, 116

Elasticity
  addictive substances and, 124
  along linear demand curve, 120
  of demand, 116, 195–196
  demand curve and, 116, 119
  marginal revenue and, 409–410
  of supply, 126, 196

Elastic supply, 126

Electronic Arts, 448

Electronic cash, 696

Emerging market economy, 41–42

Employment. *See also* Full employ-
    ment; Unemployment
  education and abilities for, 313
  human capital in, 520–522
  labor income taxes and, 198–199
  labor market equilibrium deter-
    mining, 496–497
  labor unions influencing, 498–499
  maximum, 851
  minimum wage and, 179
  part-time, 576
  production efficiency and, 62–63
  social security tax and, 202–203, 301
  taxes and, 198–199, 841–842

**Employment-population ratio,
    569**–570

Energy. *See* Natural resources

England, 280

Entrepreneurial ability, 524

Entrepreneurship, 38, 524

Environmental Protection Agency
    (EPA), 251, 253, 255

Environmental standards, 236. *See
    also* Pollution

Equation of exchange, 735

Equilibrium. *See also* Market
    equilibrium
  advertising and, 453
  consumer, 343–344
  convergence to, 785
  efficient, 283
  exchange rate, 892
  forces creating, 100–101

  full-employment, 763
  in insurance markets, 303
  of labor markets, 496–497,
    622–623, 750
  in loanable funds market,
    678–679
  long-run, 390, 394
  macroeconomic, 762, 763
  money market, 726–727, 732
  Nash, 470, 472
  in nonrenewable natural
    resources, 504
  pooling, 299, 302–303
  in prisoners' dilemma, 470–471
  rent seeking, 416
  separating, 299
  short run, 386–388

Equilibrium expenditure, 784–785
  aggregate demand and,
    794–795
  aggregate expenditures
    and, 784
  price levels influencing, 794–795

Equilibrium price, 100

Equilibrium quantity, 100

Euro, 885, 896

Europe
  banking system created in, 699
  potential GDP in, 617
  United States production
    compared to, 624

Eurozone, 575, 870

Excess burden, 194, 201

Excess capacity, 445

Excess reserves, 708

Exchange rates
  buyers and sellers with, 894
  changes in, 860
  dollars and, 894
  equilibrium, 892, 894
  expectations of, 894
  expected future, 888, 891
  foreign, 759–760, 885
  in international finance, 885–891
  monetary policy and, 896
  pegging, 896–897
  volatility of, 894
  of yuan, 899

Excludable, 268–269

Expected future exchange rate,
    888, 891

Expected inflation rate, 809–810, 815

Expenditures. *See also* Aggregate
    expenditure; Aggregate
    planned expenditure;
    Consumption expenditure
  autonomous, 782
  circular flows of income and, 541
  equilibrium, 784–785, 794–795
  of federal government, 827
  goods and services, 782, 825
  government multiplier of, 792, 833
  health care, 311
  income equals, 540–541
  induced, 782
  in marketing, 449
  multipliers in, 788–792
Explicit costs, 349
Export of goods and services, 52–53,
    540
Exports, 216
  airplane, 219, 464–466
  dumping of, 234
  gains/losses from, 223
  of goods and services, 52, 540
  in international finance, 52–53
  in international trade, 52, 216–217
  market with, 219
  price levels influencing, 758
  producer surplus influenced
    by, 223
  subsidies, 231
  United States, 52–53, 216–219
  United States influenced by, 886
  voluntary restraints on, 231
Export subsidy, 231
External benefits
  of college education, 257–258
  government actions with,
    259–261
  marginal, 257–258
  underproduction with, 258
External costs
  common resources and, 282
  governments and, 252
  inefficiency with, 248
  marginal, 246–247
  output and, 247
  pollution as, 247
Externalities, 244. *See also* Negative
    externality
  in market failure, 158
  negative, 244–255
  positive, 244–245

public health, 308–309
types of, 244
Eye on the Global Economy. *See also*
    Global economy
  cocoa and chocolate market, 103
  coffee, 105
  fishing/overfishing and, 282
  global current account balance
    in, 883
  global inequality, 517
  global standard of livings in, 557
  goods and services production in, 45
  health care expenditures in, 311
  Hong Kong's economic growth
    and, 72
  inflation and unemployment in, 805
  inflation targeting in, 870
  international trade and, 54
  ITQs in, 287
  natural unemployment rate in, 628
  oil/metal prices in, 504–505
  OPEC oil cartel in, 467
  potential GDP in, 617
  PPP in, 895
  price elasticities of demand in, 121
  production quotas, 183
  real GDP per person in, 659
  tax wedges in, 839
  unemployment benefits in, 628
  unemployment rate in, 575
  women in, 575
  yuan in, 899
Eye on the Past. *See also* United
    States
  banking creation in, 699
  birth of economics as social
    science, 18
  effective demand in, 786
  England's commons, 280
  federal government debts and
    revenues in, 827
  government's growth and, 52
  hyperinflation in Germany, 739
  income tax origins in, 204
  inflation and deflation in, 594
  lighthouse as natural monopoly, 270
  natural rate hypothesis in, 811
  production changes and, 36
  real GDP per person in, 639
  tragedy of the commons and, 280
  unemployment rates in, 626
  United States tariffs in, 225

U.S. Phillips curve, 806
utility in, 327
Eye on the U.S. Economy. *See also*
    Economy; United States
  airline price discrimination in, 422
  air pollution trends in, 253
  balance of payments in, 879
  consumption function in, 780
  credit cards and money in, 728
  cyclical or structural budget
    balances, 832
  earnings differences in, 523
  e-commerce in, 156
  economic growth in, 764–765
  education in, 522
  federal funds rate and, 869
  federal minimum wage in, 631
  financial crisis in, 701
  fiscal and generational imbalances
    in, 829
  health care in, 308
  import/exports and, 217
  income inequality, 518
  inflation and quantity theory of
    money, 738
  information-age monopolies, 406
  information economy and, 38
  insurance in, 301
  interest rates changes in, 668
  invisible hand's influence in, 156
  labor productivity growth in, 648
  loanable funds market during
    financial crisis, 680
  Lucas wedge in, 616
  mergers in, 481
  minimum wage in, 179
  monopolistic competition
    and, 440
  nominal GDP and, 603
  Okun gap in, 616
  oligopoly in, 462
  population survey in, 571
  potential GDP and, 640
  PPF possibilities expanding in, 71
  price elasticities of demand in, 124
  production in, 35
  real GDP per person in, 653
  relative prices in, 324
  software in, 544
  specialization and trade in, 73
  sticky-price CPI, 600
  taxes in, 199

Eye on the U.S. Economy (*continued*)
unemployment, 579, 580
wireless provider mergers in, 481
Eye on Your Life
AS-AD model in, 768
comparative advantage and, 77
CPI rate of college students, 607
demand and supply in, 98
economic growth and, 654
externalities, 245
fiscal policy in, 843
foreign exchange transactions
in, 899
free rider problem and, 271
GDP contributions in, 556
global economy and, 47
grade point averages in, 357
income redistribution in, 531
international trade and, 237
job choice/income prospects
in, 499
labor market activity in, 583
loanable funds market in, 684
marginal utility theory and, 336
monetary policy influence in, 871
money creating in, 707
money holding in, 729
monopolies in, 428
multipliers in, 791
natural unemployment in, 631
payoff matrix in, 474
perfect competition and, 397
PPF and, 64
price elasticities of demand and, 133
price increases, 123
resource allocation in, 163
selling costs and, 452
short-run tradeoff in, 817
signaling ability in, 313
Tax Freedom Day in, 204
time allocation, 17
United States economy and, 47

Facebook, 38, 406, 453
Factor markets, **48**, **488**
capital markets in, 501
in circular flows, 49
demand for labor curve in, 491–492
demand for labor in, 490
land markets in, 502
marginal product value in, 489–490
market income in, 512

natural resources in, 488
nonrenewable natural resources
in, 504
services in, 488
Factor prices, 364–365, **488**
Factors of production, **36**
capital in, 37
entrepreneurship in, 38
labor in, 37
land in, 36
prices and, 364–365, 492
Fair Labor Standards Act of 1938,
179, 631
Fairness
ability-to-pay principle and,
206–207
benefits principle and, 206
big tradeoff and, 161, 207–209
of markets, 161–163
of minimum wage, 181
of monopolies, 415
of perfect competition, 397
of price gouging, 162
of production quotas, 185
of rent ceilings, 174
of resource allocation, 163
rules of, 161
FairTax, **209**
Fannie Mae. *See* Federal National
Mortgage Association
Federal budget
Congress' role in, 824
deficit and debt, 6
of fiscal 2017, 824–826
from Great Depression, 824
President's role in, 824
time line of, 825
of United States, 829, 832
Federal funds rate, **700**, **852**
aggregate expenditure changed
by, 861
bank loans and, 861
bank reserves and, 862–863
Federal Reserve and, 852–853
Federal government, 50, 52
expenditures/revenues of, 827
historical debts and revenues of, 827
social security and Medicare
obligations of, 825
Federal Home Loan Mortgage
Corporation (Freddie Mac),
669, 680

Federal minimum wage, 631
Federal National Mortgage Association
(Fannie Mae), 669, 680
**Federal Open Market Committee
(FOMC)**, **704**, 705, 852
Federal Reserve Act of 2000, 850
Federal Reserve System (the Fed), **703**
actions and influence of, 852
alternative monetary policy
strategies of, 868–871
banking system and, 698
Board of Governors of, 703–704
consumers selling securities to,
711–712
crisis measures of, 705
decision-making strategy of,
852–854
discount rate used by, 705
districts of, 703
expected inflation rate influenced
by, 815
federal funds rate and, 852–853
FOMC of, 704, 705, 852
full employment goal of, 851, 865
Great Depression and, 856
inflation fought by, 864–865
interest rate decisions in, 738,
852–853, 859
monetary policy of, 850–851,
865, 871
money creation by, 714
money supply changes by, 722, 733
open market operation used by, 705
policies toward inflation, 817
policy tools of, 704–705
quantity of money changes
of, 733
recession actions of, 862–863
regional banks of, 704
required reserve ratio used by,
704, 705
securities bought by, 709–712
securities sold by, 712
structure of, 703–704
Z-pop ratio employment indicator,
580–581
Federal Trade Commission (FTC), 481
Feige, Edgar L., 555
Feldstein, Martin, 843
Fiat money, **694**
Final good or service, **538**, 544
Finance, 666

Financial capital, 37, 524
  financial institutions using, 669–670
  markets for, 667–668
  physical capital compared to, 666
  taxes influence on, 841
Financial crisis
  bank reserves in, 855
  commercial banks under stress from, 701
  financial stability in, 855
  loanable funds market in, 680
  in United States, 701, 769
Financial institutions, 669–670
Financial markets
  bond markets in, 667–668
  circular flow with, 541
  financial stability of, 851
  interest rates in, 685
  loanable funds markets grouped with, 672
  loan markets in, 667
  stock markets in, 668
  types of, 667–668
Financial stability, 851
  in financial crisis, 855
  of financial markets, 851
  risk and, 851
Financial technology, 726
Firms, 48. *See also* Businesses
Fiscal imbalance, 828–829
Fiscal policy, 759, 824
  aggregate demand and, 831
  automatic, 831, 835
  discretionary, 831, 833, 835–836
  economy influenced by, 843
  full employment and income tax, 840–841
  full employment involving, 824–825
  goods and services and, 759
  long-run, 843
  potential GDP and, 838–841
  supply-side debate, 842–843
  in United States, 843
Fiscal stimulus
  in *AS-AD* model, 834
  for full employment, 834
  recession ended by, 835
  supply-side effects in, 842–843
Fiscal year, 824
Fishing/overfishing, 280–283

Fixed costs, 427
Fixed plant, 352
Flat tax, 208–209
FOMC. *See* Federal Open Market Committee
Food Stamp program, 261
Force, 142–143
Foreign exchange market, 885
  aggregate demand influence in, 759–760
  demand in, 886
  intervention in, 896–897
  law of demand in, 886–887
  law of supply in, 889–890
  market equilibrium and, 892, 894
  People's Bank of China in, 897–899
  supply in, 889–890
  transactions in, 899
  U.S. dollars in, 886–887
Foreign exchange rate, 759–760, 885
Foreign labor, 235–236
Four-firm concentration ratio, 438, 440, 462
France, 839
Freddie Mac. *See* Federal Home Loan Mortgage Corporation
Free lunch, 63–64
Free markets, 184
Free rider, 158, 271–278
Frictional unemployment, 578, 580
Friedman, Milton, 615, 811, 856, 871
Full employment, 579
  adjustment toward, 763
  expected inflation rate with, 809–810
  Federal Reserve maintaining, 851, 865
  fiscal policy involving, 824–825
  fiscal stimulus for, 834
  government intervention for, 615
  income tax and, 840–841
  inflation and, 864–865
  job rationing and, 628–630
  Keynesian macroeconomics and, 614–615
  in long run, 731
  long-run Phillips curve and, 808
  natural rate hypothesis with, 810
  potential GDP and, 583, 617, 623, 838
  price levels and, 734, 767
  real wage rate at, 722, 786

restoring, 767, 838, 862
  short-run Phillips curve and, 802–806, 813
  structural surplus or deficit with, 832
  unemployment rate and, 816–817
Full-employment equilibrium, 763
Full-time workers, 571
Functional distribution of income, 39
Future income, 676–677, 779
Future prices, 96

Games, 474
Game theory, 469–475
  duopolists' dilemma and, 471
  in oligopoly, 469–471
  prisoners' dilemma and, 469–471
Gasoline
  prices, 118
  taxes, 255, 278
Gates, Bill, 6, 38, 141, 428, 524
GDP price index, 603
General Agreement on Tariffs and Trade (GATT), 225
The General Theory of Employment, Interest, and Money (Keynes), 614–615
Generational accounting, 828–829
Generational imbalance, 829
Germany, 739
Gifts of nature, 36
Glass-Steagall Act of 1933, 669
Global economy
  advanced economies in, 41–43, 45
  average incomes in, 45–46
  career choices in, 47
  circular flows in, 52–53
  current account balance in, 883
  developing economies in, 41–43
  economic growth in, 659
  goods and services in, 44
  human capital in, 44
  income distribution in, 45–46
  income inequality in, 45–46, 517
  inflation in, 805
  inflation targeting used in, 869–870
  international trade in, 52–54
  natural unemployment rate in, 628
  physical capital in, 44
  potential GDP in, 617

Global economy (*continued*)
poverty in, 46
PPP in, 895
price elasticity of demand in, 121
production in, 43
real GDP per person and, 659
standard of living in, 554, 557
unemployment benefits in, 628
unemployment in, 805
unemployment rate in, 575
women in, 575
Globalization, 5, 221
Global oil cartel, 467
Gokhale, Jagadeesh, 828, 829
Goldsmith, Samuel, 699
Gone with the Wind, 606
Goods
bias of new, 596
capital, 34, 539
classifying, 268–269
durable, 539
GDP and import of, 556
inferior, 89
markets for, 48
nondurable, 539
normal, 89
price elasticity of demand and,
114–115, 133
price level measures of, 596–600
prices of related, 88–89
private/public, 268–269
property rights of, 656
used, 544
Goods and services, 3
account balances and, 881
AS-AD model with, 750
consumption of, 34, 539
CPI measure of, 590–594
economic growth and, 656–657
expenditures on, 782, 825
explanation of, 3–4
exports/imports of, 52,
540, 556
fiscal and monetary policies
and, 759
GDP and omitted, 555
GDP measurement of, 538–539
GDP price index and, 599
in global economy, 44
GNP and, 547
government expenditure
multiplier on, 792, 833

government expenditure on,
540, 831
Keynesian macroeconomics and,
614–615
monetary policy and, 759
money used for, 693
net exports of, 540, 882–883
nominal GDP value of, 548
physical capital and, 666
production changes in, 45
production of, 555
public, 838
quantity of money demanded
for, 723
real GDP value of, 548, 617
real interest rates and, 606–607
standard of living value of, 551,
554, 557
tax wedges influencing, 839
United States deficits from, 6
United States producing, 34–35
value, 548
value of money for, 731–732
velocity of circulation in, 734–735
Goods markets, 48, 49, 51, 53
Google, 406, 427
Government. *See also* Federal
government
aggregate expenditure and,
833, 834
budget deficit and obligations
of, 828
in circular flows, 51
consumption expenditure and, 834
external benefits and, 259–261
external costs and, 252
federal, 50
full employment intervention
by, 615
generational accounting, 828–829
goods and services expenditure
of, 540, 831
growth of, 52
import quotas imposed by,
229–231
Income distribution/redistribution
by, 526–527
investments, 882
licenses and legal monopoly, 405
limits on funding of, 277
loanable funds/budget deficit of,
683–684

loanable funds/budget surplus of,
682–684
loanable funds market involvement of, 682–684
local/state, 50
multiplier of expenditures and,
792, 833
outlay increases of, 598
productivity role of, 838
securities issued by, 700
state/local, 50
subsidies from, 426
tariff revenue of, 227
The Government Debt Iceberg
(Gokhale), 828, 829
Government expenditure multiplier,
792, **833**
**Government expenditure on goods
and services, 540**
Government sector balance, 882
Grade point average (GPA), 64, 357
Graphs
axes of, 23
ceteris paribus used in, 30
cross-section of, 24–25
economic models using, 15,
26–28
making, 23
origin of, 23
relationships/variables in, 26–28
time-series, 24
Great Compression, 514, 652
Great Convergence, 653
Great Depression, 573
classical macroeconomics
during, 614
deflation and, 768
effective demand during, 786
federal budget from, 824
Federal Reserve and, 856
inflation and unemployment
during, 805
money creation and, 714
Great Divergence, 652–654
Greenhouse gases (GHG), 254–255
Greenspan, Alan, 674, 851
Gross domestic product (GDP), 538
goods and services and, 538–539
goods and services omitted
from, 555
import of goods and, 556
income measuring, 545–546

personal contributions in, 556
price index and, 599
production and income measures in, 547
Gross investment, 666
Gross national product (GNP), 547
Growth rate
economic, 638–639
real GDP per person and, 639

Hamermesh, Daniel, 179
Health, 556
Health care
economic problems in, 307–310
expenditures, 311
global expenditures in, 311
in other countries, 311
poverty and, 309
public choice solutions, 310, 312
reform ideas in, 312–313
in United States, 308
vouchers in, 313
Health insurance, 307–313
asymmetric information in, 307
inequality in ability to pay, 309–310
moral hazards in, 307–308
underestimation of benefit, 308
in United States, 308
Health Maintenance Organizations (HMO), 308
Herfindahl-Hirschman index, 439, 440, 462, 463, 481
Hong Kong, 72
Horizontal drilling, 71
Horizontal equity, 206–207
Hotelling, Harold, 505
Hotelling Principle, 504–505
Household production, 555
Households, 48
bank loans received by, 667
in circular flows, 49, 51
credit cards used by, 728
income of, 518, 531
mortgages for, 668
production, 555
Housing market, 170–174, 680
Howitt, Peter, 743–744
Human capital, 37
in developing and global economies, 44
in employment, 520–522

expansion of, 644–646
high/low skilled labor as, 520–522
replicating activities and, 651
technology and, 645–646
Human Development Index (HDI), 557
Hydraulic fracturing, 71
Hyperinflation, 737, **739,** 742

Illegal hiring, 178
Illiquidity, 670
IMF. *See* International Monetary Fund
Implicit costs, 349
Import quota, 229
government imposing, 229–231
influence of, 229–230
international trade and, 229–231
producer surplus and, 230–231
profits from, 230–231
Imports, 216
gains/losses from, 222
of goods and services, 52, 540, 556
multiplier of income taxes and, 790
policy barriers of, 231
price levels influencing, 758
producer surplus influenced by, 222
real GDP and, 780
United States, 52–53, 216–219
United States influenced by, 889
Imports of goods and services, 540
Incentive mechanisms, 657
Incentives, 11
Income
break-even, 379
capital, 200
change in demand and, 89
circular flows of expenditure and, 541
consumption expenditure and changes in, 769
disposable, 528, 676, 776–779
disposable personal, 547
economic mobility and, 516–517
education influencing, 518
expected future, 89
expenditure equals, 540–541
functional distribution of, 39
future, 676–677, 779
GDP measured using, 545–546
GDP measures of production and, 547
household, 518, 531
inequality, 514

labor, 198–199
land, 201
maintenance programs, 526–527
market, 512
money, 512
personal distribution of, 39, 45
price elasticity of demand and, 121
profit, 545
prospects for, 499
rent, 39
taxable, 199
taxation of, 198–201
from wages, 39, 545
Income distribution
economic growth and, 652–654
in global economy, 45–46
by governments, 526–527
Income elasticity of demand, 132–133
Income redistribution
of consumers, 531
by governments, 526–527
income maintenance programs for, 526–527
income taxes for, 526
negative income tax and, 531
normative theories of, 529
positive theories of, 530
poverty and, 530–531
scale of, 527–528
subsidized services and, 527
as tradeoff, 163
Income taxes
full employment and, 840–841
income redistribution through, 163, 526
labor income and, 198–199
labor markets influenced by, 840
from land, 201
multiplier of imports and, 790
negative, 531
origins of, 204
personal, 199
proportional, 207, 526
in United States, 204, 208
Increasing marginal returns, 354
Indifference curve, 341
deriving demand curve, 344–345
marginal rate of substitution in, 342–343
preference map of, 341–342
Individual demand, 87, 330–331

Individual supply, 94
Individual transferable quota (ITQ), **286**–287
Induced expenditures, 782
Induced taxes, 831
Industrial Revolution, 5, 594, 639, 642, 645, 786
Inefficiency
    with external costs, 248
    of minimum wage, 180–181
    of monopoly, 414
    in pooling equilibrium, 303
    in production, 62–63, 74–75, 143
    of rent ceiling, 173–174
Inelastic demand, 116
Inelastic supply, 126, 196
Inequalities, 45–46, 514. *See also* Economic inequality
Infant-industry argument, 233
Inferior good, 89
Inflation
    confusion costs in, 742–743
    constant, 736
    core inflation rate, 599
    cost of, 741–742
    cost-push, 767
    cycles of, 766–767
    deflation and, 593–594, 738
    demand-pull, 766
    economic growth trends of, 764
    Federal Reserve fighting, 864–865
    Federal Reserve policies toward, 817
    full employment and, 864–865
    in global economy, 805
    during Great Depression, 805
    historical, 594
    money growth and, 737
    price levels and, 803–804
    quantity theory of money and, 734–737
    shoe-leather costs of, 742
    sticky-price CPI, 600
    taxes as, 741–742
    uncertainty costs of, 743
Inflationary gap, 763, 766, 832, 851
Inflation rate, 593
    adjusting, 736–737
    core, 599, 851
    CPI and, 594, 607
    expected, 809–810, 815

Federal Reserve influencing, 815
    fluctuations in, 815
    with full employment, 809–810
    measures of, 600
    unemployment and, 802, 805, 810–813
    unemployment rate relationship with, 808–813
    in United States, 593–594
Inflation targeting, 869–870
Information age economy, 5–6, 38, 648
Information Revolution, 5–6, 645
Insolvency, 670
Insurance
    asymmetric information in, 302–303
    auto, 304–305
    companies, 669–670
    deductibles in, 304
    health, 301, 307–313
    life, 301
    moral hazards in, 303
    no-claim bonus in, 304
    in United States economy, 301
Insurance markets
    inefficient pooling equilibrium in, 303
    screening in, 304–305
    in United States, 301–305
Interest, 39, 348, 545
Interest rate parity, 896
Interest rates. *See also* Nominal interest rate; Real interest rate
    adjusting, 727, 728–729
    asset prices and, 670
    bank loans and, 858–860
    consumption expenditure and changes in, 858–860
    in economy, 685
    Federal Reserve decisions on, 852–854, 859
    in financial markets, 685
    housing market and, 680
    long-term, 860
    monetary policy changes in, 858–860
    money and, 724
    short-term, 860
    as tax wedge, 842
    unemployment influenced by, 865

United States changes in, 668, 858–860, 888, 891
    United States decisions on, 852–853
Intermediate good or service, **538**, 544
International finance
    balance of payments accounts in, 878–879
    borrowers and lenders in, 880, 883
    circular flows in, 52–53
    current account balances in, 881
    demand for dollars in, 886–888
    demand in, 886–887
    exchange rates in, 885–891
    foreign exchange demand in, 886–887
    foreign exchange supply in, 889–890
    market equilibrium in, 892, 894
    net exports in, 882–883
    People's Bank of China and, 897–899
    PPP in, 894–895
    supply of dollars in, 889–891
International Monetary Fund (IMF), 554
International trade
    balance of payments account with, 878
    booms and slumps in, 53
    comparative advantage in, 216
    consumer/producers in, 217, 237
    with consumer/producer surplus, 227–228
    in economic growth, 658
    exports in, 52, 216–217
    in global economy, 52–54
    import quotas and, 229–231
    protection/restriction arguments in, 233–236
    regulations in, 231
    restrictions to, 225–231, 236–237
    of United States, 52, 216
Inverse relationship, 27
Investment, 539
    capital and, 667
    government, 882
    gross, 666
    net, 666
    physical capital and, 642–643

Investment banks, 669
Invisible hand, 155–156

Japan, 870
J.D. Power Consumer Center, 437
Jevons, William Stanley, 327, 336
Job choices, 499
Job rationing, 628–630
Job search, 627
  demographic changes in, 627
  structural change in, 628
  unemployment benefits and, 627
  wages and, 629–630
Job-search activity, 178

Kahn, Lawrence M., 575
Kennedy, John F., 806
Kershaw, Clayton, 12
Keynes, John Maynard, 499,
  614–615, 786
Keynesian macroeconomics, 614
  federal budget, 824
  full employment and, 614–615
  goods and services in, 614–615
  recession and, 776
Kotlikoff, Laurence, 313
k-percent rule, **871**
Krueger, Alan, 179
Krugman, Paul, 615, 654
Kuznets, Simon, 652, 654
Kydland, Finn E., 614

Labor, 37. *See also* Demand for labor;
  Quantity of labor
  division of, 18, 354–355
  in factors of production, 37
  foreign, 235–236
  high/low skilled, 520–522
  income, 198–199
  income taxes from, 198–199
  market equilibrium and, 496–497
  market supply of, 494–496
  price floor and market of, 185
  skill differentials/wage rates of, 521
  specialization of, 73, 367
  supply of, 621–622
  in United States, 37, 60, 496
  United States' productivity
    growth in, 648
  wage rates and, 494, 496, 520–522
  wage rates and skill differentials
    of, 521

Labor force, 568
  categories of, 569
  participation of, 622
  unemployment rate in, 569
Labor force participation rate, 570
Labor markets
  activity and status in, 583
  demand for labor in, 619–620
  employment and equilibrium of,
    496–497
  equilibrium of, 496–497,
    622–623, 750
  income tax influencing, 840
  indicators in, 569–570
  labor supply influences on,
    494–496
  labor unions in, 498–499
  participation rate in, 574
  with price floor, 185
  school/training in, 496
  supply of labor in, 621–622
  unemployment rate in, 573
  wage rate in, 494, 496, 520–522
  wages and, 496
Labor productivity, 642
  growth in, 646–647, 648
  physical capital and, 642–643
  United States growth in, 648
Labor unions, 498–499
Laffer, Arthur, 842–843
Land, 36
  in factors of production, 36
  income taxes from, 201
  marginal product and, 502
  market for, 502
  as natural resources, 36, 488
Law-maker discretion, 836
Law-making time lag, 836
Law of decreasing returns, 356
Law of demand, 85, 86, 98, 102–107,
  886–887
**Law of diminishing marginal
  returns, 643**–644
Law of market forces, 100
Law of supply, 92, 98, 102–107, 381,
  889–890
Legal barriers to entry, 405
Legal monopoly, 405
Leisure time, 555, 622
Lemons problem, 294–299
Lenders, 880
Life expectancy, 556

Life insurance, 301
Lighthouse, 270
Linear demand curve, 120
Linear relationships, 26
Liquid assets, 700
Loanable funds market, 672
  circular flows in, 672
  demand in, 672–674
  equilibrium in, 678–679
  in financial crisis, 680
  financial markets grouped
    with, 672
  government budget deficit
    in, 683–684
  government budget surplus
    in, 682–684
  government involved in,
    682–684
  savings and, 684
  supply changes in, 675–677
  supply in, 675–677, 685
Loans
  by banks, 700
  deposits by making, 707–708
  market for, 667
Local governments, 50
Lomborg, Bjørn, 255
Long run, 352
  demand for money in, 731
  excess capacity and, 445
  full employment in, 731
  markup in, 445
  money market in, 731–732
  output/price/profit in, 444
  plant size and cost in, 367–368
  variable plant and, 352–353
  zero economic profit in, 386, 444
**Long-run average cost curve,
  368**–369
Long-run costs, 367–369
Long-run equilibrium, 390, 394
Long-run fiscal policy, 843
Long-run Phillips curve, 808
  expected inflation rate, 809–810
  unemployment rate relationship
    with, 811–812
Long-term interest rates, 860
Long-term real interest rates,
  861, 865
Lorenz curve, 513
  disposable income and, 528
  in United States, 513, 517

Loss, 39
Lottery, 142
Lucas, Robert E., Jr., 616
Lucas wedge, 616, 842, 843
Lucky Brand, 442–446

M1, 694–695, 871
M2, 694–695, 738, 871
Macroeconomic equilibrium, 762, 763
Macroeconomics, 3
  classical, 614
  Keynesian, 614–615, 776, 824
  monetarist, 615
  nominal and real values in,
    602–603
Majority rule, 141
Malthus, Thomas Robert, 650
Malthusian theory, 650
Margin, 10
Marginal analysis, 380–381
Marginal benefits, 10
  demand curve and, 144–145
  marginal costs equal to, 144–145,
    154–155
  of public good, 272–273
  rational choices and, 11
Marginal cost, 10, 360
  average cost and, 361
  marginal benefits equal to,
    144–145, 154–155
  natural monopolies pricing and,
    424–425
  of public goods, 272
  short-run cost and, 360
  supply and, 151
  zero, 427
Marginal cost curve, 362, 410–411
Marginal cost pricing rule, 424–425
Marginal external benefit, 257
Marginal external cost, 246
Marginally attached workers, 570
Marginal private benefit, 257
Marginal private cost, 246, 252
Marginal product, 354
  average product and, 355
  curve, 491–492
  in factor markets, 489–490
  land demand and, 502
  total product and, 354, 355
  value of, 489–490, 497, 520
Marginal propensity to consume,
    778, 789–790

Marginal propensity to import, 780
Marginal rate of substitution,
    342–343
Marginal returns, 354, 643–644
Marginal revenue, 377
  curve, 408–409
  demand and, 408–409
  elasticity and, 409–410
  in perfect competition, 377–378
  price and, 408–409
  total revenue and, 408–409
Marginal social benefit, 257, 282
Marginal social cost, 246, 252
Marginal tax rate, 207, 790
Marginal utility, 326
  diminishing, 326
  efficiency/price/value, 333–336
  per dollar, 328–331
  theory, 326–336
  total, 333
  total utility and, 327, 328–330
Marginal utility per dollar, 328–331
Market demand, 87, 390
Market equilibrium, 100
  in bank reserves, 854
  demand/supply changes influ-
    encing, 102–107
  fishing/overfishing and, 283
  foreign exchange and, 892, 894
  in international finance, 892, 894
  labor and, 496–497
  law of market forces and, 100–101
  price influencing, 100–101
  with property rights, 250
  quantity of labor and, 750
  tax incidence and, 192–193
Market failure, 157–159
Market forces, law of, 100–101
Market income, 512
Marketing, 436, 449–450
Market price, 140, 545
Market(s), 48. *See also* Factor markets;
    Financial markets; Foreign ex-
    change market; Labor markets;
    Loanable funds market
  for airplanes, 219, 464–466
  alternatives to, 159
  black, 171–172
  bond, 667–668
  businesses entering, 391–392
  businesses exiting, 391–393
  buyers and sellers in, 656–657

  capital, 501
  for capital services, 488, 501
  with circular flow, 48
  for cocoa and chocolate, 103
  for coffee, 105
  competitive, 84, 155, 394–395
  domestic, 183
  economic freedom and, 656–657
  efficient, 154–159
  emerging, 41–42
  exports of, 219
  fairness of, 161–163
  for financial capital, 667–668
  free, 184
  for goods, 48
  housing, 170–174
  income, 512
  insurance, 301–305
  for land, 502
  loan, 667
  money, 701, 726–727, 731–732
  monopolies, 376
  scarce resources and prices in, 140
  stock, 668
  structure, 439
  supply and demand in, 294–297
  two-sided, 453
  types of, 376
  in used cars, 298–299
Market supply
  curve, 385, 494
  individual supply and, 94
  of labor, 494–496
  in short run, 385
Market value, 538
Markup, 445, 450
Maximum employment, 851
Maximum/minimum points, 28
McCallum, Bennett T., 868
McCallum Rule, 868, 869
Means of payment, 692
Median voter theory, 530
Medicaid, 308, 312–313, 527
Medicare, 308, 312–313, 527, 825,
    828–829
Medium of exchange, 693
Merger rules, 480–481
Metal prices, 504
Microeconomics, 2
Microsoft, 38, 406, 427, 428, 479–480
Midpoint method, 114–115
Mill, John Stuart, 614

Minimum wage
efficiency/inefficiency of, 180–181
employment and, 179
fairness of, 181
federal, 631
illegal hiring and, 178
job-search activity and, 178
law, 179
unemployment created by, 177
in United States, 179, 631
Minimum wage law, **177**, 179, **629**
Mishkin, Frederic S., 870
Mobile wallets, 696
Monetarist macroeconomics, **615**
Monetary base, **705**
banking system and, 709–712
money multiplier and, 713–715, 856
open market operations changing, 708, 712–713
Monetary policy, **759**
aggregate demand influenced by, 759
alternative strategies in, 868–871
Congress' role in, 852
discretionary, 868
exchange rate and, 896
of Federal Reserve, 850–851, 865, 871
Federal Reserve's alternative strategies of, 868–871
goods and services and, 759
individuals influenced by, 871
inflation targeting in, 869–870
interest rate changes in, 858–860
loose links in chain, 866
objectives of, 850–851
President's role in, 852
responsibilities for, 852
time lags, 866
of United States, 852
Monetary policy instrument, **852**
Money, **692**
bank loans and, 860–861
buying power of, 756–757
e-cash as, 696
economy, 722
Federal Reserve's changes and, 722, 733
Federal Reserve's creation of, 714
fiat, 694
functions of, 692–693

for goods and services, 693
Great Depression and creation of, 714
holding of, 723, 729
individual's role in creating, 707
inflation and growth of, 737
interest rates and, 724
measures of, 694–695
prices, 754
quantity of, 856
regulating quantity of, 707–715
supply of, 726
in United States, 728
value of, 731–732
Money flows, 48–49
Money income, **512**
Money market
equilibrium, 726–727, 732
funds, 701
in long run, 731–732
Money multiplier, **713**–715, 856
Money wage rate, 753–754, 763
Monopolistic competition, **376**
advertising in, 437, 448–452
businesses involved in, 436–437
concentration measures in, 440
deadweight loss created in, 446
efficiency of, 446
entry/exit in, 437
four-firm concentration ratios and, 438, 440
Herfindahl-Hirschman index and, 439, 440
identifying, 437–440
output/prices in, 436–437, 442–446
perfect competition and, 445
product differentiation in, 436, 446
quality price and marketing in, 436–437
United States economy and, 440
Monopoly, **376**, **404**. *See also* Natural monopoly
barriers to entry causing, 404–405
buying/creating, 415
cartels and, 465–467
causes of, 404
close substitutes and, 404
competition and, 413–416
consumers facing, 429
deadweight loss and, 414, 429
efficiency/inefficiency of, 414
fairness of, 415

Gates and, 428
legal, 405
market, 376
natural, 269, 404, 424–429
natural resources and, 404–405
oligopoly and, 376, 464–465
output/price decisions of, 410–411, 413
price-discriminating, 406
price-setting strategies of, 406
profits maximized by, 158, 411
regulation of, 424–429
rent seeking creating, 415–416
single-price, 406, 408–409, 419–420
Moore, Gordon, 6
Moral hazard, **303**, 307–308
Mortgage
-backed securities, 668
for households, 668
lenders, 669
Moulton, Brent, 544
Multifiber Arrangement (MFA), 235
Multiplier, **788**
in aggregate demand, 760
in aggregate planned expenditure, 788
balanced budget, 833
consumption expenditure and, 788–792
in expenditure, 788–792
government expenditure, 792, 833
imports and income taxes with, 790
marginal propensities and, 789–790
money, 713–715, 856
open market operations and effect of, 712–713
size of, 789
slope with, 791
tax, 833
transfer payments, 833
Multiplier effect, 712–713
Murphy, Kevin, 179

NAFTA. *See* North American Free Trade Agreement
Nash, John, 470
Nash equilibrium, **470**, 472
National Bureau of Economic Research (NBER), 552–553, 554
National comparative advantage, 216
National debt, **825**
National security, 233

Natural gas shale, 71
Natural monopoly, 404
  average cost pricing of, 426
  deadweight loss and, 424
  efficient regulation of, 424–429
  goods produced by, 269
  lighthouse as, 270
  marginal cost pricing in, 424–425
  price cap regulations and, 429
  regulations of, 424–429
Natural oligopoly, 460–461
Natural rate hypothesis, 810, 811
Natural resources
  capital and, 503–505
  in factor markets, 488
  land as, 36, 488
  monopolies and, 404–405
  population growth influencing, 505
  supply of, 503
Natural unemployment rate, 579,
    626–630
  changes in, 811–812
  in global economy, 628
  job rationing and, 630
  job rationing increasing, 630
  short-run Phillips curve and, 808
  tradeoff and, 811–812
  unemployment benefits and, 581
Needs-tested spending, 831
Negative externality, 244
  in consumption, 245
  pollution as, 246–255
  in production, 244
Negative income tax, 531
Negative relationship, 27
Net borrower, 880, 883
Net domestic product at factor
    cost, 545
Net exports of goods and services,
    540, 882–883
Net investment, 666
Net lender, 880
Net operating surplus, 545
Net taxes, 540
Net worth, 670, 700
Neumark, David, 179
New growth theory, 650–652
Nike, 452
Nintendo, 128
No-claim bonus, 304
Nominal GDP, 548
  calculating, 549

deflation and, 603–604
goods and services value
    expressed by, 548
real GDP and, 548
in United States, 603
Nominal interest rate, 606–607
  demand and supply determining,
    726–727
  demand for money and, 724
Nominal values, 602–603
Nominal wage rate, 604–605, 619
Nondurable goods, 539
Nonexcludable, 268–269
Nonrenewable natural resources,
    488, 504
Nonrival, 268–269
Normal good, 89
Normal profit, 349
Normative statements, 15
Normative theories of income redis-
    tribution, 529
North American Free Trade Agree-
    ment (NAFTA), 225, 234, 881
Nozick, Robert, 161, 529

Obama, Barack, 835
Obamacare. *See* Patient Protection
    and Affordable Care Act
Official settlements account, 878
Oil prices, 467, 504–505, 648
Okun, Arthur B., 616, 803
Okun gap, 616
Okun's Law, 803
Oligopoly, 376
  advertising and, 472–473
  barriers to entry in, 460–461
  cartel dilemma and, 460, 466
  collusion and, 460
  duopolists' dilemma in, 471
  efficiency of, 475
  four-firm concentration ratios
    and, 462
  game theory in, 469–471
  Herfindahl-Hirschman index and,
    462, 463
  identifying, 462
  interdependence in, 460
  monopoly outcome in, 376,
    464–465
  natural, 460–461
  research games in, 472–473
  in United States economy, 462

OPEC. *See* Organization of the
    Petroleum Exporting
    Countries
Open market operation, 705
  Federal Reserve using, 705
  monetary base changed by, 708,
    712–715
  money multiplier process with,
    713–715, 856
  multiplier effect of, 712–715
Operation Twist, 705
Opportunity cost, 8–9
  budget line slope is, 324
  comparative advantage compared
    to, 73, 74–75
  of consumption expenditure, 675
  demand for money and, 724–725
  of firm's production, 348–349
  PPF slope and, 67
  ratios in, 67
  resources with, 68
  search activity and, 172
  of smartphone production, 66–67
Orange prices, 124
Organization of the Petroleum
    Exporting Countries (OPEC),
    467, 504–505
Outlet substitution bias, 597
Output
  business prices of, 492
  changing rate of, 752
  external costs and, 247
  gaps in, 763
  long run, 444
  monopolies/price decisions of,
    410–411, 413
  in monopolistic competition,
    436–437, 442–446
  prices and, 410–411, 413
  profit-maximizing, 411
Output gap, 582, 583, 851
Overproduction, 157, 277
Ownership barriers to entry, 405

Page, Larry, 524
Part-time employment, 576
Part time for economic reasons, 571
Part-time workers, 571
Patent, 405
Patient Protection and Affordable
    Care Act of 2010, 312–313
Payoff matrix, 470, 471–472, 474

PayPal, 696
Pencil manufacturing, 73
Pension funds, 669
People's Bank of China, 897–899
Perfect competition, 376
consumers and, 397
demand/price/revenue in, 377–378
efficiency of, 396
fairness of, 397
marginal revenue and, 377–378
monopolistic competition and, 445
outcome of, 465
price taker in, 377
supply decisions in, 380–381, 385
technological change in, 364
Perfectly elastic demand, 116,
195–196
Perfectly elastic supply, 126, 196
Perfectly inelastic demand, 116, 195
Perfectly inelastic supply, 126, 196
Perfect price discrimination, 420–421
Perpetual motion, 651–652
Personal characteristics, 142, 524
**Personal Consumption Expenditures
Price Index (PCEPI), 599,**
600, 851
Personal contributions, 556
Personal distribution of income, 39, 45
Personal economic policy, 14
Personal income taxes, 199
Personal Responsibility and Work
Opportunities Reconciliation
Act of 1996, 530
Phelps, Edmund S., 811
Phillips, A. W. (Bill), 805
Phillips curve
long-run, 808–813
short-run, 802–806, 809, 813
uses of, 794–795
Physical capital, 666
economic inequality and, 524
financial capital compared to, 666
global economy and, 44
goods and services and, 666
investments and, 642–643
labor productivity and, 642–643
Pigovian taxes, 251–252, 253
Piketty, Thomas, 654
Plant size, 367–369
Policy
barriers, 231
debates, 477–479

decisions, 657–658
tools, 704–705
Political freedom, 556
Political process, 277
Political support, 174, 237, 277
Pollution
air, 251–253
cap-and-trade ceiling on, 252–253,
255
clean technologies and, 251
Coase theorem and, 249
deadweight loss caused by, 248
external costs of, 247
limits, 251
as negative externalities, 246–255
production reduction and, 248
standard of living and, 555
tax on, 251–252
in United States, 251, 253
Pooling equilibrium, 299, 302–303
Population growth, 505
Population survey, 568, 571
Positive externality, 244, 245
Positive relationship, 26
Positive statements, 15
Positive theories of income redistribution, 530
Post-industrial economy, 47
Potential GDP, 551, 583, 617
changes in, 753
estimating, 836
in European Union and United
States, 617
fiscal policy and, 838–841
full employment and, 583, 617,
623, 838
in global economy, 617
per person, 552
real GDP and, 768, 864–865
of United Kingdom, 839
of United States, 552, 617,
640, 839
Poverty, 515
duration of, 516
entrepreneurial ability and, 524
global inequity and, 46
health care and, 309
income redistribution and, 530–531
in United States, 513
Predatory pricing, 234, 479
Preferences, 89, 144, 496
Prescott, Edward C., 614, 839

President
federal budget role of, 824
monetary policy role of, 852
wage rates for, 605
Price cap, 170
Price cap regulation, 429
Price ceiling, 170
Price-discriminating monopoly, 406
Price discrimination
in airline industry, 419–422
buyers and, 418–419
consumer surplus and, 418–419
efficiency and, 422
perfect, 420–421
profiting by, 419–420
Price elasticity of demand, 114
in agriculture, 124
applying, 124
calculating, 118–119
consumers and, 133
food spending and, 121
gasoline prices and, 118
in global economy, 121
goods and, 114–115, 133
income and, 121
influences on, 116–118
interpreting, 119
midpoint method in, 114–115
price change in, 114, 116
quantity demanded changes
and, 115
ranges of, 117
total revenue and, 122–123
Price elasticity of supply, 126
calculating, 128–129
influences on, 126–128
production possibilities, 126, 128
range of, 127
storage possibilities, 128
Price floor, 176
labor market with, 185
wage rates and, 177
Price level, 593
aggregate demand and,
756–757
change in output rate and, 752
in demand for money, 725
equilibrium expenditure depends
on, 794–795
exports and imports influenced
by, 758
full employment and, 734, 767

Price level (*continued*)
  goods and measures of, 596–600
  inflation and, 803–804
Price(s)
  asset, 670
  base-year, 563
  budget line slope of, 323–324
  business' output, 492
  ceiling, 185
  changes in, 322
  equilibrium, 100–101
  factor, 364–365, 488
  factors of production and,
    364–365, 492
  future, 96
  gasoline, 118
  GDP and index of, 599
  gouging, 140, 162
  index measures of, 599
  long run, 444
  marginal revenue and, 408–409
  market, 545
  market demand and, 87, 390
  market equilibrium influenced by,
    100–101
  Microsoft, 427
  money, 754
  monopolies' decisions on,
    410–411, 413
  in monopolistic competition,
    436–437, 442–446
  monopolistic competition
    marketing and, 436–437
  oil/metal, 467, 504–505, 648
  oranges, 124
  output and, 410–411, 413
  percent change in, 114–115
  in perfect competition, 377–378
  predatory, 234
  predicting changes in, 101
  regulations, 158
  of related goods, 88–89
  relative, 324, 563
  of resources, 96
  scarce resources and, 140
  stable, 850–851
Price-setting strategies, 406
Price stability, 864–865
Price survey, 591
Price taker, 377
Prisoners' dilemma, 469

  equilibrium in, 470–471
  game theory and, 469–471
  payoffs of, 470
  rules of, 469
  strategies of, 470
Private benefits, 257–258
Private contracts, 598
Private costs, 246–247, 282
Private good, 268–269
Private information, 294
Private property, 284–286
Private provision, 274
Private sector balance, 882
Producer surplus, 152
  import quotas influencing, 230–231
  imports/exports influencing, 222
  international trade and, 227–228
  rent ceilings and, 173–174
  supply and marginal cost, 151
  tariffs influencing, 227
  taxes and, 194
  total surplus and, 155
Product curve, 365
Product development, 448
Product differentiation, 436, 446, 451
Production. *See also* Factors of
    production
  in advanced economies, 45
  changes in shoe, 36
  complement in, 95–96
  in developing economies, 43
  domestic, 227
  efficient/inefficient, 62–63,
    74–75, 143
  Europe and United States
    compared, 624
  factor prices of, 364–365, 492
  GDP measures of income and, 547
  in global economy, 43
  of goods and services, 555
  goods and services changes in, 45
  household, 555
  negative externalities in, 244
  over, 157, 248, 277
  pollution and reduction of, 248
  positive externalities in, 244
  public provisions and, 275–277
  quantity of labor and, 618–619
  quotas, 285–286
  real GDP and, 618–619
  shale gas, 71

  short-run, 353–357
  substitute in, 95–96
  technological change in, 393–395
  under, 157, 258
  underground, 555
  in United States economy, 34–35
  value, 563
Production efficiency, 62–63
Production function, 618–619
**Production possibilities frontier
    (PPF), 60**
  allocative efficiency, 143–145
  attainable/unattainable
    combinations in, 62
  budget line similar to, 321
  economic growth and, 70, 71
  efficient/inefficient production in,
    62–63, 77, 143
  opportunity costs and slope of, 67
  tradeoffs/free lunches in, 63–64
Production quota, 183
  in agriculture, 183–185
  efficiency/inefficiency of, 184–185
  fairness of, 185
  free market reference point, 184
  markets with effective, 184
Productivity, 73, 96, 838
Productivity curve, 644
Profit. *See also* Economic profit
  business decisions maximizing,
    378–379, 442–443
  businesses and, 752
  businesses maximizing, 348
  of commercial banks, 699
  cost and, 348, 350
  entrepreneurship seeking, 38
  import quota bringing, 230–231
  income, 545
  long run, 444
  maximizing, 427, 448
  maximizing output, 411
  monopolies maximizing, 158, 411
  normal, 349
  price discrimination for, 419–420
  quantity of labor and, 619
  shutdown decisions and, 381–382
  taxes on, 200
  zero economic, 386, 444
Profit (or loss), 39
Profit-maximizing decisions, 378–379,
    380, 442–443, 453, 619

Profit-maximizing output, 411
Progressive tax, **207**, 208
Property rights, **249**–250, 284–285, **656**
Proportional tax, **207**, 526
Protection, arguments for, 233–236
Public franchise, 405
Public good, **269**
    efficient quantity of, 274
    free-rider problem and, 271–278
    marginal benefit of, 272–273
    marginal cost of, 272
    productivity and, 838
Public goods and services, 838
Public health, 311
Public provision, **259**
    benefit-cost analysis, 276–277
    with efficient outcome, 259, 275–277
    overproduction and, 277
    private subsidy compared to, 260
    production and, 275–277
Purchasing power parity (PPP), 554, **894**–895

Quality
    advertising signals of, 451
    change bias, 597
    of education, 658
    in monopolistic competition, 436–437
Quantitative easing (QE), 705
Quantity demanded, **85**, 90, 115
Quantity of labor
    economic growth with, 647
    labor market equilibrium and, 750
    production function in, 618–619
    profit-maximizing, 619
    real wage rate and, 628, 751–752, 786, 810, 838
    tax wedge influencing, 839
    unemployment and, 803
Quantity of labor demanded, **619**
Quantity of labor supplied, **621**
Quantity of loanable funds demanded, 672
Quantity of loanable funds supplied, 675
Quantity of money, 733
Quantity of money demanded, **723**
Quantity supplied, **92**, 97
Quantity theory of money, **734**–738, 868

Quantity theory prediction, 735–736
Quotas. *See also* Import quota
    common resources and, 285–286
    import, 229–231
    production, 285–286

Rate of return regulation, **428**
Rational choice, **9**–10, 11
Rational expectation, **815**
Rational ignorance, **277**
Rawls, John, 529
Reagan, Ronald, 52, 842–843
Real business cycle, **765**
Real economy, 722
Real flows, 48–49
Real GDP, **548**
    aggregate demand and, 756–757
    aggregate planned expenditures and, 782–783, 785, 788, 792
    aggregate supply and, 750–751, 762
    calculating, 548–549, 564
    chained-dollar, 563, 565
    consumption expenditure and increases in, 792, 833
    CPI and, 603–604
    in demand for money, 725
    economic tracking of, 554
    goods and services value of, 548, 617
    imports and, 780
    measuring, 563–565
    nominal GDP and, 548
    potential GDP and, 768, 864–865
    production function and, 618–619
    unemployment and, 581–583, 803
Real GDP per person, 551, 639
    global economy and, 659
    growth rate and, 639
    historical, 639
    rule of 70 applied to, 640
    in United States, 552, 557, 653
Real interest rate, **606**–607
    aggregate demand and, 757–758
    aggregate planned expenditures and, 863
    consumption expenditure influenced by, 779
    goods and services and, 606–607
    long-term, 861, 865

    taxes and, 842
Real values
    CPI calculations of, 603–604
    nominal values and, 602–603
Real wage rate, **604**–605
    at full employment, 722, 786
    natural unemployment influenced by, 580
    quantity of labor and, 628, 751–752, 786, 810, 838
Recession, **552**–553
    from aggregate supply, 769
    in economy, 769
    Federal Reserve taking actions against, 862–863
    fiscal stimulus ending, 835
    impact on international trade, 54
    of United States, 573, 580, 769
Recessionary gap, **763**, 832, 834, 851
Record stores, 394–395
Reference base period, **590**
Reference base year, 548
Regressive tax, **207**
Regulation, **424**
    deadweight loss caused by, 158
    earnings sharing, 429
    efficient, 424–429
    in international trade, 231
    of monopoly, 424–429
    of natural monopolies, 424–429
    price, 158
    price cap, 429
    rate of return, 428
    second-best, 425–429
Relationships
    disposable income, 776–779
    inflation rate, 808–813
    inverse/negative, 27
    linear/positive, 26
    maximum/minimum points in, 28
    output gap's, 582
    slope of, 29
    variables in, 26–28, 30–31
Relative price, **324**, 563
Relevant comparisons, 446
Rent, **39**, 545
Rent ceiling, **170**
    black market and, 171–172
    consumer/producer surplus and, 173–174
    deadweight loss and, 173

Rent ceiling (*continued*)
efficiency/inefficiency of, 173–174
fairness of, 174
political support for, 174
shortages created by, 171
Rent income, 39
Rent seeking, 237, 415
deadweight loss and, 415
equilibrium, 416
monopolies created by, 415–416
Repeated games, 474
Required reserve ratio, 699,
704, 705
Resale price maintenance, 477–478
Research and development, 658
Research games, 472–473
Reserves, 699
Resource allocation
command system and, 141
consumers and, 163
contests and, 141
efficiency in, 143–146
fairness of, 163
first-come, first-served and,
141–142
force used in, 142–143
lotteries in, 142
majority rule and, 141
market price, 140
methods of, 140–143
personal characteristics in, 142
sharing equally, 142
Resources, 68, 84, 96, 140. *See also*
Common resources; Natural
resources; Nonrenewable natural
resources; Scarce resources
Restarts, 752
Retained earnings, 672
Revenues. *See also* Marginal revenue;
Total revenue
economic profits and concepts of,
377–378
of federal government, 827
in perfect competition, 377–378
from tariffs, 227
tax, 824–825, 841–842
Ricardo, David, 614, 650, 684
Ricardo-Barro effect, 684
Risk
of commercial banks, 699
default, 677
financial stability and, 851

Rival, 268–269
Robinson-Patman Act of 1936, 477–478
Romer, Christina, 792
Romer, Paul, 650
Rule-based monetary policy, 868
Rule of 70, 640
Rule of law, 143, 656
Running shoes, 452

Saban, Nick, 497
Saez, Emmanuel, 514
Sala-i-Martin, Xavier, 46
Samuelson, Paul A., 794–795
Saving, 540
economic growth from, 657–658
loanable funds market and, 684
wealth and, 667
Savings and loan association, 701
Savings bank, 701
Say, Jean-Baptiste, 786
Say's Law, 786
Scarce resources, 140
Scarcity, 2, 8, 61–64
Scatter diagram, 24–25
Schumpeter, Joseph, 650
Schwartz, Anna J., 856
Scientific method, 14
Screening, 304–305
Search activity, 172
Securities
commercial banks selling, 710
Federal Reserve buying, 709–712
Federal Reserve selling, 712
government issuing, 700
mortgage-backed, 668
Self-interest, 4–5
Sellers
exchange rates and, 894
markets for buyers and, 656–657
Seller's decisions, 296
Selling costs
consumers encountering, 452
demand and, 452
total costs and, 452
Separating equilibrium, 299
Services. *See* Goods and services
7-Eleven, 369
Shale gas production, 71
Shepperson, John, 162
Sherman Act of 1890, 477–478
Shoe-leather costs, of inflation, 742
Shoe production, 36

Shortage, 100, 171
Short run, 352
economic loss in, 388, 443
economic profit in, 386–388
equilibrium in bad times, 388
equilibrium in good times, 387
equilibrium/normal times, 386
market supply in, 385
Short-run costs, 359–365
average cost and, 361–363
curve, 363
marginal cost and, 360
in total costs, 359–360
Short-run Phillips curve, 802
aggregate supply and, 803–804
expected inflation rate, 809–810,
813
full employment and, 802–806
unemployment rate relationship
with, 811–812
uses of, 794–795
Short-run production, 353–357
Short-run supply curve, 382–383
Short-run tradeoff, 817
Short-term interest rates, 860
Shutdown decisions, of businesses,
381–382
Shutdown point, 381
Signal, 451
Signaling, 298, 313
Simon, Julian, 505
Single-price monopoly, 406, 408–411,
419–420
Slope, 29
calculating, 29
of consumption function, 778
with multiplier, 791
PPF, 67
prices and budget line, 323–324
of relationships, 29
Smartphones, 61–63, 66–67, 193, 451,
475, 481
Smith, Adam, 18, 155–156, 333–334,
614, 650, 786
Smoot-Hawley Act of 1930, 225
Smoothie bars, 74–77, 359–362
Social benefits, 257–258
Social costs, 282
Social interest, 4–5
Social interest theory, 424
Social justice, 556
Social science, 8, 18

Social Security
  federal government obligation
    of, 825
  fiscal imbalance and, 828–829
  programs, 50, 526
  tax, 202–203, 301
Software, 544
Solow, Robert M., 794–795
Song downloads, 334–335
Specialization
  of capital, 367
  of labor, 73, 367
  productivity gains from, 73
  trade gains from, 76
Spence, Michael, 313
Sprint, 475, 481
Stability, 236, 851, 855, 864–865
Stable prices, 850–851
Stagflation, 767
Standard of living, 517, 551
  economic growth influencing, 652
  in global economy, 554, 557
  goods and services value in, 551,
    554, 557
  influences on, 557
  pollution and, 555
Startups, 752
Star Wars: The Force Awakens, 606
State governments, 50
Statistical discrepancy, 546
Stern, Nicholas, 254–255
Sticky-price CPI, 600
Stiglitz, Joseph, 313
Stock, 668
Stock markets, 668
Store of value, 693
Strategies, 470
Structural change, 580, 628
Structural surplus or deficit, 832
Structural unemployment, 578, 580
StubHub, 397
Subsidized services, 527
Subsidy, 260
  dumping argument and, 234
  export, 231
  from governments, 426
  in market failure, 158
  private, 260
Substitute, 88, 116, 123, 404
Substitute in production, 95–96
Supplemental Nutrition Assistance
    Program (SNAP), 527

Supplemental Security Income
    program (SSI), 527
Supply, 92. *See also* Aggregate supply
  change in, 95–96, 104, 106–107,
    675–677
  consumers and, 98
  decisions, 380–381, 385
  demand and, 102–107
  demand's opposite direction
    change with, 107
  demand's same direction change
    with, 106
  of dollars, 889–891
  elastic/inelastic, 126, 196
  Federal Reserve changes in
    money, 722, 733
  in foreign exchange market,
    889–890
  individual, 94
  of labor, 621–622
  labor market, 495–496
  law of, 92, 98, 102–107, 381,
    889–890
  in loanable funds market, 675–677,
    685
  loanable funds market changes of,
    675–677
  marginal costs and, 151
  market, 94, 294–297, 385, 494–496
  market equilibrium and, 102–107
  of money, 726
  of natural resources, 503
  nominal interest rates determined
    by, 726–727
  perfect competition decisions of,
    380–381, 385
  perfectly elastic, 126, 196
  perfectly inelastic, 126, 196
  price elasticity of, 126–129
  producer surplus and, 151–152
  unit elastic, 126
  of used cars, 294–297
Supply curve, 93
Supply of dollars, 889–891
Supply of labor, 621
Supply of loanable funds, 675
Supply of money, 726
Supply schedule, 93
Supply-side effects, 838, 842–843
Surplus
  budget, 682–683, 824–825
  cyclical, 832

market equilibrium and, 100
net operating, 545
structural, 832
total, 155
Sustainable use, 280–281

Targeting rule, 871
Tariff, 225
  deadweight loss and, 228
  governmental revenue from, 227
  influence of, 226–228
  in United States, 225
Taxable income, 208
Tax credit, 203
Taxes
  burden of, 194
  capital and, 200
  on capital income, 200
  change in rate of, 840
  Congress and, 202–203
  on consumption, 658
  on consumption expenditure,
    839, 840
  credits/rebates, 203
  deadweight loss caused by, 193
  decreases in, 598
  economic growth influenced by,
    841–842
  efficiency of, 193
  elasticity of demand and, 195–196
  elasticity of supply and, 196
  employment and, 198–199,
    841–842
  fairness and, 206–209
  financial capital influenced by, 841
  flat tax, 208–209
  on income, 198–201
  induced, 831
  inflation as, 741–742
  land income and, 201
  market failure and, 158
  net, 540
  Pigovian taxes, 251–252, 253
  on pollution, 251–252
  producer surplus and, 194
  on profits, 200
  progressive, 207, 208
  real interest rates and, 842
  in United States, 199
Tax Foundation, 204
Tax Freedom Day, 204
Tax incidence, 192–193

Tax multiplier, 833
Tax revenues, 824–825, 841–842
Tax wedge, 839
  goods and services influenced
    by, 839
  interest rates as, 842
  quantity of labor influenced
    by, 839
Taylor, John B., 792, 868
Taylor Rule, 868, 869
Technology
  abatement, 249
  clean, 251
  demand for labor influenced by, 492
  financial, 726
  human capital and, 645–646
  information-age monopolies, 406
  perfect competition and, 364
  production changes of, 393–395
  short-run cost curve and, 364
  wireless industry, 475, 481
Temporary Assistance for Needy
    Families (TANF), 527, 530
Temporary shutdowns, 752
Third World debt crisis, 881
Thrift institutions, 701
Time-series graph, 24–25
T-Mobile, 475, 481
Token, 692
Total cost, 359
  average, 361
  average curve of, 362, 363, 386,
    410–411
  curve, 360
  selling costs and, 452
  short-run costs in, 359–360
  total revenue/economic profit
    and, 379
Total fixed cost, 359
Total product, 353–354
Total revenue, 122
  marginal revenue and, 408–409
  orange prices and, 124
  price elasticity of demand and,
    122–123
  total cost/economic profit and, 379
Total revenue test, 123
Total surplus, 155
Total utility, 326
  marginal utility and, 327,
    328–330, 333
  maximizing, 328–330

Total variable cost, 359
Trade. *See* International trade
Trade gains, 76
Tradeoff, 8, 63, 207–209, 811–812
Tragedy of the commons, 280–287
Training, 496
Transactions costs, 159
Transfer payments, 825, 831
Transfer payments multiplier, 833
Transportation infrastructure, 278
Treasury bills, 668, 701, 858–860
A Treatise on Political Economy
    (Say), 786
Trend, 24
T-shirts, 218, 229–231
Tying arrangements, 479

Uncertainty costs, 743
Underground production, 555
Underproduction, 157, 258, 274
Unemployment
  alternative measures of, 570–571,
    576
  compensation, 527
  cyclical, 579
  duration of, 579
  frictional, 578, 580
  global, 575
  in global economy, 805
  during Great Depression, 805
  inflation rate and, 802, 805,
    810–813
  interest rates influencing, 865
  job rationing and, 630
  marginally attached workers in, 570
  maximum employment and, 851
  measures of, 570–571
  minimum wage creating, 177
  natural, 579
  output gap's relationship with,
    582–583
  part-time workers in, 571
  quantity of labor and, 803
  real GDP and, 581–583, 803
  structural, 578, 580
  types of, 578–581
Unemployment benefits
  in global economy, 628
  job search and, 627
  natural unemployment rates
    and, 580
  as transfer payments, 825

Unemployment rate, 569. *See also*
    Natural unemployment rate
  full employment and, 816–817
  in global economy, 575
  inflation rate relationship with,
    808–813
  in labor force, 569
  in labor markets, 573–574
  measures of, 570–571, 576
  targeting, 816–817
  in United States, 573, 626, 817
Union wage, 629–630
United Kingdom, 839
United States
  aging population of, 828
  air pollution in, 251, 253
  antitrust laws in, 477–478
  average incomes and, 45–46
  balance of payments account of,
    878–879
  balance of payments in, 879
  bank reserves of, 896
  budget deficits of, 829
  business cycle in, 553–554
  circular flows in economy of,
    539–540
  consumption function in, 780
  economic growth in, 764–765
  economic mobility in, 516
  economy of, 34–35, 47
  education influencing income in,
    518, 522
  European production compared
    to, 624
  exports influence on, 886
  FairTax proposal, 209
  federal budget of, 6, 824–826,
    829, 832
  federal funds rate in, 869
  financial crisis in, 701, 769
  fiscal policy in, 843
  foreign exchange market dollars
    of, 886–887
  goods and services deficits of, 6
  goods and services produced in,
    34–35
  health care in, 308
  health insurance in, 308
  imports/exports of, 52–53, 216–219
  imports influence on, 889
  income taxes in, 204, 208
  inflation rate in, 593–594

insurance markets in, 301–305
interest rates changes in, 668, 858–860, 888, 891
international trade of, 52, 216
ITQs working in, 287
labor in, 37, 60, 496
labor productivity growth in, 648
loanable funds market during financial crisis, 680
Lorenz curves in, 513, 517
minimum wage in, 179, 631
monetary policy of, 852
money and credit cards in, 728
monopolistic competition and, 440
natural gas shale in, 71
natural rate hypothesis in, 811
as net borrower, 880, 883
nominal GDP in, 603–604
oligopoly in, 462
pollution in, 251, 253
post-industrial economy of, 47
potential GDP of, 552, 617, 839
potential GDP per person in, 552, 640
poverty in, 513
presidential wage rates in, 605
production in, 34–35
real GDP per person in, 552, 557, 653
recession of, 573, 580, 769
tariffs in, 225
taxes in, 199
transportation infrastructure, 278
unemployment rates in, 573, 626, 817
used car market in, 298–299
wealth distribution in, 512, 513
welfare challenge in, 530–531
Unit elastic demand, 116
Unit elastic supply, 126
Unit of account, 693
Universal coverage/single payer health care, 310, 313
Unrelated variables, 28
U.S. Cellular, 475

Used cars, 294–295
Used goods, 544
U.S. interest rate differential, 888
U.S. official reserves, 878
Utilitarianism, 529
Utility, 326
    birth of, 327
    diminishing marginal, 326
    marginal, 326–336
    total, 326–331, 333
Utility-maximizing rule, 328

Value
    goods and services, 548, 551, 554, 557, 617
    market, 538
    of money, 731–732
    nominal, 602–603
    nominal GDP, 548
    paradox of, 333–334
    production, 563
    real, 602–604
    real GDP, 548, 617
    standard of living, 551, 554, 557
    store of, 693
Value of marginal product, 489–490, 497, 520
Variable plant, 352–353
Variables, 26–28, 30–31
Velocity of circulation, 734–735, 738
Verizon, 475, 481
Vertical equity, 207
Voluntary export restraints, 231
von Neumann, John, 469
Voodoo economics, 843
Voucher, 261, 313

Wage gap, 499
Wage rate. *See also* Real wage rate
    at full employment, 722, 786
    job choices and, 499
    in labor markets, 494, 496, 520–522
    labor skill differentials and, 521
    money, 753–754, 763

nominal, 604–605, 619
price floor and, 177
United States presidents, 605
Wages, 39
    career choices and, 47
    efficiency, 629
    explicit cost of, 349
    income from, 39, 545
    job search and, 629–630
    labor markets and, 496
    labor union and, 498–499
    minimum, 177–179
    union, 629–630
Wal-Mart, 38, 369
Walton, Sam, 38
Warranties, 298–299
Water, 322, 328–331, 341–345
Wealth, 667, 676, 779
Wealth distribution, 512, 513
Wealth of Nations (Smith), 18, 155, 786
Welch, Finis, 179
Welfare benefits, 50
Welfare programs, 527, 530–531
Wind power, 68
Women
    earning differences, 523
    in global economy, 575
    in labor force, 496, 574, 575
    quantity of labor and, 37
    as single mothers, 530
Working-age population, 568, 580–581
World economy, 759–760
World Trade Organization (WTO), 225, 234

Yellen, Janet, 703
Yuan, 897–899

Zero economic profit, 386, 444
Zero marginal costs, 427
Z-pop ratio, 580–581
Zuckerberg, Mark, 38, 524

Photo Credits

The Pearson Series in Economics

Abel/Bernanke/Croushore
*Macroeconomics**

Bade/Parkin
*Foundations of Economics**

Berck/Helfand
The Economics of the Environment

Bierman/Fernandez
Game Theory with Economic Applications

Blanchard
*Macroeconomics**

Boyer
Principles of Transportation Economics

Branson
Macroeconomic Theory and Policy

Bruce
Public Finance and the American Economy

Carlton/Perloff
Modern Industrial Organization

Case/Fair/Oster
*Principles of Economics**

Chapman
Environmental Economics: Theory, Application, and Policy

Daniels/VanHoose
International Monetary & Financial Economics

Downs
An Economic Theory of Democracy

Farnham
Economics for Managers

Fort
Sports Economics

Froyen
Macroeconomics

Fusfeld
The Age of the Economist

Gerber
*International Economics**

Gordon
*Macroeconomics**

Greene
Econometric Analysis

Gregory/Stuart
Russian and Soviet Economic Performance and Structure

Hartwick/Olewiler
The Economics of Natural Resource Use

Heilbroner/Milberg
The Making of the Economic Society

Heyne/Boettke/Prychitko
The Economic Way of Thinking

Hubbard/O'Brien
*Economics**

*InEcon Money, Banking, and the Financial System**

Hubbard/O'Brien/Rafferty
*Macroeconomics**

Hughes/Cain
American Economic History

Husted/Melvin
International Economics

Jehle/Reny
Advanced Microeconomic Theory

Keat/Young/Erfle
Managerial Economics

Klein
Mathematical Methods for Economics

Krugman/Obstfeld/Melitz
*International Economics: Theory & Policy**

Laidler
The Demand for Money

Lynn
Economic Development: Theory and Practice for a Divided World

Miller
*Economics Today**

Understanding Modern Economics

Miller/Benjamin
The Economics of Macro Issues

Miller/Benjamin/North
The Economics of Public Issues

Mishkin
*The Economics of Money, Banking, and Financial Markets**

*The Economics of Money, Banking, and Financial Markets, Business School Edition**

*Macroeconomics: Policy and Practice**

Murray
Econometrics: A Modern Introduction

O'Sullivan/Sheffrin/Perez
*Economics: Principles, Applications and Tools**

Parkin
*Economics**

Perloff
*Microeconomics**

*Microeconomics: Theory and Applications with Calculus**

Perloff/Brander
*Managerial Economics and Strategy**

Pindyck/Rubinfeld
*Microeconomics**

Riddell/Shackelford/Stamos/Schneider
Economics: A Tool for Critically Understanding Society

Roberts
The Choice: A Fable of Free Trade and Protection

Scherer
Industry Structure, Strategy, and Public Policy

Schiller
The Economics of Poverty and Discrimination

Sherman
Market Regulation

Stock/Watson
Introduction to Econometrics

Studenmund
Using Econometrics: A Practical Guide

Todaro/Smith
Economic Development

Walters/Walters/Appel/Callahan/Centanni/Maex/O'Neill
Econversations: Today's Students Discuss Today's Issues

Williamson
Macroeconomics

*denotes MyEconLab titles

Visit www.myeconlab.com to learn more.

Macroeconomic Data

These macroeconomic data series show some of the trends in GDP and its components, the price level, and other variables that provide information about changes in the standard of living and the cost of living—the central questions of macroeconomics. You will find these data in a spreadsheet that you can download from your MyEconLab Web site.

		NATIONAL INCOME AND PRODUCT ACCOUNTS	1970	1971	1972	1973	1974	1975	1976	1977	1978	1979
		EXPENDITURES APPROACH										
the sum of	1	Personal consumption expenditure	648	701	769	851	932	1,033	1,150	1,277	1,426	1,590
	2	Gross private domestic investment	170	197	228	267	275	257	323	397	478	540
	3	Government expenditure	254	269	288	306	343	383	406	436	477	526
	4	Exports	60	63	71	95	127	139	150	159	187	230
less	5	Imports	56	62	74	91	128	123	151	182	212	253
equals	6	Gross domestic product	1,076	1,168	1,282	1,429	1,549	1,689	1,878	2,086	2,357	2,632
		INCOMES APPROACH										
	7	Compensation of employees	625	667	734	815	890	950	1,051	1,169	1,320	1,481
plus	8	Net operating surplus	222	247	280	317	323	357	405	457	526	564
equals	9	Net domestic product at factor cost	847	914	1,013	1,132	1,214	1,307	1,457	1,626	1,846	2,045
	10	Indirect taxes less subsidies	87	96	101	112	122	131	141	153	162	172
plus	11	Depreciation (capital consumption)	137	149	161	178	206	238	259	288	325	371
	12	GDP (income approach)	1,071	1,158	1,275	1,423	1,541	1,676	1,857	2,067	2,334	2,587
	13	Statistical discrepancy	5	10	7	6	7	13	21	19	23	45
equals	14	GDP (expenditure approach)	1,076	1,168	1,282	1,429	1,549	1,689	1,878	2,086	2,357	2,632
	15	Real GDP (billions of 2009 dollars)	4,722	4,878	5,134	5,424	5,396	5,385	5,675	5,937	6,267	6,466
	16	Real GDP growth rate (percent per year)	0.2	3.3	5.3	5.6	−0.5	−0.2	5.4	4.6	5.6	3.2
		OTHER DATA										
	17	Population (millions)	205	208	210	212	214	216	218	220	223	225
	18	Labor force (millions)	83	84	87	89	92	94	96	99	102	105
	19	Employment (millions)	79	79	82	85	87	86	89	92	96	99
	20	Unemployment (millions)	4	5	5	4	5	8	7	7	6	6
	21	Labor force participation rate (percent of working-age population)	60.4	60.2	60.4	60.8	61.3	61.2	61.6	62.2	63.2	63.7
	22	Unemployment rate (percent of labor force)	5.0	6.0	5.6	4.9	5.6	8.5	7.7	7.1	6.1	5.9
	23	Real GDP per person (2009 dollars per year)	23,024	23,485	24,458	25,593	25,227	24,935	26,024	26,951	28,151	28,725
	24	Growth rate of real GDP per person (percent per year)	2.9	2.0	4.1	4.6	−1.4	−1.2	4.4	3.6	4.5	2.0
	25	Quantity of money (M2, billions of dollars)	602	674	758	832	881	964	1,087	1,221	1,322	1,426
	26	GDP price index (209 = 100)	22.8	23.9	25.0	26.3	28.7	31.4	33.1	35.1	37.6	40.7
	27	GDP price index inflation rate (percent per year)	5.3	5.1	4.3	5.4	9.0	9.3	5.5	6.2	7.0	8.3
	28	Consumer price index (1982–1984 = 100)	38.8	40.5	41.8	44.4	49.3	53.8	56.9	60.6	65.2	72.6
	29	CPI inflation rate (percent per year)	5.9	4.2	3.3	6.3	11.0	9.1	5.8	6.5	7.6	11.3
	30	Current account balance (billions of dollars)	4	0	−4	9	6	20	7	−11	−13	−1

1980	1981	1982	1983	1984	1985	1986	1987	1988	1989	1990	1991	1992
1,755	1,938	2,074	2,287	2,498	2,723	2,898	3,092	3,347	3,593	3,826	3,960	4,216
530	631	581	638	820	830	849	892	937	1,000	994	944	1,013
591	655	710	766	825	908	975	1,031	1,078	1,152	1,238	1,298	1,345
281	305	283	277	302	303	321	364	445	504	552	595	633
294	318	303	329	405	417	453	509	554	591	630	624	668
2,863	3,211	3,345	3,638	4,041	4,347	4,590	4,870	5,253	5,658	5,980	6,174	6,539
1,626	1,795	1,895	2,014	2,218	2,389	2,546	2,726	2,951	3,144	3,345	3,455	3,674
576	670	684	767	921	983	987	1,059	1,175	1,242	1,258	1,270	1,341
2,202	2,465	2,578	2,782	3,139	3,372	3,533	3,785	4,126	4,386	4,603	4,725	5,015
191	224	226	242	269	287	299	317	345	372	398	430	453
426	485	534	561	594	637	682	728	782	836	887	931	960
2,819	3,174	3,338	3,584	4,002	4,296	4,513	4,830	5,253	5,594	5,888	6,086	6,428
44	37	7	54	39	51	77	41	−1	64	91	88	111
2,862	3,211	3,345	3,638	4,041	4,347	4,590	4,870	5,253	5,658	5,980	6,174	6,539
6,450	6,618	6,491	6,792	7,285	7,594	7,861	8,133	8,475	8,786	8,955	8,948	9,267
−0.2	2.6	−1.9	4.6	7.3	4.2	3.5	3.5	4.2	3.7	1.9	−0.1	3.6
228	230	232	234	236	239	241	243	245	247	250	254	257
107	109	110	112	114	115	118	120	122	124	126	126	128
99	100	100	101	105	107	110	112	115	117	119	118	118
8	8	11	11	9	8	8	7	7	7	7	9	10
63.8	63.9	64.0	64.0	64.4	64.8	65.2	65.6	65.9	66.4	66.5	66.2	66.4
7.2	7.6	9.7	9.6	7.5	7.2	7.0	6.2	5.5	5.3	5.6	6.9	7.5
28,325	28,772	27,953	28,984	30,817	31,839	32,659	33,489	34,581	35,517	35,794	35,295	36,068
−1.4	1.6	−2.8	3.7	6.3	3.3	2.6	2.5	3.3	2.7	0.8	−1.4	2.2
1,540	1,679	1,831	2,055	2,219	2,417	2,613	2,782	2,932	3,055	3,223	3,342	3,404
44.4	48.5	51.5	53.6	55.5	57.2	58.4	59.9	62.0	64.4	66.8	69.0	70.6
9.0	9.3	6.2	3.9	3.5	3.2	2.0	2.6	3.5	3.9	3.7	3.3	2.3
82.4	90.9	96.5	99.6	103.9	107.6	109.7	113.6	118.3	123.9	130.7	136.2	140.3
13.5	10.4	6.2	3.2	4.4	3.5	1.9	3.6	4.1	4.8	5.4	4.2	3.0
9	3	−3	−35	−90	−114	−143	−154	−116	−92	−75	8	−46